Schroeder's Collectible
TOYS
Antique to Modern
Price Guide

Fourth Edition

Edited by Sharon and Bob Huxford

COLLECTOR BOOKS
A Division of Schroeder Publishing Co., Inc.

The current values in this book should be used only as a guide. They are not intended to set prices, which vary from one section of the country to another. Auction prices as well as dealer prices vary greatly and are affected by condition as well as demand. Neither the Editors nor the Publisher assumes responsibility for any losses that might be incurred as a result of consulting this guide.

Searching For A Publisher?

We are always looking for knowledgeable people considered to be experts within their fields. If you feel that there is a real need for a book on your collectible subject and have a large comprehensive collection, contact us.

On The Cover:
Buddy L Oil Tank Truck, 26", 1920s, EX, $2,500.00; Ross Big Bad Wolf Doll, 14", rare, M, $2,500.00; Whirligig Aeroplane Race Game, 10", McDowell, 1930s, $275.00; Marx Tin Gas Station, 1930s, EX, $500.00 (photo courtesy Dunbar Gallery); Munsters Lunch Box, King Seeley Thermos, 1965, $195.00; J. Chein Ferris Wheel, 16½", 1930s, EX, $350.00 (photo courtesy June Moon); Mackie Platinum Barbie, 1991, NRFB, $675.00 (photo courtesy *A Decade of Barbie Dolls and Collectibles* by Beth Summers); Buck Rogers Tin Litho Spaceship, 12", Marx, 1927, EX, $895.00; Lehmann Wild West Bucking Bronco, 1903, $795.00.

Editorial Staff:
Editors: Sharon and Bob Huxford
Research and Editorial Assistants: Michael Drollinger, Nancy Drollinger, Linda Holycross, Donna Newnum, Loretta Woodrow
Cover Design: Beth Summers
Layout: Terri Stalions and Beth Ray

Additional copies of this book may be ordered from:

COLLECTOR BOOKS
P.O. Box 3009
Paducah, Kentucky 42002-3009

@$17.95. Add $2.00 for postage and handling.

Introduction

It seems that every decade will have an area of concentrated excitement when it comes to the antiques and collectibles market place. What Depression Glass was to the late sixties, Fiesta to the seventies, and cookie jars were to the eighties, toys are to the nineties. No one even vaguely involved in the field can have missed all the excitement toys have stirred up among many, many collectors. There are huge toy shows nationwide; scores of newsletters, magazines, and trade papers that deal exclusively with toys; cataloged toy auctions with wonderful color photographs and several hundred lots each; and more and more toy collector's guides are appearing in the book stores each week.

If you've been using *Schroeder's Antiques Price Guide,* you know that we try very hard not to omit categories where we find even a minor amount of market activity — being collectors ourselves, we know how frustrating it can be when you are unable to find any information on an item in question. But that book is limited to a specific number of pages, and as we watched the toy market explosion taking place, we realized that if we were to do it justice, we would have to publish a companion guide devoted entirely to toys. And following the same convictions, we decided that rather than to try to zero in on only the larger, more active fields, we'd try to represent toys of all kinds, from the 19th century up to today. This is the format we chose to pursue.

Our concept is unique in the collectibles field. Though we designed the book first and foremost to be a price guide, we wanted to make it a buying/selling guide as well. So we took many of our descriptions and values from the 'toys for sale' lists of dealers and collectors around the country. In each of those listings we included a dealer's code, so that if you were looking for the particular model kit (or whatever) that (S5) had to offer, you'd be able to match his code with his name and address in the 'Dealer's Codes' section and simply drop him a line or call him to see if it were still available. Our experiment has been very successful. Feedback indicates that many of our sellers do very well, making productive contacts with collectors who not only purchase items from them on their initial call but leave requests for other merchandise they are looking for as well.

Each edition contains about 24,000 listings, but even at that we realize that when it comes to the toy market, that only begins to scratch the surface. Our intent is to provide our readers with fresh information, issue after issue. The few categories that are repeated in their entirety in succeeding editions generally are those that were already complete or as nearly complete as we or our advisors could make them. But even those are checked to make sure that values are still current and our information up to date.

When we initially began to plan our layout, we soon discovered that organizing toys is mind-boggling. Collectors were quick to tell us that toys generally can't be sorted by manufacturer, as we were accustomed to doing in our other price guides. So we had to devise a sort that would not only be easy to use but one that our staff could work with. With this in mind, we kept our categories very broad and general. On the whole this worked very well, but we found that the character section was so large (4,000 lines) it was overwhelming to our advisors. So even though our original approach was probably the most user-friendly, we have broken the character collectibles down into several groups of collectibles and genres and created specific categories for them. But you'll find 'See Alsos' in bold, cross-references within the description lines, and a detailed index to help you locate the items you're looking for with ease.

What we want to stress is that our values are not meant to set prices. Some of them are prices realized at auction; you'll be able to recognize these by the 'A' at the end of the description line. The listings that have neither the 'A' code or the dealer code mentioned above were either sent to us for publication by very knowledgeable collectors who specialize in those specific types of toys or were originally dealer coded but altered at the suggestion of an advisor who felt that the stated price might be far enough outside the average market price range to be misleading (in which case, the dealer's code was removed). There are so many factors that bear on the market that for us to attempt to set prices is not only presumptuous, it's ludicrous. The foremost of these factors is the attitude of the individual collector — his personal view of the hobby. We've interviewed several by telephone; everyone has his own opinion. While some view auction prices as useless, others regard them as actual selling prices and prefer them to asking prices. And the dealer who needs to keep turning his merchandise over to be able to replenish and freshen his stock will of necessity sell at lower prices than a collector who will buy an item and wait for the most opportune time to turn it over for maximum profit. Where you buy affects prices as well. One of our advisors used this simple analogy: while a soda might cost you $2.50 at the ball park, you can buy the same thing for 39¢ at the corner 7-11. So all we (or anyone) can offer is whatever facts and information we can compile, and ask simply that you arrive at your own evaluations based on the data we've provided, adapted to your personal buying/selling arena, desire to own, and need to sell.

We hope you enjoy our book and that you'll be able to learn by using it. We don't presume to present it as the last word on toys or their values — there are many specialized books by authors who are able to devote an entire publication to one subject, covering it from 'A' to 'Z,' and when we're aware that such a text book exists, we'll recommend it in our narratives. If you have suggestions that you think will improve our format, let us hear from you — we value your input. Until next time — happy hunting! May you find that mint-in-the-box #1 Barbie or if you prefer that rare mechanical bank that has managed to so far elude you. But even if you never do, we hope that you'll find a generous measure of happiness and success, a treasure now and then, and new friends along the way.

The Editors

Advisory Board

The editors and staff take this opportunity to express our sincere gratitude and appreciation to each person who has contributed their time and knowledge to help us. We've found toys to be *by far* the largest, most involved field of collecting we've ever tried to analyze, but we will have to admit, it's great fun! We've been editing general price guides for fifteen years now, and before ever attempting the first one, we realized there was only one way we would presume to publish such a guide — and that would be to first enlist the help of knowledgeable collectors around the country who specialized in specific areas. We now have more than 120, and we're still looking for help in several areas. Generally, the advisors are listed following each category's narrative, so if we have mentioned no one and you feel that you are qualified to advise us, have the time, and would be willing to help us out with that subject, please contact us. We'd love to have you on our advisory board. (We want to stress that even if an advisor is credited in a category narrative, that person is in no way responsible for errors. Errors are our responsibility.) Even if we currently list an advisor for your subject, contact us so that we'll have your name on file should that person need to be replaced. This of course happens from time to time due to changing interests or because they find they no longer have the time.

While some advisors sent us listings and prices, others provided background information and photographs, checked printouts, or simply answered our questions. All are listed below. Each name is followed by their code, see the section called "Dealer and Collector Codes" for an explanation of how these are used in the listings.

Matt and Lisa Adams (A7)
Geneva Addy (A5)
Diane Albert (T6)
Sally and Stan Alekna (A1)
Jane Anderson (A2)
Pamela E. Apkarian-Russell (H9)
Bob Armstrong (A4)
Richard Belyski (B1)
Bill and Jeanne Bertoia
Larry Blodget (B2)
Bojo (B3)
Scott Bruce (B14)
Dick Borgerding (B4)
Sue and Marty Bunis (B11)

Bromer Booksellers, Inc. (B12)
Danny Bynum (B7)
Bill Campbell (C10)
Candelaine (Candace Gunther) (G16)
Casey's Collectible Corner (C1)
Brad Cassity (C13)
Mark Chase and Michael Kelly (C2)
Arlan Coffman (C4)
Joel Cohen (C12)
Cotswold Collectibles (C6)
Marilyn Cooper (C9)
Cynthia's Country Store (C14)
Rosalind Cranor (C15)
Marl Davidson (D2)

Larry DeAngelo (D3)
Doug Dezso (D6)
Donna and Ron Donnelly (D7)
George Downes (D8)
Larry Doucet (D11)
Allan Edwards (E3)
Paul Fink (F3)
Steve Fisch (F7)
Mike and Kurt Fredericks (F4)
Fun House Toy Co. (F5)
Lee Garmon
Carol Karbowiak Gilbert (G6)
Mark Giles (G2)
Joan Stryker Grumbaugh (G8)
Bill Hamburg (H1)
Don Hamm (H10)
George Hardy (H3)
Ellen and Jerry Harnish (H4)
Tim Hunter (H13)
Dan Iannotti (I3)
Roger Inouye (I1)
Kerry and Judy Irwin (K5)
Terri Ivers (I2)
Keith and Donna Kaonis (K6)
Ilene Kayne (K3)
David Kolodny-Nagy (K2)
Trina and Randy Kubeck (K1)
Tom Lastrapes (L4)
Kathy and Don Lewis (L6)
Val and Mark Macaluso (M1)
John McKenna (M2)
Nancy McMichael (M18)
Michael and Polly McQuillen (M11)
Lucky Meisenheimer (M3)
Bill Mekalian (M4)
Steven Meltzer (M9)
Bruce Middleton (M20)
Ken Mitchell (M14)
Gary Mosholder (G1)

Judith Mosholder (M7)
Peter Muldavin (M21)
Natural Way (N1)
Roger Nazeley (N4)
Dawn Parrish (P2)
Diane Patalano (P8)
Sheri and John Pavone (P3)
The Phoenix Toy Soldier Co. (P11)
Pat and Bill Poe (P10)
Gary Pollastro (P5)
Judy Posner (P6)
Lorraine Punchard (P13)
John Rammacher (S5)
Jim Rash (R3)
Robert Reeves (R4)
Charlie Reynolds (R5)
David E. Richter (R1)
David Riddle (R6)
Cindy Sabulis (S14)
Jim and Nancy Schaut (S15)
Scott Smiles (S10)
Carole and Richard Smythe (S22)
Steve Stephenson
Bill Stillman (S6)
Nate Stoller (S7)
Mark and Lynda Suozzi (S24)
Jon Thurmond (T1)
Toy Scouts, Inc. (Bill Bruegman) (T2)
Richard Trautwein (T3)
Marcie and Bob Tubbs (T5)
Judy and Art Turner (H8)
Marci Van Ausdall (V2)
Norm Vigue (V1)
Randy Welch (W4)
Dan Wells (W1)
Larry and Mary White (W7)
Mary Young (Y2)
Henri Yunes (Y1)

How to Use This Book

Concept. Our design for this book is two-fold. Primarily it is a market report compiled from many sources, meant to be studied and digested by our readers, who can then better arrive at their own conclusion regarding prices. Were you to ask ten active toy dealers for their opinion as to the value of a specific toy, you would no doubt get ten different answers, and who's to say which is correct? Quite simply, there are too many variables to consider. Where you buy is critical. Condition is certainly subjective, prices vary from one area of the country to another, and probably the most important factor is how badly you want to add the item in question to your collection or at what price you're willing to sell. So use this as a guide along with your observations at toy shows, flea markets, toy auctions, and elsewhere to arrive at an evaluation that satisfies you personally.

The second function of this book is to put buyers in touch with sellers who deal in the type of toys they want to purchase. We contact dealers all over the country, asking them to send us their 'for sale' lists and permission to use them as sources for some of our listings, which we code so as to identify the dealer from whose inventory list the price and description are taken. Even though by publication, much of their merchandise will have been sold since we entered our data early last spring, many of them tell us that they often get similar or even the same items in over and over, so if you see something listed you're interested in buying, don't hesitate to call any of them. Remember, though, they're not tied down to the price quoted in the book, since their asking price is many times influenced by what they've had to pay to restock their shelves. Let us know how well this concept works out for you.

Toys are listed by name. Every effort has been made to list a toy by the name as it appears on the original box. There have been very few exceptions made, and then only if the collector-given name is more recognizable. For instance, if we listed 'To-Night Amos 'n' Andy in Person' (as the name appears on the box lid), very few would recognize the toy as the Amos 'n' Andy Walkers. But these exceptions are few.

Descriptions and sizes may vary. When we were entering data, we often found the same toy had sold through more than one auction gallery or was listed in several dealer lists. So the same toy will often be described in various ways, but we left descriptions just as we found them, since there is usually something to be gleaned from each variation. We chose to leave duplicate lines in when various conditions were represented so that you could better understand the impact of condition on value. Depending on the source and who was doing the measuring, we found that the size of a given toy might vary by an inch or more. Not having the toy to measure ourselves, we had to leave dimensions just as they were given in auction catalogs or dealer lists.

Lines are coded as to source. Each line that represents an auction-realized price will be coded 'A' at the end, just before the price. Other letter/number codes identify the dealer who sent us that information. These codes are explained later on. Additional sources of like merchandise will be noted under the narratives. These are dealers whose lists arrived at our office too late to be included in the lines themselves.

As we said before, collectors have various viewpoints regarding auction results. You will have to decide for yourself. Some feel they're too high to be used to establish prices while others prefer them to 'asking' prices that can sometimes be speculative. We must have entered about 8,000 auction values, and here is what we found to be true: the really volatile area is in the realm of character collectibles from the '40s, '50s, and '60s — exactly where there is most interest, most collector activity, and hot competition when the bidding starts. But for the most part, auction prices were not far out of line with accepted values. Many times, compared to the general market place, toys in less-than-excellent condition actually sold under 'book.' Because the average auction-consigned toy is in especially good condition and many times even retains its original box, it will naturally bring higher prices than the norm. And auctions often offer the harder-to-find, more unusual items. Unless you take these factors into consideration, prices may seem high, when in reality, they may not be at all. Prices may be driven up by high reserves, but not all galleries have reserves. Whatever your view, you'll be able to recognize and consider the source of the values we quote and factor that into your personal evaluation.

Categories that have priority. Obviously there are thousands of toys that would work as well in one category as they would in another, depending on the preference of the collector. For instance, a Mary Poppins game would appeal to a games collector just as readily as it would to someone who bought character-related toys of all kinds. The same would be true of many other types of toys. We tried to make our decisions sensibly and keep our sorts simple. But to avoid sending our character advisors such huge printouts, we felt that it would be best to pull out specific items and genres to create specific categories, thereby reducing the size of the character category itself. We'll guide you to those specialized categories with cross-references and 'See Alsos.' If all else fails, refer to the index. It's as detailed as we know how to make it.

These categories have precedence over Character:

Action Figures
Battery-Operated Toys (also specific manufacturers)
Books
Bubble Bath Containers
Celebrity Dolls (see Dolls)
Character and Promotional Drinking Glasses
Character Clocks and Watches
Character Bobbin' Heads
Chein
Coloring, Activity, and Paint Books
Corgi
Dakins
Disney
Fisher-Price
Games
Guns
Halloween Costumes
Lunch Boxes
Marx
Model Kits

Nodders
Paper Dolls
Pez Dispensers
Pin-Back Buttons
Plastic Figures
Playsets
Puppets
Puzzles
Radios
Records
Rock 'n Roll
Snow Domes
Sporting Collectibles
Telephones
Trading Cards
Toothbrush Holders
View-Master
Western
Windups, Friction, and Other Mechanicals

Price Ranges. Once in awhile, you'll find a listing that gives a price range. These result from our having found varying prices for the same item. We've taken a mid-range — less than the highest, a little over the lowest — if the original range was too wide to really be helpful. If the range is still coded 'A' for auction, all that were averaged were auction-realized prices.

Condition, how it affects value, how to judge it. The importance of condition can't be stressed enough. Unless a toy is exceptionally rare, it must be very good or better to really have much collector value. But here's where the problem comes in: though each step downward on the grading scale drastically decreases a toy's value, as the old saying goes, 'beauty is in the eye of the beholder.' What is acceptable wear and damage to one individual may be regarded by another as entirely too degrading. Criteria used to judge condition even varies from one auction company to the next, so we had to attempt to sort them all out and arrive at some sort of standardization. Please be sure to read and comprehend what the description is telling you about condition; otherwise you can easily be mislead. Auction galleries often describe missing parts, repairs, and paint touch-ups, summing up overall appearance in the condition code. When losses and repairs were noted in the catalog, we noted them as well. Remember that a toy even in mint restored condition is never worth as much as one in mint original condition. And even though a toy may be rated 'otherwise EX' after losses and repairs are noted, it won't be worth as much as one with original paint and parts in excellent condition. Keep this in mind when you use our listings to evaluate your holdings.

These are the conditions codes we have used throughout the book and their definitions as we have applied them:

M — mint. Unplayed with, brand new, flawless.
NM — near mint. Appears brand new except on very close inspection.
EX — excellent. Has minimal wear, very minor chips and rubs, a few light scratches.
VG — very good. Played with, loss of gloss, noticeable problems, several scratches.
G — good. Some rust, considerable wear and paint loss, well used.
P — poor. Generally unacceptable except for a filler.

Because we do not use a three-level pricing structure as many of you are used to and may prefer, we offer this table to help you arrive at values for toys in conditions other than those that we give you. If you know the value of a toy in excellent condition and would like to find an approximate value for it in near mint condition, for instance, just run your finger down the column under 'EX' until you find the approximate price we've listed (or one that easily factors into it), then over to the column headed 'NM.' We'll just go to $100.00, but other values will be easy to figure by addition or multiplication. Even though at auction a toy in very good to excellent condition sometimes brings only half as much as a mint condition toy, the collectors we interviewed told us that this was not true of the general market place. Our percentages are simply an average based on their suggestions.

.G	VG	EX	NM	M
40/50%	55/65%	70/80%	85/90%	100%
5.00	6.00	7.50	9.00	10.00
7.50	9.00	11.00	12.50	15.00
10.00	12.00	15.00	18.00	20.00
12.00	15.00	18.00	22.00	25.00
14.00	18.00	22.50	26.00	30.00
18.00	25.00	30.00	35.00	40.00
22.50	30.00	37.50	45.00	50.00
27.00	35.00	45.00	52.00	60.00
32.00	42.00	52.00	62.00	70.00
34.00	45.00	55.00	65.00	75.00
35.00	48.00	60.00	70.00	80.00
40.00	55.00	68.00	80.00	90.00
45.00	60.00	75.00	90.00	100.00

Condition and value of original boxes and packaging. When no box or packaging is referred to in the line or in the narrative, assume that the quoted price is for the toy only. Please read the narratives! In some categories (Corgi, for instance), all values are given for items mint and in original boxes. Conditions for boxes (etc.) are in parenthesis immediately following the condition code for the toy itself. In fact, any information within parenthesis at that point in the line will refer to packaging. Collector interest in boxes began several years ago, and today many people will pay very high prices for them, depending on scarcity, desirability, and condition. The more colorful, graphically pleasing boxes are favored, and those with images of well-known characters are especially sought after. Just how valuable is a box? Again, this is very subjective to the individual. We asked this question to several top collectors around the country, and the answers they gave us ranged from 20% to 100% above mint-no-box prices.

Advertising. You'll notice display ads throughout the book. We hope you will contact these advertisers if they deal in the type of merchandise you're looking for. If you'd like your ad to appear in our next edition, please refer to the advertising rate chart in the back of the book for information.

Listing of Standard Abbreviations

These abbreviations have been used throughout this book in order to provide you with the most detailed descriptions possible in the limited space available. No periods are used after initials or abbreviations. When two dimensions are given, height is noted first. When only one measurement is given, it will be the greater — height if the toy is vertical, length if it is horizontal. (Remember that in the case of duplicate listings representing various conditions, we found that sizes often varied as much as an inch or more.)

Am	American
att	attributed to
bl	blue
blk	black
brn	brown
bsk	bisque
c	copyright
ca	circa
cb	cardboard
CI	cast iron
compo	composition
dbl	double
dia	diameter
dk	dark
dtd	dated
ea	each
emb	embossed
EX	excellent
F	fine
fr	frame, framed
ft, ftd	feet, foot, footed
G	good
gr	green
hdl	handle, handled
hdw	hardware
illus	illustrated, illustration
inscr	inscribed
jtd	jointed
L	long, length
litho	lithographed
lt	light, lightly
M	mint
MBP	mint in bubble pack
mc	multicolored
MIB	mint in box
MIP	mint in package
mk	marked
MOC	mint on card
MOT	mint on tree
NM	near mint
NP	nickel plated
NRFB	never removed from box
NRFP	never removed from package
orig	original
o/w	otherwise
P	poor
Pat	patented
pc	piece
pg, pgs	page, pages
pk	pink
pkg	package
pnt	paint, painted
pr	pair
prof	professional
rfn	refinished
rnd	round
rpl	replaced
rpr	repaired
rpt	repainted
rstr	restored
sq	square
sz	size
turq	turquoise
unmk	unmarked
VG	very good
W	width, wingspan
wht	white
w/	with
w/up	windup
yel	yellow

Action Figures

Back in 1964, Barbie dolls had taken the feminine side of the toy market by storm. Hasbro took a risky step in an attempt to target the male side. Their answer to the Barbie craze was GI Joe. Since no self-respecting boy would admit to playing with dolls, Hasbro called their boy dolls 'action figures,' and to the surprise of many, they were phenomenally successful. Both Barbie and GI Joe were realistically modeled (at least GI Joe was) and posable 12" vinyl dolls that their makers clothed and accessorized to the hilt. Their unprecedented successes spawned a giant industry with scores of manufacturers issuing one 'action figure' after another, many in series. Other sizes were eventually made in addition to the 12" dolls. Some are 8" to 9", others 6", and many are the 3¾" figures that have been favored in recent years.

This is one of the fastest-growing areas of toy collecting today. Manufacturers of action figures are now targeting the collector market as well as the kids themselves, simply because the adult market is so active. You will find a wide range of asking prices from dealer to dealer; most of our listings are coded and represent only a sampling. Naturally, *where* you buy will also affect values. Be critical of condition! Original packaging is extremely important. In fact, when it comes to the recent issues, loose, played-with examples are seldom worth more than a few dollars. Remember, if no box is mentioned, values are for loose (unpackaged) dolls. When no size is given, assume figures are 3¾" or standard size for the line in question.

For more information we recommend *Collectible Action Figures* by Paris and Susan Manos and *Mego Toys* by Wallace M. Crouch (all published by Collector Books).

Advisors: George Downs (D8); Robert Reeves (R4), Best of the West.

Other Sources: B3, H12, I2, J2, J7, M15, M17, O1, P3, S17, T1

See also Barbie Dolls; Character Collectibles; Dolls, Celebrity; GI Joe; Star Trek; Star Wars.

Action Jackson, figure, Action Jackson, Mego, 8", M (NM box), C1 ....$32.00
Action Jackson, outfit, Air Force Pilot, Mego, MOC, F1 .$10.00
Action Jackson, outfit, Ski Patrol, Mego, MIP, F1 ....$10.00
Advanced Dungeons & Dragons, figure, BowMarc, Grimsword or Northlord, LJN, NM, D8, ea $25.00
Advanced Dungeons & Dragons, figure, Elkhorn, Kelek, Mericon, Strongheart, Warduke or Zarak, LJN, NM, D8, ea $18.00
Advanced Dungeons & Dragons, figure, Stalwart Men-At-Arms, LJN, MOC, D8 ....$25.00
Adventures of Indiana Jones, figure, Cairo Swordsman or Toht, Kenner, MOC, ea $25.00
Adventures of Indiana Jones, figure, German Mechanic, Kenner, MOC..$35.00
Adventures of Indiana Jones, figure, Indiana Jones, Kenner, MOC..$125.00
Adventures of Indiana Jones, horse, Arabian, Kenner, MOC, J6 ....$95.00

Adventures of Indiana Jones, figure, Indiana Jones, Raiders of the Lost Ark, Kenner, 1984, 12", MIB, $350.00.

Adventures of Indiana Jones, playset, Well of the Souls, Kenner, 1982, MIB, $100.00.

Aliens, accessory, Electronic Hover Tread Vehicle, Kenner, MIB, D4 ....$10.00
Aliens, accessory, EVAC Fighter, Kenner, MIB, D4 ....$25.00
Aliens, accessory, Power Loader, Kenner, MOC, D4.......$15.00
Aliens, accessory, Queen Hive playset, Kenner, MIB.......$50.00
Aliens, accessory, Sting XT-37, Kenner, MOC, D4 ....$10.00
Aliens, figure, Alien Vs Predator, Kenner, MOC (2-pack), D4 ....$15.00
Aliens, figure, Bishop, Gorilla, Killer Crab, Mantis, Night Cougar, Panther, Ripley or Wild Boar, Kenner, MOC, D4, ea..$10.00
Aliens, figure, Colossus Rex, Colorforms, complete, EX, H4 ....$190.00
Aliens, figure, Commander Comet, Colorforms, moderate pnt wear & broken crossbow o/w VG, H4.....................$160.00
Aliens, figure, Flying Queen Alien, Kenner, MOC, D4 ...$15.00
Aliens, figure, Swarm Alien, Kenner, MOC, D4 ....$25.00
Aliens, figure, Zodiac, Colorforms, moderate pnt wear & sm stains o/w VG, H4 ....$150.00
American West, figure, Cochise, Mego, 8", M (NM box), B3..$55.00
American West, figure, Wild Bill Hickok, Mego, 8", M (NM box), B3 ....$55.00
Attack of the Killer Tomatoes, figure, Chad, Dr Gangreen or Wilbur, Mattel, MOC, D4, ea $5.00
Batman, accessory, Bat Lab Van, Mego, VG, H4 ....$70.00

Batman, accessory, Batmobile, plastic, Mego, 1974, EX, $65.00.

Batman, accessory, Batmobile, Toy Biz, EX, D4 ....$25.00

Batman, accessory, Batmobile, Toy Biz, NRFB, H4..........$50.00

Batman, accessory, Batwing vehicle, Toy Biz, NRFB, H4..$45.00

Batman, figure, Batman, Joker or Penguin, Toy Biz, MOC, D4, ea...............................$10.00

Batman, figure, Batman, Kid Biz (Australia), MOC, H4..$60.00

Batman, figure, Batman, Mego, 8", MIB $140.00

Batman, figure, Riddler or Robin, Toy Biz, MOC, D4, ea .$15.00

Batman, see also Dark Knight, DC Comics Super Heroes or Legends of Batman

Batman Forever, figure, Blastcape, Manta Ray, Nighthunter or Transforming Bruce Wayne, MOC, D4, ea................$10.00

Batman Returns, figure, Catwoman or Robin, MOC, D4, ea ...$15.00

Batman Returns, figure, Hydro Charge, Jungle Tracker or Night Climber, Kenner, 2nd series, MOC, D4, ea $10.00

Battlestar Galactica, figure, Cylon Commander, gold version, Mattel, rare, MOC, M17........................$120.00

Battlestar Galactica, figure, Daggit, Mattel, 3¾", EX, H4...$15.00

Battlestar Galactica, figure, Daggit, Mattel, 3¾", MOC (unpunched), H4 ....$25.00

Battlestar Galactica, figure, Imperious Leader, Mattel, 3¾", MOC (crushed bubble, unpunched), H4 ....$15.00

Battlestar Galactica, figure, Lieutenant Starbuck, Mattel, 3¾", MOC (unpunched), H4 ....$30.00

Beetlejuice, figure, Exploding Beetlejuice or Shipwreck Beetlejuice, Kenner, 2nd series, MOC, ea, from $10 to.......$14.00

Beetlejuice, figures, Showtime and Shipwreck, Kenner, 1989, 3¾", MOC, from $10.00 to $14.00 each.

Best of the West, figure, Bill Buck, Marx, complete, M (EX box), H4, from $500 to.............................$650.00

Best of the West, figure, Captain Maddox, Marx, complete, EX (VG box), H4 ....$80.00

Best of the West, figure, Fighting Eagle, Marx, w/accessories, EX..............................$160.00

Best of the West, figure, General Custer, Marx, missing few pcs, VG, H4 ....$40.00

Best of the West, figure, General Custer, Marx, w/20 accessory pcs, NM, F5 ....$85.00

Best of the West, figure, Geronimo, Marx, rare orange body, missing few accessories, EX, H4...............$95.00

Best of the West, figure, Jaimie West, Marx, missing tether, EX, H4 ....$35.00

Best of the West, figure, Jane West, Marx, missing few pcs, NMIB..............................$55.00

Best of the West, figure, Jane West, Marx, w/15 accessory pcs, EX+, F5 ....$25.00

Best of the West, figure, Janice West, Marx, EX, B10 ....$20.00

Best of the West, figure, Jay West, Marx, missing tether, EX, H4 ....$35.00

Best of the West, figure, Jay West, Marx, missing 1 accessory, NM (EX box)..............................$60.00

Best of the West, figure, Jed Gibson, Marx, M $125.00

Best of the West, figure, Johnny West, Marx, complete, EXIB, B10..............................$60.00

Best of the West, figure, Johnny West, Marx, EX, B10.....$20.00

Best of the West, figure, Johnny West, Marx, complete, NM, from $45.00 to $50.00.

Best of the West, figure, Johnny West, Marx, w/most accessories, EX, H4 ....$30.00

Best of the West, figure, Josie West, Marx, MIB...............$75.00

Best of the West, figure, Princess Wildflower, Marx, missing 2 pcs, NM (EX box), F5 ....$145.00

Best of the West, figure, Sam Cobra, Marx, complete, EX, H4.$40.00

Best of the West, figure, Sam Cobra, Marx, complete, EX (worn box), J5 ....$45.00

Best of the West, figure, Sam Cobra, Marx, no accessories, VG, H4 ....$20.00

Best of the West, figure, Sheriff Garrett, Marx, w/17 accessory pcs, NM, F5 ....$100.00

Best of the West, figure, Zeb Zachary, Marx, complete, NM+, from $135 to $150.00

Best of the West, figure set, Geronimo & Pinto, Marx, complete, EXIB, B3 ....$135.00

Best of the West, horse, Buckskin, Marx, dk brn, NM, F5 ..$55.00

Best of the West, horse, Comanche, Marx, M (EX Fort Apache Fighters box) $85.00

Best of the West, horse, Flame, Marx, palomino, complete, NM, F5 ....$42.00

Best of the West, horse, Pancho, Marx, chestnut w/blk tack, complete w/accessories, NM, F5 ....$35.00

Best of the West, horse, Pancho, Marx, palomino, NM, F5 ..$20.00

Best of the West, horse, Thunderbolt, Marx, blk w/blk tack, complete w/accessories, EX+, from $50 to $70.00

Best of the West, horse, Thunderbolt, Marx, cream colored, complete, VG, H4 ....$35.00

Best of the West, horse, Thunderbolt, Marx, palomino, EX+, F5 ....$25.00

Best of the West, horse, Thunderbolt, Marx, rare brn version, missing 1 reign, VG, H4 ....$45.00

Best of the West, horse, Thunderbolt, Marx, tan & wht, complete, NM (EX box) $70.00

Big Jim, accessory, Kung Fu Studio, MIP $50.00

Big Jim, accessory, outfit, Mattel, bl shirt, pants, books, rifle & helmet, MOC, J5 ....$15.00

Big Jim, accessory, Sky Commander Jet, M (VG box)......$50.00

Black Hole, figure, Booth, Durant, Holland, McCray or Reinhardt, Mego, MOC, D8, ea..$18.00

Black Hole, figure, Dr Kate McCray, Mego, 12½", M (NM box), B3 ....$60.00

Black Hole, figure, Sentry Robot, Mego, M (EX card), B3 ..$48.00

Bonanza, figure, Ben Cartwright, Am Character, 8", complete w/horse & accessories, MIB...................................$180.00

Bonanza, figure set, Hoss w/horse, Am Character, 8", MIB, H4 ....$200.00

Bonanza, horse, Am Character, no accessories, EX, H4 ...$15.00

Buck Rogers in the 25th Century, accessory, Laserscope Fighter (for sm figures), Mego, M (EX+ box), B3..................$45.00

Buck Rogers in the 25th Century, figure, Ardella, Mego, MOC..$35.00

Buck Rogers in the 25th Century, figure, Buck, Twiki or Wilma, Mego, NM, D8, ea $25.00

Buck Rogers in the 25th Century, figure, Buck Rogers, Mego, 12", MIB, F1 ....$80.00

Buck Rogers in the 25th Century, figure, Dr Huer, Mego, 12", M (EX box), B3 ....$65.00

Buck Rogers in the 25th Century, figure, Draconian Guard, Mego, 12", M (EX box), B3 ....$60.00

Buck Rogers in the 25th Century, figure, Drako, Killer Kane or or Tigerman, Mego, MOC, D8, ea $28.00

Buck Rogers in the 25th Century, figure, Drako, Mego, 12", M (EX box), B3 ....$60.00

Buck Rogers in the 25th Century, figure, Tigerman, Mego, 12", M (EX box), B3 ....$60.00

Buck Rogers in the 25th Century, figure, Walking Twiki, Mego, 7½", M (EX box), B3.....................................$50.00

Captain Action, accessory, Jet Mortar, Ideal, complete, EX (EX box)...$250.00

Captain Action in Superman outfit, Ideal, 1967, complete with accessories, 12", MIB, $950.00.

Photo courtesy June Moon.

Captain Action, accessory, Silver Streak Amphibian Car, Ideal, NM (EX+ box) $950.00

Captain Action, figure, Action Boy, Ideal, complete w/space suit, accessories & panther, NM, A $400.00

Captain Action, figure, Dr Evil, Ideal, complete, 12", NM (VG+ box), A $450.00

Captain Action, outfit, Aquaman, Ideal, complete, NMIB, A $400.00

Captain Action, outfit, Batman, Ideal, unused, NM (display card only), A $400.00

Captain Action, outfit, Captain America, Ideal, complete, NMIB...$700.00

Captain Action, outfit, Green Hornet, complete, M (EX+ box)..$300.00

Captain America, accessory, car, Mego, trigger mechanism broke o/w NMIB, H4 ....$80.00

Captain Planet & the Planeteers, figure, any character, Kenner, MOC, F1, ea $15.00

CHiPs, figure, Jimmy Squeaks, Ponch or Wheels Willy, Mego, 3¾", MOC, B3, ea $10.00

CHiPs, figure, Jon, Mego, 8", MOC $35.00

CHiPs, figure, Ponch, Mego, 8", MOC $25.00

CHiPs, figure, Sarge, Mego, 8", MOC, C1 ....$40.00

Chuck Norris, figure, Chuck Norris, Ninja Warrior, Kimo or Super Ninja, Kenner, 3¾", MOC, F1, ea..................$15.00

Clash of the Titans, figure, Charon, Mattel, NM, D8 ......$25.00

COPS, figure, 11 different, Hasbro, MOC, D4, ea............$10.00

Crash Dummies, figure, Larry or Vince, MOC, D8, ea $12.00

Dark Knight, figure, Bruce Wayne or Iron Winch Batman, Kenner, MOC, D4, ea..$10.00

DC Comics Super Heroes, figure, Aquaman, Toy Biz, MOC, D4 ....$20.00

DC Comics Super Heroes, figure, Batman, 1st or 2nd issue, Toy Biz, 3¾", MOC, F1, ea.......................................$15.00

DC Comics Super Heroes, figure, Green Lantern, Toy Biz, MOC, D4 ....$25.00

DC Comics Super Heroes, figure, Riddler, Toy Biz, MOC, D4..$15.00

DC Comics Super Heroes, figure, Robin, Toy Biz, MOC, D4 ....$15.00

Demolition Man, figure, 5 different, Mattel, MOC, D4, ea ..$8.00

Dick Tracy (Movie), figure, Al Caprice, Influence, Lips Manlis, Pruneface, Sam Catchum or Tracy, Playmates, MOC, D4, ea $6.00

Droids, figure, any character, Kenner, 3¾", MOC, F1, ea ..$20.00

Dukes of Hazzard, figure, Coy, Mego, 8", MOC, F1 ....$40.00

Dukes of Hazzard, figure, Daisy, Mego, gr shirt, 3¾", MOC, C1 ....$24.00

Dukes of Hazzard, figure, Luke, Mego, 3¾", MOC, F1 .....$20.00

Dukes of Hazzard, figures, Bo, Luke, Daisy or Boss Hogg, Mego, 8", MOC, ea $35.00

Dune, accessory, Fremen Tarpel Gun, LJN, M (EX box), B3 ..$40.00

Dune, accessory, Sand Scout, LJN, NM (VG card), D8 ...$15.00

Dune, figure, Feyd, LJN, w/accessories, EX, H4 ....$10.00

Dune, figure, Sardaukan Warrior, LJN, no accessories, EX, H4 ....$10.00

Dune, figure, Stilgar, LJN, no accessories, EX, H4 ....$8.00

Emergency, figure, fireman & nurse, EX, B10, ea................$8.00

ET, figure, LJN, 3", rare, MOC, F1 ....$20.00

Fist of the North Star, figure, Kenshiro, Jagi, Lynn, Mamiya, Rey, Rooh, Shin or Yuria, Tongda, MOC, D4, ea $10.00

Flash Gordon, accessory, Ming's Space Shuttle, Mattel, EX (VG box), H4...$30.00

Flash Gordon, figure, Dr Zarkov, Mego, 9", M (EX box), B3..$80.00

Flash Gordon, figure, Flash Gordon, Mattel, MOC, H4...$25.00

Flash Gordon, figure set, Flash, Dr Zarkov & Thun, Mattel, 3¾", MIB, H4...$40.00

Flash Gordon, figure set, Ming, Lizard Woman & Beastman, Mattel, 3¾", MIB, H4 ....$40.00

Go Bots, figure, Crasher, Flip-top, Heat Seeker, Night Ranger, Scorp, Small Foot, Vamp or Wrong Way, Tonka, MOC, D4, ea $8.00

Happy Days, figure, Fonzie, Mego, 8", MIB, M15 ....$50.00

Happy Days, figure, Potsie, Mego, 8", MOC, J6................$60.00

Happy Days, figure, Ralph, Mego, 8", MOC, J6................$45.00

Happy Days, figure, Richie, Mego, 8", NMOC (unpunched), H4 ....$50.00

Happy Days, playset, Fonzie Garage, Mego, MIB, $75.00.

Hardy Boys, figure, Joe Hardy, Kenner, 12", MIB, C1 ......$65.00

He-Man, accessory, Shuttle Pod, Mattel, EX, D4 ....$5.00

He-Man, figure, Flipshot, Flogg, Hoove, Hydron, Karatti, Optik or Vizar, Mattel, EX, D4, ea..$5.00

Honey West, figure, Honey West, Gilbert, complete w/accessories, 12", NMIB $250.00

Honey West, figure, Honey West, Gilbert, orig blk leotard outfit & boots, 12", EX, H4..$125.00

Hook (Movie), figure, Ace, Air Attack Peter Pan, Rufio, or Swashbuckling Peter Pan, Mattel, MOC, D4, ea $5.00

Hook (Movie), figure, Attack Crocodile, Mattel, MOC, D4 ..$10.00

How the West Was Won, figure, Lone Wolf or Zeb Macahan, Mattel, MIB, H4, ea..$45.00

Indiana Jones, see Adventures of Indiana Jones

Iron Man, figure, any character, Toy Biz, MOC, D4, ea...$10.00

James Bond, accessory, Oddjob karate jacket w/belt, minor stains on back o/w EX, H4...$12.00

James Bond, figure, Gilbert, with photo button, gun, and attache case, 12", NM, $200.00.

James Bond, figure, Goldfinger, Gilbert, 3¾", NMOC, C1 ....$15.00

James Bond, figure, James Bond, Gilbert, tuxedo outfit, complete, 12", spring arm not working o/w EX, H4 ....$130.00

James Bond, figure, Oddjob, Gilbert, 12", M (EX box), A ...$385.00

James Bond, figure, Thunderball, Gilbert, 12", M (NM box), A $235.00

Johnny Apollo, figure, Astronaut, Marx, complete, NM (EX box), F5...$100.00

Johnny West, see Best of the West

Justice League of America, figure set, Wonder Woman & Flash, w/Mouseman & Thunderbolt, Ideal, 3½", EX (EX card) ..$800.00

Karate Kid, figure, Remco, 6", EX, B10 ....$5.00

Land of the Lost, figure, Stink or Tiger, 1992, MOC, B10, ea..$8.00

Last Action Hero, accessory, Evil Eye Roadster, Mattel, MOC, D4...$15.00

Last Action Hero, figure, Axe Swinging Ripper or Dynamite Jack Slater, Mattel, 1st series, MOC, D4, ea $5.00

Last Action Hero, figure, Evil Eye Bandit, Mattel, MOC, D4...$10.00

Last Action Hero, figure, Heat Packing Jack, Hook Launching Dan, Undercover Jack Slater, Mattel, 2nd series, MOC, D4, ea $5.00

Legends of Batman, accessory, Batcycle w/Motorized Hyperspeed, D4...$15.00

Legends of Batman, figure, Attack Wing, Flightpak or Silver Knight, Kenner (Deluxe), MOC, D4, ea $12.00

Legends of Batman, figure, Cyboborg, Future, Knightquest or Knightsend, Kenner, MOC, D4, ea.........................$10.00

Legends of Batman, figure, Nightwing, Power Guardian, Samurai or Viking, Kenner, MOC, D4, ea.........................$10.00

Legends of the Lone Ranger, figure, Butch Cavendish, Gabriel, 3¾", MOC, S18...$20.00

Legends of the Lone Ranger, figure, General George Custer, Gabriel, 3¾", MOC, S18......................................$20.00

Legends of the Lone Ranger, figure, Lone Ranger, Gabriel, 3¾", MOC, S18..$20.00

Legends of the Lone Ranger, figure, Tonto, Gabriel, 3¾", M (NM card), B3 ....$20.00

Lone Ranger Rides Again, accessory, Apache Buffalo Hunt, Gabriel, VG $25.00

Lone Ranger Rides Again, accessory, Blizzard Adventure, Gabriel, NRFB (window cracked), H4.....................$35.00

Lone Ranger Rides Again, accessory, Hidden Silver Mine, Gabriel, NRFB, H4...$40.00

Lone Ranger Rides Again, accessory, Landslide Adventure, Gabriel, NRFB, H4...$35.00

Lone Ranger Rides Again, figure, Butch Cavendish or Little Bear, Gabriel, 9", NRFB, H4, ea...........................$50.00

Lone Ranger Rides Again, figure, Lone Ranger or Tonto, Gabriel, 9", EX, H4, ea $20.00

Lone Ranger Rides Again, horse, Smoke, Gabriel, M (VG box), H4 ....$35.00

Love Boat, figures, Mego, set of 6, MOC, B10 ....$85.00

M*A*S*H, accessory, 4077th Military Base playset, Tri-Star, complete, EX (NM box), C1 ....$130.00

M*A*S*H, figure, Klinger, Tri-Star, 3¾", MOC, M17....$12.00

M*A*S*H, figure, Klinger in Drag, Tri-Star, 3¾", MOC, M17 ....$40.00

Major Matt Mason, accessory, Gamma Ray Guard Gun, Mattel, complete, EX, H4 ....$25.00

Major Matt Mason, accessory, Gamma Ray Guard Pak, Mattel, MIB, D8 ....$95.00

Major Matt Mason, accessory, Space Bubble, Mattel, VG, H4 ....$30.00

Major Matt Mason, accessory, Space Crawler, Mattel, VG, H4 ....$30.00

Major Matt Mason, accessory, Space Power Suit, Mattel, MIB (Mexico) $75.00

Major Matt Mason, accessory, Space Shelter Pak, Mattel, complete, EX, H4 ....$25.00

Major Matt Mason, accessory, Space Shelter Pak, Mattel, MIB, D8...$95.00

Major Matt Mason, accessory, Space Travel Pak, Mattel, MIB, D8...$95.00

Major Matt Mason, accessory, Star Seeker, Mattel, EX (VG box), M17 ....$135.00

Major Matt Mason, accessory, Supernaut Power Limbs, Mattel, EX, H4 ....$25.00

Major Matt Mason, accessory, Supernaut Power Limbs, Mattel, MIB, D8 ....$95.00

Major Matt Mason, accessory, Talking Backpack, Mattel, VG, H4 ....$30.00

Major Matt Mason, figure, Calisto Space Alien, bendable, Mattel, 1968, EX, A $60.00

Major Matt Mason, figure, Doug Davis, Mattel, w/helmet, EX, H4 ....$60.00

Major Matt Mason, figure, Matt Mason, Mattel, bendable, 6", EX, A $40.00

Major Matt Mason, figure, Sgt Storm, Mattel, VG..........$45.00

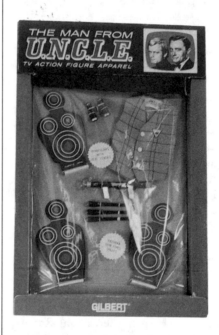

Man From UNCLE, accessory, action figure apparel, Gilbert, 1965, MIP, $65.00.

Man From UNCLE, figure, Illya Kuryakin, Gilbert, 12", VG (G+ box), H4..$90.00

Mario Bros, figure, Boomba, Koopa or Luigi, MOC, ea $18.00

Marvel Super Heroes, figure, Beast, Bishop, Blob, Caliban, Invisible Woman II, Morph or Omega Red, Toy Biz, MOC, D4, ea...$15.00

Marvel Super Heroes, figure, Slime Pore Venom w/Spider, Storm II or Tyler-Apocalypse III, Toy Biz, MOC, D4, ea......$15.00

Marvel Super Heroes, figure, Talking Marvel Venom, Toy Biz, MOC, D4...$10.00

Marvel Super Heroes, figure, Web Shooting Spider-Man, MOC, D4...$20.00

Marvel Super Heroes, figure, Wonder Woman, Mego, 8", MIB, H4...$300.00

Marvel Super Heroes Secret Wars, accessory, Tower of Doom, Mattel, M (EX+ sealed box), D8...............................$36.00

Masters of the Universe, accessory, Blasterhawk, Mattel, MIB, F1 ....$40.00

Masters of the Universe, accessory, Fright Zone playset, Mattel, MIB...$85.00

Masters of the Universe, accessory, Masters Weapon Pak, Mattel, MOC, F1...$5.00

Masters of the Universe, accessory, Road Ripper, Mattel, EX, B10...$18.00

Masters of the Universe, accessory, Spydor, Mattel, MIB, F1 ..$40.00

Masters of the Universe, figure, Buzz Saw Hordak, Mattel, 3¾", MOC, F1...$20.00

Masters of the Universe, figure, King Randor, Mattel, 3¾", MOC, F1 ....$25.00

Masters of the Universe, figure, Ram Man, Mattel, 3¾", MOC, $35.00.

Masters of the Universe, figure, Thunder Punch He-Man, Mattel, 3¾", MOC, F1 ....$20.00

Micronauts, accessory, Rocket Tubes, Mego, MIB, D8 .....$95.00

Micronauts, figure, Giant Acroyear, Mego, MIB, D8 ....$45.00

Mike Hazard, figure, Mike Hazard Double Agent, Marx, missing several accessories, EX (VG box), F5 ....$180.00

Mike Hazard, figure, Mike Hazard Double Agent, Marx, missing few accessories, NM (EX box), F5 ....$300.00

Mini Monsters, case, Remco, EX, J5 ....$15.00

Moonraker, figure, Drax, Mego, 12", NMIB, B3 ....$130.00

Moonraker, figure, Holly, Mego, 12", M (EX box), B3...$135.00

Moonraker, figure, James Bond, Mego, 12", M (NM box), B3 ....$90.00

Mortal Kombat, figure, any character, Hasbro, MOC, D4, ea $8.00

Noble Knights, figure, Sir Gordon the Gold Knight, Marx, complete, NM (EX box), F5...................................$180.00

Noble Knights, figure, Sir Gordon the Gold Knight, Marx, missing 5 of 45 accessories, NM, F5 ....$135.00

Noble Knights, figure, Sir Stuart the Silver Knight, Marx, missing few accessories, G, H4 ....$50.00

Noble Knights, horse, Bravo the Gold-Armoured Horse, Marx, complete, NM/G wheels, F5 ....$70.00

Official Scout High Adventure, accessory, Avalanche at Blizzard Ridge, Kenner, complete, EX, H4 ....$20.00

Official Scout High Adventure, accessory, Balloon Race to Devils Canyon Adventure Set, Kenner, MIB, H4............$25.00

Official Scout High Adventure, accessory, Pathfinder Jeep & Trailer Adventure Set, Kenner, EX (VG box), H4 ...$30.00

Official Scout High Adventure, accessory, Search for the Spanish Galleon, Kenner, complete, EX, H4 ....$20.00

Official Scout High Adventure, figure, Craig Cub Scout, Kenner, NRFB, H4..$30.00

Official Scout High Adventure, figure, Steve Scout, Kenner, NRFB, H4 ....$30.00

Official World's Greatest Super Heroes, accessory, Batcave, Mego, complete, NMIB, C1 ....$235.00

Official World's Greatest Super Heroes, figure, Batman, Mego Bend 'n Flex, 5", MOC (sealed), T2 ....$125.00

Official World's Greatest Super Heroes, figure, Batman, Mego, 12", MIB, D4..$75.00

Official World's Greatest Super Heroes, figure, Batman, Mego, 8", MIB $175.00

Official World's Greatest Super Heroes, figure, Catwoman, Mego, 8", missing gloves o/w M, D8.........................$85.00

Official World's Greatest Super Heroes, figure, Conan, Mego, 8", complete, M, from $150 to $160.00

Official World's Greatest Super Heroes, figure, Green Arrow, 8", no accessories o/w G, D8 ....$25.00

Official World's Greatest Super Heroes, figure, Human Torch, Mego, 8", complete, M, D8............................$30.00

Official World's Greatest Super Heroes, figure, Human Torch, Mego, 8", MOC, D8 ....$50.00

Official World's Greatest Super Heroes, figure, Human Torch, 8", NMIB, D8 ....$150.00

Official World's Greatest Super Heroes, figure, Incredible Hulk, Mego, 8", M (EX box), T2 ....$100.00

Official World's Greatest Super Heroes, figure, Joker, Mego, 8", complete, M, D8 ....$55.00

Official World's Greatest Super Heroes, figure, Mr Mxyzptlk, Mego, 8", MOC (sealed), T2..............................$175.00

Official World's Greatest Super Heroes, figure, Penguin, Mego, 8", MOC (sealed), T2..............................$125.00

Official World's Greatest Super Heroes, figure, Penguin, Mego, 8", EX (EX box) $95.00

Official World's Greatest Super Heroes, figure, Riddler, Fist Fighting; Mego, 8", M, D8..................................$150.00

Official World's Greatest Super Heroes, figure, Riddler, Mego, 8", complete, NM, D8...............................$95.00

Official World's Greatest Super Heroes, figure, Robin, Fist Fighting; Mego, 8", complete, M, D8 ....$125.00

Official World's Greatest Super Heroes, figure, Shazam!, Mego Bend 'n Flex, 5", MOC, T2 ....$150.00

Official World's Greatest Super Heroes, figure, Shazam!, Mego, 8", EX (EX box), D8 ....$120.00

Official World's Greatest Super Heroes, figure, Spider-Man, Mego Bend 'n Flex, 5", M (EX card), A $75.00

Official World's Greatest Super Heroes, figure, Spider-Man, Mego, 8", EX (VG+ box), D8................................$75.00

Official World's Greatest Super Heroes, figure, Spider-Man, Mego, 12", complete, M, D8................................$35.00

Official World's Greatest Super Heroes, figure, Spider-Man, Mego, 12", NRFB...$80.00

Official World's Greatest Super Heroes, figure, Superman, Mego Bend 'n Flex, 5", MOC (sealed), T2 ....$150.00

Official World's Greatest Super Heroes, figure, Superman, Mego, 8", VG (VG box), D8................................$125.00

Official World's Greatest Super-Gals, figure, Supergirl, Mego, 8", MOC (sealed), T2................................$200.00

Official World's Greatest Super-Gals, figure, Wonder Woman, Mego, 8", MOC (sealed), T2................................$200.00

Pee-Wee's Playhouse, figure, Pee-Wee, Matchbox, MOC $25.00
Planet of the Apes, accessory, Village, Mego, M (EX box) ..$75.00

Planet of the Apes, figure, General Ursus, Mego, 8", MOC, $155.00.

Planet of the Apes, figure, General Ursus, Mego, 8", complete, EX $75.00
Planet of the Apes, figure, Peter Burke, Mego, 8", complete, EX $75.00

Planet of the Apes, figure, Soldier Ape, Mego Bend 'n Flex, MOC, $65.00.

Planet of the Apes, figure, Soldier Ape, Mego, 8", rare all brn version w/gloves, EX, H4 ....$70.00
Planet of the Apes, horse, Stallion, Mego, M, J6 ....$85.00
Police Academy, figure, Larvelle Jones or Zed, Kenner, MOC, D8, ea...$12.00
Police Academy, figure, Numbskull, Tackleberry or Zed, Kenner, EX, D4, ea..$4.00
Power Rangers, figure, Billy (Bl Ranger), Bandai, 1st issue, MIB (triangular), H4 ....$15.00

Power Rangers, figure, Kimberly (Pk Ranger) or Trina (Yel Ranger), Bandai, 1st issue, MIB (triangular), H4, ea ...$20.00
Power Rangers, figure, Zach (Blk Ranger) or Jason (Red Ranger), Bandai, 1st issue, MIB (triangular), H4, ea............$12.00
Predator, figure, Cracked Tusk, Clan Leader, Scavage, Spiked Tail or Stalker, MOC, D4, ea...................................$10.00
Predator, figure, Ultimate Predator, Kenner, 12", MIB, D4 ....$30.00
Raiders of the Lost Ark, accessory, Arabian Horse, M, VG, J6...$40.00
Rambo, accessory, Savage Strike Cycle, Coleco, MOC, F1 ..$15.00
Rambo, figure, Rambo, Coleco, 6", MOC, F1 ....$25.00
Rambo, figure, Sgt Havoc, Gripper or Turbo, Coleco, 6", MOC, F1, ea..$20.00
Real Ghostbusters, figure, Ecto-Plasm, Nasty, Terrible Teeth or Terror Tongue, Kenner, MOC, D8, ea......................$18.00
Real Ghostbusters, figure, Stay Puft Man, Kenner, MOC, D8 ....$28.00
Robin Hood, Prince of Thieves, figure, Little John or Azeem, Kenner, MOC, F1, ea $15.00
Robin Hood Prince of Thieves, accessory, Battle Wagon, Kenner, MIP...$15.00
Robin Hood Prince of Thieves, figure, Dark Warrior or Will Scarlett, Kenner, MOC, F1, ea............................$25.00
Robin Hood Prince of Thieves, figure, Friar Tuck, Kenner, rare, MOC, F1 ....$30.00
Robin Hood Prince of Thieves, figure, Robin Hood, Kenner, MOC, B10...$8.00
RoboCop & the Ultra Police, figure, Anne Lewis, Kenner, MOC..$18.00
RoboCop & the Ultra Police, figure, Chainsaw, Dr McNamara, Headhunter or Nitro, Kenner, MOC, ea.................$15.00
Robotech, figure, Max Sterling, Matchbox, MOC, B10...$16.00
Robotech, figure, Rook Bartley, Matchbox, MOC, D8 ....$25.00
Robotech, figure, Roy Fokker, Matchbox, MOC, B10......$15.00
Rookies, accessory, Official Police Car, Fleetwood, 1975, MOC..$85.00
Rookies, figure, Lt Riker, LJN, 8", MOC, B10 ....$50.00

Spider-Man, figure, Super Heroes, Mego, 1979, 8", MOC (French), $65.00.

Six Million Dollar Man, accessory, Mission Control Center, Kenner, missing few pcs o/w EX (VG box), H4.........$60.00

Six Million Dollar Man, accessory, Porta-Communicator, Kenner, NRFB, H4..$30.00

Six Million Dollar Man, figure, Fembot, Kenner, 12", NRFB, H4..$130.00

Space: 1999, figure, Commander Koenig, Mattel, 9", M (EX box), B3 ....$50.00

Space: 1999, figure, Professor Bergman, Mattel, 9", NM (VG box), B3 ....$45.00

Spawn, figure, Badrock, Todd Toys, MOC, D8 ....$12.00

Spawn, figure, Clown, Todd Toys, MOC.........................$12.00

Spawn, figure, Overkill, Todd Toys, MOC, D8 ....$12.00

Starsky & Hutch, figure, Chopper, Mego, 8", M (EX box), B3..$35.00

Starsky and Hutch, figure, Dobey, Mego, 8", MOC, $50.00.

Starsky & Hutch, figure, Huggy Bear, Mego, 8", MOC, D8...$45.00

Starsky & Hutch, figure, Starsky or Hutch, Mego, 8", M (NM card), B3, ea...$30.00

Steve Canyon, accessory, Glider Bomb Truck, Ideal, 17", missing glider, NM, C1..$80.00

Steve Scout, see Official Scout High Adventure

Stony Smith, accessory, Stony the Sky Commando, Marx, missing few accessories, NM (NM box), F5....................$150.00

Stony Smith, figure, Paratrooper, Marx, missing 3 accessories, NM (EX box), F5 ....$175.00

Super Naturals, figure, Burnheart, Eagle Eye, Lionheart, Skull, Snakebite or Thunder Bolt, Tonka, MOC, ea.............$6.00

Super Naturals, figure, Lionwings, Tonka, MOC $15.00

Super Powers, accessory, Darkseid Destroyer, Kenner, MIB, from $35 to $45.00

Super Powers, accessory, Delta Probe 1, Kenner, MIB, from $20 to $30.00

Super Powers, accessory, Hall of Justice, Kenner, MIB.....$90.00

Super Powers, figure, Batman, Kenner, complete, NM.....$35.00

Super Powers, figure, Batman, Kenner, M (NM unpunched card), H4..$55.00

Super Powers, figure, Cyclotron, Kenner, M (EX card), H4..$50.00

Super Powers, figure, Darkseid, Kenner, M (VG card), H4...$14.00

Super Powers, figure, Fire Storm or Mantis, Kenner, complete, NM, ea $25.00

Super Powers, figure, Flash or Kalibak, Kenner, MOC, H4, ea..$10.00

Super Powers, figure, Golden Pharaoh, Kenner, complete, NM, H4 ....$50.00

Super Powers, figure, Green Arrow, Kenner, complete, NM, H4 ....$35.00

Super Powers, figure, Hawkman, complete, NM, H4........$40.00

Super Powers, figure, Mr Freeze, MOC (unpunched), H4 ..$80.00

Super Powers, figure, Penguin or Robin, Kenner, complete, NM, H4, ea...$20.00

Super Powers, figure, Plastic Man, Kenner, MOC, H4...$125.00

Super Powers, figure, Robin, Kenner, MOC (unpunched), H4...$55.00

Super Powers, figure, Steppenwolf, Kenner, complete, NM, H4...$30.00

Super Powers, figure, Superman, Kenner, complete, NM, H4..$20.00

Super Powers, figure, Wonder Woman, Kenner, M (NM card), H4...$30.00

Swamp Thing, accessory, Swamp Trap, Kenner, MIB (sealed), B10..$12.00

Swamp Thing, accessory, Transducer, Kenner, MIB (sealed), B10..$12.00

Swamp Thing, figure, any accept Camouflage Swamp Thing (pnt on arms & chest), MIP, ea..................................$8.00

Swamp Thing, figure, Camouflage Swamp Thing (pnt on arms & chest), Kenner, MIP..$18.00

SWAT, figure, McCabe, 8", MOC, H4...............................$80.00

Tales From the Crypt, figure, Cryptkeeper, Frankenstein, Gargoyle, Mummy, Vampire, Werewolf or Zombie, MOC, B10, ea $8.00

Tarzan, figure set, Young Tarzan with Kala, MOC, $45.00.

Teenage Mutant Ninja Turtles, figure, April O'Neil, Playmates, bl stripe, MOC, D8 ....$15.00

Terminator 2, figure, Blaster T1000, Damage Repair, Power Arm, Secret Weapon or Techno Punch, Kenner, MOC, ea $18.00

Terminator 2, figure, John Conner, Kenner, MOC $25.00

Terminator 2, figure, Terminator, posable, limited video offer w/release of 1st movie, 11", EX, H4 ....$20.00

Thundercats, accessory, Luna-Lasher, LJN, MIB $35.00

Thundercats, accessory, Mutant Skycutter, LJN, MIB......$35.00

Thundercats, figure, Berbil Bert or Berbil Belle, LJN, MOC, ea $45.00

Thundercats, figure, Captain Cracker or Safari Joe, LJN, MOC, ea $35.00

Thundercats, figure, Captain Shiner, Jackalman or Tusca Warrior, LJN, MOC, ea $35.00

Thundercats, figure, Lion-O, LJN, MOC, D8 ....$35.00

Thundercats, figure, Mumm-Ra, LJN, MOC $35.00

Universal Monsters, figure, Creature From the Black Lagoon, Remco, MOC, D8................................$25.00

Universal Monsters, figure, Frankenstein, Dracula or Phantom, Remco, MOC, D8, ea $18.00

Viking Warriors, figure, Brave Erik, Marx, w/accessories, NM (G box), F5 ....$165.00

Viking Warriors, figure set, Erik the Viking & horse, complete, NM (EX mailer), F5 ....$195.00

Waltons, figure, any character, Mego, 8", complete, EX, H4, ea $18.00

Waterworld, figure, Atoll Enforcer, Deacon, Hydro Stinger, Mariner, Mord or Power Bow Mariner, Kenner, MOC, D4, ea $10.00

Welcome Back Kotter, figure, Horshack, Mattel, complete, B10 ....$30.00

Welcome Back Kotter, figure, Mr. Kotter, Mattel, 9", MOC, from $35.00 to $45.00.

Who Framed Roger Rabbit?, figure, Eddie Valiant, LJN, 1988, MOC, B10................................$6.00

Who Framed Roger Rabbit?, figure, Roger Rabbit, LJN, 1988, MOC, B10................................$6.00

Willow, figure, 11 different, Tonka, MOC, D4, ea $5.00

Wizard of Oz, accessory, Munchkinland playset, Mego, complete, VG, H4 ....$150.00

Wizard of Oz, figure, Cowardly Lion, Mego, 8", M, D8 ....$25.00

Wizard of Oz, figure, Flying Monkey, Multiple Toy, 1988, MOC, H4 ....$30.00

Wizard of Oz, figures, Glinda and Wicked Witch, Multi-Toy, 1988, MOC, $18.00 each.

Wizard of Oz, figure, Scarecrow, Mego, 8", MIB, D8 ....$65.00

Wizard of Oz, figure, Scarecrow, Mego, 8", NM, D8.........$25.00

Wizard of Oz, figure, Tin Woodsman, Mego, 8", MIB $35.00

Wizard of Oz, figure, Wicked Witch, Mego, complete, B10...$45.00

Wizard of Oz, figure, Wicked Witch, Mego, 8", rare, MIB, H4 ....$65.00

Wizard of Oz, playset, Wizard of Oz and His Emerald City, Mego, 1974, MIB, $300.00.

World Wrestling Federation, figure, Andre the Giant, Hasbro, MOC (Spanish), F1................................$125.00

World Wrestling Federation, figure, Bret Hitman Hart #2 (Series 5), Hasbro, M..................$18.00

World Wrestling Federation, figure, British Bulldog (Series 3), Hasbro, MOC..................$35.00

World Wrestling Federation, figure, Brutus Beefcake, Hasbro, EX, O1 ....$10.00

World Wrestling Federation, figure, Brutus Beefcake, Hasbro, MOC, F1 ....$30.00

World Wrestling Federation, figure, Classie Freddie Blassie, LJN, EX, O1..................$8.00

World Wrestling Federation, figure, El Matador (Series 4), Hasbro, MOC..................$10.00

World Wrestling Federation, figure, Elizabeth, LJN, MOC ..$50.00

World Wrestling Federation, figure, Hulk Hogan, (Series 1), Hasbro, MOC $45.00

World Wrestling Federation, figure, Iron Sheik, LJN, EX, O1...$8.00

World Wrestling Federation, figure, Jake the Snake Roberts, Hasbro, MOC, F1 ....$20.00

World Wrestling Federation, figure, Jimmy Snuka, Hasbro, MOC, F1..................$30.00

World Wrestling Federation, figure, Mr Perfect, Hasbro, MOC, F1 ....$30.00

World Wrestling Federation, figure, Randy Savage (Series 1), orange, MOC..................$40.00

World Wrestling Federation, figure, Ricky the Dragon, LJN, MOC..................$45.00

World Wrestling Federation, figure, Sgt Slaughter, Hasbro, MOC, F1..................$30.00

World Wrestling Federation, figure, Texas Tornado (Series 2), Hasbro, MOC $25.00

World Wrestling Federation, figure, Tito Santana, EX, O1 ..$15.00

World Wrestling Federation, figure, Typhoon, Hasbro, MOC, F1 ....$30.00

World Wrestling Federation, figure, Ultimate Warrior, Hasbro, MOC, F1 ....$50.00

Zeroid, accessory, Action Set, Ideal, missing 2 rockets, G (VG box), H4..................$90.00

Zeroid, accessory, Robot Zogg Commander Set, Ideal, complete, VG, H4 ....$90.00

Zeroid, figure, Robot From Star Raiders, Ideal, EX, H4 ....$45.00

Activity Sets

Activity sets that were once enjoyed by so many as children — the Silly Putty, the Creepy Crawlers, and those Mr. Potato Heads — are finding their way back to some of those same kids, now grown up, more or less, and especially the earlier editions are carrying pretty respectable price tags when they can be found complete or reasonably so. The first Thingmaker/Creepy Crawler (Mattel, 1964) in excellent but played-with condition will sell for about $65.00 to $75.00. For more information about Tinker Toys see *Collector's Guide to Tinker Toys* by Craig Strange (Collector Books).

      Advisor: Jon Thurmond (T1).

See also Character, TV, and Movie Collectibles; Coloring, Activity, and Paint Books; Disney; Playsets; Western.

Adams' Hocus-Pocus Magic Set, SS Adams, 1962, complete & unused, NM (EX box) $85.00

Adams' Real Magic Set, SS Adams, EX (G box)............$150.00

Aristo Craft Microscope Set, 1950s, complete, MIB, H12..$45.00

Boy's World Thingmaker, Mattel, EX (EX box), T1 ......$150.00

Cartoon Charm Set, KFS, 1954, complete w/21 comic strip characters, unused, M (EX box), A..................$250.00

Colorforms, 1st issue, 1950, rare, complete, NMIB, T2 ....$80.00

Creeple Peeple Thingmaker, Mattel, 1965, complete, MIB, $95.00.

Creeple Peeple Thingmaker, Mattel, 1965, missing few minor pcs o/w EX (EX box), T2..................$80.00

Creeple Peeple Thingmaker Pak, VG, T1..................$45.00

Creepy Crawlers, Mattel, 1964, 1st issue, VG (VG box), from $65 to..................$75.00

Creepy Crawlers II, Mattel, 1978, NMIB..................$45.00

Dunkie Donut Head, NMIB, A..................$100.00

Eeeeks! Thingmaker Play-Pak, Mattel, 1968, unused, NMIB..$85.00

Etch-A-Sketch Magic Screen, Ohio Art, EX (NM box), F5..$20.00

Famous Monsters Creature From the Black Lagoon Plaster Casting Kit, Rapco, complete, M (NM box), H4 ....$110.00

Famous Monsters Frankenstein Plaster Casting Kit, Rapco, complete, M (NM box), H4..................$110.00

Federal Agent Fingerprint Set, Transogram, 1938, MIB, A ..$135.00

Fighting Men Mold Set, Ideal, NMIB, T1 ....$60.00

Formex Universal Monster Casting Set, Emenee, complete w/6 monsters, NMIB, H4 ....$700.00

Fright Factory Thingmaker Pak, Mattel, 1966, EX (EX box) ..$65.00

Fright Factory Thingmaker Pak, Mattel, 1966, VG, T1 ...$50.00

Gilbert Puzzle Tricks, ca 1935, set of 6 w/Ring-a-Peg, Radio Tube Trick, Hungry Pup, etc, EXIB (6 sm boxes in 1 lg), A..................$100.00

Great Foodini Magic Set, Pressman, 1960, complete, rare, NMIB, F8..................$150.00

Hairy Bunch Shaker Maker Set, Ideal, 1970s, complete, EX (worn box), J5..................$25.00

Johnny Toymaker, Topper, 1968, VG (orig box) $60.00

Krazy Ikes, Whitman, 1964, complete, EX (EX canister), T2..$25.00

Little Miss Hasbro Brownie Mix, w/recipe book & pans, MIP, T1 ....$35.00

Little Miss Hasbro Soup Mix, w/recipe book & bowls, MIP, T1 ....$35.00

Make Your Own Funnies, Jaymar, 1930, complete w/10 jtd wood comic characters to assemble, rare, NM (EX box), A $1,100.00

Martian Magic Tricks, Gilbert, 1963, complete, scarce, NM (EX box), T2 ....$300.00

Master Magic Set No 1, Knapp Electric, 1929, complete, NM (EX box), A $100.00

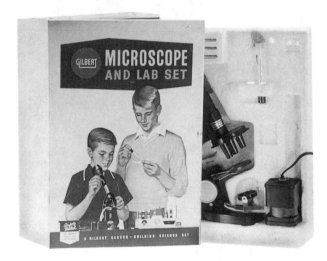

Microscope and Lab Set, Gilbert #13025, electric, MIB, $35.00.

Mini-Dragons Thingmaker Pak, Mattel, 1965, missing some bottles of goop o/w complete & VG $65.00

Motorized Monster Maker, Topper, 1960s, complete, M (EX box), H4 ....$185.00

Motorized Monster Maker, Topper, 1960s, no goop, VG (VG box), $85.00.

Mr & Mrs Potato Head & Pets, Hasbro, MIB $55.00

Mr Magic Magic Set, Adams, 1960, NMIB, J2 ....$55.00

Mr Potato Head & His Tooty Frooty Friends, Hasbro, 1950s, NMIB, J6 ....$65.00

Mr Potato Head Frenchy Fry Set, Hasbro, very rare, few pcs missing, VG (VG box) $50.00

Mr Potato Head Funny-Face Kit, Hasbro, 1950s, complete, NM (VG+ box) $65.00

Mr Tricko Magic Set, Remco, 1965, complete, NM (EX box), F8 ....$95.00

Mysto Magic Exhibition Set, Gilbert, #2½, complete, EX (VG box), A $95.00

Mysto Magic Exhibition Set, Gilbert, 1920s, NM (EX box) ..$450.00

Physique Magic Set, French, 1900, hinged box opens to reveal various tricks & papers describing them, complete, EXIB, A $650.00

Play-Doh Wood-Doh Modeling Compound, Rainbow Crafts, 1959, complete, EX (VG canister), A $30.00

Power Mite Workshop, Ideal, 1969, complete, EX (VG box), $125.00.

Power Mite Workshop, Ideal, 1969, complete, unused, M (EX+ sealed box), A $220.00

Shaker Maker Animals Set #2, Ideal, 1971, missing pnts o/w complete & unused, NM (EX box), F8 ....$30.00

Shrink Machine, Wham-O, rare, MIB, T1 ....$85.00

Shrunken Head Apple Sculpture Kit, Milton Bradley, 1975, complete, M (NM box), M17 ....$70.00

Sneaky Pete's Magic Show, Remco, 1960s, complete, NMIB, F8 ....$145.00

Space Fleet Set, Handi-Craft, complete, scarce, MIB, A ..$275.00

Space Scientist Drafting Set, Hassenfeld Bros, 1955, w/compass, protractor, triangle, etc, complete, EXIB, A $40.00

Spirofoil, Kenner, 1970, missing few pcs o/w NM (EX box), F8 ....$20.00

Spirograph, Kenner, 1968, 1st issue, complete, EX (EX box), T2 ....$25.00

Spud-ettes the Potato Head Pets, Hasbro, 1950s, VG $35.00

Strange Change Toy, Lost World, Mattel, 1967, complete, NMIB $95.00

Tinkersand Pictures, Toy Tinkers, 1936, 12 stylized pictures w/6 colored glues & sand, 8x18", EXIB, A $50.00

Travel Art Coloring Set, Hassenfield, 1950s, complete, unused, EX+ (EX box), A $175.00

Triple Thingmaker, Mattel, w/Picadoos, Fun Flowers, Zoofie Goofies molds & heater, EX (EX box), T1 ....$145.00

Trix Stix, Harry Dearly, 1952, complete, MIP, M17 ....$40.00

Vac-U-Form Casting Set, Mattel, 1960s, MIB, $95.00.

Vac-U-Form Casting Set, Mattel, 1962, orig issue, VG (VG box), F8/T1, from $65 to $75.00
Wiggly Weirdies, Hasbro, 1978, complete, NMIB, T1 .....$50.00
Winky Dinky Paint Set, Pressman, 1950s, complete, EX, A ..$75.00
Young Magician (Easy Conjuring Tricks), ca 1910, may be incomplete, EX (rpr box), A $80.00

Advertising

The assortment of advertising memorabilia geared toward children is vast — plush and cloth dolls, banks, games, puzzles, trucks, radios, watches, and much, much more. And considering the popularity of advertising memorabilia in general, when you add to it the crossover interest from the realm of toys, you have a real winning combination! Just remember to check for condition very carefully; signs of play wear are common. Think twice about investing much money in soiled items, especially cloth or plush dolls. (Stains are often impossible to remove.)

For more information we recommend *Zany Characters of the Ad World* by Mary Jane Lamphier; *Advertising Character Collectibles* by Warren Dotz; *Advertising Dolls Identification & Value Guide* by Joleen Ashman Robinson and Kay Sellers; *Huxford's Collectible Advertising* by Sharon and Bob Huxford; *Cracker Jack Toys* by Larry White; *Pepsi-Cola Collectibles, Vols I, II, and III,* by Bill Vehling and Michael Hunt; and *Collectible Coca-Cola Toy Trucks* by Gael de Courtivron.

Advisors: Jim Rash (R3), advertising dolls; Larry White (W7), Cracker Jack.

See also Bubble Bath Containers; Cereal Boxes and Premiums; Character, TV, and Movie Collectibles; Dakins; Disney; Fast-Food Collectibles; Halloween Costumes; Pin-Back Buttons; Premiums; Radios; Telephones; Western; and other specific categories.

A&P Super Markets, truck, Marx, red & silver pressed steel, 19", NM (EX box), A $400.00
Admiral Appliances, bank, Admiral figure, vinyl, M, P12..$20.00
Allied Van Lines, doll, 1970s, 18", G, M15 ....$30.00
Aunt Jemima Pancakes, see Quaker Oats
Baby Ruth, doll, beanbag body w/vinyl head & hands, EX, H4 ....$30.00

Baskin Robbins, figures, vinyl, set of 3, P12 ....$45.00
Big Boy, bank, Big Boy figure, 1970s, vinyl, slender version, MIP, H4 ....$35.00
Big Boy, bank, Big Boy figure, 1994, vinyl, MIP $15.00
Big Boy, bobbin' head doll, from $1,000 to $1,500.00
Big Boy, doll, Big Boy, 1978, stuffed printed cloth w/Big Boy lettered on chest, 14", MIP $30.00
Big Boy, doll, Dolly, 1978, stuffed printed cloth, hands on hips, dotted dress, 14", M $30.00
Big Boy, doll, Nugget the dog, 1978, stuffed printed cloth, side view in seated position, w/collar, MIP $35.00
Big Boy, game, Big Boy, w/game board...........................$200.00
Big Boy, kite, Big Boy image on paper $250.00
Big Boy, playing cards, Big Boy image, from $25 to $35.00
Big Boy, watch, from $50 to $100.00
Borden, bank, Elsie's head, 1970s, molded vinyl, ring of daisies around her neck, rnd red base, 9", EX $85.00
Borden, board game, Elsie & Her Family, 1941, Selchow & Righter Co, 1941, EXIB, from $50 to $70.00
Borden, doll, Elsie, sits or stands, stuffed body w/rubber head, high button shoes & metal neck bell, 17", EX+, A .$125.00
Borden, doll, Elsie, sitting, brn & yel plush w/vinyl head, yel neck bow w/plastic charm, 16¼", M, P6.................$135.00

Borden, doll, Elsie, stuffed cloth with vinyl head, moos when turned over, original tag, EX, $75.00.

Borden, Elsie's Funbook Cut-Out Toys & Games, 1940s, EX, P6 .$65.00
Borden, hand puppet, one of the twins, 1950s, EX $75.00
Borden, playing cards, image of Elsie, NMIB $20.00
Borden, rattle toy, Beauregard, 1950s, plastic, in diaper sucking on bottle, 5", EX $40.00
Borden, train, paper, in orig pkg, EX..............................$165.00
Breck, doll, Bonnie Breck, Hasbro, 1972, 9", MIB, M15 ..$40.00
Brillo Pads, pillow, 1960s, inflatable, designed like a giant box of Brillo, 23x23", EX, J5..$15.00
Buster Brown Shoes, bank, 1950s, bust image of Buster & Tige atop red molded plastic ball emb Buster Brown Bank, 5", M...$40.00

Buster Brown Shoes, doll, 1974, Buster Brown, stuffed cloth, 14", NM $35.00

Buster Brown Shoes, game, Buster Brown Shoe Game, ring toss, complete, MIB $70.00

Buster Brown Shoes, game, Necktie, variation of Pin the Tail on the Donkey, w/printed cloth ties, EX......................$150.00

Buster Brown Shoes, kite, 1940s, NM $38.00

Buster Brown Shoes, noisemaker, Brown Bilt Shoes..., 1915, litho tin & wood, 4", scarce, M, A $75.00

Buster Brown Stocking Co, paint box, 1902, unused, M, A..$150.00

Campbell's Soups, bank, Campbell's Vegetable Garden, tin w/paper label, Money Saving..., w/orig contents, 4½", EX $25.00

Campbell's Soups, doll, Cambell Girl as cheerleader, 1967, vinyl, 8", EX, from $70 to $75.00

Campbell's Soups, jigsaw puzzle, 1986, All Aboard, 28-pc, VG...$22.00

Campbell's Soups, lunch box, 1968, w/thermos, rare, VG ..$300.00

Campbell's Soups, spoon, yel porcelain w/Campbell's lettered on hdl, kid pictured in bowl, 7", EX $30.00

Campbell's Soups, squeeze toy, Campbell Boy, Oak Rubber, 1950s, MIB...$125.00

Campbell's Soups, storybook, 1954, Rand McNally, kids on cover, 8x6½", VG...$30.00

Campbell's Soups, tea set, 1982, plastic, kids illustrated, 4 cups, plates, tray, dish & utensils, MIB $50.00

Campbell's Soups, vacuum cleaner, Mirro Campbell Kids, Pla-Vac Electric Cleaner, 1950s, aluminum, battery-op, MIB, A $85.00

Campbell's Soups, watch, 1982, featuring Campbell Boy, 50th anniversary, EX $50.00

Campbell's Soups, doll, Campbell Boy, 1973, stuffed cloth, 15½", EX, $35.00.

Cap'n Crunch, doll, Mighty Star, 1987, stuffed cloth, 18", EX, $30.00.

Campbell's Soups, doll, Campbell Boy, 1975, vinyl, 10", EX...$65.00

Campbell's Soups, doll, Campbell Boy & Girl, 1988, special edition, MIB, pr...$100.00

Campbell's Soups, doll, Campbell Boy as chef, vinyl, 8", EX...$50.00

Campbell's Soups, doll, Campbell Boy or Girl, Product People, 1974, 10", EX, ea..................................$30.00

Campbell's Soups, doll, Campbell Girl, 1965, vinyl & rubber, 10", EX...$85.00

Campbell's Soups, doll, 1976, Bicentennial, MIB, from $60 to $70.00

Campbell's Soups, dolls, Campbell Kids, 1970s, rag-type, MIB, pr, from $100 to $125.00

Campbell's Soups, fork, kid's head engraved above M-m-m Good on hdl, EX...$15.00

Campbell's Soups, game, Alphabet Soup, kids illustrated on cb canister, tin lid, contains red plastic letters, EX........$22.00

Campbell's Soups, garden set, 1950s, 5 metal & wood tools on display card featuring kids, NM.....................$50.00

Campbell's Soups, jigsaw puzzle, Jaymar, 1960-70, M'm! M'm! Good, features the Campbell Kids, 100 pcs, EXIB, A4 ..$10.00

Ceresota Flour, doll, printed cloth, name on shirt, early, 17", EX, A $100.00

Ceresota Flour, paint book, Adventures of Ceresota, VG...$25.00

Cheetos, doll, Chester Cheeto, stuffed cloth, 22", VG, M15 ....$15.00

Chevrolet, jigsaw puzzle, 1932, 2-sided image of children running to Chevrolet school bus, rare, EX (G box), A.$350.00

Chicken of the Sea, doll, Mermaid, cloth & satin w/yarn hair, 13", MIP...$30.00

Chicken of the Sea, doll, Mermaid, cloth & satin w/yarn hair, 13", EX, B10...$15.00

Chiffon Margarine, doll, Mother Nature, stuffed cloth w/yarn hair, MIP, H4...$30.00

Chocks Vitamins, doll, Charlie Chocks, 1970-71, stuffed printed cloth, 18", EX, J5.................................$30.00

Chrysler, bank, Mr Fleet, 1970s, vinyl, NM, P12 ....$345.00

Coca-Cola, airplane, 1973-74 Albatros, red & wht w/blk markings, EX+, A $100.00

Coca-Cola, bank, Coca-Cola bear, vinyl, EX, P12 ....$20.00

Coca-Cola, Athletic Games Cutout, 1932, EX, $50.00.

Coca-Cola, bicycle, boy's, red & wht w/wht-wall tires, old store stock, NM, A $425.00

Coca-Cola, cutout, Toy Town, 1927, EX, D10 ....$75.00

Coca-Cola, doll, Buddy Lee, 1950s, composition, in uniform, w/hat, EX+ $875.00

Coca-Cola, game, cribbage, complete, NMIB, A $50.00

Coca-Cola, game, Safety & Danger, 1938, EX+ (EX box), A $100.00

Coca-Cola, game, Steps to Health, 1938, NMIB, M5 ......$60.00

Coca-Cola, game set, Milton Bradley, 1943, 2 decks of cards, cribbage board, checkers, dominos, NM (G+ box), A $450.00

Coca-Cola, truck, Buddy L #5216, 1962, A-frame, yel plastic, holds 8 gr & red plastic cases, NMIB, A $425.00

Coca-Cola, truck, Budgie, 1950s, diecast, orange w/red & wht panel atop divided open bay, orange hubs, 5", EX+, A $120.00

Coca-Cola, truck, Budgie, 1980s, VW, die-cast metal, red cab & bed w/wht bed cover, NMIB, A $70.00

Coca-Cola, truck, Budgie Toys, 1950s, diecast, yel-orange w/red trim, open side bays w/center divider, 1 case, 5", EX, A $120.00

Coca-Cola, truck, H/Japan, bright yel w/litho cases of Coke on both sides, Sign of Good Taste on back panel, 8", VG, A $250.00

Coca-Cola, truck, Linemar, 1950s, friction, yel w/lithoed driver & cases of bottles in side bays, 3", EX+, A $165.00

Coca-Cola, truck, Marx, 1954, pressed steel, yel w/red front wheel covers, 2-tiered bay w/center ad panel, VG, A............$230.00

Coca-Cola, truck, Marx, 1954-56, metal, yel w/red trim, 2-tiered bed w/center ad panel, 6 cases, 12", NM (EX box), A $650.00

Coca-Cola, truck, Marx, 1956, metal, yel w/red Sprite Boy logo on litho stake bed, rubber wheels, 19", NM+ (VG box), A $1,150.00

Coca-Cola, truck, Marx, 1956, plastic, yel, 6 plastic cases w/litho cb inserts, EX+ (EX box), A...................................$475.00

Coca-Cola, truck, Marx/Canadian, 1950-54, Chevy style, red plastic, wood wheels, 6 cases w/bottles, 11", EX+ (G box), A..$1,300.00

Coca-Cola, truck, Matchbox #37, yel, red & wht ad panel atop divided 4-tiered bay, blk tires, NMIB, A $115.00

Coca-Cola, truck, Metalcraft #171, 1932, A-frame, pressed steel, red & yel, rubber wheels, 7 bottles, 11", EX.............$600.00

Coca-Cola, truck, Sanyo, 1960s, yellow and white with red detail and logo, battery-operated, 12", NMIB, $275.00.

Cracker Jack, book, Baby Bears, 1910, EX $80.00
Cracker Jack, book, Cracker Jack Story Book, 1910, EX ..$100.00
Cracker Jack, book, Handy Andy, 1920, EX $75.00
Cracker Jack, charm, 1920, pot metal, various figures, EX, ea ..$8.00
Cracker Jack, charm, 1920, pot metal w/gold japan finish, various instruments, EX, ea..$12.00
Cracker Jack, delivery van, 1930, sheet metal, red & blk, EX $95.00
Cracker Jack, figure, skunk, squirrel, fish, etc, 1950, plastic, EX, ea $7.00
Cracker Jack, fire pumper, 1920, pot metal, EX $25.00
Cracker Jack, game, Monkey Ring Toss, 1940, paper, red & gr, EX..$30.00
Cracker Jack, hat, 1920, Me for Cracker Jack, paper, EX...$125.00
Cracker Jack, horse & wagon, 1920, USM on sides, pot metal w/japan finish, EX...$25.00
Cracker Jack, magnifier, 1960, plastic, various shapes & colors, EX, ea $5.00
Cracker Jack, mask, 1930, paper, 5 different, EX, ea.........$85.00
Cracker Jack, maze puzzles, 1980, plastic & paper, 20 different, EX, ea $8.00

Cracker Jack, first row: metal Man-in-the-Moon plate, $95.00; metal patriotic whistle, $85.00; plastic astronaut, $10.00; second row: Cracker Jack Air Corp stud, $95.00; third row: plastic and paper rising moon palm puzzle, $85.00; metal Mary Lu Quick Delivery truck, $78.00; plastic, invisible magic picture, $9.00.

Cracker Jack, pencil holder, 1940, paper, bl & yel, EX.....$45.00

Cracker Jack, pocket clip, 1970, plastic, monkey, Indian, astronaut, etc, EX, ea $6.00

Cracker Jack, puzzle books, 1910, 3 different, EX, ea......$100.00

Cracker Jack, riddle card, 1900s, paper, CJ box on front, red & bl, EX $25.00

Cracker Jack, ring, 1950, metal & plastic, split back w/colored faux jewel, EX $4.00

Cracker Jack, score counter, 1910, red & bl, EX.............$145.00

Cracker Jack, stand-up, Jack & Bingo, 1900s, sheet metal, bl, red & wht, EX $95.00

Cracker Jack, stencil, 1980, EX....................................$11.00

Cracker Jack, tattoos, 1970, 9 different, ea.........................$4.00

Cracker Jack, trophy, 1960, plastic, gold or silver w/various sayings, EX, ea, from $5 to......................................$15.00

Cracker Jack, water gun, 1900s, metal & rubber, EX........$65.00

Curity, doll, Dydee Bear, plush w/cloth diaper, EX, H4....$12.00

Dow, bank, Scrubbing Bubble, ceramic, EX, B10 ....$15.00

Dow, figure, Scrubbing Bubble, 1989, vinyl, EX, B10.......$15.00

Duracell Batteries, Bunny, plush, battery-op, 14", NM, A..$25.00

Dutch Boy Paint, hand puppet, 1950s, Dutch Boy lettered on front of bl overalls, yel yarn hair, plastic face, EX......$35.00

Entenmann's, bank, chef figure holding tray of donuts, ceramic, M, P6...$75.00

Eskimo Pie, rag doll, Eskimo Pie Man, EX $15.00

Eveready Batteries, flashlight, Energizer Bunny figure, squeezable vinyl, 4", MOC, H4 ....$10.00

Fisk Tires, bank, Fisk tire boy holding tire, ceramic, M, P12....$55.00

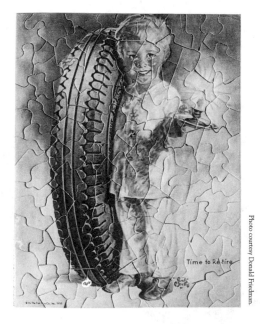

Fisk Tires, jigsaw puzzle, Time To Retire, 1933, 11x9", EX, $65.00.

Florida Orange, bank, bird, 1970s, NM, C17....................$20.00

Fox Woods Casino, figure, Foxy, resin, 6", M, P12 ....$45.00

Fruit Roll-Ups, figure, Rollupo the Wizard, bendable, 6", EX, H4 ....$12.00

Fruit Stripe Gum, doll, Yipes, plush, 15", NM, F8 ....$40.00

Fruit Stripe Gum, figure, Zebra, bendable, scarce, EX, P12...$30.00

Funny Face Drink Mix, see Pillsbury

Gerber, cup, plastic, Gerber Prod Co, plastic w/emb baby & emblem, 3¼", EX..$5.00

Grandma's Cookies, bank, Grandma, vinyl, EX, P12 ....$45.00

Green Giant, figure, Little Niblet, 1970s, vinyl, 6½", EX...$12.00

Green Giant, bank, Little Sprout, composition, plays Valley of the Jolly Green Giant, 8½" $50.00

Green Giant, clock, Little Sprout holding rnd dial in front on rnd base, w/talking alarm, 10½", EX, A $25.00

Green Giant, cookware set, Chein, 1960s, metal, complete, MIB, M17 ....$175.00

Green Giant, doll, Jolly Green Giant, 1966, cloth, 16", M (orig mailer), M17 ....$45.00

Green Giant, doll, Little Sprout, 1970s, plush w/cloth outfit, felt leaf hair, 12", NM, H4 ....$20.00

Green Giant, figure, Little Sprout, 1970s, vinyl, 6½", VG, M15 ....$12.00

Green Giant, jump rope, Little Sprout, MIP, H4.............$30.00

Green Giant, squeeze toy, Green Giant, 1970s, vinyl, w/movable upper torso, NM+ $55.00

GTA Feed Co, bank, Ernie Pig, M, P12........................$195.00

Gulf, Service Station, w/delivery & tow truck, pumps, tires, etc, unused, 15x4", MIB (box converts to station), A....$925.00

Gulf Gasoline & Motor Oils, truck, Cortland, orange & bl litho tin w/blk rubber tires, friction, 12", NM (EX box), A..$285.00

Harley-Davidson, doll, Harley Hog, plush, 6", MIP..........$10.00

Heinz, clock, talking alarm, Mr Aristocrat standing next to logo-shaped clock on rnd base, 10", NMIB, A.................$125.00

Heinz, figure, ant, bendable, 4½", M, H4.........................$10.00

Heinz, truck, Metalcraft, 1930s, wht pressed steel w/decals, 28", EX, A..$325.00

Heinz, truck, Metalcraft, 1930s, wht pressed steel w/decals, battery-op lights, 12", G, A $200.00

Hershey's Mr Goodbar, Candee Babes doll & purse playset, Nasta, 1980, MOC, H4..$10.00

Hess Fuel Oils & Gasoline, truck, Made in Hong Kong, gr, wht, yel & red plastic, blk tires, MIB.................................$65.00

Hood's Sarsaparilla, jigsaw puzzle, 1880s, EX (worn box), from $300.00 to $400.00.

Photo courtesy Donald Friedman.

Photo courtesy Dunbar Gallery.

Howard Johnson's, truck, Marx, 1950s, plastic, 11", scarce, NMIB, from $250.00 to $400.00.

Icee, bank, Icee bear seated w/cup, vinyl, EX, P12 ....$45.00

Jack Frost Sugar Company, doll, Jack Frost, stuffed cloth, 17", EX, $40.00.

Jell-O, hand puppet, Sweet Tooth Sam, 1960s premium, cloth & vinyl, EX, P12 ....$95.00
Jif Peanut Butter, periscope, 1950s, features Jifaroo the kangaroo, yel cb w/red & bl graphics, unpunched, 20", EX, J5 ....$60.00
Jordache Jeans, doll, Jordache cheerleader, Mego, 11½", NRFB, M15 ....$20.00
Keebler, bank, Ernie, ceramic, seated holding barrel, recent, from $15 to $20.00
Keebler, doll, Ernie the Keebler Elf, 1981, stuffed, VG-NM, M15/T1, from $25 to $40.00

Keebler, figure, 1970s, vinyl, 7", M......................$30.00
Kellogg's, book, Funny Jungleland, 1909, EX+, J2 ....$75.00
Kellogg's, drum, Ohio Art, 1983, 9" dia, EX, J2 ....$25.00
Kentucky Fried Chicken, bank, Colonel Sanders, plastic figure w/bucket, arm around restaurant, wht w/red & blk, 6", EX $125.00
Kentucky Fried Chicken, bank, Colonel Sanders, 1970s, plastic figure, no base, wht w/blk necktie, holding bucket, 8", EX $40.00
Kentucky Fried Chicken, finger puppet, Colonel Sanders, wht vinyl figure w/blk trim, EX $10.00
Kentucky Fried Chicken, football, rubber, image of the Colonel, 12", M $15.00
Kentucky Fried Chicken, jigsaw puzzle, We Fix Sunday Dinner 7 Days a Week, bucket of chicken shown, sealed, 9x7", M $25.00
Kentucky Fried Chicken, nodder, Colonel Sanders, 1960s, wht suit w/blk trim, cane & sunglasses, holding bucket, 7", EX $85.00
Kentucky Fried Chicken, tea set, 1970s, plastic, w/Colonel's image, MIB $110.00
Kool-Aid, doll, Kool-Aid Kid, 1989, w/pigtails & freckles, 14", VG, M15 ....$25.00
Kool-Aid, toy soft-drink dispenser, NMIB, J2 ....$30.00
Kraft, playset, Robin Hood, 1950s, 3-D castle & cb punch-out figures, unpunched, M (orig mailer), J5, from $75 to......$100.00
Kraft, pull toy, cameraman on roll-about TV camera, EX+, A $90.00
Kraft Macaroni & Cheese, bank, Cheesasarus, mail-in premium, M, P12...$35.00
Lee Jeans, teddy bear, 1988, 15", VG, M15......................$10.00
Levi's, rag doll, 1978, 16", NRFB, M15 ....$45.00
Lion Coffee, game, Our Union, 48 cards describe a state w/advertising on reverse, 3x2", VG (no box), A $40.00
Little Caesar's Pizza, figure, Pizza Man, stuffed cloth, 6", M, H4 ....$8.00
Magic Chef Ovens, bank, Chef figure, vinyl, M, P12 ....$20.00
Michelin, playing cards, image of 2 Michelin men seated at table, Michelin Tires/Tubes around border, complete, EX $85.00
Michelin, puzzle, plastic take-apart Michelin Man figure, 2", EX, A $150.00
Michelin, squeeze toy, Michelin Man holding baby, rubber, 6½", EX+, A $200.00
Michelin, windup toy, MIB $20.00
Morton Salt, airplane (glider), 1930s, EX, C10 ....$25.00

National Biscuit Company, truck, Gibbs, 13", EX, sign not included, $1,325.00.

Morton Salt, doll, Morton Girl, 10", MIB, M15 ....$50.00

Mountain Dew, doll, Hillbilly Man, vinyl w/cloth outfit, poseable, NM, T1 ....$125.00

Mr Bubble, figure, vinyl, 10", M, P12.....................$35.00

Mr Softee, van, Japan, friction, 2x4", M, P6 ....$45.00

Munsingwear, figure, penguin, 1970, vinyl, EX.............$25.00

National Crime Prevention, figure, McGruff, vinyl, 5", EX, P12 ....$20.00

Nestle, figure, Quik Bunny, bendable, 6", EX, H4 ....$12.00

Nestle, figure, Swiss Man, 1969, vinyl w/cloth clothes, rooted mustache, 13", VG, H4...$50.00

Nestle, rag doll, Little Hans, MIP, C17.....................$20.00

North American Van Lines, doll, Mary Ann, MIB, J2 .....$70.00

Northern Tissue, doll, 1986, 16", VG+ $25.00

Old Dutch Cleanser, pull toy, Hubley, 1932, pnt CI figure of Old Dutch Girl chasing dirt on emb wht base, 9", NM, A...$575.00

Oscar Mayer, bank, Wienermobile, EX, H4...................$20.00

Oscar Mayer, Weinermobile, pedal car, M, P12 ....$245.00

Oscar Mayer, Weinermobile, remote control, MIB, P12 ..$75.00

Pepsi-Cola, dolls, Pete & Pepsi the Pepsi cops, w/music box, NM, T1 ....$125.00

Pepsi-Cola, game, Big League Baseball, 1950s-60s, EX...$100.00

Pepsi-Cola, hot dog wagon, 1950s, wooden cart w/tin umbrella, MIB $150.00

Pepsi-Cola, truck, Nylint, 1950s, 16½", EX....................$400.00

Pepsodent, musical flute, MIB, C10 ....$15.00

Pepto Bismol, figure, 24-Hour Bug, vinyl, 24", M, P12.....$95.00

Peters Weatherbird Shoes, pencil holder, cb, shaped like a lg pencil, 10½", NM, A...$45.00

Pillsbury, bank, cardboard biscuit tube, 1980s, w/images of Poppin' Fresh, 7", NM $15.00

Pillsbury, bank, Poppin' Fresh, 1980s, mail-in offer, M $25.00

Pillsbury, doll, Poppin' Fresh, 1970s, wht stuffed cloth w/bl printed features, 14", VG..................................$15.00

Pillsbury, doll, Poppin' Fresh, 1972, stuffed, 11", EX, I2 ...$20.00

Pillsbury, doll, Poppin' Fresh, 1982, plush, scarce, M, P12..$50.00

Pillsbury, figure, Poppin' Fresh, 1971, vinyl, 7", EX, B10/F8..$15.00

Pillsbury, figures, Pillsbury Grandparents, vinyl, NM, pr, P12 ....$165.00

Pillsbury, finger puppet, Biscuit the Cat, EX....................$35.00

Pillsbury, finger puppet, Flapjack the Dog, EX.................$55.00

Pillsbury, finger puppet, Granmommer, EX $50.00

Pillsbury, finger puppet, Poppie Fresh, vinyl, 3½", EX......$15.00

Pillsbury, gumball machine, Poppin' Fresh, MIB, P12, from $350 to $400.00

Pillsbury, hand puppet, Poppin' Fresh, 1972, image w/name, EX..$2.50

Pillsbury, hand puppets, Poppin' or Poppie Fresh, 1974, pop out of refrigerator can, vinyl & cloth, EX, ea $10.00

Pillsbury, kite, Goofy Grape Funny Face, 1970s, MIP, P12..$45.00

Pillsbury, Poppin' Fresh Playhouse, w/4 finger puppets, missing top floor o/w G+, T1 ....$185.00

Pillsbury, record, Goofy Grape Sings, 1969, rare, M, P12.$65.00

Planters, bank, Mr Peanut, commemorative version, M, P12...$35.00

Planters, book, Fun Days With Mr Peanut, 1960s, image of children on carousel & Mr Peanut, EX $30.00

Planters, charm bracelet, 1941, 6 mc plastic figures on brass-colored chain, VG, P4 ....$45.00

Planters, charm bracelet, 1970s, Mr Peanut figure on rnd gold-tone charm w/chain-link bracelet, M........................$18.00

Planters, dart board, 1980s, wood case w/Planters lettered in yel above Mr Peanut on hinged doors opening to game, EX.............$20.00

Planters, doll, Mr Peanut, stuffed plush, salesman's sample, 26", MIP, H4..$25.00

Planters, playing cards, 1980s, Mr Peanut on wht w/bl border, complete, EX $8.00

Planters, pop gun, paper, 1930s-40s, 9", rare, G, A.........$200.00

Planters, truck, 1950s-60s, red cab w/image of Mr Peanut & Planters Peanuts lettered on wht trailer sides, 5½", NM................$90.00

Poll-Parrot Shoes, bank, golden shoe, NM, J2 ....$20.00

Poll-Parrot Shoes, clicker, litho tin, 2", NM, A................$15.00

Popsicle, Mystery Musical Truck, Mattel, red & pk plastic w/decal, press roof for music, 11", EX (EX box), A..$235.00

Quaker Oats, doll set, Aunt Jemima, Uncle Mose, Wade & Diana, stuffed printed cloth, M, ea, from $100 to....$150.00

Quaker Oats, pancake-making kit for children, 1986, featuring Aunt Jemima, complete w/instructions, EXIB $60.00

Quaker Oats, pin-back button, Aunt Jemima Pancake Club, Pancake Days Are Here Again, image of drummer, blk & red, 3", M $45.00

Raid, doll, Raid Bug, plush, rare, M, P12 ....$75.00

Photo courtesy June Moon.

Pillsbury, Funny Face mugs, set of 4, M, original mailer, J6, $85.00.

Photo courtesy Jon Thurmond.

Raid Bug, battery-operated, missing controller, otherwise EX, rare, $225.00.

Raid, remote control Raid Bug, 1 of 3,000, 14", EX, H4 ...**$400.00**

Raid, w/up Raid Bug, 5", missing antenna & key o/w VG, H4 ....**$40.00**

RCA Radiotron, figure, jtd wood & compo, orig label on foot, 17", rare, EX, H12 ....**$950.00**

Red Goose Shoes, bank, Arcade, 1910, red-pnt CI goose, 3¾", VG, A **$275.00**

Red Goose Shoes, bank, 1960s, plastic figure, 5", M **$145.00**

Red Goose Shoes, ring, glow-in-the-dark w/secret compartment, NM, C10 ....**$195.00**

Red Goose Shoes, whistle, tin, rnd, 1¼" dia, NM **$20.00**

Red Goose Shoes, whistle, wood w/paper label, cylindrical, Blow To Beat the Band, 3½", EX **$15.00**

Reddy Kilowatt, comic book, Wizard of Light, Story of Thomas Edison, 1965, Reddy illustrations **$25.00**

Reddy Kilowatt, figure, 1960s, glow-in-the-dark, lg head version, MOC (orig mail-order box), H4 ....**$200.00**

Reddy Kilowatt, nodder, 1960s, papier-mache cowboy figure w/name on sq base, 6½", M...............................**$260.00**

Reddy Kilowatt, playing cards, dbl deck, M **$40.00**

Reddy Kilowatt, suction-cup doll, Steven Smith, 1980s, vinyl head w/plush body, EX...**$35.00**

Rexall Drug Stores, puzzle, 1930s, Mountain Splendor, jigsaw, some pcs missing, VG (orig box), A4 ....**$5.00**

Richfield, gas service island, wood, bl base w/2 yel & bl gas pumps, bl & wht sgn post w/tool box, 9", EX+, A ...**$440.00**

Salamander Shoes, figures, salamander, elf, mouse or porcupine, soft vinyl, 5", H4, ea **$10.00**

Salamander Shoes, figures, salamander, frog, lizard, mouse, elf & porcupine, vinyl, set of 6, 11", rare, H4 ....**$300.00**

Sambo's, Family Funbook, Fun Games & Puzzles Featuring JT & Tiger Kids, 1978, EX, P6 ....**$50.00**

Seven-Up, truck, 1950s, tin w/clear plastic dome over cab, driver moves back & forth, lithoed ads & cases, 9", EX, A **$335.00**

Shell Oil, game, Stop & Go, 1936, unpunched, NM, J2 ..**$30.00**

Shoney's, bank, Shoney bear, vinyl, M, P12 ....**$20.00**

Snuggle Fabric Softener, bear, Snuggles, Lever Bros, 1986, glassine eyes, ear button & wrist tag, 16", M, H12 ....**$35.00**

Sprite, doll, Lucky Lymon, 1990, vinyl, talker, 7½", M, T1 ..**$20.00**

Sprite, doll, Smilin' Sprite, vinyl, talker, NMIB, T1 ....**$45.00**

Standard Oil, gas pump, American Super Premium, modern-type w/silver body, bl, gr & wht trim, 30", EX, A **$130.00**

Star Brand Shoes, racer, ca 1917, red litho tin w/simulated spoke wheels, bl trim & lettering, w/driver, 8½", EX, A ..**$1,155.00**

Star-Kist, doll, Charlie Tuna, plush, 15", MIP, H4............**$15.00**

Star-Kist, doll, Charlie Tuna, 1980, inflatable, 36", EX, H4 ....**$20.00**

Star-Kist, squeeze toy, Charlie Tuna, 1973, vinyl figure, 7½", M, from $35 to...**$40.00**

Star-Kist, wristwatch, 1977, featuring Charlie Tuna, EX .**$75.00**

Stripe Toothpaste, Rocket Balloon, MOC, C10...............**$15.00**

Sunbeam Bread, flicker ring, Little Miss Sunbeam, EX, C10...**$20.00**

Sunshine Biscuits, truck, Metalcraft, red cab & chassis w/bl stake body, 12", NM, A **$650.00**

Tango Orange Drink, figure, Tango Voodoo Doll, vinyl, MIB, P12 ....**$45.00**

Tastee Freeze, doll, Miss Tastee Freeze, plastic w/cloth clothes, name on sash, 8", G, H4 ....**$20.00**

Tastee Freeze, puppet, Little T, 1960s-70s, M, $15.00.

Photo courtesy Jon Thurmond.

Photo courtesy Dunbar Gallery.

Texaco, Fire Chief hat, Brown and Bigelow, 1950s, hard plastic, battery-operated microphone and amplifier, unused, MIB, from $200.00 to $300.00.

Texaco, truck, Fire Chief water truck, late model, 25", EXIB, A **$300.00**

Tip-Top Bread, puzzle, Tip-Top Town USA, Japan, 2x4", M, P6 ....**$45.00**

Tony's Pizza, figure, Mr Tony, vinyl, 8", minor pnt wear o/w EX, H4 ....**$35.00**

Tupperware, doll, 1988, stuffs into satin Tupperware bowl, 13", M, M15 ....**$25.00**

Wheat Puffs, puppet cereal container, Kanga & Roo, Nabisco, 1966, vinyl figure, 10", EX, P6........................**$60.00**

Wrangler, doll, Cody, Ertl, 1982, 11½", MIB, M15..........**$55.00**

Wrangler, doll, Missy, Ertl, 1982, 11½", MIB, M15 ....**$45.00**

Wrangler, doll, The Wrangler, Ertl, 11½", NRFB, J6.......**$65.00**

Wrangler, figures, Missy or Cody, Ertl, 1982, 4", MOC, M15, ea..**$6.00**

Zeller's, bank, Zeddy Bear, M, P12 ....**$45.00**

Advertising Signs, Ads, and Displays

A common advertising ploy used as far back as the late 1900s and still effective today is to catch the eye of the potential consumer with illustrations of well-known celebrities or popular fictional characters. Nowadays, with the intense passion character-collectibles buffs pour into their hobby, searching for these advertising items is a natural extension of their enthusiasm, adding even more diversity to an already multi-faceted collecting field.

Action Adventure Comics in the Standard 10¢, sign, Canadian, 1940, features Superman, Tarzan, etc, fr, 44x28", A ...**$1,255.00**
American Skyline Construction Set, display sign, 24", EX, J2 ..**$125.00**
Batman Coloring Book & Holloway Candy, poster, 1966, coloring book w/6-pack of Holloway candy (Milk Duds, etc), NM...**$85.00**
Batmobile, display, 1966, advertises Aurora Batmobile model kit as a premium for Burry's Cookies, 45x30", VG, J5 ..**$900.00**
Beatles Big Beat Guitar, display, English, 1964, diecut cb stand-up, name & signatures surround image, 16x11", EX+, A **$2,120.00**
Buck Rogers Space Ranger Kit, ad, EX, J2 ....**$20.00**
Character Watches, display, Rouan, 1969, spinning Archie & Jughead, Tinkerbell, Peter Pan, Woody Woodpecker, NM, J5...**$565.00**
Charlie McCarthy Valentine Pops, display, Rosen/McCarthy, 1938, cb, Charlie in heart on top pc, 9x6" unfolded, EX, A ..**$185.00**
Donnie & Marie Osmond String Puppets, display, 1978, 2 puppets dance on electrified stage-type box, 25", NM, A **$180.00**
Fisher-Price, pamphlet, 1940s, folds out to advertise 17 different toys including Popeye Spinach Eater, 23", EX.........**$100.00**
Green Hornet (The Official) Bike Badge, display, Burry's, 1966, 3-D Vac-u-form display, 30x45", EX, from $3,000 to........**$4,000.00**
Honey West, display, TV's Private Eyeful, 'Action Accessories That Really Work' surround doll in box, 24x20x3", EX+, A **$1,135.00**

Keystone Steam Shovels and Trucks, original ad artwork, ca 1925, mixed media on board, framed, 20x13¾", G, A, $5,465.00.

Howdy Doody Promotes Colgate Dental Cream, 1950s, Hey Kids!, Get These 2 Big Offers (Photo Printer & Disguise Kit), M, A...**$730.00**
Jazzbo Jim, display, Unique Art, 1925, lg electrified version of orig w/satin-like outfit & cap on tin cabin, 34", EX, A ..**$7,000.00**
Klik-Klak Blox, display, Pico Novelty, 1950, litho tin box w/phrases & images of kids playing w/Blox, 19x7x5", EX, A **$80.00**
Lone Ranger & Lassie at Madison Square Garden Rodeo, 4-pg fold-out poster, 1950s, 8x14", EX, J5.........................**$95.00**
Lone Ranger Badges, display, Lone Ranger Inc, 1950s, cb card w/12 metal pin-back star badges, 11x10", EX, A **$400.00**
Mickey Mouse, display, Merchants Display & Novelty, early, pnt & glittered papier-mache Mickey in rocket, 23", NM, A **$1,600.00**

Mickey Mouse Flashlight, display, cardboard, 17", EX, A, $650.00.

Roy Rogers Dream of Santa Toys, 4-pg ad, 1950s, EX, J2 ..**$35.00**
Roy Rogers Exclusive RCA Victor Recording Artist, sign, 1948, displayed in music stores, portrait w/guitar, 24", EX, A..**$725.00**
Roy Rogers Straight Shooter Gun Puzzle Key Chain, display, 1950s, w/signature design, G, from $200 to **$300.00**
Slinky, display, ca 1956, cb mechanical, ...More Fun Than a Circus..., bust image of boy holding a Slinky, 17", EX, A...**$750.00**
Snow White & the Seven Dwarfs Welcome You to Toytown, flyer, WDE, 1938, 7-pg newsprint, Misc 5 & 10¢ Store..., M, P6 ....**$40.00**
Space: 1999 & Dinky Toys, poster, 1970s, New From Space: 1999 & Dinky Toys — Eagle..., 10x18", NM.............**$75.00**
Sturditoy, newspaper ad, Evening Bulletin, Dec 14, 1928, shows 14 trucks & steam shovel, fr, 27x19", EX, A **$430.00**
Super Heroes Comics/General Mills Cereals, display, 1979, 1 comic given away w/2 boxes of cereal, VG (6 NM comics) ...**$150.00**

Super Heroes Planters, display box, Hampshire, 1976, holds 12 ceramic planters featuring the Super Heroes, M, J5...$100.00

Tinker Toy, display, ca 1940, rotating Tinker Toy paddle wheel model on board, 19x19", EX, A, $450.00.

Woody Woodpecker Animated Clocks, display, ca 1959, diecut cb w/Woody on tree limb & on animated horse, 21", EX, A $600.00

Aeronautical

Toy manufacturers seemed to take the cautious approach toward testing the waters with aeronautical toys, and it was well into the second decade of the 20th century before some of the European toy makers took the initiative. The earlier models were bulky and basically inert, but by the '50s, Japanese manufacturers were turning out battery-operated replicas with wonderful details that advanced with whirring motors and flashing lights.

See also Battery Operated; Cast Iron, Airplanes; Model Kits; Windups, Friction, and Other Mechanicals.

Air France, marked Croix du Sud across bottom, windup with battery-operated lights, cream and red lithographed tin, 21" wingspan, EX, A, $1,155.00.

Attack Bomber, Hubley #326, 2-prop, red plastic, retractable landing gear, 8" W, NM (EX box), A $165.00

Biplane, M&K/Germany, w/up, pnt tin, early wht model w/bl stripes, solo pilot seated on bottom wing, 8½" L, VG, A $1,485.00

Biplane, Mecavion/France, single-prop, red & silver tin completely riveted w/screws, 2 disk wheels, 16" W, VG, A............$275.00

Boeing Strato Cruiser, Wyandotte, pnt pressed steel, 13" W, VG+, A..$250.00

Boeing YB-52 Strato Fortress, Linemar, friction, 4-prop, mk USAF on wing, red, wht & bl tin, 13" L, NM (VG+ box), A..$345.00

Bomber, Marx, w/up, 2-prop, litho tin w/gr & brn camo design, sm protruding cockpit, graphics show gunners, 18" W, NM, A $175.00

Photo courtesy Bob and Jacquie Henry.

Bristol Bulldog Airplane, marked NF-125 on wings, Straco, battery-operated, blue with red and yellow detail, NMIB, $275.00.

China Clipper, pnt pressed steel, 13" W, rpt, VG, A........$60.00
Concorde Jet, battery-op, plastic, 20", NMIB, J2 ....$65.00

Cragstan Patrol Plane, marked Police Patrol on wings, remote control with automatic steering and blinking lights, 15½" long, NMIB, A, $175.00.

Elektro Radiant 5600, Schuco, marked Clipper Nurnberg, battery-operated, lithographed tin with plastic props and dome, 19" wingspan, NM (NM box), A, $750.00.

Fanny Passenger Airliner, France, w/up, battery-op lights, 4-prop, red & silver tin, cut-out windows, 20" W, EX+, A $525.00

Fokker, ET Co/Japan, w/up, litho tin w/chrome prop, metal wheels, 17½" W, EX+, A....................................$8,800.00

G-A MTY, Mettoy, w/up, single-prop, red & silver tin w/top wing, 16½" W, EX, A..$300.00

German Fighter Plane, Haji, friction, single prop, German cross on wings and fuselage, tin, 11" wingspan, M (EX box), A, $200.00.

GRAF Zeppelin DLZ 127, Tipp, silver & bl tin, battery-op gondola light, 17", EX, A $825.00

GRAF Zepplin, Steelcraft, 1930, 25½" L, G, A $225.00

Highway Patrol Helicopter, TN, tin, 16", EX, J2............$100.00

Ikarus #653, Lehmann, 1915, w/up, single-prop, tin, red & yel w/orig paper wings, 11", VG, A $3,500.00

JD Air Me-Donech, Spain (Isla ?), 1930s, w/up, single-prop, litho cb & tin, 10", EX, A $225.00

Jet Air Liner, Mettoy, w/up w/sparking action, litho tin w/2 plastic engines, 20" W, EX+ (EX box), A $1,000.00

Jet w/Ejecting Pilot, TN, friction, unused, 11", MIB, J2 ..$250.00

Lockheed Sirius, pressed steel, single-prop, open cockpit, covered wheels, VG $1,600.00

Lufthansa Radiant 5600 Passenger Plane, Schuco, 1955, battery-op, 4-prop, tin, see-through cockpit w/crew, 17", EX, A ...$700.00

Mammoth Zeppelin, Marx, litho tin, pull toy w/ratchet-type noisemaker, 27", G, A $475.00

Mono Coupe, Buddy L, 10", NM.................................$800.00

Monoplane, Girard, 1922, w/up, high-wing, metal, yel w/red wings, bl wheels, 9", EX, A.......................................$180.00

Monoplane, Wyandotte, low-wing, pressed steel, blk w/red wings & yel wooden wheels, 10" W, EX, A $225.00

Northwest Airlines, Japan, friction, 4-prop, red & silver tin, 11" W, EX, A...$200.00

NX-843 Boston Flyer, Marks Bros, 1930, orange silk over balsa & metal fr, celluloid wheels, w/instructions, 34", EXIB, A $230.00

Pan American Constellation, pressed steel, 28" W, G, A..$225.00

Pan American Jet Clipper America, TN, battery-op, litho tin, stop-&-go action, 20", EX (EX box), A $350.00

Pan American Strato Clipper, Japan, friction, 4-prop, red, wht & bl litho tin, 11" W, NM (EX box), A $250.00

Pan American Vertol Helicopter, battery-op, MIB, L4 ..$165.00

Pan American World Airways, 4-prop, silver tin w/wooden wheels & plastic props, 21" L, EX, A $225.00

Pan American World Airways, battery-operated, cream, blue, and gray lithographed tin, 20" wingspan, EX, A, $400.00.

Pan American 747 Boeing Jet, display model, resin, orig wood display stand, 26" L, EX, A....................................$250.00

Piasecki YH-16 Helicopter, battery-op, MIB, L4...........$175.00

Sky Taxi Cessna, TT, friction, single prop, tin, 10" wingspan, NMIB, from $150.00 to $175.00.

Spirit of Liberty Seaplane, Liberty Playthings, ca 1929, pnt wood, 22" W, G, A $85.00

Starfire FA-985, friction, red, white, and blue lithographed tin, 8½" long, NM (worn box), A, $100.00.

Top-Wing, Germany, w/up, 3-prop, red & silver tin, 20" W, VG, A $425.00

Top-Wing, Keystone, mustard-colored body w/orange wing, flaps & passenger door, 25", VG, A..................................$600.00

TWA Passenger Plane, w/up, gold tin w/emb lettering on wings, rubber tires, 6¾" W, VG, A......................................$135.00

US Air Force Boeing 707, Japan, friction, 4-prop, litho tin w/Disney characters on wings, 5½" L, EX, A $175.00

US Army Flying Fortress, Marx, 1930s, w/up, red, bl & silver tin w/celluloid props, guns spark, 19" W, NM, A..........$455.00

US Mail Plane, Marx, 1930, windup, red and yellow lithographed tin with balloon tires, 19" wingspan, EX, A, $285.00.

US Mail Plane #NX-131, Steelcraft, 3-prop, pressed steel, yel body w/red wings, 23", VG, A..................................$850.00

US Mail Plane #NZ-107, Steelcraft, bl body w/yel wings & tail, 21½", G, A $400.00

US Navy Fighter Jet, TN, friction w/battery-op lights, 8" L, NM (EX box), A $175.00

US Navy Shooting Fighter Jet #20, Japan, battery-op w/automatic launching lever, litho tin, 13½" L, EX, A $125.00

US Passenger Plane, 4-prop, wht w/red wings & trim, cut-out passenger portholes, 27" W, NM, A........................$400.00

USAF F-8A Fighter Jet, Japan, friction, w/lithoed pilot, 12x14", EX (VG box), A $165.00

USAF PF-256, Yone, friction, single-prop, litho tin w/plastic prop, 7" W, MIB, A $65.00

USAF Plane, TN, battery-op, bump-&-go action w/lights, litho tin, 11", NM (EX box), A $285.00

USAF Sky-Guard Jet, Showa, battery-op, litho tin, 12" L, NM, A $500.00

Westland G-AMHK Helicopter, battery-op, EX, L4......$200.00

Automobiles and Other Vehicle Replicas

Listed here are the model vehicles (most of which were made in Japan during the 1950s and '60s) that were designed to realistically represent the muscle cars, station wagons, convertibles, budget models, and luxury cars that were actually being shown concurrently on showroom floors and dealers' lots all over the country. Most were made of tin, many were friction powered, some were battery operated. In our descriptions, all are tin unless noted otherwise.

When at all possible, we've listed the toys by the names assigned to them by the manufacturer, just as they appear on the original boxes. Because of this, you'll find some of the same models listed by slightly different names. All vehicles are painted or painted and lithographed tin unless noted.

For more information we recommend *The Golden Age of Automotive Toys, 1925-1941*, by Ken Hutchison and Greg Johnson (Collector Books).

Advisors: Nancy and Jim Schaut (S15).

See also Promotional Cars; specific manufacturers.

BMW Convertible, Schuco #2002/Germany, w/up, wht, 5½", EX, A $65.00

Buick, KO, friction, blue with chrome trim, 10½", EX (EX box), $250.00.

Buick Sedan, Japan, friction, bl w/chrome hood ornament & detail, advances w/sound, 11", VG...........................$150.00

Cadillac, 1954, Alps, friction, dk gr w/chrome detail, red interior, 11½", scarce, NM, A.........................$1,400.00

Cadillac, 1967, Ichiko, friction, red w/chrome & red hubs, w/driver, 28", G+..............................$500.00

Cadillac (Big Shot), TN, battery-op, 9½", G (G box), A...$200.00

Cadillac Convertible, 1959, Bandai, friction, red w/chrome detail, 11", NM (VG box), A..........................$475.00

Cadillac Convertible Model #350EA, 1954, Gama/Germany, battery-op, yel w/blk top, chrome detail, wht-walls, 12", MIB, A $3,300.00

Cadillac Convertible Series 62, 1952-53, Alps, friction, bl-gray w/red interior, wht-walls, 11½", MIB.................$1,500.00

Cadillac Sedan, Marusan, blk w/bl & yel interior, 12", EX, A...$550.00

Cadillac Sedan, 1950, Marusan, battery-operated, cream with dark green top, chrome trim, 11", MIB, $2,500.00.

Cadillac Sedan, 1950, Marusan, battery-op, cream w/orange rear fenders & top, chrome trim, wht-walls, 11¼", NMIB..$1,800.00

Cadillac Sedan, 1950s, Marusan, friction, gray, 12", EX..$500.00

Cadillac Sedan, 1950s, Marusan, off-wht w/NP trim, wht-wall tires, 12½", M (worn box), A $1,000.00

Cadillac Sedan, 1950s, TN, battery-op, brn w/chrome detail & hood ornament, litho interior, 8", NM, A...............$160.00

Cadillac Sedan, 1950s(?), TN, friction, cream w/yel top, chrome detail, unused, 13¼", M, A $300.00

Cadillac Sedan, 1959, Bandai, friction, blk w/chrome detail, litho interior, plastic taillights, 11", EX, A $300.00

Cadillac Sedan, 1959, Bandai, friction, lt bl w/chrome trim, 11", EX+ (G+ box), A $430.00

Cadillac Sedan, 1962, Bandai, friction, tan w/chrome detail, 8", M (EX box)..$350.00

Cadillac Sedan, 1963, Bandai, friction, red w/chrome detail, litho interior, 8", NM (EX box) $350.00

Cadillac Sedan, 1963, Bandai, friction, red w/chrome detail, 8", EX+, A...$115.00

Chevrolet, 1956, Bandai, friction, cream w/chrome detail, 9½", EX (EX box), A $425.00

Chevrolet Corvair Compact Convertible, Y, friction, cream w/red interior, trunk opens to show motor, 9", NM (EX box), A...$400.00

Chevrolet, 1954, Marusan, battery-operated, red with yellow top, chrome trim, 11", MIB, $2,000.00.

Chevrolet Corvette, 1965, Bandai, friction, cream, 8", EX ..$150.00

Chevrolet Corvette Stingray, 1964, Bandai, friction, bl w/chrome detail, litho interior, fancy hubs, 8", EX, A $150.00

Chevrolet 2-Door, 1954, Linemar, friction, gray w/blk top, chrome detail, wht-walls, 11½", MIB, A..............$3,200.00

Chevrolet 2-Door, 1954, Linemar, friction, lt gray w/blk top, wht-walls w/red & chrome hubs, 11½", M, A $880.00

Chrysler Airflow X, KT, w/up, red w/chrome detail, advances w/non-fall action, 5", EX+ (VG box), A $400.00

Chrysler Imperial, 1962, ATC, red with chrome trim and gold detail, 16", MIB, $7,500.00. (This is the only red version known to exist.)

Chrysler Imperial Hardtop Sedan, Cragstan, friction, red w/blk top, chrome detail, rear spare, 8", NM (NM box), A $200.00

Chrysler Imperial Sedan, 1961, Bandai, friction, red w/blk top, chrome detail, plastic taillights, 8", NM (NM box), A ..$275.00

Citroen Car, Bandai, friction, gr & cream, 8½", VG, A .$125.00

Citroen DS 19, Bandai #740, friction, bl w/chrome detail, litho interior, 8", EX (EX box), A....................................$300.00

Continental III, Sanyo, friction, gr w/wht top, chrome detail, plastic windshield, 9", EX+ (EX box), A $200.00

Dodge Sedan, 1959, TN, friction, red w/wht top, chrome detail, litho interior, fancy hubs, mk D on fins, 9", EX, A..$325.00

Ferrari GT 250 Convertible, Japan, friction, wht w/chrome detail, litho interior, 9¾", rare, EX, A $750.00

Datsun Fair Lady Z, Ichiko, friction, bright yellow with chrome trim, 18", NM (EX box), $250.00.

Fire Bird Racer, 1960s, TN, battery-op, litho tin & plastic, 14", VG (G box), A $175.00
Ford Ambulance, Bandai, wht w/lg red cross on top, 2 red lights on front fenders, chrome detail, 11¾", EX, A $225.00
Ford Convertible, 1956, Haji, friction, cream over red w/chrome detail, wht-walls, 11½", M, A..............................$1,375.00

Ford Convertible, 1956, Irco, yellow and red with chrome trim, 7", VG, A, $275.00.

Ford Custom Ranch Wagon, 1955, Bandai, friction, red with black top, chrome trim, 11½", MIB, $375.00.

Ford Crown Victoria, 1956, Yonezawa, friction, wht over red w/deep bl roof, chrome trim, wht-walls, 12", MIB..$1,500.00
Ford Fairlane 500 Sunliner, 1957, Bandai, friction, red w/chrome detail, movable bucket seats, 12", NM (EX box), A ...$1,700.00
Ford Falcon Sedan, 1960, Bandai, friction, red w/blk top, litho interior, 8", NM (EX box), A...................................$110.00
Ford Hardtop, 1956, Marusan, battery-op, wht over red w/red top, chrome detail, wht-walls, 13", MIB, A..........$2,200.00
Ford Mustang Coupe, 1965, Bandai, friction, metallic bl w/blk top, chrome detail, litho interior, 8", NM, A $200.00
Ford Rancher, Bandai, friction, lt bl w/dk bl top, Ford Lasts Longer elephant decals on doors, chrome trim, 12", EX, A....$350.00

Ford Fairlane, 1956, SAN, friction, scarce chrome version, 13", EX (G box), $750.00.

Ford Sedan, 1957, Schuco #1045, w/up, red & cream, 4½", EX+, A $135.00
Ford Station Wagon, 1960, Japan, friction, deep yel over blk w/Standard Fresh Coffee advertising, 11½", MIB, A..............$2,420.00
Ford Thunderbird, 1955, TN, friction, red w/see-through tinted gr roof, 8", M (EX box mk Sports Car) $375.00
Ford Thunderbird Retractable Hardtop, 1962 or 1963, Yonezawa, battery-op, 11", M, L4 ....$250.00
Ford Thunderbird w/Sunroof, 1960, Bandai, friction, red w/blk top, litho interior, fancy hubs, 8", NM, A $115.00
Ford 2-Door Hardtop, 1957, Ichiko, friction, bl & wht w/chrome detail, 9½", VG+, A...$300.00
Isetta, Bandai, friction, wht over red w/opening door in front, blk tires w/chrome wheels, 6¾", EX (EX+ box), A..........$400.00
Jaguar, 1960s, TT, friction, red E-type w/chrome detail, 11", M (VG box), A $300.00
Lincoln Mark III w/Shasta Trailer, 1958, Bandai, friction, gr & wht, 22", M, A...$650.00
Lotus Elan, Bandai, friction, bl w/blk top, chrome detail, fancy hubs, 8", NM (EX box), A $165.00
Mercedes Benz Racer #8, Marusan, friction, red w/wht number on hood, w/driver, 10", EX, A $225.00
Mercedes Coupe, 1960s, TN, battery-op, cream w/maroon roof, 15½", VG+, A...$175.00
Mercedes 190 SL Coupe, Gama, w/up, non-fall action, red & blk, w/compo driver, 9", VG, A $155.00
Mercedes 219 Sedan, Bandai, friction, bl w/chrome detail, plastic hood ornament, litho interior, 8", NM..............$235.00

Mercedes 220 S, Schuco, windup, red with white top, chrome trim, 5", EX (VG box), A, $125.00.

Mercedes 300 SE Coupe, Ichiko, friction, red w/chrome detail, 24", EX (G box), A...$150.00

Mercedes 300 SL Gullwing Coupe, 1955, Marklin, w/up, chrome, steerable front end, 13", MIB, A................$325.00

MG Magnette Mark III Convertible, Japan, friction, 8", EX (EX box), A, $325.00.

MG Magnette Sedan, Bandai, friction, wht w/dk red top, trunk & rear fenders, dk red hubs, chrome trim, 8", EX, A...$250.00

MGA 1600 Mark II, Bandai, friction, red w/blk top, chrome detail, litho interior, fancy hubs, 8", NM, A.............$200.00

Oldsmobile, 1959, Ichiko, friction, red, wht & pk w/gold detail on front, 13", EX (VG box) $250.00

Oldsmobile Convertible, 1952, Y, friction, red with chrome trim, 10", EX (EX box), $500.00.

Oldsmobile Station Wagon, Bandai, friction, red w/blk top, chrome detail, litho interior, working wipers, 12", NM $225.00

Oldsmobile Toronado, Asahi (ATC), red w/bl-tinted windows, chrome detail, blk-walls, 15½", EX, A....................$250.00

Oldsmobile 88 '59' Highway Patrol Car, Japan, friction, 13", EX, J2..$225.00

Oldsmobile 98, Ichiko, friction, 2-tone bl w/chrome detail, 8½", NM (EX box), A $300.00

Packard 52, Japan, friction, red with bright blue tires, chrome trim, 7", EX (EX box), A, $150.00.

Packard Convertible, JNF/Germany, w/up w/battery-op lights, red, 11½", EX (EX box), A $350.00

Packard Hawk Convertible, 1957, Schuco/Germany, battery-op, 10½", EX (VG box), A $900.00

Packard Sedan, Alps, friction, bl-gray w/chrome detail, wht-walls w/chrome hubs, 16½", rare, EX, A $2,530.00

Plymouth Convertible, 1959, friction, red w/wht tail fins, chrome detail, wht-walls, 11¼", EX, A....................$600.00

Plymouth Valiant Sedan, 1963, Bandai, friction, bl w/chrome detail, litho interior, 8", NM (EX box), A $75.00

Porsche Electromatic 7500 Convertible, Distler, w/up, red, wht-walls w/red trim & chrome hubs, 10", VG, A..........$380.00

Porsche Sportomatic Coupe, TT, battery operated, red and blue, 11", EX (EX box), A, $185.00.

Rambler Classic Sedan, 1960s, Cragstan, friction, red w/mc interior, wht-wall tires, 8", MIB, A $75.00

Rambler Sedan, Y, 1950s, friction, brn w/wht top, working wipers, 8", M $75.00

Renault Floride, ATC, friction, red with chrome trim, removable plastic roof, 9", NM (EX box), A, $400.00.

Renault Floride Sedan, ATC, friction, wht w/chrome trim, 9½", VG+..$175.00

Renault Sedan, Japan, friction, red w/chrome extended bumpers & detail, advances w/loud machine noise, 7", NM..$200.00

Rolls Royce Silver Cloud, Bandai, friction, bl w/wht top, chrome detail, 12", scarce, NM (EX box) $350.00

Valiant Sedan, Cragstan, friction, bl w/mc interior, wht-wall tires, 8", MIB, A...$75.00

Volkswagen Bug, KO, friction, yel & blk, mk PTT w/wht cross above on doors, litho interior, 6", NM (NM box), A ...$185.00

Volkswagen Bug, 1963, Bandai, friction, bl w/chrome detail, litho interior, 8", NM (EX box), A..........................$150.00

Volkswagen Convertible, Japan, friction, lighted piston action, bl w/cream top, red plastic seats, 9½", EXIB, A.......$100.00

Volkswagen Pickup Truck, Bandai, battery-op w/remote control, bl w/VW hubs on blk rubber tires, 8", NMIB, A $300.00

Volvo Amazon Sedan, Bandai, friction, gr w/wht top, chrome trim, 8¼", EX+, A $325.00

Banks

The impact of condition on the value of a bank cannot be overrated. Cast iron banks in near-mint condition with very little paint wear and all original parts are seldom found and might bring twice as much (if the bank is especially rare, up to five times as much) as one in average, very-good original condition with no restoration and no repairs. Overpainting and replacement parts (even screws) have a very negative effect on value. Mechanicals dominate the market, and some of the hard-to-find banks in outstanding, near-mint condition may exceed $20,000.00! (Here's a few examples: Girl Skipping Rope, Calamity, and Mikado.) Modern mechanical banks are also emerging on the collectibles market, including Book of Knowledge and James D. Capron, which are reproductions with full inscriptions stating that the piece is a replica of the original. Still banks are widely collected as well, with more than 3,000 varieties having been documented. Beware of unmarked modern reproductions.

For more information we recommend *The Dictionary of Still Banks* by Long and Pitman; *The Penny Bank Book* by Moore; *The Bank Book* by Norman; and *Penny Lane* by Davidson.

Advisors: Bill Bertoia, mechanicals; Dan Iannotti (I3), modern mechanicals; and Diane Patalano (P8).

See also Advertising; Battery-Operated; Character, TV and Movie Collectibles; Disney; Diecast Collector Banks; Reynolds Toys; Rock 'n Roll; Santa; Western.

MECHANICAL BANKS

Volkswagen Karmann Ghia, ATC, friction, red with black roof, 9½", NM (EX box), $250.00.

Photo courtesy Dan Iannotti.

Auto Bank, John Wright, 1 of 250, 1974, NM, I3, $700.00.

Always Did 'Spise a Mule (Jockey), Book of Knowledge, Medallion series, pnt CI, MIB, I3 ....$365.00

Always Did 'Spise a Mule (Jockey), Book of Knowledge, pnt CI, NM, I3 ....$265.00

Always Did 'Spise a Mule (Jockey), J&E Stevens, pnt CI, EX $2,600.00

Always Did 'Spise a Mule (Jockey), J&E Stevens, pnt CI, VG, A $1,150.00

Artillery Bank, J&E Stevens, bronze-pnt CI, soldier shoots coins from mortar into fortress, rpt $350.00

Artillery Bank, J&E Stevens, mc-pnt CI, soldier shoots coins from mortar into fortress, VG, A, from $850 to.......$950.00

Birdie Putt, Richards/Utexiqual, EX+, I3 ....$375.00

Bobby Clarke Slap Shot, John Wright, 1977, 1 of 141, rare, NM, I3...$3,500.00

Bowler's Strike, Richards/Utexiqual, NM, I3.................$725.00

Boy on Trapeze, Book of Knowledge, pnt CI, NM, I3 ....$750.00

Boy Scout Camp, J&E Stevens, pnt CI, EX, A $6,600.00

Boy Scout Camp, J&E Stevens, pnt CI, rpt $900.00

Buffalo Bank (Twist Head), brn-pnt CI, rpl tail, EX $325.00

Bull Dog Bank, Book of Knowledge, pnt CI, NM, I3 .....$300.00

Bull Dog Bank, J&E Stevens, pnt CI, EX $1,250.00

Bull Dog Bank, J&E Stevens, pnt CI, G, from $325 to ..$400.00

Bad Accident, James D. Capron, painted cast iron, boy darts in front of man on mule, NM, I3, $1,150.00.

Bad Accident, J&E Stevens, pnt CI, boy darts in front of Black man on mule, NM-, A $3,750.00

Beehive, NP CI, VG, A..$225.00

Butting Buffalo, Book of Knowledge, painted cast iron, NM, I3, $385.00.

Cabin Bank, Book of Knowledge, pnt CI, MIB, I3 ....$365.00

Cabin Bank, Book of Knowledge, pnt CI, NM, I3...........$300.00

Cabin Bank, J&E Stevens, pnt CI, EX+, A $825.00

Cabin Bank, J&E Stevens, pnt CI, G, A $175.00

Calamity, J&E Stevens, pnt CI, 3 football players on platform, VG, A...$9,900.00

Cat & Mouse Bank (Cat Balancing), Book of Knowledge, pnt CI, M, I3 ....$425.00

Cat & Mouse Bank (Cat Balancing), J&E Stevens, pnt CI, EX, A...$2,875.00

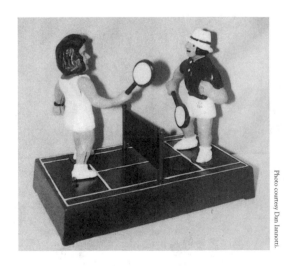

Bobby Riggs and Billie Jean King, John Wright, 1975, M, I3, $1,400.00.

Cat & Mouse Bank (Cat Balancing), J&E Stevens, pnt CI, rpt, A $1,150.00

Cat Boat, Richards/Utexiqual, NM, I3 ....$900.00

Chief Big Moon, J&E Stevens, pnt CI, NM, A, from $3,200 to $3,800.00

Chief Big Moon, J&E Stevens, pnt CI, VG.................$2,200.00

Circus Ticket Collector, Judd, pnt CI, insert coin into top of barrel & man nods thanks, EX, A.........................$1,925.00

Clown on Globe, James D. Capron, painted cast iron, NM, I3, $1,200.00.

Photo courtesy Dan Iannotti.

Cottage Bank, Germany, litho tin house, lever action w/compo hen appearing through opening shutters, 5", EX+...$200.00

Cottage w/Old Lady, litho tin w/graphics of old lady at well, pull lever & window opens, sm bird pops out, EX $200.00

Creedmore, Book of Knowledge, pnt CI, man shoots coin into tree trunk, NM, I3 ....$380.00

Darktown Battery, J&E Stevens, pnt CI, NM $4,850.00

Darktown Battery, J&E Stevens, pnt CI, rpl bat & arms, VG, A...$2,200.00

Dentist Bank, Book of Knowledge, Medallion series, pnt CI, M, I3 ....$315.00

Dentist Bank, Book of Knowledge, pnt CI, EX, I3 ....$200.00

Dentist Bank, J&E Stevens, pnt CI, EX+, A.............$12,100.00

Dinah, John Harper, pnt CI, bust of Black girl, rolls eyes as she swallows coin, EX+, A..$990.00

Dog on Turntable, Judd, CI, G, A....................................$80.00

Dog on Turntable, Judd, japanned CI, dog carries coin on dish into bank building & returns, VG+, A $400.00

Drumming Pig, Schuco/Disney, litho tin pig w/felt pants playing drum w/slot in top, clockwork mechanism, NMIB..$3,200.00

Eagle & Eaglets, Book of Knowledge, pnt CI, NM, I3 ....$420.00

Eagle & Eaglets, J&E Stevens, pnt CI, EX-, A, from $1,000 to $1,200.00

Eagle & Eaglets, J&E Stevens, pnt CI, G, from $400 to.$500.00

Electric Safe, Louis Mfg Co, blk w/rotating dial that causes coin to fall into safe, EX $50.00

Elephant (Swings Trunk), AC Williams, pnt CI, scarce gold version, EX+, I3 ....$325.00

Elephant & Three Clowns, J&E Stevens, pnt CI, EX, A..$2,420.00

Elephant Bank, John Wright, M, I3 ....$195.00

Elephant Bank, John Wright, MIB, I3 ....$245.00

Elephant w/Howdah (Pull-Tail), Hubley, 1930s, pnt CI, gray w/red howdah, G $150.00

Ferris Wheel Bank, Hubley, metal w/CI figures in gondolas, wind mechanism, press lever & coin activates wheel, EX, A..$6,700.00

Fortune Wheel Biscuit Tin Bank, Jacob & Co/England, litho fortune wheel w/rabbits around Christmas tree, 8", EX, A $415.00

Photo courtesy Dunbar Gallery.

Frog Bank (2 Frogs), J&E Stevens, Pat. 1882, painted cast iron, EX, D10, $2,500.00.

Frog Bank (2 Frogs), J&E Stevens, pnt CI, rpl leg, o/w VG, A...$700.00

Girl Skipping Rope, J&E Stevens, pnt CI, 9", VG, A.$14,000.00

Hall's Excelsior Bank, J&E Stevens, pnt CI, scarce tan version, G, I3 ....$350.00

Hall's Liliput Bank, J&E Stevens, pnt CI, NM, A..........$925.00

Hall's Liliput Bank, J&E Stevens, pnt CI, VG, A $550.00

Photo courtesy Dunbar Gallery.

Creedmore, J&E Stevens, painted cast iron, man shoots gun into tree trunk, EX, from $700.00 to $800.00.

Home Bank, Wm Morrison, pnt CI building, G-, A $500.00

Hoopla Bank, John Harper, pnt CI, dog jumps through hoop held by clown & deposits coin into barrel, EX $1,200.00

Humpty Dumpty, Book of Knowledge, Medallion series, pnt CI clown bust, M, I3 ....$335.00

Humpty Dumpty, Shepard Hardware, pnt CI clown bust, NM, A $4,000.00

Humpty Dumpty, Shepard Hardware, pnt CI clown bust, VG, A $1,000.00

Indian & Bear, Book of Knowledge, pnt CI, NM, I3......$385.00

Indian Shooting Bear, J&E Stevens, painted cast iron, EX, from $3,500.00 to $4,000.00.

John Paul Jones, Franklin Mint, 1986, I Have Not Yet Begun To Fight, M, I3, $850.00.

Jolly 'N' Bank, ca 1920, aluminum, VG+, I3 ....$400.00

Jolly 'N' Bank, John Harper, pnt CI, red jacket w/wht collar, bl butterfly tie, VG $150.00

Jolly 'N' Bank, Starkies, cocked hat, pnt CI bust of Black man in wht top hat, eyes roll as he swallows coin, EX, A $400.00

Jolly 'N' Bank, Starkies, pnt CI, moves ears, red jacket w/wht collar, bl butterfly tie, red lips, EX $125.00

Jolly 'N' Bank, Starkies, straight hat, pnt CI bust of Black man in wht top hat, eyes roll as he swallows coin, EX+, A $875.00

Jolly 'N' With High Hat, Sydenham and McOustra, England, 1920s, painted cast iron, EX, $500.00.

Jonah & the Whale, Book of Knowledge, pnt CI, NM, I3..$300.00

Jonah & the Whale, Shepard Hardware, pnt CI, EX+, from $5,000 to..$5,500.00

Jonah & the Whale, Shepard Hardware, pnt CI, G, A ..$2,200.00

Leap Frog, Book of Knowledge, Medallion series, painted cast iron, MIB, I3, $400.00.

Leap Frog, Shepard Hardware, pnt CI, G $1,600.00

Leap Frog, Shepard Hardware, pnt CI, NM, A............$4,950.00

Lighthouse, unknown mfg, pnt CI, no trap o/w EX, A ..$2,970.00

Lion & Monkeys, Kyser & Rex, pnt CI, VG $1,200.00

Little Joe, att John Harper, pnt CI bust of Black man, lifts hand to mouth, eyes roll as tongue flips coin, VG $225.00

Magic Bank, J&E Stevens, pnt CI, NM, A $4,000.00

Magic Bank, J&E Stevens, pnt CI, VG+, A......!.........$1,650.00

Magician, Book of Knowledge, pnt CI, NM, I3 ....$330.00

Mammy, Kyser & Rex, pnt CI, red dress, EX, A $4,500.00

Mason Bank, Classic Iron, M, I3, $925.00.

Memorial Money Box, Enterprise, ca 1876, CI, insert coin, release lever & it snaps back to ring bell, VG, A $500.00

Milking Cow, Book of Knowledge, pnt CI, NM, I3........$350.00

Monkey & Coconut, J&E Stevens, pnt CI, NM, A, from $3,200 to $3,800.00

Monkey & Coconut, J&E Stevens, pnt CI, VG, A.....$2,640.00

Monkey Bank, Chein, litho tin, seated monkey drops coin into container & tips hat, 5½", M...................................$125.00

Monkey Bank, Hubley, pnt CI, EX+, A $1,150.00

Monkey Bank, James D Capron, pnt CI, NM, I3 ....$265.00

Mosque, Judd, CI, japanned, rotating gorilla w/woman finial atop domed building, 9", EX, A, from $800 to $1,200.00

Mule Entering Barn, J&E Stevens, pnt CI, EX, A...........$950.00

Mule Entering Barn, James D Capron, pnt CI, NM, I3 ..$650.00

Novelty Bank, J&E Stevens, pnt CI building, EX, A..$1,000.00

Organ Bank (Boy & Girl), Book of Knowledge, pnt CI, NM, I3...$320.00

Organ Bank (Boy & Girl), Kyser & Rex, pnt CI, NM, A..$3,200.00

Organ Bank (Boy & Girl), Kyser & Rex, pnt CI, no trap o/w VG, A...$1,375.00

Organ Bank (Cat & Dog), Kyser & Rex, pnt CI, G, A..$500.00

Organ Bank (Monkey), Kyser & Rex, pnt CI, 6¼", VG, A..$230.00

Organ Grinder & Bear, Kyser & Rex, pnt CI, organ grinder next to house w/other figure at fence & performing bear, NM, A...$7,250.00

Organ Grinder & Bear, Kyser & Rex, pnt CI, organ grinder next to house w/other figure at fence & performing bear, VG, A...$2,850.00

Organ Grinder, Kyser and Rex, miniature, EX, D10, $700.00.

Owl (Slot in Head), Kilgore, 1930, pnt CI, G+, A.........$230.00

Owl (Turns Head), Book of Knowledge, pnt CI, EX, I3.$165.00

Owl (Turns Head), Book of Knowledge, pnt CI, NM+, I3....$235.00

Owl (Turns Head), J&E Stevens, pnt CI, glass eyes, EX, A ..$500.00

Owl (Turns Head), J&E Stevens, pnt CI, glass eyes, G..$300.00

Paddy & the Pig, Book of Knowledge, pnt CI, NM+, I3 .$385.00

Paddy & the Pig, J&E Stevens, pnt CI, EX+ $3,000.00

Paddy & the Pig, J&E Stevens, pnt CI, VG, A, from $1,300 to..$1,500.00

Panorama Bank, J&E Stevens, pnt CI building, G, A ...$1,650.00

Panorama Bank, J&E Stevens, pnt CI building, VG+, A ..$2,630.00

Pelican Bank, J&E Stevens, CI, EX $450.00

Penny Pineapple, Wilton, repro, NM, I3 ....$175.00

Penny Pineapple, Wilton, 2nd edition, NM, I3.............$475.00

Popeye Knockout Bank, Straits, litho tin, diecut Popeye & opponent boxing on rectangular base, VG $450.00

Presto Bank, Kyser and Rex, 1890s, painted cast iron, EX, D10, $550.00.

Professor Pug Frog, James D Capron, pnt CI, NM, I3...**$1,095.00**

Prussian Drummer, Schuco, litho tin soldier w/cloth suit beats on drum bank, EX, A **$3,300.00**

Pump & Bucket, pnt CI, rpl hdl, crack in base, A..........**$550.00**

Punch & Judy, Book of Knowledge, pnt CI, M, I3 ....**$300.00**

Punch & Judy, Book of Knowledge, pnt CI, MIB, I3......**$350.00**

Punch & Judy, Shepard Hardware, pnt CI, NM, A.....**$4,625.00**

Punch & Judy, Shepard Hardware, pnt CI, VG+, A...**$1,760.00**

Race Course Runners, James D Capron, NM, I3 ....**$875.00**

Reclining Chinaman, J&E Stevens, pnt CI, rpl hands & face, A...**$1,980.00**

Santa Bank, Noel Decoration/Japan, coin & battery-op, cloth-dressed Santa seated on litho tin house, 10½", EX..**$100.00**

Santa Claus, John Wright, M, I3 ....**$250.00**

Santa Claus, John Wright, MIB, I3................................**$300.00**

Santa Claus, Shepard Hardware, pnt CI, place coin into Santa's hand & he tosses it into chimney, VG, A............**$1,050.00**

Speaking Dog, J&E Stevens, pnt CI, girl in bl dress seated in front of dog, NM, A **$1,200.00**

Stump Speaker, Shepard Hardware, pnt CI, EX, A.....**$1,815.00**

Tammany Bank, Book of Knowledge, pnt CI, man seated in chair deposits coin into pocket & nods thanks, NM, I3 .....**$295.00**

Tammany Bank, J&E Stevens, pnt CI, man seated in chair deposits coin into pocket & nods thanks, VG, A....**$400.00**

Teddy & the Bear, Book of Knowledge, pnt CI, NM, I3 .**$315.00**

Toutou Bank, Germany, litho tin doghouse, place coin in dog's mouth, pull string & dog withdraws into doghouse, VG, A **$165.00**

Trick Dog, James D. Capron, painted cast iron, NM, I3, $625.00.

Snapping Bulldog, Ives, Pat. 1878, clockwork, NM, $8,500.00.

Trick Dog, James D Capron, pnt CI, no trap o/w EX+, I3 ..**$385.00**

Trick Dog, pnt CI, Hubley, NM, I3 ....**$800.00**

Trick Dog, pnt CI, Hubley, VG, A **$375.00**

Trick Pony, Book of Knowledge, pnt CI, EX, I3............**$235.00**

Trick Pony, Book of Knowledge, pnt CI, NMIB, I3 ....**$350.00**

Trick Pony, Shepard Hardware, pnt CI, EX, A **$1,155.00**

Trick Pony, Shepard Hardware, pnt CI, VG, A **$850.00**

Two Frogs, James D Capron, pnt CI, NM, I3 ....**$560.00**

Uncle Remus, Book of Knowledge, pnt CI, NM, I3 ....**$450.00**

Uncle Sam, Book of Knowledge, pnt CI, NM, I3 ....**$350.00**

Uncle Sam, John Wright, pnt CI, MIB, I3 ....**$235.00**

Uncle Sam, Shepard Hardware, pnt CI, VG, A **$1,250.00**

Uncle Sam, Wilton, pnt CI, M, I3 ....**$500.00**

Uncle Sam & Arab, John Wright, 1975, 1 of 250, NM, I3 ..**$1,200.00**

Uncle Tom (Star & Lapel), Kyser & Rex, pnt CI bust, NM, A...**$775.00**

Uncle Tom (Star & Lapel), Kyser & Rex, pnt CI bust, VG, A...**$400.00**

US & Spain, Book of Knowledge, pnt CI, M, I3 ....**$325.00**

Washington at Rappahannock, John Wright, 1977, NM, I3...**$675.00**

Watchdog Safe, J&E Stevens, pnt CI, wht-pnt dog on front of blk safe w/gold trim, dog barks, VG, A **$350.00**

Wild West Bank, Duro Mold, CI w/plastic figure, gun shoots coin into building, 7⅞", MIB, A **$65.00**

Speaking Dog, Shepherd Hardware, 1880s, painted cast iron, EX, D10, $1,750.00.

William Tell, Australian, aluminum & sheet metal, EX...**$400.00**
William Tell, J&E Stevens, pnt CI, EX+ **$1,400.00**
William Tell, J&E Stevens, pnt CI, G...........................**$550.00**
Wireless Bank, John Hugo Mfg, metal bank building on base, battery-op, clap hands & coin deposits into bank, EX, A **$220.00**

REGISTERING BANKS

Bean Pot, pnt CI, reads Nickel Register 5¢, G, A **$150.00**
Ben Franklin Bank, Marx, tin, MIB, I3.........................**$450.00**
Captain Kidd, US, pnt CI, 5⅝", rpt, A...........................**$150.00**

Daily Dime Bank, circus scene with clown and monkey, lithographed tin, EX, J6, $65.00.

Popeye Daily Dime Bank, 1956, lithographed tin, EX, D10, $65.00.

Daily Dime Cowboy Bank, Kalon, metal box w/canted corners, press-down trap, mc image on front, 2⅝" sq, G+.......**$75.00**
Daily Dime Piggy Bank, Kalon, metal box w/canted corners, press-down trap, mc image on front, 2⅝" sq, NM, A..**$90.00**
Daily Dime Vacation Bank, Kalon, metal box w/canted corners, press-down trap, mc image on front, 2⅝" sq, EX, A ..**$85.00**
Dime Register Bank (Battleship), metal box w/canted corners, slide trap, battleship image on front, 2½" sq, G- **$50.00**
Dime Register Bank (Boy & Girl), rnd w/polished chrome finish, flat trap, 3" dia, EX, A **$100.00**
Transvaal Money Box, England, pnt CI, mc roly-type bearded figure w/lettered top hat & pipe, 6", 2nd casting, EX, A.........**$200.00**
10¢ Bank, Bell, Italy, litho tin, rectangular container w/graphics of boy reaching to deposit coin, yel & gr, 5", EX, A.**$200.00**

STILL BANKS

Administration Building, Magic Introduction Co, NP CI, 5¼", EX **$300.00**
Alamo Bank, Alamo Iron Works, CI w/emb lettering, 3⅜", VG, A **$385.00**
Alphabet Cube, US, gold-pnt CI, emb letters on 26-sided cube, 3⅞", EX, A **$2,750.00**
Andy Gump, Arcade, standing reading paper, pnt CI, 4⅜", EX, A **$690.00**

Apple, Kyser and Rex, 1882, rare, EX, D10, $1,500.00.

Baseball Player, AC Williams, standing w/bat, pnt CI, gold w/red stockings, 5¾", EX, A....................................**$250.00**
Battleship Maine, Grey Iron, japanned CI w/gold trim, 4½", VG, A **$225.00**
Bear, Hubley, w/honey pot, pnt CI, brn bear w/bl & yel pot, 6½", NM, A..**$450.00**
Bear, John Harper, standing on hind legs, aluminum on wooden base, brn, 6", EX, A **$230.00**
Bear, US, standing on hind legs begging, gold-pnt CI, 5⅜", G, A **$35.00**

Beehive (Bear Stealing Honey), Sydenham and McOustra, England, 1908, painted cast iron, 7", EX, $265.00.

Beehive, Kyser & Rex, ca 1882, yel-pnt CI w/gr base, 2⅜", EX, A $1,100.00

Bell, Germany, brn-pnt lead, allover emb floral design, open 5-sided hdl, base unscrews, 6", EX, A $130.00

Betsy Ross Bicentennial Bank, Modern, pnt CI, Betsy in gr dress seated w/flag on brn base, limited edition, 11", M, A $300.00

Billiken, AC Williams, ca 1909, painted cast iron, 4¼", EX, $250.00.

Photo courtesy Dunbar Gallery.

Billy Bounce, Hubley, silver-pnt CI w/red trim, 4¾", EX, A .$770.00

Bird Perched on House, Germany, silvered lead, ornate ftd birdhouse w/emb dogwood decor, 4⅞", EX+, A $700.00

Boston State House, Smith & Egge, bl-pnt CI w/red roof & base, gold highlights, 6¾", rpr roof, o/w EX, A $3,630.00

Boston State House, Smith & Egge, gold-pnt CI w/red trim, 5⅛", EX, A $5,720.00

Boy Scout, AC Williams, gold-pnt CI w/red hat, 5⅞", EX+, A $175.00

Boy w/Football, AC Williams, kneeling, holding lg football overhead, pnt CI, red & silver, 5⅛", EX, A $2,300.00

Buffalo, US, gold-pnt CI, 4⅜", EX, A.............................$200.00

Bulldog Seated, mk Made in Canada, pnt CI, gr, 3⅞", rpt, A $100.00

Bulldog Seated w/Sailor Cap, Germany, pnt lead, blk w/wht & brn eyes, bl cap, 4⅜", no trap o/w EX, A $875.00

Buster Brown & Tige, bl- & red-pnt CI figure of Buster standing w/hand on hip & arm around Tige's neck, 5½", VG, A .$300.00

Cadet Marching, Hubley, bright bl-pnt CI w/gold trim, 5¾", G, A $275.00

Photo courtesy Bob and Jacquie Henry.

Camel, AC Williams, gold-painted cast iron, 7¼", EX, $300.00.

Camel (Oriental), US, blk-pnt CI w/gr rocking base, emb lettering, 5⅜", EX+, A....................................$1,200.00

Campbell Kids, AC Williams, gold-pnt CI, 3¼", VG, A....$220.00

Capitalist, US, ca 1890, pnt CI, man standing in gold pants w/blk jacket, wht face, 5", EX, A, from $2,200 to $2,750.00

Captain Kidd, US, pnt CI, caped figure w/shovel standing next to tree trunk on base, 5⅝", EX+, A $415.00

Castle Bank, Kyser & Rex, bl-pnt CI, 3", EX, A $580.00

Cat Seated on Tub, AC Williams, gold-pnt CI, 4", VG, A...$220.00

Cat Standing w/Long Tail, US, gold-pnt CI, 6¾", EX+, A...$1,600.00

Cat w/Ball, AC Williams, gray-pnt CI w/gold ball, 5¾", VG+, A $250.00

Church, Germany, pnt & stenciled tin church w/tall clock steeple, wht w/red roof, gr base, 6½", EX, A............$250.00

City Bank, Grey Iron, japanned CI, 3¼", VG, A $500.00

City Bank w/Director's Room on Top, England, CI, 4⅛", EX+, A $175.00

Clock (Street), AC Williams, red-pnt CI w/gold trim, rnd clock on pedestal base, 6", VG, A $635.00

Clown (Round), tin ball mounted on knob ft, litho image of clown playing mandolin, 2½" dia, EX....................$150.00

Clown Bank, litho face on tin container w/arched top, deposit coin through mouth, 4¼", EX, A..............................$100.00

Clown w/Crooked Pointed Hat, US, pnt CI, gold w/wht face & red collar, 6¾", VG, A $550.00

Colonial House w/Porch, AC Williams, gold-pnt CI w/gr roof, 3", G...$65.00

Columbia Magic Savings Bank, Magic Introduction Co, NP CI, 5¼", EX, A $250.00

County Bank, John Harper, japanned CI, 4¼", VG, A..$165.00

Crown Bank (Footed), US, pnt CI, gr & red, 4⅞", EX, A ..$1,100.00

Cupola Bank, England, japanned CI, 6", EX+, A...........$415.00

Cupola Bank, J&E Stevens, pnt CI, red & wht, 3¼", VG, A..$290.00

Daisy Safe, Shimer Toy, pnt CI, red w/gold highlights, 2⅛", EX $125.00

Darky Sharecropper, AC Williams, CI, gold w/red trim, toes visible on both ft, 5¼", NM, A $1,650.00

Darky Sharecropper, AC Williams, CI, mc, toes visible on 1 ft, 5½", G+, A..$150.00

Deckers Iowana Pig, pnt CI, gold pig w/lettering incised on sides, 4¼", EX, A $250.00

Dirigible, AC Williams, silver-pnt CI, 6½", EX, A $275.00

Dog in Doghouse, Saxony, litho tin, dog standing in doorway of wood-look doghouse, 2", EX+, A $300.00

Dog Seated on Tub, AC Williams, gold-pnt CI, 4", G, A ..$150.00

Dog's Head Bank, bronze head on wooden box w/viewing glass, dog's mouth takes coins, 6½", EX $1,550.00

Dolphin, US, gold-pnt CI, sailor in boat w/emb name, 4½", EX+, A...$880.00

Domed Bank, AC Williams, pnt CI, silver building w/gold dome & trim, 3", EX, A..$55.00

Double-Decker Bus, US, pnt CI, orange & blk, 3½", EX, A ...$1,870.00

Dough Boy, Grey Iron, pnt CI figure standing in brn uniform w/brimmed hat, 7", VG, A $525.00

Dutch Boy, Grey Iron, gold-pnt CI figure standing w/hands in pockets, 6¾", G, A $250.00

Dutch Girl, Grey Iron, standing w/hands on hips, CI, gold, 6½", G+, A...$300.00

Eiffel Tower, Sydenham & McOustra/England, japanned CI w/gold highlights, 8¾", EX+, A............................$1,100.00

Electric Railroad, Shimer Toy Co, japanned CI w/gold highlights, figure standing at rear, 8¼", VG+, A $1,700.00

Elephant, Arcade, trunk curled down, gr-pnt CI, 4½", VG, A...$120.00

Elephant, Germany, standing w/trunk down, silvered lead w/emb blanket, hinged back, 5", EX, A $100.00

Elephant, Kenton, trunk turned down, pnt CI, gray w/wht tusks, red blanket, NM, A..$1,000.00

Elephant, Kenton, w/bent knee, gold-pnt CI, 4⅞", G-, A ...$200.00

Elephant, US, seated w/trunk turned, gold-pnt CI, 4¼", rpt, A $190.00

Elephant, US, trunk raised high (Art Deco), orange-pnt CI, 4⅜", G, A $75.00

Elephant, US, w/raised slot on back & blanket, CI, traces of gold on blanket & slot top, 6⅛", VG.............................$90.00

Elephant on Tub, AC Williams, seated on bench, gold-pnt CI, 3⅞", G, A $110.00

Elephant on Tub, AC Williams, standing on hind legs, trunk down, gold-pnt CI, 5⅜", VG, A $110.00

Elephant w/Howdah, AC Williams, pnt CI, gray w/red howdah & blanket, gr strap, 4¼", EX, A $200.00

Elephant w/Howdah, Harris Toy, walking stiff legged w/trunk down, gold-pnt CI w/red highlights, 4½", G, A $475.00

Donkey, AC Williams, ca 1920s, painted cast iron, 6¼" long, EX, $175.00.

Donkey, US, red-pnt CI, 4½", VG, A $50.00

Elephant With Swivel Trunk, Ives, ca 1890s, painted cast iron, 4" long, rare, EX, from $325.00 to $450.00.

Fido, Hubley, pnt CI, wht dog seated w/head cocked & blk ears flared, red collar, 5", EX, A $100.00

Fish (IFC), US, gr-pnt CI w/emb lettering, 7", VG.....$1,400.00

Flat Iron Bank, Kenton, CI, silver, 3¼", EX+, A...........$700.00

Flat Iron Bank, Kenton, CI, silver, 5¾", VG+, A $450.00

Fonderie de Lislet (Furnace), chrome-finished CI, 8½", EX, A $150.00

Football Player w/Large Football, Hubley, pnt CI, red kneeling player holding silver football above head, 5⅛", VG, A $1,650.00

Fort, Kenton, blk-pnt CI w/emb lettering, 4⅛", G, A $330.00

Fort Mt Hope, US, brn-pnt CI, emb logs w/red roof, 2⅞", EX+, A $600.00

Four-Gabled Dome Bank, gold-pnt CI, 3½", EX, A $415.00

Foxy Grandpa (Turnpin), Wing, silver-pnt CI figure w/red vest, derby hat, 5½", VG, A $300.00

Garage, AC Williams, 1-car, pnt CI, gold w/red roof, emb doors, 2", G, A $120.00

Garage, AC Williams, 2-car, CI, silver w/red roof, 2½", EX, A $200.00

General Butler, J&E Stevens, pnt CI figure appearing to have a human head on a frog body, blk & wht, 6½", EX, A .. $3,080.00

General George Washington (Solid Base), US, pnt CI figure standing w/outstretched arm, 4⅜", EX, A $220.00

General Sheridan on Rearing Horse, Arcade, gold-pnt CI, rectangular base, 6", EX, A $360.00

Globe on Arc, Grey Iron, pnt CI, bl, 5¼", EX $350.00

Globe on Arc, Grey Iron, pnt CI, red, 5¼", VG, A $135.00

Globe w/Eagle, Enterprise, 1883, for Columbia Exposition, CI w/3 profile transfers, red base, 5¾", scarce, EX, A ... $175.00

Globe w/Eagle Atop, Enterprise Mfg, ca 1875, gold-pnt CI, pedestal base, 5¾", EX, A $165.00

Gold Dollar Eagle Clock, Arcade, pnt CI & steel, allover goldtone, resembles ftd gold eagle dollar, 3", VG, A $150.00

Golliwog, John Harper, pnt CI googly-eyed figure standing in blk waist coat w/red pants & tie, 6¼", EX+ $650.00

Goose Bank, Arcade, gold-pnt CI, 3¾", G, A $110.00

Grandpa Dukes, Germany, litho tin bust figure in straw hat & bow tie, 2¼", EX, A $230.00

Grandpa's Hat, US, blk-pnt CI w/red interior & emb lettering, 3⅞", VG, A, from $250 to $350.00

Gunboat, Kenton (?), CI, bl w/wht upper deck & bl-trimmed masts, 8½" L, EX, A $880.00

Hamburg Touring Boat, Germany, silvered lead, ocean wave pedestal, 4", NM, A $400.00

Harleysville Bank, Unicast Foundry, 1959, gold-pnt CI w/emb lettering, 2⅝", EX, A $85.00

Hen on Nest, US, gold-pnt CI w/red highlights, 3⅜", G, A .. $550.00

Holstein Cow, Arcade, blk- & wht-pnt CI, 4½", EX+, A .. $400.00

Home Bank, Judd, japanned CI, 3½", VG, A $275.00

Home Savings Bank w/Finial, J&E Stevens, yel-pnt CI w/red lettering, 3½", EX, A $550.00

Horse, AC Williams, rearing on platform, CI, gold, 7¼", EX, A $150.00

Horse, AC Williams, w/forelegs on tub, CI, gold, 5¼", VG, A $150.00

Horse, Arcade, Beauty, CI, blk, 4¾", G, A $50.00

Horse, Arcade, in Good Luck horseshoe w/Buster Brown & Tige, CI, blk & gold, 4½", EX, A $275.00

Horse, Arcade, My Pet, CI, blk w/emb lettering, 5", G-, A.. $50.00

Horse, Canada, prancing, CI, blk, 4⅛", EX, A $200.00

Horse, Canada, rearing, CI, gold, rectangular base, 4¼", EX, A $150.00

Horse, Grey Iron, w/saddle, CI, gold, 5½", EX, A $200.00

House, Ohio Foundry, w/basement, CI, red & blk, 4⅝", EX+, A $4,620.00

House, US, w/bay windows, CI, red, 4", G, A $200.00

House, US, w/chimney slot, CI, red & yel highlights, 2¾", VG, A $525.00

House, US, 1-story, CI, gr w/red trim, 3", EX, A $165.00

Humpty Dumpty, England, pnt ceramic, molded facial features on egg head w/cocked hat, collar & bow tie, 5½", EX, A $330.00

Husky Dog, Grey Iron, brn-pnt CI w/blk eyes & nose, 5", EX+, A $775.00

Independence Hall, US, aluminum, red & wht, 5", EX.... $75.00

Independence Hall, US, gold-pnt CI, 6⅜", EX $4,350.00

Indian Bust, Japan, pnt china, bust image in full headdress, slot in back, 4", EX+, A.. $40.00

Indian With Tomahawk, Hubley, 1920s, painted cast iron, 5", EX, D10, $350.00.

Iron Master's House, Kyser & Rex, brn-pnt emb CI cabin w/red roof, 4½", EX+, A $990.00

Jr Savings Bank & Clock, Baby Barry Products, pressed cb figure of Uncle Sam w/clock next to tin box bank, 7½", M .. $85.00

Junior Cash Register, J&E Stevens, emb CI, 4¼", G, A ... $100.00

Kitten Seated w/Neck Bow, Hubley, wht-pnt CI, 4¾", EX, A, from $90 to $110.00

Labrador Retriever Standing, US, gold-pnt CI, 6", rpt, A .. $80.00

Lion, Arcade, standing on wheeled platform, gold, wht rubber wheels, 4½", VG, A $150.00

Lion, Hubley, tail at left, CI, gold w/red eyes, 5⅜", G, A .. $40.00

Lion, John Harper, seated, aluminum, 5", EX+, A $75.00

Lion, US, quilted, CI, gold w/red mouth, 4¾", G- $250.00

Lion, US, tail at right, gold-pnt CI, 4⅞", EX, A $50.00

Lion, US, tail between legs, gold-pnt CI, 5¼", G, A $75.00

Log Cabin, Kyser & Rex, chimney at left, CI, red, 3¼", rpl pin, A $130.00

Log Cabin, US, chimney in center, CI, japanned, 2½", EX, A, from $225 to $250.00

Lost Dog, US, blk-pnt dog seated on haunches w/head up howling, w/base, 5⅜", VG, A..................................$580.00

Mammy, AC Williams, w/spoon, pnt CI, 5⅞", EX, A....$230.00

Man on Cotton Bale (Coon Bank), US, ca 1898, pnt CI, 4⅞", rare, G, A $1,430.00

Mellow Furnace, Liberty Toy Co, CI, emb lettering, hinged front door, 4", VG, A $120.00

Mermaid, US, gold-pnt CI, girl in boat w/emb name, 4½", EX, A..$880.00

Middy Bank, US, ca 1887, CI standing figure, 4⅛", VG, A..$120.00

Minuteman Holding Rifle, Hubley, CI, 6", G-, A $150.00

Money Bag ($100,000), US, chrome-plated CI, 3¼", EX+, A...$525.00

Money Bag w/2 Dogs, Germany, silver-pnt lead bag emb w/2 dog heads peering from side of bag, 3¼", VG, A............$275.00

Money Saver, Arcade, pnt CI & steel, blk w/gold trim, resembles rnd ftd alarm clock w/Roman Numerals, 3", EX+, A..$110.00

Mosque (Combination Door), Grey Iron, gold- & bronze-pnt CI, 5⅛", EX+, A...$660.00

Mosque (3-Story), AC Williams, gold-pnt CI, 3½", VG, A...$110.00

Mother Hubbard, Germany, lead, standing figure, 4⅝", VG, A $110.00

Mulligan, AC Williams, bl-pnt CI policeman standing w/hand on hip & club, stamped Bennet & Fish on rear, 5¾", VG, A..$635.00

Multiplying Bank, J&E Stevens, pnt CI building, 6½", rpt, A..$470.00

Mutt and Jeff, AC Williams, 1920s, gold-painted cast iron, 4", EX, D10, $250.00.

Photo courtesy Dunbar Gallery.

Mutt & Jeff, AC Williams, comical pose, CI, gold, 4", VG, A..$150.00

Old Lady's Head in Bonnet, English, brn-glazed pottery, 4", EX, A...$75.00

Old Man Seated, England, brn-glazed pottery, back lettered Money Taken In Here, 4¼" $85.00

Old South Church, US, wht-pnt CI w/gray roof, 9¾", EX, A...$6,820.00

Oregon Battleship, J&E Stevens, pnt CI, gray w/gold guns & red-trimmed stacks, 4⅞", VG, A..........................$250.00

Oregon Battleship, J&E Stevens, pnt CI, olive brn w/gold guns, red-trimmed stacks, 4⅞", EX, A........................$400.00

Oriental Bank (Oval), Kyser & Rex, bl-pnt CI w/yel roof & base, 3", EX, A...$750.00

Our Kitchener, England, 1914, japanned CI, 6¾", scarce, EX+ $200.00

Owl (Be Wise Save Money), AC Williams, pnt CI, gold w/red lettering, 4⅞", EX+, A..................................$300.00

Pagoda Bank (Footed), England, ca 1889, gr-pnt CI w/gold trim, 5", EX+, A..$750.00

Palace, Ives, japanned CI w/gold highlights, 7½", EX+ $1,900.00

Pass Around the Hat, US, Derby, CI, red, 3⅛", EX, A ..$250.00

Pass Around the Hat, US, Lincoln High Hat, CI, blk, 3", G, A...$50.00

Pelican Nesting on Rooftop Chimney, wht metal w/electro-plated copper finish, marble base, 5", EX.............$300.00

Pig (Christmas Roast), US, gold-pnt CI w/emb lettering, 7⅛", rpt, A $200.00

Pig Flutist & Money Bag, pnt lead, flesh-colored pig next to gray money bag, 2¾", EX+ $1,000.00

Pig Standing, Shimer Toy, gold-pnt CI, 5¼", VG............$75.00

Policeman, Arcade, pnt CI, standing figure in dk bl uniform w/gold buttons on jacket, 5½", G, A.....................$220.00

Policeman (Round), Germany, late 1800s, litho tin, ball-shaped w/ftd base, 2⅜", EX, A................................$440.00

Polish Rooster, US, gold-pnt CI, 5½", rpt, A.................$360.00

Porky Pig, Hubley, ca 1930, CI, mc, sq base emb w/name, G, A..$150.00

Presto Bank, US, silver-pnt CI, 3¼", VG, A....................$30.00

Presto Bank (Jewel), Kenton, blk-pnt CI w/emb jewel on top, 4", G, A..$125.00

Princess Di & Charles Bank, 1981, copper-plated CI medallion w/images of Charles & Di, 7", M, A........................$100.00

Professor Pug Frog (Frog Bank), AC Williams, gold-pnt CI, bl jacket, 3¼", EX, A...$450.00

Pug Dog Seated, Kyser & Rex, pnt CI, wht & blk w/red collar, 3½", G, A...$80.00

Rabbit, AC Williams, sitting, CI, gold, 5⅛", rpt, A.......$130.00

Rabbit, AC Williams, standing, CI, gold, 6¼", EX, A ...$300.00

Rabbit, US, seated on base, CI, wht w/gr base, dated 1884, 2¾", VG, A...$770.00

Rabbit, US, sitting, CI, wht w/pk highlights on ears, nose & tail, 4⅜", VG, A...$100.00

Reid Library of Lake Forest College, CI, 5¼", G, A.......$220.00

Rhino, Arcade, gold-pnt CI, 5", EX, A.........................$635.00

Roof Bank, J&E Stevens, 1897, japanned CI w/gold trim, 5¼", NM, A...$250.00

Rose Window, England, japanned CI, 2⅜", rpl screw, A..$100.00

Rooster, Hubley, ca 1920s, gold-painted cast iron with red waddle, 4¾" long, EX, $175.00.

Royal Safe Deposit, blk-pnt CI w/paper litho pictures on sides, 6", VG, A...$155.00

Rumplestiltskin, US, ca 1910, gold-pnt CI figure w/emb lettering, 6", G, A $150.00

Safe Deposit, pnt CI, blk w/gold highlights on emb front door, 5¼", EX+, A...$120.00

Safe w/Animals, Pat 1881, pnt CI, blk w/gold emb animals & dial on front, 3⅛", EX+, A.....................................$275.00

Sharecropper, AC Williams, ca 1901, painted cast iron, NM, $275.00.

Safe w/Hinged Door, USA, pnt CI, gr & blk w/gold stenciled design on door & gold-trimmed hinges, 4¾", EX+, A..............$175.00

Sailor Saluting, Hubley, silver-pnt CI w/bl scarf, 5¼", G, A .$110.00

Santa w/Tree, Hubley, pnt CI, red figure w/wht beard & gr tree, 5⅞", VG, A $385.00

Save & Smile, England, pnt CI, blk face w/googly eyes & red smiling mouth, gold hat w/emb lettering, 4", EX+, A $600.00

Seal on Rock, Arcade, gold-pnt CI, 4¼", G, A $250.00

Security Safe, US, 1894, CI w/wood drawers & hdls, 6", NM, A $175.00

Self-Denial Missionary Fund Bank, red CI w/wht roof, 5⅛", EX, A $300.00

Shell, J&E Stevens, CI, wht-pnt shell form on oval base, 4¾", EX, A $450.00

Six-Sided Building, US, blk-pnt CI, 3", rpl pin, EX, A ..$120.00

Skyscraper, AC Williams, pnt CI, gold & silver, 5½", VG, A $150.00

SNCCA Soldier, Laverne Worley, 1982, pnt CI, soldier saluting on rnd base, 7½", M, A $10.00

Songbird on Stump, AC Williams, gold-pnt CI w/blk beak, 4¾", some rpt, A $175.00

Sound Money Bank, gold-pnt CI house w/emb profile on front, 5½", extremely rare, EX, A..................................$1,650.00

Space Heater (Birds), England, brn-pnt CI, 6½", EX+, A ..$110.00

Spaniel Begging, Europe, pnt lead, wht w/blk ears & eyes, separates at neck, 4⅜", EX+, A.....................................$200.00

Spitz Dog, Grey Iron, gold-pnt CI, 4½", EX+, A............$500.00

Squirrel w/Nut, US, gold-pnt CI, 4⅛", rpt, A $360.00

State Bank, Kenton, japanned CI building w/gold & bronze highlights, 5", NM, A...$200.00

State Bank, Kenton, japanned CI building w/gold & bronze highlights, 8¾", EX+, A $1,050.00

Steamboat, AC Williams, CI, red side-wheeler w/gold stacks, 7⅝", VG, A $125.00

Steamboat, Arcade, silver-pnt CI side-wheeler w/emb Arcade, 7½", EX...$550.00

Terrier, Vindex, ca 1931, painted cast iron, 5½" long, EX, $250.00.

Stop Signal, Dent, pnt CI, bl sq post w/gold highlights, emb lettering, light signal atop & on front, 4½", EX+, A...$775.00

Stop Signal, Dent, pnt CI, red sq post w/gold highlights, emb lettering w/light signal atop & on front, 5⅝", EX, A......$550.00

Sundial, Arcade, gold-pnt CI, letters on dial, pedestal base, 4¼", VG...$3,100.00

Tally Ho Bank, Chamberlain & Hill/England, CI w/gold highlights, Horse emb inside horseshoe, 4½", EX..........$165.00

Tank, England, ca 1918, brn-pnt CI, 8¼", EX+, A........$360.00

Taxi Cab, Arcade, pnt CI, wht body w/brn top, hood & fenders, rear spare tire, rear mesh windows, w/driver, 8", EX, A......$2,200.00

Teddy, AC Williams, ca 1919, gold-pnt CI bust of Theodore Roosevelt on pedestal, 5", EX, A, from $275 to.......$325.00

Three Wise Monkeys, AC Williams, gold-pnt CI, See No Evil, Hear No Evil & Speak No Evil, 3½", VG, A..........$200.00

Throne, John Harper, japanned CI English throne w/ornate trim, 8⅛", EX, A...$165.00

Time Is Money, Arcade, pnt CI & steel, allover gold-tone, resembles rnd ftd alarm clock w/Roman numerals, 3", G, A...$35.00

Traders Bank, Canada, bronze-tone CI building, 8½", missing finials o/w EX, A...$1,000.00

Transvaal, John Harper, pnt CI squatty figure w/wht beard, blk suit & top hat, 6¼", rpt, A......................................$360.00

Turkey, AC Williams, gold-pnt CI, 3⅜", VG, A...........$110.00

Two Kids, John Harper, 2 blk-pnt CI goats w/horns locked over silver tree trunk, gr base, emb lettering, 4½", EX+, A $1,650.00

United Bank, AC Williams, gold-pnt CI, 2¾", VG+, A..$215.00

US Mailbox (Hanging), AC Williams, ca 1921-34, EX-, $110.00.

US Mailbox, Hubley, w/eagle, NP CI, 4", VG, A.............$40.00

US Mailbox, Kenton, w/combination lock, CI, silver w/red emb lettering, 4¾", EX, A...$100.00

US Mailbox, Kenton, w/eagle, CI, gr, 3⅝", G-, A.............$90.00

US Treasury Bank, Grey Iron, pnt CI, wht building w/red roof & trim, sheet-metal base, 3¾", EX, A..........................$135.00

Villa Church, Kyser & Rex, 1882, japanned CI w/gold highlights, 5¾", scarce, NM, A.......................................$400.00

Washington Bell w/Yoke, Grey Iron, pnt CI, red w/emb profile of George Washington, gold highlights, 3", VG, A......$120.00

Weight Scale (The Record Money Bank), Germany, 1906, litho tin, 6½", VG+, A...$520.00

Weight Scale (Try Your Weight & Save Money), Germany, 1906, litho tin, 6½", VG+, A $520.00

When My Ship Comes In (Sailing Ship), Brighton, brn-pnt CI, 5⅜", EX+, A...$1,760.00

Wise Pig, Hubley, 1930s, pnt CI, wht upright pig holding placard w/short poem, Thrifty on base, 6⅝", VG, A......$100.00

Woolworth Building, Kenton, ca 1915, CI, 5¾", VG, A .$130.00

Workhorse, Arcade, CI, bl, 4¾", EX, A.........................$150.00

Workhorse, Arcade, CI, blk, 4¾", VG.............................$100.00

1876 Bank, Judd, japanned CI, 2⅞", EX+, A $150.00

1876 Bank, Judd, japanned CI, 3⅜", EX+ $200.00

Barbie and Friends

No one could argue the fact that vintage Barbies are holding their own as one of the hottest areas of toy collecting on today's market. Barbie was first introduced in 1959, and since then her face has changed three times. She's been blond and brunette; her hair has been restyled over and over, and it's varied in length from above her shoulders to the tips of her toes. She's worn high-fashion designer clothing and pedal pushers. She's been everything from an astronaut to a veterinarian, and no matter what her changing lifestyle required, Mattel (her 'maker') has provided it for her.

Though even Barbie items from recent years are bought and sold with fervor, those made before 1970 are the most sought after. You'll need to do a lot of studying and comparisons to learn to distinguish one Barbie from another, but it will pay off in terms of making wise investments. There are several books available; we recommend them all: *The Wonder of Barbie* and *The World of Barbie Dolls* by Paris and Susan Manos; *The Collector's Encyclopedia of Barbie Dolls and Collectibles* by Sibyl DeWein and Joan Ashabraner; *The Story of Barbie* by Kitturah B. Westenhouser; *Barbie Doll Fashion, Vol. 1, 1959-1967*, and *Barbie Doll Fashion, Vol. II, 1968-1974*, by Sarah Sink Eames; *Barbie Exclusives, Books I and II*, by Margo Rana; *Barbie, The First 30 Years, 1959 Through 1989*, by Stefanie Deutsch; *A Decade of Barbie Dolls and Collectibles, 1981-1991*, by Beth Summers; *The Barbie Doll Boom, 1986-1995*, and *Collector's Encyclopedia of Barbie Doll Exclusives and More* by J. Michael Augustyniak; *The Barbie Years, 1959 to 1996*, by Patrick C. Olds; and *Collector's Guide to Barbie Doll Paper Dolls* by Lorraine Mieszala (all published by Collector Books).

Remember that unless the box is mentioned in the line (orig box, MIB, MIP, NRFB, etc), values are given for loose items. As a general rule, a mint-in-the box doll is worth twice as much (or there about) as one mint, no box. The same doll, played with and in only good condition, is worth half as much (or even less). Never-removed-from-box examples sell at a premium.

Advisor: Marl Davidson (D2).

DOLLS

Allan, 1963, pnt red hair, straight legs, NRFB, D2.........$165.00

Allan, 1963, pnt red hair, straight legs, orig swimsuit & sandals, VG, M15...$65.00

Barbie, #1, 1958-59, blond hair, MIB, D2 ....$8,000.00

Barbie, #1, 1958-59, blond hair, orig swimsuit & shoes, NM, D2...$5,500.00

Barbie, #1, 1958-59, brunette hair, replica stand, MIB, D2 ..$8,750.00

Barbie, #2, 1959, brunette hair, MIB, D2 ....$7,000.00

Barbie, #3, 1960, blond hair, MIB, D2........................$1,350.00

Barbie, #3, 1960, blond hair, orig swimsuit, NM, D2 .....$800.00

Barbie, #3, 1960, brunette hair, MIB, D2 ....$1,550.00

Barbie, #3, 1960, brunette hair, orig swimsuit, NM, D2 .$950.00

Barbie, #4, 1960, blond or brunette hair, orig swimsuit, NM, D2..$400.00

Barbie, #5, 1961, blond hair, MIB, D2 ....$550.00

Barbie, #5, 1961, blond hair, replica swimsuit, EX, D2...$300.00

Barbie, #5, 1961, brunette hair, MIB, D2......................$625.00

Barbie, #5, 1961, brunette hair, orig swimsuit, NM, D2 .$400.00

Barbie, #5, 1961, red hair, MIB, D2 ....$900.00

Barbie, American Girl, 1964, blond hair, bendable legs, orig swimsuit, M, D2 ....$1,300.00

Barbie, Angel Lights (tree topper), 1993, M, $125.00.

Barbie, Astronaut, 1994 department store special, NRFB, D2..$45.00

Barbie, Benefit Ball, 1992, Classique Collection, NRFB, D2...$150.00

Barbie, Benefit Performance, porcelain, 1987, NRFB, D2 ..$600.00

Barbie, Bicyclin', 1993 department store special, NRFB, D2..$35.00

Barbie, Brazilian, 1989, Dolls of the World series, NRFB, D2..$75.00

Barbie, Bubble-Cut, 1961, blond hair, MIB, D2 ....$500.00

Barbie, Bubble-Cut, 1961, blond hair, replica swimsuit, NM, D2..$175.00

Barbie, Bubble-Cut, 1961, brunette hair, MIB, D2.........$500.00

Barbie, Bubble-Cut, 1961, brunette hair, NM, D2 ....$200.00

Barbie, Bubble-Cut, 1961, red hair, MIB, D2 ....$700.00

Barbie, Bubble-Cut, 1961, red hair, orig swimsuit, NM, D2 ..$500.00

Barbie, Bubble-Cut w/side part, 1962-64, brunette hair, orig red swimsuit & shoes, VG, M15...$125.00

Barbie, Bubble-Cut w/side part, 1962-64, red hair, extremely rare, MIB, D2 ....$850.00

Barbie, Bubble-Cut w/side part, 1962-64, red hair, replica swimsuit, VG, M15...$250.00

Barbie, California Dream, 1987 department store special, NRFB, D2..$45.00

Barbie, Canadian, 1987, Dolls of the World series, NRFB, D2..$75.00

Barbie, Circus Star, FAO Schwarz, 1994 department store special, NRFB, D2 ....$95.00

Barbie, Color Magic, 1966, blond hair, NRFB, D2 .....$1,500.00

Barbie, Color Magic, 1966, brunette hair, NRFB, D2 .$1,800.00

Barbie, Crystal Rhapsody, porcelain, 1992, NRFB, D2 ..$500.00

Barbie, Cute 'N Cool, 1991 department store special, NRFB, D2..$50.00

Barbie, Dazzlin' Date, 1992, Target, NRFB, D2 ....$35.00

Barbie, Dr, 1987 department store special, NRFB, D2......$50.00

Barbie, Dreamglow (Black), 1986, orig outfit, VG, M15 ..$20.00

Barbie, Easter Fun, 1993 department store special, NRFB, D2..$35.00

Barbie, Egyptian Queen, 1993, Great Eras series, NRFB, D2..$150.00

Barbie, Empress Bride, Bob Mackie, 1992, MIB, D2.......$800.00

Barbie, Enchanted Princess, foreign, 1993, NRFB, D2 .....$70.00

Barbie, English, 1991, Dolls of the World series, NRFB, D2..$75.00

Barbie, Eskimo, 1981, Dolls of the World series, NRFB, D2..$75.00

Barbie, Evening Extravaganza, 1993, Classique Collection, NRFB, D2 ....$65.00

Barbie, Evening Flame, 1991 department store special, NRFB, D2..$200.00

Barbie, Evergreen Princess, 1994, Princess series, red hair, NRFB, D2 ....$600.00

Barbie, Fashion Queen, 1963, pnt hair, orig swimsuit, complete w/3 wigs & stand, EX, D2/M15, from $200 to $250.00

Barbie, Frills & Fantasy, 1988, Walmart, NRFB, D2 ....$40.00

Barbie, Gay Parisian, porcelain, 1991, brunette hair, NRFB, D2..$200.00

Barbie, Goddess of the Sun, Bob Mackie, 1995, NRFB, D2 ..$200.00

Barbie, Gold & Lace, 1989, Target, NRFB, D2 ....$35.00

Barbie, Gold Sensation, porcelain, 1993, MIB, D2 ....$450.00

Barbie, Golden Greetings, FAO Schwarz, 1989 department store special, NRFB, D2 ....$250.00

Barbie, Grecian Goddess, 1995, Great Eras series, NRFB, D2 ..$55.00

Barbie, Hair Happenin's, Sears Exclusive, 1971, red hair, MIB, D2...$1,200.00

Barbie, Hawaiian, 1975, orig outfit, rare, VG, M15.........$65.00

Barbie, Holiday, 1988, NRFB, D2 ....$900.00

Barbie, Holiday, 1988, orig dress, EX, M15....................$325.00

Barbie, Holiday, 1989, NRFB, D2 ....$250.00

Barbie, Holiday, 1989, orig dress, VG, M15...................$100.00

Photo courtesy Lee Garmon.

Barbie, Holiday, 1989, M, $150.00.

Barbie, Holiday, 1990, NRFB, D2 ....$200.00
Barbie, Holiday, 1990, orig dress, VG, M15.....................$85.00
Barbie, Holiday, 1991, NRFB, D2 ....$200.00
Barbie, Holiday, 1991, orig dress, VG (VG box), M15 ..$100.00
Barbie, Holiday, 1992, NRFB, D2 ....$125.00
Barbie, Holiday, 1992, orig dress, M, M15 ....$85.00
Barbie, Holiday, 1993, Black, MIB, M15 ....$50.00
Barbie, Holiday, 1994, Festival series, NRFB, D2 ....$1,500.00
Barbie, Holiday, 1994, NRFB, D2 ....$175.00
Barbie, Icelandic, 1986, Dolls of the World series, NRFB,
      D2 ....$110.00

Barbie, Living, 1970, bendable arms and legs, MIB, $150.00.

Barbie, Irish, 1994, Dolls of the World series, NRFB, D2 .$22.00
Barbie, Italian, 1992, Dolls of the World series, NRFB, D2 ..$50.00
Barbie, Japanese, 1984, Dolls of the World series, NRFB,
      D2 ....$150.00
Barbie, Kenyan, 1993, Dolls of the World series, NRFB,
      D2 ....$35.00
Barbie, Kissing, 1979, orig outfit, M, M15 ....$20.00
Barbie, Live Action, 1971, NRFB, D2 ....$200.00
Barbie, Madison Avenue, FAO Schwarz, 1991 department store
      special, NRFB, D2 ....$265.00
Barbie, Magic Moves, 1986, orig outfit, M, M15 ....$20.00
Barbie, Malaysian, 1990, Dolls of the World series, NRFB,
      D2 ....$60.00
Barbie, Malibu, 1971, orig bl swimsuit, VG, M15.............$20.00

Barbie, Masquerade Ball, Bob Mackie, 1993, M, $300.00.

Barbie, Masquerade Ball, Bob Mackie, 1993, NRFB, D2 ..$450.00
Barbie, Medieval, 1994, Great Eras series, NRFB, D2 ......$55.00
Barbie, Midnight Gala, 1994, Classique Collection, NRFB,
      D2 ....$75.00
Barbie, Miss, 1964, pnt hair w/orange headband, complete w/3
      wigs & stand, NM, D2...$400.00
Barbie, Moonlight Magic, 1993 department store special, NRFB,
      D2 ....$90.00
Barbie, Neptune Fantasy, Bob Mackie, 1992, NRFB, D2..$1,000.00
Barbie, Nigerian, 1989, Dolls of the World series, NRFB,
      D2 ....$65.00
Barbie, Night Sensation, FAO Schwarz, 1991 department store
      special, NRFB, D2 ....$200.00
Barbie, Nutcracker, 1991 department store special, MIB,
      D2 ....$250.00
Barbie, Oriental, 1980, Dolls of the World series, NRFB,
      D2 ....$150.00

Barbie, Peaches & Cream, 1984, orig outfit, M, M15.......$20.00
Barbie, Pink & Pretty, 1982, orig outfit, M, M15 ....$15.00
Barbie, Pink Jubilee, 1987, Walmart 25th Anniversary, NRFB, D2 ....$75.00
Barbie, Platinum, Bob Mackie, 1991, NRFB, D2 ....$700.00

Barbie, Ponytail, 1962, MIB, $450.00.

Barbie, Pretty in Purple, 1992, K-Mart, NRFB, D2 ....$25.00
Barbie, Queen of Hearts, Bob Mackie, 1994, NRFB, D2 ..$225.00
Barbie, Quick Curl, 1973, blond hair, orig dress, G, M15 ...$25.00
Barbie, Quick Curl Miss America, 1972, Kellogg's mail-in premium, brunette hair, orig outfit, M, M15 ....$125.00
Barbie, Royal Invitation, 1993, Spiegel, NRFB, D2 ....$100.00
Barbie, Royal Splendor, porcelain, 1993, MIB, D2.........$300.00
Barbie, Savvy Shopper, 1994, Bloomingdales, NRFB, D2 ..$150.00
Barbie, Scottish, 1980, Dolls of the World series, NRFB, D2 ....$125.00
Barbie, Shopping Spree, FAO Schwarz, 1994 department store special, NRFB, D2 ....$40.00
Barbie, Silken Flame, porcelain, 1992, Disney Exclusive, blond hair, NRFB, D2...$700.00
Barbie, Silver Screen, FAO Schwarz, 1993 department store special, NRFB, D2 ....$300.00
Barbie, Snow Princess, 1994 department store special, blond hair, NRFB, D2..$150.00
Barbie, Solo in the Spotlight, porcelain, 1989, NRFB, D2 .$200.00
Barbie, Sophisticated Lady, porcelain, 1990, NRFB, D2...$200.00
Barbie, Spanish, 1991, Dolls of the World series, NRFB, D2 ....$50.00
Barbie, Standard, 1970, blond hair, NRFB, D2 ....$700.00
Barbie, Standard, 1970, brunette hair, MIB, D2 ....$550.00
Barbie, Starlight Splendor, Bob Mackie, 1991, NRFB, D2...$700.00
Barbie, Starlily Bride, porcelain, 1994, NRFB, D2 ....$300.00
Barbie, Sterling Wishes, 1991, Spiegel, NRFB, D2 ....$175.00

Photo courtesy Lee Garmon

Barbie, Starlight Splendor, Bob Mackie, 1991, M, $400.00.

Barbie, Style Magic, 1988 department store special, NRFB, D2 ....$25.00
Barbie, Superstar, 1976, orig outfit, M, M15.....................$25.00
Barbie, Superstar, 1993, Walmart, NRFB, D2..................$35.00
Barbie, Swan Lake Ballerina, 1991 department store special, NRFB, D2 ....$300.00
Barbie, Swedish, 1982, Dolls of the World series, NRFB, D2 ..$100.00
Barbie, Sweet 16, blond hair, orig pk dress, NM, D2 ....$50.00
Barbie, Swirl Ponytail, 1964, blond hair, MIB, D2 ....$600.00
Barbie, Swirl Ponytail, 1964, blond hair, orig red swimsuit & shoes, VG, D2/M15, from $250 to $300.00
Barbie, Swirl Ponytail, 1964, red hair, orig swimsuit, NM, D2 ....$450.00
Barbie, Swiss, 1983, Dolls of the World series, NRFB, D2 ....$85.00
Barbie, Talking, 1969, brunette hair, orig outfit, NM, D2 ..$150.00
Barbie, Totally Hair, 1991 department store special, brunette hair, NRFB, D2...$45.00
Barbie, Truly Scrumptious, 1968, orig outfit, NM, D2 ...$300.00
Barbie, Twist 'N Turn, 1966, blond hair, rare paisley swimsuit, M, D2..$400.00
Barbie, Twist 'N Turn, 1966, brunette hair, NRFB, D2 .$900.00
Barbie, Twist 'N Turn, 1966, brunette hair, orig swimsuit, NM, D2 ....$300.00
Barbie, Twist 'N Turn, 1966, brunette hair, redressed, G, M15...$45.00
Barbie, Twist 'N Turn, 1967, blond hair, orig pk swimsuit, NM, D2 ....$225.00
Barbie, Twist 'N Turn, 1967, brunette hair, orig pk swimsuit & hair ribbon, VG, M15...$125.00
Barbie, Twist 'N Turn, 1969, auburn hair, NRFB, D2....$700.00
Barbie, Uptown Chic, 1993, Classique Collection, NRFB, D2 ....$65.00

Barbie, Valentine, 1994 department store special, NRFB, D2 ....$50.00

Barbie, Wedding Fantasy, 1989 department store special, NRFB, D2 ....$40.00

Barbie, Western, 1980, orig outfit, MIB, M15 ....$20.00

Barbie, Winter Fantasy, FAO Schwarz, 1990 department store special, NRFB, D2 ....$300.00

Barbie as Dorothy, Hollywood Legend series, 1994, NRFB, D2 ....$65.00

Barbie as Scarlett, Hollywood Legend series, 1994, gr & wht picnic dress, NRFB, D2/M15, from $55 to $75.00

Barbie as Scarlett, Hollywood Legend series, 1994, red dress, NRFB, D2 ....$75.00

Cara, Deluxe Quick Curl, 1976, MIB..............................$60.00

Casey, 1967, blond hair, redressed, VG, M15 ....$100.00

Chris, 1967, brunette hair, orig outfit & bows, M, D2 ...$110.00

Christie, Pink & Pretty, 1982, orig outfit, VG, M15 ....$20.00

Christie, Talking, 1968, MIB $150.00

Curtis, Free Moving, 1975, MIB.....................................$50.00

Ken, Earring Magic, 1992, NRFB, $50.00.

Ken, Mod Hair, 1973, rooted brn hair, orig outfit, VG, M15 ..$35.00

Ken, Rollerblade, 1991 department store special, NRFB, D2 ..$30.00

Ken, Spanish Talking, 1970, MIB...................................$200.00

Ken, Superstar, 1976, orig outfit, VG, M15 ....$25.00

Ken, Western, 1980, orig outfit, VG, M15........................$20.00

Ken, 1961, flocked blond or brunette hair, straight legs, M, D2..$160.00

Ken, 1961, flocked blond or brunette hair, straight legs, NRFB, D2 ....$350.00

Ken, 1962, pnt brunette hair, straight legs, dressed in Prince outfit, NM, D2 ....$325.00

Francie, 1966, blond hair, straight legs, MIB (dress is not original), $450.00.

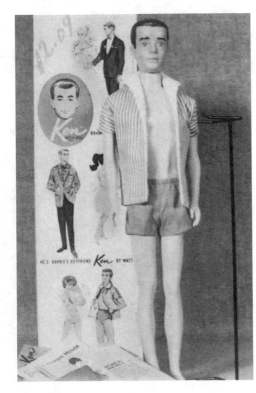

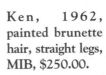

Ken, 1962, painted brunette hair, straight legs, MIB, $250.00.

Francie, Growin' Pretty Hair, 1970, MIB.........................$200.00

Francie, Hair Happenin's, 1970, nude, w/3 of 4 hairpcs, NM, D2 ....$200.00

Francie, Malibu, 1970, orig swimsuit, VG, M15 ....$45.00

Francie, Twist 'N Turn, 1967, brunette hair, nude, NM, D2..$275.00

Francie, Twist 'N Turn, 1967, brunette hair, orig swimsuit, M, D2 ....$325.00

Francie, 1966, blond hair, straight legs, MIB, D2 ....$500.00

Ken, Busy, 1972, pnt brn hair, orig outfit & accessories, VG, M15..$65.00

Ken, Dreamglow (Black), 1986, orig outfit, VG, M15......$40.00

Ken, Hot Skating, 1994 department store special, NRFB, D2..$25.00

Ken, Malibu, 1971, orig swimsuit, VG, M15....................$20.00

Ken, 1965, pnt brunette hair, bendable legs, orig swimsuit, M, D2 ....$300.00

Ken, 30th Anniversary, porcelain, 1991, NRFB, D2......$175.00

Ken as Rhett, Hollywood Legend series, 1994, NRFB, D2/M15, from $65 to..$75.00

Ken as Tin Man, Hollywood Legend series, 1995, NRFB, D2 ....$65.00

Midge, Earring Magic, 1993, MIB $25.00

Midge, Sea Holiday, foreign, 1992 department store special, NRFB, D2 ....$50.00

Midge, Ski Fun, 1991 department store special, NRFB, D2 ..$30.00

Midge, 1963, brunette hair, straight legs, orig swimsuit, NM, D2 ....$125.00

Midge, 1963, pnt hair, replica swimsuit, complete w/3 wigs & stand, D2..$400.00

Midge, 1963, red hair, straight legs, MIB, D2 ....$225.00

Midge, 1963, red hair, straight legs, nude, EX, D2..........$125.00

Midge, 1965, blond or brunette hair, bendable legs, MIB, D2..$700.00

Midge, 1965, red hair, bendable legs, orig swimsuit, EX, D2..$300.00

Midge, 30th Anniversary, porcelain, 1992, NRFB, D2 ..$300.00

PJ, Gold Medal Gymnast, 1975, MIB..$85.00

PJ, Live Action, 1971, nude, EX, D2..$75.00

PJ, Live Action, 1971, orig orange & purple outfit, NM, D2 ....$125.00

PJ, Malibu, 1971, orig lavender swimsuit, VG, M15........$20.00

PJ, Twist 'N Turn, 1970, orig swimsuit, NM, D2............$150.00

Ricky, 1965, MIB, D2..$125.00

Ricky, 1965, orig outfit, NM, D2..$65.00

Skipper, Cool Tops, 1990 department store special, NRFB, D2..$20.00

Skipper, Dramatic New Living, 1970, orig swimsuit, M, D2 ..$55.00

Skipper, Growing Up, 1975, orig outfit, VG, M15 ....$35.00

Skipper, Pepsi Spirit, 1989 department store special, NRFB, D2..$65.00

Skipper, Super Teen, 1980, MIB..$30.00

Skipper, Twist 'N Turn, 1969, blond hair w/banana curls, orig swimsuit, EX, D2 ....$150.00

Skipper, Twist 'N Turn, 1969, brunette hair w/banana curls, orig swimsuit, NM, D2..$200.00

Skipper, 1963, brunette hair, straight legs, MIB, D2 ......$300.00

Skipper, 1965, titian hair, orig swimsuit, bendable legs, G, M15..$65.00

Skipper, 1970, red hair, straight legs, MIB, D2 ....$250.00

Skipper, 30th Anniversary, porcelain, 1993, NRFB, D2..$150.00

Skooter, 1963, blond or titian hair, replica swimsuit, straight legs, VG, M15 ....$50.00

Skooter, 1963, brunette hair, straight legs, orig swimsuit, NM, D2..$65.00

Skooter, 1965, blond hair, bendable legs, orig outfit, NM, D2 ....$100.00

Stacey, Talking, 1968, blond hair, MIB, D2 ....$385.00

Stacey, Twist 'N Turn, 1968, blond hair, orig red swimsuit, NM, D2..$150.00

Stacey, Twist 'N Turn, 1968, red hair, orig red swimsuit, NM, D2..$225.00

Stacey, Twist 'N Turn, 1969, blond hair, orig mc swimsuit, NM, D2..$250.00

Teresa, Baywatch, 1994 department store special, NRFB, D2 ....$40.00

Tutti, 1966, blond hair, dressed in Me & My Dog, M, D2 ..$350.00

Tutti, 1966, blond or brunette hair, MIB, D2.................$175.00

Tutti, 1966, blond or brunette hair, orig outfit, EX, D2 ...$75.00

Twiggy, 1967, NRFB, D2..$500.00

Whitney, Perfume Pretty, 1987 department store special, NRFB, D2 ....$110.00

Whitney, Style Magic, 1989, orig outfit, VG, M15 ....$35.00

CASES

Skipper, Dramatic New Living, 1970, MIB, $100.00.

Barbie, 1963, blue background, EX, $25.00.

Barbie, Francie & Skipper, 1965, Barbie wearing International Fair, rare, EX, D2 ....$25.00

Barbie, 1967, lavender w/wht cover, G, M15.....................$12.00

Barbie & Ken, 1963, bl, rectangular, orig hangers & drawers, VG, M15...$40.00

Barbie & Ken, 1964, red, EX, D2 ....$25.00

Barbie & Midge Travel Pals, 1963, blk, G, D2 ....$25.00

Barbie & Skipper, 1964, yel, dbl opening, EX, D2............$15.00

Barbie & Steffie, 1972, makes into 2 beds, G, M15 ....$15.00

Barbie & the Rockers, 1985, dbl opening, VG, M15........$30.00

Barbie in Fashion Shiner, 1965, wht, hdl broken o/w NM, D2 ....$10.00

Barbie's Playhouse Pavillion, Europe, 1978, plastic 2-room carrying case, NRFB, D2...$65.00

Black Barbie in Evening Extravaganza & Movie Date, 1962, VG, M15 ....$25.00

Francie & Casey, 1966, G, M15.....................................$20.00

Ken in Rally Days, 1962, teal, VG, M15 ....$20.00

Madison Avenue, FAO Schwarz, 1991, EX, D2 ....$75.00

Miss Barbie, 1963, blk patent leather w/zipper closure, no mirror o/w EX, D2...$100.00

Ponytail Barbie, 1961, blk, dbl opening, rpl drawers, G....$25.00

Silver Screen Barbie, FAO Schwarz, 1994, EX, D2 ....$55.00

Tutti and Chris Patio Picnic Case, from $125.00 to $150.00.

World of Barbie, 1965, wht flowers & 2 pictures of Barbie, dbl opening, EX, D2 ....$20.00

World of Barbie, 1968, lime gr, G, M15............................$10.00

CLOTHING AND ACCESSORIES

After Five, Barbie, #934, complete, VG, D2.....................$50.00

American Airlines, Barbie, #984, complete, NM, D2 ......$70.00

American Airlines Captain, Ken, #779, NRFB, D2 ....$400.00

Antifreezers, Barbie, #1464, NRFB, D2 ....$125.00

Arabian Nights, Barbie, #874-2, missing 2 bracelets & booklet, NM, D2...$165.00

Arabian Nights, Ken, #774, replica stone on hat, missing booklet, EX, D2 ....$75.00

Ballet Lessons, Skipper, #1905, complete, NM, D2 ....$45.00

Barbie Babysits, #953-2, replica bottle, EX, D2.................$85.00

Barbie Hair Do's Fashion Pak, #100, MOC, D2...............$95.00

Barbie in Hawaii, #1605, missing anklet & booklet, EX, D2 ..$60.00

Barbie in Holland, #823, missing booklet, NM, D2..........$85.00

Barbie in Japan, #821-2, missing booklet, M, D2............$225.00

Barbie Lingerie Fashion Pak, #90, complete, M, D2 ....$30.00

Barbie Shoe Wardrobe Fashion Pak, #1833, complete w/13 pairs of shoes, MOC, D2...$195.00

Barbie-Q, #962, complete, NM, D2 ....$55.00

Big Business, Ken, #1434, complete, EX, D2 ....$25.00

Bloom Zoom, Francie, #1239, NRFB, D2 ....$135.00

Bold Gold, Ken, #1436, complete, NM, D2 ....$25.00

Bride's Dream, Barbie, #947, dress only, G, D2...............$25.00

Busy Gal, Barbie, #981, replica sketches, EX, D2 ....$150.00

Campus Hero, Ken, #770, NRFB, D2..............................$95.00

Campus Sweetheart, Barbie, #1616-1, complete, NM, D2..$500.00

Candy Striper, Barbie, #889-1, complete, M, D2............$275.00

Casuals, Ken, #782-1, complete, NM, D2 ....$40.00

Checkmates, Francie, #1259, complete, M, D2 ....$95.00

Cheerleader, Barbie, #876, complete, M, D2 ....$100.00

Chill Chasers, Skipper, #1926-1, complete, NM, D2 ....$50.00

Cinderella, Barbie, #872-1, complete, NM, D2 ....$200.00

Clam Diggers, Francie, #1258, missing glasses, M, D2 ......$75.00

Clowning Around, Tutti, #3306, complete, M, D2 ....$95.00

College Student, Ken, #1416, complete, M, D2 ....$300.00

Commuter Set, Barbie, #916-4, replica hat & box, NM, D2 ...$225.00

Cotton Casual, Barbie, #912, complete, M, D2 ....$55.00

Country Club, Ken, #1400, complete, NM, D2 ....$60.00

Country Fair, Barbie, #1603, NRFB, D2 ....$200.00

Country Fair, Barbie, #1603-1, complete, NM, D2...........$45.00

Country Music Fashion 'N Sound, Barbie, #1055, missing record, NM, D2..$95.00

Cruise Stripes, Barbie, #918, complete, NM, D2 ....$65.00

Day at the Fair, Skipper, #1911, complete, NM, D2 ......$110.00

Dinner at Eight, Barbie, #946, complete, NM, D2 ....$85.00

Disco Date, Barbie, #1633, complete, NM, D2................$150.00

Dr Ken, #793, NRFB, D2 ....$150.00

Drum Majorette, Barbie, #875, complete, M, $95.00.

Dream Boat, Ken, #785, complete, NM, D2 ....$55.00
Dream Time, Skipper, #1909, complete, NM, D2 ....$45.00
Dream Wraps, Barbie, #1476, complete, M, D2................$35.00
Dreamy Duo, Francie, #3434, missing pants & slip, M, D2...$25.00
Dreamy Pink, Barbie, #1857, complete, M, D2................$45.00
Drum Major, Ken, #775-2, complete, NM, D2 ....$85.00
Drum Majorette, Barbie, #875, jacket only, NM, D2 ....$12.00
Easter Parade, Barbie, #971, replica hat, NM, D2...........$700.00
Enchanted Evening, Barbie, #983-4, complete, NM, D2..$300.00
Evening Gala, Barbie, #1660-2, missing skirt, NM, D2 ..$100.00
Evening Splendor, Barbie, #961-2, complete, M, D2 .....$200.00
Fab City, Barbie, #1874-1, shawl only, M, D2 ....$15.00
Fab Fur, Barbie, #1493-3, jacket only, EX, D2 ....$15.00
Fashion Shiner, Barbie, #1691, complete, M, D2 ....$125.00
Floating Garden, Barbie, #1696-1, complete, NM, D2...$225.00
Floating In, Francie, #1207-1, complete, NM, D2 ....$95.00
Flower Girl, Skipper, #1904-1, complete, NM, D2...........$50.00
Flower Girl, Tutti, #3615, complete, M, D2 ....$125.00
Fraternity Dance, Barbie, #1638-2, complete, EX, D2 ...$250.00
Fraternity Meeting, Ken, #1408, complete, NM, D2 ....$40.00
Fresh as a Daisy, Francie, #1254, complete, NM, D2........$75.00
Friday Night Date, Barbie, #979-1, complete, NM, D2..$100.00
Fun at the Fair, Barbie, #1624-1, complete, NM, D2 .....$125.00
Fun on Ice, Ken, #791, complete, NM, D2 ....$45.00
Fur Out, Francie, #1262, coat only, EX, D2 ....$35.00
Furry Go Round, Francie, #1296, complete, M, D2..........$350.00
Gad Abouts, Francie, #1250, complete, NM, D2 ....$125.00
Garden Party, Barbie, #931, complete, NM, D2 ....$55.00
Garden Wedding, Barbie, #1658-1, complete, NM, D2 .$200.00
Glimmer Glamour, Barbie, #1547, coat only, EX, D2 ......$95.00
Going Bowling, Ken, #1403, complete, NM, D2 ....$25.00

Guinevere, Barbie, #873, complete, NM, D2 ....$175.00
Happy Birthday, Skipper, #1919, dress only, NM, D2 ......$25.00
Here Comes the Groom, Ken, #1426-1, missing hat & gloves,
NM, D2..$500.00
Hill Riders, Francie, #1210-1, complete, NM, D2 ....$60.00
Hip Knits, Francie, #1265, complete, M, D2 ....$75.00
Hot Togs, Barbie, #1063, jacket only, EX, D2 ....$25.00
Iced Blue, Francie, #1274-1, complete, NM, D2...............$65.00
It's Cold Outside, Barbie, #819, complete, NM, D2 ....$35.00
Jump Into Lace, Barbie, #1823-1, complete, NM, D2.......$45.00
Junior Designer, Barbie, #1620-1, missing appliques & booklet,
EX, D2...$75.00
Junior Prom, Barbie, #1614-1, complete, M, D2.............$350.00

Just for Fun, Skipper and Skooter, MOC, $195.00.

Going Huntin', Ken, #1409, complete, M, $45.00.

Gold 'N Glamour, Barbie, #1647, complete, NM, D2....$700.00
Golden Girl, Barbie, #911-1, complete, NM, D2..............$70.00
Golf Gear Fashion Pak, Ken, #13, MOC, D2....................$25.00

Ken in Hawaii, #1404-2, shirt only, NM, D2....................$15.00
Ken in Switzerland, #776-3, missing booklet, NM, D2 ..$110.00
Knit Hit, Barbie, #1804-2, dress only, NM, D2.................$20.00
Knitting Pretty, Barbie, #957-5, complete, VG, D2 ....$125.00
Lace Pace, Francie, #1216, complete, NM, D2 ....$125.00
Lamb 'N Leather, Barbie, #1467, coat only, NM, D2 ....$25.00
Land & Sea, Skipper, #1917, complete, M, D2.................$95.00
Land Ho, Francie, #1220, complete, NM, D2 ....$50.00
Learning To Ride, Skipper, #1935, NRFB, D2 ....$250.00
Leather Limelight, Francie, #1269, complete, NM, D2..$125.00
Leather Weather, Barbie, #1751, complete, NM, D2 ....$85.00
Lemon Fluff, Skipper, #1749, complete, NM, D2 ....$35.00
Let's Dance, Barbie, #978-1, replica necklace, NM, D2 ...$55.00
Let's Play House, Skipper, #1932, complete, EX, D2......$110.00
Little Red Riding Hood, Barbie, #880-1, missing basket & hat,
EX, D2 ....$150.00
Lollapaloozas, Skipper, #1947, complete, M, D2 ....$75.00
Masquerade, Barbie, #944, complete, NM, D2 ....$85.00
Masquerade, Ken, #794-2, complete, NM, D2 ....$55.00
Me 'N My Doll, Skipper, #1913-2, complete, NM, D2 ..$125.00
Midi Plaid, Francie, #3444, NRFB, D2.............................$50.00

Mood Matchers, Barbie, #1792, missing dress & belt, NM, D2 ....$45.00

Moonbeams, Barbie, #1694-1, complete, NM, D2 ....$125.00

Music Center Matinee, Barbie, #1663-1, complete, M, D2 ...$450.00

Night Clouds, Barbie, #1841, complete, NM, D2 ....$35.00

Nightly Negligee, Barbie, #965, complete, NM, D2 ....$45.00

O-Boy Corduroy, Barbie, #3486, complete, NM, D2 ....$50.00

On the Avenue, Barbie, #1644, complete, NM, D2 ....$300.00

Open Road, Barbie, #985-7, missing glasses, EX, D2 ......$150.00

Orange Blossom, Barbie, #987, NRFB, D2 ....$250.00

Outdoor Casuals, Skipper, #1915, complete, M, D2 ....$50.00

Partners in Print, Francie, #1293, Sears Exclusive, complete, NM, D2 ....$600.00

Patio Party, Barbie, #1692-1, complete, NM, D2 ....$125.00

Pazam, Francie, #1213, complete, NM, D2 ....$150.00

Peachy Fleecy, Barbie, #915, complete, NM, D2 ....$65.00

Picnic Set, Barbie, #967-1, complete, NM, D2 ....$125.00

Pinky PJ's, Tutti, #3616, complete, M, D2 ....$75.00

Plantation Belle, Barbie, #966, complete, M, D2 ....$300.00

Polka Dots & Rainbows, Francie, #1255-1, complete, NM, D2 ....$35.00

Poodle Parade, Barbie, #1643, dress & jacket only, EX, D2 ..$50.00

Posy Party, Skipper, #1955, complete, NM, D2 ....$85.00

Pretty as a Picture, Barbie, #1652, complete, M, D2 ......$175.00

Prince, Ken, #772-4, missing slipper & booklet, EX, D2 ..$95.00

Prom Pinks, Francie, #1295, dress & coat only, VG, D2 ..$95.00

Puddle Jumpers, Tutti, #3601, complete, M, D2 ....$20.00

Quick Shift, Francie, #1266, complete, NM, D2 ....$125.00

Rainy Day Checkers, Skipper, #1928-1, complete, NM, D2 ..$175.00

Rally Days, Ken, #788-2, missing keys, NM, D2 ....$25.00

Red Flare, Barbie, #939-2, complete, NM, D2 ....$50.00

Red Sensation, Skipper, #1901, complete, M, D2 ....$55.00

Registered Nurse, Barbie, #991, complete, NM, D2 ....$90.00

Resort Set, Barbie, #963-1, complete, EX, D2 ....$65.00

Roller Skate Date, Ken, #1406, complete, NM, D2 ....$55.00

Roman Holiday, Barbie, #968, complete, NM, D2 ......$1,500.00

Romantic Ruffles, Barbie, #1871, complete, NM, D2.......$95.00

Rovin' Reporter, Ken, #1417, NRFB, D2.....................$300.00

Sailor, Ken, #796, NRFB, D2 ....$125.00

Sand Castle, Tutti, #3603, complete, EX, D2 ....$50.00

Satin 'N Rose, Barbie, #1611-2, complete, EX, D2.........$125.00

Saturday Night Date, Ken, #786, complete, NM, D2 ....$45.00

School Days, Skipper, #1907-1, complete, NM, D2 ....$40.00

School Girl, Skipper, #1921, complete, M, D2 ....$150.00

Senior Prom, Barbie, #951-1, complete, NM, D2 ....$85.00

Shape Ups, Barbie, #1782-1, missing shoes, M, D2 ....$30.00

Sheath Sensation, Barbie, #986-1, complete, EX, D2 ....$50.00

Shore Lines, Ken, #1435, NRFB, D2..............................$50.00

Silken Flame, Barbie, #977-1, complete, NM, D2 ....$75.00

Singing in the Shower, Barbie, #988-2, complete, M, D2 ...$40.00

Skate Mates, Francie, #1793-1, complete, EX, D2 ....$45.00

Skating Fun, Skipper, #1908, complete, NM, D2 ....$45.00

Ski Champ, Ken, #798, NRFB, D2 ....$125.00

Ski Queen, Barbie, #948-1, complete, EX, D2 ....$65.00

Ski Scene, Barbie, #1797, NRFB, D2 ....$110.00

Skimmy Stripes, Skipper, #1956, complete, NM, D2 .....$150.00

Skin Diver, Ken, #1406, complete, NM, D2 ....$15.00

Skippin' Rope, Tutti, #3604-4, complete, M, D2 ....$30.00

Sledding Fun, Skipper, #1939, NRFB, D2 ....$300.00

Sleeper Set, Ken, #781-2, pajamas only, EX, D2 ....$10.00

Sleeping Pretty, Barbie, #1636-2, complete, EX, D2 ....$75.00

Sleepy Time Gal, Barbie, #1674-1, robe only, NM, D2 ....$25.00

Snake Charmers, Francie, #1245-1, jacket only, EX, D2 ..$10.00

Snazz, Francie, #1225, complete, EX, D2 ....$65.00

Snugg Fuzz, Barbie, #1913-1, complete, NM, D2 ....$125.00

Solo in the Spotlight, Barbie, #982, complete, NM, D2 ...$200.00

Sorority Meeting, Barbie, #937, complete, NM, D2 ....$70.00

Special Date, Ken, #1401, complete, NM, D2 ....$85.00

Sports Man Fashion Pak, Ken, #1802, MOC, D2 ....$75.00

Stormy Weather, Barbie, #949-2, complete, M, D2.........$45.00

Stripes Away, Barbie, #1775, complete, NM, D2 ....$150.00

Style Setters, Francie, #1268, complete, NM, D2...........$125.00

Suburban Shopper, Barbie, #969, dress only, NM, D2......$25.00

Summer Coolers, Francie, #1292-1, missing umbrella, NM, D2 ....$125.00

Sweater Girl, Barbie, #976-2, complete, EX, D2 ....$55.00

Sweet 'N Swingin', Francie, #1283, complete, NM, D2 .$275.00

Sweet Dreams, Barbie, #973, complete, NM, D2 ....$40.00

Swirly Cue, Barbie, #1822, complete, M, D2 ....$125.00

Tangerine Scene, Barbie, #1451, complete, M, D2 ....$40.00

Tennis Anyone, Barbie, #941, complete, EX, D2 ....$35.00

Tenterrific, Francie, #1211, complete, NM, D2 ....$125.00

Terry Togs, Ken, #784, NRFB, D2 ....$100.00

Tickled Pink, Barbie, #1681-1, complete, G, D2 ....$150.00

Time for Tennis, Ken, #790, NRFB, D2 ....$120.00

Togetherness, Barbie, #1842-1, complete, NM, D2..........$75.00

Top It Off Fashion Pak, Ken, #1800, MOC, D2 ....$75.00

Touchdown, Ken, #799, NRFB, D2 ....$125.00

Travel Togethers, Barbie, #1688-2, complete, NM, D2....$75.00

Tropicana, Barbie, #1460, dress only, EX, D2 ....$25.00

Tweed Somes, Francie, #1286, complete, NM, D2.........$300.00

Twiggy Gear, #1728, NRFB, D2....................................$325.00

Twigsters, Twiggy, #1727, NRFB, D2 ....$325.00

Twinkle Togs, Barbie, #1854, complete, EX, D2 ....$95.00

Saturday Matinee, Barbie, #1615, complete, M, $500.00.

Two Way Tiger, Barbie, #3402, complete, NM, D2 ....$45.00
Under Pretties, Skipper, #1900, complete, NM, D2 ....$25.00
Velvet 'N Lace, Skipper, #1948-1, complete, EX, D2 ....$75.00
Velveteens, Barbie, #1818, Sears Exclusive, complete, VG,
    D2 ....$250.00
Victory Dance, Ken, #1411-1, blazer only, NM, D2 ....$10.00
Wedding Day, Barbie, #972-4, missing garter, EX, D2 ...$100.00
Wedding Wonder, Barbie, #1849-1, dress only, NM, D2 .$35.00
Wedding Wonder, Francie, #1244-1, complete, NM, D2 ...$125.00
Winter Holiday, Barbie, #975-2, complete, EX, D2 ....$65.00
Winter Wows, Barbie, #1486-1, boots not orig, NM, D2 .$75.00
Yachtsman, Ken, #789, NRFB, D2 ....$100.00

FURNITURE, ROOMS, AND HOUSES

Barbie & Francie Campus, #4093, 1966, MIB $700.00
Barbie & Ken Little Theater, 1964, MIB $600.00
Barbie Dream Canopy Bed, #5641, 1987, NRFB, D2 ....$15.00
Barbie Dream Furniture, sofa & coffee table, #2475, 1978, M
    (worn box), D2 ....$10.00
Barbie Dream Furniture, vanity & stool, #2469, 1978, NRFB,
    D2 ....$15.00
Barbie Dream House, 1961, 1st edition, complete, NM, D2...$150.00
Barbie Dream House Finishing Touches, bedroom set, #3769,
    MOC, D2 ....$6.00
Barbie Dream House Finishing Touches, living room set, #3769,
    MOC, D2 ....$6.00

Barbie Lawn Swing and Planter, Go-Together Furniture, MIB, $150.00.

Barbie's Cookin' Fun Kitchen, #4987, 1971, MIB $100.00
Barbie's Family House, 'Carnaby St,' 1966, 3 open rooms
    w/round table & 2 chairs, G, M15 ....$35.00
Barbie's Room-Fulls Country Kitchen, #7407, 1974, NRFB,
    D2 ....$50.00
Barbie's Room-Fulls Studio Bedroom, #7405, 1974, NRFB,
    D2 ....$50.00
Barbie's Teen Dream Bedroom, #4985, 1971, MIB, from $35
    to $50.00
Skipper's Dream Room, #4094, 1964, NRFB, D2 ....$600.00
Skipper's 2-in-1 Bedroom, #9282, 1975, NRFB, D2 ....$100.00

Skipper 'n Skooter Double Bunk Beds and Ladder, Go-Together Furniture, MIB, $150.00.

Suzy Goose, Skipper's Jeweled Bed, 1965, MIB, D2 ....$150.00
Suzy Goose, Skipper's Jeweled Vanity, 1965, NRFB, D2 ..$250.00
Suzy Goose Hope Chest, 1961, EX, D2 ....$5.00
Suzy Goose Vanity, 1963, G, D2 ....$25.00
Suzy Goose Wardrobe, 1961, EX, D2 ....$25.00
World of Barbie House, #1048, 1968, M $175.00

GIFT SETS

Air Force Barbie & Ken, 1993, NRFB, D2 ....$50.00
Ballerina Barbie on Tour, 1976, MIB $150.00
Barbie & Ken Campin' Out, 1983, MIB $75.00
Barbie Around the Clock, 1963, complete, NMIB, from $3,500
    to $4,500.00
Barbie Around the Clock, 1963, NRFB, D2 ....$5,500.00
Barbie Denim Fun, #4893, 1989, MIB, D2 ....$50.00
Barbie for President, 1991 department store special, NRFB,
    D2 ....$75.00
Barbie Golden Groove, 1969, Sears, MIB $1,000.00
Barbie on the Go, 1990, MIB $70.00
Barbie Twinkle Town, 1969, Sears, MIB $1,000.00

Barbie, Ken, and Midge on Parade, MIB, from $1,500.00 to $1,800.00.

Barbie's 35th Anniversary, 1993, brunette hair w/curly bangs, NRFB, D2 ....**$175.00**

Barbie's 35th Anniversary, 1993, blond hair, NRFB, D2 ..**$135.00**

Beach Fun Barbie & Ken, 1993, NRFB, D2 ....**$35.00**

Beautiful Blues, 1967, MIB, from $2,500 to **$3,000.00**

Birthday Fun at McDonald's, 1993, NRFB, D2 ....**$50.00**

Dance Club Barbie w/Tape Player, 1989, NRFB, D2 ....**$50.00**

Dance Magic Barbie and Ken, 1990, MIB, **$45.00.**

Disney Barbie & Friends, 1991, NRFB, D2 ....**$65.00**

Francie & Her Swingin' Separates, 1966, Sears, MIB ..**$1,000.00**

Francie Rise & Shine, 1971, NRFB **$1,000.00**

Jamie Strollin' in Style, 1972, Sears, MIB.....................**$425.00**

Ken Red, White & Wild, 1970, Sears, MIB **$250.00**

Little Theater, rare, complete, M (NM box), D2 ....**$6,500.00**

Marine Barbie & Ken, 1992, MIB.................................**$40.00**

PJ Fashion in Motion, 1971, Sears, MIB.......................**$500.00**

PJ Swingin' in Silver, 1970, Sears, MIB.......................**$800.00**

Pose 'N Play Skipper & Her Swing-a-Rounder Gym, 1971, NRFB, D2 ....**$150.00**

Skipper Bright & Breezy, 1969, MIB............................**$725.00**

Skipper Perfectly Pretty, 1968, MIB.............................**$350.00**

Sparkling Pink Barbie, NRFB, D2 ....**$2,650.00**

Stacey Nite Lightning, 1969, Sears, MIB **$1,200.00**

Super Star Barbie & Ken, 1978, MIB............................**$200.00**

Tennis Star Barbie & Ken, 1988, NRFB, D2 ....**$50.00**

Tutti Walking My Dolly, NRFB, D2...............................**$400.00**

Wedding Party Midge, 1990, NRFB, D2 ....**$150.00**

Vehicles

Airplane, Barbie & Ken, Irwin, 1963, steering wheel missing o/w EX, rare, D2 ....**$500.00**

Austin Healy, Irwin, 1962, MIB, D2.............................**$300.00**

Barbie Goin' Boating, Sears Exclusive, 1973, NM, D2 .....**$50.00**

California Dream Beach Taxi, #4520, 1988, MIB **$25.00**

Classy Corvette, 1976, NRFB, D2 ....**$35.00**

Country Camper, #4994, 1971, MIB...............................**$35.00**

Country Camper, 1970, NMIB, D2 ....**$25.00**

Dream Carriage w/Dapple Gray Horses, Europe, 1982, M (separate boxes), D2 ....**$125.00**

Dune Buggy, Barbie and Ken, pink, 1970, NRFB, **$300.00.**

Ferrari, 1987, red, MIB, D2......................................**$50.00**

Ferrari, 1988, wht, MIB, D2......................................**$50.00**

Jaguar XJS, 1994, pk, NRFB, D2 ....**$50.00**

Ken's Hot Rod, Irwin, 1961, NM, D2 ....**$165.00**

Mercedes, 1963, gr, NMIB, D2...................................**$150.00**

Mercedes, 1963, gr, VG, M15 ....**$115.00**

Snowmobile, 1972, Montgomery Ward, MIB **$50.00**

Star Traveler Motorhome, #9794, 1980, MIB...................**$75.00**

Sun 'N Fun Buggy, 1970, orange, MIB, D2 ....**$75.00**

Super Corvette, 1979, remote control, NRFB, D2............**$75.00**

Ten Speeder, 1973, MIB, D2......................................**$15.00**

Travelin' Trailer Deluxe Set, #5514, 1983, MIB **$25.00**

Volkswagen Cabriolet, #3804, 1988, MIB **$35.00**

1957 Belair Chevy, 1989, 1st edition, aqua, MIB, **$150.00.**

1957 Belair Chevy, 1990, 2nd edition, pk, MIB, D2 ......**$125.00**

MISCELLANEOUS

Barbie & Francie Magic Stay-On Fashions, 1966, MIB....$75.00
Book, Barbie & Ken, Random House, 1962, EX, D2........$25.00
Book, Barbie's Fashion Success, Random House, 1962, NM, D2 ....$35.00
Book, Here's Barbie, Random House, 1962, EX, D2.........$25.00
Book & Record Set, Barbie Sings: My First Date & Busy Buzz, 1961, VG, M15...$15.00
Booklet, Skipper, Skooter & Ricky, EX, D2.....................$8.00
Booklet, World of Barbie, EX, D2 ....$30.00
Booklet, World of Barbie Fashions #1, EX, D2 ....$10.00
Box, Color Magic Barbie, 1958, G, D2 ....$150.00
Box, Ken, 1962, EX, D2...$50.00
Box, Midge, 1962, G, D2 ....$50.00
Box, Miss Barbie, 1964, no liner, VG, D2 ....$195.00
Box, Twiggy, 1967, G, D2 ....$65.00
Bubbling Milk Bath, 1961, M, D2 ....$50.00
Calendar, 1989, 30th Anniversary, M...............................$20.00
Catalog, Timeless Creations, 1990, EX, D2 ....$10.00
Colorforms Dress-Up Kit, Barbie, 1970, complete, EX (EX box), F8 ....$25.00
Embroidery Set, Barbie, Ken & Midge, #7686, 1963, complete, MIB, from $200 to.......................................$250.00
Embroidery Set, Midge, #7538A, 1964, MIB, from $200 to $250.00
Francie & Barbie Electric Drawing Set, Lakeside, 1967, NMIB, D2 ....$50.00
Game, Barbie Queen of the Prom, Mattel, 1960, complete, EX (G box), M15..$35.00
Lunch Box, see Lunch Box Category
Magazine, Barbie Bazaar, January/February, 1989, EX, D2..$75.00
Magazine, Barbie Bazaar, May/June, 1990, EX, D2 ....$25.00
Magazine, Barbie Bazaar, September, 1988, EX, D2 ....$125.00
Magazine, World of Barbie, 1964, NM, D2......................$85.00
Ornament, Barbie in sled, McDonald's, 1995, NRFB, D2 .$50.00

Photo courtesy Lee Garmon.

Ornaments, Holiday Barbies, Hallmark, 1993, 1st in series, NRFB, $100.00; 1994, 2nd in series, NRFB, 50.00; 1995, 3rd in series, NRFB, $35.00.

Ornament, Solo in the Spotlight, Hallmark, 1995, 2nd in series, NRFB, M15..$40.00
Paper Dolls, Barbie & Skipper, Whitman #1944, 1964, uncut, M $80.00
Paper Dolls, Barbie Has a New Look!, Whitman #1976, 1967, uncut, M..$90.00

Paper Dolls, Barbie's Beach Bus, Whitman #1996-1, 1976, uncut, M..$15.00
Paper Dolls, Growing Up Skipper, Whitman #1990, 1976, uncut, M..$20.00
Paper Dolls, Pink & Pretty Barbie, Golden #1836-43, 1983, uncut, M..$20.00
Pattern, Barbie, Sightseeing, Sew-Free Fashion Fun #1713, M, D2...$30.00
Pattern, Skipper, Simplicity #6275, MIP, D2...................$25.00
Photo Album, Barbie, 1963, M.......................................$50.00
Tea Set, Barbie's 35th Anniversary, 1994, NRFB, D2......$50.00
Travel Case, Barbie, 1979, w/comb & mirror, VG, M15 ..$15.00
Wallet, pictures Bubble-Cut Barbie, 1962, blk vinyl, G, D2 ..$40.00
Wallet, pictures Skipper, 1964, bl, M...............................$30.00

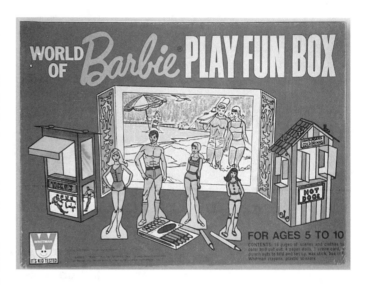

World of Barbie Play Fun Box, Whitman, 1972, complete, NMIB, from $25.00 to $35.00.

Wristwatch, Barbie's 30th Anniversary, Armitron, 1989, pk band, EX, D2..$75.00
Wristwatch, Ponytail Barbie, 1963, bl band, NM, D2....$150.00

Battery-Operated Toys

From the standpoint of being visually entertaining, nothing can compare with the battery-operated toy. Most (probably as much as 95%) were made in Japan from the '40s through the '60s, though some were distributed by American companies — Marx, Ideal, and Daisy, for instance — who often sold them under their own names. So even if they're marked, sometimes it's just about impossible to identify the actual manufacturer. Though batteries had been used to power trains and provide simple illumination in earlier toys, the Japanese toys could smoke, walk, talk, drink, play instruments, blow soap bubbles, and do just about anything else humanly possible to dream up and engineer. Generally, the more antics the toy performs, the more collectible it is. Rarity is important as well, but first and foremost to consider is condition. Because of their complex mechanisms, many will no longer work. Children often stopped them in mid-cycle, rubber hoses and bellows aged and cracked, and leaking batteries caused them to corrode, so very few have survived to the present intact and in good enough condition to interest a collector. Though it's sometimes possible to have them repaired, unless you can buy them cheap enough to allow for the extra expense involved, it is probably better to wait on a better example. Original boxes are a definite plus in assessing the value of a battery-op and can be counted on to add from 30% to 50% (and up), depending on the box's condition, of course, as well as the toy's age and rarity.

We have made every attempt to list these toys by the name as it appears on the original box. Some will sound very similar. Many toys were reissued with only minor changes and subsequently renamed. For more information we recommend *Collecting Toys* by Richard O'Brien and *Collecting Battery Toys* by Don Hultzman (Books Americana).

Advisor: Tom Lastrapes (L4).

See also Aeronautical; Automobiles and Other Vehicle Replicas; Boats; Marx; Robots and Space Toys.

Accordion Bear, Alps, bear w/microphone plays accordion & sways w/light-up eyes, 11", NMIB $900.00
Accordion Player Hobo w/Monkey, Alps, seated hobo plays accordion while monkey plays cymbals, MIB, L4 ....$575.00
Acrobat Police Car, TPS, blk & wht w/flashing light, 10", EX, A $55.00
Acrobot, Y, robot does acrobatics, plastic, MIB, L4 ....$525.00
Aerial Ropeway, TN, EXIB, L4 ....$165.00
Air Control Tower #783, Cragstan, remote control, NMIB, A $200.00
Air Fighter w/Bombing Action, Bandai, advances w/lights & sound, tin w/vinyl-headed pilot, remote control, 10", NMIB, A $260.00
Airmail Helicopter, KO, mystery action w/spinning rotors & sound, MIB, L4 ....$200.00
Albino Gorilla, TN, MIB, L4 ....$525.00
Animal Train, MT, MIB, L4 ....$575.00
Animated Squirrel, S&E, 1950s, 8½", MIB, L4..............$250.00
Anti-Aircraft Jeep, K, advances w/turning turret & light-up guns, 2 figures, litho tin, 9", EX (G box), A...............$85.00
Antique Gooney Car, Alps, 1960s, wht open touring car w/animated driver, 4 actions, NMIB................................$330.00
Arthur-A-Go-Go Drummer, Alps, 1960s, 10", M, L4 ....$475.00
Atomic Armored Train Set, Bandai, litho tin, complete w/track & station, EX (VG box), A $285.00
Atomic Generator, Linemar, NMIB, L4 ....$575.00
Automatic Train Station & Rubber Track, Cragstan, train travels track & conductor moves on platform, scarce, MIB, A.$165.00
B-Z Porter, MT, 1950s, figure on platform truck w/3 pcs of luggage, 7", MIB, L4 ....$375.00
Baby Bertha, Mego, rare, MIB, L4 ....$1,250.00
Ball Blowing Clown, TN, 1950s, 3 actions, litho tin w/cloth clothes, 9", MIB, L4..$350.00
Ball Playing Dog, Linemar, 1950s, 3 actions, tin & plush, 9", M, L4 ....$175.00
Balloon Blowing Monkey, Alps, 1950s, 11", MIB, L4 ....$225.00
Balloon Bunny, Y, remote control, rare, MIB, L4..........$375.00

Balloon Vendor, Japan, 1961, clown w/balloons & bell, tin, cloth & vinyl, 11", MIB, L4 ....$300.00
Bambi, see Walking Bambi
Barber Bear, TN, 1950s, barber clips & combs child's hair w/several other actions, tin & plush, 10", NMIB, L4 ....$525.00
Barney Bear the Drummer Boy, Cragstan, plush & tin w/cloth clothes, remote control, MIB, L4 ....$250.00
Bartender, Rosko, several actions, litho tin & vinyl w/cloth clothes, 11½", MIB, L4..$85.00
Bartender, Rosko, 11½", EX (EX box), A $65.00
Batmobile, Taiwan, bump-&-go w/lights & sound, litho tin w/plastic figures, 10", NMIB, A................................$275.00
Bear the Cashier, Modern Toys, 7½", MIB, L4 ....$425.00
Beauty Parlor Bear, works w/curling iron & comb as bear child squeals & kicks, tin & plush, 10", NMIB.................$825.00
Beethoven the Piano Playing Dog, TN, plays piano & moves head, litho tin & plush, 8½", scarce, NMIB............$265.00
Big Machine Race Car, Taiyo, NMIB, L4 ....$175.00
Bimbo the Clown, Cragstan, MIB, L4............................$675.00
Bingo the Clown, TN, 1950s, 13", rare, NM, L4 ....$375.00
Black Smithy Bear, TN, litho tin & plush, 9", MIB, L4 .$375.00

Blacksmith Bear, AI, 1950s, several actions, lithographed tin and plush, 10", NM (EX box), A, $350.00.

Blinky the Clown, Amico, advances & plays xylophone, light-up eyes, remote control, 10", EX, L4......................$225.00
Blushing Cowboy, Y, 1960s, 4 actions, NM....................$125.00
Blushing Frankenstein, TN, sways, growls & loses his pants, tin, cloth & vinyl, 12", MIB, L4 ....$275.00
Blushing Willie, Y, 1960, man pours drink, face lights up & eyes twirl, tin & plastic, 10", NM, K4................................$70.00
Bobby the Drinking Bear, Y, 1950s, wht, 10", MIB, L4 ..$675.00
Bombadier, Waco, NMIB, L4..$375.00
Bongo the Drumming Monkey, Alps, 1960s, 3 actions, MIB, L4..$250.00
Bongo the Drumming Monkey, Alps, 1960s, 3 actions, VG+, L4..$65.00
Bowling Bank, MB Daniel, 1960s, 3 actions, 10" L, M, L4....$125.00
Brave Eagle, TN, 1950s, beats drum, sways & makes war-whoop sounds, tin & plastic w/cloth clothes, 12", EX, L4.....$65.00

Bruno Accordion Bear, Y, 1950s, slides side to side while playing, tin & plush, remote control, 10", M, L4 ....$225.00

Bubble Blowing Boy, Y, litho tin, 7½", MIB, L4 ....$375.00

Bubble Blowing Dog, Y, 1950s, 8", M, L4 ....$300.00

Bubble Blowing Kangaroo, MT, mama w/baby in pouch, litho tin, 8½", MIB, L4 ....$500.00

Bubble Blowing Lion, MT, 1950s, litho tin, 7½", MIB, L4 ..$200.00

Bubble Blowing Monkey, Alps, 1959, dips wand in solution & blows bubbles, 10", NMIB, L4 ....$150.00

Bubble Blowing Monkey, Alps, 1959, monkey dips wand in solution and blows bubbles, eyes light, 10", VG (VG box), A, $85.00.

Bubble Blowing Musician, Y, 1950s, man blows bubbles w/trumpet behind podium, 11", NMIB..............................$175.00

Bubble Blowing Popeye, Linemar, litho tin, NMIB, A..$1,430.00

Bulldozer, Japan, 1950s, bump-and-go action, lithographed tin, EX, J6, $85.00.

Bunny the Magician, Japan, turns head & tips hat while performing card trick, plush, litho tin & cloth, 13", NMIB, A $275.00

Burger Chef, Y, dog shakes pan & flips burger over barbecue pit, ears raise & eyes roll, tin & plush, 10", MIB............$275.00

Busy Housekeeper Bear, Alps, pushes vacuum cleaner w/lights & sound, litho tin & plush, 8", NM, L4 ....$225.00

Busy Housekeeper Rabbit, Alps, pushes vacuum cleaner w/lights & sound, litho tin & plush, 8", MIB, L4 ....$425.00

Cable Express Train, TN, locomotive & coal car travel on cable, litho tin, 8", MIB, A $95.00

Cappy the Baggage Porter Dog, Alps, 1960s, 12", NM, L4 .$175.00

Captain Blushwell, Y, several actions, tin, vinyl & cloth, 11", MIB, L4...$165.00

Captain Kidd Pirate Ship, Frankonia, bump-&-go, cannon shoots caps w/smoking action, tin, 13", rare, NM (EX box)...$300.00

Casino King Slot Machine, Waco, EX, L4...............$100.00

Champion Weight Lifter, YM, 1960s, monkey lifts barbell & face turns red, 10", NM (EX box), M5.....................$140.00

Chap the Obedient Dog, Rosko, MIB, L4......................$275.00

Charlie the Drumming Clown, Alps, 9½", MIB, L4.......$300.00

Charlie Weaver Bartender, TN, 1962, makes drinks w/several actions, 12", MIB, L4...$125.00

Charm the Cobra, Alps, 1960s, 6", MIB, L4...............$1,250.00

Chef Cook, Y, 1960s, 11½", MIB, L4 ....$275.00

Chevy Police Car, Linemar, tin, 9", EX, J2.....................$110.00

Chimp and Pup Rail Car, Cragstan/Y, chimp and pup work handlebars as eyes light up, lithographed tin, 9", NM (EX box), A, $275.00.

Chimpy the Drumming Monkey, Alps, 1960s, 6 actions, w/drum & cymbals, 9", NM, L4...$125.00

Chippy the Chipmunk, Alps, 1950s, 12", M, L4 ....$125.00

Chippy the Chipmunk, Alps, 1950s, 12", MIB, L4.........$225.00

Circus Elephant, TN, 1950s, plush over tin, 10", MIB, L4 ....$200.00

Circus Fire Engine, MT, 1960s, 10", EX, L4 ....$225.00

Circus Jet, TN, circles & fires machine gun, MIB, L4 ....$150.00

Circus Lion, VIA, hit circus mat with wand for several actions, lithographed tin and plush, 10", M (EX box), A, $475.00.

Circus Queen Seal, rare, MIB, L4 ....$575.00

Claney the Great, Ideal, MIB, L4....................................$375.00

Climbing Donald Duck on His Friction Fire Engine, Linemar, Pluto driving, 18", EX (EX box) $1,500.00

Climbing Linesman, TPS, climbs up & down telephone pole, head lamp lights up, litho tin, 24", EX (EX box).....$300.00

Clown Car, Y, EX, L4 ....$100.00

Clown Magician, Alps, tips hat & flips stack of cards, tin, cloth & vinyl, 12", EX (VG box) $175.00

Clucking Clara, CK, MIB, L4...$225.00

Cock-A-Doodle-Doo Rooster, Mukuni, advances & crows, tin & cloth, 8", NM (EX box), A...............................$100.00

Cock-A-Doodle-Doo Rooster, Mukuni, 8", VG+, L4.......$50.00

Coffeetime Bear, TN, pours & drinks cup of coffee, plush & tin, not working o/w EX (EX box), A...........................$150.00

Cola Drinking Bear, Alps, 1950s, rare yel version, 3 actions, NMIB..$185.00

Combination Volkswagen, nonfall mystery bump-&-go action, 9½", NMIB, A...$150.00

Comic Police Car, Bandai, bump-&-go action w/flashing lights, litho tin w/vinyl-headed driver, 9½", EX (G box), A..$100.00

Comic Tank, Tomy, mystery action, rare, MIB, L4........$350.00

Coney Island Bumper Car, Alps, EX, L4.....................$250.00

Coney Island Penny Machine, Remco, 15", NMIB, L4..$185.00

Coney Island Rocket Ride, Alps, 1950s, spins w/ringing bell & flashing lights, litho tin, 14", rare, EX+, M5............$375.00

Cragstan Bullfighter, TN, 1950s, litho tin, EX $100.00

Cragstan Circus Jet, NMIB, J2.......................................$225.00

Cragstan Crapshooter, Japan, 9", VG (G box), A $50.00

Cragstan Crapshooting Monkey, NM, L4 ....$75.00

Cragstan Dilly Dalmatian, MIB, L4 ....$250.00

Cragstan Melody Band Clown, tin, EX, J2.....................$115.00

Cragstan One-Armed Bandit, Y, 1960s, 3 actions, 6", MIB, L4...$250.00

Cragstan Playboy, NM, L4 ....$200.00

Cragstan Telly Bear, S&E, 1950s, 6 actions, 9", MIB, L4 ..$500.00

Cragstan Tugboat, SAN, 13", MIB, L4............................$225.00

Cragstan Two-Gun Sheriff, Y, 1950s, 5 actions, EX (G box) ..$200.00

Crawling Baby (Call Me Baby), Rosko, NMIB, L4.........$275.00

Cuty Cook (Elephant Chef), Y, 1960s, NMIB, L4......$1,275.00

Cuty Cook (Hippo Chef), Y, 1960s, 10", NMIB, L4...$1,275.00

Cycling Daddy, Bandai, 1960s, vinyl figure rides tricycle, 10", MIB, L4...$225.00

Cycling Daddy, Bandai, 1960s, 10", NM, L4 ....$125.00

Cyclist Clown, K, advances w/flashing light, tin & cloth, remote control, 7", NMIB, L4 ....$750.00

Daisy the Jolly Drumming Duck, Alps, 1950s, 9", MIB, L4..$375.00

Daisymatic No 60 Tractor 'N Trailer, MIB, L4 ....$165.00

College Jalopy, Linemar, advances with lights and sound, lithographed tin with 4 figures, remote control, 9½", EX (VG box), A, $450.00.

Photo courtesy June Moon.

Dandy the Happy Drumming Pup, Cragstan, 1950s, lithographed tin and plush, MIB, J6, $200.00.

Dennis the Menace Playing Xylophone, Rosko, 1950s, 3 actions, MIB, from $250 to $350.00

Dick Tracy Police Car, Linemar, 1950s, tin, remote control, 8", EX (VG box), A $300.00

Dip-ie the Whale, Japan, shoots water w/plastic spout, ears flap, litho tin w/rubber ears, 13", EX (EX box), A $225.00

Disney Acrobats, Linemar, 3 different versions w/Mickey, Pluto or Donald, 9", MIB, L4, ea $875.00

Disneyland's Haunted House Bank, 1960s, tin & plastic, EX, T1 ....$150.00

Dolly Dressmaker (Dolly Seamstress), TN, 1950s, dolly at sewing machine, 10 actions, 7", NMIB, A...............$200.00

Donald Duck, see Climbing Donald Duck on His Friction Fire Engine and Disney Acrobats

Dozo the Steaming Clown, Rosko, 1960s, litho tin w/cloth clothes, 10", MIB, L4..$575.00

Dream Boat, Japan, 1950s, lithographed tin, 7", EX, $275.00.

Photo courtesy Dunbar Gallery.

Drinker's Savings Bank, Illfelder, 1960s, 9", M, L4 ....$125.00

Drinking Captain, S&E, 1950, EX, L4.............................$75.00

Drinking Captain, S&E, 1950, MIB, L4 ....$185.00

Drinking Dog, Y, 1950s, M, L4 ....$125.00

Drinking Licking Cat, TN, 1950s, pours & drinks from cup, plastic, plush & litho tin, 10", MIB, L4 ....$325.00

Drinking Monkey, Alps, 1960s, 8", NM, L4 ....$100.00

Drinking Sheriff, Y, NM, L4 ....$100.00

Drumming Bear, Alps, 1950s, Y, plays drum & eyes light, 12½", rare, NMIB, L4..$1,600.00

Drumming Bunny, Alps, MIB, L4 ....$125.00

Drumming Happy Santa, plastic w/red cloth costume, wht fur trim, 11½", new old stock, A $50.00

Drumming Mickey Mouse, Linemar, advances & plays drum, litho tin w/cloth clothes, remote control, 11", NM (EX box), A...$1,200.00

Drumming Target Bear, MT, EX, L4 ....$275.00

Dune Buggy, TPS, tin & plastic, 11", EX+, J2 ....$100.00

Electric Cable Car, MIB, L4..$125.00

Electro Toy Fire Engine, Linemar, MIB, L4....................$175.00

Electro Toy Sand Loader w/Conveyor, Linemar, MIB, L4 ....$225.00

Elephant Chef, see Cuty Cook

Expert Motorcyclist, Modern Toys, rider mounts & dismounts, litho tin, 11½", MIB, L4 ....$1,000.00

Father Bear, MT, rare, MIB, L4..................................$500.00

Feeding Baby Bear, Y, EX, L4.....................................$175.00

Feeding Bird Watcher, Linemar, baby birds chirp as mother bird swings around to feed them, tin & plush, 10", MIB, L4 ..$675.00

Feeding Bird Watcher, Linemar, 10", NM, A.................$400.00

Fido the Xylophone Player, Alps, litho tin & plush dog, 9", scarce, MIB, L4...$475.00

Fighting Bull, Alps, EXIB, T1.......................................$35.00

Fire Chief Car, Cragstan, 1957, red Cadillac Sedan advances w/lights & sound, remote control, 7", EX (G box), A ..$45.00

Fire Ladder Truck, TN, tin, 13", unused, NMIB, J2 ....$250.00

Fire Tricycle, TN, advances w/siren & lights, litho tin, 10", NM (EX box), A $475.00

Fishing Polar Bear, Alps, bear pulls fish out of pond, throws it in basket & squeals, plush & tin, 10", NMIB, A..........$250.00

Fishing Polar Bear, Alps, 10", NM, L4 ....$200.00

Flexie Pocket Monkey, Alps, MIB, L4 ....$100.00

Flipper the Spouting Dolphin, Bandai, MIB, L4.............$125.00

Flutterbirds, Alps, 2 birds fly above birdhouse as 1 chirps in door, litho tin & plush, 27", MIB, L4..................................$550.00

Flying Dutchman, Remco, EXIB, T1 ....$125.00

Fork-Lift S-1002, NM, L4...$145.00

Foto Finish Racehorse, MT, 1950s, 12", rare, VG+, L4..$275.00

Frankie the Roller Skating Monkey, Alps, 1950s, remote control, 12", MIB, L4 ....$250.00

Fred & Barney Car, AHI, 1974, rare, NM $175.00

Fred Flintstone's Bedrock Band, Alps, 1962, Fred plays drum & cymbals, litho tin & vinyl, 8", EX (EX box), A.......$825.00

Fred Flintstone's Bedrock Band, Alps, 1962, 8", NM, L4...$600.00

Friendly Jocko My Favorite Pet, Alps, 1950s, 8", NMIB, L4 ....$400.00

Frontline Army Jeep, Daishin, MIB, L4 ....$150.00

Funland Cup Ride, Sonsco, kids spin around in cups, MIB, from $300 to $375.00

Futurmatic Airport, Automatic Toy Co, remote control, complete, M (worn box), A $300.00

Gino Neopolitan Balloon Blower, Tomiyama, 10", MIB, L4 .$225.00

GM Coach Bus, Yone, bump-&-go action as door swings open & attendant directs passengers out, 16", VG, A $150.00

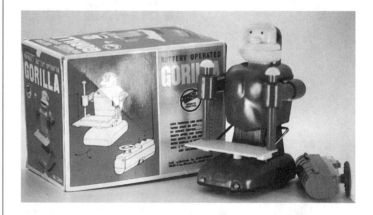

Gorilla, Bandai, Montgomery Ward store special, plastic, remote control, 8", MIB, $45.00.

Go Go Fireman, Toplay, 1982, cat-like fireman climbs ladder, NMIB, M17 ....$70.00

Godzilla, Bandai, gr version, remote control, 6", MIB, A $135.00

Godzilla, Bandai, silver version, remote control, 7", MIB, A.$125.00

Good Time Charlie, MT, 1960s, 12", EX, L4 ....$125.00

Grand Prix Raceway, Merzbach, remote control, NMIB, L4..$375.00

Grand-Pa Panda, MT, sits in rocking chair & eats popcorn, eyes light, 9", MIB $450.00

Growling Tiger Trophy Plaque, Cragstan, tiger head mounted on plaque, pull-string action, 10", rare, NM (EX box)....$335.00

Happy 'N Sad Magic Face Clown, Y, moves side to side & plays accordion, face changes expression, 10", NMIB, L4 ..$275.00

Happy Band Trio, MT, 1970s, dog, rabbit & bear play instruments on litho tin stage w/cb backdrop, 11", MIB, L4...........$675.00

Happy Clown Theatre, Y, 1950s, w/puppet, 3 actions, 10", MIB, L4 ....$425.00

Happy Dog Family, MT, MIB, L4 ....$125.00

Happy Fiddler Clown, Alps, litho tin w/cloth clothes, 10", MIB, L4 ....$600.00

Happy Miner, Bandai, 1960s, 11", MIB, L4.................$1,350.00

Happy Naughty Chimp, Daishin, 1960, MIB, L4 ....$100.00

Happy Santa, Moran #708, MIB, L4 ....$325.00

Happy Santa One-Man Band, Alps, 9", MIB, L4 ....$300.00

Happy Singing Bird, MT, 1950s, 9", MIB, L4.................$200.00

Hasty Chimp, Y, 1960s, 9", MIB, L4 ....$125.00

High Jinks at the Circus, Alps, clown w/performing monkey, 6 actions, MIB, L4 ....$375.00

High Jinks at the Circus, Alps, 6 actions, EX, L4 ....$150.00

Highway Drive, TN, car maneuvers through highway obstacles, MIB, L4...$125.00

Hippo Chef, see Cuty Cook

Hoop Zing Girl, Linemar, girl wiggles w/Hula Hoop, celluloid figure on tin base, 12", scarce, NM, L4 ....$275.00

Hoopy the Fishing Duck, Alps, 10", MIB, L4 ....$575.00

Hooty the Happy Owl, Alps, 1960s, 6 actions, 9", MIB, L4 ..$185.00

Hopping Pup w/Cart, VIA, MIB, L4 ....$125.00

Hot Rod Custom T Ford, Alps, 1960s, 4 actions, 10½", MIB, L4..$200.00

Housekeeping Rabbit, Alps, MIB, L4..............................$325.00

HR-47 Army Helicopter, EX, L4.....................................$100.00

Huey Helicopter, MIB, L4...$100.00

Hungry Baby Bear, Y, 1950s, mama bear feeds baby bear, several actions, tin & plush, 10", MIB, L4......................$275.00

Hungry Baby Bear, Y, 1950s, 10", VG+, L4......................$100.00

Hungry Cat, Linemar, 1960s, 7 actions, w/tray & fish, 9", MIB, L4..$700.00

Ice Cream Vendor, TN, travels w/ringing bell & lights, litho tin, 10", rare, NM (EX box), A $1,425.00

Jalopy, Linemar, 1950s style w/allover graffiti, tin w/celluloid driver, 7", driver missing arm o/w EX (G box), A......$75.00

Photo courtesy Bill Bruegman.

James Bond's Aston-Martin, Gilbert/Glidrose, 1965, advances with several actions as figure pops up, tin, 11", NMIB, $475.00.

Japanese Bullet Train, MT, litho tin train w/plastic track, MIB, L4 ....$175.00

Jocko the Drinking Monkey, Linemar, pours drink & lifts to mouth, light-up eyes, litho tin, 11", NM (EX box), A...............$150.00

Photo courtesy Dunbar Gallery.

Hot Rod Racer, Cragstan/K, 1950s, lithographed tin, 8", D10, $325.00.

Jolly Bambino the Eating Monkey, Alps, monkey eats candy with several actions, tin and plush, 10", NMIB, $575.00.

Jolly Bambino the Eating Monkey, Alps, 10", EX, A $255.00

Jolly Bear the Drummer Boy, K, NMIB, L4 ....$250.00

Jolly Bear w/Robin, MT, 10", MIB, L4..........................$975.00

Jolly Bear w/Robin, MT, 10", VG+, L4..........................$575.00

Jolly Daddy Elephant, Marusan, 1950s, MIB, L4 ....$350.00

Jolly Daddy Elephant, Marusan, 1950s, NM, L4.............$175.00

Jolly Peanut Vendor, TN, NMIB, L4 ....$525.00

Jolly Pianist, TN, 1950s, dogs plays piano, tin & plush, 8", NM, L4 ....$150.00

Jolly Santa on Snow, Alps, 1950, 13", MIB, L4..............$400.00

Josie the Walking Cow, Daiya, 1950s, 14", MIB, L4 ......$275.00

Josie the Walking Cow, Daiya, 1950s, 14", NM, L4.......$150.00

Jumbo the Bubble Blowing Elephant, Yonezawa, 1950, plush elephant on litho tin base, 7", MIB $185.00

Jumbo the Roaring Elephant, Alps, MIB, L4 ....$175.00

Jungle Jumbo, BC, 1950s, 6 actions, 10", MIB, L4..........$775.00

Jungle Trio, Linemar, 1950s, monkeys & elephant play instruments on platform, M, L4..$575.00

Kissing Couple, Ichida, 1950s, bump-&-go car rolls as bird spins & chirps on hood, 10½", NMIB, L4 ....$225.00

Knitting Grandma, TN, 8½", M, L4 ....$250.00

Ladder Fire Engine, Linemar, forward & reverse action w/ringing bell & telescoping ladder, 3 figures, 12", EX (G box), A.......$175.00

Lady Pup Tending Her Garden, Cragstan, 1950s, several actions, litho tin w/cloth clothes, 8", MIB, L4 ....$500.00

Lady Pup Tending Her Garden, Cragstan, 1950s, 8", NM, A..$250.00

Lambo, Alps, elephant picks up logs, remote control, MIB, L4..$675.00

Laughing Head Leprechaun, Peter/Korean, EX, L4 ....$100.00

Linus the Lovable Lion, Illco, 1970, MIB $40.00

Lion, Linemar, advances & roars, plush over tin, remote control, 10", NM (EX box), A $95.00

Lite-O-Wheel Go Kart, Rosko, MIB, L4..........................$185.00

Loop the Loop Monkey, TN, MIB, L4 ....$100.00

Magic Man Clown, Marusan, advances while smoking pipe and tipping hat, lithographed tin with cloth clothes, 11", MIB, $575.00.

Lucky Car, Marusan, rare, VG+, L4................................$250.00

Lucky Crane, Japan, slot machine w/3 prizes, move lever & push buttons to pick up prize, tin, 9", NM (EX box), A .$1,025.00

Lucky Seven Dice Throwing Monkey, Alps, 1960, MIB, L4 ....$165.00

Luncheonette Bank, Alps, 1960, 12", MIB, L4...............$450.00

M-4 Tank, Taiyo, MIB, L4..$225.00

M-66 Tank, MIB, L4 ....$250.00

Mac the Turtle, Y, rolls over barrel w/several actions, MIB, L4..$250.00

Magic Bulldozer, Y, bump-&-go action, w/driver, 5", MIB, L4..$175.00

Major Tooty, Alps, drum major plays drum, 14", MIB, L4..$275.00

Make-Up Bear, MT, 1960s, 9", EX, L4 ....$375.00

Make-Up Bear, MT, 1960s, 9", MIB, L4..........................$750.00

Mambo the Jolly Drumming Elephant, Alps, 1950s, plays drum & cymbals, tin & plush, 9½", MIB, L4 ....$375.00

Mambo the Jolly Drumming Elephant, Alps, 1950s, 9½", EX, L4..$225.00

Maxwell Coffee-Loving Bear, TN, 10", NMIB, L4.........$250.00

Merry-Go-Round Truck, TN, advances & stops as merry-go-round spins, litho tin, 11", NM (EX box), A...........$800.00

Mickey Mouse, see also Disney Acrobats and Drumming Mickey Mouse

Mickey Mouse & Donald Duck Fire Engine, MT, bump-&-go action w/lights & sound, litho tin w/plastic figures, 16", MIB, A..$425.00

Mickey Mouse Club Dance-A-Tune, Jaymar #800/WDP, unused, MIB, P6...$85.00

Mickey Mouse Flying Saucer, MT, MIB, L4 ....$275.00

Mickey Mouse Loop the Loop, Illco, MIB, L4 ....$175.00

Mickey Mouse Melody Railroad, Frankonia/WDP, 1967, rare, MIB, L4 ....$1,600.00

Mickey Mouse on Handcar, MT, bump-&-go, litho tin w/vinyl head, 10", NM (EX box), A $365.00

Mickey Mouse Sand Buggy, TN, NMIB....................$225.00

Mickey the Magician, Linemar, tin, 10", NMIB, L4 ...$2,500.00

Mighty Mike the Barbell Lifter, K, litho tin & plush, 12", M, L4..$250.00

Minnie Mouse Shopping Cart, Illco/WDP, 1960s-70s, bump-&-go action, plastic, 10", EX (EX box)............................$65.00

Mischievous Monkey, MT, monkey scoots up & down tree w/bone in front of doghouse, litho tin, 18", NM (EX box), A $300.00

Mischievous Monkey, MT, 18", non-working, VG (VG box), A $125.00

Miss Friday the Typist, TN, girl types & bell rings, tin & vinyl, 7", NMIB, M5..$275.00

Miss Friday the Typist, TN, 7", EX, A $175.00

Mobile Artillery Unit, Cragstan, complete, 10", NM (EX box), A $365.00

Moby Dick Boat, Linemar, EX, L4 ....$175.00

Monkey the Shoe Maker, TN, seated monkey smokes pipe & hammers on shoe, MIB, rare, L4 ....$875.00

Mother Bear, MT, sits in rocking chair & knits, head nods & eyes light, tin & plush, 10", MIB, L4 ....$300.00

Mother Bear, MT, 10", EX, L4....................................$185.00

Mr Fox the Magician, Cragstan, fox lifts hat to reveal rabbit, litho tin, 9", NM (EX box), A..................$950.00

Mr MacPooch, SAN, dog advances & lifts pipe to mouth as it lights & puffs smoke, remote control, 8", M (EX box), A $350.00

Mr Magoo Car, Hubley, 1961, Mr Magoo steers as car rocks & rattles, tin w/cloth top, 9", EX (VG box), A $250.00

Mr Strong Pup, K, 1950s, MIB, L4..........................$475.00

Mumbo Jumbo the Hawaiian Drummer, Alps, 3 actions, 10", NM, L4 ....$175.00

Musical Bulldog, Marusan, EX, L4 ....$975.00

Musical Cadillac, Irco, 1955 Cadillac advances & plays 'Home on the Range,' 8½", NM (EX box), A $350.00

Musical Comic Jumping Jeep, Alps, 1970s, 12", M, L4 ..$175.00

Musical Jackal, Linemar, 1950s, 10", rare, MIB, L4 ....$1,075.00

Musical Vegetable Truck, Bandai, MIB, L4...................$275.00

Mustang Fastback Swinger, TPS, advances & circles, lime gr litho tin, 10", NM (EX box), A...............................$65.00

Nautilus Periscope, Cragstan, MIB, L4 ....$225.00

Non-Stop Boat, AHI, MIB, L4......................................$225.00

Nutty Mads Car, Linemar, MIB, L4 ....$675.00

Nutty Nibs, Linemar, pnt tin w/red, wht & blk paper skirt, 12", EX, L4 ....$975.00

Ol' Sleepy Head Rip, Y, 9", MIB, L4 ....$450.00

Old Fashioned Fire Engine, SH, MIB, L4 ....$300.00

Old Fashioned Grandpa's Car, MIB, L4 ....$125.00

Old Time Automobile, Y, 1950s, 9", M, L4 ....$100.00

Open Sleigh, MT, bump-and-go action with light-up lantern, lithographed tin and vinyl, 15", NM (EX box), A, $500.00.

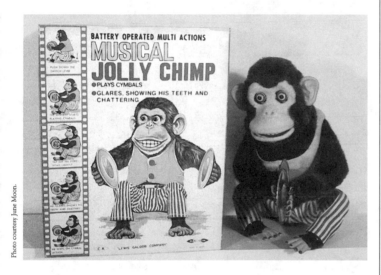

Musical Jolly Chimp, Lewis Galoob Co., 1960s, plays cymbals, shows teeth and chatters, MIB, $95.00.

Musical Marching Bear, Alps, 1950s, beats drum & blows horn, plush & tin w/cloth clothes, MIB, L4 ....$700.00

Musical Showboat, Gakken, plays 'Oh Suzanna', 13½", NMIB, J2 ....$200.00

Overland Stagecoach, Ichida, horse-drawn stagecoach w/driver, litho tin, 18", MIB, L4...$275.00

Pat O'Neill the Fun Loving Irishman, TN, hold flame to glass cigar tip for several actions, 11", rare, MIB, L4........$600.00

Pat the Dog, Alps, MIB, L4..$175.00

Patrol Auto-Tricycle, TN, advances as policeman blows whistle, litho tin, NM (EX box), A $365.00

Pepi the Tumbling Monkey, Yanoman, MIB, L4............$100.00

Performing Circus Lion, VIA, MIB, L4.........................$500.00

Pete the Spaceman, Bandai, 1960s, MIB, L4 ....$200.00

Pete the Talking Parrot, TN, repeats messages, 17", NM, L4 ....$375.00

Peter the Drumming Rabbit, Alps, 1950s, 5 actions, 13", MIB, L4 ....$250.00

Piano Pooch, TN, plays piano w/several actions, tin & plush, 7", NMIB, A...$150.00

Picnic Bear, Alps, 1950s, plush & tin, 10", EX, L4 ....$75.00

Picnic Bunny, Alps, 1950s, plush & tin, 10", MIB, L4 ...$150.00

Pierrot-Monkey Cycle, MT, clown drives erratic cycle w/bell as monkey rider waves hat, litho tin, 10", NM (EX box)..$475.00

Piggy Cook, Yonezawa, squealing pig flips egg in pan & shakes pepper shaker, litho tin & vinyl, 11", MIB, L4........$275.00

Piggy Cook, Yonezawa, 11", VG, A.................................$85.00

Pinky the Clown, Alps, clown blows whistle, balances ball on nose & juggles, 10½", MIB, L4 ....$500.00

Pinky the Clown, Alps, 10½", NM, L4..........................$225.00

Oldtimer Train Set, Cragstan, 1950s, lithographed tin, MIB, J6, $300.00.

Pinocchio Xylophone Player, TN, 1962, plays 'London Bridge,' tin w/rubber head, 9", NM (EX box) $300.00

Pistol Pete, Marusan, litho tin w/cloth clothes, remote control, 11", NMIB, A $250.00

Playful Puppy, MT, 1950s, 4 actions, 5", MIB, L4 ....$300.00

Playful Pussy, MT, MIB, L4...$250.00

Playland Octopus, Alps, gondolas undulate up & down as they spin, lights & sound, tin, 19", scarce, EX (VG box), A $1,000.00

Pluto, Frankonia, advances w/several actions, plush, bone-shaped remote control box, 11", scarce, M (EX box), A........$430.00

Pluto, see also Disney Acrobats

Pluto Hopper, Linemar, litho tin w/rubber tail, remote control, 5x5", EX, A...$385.00

Popcorn Vendor, S&E/Cragstan, bear pedals cart while umbrella spins & popcorn pops, litho tin & plush, 8", MIB, L4 ..$575.00

Popcorn Vendor, S&E/Cragstan, 8", VG, A...................$125.00

Popcorn Vendor, TN, duck pushes wagon w/bump-&-go action as popcorn pops, 8", MIB, L4 ....$575.00

Popeye, see also Bubble Blowing Popeye

Popeye in Rowboat, Linemar, remote control, 10", NMIB .$9,000.00

Porsche Rally Car #17, 9½", M (EX box), A.....................$50.00

Portable Mixmaster, Daiya, MIB, L4................................$65.00

Pretty Peggy Parrot, Rosko, several actions, lithographed tin and plush, 10", NM (VG box), $300.00.

Professor Owl, Y, turns, chirps & raises pointer to chalkboard, litho tin, 8", NMIB, A..$425.00

Puffy Morris, Y, 1960s, smokes real cigarette, 10", EX, L4....$175.00

Rabbits & Carriage, S&E, mama pushes baby in carriage, MIB, L4 ....$425.00

Radar 'N Scope, MT, features screen that shows images of airplanes, flashing lights & sound, litho tin, 10", NM, A $165.00

Radicon Boat, MT, remote control, rare, MIB, L4 ....$675.00

Radio Rex, Elmwood Button Co, 1920s, w/instructions, EX+ (partial box), J2 ....$250.00

Randy the Walking Monkey, AI, NMIB, L4 ....$175.00

RCA-NBC Mobile Color TV Truck, Y, forward & reverse action w/circus scene on lighted TV screen, tin, 9", NM (EX box), A...$1,350.00

Radio Televisione Italiana, Ichiko, bump-and-go action, 12", rare, NM (NM box), A, $935.00.

Reading Bear, Alps, 1950s, 5 actions, 9", M, L4 ....$525.00

Riverboat Queen Mary, Marusan, NM, L4 ....$125.00

Rock 'N Roll Monkey, Rosko, 1950s, monkey plays guitar & sways, 13", MIB, L4 ....$350.00

Rocky (Fred Flintstones look-alike), Japan, bump-&-go action, carries club & hatchet, litho tin, 4", MIB, L4..........$275.00

Romance Car, M, caddy-style car advances as driver waves hat, tin, 8", MIB, A..$250.00

Royal Cub, S&E, mama bear pushes baby bear in buggy w/6 other actions, 8", MIB, L4 ....$450.00

Sam the Shaving Man, Plaything Toy, 1960s, 12", MIB, L4..$325.00

Sammy Wong the Tea Totaler, TN, several actions, litho tin, 10", NM (EX+ box), A...$300.00

Santa Bank, Trim-A-Tree, shakes presents & rings bell w/nodding head & light-up eyes, tin & plush, 11", NMIB, A......$300.00

Santa Claus Phone Bank, S&E, w/pay phone, 8", rare, EX, L4 ....$500.00

Santa Copter, MT, 1960, 8½", MIB, L4 ....$150.00

Santa in Rocking Chair, Alps, 1950s, 4 actions, w/tree & stocking, rare, EX, L4...$750.00

Santa on Rooftop, MIB, L4 ....$225.00

Santa on Rotating Globe, HTC, 15", M, L4....................$350.00

Santa on Scooter, MT, bump-&-go action w/flashing lights & sound, litho tin & vinyl, MIB $125.00

Santa Sled, TN, 1950s, 4 actions, 14" L, M, L4..............$350.00

Santa w/Lighted Star, NM, L4 ....$275.00

Secret Agents Car, Japan, plates mk Chevrolet, mystery action w/flashing lights, bl tin w/blk rubber tires, 14", NMIB, A...$235.00

Shark-U-Control Racing Car, Remco, plastic, 19", NMIB, L4 ....$100.00

Shoe Shine Joe w/Lighted Pipe, Alps, 1950s, monkey buffs shoe, 11", MIB, L4 ....$300.00

Shootin' Bear, SAN, advances w/several actions, litho tin, remote control, 11", NM, A..$345.00

Shooting Gallery Gorilla, MT, shoot gorilla & he raises hands & growls, litho tin, w/orig cork gun, 10", rare, NMIB, A.$350.00

Shutter Bug, TN, boy shuffles along & takes pictures, bulb flashes, tin, 9", NM (EX box), A.............................$850.00

Ski Lift, Alps, goes to end of cable & changes direction, litho tin, 7", NM, M5..$150.00

Skipping Monkey, TN, 1960s, 9½", MIB, L4 ....$100.00

Sky Sweeper, Ideal, rocket launcher fires darts at projected images from truck, plastic, 25", NM (EX box), A....$175.00

Sleeping Baby Bear, Linemar, bear sits up in bed, yawns & squeals, tin & plush, 9", EX (EX box) $300.00

Slurpy Puppy, TN, 1960s, 6½", MIB, L4 ....$125.00

Smarty Bird, Ideal, 1964, EX, V1 ....$60.00

Smokey Bear Jeep, TN, 10", rare, EX, L4 ....$675.00

Smokey Bear Jeep, TN, 1950s, advances w/lights & sound, litho tin, 10", rare, MIB, L4.......................................$1,250.00

Smokey Joe Car, Marusan, 8½", MIB, L4 ....$375.00

Smoking and Shoe Shining Panda Bear, Alps, smokes pipe and shines his shoes, plush and lithographed tin, 10", NM (EX box), A, $275.00.

Smoking Grandpa, SAN, 1950s, eyes closed, 9", rare, MIB, L4 ....$375.00

Smoking Grandpa, SAN, 1950s, eyes open, 9", EX (EX box)..$150.00

Smoking Pa Pa Bear, SAN, 8", MIB, L4 ....$175.00

Snake Charmer (Casey the Charmed Cobra), Linemar, 1950s, 4 actions, 8", EX, L4..$300.00

Snappy the Dragon, TN, 1960s, 6 actions, 30", rare, EX (repro box), L4..$4,500.00

Sneezing Bear, Linemar, raises tissue & sneezes, light-up eyes, plush & tin, 9½", not working o/w EX, A $100.00

Snoopy, see Surfing Snoopy

Snowman, Santa Creations, blows styrofoam ball on head, MIB, L4..$275.00

Snowman, Santa Creations, EX, L4.............................$175.00

Space Traveling Monkey, Y, MIB, L4.............................$225.00

Spanking Bear, Linemar, 1950s, mama bear spanks baby, several actions, litho tin & plush, 9", NMIB, L4 ....$475.00

Spanking Bear, Linemar, 9", EX, L4.............................$250.00

Sparky Savings Bank, Byron, 1930s, MIB, L4.................$175.00

Sparky the Seal, MT, plush over tin, 8", M, L4 ....$100.00

Spin-A-Disk Monkey, Rosko, NMIB, L4.........................$225.00

State Trooper Motorcycle, Japan, litho tin w/rubber front tire, 10¼", EX (EX box), A $925.00

Stick-Shift Army Tank, TN, MIB, L4 ....$150.00

Strange Explorer, DSK, tank advances as gorilla forces it to turn over, litho tin, 8", EX (EX box), A.........................$125.00

Strutting My Fair Dancer, Haji, 1950s, sailor girl does jig on platform, litho tin & celluloid, 11", MIB, L4...........$275.00

Strutting Sam, Haji, Black man dances atop platform, litho tin, 11", EX (VG box), A...$325.00

Sunbeam Motorcycle w/Sidecar, Marusan, advances w/lights & sound, litho tin w/blk rubber tires, 9½", EX, A $350.00

Super Susie, Linemar, bear pushes groceries on conveyor belt & several other actions, litho tin & plush, 8", NMIB, A $650.00

Superman Tank, Linemar, Superman pushes tank forward & backward & lifts front end, litho tin, 11", rare, VG (G box), A..$2,450.00

Surfing Snoopy, Mattel #3477, M, H11 ....$60.00

Suzette the Eating Monkey, Linemar, sets at table & takes bite of meat, tin w/cloth outfit, 9", rare, NM (EX box), A ...$425.00

Swimming Duck w/Ball, Bandai, MIB, L4 ....$150.00

Swimming Fish, Bandai, rare, MIB, L4 ....$275.00

Switchboard Operator, Linemar, 1950s, 7½", MIB, L4 ..$875.00

Talking Police Car, Yone, bump-&-go mystery action, litho tin, 13½", EX, A...$150.00

Teddy Balloon Blowing Bear, Alps, 11", MIB, L4 ....$200.00

Teddy Bear Swing, Yonezawa, plush bear does flips on litho tin bar, 13", MIB, L4...$425.00

Teddy Go-Kart, Alps, EX, L4 ....$175.00

Teddy the Artist, Yonezawa, Teddy simulates drawing, complete w/9 templates, MIB, L4..$500.00

Teddy the Boxing Bear, Y, 1950s, 9", MIB, L4 ....$500.00

Telephone Bear, Linemar, 1950s, bear picks up phone & chatters w/several other actions, plush & tin, 7½", MIB, L4 .$375.00

Traveler Bear, K, advances with light-up eyes, plush and lithographed tin, 8", EX (EX box), A, $400.00.

Telephone Bear, Linemar, 1950s, 7½", VG, A...............$150.00
Telephone Rabbit, MT, sits in rocking chair & picks up phone, MIB, L4...............$275.00
Tinkling Trolley, MT, 10½", MIB, L4...........................$200.00
Tom & Jerry Helicopter, MT, bump-&-go action w/spinning rotor blade, NMIB, L4...............$325.00
Tom & Jerry Locomotive, MT, bump-&-go action w/ringing bell, litho tin w/vinyl figures, 9", NMIB..................$275.00
Topo Gigio Xylophone Player, TN, 1960s, MIB, L4...$1,450.00
Traffic Policeman, AI, policeman blows whistle & turns as light changes, 13", MIB, L4.............................$525.00
Traveler Bear, K, 8", NM, L4...........................$375.00
Treasure Chest Bank, Illfelder, 1960s, 11", MIB, L4......$150.00
Tric-Cycling Clown, MT, 1960s, 12", rare, MIB, L4......$875.00
Trumpet Playing Monkey, Alps, 1950s, 9", MIB, L4......$250.00
Tugboat Neptune, MT, bump-&-go action w/lights & sound, litho tin, 14", NM (EX box), A...............$200.00
Turn-O-Matic Gun Jeep, TN, 10", NMIB, L4.................$175.00
Twin Racing Cars, Alps, 1950s, MIB, L4.......................$675.00
Union Mountain Cable Lines Monorail, TN, 1950s, MIB, L4 ....$225.00
Vibraphone, Rosko, MIB, L4...............................$150.00
VIP Busy Boss Bear, S&E, 1950s, 8", EX, L4.................$275.00
Volkswagen, Taiyo, non-fall mystery action w/flashing lights, litho tin, 9½", EX (EX box), A...............$150.00
Volkswagen w/Visible Engine, KO, 7", MIB, L4.............$175.00
VW Micro Bus, Bandai, MIB, L4...................................$575.00
Waddles Family Car, Y, EX, L4...............................$100.00
Wagon Master, MT, 1960s, 4 actions, 18", MIB, L4......$375.00
Walking Bambi, Yanoman, MIB, L4........................$675.00
Walking Elephant, Linemar, 1950s, 8½", MIB, L4.........$175.00
Walking Gorilla, MT, rare, NMIB, L4........................$1,800.00
Walking Knight in Armour, MT, rare, NMIB, L4......$3,000.00
Waltzing Matilda, TN, rare, MIB, L4.............................$875.00
Western Bad Man at Red Gulch Bar, Japan, outlaw takes drink from bartender then fires gun, EX...............$375.00
Western Special Locomotive, Modern Toys, 1950s, bump-&-go w/several other actions, litho tin, NM (EX box), A..$45.00
Whirly Twirly Rocket Ride, Alps, rockets spin w/flashing lights & bell sound, litho tin, 13", NM...............$325.00
Wild West Rodeo Bubbling Bull, Linemar, 6½", MIB, L4..$375.00
Willie the Walking Car, Y, MIB, L4.............................$325.00
Windy the Juggling Elephant, TN, w/celluloid ball & litho tin umbrella, 10½", MIB, L4...............$325.00
Windy the Juggling Elephant, TN, 10½", EX, L4.............$85.00
Worried Mother Duck, TN, 11", MIB, L4.......................$225.00
Xylophone Bear, Linemar, rare, NM, L4.........................$275.00
Yo-Yo Clown, Alps, 1960s, 9", NM, L4...........................$375.00
Yo-Yo Monkey, Alps, 1960s, 9", MIB, L4.......................$300.00

Bicycles, Motorbikes, and Tricycles

The most interesting of the vintage bicycles are those made from the 1920s into the '60s, though a few even later models are collectible as well. Some from the '50s were very futuristic and styled with sweeping Art Deco lines; others had wonderful features such as built-in radios and brake lights, and some were decked out with saddlebags and holsters to appeal to fans of Hoppy, Gene, and many other western heroes. Watch for reproductions.

Condition is everything when evaluating bicycles, and one worth $2,500.00 in excellent or better condition might be worth as little as $50.00 in unrestored, poor condition. But here are a few values to suggest a range.

Advisor: Richard Trautwein (T3).

BICYCLES

Cleveland Tandem, 1897, Lozier Manufacturing Co., EX, A, $1,000.00.

Colson Firestone, 1939, boy's, wht-walls, EX, A.........$2,600.00
Colson Firestone, 1939, girl's, wht-walls, EX, A.............$900.00
Colson Firestone Super Cruiser, 1950, girl's, EX, A.......$325.00
Columbia, 1940, boy's, maroon & cream, wht-walls, EX, A $700.00
Columbia Chainless 2-Speed Safety, 1903, boy's, cushion fr, NP front forks, pneumatic tires, EX...............$2,000.00
Columbia Deluxe, 1949, boy's, orig, 24", EX, A.............$250.00
Columbia Expert Ordinary, 1886, 52", EX, A.............$1,600.00
Columbia Motobike, 1937, boy's, w/speedometer & clock dashboard, fender headlight, rear carrier, EX...............$1,900.00
Columbia Ordinary, 1890, 58", VG, A........................$1,200.00
Columbia Roadster Ordinary, 1886, 57", EX, A..........$3,200.00
Columbia Roadster Ordinary, 1890-91, 50", VG, A ...$1,700.00
Columbia 1952 RX5 5 Star, boy's, 75th anniversary replica, used, A...............$350.00
Columbia 5-Star Model R9T, 1950, wht-walls, rstr, A.$1,000.00
Elgin Blackhawk, 1934, boy's, rstr, A...............$2,000.00
Elgin Twin 20, 1938, boy's, VG, A...............$250.00
Grendon #7 Hard-Tire Safety, Iron Wheel Co, boy's, EX, A $2,200.00
Hartford Hard-Tire Safety, 1891, boy's, w/brake hardware, coasting pegs & nameplate, EX, A...............$1,700.00
Hawthorne 2-Speed, Montgomery Ward, 1937, boy's, red & wht w/wht-walls, EX, A...............$425.00
Hawthorne Comet, Montgomery Ward, 1938, boy's, fender light, rear carrier, rear-wheel kickstand, wht-walls, EX, A..$500.00
Hopalong Cassidy, girl's, fender headlight, rear carrier, wht-walls, 26", EX, A...............$800.00
Huffy Radio w/Power Pack, ca 1955, boy's, front torpedo headlight, rear carrier, wht-walls, G+, A...............$1,400.00

JC Higgins, Sears, boy's, maroon w/gold tank, shock-absorber springs, rstr, EX+ $600.00

JC Higgins, 1951, boy's, jeweled tank, batwing headlight, EX, A..$800.00

JC Higgins, 1951, girl's, full-skirted springer, wht-walls, rstr, A..$425.00

JC Higgins Deluxe, 1947, girl's, NM, A.........................$450.00

Lozier & Yost Little Giant #4 Hard-Tire Safety, 1891, man's, VG, A..$4,750.00

Mercury Deluxe, 1954, boy's, red & wht w/chrome trim, fender headlight, rear carrier, wht-walls, rstr, A $650.00

Monarch (Westfield), girl's, orig, EX, A $350.00

Monarch Super Cruiser, boy's, fender headlight, rear carrier, wht-walls, G+, A $650.00

Monark Hex Custom Boardwalk Cruiser, 1947, boy's, G, A .$650.00

Pierce Arrow Spring-Fork Pneumatic Safety, 1919, boy's, w/orig tires, rstr..$950.00

Pierce Arrow Spring-Fork Pneumatic Safety, 1900, boy's, cushion fr, EX $1,200.00

Roadmaster Luxury Liner, girl's, metallic gr w/chrome fenders, 26", EX, A $500.00

Schwinn B-6, 1946, boy's, rstr, A.................................$750.00

Schwinn B-6, 1948, boy's, EX, A $550.00

Schwinn Black Phantom boy's bike, EX original condition, $600.00.

Schwinn Black Phantom, boy's, 26", rstr, A $850.00

Schwinn Black Phantom, girl's, 26", rstr, A $400.00

Schwinn Cycle Truck, boy's, red w/chrome fenders, lg front wire basket, sm front tire w/lg back tire, EX, A $300.00

Schwinn Green Phantom, 1951, boy's, 26", EX, A $700.00

Schwinn Hornet, boy's, wht-walls, EX, A.......................$200.00

Schwinn Hornet, girl's, torpedo headlight, rear carrier, wht-walls, G+, A..$30.00

Schwinn Panther, 1952, boy's, EX, A $650.00

Schwinn Starlet, 1955, girl's, gr & cream, VG, A $175.00

Shelby Airflow, boy's, red w/bl trim, wht-walls, 26", rstr, A ..$200.00

Shelby Streamline, 1953, girl's, bl & wht springer w/rear carrier, Delta triple light, orig condition, A $200.00

Silver King, 1934, girl's, light on front fender, EX, A $350.00

Silver King Flo, 1936, boy's, w/tool-box seat, horn on front fender, wht-wall tries, EX, A $1,700.00

Silver King Wingbar, 1939, girl's, tool-box seat, jeweled light on front fender, wht-walls, butterfly kickstand, EX, A..$600.00

Shelby Donald Duck girl's bike, 1949, 24", EX, A, $1,600.00.

Shelby Western Flyer Speedline Airflow boy's bike, 1937, restored, $3,800.00.

Springfield Roadster Ordinary, 1899, 50", rstr, A........$6,500.00

Western Flyer Roadmaster Deluxe, 1941, girl's, orig pnt & chrome, EX, A $350.00

Western Flyer X53, boy's, blk & gold, VG, A.................$450.00

Wolf American lady's bike, 1898, EX original condition, A, $450.00.

MOTOR VEHICLES

Elgin Motorbike/Bicycle, rear-wheel kickstand, rpl tires, G-, A $800.00

Monarch Super-Twin, ca 1949, blk w/red-orange trim, chrome fender headlight, rear-wheel kickstand, EX+, A ..$3,200.00

Spaceliner, Sears, girl's, bl-gr w/chrome fenders, wht seat & grips, electric light & horn, wht-walls, 67", EX, A ..$200.00

Speed Bike, Metal Specialties, ca 1930, red, rear-wheel kickstand, 12" pneumatic tires w/red spokes, G, A.........$850.00

Whizzer Sportsman, w/windshield & spring seat, rear carrier, wht-walls, 20", rstr, A $5,000.00

TRICYCLES

Canterpony Riding Horse, Deeks Engineering Corp, 1930, pnt wood & aluminum w/glass eyes, 40", VG, A $400.00

Colson adult tricycle, 1900, 2-wheel drive with rear differential, EX, A, $525.00.

Dandy Dan Horse-Drawn Sulky, Dan Patch Co, late 1800s-early 1900s, pnt iron & wood, 44", VG, A $635.00

Velocipede, 1870, green, 16", restored, A, $600.00.

Ferbo, blk body w/bicycle chain, no fenders, 12" wide-spoked front wheel, G, A $225.00

Good Humor Trike, ca 1955, chain drive, opening door in rear compartment, 36", EX, A.................................$1,050.00

Grendon Pioneer, red, no fenders, 19½" wide-spoked front wheel, G, A $375.00

Horse, articulated wooden horse w/stuffed saddle on CI fr, 3 spoke wheels, front pedals, 36", VG+, A $850.00

Iron Horse, 1940, child's, blk cast aluminum horse w/curved handlebars, red saddle & grips, EX, A....................$400.00

Murry Airflow Jr, pnt pressed steel w/steel seat, 17½", G, A..$200.00

Black Americana

Black subjects were commonly depicted in children's toys as long ago as the late 1870s. Among the most widely collected today are the fine windup toys made both here and in Germany. Early cloth and later composition and vinyl dolls are favorites of many; others enjoy ceramic figurines. Many factors enter into evaluating Black Americana, especially in regard to the handmade dolls and toys, since quality is subjective to individual standards. Because of this you may find wide ranges in dealers' asking prices. In order to better understand this field of collecting, we recommend *Black Collectibles Sold in America* by P.J. Gibbs and *Black Dolls, Books I and II*, both by Myla Perkins.

Advisor: Judy Posner (P6).

See also Banks; Battery-Operated Toys; Schoenhut; Windups, Friction, and Other Mechanicals.

Acrobat Toy, 1930s, articulated pnt-wood pickaninny does tricks by squeezing sticks, 7½", EX, P6......................$95.00

Bank, 1940s, bsk, nude native boy seated w/drum, blk skin tone, 7", EX, P6..$95.00

Book, *Little Black Sambo*, Rand McNally, worn spine, $125.00.

Book, All About Little Black Sambo, Cupples & Leon, 1917, illus by John Gruelle (creator of Raggedy Ann), 48 pgs, EX, P6..$200.00

Book, Little Black Sambo, Saalfield, 1942, color illus by Ethel Hays, cloth-like throughout, EX, P6 ....$80.00

Book, Little Black Sambo, Samuel Gabriel Publishing #528, 1939, linen-type, 12 pgs, EX, P6.................................$85.00

Book, Little Black Sambo & the Tiger Kitten, by Frank Ver Beck, Platt & Monk, 1935, w/illus by author, 62 pgs, EX, P6..$125.00

Book, Little Black Sambo Calico Classics, Saalfield, 1932, color illus by Fern Peat, 20 pgs, hardbound, EX, P6..........$145.00

Book, Little Black Sambo Story Book, Platt & Munk, 1935, illus by H Bannerman & F Ver Beck, 6 stories, 63 pgs, EX, P6..$125.00

Book, Little Black Sambo w/'Pop-Up' Pictures, Blue Ribbon Press, 1934, 60 pgs, rare, EX, P6.............................$150.00

Book, Little Black Sambo: The Story of Topsy, Reilly, 1908, John Neill illus (orig Wizard of Oz books), 57 pgs, EX, P6..$275.00

Book, Pickaninnies Little Redskins, 1800s, blk & red graphics on ivory ground, 15 pgs, rare, intact but brittle, P6.$250.00

Book, Ten Little Pickaninnies, Faultless Starch Co premium, ca 1920, 15 pgs, 5x3", rare, EX, P6 ....$125.00

Book, The 'Pop-Up' Little Black Sambo, Blue Ribbon Press, 1934, EX, P6 ....$125.00

Book, The Adventures of Rufus Rastus Brown in Darktown, JI Auston & Co, 1906, blk & wht & color images, 14 pgs, EX, P6..$200.00

Book, The Pickaninny Twins, by Lucy Fitch Perkins, 1931, illus by author, 149 pgs, EX, P6.................................$165.00

Book, Watermelon Pete, by Elizabeth Gordon, Rand McNally, 1937, illus by Clara Powers Willson, EX, P6..............$85.00

Candy Container, 1920s, cardboard fold-up, from $65.00 to $85.00.

Card Game, Game of Dixieland, Fireside Game Co, 1897, EX (worn box), P6...$255.00

Cinelin Theatre, Spain, 1920s, graphic stories with performers on turning roller, multicolored cardboard stage, 8x7½", EX, A, $155.00.

Coloring Book, Little Brown Koko, 1941, illus by Dorothy Wadstaff, 22 pgs, unused, EX, P6...................................$125.00

Dice Toy, Alco/Britain, image of man's head, plunger activated, 2" dia, NM, A $125.00

Dice Toy, Kobe/Japan, 1930s, top hat of man unscrews to reveal miniature dice for crapshooting, 3½", EX, P6..........$150.00

Doll, Belindy (Raggedy Ann's Mammy friend), 1950s, stocking-knit head & torso w/stuffed cotton legs & arms, 14", EX, P6..$75.00

Doll, bsk, Japan, 1920s, dk-brn skin tone w/googly eyes, 3 tufts of hair w/red bows, 4¼", NM, P6 ....$70.00

Doll, golliwog, hand-knitted in striped sweater & striped pants, blk skin tone w/appliqued felt features, 17", EX, P6 ..$75.00

Doll, golliwog, 1930s, hand-knitted in wool suit & bow tie, blk skin tone, 16¼", EX, P6...$85.00

Doll, Norah Wellings artist, England, late 1940s, dk brn velvet body w/pnt features on molded velvet face, 7", EX, P6..$85.00

Doll, stuffed cloth, red & bl dress & pants w/red shoes, bandanna on head, 15", G, A..$50.00

Doll, topsy-turvy, 1930s, changes to wht girl, stuffed cotton w/yarn hair, 14", EX, P6...$95.00

Game, Alabama Coon, JW Spear & Son/Bavaria, EX, P6..$300.00

Game, Amos 'n Andy Card Party, AM Davis, 1930, complete, NM (NM box), A...$165.00

Game, Gold Bug (Edgar Allen Poe), Einson-Freeman, 1934, complete, EX (EX box), A $275.00

Game, Little Black Sambo, Parker Bros, 1920s, EXIB, F3...$500.00

Game, Old Barn Door Target w/Harmless Air Rifle, Parker Bros, EXIB, A $300.00

Game, Sambo Target, Wyandotte, 1930s, VG+, A........$100.00

Game, Black Sambo, Stoll and Einson, 1934, missing few pieces, EX (VG box), $150.00.

Game, Skillets & Cakes, Milton Bradley, 1946, complete, EX (EX box), from $150 to $200.00

Game, White-Eyed Coon the New Ring Game, Spear, EXIB, A...$400.00

Gravity Toy, 2 celluloid babies on tin seesaw revolve to bottom of spring-wound rod, 11", EX, A $230.00

Noisemaker, 1940s, litho tin, shows strutting minstrel w/party design, EX, P6 ....$55.00

Phonograph Toy, Dancing Dandy jigger, wood figure dances on platform that attaches to phonograph, EX..............$225.00

Phonograph Toy, 1900, wood & metal, dapper referee instructs boxers on platform that attaches to phonograph, M, A $265.00

Platform Waltzers, Ives, Pat. 1876, Jubilee, 3 dancers in cloth outfits on round wooden pedestal atop box, NM, A, $9,500.00.

Premium, Aunt Jemima Breakfast Bear, stuffed bl velour w/chef's hat & apron, checked neckerchief, 13", M, P6........$175.00

Premium, Aunt Jemima doll, oilcloth, unstuffed, 14", M (orig mailing envelope), P6..$140.00

Premium, Cream of Wheat's Rastus doll, 1910s, litho image & directions on uncut cloth, 28x20", M, P6.................$300.00

Premium, Junior Chef Pancake Set, Aunt Jemima Pancake Mix/Argo Industries, 1949, EX, P6 ....$150.00

Premium, Turkey Doodle Dart Game, Jimmy Scribner & His Johnson family radio show, 1936, VG, P6 ....$225.00

Pull Toy, Snowflakes & Swipes, Nifty, 1920s, 8", NMIB $1,850.00

Puppet, Lucifer, Effanbee, wood & compo marionette w/cloth outfit, 14", EX (G box mk FAO Schwarz) $150.00

Puzzle, fr-tray, Black Sambo, Sambo w/umbrella meets tiger (Sam Gabriel design from book dated 1939), 8½x7", EX, P6...$60.00

Puzzle, jigsaw, Ullman's Society Picture Puzzle 'Pleasant Anticipations,' 1880s, 3½x5½", rare, EXIB, P6 ....$145.00

Puzzle, Pick the Pickaninnies, USA, 1907, 10x15", NM, A...$100.00

Record, Blue Tail Fly/Carry Me Back to Old Virginny, 1940s, sides feature colorful images, 78 rpm, 6½", EX, P6..$95.00

Record, Little Black Sambo, RCA Victor Y333, 1947, 78 rpm, set of 2 in album, EX, from $50 to..........................$75.00

Record, Little Brave Sambo, 45 rpm, 1950s, VG (full-color sleeve w/Sambo & 3 tigers), P6 ....$42.00

Tea Set, ca 1904, matt porcelain w/golliwog graphics by Florence Upton, teapot, creamer & sugar, cup & saucer, M, A...$240.00

Ventriloquist Doll, compo head w/red lips, red jacket, vest & top hat, wht shirt, blk & wht plaid pants, 28", EX, A $770.00

View-Master Reel & Booklet, Little Black Sambo, 1948, EX (orig envelope), P6 ....$65.00

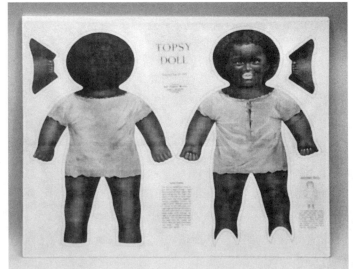

Photo courtesy Dunbar Gallery.

Topsy Doll, Pat. 1900, cloth, uncut, M, D10, from $400.00 to $600.00.

Boats

Though some commercially made boats date as far back as the late 1800s, they were produced on a much larger scale during WWI and the decade that followed and again during the years that spanned WWII. Some were scaled-down models of battleships measuring nearly three feet in length. While a few were actually seaworthy, many were designed with small wheels to be pulled along the carpet or out of doors on dry land. Others were motor-driven windups, and later a few were even battery operated. Some of the larger manufacturers were Bing (Germany), Dent (Pennsylvania), Orkin Craft (California), Liberty Playthings (New York), and Arnold (West Germany).

Advisors: Richard Trautwein (T3); Dick Borgerding (B4).

See also Cast Iron, Boats; Battery-Operated Toys; Tootsietoys; Windups, Friction, and Other Mechanicals; and other specific manufacturers.

Battleship, Fleischmann (?), w/up, pnt tin, gray & blk w/deck rail, 4 red & wht flags, guns fore & aft, 14", EX, A..$775.00

Battleship, Hillclimber, flywheel mechanism, pnt pressed steel, 15½", pnt loss o/w VG, A $135.00

Battleship, Wolverine, w/up, litho tin, guns spark & props turn, 14½", scarce, EX (G- box), A $200.00

Battleship Indiana, litho tin hull, crew station & pilot's house w/wooden deck, cannons & 2 smoke stacks, 31", EX+, A......................$1,375.00

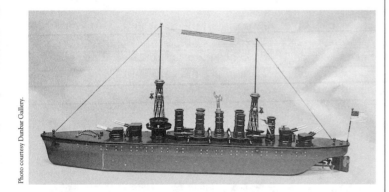

Battleship Constitution, Orkin, minor restoration, 35", D10, $2,500.00.

Battleship Invincible, windup, red, white, and blue, 13", EX, A, $1,200.00.

Battleship Kaiser Karl Dar Grosse, Bing, w/up, pnt tin, 2-tone gray w/railed red deck & trim, 2-masted, 32", NM, A ..$17,600.00

Battleship Leipszig, Bing (?), w/up, pnt tin, gray & blk, 12", EX, A $700.00

Bluebird Speedboat, Sutcliffe/England, w/up, pressed steel, wht w/red trim, hydroplane w/2 lg pontoons, 12", MIB, A..$475.00

Cabin Cruiser, French, 1950s, battery-op, pnt tin, 20", EXIB, A......................$175.00

Cabin Cruiser Miss America, may be Orkin or Seaworthy, 1930s, clockwork mechanism, yellow hull, 18", NM, D10, from $500.00 to $650.00.

Cruise Ship/Battleship, Japan, tin, w/interchangable deck, 12", EX, J2 ....$110.00

Destroyer (US), Ideal, plastic, red, yel & bl, moving parts, 15", NM (EX box), A $135.00

Destroyer Taku, w/up, litho tin, blk w/red trim, EX, A ..$250.00

Gunboat, Carette, pnt tin, tan & cream, 2 stacks, 4 guns, railed deck, 11", rpt, A $325.00

Gunboat, Carette, w/up, pnt tin, red & wht, 11", EX (EX box), A $650.00

Gunboat, Fleischmann, ca 1915, w/up, pnt tin, brn & gray hull, red deck w/rail, blk trim, 2 stacks, 17", NM, A $3,850.00

Gunboat, Orobr, w/up, litho tin, wht w/red & blk trim, guns fore & aft, 2 stacks, 11", VG+, A $600.00

Gunboat Liberty, Liberty Playthings, wood w/4 wooden wheels, 2-tone w/3 stacks, 25", G, A......................$550.00

Gunboat Mars, Bing, 1908, live steam, pnt tin, gray w/red trim, 2-masted w/3 stacks & 6 funnels, railed deck, 24", NM, A $7,150.00

Gunboat Massena, Bing, windup, light blue and gray with red trim, 24", NM, A, $10,450.00.

Japanese Gunboat, Bliss (?), ca 1895, paper litho on wood, geisha girls lithoed in cabin, 15½", EX, A $900.00

Ocean Liner, Arnold, w/up, pnt tin, red & bl w/wht upper deck, 2-masted w/2 stacks, 2 tiers of lifeboats, 13½", EX, A $990.00

Ocean Liner, Arnold, w/up, pnt tin, red & bl w/wht upper deck, 2-masted w/3 red, wht & bl stacks, 16¾", EX, A ..$1,650.00

Ocean Liner, Arnold, w/up, pnt tin, wht w/wide red stripe on hull, 2-masted w/single stack, 11¾", EX, A $130.00

Ocean Liner, Arnold, w/up, pnt tin, 3 center stacks, 12", G, A $225.00

Ocean Liner, Arnold, w/up, pnt tin, 3 stacks, 2 decks, 12", missing 3 flags o/w VG, A $375.00

Ocean Liner, Arnold, 1930s, flywheel mechanism, pnt tin, red & bl w/wht striping, 4 stacks, railed deck, 12½", EX, A .$690.00

Ocean Liner, Bing, 1912, pnt metal, red & blk hull, yel stacks, 10 lifeboats, 6 ventilators, spring mechanism, 40", G, A.$4,025.00

Ocean Liner, Carette, w/up, red, wht & blk w/gold trim, 2-masted w/4 stacks, railed deck, 11½", EX, A $825.00

Ocean Liner, Falk, 1905, pnt tin, 4 stacks, railed deck, includes extra hull, 17", G, A $1,150.00

Ocean Liner, Falk, 1910, w/up, pnt tin, 3 stacks atop 2 windowed decks, 12", G+, A...$500.00

Ocean Liner, Fleischmann, w/up, pnt tin, 2 stacks, 10½", NM, A $525.00

Ocean Liner, Fleischmann, 1920, w/up, pnt tin, cream, brn & red w/blk trim, 2 stacks, masts & lifeboats, 16", EX, A...$2,100.00

Ocean Liner, Orobr, pnt tin, 4 decks & 3 stacks, 11", VG, A $300.00

Ocean Liner, Orobr, w/up, pnt tin, 4 decks & 3 stacks, 4 suspended lifeboats, 11", flag missing o/w VG, A.........$500.00

Oil-Powered Boat, Japan, litho tin, oil lamp burner in cabin w/2 sailors on deck, red, wht & blk, 9", VG (VG box), A .$580.00

Power Boat, battery-op, wood & plastic, bl & wht, wood-tone & bl cabin, Johnson 80 motor, 12", NM (EX box), from $150 to...$180.00

Power Boat, battery-op, wood & plastic, red & wht, Mercury Zoom motor, 14", unused, NM (EX+ box), from $150 to $180.00

Racing Boat, Lionel, w/up, pnt steel w/2 compo figures, 18", G...$520.00

Racing Boat BW Bavaria, Bing, w/up, litho tin, w/2 passengers, 5", EX, A...$950.00

Side-Wheeler Atlantic, Althof Bergmann, painted tin, 10", NM, D10, $4,500.00.

Side-Wheeler, Carette, clockwork mechanism, painted tin with lead figure, 8", EX, A, $1,650.00.

Speedboat, Bing, 1910, w/up, pnt tin, lt gr & gray w/red trim, compo figure, 11", VG+, A $550.00

Speedboat, ca 1920, steam-powered, pressed steel, gray hull w/brn deck, 26", EX, from $800 to........................$1,000.00

Speedboat, Carette, 1910, cream w/red trim, 8", VG (partial box), A..$425.00

Racing Shell, windup, painted and lithographed tin with 8-man rowing team and helmsman, 27", NM, A, $12,000.00.

Riverboat, Carette, w/up, pnt tin metallic gold & blk w/red sidewheels, lead sailor, 8", EX, A $1,650.00

Riverboat, Fischer, litho tin, wht w/bl trim, w/pilot, 7½", EX, A...$950.00

Riverboat Queen Mary, battery-op, NM, L4 ....$125.00

Speedboat, Fleet Line the Marlin, 1950s, battery operated, green and white hard plastic hull, varnished wood deck, metal trim and canvas cover, 16", NM, from $200.00 to $300.00.

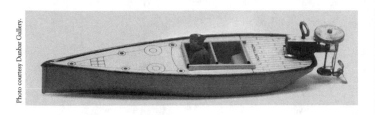

Photo courtesy Dunbar Gallery.

Speedboat, Lindstrom, windup, 11½", M, D10, $750.00.

Speedboat, Lionel, 1930s, w/up, tin, red & wht, compo figure, 17", EX, A...$600.00

Speedboat, Metalcraft, battery-op, pnt metal, blk & red, 24", G, A...$150.00

Speedboat, Schuco #1015, w/up, tin, wht & burgundy, w/driver, 5", NM (EX box), A..$400.00

Speedboat Greyhound, battery-op, wood w/gr-pnt hull, celluloid windshield, 20", EX, A...$550.00

Speedboat Miss America, Mengel Playthings, w/up, wood w/brass screws & lever controls, 14½", EX, A.........$385.00

Speedboat Sea Wolf, Fleet Line, battery-op, wood & plastic, red, wht & bl, 16½", EX+ (EX box), A..............................$85.00

Speedboat Seamaid, TKK/Japan, battery-op, 18", EX (EX box), A...$225.00

SSN 571 Skate Submarine, Marusan, battery-op, litho tin, 18½", EX+ (VG box), A....................................$250.00

Steam Launch, Carette, pnt tin, cream w/red & blk trim, yel deck, 16", VG (worn box), A..................................$900.00

Steam Launch, Union, pnt tin, metallic gold, steam boiler activates rear prop, 9", VG, A.......................................$265.00

Submarine, Bing, w/up, pnt tin, gray w/blk trim, 7½", non-working o/w VG, A...$135.00

Submarine, Kuramochi/Japan, flywheel mechanism, pnt tin, gray w/wht upper deck, top cannon, 12¼", EX, A..........$110.00

Submarine (Catalog #5081/57), Marklin, w/up, pnt tin, olive gr, railed deck w/periscope on upper deck, 22½", EX, A..$2,860.00

Submarine Courseaire, JEP/France, w/up, pnt tin, bl & wht, 16", G, A...$315.00

Submarine Le Berrob, France, dives & rises when air is squeezed into tube, pnt tin, gray w/wht & red hatch, 9", EXIB, A........$700.00

Torpedo Boat, Bing, pnt tin, deep gray & red w/blk trim, 4 stacks, railed deck, mast w/crow's nest, 21", NM, A...........$1,760.00

Torpedo Boat, Bing, w/up, pnt tin, gray & blk w/deck rail, red & yel flags fore & aft, GBN emb on deck, 17", EX, A..$1,265.00

Yacht, steam-powered, pnt tin, red & wht w/blk trim, gr interior, boiler on deck, 10", G, A..$550.00

76 Wonder, Union, late 1800s, steam-powered, brass, 10", G (wood box), A...$575.00

Books

Books have always captured and fired the imagination of children, and today books from every era are being collected. No longer is it just the beautifully illustrated Victorian examples or first editions of books written by well-known children's authors, but more modern books as well.

One of the first classics to achieve unprecedented success was *The Wizard of Oz* by author L. Frank Baum — such success, in fact, that far from his original intentions, it became a series. Even after Baum's death, other authors wrote Oz books until the decade of the 1960s, for a total of more than forty different titles. Other early authors were Beatrix Potter, Kate Greenaway, Palmer Cox (who invented the Brownies), and Johnny Gruelle (creator of Raggedy Ann and Andy). All were acomplished illustrators as well.

Everyone remembers a special series of books they grew up with, the Hardy Boys, Nancy Drew Mysteries, Tarzan — there were countless others. And though these are becoming very collectible today, there were many editions of each, and most are very easy to find. Generally the last few in any series will be most difficult to locate, since fewer were printed than the earlier stories which were likely to have been reprinted many times. As is true of any type of book, first editions or the earliest printing will have more collector value. For more information on series books as well as others, we recommend *Collector's Guide to Children's Books, 1850-1950*, by Diane McClure Jones and Rosemary Jones (Collector Books).

Big Little Books came along in 1933 and until edged out by the comic-book format in the mid-1950s sold in huge volumes, first for a dime and never more than 20¢ a copy. They were printed by Whitman, Saalfield, Goldsmith, Van Wiseman, Lynn, and World Syndicate, and all stuck to Whitman's original layout — thick hand-sized sagas of adventure, the right-hand page with an exciting cartoon, well illustated and contrived so as to bring the text on the left alive. The first hero to be immortalized in this arena was Dick Tracy, but many more were to follow. Some of the more collectible today feature well-known characters like G-Men, Tarzan, Flash Gordon, Little Orphan Annie, Mickey Mouse, and Western heroes by the dozens. (Note: At the present time, the market for these books is fairly stable — values for common titles are actually dropping. Only the rare, character-related titles are increasing.) For more information we recommend *Big Little Books*, by Larry Jacobs (Collector Books).

Little Golden Books were first published in 1942 by Western Publishing Co. Inc. The earliest had spines of blue paper that were later replaced with gold foil. Until the 1970s the books were numbered from 1 to 600, while later books had no numerical order. The most valuable are those with dust jackets from the early '40s or books with paper dolls and activities. The three primary series of books are Regular (1-600), Disney (1-140), and Activity (1-52). Books with the blue or gold paper spine (not foil) often sell at $8.00 to $15.00. Dust jackets alone are worth $20.00 and up in good condition. Paper doll books are generally valued at about $30.00 to $35.00, and stories about TV Western heroes at $12.00 to $18.00. First editions of the 25¢ and 29¢ cover-price books can be identified by a code (either on the title page or the last page); '1/A' indicates a first edition while a number '/Z' will refer to the twenty-sixth printing. Condition is important but subjective to personal standards. For more information we recommend *Collecting Little Golden Books, Vols I and II*, by Steve Santi (S8). The second edition also includes information on Wonder and Elf books. For further study we recommend *Whitman Juvenile Books* by David and Virginia Brown (Collector Books).

See also Black Americana; Coloring, Activity, and Paint Books; Rock 'n Roll.

BIG LITTLE BOOKS

Ace Drummond, #1177, 1935, EX, P3 ....$40.00
Aquaman Scourge of the Sea, 1968, 260 pgs, EX, T2 ....$10.00
Arizona Kid on the Bandit Trail, 1936, EX.......................$20.00
Bambi's Children, Whitman, 1943, VG............................$45.00
Barney Baxter in the Air With Eagle Squadron, #1459, 1937, EX, P3 ....$44.00
Blaze Brandon Foreign Legion, 1938, EX $20.00
Blondie & Baby Dumpling, #1415, EX+, P3 ....$38.00
Bob Stone Young Detective, #1432, EX+, P3 ....$35.00
Brenda Starr & the Masked Imposter, Whitman #1427, 1943, NM...$45.00
Bronc Peeler the Lone Cowboy, #1417, 1937, EX, P3 ......$30.00
Buck Jones & the Rock Creek Cattle War, 1938, VG+, J5 ..$25.00
Buck Rogers & the Doom Comet, Whitman, 1935, VG+, J5 ..$45.00
Buck Rogers in the 25th Century AD, Whitman #742, 1933, VG, P4 ....$55.00
Buck Rogers on the Moons of Saturn, 1934, EX- $60.00
Burn 'Em Up Barns, 1935, EX, P3 ....$24.00
Captain Easy Behind Enemy Lines, Whitman #1474, 1943, NM...$60.00
Chester Gump, Pole to Pole Flight, #1402, 1937, EX, P3.$28.00
Chester Gump, Silver Creek Ranch, #734, 1933, EX, P3.$30.00
Dan Dunn, Crime Never Pays, #1116, EX, P3 ....$33.00
Dan Dunn & the Crime Master, #1171, 1937, EX, P3 .....$35.00
Dan Dunn Secret Operative 48 & the Border Smugglers, Whitman #1481, 1938, NM..$50.00
Danger Trails in Africa, #1151, EX, P3 ....$27.00
Dick Tracy & Yogee Yamma, 1946, EX $40.00

Don Winslow, USN #1107, 1935, EX, P3........................$30.00

Felix the Cat, Whitman, 1936, VG, $32.00; *Li'l Abner in New York*, Whitman, 1936, EX, $60.00.

Felix the Cat, Whitman #1439, 1943, VG+, F8 ....$50.00
Flash Gordon Forest Kingdom of Mongo, 1938, Alex Raymond, VG+, J5..$45.00
Flash Gordon in the Water World of Mongo, Whitman, 1937, EX+ $50.00
Flash Gordon on the Planet Mongo, #1110, VG, P3........$25.00
Flash Gordon Power Men of Mongo, Whitman #1469, 1943, NM...$95.00
Frank Merriwell at Yale, 1935, G, J5 ....$15.00
Frankenstein Jr, Whitman, 1968, EX+............................$15.00
G-Man Breaking the Gambling Ring, #1493, 1938, EX, P3 ...$30.00
Gene Autry Raiders of the Range, 1946, VG+, J5............$15.00

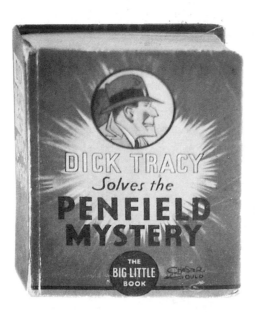

Dick Tracy Solves the Penfield Mystery, VG, $30.00.

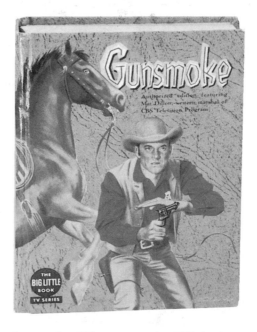

Gunsmoke, Whitman, 1958, EX, $25.00.

Inspector Wade Solves the Mystery of Red Aces, 1937, VG, J5 ....$15.00

International Spy, Doctor Doom Faces Death at Dawn, 1937, VG+, J5..$25.00

Jack Armstrong & the Ivory Treasure, Whitman #1435, 1937, EX, F8..$40.00

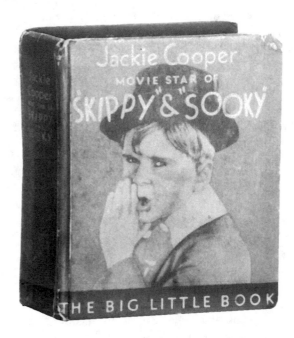

Jackie Cooper Movie Star of Skippy and Sooky, G, $18.00.

Just Kids Deep-Sea Dan, Saalfield #1184, 1940, EX $30.00

Little Men, #1150, 1934, VG $15.00

Little Orphan Annie & the Junior Commandos, Whitman #1457, 1943, EX, F8 ....$45.00

Lost Patrol, Whitman, 1934, EX $40.00

Man From UNCLE, Calcutta Affair, Whitman, 1960s, EX, J5 ....$10.00

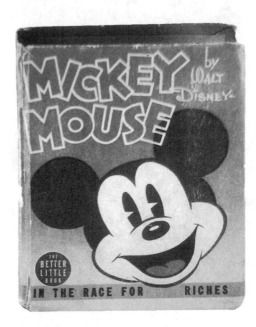

***Mickey Mouse in the Race for Riches**, Better Little Book, 1938, VG, $32.00.*

Mandrake the Magician, Whitman #1167, 1935, EX+, F8 ...$40.00

Mickey Mouse Mail Pilot, 1933, softcover, EX+ $70.00

Mickey Mouse on Cave-Man Island, Whitman #1499, 1944, EX+...$40.00

Polly & Her Pals on the Farm, Saalfield, 1934, EX...........$30.00

Popeye Sees the Sea, Whitman #1163, 1936, EX, F8 ....$45.00

Prairie Bill & the Covered Wagon, #758, 1934, VG, P3..$27.00

Radio Patrol Trailing the Safe Blowers, #1173, 1937, EX, P3..$36.00

Red Ryder Circus Luck, Whitman #1466, 1947, EX, F8...$25.00

Scrappy, Whitman #1122, 1934, EX, F8 ....$35.00

Sequoia, Whitman #1161, 1935, VG $15.00

Skeezix at the Military Academy, #1408, 1938, EX, P3 ...$29.00

Skippy, Whitman #761, 1934, EX, F8 ....$25.00

Smitty & Herby Lost Among the Indians, Whitman #1404, 1941, EX, F8...$25.00

Smokey Stover, Whitman #1413, 1942, EX, F8 ....$35.00

Speed Douglas & the Mole Gang, #1455, 1941, VG, P3..$20.00

Spike Kelly of the Commandos, Whitman #1467, 1943, EX...$20.00

Tarzan Twins, Whitman, #770, G+ $40.00

***Tarzan Twins**, 1934, 1st edition, rare, NM, $250.00.*

Texas Ranger, #1135, EX, P3 ....$32.00

Tim Tyler's Luck in the Ivory Patrol Adventures, Whitman, #1140, 1937, EX, F8..$25.00

Tiny Tim in the Big Big World, Whitman, 1945, EX.......$30.00

Treasure Island, #720, 1933, VG+, P3 ....$20.00

Walt Disney's Story of Clarabelle Cow, Whitman, 1938, EX, F8 ....$40.00

Zip Saunders King of the Speedway, 1939, VG+ $18.00

BIG GOLDEN BOOKS

Alice in Wonderland, #10426, 23rd edition, VG-EX, K3 ..$6.00

Animals & Me, #10888, 3rd edition, VG-EX, K3...............$7.00

Animals Merry Christmas, #10315, Christmas spine, VG-EX, K3..$15.00

Animals Merry Christmas, #10315, 1st (?) edition, Golden spine, VG-EX, K3 ....$40.00

Around the Year Storybook, #15769, J edition, VG-EX, K3 ...$10.00

Baby Farm Animals, #10545, 23rd edition, VG-EX, K3 .....$6.00

Bambi, #10450, 9th edition, VG-EX, K3 ....$8.00

Bedknobs & Broomsticks, #10489, 1st edition, VG-EX, K3 ...$12.00

Big Golden Animal ABC, #10457, 22nd edition, VG-EX, K3 ..$6.00

Child's Garden of Verses, #12557, M edition, VG-EX, K3......$20.00

Chinese Fairy Tales, 1st edition (revised), 1973, VG, K3..$30.00

Cowboys & Indians, 1st edition, VG, K3...........................$30.00

Cyndy Szekere's Book of Nursery Tales, #15597, C edition, VG-EX, K3 ....$15.00

Detective Arthur Master Slueth, #15790, 2nd edition, VG-EX, K3..$14.00

Dog Stories, A edition, VG, K3.......................................$15.00

Gay Purr-ee, #10408, A edition, Golden spine, VG-EX, K3 ..$24.00

Gingerbread Man, #10460, 2nd edition, VG-EX, K3 ....$8.00

Golden Almanac, 3rd edition, VG-EX (w/dust jacket), K3 ..$55.00

Golden Bible, 1st edition, VG-EX, K3 ....$45.00

Golden Book of 365 Stories, #15557, 18th edition, VG-EX, K3..$12.00

Golden Christmas Book, D edition, VG-EX, K3 ....$25.00

Golden Dictionary, 3rd edition, VG-EX, K3 ....$15.00

Golden Egg Book, #10853, 14th edition, VG-EX, K3 ....$7.00

Golden Song Book, 2nd edition, VG, K3 ....$45.00

Golden Treasury of Prayers for Boys & Girls, #1344, 4th edition, E Wilkin, VG-EX, K3 ....$30.00

Great Big Car & Truck Book, #10473, 17th edition, VG-EX, K3..$6.00

Iliad & the Odyssey, #13581, 1964, VG-EX, K3...............$30.00

Joe Kaufman's What Makes It Go?, #15767, VG, K3 ....$15.00

Lassie Finds a Way, #456, A edition, VG-EX, K3.............$18.00

Mickey Mouse Cookbook, #16812, J edition, VG-EX, K3..$30.00

My Big Book of Seasons, #10309, A edition, VG-EX, K3...$30.00

My First Golden Dictionary, #10417, 9th edition, VG-EX, K3..$7.00

New Golden Dictionary, #16837, A edition, VG, K3 ......$18.00

New Testament Bible Stories, #10502, 2nd edition, VG-EX, K3..$8.00

New Walt Disney Treasury, #15546, VG-EX, K3.............$14.00

Peter Pan, #10453, 43rd edition, VG-EX, K3 ....$6.00

Piggy Wiglet, #10493, 3rd edition, VG-EX, K3 ....$10.00

Poky Little Puppy & Patchwork Blanket, #10387, B edition, VG-EX, K3..$10.00

Poky Little Puppy's First Christmas, 6th edition, VG-EX, K3 ....$10.00

Prayers for Children, #10432, 7th edition, VG-EX, K3 ....$10.00

Professor Wormbog in Search for the Zipperump-A-Z, D edition, Mercer Mayer, VG-EX, K3..$18.00

Raggedy Ann, Thank You, Please & I Love You, 2nd edition, VG-EX, K3..$9.00

Road Runner, Very Scary Lesson, #10825, 2nd edition, VG-EX, K3 ....$9.00

Rudolph the Red-Nosed Reindeer, #10849, 11th edition, VG-EX, K3 ....$9.00

Savage Sam, #10359, A edition, VG, K3..........................$12.00

Selections From Child's Garden of Verses, #10873, 8th edition, VG-EX, K3..$15.00

Sleeping Beauty, #10390, E edition, no Golden spine, VG-EX, K3 ....$12.00

Snowy the Little White Horse, A edition, VG, K3 ....$16.00

Tale of Peter Rabbit, #10486, 6th edition, VG-EX, K3 ......$8.00

Tales From the Ballet, #17852, A edition, VG-EX, K3 ....$25.00

Tenggren's Pirates Ships & Sailors, #13580, 1st edition, VG-EX, K3..$30.00

Treasury of Little Golden Books, #16540-2, D edition, 30 stories, VG-EX, K3..$20.00

Walt Disney's Mickey Mouse Birthday Book, #482, A edition, VG-EX, K3..$30.00

Whatever Happened to Baby Horses, #10851, 8th edition, VG-EX, K3 ....$6.00

Wheels Sails & Wings, #15701, A edition, VG-EX, K3...$20.00

Wild Animals & Their Babies, #15768, 1971, VG-EX, K3 .$30.00

Wonderful Storybook, #15777, B edition, 1974, MW Brown/JP Miller, VG-EX, K3..$20.00

Woody Woodpecker Pirate Treasure, #10505, 3rd edition, VG-EX, K3 ....$10.00

LITTLE GOLDEN BOOKS

All My Chickens, #200-67, A edition, VG-EX, K3 ....$5.00

Alphabet From A to Z, #3, P edition, VG, K3.................$10.00

Animal Daddies & My Daddy, #576, 3rd edition, VG-EX, K3..$4.00

Animal Dictionary, #533, 4th edition, VG-EX, K3 ....$2.00

Baby Bear, #466, 3rd edition, VG-EX, K3.......................$12.00

Baby's Book, #10, 1992, commemorative edition, EX, K3 ..$12.00

Baby's First Book, #358, 7th edition, VG-EX, K3 ....$3.00

Baby's House, #80, B edition, VG-EX, K3 ....$10.00

Baby's Mother Goose, #422, 10th edition, VG-EX, K3 ......$6.00

Bambi, #106-9, F edition, VG-EX, K3..............................$2.00

Bambi, Walt Disney, #7, 1948, NM, $12.00.

Beany Goes to Sea, #572, B edition, G, K3.........................$9.00

Beauty & the Beast, #104-65, A edition, VG-EX, K3.........$5.00

Bedknobs & Broomsticks, #D93, 1st edition, K3 ....$8.00

Bert's Hall of Fame, #321, 1st edition, VG-EX, K3 ....$2.00

Big Bird Brings Spring to Sesame Street, #108-63, 1992, VG-EX, K3 ....$3.00

Blue Book of Fairy Tales, #374, 2nd edition, VG, K3 ....$8.00

Bobby the Dog, #440, A edition, VG-EX, K3 ....$28.00

Brave Cowboy Bill, #93, B edition, VG-EX, K3 ....$14.00

Bugs Bunny Birthday, #98, A edition, VG-EX, K3 ....$14.00

Bugs Bunny the Carrot Machine, #111-65, B edition, VG-EX, K3 ....$2.00

Bullwinkle, #462, A edition, VG-EX, K3.....................$20.00

Busy Timmy, #452, 8th edition, VG-EX, K3 ....$8.00

Child's Garden of Verses, #493, C edition, VG, K3 ....$9.00

Christmas in the Country, #95, A edition, VG-EX, K3 ...$15.00

Cinderella's Friends, #D115, F edition, K3 ....$12.00

Come Play House, #44, D edition, edge wear, K3.............$40.00

Crispy in the Birthday Band, Special Edition, softcover, VG-EX, K3.......................$10.00

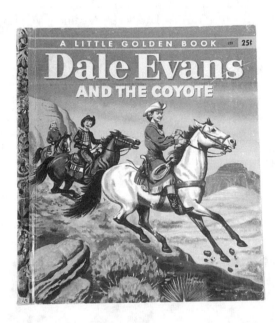

Dale Evans and the Coyote, #253, A edition, EX, $22.00.

Darby O'Gill, #D81, A edition, VG-EX, K3 ....$15.00

Doctor Dan Circus, #399, A edition, no bandages o/w VG-EX, K3.......................$14.00

Donald Duck Christmas Tree, #460-13, 1993, VG-EX, K3 ..$3.00

Donald Duck in America on Parade, #D131, 3rd edition, VG-EX, K3 ....$6.00

Donald Duck Toy Train, #D18, 14th edition, VG-EX, K3.$6.00

Dumbo, B edition, bl spine, EX+, M8 ....$18.00

Exploring Space, #342, A edition, VG-EX, K3 ....$13.00

First Bible Stories, #198, A edition, VG-EX, K3 ....$22.00

Five Little Firemen, #301, P edition, VG-EX, K3 ....$7.00

Four Little Kittens, #322, 6th edition, VG-EX, K3 ....$3.00

From Trash to Treasure, #108-70, 1993, VG-EX, K3..........$5.00

Gene Autry, #230, A edition, VG-EX, K3 ....$14.00

Gingerbread Man, #437, F edition, VG-EX, K3 ....$6.00

Goodbye Tonsils, #327, 4th edition, VG-EX, K3 ....$3.00

Happy Little Whale, #393, 6th edition, VG-EX, K3 ....$6.00

Hiawatha, #D31, B edition, VG, K3.......................$8.00

Howdy Doody & Santa Claus, #237, A edition, VG-EX, K3 ....$30.00

I Have a Secret, #494, A edition, VG-EX, K3 ....$14.00

Jack & the Beanstalk, #545, 2nd edition, G, K3 ....$3.00

Jiminy Cricket Fire Fighter, A edition, EX, M8 ....$18.00

Lady Lovely Locks, #107-57, A edition, VG-EX, K3 ....$8.00

Little Book, #583, 3rd edition, VG-EX, K3.....................$5.00

Little Galoshes, #68, B edition, tears, K3.....................$12.00

Little Pond in the Woods, #42, A edition, VG-EX, K3....$22.00

Little Red Riding Hood, #42, Z edition, VG, K3 ....$6.00

Magilla Gorilla, #547, A edition, EX, J6, $12.00.

Mickey Mouse & Goofy — The Big Bear Scare, #100-44, I edition, VG-EX, K3 ....$3.00

Mickey Mouse & the Missing Mousketeers, #D57, 4th edition, VG-EX, K3 ....$3.00

Mickey's Christmas Carol, #459-09, H edition, VG-EX, K3..$2.00

Monster at the End of This Book, #316, 1st edition, VG-EX, K3 ....$4.00

Mother Goose, #4, 2nd (war) edition, bl spine, VG-EX, K3 ....$20.00

My Christmas Treasury, #455, A edition, VG-EX, K3 .....$14.00

My Little Golden Picture Dictionary, #90, A edition, VG-EX, K3 ....$15.00

My Puppy, #469, 5th edition, VG-EX, K3 ....$12.00

Noel, #456-16, A edition, VG-EX, K3 ....$4.00

Our Baby, #DIN8, A edition, VG-EX, K3 ....$24.00

Pebbles Flintstone, #531, A edition, VG-EX, K3 ....$24.00

Peter Rabbit, #131, A edition, VG-EX, K3 ....$18.00

Peter Rabbit, #505, 9th edition, VG-EX, K3.....................$7.00

Pierrot's ABC Garden, #312-24, A (50th Anniversary) edition, VG-EX, K3 ....$4.00

Pluto the Pup Goes to Sea, A edition, 1952, NM, M8 .....$12.00

Porky Pig & Bugs Bunny — Just Like Magic, #110-65, A edition, VG-EX, K3 ....$8.00

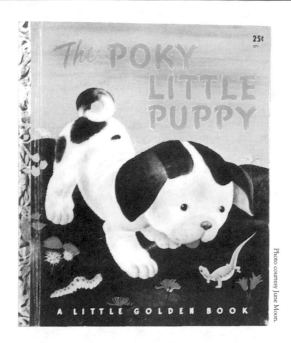

Poky Little Puppy, 1942, 1st edition, NM, J6, $24.00.

Raggedy Ann & Andy Help Santa Claus, #156, 1st edition, VG-EX, K3 ....$6.00
Rin-Tin-Tin & Rusty, #246, B edition, VG-EX, K3.........$12.00

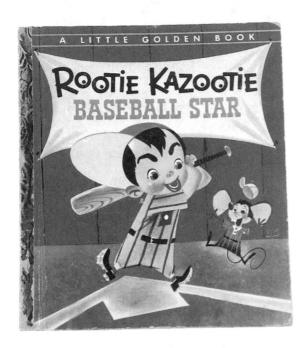

Rootie Kazootie Baseball Star, #190, A edition, EX, $20.00.

Saggy Baggy Elephant, #38, C edition, no title pg, K3 ....$6.00
Shazam, #110-36, B edition, VG-EX, K3 ....$5.00
Smokey the Bear, #224, 9th edition, VG-EX, K3 ....$12.00
Sorcerer's Apprentice, #100-79, A edition, VG-EX, K3.....$6.00
Tailspin Ghost Ship, #104-62, 1992, VG-EX, K3...............$3.00
Tex & His Toys, #129, A edition, VG-EX, K3 ....$16.00
This Is My Family, #312-22, A (50th Anniversary) edition, VG-EX, K3 ....$9.00

Three Bedtime Stories, #309, H edition, VG-EX, K3 ....$7.00
Toad Flies High, #103-44, A edition, VG-EX, K3 ....$9.00
Tom & Jerry Christmas, #197, F edition, VG-EX, K3 ....$6.00
Tootle, #210-87, CC (Fisher-Price) edition, VG-EX, K3 ...$6.00
Tweety's Global Patrol, #110-82, A edition, VG-EX, K3 ...$5.00
Velveteen Rabbit, #307-68, 1993, VG-EX, K3 ....$3.00
Wally Gator, #502, A edition, VG-EX, K3......................$20.00
Waltons, #134, 2nd edition, VG-EX, K3 ....$9.00
We Help Mommy, #352, C edition, VG-EX, K3 ....$30.00
We Help Mommy, #352, 7th edition, VG-EX, K3 ....$14.00
We Like Kindergarten, #205-53, E edition, blk background, VG-EX, K3 ....$4.00
What's Up in the Attic, #108-58, B edition, VG-EX, K3...$4.00
Where's Woodstock, #111-63, A edition, VG-EX, K3 ....$9.00
Whistling Wizard, #132, A edition, VG-EX, K3 ....$18.00
Winnie the Pooh, #101-24, 2nd edition, VG-EX, K3.........$3.00
Wonderful School, #582, 3rd edition, VG-EX, K3 ....$3.00
Woody Woodpecker & Andy Panda at the Circus, 1952, 1st edition, EX, F8 ....$12.00
Woody Woodpecker Takes a Trip, #445, A edition, VG, K3 .$5.00
Zorro & the Secret Plan, #D77, B edition, VG-EX, K3....$12.00

POP-UP BOOKS

Alice in Wonderland, Modern Publishers, 4 pop-ups, 8 pgs, EX, K3 ....$12.00
Anne of Green Gables, Big Imagination, 1993, 12 pop-ups, EX, K3 ....$10.00
Anne of Green Gables Adventures at School, 1993, 12 pop-ups, 6 movable, EX, K3 ....$12.00
Barbie Rockin' Rappin' Dancin' World Tour, Western Publishers, 1st edition, 5 pop-ups, EX, A $20.00

Bobby Bear Magic-Action Book, EX, D10, $100.00.

Buck Rogers in a Dangerous Mission, 1934, Blue Ribbon Press/Dille, blk & wht illus, 60 pgs, VG.................$200.00

Buck Rogers Strange Adventures in the Spider-Ship, Blue Ribbon/Dille, 1935, 3 pop-ups, EX $475.00

Christmas on Stage, 1950s, 5 pop-ups, 14 pgs, spiral-bound, EX (orig brn box), K3 ....$40.00

Dick Tracy Capture of Boris Arson, 1935, Pleasure Books, 3 pop-ups, NM..$375.00

Dino the Mouse Who Had Hiccups, 1974, 4 pop-ups, EX, K3 ....$22.00

First Christmas, Brown-Watson, 1988, 6 pop-ups, 12 pgs, K3...$12.00

Flash Gordon Tournament of Death, **Pleasure, 1935, Raymond Art, EX, $525.00.**

Flying Fun, 1982, 5 pop-ups, 10 pgs, cover tear, K3 ....$3.00

Gene Autry in Prairie Fire, British, 1950s, 5 pop-ups, EX+, A $75.00

Goldilocks & the Three Bears, Blue Ribbon Press, 1934, 3 pop-ups, 14 pgs, EX, B12 ....$275.00

Hocus Pocus, 1991, 1 pop-up, 14 pgs, 11 movable, EX, K3 ...$14.00

Hopalong Cassidy & Lucky at the Double X Ranch, 1950, 2 pop-ups, NM, A..$72.00

Hopalong Cassidy Lends a Helping Hand, Bonnie Books, 2-pop-ups, VG, J5..$25.00

Into Space with Ace Brave!, 1950s, 4 pop-ups, NM, A .$255.00

Jack & the Beanstalk, illus by Julian Wehr, 1944, 5 pop-ups, 20 pgs, minor tears, K3 ....$45.00

Jolly Old St Nicholas, 1st edition, 1 pop-up, musical, 12 pgs, EX, K3 ....$15.00

Jumping, Random House, 1st edition, 6 pop-ups, 12 pgs, K3 ..$5.00

Little Orphan Annie & Jumbo the Circus Elephant, FAS, 1935, 3 pop-ups, EX+, A $210.00

Little Red Riding Hood, Blue Ribbon Press, 1934, 3 pop-ups, blk & wht illus, 10 pgs, EX, B12 ....$275.00

Mickey Mouse Waddle Book, **1930s, M, rare, $6,500.00.**

Mickey Mouse Waddle Book, Blue Ribbon Books, 1934, some rpr & rpl parts o/w EX (w/dust jacket), M8 ....$1,000.00

Minnie Mouse, **VG, M5, $125.00.**

My Pop Up Book of Sleeping Beauty, 4 pop-ups, 10 pgs, EX, K3 .$8.00

New Adventures of Tarzan, Pleasure Books, 1935, 3 pop-ups, EX $600.00

New at the Zoo, Random House, 5 pop-ups, 10 pgs, EX, K3 ..$10.00

Night Before Christmas, 1st edition, 1993, 3 pop-ups, 1 movable, slight tear in back binding, K3........................$10.00

Pinocchio, Blue Ribbon Books, pre-Disney, 1932, illus by Lentz, 4 pop-ups, EX+, A $375.00

Pop-Up Mickey Mouse, Blue Ribbon, 1933, 3 pop-ups, 32 pgs, VG+, A..$250.00

Popeye With the Hag of the Seven Seas, FAS, 1935, 3 pop-ups, EX+ $450.00

Rainbow Round-a-Bout, 1992, 2 pop-ups & 2 revolving pictures, EX, K3..$12.00

Seven Natural Wonders of the World, 1991, 7 pop-ups, 30 pgs, EX, K3...$12.00

Smurf Catching Trip, Random House, 6 pop-ups, 12 pgs, VG, K3...$4.00

Tale of Two Bad Mice, by Frederick Warne, 1990, 5 pop-ups, 10 pgs open to form carousel, EX, K3 ....$12.00

Terry & the Pirates, FAS, 1935, 3 pop-ups, scarce, EX+, A.....$250.00

Tom & Jerry Book of Numbers, 11 lift-up flaps, 28 pgs, EX, K3.$12.00

Visions of St Nick, 1950, 5 pop-ups connect to form star, scarce, MIB, A...$110.00

Winnie the Pooh & Eeyore's Tail, Methuen/London, EH Shepard artist, 4 pop-ups, EX, B12 ....$300.00

TELL-A-TALE

Bedknobs & Broomsticks, Whitman #2541, 1971, VG-EX, K3 ....$5.00

Brown Puppy & a Falling Star, #2560, 1965, VG, K3.........$3.00

Child's Garden of Verses, Whitman #2497, 1964, VG-EX, K3 ....$4.00

Cinderella, Whitman #22, 1972, VG-EX, K3 ....$3.00

Circus Alphabet, Whitman, #2531, 1974, VG-EX, K3 ......$5.00

Daktari — Judy & the Kitten, Whitman #2506, 1969, VG-EX, K3 ....$7.00

Disneyland, Whitman, 1964, 28 pgs, NM, A...................$25.00

Donald Duck & the New Birdhouse, Whitman #2520, 1956, VG-EX, K3...$8.00

Donald Duck Chip & Dale, Whitman #2455-33, 1954, VG-EX, K3 ....$5.00

Duck Tales — Silver Dollars for Uncle Scrooge, #2354-49, A edition, VG-EX, K3 ....$3.00

Frisker, Whitman #2426, 1956, VG-EX, K3 ....$5.00

Goby Goat & the Birthday Gift, Whitman #2595, 1975, VG-EX, K3 ....$4.00

Great Fort, Whitman #2564, 1970, VG-EX, K3 ....$3.00

House My Grandpa Built, Whitman #2404, 1971, VG-EX, K3 ....$3.00

How To Be a Grouch, Whitman #2618 or #2452-31, 1976, VG-EX, K3 ....$4.00

Lady, Whitman, #2456-35, 1954, VG-EX, K3 ....$5.00

Learning To Count w/Twelve Elves, Whitman #2407-1, 1972, VG-EX, K3 ....$4.00

Little Miss Muffet, Whitman #2464-33, 1958, VG-EX, K3 ..$4.00

Mickey Mouse & the Mousketeers, Whitman #2454-35, 1977, VG-EX, K3 ....$5.00

Mother Goose, Whitman #2511, 1961, VG-EX, K3...........$6.00

My Little Book of Cars & Trucks, Whitman #2414-1, 1973, VG-EX, K3 ....$5.00

Night Before Christmas, Whitman #2517, 1953, illus by Zillah Lesko, VG-EX, K3 ....$6.00

Pete's Dragon, Whitman #2428-3, 1977, VG-EX, K3.........$3.00

Princess Who Never Laughed, Whitman #2610, 1961, VG-EX, K3 ....$5.00

Raggedy Ann & the Tagabout Present, Golden #2451-43, B edition, VG-EX, K3 ....$4.00

Road Runner & the Birdwatchers, Whitman #2518, 1968, VG-EX, K3 ....$5.00

Sesame Street — The Invention of Paper, Whitman #2402-3, 1975, VG-EX, K3 ....$3.00

Slowpoke at the Circus, Whitman #2457, 1973, VG-EX, K3 ..$8.00

Snow White & the Seven Dwarfs, Whitman #2533, 1957, VG-EX, K3 ....$5.00

Surprise for Howdy Doody, Whitman #2573, 1950, VG-EX, K3...$28.00

Three Bears, Whitman #2551, 1955, VG-EX, K3.............$10.00

Three Little Pigs, Whitman #921, 1958, VG-EX, K3 ....$5.00

Tom & Jerry's Big Move, Golden #2451-38, A edition, VG-EX, K3 ....$3.00

Tuffy the Tugboat, Whitman #880, 1947, VG-EX, K3.......$3.00

Where Is the Keeper?, Whitman #2441, 1966, illus by Art Seiden, VG-EX, K3 ....$4.00

Winnie the Pooh the Blustery Day, Golden #2456-52, 1975, VG-EX, K3...$3.00

Yippee Kiyi & Whoa Boy, Whitman #2514, 1954, VG-EX, K3 ....$5.00

101 Dalmatians, Whitman #2622, 1960, VG-EX, K3.........$5.00

WHITMAN

Bible Stories, #2029, 1952, Cozy Corner, VG-EX, K3......$12.00

Cinderella, 1950, Cozy Corner, VG, P6..........................$28.00

Dick Tracy Meets the Night Crawler, 1945, hardcover, EX, D11 ....$15.00

Donald Duck & His Cat Troubles, 1948, hardcover, EX, P6...$35.00

Donald Duck & the Boys, 1948, hardcover, EX, P6 ....$35.00

Donald Duck in Bringing Up the Boys, 1948, softcover, NM, F8 ....$18.00

Family Affair, Buffy Finds a Star, 1971, TV Adventure series, hardcover, EX, A $25.00

Flipper Mystery of the Black Schooner, 1966, blk & wht illus, 190 pgs, EX, T2 ....$5.00

Johnny Appleseed, 1949, softcover, EX, F8 ....$16.00

Lady the Little Blue Mare, #2027, 1950, Cozy Corner, VG-EX, K3 ....$12.00

Mickey Mouse Fire Brigade, 1936, EX+ (w/dust jacket), M8..$145.00

Mr Jinks & Pixie & Dixie, 1962, hardcover, EX, F8.........$25.00

Popeye Borrows a Baby Nurse, 1937, illus, scarce, EX+, A.....$90.00

Rootie Kazootie & the Pineapple Pies, 1935, illus, NM, T2...$14.00

Snooper & Blabber & Quick Draw McGraw, 1962, hardcover, EX, F8 ....$40.00

Snow White & the Seven Dwarfs, #933, An Authorized Book of the Walt Disney Movie, paper cover, 12x13", rare, EX, P6 ....$80.00

Story of Doc, #1044, EX+, M8 ....$80.00

Story of Grumpy, #1044, 1938, EX+, M8.......................$80.00

Story of Happy, #1044, 1938, EX+, M8.........................$80.00

Story of Sneezy, #1044, 1938, EX+, M8.......................$80.00

Three Orphan Kitties, 1949, softcover, EX, F8 ....$12.00

Wally Gator, Guess What's Hiding at the Zoo, 1963, EX, F8..$15.00

Walt Disney's Pinocchio, #709, 1939, softcover, EX, M8.$45.00

Walt Disney's Story of Dippy the Goof, #1006, 1938, VG, M8...$37.00

WONDER BOOKS

ABC & Counting Rhymes, #823, VG-EX, K3 ....$3.00

Alice in Wonderland, #574, 1951, VG-EX, K3 ....$7.00

Babar the King, #602, VG, K3.......................................$10.00

Bambi's Children, 1951, 1st edition, EX, F8 ....$12.00

Bedtime Stories, #507, 1946, illus by Masha, VG-EX, K3 .$15.00

Billy & His Steam Roller, #537, 1951, VG-EX, K3 ....$5.00

Blondie's Family, 1954, EX+.......................................$5.00

Blowaway Hat, #554, 1946, VG-EX, K3.........................$8.00

Boy Who Wouldn't Eat His Breakfast, #815, 1963, VG-EX, K3 ....$6.00

Brave Little Steamshovel, #555, 1951, VG-EX, K3 ....$5.00

Can You Guess?, #701R, 1953, Romper Room, VG-EX, K3 ...$5.00

Casper & Wendy Adventures, #855, 1969, VG, K3 ....$9.00

Christmas Favorites, #869, 1951, VG-EX, K3 ....$6.00

Christmas in Song & Story, #586, 1953, illus by Catherine Scholz, VG-EX, K3 ....$6.00

Cinderella, #640, 1954, illus by Ruth Ives, VG-EX, K3......$9.00

Come & See the Rainbow, #743, 1960, VG-EX, K3 ....$4.00

Copycat Colt, #545, 1951, illus by Charlotte Steiner, VG-EX, K3 ....$10.00

Costume Party, #0800, 1962, VG-EX, K3 ....$5.00

Counting Book, #0692, 1957, VG-EX, K3 ....$7.00

Crusader Rabbit, 1958, EX, F8 ....$20.00

Do You Know the Magic Word?, #0578, 1952, VG-EX, K3 .$5.00

Doll Family, #802, 1962, photos by Martin Harris, VG-EX, K3 ...$12.00

Famous Fairy Tales, #505, 1949, VG-EX, K3 ....$10.00

Favorite Nursery Tales, #1504, 1953, sculptured cover, VG-EX, K3 ....$9.00

Five Little Finger Playmates, #522, 1949, VG-EX, K3......$14.00

Fixit Man, #756, 1952, VG-EX, K3 ....$5.00

Fred Flintstone The Fix-It Man, #917, 1976, VG-EX, K3 ..$8.00

Giraffe Who Went to School, #551, 1951, VG-EX, K3 .....$7.00

Guess What?, #605, 1953, VG-EX, K3 ....$6.00

Hans Christian Andersen's Fairy Tales, #599, 1952, VG-EX, K3 ....$8.00

Happy Birthday Present, #564, 1951, VG-EX, K3 ....$4.00

Heidi, #532, 1950, VG-EX, K3 ....$10.00

Hide & Seek Duck, #568, 1952, VG-EX, K3 ....$5.00

Hoppy the Curious Kangaroo, #579, 1952, VG-EX, K3 ...$10.00

How the Clown Got His Smile, #566, 1951, VG-EX, K3...$12.00

It's a Lovely Day, #632, 1956, VG-EX, K3 ....$5.00

It's a Secret, #540, 1950, VG-EX, K3 ....$10.00

Just Like Mommy/Just Like Daddy, #589, 1952, 2-in-1 book, VG-EX, K3 ....$5.00

Kewtee Bear's Christmas, #867, 1956, rounded corners, VG-EX, K3 ....$8.00

Let's Go Shopping, #693, 1958, VG-EX, K3 ....$10.00

Let's Go to School, #961, 1954, w/full-color cutouts, VG-EX, K3 ....$9.00

Let's Play Indian, #538, 1950, VG-EX, K3 ....$4.00

Little Audrey & the Moon Lady, #759, 1977, VG, K3 ....$7.00

Little Dog Who Forgot How To Bark, #504, 1946, VG-EX, K3 ....$6.00

Little Garage Man, #744, 1960, VG-EX, K3 ....$6.00

Little John Little, #558, 1951, VG-EX, K3 ....$5.00

Little Lost Puppy, #528, 1976, VG-EX, K3 ....$6.00

Little Peter Cottontail, #641, 1956, by Thorton W Burgess, VG-EX, K3 ....$7.00

Little Puppy Who Would Not Mind His Mother, #515, 1949, 44 pgs, VG, K3 ....$7.00

Little Train That Saved the Day, #571, 1952, VG-EX, K3 ...$7.00

Magic Word, #578, 1952, VG-EX, K3 ....$7.00

Make-Believe Parade, #520, 1949, VG-EX, K3 ....$15.00

Mary Alden's Cook Book for Children, #2518, 1955, softcover, VG-EX, K3 ....$24.00

Morning Noises, #795, 1962, VG-EX, K3 ....$7.00

Mother Goose, #501, 1946, Mother Goose in bonnet on cover, VG-EX, K3 ....$5.00

My First Book of Riddles, #745, 1960, VG-EX, K3 ....$5.00

Night Before Christmas, #858, 1974, VG-EX, K3 ....$4.00

Pecos Bill, #767, 1961, VG-EX, K3 ....$12.00

Peter Cottontail & Reddy Fox, #743, 1954, VG-EX, K3 ..$10.00

Peter Goes to School, #600, 1953, VG-EX, K3 ....$5.00

Peter Pan, #597, 1952, VG-EX, K3 ....$5.00

Peter Rabbit & Reddy Fox, #611, 1954, VG-EX, K3 ....$6.00

Pinocchio, #615, 1954, VG-EX, K3 ....$6.00

Puppy Who Found a Boy, #561, 1951, VG-EX, K3............$8.00

Quiet Little Indian, #709, 1958, VG-EX, K3 ....$5.00

Raggedy Andy's Surprise, #604, 1953, VG, K3 ....$8.00

Raggedy Ann & Marcella's First Day at School, 1952, by J Gruelle, rpr, K3 ....$10.00

Rattle-Rattle Train, #655, 1974, VG-EX, K3........................$3.00

Roly-Poly Puppy, #549, 1950, VG-EX, K3 ....$7.00

Romper Room Book of Happy Animals, #687R, 1957, VG-EX, K3 ....$8.00

Romper Room Safety Book, #854, 1974, VG-EX, K3 ....$5.00

Runaway Baby Bird, #748, 1960, VG-EX, K3 ....$6.00

See How It Grows, #630, 1954, VG-EX, K3 ....$5.00

Shy Little Horse, #1509, 1947, sculptured cover, VG-EX, K3 ....$15.00

Sleeping Beauty, #635, 1956, VG-EX, K3 ....$5.00

Sonny the Bunny, #591, 1952, VG-EX, K3 ....$6.00

Soupy Sales & the Talking Turtle, #860, 1965, VG-EX, K3 ...$10.00

Storytime Favorites, #514, 1947, VG-EX, K3 ....$6.00

Surprise for Mrs Bunny, #601, VG-EX, K3 ....$5.00

Three Little Pigs/Red Riding Hood, #609, 1975, 2-in-1 book, VG-EX, K3..$14.00

Tom Terrific's Greatest Adventure, 1959, 1st edition, EX, F8 ....$18.00

Too Little Fire Engine, #526, 1950, VG-EX, K3 ....$4.00

Traveling Twins, #596, 1953, no play money, VG-EX, K3..$8.00

Twelve Days of Christmas, #651, 1956, VG-EX, K3..........$8.00

Visit to a Hospital, #690, VG-EX, K3 ....$5.00

Who Lives Here?, #669, 1958, VG-EX, K3 ....$8.00

Who Lives on the Farm?, #518, 1949, VG-EX, K3 ....$6.00

Why the Bear Has a Short Tail, #508, 1946, VG-EX, K3..$10.00

Wild Bill Hickok, #549, 1956, VG, K3 ....$7.00

Wizard of Oz, #543, 1951, VG, K3 ....$8.00

Wonder Book of Bible Stories, #577, 1951, VG-EX, K3.....$8.00

Wonder Book of Cowboys, #640, 1956, VG-EX, K3 ....$8.00

Wonder Book of Favorite Nursery Tales, #730, 1953, VG-EX, K3 ....$5.00

Wonder Book of Fun, #576, 1951, illus by Dellwyn Cunningham, VG-EX, K3..$8.00

Yogi Bear Mosquito Flying Day, #924, 1976, VG-EX, K3...$5.00

MISCELLANEOUS

Alice in Wonderland, **Juvenile Productions Ltd., inscribed 1938, 190 pages, edge wear otherwise EX, $110.00.**

Photo courtesy Marvelous Books.

A Friend Is Someone Who Likes You, Joan Walsh Anglund, 1967, VG-EX (w/dust jacket), K3 ....$8.00

Addams Family Homebodies, 1965, 1st ed, EX $8.00

Alice Through the Looking Glass, Maxton, 1947, hardcover, w/dust jacket, EX, F8 ....$15.00

Baby Bunny, Joan Walsh Anglund, 1967, Golden sturdy shape, VG-EX, K3 ....$4.00

Bambi Picture Book, Simon & Schuster, 1942, fabric pgs, EX, F8 ....$18.00

Babar Visits Another Planet, Random House, 1972, VG-EX, K3 ....$7.00

Berenstains' Baby Book, MacMillan, 1951, 1st edition, hardcover, EX, F8 ....$25.00

Bible Stories for Children, #1078, 1945, Samuel Lowe, VG-EX, K3 ....$10.00

Big Locomotive Number One, Saalfield #4207, 1952, VG-EX, K3 ....$6.00

Bobby Bear's Busy Day, Saalfield #4212, 1952, VG-EX, K3..$14.00

Book of Food, First Experience in Reading, Grosset & Dunlap, 1938, Josephine Van Dolzen Pease, VG-EX, K3........$12.00

Book of Heat & Light, First Experience in Reading, Grosset & Dunlap, 1938, Josephine Van Dolzen Pease, VG-EX, K3...$12.00

Book of Houses, First Experience in Reading, Grosset & Dunlap, 1938, Josephine Van Dolzen Pease, VG-EX, K3........$12.00

Buffalo Bill's Wild West, McLoughlin Bros, 1887, 12x10", EX, A $300.00

Buster Brown Goes Fishing, Saalfield, 1905, cloth cover, EX, A $100.00

Buster Brown Plays Cowboy, Saalfield, 1905, cloth cover, EX, A $75.00

Buster Brown's Antics, 1906, cb cover, 32 pgs, NM, A..$200.00

Choo-Choo Train, Bonnie Books #4027, 1946, VG-EX (w/dust jacket), K3 ....$35.00

Dick Whittington, 1944, Samuel Lowe, softcover, VG-EX, K3 ....$10.00

Donald Duck, Harmony, 1979, by Marcia Blitz, NM (w/dust jacket), M8 ....$125.00

Donald Duck & the Hidden Gold, Sandpiper #S2, VG (torn dust jacket), K3 ....$20.00

Donald Duck & the Hidden Gold, Sandpiper #S2, VG-EX (w/dust jacket), K3 ....$30.00

Donald Duck & the Mystery of the Double X, 1949, VG, M8...$12.00

Dopey He Don't Talk Much, 1938, linen-like cover, EX+, M8...$50.00

Elmer Elephant, 1938, linen-like cover, EX, M8 ....$50.00

Farmer Collins, Star-Bright #S-305, VG-EX, K3...........$8.00

Fox Grows Old, 1946, Samuel Lowe, VG-EX, K3 ....$10.00

Gene Autry & Red Shirt, Sandpiper, 1951, 1st edition, M (w/dust jacket), P6...$35.00

Goody Two Shoes, 1944, Samuel Lowe, softcover, VG-EX, K3 ....$10.00

Granny's Birds, A Story of Russia, Saalfield #448, 1947, VG-EX, (w/dust jacket), K3 ....$30.00

Grimm's Fairy Tales, Sturdibuilt, 1948, VG-EX, K3.........$12.00

Hans Andersen's Fairy Tales, Hans Andersen, 8vo, A. Duncan Carse illustrator, EX, $60.00.

Hansel & Gretel, 1944, Samuel Lowe, softcover, VG-EX, K3 ....$10.00

Henry in Lollipop Land, Treasure, 1953, 1st edition, EX, F8 ....$15.00

Hopalong Cassidy's Private War, Grosset & Dunlap, 1950s, hardcover, EX, F8 ....$10.00

I Go Pogo, Simon & Schuster, 1952, 8th edition, NM, F8 ....$12.00

Joan Walsh Anglund Storybook, 3rd edition, VG-EX (w/dust jacket), K3 ....$20.00

Lone Ranger's New Deputy, Sandpiper, 1951, 1st edition, M (w/dust jacket), P6...$35.00

Dolly in the Country, Father Tuck's Doll Series, ca 1901-1910, 12 pages, minor edge wear otherwise VG, $175.00.

Mickey Mouse Goes Christmas Shopping, Golden, 1953, EX, F8 ....$8.00

Mickey Mouse in Pigmy Land, by Walt Disney, 1956, EX, $58.00.

Mickey Mouse Stories Book #2, David McKay Co, 1934, softcover, EX, M8 ....$80.00

New Neighborhood, Bonnie Books #4826, 1954, VG-EX, K3.$9.00

Puss in Boots, Samuel Lowe, 1944, softcover, VG-EX, K3 .$10.00

Roy Rogers on the Double-R Ranch, Sandpiper, 1951, 1st edition, M (w/dust jacket), P6...$35.00

Stories for Bedtime, Saalfield #4201, 1952, VG-EX, K3 .....$5.00

Story of Davy Crockett, Grosset & Dunlap, VG-EX, K3....$8.00

Story of Lafayette, Grosset & Dunlap, VG-EX, (w/dust jacket), VG-EX, K3...$8.00

Surprise for a Lunchbox (Critter Country), Happy Day #3434, 1986, VG-EX, K3..$3.00

Teddy Bear Tales, Joan Walsh Anglund, 1st edition, 1985, VG-EX, K3..$20.00

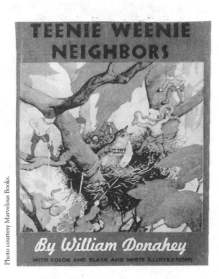

Teenie Weenie Neighbors, William Donahey, Whittlesey House publisher, 1945, 2nd printing, illustrated by author, EX, $125.00.

That Girl, Pyramid, 1971, softcover, 125 pgs, EX, A $10.00

Toonerville Trolley & Other Cartoons by Fontaine Fox, 1921, EX, A $300.00

Walt Disney's Donald Duck, Story Written & Illustrated by the Staff of Walt Disney Studios, 13x9½", EX, A............$75.00

Walt Disney's Dumbo of the Circus, Garden City Publishing, 1941, scarce, EX, M8 ....$55.00

We Were There on the Oregon Trail, Grosset & Dunlap, VG-EX, K3 ....$7.00

What Are Babies Like?, Happy Day #2012 (1st Happy Day book), 1987, VG-EX, K3 ....$9.00

Wizard of Oz, Storytime #B120, 1978, VG-EX, K3 ....$7.00

Breyer

Breyer collecting seems to be growing in popularity, and though the horses dominate the market, the company also made dogs, cats, farm animals, wildlife figures, dolls, and tack and accessories such as barns for their models. They've been in continuous production since the '50s, all strikingly beautiful and lifelike in both modeling and color. Earlier models were glossy, but since 1968 a matt finish has been used, though glossy and semiglossy colors are now being re-introduced, especially in special runs. (A special run of Family Arabians was done in the glossy finish in 1988.)

One of the hardest things for any model collector is to determine the value of his or her collection. The values listed below are for models in excellent to near mint condition. This means no rubs, no scratches, no chipped paint, and no breaks — nothing that cannot be cleaned off with a rag and little effort. Any model which has been altered in any way, including having the paint touched up, is considered a customized model and has an altogether different set of values from an original finish model. The models listed herein have their original finishes, meaning they have not been altered or customized in any way.

Advisor: Carol Karbowiak Gilbert (G6), author of a continually updated value guide as well as several articles on model collecting, values, and care for *The Model Horse Gazette*.

CLASSIC SCALE MODELS

Andalusian Foal, matt dk chestnut, 1973-93, G6 ....$15.00

Andalusian Mare, matt alabaster, 1984, Sears, G6 ....$25.00

Andalusian Stallion, matt dapple gray, 1984, Sears, G6...$25.00

Arabian Foal, matt lt bl, complete w/cookie tin, 1988 (signing parties), G6 ....$65.00

Arabian Mare, matt chestnut, 1973-91, G6 ....$15.00

Arabian Stallion, matt sorrel, 1973-91, G6......................$15.00

Black Beauty, matt blk, 1980-93, G6 ....$15.00

Black Stallion, matt blk, 1983-93, G6...............................$15.00

Bucking Bronco, matt gray, 1961-67, G6, from $150 to.$200.00

Duchess, matt bay, 1980-93, G6.......................................$15.00

Ginger, matt chestnut, 1980-93, G6 ....$15.00

Hobo (on base), matt buckskin, w/book & carrying case, G6 .$60.00

Jet Run, matt bay, 1980-93, G6...$15.00

Johar, matt alabaster, 1983-93, G6....................................$15.00

Keen, matt chestnut, 1980-93, G6 ....$15.00
Kelso, matt or semi-gloss bay, 1975-90, G6, ea, from $20 to....$30.00
Lipizzan Stallion, matt alabaster, 1975-80, G6 ....$50.00
Man O' War, matt red chestnut, 1975-95, G6, from $25 to ..$30.00
Merrylegs, matt dapple gray, 1980-93, G6 ....$15.00
Mesteno, Charging; matt dk buckskin, 1995-present, G6...$15.00
Mesteno, Fighting; matt dk buckskin, 1994-present, G6..$15.00
Mesteno, matt dk buckskin, 1992-present, G6 ....$15.00
Mesteno's Mother, matt buckskin, 1993-present, G6.......$15.00
Mighty Tango, matt dapple gray, 1980-91, G6, from $15 to.$20.00
Mustang Foal, matt chestnut, 1976-90, G6, from $10 to..$15.00
Mustang Mare, matt chestnut pinto, 1976-90, G6 ....$20.00
Mustang Stallion, matt chestnut, 1976-90, G6, from $15 to ...$20.00
Polo Pony (on base), matt bay, 1976-82, G6 ....$60.00
Quarter Horse, matt lt bay, 1974-93, G6 ....$15.00
Quarter Horse Mare, matt bay, 1974-93, G6, from $20 to..$25.00
Quarter Horse Stallion, matt palomino, 1974-93, G6, $15 to ..$25.00
Rearing Stallion, matt palomino, 1965-85, G6, $25.........$30.00
Rojo, matt red dun, 1995-present, G6..............................$15.00
Ruffian, matt dk bay, 1977-90, G6, from $30 to $35.00
Sagr, matt sorrel, 1983-93, G6, from $15 to......................$20.00
Silky Sullivan, matt brn, 1975-90, G6, from $25 to $30.00
Sombra, matt grulla, 1994-present, G6 ....$15.00
Swaps, matt chestnut, 1975-90, G6, from $25 to..............$30.00
Terrang, matt dk brn, 1975-90, G6, from $25 to $30.00

TRADITIONAL SCALE

Action Stock Horse Foal, matt chestnut, 1984-86, G6 ....$22.00
Appaloosa Gelding, #97, 1971-80, G6..............................$35.00
Appaloosa Performance Horse, matt chestnut roan appaloosa, G6 ....$44.00
Balking Mule, seal brn, 1968-71, G6 ....$150.00
Belgian, glossy dapple gray, 1964-67, G6, from $500 to ..$650.00
Belgian, matt chestnut w/red & yel ribbon, 1965-80, G6 ..$100.00

Brahma Bull, #70, 1958-93, glossy, $35.00.

Brighty Burro, matt gray, 1982-87, G6, from $35 to $40.00
Buckshot, matt grulla, 1971-73, G6 ....$45.00
Cantering Welsh Pony, matt bay w/yel ribbons, 1971-73, G6 ..$100.00
Cantering Welsh Pony, matt chestnut w/no ribbon, 1979-81, G6, from $30 to $50.00
Clydesdale Foal, matt chestnut, 1969-89, G6, from $15 to ...$20.00
Clydesdale Mare, matt chestnut, 1969-89, G6..................$25.00
Clydesdale Stallion, glossy bay w/gold ribbons, muscular, 1958-63, G6, from $140 to $200.00
Family Arabian Foal, matt palomino, 1967-87, G6 ....$15.00
Family Arabian Mare, matt alabaster, 1967-73, G6..........$30.00
Fighting Stallion, glossy charcoal, 1961-71, G6 ....$150.00
Foal, #909, woodgrain, G6..$75.00

Black Beauty, #89, 1979-88, $30.00.

Black Stallion, semi-gloss blk, G6, from $30 to $35.00

Foal, JC Penney, 1991, sorrel, $25.00.

Foundation Stallion, matt blk, 1977-87, G6 ....$40.00
Friesian, matt blk, 1992-95, G6.......................................$25.00
Fury Prancer, glossy blk pinto, 1965-63, G6, from $90 to..$100.00
Galiceno, matt bay, 1978-82, G6 ....$50.00
Gem Twist, matt alabaster, 1993-95, G6 ....$25.00

Grazing Foal, matt bay, 1964-76 & 1978-81, G1 ....$35.00
Grazing Mare, matt bay, 1961-80, G6 ....$50.00
Hackney Pony, matt bay, 1995-present, G6 ....$20.00
Halla, matt bay, 1977-85, G6 ....$60.00
Ideal American Quarter Horse, matt chestnut, Special Run,
    1995, G6, from $25 to $40.00
Indian Pony, matt alabaster, 1970-71, G6 ....$225.00
John Henry, matt dk bay, 1988-90, G6 ....$40.00
Justin Morgan, matt red bay, 1977-89, G6 ....$40.00
Khemosabi, matt red bay, 1990-95, G6 ....$25.00
Kipper, matt chocolate brn, 1986, G6 ....$80.00
Lady Phase, matt chestnut, 1976-85, G6 ....$55.00
Lady Roxana, matt alabaster, 1986-88, G6 ....$40.00

Lassie, #65, 1958-65, $40.00.

Man O' War, #47, 1969-95, $18.00.

Midnight Sun, matt blk, red & wht ribbon, 1972-87, G6...$40.00

Misty, matt palomino pinto, 1972-95, G6.....................$20.00
Misty's Twilight, matt chestnut pinto, 1991-95, G6, from $20
    to...$25.00
Morgan, matt blk w/diamond star, 1965-87, G6 ....$40.00
Mustang, glossy alabaster w/red eyes, semi-rearing, 1961-66, G6,
    from $150 to $200.00
Pacer, matt or semi-gloss, dk bay, 1967-87, G6................$45.00
Performing Misty, ceramic, glossy palomino w/stool, 1993,
    G6...$40.00
Pluto, matt lt gray, 1991-95, G6, from $20 to $40.00
Pony of the Americas, matt chestnut leopard appaloosa, 1976-
    80, G6 ....$50.00
Porcelain Icelandic Horse, matt buckskin pinto, 1992, G6, from
    $150 to $250.00
Porcelain Shire, matt bay, 1993, G6 ....$140.00
Proud Arabian Stallion, matt or semi-gloss mahogany bay, 1971-
    80, G6 ....$50.00
Quarter Horse Gelding, glossy bay, 1959-66, G6, from $125
    to $125.00
Quarter Horse Yearling, matt liver chestnut, 1970-80, G6 ...$40.00
Racehorse, glossy chestnut, 1956-67, G6, from $120 to .$150.00
Racehorse, matt woodgrain, 1958-66, G6 ....$200.00
Roy the Belgian, matt sorrel, 1989-90, G6 ....$45.00
Running Foal, glossy Copenhagen (rare), 1963-65, G6, from
    $800 to..$1,000.00
Running Foal, matt bay, 1963-87, G6 ....$20.00
Running Foal, 1963-73, glossy dapple gray, G6 ....$45.00
Running Mare, glossy Florentine (rare), 1963-64, G6, from
    $1,100 to...$1,500.00
Running Mare, 1963-73, glossy dapple gray, G6.............$75.00
Running Stallion, glossy charcoal, 1968-71, G6, from $225 to..$250.00
San Domingo, matt chestnut pinto, 1978-87, G6.............$40.00
Sea Star, matt chestnut, 1980-87, G6 ....$20.00
Secretariat, matt chestnut, 1987-95, G6 ....$25.00

Sham, #410, wheat ear version, 1984-88, $40.00.

Sherman Morgan, matt chestnut, 1989-90, G6 ....$50.00
Shetland Pony, matt bay, 1973-88, G6 ....$25.00
Shire, matt honey sorrel, 1972-76 & 1978-80, G6 ....$60.00
St Bernard, #328, 1972-80...$40.00
Stock Horse Foal, smooth coat, matt bay, 1983-88, G6 ...$25.00
Stock Horse Stallion, matt bay blanket appaloosa, 1981-86,
     G6..$40.00
Stormy, matt chestnut pinto, 1977-95, G6 ....$15.00

Stud Spider, #66, 1978-89, $40.00.

Touch of Class, matt bay, 1986-88, G6............................$40.00
Trakehner, matt bay, 1979-84, G6 ....$60.00
Western Horse, glossy palomino, 1950-70, G6 ....$40.00
Western Pony, glossy blk, 1956-63, G6............................$75.00
Western Prancing Horse, matt bay, 1961-71, G6 ....$75.00

Bubble Bath Containers

Since back in the 1960s when the Colgate-Palmolive Company produced the first Soaky, hundreds of different characters and variations have been marketed, bought on demand of the kids who saw these characters day to day on TV by parents willing to try anything that might make bathtime more appealing. Purex made their Bubble Club characters, and Avon and others followed suit. Most Soaky bottles came with detachable heads made of brittle plastic which cracked easily. Purex bottles were made of a softer plastic but tended to loose their paint.

Rising interest in US bubble bath containers has created a collector market for those made in foreign countries, i.e, UK, Canada, Italy, Germany, and Japan. Licensing in other countries creates completely different designs and many characters that are never issued here. Foreign containers are generally larger and are modeled in great detail, reminiscent of the bottles that were made in the US in the '60s. Prices may seem high, considering that some of these are of fairly recent manufacture, but this is

due to their limited availablity and the costs associated with obtaining them in the United States. We believe these prices are realistic, though many have been reported much higher. Rule of thumb: pay what you feel comfortable with — after all, it's meant to be fun. And remember, value is affected to a great extent by condition. Unless noted otherwise, our values are for examples in near-mint condition. Bottles in very good condition are worth only about 60% to 65% of these prices. For slip-over styles, add 100% if the bottle is present.

Advisors: Matt and Lisa Adams (A7); Jon Thurmond (T1).

Alvin (Chipmunks), Soaky, red w/wht A, w/contents, neck tag
     & puppet, M, A7 ....$75.00
Alvin (Chipmunks), Soaky, yel w/red A, EX, A7.............$35.00
Atom Ant, Purex, orange body w/red accents, EX+, A7 ..$50.00
Augie Doggie, Purex, orange body w/gr shirt, orig tag & card,
     EX+, A7 ....$50.00
Baba Louie, Soaky, w/orig tag, M, H4 ....$20.00
Baloo Bear (Jungle Book), Colgate-Palmolive, 1960s, slipover
     only, NM, A7...$25.00
Bambi, EX $30.00
Bamm-Bamm, Purex, 1960s, blk & wht, NM, A7/J2........$30.00
Barney Rubble, Purex, 1960s, brn & yel, NM, A7............$30.00
Barney Rubble, Soaky, MIB, H4.......................................$20.00
Batman, Avon, MIB $25.00
Batman, Soaky, VG $50.00
Batmobile, Avon, 1978, bl & silver w/decals, EX+, A7....$25.00
Beatles, Paul McCartney, Colgate-Palmolive, red, EX, from $100
     to..$125.00
Beatles, Ringo Starr, bl, EX, B3/R2, from $100 to $125.00
Big Bad Wolf, Tubby Time, gray & red w/cap head, NM, A7 ...$40.00
Bozo the Clown, Soaky, NM, A7......................................$35.00
Broom Hilda, Lander, 1977, EX, A7 ....$25.00
Brutus (Popeye), Soaky, red shorts w/red & wht striped shirt,
     EX+, A7 ....$40.00

Bullwinkle, striped shirt, Colgate-Palmolive, NM, $50.00.

Bugs Bunny, Colgate-Palmolive, slipover only, NM, A7..$25.00

Bugs Bunny, Colgate-Palmolive, 1960s, gray, wht & orange, cap ears, NM, A7...$30.00

Bugs Bunny, Colgate-Palmolive, 1960s, lt bl & wht, NM, A7...$35.00

Bugs Bunny, leaning against egg, VG.............................$15.00

Bullwinkle, Soaky, all brn, NM+, A7.............................$40.00

Casper the Friendly Ghost, EX, T1 ....$30.00

Cecil Sea Serpent, Purex, 1960s, gr, w/contents & hula skirt disguise, MIB, A7...$75.00

Cement Truck, Colgate-Palmolive, 1960s, bl & gray w/movable wheels, NM, A7...$40.00

Charlie Brown, Avon, in red baseball outfit, NM, A7 .....$20.00

Cinderella, Colgate-Palmolive, 1960s, movable arms, NM, A7...$35.00

Creature From the Black Lagoon, NM...........................$125.00

Deputy Dawg, Colgate-Palmolive, gray, yel & bl, cap hat, sm, NM, A7...$30.00

Deputy Dawg, Colgate-Palmolive, 1960s, brn & yel outfit, lg, NM, A7/C17..$30.00

Dick Tracy, Soaky, 1965, 10", EX+, D11 ....$45.00

Dino (Flintstones), Purex, purple body, NM+, A7...........$60.00

Donald Duck, Colgate-Palmolive, 1960s, wht, bl & yel w/cap head, NM, A7...$25.00

Donald Duck, Colgate-Palmolive, 1960s, wht & bl, NM, A7 ..$30.00

Dopey, Colgate-Palmolive, 1960s, bank, purple & yel, NM, A7...$30.00

Dopey, Colgate-Palmolive, 1960s, purple, yel & red, NM, A7...$30.00

Droop-A-Long Coyote, Purex, pk w/bl & orange accents, gr hat, EX+, A7...$40.00

Dum Dum, Purex, 1966, scarce, NMIB..........................$145.00

El Cabong, Knickerbocker, 1960s, blk, yel & wht, rare, VG, A7...$75.00

Elmer Fudd, Soaky, in hunting outfit, NM, A7 ....$30.00

Explosives Truck, Colgate-Palmolive, 1960s, red & gray w/movable wheels, NM, A7...$40.00

Felix the Cat, Soaky, red body, EX+, A7 ....$35.00

Fire Truck, Colgate-Palmolive, 1960s, red w/hose & movable wheels, NM, A7...$40.00

Flintstones Fun Bath, Roclar (Purex), 1970s, MIB (unopened), A7...$75.00

Frankenstein, Soaky, 1960s, 10", EX, F8 ....$90.00

Fred Flintstone, Colgate-Palmolive, EX, C17 ....$20.00

Fred Flintstone, Purex, 1960s, blk & red, NM, A7 ....$30.00

GI Joe, NM $15.00

Goofy, Colgate-Palmolive, 1960s, red, wht & blk w/cap head, NM, A7...$25.00

Gravel Truck, Colgate-Palmolive, 1960s, orange & gray w/movable wheels, NM, A7...$40.00

Gumby, Perma Toy, No More Tears, 1987, 9½", M (sealed) ..$20.00

Gumby & Pokey, M&L, shampoo & conditioner, orig shrinkwrap & stickers, M, A7..$40.00

Huckleberry Hound, Knickerbocker, 1960s, powder/bank, red & blk, 15", NM, A7...$50.00

Jack Skellington (Nightmare Before Christmas), Canadian, NM...$25.00

Jiminy Cricket, Colgate-Palmolive, 1960s, gr, blk & red, NM, A7...$30.00

Jurassic Park Dinosaur, Cosrich, orig tag, M, A7 ....$10.00

King Louie (Jungle Book), Colgate-Palmolive, 1960s, slipover only, NM, A7...$25.00

Lippy the Lion, Purex, purple vest, EX, A7......................$40.00

Little Orphan Annie, Lander, 1977, NM, A7....................$25.00

Lucy (Peanuts), Avon, 1970, red dress w/hat top, MIB, A7..$25.00

Mad Hatter, Avon, 1970, bronze plastic w/pk hat & clock, EX, A7...$20.00

Magilla Gorilla, Purex, 1960s, movable or non-movable arms, NM, A7, ea $60.00

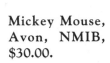

Mickey Mouse, Avon, NMIB, $30.00.

Mickey Mouse, Soaky, in red shirt & wht pants, cap head, M, A7 ....$30.00

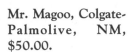

Mr. Magoo, Colgate-Palmolive, NM, $50.00.

Mickey Mouse, Soaky, 1960s, Mickey as band leader in red uniform, NM, A7 ....$30.00

Mighty Mouse, Soaky, NM...$25.00

Mousketeer Girl, Colgate-Palmolive, 1960s, red outfit w/orange or yel hair, NM, A7, ea...$30.00

Mr Do Bee (Romper Room), Manon F Inc, w/sticker, rare, NM, A7 ....$75.00

Mr Jinx w/Pixie & Dixie, Colgate-Palmolive, EX, B10/T2, from $30 to $35.00

Mr Jinx w/Pixie & Dixie, Purex, 1960s, orange w/gray mice, NM, A7..$30.00

Mr Magoo, Soaky, red or bl outfit, VG, A7, ea................$25.00

Mummy, Colgate-Palmolive, 1960s, NM, $100.00.

Mummy, Soaky, wht & gr, EX, A7......................................$85.00

Mush Mouse, Purex, purple vest, head & hat, EX, A7 .....$30.00

Muskie, Soaky, 1960s, NM, C1/J2, from $25 to.................$35.00

Oil Truck, Colgate-Palmolive, 1960s, gr & gray w/movable wheels, NM, A7...$40.00

Panda Bear, Tubby Time, 1960s, wht & blk w/cap head, NM, A7 ....$30.00

Pebbles Flintstone, Purex, 1960s, gr shirt w/yel shorts or purple shirt w/bl shorts, EX, A7, ea $40.00

Peter Potomus, Soaky, w/orig tag, M $25.00

Pinocchio, Colgate-Palmolive, 1960s, red w/removable head, EX, C17...$20.00

Pluto, Colgate-Palmolive, 1960s, orange w/cap head, NM, A7...$25.00

Pokey, 1987, M (sealed) $20.00

Popeye, Soaky, 1960s, wht suit w/bl accents, MIB, A7.....$55.00

Popeye, Soaky, 1970s, bl suit w/wht accents, NM, A7 .....$35.00

Porky Pig, Colgate-Palmolive, w/removable head, EX, C17/T2...$20.00

Power Rangers, Kid Care, any character, w/contents, M, A7, ea...$6.00

Punkin' Puss, Purex, orange body w/bl clothing, VG, A7.$30.00

Quick Draw McGraw, Purex, 1960s, orange & bl or orange only, NM, A7, ea $40.00

Ricochet Rabbit, Purex, 1960s, movable or non-movable arm, NM, A7, ea $50.00

Robin (Batman), Soaky, EX, A7 ....$75.00

Rocky Squirrel, Soaky, 1960s, w/removable head, NM $35.00

Sailor, Avon, VG...$10.00

Santa, Colgate-Palmolive, NMIB, $30.00.

Schroeder (Peanuts), Avon, 1970, MIB, A7......................$35.00

Secret Squirrel, Purex, 1960s, yel & purple, NM, A7.......$60.00

Simba (Lion King), Kid Care, head squirts, M, A7.............$6.00

Simon (Chipmunks), Colgate-Palmolive, 1960s, bl shirt, NM, A7 ....$35.00

Smokey the Bear, Colgate-Palmolive, bl pants, yel cap hat, NM, A7 ....$30.00

Snaggle Puss, Purex, 1960s, pk w/gr hat, NM, A7 ....$65.00

Snoopy, Avon, retains orig label, 5½", EX, D9.................$15.00

Snoopy & Woodstock, Avon, 1974, on red skis, MIB, A7...$30.00

Snow White, Colgate-Palmolive, 1960s, bank, bl & yel, NM, A7 ....$30.00

Speedy Gonzales, Colgate-Palmolive, 1960s, bl & red, NM, A7/T1..$30.00

Spouty the Whale, retains orig tag, M...............................$25.00

Squiddly Diddly, Purex, 1960s, purple & pk, NM, A7......$75.00

Superman, Avon, 1978, 8", NM, minimum value $35.00

Superman, Soaky, bl w/red outfit, EX+, A7 ....$50.00

Sylvester, Soaky, holding microphone, EX+, A7..............$30.00

Tasmanian Devil, Kid Care, standing in inner tube, EX, A7....$7.00

Teenage Mutant Ninja Turtles, Kid Care, any character, M, A7, ea $7.00

Tennessee Tuxedo, Soaky, holding ice-cream cone, NM, A7 ....$35.00

Spider-Man, Colgate-Palmolive, NMIB, $55.00.

Theodore (Chipmunks), Soaky, wht w/bl T, w/contents, neck tag & puppet, M, A7 ....$75.00

Three Little Pigs, Tubby Time, 1960s, bl, red or yel overalls, NM, A7, ea $35.00

Thumper (Bambi), Colgate-Palmolive, 1960s, lt bl & wht, NM, A7 ....$30.00

Tidy Toy Race Car, red or bl w/movable wheels, NM, A7, ea..$50.00

Top Cat, Soaky, NM, T1 ....$35.00

Touche Turtle, Purex, 1960s, turquoise or red w/purple feathers, lying down, NM, A7, ea $50.00

Tweety Bird, Colgate-Palmolive, 1960s, slipover only, NM, A7 ....$25.00

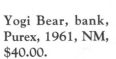

Yogi Bear, bank, Purex, 1961, NM, $40.00.

Wally Gator, Purex, 1960s, powder, lying on stomach, gr, NM, A7 ....$50.00

Wendy the Witch (Casper), Soaky, red & yel, NM, A7 ..$30.00

Whitey the Whale, Avon, 1959, wht, EX, A7..................$20.00

Winsome Witch, Purex, 1960s, bl & blk, NM, A7...........$30.00

Wolfman, Soaky, red pants, NM, A7 ....$110.00

Woodsy Owl, Lander Co, early 1970s, brn, gr & yel, NM, A7 ....$45.00

Woody Woodpecker, Colgate-Palmolive, 1960s, bl, yel & wht w/red flume cap, NM, A7 ....$25.00

Yakky Doodle Duck, Roclar (Purex), w/contents & neck card, M, A7..$25.00

Yogi Bear, Knickerbocker (Purex), 1960s, powder/bank, brn, w/tag & card, 14", VG+, A7.................................$35.00

FOREIGN

Action Man (Battle Force), Rosedew Ltd/UK, 1994, camo out-fit, kneeling w/machine gun, 8½", NM, A7..............$25.00

Action Man (Dr X), Rosedew Ltd/UK, 1994, Topper, bald man w/X on back of head, 8", NM, A7 ....$15.00

Aladdin, Grosvenor/UK, on flying carpet w/Jasmin & monkey, M, A7..$20.00

Aladdin, Prelude/UK, holding lamp, comes apart at waist, M, A7 ....$20.00

Alf, PE/Germany, unknown date, brn & tan, opens at neck, 7", NM, A7 ....$40.00

Alice in Wonderland, Aidee International Ltd/UK, 1993, stand-ing in grass w/rabbit, 10", NM, A7......................$35.00

Aliens, Grosvenor/UK, 1993, Topper, Plasma Foam Bath, 9", NM, A7 ....$25.00

Ariel (Little Mermaid), Damascar/Italy, 1995, sitting on purple rock, 8", NM, A7 ....$25.00

Ariel (Little Mermaid), Prelude/UK, sitting in clear bubbles, opens at center, NM, A7 ....$25.00

Asterix, Euromark/Switzerland, 1992, wing-headed man w/yel moustache & gr belt, 9½", NM, A7.....................$75.00

Baloo (Jungle Book), Prelude/UK, dancing, M, A7 ....$20.00

Barbie, Grosvenor/UK, w/butterfly in hand & on shoulder, pk, lavender & wht dress, M, A7 ....$20.00

Barbie, Grosvenor/UK, 1995, pk & wht wedding dress w/heart tag, 9", NM, A7 ....$25.00

Barney Rubble, Damascar/Italy, 1995, wearing Water Buffalo hat w/bowling ball, 9", NM, A7.................................$45.00

Barney Rubble, Rosedew/UK, standing at attention, M, A7 ....$40.00

Bart Simpson, Grosvenor/UK, standing nude w/wht towel & soap, M, A7..$35.00

Batman, Grosvenor/UK, 1992, c DC Comics, gray suit & blk cape, 11", NM, A7 ....$30.00

Batman Forever, Prelude/UK, 1995, blk w/beige face, movable arms, comes apart at waist, 11", NM, A7 ....$30.00

Bear (Forever Friends), Grosvenor/UK, 1995, in tub of bubbles, 5", NM, A7 ....$20.00

Beast (Beauty & the Beast), Prelude/UK, 1994, movable arms, comes apart at waist, lg, NM, A7 ....$30.00

Belle (Beauty & the Beast), Centura/Canada, 1994, yel gown & gloves, 10", NM, A7 ....$20.00

Benjamin Bunny (Beatrix Potter), Grosvenor/UK & Canada, 1991, Topper, gr & red hat, holding bag & onion, 7", NM, A7 ....$20.00

Big Bird (Sesame Street), Grosvenor/UK, 1995, Topper, sitting in bubbles w/teddy bear, 8", NM, A7 ....$15.00

Boo Boo Bear, Damascar/Italy, sitting on 3 picnic baskets eating an apple, M, A7 ....$50.00

Bugs Bunny, Centura/Canada, 1994, purple robe, holds carrot, 11", NM, A7 ....$25.00

Captain Scarlet (Thunderbirds), Euromark/UK, 1993, red & blk outfit, kneeling w/blk gun, 9½", NM, A7 ....$35.00

Casper the Friendly Ghost, Damascar/Italy, 1995, sitting on pumpkin, glow-in-the-dark, 7½", NM, A7 ....$35.00

Catwoman, Damascar Jr/Italy, standing w/3 cats, M, A7..$45.00

Cinderella, Damascar/Italy, 1994, gray & wht gown, 9½", NM, A7 ....$25.00

Cindy Bear (Yogi Bear), Damascar/Italy, sitting on purple rock, gray head & body, M, A7 ....$50.00

Cookie Monster (Sesame Street), Jim Henson, PI/UK, 1995, w/bl & wht cloth towel, 8½", NM, A7 ....$20.00

Daffy Duck, Prelude/UK, 1994, wearing shark suit, 10½", NM, A7 ....$30.00

Dennis the Menace, Rosedew/UK, red & blk striped outfit w/blk curly hair, M, A7 ....$20.00

Desperate Dan, DC Thompson/UK, 1991, lumberjack w/dog, 10½", NM, A7 ....$30.00

Dewey (Donald Duck's nephew), Rosedew Ltd/UK, 1990s, bl outfit & hat, 8½", NM, A7 ....$30.00

Dino (Flintstones), Damascar/Italy, 1995, standing on food dish w/giant bone, 9½", M, A7 ....$50.00

Dino (Flintstones), Rosedew Ltd/UK, 1993, w/collar, 9", NM, A7 ....$35.00

Dirt Movers, Prelude/UK, yel construction vehicle w/movable wheels, 7", NM, A7 ....$25.00

Donald Duck, Centura/Canada, 1994, standing on red base, 9½", NM, A7..$25.00

Donald Duck, Mann & Schroder/German, 1970s, standing w/arms on hips, M, A7................................$45.00

Donald Duck (Mickey & Pals), Centura/Canada, 1995, driving yel boat, 9", NM, A7 ....$25.00

Dopey & Sneezy, Grosvenor/UK, Dopey on Sneezy's shoulders, M, A7...$25.00

Fairy, Delagar/UK & Canada, 1994, bl dress w/3 yel stars, holds wand, wings at back, 10", NM, A7.........................$25.00

Flipper, Euromark/UK, riding a wave, M, A7 ....$20.00

Fozzie Bear (Muppets), Prelude/UK, hand puppet that slips over bottle, M, A7 ....$30.00

Fred Flintstone, Damascar/Italy, 1994, standing w/golf club, M, A7 ....$50.00

Garfield, Grosvenor/UK, lying on stomach, M, A7.........$25.00

Genie (Aladdin), Prelude/UK, 1994, sitting w/arms crossed, 10", NM, A7...$25.00

Goofy, Mann & Schroder/German, 1970s, hitchhiking pose, M, A7 ....$45.00

Hello Kitty, Bandai/Japan, 1992, wht cat w/red ribbons, 5", NM, A7 ....$25.00

Hulk Hogan, Grosvenor/UK, bath beads, flexing muscles, M, A7 ....$25.00

Hunchback of Notre Dame, Grosvenor/UK, sitting on gold bell w/pigeon in hand, M, A7.......................................$20.00

Jafar (Aladdin), Grosvenor/UK, standing w/scepter & bird on shoulder, M, A7...$25.00

Jasmin (Aladdin), Prelude/UK, 1994, gr outfit, holds bird in hand, 9", NM, A7...$25.00

Jerry (Tom & Jerry), Euromark/UK, 1989, standing on Swiss cheese, holding his full stomach, 7½", NM, A7 ....$35.00

John Smith (Pocahontas), Centura/Canada, 1995, sitting on gray rock, opens at waist, 8½", NM, A7 ....$25.00

Mario (Mario Brothers), Grosvenor/UK, 1992 red & bl outfit w/red hat, 8", NM, A7...$25.00

Martin the Pig (Creature Comforts), Rosedew Ltd/UK, 1995, pk pig w/yel shower cap & beige towel, 6½", NM, A7...$25.00

Mickey Mouse, Disney/Canada, 1994, blk tuxedo, red pants & yel tie, 8½", NM, A7...$30.00

Mickey Mouse, Prelude/UK, 1994, Topper, pie-eyed w/legs crossed, 7½", NM, A7.......................................$15.00

Mickey Mouse (Fantasia), Centura/Canada, 1994, red robe, bl star & moon hat, 9½", NM, A7 ....$30.00

Minnie Mouse, Disney/Canada, 1994, pie-eyed, traditional 1930s outfit, 8½", NM, A7....................................$30.00

Mowgli & Kaa (Jungle Book), Prelude/UK, 1994, snake wrapped around boy, 7", NM, A7....................................$30.00

Mumfie (Magic Adventures of Mumfie), Euromark/UK, 1995, gray & pk elephant waving bl scarf w/trunk, 9½", NM, A7 ....$25.00

Musical Bears, Delagar/Canada & US, 1989, band leader, accordion or drummer, 7", NM, A7, ea $15.00

Nala (Lion King), Centura/Canada, 1994, sitting on pk base, 8", NM, A7...$20.00

Olive Oyl, Damascar/Italy, 1995, sitting w/hands clasped, M, A7 ....$50.00

Olive Oyl and Popeye, Damascar/Italy, 1995, NM, A7, $35.00 each.

Photo courtesy Matt and Lisa Adams.

Oscar the Grouch (Sesame Street), Grosvenor/UK, 1995, Topper, in trash can w/I Hate Baths sign, 8½", NM, A7 ....$15.00

Pablo the Parrot (Creature Comforts), Rosedew Ltd/UK, 1995, Topper, gr, yel, red, purple & bl, 8½", NM, A7.........$15.00

Paddington Bear, Cottsmore Ltd/UK, 1995, Topper, bl or red raincoat w/suitcase & sandwich, 9", NM, A7, ea.......$30.00

Papa Smurf, IMPS Brussels/Germany, 1991, bl w/red pants & hat, wht beard, 9½", NM, A7 ....$30.00

Pebbles & Bamm-Bamm, Damascar/Italy, sitting on sabertooth tiger, M, A7 ....$50.00

Percy (Thomas the Tank), Grosvenor/UK, 1994, Topper, sitting on blk tracks w/gray bricks, 6½", NM, A7 ....$15.00

Peter Rabbit (Beatrix Potter), Grosvenor/US & Canada, 1991, bl coat, 8½", NM, A7..$20.00

Piglet (Winnie the Pooh), Prelude/UK, 1990s, Topper, waving w/scarf flapping in wind, 10", NM, A7.....................$20.00

Pink Panther, UK, 1972, standing at attention, M, A7....$75.00

Pocahontas, Centura/Canada, 1995, sitting on rock in grass, 8½", NM, A7 ....$25.00

Pocahontas, Grosvenor/UK, 1995, Topper, in canoe w/racoon, 10", NM, A7 ....$15.00

Pogo (101 Dalmatians), Grosvenor/UK, 1994, father dog w/pup on head & between legs, 9½", NM, A7 ....$25.00

Polly Pocket Castle, Euromark/UK, gray & purple w/gr grass & tiny figure, M, A7 ....$15.00

Popeye, Rosedew Ltd/UK, 1987, holds spinach can, blk base, 10", NM, A7 ....$40.00

Postman Pat, Rosedew Ltd/UK, 1991, mailman w/lg brn bag, 9", NM, A7...$30.00

Power Rangers, Euromark/UK, wht & gold outfit w/yel bolt at legs, movable arm, M, A7.......................................$20.00

Pumba (Lion King), Centura/Canada, 1994, Topper, warthog eating worm, 9", NM, A7 ....$15.00

Pumba (Lion King), Prelude/UK, 1994, warthog, 7", NM, A7..$25.00

Robin (Batman), Damascar/Italy, squatting on eagle-head statue, M, A7 ....$40.00

RoboCop, Euromark/UK, 1995, movable, standing on gray bricks, 12", NM, A7...$30.00

Scooby Doo, Damascar/Italy, sitting, M, A7.....................$60.00

Scrappy Doo (Scooby Doo), Damascar/Italy, 1995, dog coming out of well w/water creature, 7", NM, A7 ....$35.00

Simba (Lion King), Prelude/UK, 1994, cub w/paw raised, sitting on gray rock, 8", NM, A7 ....$25.00

Skates, unknown maker/Canada, 1990s, turtle on skates w/bl hat, mk #1 on back, 8", NM, A7 ....$20.00

Sleeping Beauty, Damascar/Italy, 1994, standing w/rose, 10½", NM, A7...$30.00

Smurf, IMPS Brussels/Germany, 1991, w/wht pants & hat, 9½", NM, A7...$30.00

Sneezy & Sleepy, Grosvenor/UK, 1994, Topper, Fairy Tale Fragrance Foam Bath, 7½", NM, A7.............................$15.00

Snoopy, Grosvenor/UK, 1990s, on stomach w/cap nose, 8½", NM (clear box w/card), A7 ....$30.00

Snow White, Rosedew Ltd/UK, 1994, standing w/crossed arms & long dress, 10", NM, A7 ....$30.00

Sonic Hedgehog, Matey/UK, 1990s, standing on red & bl game button, 9", NM, A7 ....$30.00

Spider-Man, Euromark/UK, 1995, walking over trash can & tire, 9", NM, A7 ....$30.00

SPV (Thunderbirds), Euromark/UK, 1993, gray, bl, wht & blk vehicle from cartoon, 8", NM, A7 ....$35.00

Super Soaker Gun, Larami/Cosrich/Canada, 1992, 7", NM, A7 ....$25.00

Superman, Euromark/UK, flying pose, comes apart at waist, M, A7 ....$30.00

Sylvester & Tweety, Prelude/UK, 1995, cat w/mean look holds bird, 10", NM, A7...$25.00

Tasmanian Devil, Centura/Canada, 1994, gray whirlwind on rock, opens at waist, 7", NM, A7 ....$25.00

Thomas the Tank, Bandai/Japan, 1991, red & bl engine, 3½", NM, A7...$25.00

Tom (Tom & Jerry), Euromark/UK, holding microphone & stand, M, A7 ....$30.00

Troll, German, bl, pk or yel hair, M, A7, ea $30.00

Truck (4x4 Matchbox), Grosvenor/UK, 1995, Topper, Fast Lane, on lg rock, 6½", NM, A7 ....$15.00

Vampire (Horror Bubbles!), Jackel International/UK, 1994, cartoon-like child vampire, 7½", NM, A7....................$25.00

Wakko (Animaniacs), Prelude/UK, 1995, Topper, baseball cap, 10½", NM, A7...$15.00

Wile E Coyote, Prelude Ltd/UK, w/rocket backpack, M, A7 ..$20.00

Wilma Flintstone, Damascar/Italy, 1995, washing clothes in pelican's bill, 9", NM, A7..$35.00

Wilma Flintstone, Rosedew Ltd/UK, 1993, Topper, cartoon outfit, 8½", NM, A7 ....$20.00

Photo courtesy Matt and Lisa Adams.

Winnie the Pooh, left to right: United Kingdom/Canada, NM, $30.00; United Kingdom, NM, $25.00; Topper/Canada, NM, $20.00.

Wombles (Uncle Bulgaria), Euromark/UK, 1994, full figure, 8", NM, A7...$25.00

Woodstock (Peanuts), unknown maker/UK, flying red plane, yel w/blk heart-shaped glasses, M, A7.............................$20.00

Yakko (Animaniacs), Prelude/UK, 1995, Topper, blk & wht w/red nose, 10½", NM, A7...$15.00

Yogi Bear, Damascar/Italy, standing on gr & purple grass, brn w/gr hat & tie, M, A7...$50.00

101 Dalmatians, Grosvenor/UK, pups on pillow w/red sunglasses, M, A7 ....$15.00

Buddy L

First produced in 1921, Buddy L toys have escalated in value over the past few years until now early models in good original condition (or restored, for that matter) often bring prices well into the four figures when they hit the auction block. The business was started by Fred Lundahl, founder of Moline Pressed Steel Co., who at first designed toys for his young son, Buddy. They were advertised as being 'Guaranteed Indestructible,' and indeed they were so sturdy and well built that they just about were. Until wartime caused a shortage, they were made of heavy-gauge pressed steel. Many were based on actual truck models; some were ride-ons, capable of supporting a grownup's weight. Fire trucks with hydraulically activated water towers and hoisting towers that actually worked kept little boys entertained for hours. After the war, the quality of Buddy Ls began to decline, and wood was used to some extent. Condition is everything. Remember that unless the work is done by a professional restorer, overpainting and amateur repairs do nothing to enhance the value of a toy in poor condition. Professional restorations may be expensive, but they may be viable alternatives when compared to the extremely high prices we're seeing today. In the listings that follow, toys are all pressed steel unless noted.

See also Advertising; Boats.

CARS AND BUSSES

Country Squire Station Wagon, 1964, EX....................$200.00

Flivver Coupe, 1920s, black with red spoked wheels, 12", EX+, from $950.00 to $1,250.00.

Flivver Coupe #210B, 1920s, blk w/balloon tires & red spoked wheels, 11", EX-, A..................................$700.00
Greyhound Bus #755, MIB, from $550 to $600.00

Passenger Bus, ca 1929, 30", scarce, paint worn otherwise VG, from $3,500.00 to $3,800.00.

Scarab #711, red futuristic vehicle w/chrome lights & grille, blk rubber tires, w/up, 10", VG.....................................$350.00
Town & Country Convertible, pnt & varnished wood w/flip-back top, 19", EX.....................................$150.00
Transportation Bus, lt gr, 28", NM, A.........................$4,300.00
Transportation Bus, maroon w/blk & gold, 28", rstr, EX, A.....................................$3,000.00
Volkswagen Bus, no plastic sunroof o/w EX...................$125.00

CONSTRUCTION

Cement Mixer, gr, 9", VG, A...$135.00
Cement Mixer, 18x12x12", EX, A $525.00
Excavator Truck, 1940, bl & gray slant cab, clockwork wench, 20", no shovel or ramp, G, A $100.00
Hi-Lift Scoop Dump Truck, orange cab & chassis w/cream dump bed, VG+ $130.00

Mobile Power Digger, orange and yellow with red chassis, green crane, 20", EX, A, $250.00.

Overhead Crane, 27x46", EX, A.................................$1,500.00
Pile Driver #260, 1924-27, 19", G, A..........................$425.00
Road Roller #290, 1930, 29", G, A...............................$2,400.00

Sand & Gravel Truck, doorless cab w/divided bed, orig decals, 26", some overpnt, VG+, A $1,750.00
Sand Loader, yel w/blk buckets, 15", G, A.....................$275.00
Stationary Crane, 17", G, A..$250.00
Steam Roller, 19", G, A...$175.00

Steam Shovel, black with red roof, upright boiler, crank-operated shovel and boom, cast-iron wheels, 24", VG+, A, $325.00.

Trench Digger #400, 1928-31, yellow and red, 24", VG, A, $4,300.00.

FIREFIGHTING

Aerial Ladder Truck, red with nickel-plated ladders, hydraulic lift, 40", restored, minimum value, $2,000.00.

Aerial Ladder Truck, 1960, mk BLFD, w/2 extension ladders, 24", EX, A...$100.00
Aerial Ladder Truck, 39", VG, A.................................$975.00
Hook & Ladder Truck #205, 1920s, 24", missing ladders, rpt, A $500.00
Pumper Truck #205A, 1925, 23", rpt, A........................$700.00
Pumper Truck #29, ride-on, 26", rstr, VG, A $1,200.00
Texaco Fire Chief Water Truck, 25", EXIB, A..............$300.00

OUTDOOR TRAINS

Boxcar #35407, red w/blk trucks, sliding center doors, ladders on 1 end, 22½", NM $1,550.00
Caboose, red w/blk trucks, opening door at ea end, 20¼", EX $1,650.00
Coal Car (Gondola) #96834, blk w/ladders on 1 end, 22½", rare, EX, from $1,100 to $1,200.00

Freight Car, red, 21", EX, A, $650.00.

Locomotive & Tender #1000, 1920s, w/5 pcs of track, 43", VG+, A $175.00
Pile Driver, blk w/corrugated roof, geared hand wheel rotates cab on flatcar case, 22½", rstr, from $900 to...............$1,300.00
Railway Improved Steam Shovel, blk w/red corrugated roof, rotating cab on flat bed, 22½", VG $4,400.00
Stock Car #12457, red w/blk trucks, sliding center doors w/ladders on 1 end, 22½", EX..$1,100.00

TRUCKS AND VANS

Allied Van Lines Tractor-Trailer, pull toy, yel & blk, 30", VG, A $400.00
Baby Truck, 1920s, red w/red spoke wheels, 24", G, A...$750.00
Baggage Line Truck, blk cab & chassis w/yel bed, 27", VG, A...$2,300.00

City Dray Truck #439, 1934, green and yellow, 19", EX, A, $500.00.

Photo courtesy Dunbar Gallery.

City Dray Truck, blk cab, yel stake bed w/open tailgate, 24",
rare, VG, A...$2,250.00

**Coal Truck, black with red chassis, white rubber tires, 25",
G, A, $850.00.**

Coal Truck, opening doors, front fenders & running boards, rub-
ber tires w/simulated spoke wheels, 26", rpt, G, ...$4,850.00
Delivery Truck, C-style cab w/removable screened van, 25", G,
A...$675.00
Delivery Truck, early open cab & bed, spoke wheels, 24", G,
A...$500.00
Dump Truck, open cab & bed, crank-operated chain dump, 25",
partial rpt, VG+, A...................................$375.00
Dump Truck, open cab & bed, piston mechanism, 24", rstr,
A...$400.00
Express Line Truck, enclosed cab, trailer w/open top, 24", EX+,
A...$2,500.00
Express Line Van, open C-style cab w/extended van roof, gr &
blk, 25", rstr, A.......................................$550.00
Express Van, blk w/red chassis, removable blk mesh van top, alu-
minum tires w/red disk hubs, 25", G.....................$1,450.00
Flivver Dump Truck, blk w/open cab, aluminum tires w/spoked
wheels, lever-action dump bed, 12", EX, A..........$2,500.00
Flivver Pickup Truck #210, 1920s, 12", EX+, A..........$1,320.00
Huckster Truck, blk, 14", EX, A..................................$4,000.00
Hydraulic Dumper, wht & gr w/decals, rubber tires, 22", EX+,
A...$500.00
Ice Truck #602, 1930s, orig canvas top, 21", EXIB, A....$700.00

International Dump Truck, rider, 25", NM, A, $550.00.

Ice Truck #602, 1930s, orig canvas top, 21", G, A.........$150.00
International Harvester Sales & Service Truck, red, 6 bales of
hay in back, 24", EX, A...............................$2,300.00
Lumber Truck #203A, 1927, blk w/red chassis & wheels, 24",
G+, A..$3,675.00

**Merry-Go-Round Truck, red with black tires, wooden
carousel with plastic horses, 12", VG, $165.00.**

Milk Delivery Truck, 24", VG-, A...............................$1,500.00
Moving Van #204, 1920s, 25", G, A..............................$575.00
Railway Express Truck, blk w/screen side body, 24", EX, A..$1,900.00
Repair-It Unit Truck, late version, red cab & chassis w/wht
body, 6 wheels, 21", EX, A...........................$175.00

**Robotoy Truck #72, 1932, red and green, 21", EX, A,
$1,250.00.**

Sand Loader & Dump Truck, yel & bl w/blk tires, 23", EX,
A...$450.00
Shell Fuel Oil Delivery Truck, 1930s, yel & red, 22",
NMIB..$2,400.00
Standard Oil Tanker #14, 1934, red cab & tank w/brass spigot,
blk pull rod, 27", VG+, A............................$4,025.00
Supermarket Delivery Truck, wht w/decals on open bed, chrome
grille, blk rubber tires, 12½", EX+, A.................$300.00
Tank Truck #206, 1924, 25", EX, A.............................$1,400.00
Telephone Maintenance Repair Truck & Trailer #450, 1930s,
2-tone gr w/red trailer, complete w/accessories, 15", NMIB,
A...$350.00
US Mail Truck, brn w/wht van roof, Buy Defense Bonds decal,
blk tires w/chrome hubs, 21", M.........................$850.00

US Mail Truck #5345, 1964, EX......................................$250.00
Van Lines Tractor-Trailer, yel & blk, 29", rear doors missing, G,
    A..$250.00
Wrecker, wht & gr w/Buddy L Towing Service decal, 25",
    EX..$385.00
Wrecker, yel & red cab w/yel winch in red open bed, 28", G,
    A...$2,150.00
Wrecker Van, red cab & chassis w/wht body, 15", G, A...$375.00
Wrigley Spearmint Gum Railway Express Agency Truck, red &
    gr, blk tires w/red hubs, battery-op lights, 23", G, A..$750.00

Building Blocks and Construction Toys

Toy building sets were popular with children well before television worked its mesmerizing influence on young minds; in fact, some were made as early as the end of the eighteenth century. Important manfacturers include Milton Bradley, Joel Ellis, Charles M. Crandall, William S. Tower, W.S. Read, Ives Manufacturing Corporation, S.L. Hill, Frank Hornby (Meccano), A.C. Gilbert Brothers, The Toy Tinkers, Gebruder Bing, R. Bliss, S.F. Fischer, Carl Brandt Jr., and F. Ad. Richter (see Richter Anchor Stone Building Sets). Whether made of wood, paper, metal, glass, or 'stone,' these toys are highly prized today for their profusion of historical, educational, artistic, and creative features. For further information on Tinker Toys, read *Collector's Guide to Tinker Toys* by Craig Strange (Collector Books).

Richter's Anchor (Union) Stone Building Blocks were the most popular building toy at the beginning of the twentieth century. As early as 1880, they were patented in both Germany and the USA. Though the company produced more than six hundred different sets, only their New Series is commonly found today (these are listed below). Their blocks remained popular until WWI, and Anchor sets were one of the first toys to achieve international 'brand name' acceptance. They were produced both as basic sets and supplement sets (identified by letters A, B, C, or D) which increased a basic set to a higher level. There were dozens of stone block competitors, though none were very successful. During WWI the trade name Anchor was lost to A.C. Gilbert (Connecticut) who produced Anchor blocks for a short time. Richter responded by using the new trade name 'Union' or 'Stone Buiilding Blocks,' sets considered today to be Anchor blocks despite the lack of the Richter's Anchor trademark. The A.C. Gilbert Company also produced the famous Erector sets which were made from about 1913 through the late 1950s.

Note: Values for Richter's blocks are for sets in very good condition; (+) at the end of the line indicates these sets are being reproduced today.

Advisors: Arlan Coffman (C4); George Hardy (H3), Richter's Building Blocks.

Aeroplane Constructor, Meccano, G (orig box), A.......$300.00
American Plastic Bricks #705, Halsam, w/brochure, NM (w/canister), J6..$35.00
American Plastic Bricks #735, Halsam, 1960s, complete, EX (EX canister), T2..$40.00

American Skyline, Elgo, 1950s, complete, NM (VG box),
    T2...$35.00
Astrolite, 1960s, builds futuristic city w/lights, missing few pcs,
    EX (EX box), T1...$65.00
Auto-Baukasten Construction Kit, Marklin, ca 1935, for building a gr & red truck, EXIB, A $3,200.00
Auto-Bouwdoos, Marklin, 2-door limousine, lt gr, completely assembled, w/up, 14½", M (orig box w/extra parts), A.........$4,400.00
Block City #B-500, Plastic Block City Inc, 1960, complete, EX
    (EX canister), T2 ....$40.00
Building Bricks, Auburn Rubber, 1950s, complete, EX (EX canister), T2 ....$35.00

Bilding Boats With Blocks, Artwood #6050, complete, EX (EX box), P3, $25.00.

Construct-All #100, Transogram, plastic, complete, NMIB,
    T1..$45.00
Construx Action Building System #6331, Mobile Missiles Military series, Fisher-Price, NMIB, from $50 to..............$60.00

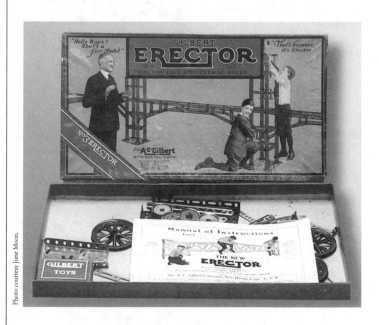

Erector Set, Gilbert, No. 3, MIB, $175.00.

Curtain Wall Builder No 630, Spalding Tinkertoy, NM (NM canister) $75.00

Drawbridge Set, Renwal #155, complete, scarce, NM (EX box), A...$245.00

Dux Airplane Construction Set, Germany, metal, EX (EX box), A...$100.00

Erector Set, Gilbert, #4, complete, VG (VG box), A $125.00

Photo courtesy John and Sheri Pavone.

Erector Set, Gilbert, No. 6½, MIB, $160.00.

Erector Set, Gilbert, #7, EX (orig wooden box), A $250.00

Erector Set, Gilbert, #8, Zeppelin, EX (orig box), A......$860.00

Giant Building Set, Ideal, 1960s, scaled to fit Motorific cars, complete, EX (EX box), J6, $145.00.

Girder & Panel Bridge & Turnpike, Kenner, 1959, complete, NMIB..$40.00

Girder & Panel Build-A-Home Set, Kenner, 1962, complete, EX (EX canister), T2 ....$35.00

Girder & Panel Building Set No 3, Kenner, 1957, missing platform, EX (EX box), A..................................$30.00

Girder & Panel Constructioneer Set #8, Kenner, VG (VG box), T1...$85.00

Girder & Panel Build-A-Home Set, Kenner No. 14, M (VG box), J6, $85.00.

Girder & Panel Hydro-Dynamic Double Set #18, Kenner, VG (VG box), T1 ....$175.00

Girder & Panel Hydro-Dynamic Single Set #17, Kenner, VG (VG box), T1 ....$150.00

Girder & Panel Monorail Skyway Set #11, Kenner, VG (VG box), T1 ....$150.00

Girder & Panel Skyscraper Set #72050, Kenner, complete w/elevator, EX (rpr box), S15 ....$40.00

Lincoln Logs, lg canister set, VG, T1 ....$45.00

Masterbuilder Kit of the White House, Marx, complete, M (EX box), T1 ....$185.00

Match Box Construction Set, Marx, complete, scarce, MIB, A...$65.00

Photo courtesy June Moon.

Tru Model Erector Set, Gilbert, No. 1, complete, EX (G box), $175.00.

Motor Car Constructor, Meccano, complete, EX (EX box), A $500.00

Roadster Constructor, Meccano, complete, MIB, A ...$1,100.00

Skyport Building Set, Ideal, 1968, complete, EX (EX box), F8 ....$85.00

Super City Skyscraper Building Set, Ideal, 1960s, NM (VG box), T1 ....$135.00

Tinker Zoo, Tinkertoy, 1961, complete, NM (NM canister), T2...$20.00

Tinkertoy Big Boy No 155, 1950s, complete, EX (EX canister), T2...$30.00

ANCHOR STONE BUILDING SETS BY RICHTER

DS, Set, #05, w/metal parts & roof stones, VG, H3 ....$100.00
DS, Set, #07, w/metal parts & roof stones, VG, H3 ....$250.00
DS, Set, #15, w/metal parts & roof stones, VG, H3 ....$1,500.00
DS, Set #E3, w/metal parts & roof stones, VG, H3 ....$60.00
DS, Set #03A, w/metal parts & roof stones, VG, H3........$50.00
DS, Set #05A, w/metal parts & roof stones, VG, H3 .....$150.00
DS, Set #07A, w/metal parts & roof stones, VG, H3 .....$200.00
DS, Set #09A, w/metal parts & roof stones, VG, H3 .....$250.00
DS, Set #11, w/metal parts & roof stones, VG, H3 ....$675.00
DS, Set #11A, w/metal parts & roof stones, VG, H3 .....$300.00
DS, Set #13A, w/metal parts & roof stones, VG, H3 .....$325.00
DS, Set #15A, w/metal parts & roof stones, VG, H3 .....$475.00
DS, Set #19A, w/metal parts & roof stones, VG, H3 .....$475.00
DS, Set #21A, w/metal parts & roof stones, VG, H3 .....$975.00
DS, Set #23A, w/metal parts & roof stones, VG, H3 .....$750.00
DS, Set #25A, w/metal parts & roof stones, VG, H3 ..$1,500.00
DS, Set #27, w/metal parts & roof stones, VG, H3 .....$6,000.00
Fortress Set, #406, VG, H3.................................$500.00
Fortress Set #402, VG, H3.................................$100.00
Fortress Set #402A, VG, H3.................................$130.00
Fortress Set #404, VG, H3.................................$250.00
Fortress Set #404A, VG, H3.................................$275.00
Fortress Set #406, VG, H3.................................$550.00
Fortress Set #406A, VG, H3.................................$400.00
Fortress Set #408, VG, H3 ....$1,000.00
Fortress Set #408A, VG, H3.................................$800.00
Fortress Set #410, VG, H3.................................$1,800.00
Fortress Set #410A, VG, H3.................................$1,000.00
Fortress Set #412A, VG, H3.................................$1,500.00
Fortress Set #414, VG, H3.................................$5,000.00
GK-BK, Great-Castle, VG, H3.................................$9,950.00
GK-NF, Set #06, VG, H3 (+) $120.00
GK-NF, Set #06A, VG, H3 (+) $120.00
GK-NF, Set #08, VG, H3.................................$240.00
GK-NF, Set #08A, VG, H3 (+) $120.00
GK-NF, Set #10, VG, H3.................................$360.00
GK-NF, Set #10A, VG, H3 (+) $140.00
GK-NF, Set #12, VG, H3.................................$550.00
GK-NF, Set #12A, VG, H3 (+) $195.00
GK-NF, Set #14A, VG, H3.................................$200.00
GK-NF, Set #16, VG, H3.................................$900.00
GK-NF, Set #16A, VG, H3.................................$240.00
GK-NF, Set #18A, VG, H3.................................$375.00
GK-NF, Set #20, VG, H3 ....$1,600.00

GK-NF, Set #20A, VG, H3.................................$450.00
GK-NF, Set #22A, VG, H3.................................$450.00
GK-NF, Set #24A, VG, H3.................................$500.00
GK-NF, Set #28, VG, H3.................................$1,125.00
GK-NF, Set #28, VG, H3 ....$3,875.00
GK-NF, Set #28A, VG, H3.................................$1,000.00
GK-NF, Set #30A, VG, H3.................................$1,125.00
GK-NF, Set #32B, VG, H3.................................$1,600.00
GK-NF, Set #34, VG, H3 ....$6,000.00
KK-NF, Set #05, VG, H3.................................$45.00
KK-NF, Set #05A, VG, H3.................................$55.00
KK-NF, Set #07, VG, H3.................................$100.00
KK-NF, Set #07A, VG, H3.................................$90.00
KK-NF, Set #09A, VG, H3.................................$100.00
KK-NF, Set #11, VG, H3.................................$275.00
KK-NF, Set #11A, VG, H3.................................$275.00
KK-NF, Set #13A, VG, H3.................................$300.00
KK-NF, Set #15A, VG, H3.................................$450.00
KK-NF, Set #17A, VG, H3.................................$750.00
KK-NF, Set #19A, VG, H3.................................$1,500.00
KK-NF, Set #21, VG, H3.................................$3,500.00
Modern House & Country House Set #206, VG, H3.....$600.00
Modern House & Country House Set #208, VG, H3.....$600.00
Modern House & Country House Set #210, VG, H3.....$700.00
Modern House & Country House Set #301, VG, H3.....$500.00
Modern House & Country House Set #301A, VG, H3..$500.00
Modern House & Country House Set #303, VG, H3.....$800.00
Modern House & Country House Set #303A, VG, H3..$2,000.00
Modern House & Country House Set #305, VG, H3 .$2,500.00
Neue Reihe, Set #102, VG, H3.................................$75.00
Neue Reihe, Set #104, VG, H3.................................$100.00
Neue Reihe, Set #106, VG, H3.................................$150.00
Neue Reihe, Set #108, VG, H3.................................$250.00
Neue Reihe, Set #110, VG, H3.................................$500.00
Neue Reihe, Set #112, VG, H3.................................$600.00
Neue Reihe, Set #114, VG, H3.................................$1,000.00
Neue Reihe, Set #116, VG, H3 ....$1,500.00

California Raisins

The California Raisins made their first TV commercials in the fall of 1986. The first four PVC figures were introduced in 1987, the same year Hardee's issued similar but smaller figures, and three 5½" Bendees became available on the retail market. In 1988 twenty-one more Raisins were made for retail as well as promotional efforts in grocery stores. Four were graduates identical to the original four characters except standing on yellow pedestals and wearing blue graduation caps with yellow tassels. Hardee's increased their line by six.

In 1989 they starred in two movies: *Meet the Raisins* and *The California Raisins — Sold Out*, and eight additional characters were joined in figurine production by five of their fruit and vegetable friends from the movies. Hardee's latest release was in 1991, when they added still four more. All Raisins issued for retail sales and promotions in 1987 and 1988 (including Hardee's) are dated with the year of production (usually on the bottom of one foot). Of those released for retail sales in 1989, only the Beach Scene characters are dated, and these are actually dated 1988. Hardee's 1991 series are also undated.

Advisors: Ken Clee (C3) and Larry DeAngelo (D3).
Other Sources: W6

Applause, Captain Toonz, w/bl boom box, yel glasses & sneakers, Hardee's Second Promotion, 1988, sm, M **$3.00**
Applause, FF Strings, w/bl guitar & orange sneakers, Hardee's Second Promotion, 1988, sm, M **$3.00**

Photo courtesy Larry DeAngelo.

Applause, Michael Raisin, Special Edition, 1989, M, $15.00.

Applause, Rollin' Rollo, w/roller skates, yel sneakers & hat mk H, Hardee's Second Promotion, 1988, sm, M **$3.00**
Applause, SB Stuntz, w/yel skateboard & bl sneakers, Hardee's Second Promotion, 1988, sm, M **$3.00**
Applause, Trumpy Trunote, w/trumpet & bl sneakers, Hardee's Second Promotion, 1988, sm, M **$3.00**
Applause, Waves Weaver I, w/yel surfboard connected to foot, Hardee's Second Promotion, 1988, sm, M **$4.00**
Applause, Waves Weaver II, w/yel surfboard not connected to foot, Hardee's Second Promotion, 1988, sm, M...........**$6.00**
Applause-Claymation, Banana White, yel dress, Meet the Raisins First Edition, 1989, M **$15.00**
Applause-Claymation, Lick Broccoli, gr & blk w/red & orange guitar, Meet the Raisins First Edition, 1989, M **$15.00**
Applause-Claymation, Rudy Bagaman, w/cigar, purple shirt & flipflops, Meet the Raisins First Edition, 1989, M......**$15.00**
CALRAB, Blue Surfboard, board connected to foot, Unknown Promotion, 1988, M..**$35.00**
CALRAB, Blue Surfboard, board in right hand, not connected to foot, Unknown Promotion, 1987, M **$50.00**
CALRAB, Guitar, red guitar, First Commercial Issue, 1988, M .**$8.00**
CALRAB, Hands, left hand points up, right hand points down, Post Raisin Bran Issue, 1987, M **$4.00**

CALRAB, Hands, pointing up w/thumbs touching head, First Key Chains, 1987, M **$5.00**
CALRAB, Hands, pointing up w/thumbs touching head, Hardee's First Promotion, 1987, sm, M **$3.00**
CALRAB, Microphone, right hand in fist w/microphone in left, Post Raisin Bran Issue, 1987, M **$6.00**
CALRAB, Microphone, right hand points up w/microphone in left, Hardee's First Promotion, 1987, M **$3.00**
CALRAB, Microphone, right hand points up w/microphone in left, First Key Chains, 1987, M....................................**$7.00**

CALRAB, Santa, Christmas Issue, 1988, M, $9.00.

CALRAB, Saxophone, gold sax, no hat, First Key Chains, 1987, M **$5.00**
CALRAB, Saxophone, gold sax, no hat, Hardee's First Promotion, 1987, sm, M **$3.00**
CALRAB, Saxophone, inside of sax pnt red, Post Raisin Bran Issue, 1987, M **$4.00**
CALRAB, Singer, microphone in left hand not connected to face, First Commercial Issue, 1988, M........................**$6.00**
CALRAB, Sunglasses, holding candy cane, gr glasses, red sneakers, Christmas Issue, 1988, M **$9.00**
CALRAB, Sunglasses, index finger touching face, First Key Chains, 1987, M..**$5.00**
CALRAB, Sunglasses, index fingers touching face, orange glasses, Hardee's First Promotion, 1987, M **$3.00**
CALRAB, Sunglasses, right hand points up, left hand points down, orange glasses, Post Raisin Bran Issue, 1987, M...**$4.00**
CALRAB, Sunglasses II, eyes not visible, aqua glasses & sneakers, First Commercial Issue, 1988, M..........................**$6.00**
CALRAB, Sunglasses II, eyes visible, aqua glasses & sneakers, First Commercial Issue, 1988, M **$16.00**
CALRAB, Winky, in hitchhiking pose & winking, First Commercial Issue, 1988, M **$6.00**

Photo courtesy Larry DeAngelo.

CALRAB-Applause, AC, 'Gimme-5' pose, Meet the Raisins Second Edition, 1989, M, $150.00.

CALRAB-Applause, Alotta Stile, w/purple boom box, pk boots, Hardee's Fourth Promotion, 1991, sm, MIP..............$12.00

CALRAB-Applause, Anita Break, shopping w/Hardee's bags, Hardee's Fourth Promotion, 1991, sm, MIP..............$12.00

CALRAB-Applause, Bass Player, w/gray slippers, Second Commercial Issue, 1988, M $8.00

Photo courtesy Larry DeAngelo.

CALRAB-Applause, Benny, with bowling ball and bag, Hardee's Fourth Promotion, 1991, small, MIP, $20.00.

CALRAB-Applause, Boy in Beach Chair, orange glasses, brn base, Beach Theme Edition, 1988, M $10.00

CALRAB-Applause, Boy w/Surfboard, purple board, brn base, Beach Theme Edition, 1988, M $10.00

CALRAB-Applause, Cecil Tyme (Carrot), Meet the Raisins Second Promotion, 1989, M, C3 ....$175.00

Photo courtesy Larry DeAngelo.

CALRAB-Applause, Drummer, Second Commercial Issue, 1988, M, $8.00.

CALRAB-Applause, Girl w/Boom Box, purple glasses, gr shoes, brn base, Beach Theme Edition, 1988, M..................$10.00

CALRAB-Applause, Girl w/Tambourine, gr shoes & bracelet, Raisin Club Issue, 1988, M......................................$12.00

CALRAB-Applause, Girl w/Tambourine (Ms Delicious), yel shoes, Second Commercial Issue, 1988, M $12.00

CALRAB-Applause, Hands, Graduate w/both hands pointing up & thumbs touching head, Graduate Key Chains, 1988, M .$85.00

CALRAB-Applause, Hip Band Guitarist (Hendrix), w/headband & yel guitar, Third Commercial Issue, 1988, M..........$22.00

CALRAB-Applause, Hip Band Guitarist (Hendrix), w/headband & yel guitar, Second Key Chains, 1988, sm, M...........$65.00

CALRAB-Applause, Hula Girl, yel shoes & bracelet, gr skirt, Beach Theme Edition, 1988, M $10.00

CALRAB-Applause, Lenny Lima Bean, purple suit, Meet the Raisins Second Promotion, 1989, M.........................$125.00

CALRAB-Applause, Microphone (female), yel shoes & bracelet, Third Commercial Issue, 1988, M $9.00

CALRAB-Applause, Microphone (female), yel shoes & bracelet, Second Key Chains, 1988, sm, M.................$45.00

CALRAB-Applause, Microphone (male), left hand extended w/open palm, Third Commercial Issue, 1988, M $9.00

CALRAB-Applause, Microphone (male), left hand extended w/open palm, Second Key Chains, 1988, sm, M........$45.00

CALRAB-Applause, Mom, yel hair, pk apron, Meet the Raisins Second Promotion, 1989, M $125.00

CALRAB-Applause, Piano, bl piano, red hair, gr sneakers, Meet the Raisins First Edition, 1989, M..............................$25.00

CALRAB-Applause, Saxophone, blk beret, bl eyelids, Third Commercial Issue, 1988, M $15.00

CALRAB-Applause, Saxophone, Graduate w/gold sax, no hat, Graduate Key Chain, 1988, M $85.00

CALRAB-Applause, Singer (female), reddish purple shoes & bracelet, Second Commercial Issue, 1988, M $12.00

CALRAB-Applause, Sunglasses, Graduate w/index fingers touching face, orange glasses, Graduate Key Chains, 1988, M..$85.00

CALRAB-Applause, Valentine, girl holding heart, Special Lover's Edition, 1988, M, $8.00.

CALRAB-Applause, Valentine, I'm Yours, boy holding heart, Special Lover's Issue, 1988, M $8.00
CALRAB-Claymation, Sunglasses, Singer, Hands, Saxophone, Graduate on yel base, Post Raisin Bran, 1988, ea, from $45 to $65.00

MISCELLANEOUS

Activity Book, by Helen Hovanec, 1988, EX, W6..............$6.00
Address Book, Conga Line, yel, 1988, EX, W6.................$10.00
Air Freshener, several styles, M, C3, ea...............................$5.00
Backpack, w/3 figures, maroon & yel, 1987, EX, W6........$35.00
Balloon, Conga Line, 1987, M $12.00
Bank, cereal box w/lid, plastic, EX, W6 ....$15.00
Bank, Sunmaid, plastic, 1987, MIP, D3/W6 ....$35.00
Belt, lead singer w/mike on buckle, 1987, EX, W6 ....$15.00
Book, Birthday Boo Boo, 1988, EX, W6 ....$10.00
Book, Raisin in Motion, illus by Pat Paris Productions, 1988, NM, W6...$20.00
Book, Raisin the Roof, 1988, EX, W6 ....$10.00
Book, What's Cool, 1988, EX, W6 ....$5.00
Book Tote, w/tag, P12..$30.00
Booklet, The Great Raisin Family Fitness Caper, 1990, M, W6 ....$5.00
Bookmark, 10 different styles, D3, ea $2.50
Bubble Bath, Rockin' Raisin, 24-oz, M, W6......................$4.00
Bulletin Board, Singer & Conga Line or Beach Scene, Rose Art Presents, 1988, MIP, W6, ea $35.00
Cake Topper, Michael Raisin or Piano Player & Drummer, 1988, MIP, C3, ea..$60.00
Can, product label w/1 California Raisin on side, M, C3 .$12.00
Candy Dish, 7 Raisin figures w/bl lettering, 1989, sm, M, W6..$15.00
Canister, glass, C3 ....$125.00
Cap, 1988, EX, W6 ....$5.00
Card Game, 1987, EX, W6 ....$6.00

Chalkboard, Singer & Conga Line or Beach Scene, Rose Art Presents, 1988, MIP, W6, ea $35.00
Clock, wall-type wristwatch, 1987, M, W6......................$95.00
Colorforms, MIB (sealed), M, C3......................................$30.00
Coloring Book, Sports Crazy, 1988, EX, W6......................$5.00
Comic Books, 3-D, #1, #2, #3, #4 or #5, Hawthorne, 1987-88, MIP, W6, ea..$25.00
Computer Game, IBM, M, C3/D3......................................$22.00
Costume, Collegeville, 1988, MIB, W6 ....$10.00
Display, w/38 pin-back buttons, 1987, complete, W6 ....$150.00
Display Box, for Christmas figurines, 1988, EX, W6.........$55.00
Display Box, for Meet the Raisins II figures, 1989, EX, C3 ....$150.00
Display Box, for Michael Raisin figures, 1988, EX, W6....$50.00
Display Figure, stage w/bl drapes, 1987, EX, W6 ....$150.00
Doll, vinyl, w/suctions cups, 1987, M, W6.........................$9.00
Doorknob Hangers, 6 different styles, M, C3, ea................$6.00
Earmuffs, bl, purple or wht, 1987, EX, W6, ea $12.00
Eraser, rubber, set of 2, MOC, C3 ....$15.00
Figure, bendable flat body, bl sneakers, orange sunglasses or microphone, C3, ea...$7.00
Figures, bendable plush, set of 4, 5", M, D3......................$20.00

Fingertronic Puppet Theatre, Bendy Toys Ltd., 1987, MIB, J6, $25.00.

Game, California Raisin board game, MIB, D3 ....$25.00
Iron-on Patches, Applause/Italy, 1988, MIP, W6 ....$5.00
Juice Jar, Conga Line w/Singers, gray cap, 1989, EX, W6..$25.00
Lapel Pin, PVC figure, set of 3, MOC, C3 ....$19.00

Library Set, w/certificate, sticker, bookmark & 4 trading cards, C3...$20.00

Mugs, Christmas Issue, 1988, set of 4, MIB, W6...............$60.00

Ornament, Christmas tree or star shape w/Raisin, 1987, EX, W6, ea...$10.00

Paper Plates, MIP, C3...$15.00

Party Invitations, M, C3...$15.00

Pens, orange, wht or blk ballpoints w/sm PVC figure on top, set of 3, M, C3...$40.00

Pillow Sham, Sears, 1987, MIP, W6.................................$12.00

Place Mat, Raisins in profile, Hardee's, 1987, EX, W6 .....$20.00

Postcard, Claymation/Will Vinton, 1988, M, W6..............$5.00

Poster, California Raisin Band, 22x28", M, D3 ....$8.00

Poster, Heard It Through the Grapevine, Straytech Graphics, 1988, fr, NM, W6 ....$30.00

Puppet, male or female, Bendy/Sutton Happenings, 1987, MIB, ea...$10.00

Puzzle, American Publishing, 1988, 75 pcs, 7x9", MIB, W6 .$15.00

Radio, AM/FM, 1987, MIB (w/inserts), C3/D3 ....$150.00

Record, Rudolph the Red-Nosed Reindeer, 45 rpm, M (w/picture sleeve), C3...$20.00

Record, Signed Sealed Delivered I'm Yours, 45 rpm, M (w/picture sleeve), C3...$20.00

Record, When a Man Loves a Woman, 45 rpm, M (w/picture sleeve), C3 ....$20.00

Refrigerator Magnets, Microphone, Hands, Saxophone or Orange Sunglasses, CALRAB-Applause, 1988, C3, ea.............$55.00

Sandwich Music Box, Hands, both hands out to side pointing, mk 1987 CALRAB, M $25.00

Sandwich Music Box, Microphone, both hands out as if to hug, mk 1987 CALRAB, M $25.00

Sandwich Music Box, Sunglasses, both hands out as if to hug, mk 1987 CALRAB, M $25.00

Scarf, Raisin Chorus Line printed on fabric, M, C3..........$20.00

School Kit, w/ruler, pencil sharpener, eraser & pencil holder, 1988, MOC, W6...$40.00

Stadium Cups, Tiny Good Bite, Justin X Grape, & Ben Inda Sun, M, D3...$15.00

Sticker Album, Diamond Publishing, 1988, M, W6.........$15.00

Stir Stick, w/orange sunglasses or microphone, 1988, M, W6, ea...$3.00

Sunglasses, w/figure on ea side, 4 colors, MOC, C3, ea $15.00

Sunshield, Conga Line, 1988, EX.................................$10.00

Thank You Notes, 1988, MIP, C3.................................$12.00

Trading Cards, World Tour Series #1, complete set, M, C3 ....$22.00

Video, Hip To Be Fit, M, C3...$18.00

Wallet, fabric, maroon, 1987, EX, W6.................................$20.00

Wallet, yel plastic, 1988, EX, W6.................................$20.00

Welcome Mat, 1988, M, W6...$95.00

Wind-up Toy, figure, w/left hand up & right hand down, plastic, 1987, MIB $8.00

Wind-up Toy, figure w/orange tennis shoes & glasses, 1987, sm, EX...$8.00

Wind-up Toy, figure w/right hand up & orange glasses, 1987, MIB $8.00

Winross Truck (Champion Raisins), 1989, red Ford long nose tandem axle w/dual stacks, approximately 600 made, M, D3 ....$140.00

Wrapping Paper, M, C3...$15.00

Wristwatch, Official Fan Club, w/3 different bands, Nelsonic, 1987, MIB $50.00

Candy Containers

As early as 1876, candy manufacturers used figural glass containers to package their candy. They found the idea so successful that they continued to use them until the 1960s. The major producers of these glass containers were Westmoreland, West Bros., Victory Glass, J.H. Millstein, J.C. Crosetti, L.E. Smith, and Jack and T.H. Stough. Some of the most collectible and sought after today are the character-related figurals such as Amos 'N Andy, Barney Google, Santa Claus, and Jackie Coogan, but there are other rare examples that have been known to command prices of $1,000.00 and more. Some of these are Black Cat for Luck, Black Cat Sitting, Quick Firer Cannon (with original carriage), and Mr. Rabbit with Hat (that books for $1,800.00, even in worn paint). There are many reproductions; know your dealer. For a listing of these reproductions, refer to Schroeder's Antiques Price Guide.

'L' numbers in the listings that follow refer to An Album of Candy Containers, Vols 1 and 2, by Jennie Long; 'E&A' numbers correlate with The Compleat American Glass Candy Containers Handbook by Eikelberner and Agadjanian, revised by Adele Bowden. Watch for a soon-to-be released comprehensive information and value guide, The Collector's Guide to Candy Containers, written by our advisor Doug Dezso and Leon and Rose Poirier (Collector Books).

Advisor: Doug Dezso (D6).

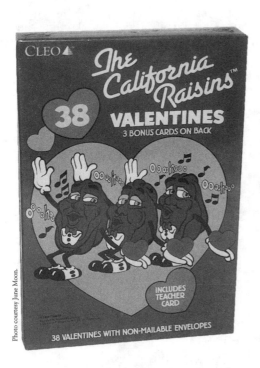

Photo courtesy June Moon.

Valentines, Cleo, 1988, MIB (sealed), $32.00.

For other types of candy containers, see Halloween; Pez Dispensers; Santa Claus.

Airplane, US Army B-51, w/wings, L #591 ....$120.00
Amos 'N Andy Fresh Air Taxi, clear glass w/pnt figures & wheels, EX $450.00
Basket, clear glass w/grape design, L #223 (E&A #81) $45.00
Bear on Circus Tub, orig blades, L #1 (E&A #83)..........$425.00
Black Cat Sitting, L #5..$3,500.00
Bureau, L #125 (E&A #112) $200.00
Candlestick, L #201..$300.00
Car, Long Hood Coupe #3, L #359 (E&A #51) $110.00
Chicken, fancy closure, L #9 ....$900.00
Coal Car, w/tender, L #402, (E&A #170) $350.00
Decorettes, L #655..$200.00
Felix by Barrel, L #85 (E&A #211)...............................$625.00

Fire Engine, Victory Glass, L #386, $35.00.

Fish, L #34 ....$225.00
Flossie Fisher's Bed, L #127 (E&A #234), EX $2,600.00
Gas Pump, metal base, L #316.....................................$300.00
Horn, Millstein's, L #282 (E&A #311) $25.00
Ice Truck, all orig, L #458 (E&A #784) $1,200.00
Jack-O-Lantern, blk cat, L #158 (E&A #349-1) $450.00

Kiddie Kar (E&A #360), $225.00.

Kiddies' Band, complete, L #277 (E&A #314) $325.00

Little Express, L #405 ....$600.00
Locomotive 888, no wheels, L #395 (E&A #485) $50.00
Maud Muller Milk Carrier, L #69..................................$125.00
Mule Pulling Barrel, L #38 (E&A #539) $85.00
Naked Child, Victory Glass, L #94 ....$100.00
Nurser Bottle, L #71 (E&A #548) $25.00
Peter Rabbit, L #55 (E&A #618) $25.00
Poodle Dog, glass head, L #471, from $20 to....................$30.00

Pumpkin-Head Policeman, NM, $2,000.00.

Pumpkin-Head Witch, L #165 (E&A #594) $600.00
Rabbit Crouching, L #41 (E&A #615), EX pnt.............$105.00
Rabbit Nibbling Carrot, L #53 (E&A #609), w/orig candy...$60.00
Rabbit on Dome, gold pnt, L #46 (E&A #607) $450.00

Rabbit on Eggshell, gold-painted top, L #48, 5½", $75.00.

Photo courtesy Doug Deso.

Racer #12 (E&A #642), $200.00.

Rooster Crowing, orig pnt, L #56 (E&A #151) $275.00
Scottie Dog, L #17 (E&A #184) $15.00
Spark Plug, dated 1923 (E&A #699) $100.00

Taxi, L #366, 4¼" long, $100.00.

Telephone, Redlich's No 3, L #294 (E&A #752)...........$325.00
Telephone, Victory Glass #1, L 298 (E&A #746-1).......$250.00

Telephone, Victory Glass (E&A #379), 5", $50.00.

Toonerville Trolley, L #111 (E&A #767), orig closure &
    pnt $800.00
Trunk, L #218 (E&A #789) $125.00
Wagon or Stagecoach, L #441..$125.00
Willy's Jeep Scout Car, L #391 (E&A #350) $30.00
Windmill, shaker top, orig blades, L #445 (E&A #842).$200.00

Cast Iron

Realistically modeled and carefully detailed cast-iron toys enjoyed their heyday from about the turn of the century (some companies began production a little earlier) until about the 1940s when they were gradually edged out by lighter-weight toys that were less costly to produce and to ship. (Some of the cast irons were more than 20" in length and very heavy.) Many were vehicles faithfully patterned after actual models seen on city streets at the time. Horse-drawn carriages were phased out when motorized vehicles came into use.

Some of the larger manufacturers were Arcade (Illinois), who by the 1920s was recognized as a leader in the industry; Dent (Pennsylvania); Hubley (Pennsylvania); and Kenton (Ohio). In the 1940s Kenton came out with a few horse-drawn toys which are collectible in their own right but naturally much less valuable than the older ones. In addition to those already noted, there were many minor makers; you will see them mentioned in the listings.

For more detailed information on these companies, we recommend *Collecting Toys* by Richard O'Brien (Books Americana).

Advisor: John McKenna (M2).

See also Banks; Pull and Push Toys.

AIRPLANES

Photo courtesy Dunbar Gallery.

Air Ford Monoplane, Hubley, 1930s, green with nickel-plated propeller and wheels, 4" wingspan, EX, $185.00.

America, Hubley, gray & red w/NP prop, 2 pilots in open cock-
    pit, 13" L, EX+, A $4,400.00
Fokker Airplane, Vindex, red w/gr undercarriage, NP prop, 8¼"
    wingspan, NM, A $6,160.00
Lindy NX 211 Ryan NYP, Hubley, spring-wind single prop,
    unpnt version, 11" L, EX, A $875.00

Monocoupe, Arcade, blk w/orange wings, NP prop, 8½"
wingspan, rpt wing, A..$500.00
Navy Fighter #467, Hubley, 1948, silver w/red wings, retractable
wheels, folding wings, plastic dome, 6½", EXIB, A..$550.00
Sea Gull, Kilgore, orange w/gray wings, NP wing prop & wheels,
emb lettering, 7¾" L, VG, A $1,050.00

Photo courtesy Dunbar Gallery.

UX-99 Monoplane, Hubley, 1930s, red with nickel-plated propeller and wheels, 4" wingspan, NM, $250.00.

Boats

Chris-Craft Commuter, Kilgore, 1930, yel & gr, 11", EX, A..$6,820.00
Racing Boat, Hubley, 1929, yel w/bl cast waves, wht & blk
driver holding motor throttle, 10", VG, A...........$6,275.00
Speedboat, Hubley, 1930s, red w/2 NP wheels, integral driver,
5½", G, A...$200.00
Static Boat, Hubley, gr, on wheels, no wave, w/driver, 9½", G,
A $3,000.00
Static Boat, Hubley, gr, on wheels, no wave, w/driver, 9½",
EX+, A $11,550.00
Static Boat, Hubley, yel, orange & bl, on wheels, w/wave,
w/driver, 9½", VG+, A $9,750.00
Steamboat, Wilkins, wht w/bl & red trim, on 3 spoked wheels,
7½", G-, A...$135.00

Character

Photo courtesy Dunbar Gallery.

**Popeye Spinach Wagon, red with multicolored figure,
5½" long, EX, $950.00.**

Buster Brown Cart Pulled by Tige, Dent, early 1900s, 5½",
VG+, A..$475.00
Chester Gump Cart, Arcade, yel cart w/2 red spoke wheels, gray
horse, w/Gump figure, 7½", VG, A.....................$500.00
Mama Katzenjammer Spanking Child in Mule Cart, Kenton, 1910,
Captain driving 2-wheeled cart, 12", VG, A...........$1,600.00
Sight Seeing Auto #899, Kenton, w/Happy Hooligan & 4 other
characters, 10½", rpt, A................................$2,530.00
Yellow Kid Goat Cart, late 1890s, blk, wht & red removable
Kid, 5", VG, A...$1,500.00

Circus and Accessories

Express Wagon, Wilkins, red wagon w/yel spoke wheels, single
blk horse, mc-pnt driver, 12½", VG, A $550.00
Overland Circus Band Wagon, Kenton, 6 band members
w/driver & rider on 1 of 2 horses, 15½", EX+, A $600.00
Overland Circus Cage Truck, Kenton, red w/gold trim, wht-pnt
tires w/gold hubs, wht bear, no driver, 10", EX, A..$1,760.00
Overland Circus Cage Wagon, Kenton, w/2 bears, 2 horses
w/riders & driver, 14", VG, A $400.00
Overland Circus Cage Wagon, Kenton, 1940s, w/wht bear, 2
wht horses w/riders & driver, 14", NMIB (#231 on box),
A..$400.00
Overland Circus Calliope Truck, Kenton, orange, no driver, 9",
G, A..$850.00
Overland Circus Calliope Wagon, Kenton, w/2 wht horses & 4
figures, 14", G, A..$300.00

**Royal Circus Band Wagon, Hubley, red with blue and gold
spoked wheels, complete with 4 gray horses and 6 musicians,
repainted figures, EX, A, $2,100.00.**

Royal Circus Cage Wagon, Hubley, bl w/gold trim & yel
spoke wheels, w/lion, 2 gray horses, blk-pnt driver, 9½",
VG, A..$325.00

Construction

Caterpillar Ten Tractor, Arcade, gr, enclosed motor, red spoke
wheels w/steel treads, NP driver, 7½", EX, A..........$700.00
Caterpillar Tractor, Arcade, yel, aluminum motor, blk spoke wheels
w/steel treads, NP radiator & driver, 7¾", NM, A......$2,800.00
Caterpillar Tractor, Arcade, yel, aluminum motor, spoke wheels
w/blk rubber treads, pnt driver, 7¾", MIB, A.......$3,200.00
Caterpillar Tractor, Arcade, yel, aluminum motor, spoke wheels w/blk
rubber treads, NP radiator & driver, 7¾", VG, A............$600.00

Huber Road Roller, Hubley, 1930, gr w/NP wheels, w/driver, 4½", VG, A $175.00

Huber Road Roller, Hubley, 1930, gr w/red wheels, w/driver, 14", G, A $400.00

Jaeger Cement Mixer, Kenton, red with white rubber tires, 9½", EX, $1,950.00.

Jaeger Cement Mixer, Kenton, 1930s, red, bl & gr w/NP mixing drum, bucket & wheels, 6½", VG, A $290.00

Mack Steam Shovel Truck, Hubley, 1930s, gr cab, red shovel w/NP bucket, rubber wheels, 10", VG+, A $375.00

Road Scraper, Hubley, yel w/blk rubber tires, 10", MIB .$135.00

Rotary Concrete Mixer, Kenton, red with white rubber tires, nickel-plated mixer, M, $2,800.00.

Trac-Tractor (Diesel), Arcade, red w/blk radiator, red spoke wheels w/blk rubber treads, NP driver, 8¼", EX+, A $2,300.00

Trac-Tractor (ID Model), Arcade, red w/red disk wheels, blk rubber treads, NP drawbar & driver, 7½", MIB, A $5,725.00

Trac-Tractor (ID Model), Arcade, red w/red disk wheels, blk rubber treads, NP drawbar & driver, 7½", VG, A ...$700.00

FARM TOYS

See also Horse-Drawn.

Allis-Chalmers Farmall Regular Tractor, Arcade, orange w/blk rubber tires, orange hubs, NP driver, 7", NM, A $925.00

Case 3-Bottom Plow, Vindex, red w/gr spoke wheels, 10¼", EX+, A $1,750.00

Cultivision Tractor, Arcade, red w/gold trim, blk rubber tires w/red hubs, NP steering post & driver, 7½", MIB, A $2,850.00

Farmall Tractor, Arcade, gray w/red spoke wheels, NP front & dual front tire axle, NP driver, 6", EX+, A $1,000.00

Ford Model 9N Tractor, 1939 model, Arcade, gray w/blk rubber tires, integral driver, 6⅜", EX+, A $800.00

Fordson Tractor, Arcade, gray w/simulated tread on rear red spoke wheels, NP driver, 6", EX+, A $330.00

Fordson Tractor, Arcade, red w/gr spoke wheels, red-pnt driver, 5½", EX+, A $385.00

John Deere Manure Spreader, Vindex, red w/gr shafts, yel spoke wheels, working, 9¼", very rare, M, A $3,525.00

John Deere Model A Tractor, Arcade, gr, blk rubber tires w/yel hubs, NP driver, 7", NM, A..................................$875.00

John Deere Model D Tractor, Vindex, gr w/yel spoke wheels, NP driver, 6½", EX+, A $3,750.00

John Deere Thresher, Vindex, gray & gr w/yel spoke wheels, removable straw stacker & grain pipe, 7½", rare, EX+, A $6,000.00

John Deere Van Brunt Drill, Vindex, NP disks, 9¾", very rare, EX+, A $3,525.00

John Deere 3-Bottom Plow, Vindex, gr w/yel spoke wheels, 9", EX+, A $2,400.00

McCormick-Deering Model 10-20 Tractor, Arcade, red, blk rubber tires w/red hubs, NP driver, 7½", EX, A $250.00

McCormick-Deering Thresher, Arcade, bl w/red trim, NP spoke wheels, 9½", VG, A $350.00

McCormick-Deering Thresher, Arcade, gray w/red trim, yel spoke wheels, movable grain spout, 12", EX+, A $325.00

McCormick-Deering Thresher, Arcade, yel w/red trim, NP spoke wheels, 9½", rpl straw shoot, EX, A...............$250.00

McCormick-Deering 10-20 Tractor, Arcade, gr, red spoke wheels, NP driver, 7", NM, A..............................$1,875.00

McCormick-Deering 10-20 Tractor, Arcade, gray w/red disk wheels & blk rubber tires, NP driver, 7", G, A........$250.00

McCormick-Deering 10-20 Tractor, Arcade, gray w/red spoke wheels, NP driver, 7", EX, A $750.00

McCormick-Deering 10-20 Tractor, Arcade, red w/red spoke wheels, NP driver, 7", VG+, A $350.00

McCormick-Deering 10-20 Tractor w/Dump Rake, Arcade, bl w/gold trim, red spoke wheels, NP driver, 7", rpt, A...$250.00

Oliver Tractor, Hubley, green with red integral driver, 5½", EX, D10, from $200.00 to $400.00.

Oliver Row Crop Tractor, Arcade, 1939, gr w/red striping, blk rubber tires w/red hubs, NP driver, 7", MIB, A **$2,530.00**

Oliver Row Crop Tractor, Arcade, 1939, red, blk rubber tires w/silver hubs, red-pnt driver, 5½", EX, A **$150.00**

Oliver Row Crop Tractor, Arcade, 1939, red, blk rubber tires w/yel hubs, NP driver, 7", EX+, A **$325.00**

Oliver Superior Manure Spreader, Arcade, yel w/NP shafts & blk trim, 2 blk rubber tires, 9½", MIB, A **$2,850.00**

Oliver Superior Manure Spreader, Arcade, yel w/NP shafts & blk trim, 2 blk rubber tires, 9½", VG, A **$635.00**

Oliver 70 Tractor, Arcade, red, blk rubber tires w/orange hubs, NP driver, 7", EX, A **$400.00**

Tractor, Arcade, 1930s, 2 lg & 2 sm wht rubber tires, w/driver, 5¼" w/4¼" side-dump trailer, G, A **$175.00**

FIREFIGHTING

Only motor vehicles are listed here; see also **Horse-Drawn.**

Burning Building, Carpenter, 1892, CI & wood building w/fireman climbing ladder to save woman (missing), 16¾", EX, A..**$29,900.00**

Photo courtesy Dunbar Gallery.

Chemical Truck, Hubley, red with nickel-plated figure and ladder, white rubber tires, 14", M, $1,850.00.

Fire Engine House, Ives, 1893, clockwork mechanism rings bell & opens door to horse-drawn pumper, 12", rpr, A......**$3,900.00**

Photo courtesy Dunbar Gallery.

Fire Pumper, Hubley, red with nickel-plated figures, black rubber tires with nickel-plated spokes, 13", NM, $1,350.00.

Hose Truck, Kenton, early red model, yel spoke wheels, w/driver, no sz given, VG, A **$470.00**

Ladder Truck, Hubley, no ladders, NP grille, 2 firemen, 6½", EX, A **$115.00**

Ladder Truck, Hubley, 4 metal ladders, rubber tires, 13", rpl driver, G, A **$200.00**

Ladder Truck, Kenton, red w/2 gray metal ladders, NP bumper, blk tires w/red spokes, NP driver, 12", rpl ladders, G, A **$470.00**

Ladder Truck, Kenton, red w/2 wooden ladders, disk wheels, gold-pnt emb water cans on sides, w/driver, 11½", EX, A..**$500.00**

Mack Ladder Truck, Arcade, red w/open C-style cab, 3 yel ladders, hose reel, blk tires, NP driver, 17¾", EX, A...**$1,075.00**

Patrol Truck, Hubley, 1920s, bl w/yel emb lettering, yel spoke wheels, 5 firemen w/driver, 11½", VG, A **$935.00**

Patrol Wagon, Kenton, bl w/yel emb lettering, yel spoke wheels, 2 NP passengers w/mc driver, 9", rpl passengers, G, A **$470.00**

Pumper Truck, Arcade, red w/blk rubber tires, red driver, 6½", EX, A **$90.00**

Pumper Truck, Hubley, red w/silver trim on boiler, blk rubber tires w/spoke wheels, NP driver, 11", VG, A **$385.00**

Pumper Truck, Hubley, 1930s, NP boiler & grille, wht rubber tires, 2 firemen, 6½", EX, A **$350.00**

Water Tower Truck, red open cab & bed w/bl tower, red-pnt driver, 23¼", missing rear support o/w VG, A.........**$745.00**

HORSE-DRAWN (AND OTHER ANIMALS)

Back-to-Back Trap, Wilkins, yel sheet metal trap w/2 yel spoke wheels, blk horse, blk-pnt driver, 9", VG, A **$190.00**

Bakery Wagon, Kenton, wht enclosed body w/open doors & windows, 4 red spoke wheels, blk horse, no driver, 12¾", G, A..**$300.00**

Brake (4-Seat), Pratt & Letchworth, 1890, w/4 horses & 7 orig figures, 28", few pcs missing, EX finish, A..........**$18,400.00**

Buckboard, Ideal, NP wagon w/spoke wheels, 2 removable seats, single NP horse, rpl bl-pnt driver, 13", EX, A **$600.00**

Buckboard, Pratt & Letchworth, blk w/red spoke wheels, wht horse, lady driver in yel w/blk hat, 11¼", G, A **$385.00**

City Express Wagon, Kenton, bl wagon w/yel spoke wheels & hitch, single blk horse, blk-pnt driver, 17", G, A **$475.00**

City Truck Dray Wagon, Harris, red w/4 yel spoke wheels, wht horse, red-pnt driver, 15", VG, A **$1,050.00**

Coach, Hubley, bl scalloped shape w/2 red spoke wheels, single blk horse, mc-pnt driver, 7¾", EX, A **$300.00**

Coal Wagon, Hubley, blk w/2 yel spoke wheels, single blk horse, blk-pnt driver, 11¾", G+, A **$350.00**

Coal Wagon, Hubley, 1920, gr w/spoke wheels, 2 blk horses, blk-pnt driver, 16¼", G, A **$230.00**

Consolidated Street Trolley, Wilkins, ca 1895, red w/single blk horse, 13", EX, A **$750.00**

Contractor's Dump Wagon, Arcade, gr w/blk rubber tires, 1 blk/1 wht horse w/gold trim, pnt driver, 13", VG, A **$425.00**

Contractor's Dump Wagon, Arcade, gr w/NP spoke wheels, 2 blk horses w/gold trim, NP driver, 13½", VG+, A ..**$525.00**

Covered Wagon, Kenton, 1940s, 1 wht & 1 blk horse, w/driver, NMIB (#170 on box), A **$175.00**

Doctor's Buggy, Wilkins, blk w/4 red spoke wheels, orange horse w/wht mane & tail, doctor in blk, 10½", EX, A **$600.00**

Doctor's Buggy, Wilkins, blk w/4 yel spoke wheels, 2 blk horses w/gold trim, doctor in blk, 13", VG, A $525.00

Dog-Meet Cart, Welker & Crosby, blk w/gr sides, 2 red spoke wheels, blk horse w/red harness, no driver, 10", rpt, A $1,100.00

Dray Wagon, Kenton, gr w/red spoke wheels, single wht horse w/gold trim, blk-pnt driver, 15", EX, A....................$175.00

Dray Wagon, Kenton, gr w/red spoke wheels, 2 blk horses w/gold trim, no driver, 11", M, A $550.00

Dray Wagon, Kenton, gr w/red spoke wheels, 2 blk horses w/silver tails, gold trim, bl-pnt driver w/red cap, 15", EX, A...$450.00

Dray Wagon, Welker & Crosby, gr w/4 red spoke wheels & 2 red side nameplates, blk horse, no driver, 14½", EX, A...$1,155.00

Dray Wagon, Wilkins, red sheet-metal wagon w/4 yel spoke wheels, blk horse, blk-pnt driver, 12", EX, A...........$550.00

English Trap, Kenton, blk w/4 yel spoke wheels, 2 wht horses w/red trim, w/driver & lady passenger, 14", EX, A ..$2,640.00

Farm Wagon, Arcade, 1939, red wagon w/gr chassis, blk rubber tires, 2 gray horses, pnt driver, w/label, 10¾", M, A ...$525.00

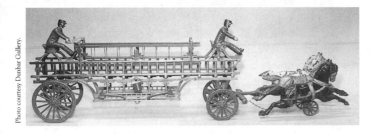

Photo courtesy Dunbar Gallery.

Fire Hook and Ladder Wagon, 1880s, 2 figures in wagon pulled by 3 horses, 32", EX, $1,950.00.

Fire Hose Carriage #35, Carpenter, 1890, w/horse & 2 removable firemen, 14½", EXIB (lid missing on wood box), A ..$5,465.00

Fire Hose-Reel Wagon, Dent, brn w/gold reel, 4 NP wheels w/red spokes, 1 blk & 1 wht horse, 2 firemen, 23½", M, A...$6,600.00

Fire Hose-Reel Wagon, Dent, gold w/wht horse, 4 NP wheels w/yel spokes, 1 wht & 1 blk horse, 2 firemen, 20", NM, A $3,630.00

Fire Hose-Reel Wagon, Dent, w/2 horses & driver, spoke wheels, rpl driver, 18", VG, A...$900.00

Fire Hose-Reel Wagon, Welker & Crosby, blk w/5 spoke wheels, blk horse & driver, 14", G, A...................................$880.00

Fire Ladder Wagon, Dent, brn, red & bl ladders, NP wheels w/red spokes, 1 blk & 1 wht horse, 2 firemen, 33", M, A...$7,370.00

Fire Ladder Wagon, Dent, tan w/2 ladders, 3 blk horses, 2 firemen, 32", VG, A $1,025.00

Fire Ladder Wagon, Hubley, red w/yel ladders & spoke wheels, 1 wht & 2 blk horses, front & rear drivers, VG, A $575.00

Fire Ladder Wagon, Ives, blk & red w/4 spoke wheels, yel ladders, 1 blk & 1 wht horse, 2 firemen, 28", EX, A.....$715.00

Fire Ladder Wagon, Kenton, red w/yel ladders & spoke wheels, 1 wht & 2 blk horses, red-pnt driver, 12", NM, A......$150.00

Fire Ladder Wagon, Kenton, 1950, red w/2 ladders, spoke wheels, 1 wht & 2 blk horses, 2 firemen, 16", G+, A $300.00

Fire Ladder Wagon, Kenton, 3 horses, w/driver, 16", EX, A..$200.00

Fire Patrol #408-2, IB&W Co, ca 1890, 1 wht & 1 blk horse, 7 firemen, 20½", EXIB (wood box), A $8,340.00

Fire Patrol Wagon, Dent, w/2 horses & 7 firemen, spoke wheels, 19", G, A..$800.00

Fire Pumper, Dent, tan w/gold & blk trim, 4 NP wheels w/red spokes, 1 blk & 1 wht horse, 2 firemen, 24", M, A ..$7,150.00

Fire Pumper, Hubley, red w/gold trim & yel spoke wheels, 1 blk & 1 wht horse, red-pnt driver, 16", EX+, A.............$650.00

Fire Pumper, Hubley, wht w/4 red spoke wheels, 1 wht & 2 blk horses, w/driver, 14½", VG, A $275.00

Fire Pumper, IB&W Co, 1890, 1 wht & 1 blk horse, 2 firemen, 18¾", EX (EX orig wooden box), A $7,475.00

Fire Pumper, Ives, w/2 horses, 13", G, A.........................$230.00

Fire Pumper, Ives, w/3 horses, 3 firemen, 20", rpt, A......$175.00

Fire Pumper, Pratt & Letchworth, blk & gr w/gold boiler, 4 red spoke wheels, 1 blk & 1 tan horse, w/driver, 17", EX, A..$1,760.00

Fire Pumper #33, Carpenter, 1890, w/2 horses & driver, EXIB (lid missing on wood box), A..............................$7,250.00

Goat Cart, Harris, red cart w/emb upholstered seat & 2 yel spoke wheels, wht goat, mc-pnt driver, 9¼", G-, A...........$400.00

Hansom Cab, Kenton, rear driver, red w/2 yel spoke wheels, silver horse, 11¼", EX, A..$880.00

Hansom Cab, Kenton, 1940s, front driver, wht horse, NMIB (#162 on box), A..$300.00

Hansom Cab, Wilkins, brn w/2 spoke wheels, blk horse w/gold trim, rear driver in blk suit & hat, 9", EX, A...........$155.00

Horse Cart, Shiner, blk w/upholstered arm seat, gold trim, 2 spoke wheels, blk horse, red lady driver, 10½", rpt, A.........$330.00

Ice Wagon, Hubley, 1920, red w/yel top, 4 yel spoke wheels, 2 blk horses, NP driver, 15", VG, A...........................$635.00

Ice Wagon, Hubley, 1920, red w/yel top, 4 yel spoke wheels, 2 blk horses, no driver, 15", G, A.................................$385.00

Ice Wagon, Ives, 1900, w/horse, 8½", G, A.....................$175.00

John Deere Farm Wagon, Vindex, dk gr w/red spoke wheels, removable seat, 2 blk horses, no driver, 12½", VG, A...........$1,250.00

John Deere Farm Wagon, Vindex, gr w/red spoke wheels, removable seat, 2 blk horses, no driver, 12½", NM, A...$3,525.00

Log Cart, Kenton, log on cart w/4 spoke wheels, 2 blk & wht oxen, w/driver, 15½", EX, A................................$1,100.00

Log Wagon, Hubley, log on yel fr w/4 red spoke wheels, 2 blk oxen, w/Black driver seated sideways, 15", VG, A ..$825.00

McCormick-Deering Farm Wagon, Arcade, gr w/red spoke wheels, 2 blk horses w/gold trim, no driver, 12", VG, A...........$350.00

McCormick-Deering Hay Rake, Arcade, CI, yel & red w/NP spoke wheels, solo seat, 2 blk horses w/red trim, 9½", EX, A..$775.00

McCormick-Deering Manure Spreader, Arcade, red w/blk rubber tires, NP gears, 2 blk horses, 14", NM, A $2,200.00

McCormick-Deering Weber Farm Wagon, Arcade, gr w/red spoke wheels, 2 blk horses w/gold trim, no driver, 12", VG, A..$600.00

Ox Cart, Ives, 1883, gr cart w/2 red spoke wheels, 2 oxen, 11", G, A..$375.00

Patrol Wagon, Dent, bl w/4 red spoke wheels, 1 blk & 1 wht horse, w/4 riders & driver, 21", VG, A $935.00

Patrol Wagon, Ives, wht w/4 red spoke wheels, 1 blk & 1 wht horse, w/6 riders & driver, 21", G, A $550.00

Phaeton, Hubley, 1890s, red carriage, 4 yel spoke wheels, 2 blk horses w/gold trim, mc-pnt lady driver, 17", some rpt, A...........$770.00

Phoenix Fire Pumper, Ives, 1890, w/driver, 19½", rpt, A ..$450.00

Police Patrol, Kenton, 2 horses, 4 policemen (2 not orig), 19", horse w/broken leg o/w EX, A $400.00

Pony Cart, Hubley, red body w/2 yel spoke wheels, blk horse w/gold trim, driver in blk suit & hat, 11", VG, A....$360.00

Pony Phaeton, Pratt & Letchworth, 1892, blk carriage w/yel spoke wheels, single wht horse, female passenger, 15", VG, A $700.00

Sand & Gravel Wagon, Kenton, gr w/4 red spoke wheels, 1 wht & 1 blk horse, w/bl driver, dumping action, 15", EX+, A $220.00

Sand & Gravel Wagon, Kenton, red w/4 gr spoke wheels, 1 wht & 1 blk horse, w/NP driver, dumping action, 10", EX+, A $160.00

Stake Cart, Wilkins, red w/3 yel spoke wheels, blk mule w/gold & red trim, w/driver, 11", EX, A $360.00

Stake Wagon, Kenton, 1920s, red wagon w/gr hitch, blk horse, w/driver, 14", VG, A $175.00

Sulky, Canada, 2 spoke wheels, blk horse, silver-tone driver, 8", VG, A $150.00

Sulky, Champion, red spoked wheels, yel horse & driver, 8½", EX, A $175.00

Sulky, Kenton, yel w/spoke wheels, blk horse, red-pnt driver, 7", EX, A $200.00

Sulky, Pratt & Letchworth, 2 yel spoke wheels, blk horse, w/red, wht & bl driver, 8", G, A $300.00

Surrey, Kenton, bl w/yel fringed top, 4 spoke wheels, single wht horse, red driver w/yel passenger, 13", M, A $300.00

Surrey, Pratt & Letchworth, single seat, blk w/4 yel spoke wheels, tan & wht horse, w/driver, no top, 15", VG,............$880.00

Surrey, Pratt & Letchworth, 2-seat, blk w/4 yel spoke wheels, tan & wht horse, w/driver, no top, 14", EX, A $1,375.00

Transfer Wagon, Dent, NP w/4 red spoke wheels, 4 blk horses w/red trim, no driver, 17", EX, A $715.00

Trap, Kenton, red w/emb upholstered arm seat, 2 yel spoke wheels, blk horse, lady driver, 9¼", VG, A $880.00

Whitewater Farm Wagon, Vindex, gr w/red spoke wheels, working running gear, 2 blk horses, no driver, 7½", rare, EX, A $2,425.00

MOTOR VEHICLES

Note: Description lines for generic vehicles may simply begin with 'Bus,' 'Coupe,' or 'Motorcycle,' for example. But more busses will be listed as 'Coach Bus,' 'Coast-To-Coast,' 'Greyhound,' 'Interurban,' 'Mack,' or 'Public Service' (and there are other instances); coupes may be listed under 'Ford,' 'Packard,' or some other specific car company; and lines describing motorcycles might be also start 'Armored,' 'Excelsior-Henderson,' 'Delivery,' 'Policeman,' 'Harley-Davidson,' and so on. Look under 'Yellow Cab' or 'Checker Cab' and other cab companies for additional 'Taxi Cab' descriptions. We often gave any lettering or logo on the vehicle priority when we entered descriptions, so with this in mind, you should have a good idea where to look for your particular toy. Body styles (Double-Decker Bus, Cape-Top Roadster, etc.) were also given priority.

Photo courtesy Dunbar Gallery.

Airflow Coupe, AC Williams, blue with nickel-plated bumpers and grille, white rubber tires, 6½", EX, $950.00.

Army Motor Truck, J&B, gr open body w/stake bed, spoke wheels, w/driver, 14¾", EX, A $1,265.00

Bell Telephone Truck, Hubley, gr C-style cab w/wht rubber tires, no winch, 5¼", EX, A $250.00

Bell Telephone Truck, Hubley, gr C-style cab w/wht rubber tires, red winch, 9¼", EX, A $660.00

Bell Telephone Truck, Hubley, gr C-style cab w/wht rubber tires, w/winch, pole trailer & post digger, 9½", VG, A $600.00

Bell Telephone Truck, Hubley, gr enclosed cab w/blk rubber tires, w/red winch & pole carrier, 8", NMIB, A.......$140.00

Bell Telephone Truck, Hubley, red C-style cab w/wht rubber tires, w/winch, trailer, NP ladders, 14", VG, A........$750.00

Buick Coupe, Arcade, gr w/blk top, rubber tires w/rear spare, 8½", VG, A $5,500.00

Buick Sedan, Arcade, bl-gr & blk w/NP grille, wht rubber tires w/blk spokes, rear spare, NP driver, 8½", G, A $2,530.00

Buick Sedan, Arcade, bl-gr & blk w/NP grille, wht rubber tires w/blk spokes, rear spare, NP driver, 8½", EX+, A ..$8,470.00

Buick Sedan, Arcade, bl-gr & blk w/NP grille, wht rubber tires w/blk spokes, rear spare, NP driver, 8½", VG, A .$4,500.00

Bus, Arcade, bl w/NP tires, 6", EX, A $175.00

Car Carrier, AC Williams, red w/NP spoke wheels, w/bus & 2 cars, 12½", EX+, A...$635.00

Car Carrier, Arcade, 1939, gr truck cab w/red trailer, wht rubber tires w/red hubs, 1 bl car, 15½", EX+, A.................$775.00

Car Carrier, Hubley, 1938, red w/gray front fenders, 4 mc wreckers, wht rubber tires, 10½", 1 tire missing, VG, A...$425.00

Central Garage Wrecker, Skoglund & Olsen/Sweden, wht w/red winch & crane, wht rubber tires w/red hubs, 11¾", EX, A $2,420.00

Century of Progress Ford Taxi, Arcade, 1933, orange & blk w/NP grille, wht rubber tires, no driver, 6½", VG, A $580.00

Century of Progress Greyhound Bus, Arcade, 1933, bl cab pulls beige bus, wht rubber tires, 7½", EX, A $125.00

Century of Progress Greyhound Bus, Arcade, 1933, bl cab pulls beige bus, wht rubber tires, 11⅝", EX+, A...............$750.00

Century of Progress Greyhound Bus, Arcade, 1933, bl truck cab w/wht & bl bus trailer, wht rubber tires, 14", EX, A $1,430.00

Century of Progress Yellow Cab, Arcade, yel-orange & blk, wht rubber tires, no driver, 6½", EX+, A....................$1,760.00

Checker Cab Co, Arcade, 1925-28, gr & blk w/blk & wht check striping, wht-pnt tires w/gr hubs, w/driver, 9", EX, A $10,450.00

Photo courtesy Dunbar Gallery.

Chevrolet Coupe, Arcade, 2-tone brown with nickel-plated tires, 8", NM, $2,950.00.

Chevrolet Coupe, Arcade, 1928, gray & blk w/aluminum grille, NP spoke wheels & rear spare mk Imperial..., 8", NM, A $4,950.00

Chevrolet Coupe, Arcade, 1928, gray & blk w/silver-pnt grille, NP spoke wheels & rear spare, w/driver, 8", EX+, A $3,520.00

Chevrolet Coupe, Arcade, 1928, gray & blk w/silver-pnt grille, wht rubber tires, rear NP spare, no driver, 8", VG, A $1,870.00

Chevrolet Sedan, Arcade, 1928, bl & blk w/gold striping, silver-pnt grille, NP tires, blk hubs, w/driver, 8¼", EX+, A $5,720.00

Chevrolet Sedan, Arcade, 1928, blk, wht rubber tires w/blk spokes, no driver, 7", EX, A.......................................$525.00

Chevrolet Superior Sedan, Arcade, 1925, blk w/NP spoke wheels & driver, 7", VG, A...$825.00

Chevrolet Utility Coupe, Arcade, 1925, blk w/gold trim, mesh front radiator, blk spoke wheels, NP driver, 6¾", EX+, A $1,875.00

Chrysler Airflow, Hubley, putty beige w/NP grille & bumpers, wht tires w/red hubs, rear spare, no driver, 4½", EX, A......$200.00

Chrysler Airflow, Hubley, putty beige w/NP grille & bumpers, wht tires w/red hubs, rear spare, no driver, 6", EX, A........$440.00

Chrysler Airflow, Hubley, putty beige w/NP grille & bumpers, electric lights, rear spare, no driver, 8", EX, A $2,310.00

City Ambulance, Arcade, 1932, wht w/blk rubber tires, 5¾", G, A $165.00

Coal Truck, Hubley, red open body w/gray dump bed w/COAL emb on sides, yel spoke wheels, w/driver, 14½", EX, A $990.00

Coal Truck, Kenton, red open body, disk wheels, w/NP driver, 6½", EX, A $300.00

Contractor's Auto Wagon, Kenton, red w/3 separate compartments, open cab, spoke wheels, 8½", EX, A $440.00

Convertible, Kilgore, yel 2-seater w/red running boards & fenders, extensive NP trim & tires, no driver, 10½", EX+, A...$8,250.00

Coupe, AC Williams, long bl body w/NP spoke wheels, molded rear spare, 5", EX+, A...$145.00

Coupe, AC Williams, 1930, red, NP tires w/red hubs, rear spare, w/driver, 4½", VG, A $150.00

Coupe, Kilgore, bronze w/NP spoke wheels, trunk lid opens, spring-mounted passenger, 6¾", VG, A $200.00

Coupe, Kilgore, orange w/NP spoke wheels, 2 spring-mounted NP passengers, 6¼", EX, A $400.00

Coupe w/Rumble Seat, Arcade, gr w/wht rubber tires, 5⅛", G, A $150.00

Coupe w/Rumble Seat, Arcade, red w/NP tires, 5⅛", VG, A ..$300.00

Crash Car Motorcycle, Hubley, gr & red w/gold trim, wht rubber tires, gr driver, 9½", EX, A $1,650.00

Delivery Van, Arcade, w/driver, tan w/red hood & stripes, wht rubber tires w/2 side mounts, 13¼", EX, A.........$18,000.00

Photo courtesy Dunbar Gallery.

Double-decker Bus, Arcade, green with black tires, 8", EX, $500.00.

Double-Decker Bus, Arcade, gr w/NP grille, blk rubber tires, 8", G, A $225.00

Double-Decker Bus, Kenton, bl w/orange stripe, disk wheels, rear stairs, 10", G, A $660.00

Double-Decker Bus, Kenton, dk gr w/open cab, yel spoke wheels, rear stairs, 8", rpt, A.....................................$600.00

Double-Decker Bus, Kenton, gr w/red stripe, gold trim, wht rubber tires, rear stairs, 10", EX, A $880.00

Dump Truck, Arcade, bl w/red dump bed, NP spoke wheels, 7", EX, A $300.00

Dump Truck, Champion, red w/C-style cab, bl dump bed, wht rubber tires, no driver, 6", VG, A...............................$130.00

Dump Truck, Hubley, open silver body w/red spoke wheels, w/driver, 6", VG, A $200.00

Dump Truck, Kilgore, bl body w/red dump bed, NP disk wheels, 6", EX, A $220.00

Elgin Street Sweeper, Hubley, 1930, gray w/NP trim & blk side brush, w/driver, 8½", EX, A..............................$5,500.00

Faegol Bus, Arcade, 1920s, gr w/gold striping, NP disk wheels & driver, 12", EX, A $600.00

Faegol Bus, Arcade, 1920s, red w/gold stripe, NP disk wheels, no driver, 8", rpt, A $260.00

Five-Ton Stake Truck, open cab, yel w/red spoke wheels, w/driver, 16", G, A $700.00

Ford Coupe, Arcade, 1925, blk w/blk spoke wheels, NP driver, 6½", VG, A $475.00

Ford Coupe, Arcade, 1925, blk w/gold striping, wht-pnt tires w/blk spokes, NP driver, 6½", EX+, A....................$775.00

Ford Coupe, Arcade, 1927, gr w/blk top, blk spoke wheels, NP driver, 6", G, A $275.00

Ford Dump Truck, Arcade, 1929, bl w/red dump bed, NP spoke wheels, no driver, 7", EX, A $360.00

Ford Model A Coupe, Arcade, 1928, red w/gold striping, hinged rumble seat, NP daisy-spoked wheels & driver, 6¾", M, A $2,200.00

Ford Model A Coupe, Arcade, 1930, gr w/rumble seat, wht-pnt tires w/daisy-spoked wheels, no driver, 6½", G, A ..$400.00

Ford Model A Stake Truck w/2 Trailers, Arcade, 1931, gr cab w/2 red stake beds, NP spoke wheels, no driver, 18", VG, A................$575.00

Ford Model A Weaver Wrecker, Arcade, 1933, red body w/gr & NP crank, NP spoke wheels, no driver, 11", G, A ...$600.00

Ford Model A Weaver Wrecker, Arcade, 1933, red w/gr & chrome crank, NP spoke wheels, no driver, 7", NM, A $855.00

Ford Model T Anchor Truck Co Stake Truck, North & Judd, blk w/gray stake body, NP spoke wheels, 8¾", rpt, A $880.00

Ford Model T Anthony Dump Truck, Arcade, 1927, gray & blk w/open cab, NP spoke wheels, 8", rpt, A $1,320.00

Ford Model T Coupe, AC Williams, blk w/silver-pnt spoke wheels, no driver, 6", EX, A $140.00

Ford Model T Pickup Truck, Arcade, blk w/low bed, spoke wheels, NP driver, 8½", EX+, A $660.00

Ford Model T Sedan w/Center Door, Arcade, 1923, blk w/gold striping, wht tires, NP driver, Hale Motors, 6½", NM, A $2,420.00

Ford Model T Sedan w/Center Door, Arcade, 1924, blk w/gold striping, blk spoke wheels, NP driver, 6½", EX, A ..$650.00

Ford Model T Sedan w/Center Door, Arcade, 1924, blk w/gold striping, blk spoke wheels, no driver, 6½", G+, A...$275.00

Ford Model T Stake Truck, Arcade, blk body w/gray stake bed, NP spoke wheels, w/driver, 9", rpt, A $330.00

Ford Model T Stake Truck, Arcade, orange w/NP spoke wheels, removable rear stake, NP driver, 7½", NM, A $1,475.00

Ford Taxi, Arcade, orange w/NP grille, wht rubber tires, 6½", VG, A $500.00

Ford Touring Car, Arcade, blk, wht tires w/blk spokes, NP driver, 6½", EX+, A $1,100.00

Ford Touring Car, Arcade, 1923, blk w/NP spoke wheels & driver, 6½", EX, A....................................$625.00

Ford Touring Car (1923), Arcade, blk, open sides, wht-pnt spoke wheels, no driver, 6½", G, A $250.00

Ford 2-Door Sedan, Arcade, 1925, blk w/gold stripe, wht spoke wheels, no driver, 6½", VG+, A $300.00

Ford 4-Door Sedan, Arcade, 1924, blk w/gold stripe, gold-pnt spoke wheels, w/driver, 6½", EX, A $440.00

Ford 4-Door Sedan, Arcade, 1924, blk w/gold stripe, wht-pnt spoke wheels, w/driver, 6½", VG, A $250.00

Galion Master Road Roller, Kenton, red w/wooden front roller, 2 lg NP spoke wheels, 7", NM, A...........$250.00

Greyhound, see also Century of Progress or New York World's Fair

Greyhound Bus, Arcade, bl & wht w/wht greyhound dog trademark on sides & lettering on roof, wht rubber tires, 9", EX, A $650.00

Greyhound GMC Bus, Arcade, bl truck cab w/wht bus trailer, wht rubber tires, cut-out windows, 11½", EX+ (orig box), A $500.00

Photo courtesy Dunbar Gallery.

Greyhound Lines Bus, Arcade, 1940, 9", NM, $650.00.

Harley-Davidson Motorcycle w/Policeman, Hubley, khaki w/gold trim, rubber tires w/NP spokes, blk-pnt driver, 9", EX+, A $1,750.00

Harley-Davidson Motorcycle w/Policeman, Hubley, khaki w/NP spoke wheels, 7", EX, A $1,000.00

I-H Baby Model Yellow Cab Co Truck, Arcade, orange & blk w/wht rubber tires, NP driver, 10", rpt, A...............$250.00

I-H Delivery Van, Arcade, red w/NP grille & bumper, wht rubber tires w/gray hubs, curved top, no driver, 9½", NM, A $10,100.00

I-H Delivery Van, Arcade, 1932, wht & blk w/yel trim, wht rubber tires, yel hubs, flat top, NP driver, 9½", VG, A.......$1,000.00

I-H Dugan Sand & Gravel Dump Truck, Arcade, 1923, bl & blk fenders, NP driver, 10½", rpt, A $275.00

I-H Dump Truck, Arcade, red & silver w/rear dual tires, decals on doors, 3½", VG, A $375.00

I-H Pickup Truck, Arcade, 1941, yel w/blk rubber tires, decal on doors, no driver, 9", NM, A $1,650.00

I-H Red Baby Dump Truck, Arcade, 1923, decaled doors, NP tires w/red hubs, NP driver, 10½", NM, A $1,100.00

I-H Red Baby Dump Truck, Arcade, 1923, decaled doors, wht rubber tires w/red hubs, NP driver, 10½", EX+, A ..$900.00

I-H Red Baby Dump Truck, Arcade, 1923, plain doors, wht rubber tires w/red hubs, NP driver, 10½", VG, A $700.00

I-H Red Baby Dump Truck, Arcade, 1923, stenciled doors, wht rubber tires w/red hubs, NP driver, 10½", rpt, A $200.00

I-H Red Baby Model Gold's Dairy Truck, Arcade, red & blk w/NP tires, blk hubs, NP driver, 10", rpt, A $250.00

I-H Red Baby Pickup Truck, Arcade, stationary bed, decaled doors, wht rubber tires w/red hubs, NP driver, 10", VG, A $700.00

I-H Red Baby Weaver Wrecker, Arcade, 1929, decaled doors, gr crank, NP wheels w/red hubs, NP driver, 12", EX+, A $4,400.00

Photo courtesy Dunbar Gallery.

Gasoline Truck with Standard Oil Co. advertising, Arcade, 1925, blue with nickel-plated driver, spoked wheels, 13¼", EX, $2,250.00.

I-H Red Baby Weaver Wrecker, Arcade, 1929, stenciled door, gr crank, wht-pnt tires w/red hubs, NP driver, 12", G, A..**$1,750.00**

I-H Stake Truck, Arcade, 1935, gr, wht rubber tires w/red hubs, no driver, 12", G, A...**$1,000.00**

I-H Stake Truck, Arcade, 1935, gr, wht rubber tires w/red hubs, no driver, 12", EX, A...**$3,000.00**

I-H Yellow Baby Dump Truck, Arcade, 1923, yel, stenciled doors, wht-pnt tires w/yel hubs, NP driver, 10½", rpt, A **$275.00**

I-H Yellow Baby Dump Truck, Arcade, 1923, yel-orange, stenciled doors, NP tires w/yel-orange hubs, 10½", EX, A **$1,375.00**

Indian Crash Car, Hubley, 1930s, 3-wheeled cart w/removable policeman driver, 11½", EX, A...........................**$2,500.00**

Indian Crash Car, Hubley, 1930s, 3-wheeled hose cart w/removable policeman driver, 11½", EX, A **$3,550.00**

Indian Crash Car, Hubley, red with white rubber tires, integral driver, 6½", EX, $750.00.

Lincoln Touring Car, AC Williams, 1924, gr, blk tires w/lg spoke wheels, no driver, 8¾", rpt, A.........................**$250.00**

Lincoln Touring Car, AC Williams, 1924, red w/spoke wheels & rear spare, 7", VG, A **$300.00**

Lincoln Zephyr, Hubley, light blue with nickel-plated bumpers and grille, white rubber tires, 7½", NM, $850.00.

Machinery Hauler Truck, AC Williams, red truck w/2 gr flatbed trailers hauling yel grader & red roller, 21¼", EX, A ..**$2,860.00**

Mack Coal Truck, Arcade, red w/COAL stenciled in wht, wht rubber tires w/red hubs, w/driver, 10", rpl tires, VG, A **$965.00**

Mack Dump Truck, Arcade, red w/gr dump bed, NP spoke wheels, integral driver, 6", G, A................................**$115.00**

Mack Dump Truck, Arcade, red w/lift-down dump bed, gr tow hitch, NP spoke wheels & driver, 8", G, A..............**$500.00**

Mack Dump Truck, Arcade, tan, nickel-plated driver, 12", EX, $1,750.00.

Mack Dump Truck, Dent, red, gr dump bed w/opening tailgate, gold trim, yel spoke wheels, no driver, 15¼", VG, A **$1,650.00**

Mack Dump Truck, Hubley, gr w/red dump bed, wht rubber tires w/dual rears, rpl driver, 11", EX, A...........................**$650.00**

Mack Dump Truck, Hubley, gr w/red dump bed, wht rubber tires w/red hubs, w/driver, 5", VG, A...............................**$165.00**

Mack Dump Truck, Hubley, gr w/red dump bed, wht rubber tires w/rear duals, red hubs, w/driver, 11", EX, A **$1,650.00**

Mack Dump Truck, Hubley, gr w/red dump bed, wht rubber tires w/red hubs (rpl), w/driver, 11", G+ pnt, A **$360.00**

Mack Dump Truck, Walker Stuart, red w/yel disk wheels, no sz given, VG, A **$55.00**

Mack Gasoline Truck, Arcade, 1925, bl w/NP spoke wheels, 3 fill caps, w/driver, 13", VG, A...................................**$1,485.00**

Mack Gasoline Truck, Arcade, 1929, gr w/tin tank, gold trim, NP spoke wheels, w/driver, 12½", EX, A **$1,265.00**

Mack Ice Truck, Arcade, 1930, bl, NP spoke wheels & driver, w/orig ice & tongs, 10½", EX, A **$1,925.00**

Mack Stake Truck, Arcade, gr w/gold trim, wht dual rubber tires w/gr hubs, chain drive, NP driver, 11½", EX, A ..**$2,200.00**

Mack Stake Truck, Hubley, deep bl, wht rubber tires w/red hubs, w/driver, 5½", VG, A **$120.00**

Mack Stake Truck, Hubley, orange w/wht rubber tires, w/driver, 5½", EX, A **$165.00**

Mack T-Bar Dump Truck, Arcade, 1928, lt bl, gold trim, NP spoke wheels, 12", rpt, A **$600.00**

Mack Truck, Walker Stuart, red w/boxcar-type trailer, spoke wheels, no driver, 5", G, A **$100.00**

Mack Wrecker & Service Truck, Arcade, red w/gr crane, NP tires w/red spokes, w/driver, 12½", VG, A **$1,980.00**

Merchants Delivery Van, Hubley, orange w/NP spoke wheels, 6", rare, EX, A...**$800.00**

Motorcycle, Champion, bl, wht rubber tires w/red hubs, bl integral driver, 5", EX, A **$150.00**

Motorcycle, Hubley, orange, wht rubber tires, w/driver, 6", EX, A **$550.00**

Motorcycle, Hubley, red w/gold tank decoration, battery-op lights, rubber wheels, w/driver, 6", EX, A **$520.00**

Motorcycle & Sidecar, Hubley, olive gr, w/driver, 9", VG,
A..$1,000.00

Motorcycle & Sidecar w/Armored Shield, Hubley, red, rubber
tires w/spoke wheels, 2 riders, 8½", rpt, A............$1,100.00

Racer, AC Williams, red, NP spoke wheels, red driver, 5½", VG,
A..$150.00

Motor Express Truck, Hubley, 1930s, red and green with white rubber tires, 9", EX, $500.00.

Racer, AC Williams, red with nickel-plated spoked wheels, 5½", NM, $350.00.

New York World's Fair Greyhound Sight-Seeing Trolley,
Arcade, driver in open car pulls 3 canopied cars, 15½", NM,
A..$850.00

New York World's Fair Greyhound Trolley Bus, Arcade, bl w/wht
top, decaled sides, blk rubber tires, 6¾", EX, A.........$250.00

Nu Car Transport, Hubley, 1932, red & silver, wht rubber tires
w/red hubs, 17¼", NM, A......................................$1,100.00

Panel Van, Champion, red, blk rubber tires w/red spokes, 7¾",
VG, A..$660.00

Pennsylvania Independent Oil Co Mack Truck, Arcade, red,
enclosed C-style cab, blk fr, rubber tires, driver, 13", EX,
A..$3,850.00

Phaeton, Dent, red w/silver trim, 4 cast lanterns, curved hood, spoke
wheels, w/lady passenger & driver, 8½", VG, A........$1,210.00

Pickup Truck, Arcade, red w/rear bed corners curving down, blk
rubber tires, orig Arcade sticker on door, 5½", EX, A...$200.00

Pickwick Nite Coach, Kenton, gr dbl-decker bus w/orange
stripe, NP front, wht rubber tires w/red hubs, 9½", rpt,
A..$2,420.00

Pickwick Nite Coach, Kenton, gr w/NP tires, 6", EX, A ..$900.00

Pierce Arrow, AC Williams, bl & red w/wht rubber tires, 7",
EX-, A..$350.00

Police Motorcycle, Champion, 1930s, 7", EX, A............$400.00

Racer, Hubley, bl, wht rubber tires, w/driver, 6½", EX, A..$300.00

Racer, Hubley, red boat-tail style w/wht rubber tires, w/driver,
7", VG, A..$175.00

Racer, Hubley, 12 moving cyclinders, bl w/gold trim, blk rubber tires
w/spoke wheels, blk-pnt driver, 10½", EX+, A..........$2,300.00

Racer, Hubley, 12 moving cyclinders, silver w/red trim, blk rubber tires w/spoke wheels, red driver, 10½", EX, A ..$1,815.00

Racer, Hubley, 12 simulated cylinders, yel w/red trim & tail fin,
NP tires, blk-pnt driver, 10½", NM, A................$2,540.00

Racer #2, Vindex, silver, blk rubber tires w/silver spokes, w/blk-
pnt driver, EX+, A..$2,970.00

Racer #5, Arcade, red, wht rubber tires, w/driver, 7¾", NM,
A..$1,100.00

Racer #5, Hubley, bl & blk, NP grille & trim, blk rubber
tires w/spoke wheels, hood opens, w/driver, 9½", EX,
A..$1,980.00

Racer #5, Hubley, orange, wht rubber tires, NP driver, 5", NM,
A..$235.00

Police Patrol Wagon, Kenton, blue with white rubber tires, complete with 4 figures, EX, $1,650.00.

Railway Express Truck, Hubley, 1930s, green with white rubber tires, 4", EX, $275.00.

Racer #5, Hubley, red, w/NP grille, trim & tires, pnt hubs, w/driver, 9½", EX, A..................................$1,250.00

Racer #5, Hubley, yel, wht-pnt tires w/red hubs, blk-pnt driver, w/pull cord, 10", EX+, A..$6,600.00

Red Top Cab, Arcade, wht body & red top w/blk hood & fenders, rear spare tire, wht hubs, 8", rpt, A....................$360.00

REO Coupe, Arcade, gray w/red trim, wht rubber tires & spare w/red spokes, NP grille, w/driver, 9½", VG+, A ..$4,300.00

REO Coupe, Arcade, gray w/red trim, wht rubber tires & spare w/red spokes, NP grille, w/driver, 9½", NM, A..$11,000.00

REO Coupe, Arcade, yel w/blk fenders, NP tires w/red spokes, NP grille & driver, 9½", G, A $1,875.00

Roadster, Arcade, gr w/gold trim, w/rumble seat & NP spoke wheels, no driver, 6½", VG, A..............................$650.00

Roadster, Hubley, take-apart model, yel & blk w/wht rubber tires, 6⅛", EX, A..$250.00

Sedan, Arcade, wht rubber tires, no driver, 5", VG, A...$165.00

Sedan, Hubley, bl w/NP grille & bumper, wht rubber tires, 4⅛", EX, A..$250.00

Stake Truck, AC Williams, bl w/NP tires, interchangable tractor & trailer, 7", EX+, A...$300.00

Stake Truck, Arcade, bl, NP spoke wheels, no driver, 7", NM, A $475.00

Stake Truck, Arcade, dk gr, wht rubber tires, no driver, 4½", VG, A $90.00

Stake Truck, Arcade, red, NP spoke wheels, no driver, 7", VG, A $200.00

Stake Truck, Champion, red w/C-style cab, spoke wheels, 7½", VG, A $275.00

Stake Truck, Hubley, take-apart model, orange & blk w/wht rubber tires, 4¾", NM, A $215.00

Stake Truck, Kenton, gr, rpl tires, 8", NM, A.................$365.00

Stop-1926 Coupe, Kenton, red w/blk running boards & red & gr stoplights, blk tires w/red hubs, w/driver, 10", EX, A $4,070.00

Studebaker Sedan, Champion, blue with white rubber tires, 8", EX, $950.00.

Tank, Arcade, camo colors, rubber treads, 7¼", EX+, A..$745.00

Taxi Cab, Hubley, 1930s, orange w/blk trim, separate luggage rack, wht rubber tires, w/driver, 8", EX, A $550.00

Touring Car, Kenton, red w/yel spoke wheels, open sides w/roof, w/passenger & driver, 9¼", rpt, A..........................$575.00

Truck #675, Arcade, red & gold open-cab w/NP spoke wheels, upright steering wheel, no driver, 6½", EX, A.........$330.00

Valley View Dairy Van, Dent, bl & blk w/silver trim, wht rubber tires w/red hubs, no driver, new old stock, 8¼", A ..$350.00

Van, Hubley, red & bl w/NP grille & bumper, wht rubber tires, no driver, 4", NM, A $400.00

White Delivery Van, Arcade, bl, wht rubber tires, no side spare, w/driver, 8½", partial rpt, A................................$1,700.00

White Delivery Van, Arcade, gr, wht rubber tires w/side spare, w/driver, 8½", VG, A..$2,750.00

White Moving Van, Arcade, beige w/red trim, silver-pnt grille & bumper, wht rubber tires, NP driver, 13", EX, A..$12,100.00

White Moving Van, Arcade, blk w/silver trim, Lammert's Furniture & Draperies, NP tires & driver, 13", VG, A .$9,350.00

Wrecker, Champion, red w/C-style cab, wht rubber tires, NP crank, 8", G, A $330.00

Wrecker, Champion, red with white rubber tires, 8½", EX, from $500.00 to $550.00.

Wrecker, Hubley, red & bl, wht rubber tires w/red hubs, NP hook, 5", EX, A...$155.00

Yellow Cab, Arcade, yel-orange & blk, blk-pnt tires w/yel-orange hubs, w/driver, 8", EX, A $725.00

Yellow Cab, Arcade, yel-orange & blk, blk-pnt tires w/yel-orange hubs, w/driver, 8", G, A $500.00

Yellow Cab, Arcade, yel-orange & blk, blk-pnt tires w/yel-orange hubs, w/driver, 9", EX+, A $3,190.00

Yellow Cab, Arcade, yel-orange & blk, wht-pnt tires w/yel-orange hubs, w/driver, 9", VG, A........................$1,100.00

Yellow Cab, Hubley, yel-orange Sky View w/chrome trim, wht rubber tires, w/driver, 8½", NM, A......................$2,530.00

Yellow Cab, Hubley, yel-orange w/blk trim, blk-pnt tires w/yel-orange hubs, w/driver, 8", EX, A..........................$1,200.00

Yellow Cab, Kenton, orange & blk, wht-pnt tires w/orange hubs, no driver, 8", NM, A..................................$3,520.00

Yellow Cab Co Baggage Express Truck, Arcade, yel-orange & blk, wht rubber tires, yel-orange hubs, w/driver, EX, A..$17,600.00

Yellow Cab Co Main 7171, Arcade, yel-orange & blk, wht-pnt tires w/yel-orange hubs, no driver, 5¼", EX+, A..$2,200.00

Yellow Cab Delivery Van, Arcade, yel-orange & blk, blk-pnt tires w/yel-orange hubs, side spare, w/driver, 8½", VG, A $3,080.00

Yellow Cab Grant 81001, yel-orange & blk Parmalee, wht rubber tires, 8", EX+, A.............................$13,750.00

Yellow Cab Limousine, yel-orange & blk, NP tires w/yel-orange hubs, NP driver, no spare, 8½", NM, A $13,200.00

Yellow Coach Double-Decker Bus, Arcade, gr, wht rubber tires, NP driver, 13", EX, A.............................$3,200.00

TRAINS

Baer, German, ca 1840, locomotive & tender w/3 enclosed passenger cars, 1 open & 1 cage car, w/passengers, 23", VG, A...$1,840.00

Baggage Car, Harris, ca 1903, red w/rubber-stamped stenciling on sides, cut-out windows, 13⅜", EX, A...................$360.00

Canadian Pacific, blk locomotive w/spoke wheels, coach mk Made in Canada, 15", rpt, A $75.00

Floor Train, Kenton, 1900, #642 locomotive w/CRI & PRY tender, #1020 Pullman, G, A $375.00

Lake Shore-Michigan Southern, NP, w/locomotive, coal car & 2 passenger cars, also mk Bonvoyage & US Mail, 34", EX, A...$525.00

Locomotive, Ives, Blakeslee & Co, 1884, clockwork, blk w/red stack & spoke wheels, gold trim, 7", EX, A..........$2,070.00

Locomotive, Tender & 2 Gondolas #104, WIW Co (Watson Iron Works ?), 1880, blk & red w/gold trim, 34", EXIB (wood box), A...$6,325.00

Narcissus, blk locomotive & tender w/spoke wheels, 2 gr passenger cars, gold trim, 32", EX+, A $715.00

Pullman Railplane, Arcade, red w/yel stenciled lettering, 8¾", EX, A...$330.00

Royal Blue Line, Harris, blk loco & tender w/red & gold trim, red passenger car w/stenciling, 34", VG, A $1,430.00

Victory Train, Dent, 1900, locomotive w/integral tender & 2 red passenger cars, 16", EX, A $325.00

2-4-0 Locomotive w/Tender & 3 Passenger Cars, Kenton, 1920, G, A...$115.00

4-4-0 Locomotive w/8-Wheeled Tender, Wilkins, 12", G, A $60.00

MISCELLANEOUS

Alphabet Man/Yankee Schoolmaster, Pat EA Cooper & F Sibley, 1884, lever action, man displays letters of alphabet, 10", A...$23,575.00

Anti-Aircraft Rapid-Fire Machine Gun, Gray Iron, 1930, 7½", VG, A..$150.00

Champion Express Wagon, bl w/red pull hdl, wht rubber tires w/red hubs, 8", rpt, A...$85.00

Champion Express Wagon, gr w/red pull hdl, wht rubber tires w/red hubs, 8", M, A..$550.00

Gas Pump, Arcade, bl w/gold base, emb GAS, gallon dial revolves when crank is turned, rope hose, 6", EX+, A...........$1,150.00

Gas Pump, Arcade, gr w/gold base, emb GAS, gallon dial revolves when crank is turned, rope hose, 6", NM, A............$2,600.00

Gas Pump, Arcade, red w/red base, emb GAS, gallon dial revolves when crank is turned, rope hose, 4¾", EX, A $440.00

Gas Pump, Arcade, red w/red base, emb GAS, gallon dial revolves when crank is turned, rope hose, 7", EX+, A..........$1,155.00

GE Ice Box, Hubley, wht w/bl & wht logo on door & bl hinges, compressor on top, 7¼", EX+, A $500.00

Morse 'Z' Engine, Fairbanks/Arcade, gr w/red flywheels, 8¾", EX, A..$350.00

Road Signs, Hubley, 1930, Men Working Ahead, Slow, Road Closed & Flag, set of 4, VG+, A $150.00

Service Station, Arcade, wooden building w/Arcade Service stenciled on front, w/triple red CI gas pumps, 7x13", EX, A...$650.00

Sign, Don't Park Here, 5", G-, A $120.00

Sign, RR, Arcade, wht w/blk lettering, 4¾", VG, A $250.00

Sign, US 30, Arcade, wht, 4¼", VG, A $200.00

Toonerville Trolley, Dent/G Borgfeldt, 1930s, red, yel & blk version, 5½", M (EX box), A..............................$1,400.00

Catalogs

In any area of collecting, old catalogs are a wonderful source for information. Toy collectors value buyers' catalogs, those from toy fairs, and Christmas 'wish books.' Montgomery Ward issued their first Christmas catalog in 1932, and Sears followed a year later. When they can be found, these 'first editions' in excellent condition are valued at a minimum of $200.00 each. Even later issues may sell for upwards of $75.00, since it's those from the '50s and '60s that contain the toys that are now so collectible.

Advisor: Bill Mekalian (M4).

American Character Doll Catalog, 1965, features Tiny Tears, Cricket, Tressy, etc, 31 pgs, M, H12 ....$45.00

American Flyer, 1924, w/supplements, G, A $175.00

Aurora Model Kits, 1960, EX, G5 ....$70.00

Aurora Model Kits, 1970, EX, from $50 to $75.00

Aurora, 1970, M, $120.00.

Aurora Model Kits, 1975, EX, G5 ....$20.00

BCM Die Cast Toys, 1965-67 (?), blk & wht, 18 pgs, EX, P4...$20.00

Carnell Manufacturing Co Authentic Western Holsters, 1956 dealer catalog, blk & wht illus, 16 pgs, EX, P4 ....$35.00

Colorforms, 1980, w/Mork & Mindy, Spider-Man, Barbie, Black Hole, Wonder Woman, etc, EX $40.00

Corgi Toys, 1969, M, $10.00.

Cragstan, 1959, EX, A $145.00

Dakin, 1973, featuring plastic & stuffed figures, store displays pictured, EX $50.00

Dent Toys Catalogue No 10, EX, A $30.00

Fisher-Price, 1950, EX, A $135.00

Gabriel Year Round Favorites, 1977, features Disney toys, 8 pgs, EX $40.00

Hasbro, 1978, features Charlie's Angels dolls & accessories, Super Joe & his creatures, etc, 10 pgs, EX.................$60.00

Horseman, 1963, features Poor Pitiful Pearl, Gloria Jean & Baby Buttercup, NM, H12...........................$35.00

Hubley Cap Pistols, 1950 dealer catalog, 8 pgs, EX, P4 ....$25.00

Hubley Cap Shooting Rifles & Pistols, 1954 dealer catalog, 12 pgs, EX, P4 ....$30.00

Ideal Shaker Makers, 1979, features Evel Knievel, 7 pgs, EX .$50.00

Imperial Bicycles, Ames & Frost Co, 1897, EX, A $35.00

Iroquois Cycle Works, 1897, EX, A $90.00

Ives Toys, 1924, w/wholesale price list, VG, A...............$115.00

Ives Trains, 1931, VG, A.................................$85.00

Kenner, 1976, Bionic Woman & Six Million Dollar Man on cover, EX $150.00

Kenner, 1978, 28 pgs of Star Wars, w/Bionic Woman, Six Million Dollar Man, Stretch Armstrong, Play Doh, etc, EX ...$175.00

Knickerbocker, 1982, Annie (movie) on the cover, features Annie dolls & toys, EX.............................$40.00

LJN, 1982, w/diecut foldout cover of Brooke Shields, 6-pg spread of her dolls, cars & motorcycles, EX.........................$40.00

Matchbox Aircraft Kits, 1977, EX...................$30.00

Mattel, 1966, 30 pgs of Barbie & Friends w/5 pgs of Kiddles, etc, VG $250.00

Marx, 1965 Toy Line, NM, A, $140.00.

McLoughlin Bros, July 1895, ...Illustrated Catalogue, 105 pgs, G+...$825.00

Mego, 1976, features Star Trek, Wizard of Oz, Super Heroes, etc, VG $250.00

Miro, 1977, features eating & cooking toys such as Real Refridge, First Bakery, Sweet Shoppe, Cookie Factory, etc, EX $40.00

Ohio Art, 1974, Woody Woodpecker on cover, EX $50.00

Parker Bros, 1978, Monopoly on cover, EX $40.00

Playthings, Kay Kayman/WDP, 1947, 430 pgs, binding loose o/w EX, A $200.00

Regal Toy, 1977, Luv & Kisses doll on cover, EX.............$35.00

Remco, 1979, features the Energized Spider-Man, Hulk, I Dream of Jeannie doll, etc, EX $60.00

Revell Toys, 1953, EX, H12 ....$35.00

Schoenhut's Marvelous Toys/The Humpty Dumpty Circus, 1918, 50 pgs, M, A $400.00

Tootsietoy, 1968, $75.00; Fisher-Price Toys, 1950, EX, $135.00.

Schoenhut's Marvelous Toys/The Humpty Dumpty Circus, 1918, 50 pgs, VG, A..$185.00

Superhero Catalog of Games, Books, Toys & Puzzles, 1977, EX+, A $45.00

Tom Mix Premium Catalog, orig mailer, C10..................$85.00

Tonka, 1963, NM, A...$100.00

Transogram, 1948, blk & wht, EX....................................$50.00

View-Master, 1988, EX..$30.00

Vogue Dolls, 1978, EX...$40.00

Cereal Boxes and Premiums

This is an area of collecting that attracts crossover interest from fans of advertising as well as character-related toys. What makes a cereal box interesting? Look for Batman, Huckleberry Hound, or a well-known sports figure like Larry Bird or Roger Maris on the front or back. Boxes don't have to be old to be collectible, but the basic law of supply and demand dictates that the older ones are going to be expensive! After all, who saved cereal boxes from 1910? By chance if Grandma did, the 1910 Corn Flakes box with a printed-on baseball game could get her $750.00. Unless you're not concerned with bugs, it will probably be best to empty the box and very carefully pull apart the glued flaps. Then you can store it flat. Be sure to save any prize that might have been packed inside. For more information we recommend *Cereal Box Bonanza, The 1950s, ID and Values* by Scott Bruce (Collector Books). Unless noted, our values are for boxes in mint condition, whether full or folded.

Advisor: Scott Bruce (B14); Larry Blodget (B2), Post Cereal cars.

General Mills Cheerios, 1957, Lone Ranger Rapid-Fire Revolving premium on front, scarce, EX, A........................$265.00

General Mills Cheerios, 1980, Lone Ranger on Silver, EX, from $35 to $50.00

General Mills Count Chocula, Mystery Drawing Disk premium, flat, EX, B14..$15.00

General Mills Count Chocula, 1988, flicker eye cover, door sign on back, flat, EX, B14..$15.00

General Mills Crunch Berries, 1982, Cap'n Crunch & the Crunch Berry Beast, bowling contest on back, 15-oz, EX $15.00

General Mills Franken Berry, 1985, free Wacky Racers offer, NM, T1 ....$5.00

General Mills Frosty O's, 1970, features Dudley DoRight, B14, from $400 to $600.00

General Mills Trix, 1960, Corvair Sweepstakes offer, EX, from $100 to $150.00

General Mills Wheaties, Bob Richards track & field game, front & back only, EX, J2 ....$15.00

General Mills Wheaties, 1960s, Bob Richards sports fitness, VG+, J2..$10.00

General Mills Wheaties, 1988, Redskins NFL Champs....$20.00

General Mills Wheaties, 1992, features Lou Gehrig, NM, T1 ..$10.00

Kellogg's Cocoa Krispies, 1980, Tusk the Elephant on front, Fun Games on back, 13-oz, EX $25.00

Kellogg's Cocoa Krispies, 1991, River Run game on back, flat, EX, B14 ....$5.00

Kellogg's Cocoa Puffs, 1980s, Popeye & Sonny on cover, Even I's Can't Resist Cocoa Puffs!, bubble gum inside, EX.$25.00

Kellogg's Cookie Crisp, Teenage Mutant Ninja Turtles collector cards on back, w/bowl, EX, B14................................$15.00

Kellogg's Corn Flakes, Canadian, 1950s, Tom Corbett cutouts on back, Space Patrol Ray Gun offer on side, 12-oz, EX, J5 ....$250.00

Kellogg's Corn Flakes, 1956, Superman Satellite launcher offer, EX, B14, from $300 to...$400.00

Kellogg's Corn Flakes, 1960, Yogi Bear cup offer, EX, from $50 to $75.00

Kellogg's Corn Flakes, 1962, Yogi Bear Birthday Party, B14...$420.00

Kellogg's Corn Flakes, 1973, biography scenes, Clark Button, EX, J2 ....$10.00

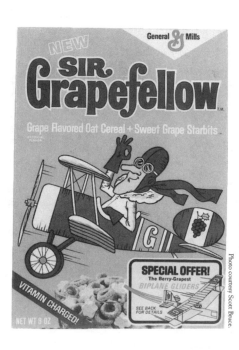

General Mills Sir Grapefellow, features Biplane Glider offer, M, from $125.00 to $200.00.

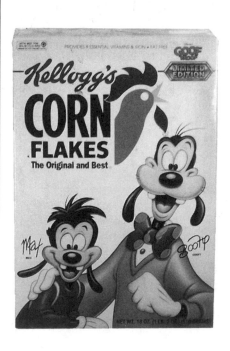

Kellogg's Corn Flakes, features Max and Goofy, limited edition, M, from $5.00 to $10.00.

Kellogg's Corn Flakes, 1984, Vanessa Williams (Miss America) on front, EX, from $50 to $65.00

Kellogg's Corn Flakes, 1988, Duck Tales mask on back, flat, EX, B14 ....$7.00

Kellogg's Corn Flakes, 1991, 85th Anniversary, NM..........$3.00

Kellogg's Corn Pops, 1991, table-top soccer game on back, flat, EX, B14 ....$5.00

Kellogg's Froot Loops, with mail-in coupon for Toucan Sam stuffed toy, M, box: from $300.00 to $400.00; doll: from $20.00 to $30.00.

Kellogg's Froot Loops, 1991, Disney Gummi Bear Stamper premium, EX, B14................................$5.00

Kellogg's Frosted Flakes, 1966, ad for Batman Printing Set on front, image on back, EX, A................$500.00

Kellogg's Honey Nut Cheerios, 1990, w/Magic Motion sticker, EX, T1 ....$3.00

Kellogg's Honey Smacks, European, 1967, Bertie the Bee on front, Pepsi sweepstakes on back, NM $25.00

Kellogg's Honey Smacks, 1980s, Dig'em mask on back, flat, EX, B14 ....$5.00

Kellogg's Honey Smacks, 1989, ghost detector premium, flat, EX $5.00

Kellogg's OKs, 1963, Yogi flexing muscles, Pin-M-Up In a 3-D Frame & picture of Yogi on back, 8¼-oz, VG, from $200 to................................$225.00

Kellogg's Pep, Canadian, 1952, French/English text, Tom Corbett space scene on front, goggles offer on back, NM, J5 ....$350.00

Kellogg's Pep Wheat Flakes, 1969, box back only, Linda Lou doll offer, EX $5.00

Kellogg's Raisin Bran, 1958, Woody Woodpecker & Turbo Beam Car, VG $55.00

Kellogg's Rice Krispies, 1961, Dennis the Menace fan club offer, EX................................$65.00

Kellogg's Rice Krispies, 1967, features Monkeemobile, NM, B14................................$250.00

Kellogg's Rice Krispies, 1988, Win, Lose or Draw, NM, T1 ..$4.00

Kellogg's Rice Krispies, 1990, 60 Years, Matchbox offer, NM ..$7.00

Kellogg's Sugar Pops, Canadian, 1952-57, features Wild Bill Hickok, rare, EX $75.00

Kellogg's Sugar Pops, 1958-59, Sugar Pop Pete shooting cereal bowl on front, cartoon cutout on back, EX, J5...........$80.00

Kellogg's Sugar Smacks, British, 1970, features Mr Spock, NM, B14 ....$1,000.00

Nabisco Rice Honeys, 1960, Frontier Hero medal, unopened, EX, B14 ....$75.00

Nabisco Rice Honeys, 1963, Buffalo Bee on front w/lasso around prize offered (patches), flat, M................$95.00

Nabisco Shredded Wheat, 1956, Rin-Tin-Tin Televiewer offer on back, 12-oz, flat, NM................$125.00

Nabisco Wheat Honeys, 1956, Buffalo Bee on front w/gun drawn, Rin-Tin-Tin 12-ring set offer on back, flat, M...........$125.00

Kellogg's Raisin Bran, features 1992 Dream Team, M, from $7.00 to $12.00.

Nabisco Winnie-the-Pooh Great Honey Crunchers, M, from $275.00 to $375.00.

Post Rice Krinkles, early 1960s, So-Hi w/cereal bowl on front, So-Hi & Tumbling Turtles cutouts on back, EX, J5........$100.00

Post Sugar Crisp, 1961, Sugar Bear & Bugs Bunny on front, Sylvester mask on back, EX......................................$125.00

Post Sugar Rice Krinkles, 1955, clown & top offer on front, EX $45.00

Post Sugar-Crisp Corn Flakes, Canadian, 1935, Mickey's Steam Roller cutouts, EX...$175.00

Post Toasties, late 1930s, Pied Piper featured on back & 2 side panels attached as 1, EX, M8......................................$25.00

Post Toasties, late 1930s, red & yel w/Mickey Mouse Presents Ferdinand the Bull on back, EX, from $125 to $150.00

Post Toasties, 1934, features Mickey Out West cutouts, EX, from $250 to..$300.00

Post Toasties, 1935, Mickey Mouse Band Concert, back only, VG+ $25.00

Post Toasties, 1937, Snow White & the Seven Dwarfs, back panel only, EX...$25.00

Post Toasties, 1939, features Pinocchio, EX, J2 ....$180.00

Quaker Oats, 1950, advertises Roy Rogers Microscope Ring ...$75.00

Quaker Oats/Mother's Oats, 1950, rnd box w/ad for Roy Rogers Branding Iron Ring on lid, shows Roy on side, EX+, A ..$90.00

Quaker Quisp, ray gun offer, 1968, from $750 to $1,000.00

Quaker Quisp, Space Trivia, flat, 1990, EX, B14 ....$5.00

Quaker Quisp, 1970s, Quisp Zoo on Planet Q cutouts on back, missing top o/w VG, J5...$50.00

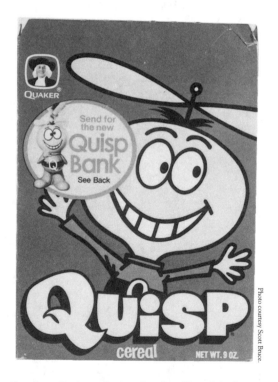

Quaker Quisp, Quisp bank offer, M, from $600.00 to $750.00.

Ralston Batman Cereal, 1989, w/7" plastic Batman bank, unused, M (shrink-wrapped) $10.00

Ralston Hot Wheels Cereal, 1990, Super Changers offer, NM, T1..$10.00

Ralston Prince of Thieves, 1991, free target game, NM, T1 ..$4.00

Ralston Rice Chex, Charlie Brown in chef hat holding bowl, flat, 1990, EX, B14..$3.00

Ralston Teenage Mutant Ninja Turtles, 1989, free comic book offer, NM, T1..$6.00

Ralston Wheat Chex, 1953, Space Patrol w/magic photo of Cadet Happy, NM, C10 ....$200.00

Ralston Wheat Chex, 1953-55, back only, Space Patrol contest w/rules & list of prizes, from $15 to $25.00

PREMIUMS

Sure, the kids liked the taste of the cereal too, but in families with more than one child there was more clammoring over the prize inside than there was over the last bowlfull! In addition to the 'freebies' included in the boxes, many other items were made available — rings, decoders, watches, games, books, etc. — often for just mailing in boxtops or coupons. If these premiums weren't free, their prices were minimal. Most of them were easily broken, and children had no qualms about throwing them away, so few survive to the present. Who would have ever thought those kids would be trying again in the '90s to get their hands on those very same prizes, and at considerably more trouble and expense. Note: Only premiums that specifically relate to cereal companies or their character logos are listed here. Other character-related premiums are listed in the Premiums category.

Apple Jack Kids, secret decoder, 1985, red plastic, NM, B14 ..$5.00

Archies, rub-ons, 1971, MIP, B14 ....$12.00

Booberry, pencil topper, 1973, pk rubber, NM, B14.........$10.00

Cap'n Crunch, Chockle stickers, 1980s, sheet B, set of 8, M, B14...$15.00

Cap'n Crunch, Rescue Kit, 1986, paper, MIP, B14.............$5.00

Cap'n Crunch, Seadog Spy Kit, plastic & paper instructions, MIP, B14..$45.00

Cap'n Crunch, Storyscope, 1972, plastic, w/cutout story disk, NM, B14 ....$25.00

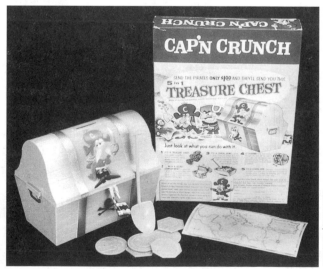

Cap'n Crunch, treasure chest bank: from $100.00 to $150.00; box: from $200.00 to $300.00.

Count Chocula, figure, ceramic, NM, T1 ....$16.00
Count Chocula, memo pad, crayons & eraser, MIP, H4.....$6.00
Count Chocula, mini-mug, 1973, plastic, M, B14 ....$25.00
Count Chocula, pencil topper, 1973, wht or bl rubber, NM, B14,
 ea...$15.00
Count Chocula, Puff-a-plane, 1971, plastic tube w/cb wings, M,
 B14 ....$15.00
Frankenberry, mug, 1973, yel or bl plastic, miniature, M, B14,
 ea $25.00
Freakies, figure, Goody-Goody, 1971, pk plastic, NM, B14 .$15.00
Freakies, figure, Grumble, 1971, orange plastic, MIB, B14...$20.00
Freakies, Freakmobile, Gargle, Bossmoss or Snorkeldorf, 1974,
 plastic, MIB, B14, ea from $3 to $5.00
General Mills, Crazy Eights card game, 1981, features all of the
 General Mills characters, MIB (sealed), J2 ....$20.00
Grins & Giggles, refrigerator magnet, 1976, MIP, B14, ea, from
 $15 to $20.00
King Vitamin, racing coach, 1970s, plastic w/metal drive wheel,
 MIP, B14, ea, from $25 to $30.00
King Vitamin, 3-D Hologram ring, 1972, red plastic, M, B14 ..$65.00
Lucky the Leprechaun, figure, on skateboard, 1977, red plastic,
 M, B14 ....$10.00
Lucky the Leprechaun, iron-on decal, 1979, NM, B14.....$10.00
Ogg, bicycle license plate, 1973, bl plastic, EX, B14.........$15.00
Pop!, canteen, 1973, yel, wht & red plastic, NM, B14 .....$15.00
Pop!, squeeze toy, 1978, plastic, EX, B14 ....$25.00
Poppy, secret decoder, 1985, yel plastic, NM, B14..............$5.00
Post Vehicle, F&F Mold, 1950 Ford, bl, no magnet, EX...$40.00

Photo courtesy Pat Webb.

Post Vehicle, F&F Mold, 1950 Ford Custom Fordor, Magno-Power, red, M, original mailer, $50.00.

Post Vehicle, F&F Mold, 1954 Club Coupe, Sierra Brown, M..$30.00
Post Vehicle, F&F Mold, 1954 Mercury 2-door, yel w/silver-pnt
 bumpers, EX $30.00
Post Vehicle, F&F Mold, 1954 Mercury 4-door, yel, rpl posts,
 EX $20.00
Post Vehicle, F&F Mold, 1954 Rancho Wagon, Bloomfield,
 EX $30.00

Post Vehicle, F&F Mold, 1954 Sunliner, Torch Red, EX.$30.00
Post Vehicle, F&F Mold, 1955 Crown Victoria, Sea Sprite,
 EX $15.00
Post Vehicle, F&F Mold, 1955 Sunliner, buckskin, EX......$5.00
Post Vehicle, F&F Mold, 1955 Thunderbird, red, EX $10.00
Post Vehicle, F&F Mold, 1956 Ford/Fruehauf gasoline transport,
 aluminum, EX $20.00
Post Vehicle, F&F Mold, 1956 Greyhound Highway Traveler,
 bl, rare, EX $35.00
Post Vehicle, F&F Mold, 1956 Greyhound Super Sceni-cruiser,
 bl, rare, EX $35.00
Post Vehicle, F&F Mold, 1957 Custom 4-door, Inca Gold,
 M $25.00
Post Vehicle, F&F Mold, 1960 Plymouth Hardtop, Twilight Bl,
 EX $15.00
Post Vehicle, F&F Mold, 1966 Mustang Convertible, Spring-
 time Yel, EX $10.00
Post Vehicle, F&F Mold, 1967 Cougar, Fawn, lg early tires, EX
 finish $35.00
Quisp, Gyro Trail Blazer, 1960s, bl plastic, EX, B14.........$25.00
Quisp, Gyro Unicycle, 1970s, bl plastic, MIP, B14...........$50.00
Quisp, ray gun, 1960s, red plastic, shoots sugar, 5", EX, J5 ..$80.00
Snap!, Crackle! & Pop!, binoculars, 1980s, paper & plastic,
 MIP, B14..$3.00
Snap!, Crackle! & Pop!, drawing template, 1970s, yel plastic,
 3x5", NM, B14...$15.00
Snap!, Crackle! & Pop!, figures, 1975, vinyl, 8", EX, ea...$30.00
Snap!, Crackle! & Pop!, hand puppets, 1950s, cloth w/vinyl
 heads, EX, ea $40.00
Snap!, Crackle! & Pop!, iron-on patch, 1974, glow-in-the-dark,
 2", MIB, B14, ea $7.00
Snap!, Crackle! & Pop!, sticker, 1971, glow-in-the-dark, M,
 B14..$5.00
Snap!, Crackle! & Pop!, sticker, 1973, Don't Pollute!, NM,
 B14 ....$10.00
Snorky the Elephant, hand puppet, Kellogg's, 1968, plastic, VG,
 B13 ....$12.00
Sonny the Cuckoo Bird, bicycle spinner, 1970s, brn plastic, M,
 B14 ....$25.00
Sugar Bear, doll, cloth, 4", EX, B10 ....$8.00
Sugar Bear, padlock & key, 1970s, plastic, MIP, B14, from $10
 to $15.00
Sugar Bear, yo-yo, 1970s, 3-in-1, plastic, MIP, B14, from $10
 to $15.00
Tony the Tiger, bank, 1970s, plastic figure, 8½", NM......$45.00
Tony the Tiger, bowling set, NMIB, T1............................$65.00
Tony the Tiger, doll, 1960s, stuffed cloth, Tony printed on red
 scarf, 25", EX, J5 ....$45.00
Tony the Tiger, doll, 1973, stuffed cloth, 14", NM...........$25.00
Tony the Tiger, figure, 1950s, inflatable vinyl, 5", NM....$40.00
Tony the Tiger, padlock, 1987, plastic, MIP, B14..............$3.00
Tony the Tiger, patch, 1965, glow-in-the-dark, 4", NM,
 B14 ....$20.00
Toucan Sam, bicycle license plate, 1973, bl plastic, 3x6",
 EX...$20.00
Toucan Sam, paper clip/page marker, 1979, bl plastic, NM,
 B14..$2.00
Toucan Sam, soccer ball, 1982, bl plastic, M, B14.............$5.00

Toucan Sam, Tony & Cornelius, stickers, 1971, glow-in-the-dark, M, B14..$5.00

Trix Rabbit, figure, 1970s, vinyl, 10", EX+, B10/C17.......$30.00

Trix Vehicle, 1970 Allied Cross Country Moving Van, orange w/decals, EX $5.00

Trix Vehicle, 1970 Allied Moving Van, tilt cab, orange w/decals, EX $5.00

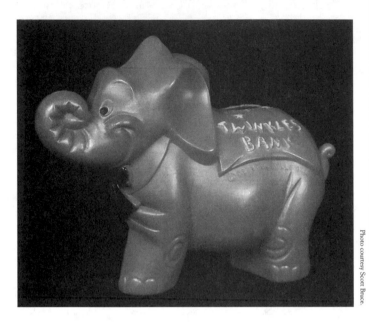

Photo courtesy Scott Bruce.

Twinkles, bank, 1960, red, NM, from $400.00 to $500.00.

Whippersnapper & Smacks Indian Brave, drawing template, 1970, gr plastic, 3x6", M, B14 ....$15.00

Character and Promotional Drinking Glasses

Once given away by fast-food chains and gas stations, a few years ago you could find these at garage sales everywhere for a dime or even less. Then, when it became obvious to collectors that these glass giveaways were being replaced by plastic, as is always the case when we realize no more (of anything) will be forthcoming, we all decided we wanted them. Since many were character-related and part of a series, we felt the need to begin to organize these garage-sale castaways, building sets and completing series. Out of the thousands available, the better ones are those with super heroes, sports stars, old movie stars, Star Trek, and Disney and Walter Lantz cartoon characters. Pass up those whose colors are worn and faded. Unless another condition or material is indicated in the description, values are for glass tumblers in mint condition. Cups are plastic unless noted otherwise.

There are some terms used in our listings that may be confusing if you're not familiar with this collecting field. 'Brockway' style tumblers are thick and heavy, and they taper at the bottom. 'Federal' is thinner, and top and diameters are equal. For more information we recommend *Collectible Drinking Glasses, Identification and Values* by Mark E. Chase and Michael J. Kelly

(Collector Books) and *The Collector's Guide to Cartoon and Promotional Drinking Glasses* by John Hervey.

Advisors: Mark E. Chase and Michael J. Kelly (C2).

Other Sources: B3, C1, C10, C11, D9, D11, F8, J2, H11, I2, J7, M8, M16, P3, P6, P10, R2, S20, T1, T2

See also Clubs, Newsletters, and Other Publications.

Abbott & Costello, see Arby's Actor Series

Al Capp, Brockway, 1975, 16-oz, flat bottom, Joe Btsptflk, from $40 to $60.00

Al Capp, Brockway, 1975, 16-oz, flat bottom, Mammy, Pappy, Sadie, Lil' Abner, Daisy Mae, ea, from $30 to $50.00

Al Capp, Brockway, 1975, 16-oz, ftd, Joe Btsptflk, from $40 to $60.00

Al Capp, Brockway, 1975, 16-oz, ftd, Mammy, Pappy, Sadie, Lil' Abner, Daisy Mae, ea, from $30 to............................$50.00

Animal Crackers, Chicago Tribune/NY News Syndicate, 1978, Louis, scarce, from $50 to $75.00

Animal Crackers, Chicago Tribune/NY News Syndicate, 1978, Lyle, Dodo, Gnu, Lana, Eugene, ea, from $7 to $10.00

Apollo Series, Marathon Oil, Apollo 11, Apollo 12, Apollo 13, Apollo 14, ea, from $2 ....$4.00

Apollo Series, Marathon oil, carafe, from $6 to $10.00

Aquaman, see Super Heroes

Arby's, Actor Series, 1979, 6 different, smoke-colored glass w/blk & wht images, silver trim, numbered, ea, from $5 to $7.00

Arby's, Bicentennial Cartoon Character Series, 1976, 10 different, 5", ea, from $10 to $12.00

Arby's, Bicentennial Cartoon Character Series, 1976, 10 different, 6", ea, from $15 to $18.00

Arby's, see also a specific name or series

Archies, Welch's, 1971, 6 different, w/many variations, ea...$2.00

Archies, Welch's, 1973, 6 different, w/many variations, ea...$2.00

Avon, Christmas Issues, 1969-72, 4 different, ea, from $2 to $5.00

Baby Huey & Related Characters, see Harvey Cartoon Characters

Batman & Related Characters, see Super Heroes

Battlestar Galactica, Universal Studios, 1979, 4 different, ea, from $7 to..$10.00

BC Ice Age, Arby's, 1981, 6 different, ea, from $3 to $5.00

Beatles, Dairy Queen, group photo & signatures in wht starburst, gold trim, Canadian, from $75 to $100.00

Beatles, United Kingdom, George Harrison, full-color decal, gold trim, 4", B3 ....$160.00

Beatles, United Kingdom, John Lennon or Paul McCartney, full-color decal, gold trim, 4", B3, ea.........................$170.00

Bugs Bunny & Related Characters, see Warner Bros

Bullwinkle, Rocky & Related Characters, see Arby's Bicentennial or PAT Ward

Burger Chef, Burger Chef & Jeff, Now We're Glassified!, from $15 to $25.00

Burger Chef, Endangered Species Collector's Series, 1978, Tiger, Orang-Utan, Bald Eagle, ea, from $5 to $7.00

Burger Chef, Endangered Species Collector's Series, 1979, Giant Panda, from $7 to.....................................$9.00

Burger Chef, Friendly Monsters Series, 1977, 6 different, ea, from $25 to $35.00

Burger Chef, Presidents & Patriots, 1975, 6 different, ea, from $3 to $5.00

Burger King, Collector Series, 1979, 5 different Burger King characters featuring Burger Thing, etc, ea, from $4 to $6.00

Burger King, Dallas Cowboys, Dr Pepper, 2 sets ea w/6 different, ea, from $7 to $10.00

Burger King, Have It Your Way 1776-1976 Series, 1976, 4 different, ea, from $4 to.....................................$6.00

Burger King, see also a specific name or series

Captain America, see Super Heroes

Casper the Friendly Ghost & Related Characters, see Arby's Bicentennial or Harvey Cartoon Characters

Chilly Willy, see Walter Lantz

Cinderella, Disney/Libbey, 1950s-1960s, set of 8, 4⅝"...$120.00

Cinderella, see also Disney Collector's Series or Disney Film Classics

Clarabell, see Howdy Doody

Coca-Cola, Christmas, McCrory's, 1982-89, 8 different, various styles, ea, from $2 to.....................................$4.00

Coca-Cola, Haddon Sundblom Coca-Cola Santas, 3 different in series 1 or 2, ea, from $4 to $6.00

Coca-Cola, Heritage Collector Series, 1976, 4 different, tall pedestal bottom, ea, from $3 to $6.00

Coca-Cola, Heritage Collector Series (Spirit of 1776), 4 different, short pedestal bottom, ea, from $4 to...................$7.00

Coca-Cola, Wild West Series, Buffalo Bill, Annie Oakley or Calamity Jane, ea, from $12 to $15.00

Coca-Cola, see also a specific name or series

Currier & Ives, Arby's, 1975-76, 4 different, titled, ea, from $3 to $5.00

Currier & Ives, Arby's, 1978, 4 different, numbered, ea, from $3 to $5.00

Daffy Duck, see Warner Bros

Daisy Mae, see Al Capp

Dick Tracy, 1940s, 8 different characters, frosted, 3" or 5", ea, from $50 to.....................................$75.00

Dilly Dally, see Howdy Doody

Disney, see also Wonderful World of Disney

Disney Characters, 1936, Mickey, Minnie, Donald, Pluto, Clarabelle, Horace, F Bunny, 4¼" or 4¾", ea, from $30 to..$60.00

Disney Collector's Series, Burger King, 1994, mc images on clear plastic, 8 different, MIB, ea.............................$3.00

Disney Double Character, Goofy and Pluto, 1950s or early '60s, $15.00.

Disney Film Classics, McDonald's/Coca-Cola/Canada, Peter Pan, Cinderella, Fantasia or Snow White & the Seven Dwarfs, ea...$15.00

Disney's All-Star Parade, 1939, 10 different, ea, from $25 to...$60.00

Domino's Pizza, Avoid the Noid, 1988, set of 4, ea.............$7.00

Donald Duck or Daisy, see Disney Characters or Mickey Mouse (Happy Birthday)

Dudley Do-Right, see Arby's Bicentennial or PAT Ward

Dynomutt, see Hanna-Barbera

Flintstones, First 30 Years, Snorkasaurus Story, Hardee's/Roy Rogers, 1990, from $3.00 to $5.00.

Elmer Fudd, see Warner Bros

Elsie the Cow, Borden, Elsie & Family in 1976 Bicentennial parade, red, wht & bl graphics, from $5 to $7.00

Elsie the Cow, Borden, 1950s, wht head image on waisted style, from $10 to..$12.00

Elsie the Cow, Borden, 1960s, yel daisy image, from $10 to..$12.00

Empire Strikes Back, see Star Wars Trilogy

ET, Army & Air Force Exchange Service, 1982, 4 different mc images, rnd bottom, ea, from $5 to............................$10.00

ET, Pepsi/MCA Home Video, 1988, 6 different, ea, from $15 to..$25.00

ET, Pizza Hut, 1982, 4 different mc images, ftd, from $2 to...$4.00

Fantasia, see Disney Film Classics

Flintstone Kids, Pizza Hut, 1986, Freddy, Wilma, Barney or Betty, ea, from $2 to..$4.00

Flintstones, see also Hanna-Barbera

Flintstones, Welch's, 1962 (6 different), 1963 (2 different), 1964 (6 different), ea, from $4 to $8.00

Foghorn Leghorn, see Warner Bros

Ghostbusters II, Sunoco/Canada, 1989, 6 different, ea, from $5 to $7.00

Goonies, Godfather's Pizza/Warner Bros, 1985, 4 different, ea, from $4 to $8.00

Great Muppet Caper, McDonald's, 1981, 4 different, 6", ea ..$2.00

Green Arrow, see Super Heroes

Green Lantern, see Super Heroes

Gulf Oil, Collector Series Limited Edition, Indiana Glass Co, early 1980s, 6 different, tall or rocks, ea, from $3 to $5.00

H Salt Historic Ships, Brockway, 1970s, 6 different, ea, from $7 to..$10.00

Hanna-Barbera, Pepsi/Brockway, 1977, Yogi/Huck, Josie/Pussycats, Mumbly, Scooby Doo, Flintstones, Dynomutt, ea, from $20 to $30.00

Hanna-Barbera, 1960s, jam glasses featuring Flintstones, Yogi Bear, Quick Draw, Cindy Bear, Huck, rare, ea, from $90 to .$110.00

Happy Days, Dr Pepper, 1977, Ralph, Joanie, Potsie, ea, from $6 to..$8.00

Happy Days, Dr Pepper, 1977, the Fonz, from $7 to $10.00

Happy Days, Dr Pepper, 1977, the Fonz on a motorcycle or Richie, ea, from $8 to $12.00

Happy Days, Dr Pepper/Pizza Hut, 1977, Ralph, Joanie, Potsie, ea, from $8 to $10.00

Happy Days, Dr Pepper/Pizza Hut, 1977, the Fonz, from $10 to..$15.00

Happy Days, Dr Pepper/Pizza Hut, 1977, the Fonz on a motorcycle or Richie, ea, from $12 to $15.00

Harvey Cartoon Characters, Pepsi, 1970s, 5", action poses, Casper, Baby Huey, Wendy or Hot Stuff, ea, from $8 to..$12.00

Harvey Cartoon Characters, Pepsi, 1970s, 5", static poses, Casper, Baby Huey, Wendy or Hot Stuff, ea, from $12 to..$15.00

Harvey Cartoon Characters, Pepsi, 1970s, 6", static poses, Casper, Baby Huey, Wendy, or Hot Stuff, ea, from $12 to..$15.00

Harvey Cartoon Characters, Pepsi, 1970s, 6", static pose, Richie Rich, from $15 to..$20.00

Harvey Cartoon Characters, Pepsi, 1970s, 6", static pose, Sad Sack, scarce, from $25 to...$30.00

Harvey Cartoon Characters, see also Arby's Bicentennial Series

He-Man & Related Characters, see Masters of the Universe

Heinz, Product Labels, late 1970s-early 1980s, 2-sided, 3 different, ea, from $4 to..$7.00

Hopalong Cassidy's Western Series, 4½", ea, from $25 to ..$30.00

Hot Stuff, see Arby's Bicentennial

Howard the Duck, see Super Heroes

Howdy Doody, Welch's, 1953, 6 different w/Welch's sayings around top, many color variations, ea, from $10 to ...$15.00

Howdy Doody, Welch's/Kagran, early 1950s, 6 different w/many color variations & bottom embossings, ea, from $15 to..$20.00

Huckleberry Hound, see Hanna-Barbera

Incredible Hulk, see Super Heroes

Indiana Jones & the Temple of Doom, 7-Up (w/4 different co-sponsors), 1984, set of 4, ea, from $8 to....................$12.00

Indiana Jones: The Last Crusade, wht plastic w/4 different images, ea, from $2 to $4.00

James Bond 007, 1985, 4 different, ea, from $10 to $15.00

Joe Btsptflk, see Al Capp

Joker, see Super Heroes

Josie & the Pussycats, see Hanna-Barbera

Jungle Book, Disney/Canada, 1966, 6 different, numbered, 4⅞", ea, from $40 to...$60.00

Jungle Book, Disney/Canada, 1966, 6 different, numbered, 6½", ea, from $30 to...$50.00

Jungle Book, Disney/Pepsi, 1970s, King Looie, Baloo, Kaa or Colonel Hathi, unmk, ea, from $50 to $65.00

Jungle Book, Disney/Pepsi, 1970s, Mowgli, unmk, from $40 to..$50.00

Jungle Book, Disney/Pepsi, 1970s, Rama, unmk, from $45 to..$60.00

Jungle Book, Disney/Pepsi, 1970s, unmk, Bagheera or Shere Kahn, ea, from $60 to $90.00

Keebler, Soft Batch Cookie, 1984, 4 different, ea, from $7 to...$10.00

Keebler, 135th Birthday, 1988..$3.00

Kellogg's Collector Series, Big Yella, 1977, 1 of 6, $10.00.

Kellogg's, 1977, 6 different, Tony, Tony Jr, Big Yella, Snap!, Crackle! & Pop!, Dig 'Em, Toucan Sam, ea, from $7 to $10.00

King Kong, Coca-Cola/Dino De Laurentis Corp., 1976, from $5.00 to $8.00.

Laurel & Hardy, see Arby's Actor Series

Leonardo TTV, see also Arby's Bicentennial Series

Leonardo TTV Collector Series, Pepsi, 5", Underdog, Sweet Polly or Simon Bar Sinister, ea, from $8 to $12.00

Leonardo TTV Collector Series, Pepsi, 6", Underdog, bl lettering, w/or w/o logo, from $20 to......................$25.00

Leonardo TTV Collector Series, Pepsi, 6", Underdog, Go-Go Gophers, Sweet Polly or Simon Bar Sinister, ea, from $15 to.......................$20.00

Lil' Abner & Related Characters, see Al Capp

Little Rascals, see Arby's Actor Series

Looney Tunes/Warner Bros, Pepsi, 1973, 16-oz, Bugs, Daffy, Porky, Road Runner, Sylvester, Tweety, ea, from $5 to $10.00

Mae West, see Arby's Actor Series

Mark Twain Country Series, Burger King, 1985, 4 different, ea, from $8 to...$10.00

Masters of the Universe, Mattel, plastic, 4 different, ea......$3.00

Masters of the Universe, Mattel, 1983, Teela, He-Man, Skeletor, Man-at-Arms, ea, from $5 to.....................................$10.00

Masters of the Universe, Mattel, 1986, Orko, He-Man/Battle Cat, Skeletor/Panthor, Man-at-Arms, ea, from $3 to ..$5.00

McDonald's, All-Time Greatest Steelers Team, 1982, 4 different, ea, from $5 to...$8.00

McDonald's, Atlanta Falcons, Dr Pepper, 1980-81, 4 different, ea, from $4 to $6.00

McDonald's, McDonaldland Action Series, 1977, 6 different, 5⅝", P10, ea...$5.00

McDonald's, McDonaldland Collector Series, 1970s, 6 different, 5⅝", P10, ea..$4.00

McDonald's, McVote, 1986, 3 different, 5⅞", P10, ea $10.00

McDonald's, Philadelphia Eagles, 1980, 5 different, ea, from $4 to $6.00

McDonald's, Pittsburgh Steelers Superbowl 13, 1978, 4 different, ea, from $5 to $8.00

McDonald's, Pittsburgh Steelers Superbowl 14, 1979, 4 different, ea, from $3 to $5.00

MGM Collector Series, Pepsi, 1975, 5", Tom chasing Jerry or Jerry catching Tom's tail in trap, ea, from $6 to $10.00

MGM Collector Series, Pepsi, 1975, 6", Tom, Jerry, Tuffy, Barney, Droopy or Spike, ea, from $10 to......................$12.00

Mickey Mouse, Happy Birthday, Pepsi, 1978, Daisy & Donald, from $12 to..$15.00

Mickey Mouse, Happy Birthday, Pepsi, 1978, Horace & Clarabelle, from $15 to...$20.00

Mickey Mouse, Happy Birthday, Pepsi, 1978, Mickey, Minnie, Donald, Goofy, Pluto, Uncle Scrooge, ea, from $6 to..$8.00

Mickey Mouse, Mickey's Christmas Carol, Coca-Cola, 1982, 3 different, ea...$10.00

Mickey Mouse, Through the Years, Sunoco/Canada, 1988, 6 different (1928, 1938, 1940, 1955, 1983 & 1988), ea, from $5 to $10.00

Mickey Mouse, see also Disney Characters

Mister Magoo, unknown promotion, many different variations & styles, ea, from $25 to...$35.00

NFL, Mobil Oil, helmets on colored bands, rocks, flat, Colts, Oilers, Steelers, Cowboys, ea, from $2 to $4.00

NFL, Mobil Oil, helmets on wht bands, rocks, ftd, Redskins, Bills, Steelers, Eagles, Buccaneers, ea from $3 to $5.00

NFL, Mobil Oil, 1988, single band, tall, ftd, ea, from #3 to...$5.00

NFL, Mobil Oil, 1989, dbl bands, tall, ftd, ea, from $3 to...$5.00

Norman Rockwell, Arby's, early 1980s, Saturday Evening Post Series, 6 different, numbered, ea, from, $2 to...............$4.00

Norman Rockwell, Arby's, 1987, Summer Scenes, 4 different, tall, ea, from $3 to..$5.00

Norman Rockwell, Arby's/Pepsi, 1979, Winter Scenes, 4 different, short, ea, from $3 to..$5.00

Norman Rockwell, Coca-Cola, boy w/hoe, boy w/sandwich or boy w/fishing pole, 2 different styles, ea, from $3 to.....$5.00

Norman Rockwell, Country Time Lemonade, Saturday Evening Post Series, 4 different, w/authorized logo, ea, from $7 to $10.00

Norman Rockwell, Country Time Lemonade, Saturday Evening Post covers, 4 different, no logo, ea, from $5...............$7.00

PAT Ward, see also Arby's Bicentennial Series

PAT Ward Collector Series, Holly Farms Restaurants, 1975, Bullwinkle, Rocky, Natasha, Boris, ea, from $50 to...$75.00

Peanuts Characters, Camp Snoopy, McDonald's, 1983, wht plastic, Lucy or Snoopy, ea, from $5 to..............................$8.00

Peanuts Characters, I Have a Strange Team, Let's Break for Lunch!, I Got It! I Got It!, wht plastic, ea, from $5 to...$8.00

Peanuts Characters, Kraft, 1988, Snoopy in pool, Lucy on swing, Snoopy on surfboard, Charlie Brown flying a kite, ea..$2.00

Peanuts Characters, Snoopy for President, Dolly Madison Bakery, 4 different, ea, from $4 to................................$6.00

Peanuts Characters, Snoopy sitting on lemon or Snoopy sitting by lg red apple, pedestal bottom, ea, from $2 to...........$3.00

Peanuts Characters, Snoopy Sports Series, Dolly Madison Bakery, 4 different, ea, from $4 to..................................$6.00

Penguin, see Super Heroes

Pepsi, Caterpillar D-10 Tractor, 5⅛", NM, A..................$10.00

Pepsi, Historical Advertising Posters, 1979, 4 different, blk & wht, ea, from $8 to..$10.00

Pepsi, Night Before Christmas, 1982-83, 4 different, ea, from $4 to $6.00

Pepsi, Twelve Days of Christmas, 1976, ea, from $1 to.......$3.00

Pepsi, see also specific names or series

Peter Pan, see Disney Film Classics

Pinocchio, Dairy Promo/Libbey, 1938-40, 12 different, 4¾", ea..$20.00

Pinocchio, see also Disney Collector's Series or Wonderful World of Disney

Pluto, see Disney Characters

Pocahontas, Burger King, 1995, 4 different, MIB, P10, ea..$4.00

Popeye, Kollect-A-Set, Coca-Cola, 1975, any of 6 except Popeye, ea..$5.00

Popeye, Kollect-A-Set, Coca-Cola, 1975, Popeye $7.00

Popeye, Pals, Popeyes Famous Fried Chicken, 1979, 4 different, ea, from $10 to..$20.00

Popeye, 10th Anniversary Series, Popeye's Famous Fried Chicken/Pepsi, 1982, 4 different, ea, from $10 to......$15.00

Porky Pig, see Looney Tunes/Warner Bros

Quick Draw McGraw, see Hanna-Barbera

Rescuers, Pepsi/Brockway, 1977, 8 different, 6¼", ea, from $5 to $10.00

Return of the Jedi, see Star Wars Trilogy

Richie Rich, see Harvey Cartoon Characters

Riddler, see Super Heroes

Ringling Bros Circus Clowns Series, Pepsi/Federal, 1976, 8 different, ea $12.00

Ringling Bros Circus Poster Series, Pepsi/Federal, 1975, 6 different, ea...$20.00

Road Runner & Related Characters, see Warner Bros

Robin, see Super Heroes

Rocky & Bullwinkle, see Arby's Bicentennial or PAT Ward

Sad Sack, see Harvey Cartoon Characters

Sadie Hawkins, see Al Capp

Scooby Doo, see Hanna-Barbera

Sleeping Beauty, American, late 1950s, 6 different, ea.....$15.00

Sleeping Beauty, Canadian, late 1950s, 12 different, ea ...$20.00

Smurfs, Hardee's, 1982, 8 different, ea, from $1 to.............$3.00

Smurfs, Hardee's, 1983, 6 different, ea, from $1 to.............$3.00

Snidley Whiplash, see PAT Ward

Snoopy & Related Characters, see Peanuts Characters

Snow White & the Seven Dwarfs, Bosco, 1938, 3", ea, from $25 to $45.00

Snow White & the Seven Dwarfs, Libbey, 1937-38, 3½", ea.$24.00

Snow White & the Seven Dwarfs, Libbey, 1937-38, 4¾", verses on back, various colors, set of 8................................$165.00

Snow White & the Seven Dwarfs, see also Disney Collector's Series or Disney Film Classics

Spider-Man or Spider-Woman, see Super Heroes

Sports Related, see McDonald's or NFL

Star Trek, Dr Pepper, 1976, 4 different, ea, from $15 to...$20.00

Star Trek, Dr Pepper, 1978, 4 different, ea, from $20 to...$30.00

Star Trek III: The Search for Spock, Taco Bell, 1984, 4 different, ea, from $3 to..$5.00

Star Trek: The Motion Pitcure, Coca-Cola, 1980, 3 different, ea, from $10 to...$15.00

Star Wars Trilogy, Darth Vader, Burger King, 1977, J6, from $12.00 to $15.00.

Star Wars Trilogy: Star Wars; Burger King/Coca-Cola, 1977, 4 different, ea, from $12 to $15.00

Star Wars Trilogy: The Empire Strikes Back; Burger King/Coca-Cola, 1980, 4 different, ea, from $7 to $10.00

Star Wars Trilogy: The Return of the Jedi; Burger King/Coca-Cola, 1983, 4 different, ea, from $4 to........................$6.00

Sunday Funnies, 1976, Broom Hilda, from $100 to........$150.00

Sunday Funnies, 1976, O Annie, Smilin' Jack, Moon Mullins, Gasoline Alley, Terry & Pirates, Brenda Starr, ea, from $8 to $15.00

Super Heroes, DC Comics, Supergirl, Pepsi, 1976, $15.00.

Super Heroes, Marvel/Federal, 1978, Captain America, Hulk, Spider-Man, Thor, ea $100.00

Super Heroes, Marvel/Federal, 1978, Spider-Woman $140.00

Super Heroes, Marvel/7-Eleven, 1977, Captain America, Fantastic Four, Howard the Duck, Thor, ea $20.00

Super Heroes, Marvel/7-Eleven, 1977, Incredible Hulk...........**$25.00**

Super Heroes, Marvel/7-Eleven, 1978, Amazing Spider-Man...**$30.00**

Super Heroes (Moon) Series, Pepsi/DC Comics, 1976, Green Arrow, from $20 to..**$30.00**

Super Heroes (Moon) Series, Pepsi/DC Comics, 1976, Riddler, Green Lantern, Joker, Penguin, ea, from $40 to........**$60.00**

Super Heroes (Moon) Series, Pepsi/DC Comics or NPP, 1976, Aquaman, Wonder Woman, Superman, Supergirl, Flash, ea **$15.00**

Super Heroes (Moon) Series, Pepsi/DC Comics or NPP, 1976, Batman, Batgirl, Robin or Shazam!, ea, from $10 to .**$15.00**

Super Heroes (Moon) Series, Pepsi/NPP, 1976, Green Arrow, ea, from $10 to..**$15.00**

Super Heroes (Moon) Series, Pepsi/NPP, 1976, Riddler, Green Lantern, Joker or Penguin, ea, from $20 to...............**$40.00**

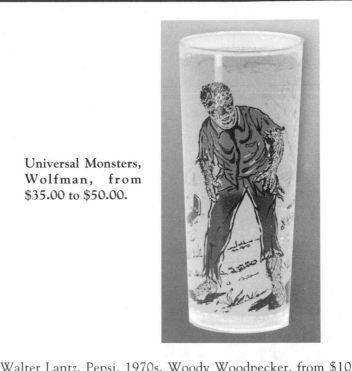

Universal Monsters, Wolfman, from $35.00 to $50.00.

Super Heroes, National Periodical Publications, Batman, 1960s, blue and gray, $15.00.

Superman, National Periodical/M Polaner & Son, 1964, 6 different, various colors, 4¼" or 5¾", ea, from $20 to........**$35.00**

Superman, see also Super Heroes (Moon) Series

Superman the Movie, Pepsi, 1978, 6 different, ea, from $7 to **$10.00**

Sylvester the Cat, see Warner Bros

Tasmanian Devil, see Warner Bros

Tom & Jerry & Related Characters, see MGM Collector Series

Tweety Bird, see Warner Bros

Underdog & Related Characters, see Arby's Bicentennial or Leonardo TTV

Urchins, Coca-Cola/American Greetings, 1976-78, swimming, baseball, skating, tennis, golf, bicycling, ea, from $3 to .**$5.00**

Walter Lantz, Pepsi, 1970s, Chilly Willie or Wally Walrus, ea, from $35 to...**$55.00**

Walter Lantz, Pepsi, 1970s, Cuddles, from $40 to.............**$60.00**

Walter Lantz, Pepsi, 1970s, Space Mouse, from $150 to...**$200.00**

Walter Lantz, Pepsi, 1970s, Woody Woodpecker, from $10 to **$20.00**

Walter Lantz, Pepsi, 1970s-80s, 2-sided, Andy/Miranda, Chilly/Smedly, Wally/Homer, Cuddles/Oswald, ea, from $20 to **$30.00**

Walter Lantz, Pepsi, 1970s-80s, 2-sided, Buzz Buzzard/Space Mouse, from $25 to..**$35.00**

Walter Lantz, Pepsi, 1970s-80s, 2-sided, Woody Woodpecker/Knothead & Splinter, ea, from $15 to..**$20.00**

Walter Lantz, see also Arby's Bicentennial Series

Warner Bros, Arby's, 1988, Adventures Series, ftd, 4 different, Bugs, Daffy, Porky, Sylvester & Tweety, ea, from $15 to **$20.00**

Warner Bros, Marriott's Great America, 1975, 12-oz, 6 different, Bugs & related characters, ea, from $25 to.................**$30.00**

Warner Bros, Marriott's Great America, 1989, 4 different, Porky, Bugs, Taz, Sylvester, ea, from $5 to.................**$10.00**

Warner Bros, Pepsi, 1973, wht plastic, 6 different, Bugs, Daffy, Porky, Sylvester, Tweety, Road Runner, ea, from $3 to..**$5.00**

Warner Bros, Pepsi, 1973, 12-oz, bottom logo, Bugs, Daffy, Porky, Sylvester, Tweety, Road Runner, ea, from $10 to **$15.00**

Warner Bros, Pepsi, 1979, Collector's Series, rnd bottom, Bugs, Daffy, Porky, Sylvester, Tweety, Road Runner, ea $7 to ..**$10.00**

Warner Bros, Welch's, 1974, action poses, 8 different, sayings around top, ea, from $2 to...**$4.00**

Warner Bros, Welch's, 1976-77, 8 different, w/names around bottom, ea, from $5 to **$7.00**

WC Fields, see Arby's Actor Series

Welch's, Dinosaur Series, 1989, 4 different, ea **$2.00**

Welch's, see also Archies, Howdy Doody or Warner Bros

Wendy's, Cleveland Browns, Dr Pepper, 1981, 4 different, ea, from $5 to..**$8.00**

Wendy's, New York Times, 1981, 4 different, ea, from $3 to ..**$5.00**

Wendy's, Pittsburgh Press, 8 different, ea, from $2 to.........**$4.00**

Wile E Coyote, see Warner Bros

Winnie the Pooh, Sears/WDP, 1970s, 4 different, ea from $7 to **$10.00**

Wizard of Id, Arby's, 1983, 6 different, ea, from $7 to **$10.00**

Wizard of Oz, Coca-Cola/Krystal, 1989, 50th Anniversary Series, 6 different, ea, from $6 to...................................$8.00

Wizard of Oz, Swift's, Dorothy, Toto, Scarecrow, Lion, Tin-man, Wizard, plain, wavy or fluted bottoms, ea, from $12 to $18.00

Wizard of Oz, Swift's, 1950-60s, fluted bottom, Glinda, from $15 to $25.00

Wizard of Oz, Swift's, 1950s-60s, fluted bottom, Flying Monkies, Winkies, Emerald City, ea, from $15 to......................$20.00

Wizard of Oz, Swift's, 1950s-60s, fluted bottom, Wicked Witch of the West, from $35 to...$50.00

Wizard of Oz, Swift's, 1950s-60s, fluted bottom, Witch of the North, from $25 to..$40.00

Wonder Woman, see Super Heroes

Wonderful World of Disney, Pepsi, 1980s, Snow White, Pinocchio, Alice, Lady & the Tramp, Bambi, 101 Dalma-tians, ea $25.00

Woody Woodpecker & Related Characters, see Arby's Bicen-tennial or Walter Lantz

Yogi Bear, see Hanna-Barbera

Yosemite Sam, Warner Bros

Ziggy, 7-Up Collector Series, 4 different, ea, from $4 to.....$7.00

CHARACTER AND PROMOTIONAL MUGS

Bat Mug, Robin the Boy Wonder, wht glass w/bl image & letter-ing, Anchor Hocking, 1966, from $20 to...................$30.00

Batman, Bat-Man w/Robin logo on wrap-around sheet, plastic, 1966, A $20.00

Batman & Robin, wht plastic w/decal, 1 in series of 4, Arrow Plastics, 1966, A $15.00

Batman Forever, Batman, Riddler, Robin or Two Face, plastic figural heads, Applause, ea...$6.00

Batman Returns, Batman, ceramic figural head $10.00

Burger King, Mardi Gras, 1988 or 1989, blk or wht glass w/letter-ing, pedestal bottom, ea, from $8 to $10.00

Captain Midnight, Ovaltine, 1953, NM, J2......................$55.00

Casper (Movie), Casper, Fatso, Stretch or Stinky, decaled, ea...$7.00

Casper (Movie), plastic figural head of Casper, ea............$12.00

Cheerios, set of 6 w/Scooby Doo, Jabberjaw, Speed Buggy, Mumbly, Dynomutt & Grape Ape, wht plastic, 1970s, EXIB, J5 ....$45.00

Disney, Pepsi Collector Series, 4 different featuring Mickey, Minnie, Donald & Daisy, milk glass, ea, from $8 to ..$10.00

Donald Duck, Enesco, 1960s, emb pnt image of Donald's head w/name above, EX, P6 ....$50.00

Garfield, I'm a Vikings Fan-Atic!, ceramic, 1978, 3½", A .$3.00

Garfield, McDonald's, 1987, 4 different, ea.........................$2.00

Gulf Oil, Collector Series Limited Edition, Indiana Glass Co, 1980s, clear glass w/images, 6 different, ea, from $3 to..$5.00

Howdy Doody, ...Be Keen Drink Chocolate Flavored Ovaltine!, red plastic w/decal, 1950s, EX $60.00

Jetsons, Wendy's, set of 4 ....$8.00

Little Orphan Annie, Ovaltine, Beetleware, complete w/red lid, NM, A..$65.00

Ludwig Von Drake, ceramic, 1961, 4", NM, J2.................$23.00

McDonald's, Captain Crook (baseball), Grimace (basketball) or Ronald (football), smoked glass, ea $8.00

McDonald's, French Roast or Irish Cream, 1989, ea, from $3 to $5.00

McDonald's, Good Morning, milk glass $2.00

McDonald's, Olympics, 1984, 4 different, ea, from $3 to....$5.00

McDonald's, Slippery Rock, PA, bl ceramic w/wht lettering, A...$8.00

Mickey Mouse, Through the Years, department store issue, early 1990s, 4 different, clear glass, ea, from $3 to $5.00

Mickey Mouse, Through the Years, Pepsi, 1980, 4 different, milk glass, ea, from $8 to...$10.00

Mickey Mouse Club, milk glass, 1955................................$6.00

Munsters, any character, ceramic, 12-oz, EX, F1, ea $10.00

Nestle Quik, bunny head w/ear hdls, plastic, 1970s, 4" $20.00

Pink Panther, figural head, ceramic..................................$15.00

Roy Rogers, cowboy hat w/lid, Quaker, plastic, NM, C1..$65.00

Snoopy, At Times Life Is Pure Joy!, shows Snoopy & Wood-stock, wht milk glass, from $3 to $5.00

Snoopy for President, 4 different, milk glass, ea, from $5 to..$8.00

Three Little Pigs, china, pigs singing Who's Afraid... & dancing on wolfskin rug, Patriot China/WDE, 1930s, 3", A ...$80.00

Welch's Donuts, As you ramble on through life, brother, what-ever be your goal..., milk glass, ftd, 5½" $3.00

Character Bobbin' Heads

Frequently referred to as nodders, these papier-mache dolls reflect accurate likenesses of the characters they portray and have become popular collectibles. Made in Japan throughout the 1960s, they were sold as souvenirs at Disney, Universal Studios, and Six Flags amusement parks, and they were often available at roadside concessions as well. Papier-mache was was used until the mid-'70s when ceramic composition came into use. They were very susceptible to cracking and breaking, and it's difficult to find mint specimens — little wonder, since these nodders were commonly displayed on car dashboards!

Our values are for nodders in near-mint condition. To cal-culate values for examples in very-good condition, reduce our prices by 25% to 40%.

Advisors: Matt and Lisa Adams (A7).

Beetle Bailey, NM, A7, from $100 to.............................$150.00

Bugs Bunny, NM, A7, from $100 to................................$175.00

Charlie Brown, Japan, ceramic w/gr baseball cap & mitt, NM, A7 ....$60.00

Charlie Brown, 1970s, no base, sm, NM, A7 ....$45.00

Colonel Sanders, Kentucky Fried Chicken, 2 different styles, NM, A7, ea, from $100 to $125.00

Danny Kaye, kissing, NM, A7......................................$100.00

Danny Kaye & Girl, kissing, NM, A7, pr.......................$150.00

Dobie Gillis, NM, A7, from $250 to...............................$300.00

Donald Duck, Walt Disney World, sq wht base, NM, A7 ..$75.00

Donald Duck, 1970s, rnd gr base, NM, A7 ....$75.00

Donny Osmond, wht jumpsuit w/microphone, NM, A7, from $100 to...$150.00

Dr Ben Casey, from 1960s TV show, NM, A7, from $100 to ..$125.00

Dr Kildare, from 1960s TV show, NM, A7, from $100 to........$125.00

Charlie Brown, Lego, black square base, NM, $95.00.

Photo courtesy June Moon.

Photo courtesy Matt and Lisa Adams.

Phantom of the Opera and Wolfman, rare, NM, A7, $500.00 each.

Dumbo, rnd red base, NM, A7 ....$100.00

Eisenhower, bl coat, NM, A7, from $100 to $125.00

Elmer Fudd, NM, A7, from $100 to $175.00

Foghorn Leghorn, NM, A7, from $100 to.......................$175.00

Goofy, Disneyland, arms at side, wht base, NM, A7.........$75.00

Goofy, Walt Disney World, arms folded, sq wht base, NM, A7 ....$75.00

Linus, Japan, ceramic, baseball catcher w/gr cap, NM, A7 ..$60.00

Linus, Lego, sq blk base, NM, A7.....................................$95.00

Little Audrey, NM, A7, from $100 to..............................$150.00

Lt Fuzz (Beetle Bailey), NM, A7, from $100 to $150.00

Lucy (Peanuts), Japan, ceramic, gr baseball cap & bat, NM, A7...$60.00

Lucy (Peanuts), Lego, sq blk base, lg, NM, A7.................$95.00

Lucy (Peanuts), 1970s, no base, sm, NM, A7 ....$45.00

Mammy (Dogpatch USA), NM, A7 ....$75.00

Mary Poppins, Disneyland, 1960s, wooden figure w/umbrella & satchel, 5¾", M, P6...$95.00

Maynard Krebs (Dobie Gillis), holds bongos, NM, A7, from $250 to...$350.00

Mickey Mouse, Disneyland, red, wht & bl outfit, sq wht base, NM, A7...$100.00

Mickey Mouse, Walt Disney World, bl shirt & red pants, NM, A7 ....$75.00

Mickey Mouse, yel shirt & red pants, rnd gr base, NM, A7 .....$75.00

Mr Peanut, moves at waist, w/cane, NM, A7, from $150 to ..$200.00

New York World's Fair, boy & girl in fair outfits, kissing, NM, A7 ....$125.00

New York World's Fair, 1964, globe, NM, A7...................$75.00

Oodles the Duck (Bozo the Clown), NM, A7, from $150 to..$200.00

Pappy (Dogpatch USA), NM, A7.....................................$75.00

Peppermint Patti, Japan, ceramic, gr baseball cap & bat, NM, A7 ....$60.00

Phantom of the Opera, Universal Studios of California, gr face, NM, A7 ....$150.00

Pluto, 1970s, rnd gr base, NM, A7 ....$75.00

Porky Pig, NM, A7, from $100 to $175.00

Raggedy Andy, bank, mk A Penny Earned, NM, A7 ....$75.00

Raggedy Ann, bank, mk A Penny Saved, NM, A7...........$75.00

Roy Rogers, Japan, 1962, compo, name on gr sq base, 6½", M, from $150 to $200.00

Roy Rogers, NM, A7, from $150 to $200.00

Roy Rogers, 1950s, compo figure on gr decaled base, EX+..$250.00

Schroeder (Peanuts), Lego, sq blk base, lg, NM, A7........$95.00

Sgt Snorkel (Beetle Bailey), NM, A7, from $100 to $150.00

Smokey the Bear, holds shovel, rnd base, NM, A7, from $125 to..$200.00

Smokey the Bear, holds shovel, sq base, NM, A7, from $125 to..$200.00

Snoopy, as Flying Ace, 1970s, no base, sm, NM, A7 ....$45.00

Snoopy, as Joe Cool, 1970s, no base, sm, NM, A7...........$45.00

Snoopy, in Christmas outfit, 1970s, no base, sm, NM, A7..$45.00

Snoopy, Japan, ceramic, gr baseball cap & mitt, NM, A7...$60.00

Snoopy, Lego, sq blk base, lg, NM, A7.............................$95.00

Space Boy, blk space suit & helmet, NM, A7 ....$75.00

Speedy Gonzales, NM, A7, from $100 to.........................$175.00

Three Little Pigs, bl overalls & yel cap, rnd red base, NM, A7, ea..$100.00

Topo Gigio, standing w/out fruit, standing w/apple, orange or pineapple, NM, A7, ea..$75.00

Tweety, NM, A7, from $100 to $175.00

Wile E Coyote, NM, A7, from $100 to............................$175.00

Winnie the Pooh, 1970s, rnd gr base, NM, A7, from $100 to...$150.00

Woodstock, Japan, ceramic, w/bat, NM, A7....................$60.00

Woodstock, 1970s, no base, sm, NM, A7.........................$45.00
Yosemite Sam, NM, A7, from $100 to.............................$175.00
Zero (Beetle Bailey), NM, A7, from $100 to..................$150.00

Character Clocks and Watches

Clocks and watches whose dials depict favorite sports and TV stars have been manufactured with the kids in mind since the 1930s, when Ingersoll made a clock, a wristwatch, and a pocket watch featuring Mickey Mouse. The #1 Mickey wristwatch came in the now-famous orange box commonly known as the 'critter box,' illustrated with a variety of Disney characters. There is also a blue display box from the same time period. The watch itself featured a second hand with three revolving Mickey figures. It was available with either a metal or leather band. Babe Ruth stared on an Exacta Time watch in 1949, and the original box contained not only the watch but a baseball with a facsimilie signature.

Collectors prize the boxes about as highly as they do the watches. Many were well illustrated and colorful, but most were promptly thrown away, so they're hard to find today. Be sure you buy only watches in very good condition. Rust, fading, scratches, or other signs of wear sharply devalue a clock or a watch. Hundreds have been produced, and if you're going to collect them, you'll need to study *Comic Character Clocks and Watches* by Howard S. Brenner (Books Americana) for more information.

Note: Our values are typical of high retail. A watch in exceptional condition, especially an earlier model, may bring even more. Dealers (who will generally pay about half of book when they buy for resale) many times offer discounts on the more pricey items, and package deals involving more than one watch may sometimes be made for as much as a 15% discount.

Advisor: Bill Campbell (C10).

See also Advertising; California Raisins.

CLOCKS

Photo courtesy June Moon.

Batman and Robin Talking Alarm Clock, Janex Corp., 1974, VG+, from $40.00 to $50.00.

Bambi Alarm Clock, Bayard/France, image of Bambi & Thumper looking at butterfly, rnd chrome case, bl base, 5", EXIB, A $125.00
Batman, Electro-Optix, 1989, lg image of Batman in center, other characters at 12, 3, 6 & 9, plastic, 9" dia, NM, M17...$40.00
Betty Boop Pendulum Clock, Poppo, pnt wood figure w/dial in middle, eyes move, 14½", EX, A..............................$500.00
Big Bad Wolf Alarm Clock, Ingersoll, image of wolf w/nodding head pointing at the 3 pigs, rnd red case, 4½", EX, A $650.00
Big Bird Alarm Clock, Bradley, 1970s, VG, J5.................$35.00
Cinderella Alarm Clock, Bradley/Japan, image of Cinderella leaving slipper on steps, 3" dia, scarce, MIB, A.......$125.00
Disneyland Alarm Clock, Bradley, musical analog, wht plastic body, Mickey as band leader w/parade of characters, EX, P6..$125.00
Doc (Snow White & the Seven Dwarfs), 1970s, plastic figure w/dial in stomach, w/up w/pendulum, 7", unused, A .$50.00
Donald Duck Alarm Clock, Bayard/France, image of Donald w/lg arms, rnd lt bl case, 5", EXIB...........................$200.00
Donald Duck Alarm Clock, Glen Clock/Scotland, farm scene w/Donald holding bird, metal case, 5x5", scarce, EX (NM box), A..$500.00
Flintstones Alarm Clock, Sheffield, 1960s, ceramic standing figure of Fred w/dial in middle, 8½", VG+, A.............$185.00
Heinz Talking Alarm Clock, Mr Aristocrat (Tomato Man) standing next to Heinz logo clock on rnd base, 10", NMIB, A $125.00
Howdy Doody Talking Alarm Clock, It's Howdy Doody Time on rnd dial next to Howdy sitting on Clarabell's feet, 7", EX, A $200.00
Lady & the Tramp, 1970s, plastic figure of Lady w/dial under chin, w/up w/pendulum, unused, 7", NM, A..............$50.00
Little Sprout Talking Alarm Clock, Little Sprout holds rnd dial in front on rnd base, 10½", EX, A...............................$25.00
Mickey Mouse Alarm Clock, Bayard/France, image of Mickey w/lg dial arms & nodding head, rnd red case, 5", MIB.........$330.00
Mickey Mouse Alarm Clock, Bayard/France, image of Mickey w/lg dial arms & nodding head, rnd red case, 5", EX, A......$135.00
Mickey Mouse Alarm Clock, Bradley, 1970s, MIB, P6.....$90.00
Mickey Mouse Alarm Clock, Bradley, 1970s, Mickey's lg face on dial, red rnd case w/lg blk ears atop, ftd, NM, A........$50.00

Mickey Mouse Alarm Clock, Ingersoll, 1930s, electric, lg rotating Mickey, gr case, 4x4", NMIB, A $2,200.00

Mickey Mouse Alarm Clock, Ingersoll, 1930s, w/up, lg Mickey & seconds dial w/3 rotating Mickeys, gr case, 4x4", MIB.......$2,200.00

Mickey Mouse Alarm Clock, Vantage, Mickey figure w/stationary arms, rnd red case w/dbl gold-tone bells, ftd, 4", NM, A..$50.00

Mickey Mouse Choo-Choo Talking Alarm Clock, Bradley, plastic case resembling train engine w/Mickey atop, 8½", MIB, A $50.00

Mickey Mouse Wall Clock, lg wristwatch w/plastic strap, image of Mickey w/arms as clock hands, 9" dia w/30" strap, M, A...$85.00

Mickey Mouse Wall Clock, W Germany/WDP, 1960s, mc diecut wooden image of Mickey w/pendulum, 11½", EXIB, P6 ....$175.00

Minnie Mouse Travel Alarm Clock, Bradley/WDP, 1970s, metal case holds 2" dia clock, MIB, A $100.00

Peanuts Alarm Clock, Janex, 1974, rnd dial next to Charlie Brown & Snoopy sleeping, EX, A $25.00

Pinocchio Alarm Clock, Bayard/France, 1940, bust image by characters dial, rnd chrome case, bl base, 5", EXIB, A........$225.00

Planters Peanuts Alarm Clock, Mr. Peanut on face, EX, $50.00.

Pluto Alarm Clock, Bayard/France, 1978, image of Pluto in front of doghouse on rnd dial, 5", MIB, A $265.00

Pluto Wall Clock, Allied, plastic figure w/clock attached to his chest, hands shaped as dog bones, 8", EX (EX box), A $440.00

Popeye Alarm Clock, Smith Alarm/Great Britian, Popeye & Sweet Pea at play, rnd wht case, EX (EX box), A ...$385.00

Popeye Alarm Clock, Smith Alarm/Great Britian, Popeye & Sweet Pea at play, rnd wht case, 5", VG (VG box), A $250.00

Roy Rogers Alarm Clock, Ingraham, 1940, Roy on Trigger riding through canyon, sq gr case, 5", EX (EX box), A $385.00

Roy Rogers Alarm Clock, Ingraham, 1940, Roy on Trigger riding through canyon, sq gr case, 5", VG (VG box), A $225.00

Sesame Street Talking Alarm Clock, rnd dial in building w/Big Bird reading to Ernie & Oscar the Grouch, 11", EX, A $25.00

Raggedy Ann and Andy Talking Alarm Clock, NM, from $25.00 to $35.00.

Shmoo Pendulette Alarm Clock, Lux, ca 1950, figural w/dial in middle, 8", EX+ (EX box), A $200.00

Sleepy (Snow White & the Seven Dwarfs), Miken, 1950s (?), plastic figure w/dial in middle, eyes move, 8½", VG, A.....$100.00

Snow White Alarm Clock, Bayard/France, 1960s, Snow White w/bird in center, dwarfs, etc next to numbers, 4½", MIB, A..$350.00

Star Wars Talking Alarm Clock, rnd dial on base next to figures of R2-D2 & C-3PO, 8½x6½", EX+ (EX+ box), A .$175.00

Thunder Cats Talking Alarm Clock, molded characters on base w/rnd dial, 7", EX, A..$25.00

Woody Woodpecker Alarm Clock, Westclox, image of nodding Woody w/spatula at Cafe tree, rnd wht case, 5½", EXIB..$400.00

POCKET WATCHES

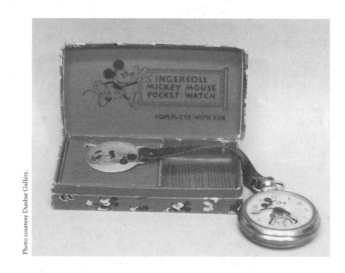

Mickey Mouse, Ingersoll, 1935, complete with fob, EX (EX box), $1,250.00.

GI Joe Combat Watch, Gilbert, w/compass & sighting lenses, EXIB..$250.00

Mickey Mouse, Bradley, 1970s, name flanks image w/moving arms, rnd gold-tone case w/train emb on back, 2", EX, A...$125.00

Mickey Mouse, Bradley, 1970s, name flanks image w/moving arms, rnd gold-tone case w/train emb on back, 2", MIB, A...$300.00

Mickey Mouse, Ingersoll, 1933, lg image w/sm Mickeys on seconds dial, rnd chrome case, w/fob, rare, VG (VG box), A..$950.00

Mickey Mouse, Lorus, 1980s, full-figure Mickey on dial, rnd gold case w/chain, MIB, A...$100.00

Mickey Mouse, USA/WDP, image w/lg dial arms, rnd chrome case, MIB, A $75.00

Mighty Mouse, flexing his muscles, NP case, 1⅞" dia, EX+ ..$100.00

Roy Rogers, Bradley, 1959, lg image of Roy w/sm image of Roy on rearing Trigger in background, EX......................$200.00

007 Spy Watch, Gilbert, w/secret lenses, EXIB $295.00

WRISTWATCHES

Alice in Wonderland, Ingersoll, image of Alice on dial, pk fabric strap, EXIB (rnd pk box w/clear plastic teacup), A .$250.00

Archie, Rowan, 1970s, Archie's face spins around on clear plastic disk, red band, MIB (w/Archie & Jughead insert) $75.00

Babe Ruth, Exacta Time, image in baseball diamond, rnd chrome case, chrome stretch band, EX, A $135.00

Bambi, Ingersoll, Shines in the Dark, image of Bambi on dial, chrome case, gr vinyl strap, EXIB (w/gr pen), A......$325.00

Big Jim, Bradley, 1973, figure in red shorts w/arms as hands, Big Jim in bl & red lettering, blk vinyl band, NM, J5....$150.00

Bozo the Clown, 1960s, Bozo's arm stretched across yel dial, gives illusion of Bozo juggling, rpl red band, NM, J5 ....$80.00

Bugs Bunny, Timex/Warner Bros, image w/lg carrots for hands, chrome case, red leather strap, EX, A $100.00

Captain Marvel, Fawcett, 1948, Captain Marvel holding airplane, rnd chrome case, vinyl strap, NMIB, A $600.00

Captain Marvel, Fawcett, 1948, Captain Marvel holding airplane, rnd chrome case, vinyl strap, EX $300.00

Casper the Friendly Ghost, Bradley, 1960s, Casper flies over mountains on bl dial, wht vinyl band, NM, J5 ....$150.00

Chitty-Chitty Bang-Bang, Sheffield, 1960s, mc image of vehicle, orig red, wht & bl vinyl band, NM, from $150 to ...$200.00

Cinderella, US Time, 1951, on plastic figure, EX..........$115.00

Cool Cat, Sheffield/Warner Bros, 1960s, rpl red band, NM, J5..$80.00

Dale Evans, Bradley, 1950s, rectangular horseshoe image, rectangular chrome case, leather strap, NM (NM pop-up box).$400.00

Dale Evans, Bradley, 1950s, rnd horseshoe image, rectangular chrome case, leather strap, EXIB (missing lid), A ...$165.00

Dale Evans, Bradley, 1950s, rnd horseshoe image, rectangular gold-tone case, tan leather strap, EXIB, A...............$265.00

Daniel Boone, 1960s, cream w/blk image of powder horn below name, rpl band, EX $50.00

Davy Crockett, USA/WDP, image of Davy w/gun on dial, tan leather strap w/silver stenciling, EXIB (w/powder horn), A...$300.00

Dennis the Menace, 1960s, cartoon image of Dennis & Ruff w/name in red, rpl band, EX $75.00

Dick Tracy, New Haven, 1948, rectangular case, NMIB, from $250.00 to $300.00.

Dick Tracy, New Haven, 1948, Tracy pointing gun, rectangular chrome case, tan leather strap, VG (EX box), A.....$165.00

Dick Tracy, New Haven, 1948, Tracy pointing gun, rnd chrome case, leather strap, EXIB, A.....................................$350.00

Donald Duck, Bradley, 1985, 50th Birthday Registered Edition, battery-op, MIB (w/paperwork), P6 ....$150.00

Donald Duck, Ingersoll/US Time, image of Donald w/lg dial arms, chrome case, bl strap, EXIB, A $635.00

Donald Duck, Topolino/Swiss, WDP, image w/lg dial arms, rnd chrome case, red leather strap, EXIB, A.....................$30.00

Dukes of Hazzard, LCD Quartz, Unisonic, 1981, stainless steel band, NRFB, H4 ....$40.00

Hopalong Cassidy, US Time, ca 1950, Hoppy portrait on gray dial, original band, Hoppy pin with miniature 6-shooter and message from pamphlet, MIB, A, $350.00.

Elmer Fudd, Sheffield, 1960s, Elmer waving hand & holding shotgun, MIB, J5 ....$150.00

Flash Gordon, 1960s, Gary Morrow artwork on dial & box, EXIB, A $200.00

Gene Autry, Wilane, Champion, portrait image on dial, alligator-look strap, EXIB, A..$350.00

Goofy, Helbros, 1971, numbers run backwards as does Goofy, rare, NM (NM plastic box w/orig price tag) $1,000.00

Hopalong Cassidy, US Time, 1950s, bust image, rnd chrome case, blk leather western strap, EXIB (w/cb saddle display), A $400.00

Hopalong Cassidy, US Time, 1950s, bust image, rnd chrome case, blk leather western strap, EX, A $150.00

Hopalong Cassidy, US Time, 1950s, Hoppy & Topper, blk leather western strap, MIB (w/cb saddle display), A $475.00

Huckleberry Hound, Bradley, 1950s, Huck in top hat, EX (EX display box w/pop-up circus & see-through top), A $380.00

Huckleberry Hound, Bradley, 1950s, Huck in top hat, VG (G display box w/pop-up circus & see-through top), A $200.00

Jiminy Cricket, Ingersoll, Shines in the Dark, image of Jiminy on dial, chrome case, bl vinyl strap, NMIB (w/bl pen), A $475.00

Josie & the Pussycats, 1971, Josie playing guitar, red & yel lettering w/musical notes at 12, 3, 6 & 9, EX, J5 ....$250.00

Lassie, 1960s, image of Lassie sitting, wht w/name in bl, EX ..$60.00

Little Pig, US Time, image of Little Pig, rectangular chrome case, red strap, NMIB, A $500.00

Lone Ranger, Hi-Yo Silver, image of Lone Ranger on Silver, rectangular chrome case, tan leather strap, VG, A..$125.00

Lone Ranger, 1950s, flasher image of Roy on rearing Trigger & waving hat, Many Happy Trails..., leather band, EX+ $200.00

Man From UNCLE, 1966, bl w/blk & wht line drawing of Napolean talking on communicator, UNCLE Secret Agent in wht, EX...$100.00

Mary Marvel, orig band, NM..$200.00

Mickey Mouse, box only, 1933, bl w/Mickey standing atop red banner reading Ingersoll Mickey Mouse Wrist Watch, VG, A $60.00

Mickey Mouse, Bradley, 50th Anniversary, image w/lg dial arms, rnd chrome case, blk lizard strap, NMIB, A $85.00

Mickey Mouse, Ingersoll, Mickey Mouse Electric, Mickey w/lg dial arms, rectangular chrome case, blk vinyl strap, NMIB...$100.00

Mickey Mouse, Ingersoll, 1933, Mickey w/lg dial hands & seconds dial, rnd chrome case, chrome bracelet strap, EX, A $550.00

Mickey Mouse, Ingersoll, 1947, Mickey w/lg dial arms & seconds dial, rectangular case, leather strap, VG (VG box), A..$185.00

Mickey Mouse, Ingersoll, 1948, Happy Birthday Mickey, red band, MIB (complete w/silverplated ring & pen), A $735.00

Mickey Mouse, Ingersoll, 1950s, Mickey on face, red band, NM (NM box w/5" plastic Mickey figure), A..................$225.00

Mickey Mouse, Ingersoll/Great Britain, lg image w/sm Mickeys on seconds dial, rnd chrome case, blk leather band, VG, A...$1,000.00

Mickey Mouse, Ingersoll/US Time, 1947, Mickey on rectangular face, vinyl band, complete w/paperwork, NM (EX box)...$300.00

Mickey Mouse, Timex, Mickey w/lg dial arms, red strap, EXIB (missing plastic display figure)...................................$50.00

Mickey Mouse, Topolino/Swiss, WDP, image w/lg dial arms, rnd chrome case, red leather strap, EXIB, A...................$35.00

Mickey Mouse, US Time, 1955, Mickey on rnd face, red band, NMIB (pop-up box w/cb Mickey & Mousketeers sign), A..$265.00

Mighty Mouse, Bradley, Mighty Mouse w/lg dial arms, red strap, EXIB (lt bl cylindrical box), A................................$100.00

Minnie Mouse, Topolino/Swiss, WDP, image w/lg dial arms, rnd chrome case, yel leather strap, EXIB, A $30.00

Photo courtesy Plymouth Rock Toy Co.

Orphan Annie, New Syndicate/New Haven, 1948, replaced brown band, NMIB, from $250.00 to $300.00.

Pluto, Ingersoll, Shines in the Dark, image of Pluto on dial, chrome case, vinyl strap, NMIB (w/pen), A............$500.00

Popeye, 1960s, Popeye opening a can of spinach w/name in red, rpl band, EX $60.00

Porky Pig, Ingraham, 1949, red band, MIB, $345.00.

Porky Pig, Sheffield, 1960s, Porky tipping hat, bl leather band, MIB, J5..$150.00

Raggedy Ann, Bobbs-Merrill, 1971, image of Raggedy Ann w/arms as hands, rpl band, EX $50.00

Red Ryder, Stephen Slesinger, 1949, Red Ryder on horse, rnd gold-plated case, tan cordovan strap, EX, A $600.00

Robin Hood, Viking/Swiss, image of Robin w/bow on dial, rnd chrome case, tan leather strap, EXIB, A $100.00

Rocketeer, Hope, 1991, unused, MOC, J2 ....$35.00

Rocky Jones Space Ranger, image of Ranger climbing into rocketship, rectangular chrome case, blk leather strap, EX, A .$225.00

Roy Rogers, Ingraham, 1951, Roy & Trigger on rectangular face, brn strap, NM (NM box) $400.00

Rudolph the Red-Nosed Reindeer, USA, rectangular chrome case, red vinyl strap, EX..$75.00

Smitty, New Haven, 1935, rectangular chrome case & back, brn leather band, rare, VG, P4 ....$425.00

Smokey the Bear, Bradley, 1960s, Smokey standing w/shovels as hands, slogan at 3 o'clock, EX, J5............................$100.00

Snow White, USA/WDP, image of Snow White, rnd chrome case, red fabric strap, EXIB (missing Snow White figure), A..$60.00

Snow White, USA/WDP, image of Snow White on dial, rnd plastic case, yel strap, EXIB (w/wall hanging of Snow White), A $175.00

Space Patrol, w/compass, EXIB $650.00

Superman, Bradley, Superman image, rnd gold-tone case, gold-tone stretch band, EXIB (lt bl cylindrical box), A ..$165.00

Superman, Dabs/DC Comics, 1977, half-figure on rnd dial, bl leather strap, MIB, A..$130.00

Tom Corbett Space Cadet, Ingraham, 1951, rocket & planet on band, complete w/rocket ship display card, NM, A .$575.00

Tweety Bird, Topolino/Swiss, image w/lg dial arms, rnd chrome case, red leather strap, EXIB, A..................................$50.00

Underdog, Lafayette, 1973, Undersdog's hands point out the time, bl vinyl band, MIB (w/Underdog insert), J5...$250.00

Winnie the Pooh, Bradley, 1960s, Pooh points out the time w/hands, rpl band, EX..$65.00

Woody Woodpecker, Ingraham, image of Woody on dial, chrome case, red strap, NMIB, A $475.00

Yogi Bear, Swiss/Hanna-Barbera, image w/lg dial arms, rnd chrome case, bl leather strap, EXIB, A........................$50.00

Zorro, Fossil, limited edition, MIB (blk w/Zorro logo), W6...$80.00

Zorro, US Time, name in script, chrome case, blk leather strap w/silver-stamped designs, EXIB (w/display hat).......$400.00

Character, TV, and Movie Collectibles

To the baby boomers who grew up glued to the TV set and addicted to Saturday matinees, the faces they saw on the screen were as familiar to them as family. Just about any character you could name has been promoted through retail merchandising to some extent; depending on the popularity they attain, exposure may continue for weeks, months, even years. It's no wonder, then, that the secondary market abounds with these items or that there is such wide-spread collector interest. For more information, we recommend *Collector's Guide to TV Memorabilia, 1960s & 1970s*, by Greg Davis and Bill Morgan; *Howdy Doody* by Jack Koch;

Character Toys and Collectibles, Vols I and II, by David Longest; and *Cartoon Friends of the Baby Boom Era* by Bill Bruegman.

Note: Though most characters are listed by their own names, some will be found under the title of the group, movie, comic strip, or dominate character they're commonly identified with. The Joker, for instance, will be found in the Batman listings.

Advisors: Lisa Adams (A7), Dr. Dolittle; Jerry and Ellen Harnish (H4); Larry Doucet (D11), Dick Tracy; Trina and Randy Kubeck (K1), The Simpsons; Norm Vigue (V1); TV Collector (T6); Casey's Collectible Corner (C1); Bill Stillman (S6), Wizard of Oz.

See also Action Figures; Battery-Operated; Books; Chein; Character Clocks and Watches; Coloring, Activity, and Paint Books; Dakins; Disney; Dolls, Celebrity; Fisher-Price; Games; Guns; Halloween Costumes; Lunch Boxes; Marx; Model Kits; Paper Dolls; Pin-Back Buttons; Plastic Figures; Playsets; Puppets; Puzzles; Records; Toothbrush Holders; View-Master; Western; Windups, Friction, and Other Mechanicals.

Addams Family, doll, Uncle Fester, Remco, 1964, NM, C1..$345.00

Addams Family, key chain, Thing, EX, F1 ....$5.00

Alf, bank, head figure, NMIP, J8 ....$25.00

Alf, doll, stuffed, 18", EX, B10/I2, from $10 to $15.00

Alf, doll, talker, battery-op, 18", B10 ....$25.00

Alf, figures, all characters, Coleco, NMOC, J8, ea $12.00

Alf, lap tray, Let's Do Lunch!, How About Yours?, 1987, EX, I2 ....$15.00

Alfred E Neuman, doll, mk Baby Barry, 1961, vinyl w/HP features, features What Me Worry? tie, 20", scarce, EX .$900.00

Alfred E Neuman, statue, Warner Exclusive, resin, 14", MIB, P12 ....$95.00

Alien, face ring, EX, B10 ....$28.00

Alvin & the Chipmunks, bank, Alvin, 1984, vinyl figure w/harmonica in hand & slot in hat, 9", EX, J5 ....$15.00

Alvin & the Chipmunks, Curtain Call Theater, Ideal, 1983, MIB, B10..$25.00

Alvin & the Chipmunks, doll, Alvin, Ideal, 1983, talker, plush, NM, J8 ....$25.00

Alvin & the Chipmunks, doll, Simon, Ideal, 1964, inflatable vinyl, 16", NMOC, T2 ....$20.00

Alvin & the Chipmunks, On Tour Van, Ideal, 1983, MIB, B10..$28.00

Alvin & the Chipmunks, outfit, Ideal, 1983, for 10" doll, MOC, B10..$8.00

Alvin & the Chipmunks, soap dispenser, Alvin, figure, Helm Products, 1984, MIB, B10/T1, from $8 to $10.00

Andre the Giant, Wrestling Superstars, clip-on figure, MOC, B10..$8.00

Andy Gump & Min, pencil holder, FAS/S2, 1920s, bsk figures standing against sq holder, 5", EX, A $60.00

Annie Rooney, figure, Germany, bsk w/blond yarn braids & felt hat, molded clothes, 4½", EX, H12..........................$155.00

Arachnophobia, figure, Big Bob Spider, Remco, 1990, MOC, H4..$8.00

Archies, activity set, Archies Gang at Pops, Whitman, 1970, complete, MIB, H4 ....$30.00

Archies, tattoos, Topps, 1969, MIP, T2.........................$20.00

Aristocats, doll case, 1970, vinyl, for Barbie-type dolls, 12x9", EX, F8..$30.00

Astro Boy, figure, Japan, 1960s, ceramic, 8", NM, F8.....$200.00

Astro Boy, music box, Japan, 1980s, red ceramic w/blk specks, gold trim, plays theme song, NM, C1 ....$175.00

Astro Boy, squirt gun, plastic, VG, H4.............................$12.00

Baba Louie, bank, plastic figure w/removable hat, EX, H4..$10.00

Baby Huey, Deep View Paint Set, Pressman, 1950s-60s, complete, NM (EX box), F8.......................................$60.00

Back to the Future II, postcards, set of 10 w/different images, 4x6", EX, F1 ....$10.00

Banana Splits, doll, Fleegle, 1970, stuffed pillow-type, 10", EX, F8 ....$35.00

Barney Google, figure, Spark Plug, plaster, 1930s, unauthorized carnival pc, 10" L, EX+, A $100.00

Batman, bank, ceramic figure w/bobbing head, unmk, 5", scarce, NM, A $450.00

Batman, bank, plastic figure standing, Transogram, 1966, bl, yel & flesh-tone pnt accents, 19", VG+ $120.00

Batman, Bat Cave/Carrying Case, Ideal, 1966, accessory for 3" figures, w/6" Vacuform Batmobile, complete, EX $450.00

Batman, Bat Chute, CDC, 1966, metallic bl figure & working parachute, NMOC...$55.00

Batman, Bat Memos, Hallmark, 1966, about 50 pgs w/4 different corner images & words of wisdom, unused, NM, A ...$20.00

Batman, Batarang, Ideal, 1966, 8", NM $80.00

Batman, Batboat, Duncan, early 1970s, blk plastic w/red fin & decals, 8" L, VG+, A $85.00

Batman, Batcuffs, Ideal, 1966, NM, A $100.00

Batman, bath mat, 1976, yel foam w/color graphics of Batman & Robin in the Batboat, EX+, A.............................$40.00

Batman, Batman Helmet & Cape, Ideal, 1966, NM (EX box) ..$150.00

Batman, Batman Utility Belt, Ideal, 1966, EX, A..........$400.00

Batman, Batman Utility Belt, Ideal, 1966, unused, M (NM box)...$2,500.00

Batman, Batmobile slot car, BZ, 1966, plastic w/rubber wht-wall tires, red & silver trim, clear plastic dome, 8", EX...$150.00

Batman, Batmobile w/figures, Duncan, 1970s, blk plastic w/bl Batman & yel Robin, 8", EX, J5 ....$35.00

Batman, bicycle license plate, Gross Signs, 1966, Batman & bats against Gotham skyline, metal, 6x12", EX, A............$30.00

Batman, bicycle license plate, 1966, Bat-Man in red lettering over blk image, metal, 6x12", NM $70.00

Batman, bicycle license plate, 1966, Batmobile #2F3567, yel diecut metal w/bl lettering, red border, 6x12", EX.....$30.00

Batman, bicycle ornament, 1966, 10", EX, A $45.00

Batman, bowl, Joker, Sun Valley, 1966, plastic, 5", EX, A...$20.00

Batman, bumper stickers, 1982, set of 6 w/different images, EX, F1 ....$10.00

Batman, cake topper, Wilton, 1966, plastic figure, 4", NM, very scarce $290.00

Batman, centerpiece, Hallmark, 1966, diecut free-standing Batman & Robin running w/capes flying, NM (NM envelope), A $25.00

Batman, charm bracelet, National Periodical Publications, 1966, MOC, J6, $125.00.

Batman, coins, Transogram, 1966, MIP (sealed), T2........$95.00

Batman, cuff links & tie clip, 1966, card reads Batboy for the All-American Boy, gold-tone, NMOC....................$175.00

Batman, figure, Batman & Robin, Italy, 1966, puffy foam-filled vinyl, pnt fronts w/wht backs, 3½", M, A, pr.............$30.00

Batman, figure set, Ideal, 1966, 3 molded figures of Batman, Robin & the Joker in action poses, NMOC, A $100.00

Batman, Follow the Color Magic Rub-Off Set, Whitman, 1966, 8 wipe-off pictures w/set of 6 crayons, EX (VG+ box), A $75.00

Batman, gloves, Wells Lamont, 1966, imitation leather, unused, MIP, A $85.00

Batman, hat, Joker, 1989, replica of hat worn in movie, EX, F1...$15.00

Batman, helmet & cape, Ideal/NPPI, 1966, vinyl, EX (EX box), A $150.00

Batman, jackknife, 1972, yel plastic w/Batman logo, 3½", NM...$90.00

Batman, kite, Canadian, 1979, vinyl w/Batman graphics, unused, EX (orig pkg) $15.00

Batman, kite, Sky-Way, 1974, inflatable, 45x36", MIP (sealed) $30.00

Batman, magic slate, Watkins/Strathmore, 1966, diecut top w/Batman logo & images of Batman & Robin, no stylus, VG+, A...$35.00

Batman, magic slate, Whitman, 1966, diecut top w/image of Batmobile, EX+ $80.00

Batman, night light, Snap-it, 1966, plastic Batman head w/wings, NM, A...$25.00

Batman, Official Directional Finder, 1966, NMOC, A $30.00

Batman, paddle ball, 1966, wht plastic w/bl outline of Batman & red outline of the Joker on reverse, 10", EX, A..........$20.00

Batman, party hat, Amscan/Canada, 1972, cb w/image of Batman & Robin & Gotham City beyond, M, T2 ....$10.00

Batman, pencil case, 1977, pk vinyl w/colorful image of Batman & Robin in Batmobile, 5x8", NM $30.00

Batman, pillow, 1966, red cloth w/blk, bl & yel lettering & images, standard sz, EX $150.00

Batman, Punch-A-Loon, Riddler, National Latex Products, 1966, red inflatable balloon w/rubber band, EX (EX card)..$45.00

Batman, record & book set, Batman Meets Man Bat, 45 rpm record w/20-pg booklet, EX, F1 ....$10.00

Batman, roller skates, 1966, EX, B10 ....$15.00

Batman, school pouch, 1966, yel plastic trifold in likeness of Batman w/scalloped bottom, EX+, A.......................$40.00

Batman, statue, Robin, cold-cast resin, 15", MIB, F1 ....$50.00

Batman, String Art Kit, Smith, 1976, MIB (sealed).........$35.00

Batman, walkie-talkies, Lone Star, 1966, w/pin-back button, unused, NM (EX box) $300.00

Batman, wallet, Mattel, 1966, yel vinyl w/full-color image of Batman & name, EX, A...$15.00

Batman, wastebasket, 1966, metal w/litho scenes, 10", VG+, A...$55.00

Batman, watch (toy), Bat-Watch, Amsco, 1966, MOC, A..$300.00

Batman, Wrist Radios, Remco/NPPI, 1966, bright bl plastic w/decals, set of 2, NM, A $125.00

Batman, Wrist Radios, Remco/NPPI, 1966, bright bl plastic w/decals, set of 2, NM (EX box) $175.00

Batman & Robin, bookends, National Periodical, 1966, plaster figures against Gotham on bases w/names, 6½", NM, pr..$225.00

Batman & Robin, pennant, 1966, bl felt w/mc image of Batman & Robin swinging down on ropes, 28", EX $40.00

Batman & Robin, toy watch, Occupied Japan, 1953, diecut tin case w/head images, paper face, ribbon band, M, A..$80.00

Batman Returns, Colorforms, Sparkle Art, MIB, J8 ....$10.00

Batman Returns, dolls, Penguin or Catwoman, Applause, MIP, J8, ea...$12.50

Batman Returns, pencil topper, Penguin, MOC, J8............$6.00

Battlestar Galactica, Colorforms Adventure Set, 1978, no booklet o/w complete & NM (NM box)...........................$20.00

Battlestar Galactica, ID set, wallet-sz, MOC, B10 ....$8.00

Battlestar Galactica, party masks, set of 4, MIP, T1..........$10.00

Battlestar Galactica, Poster Art Set, Craft Master, 1978, complete, NRFP, H4 ....$30.00

Battlestar Galactica, tablecloth, paper, EX, D4..................$3.00

Battlestar Galactica, vehicle, Galactic Cruiser, Larami, 1970s, diecast, MOC, J5 ....$10.00

Battlestar Galactica, wallet, w/Cylon Raider, EX, D4.......$10.00

Beany & Cecil, Beany-Copter, Mattel, 1961, w/3 props, EX, B10..$42.00

Beany & Cecil, Disguise Kit, Mattel, 1962, complete w/18" doll, NM (EX box), F8 ....$80.00

Beany & Cecil, jack-in-the-box, Mattel, 1961, litho tin, music not working o/w NM, F8 ....$90.00

Beetle Bailey, doll, Sarge's dog, plush, NM, T1 ....$45.00

Beetlejuice, doll, talker, EX, B10...................................$28.00

Ben Casey, charm bracelet, 1960s, NMOC.....................$30.00

Ben Casey, Paint-by-Number Set, Transogram, 1960s, unused, EX, J5..$15.00

Ben Casey, sweater guard, 1962, chain w/5 charms & clasp at ea end, MOC, A...$20.00

Betty Boop, doll, Vandor, 1981, bsk, movable head w/jtd arms & legs, 10¼", NM, A $250.00

Betty Boop, fan, Japan, prewar, image of Betty w/movable eyes, 12", NM, A $400.00

Betty Boop, fan, Japan, 1930s, paper foldout-type w/image of Bimbo & 3 images of Betty, 12", EX, A $850.00

Betty Boop, figure, Bimbo, bsk, Japan, ca 1930, jtd, 6", EX+, A...$600.00

Betty Boop, figure, Bimbo Orchestra, bsk, Fleischer Studios/Japan, 3 figures in different musical poses, MIB, A...$500.00

Betty Boop, figure, chalkware, classic pose, 14", NM, A..$275.00

Betty Boop, figure, 1989, bendable, MOC, J8..................$10.00

Betty Boop, mask, Bimbo, celluloid, 6x6", NM, A $175.00

Betty Boop, mask, celluloid, 6x6", NM, A.....................$250.00

Betty Boop, tambourine, Japan, colorful image of Betty surrounded by musical notes, litho tin, 6" dia, VG, A .$315.00

Beverly Hillbillies Car, Ideal, blue and red plastic with seated figures, 23", EX (original box), A, $470.00.

Beverly Hillbillies, Colorforms, 1963, missing booklet & few pcs, EX (VG box) $25.00

Bewitched, tablet, 1964, full-color photo cover, unused, M, T2...$15.00

Big Bird, see Sesame Street

Bionic Woman, bank, Animals Plus, 1970s, Jamie in running suit posed on pile of rocks, NM, C1 ....$40.00

Bionic Woman, slide-tile puzzle, Am Publishing, 1977, MOC, M17 ....$30.00

Blondie, paint set, Am Crayon, 1940, MIB, A $75.00

Blondie, paint set, Dagwood — World's Champ Snake Artist, 1946, EXIB (litho tin), P6................................$40.00

Blondie & Dagwood, apron, King Features, 1959, Cooking Capers w/Blondie & Dagwood, illus w/7 scenes, adult sz, NM, A..$75.00

Blondie & Dagwood, figure, Daisy, Ucagco, ceramic w/hand-pnt features, 4" L, NM, A..$55.00

Bluto, see Popeye

Bonanza, see Western category

Bozo the Clown, Bozo's Pocket Watch, Japan, 1960s, plastic, tin & paper, MIP, P4 ....$6.00

Bozo the Clown, doll, Knickerbocker, 1960, bendable, MIP (sealed), F8..$45.00

Bozo the Clown, doll, Knickerbocker, 1960s, 18", EX, C17..$35.00

Bozo the Clown, doll, Mattel, talker, non-working o/w EX, B10...$18.00

Bozo the Clown, figure, Lakeside, 1966, bendable, 6", EX, T2...$10.00

Breezely the Polar Bear, doll, Ideal, 1964, stuffed cloth w/wire arms & legs, vinyl face, cloth outfit, 8", M, A $115.00

Buck Rogers, printing set, Stamper Kraft #4080, 1930s, complete, EX (EX box), A $400.00

Buck Rogers, Strato-Kite Kit, NMIB, T1 ....$100.00

Buck Rogers, Super Sonic Glasses, 1950s, NMIB, T1 ....$125.00

Buck Rogers, tablet, John F Dille, 1928, image of Wilma & Buck w/Tootsietoy rocket beyond, unused, scarce, A...$350.00

Buck Rogers, walkie-talkies, Remco/Dille, plastic w/secret decoder, EX (EX box), A.......................................$150.00

Bugs Bunny, candle holder, ceramic, NMIB, T1..............$25.00

Bugs Bunny, doll, Mattel, rubber face, VG, T1.................$20.00

Bugs Bunny, doll, Mattel, 1971, talker, 12", VG, M15.....$25.00

Bugs Bunny, pencil sharpener, figural, NM, T1 ....$15.00

Bugs Bunny, soap dish, vinyl, NM, T1 ....$15.00

Bugs Bunny, tattoos, Topps, 1971, MIP, T2....................$25.00

Bullwinkle, see Rocky & Bullwinkle

Buster Brown, locket, 1920s (?), silver w/encircled emb image of Buster & Tige, rare, NM, A $200.00

Buster Brown, squeeze toy, Froggie the Gremlin, Rempel, 1950s, vinyl, 10", EX, A..$85.00

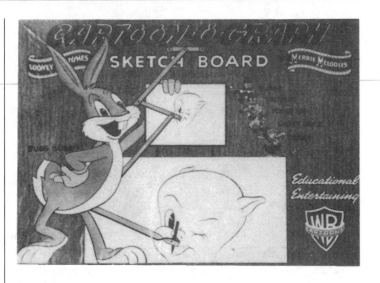

Bugs Bunny, Cartoon-O-Graph Sketch Board, 1950s, NMIB, A, $50.00.

Buster Brown, Yankee Circus Junior Sign Maker, c 1917, complete, VG, A $55.00

Captain America, kite, Pressman, 1966, red & bl graphics, EX (orig pkg), EX, J5..$35.00

Captain America, pennant, Marvel Comics, 1966, cb in plastic sleeve, 3x7", unused, M, A $60.00

Captain Kangaroo, doll, Baby Barry Toys, 1956, stuffed cloth w/vinyl head & hands, glass eyes, 21", scarce, MIB.$200.00

Captain Kangaroo, doll, Mattel, 1960s, stuffed, non-working, 18", EX, J5...$45.00

Captain Kangaroo, Fundamental Activity Set, Lowe, 1977, MIB (sealed), T2...$20.00

Captain Kangaroo, party dress, RKA Inc, 1966, paper w/full-color image of characters on balloons, 23", scarce, M, T2...$10.00

Captain Kangaroo, party dress, 1966, cheesecloth w/full-color illus of various characters, 18", NM...........................$15.00

Captain Kangaroo, Paste Without Paste Set, Jaymar, 1960, 1 picture started o/w unused & NMIB, T2....................$12.00

Captain Kangaroo, Treasure House tent, 1958, canvas w/full-color illus, rare, NM..$75.00

Captain Kangaroo, TV Eras-O-Board Set, Hasbro, 1956, complete, M (EX box), T2 ....$30.00

Captain Marvel, bank, dime register, Fawcett, ca 1948, metal box w/canted corners, press-down trap, 2⅝" sq, G, A........$90.00

Captain Marvel, Magic Flute, 1946, MOC, H12 ....$45.00

Captain Marvel, music box, DC Comics, 1978, ceramic figure on rnd base mk Shazam!, 8", MIB, A.......................$125.00

Casper (Movie), doll, plush, 16", M, D4 ....$20.00

Casper (Movie), figure, Casper on Train, Casper in Treasure Chest, Fatso, Stinky or Stretch, PVC, 3", M, D4, ea ...$4.00

Casper (Movie), figure, Casper or Fatso (flying), PVC, M, D4, ea...$5.00

Casper the Ghost, figure, 1981, inflatable vinyl, 12", MIP, J8 .$12.00

Casper the Ghost, key chains, head figures, set of 4, M, J8 ......$12.00

Casper the Ghost, mobile, Hallmark, 1965, fold-out card w/5 full-color figures, unused, M, T2................................$20.00

Cat in the Hat, doll, talker, sm, NM, T1 ....$60.00

Charlie Brown, see Peanuts

Charlie Chaplin, figure, Germany, 1920, flat tin, 2¼", EX, A $155.00

Charlie Chaplin, figure, Japan, prewar, Charlie holding cane, celluloid, 3¾", NM, A................................$150.00

Charlie Chaplin, musical statue, Hamilton, 1992, plays The Entertainer, MIB, F1..................................$20.00

Charlie McCarthy, bank, compo & tin, standing w/head tilted & hands in pockets wearing blk tux & hat, no monocle, 10", EX....$250.00

Charlie McCarthy, bank, pot metal, seated on trunk in blk tux & top hat, red hair, movable jaw, no monocle, 5¾", EX, A $275.00

Charlie McCarthy, bank, pot metal, standing next to trunk in blk tux & top hat, 7¾", no trap, VG.....................$110.00

Charlie McCarthy, doll, Effanbee, pnt rubber standing figure in blk attire w/decal on lapel, w/monocle, 8¾", EX, A...$525.00

Charlie McCarthy, figure, compo, standing w/hands in pocket, blk attire, no monocle, string-activated jaw, 13", EX, A.......$50.00

Charlie McCarthy, figure, plaster, Bo-hunkin', 1940s, 15", EX, A...$35.00

Charlie McCarthy, figure, wood, seated in blk & wht cloth attire, wht face w/rosy cheeks, blk hat, w/monocle, 7", EX, A $635.00

Charlie McCarthy, pencil sharpener, 1930s, orange Bakelite w/decal, 1¼" dia, scarce, NM, from $65 to $85.00

Charlie McCarthy, spoon, 1940s, silverplate, EX, C1 ......$20.00

Charlie's Angels, beauty kit, 1970s, complete w/cosmetics, mirror & bag, MIB, H12 ....$65.00

Charlie's Angels, beauty set, features Kate Jackson, MOC, B10...$12.00

Charlie's Angels, carrying cases, 1970s, cream vinyl w/show & names in brn repeated design, 3-pc set, EX................$50.00

Charlie's Angels, jewelry set, 1977, complete w/headband, earrings & necklace, MOC, B3 ....$10.00

Charlie's Angels, Talk Time Telephone, Fleetwood, 1977, MOC, M15 ....$45.00

Child's Play, doll, Chucky, Play by Play, 1992, stuffed cloth w/suction cups on hands & feet, real hair, 12", EX, F1 ....$30.00

Child's Play, doll, Chucky, PMI, 1991, MIB, H4..............$20.00

Child's Play, doll, Chucky, stuffed cloth w/vinyl face & real hair, 24", rare, EX, F1 ....$50.00

Child's Play, postcards, set of 3, 4x6", EX, F1.....................$5.00

Child's Play II, doll, Chucky, unused, M, T1 ....$22.00

Chipmunks, see Alvin & the Chipmunks

CHiPs, Colorforms, 1981, MIB, C1................................$20.00

CHiPs, motorcycle, Empire Toys, 1977, riding toy w/pedals, NMIB, M17 ....$165.00

Chucky, see Child's Play

Clarabell, see Howdy Doody

Comic Heroes, iron-on transfers, Fawcett, ca 1944, set of 24 (1 missing), unused, NM (EX+ envelope), A..................$70.00

Creature from the Black Lagoon, figure, Remco, 1980, 9", NM, H4 ....$125.00

Daffy Duck, figure, jtd wood, 1930s, 6½", rare, EX, H12 ..$125.00

Dagwood, see Blondie

Daredevil, pennant, Marvel Comics, 1966, The Man Without Fear!, cb in plastic sleeve, unused, 3x7", M, A $40.00

Dennis the Menace, Crayon By Number Set, Standard Toycraft, 1950s, missing few crayons, EX (EX box), F8 ....$50.00

Dennis the Menace, mug, 1962, red-pnt plastic, minor chips on bk o/w EX, B14 ....$12.00

Dick Tracy, bank, Sparkle Plenty, plaster figure in highchair w/emb profile of Tracy, 12", EX+, A.......................$675.00

Dick Tracy, Braces (suspenders), Deluxe, 1950s, w/badge, magnifying glass & whistle, NM, D11 ....$90.00

Dick Tracy, camera, Seymour Sales, 1950s, NMIB, $75.00.

Dick Tracy, Cartoon Kit, Colorforms, 1962, complete, NM (NM box), T2 ....$60.00

Dick Tracy, charm, from gumball machine, Sam Catchem, Gravel Gertie or Sparkle Plenty, D11, ea...................$20.00

Dick Tracy, charm, from gumball machine, Tracy, D11...$25.00

Dick Tracy, Crime Stopper Set, John Henry #812, 1950s, w/badge, handcuffs, wooden nightstick & card, VG, D11 ....$30.00

Dick Tracy, Dick Tracy Special Agent, Larami, 1972, w/badge & handcuffs, NMOC, D11 ....$35.00

Dick Tracy, Dick Tracy's Handcuffs for Jr, John Henry #800, 1940s, EX (orig card), D11 ....$50.00

Dick Tracy, figure, Rubb'r Niks, bendable, w/gun, wrist radio & shoulder holster, M (NM card), D11 ....$45.00

Dick Tracy, Fingerprint Lab, Parliament Toy, 1953, complete, EX (EX box), A $135.00

Dick Tracy, flashlight, 1950s, bl w/red top, image of Tracy on side, EXIB, D11...$50.00

Dick Tracy, lamp, Plasto, 1940s, bust form on rnd base w/name, 12", EX, A $750.00

Dick Tracy, mechanical pen, 1940s, celluloid w/floating images of Tracy, Tess & Jr, EX+, A $145.00

Dick Tracy, Mini Color Televiewer, Larami, 1972, VG+, D11 ....$25.00

Dick Tracy, pocketknife, 1950s, Dick Tracy Detective, single blade, wht case w/Tracy holding gun, 2¾", EX, D11.$75.00

Dick Tracy, Radio Receiver, 1961, holster set w/earpiece, MIB, A $100.00

Dick Tracy, tie tack, 1930s, Dick Tracy Jr Detective Agency, scarce, EX, D11 ....$90.00

Dick Tracy, TV Watch, plastic wristwatch viewer w/2 boxes of paper film strips, EX, D11 ....$20.00

Dick Tracy, wallet, 1973, blk vinyl w/profile image of Tracy, NM, D11 ....$20.00

Dick Tracy, wrist radio, Da Mayco, 1947, scarce, unused, MIB, D11 ....$1,000.00

Dick Tracy, wrist radios, Remco, 1960s, plastic, complete, NMIB, J5 .... $95.00

Dick Tracy, yo-yo, MOC, J8 .... $8.00

Dick Tracy (Movie), place mat, MOC, B10 .... $8.00

Ding Dong School, Finger Paints, 1950s, MIB, H12 .... $55.00

Ding Dong School, Mr Bumps figure set, Barry Products, 1955, MIB, T2 .... $60.00

Ding Dong School, record player, RCA Victor, 1953, wht plastic w/slot for 45-rpm record, Miss Frances on front, EX, T2 .... $130.00

Ding Dong School, Spools & Corks & Pipe Cleaners Set, Space-Master, 1953, complete, M (EX box), A $45.00

Dr Dolittle, bath toy, Fun Sponge, Amsco #1591, NM, A7 .... $30.00

Dr Dolittle, card game, Post Cereal premium, NM, A7 .... $15.00

Dr Dolittle, Cartoon Kit, Colorforms, 1967, complete, NM (EX box), A $15.00

Dr Dolittle, doll, Pushmi-Pullyu, 1960s, 2 stuffed bodies as 1 going in different directions, 5", EX, J5 .... $25.00

Dr Dolittle, lawn shower spray, AJ Renzi, 1975, pk sea snail, NM $50.00

Dr Dolittle, medical playset, Hasbro #1345, NM, A7 .... $75.00

Dr Dolittle, Mystery Chamber Magic Set, Remco, 1939, NMIB, A7 .... $30.00

Dr Dolittle, Paint- & Pencil-by-Number Set, Hasbro #3673, EX, A7, from $20 to $25.00

Dr Dolittle, party cup, Hallmark, plastic, NM, A7 .... $10.00

Dr Dolittle, playhouse, Mattel #5125, vinyl w/characters pictured, NM, A7 .... $60.00

Dr Dolittle, Ride-Em Rocker, Pushmi-Pullyu, AJ Renzi, 1974, NM, A7 .... $50.00

Dr Dolittle, Ride-Em Stick, Pushmi-Pullyu, AJ Renzi, plastic, 1972, NM, A7 .... $40.00

Dr Dolittle, Stamp & Paint Set, School House #D-100, NMIB, A7 .... $25.00

Dr Dolittle, wrist flashlight, Bantamlite #DW-30, NM, A7 .. $30.00

Dr Kildare, magic slate, Lowe, 1962, cb w/lift-up erasable film sheet, 12x8", unused, NM, A $50.00

Dr Kildare, Pencil-by-Number Coloring Set, Standard Toykraft, 1962, complete, NMIB, A $20.00

Dr Seuss, book bag, Horton the Elephant, cloth w/yel, red & blk graphics, 12x10", EX+ $50.00

Dracula, doll, Commonwealth, 1970s, beanbag body w/cloth face & plush hair, 8", EX, F8 .... $25.00

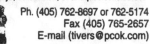

Dr. Suess, Yertle the Turtle and Horton the Elephant, Coleco, 1983, plush, EX+, $35.00 each.

Dracula, doll, Hamilton Presents, 1992, vinyl w/cloth cape, 14", EX, F1 .... $30.00

Dracula, doll, Presents, 1992, vinyl w/cloth cape, 14", MIB, H4 .... $25.00

Dudley Do-Right, figure, Fun-E-Flex, 1972, 5", MOC $25.00

Dukes of Hazard, bank, General Lee, plastic, 14" L, EX, D4 .. $15.00

Dukes of Hazzard, Wrist Racer, Knickerbocker, 1980, Police Cruiser, MOC, P3 .... $10.00

Dum Dum, figure, Kaplast, 1960s, vinyl w/hand-pnt features, movable head, 8", rare, NM, A $425.00

Elmer Fudd, pencil holder, 1940s, diecast figure, NM, T1 .. $125.00

Elmer Fudd, ring, 1970s, cloisonne, M, J8 .... $12.00

Elvira, belt, 1986, MIP, M17 .... $18.00

Elvira, earrings, 1986, MOC, M17 .... $28.00

Elvira, eyelashes, MOC, H4 .... $5.00

Elvira, make-up kit w/earrings, MOC, H4 .... $10.00

Emergency, Rescue Truck, LJN, 1975, red plastic, 14", MIB, M17 .... $135.00

ET, bank, 1982, ceramic figure, 6", EX, F1 .... $15.00

ET, doll, Showtime, 1982, plush, 8", NM, P3 .... $6.00

ET, postcards, 1982, full color, set of 10 w/different images, EX, F1 .... $10.00

ET, sponge ball, 1982, EX, F1 .... $6.00

ET, sticker, Diamond Toymakers, 1982, 6x6", MIP, F1 .... $10.00

ET, sticker sheet, Topps, 1982, uncut, EX, F1 .... $15.00

Evel Knievel, Sky Cycle, Ideal, 1976, diecast metal & plastic, MIB, M17 .... $60.00

Fall Guy, truck, Fleetwood, 1981, motorized take-apart model, NMOC, H4 .... $8.00

Fantastic Four, notebook binder, Marvel Comics, 1975, mc image of comic book #159, Havoc in the Hidden Land, EX+, A $35.00

Fat Albert, figure, PVC, 1980s, NM, J8 .... $8.00

Fat Albert, wrist TV, 1981, MOC (stapled), B10 .... $8.00

Felix the Cat, bank, cast image of Felix w/nodding head atop soccer ball, 5½", rare, EX, A $850.00

Felix the Cat, bop bag, Dartmore Corp, 1950s, inflatable vinyl w/image of Felix, 11", EX $25.00

Felix the Cat, bowl, Germany, 1920s, ceramic, wht w/early version of Felix, blk rim band, 6½" dia, EX+, A...........$350.00

Felix the Cat, figure, bsk, standing w/hands behind back, 6", EX, A..$165.00

Felix the Cat, figure, cb, 1950s, Felix holding fish, diecut, 10", EX, T2...$20.00

Felix the Cat, figure, compo, 1930, movable arms, 13", EX+, A..$575.00

Felix the Cat, figure, terra cotta, enameled, 1920s, walking pose w/hands behind back on rectangular base, 3½", EX, A..$165.00

Felix the Cat, figure, wood, Ideal, 1940s, jtd figure, 9", EX+, A..$350.00

Felix the Cat, figure, wood, jtd, posed as skier w/Mio Mao (French) lettered on chest, 4", EX+, from $300 to ..$450.00

Felix the Cat, Magna-Slide Cartoon Drawing Set, Multiple Toys, 1960s, EX, F8 ....$70.00

Felix the Cat, note holder, Germany, 1930s, celluloid figure, 2", rare, M, A..$80.00

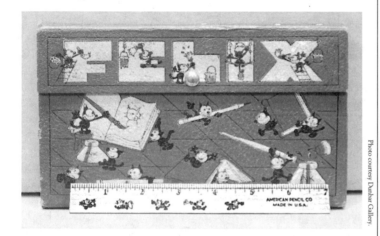

Felix the Cat, pencil box, American Pencil Co., Felix in various activities and poses, complete, 5x8", NM, $175.00.

Felix the Cat, pencil boxes, tin, set of 3 w/different images, M, P12 ....$35.00

Felix the Cat, pillowcase, Vogue Needlecraft #196, 1930s, 18x36", VG+, A $115.00

Felix the Cat, TV Color Set, Lido, 1950s, complete w/viewer & 8 films, NM (EX box), A.................................$140.00

Felix the Cat, walker toy, 1920s, wood figure w/metal legs, pushed by attached rod, 11", NM, A $130.00

Fish Police, figures, Angel, Crabby or Inspector, bendable, MOC, B10, ea...$15.00

Flash Gordon, beanie w/fins & goggles, 1950s, NM, J2..$400.00

Flash Gordon, figure, chalkware, EX, C10.....................$500.00

Flash Gordon, postcard, 1967, M, C10 ....$15.00

Flash Gordon, space outfit, Esquire Novelty, unused, MOC, J2...$190.00

Flash Gordon, Strato-Kite Kit, MIP, T1 ....$85.00

Flash/Whiz Comics, bedspread, 1970-72, cloth w/images of comic book covers, 90x54", NM, A.....................$1,000.00

Flash/Whiz Comics, pillow, 1960s-70s, cloth w/reversible images of comic book covers, NM, A $450.00

Flintstones, bank, Barney & Bamm-Bamm, plaster, 1960s, NM...$85.00

Flintstones, bank, Fred, 1973, plastic figure, EX, B10.......$30.00

Flintstones, bank, Pebbles, vinyl, sleeping, EX, T1...........$22.00

Flintstones, bank, Pebbles & Dino, bl vinyl, 13", EX, J2 ..$45.00

Flintstones, barometer, Bamm-Bamm, Schall, 1966, stone-like figure in tube, changes color w/weather change, 4", NMIB, A $75.00

Flintstones, bubble pipe, Bamm-Bamm, Transogram, 1960s, EX, C17/J2, from $20 to $30.00

Flintstones, Building Boulders, Kenner, 1963, complete, EX (VG box), T2 ....$30.00

Flintstones, Cockamamies skin transfers, 1961, MIB, A...$35.00

Flintstones, coin holder, Fred, 1975, yel or bl plastic, NM, B14 ....$5.00

Flintstones, coin purse, 1975, NM, J2 ....$23.00

Flintstones, doll, Bamm-Bamm, w/cloth clothes & club, 18", VG+, T1 ....$45.00

Flintstones, doll, Barney, Knickerbocker, cloth, 7", MIB (sealed), J2 ....$20.00

Flintstones, doll, Barney, Knickerbocker, 1960s, plush & vinyl, 12", EX, C17 ....$75.00

Flintstones, doll, Barney, 1962, squeeze vinyl w/gr hair, 6", EX, B10 ....$12.00

Flintstones, doll, Dino, Knickerbocker, 1960s, vinyl head w/plush body, NM, T1 ....$85.00

Flintstones, doll, Pebbles, Knickerbocker, 1970s, stuffed, 6", NM (worn box), J5 ....$25.00

Flintstones, doll, Pebbles, Mighty Star Ltd, 1982, cloth body w/vinyl head & limbs, 12", MIB, H4......................$55.00

Flintstones, Electric Drawing Set, Lakeside, 1962, complete, NM (VG box) $70.00

Flintstones, figure, Fred, pop-up, NM, T1 ....$20.00

Flintstones, figures, all characters, Just Toys, bendable, MOC, J8, ea..$10.00

Flintstones, Fred Flintstone Wonder Whiskers, Henry Gordy, 1988, magnetic drawing toy, EX, H4............................$5.00

Flintstones, gumball bank, Fred, Hasbro, 1968, plastic head figure, 8", EX, F8 ....$50.00

Flintstones, Pebbles and Bamm-Bamm in cradle, Ideal, plastic, 14½" long, EX, $125.00.

Flintstones, lamp, 1960-61, plastic full-figure of Fred as base, image of Fred & Barney fishing on shade, 10", NMIB, A $650.00

Flintstones, night light, Barney, Electricord, 1979, MOC, H4..$6.00

Flintstones, party horn, 1960s, yel plastic w/raised images, 8", scarce, NM, A...$140.00

Flintstones, pencil holder, Fred, 1974, plastic, various colors, M, B14, ea...$5.00

Flintstones, slippers, mk Worlds Largest Mfg of Soft-Sole Slippers, blk vinyl w/mc graphics, NM (EX box), A......$200.00

Flintstones, squeeze toy, Barney, Lanco, 1960s, 6", NMIP, A $135.00

Flintstones, squeeze toy, Wilma, Lanco, 1960s, 5", NMIP, A ..$135.00

Flintstones, sticker & iron-on set, 1976, various designs, MIP, B14, ea $10.00

Flintstones, wallet, features Dino, Estelle, 1964, vinyl, NMOC...$35.00

Flintstones (Movie), doll, Mattel, 1993, talker, MIB, B10..$18.00

Flintstones (Movie), figures, any character, 1993, MOC, B10, ea..$5.00

Flintstones (Movie), Flintmobile, Mattel, 1993, unused, MIB, B10 ....$10.00

Flipper, magic slate, Lowe, 1963, cb w/lift-up erasable film sheet, 12x8", M, A..$45.00

Flipper, music box, Mattel, 1960s, plastic Flipper pops up, VG, J5...$15.00

Flipper, Stardust Paint Set, Hasbro, 1966, missing 1 pnt vial & picture o/w NMIB, A...$50.00

Flying Nun, Oil Painting by Numbers, Hasbro, 1967, MIB (sealed), A $140.00

Frankenstein, doll, Remco, 1979, w/pants & shirt, EX, B10 .$18.00

Freddy Krueger, doll, talker, Matchbox, 18", NRFB, H4 ..$50.00

Freddy Krueger, glove, adjustable wrist & finger straps w/bendable fingers, MOC, F1...$25.00

Freddy Krueger, see also Nightmare on Elm Street

Froggie the Gremlin, see Buster Brown

G-Man, pencil sharpener, 1930s, red Bakelite pistol-shape w/decal, 2", NM, A..$75.00

G-Man, pocket siren, Cortland, litho tin, crank action, 2x3", NM, A $125.00

G-Men, pencil box, mk G-Men Clues, 1930s, red, blk & silver cb, 11x6", EX, A $85.00

G-Men, tablet, 1952, full-color photo of Jackie Coogan & Russell Hayden, unused, 10x8", EX, A.........................$12.00

Garfield, bank, vinyl, w/San Diego Chargers helmet or Denver Broncos helmet, MIB, W2, ea $16.00

Garfield, bib, image of Garfield riding in sleigh, MOC, W2 ..$2.00

Garfield, Big Birthday Party, Colorforms, MIP, W2 ....$6.00

Garfield, bubble necklace, pk lid & cord, MIP, W2.............$5.00

Garfield, clip-on, Fool for a Hug, EX, W2 ....$2.00

Garfield, clip-on w/bayberry scent, Garfield dressed as Santa, MIP, W2...$4.00

Garfield, doll, dressed as baseball player, plush, orig tag, M......$14.00

Garfield, doll, dressed as Santa Claus, plush, orig tag, M, W2 .$16.00

Garfield, doll, dressed as tennis player, plush, missing racket o/w M, W2...$5.00

Garfield, doll, Mattel, 1980s, talker, eyes move, NM, J8..$25.00

Garfield, figure, ceramic, Garfield as Graduate, Look Out World Here I Come, EX, W2 ....$12.00

Garfield, figure, ceramic, Garfield on roller skates, 2", EX, W2..$10.00

Garfield, figure, ceramic, Garfield w/toothy grin, 4", EX, W2..$25.00

Garfield, figure, ceramic, To Dad From a Chip Off the Old Block, Garfield wearing a tie, EX, W2 ....$12.00

Garfield, figure, PVC, dressed in football uniform, MIP, W2..$5.00

Garfield, figure, PVC w/suction cup, dressed as Santa w/candy canes, EX, W2...$5.00

Garfield, figure, PVC w/suction cup, in Santa hat w/snowball, EX, W2..$5.00

Garfield, growth chart, 3 sheets, MIB, W2 ....$16.00

Garfield, marbles, Qualatex, 1 Garfield & 1 Odie, MIP, W2 ..$5.00

Garfield, music box, Baby's First Christmas, train circles Garfield & plays 'Toyland,' M, W2 ....$20.00

Garfield, ornament, Hallmark, 1991, Garfield on a star, MIB, W2..$20.00

Garfield, ornament, Nutcracker, 1988, MIB, W2 ....$35.00

Garfield, pencil case, Empire, shows Garfield & Odie playing tug o' war, MIP, W2...$6.00

Garfield, pencil pouch, Empire, shows Garfield surfing on a pencil, M, W2 ....$2.50

Garfield, pencil topper, in Hawaiian shirt w/suitcase, EX, W2 ..$2.00

Garfield, play money, 80 pcs, MIP, W2.............................$3.00

Garfield, slide-tile puzzle, MIP, W2 ....$4.00

Garfield, slippers, orange plush w/image of Garfield, M, W2 .$10.00

Garfield, soap, Twincraft/Canada, MIB, W2.....................$4.00

Garfield, tile, 'Out to Lunch,' shows Garfield sleeping, ceramic, EX, W2...$16.00

Garfield, tote bag, image of Garfield & Odie in Christmas stockings, red & gr vinyl, EX, W2.....................................$5.00

Garfield, tray, Garfield's Cafe, tin, EX, W2........................$8.00

Garfield, trinket box, Garfield on top holding Be My Valentine heart, ceramic, EX, W2 ....$25.00

Garfield & Odie, jack-in-the-box, Pop Goes the Odie, MIB, W2..$30.00

Gentle Ben, doll, Mattel, 1967, talker, 18", VG, M15 .....$50.00

Ghostriders, figure, Blackout, Skinner, Ghostrider, Ghostrider II or Vengeance, Toybiz, 1995, MOC, B10, ea..............$10.00

Gilligan's Island, figure, Gilligan, 1977, vinyl, 3", EX, B10...$8.00

Gilligan's Island, figure, Skipper, 1977, vinyl, 3", VG, B10...$6.00

Gilligan's Island, tablet, 1965, full-color photo of Gilligan & Skipper, unused, 10x8", NM, A $20.00

Gizmo, see Gremlins

Godzilla, doll, Toho, 1985, fully articulated, w/tag, 13", NM, P3..$20.00

Great Ape, picture kit, Arrow, 1970s, felt cut & paste coloring set, MIB (sealed), J5...$15.00

Green Hornet, charm bracelet, 1966, complete w/5 charms, MOC, B3 ....$90.00

Green Hornet, ring, figural, NM, J2 ....$38.00

Green Hornet, ring, flicker type, NM, J2 ....$25.00

Green Hornet, ring, 1966, from bubble gum machine, adjustable gr plastic w/removable hornet mounted on peg, M, A......$35.00

Green Hornet, spoon, silverplated, C10............................$15.00

Green Hornet, wallet, Mattel, vinyl, M, P12 ....$95.00

Green Hornet, whistle, Chicken of the Sea premium, 1966, replica of the Hornet's Sting, plastic, 3", VG+, from $400 to...$600.00

Gremlins, doll, Gizmo, Spain, plush, 14", MIB, D4........$200.00

Gremlins, doll, Gizmo, Spain, plush, 8", MIB, D4..........$100.00

Gremlins, doll, Gizmo, vinyl, MIB, T1 ....$20.00

Gremlins, pencil topper, Stripe, M, D4...........................$4.00

Gremlins, sticker book, hardcover, rare, EX, J8 ....$15.00

Gulliver's Travels, drum, Paramount, 1939, 6", EX+, A.$100.00

Gumby, doll, Applause, 1989, stuffed cloth, w/guitar & headband, 6", M, J8..$10.00

Gumby, figure, Pokey, bendable, 3", EX, B10...............$4.00

Gumby, figure, Pokey, bendable, 6", EX, B10...............$6.00

Gumby, figure, Pokey, Prema Toys, 1984, bendable, 12", EX, B10...$10.00

Gumby, paddle ball, Imperial Toys, 1980s, MIP, J8..........$15.00

Happy Face, pencil sharpener, M, J2 ....$25.00

Harry & the Hendersons, doll, Harry, Galoob, 1990, talker, 24", NRFB, M15..$50.00

Harry & the Hendersons, doll, Harry, plush, 18", MIB, T1 .$25.00

Harry & the Hendersons, figure, Harry, bendable, 6", MOC, B10...$8.00

He-Man, see Masters of the Universe

Heathcliffe, bank, plastic, figural, EX, T1 ....$10.00

Hector Heathcote, magic slate, Lowe, 1964, 12x8", scarce, EX, T2 ....$60.00

Henry, squeeze toy, 1950s, NM, T1...............................$85.00

Herman & Katnip, Deep View Paint Set, Pressman, 1961, complete, M (EX box), T2 ....$60.00

Honeymooners, slide-tile puzzle, 1950s, EX (on card w/photo image of Ralph Kramden & caricatures of Trixie & Norton), A...$115.00

Hong Kong Phooey, candle, 1976, MIP, J2.....................$25.00

Howdy Doody, barrette, Clarabell, Nemo/Kagran, 1952, plastic, NMOC, A..$100.00

Howdy Doody, boxing gloves, Parvey Mfg Co, 1950s, M (EX box), A...$150.00

Howdy Doody, Color Television Set, Am Plastic Toy, complete w/viewer & 5 rolls of film, NM (VG box), A.........$525.00

Howdy Doody, cookbook, Welch's, 1950s, characters pictured on cover & throughout, EX, J5.................................$45.00

Howdy Doody, costume, Princess, Bland Chamas/Kagran, VG+ (EX box), A..$150.00

Howdy Doody, crayon set, Milton Bradley, 1950, complete w/16 lg crayons, pages to color & color guide, VG (VG box), J5..$65.00

Howdy Doody, doctor set, Ja-Ru, 1980s, MOC, J5 ....$15.00

Howdy Doody, doll, Goldberger, 1982, stuffed cloth w/vinyl head & hands, 11", NRFB, M15..................................$25.00

Howdy Doody, doll, Ideal, 1950s, talker, stuffed cloth w/plastic head, movable eyes & jaw, 19", no boots or belt, EX, A $315.00

Howdy Doody, doll, Ideal, 1950s, talker, stuffed cloth w/plastic head, movable eyes & jaw, 19", EX (EX box), A ..$1,800.00

Howdy Doody, doll, Ideal, 1965, molded plastic w/movable head & arms, blk cloth jacket & pants, 9", scarce, NM, A...$60.00

Howdy Doody, doll, 1950s, plastic w/cloth clothes, lever on back of head moves jaw, 8", EX, A $185.00

Howdy Doody, doll, 1970, stuffed body w/hard plastic head & vinyl hands, 12", EX, J5...$45.00

Howdy Doody, doll (box only), Howdy Doody, Peter Puppet Playthings, 1950s, NM, J5...$45.00

Howdy Doody, Doodyville Village, 6 Welch's Grape Juice boxes make up houses, uncut, EX+, A $260.00

Howdy Doody, earmuffs, 1950s, shaped like Howdy's face, EX+, J5 ....$95.00

Howdy Doody, Ever Ticking Toy Watch, Ever Tick/Kagran, 1950, Howdy's head bob's back & forth w/ticking sound, NMOC, A...$250.00

Howdy Doody, face ring, C10 ....$100.00

Howdy Doody, figure, Clarabell, Ben-Her/Kagran, latex w/music box on waist, 12", rare, NM (EX card mk Bend-Me Toy), A...$250.00

Howdy Doody, figures, Tee-Vee, 1950s, red & bl plastic, Howdy, Mr Bluster, Dilly, Princess & Clarabell, set of 5, EX, J5..$150.00

Howdy Doody, football, 1950s, wht kids-sz w/blk line drawing of Howdy, 7", EX, J5..$85.00

Howdy Doody, jack-in-the-box, c Bob Smith, figure of Howdy standing at microphone pops out of plastic box, EX+, A...$310.00

Howdy Doody, Magic Twinkle Doll, AHMCO Prod/Bob Smith, 6" plastic figure of Howdy sitting on rnd wooden base, NMIB, A...$500.00

Howdy Doody, Make Your Own Puppet Show, Whitman/Kagran, 1952, cb, missing 2 pcs, EX, A....................$125.00

Howdy Doody, musical toy, Clarabell, 1950s, mk Howdy Doody's Clarabell, twist nose for action, diecut cb, 9x7", EX, A...$1,900.00

Howdy Doody, night light, Nor'east Nauticak, 1950s, plastic figure w/movable head sitting on rnd wood base, 6", NM, A...$60.00

Howdy Doody, Oil Painting Set for Beginners, Kagran, 1950, Simple as ABC, unused, MIB, A..................................$120.00

Howdy Doody, pencil case, 1950s, clear vinyl w/Howdy on front, w/pencils, crayon & sharpener, VG, J5.....................$45.00

Howdy Doody, pencil cup, Leadworks, 1988, ceramic figure, MIB, J8..$30.00

Howdy Doody, pencil holder, Leadworks, 1980s, ceramic bust of Cowboy Howdy, 6", M, J5...$15.00

Howdy Doody, pencil topper, Leadworks, 1988, vinyl head figure, 1½", M, P4...$5.00

Howdy Doody, pillow case, 1950s, wht fabric w/mc name, Howdy's bust image & full-figure friends, 19x31", NM, A.........$525.00

Howdy Doody, playsuit, Clarabell, 1950s, gr & wht w/front pouch, VG+, J5..$65.00

Howdy Doody, pull toy, Howdy on tricycle, Kohner, 1950s, jtd wood body w/plastic head, felt scarf, 8", EX.............$500.00

Howdy Doody, Put on Your Own Tee-Vee Show, 5 ventriloquist figures, plastic, 3", EXIB, A......................................$270.00

Howdy Doody, Ranch House Tool Box, Kagran, 1950s, metal, EX, A...$200.00

Howdy Doody, Sand Forms, Kagran, 1952, plastic heads of Howdy, Clarabell, Flub-a-Dub & Mr Bluster w/hand shovel, NMOC, A...$130.00

Howdy Doody, squeak toy, 13", J6, $85.00.

Photo courtesy June Moon.

Howdy Doody, stationery, Graphic Products, 1971, individual characters on ea sheet, w/envelopes, MIB, J5 ....$25.00

Howdy Doody, straw holder, 1950s, plastic Howdy head w/50 cellophane straws, EX+ (EX+ box), A......................$240.00

Howdy Doody, Sun-Ray Camera, w/attached envelope of developing papers, EX (EX card), A $190.00

Howdy Doody, target set, Ja-Ru, 1980s, MOC, J5 ....$15.00

Howdy Doody, top, Portillo/Mexico, 1950s, litho tin, 10", rare, VG, A $800.00

Howdy Doody, toy watch set, Ja-Ru, 1980s, w/wristwatch & pocket watch, MOC, J5 ....$15.00

Howdy Doody, wallpaper, 1950s, circus design w/characters, 18x24", EX, J5 ....$65.00

Howdy Doody & Clarabell, Slipper Sock Kit, Kagran, 1950s, complete, NM (EX box), A......................................$245.00

Huckleberry Hound, club ring, C10 ....$65.00

Huckleberry Hound, doll, Knickerbocker, red plush tuxedo body w/blk felt hat, rubber face, orig tag, 18", EX+, A $30.00

Huckleberry Hound, flashlight, MIP, T1 ....$20.00

Huckleberry Hound, Lovable Smoking Traveler's Pet, plastic, MOC, P6..$18.00

Huckleberry Hound, pencil case, EX, J2 ....$40.00

Huckleberry Hound, squeeze toy, as fireman, vinyl, VG+, T1 ....$35.00

Huckleberry Hound, tablecloth, paper, 1960s, MIP (sealed) $35.00

Huckleberry Hound, wastebasket, litho tin, yel w/random images of TV friends, 12", EX, A $60.00

Huckleberry Hound & Yogi Bear, breakfast set, Randall & Wood, 1960s, litho plastic, 6 pcs, NM (EX box), A $395.00

I Love Lucy, doll, Ricky Jr, Am Character, 1950s, vinyl w/bl overalls, wht shirt, blk tie & wht shoes, 20", EX+ (EX box)..$500.00

I Love Lucy, doll, Ricky Jr, Am Character, 1953, vinyl w/molded hair, bl sleep eyes, yel cloth outfit, 20", NMIB, A ..$1,300.00

I Love Lucy, Ricky Jr's Layette, Am Character, 1952, sold as accessory to Ricky Jr doll, EXIB, A $800.00

In Living Color, doll, Homey the Clown, Acme, 1992, 24", MIB, F1..$20.00

Incredible Hulk, bank, head form, vinyl, M, T1 ....$20.00

Incredible Hulk, book & record set, Peter Pan, 1981, EX, F1..$10.00

Incredible Hulk, roller skates, Larami, 1970s, gr, MIB......$25.00

Incredible Hulk, switchplate, 1976, glow-in-the-dark, MIP (sealed), C1..$25.00

Incredible Hulk, wallet, 1976, vinyl, unused, NM, C1 .....$18.00

Incredible Hulk & Spider-Man, Shrinky Dinks, Cadence Industries, 1979, M (VG+ box), T2..$12.00

Indiana Jones & the Temple of Doom, sticker sheet, Topps, uncut, F1 ....$15.00

Inspector Gadget, Shrinky Dinks, Colorforms, 1983, MIB, C1..$28.00

Iron Man, pennant, Marvel Comics, 1966, cb in plastic sleeve, unused, 3x7", M, A..$100.00

Jack in the Beanstalk, Magic Bean Bowl, Miracle Bowl/Dell Comics premium, 1950s, w/storybook & figures, M (EX+ box), A..$10.00

James Bond, Electric Drawing Set, Lakeside, 1966, complete, EX (EX box), A $50.00

James Bond, quilt, 1960s, soft wht fabric w/mc illus on both sides, red piping, 52x75", EX, A................................$165.00

James Bond, transistor tape recorder, Bandai, scarce, NM (EX box), A..$525.00

Jerry Mahoney & Paul Winchell, TV Fun Kit, Transogram, 1950s, w/games, toys & cb masks, some contents sealed, EXIB, J5 ....$150.00

Photo courtesy Jon Thurmond.

Jetsons, Slate and Chalk Set, 1960s, unused, MIB, T1, $95.00.

Jetsons, doll, Elroy, 1985, plush w/plastic hat, orig tag, 14", NM, J8 ....$15.00

Jetsons, doll, George, stuffed, M, T1 ....$6.00

Jetsons, figure, any character, Just Toys, bendable, MOC, J8, ea $10.00

Jetsons, magic slate, Watkins-Strathmore, 1962, 12x8", NM, T2 ....$30.00

Jetsons, tote bag, 1960s, bl vinyl, image of Jetson family traveling in space saucer, Astro following, 14x15", NM, A $365.00

Joe Palooka, figure, mk Germany, bsk, 7", EX, H12..........$65.00

Johnny Seven, Combat Phone Set, Topper, 1964, EXIB, J2 ..$40.00

Joker, see Batman

Kermit the Frog, see Muppets

King Leonardo, pencil sharpener, vinyl, MIB, T1.............$20.00

Knight Rider, wrist communicator, MOC.........................$10.00

Krazy Cat, doll, Knickerbocker, 1930, blk velveteen w/blk felt ears & wht face & hands, yel felt boots, 10½", EX, A $1,265.00

Krazy Kat, figure on scooter, Nifty/International Service, 1932, pnt wood, 7", EX, A...$450.00

Land Before Time, doll, Little Foot, JC Penney Exclusive, stuffed cloth, 8", EX, H4..$35.00

Land of the Lost, figures, Christa or Stink, Krofft, 1991, bendable, MOC, B10 ....$8.00

Lassie, doll, Knickerbocker, 1960s, plush w/vinyl face & glass eyes, 12", VG, T2..$12.00

Lassie, Trick Trainer, Mousely Inc, 1956, complete, scarce, NM (EX box), A $275.00

Laurel & Hardy, belt, 1970s, wht vinyl w/blk images, EX, J5...$15.00

Li'l Abner, Paint Set, Gem Color, 1948, complete, unused, NM (VG+ box), A..$50.00

Linus, see Peanuts

Linus the Lionhearted, doll, Mattel, 1965, talker, 21", non-working o/w VG, J2 ....$90.00

Little House on the Prairie, Colorforms, 1978, complete, EX (VG box), A $15.00

Little Lulu, jewelry set, Little Lulu Goes to a Party, 1970s, MOC, J5...$15.00

Little Lulu, ring, 1970s, cloisonne, M, J8 ....$15.00

Little Orphan Annie, dish set, Japan, lustreware, images of Annie & Sandy on wht w/orange border, 22-pc set, EX+, A $175.00

Little Orphan Annie, doll, Knickerbocker, 1982, 6", MIB (sealed), B10 ....$20.00

Little Orphan Annie, doll, Live Long Toys, 1930, jtd compo w/pnt hair & cloth dress, 10½", EX, A $200.00

Little Orphan Annie, doll, Ralph Freundlich/Harold Gray, HP compo w/red cloth dress & blk shoes, 10", EX (EX box), A $575.00

Little Orphan Annie, figure, celluloid, Japan, 1930s, name & Harold Gray on paper band around waist, 7½", NM, A $350.00

Little Orphan Annie, pull toy, mk Lic Bu Ham Arts Syn, 1930s, Annie pulled by Sandy, 7", EX, J5 ....$150.00

Little Orphan Annie and Sandy, figure, plaster, copyright 1973, scarce, M, D10, from $300.00 to $400.00.

Little Lulu, bank, Play Pal Plastics, 7½", no trap otherwise NM, $30.00.

Lost in Space, tablet, 1965, June Lockhart in silver flight uniform on front, unused, NM.......................................$75.00

Love Boat, doctor's set, Fleetwood, 1979, unused, MOC (header card shows Love Boat cast)..$30.00

Lucy, see Peanuts

M*A*S*H, dog tags, NMOC, J2.......................................$20.00

M*A*S*H, sunglasses, plastic, MOC..............................$10.00

Magilla Gorilla, doll, Nanco, 1990, plush, 15", M, C17 ...$15.00

Magilla Gorilla, Paint-by-Number Set, Whitman, 1974, complete w/styrofoam frame, unused, EX (EX box), J5 ....$25.00

Mammy & Pappy Yokum, ceramic, UFS Inc/Al Capp, 1950s, figural heads, 3", EX, A, pr $85.00

Man From UNCLE, flasher ring, Vari-Vue, 1965, silver-colored base w/blk & wht flasher, NM, A................................$30.00

Man From UNCLE, Foto Fantastiks coloring set, Eberhard Faber/MGM, 1965, complete, NM (EX box), A $145.00

Masters of the Universe, invitations, Unique/Mattel, 1983, 8-pack, M (sealed), P3 ....$7.00

Masters of the Universe, Paint & Play Set, diecast figures w/paints, MIB, T1 ....$15.00

Masters of the Universe, party hats, He-Man, Unique/Mattel, 1983, M (sealed bag w/unpunched header), P3............$6.00

Masters of the Universe, Skeletor Staff, electronic, 36", D4 .$12.00

Mighty Mouse, doll, Ideal, 1960s, rubber face w/stuffed body, 11", VG+, T1 ....$25.00

Mighty Mouse, magic slate, Lowe, 1950s, cb w/erasable lift-up film sheet, 11x8", NM, T2......................................$30.00

Miss Piggy, see Muppets

Moon Mullins, figure, bsk, 1930s, standing w/hands in pockets, 7½", VG+, A $75.00

Mork & Mindy, doll, Mork, Mattel, 1979, w/talking space pack, 8", NRFB, H4..$35.00

Mortimer Snerd, doll, Ideal, 1930s, 12", EX, D10, from $375.00 to $450.00.

Mortimer Snerd, doll, Ideal, w/spring arms & legs, brn cloth jacket & pants, wht shirt & tie, w/tag, 12½", M, A...$550.00

Mother Goose, dishes, Ideal, 1940s, plastic, 16-pc set, MIB, A $135.00

Mother Goose, dishes, Ideal, 1940s, plastic, 26-pc set, MIB, A $150.00

Mr Jinx, doll, Knickerbocker, Hanna-Barbera, plush & vinyl, EX, C17..$60.00

Mr Magoo, doll, Ideal, 1962, plush & vinyl w/cloth clothes, 14", EX, A..$50.00

Mr Magoo, doll, stuffed body w/rubber head, felt hands & feet, VG, T1..$75.00

Mr Smith, slide-tile puzzle, Ja-Ru, 1983, MOC, M17.......$20.00

Mr Smith, sunglasses, Ja-Ru, 1983, MOC, M17..............$20.00

Mummy, figure, Playco, 1991, 10", MIB, B10 ....$12.00

Muppets, doll, Kermit the Frog, Fisher-Price, 1981, stuffed cloth, 14", MIB, M15 ....$20.00

Muppets, doll, Miss Piggy, Fisher-Price, 1981, stuffed cloth, 14", MIB, M15..$20.00

Mutt & Jeff, dolls, Switzerland, late 1940s, plaster heads w/jtd body, cloth clothing, 6½"-8", EX, A......................$350.00

Mutt & Jeff, figures, celluloid, HC Fischer/Stasco, 1920s, 5½"-5¾", EX+, A..$225.00

Nancy & Sluggo, dolls, Georgene Novelties, 1944, cloth, 14", M (separate boxes), A $1,000.00

Nancy & Sluggo, music box, Sluggo, Schmid, 1970s, figural, EX, C10 ....$125.00

Nanny & the Professor, Cartoon Kit, Colorforms, 1966, complete, scarce, NMIB, A $60.00

Natasha, see Rocky & Bullwinkle

Nightmare on Elm Street, postcards, set of 15 w/different images, 4x6", EX, F1..$20.00

Olive Oyl, see Popeye

Peanuts, bank, Snoopy on basketball, ceramic, EX...........$20.00

Peanuts, banks, Charlie Brown & Lucy, ceramic, United Feature/Italy, 1968, 7", EX+, pr $45.00

Peanuts, beach bag, Beagle Beach, Colgate premium, wht w/zipper, 9x8", M, H11 ....$20.00

Peanuts, beach bag, Snoopy, Pride of the Beach, 2-hdl, EX, B 10 ....$8.00

Peanuts, belt, Lee/USA, Snoopy & Friends on bl leather, youth sz, G, H11..$4.00

Peanuts, Colorforms, How's the Weather Lucy, EXIB......$20.00

Peanuts, Colorforms, What's on Sale Snoopy?, Snoopy in Store, EXIB, H11 ....$25.00

Peanuts, doll, Baby Sally, Hungerford, vinyl, in red pajamas w/open flap, rare, VG $65.00

Peanuts, doll, Charlie Brown, Hungerford, red shirt, blk pants, 10", EX $55.00

Peanuts, doll, Charlie Brown, 1960, flat rubber, 6", EX, B10....$8.00

Peanuts, doll, Charlie Brown, 1969, inflatable, 16", EX, B10..$12.00

Peanuts, doll, Charlie Brown or Linus, vinyl w/cloth clothes, 7", EX, H4, ea..$20.00

Peanuts, doll, Linus, Hungerford, w/hand out, red shirt, 8½", EX $60.00

Peanuts, doll, Lucy, Determined Toys, 1970s, rag type, 14", MIB, H4..$25.00

Peanuts, doll, Lucy, Hungerford, yel dress & red hat, rare, 7", EX $65.00

Peanuts, doll, Peppermint Pattie, Determined Toys, 1970s, rag type, 14", MIB, H4..$20.00

Peanuts, doll, Snoopy, Determined Toys, plush, jtd, sits or stands, 12", M, H11 ....$15.00

Peanuts, doll, Snoopy, Hasbro, movable head, 12", EX, B10 ...$12.00

Peanuts, doll, Snoopy, Ideal, 1950s, stuffed cloth, MIB, H12 ..$35.00

Peanuts, doll, Snoopy, United Features Syndicate, 1968, cloth, 6½", EX, H4..$15.00

Peanuts, doll, Snoopy, 1966, vinyl w/red plastic collar, 10", EX, B10...$18.00

Peanuts, doll, Snoopy, 1969, inflatable, 18", VG, B10........$8.00

Peanuts, doll, Woodstock, Gund, plush, 36", EX+, P3 .....$20.00

Peanuts, iron-on patch, golf, You're Away, Snoopy at tee, 3" dia, EX, H11...$6.00

Peanuts, jump rope, Snoopy, wht plastic, M $10.00

Peanuts, kaleidoscope, 1971, 9", VG, H11 ....$12.00

Peanuts, kitchen set, Ohio Art, w/3 metal plates & 3 pots & pans featuring Charlie Brown & Snoopy, VG $65.00

Peanuts, napkins, Hallmark, Snoopy for President, MIB $8.00

Peanuts, night light, Monogram, EX, B10.........................$4.00

Peanuts, pencil holder, Snoopy, World's Greatest Tennis Player, ceramic, 3½", EX $18.00

Peanuts, plaques, Snoopy, 1960s, molded plastic, set of 4, rare, 14x8", EX...$20.00

Peanuts, soap holder, Linus, Avon, 1952, vinyl, no soap, EXIB, B10...$14.00

Peanuts, wall plaques, set of 4, EX, B10 ....$12.00

Peanuts, waste can, Charlie Brown & Snoopy, 1969, tin, EX, B10...$14.00

Pee Wee Herman, doll, Vance Pig, talker, MIB, T1 ....$20.00

Peg Leg, doll, Lesney, 1973, w/outfit & map in leg, 8", EX, B10...$25.00

Peter Potamus, doll, Ideal, 1964, stuffed cloth with wire arms and legs, vinyl face, 8", M, $115.00.

Photo courtesy Bill Bruegman.

Peppermint Pattie, see Peanuts

Phantom, iron-on transfer, thin paper, 1965, 8x4", NM, T2 ..$20.00

Pink Panther, doll, plush, 6", M, D4................................$8.00

Pinky Lee, shoe laces, 1950s, pk, NM (w/wrapper), J5 .....$15.00

Planet of the Apes, bank, General Ursus, Apac Productions, 1967, 18", NM, $30.00.

Photo courtesy June Moon.

Planet of the Apes, Colorforms Adventure Set, 1967, EXIB, T1..$25.00

Planet of the Apes, squirt gun, AHI, 1967, plastic, VG ...$55.00

Planet of the Apes, wastebasket, metal w/mc images, 20", EX..$25.00

Pogo, figures, Pogo or Albert Alligator, 1969, EX, ea $8.00

Popeye, Band Box, complete w/4 litho tin instruments & covering sleeve, scarce, NM (EX box) $450.00

Popeye, bank, Daily Dime, KFS, 1956, metal box w/canted corners, image & name on front, 2⅝", EX, A..............$100.00

Popeye, bank, Daily Quarter, Kalon Mfg, 1950, litho tin, 5", scarce, NMIB, A..$450.00

Popeye, bank, Knockout, Straits, litho tin, diecut Popeye & opponent boxing on rectangular base, VG $450.00

Popeye, crayon set, Am Crayon, 1933, MIP, A $80.00

Popeye, doll, Cameo/KFS, 1960s, squeezable vinyl w/jtd limbs & head, 14", NM (EX box), A $450.00

Popeye, doll, Cameo/KFS, 1960s, squeezable vinyl w/jtd limbs & head, 14", EX+..$150.00

Popeye, doll, Gund, vinyl w/cloth outfit, crank lever in back & he laughs, 21", NM...$110.00

Popeye, fan, Japan, prewar, heavy paper w/wood hdl, movable eyes, 7", NM, A $125.00

Popeye, figure, Bluto, squeeze rubber, European, 1940s, flexing muscles on 1 arm, 8", EX, A.....................................$100.00

Popeye, figure, Olive Oyl, squeeze rubber, European, 1940s, standing w/hand on hip, red & blk dress, 7", EX+, A..........$155.00

Popeye, figure, Popeye, celluloid, Japan, prewar, w/string & finger loop, 5½", M, A..........$185.00

Popeye, figure, Popeye, chalkware, 1930s, 12", EX, D10, from $300.00 to $500.00.

Photo courtesy Dunbar Gallery.

Popeye, figure, Popeye, wood, Chein/KFS, 1932, jtd & pnt, w/insignias on arms & feet, 11", VG+, A.........$715.00

Popeye, figure, Popeye & Wimpy, rubber, KFS, 1935, 6"-6½", VG, A, pr..........$75.00

Popeye, figure, Popeye, rubber, KFS, 1935, standing w/arms down at sides, 7", EX, A..........$125.00

Popeye, figure, Wimpy, ceramic, 1980s, M, P12..........$45.00

Popeye, figure, Wimpy, squeeze rubber, standing w/hands behind back, 8", EX, A..........$130.00

Popeye, Flexee-Forms, Shimmel Sons/KFS, 1978, bendable figure inside 14" plastic tray, M..........$18.00

Popeye, flicker rings, Popeye/Sweet Pea, Popeye/Goofy or Popeye/Wimpy, ea..........$10.00

Popeye, kaleidoscope, Largo, 1978, complete w/4 changeable lenses, MOC..........$15.00

Popeye, lamp, KFS, 1935, jtd-wood figure on ship's wheel base, orig shade, 15", EX..........$525.00

Popeye, muffler box, KFS, 1935, snow scene, Blow Me Down Kids! I Ain't Never Cold..., 10x11", EX+, A..........$200.00

Popeye, night light, English, short stubby figure on sq platform, bulb eyes, battery-op, 4½", G, A..........$150.00

Popeye, paint set, Am Crayon, 1933, MIP, A..........$100.00

Popeye, paint set, Hasbro, 1950, Oil Painting by Numbers, complete, NMIB, T2..........$90.00

Popeye, paint set, Kenner, 1961, Presto-Paints, complete & unused, NM (EX box), F8..........$45.00

Popeye, pencil sharpener, KFS, 1930s, Bakelite, 1¾", NM, A..........$85.00

Popeye, Popeye's Spinach Boat, Multiple, 1950s, Popeye & friends in plastic boat, NM (VG box)..........$125.00

Popeye, ring, Olive Oyl, 1970s, cloisonne, M, J8..........$12.00

Photo courtesy Dunbar Gallery.

Popeye, soap, 1930s, complete with Popeye, Olive Oyl and Wimpy, VG (original box), $275.00.

Porky Pig, bank, AJ Renzi, 1964, 15½", rare, EX..........$45.00

Porky Pig, figure, chalkware, 1930s, 7", EX, H12..........$75.00

Porky Pig, figure, Sun Rubber, 1950s, rubber, 6", VG (EX box).$95.00

Porky Pig, ring, 1970s, cloisonne, M, J8..........$12.00

Prince Valiant, bank, Dime Register, King Features, 1954, metal w/canted corners, press-down trap, 2⅝" sq, G.........$200.00

Punky Brewster, doll, Galoob, 1984, 18", NRFB, M15.....$40.00

Quick Draw McGraw, bath soap, MIP, J2..........$15.00

Quick Draw McGraw, doll, Nanco, 1989, plush w/felt hat, 12", NM, F8..........$12.00

Quick Draw McGraw, Lovable Smoking Traveler's Pet, plastic, P6..........$18.00

Raggedy Ann, doll, Knickerbocker, 1970s, stuffed cloth, 12", VG, J5..........$10.00

Raggedy Ann & Andy, kaleidoscope, VG+..........$15.00

Rat Fink, decal, 1990, blk & wht, 6", NM..........$5.00

Rat Fink, decal, 1990, mc, 8", NM..........$5.00

Rat Fink, ring, Macman Ent, 1963, plastic w/detachable figure, MIP, T2..........$30.00

Rat Fink, Rockin' Roadster, Kenner, 1990, MOC, B10....$15.00

Red Baron, musical plane, Schmid Bros, 1968, figure in wooden biplane, wind prop & it plays Auf Weidersehen, 8", NMIB, A..........$75.00

Reginald G Racoon, soap dish, Avon, EX, B10..........$12.00

Ricochet Rabbit, doll, Ideal, 1960s, stuffed plush w/vinyl face, felt hat & vest, 16", rare, EX..........$85.00

Roadrunner, bank, compo, VG+, T1 ....$25.00
Robin, see Batman
RoboCop, doll, w/weapons, 12", MIB (mailer), T1...........$15.00
RoboCop, pencil sharpener, MIP, J8 ....$5.00

Rocky & His Friends, Cartoon Kit, Colorforms, 1961, complete, NMIB, A, 90.00.

Rocky & Bullwinkle, doll, Bullwinkle, plush, 22", NM, J8.$12.00
Rocky & Bullwinkle, doll, Rocky, 1991, stuffed cloth w/vinyl
    cap & goggles, EX, B10..$12.00
Rocky & Bullwinkle, figure, Natasha, Wham-O, MOC, T1 ..$25.00
Rocky & Bullwinkle, figure, Rocky, Wham-O, MOC, T1 ..$25.00
Rocky & Bullwinkle, figure, Snydley Whiplash, bendable,
    Wham-O, EX, H4 ....$28.00
Rocky & Bullwinkle, magic slate, Whitman, 1972, NM ..$18.00
Rocky & Bullwinkle, Pick-Up Stix, MOC, T1 ....$5.00
Rocky & Bullwinkle, wastebasket, litho tin, yel w/random
    images of TV characters, VG, A $145.00
Romper Room, bank, circus clown jack-in-the-box mascot,
    1960s, yel plastic w/pnt accents, 7", EX, A $75.00
Romper Room, bank, Do-Bee sitting on flowering meadow base,
    full-color plastic w/clear wings, 5", NM, A $55.00
Schmoo, figure, vinyl, VG, T1 ....$12.00
Scooby Doo, bank, vinyl, w/sheriff's badge, NM, T1 ....$25.00
Scooby Doo, doll, 1970, stuffed cloth, paper label w/Scooby
    image, 11", EX, A $22.00
Scooby Doo, stamper, Hanna-Barbera, 1983, MOC, B10...$5.00
Scrappy Rainbow, Water Colors, Peterson, complete w/8 vials &
    2 cups, EX (EX box), A $110.00
Sesame Street, bank, Big Bird, plastic, Big Bird sitting on nest,
    8", NM, J8 ....$12.00
Sesame Street, doll, Big Bird, Ideal, complete w/cassette, 25",
    VG, M15 ....$50.00
Sesame Street, doll, Big Bird, Playskool, 1970s, talker, 22", VG,
    M15 ....$25.00
Sesame Street, figure, Big Bird, squeeze vinyl, 3", VG, M15.....$3.00
Sesame Street, figure, Kermit the Frog, Bend 'Ems, MOC,
    J8 ....$8.00
Sesame Street, figures, Applause, 1993, PVC, set of 8, F1 .$20.00

Simpsons, bank, Bart, Street Kids, plastic, any color variation,
    MIB, K1, ea..$12.00
Simpsons, book, Simpsons Fun in the Sun, Harper Perennial,
    softcover, EX, K1 ....$12.00
Simpsons, bulletin board, Roseart, 1990, cork, 16x20", EX,
    F1 ....$15.00
Simpsons, doll, Bart, Dandee, rag-type w/suction cups on hands
    & feet, 8", MIB, K1..$10.00
Simpsons, doll, Bart, Dandee, soft vinyl, 10", MIB, K1 ....$10.00
Simpsons, doll, Bubble Blowin' Lisa, Mattel, blows bubbles
    w/saxaphone, 18", MIB, K1 ....$35.00
Simpsons, dolls, Homer, Marge, Bart or Lisa, cloth bodies
    w/vinyl heads, EX, B10, ea $6.00
Simpsons, figure, Lisa, Jesco, bendable, 3½", MOC, K1 .....$6.00
Simpsons, figure, Maggie, Jesco, bendable, 2", MOC, K1 ...$6.00
Simpsons, figures, Bart in various poses, PVC, MIP, ea $3.00
Simpsons, figures, Homer or Marge, Jesco, bendable, 6", MOC,
    K1, ea $6.00
Simpsons, frisbee, Betras Plastics, wht w/image of Bart's head &
    Radical Dude!, K1 ....$5.00
Simpsons, Homer Simpson Pop Gun Target Set, Ja-Ru, MOC,
    K1 ....$4.00
Simpsons, key chain, Bart, Street Kids, PVC figure on silver
    ring, 3", any color variation, M, K1, ea $3.00
Simpsons, license plate fr, NJ Croce Co, features Bart w/various
    sayings, wht plastic, 6x12", K1, ea $5.00
Simpsons, magazine, Simpsons Illustrated, Spring 1991,
    K1 ....$10.00
Simpsons, magazine, Simpsons Illustrated, Summer 1993,
    K1 ....$8.00
Simpsons, magnet, Marge dancing w/her jello salad, Presents,
    ceramic, 2¾x1¾", K1 ....$4.00
Simpsons, magnets, Homer or Marge, ceramic, 2x3", EX, F1,
    ea..$6.00
Simpsons, pencil sharpener, Noteworthy, 3-D characters in 2"
    snow dome, any character, MOC, K1, ea......................$5.00
Simpsons, pogs, complete set of 50, EX, F1 ....$15.00
Simpsons, poster, features Bart, Western Graphics Corp, Don't
    Have a Cow Man!, 32x21", K1 ....$5.00
Simpsons, Rad Rollers, Spectra Star, set of 6 marbles w/different
    characters magnified in center, MOC, K1....................$8.00
Simpsons, Stamper Pak, Rubber Stampede, set of 4, 1x1", MIP
    (sealed), K1 ....$6.00
Simpsons, valentine stickers, Cleo, set of 36, MOC (sealed),
    K1..$4.00
Simpsons, yo-yo, Spectra Star, wht w/image of Bart on Skate-
    board, MOC, K1 ....$8.00
Simpsons, 1992 Fun Calendar, Random House, M (sealed),
    K1...$25.00
Sinbad Jr, Magic Belt, Voplex, 1965, red plastic w/bl & wht diamond-
    shaped buckle, battery-op light, M (NM box), A $100.00
Six Million Dollar Man, Bionic Video Center, Kenner, EX (EX
    box), H4...$50.00
Six Million Dollar Man, Give-A-Show Projector, Kenner, 1977,
    EXIB, B10 ....$25.00
Six Million Dollar Man, slide-tile puzzle, Am Publishing, 1977,
    MOC, M17 ....$30.00
Skeletor, see Masters of the Universe

Smitty & Spot, figures, bsk, Japan, 1930s, 2½"-¾", EX+ (EX+ box), A..$160.00

Smitty & Spot, figures, bsk, Japan, 1930s, 5"-1½", EX $95.00

Smokey the Bear, doll, Ideal, 1960s, 13", missing 1 eye & hat o/w EX, J5 ....$15.00

Smokey the Bear, doll, inflatable, MIP, T1 ....$15.00

Smokey the Bear, doll, talker, no hat, VG, T1 ....$35.00

Smokey the Bear, hat, felt, EX, T1 ....$12.00

Smokey the Bear, ruler, wooden, M, T1 ....$7.00

Smurfs, doll, Have a Smurfy Birthday, stuffed cloth, 6", EX, B10 ....$6.00

Smurfs, doll, Smurf boy, 1981, stuffed, 12", VG, B10 ....$8.00

Smurfs, doll, Smurf boy, 1981, stuffed, 8", VG, B10 ....$6.00

Smurfs, doll, Smurfette, 1981, stuffed, 12", EX, B10........$12.00

Smurfs, doll, Smurfette, 1981, stuffed, 8", EX, B10..........$10.00

Sneezely the Seal, doll, Ideal, 1964, stuffed cloth w/wire arms & legs, vinyl face, cloth outfit, 8", M, from $85 to........$95.00

Snoopy, see Peanuts

Snydley Whiplash, see Rocky & Bullwinkle

Space Academy, doll, Loki, Hasbro, 1977, EXIB, B10......$28.00

Space Kidettes, magic slate, Watkins-Strathmore, 1967, rare, NM, F8...$40.00

Space Patrol, costume, Boys Wear by Billy the Kid, 1950s, coat, pants, cap & belt w/decoder buckle, VG, A $135.00

Spark Plug, see Barney Google

Sparkle Plenty, see Dick Tracy

Speedy Gonzales, doll, Mighty Star/Looney Tunes, 1971, cloth, EX+, J2 ....$15.00

Spider-Man, bank, plastic bust, Renzi, 1979, red, 15", VG+, A $10.00

Spider-Man, bank, plastic full-figure in action, Renzi, 1979, emb lettering at bottom, 12", NM...................................$18.00

Spider-Man, book & record set, Peter Pan, 1981, EX........$5.00

Spider-Man, brush & comb set, 1970s, MIB....................$25.00

Spider-Man, Colorforms Adventure Set, 1974, unused, M (VG+ box), A $15.00

Spider-Man, doll, cloth, 24", EX+ $15.00

Spider-Man, Fly 'Em High Parachutist & Launcher, AHI, 1976, M (VG card), C1 ....$30.00

Spider-Man, iron-on transfer, 1965, Spider-Man ready to leap, thin paper, 8x4", scarce, M, T2 ....$30.00

Spider-Man, party masks, 1970s, MIP, J8 ....$10.00

Spider-Man, postcards, set of 10 w/different images, EX, F1 ....$10.00

Spider-Man, ring, plastic, red & blk, C10 ....$15.00

Spider-Man, sunglasses, Nasta, 1986, MOC, M17 ....$10.00

Spider-Man, TV tray, Cadence Industries, 1979, image of Spi-der-Man on roof, metal w/fold-out legs, 12x17", EX..$18.00

Spider-Man, walkie-talkies, Marvel Super Heroes Secret Wars, plastic, battery-op, scarce, MIB $35.00

Steve Canyon, helmet, box only, VG $35.00

Steve Canyon, helmet, Ideal, EXIB..............................$65.00

Steve Canyon, scarf & goggles, 1950s, silver plastic goggles & red scarf, EX+ (diecut card of Canyon)......................$65.00

Steve Uerkel, doll, 18", EX, B10 ....$10.00

Super Heroes, see also individual characters

Super Heroes (DC), calendar, 1976, Neal Adams artwork, Super-man, Batman, Wonder Woman, etc, 12x11", M, J5 ....$15.00

Super Heroes (DC), postcard book, Mark IV, 1981, 28 mc detachable cards featuring all of the Super Heroes, unused, M $20.00

Super Heroes (DC), Super Shakers, Ideal, 1979, Superman, Bat-man, Wonder Woman, complete, unused, MIB, J5 ...$35.00

Super Heroes (Marvel), bumper sticker, Marvel Comics, 1978, Warn-ing: I Brake for Marvel Super Heroes, 4x14", M, A $15.00

Super Heroes (Marvel), Colorforms, 1983, complete, NMIB, T2 ....$10.00

Super Heroes (Marvel), pennants, RNS Sales Co, 1966, felt, set of 5, 3x5", unused, MIP $45.00

Super Heroes (Marvel), 3-ring binder, Mead, 1975, plastic tri-fold w/collage of Super-Heroes, NM+, A...................$65.00

Supergirl, doll, Super Queen, Ideal, 1967, vinyl w/cloth dress, red vinyl cape & boots, 12", M, from $275 to.........$325.00

Superman, bank, Dime Register, DC Comics, metal box w/canted corners, 2½", EX-NM, A, from $200 to...$275.00

Superman, belt, Pioneer, 1940s, tan leather w/repeated emb images of Superman, rnd metal buckle w/image & name, NM, A $150.00

Superman, belt buckle, Pioneer, 1940s, bronze, rectangular w/emb image & name below, 1½", VG+, A............$450.00

Superman, Cartoonist Stamp Set, 1966, complete, M (EX+ card)..$35.00

Superman, coloring cloth, Howe, 1966, wht plastic w/line draw-ings to be colored w/wipe-off crayons, 30x28", MIP ..$18.00

Superman, doll, Applause, 1988, 18", NM, B10 ....$25.00

Superman, doll, Mego, 16", EX, B10 ....$35.00

Superman, Flip Flashlight, Bantamlite, 1966, M (EX card)..$85.00

Superman, hairbrush, Avon, MIB, T1................................$10.00

Superman, iron-on transfer, 1950, red & blk w/image of Super-man in front of rocketship, 13x9", EX................$45.00

Superman, magic slate, Whitman, 1965, diecut top w/Superman in action pose & 4 characters down sides, EX...........$45.00

Superman, paddle ball, Imperial Toys, MIP, J8................$12.00

Superman, paint set, Am Toy, ca 1940, used, EXIB, A ..$290.00

Superman, paint set, Transogram, 1954, paint-by-number w/4 canvas sketches & 16 watercolor tablets, unused, NMIB, A $200.00

Superman, paint set, 1966, Sparkle Paints w/5 pictures to paint, NMIB...$65.00

Superman, pencil box, ca 1940, bl image of Superman in flight & name against wood-grain background, VG+, A ..$110.00

Superman, pencil case, 1930s, G+, J2 ....$165.00

Superman, pencils, National Periodical, 1966, set of 12, EX (VG pkg), A $30.00

Superman, pillow, National Periodical, 1966, cloth w/name above Superman flying over Metropolis, 13x13", NM............$30.00

Superman, record & story set, The Flying Train, Musette, 1947, complete, EX, A...$75.00

Superman, slide-tile puzzle, Tot Guidance, 1966, image of Superman flying over Metropolis, EX+, A................$40.00

Superman, Thingmaker Accessory Kit, Mattel, 1960s, complete w/mold, Plastigoop, pnt, brush & pins, MOC, J5 ......$85.00

SWAT, telescope, 1970s, MOC, J8.................................$8.00

Sweet Pea, see Popeye

Sylvester the Cat, doll, velour, 5", VG, B10......................$8.00

Tarzan, belt buckles, from animated show, 1970s, metal, 2 styles, M, J8, ea $10.00

Tarzan, Cartoon Kit, Colorforms, 1966, complete, EX (EX box), A $20.00

Teddy Ruxpin, doll, 1989, complete w/cassette, 14", M, M15 ..$50.00

Terminator, doll, Kenner, 1991, talker, MIB $65.00

Thor, see Super Heroes

Three Stooges, Colorforms, Maurer, 1959, complete, NM (EX box), A, $80.00.

Three Stooges, doll set, Collins, 1982, stuffed cloth, 13", M (separate cards), A $200.00

Three Stooges, flasher rings, Larry, Curly or Moe, Vari-Vue, 1960s, silver-colored plastic, NM, H4, ea $20.00

Three Stooges, Photo Printing Set, Yankee/Maurer, complete, EX+ (VG+ box), from $500 to $600.00

Tom and Jerry, dolls, Georgene, 1949, stuffed cloth, original tag, 16" and 7", M, D10, from $375.00 to $400.00 for the pair.

Three Stooges, puffy stickers, 1984, 2 different pkgs, MIP (sealed), C1 ....$16.00

Tom & Jerry, figure, any character, bendable, MOC, J8, ea ..$10.00

Tom & Jerry, guitar, Mattel, 1965, musical w/up, EX, B10 ...$40.00

Tom & Jerry, jewelry box, Loew's Inc, 1957, full-color paper label on wood, EX $95.00

Tom & Jerry, ring, Jerry, 1970s, cloisonne, M, J8 ....$12.00

Tom & Jerry, water pistols, Marx, 1960s, M, P12 ....$65.00

Tom Corbett Space Cadet, Model-Craft Kit, Kay Stanley, 1950s, complete, NMIB $225.00

Top Cat, bank, 1962, Top Cat standing in trash can, plastic, 10", NM $45.00

Top Cat, doll, Ideal, 1960s, sitting, stuffed cloth body, soft vinyl head w/tongue sticking out, 6", MIB $150.00

Topcats, bank, Benny the Ball, ceramic, NM, T1 ....$65.00

Tweety Bird, doll, Chatter Chum, talker, MIB, T1 ....$25.00

Underdog, harmonica, 1975, yel & gr plastic w/raised image of Underdog on 1 end, 7", NM $15.00

Underdog, pillow, inflatable wht vinyl, EX $15.00

Universal Monsters, stickers, 1960s, cb card features Frankenstein, set of 8, scarce, MOC, A $265.00

Vance Pig, see Pee Wee Herman

Waldo, doll, Mattel, 1991, vinyl, 18", EX, B10 ....$12.00

Weird-Ohs, magic slate, Davey the Way Out Cyclist, 1963, MIP (sealed), T2 ....$30.00

Winky Dink, Paint Set, unused, MIB $65.00

Winky Dink, Super Magic TV Kit, Winky Dink & You!, Standard Toycraft, 1968, unused, NM (M box) $125.00

Wizard of Oz, bank, Dorothy, Arnart Imports, 1960s, hand-pnt, orig paper tag, 7", NMIB, S6 ....$825.00

Wizard of Oz, bank, Scarecrow, Arnart Imports, 1960s, hand-pnt, w/orig tag, 7", NMIB, S6 ....$100.00

Wizard of Oz, bank, Tin Woodsman, Arnart Imports, 1960s, hand-pnt, 7", MIB, S6 ....$135.00

Wizard of Oz, bath beads, Ansehi, 1976, set of 12 in plastic tray, EX (EX window box), S6 ....$75.00

Wizard of Oz, figurine, Dorothy, Avon, 1985, Images of Hollywood series, porcelain, 5½", NM, S6 ....$45.00

Wizard of Oz, flicker rings, Cowardly Lion or Tin Man, C10, ea $100.00

Wizard of Oz, magic wand, Presents, 1989, MOC $5.00

Wizard of Oz, music box lid, 1960s, pnt ceramic, 4x4", NM, S6 ....$50.00

Wizard of Oz, night light, Scarecrow, 1989, MIB $25.00

Wizard of Oz, program, Ice Capades, 1960, Petty cover artist, EX, S6 ....$30.00

Wizard of Oz, puppet, Proctor & Gamble premium, 1965-69, molded plastic head w/vinyl hand cover, 7x10", EX, S6 ....$52.00

Wizard of Oz, toy watch, Occupied Japan, 1940s, features Scarecrow & Tin Woodsman, red fabric band, M, S6 ....$50.00

Wizard of Oz, trinket box, Presents, 1989, ruby slipper, MIB ...$15.00

Wizard of Oz, valentine, Am Colortype, 1940-41, Dorothy, Toto & Scarecrow on yel brick road, 3x5", EX, S6 ....$120.00

Wizard of Oz, wastebasket, Cheinco, 1975, image of characters & map of Oz, 13", G, S6 ....$265.00

Wolfman, doll, Hamilton Presents, 1992, vinyl w/cloth outfit, 14", EX, F1 ....$30.00

Wolfman, figure, Playco Products, 1991, 10", MIB, B10 ..$12.00

Wonder Woman, Colorforms, 1976, MIB........................$25.00

Wonder Woman, mirror, Avon, 1978, plastic hand mirror w/figural Wonder Woman hdl, NMIB................................$15.00

Wonder Woman, sunglasses, 1976, M (VG card), C17....$15.00

Woodsy Owl, doll, stuffed cloth, Don't Pollute, 16", EX ..$25.00

Woody Woodpecker, bank, ceramic, NM, T1 ....$18.00

Woody Woodpecker, cup & bowl set, NM, T1.................$20.00

Woody Woodpecker, harmonica, figural, plastic, early, 6", EX, J2...$30.00

Woody Woodpecker, kazoo, Linden, 1960s, red plastic figure w/adjustable airflow lever, 7", NM, F8 ....$25.00

Woody Woodpecker, movie, Castle Films, 1950s, 8mm, VG (VG box), J8...$8.00

Woody Woodpecker, purse, 1970s, vinyl w/image of Woody as Uncle Sam, NM...$18.00

Woody Woodpecker, ring, 1970s, cloisonne, M, J8 ....$12.00

X-Men, postcards, set of 10 w/different images, EX, F1 ....$10.00

Yellow Kid, doll, Arnold Print Works, 1896, by RF Outcault, yel stuffed cloth w/'Word of Wisdom' on front, 15", EX, A...$1,220.00

Yogi Bear, doll, Huckleberry Hound Products/Hanna-Barbera, 1959, plush, 24", VG+, P3...$25.00

Yogi Bear, doll, 1977, pillow-type w/bells inside, 15", EX, J8 ...$20.00

Yogi Bear, Field Set, w/binoculars, whistle & compass, MOC, T1 ....$10.00

Yogi Bear, figure, Dell, 1960, Yogi sitting on a log, vinyl, 6", EX, T2 ....$30.00

Yogi Bear, figure, Japan, 1962, rubber w/movable head & arms, 6", NM, F8 ....$45.00

Yogi Bear, flashlight, MIP, T1 ....$20.00

Yogi Bear, lamp, plastic figure on rnd base, cb shade lithoed w/various characters, NM, A...................................$130.00

Yogi Bear, lamp shade, Arch, 1962, yel plastic head figure of Yogi grinning, 9", NM, F8 ....$50.00

Yogi Bear, Lovable Smoking Traveler's Pet, plastic, MOC, P6..$18.00

Yogi Bear & Boo Boo, handkerchief, 1960s, 8" sq, EX, J5...$10.00

Yogi Bear & Huckleberry Hound, Cockamamies skin transfers, 1961, MIB...$15.00

Ziggy, mirror, 1970s, MIP (sealed), J8 ....$10.00

Chein

Though the company was founded shortly after the turn of the century, this New Jersey-based manufacturer is probably best known for the toys it made during the '30s and '40s. Wind-up merry-go-rounds and Ferris wheels as well as many other carnival-type rides were made of beautifully lithographed tin even into the '50s, some in several variations. The company also made banks, a few of which were mechanical and some that were character related. Mechanical, sea-worthy cabin cruisers, space guns, sand toys, and some Disney toys as well were made by this giant company; they continued in production until 1979.

Advisor: Scott Smiles (S10).

See also Banks; Disney; Sand Toys.

WINDUPS, FRICTIONS, AND OTHER MECHANICALS

Alligator w/Native Rider, 15", VG, A $200.00

Aquaplane, advances w/spinning prop, passengers litho in windows, 8", NM (EX box), A...................................$525.00

Barnacle Bill Floor Puncher, figure punches bag on rectangular base, litho tin & celluloid, 7", EX $700.00

Barnacle Bill in Barrel, advances in waddling motion w/swaying head, 7", EX, A...$350.00

Bonzo on Scooter, dog on gr & red scooter, 7", VG, A ..$300.00

Cabin Cruiser, 1950s, 15", MIB, H12 ....$100.00

Checkered Cab, 1924, 6", scarce, EX, A.........................$400.00

Clown Floor Puncher, clown hits punching bag, litho tin, 8½", EX, A...$725.00

Disneyland Ferris Wheel, spins w/bell sound, litho tin, 17", NM (G box) $750.00

Disneyland Melody Player, litho tin, complete w/paper cartridge, 7x7", NM (EX box), A..$150.00

Drummer Boy, 1930s, 9", NM, J6, $275.00.

Photo courtesy June Moon.

Happy Hooligan, 1932, 6", NM, $1,700.00.

Photo courtesy Dunbar Gallery.

Greyhound Bus, plate mk Coast To Coast, 2-tone gr w/red tires, 9", EX, A..$325.00

Hand-Standing Clown, balances on hands & moves back & forth, 5", EX, from $125 to.....................................$150.00

Helicopter, 12", NMIB, J2..$250.00

Hercules Jazz Band, early, complete, 13", rare, EX (G box), A..$850.00

Limousine, 1925, passengers & child w/dog in windows, litho tin, 6", EX, A...$200.00

Merry-Go-Round, kids spin around on horses w/bell sound, 10", NM (EX box), A..$800.00

Musical Aero Swing, 4 gondolas spin & fly around center pole, litho tin, 11", scarce, NM (EX box), A $1,000.00

Peggy Jane Sailboat, mk Hercules, 23", scarce, VG $250.00

Indian in Headdress, 1930s, EX, from $150.00 to $175.00.

Photo courtesy Scott Smiles.

Pig, 1938, 5", EX, S10, from $125.00 to $150.00.

Photo courtesy Scott Smiles.

Junior Truck, mk 220 on doors, gr & red w/yel tires, half-figure driver, 8", EX.................................$275.00

Junior Truck, mk 420 on doors, gr w/red tires, half-figure driver, 8", EX..$350.00

Playland Merry-Go-Round, 5 carousel horses w/riders & 5 swans around perimeter, 11" dia, EX (EX box), A.............$800.00

Monkey Bank, 1930s, tips hat when coin is dropped in slot, 5", EX, $100.00.

Photo courtesy June Moon.

Rabbit with Cart, rabbit pulls cart with lithographed rabbits carrying a pumpkin and other animal scenes, 8", NM, from $125.00 to $150.00.

Playland Whip, 4 kids in cars fly around base w/bobbing heads, litho tin, 20" base, NM (EX box), A $1,000.00

Popeye Floor Puncher, litho tin figure on platform hits celluloid bag on rod, 7½", EX, A $850.00

Popeye in Barrel, Popeye waddles back & forth in barrel, litho tin, 7", EX, A $675.00

Popeye Overhead Puncher, litho tin, 10", rare, EX, A .$2,200.00

Popeye Waddler, 1932, advances in waddling motion, litho tin, 6", NM, A $725.00

Rabbit w/Cart, rabbit pulls cart w/litho ducks riding in Express vehicle & rabbit riding an airplane, 8", NM............$175.00

Ride-A-Rocket Carousel, 18", G, A................................$100.00

Ride-A-Rocket Carousel, 4 rockets w/figures circle tower, litho tin w/celluloid props, 18", NM (G box), A $1,100.00

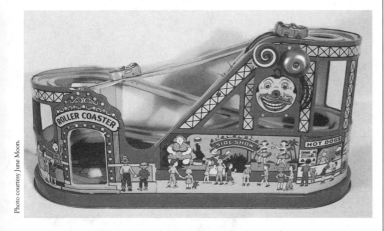

Photo courtesy June Moon.

Roller Coaster, 1930s, complete with 2 cars, EX, from $275.00 to 325.00.

Roller Coaster, 1930s, w/2 cars & bell, 19", NMIB, from $325 to...$375.00

Roller Coaster, 1950s, w/2 cars & bell, 19", EXIB, from $250 to...$300.00

Royal Blue Line Bus, 1927, yel w/red hood & blk fenders, red & bl striping & lettering, 18", G, A $525.00

Seaplane, 1930s, advances w/spinning prop, litho tin, 9", EX+ (G box), A...$250.00

Ski Boy, advances w/ski poles, 8", NM (G box), A $250.00

Ski Ride, kids travel to top of ride, 19½", NM (EX box), A $1,100.00

Space Ride, 1940s, lever action, 9", NM (EX box), A ...$750.00

Toy Town Helicopter, advances w/spinning blades, litho tin & plastic w/blk rubber tires, 13", NM (EX box), A $100.00

MISCELLANEOUS

Army Transport Truck, litho tin w/raised side grille, 8", EX, A $165.00

Cathedral Organ, turn crank & music plays, litho tin, 9½", NMIB...$175.00

Easter Egg, 1930s, take-apart egg w/litho scenes, 5", NM, A $75.00

Lawn Mower, red & yel litho tin, 34", EX, A $85.00

Log Truck, 1925, red & yel litho tin, w/2 logs, 8½", EX, A .$175.00

Popeye Sparkler, 1959, sparks fly behind clear red window inserts, plunger action, EX (VG box), A $265.00

Rabbit Roly Poly, 6", EX..$75.00

Chinese Tin Toys

China has produced toys for export since the 1920s, but most of their tin toys were made from the 1970s to the present. Collectors are buying them with an eye to the future, since right now, at least, they are relatively inexpensive.

Government-operated factories are located in various parts of China. They use various numbering systems to identify types of toys, for instance, ME (metal-electric — battery operated), MS (metal-spring — windup), MF (metal friction), and others. Most toys and boxes are marked, but some aren't; and since many of the toys are reproductions of earlier Japanese models, it is often difficult to tell the difference if no numbers can be found.

Prices vary greatly depending on age, condition, availability, and dealer knowledge of origin. Toys currently in production may be discontinued at any time and may often be as hard to find as the earlier toys. Records are so scarce that it is difficult to pinpoint the start of production, but at least some manufacture began in the 1970s and '80s. If you have additional information (toy name and number; description as to size, color variations, actions, type, etc.; and current market), please contact our advisor. In the listings below, values are for new-in-the-box items.

Advisor: Steve Fisch (F7).

#ME021, police car, current, 16½x5x5", F7, from $55 to .$125.00

#ME060, tank, remote control, 1970s, 7x4x4", F7, from $35 to $75.00

#ME084, jet plane, current, 12½x13x5", F7, from $35 to..$75.00

#ME086, Shanghai bus, MIB, F7, from $85 to................$150.00

#ME087, jetliner, 1980s, 19x18x3", F7, from $55 to $125.00

#ME089, Universe car, 1970s, MIB, F7, from $85 to......$150.00

#ME093, open-door trolley, discontinued, 10x5x4", F7, from $25 to $35.00

#ME095, fire chief car, current, 12½x5x5", F7, from $35 to ..$75.00

Photo courtesy Steve Fisch.

#ME630, Photo car, older version, 12½x5x5", from $35.00 to $125.00.

#ME097, Police car, 13x5x5", F7, from $35 to.................**$75.00**

#ME099, UFO spaceship, current, 8x8x5", F7, from $35 to..**$75.00**

#ME100, robot (resembles 1980s Star Strider robot), current, 12x4x6", F7, from $35 to.............................**$125.00**

#ME102, spaceship, blows air, current, 13x5x4", F7, from $35 to **$75.00**

#ME104, locomotive, 15½x4x7", F7, from $35 to............**$75.00**

#ME105, locomotive, 9½x5½x5½", F7, from $35 to **$75.00**

#ME603, hen & chickens, MIB, F7, from $25 to..............**$50.00**

#ME610, hen laying eggs, current, 7x4x6", F7, from $25 to .**$50.00**

#ME611, News Car or World Cap Car, 5x16½x5", MIB, F7, ea, from $55 to **$125.00**

#ME614, automatic rifle, current, 23x2x8", F7, from $25 to ..**$35.00**

#ME677, Shanghai convertible, 1970s, 12x5x3", F7, from $60 to..**$100.00**

#ME679, dump truck, discontinued, 13x4x3", F7, from $25 to...**$50.00**

#ME699, fire chief car, current, 10x5x2", F7, from $25 to ..**$50.00**

#ME756, anti-aircraft armoured tank, MIB, F7, from $35 to .**$75.00**

#ME767, Universe boat, current, 10x5x6", F7, from $35 to...**$75.00**

#ME767, Universe boat, 1970s, 10x5x6", F7, from $75 to...**$150.00**

#ME770, Mr Duck, current, 9x7x5", F7, from $25 to **$50.00**

#ME774, tank, remote control, 1970s, 9x4x3", F7, from $45 to **$75.00**

#ME777, Universe Televiboat, current, 15x4x7", F7, from $35 to **$75.00**

#ME777, Universe Televiboat, 1970s, 15x4x7", F7, from $75.00 to $150.00.

#ME801, Lunar explorer, 1970s, 12x6x4", F7, from $75 to..**$125.00**

#ME809, anti-aircraft armoured car, 1970s, 12x6x6", F7, from $75 to **$100.00**

#ME821, Cicada, 1970s, 10x4x4", F7, from $50 to.........**$125.00**

#ME842, camel, discontinued, 10x4x7", F7, from $35 to .**$50.00**

#ME884, Police car, VW bug style, current, 11½x5x5", F7, from $35 to **$75.00**

#ME895, fire engine, 1970s, 10x4x4", F7, from $50 to.....**$85.00**

#ME972, open-door police car, 9½x4x4", F7, from $35 to..**$100.00**

#ME782, Locomotive, 1970s-80s, battery operated, 10x4x7", from $35.00 to $75.00.

#ME824, Patrol car, 1970s, 11x4x3½", F7, from $35.00 to $75.00.

#MF294, Mercedes sedan, friction, 7x3x2", F7, from $12.00 to $20.00.

#ME984, jet plane, 13x14x4½", F7, from $35 to $75.00
#MF 254, Mercedes sedan, current, 8x4x3", F7, from $15 to ..$25.00
#MF032, Eastwind sedan, current, 6x2x2", F7, from $8 to..$15.00
#MF033, pickup truck, current, 6x2x2", F7, from $8 to....$15.00
#MF044, sedan, Nissan style, 9x3½x3", F7, from $10 to ..$25.00
#MF046, sparking carbine, 18x5x1", F7, from $20 to $35.00
#MF052, sedan, 8x3x2", F7, from $15 to............................$25.00
#MF083, sedan, current, 6x2x2", F7, from $8 to $15.00
#MF107, airplane, 6x6x2", F7, from $20 to.......................$35.00
#MF111, ambulance, current, 8x3x3", F7, from $15 to $20.00
#MF127, Highway patrol car, 9½x4x3", F7, from $20 to..$50.00
#MF132, ambulance, 1980s, 10x4x4", F7, from $15 to.....$35.00
#MF134, tourist bus, current, 6x2x3", F7, from $15 to $25.00
#MF135, red flag convertible, current, MIB, F7, from $35 to ..$75.00
#MF136, double-decker train, current, 8x2x3", F7, from $15
    to...$20.00
#MF146, VW, 5x2x2", F7, from $10 to $20.00
#MF151, Shanghai pickup, 1970s, 12x4x4", F7, from $50 to...$100.00
#MF154, tractor, 1970s, 5x3x4", F7, from $25 to..............$50.00
#MF155, airplane, 14x11"/12x4", F7, from $30 to $35.00
#MF162, motorcycle, 6x2x4", F7, from $15 to...................$35.00
#MF163, fire truck, current, 6x2x3", F7, from $35 to $75.00
#MF164, construction truck, 1970s, 7x3x5", F7, from $35 to ..$75.00
#MF164, VW, current, 4x2x3", F7, from $10 to $15.00
#MF170, train, current, 10x2x4", F7, from $15 to $25.00
#MF171, convertible, current, 5x2x2", F7, from $8 to......$15.00
#MF184, coach bus, 12½x4x4", F7, from $15 to...............$30.00
#MF193, soft-cover truck, 1970s, 11x3x4", F7, from $50 to..$75.00
#MF201, 1970s, 14x4x4", F7, from $15 to $25.00
#MF203, sedan, 10½x4x2½", F7, from $20 to....................$50.00
#MF206, panda truck, current, 6x3x2", F7, from $10 to...$20.00
#MF216, airplane, discontinued, 9x9x3", F7, from $15 to ..$35.00
#MF234, sedan, 6x2x2", F7, from $15 to............................$25.00
#MF239, tiger truck, 10x3x4", F7, from $15 to.................$30.00
#MF240, passenger jet, 13x11x4", F7, from $30 to $35.00
#MF249, flying boat, 1070s, 6x6x2", F7, from $35 to $75.00
#MF274, tank, 1970s, 3x2xx2", F7, from $8 to $15.00
#MF298, traveling car, 8½x4x3½", F7, from $15 to.........$25.00
#MF304, race car, discontinued, 10x4x3", F7, from $15 to...$35.00
#MF309, sedan, 9x2x3½", F7, from $20 to $35.00
#MF310, Corvette, 3x2x3", F7, from $10 to $15.00
#MF316, 1953 Corvette, current, F7, from $20 to $50.00
#MF317, Corvette convertible, current, 10x4x3", F7, from $20
    to...$50.00
#MF320, Mercedes sedan, current, 7x3x2", F7, from $10 to...$20.00
#MF321, Buick convertible, current, 11x4x3", F7, from $20
    to $50.00
#MF322, Buick sedan, current, 11x4x3", F7, from $20 to.$50.00
#MF326, Mercedes gull-wing sedan, current, 9x3x2", F7, from
    $15 to...$25.00
#MF329, 1956 Corvette convertible, current, 10x4x4", F7, from
    $20 to...$50.00
#MF330, Cadillac sedan, current, 11x4x3", F7, from $15 to ..$35.00
#MF339, 1956 Corvette sedan, current, 10x4x4", F7, from $20
    to $50.00
#MF340, Cadillac convertible, current, 11x4x3", F7, from $20
    to...$50.00
#MF341, convertible, 12x4x3", F7, from $20 to $50.00

#MF342, sedan, 12x4x3", F7, from $20 to.........................$50.00
#MF712, locomotive, current, 7x2x3", F7, from $10 to....$15.00
#MF713, taxi, current, 5x2x2", F7, from $8 to..................$15.00
#MF714, fire chief car, current, 5x2x2", F7, from $8 to....$15.00
#MF716, ambulance, 1970s, 8x3x3", F7, from $15 to.......$30.00
#MF717, dump truck, discontinued, 10x3x5", F7, from $15
    to $35.00
#MF718, ladder truck, 10x3x4", F7, from $15 to $35.00
#MF721, light tank, current, 6x3x3", F7, from $15 to......$20.00

#MF722, Jeep, current, 6x3x3", F7, from $15.00 to $20.00.

#MF731, station wagon, current, 5x2x2", F7, from $8 to .$15.00
#MF735, rocket racer, current, 7x3x3", F7, from $15 to...$35.00
#MF742, flying boat, current, 13x4x4", F7, from $15 to...$35.00
#MF743, Karmann Ghia sedan, current, 10x3x4", F7, from $15
    to $45.00
#MF753, sports car, current, 8x3x2", F7, from $15 to.......$25.00
#MF782, circus truck, current, 9x3x4", F7, from $15 to...$25.00
#MF787, Lucky open car, current, 8x3x2", F7, from $15 to..$25.00
#MF798, patrol car, current, 8x3x3", F7, from $15 to.......$25.00
#MF800, race car #5, current, 6x2x2", F7, from $10 to $20.00
#MF804, locomotive, current, 16x3x5", F7, from $15 to..$25.00
#MF832, ambulance, current, 5x2x2", F7, from $8 to $15.00
#MF844, double-decker bus, current, 8x4x3", F7, from $15 to...$20.00

#MF861, Space gun, 1970s, 10x2x6", F7, from $45.00 to $75.00.

#MF893, animal van, current, 6x2x3", from $15 to..........$20.00
#MF900, police car, current, 6x3x2", F7, from $8 to $15.00

#MF910, airport limo bus, current, 15x4x5", F7, from $20 to ..**$35.00**
#MF923, torpedo boat, 8x3x3", F7, from $15 to **$25.00**
#MF951, fighter jet, 1970s, 5x4x2", F7, from $15 to.........**$20.00**
#MF956, sparking tank, current, 8x4x3", F7, from $15 to....**$20.00**
#MF957, ambulance helicopter, 7½x2x4", F7, from $15 to..**$35.00**
#MF958, poultry truck, current, 6x2x2", F7, from $15 to .**$20.00**
#MF959, jeep, discontinued, 9x4x4", F7, from $15 to **$20.00**
#MF962, station wagon, 1970s, 9x3x3", F7, from $25 to..**$45.00**
#MF974, circus truck, 6x2x4", F7, from $15 to **$20.00**
#MF985, fowl transporter, current, 12x3x4", F7, from $25 to..**$50.00**
#MF989, noisy locomotive, 1970s, 12x3x4", F7, from $25 to..**$50.00**
#MF993, mini car, current, 5x2x2", F7, from $8 to...........**$15.00**
#MF998, sedan, current, 5x2x2", F7, from $8 to...............**$15.00**
#MS002, jumping frog, current, 2x2x2", F7, from $8 to ...**$15.00**
#MS006, pecking chicken, 1970s, 2x1x1", F7, from $8 to ..**$15.00**
#MS011, roll-over plane, current, 3x4x2", F7, from $10 to..**$18.00**
#MS014, single-bar exerciser, 1970s, 7x6x6", F7, from $25 to **$50.00**
#MS057, horse & rider, 1970s, 6x2x5", F7, from $18 to...**$35.00**
#MS058, old-fashion car, current, 3x3x4", F7, from $12 to..**$20.00**
#MS082, jumping frog, current, 2x2x2", F7, from $8 to ...**$15.00**
#MS083, jumping rabbit, current, 3x3x2", F7, from $8 to.**$15.00**
#MS085, xylophone girl, current, 7x3x9", F7, from $18 to..**$35.00**
#MS107, jumping Bambi, current, 5½x6", F7, from $12 to .**$20.00**
#MS134, sparking jet, current, F7, from $15 to **$30.00**
#MS166, crawling baby, vinyl head, current, 5x4x5", F7, from $12 to **$20.00**
#MS405, ice cream vendor, current, F7, from $8 to **$20.00**
#MS405, jumping zebra, current, 5x2x4", F7, from $8 to .**$20.00**
#MS565, drumming panda/wheel, current, 5x3x5", F7, from $8 to **$20.00**
#MS568, sparrow, current, 5x2x2", F7, from $8 to **$15.00**
#MS569, oriole, current, 5x2x2", F7, from $8 to **$15.00**
#MS702, motorcycle, current, 7x4x5", F7, from $15 to....**$35.00**
#MS704, bird music cart, 1970s, 3x2x5", F7, from $15 to...**$25.00**

#MS709, motorcycle w/sidecar, current, 7x4x5", F7, from $15 to **$35.00**
#MS710, tricycle, current, 5x3x5", F7, from $15 to..........**$20.00**
#MS713, washing machine, 3x3x5", F7, from $15 to **$20.00**
#MS765, drummer, 5x3x6", F7, from $15 to.....................**$25.00**
#MS827, sedan, steering, 1970s, 9x3x3", F7, from $50 to **$75.00**
#MS858, girl on goose, current, 5x3x3", F7, from $15 to .**$25.00**
#PMS102, rolling cart, current, 3x2x1", F7, from $15 to..**$20.00**
#PMS105, jumping dog, current, 3x2x6", F7, from $15 to **$25.00**
#PMS106, jumping parrot, current, 3x2x6", F7, from $15 to..**$25.00**
#PMS108, duck family, current, 10x2x3", F7, from $15 to .**$25.00**
#PMS113, Fu dog, current, 4x2x3", F7, from $15 to.........**$25.00**
#PMS119, woodpecker, current, 3x2x6", F7, from $15 to...**$25.00**
#PMS210, clown riding bike, current, 4x2x5", F7, from $15 to **$25.00**
#PMS212, elephant on bike, current, 6x3x8", F7, from $15 to **$35.00**
#PMS213, duck on bike, current, 6x3x8", F7, from $15 to **$35.00**
#PMS214, lady bug family, current, 13x3x1", F7, from $15 to **$25.00**
#PMS215, crocodile, current, 9x3x1", F7, from $12 to.....**$20.00**
#PMS217, jumping rabbit, current, 3x2x6", F7, from $15 to **$25.00**
#PMS218, penguin, current, 3x2x6", F7, from $15 to **$30.00**
#PS013, boy on tricycle, current, 2x4x4", F7, from $12 to...**$25.00**

Circus Toys

If you ever had the opportunity to go to one of the giant circuses as a child, no doubt you still have very vivid recollections of the huge elephants, the daring trapeze artists, the clowns and their trick dogs, and the booming voice of the ringmaster, even if that experience was a half century ago. Most of our circus toys are listed in other categories.

See also Battery-Operated Toys; Cast Iron, Circus; Chein, Windups; Marx, Windups; Schoenhut; Windups, Friction, and Other Mechanicals.

Acrobats Gravity Toy, Germany, 2 tin acrobats descend rod which can be reversed for continuous play, 11", EX **$475.00**
Britain's Mammoth Circus, complete, NM (EX box).....**$800.00**
Clever Clowns, Greycraft, Grey Iron Casting Co, 1930s, diecast figures, EX (EX box), D10 ....**$750.00**
Clicker, circus elephant, mk Made in Japan, litho tin elephant balancing on a log, 2½", NM **$125.00**
Hoop Toy, att Hull & Stafford, circus rider on horse w/acrobat on back of horse, pnt tin, G **$1,550.00**
Hoop Toy, Fallows, circus elephant w/red blanket in blk-pnt hoop, tin, 11½" dia, rstr **$450.00**
Ringling Bros Performing Animals on Circus Wagon, wooden clown & bear balancing ball spin on tin wheels, EX (VG box)..**$200.00**
Ringling Bros Toy Circus, Mattel, MIB, W5 ....**$85.00**

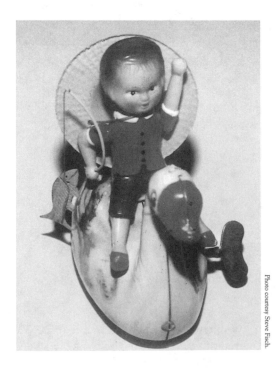

#MS858, Girl on goose, older style, 5x3x3", F7, from $25.00 to $50.00.

Photo courtesy Steve Fisch.

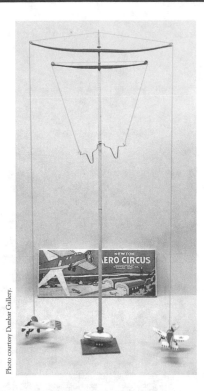

Aero Circus, Newton, 1930s, MIB, $475.00.

Photo courtesy Dunbar Gallery.

Photo courtesy Dunbar Gallery.

One-Ring Circus, probably Gibbs, 1920s, carved wood with cloth clothes on people, 21 pieces, EX, D10, from $1,200.00 to $1,600.00.

Coloring, Activity, and Paint Books

Coloring and activity books from the early years of the twentieth century are scarce indeed and when found can be expensive if they are tied into another collectibles field such as Black Americana or advertising; but the ones most in demand are those that represent familiar movie and TV stars of the 1950s and '60s. Condition plays a very important part in assessing worth, and though hard to find, unused examples are the ones that bring top dollar — in fact, as much as 50% to 75% more than one even partially used.

Advisor: Diane Albert (T6).

See also Advertising.

Addams Family, activity book, Saalfield, 1965, missing 1st pg o/w EX, T2 ....$25.00
Adventures of Rin-Tin-Tin, coloring book, Whitman, 1955, few pgs colored, EX, T2 ....$15.00
Aladdin & His Magic Lamp, coloring book, Saalfield, 1970, unused, EX, T2...$20.00

Alice in Wonderland, coloring book, Whitman, 1951, most pgs colored, NM, F8..................................$22.00
Alice in Wonderland, punch-out book, Whitman/WDP, 1951, unused, EX, P6...$175.00
Alley Oop, coloring book, Treasure, 1962, unused, NM, F8 ....$30.00
Alvin & the Chipmunks, coloring book, Saalfield, 1963, unused, NM, T2 ....$32.00
Andy Panda, coloring book, Whitman, 1944, few pgs colored, EX+, F8 ....$25.00
Animal Paint Book, Little Golden Activity Series #A4, 1st edition, partially pnt, EX, K3...............................$9.00
Animal Stamps, stamp book, Golden #6102, 1980, unused, EX, K3...$18.00
Annette, coloring book, Whitman, 1961, unused, NM, F8..$25.00
Archie & Jughead, coloring book, Whitman, 1972, few pgs colored, EX+, F8 ....$15.00
Around the World Cutout Book, Wonder #626, 1964, EX, K3 ....$5.00
Baby Moses Bible Stories, coloring book, Merrill, 1940s, unused, missing 1st pg o/w VG, F8 ....$8.00
Baby Wild Animals, stamp book, Golden #6124, 1980, unused, VG+, K3 ....$18.00
Barbie Teen Queen, coloring book, Whitman, 1969, few pgs colored, NM, T2.......................................$20.00
Barney Rubble, coloring book, Watkins-Strathmore, 1962, few pgs colored, NM, T2 ....$20.00
Batman, coloring book, Whitman, 1966, unused, M, J5, from $25 to $50.00
Batman, coloring book, Whitman, 1967, few pgs colored, EX, H4 ....$30.00
Batman, Robin & Penguin Giant Comics To Color, Whitman, 1976, unused, NM, A $10.00
Batman & Robin, dot-to-dot & coloring book, Bertand, 1967, unused, NM, A $20.00
Batman Saves the Town, coloring book, Holloway Candy premium, 1966, packaged in family-sz boxes of candy, EX+, A...$125.00
Beatles, coloring book, Saalfield, 1964, unused, EX, R2 ...$75.00
Beetle Bailey, coloring book, Lowe, 1961, unused, NM, T2 ....$25.00
Ben-Hur, coloring book, Lowe, 1959, few pgs colored, EX+, T2..$15.00
Ben-Hur, punch-out book, Golden, 1959, unused, NM, F8..$45.00
Benny the Beaver, Funny Animal Paint Book, Fawcett, 1945, unused, NM, F8 ....$18.00
Beverly Hillbillies, coloring book, Whitman, 1963, few pgs colored, EX $35.00
Billy the Kid & Oscar, Funny Animal Paint Book, Fawcett, 1945, unused, NM, F8 ....$25.00
Bird Stamps, stamp book, Golden, 1980, unused, VG+, K3 .$18.00
Black Beard's Ghost, coloring book, Whitman, 1968, VG+, P3 ....$15.00
Bob Hope, coloring book, Saalfield, 1954, unused file copy, rare, NM, A...$55.00
Bobby Benson's B-Bar-Riders, coloring book, Whitman, 1950, unused, EX, J5 ....$15.00

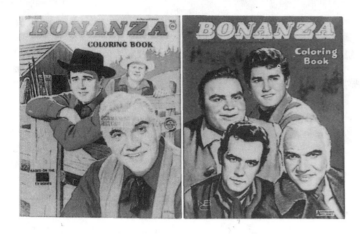

Bonanza, coloring books, Saalfield, 1957 and 1958, unused file copies, NM, $65.00 each.

Bozo the Clown, Circus Press-Out Book, Whitman, 1966, few pcs punched out, NM, T2..........................$20.00

Brady Bunch, coloring book, Whitman, 1973, few pgs colored, EX..$50.00

Brave Eagle, coloring book, Whitman, 1955, unused, NM, F8...$25.00

Bronco, coloring book, Saalfield, 1959, unused file copy, NM, A...$30.00

Bronco, coloring book, Saalfield, 1961, missing 1st pg o/w NM, F8...$25.00

Buccaneer, coloring book, Saalfield, 1959, 1 pg colored, EX, T2...$15.00

Buffalo Bill Jr & Calamity, coloring book, Whitman, 1957, few pgs colored, VG, T2..............................$20.00

Bugaloos, coloring book, Saalfield, 1971, few pgs colored, missing 1st pg o/w EX, F8...........................$28.00

Bugs Bunny Private Eye, coloring book, Whitman, 1957, unused, EX, T2..$14.00

Bullwinkle & Dudley Do-Right, coloring book, Artcraft, 1970, lg sz, unused, NM, F8..............................$25.00

Bullwinkle Paintless Paint Book, Whitman, 1960, few pgs colored, EX, F8...$25.00

Bullwinkle's How To Have Fun Outdoors Without Getting Clobbered, coloring book, General Mills, 1963, unused, EX, J5...$50.00

Buster & Mary Jane's Painting Book, Stokes, 1907, illus by RF Outcault, cloth-bound hardcover, pnt, EX, A......$145.00

Captain Gallant, coloring book, Lowe, 1956, unused, NM, C1..$45.00

Car 54 Where Are You?, Whitman, 1962, few pgs colored, EX..$25.00

Charlie McCarthy, coloring book, Whitman, 1938, most pgs colored, NM, F8..$40.00

Charlie McCarthy Coloring Set, Whitman, 1938, complete, unused, MIB, from $100 to..............................$150.00

Chilly Willy, coloring book, 1955, VG+, J2.....................$15.00

Chitty-Chitty Bang-Bang, coloring book, Watkins-Strathmore, EX, F8..$12.00

Circus Boy, coloring book, Whitman, 1957, few pgs colored, VG, R2...$45.00

Circus Boy, coloring book, Whitman, 1957, unused, EX, A .$55.00

Cisco Kid and Pancho, coloring book, Saalfield, 1951, unused file copy, NM, $50.00.

Cisco Kid, coloring book, Saalfield, 1954, few pgs colored, VG, J5..$25.00

Connect the Dots — The Three Bears, Bonnie Books #4291, 1952, diecut, VG+, K3..................................$20.00

Connect the Dots Story Book, Bonnie Books #4279, 1954, diecut, VG+, K3...$15.00

David Cassidy Paint & Color Album, Artcraft, 1971, unused, NM, H4...$30.00

Dennis the Menace, Cut-Out Coloring Book, Golden Press, 1964, few figures cut & colored, EX, T2...............$20.00

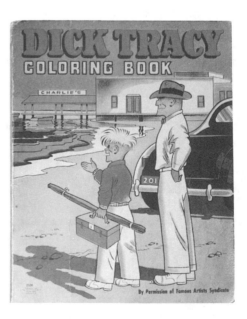

Dick Tracy, coloring book, Saalfield #2536, 1946, unused, EX, $60.00.

Dick Tracy Junior Detective Kit, punch-out book, 1962, unpunched, M, D11.................................$25.00

Dino the Dinosaur, coloring book, Whitman, 1961, few pgs colored, EX $22.00

Disneyland, coloring book, Whitman, 1964, full-color photo cover, unused, NM, T2.................................$20.00

Doris Day, coloring book, Whitman, 1954, all pgs colored, VG $15.00

Dr Dolittle, punch-out book, Whitman, 1935, unpunched, NM, A7...$30.00

Dr Dolittle & His Animals, coloring book, Watkins-Strathmore, 1967, unused, NM, A $25.00

Duck Tales, sticker book, Panini, 1987, w/set of 140 unapplied stickers, NM, M8 ....$28.00

Electro-Man, coloring book, Lowe, 1967, unused, M, A ..$10.00

Elizabeth Taylor, coloring book, Whitman, 1952, few pgs colored, EX $45.00

Ellsworth Elephant, activity book, Saalfield, 1962, several pgs colored, VG+, T2.................................$12.00

Emergency!, coloring book, Lowe, 1977, unused, NM......$35.00

Eve Arden, coloring book, Treasure Books, 1958, few pgs colored, EX $40.00

Family Affair, coloring book, Whitman, 1974, few pgs colored, EX...$20.00

Farm Animals, punch-out book, Lowe, 1961, unused, NM, T2 ....$12.00

Fire Department, punch-out book, Lowe, 1961, unused, NM, T2 ....$18.00

Fireball XL5, cut-out coloring book, Golden Funtime, 1964, several pgs colored, VG+, T2 ....$12.00

Flash Gordon, coloring book, Whitman, 1952, A McWilliams cover, unused, EX+ $40.00

Flash Gordon, paint book, Whitman #671, 1936, EX $45.00

Flintstones, coloring book, Whitman, 1962, few pgs colored, EX, T2...$20.00

Flipper, coloring book, Lowe, 1963, unused, NM, A $30.00

Flipper, coloring book, Whitman, 1965, few pgs colored, EX, A $20.00

Flipper, coloring book, Whitman, 1965, unused, EX, M17 ..$30.00

Flying Nun, coloring book, Artcraft, 1968, few pgs colored, EX, F8 ....$18.00

Gene Autry, coloring book, Whitman, 1950, unused, M, J5, from $50 to...$75.00

Gene Autry at Melody Ranch, cut-out book, Gene Autry, 1951, complete, NM, A.......................................$100.00

Gentle Ben, coloring book, Whitman, 1968, unused, EX, F8 ..$18.00

Get Smart, coloring book, Saalfield, 1965, unused, M, A ...$40.00

Gilligan's Island, coloring book, Whitman, 1965, scarce, unused, M, A...$135.00

Goonies, dot-to-dot book, Simon & Schuster, 1985, w/crayons in sealed bag, M, P3 ....$6.00

Green Hornet, coloring book, Watkins-Strathmore #1824-4, 1966, unused, M, from $25 to.............................$50.00

Green Hornet, coloring book, Whitman #1190, 1966, unused, M, from $25 to...$50.00

Green Hornet Playbook, punch-out book, 1966, Van Williams cover, stand-up figures, car, etc, unpunched, EX+, A ..$290.00

Gremlins II, sticker book, NM, unused, J8 ....$8.00

Groovie Goolies, coloring book, Whitman, 1969, missing 1st pg o/w EX, T2 ....$8.00

Gulliver's Travels, coloring book, Saalfield, 1939, few pgs colored, EX, F8...$24.00

Gumby & Pokey, sticker book, Whitman, 1968, unused, NM, F8 ..$35.00

Hee Haw, coloring book, Artcraft, 1963, unused, EX, J5 .$15.00

Heroes of the West, coloring book, Lowe, 1959, unused, NM, T2...$8.00

Hocus Pocus Magic, activity book, Bonnie Books #4161, 1953, wheel not attached, K3.................................$10.00

Flintstones, punch-out book, A Great Big Punchout, Whitman, 1961, unused, NM, A, $35.00.

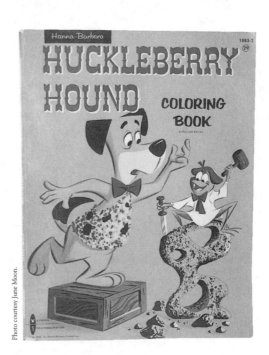

Huckleberry Hound, coloring book, Western Printing, 1962, few pages colored otherwise EX, J6, $12.00.

Hokey Wolf & Ding-A-Ling, coloring book, Golden, 1961, few pgs colored, EX, F8 ....$40.00

Hot Wheels, sticker book, Whitman, 1968, several stickers applied, NM, T2 ....$12.00

Howdy Doody, coloring book, Whitman #2093-3, 1950, pc of spine missing o/w EX, J5 ....$15.00

Howdy Doody, dot-to-dot book, Whitman, 1955, unused, EX, J5 ....$35.00

Humpty Dumpty, coloring book, Lowe, 1950s, unused, NM, T2 ....$10.00

I Love Lucy, coloring book, Whitman, 1954, unused, EX, J5...$150.00

Indian Scout Buffalo Bill, coloring book, Lowe, 1958, unused, NM, T2 ....$8.00

It's About Time, coloring book, Whitman, 1967, unused, scarce, NM..................................$35.00

Jack & Jill, coloring book, Abbott, 1959, unused, M, T2 .$10.00

Jack & the Beanstalk, coloring book, Clover Pub, 1964, unused, NM, T2 ....$12.00

Jack Webb's Safety Squad, coloring book, Lowe, 1956, unused, NM, T2 ....$25.00

Jetsons, color-by-number book, Whitman, 1963, few pgs colored, EX, F8..................................$30.00

Jetsons, coloring book, Rand McNally, 1986, unused, NM, H4 ....$6.00

Jimmy Dodd Magic Carpet, coloring book, Whitman, 1957, several pgs colored, EX, F8 ....$18.00

Julia, coloring book, Saalfield, 1968, several pgs colored, EX, F8..................................$22.00

Jungle Boy, coloring book, Artcraft, 1967, unused, EX+, T2 .....$12.00

Kidnapped!, coloring book, Treasure, 1950, unused, EX+, T2..................................$12.00

Korg, coloring book, Artcraft, 1975, unused, EX, H4 ....$15.00

Land of the Giants, coloring book, Whitman, 1969, few pgs colored, EX, A $25.00

Lassie, Magic Paint Book, Whitman, 1957, few pgs pnt, EX, T2..................................$25.00

Laugh-In, coloring book, Artcraft, 1968, few pgs colored, NM, F8 ....$25.00

Laverne & Shirley, coloring book, Playmore, 1983, unused, NM..................................$15.00

Leave It to Beaver, coloring book, Saalfield, 1958, few pgs colored, EX+, A $30.00

Lieutenant, coloring book, Saalfield, 1964, scarce, unused, NM..................................$40.00

Little Lulu, coloring book, Whitman, 1952, few pgs colored, EX, F8 ....$25.00

Little Monsters, coloring book, Watkins-Strathmore, 1965, few pgs colored, EX, F8 ....$40.00

Lone Ranger, coloring book, Whitman, 1957, few pgs colored, NM..................................$25.00

Love Bug, coloring book, WDP, 1969, Hunts Catsup premium, unused, M, P6 ....$22.00

Mackenzies Raiders, coloring book, Saalfield, 1955, unused file copy, NM, A $45.00

Make Way for Bullwinkle, coloring book, Whitman, 1972, lg diecut, unused, EX, J5..................................$15.00

Man From UNCLE, coloring book, Watkins-Strathmore, 1965, unused, NM, A $40.00

Marlin Perkins Trip to the Zoo, coloring book, Lowe, 1954, few pgs colored, EX+, F8 ....$15.00

Mickey Mouse, coloring book, Saalfield, 1936, diecut cover shows Mickey ice skating, VG+, A $100.00

Mickey Mouse in Numberland, activity book, Whitman, 1938, EX, A $40.00

Mighty Mouse, activity book, Lowe, 1954, unused, NM, T2..$60.00

Mighty Mouse, sticker book, Whitman, 1967, several stickers applied, EX, T2 ....$15.00

Mister Ed, coloring book, Whitman, 1963, few pgs colored, EX+, F8 ....$25.00

Monkees Big Beat Fun Book, activity book, unused, rare, B3 ....$130.00

Monroes, coloring book, Saalfield, 1966, unused, EX, T2...$30.00

Monster Squad, coloring book, Rand McNally, 1977, unused, EX, J5 ....$15.00

Mr Peabody, coloring book, Whitman, 1977, few pgs colored, EX, F8..................................$28.00

Mrs Beasley, coloring book, Whitman, 1970, unused, EX, J5 ..$15.00

My Favorite Martian, coloring book, Golden, 1964, unused, EX+, P3 ....$40.00

My Mother the Car, coloring book, Saalfield, 1965, unused, M, A $70.00

My Three Sons, coloring book, Whitman, 1967, few pgs colored, EX+, A $35.00

My Three Sons, coloring book, Whitman, 1967, unused, NM, C1..................................$45.00

Nanny & the Professor, coloring book, Artcraft, 1971, several pgs colored, EX+, F8 ....$25.00

Old Yeller, coloring book, Whitman, 1957, few pgs colored, scarce, VG, T2 ....$15.00

Ozzie and Harriet — David and Ricky, coloring book, Saalfield, 1954, unused file copy, EX, A, $45.00.

Parade of Comics, sticker book, Saalfield, 1968, features various comic-strip characters, unused, M, A $30.00

Partridge Family Pictorial Activity Album, Artcraft, 1973, unused, NM, J5/F8, from $25 to $35.00

Patience & Prudence, coloring book, Lowe, 1957, unused, NM, T2..$20.00

Peanuts, coloring book, Saalfield, Canadian issue, 1970s, unused, EX, J8 ....$8.00

Picture Sticker Story Book, Bonnie Books #4375, 1955, VG+, K3 ....$50.00

Pinocchio, coloring book, Whitman, 1939, Cocomalt mail-order premium, few pgs colored, EX, T2............................$15.00

Pip the Piper, coloring book, Whitman, 1962, few pgs colored, scarce, EX, T2 ....$12.00

Planet of the Apes, coloring book, Artcraft, 1974, unused, NM, J5 ....$10.00

Planet of the Apes Picture Activity Album, Saalfield, 1974, unused, EX, A $25.00

Pollyanna, coloring book, Watkins-Strathmore, 1960, several pgs colored, EX, A $10.00

Popeye, color & paint book, Whitman, 1951, unused, VG+, T2..$50.00

Popeye, coloring book, Lowe, 1964, unused, EX, T2 ....$20.00

Porky Pig, coloring book, Saalfield, 1938, unused file copy, NM, A $65.00

Presidents of the United States, stamp book, Golden #2511, 1966, unused, EX, K3..$18.00

Quick Draw McGraw, coloring book, Whitman, 1962, few pgs colored, EX, T2 ....$20.00

Racing Cars, coloring book, Lowe, unused, NM, T2 ....$10.00

Raggedy Ann, coloring book, Whitman, 1968, w/Dolls of All Nations, EX, J5 ....$10.00

Raggedy Ann and Andy Paper Dolls and Coloring Book, Saalfield, 1944, unused file copy, NM, A, $65.00.

Ramar of the Jungle, coloring book, Saalfield, 1955, 1st pg colored, EX, T2..$20.00

Rango Texas Ranger, coloring book, Saalfield, 1965, scarce, unused, NM, A $25.00

Rat Patrol, coloring book, Artcraft, 1960s, unused, EX, J5...$15.00

Red Rider & Little Beaver, coloring book, Whitman, 1947, Fred Harman cover art, unused, NM, J5, from $40 to........$60.00

Reluctant Astronaut, coloring book, Artcraft, 1967, few pgs colored, scarce, EX+, T2..$20.00

Return of the Jedi, Kenner, 1983, Luke Skywalker, unused, NM+, G7 ....$5.00

Ripley's Believe It or Not, coloring book, Lowe, 1961, unused, NM, T2..$30.00

Road Runner, coloring book, Golden, 1981, NM, F8.......$12.00

Rockets Away, coloring book, 1950s, few pgs colored, VG+, J2..$24.00

Rocks & Animals, stamp book, Golden, 1974, EX, K3 ....$14.00

Rocks & Minerals, stamp book, Golden, 1976, 4 stamps missing, VG, K3 ....$12.00

Rocky & Bullwinkle, coloring book, Watkins-Strathmore, 1962, few pgs colored, EX, J5..$15.00

Rocky Jones, coloring book, Whitman, 1951, unused, NM, F8 ....$45.00

Roger & Anita, coloring book, Watkins-Strathmore, 1961, few pgs colored, 1st page missing o/w EX, F8....................$15.00

Roy Rogers & Dale Evans, coloring book, Whitman #1116, 1950, all pgs colored, VG, J5 ....$25.00

Roy Rogers' Pal Pat Brady, coloring book, Whitman, 1956, few pgs colored, EX+, F8 ....$45.00

Rudolph the Red-Nosed Reindeer, coloring book, Lowe, 1963, unused, EX, T2...$15.00

Satellite Rocket Launcher, punch-out book, Dell, 1959, unused, NM, P4..$45.00

Scooby-Doo's All-Star Laff-a-Lympics, coloring book, Rand McNally, 1978, NM, C1...$28.00

Sgt Bilko, coloring book, Treasure Books, 1959, unused, EX, A $55.00

Shoofly! Fun Book, activity book, Bonnie Books #4436, 1956, diecut, VG+, K3 ....$30.00

Simpsons Rainy Day Fun Book, unused, NM, J8 ....$15.00

Smilin' Jack, coloring book, Saalfield, 1946, few pgs colored, EX+, T2...$20.00

Smokey the Bear, coloring book, Whitman, 1958, few pgs colored, EX, J5 ....$15.00

Soupy Sales, activity book, Treasure Books, 1965, unused, most pgs have sm tear o/w NM, A $10.00

Spider-Man, coloring book, Whitman, 1976, unused, M, A ...$15.00

Spin & Marty, coloring book, Whitman, 1956, several pgs colored, EX+, F8 ....$30.00

Star Trek, coloring book, Saalfield, 1967, scarce, M, A ...$35.00

Stars & Planets, Golden, 1982, unused, EX, K3 ....$18.00

Steve Canyon, coloring book, Saalfield, 1952, few pgs colored, EX+, T2..$30.00

Stingray, coloring book, Whitman, 1966, few pgs colored, EX, F8 ....$30.00

Sugarfoot, coloring book, Saalfield, 1959, few pgs colored, G..$15.00

Sugarfoot, coloring book, Saalfield, 1959, unused file copy, NM, A $35.00

Superman, coloring book, Saalfield, 1955, unused file copy, NM, A $150.00

Superman, sticker book, Whitman, 1977, unused, M, P6..$25.00

Tales of the Vikings, coloring book, Saalfield, 1960, unused, EX, T2...$22.00

Tarzan, coloring book, Whitman, 1966, few pgs colored, EX+, F8...$15.00

That Girl, coloring book, Saalfield, 1967, few pgs colored, EX+, A...$35.00

That Girl, coloring book, Saalfield, 1970, few pgs colored, EX+, F8...$25.00

Three Stooges, activity book, Playmore, 1983, few pgs colored, EX, H4..$12.00

Three Stooges, coloring book, Lowe, 1959, unused, EX, F8..$45.00

Thunderbirds, coloring book, Whitman, 1968, few pgs colored, NM, F8...$35.00

Tom & Jerry, coloring book, Whitman, 1952, few pgs colored, EX, F8...$25.00

Tom Corbett Space Cadet, coloring book, Saalfield, 1952, unused file copy, scarce, NM, A...............................$125.00

Tom Corbett Space Cadet, punch-out book, Saalfield, 1952, unpunched, EX+, from $80 to..................................$100.00

Tommy Tortoise & Moe Hare, coloring book, Saalfield, 1966, few pgs colored, EX, T2..$12.00

Tonto, coloring book, Whitman, 1957, few pgs colored, VG+, J5/T2, from $12 to...$15.00

Treasure Hunt, coloring book, EX+, J2.........................$15.00

Treasure Island Adventure, coloring book, Lowe, 1950s, unused, NM, T2...$8.00

Trolls, coloring book, Treasure, 1965, unused, NM, F8....$50.00

TV Roundup of Western Heroes, coloring book, Whitman, 1961, unused, EX, A...$50.00

Tweety, coloring book, Whitman, 1955, few pgs colored, EX, T2...$20.00

Uncle Scrooge, coloring book, Watkins-Strathmore, 1964, unused, NM, A..$15.00

Underdog, coloring book, Whitman, 1972, several pgs colored, EX, F8...$18.00

Underdog, coloring book, Whitman, 1974, unused, NM, J5..$15.00

Universal City Studio, coloring book, Saalfield, 1964, scarce, few pgs colored, NM, F8.......................................$30.00

Universal City Studio, coloring book, Saalfield, 1964, scarce, unused, M, A..$60.00

Voyage to the Bottom of the Sea, coloring book, Whitman, 1965, unused, EX, from $25 to...................................$50.00

Wagon Train, coloring book, Whitman, 1959, few pgs colored, EX, T2..$20.00

Wally Walrus, coloring book, Saalfield, 1964, several pgs colored, EX, F8..$18.00

Walt Disney, coloring book, Dell, 1963, few pgs colored, EX, J2...$15.00

Walt Disney's Magic Forest, coloring book, Watkins-Strathmore, 1959, few pgs colored, EX, T2.........................$15.00

Walt Disney's Vacationland, coloring book, Dell, 1955, features Scrooge McDuck & Nephews, unused, NM, A.........$25.00

Willie the Worm & Sammy, Funny Animal Paint Book, Fawcett, 1945, unused, NM, F8..................................$15.00

Wizard of Oz, activity book, Whitman, 1976, unused, M, H4..$12.00

Wonders of the Animal Kingdom, sticker book, Golden Glow, 1959, few stickers applied, rare, EX, T2.....................$20.00

Woody Woodpecker Magic Paintless Paint Book, Whitman, 1959, few pgs colored, EX, F8.......................................$12.00

Wyatt Earp, coloring book, Saalfield, 1957, few pgs colored, VG, T2...$12.00

Zoo Punchout Animals, Lowe, 1968, unused, NM, T2.....$12.00

Zorro, Whitman/WD, 1958, unused, EX, W6..................$40.00

Zorro, Whitman/WD, 1965, unused, EX, W6..................$25.00

101 Dalmatians, coloring book, Whitman, 1960, few pgs colored, EX, T2..$15.00

20,000 Leagues Under the Sea, coloring book, Whitman, 1954, unused, EX, A $85.00

Comic Books

For more than a half a century, kids of America raced to the bookstand as soon as the new comics came in for the month and for 10¢ an issue kept up on the adventures of their favorite super heroes, cowboys, space explorers, and cartoon characters. By far most were eventually discarded — after they were traded one friend to another, stacked on closet shelves, and finally confiscated by Mom. Discount the survivors that were torn or otherwise damaged over the years and those about the mundane, and of those remaining, some could be quite valuable. In fact, first editions of high-grade comics books or those showcasing the first appearance of a major character often bring $500.00 and more. Rarity, age, and quality of the artwork are prime factors in determining value, and condition is critical. If you want to seriously collect comic books, you'll need to refer to a good comic book price guide such as Overstreet's. The examples we've listed here are worth from $4.00 and up; many are worth much less.

Advisor: Ken Mitchell (M14).

Other Sources: A3, P3, K1 (for Simpson's Comics)

Avengers, Captain America Lives Again! Marvel #4, 1963, NM, $450.00.

Adventures in Paradise, Dell Four-Color #1301, 1962, EX ...$15.00
Adventures Into the Unknown, #102, VG+, M14 ....$8.00
Adventures of Bob Hope, #28, EX, M14..........................$36.00
Adventures of the Jaguar, #1, VG, M14..........................$35.00

Bewitched, Dell file copy, 1965, NM, from $30.00 to $40.00.

Adventures of the Jaguar, #7, 1962, NM..........................$30.00
Andy Panda, Dell Four-Color #280, 1950, EX+ $20.00
Annie Oakley & Tagg, #575, EX, M14............................$25.00
Aquaman, DC Comics #26, 1966, EX...............................$20.00
Archie's Mad House, Comic Book Annual #9, VG, M14...$10.00
Avengers, Gold Key #1, 1968, EX, T2 ....$45.00
Avengers, Marvel #1, 1963, G+..$225.00
Bat Masterson, Dell Four-Color #1013, 1959, G+, T2 .....$10.00
Ben Bowie & Mountain Men, #11, VG, M14....................$6.00
Ben Casey, Dell #1, 1962, photo cover, EX, F8 ....$15.00
Bionic Woman, Carlton #1, 1977, EX, from $15 to $25.00
Blazing West, #10, VG, M14 ....$8.00
Bonanza, Gold Key #27, G..$5.00
Brave & Bold, DC Comics #28, 1960, G+.......................$370.00
Brave Eagle, Dell Four-Color #929, 1958, EX, T2 ....$8.00
Bugaloos, Charlton #1, 1971, EX, F8 ....$15.00
Bugs Bunny Christmas Funnies, Dell Giant #4, EX, M14...$30.00
Bugs Bunny Finds the Frozen Kingdom, Dell Four-Color #164,
    VG, M14...$15.00
Bullwinkle, Gold Key #1, 1962, EX, F8............................$35.00
Bullwinkle & Rocky, Whitman #5, 1972, EX, F8.............$10.00
Captain Midnight, Fawcett #37, NM, M14 ....$150.00
Casper the Friendly Ghost, #18, VG, M14 ....$18.00
Cat (The), Dell #1, EX, J2..$10.00
Cave Kids, Gold Key #2, EX $6.00
Cheyenne, Dell #16, G $5.00
Christmas w/Mother Goose, Dell #201, EX, J5 ....$35.00
Circus Boy, Dell Four-Color #759, 1956, VG, T2 ....$18.00
Colt .45, Dell #5, 1960, EX, T2..$20.00
Comic Cavalcade, #16, 1946, Green Lantern, Flash, Wonder
    Woman & others, NM, M14......................................$500.00
Daisy Duck's Diary, #659, EX+, M14 ....$15.00
Daniel Boone, Gold Key #10, 1967, EX, F8 ....$5.00
Daredevil, Marvel #1, 1964, VG, A $155.00
David & Goliath, Dell Four-Color #1205, 1961, photo cover,
    EX...$17.00
David Cassidy, Charlton #1, 1972, photo cover, NM.......$18.00
Dennis the Menace, #20, EX, M14 ....$10.00
Doc Savage, #12, 1943, NM...$300.00
Doctor Solar, #5, VG+, M14..$15.00
Don Winslow, #61, 1948, EX, C1 ....$25.00
Donald & Mickey in Disneyland, Dell Giant #1, EX,
    M14...$30.00
Donald Duck Beach Party, Dell Giant #1, EX, M14.........$30.00
Donald Duck in Ghost of the Grotto, Dell Four-Color #159,
    1947, EX, M14..$200.00
Donald Duck the Crocodile Collector, Dell, 1951, VG+,
    M8...$25.00
Donald Duck's Beach Party, Dell Giant #6, 1959, EX, J5 ..$35.00
Donald in Mathmagic Land, #1198, VG, M14 ....$12.00
Dr Who & the Daleks, Dell #1, 1966, photo cover, VG, T2 ..$15.00
Elmer Fudd, Dell #689, EX, M14 ....$8.00
Fantastic Voyage, Gold Key #2, 1969, EX, T2 ....$10.00
Felix the Cat, Dell #6, 1964, EX.......................................$20.00
Felix the Cat, Toby Press #58, 1954, VG $25.00
Flintstones, Dell #6, 1962, EX $20.00
Flintstones, Gold Key #33, 1966, VG+ $6.00
Flintstones, March of Comics #243, 1963, NM $50.00

Flash, Why? DC Comics, 1965, NM, from $30.00 to $40.00.

Flying Nun, Dell #3, 1968, photo cover, EX, F8 ....$8.00
Gang Busters, DC Comics #58, VG, M14.........................$14.00
Gene Autry Comics, Dell #48, 1951, G, T2 ....$5.00
Gene Autry's Horse Champion, Dell #9, 1952, G $3.00
Gentle Ben, Dell #4, 1968, photo cover, EX, F8.................$5.00
Get Smart, Dell #1, 1965, VG+ $20.00
Girl From UNCLE, Gold Key #2, 1967, VG+, T2..............$5.00
Great Locomotive Chase, Dell Four-Color #712, Fess Parker
    photo cover, EX $20.00

Green Lantern, DC Comics #7, 1960, NM, from $175.00 to $200.00.

Hardy Boys, Dell Four-Color #760, 1956, photo cover, EX,
    F8 ....$25.00

Hardy Boys, Gold Key #2, 1970, photo cover, NM.............$8.00
Heckle & Jeckle, Dell #3, 1967, VG $4.00
Hennesey, Dell Four-Color #1200, 1961, VG+ $15.00
High Chaparral, Gold Key #1, 1968, VG+.........................$6.00
Hogan's Heroes, Dell #4, 1966, EX+ $6.00
Honey West, Gold Key #1, 1966, NM, M14.....................$70.00
Hooded Horseman, Ace #22, VG, M14...........................$10.00
Hopalong Cassidy, Fawcett #54, 1951, VG, F8 ....$8.00
Horse Soldiers, Dell Four-Color #1048, 1959, photo cover, G,
    F8 ....$45.00
House of Secrets, Dell #50, EX, M14 ....$38.00
HR Pufnstuf, Gold Key #2, 1971, photo cover, NM $40.00
HR Pufnstuf, Whitman #6, 1972, VG..............................$12.00
Huckleberry Hound, Dell #3, EX+, T2 ....$15.00
Huckleberry Hound & Yakky Doodle, Gold Key #35, 1968,
    VG+ $5.00
Huey, Dewey & Louie Back to School, Dell Giant #1, VG,
    M14 ....$15.00
I Dream of Jeannie, Dell #1, photo cover, EX+, M14.......$60.00
I Love Lucy, Dell #11, 1956, EX......................................$40.00
I Love Lucy, Dell #35, 1962, EX, J5 ....$30.00
I Love Lucy, Dell Four-Color #559, EX...........................$100.00
I Spy, Gold Key #1, 1966, photo cover, VG+, F8 ....$15.00
Incredible Hulk, Marvel #3, 1962, VG+.........................$200.00
Incredible Hulk, Marvel #6, 1963, VG+, A....................$200.00
It's About Time, Gold Key #1, EX $12.00
Jetsons, Gold Key #6, 1963, VG+, T2 ....$15.00
Journey Into Mystery, Dell #116, VG, M14 ....$15.00
Journey to the Center of the Earth, Dell Four-Color #1060,
    1959, corner missing from back cover o/w VG $10.00
King of Kings, Dell Four-Color #1236, 1961, EX, F8........$30.00
Lady & the Tramp, Dell Giant #1, 1955, VG+, M14.......$35.00
Lady & the Tramp, Whitman, 1972, EX $4.00
Lancer, Gold Key #1, EX, T2...$10.00
Lassie, Dell #11, VG+, M14 ....$8.00
Lassie, Dell #45, 1959, G, T2 ....$5.00
Little Lulu, Dell #209, EX+, M14......................................$3.00
Little Lulu Christmas Diary, Gold Key #166, 1963, EX....$40.00
Little Monsters, Gold Key #21, 1973, NM, F8 ....$5.00
Lone Ranger, Dell #6, 1948, EX+ $60.00
Lone Ranger, Dell #69, EX $18.00
Looney Tunes & Merry Melodies, Dell #15, 1942, VG,
    M14 ....$125.00
Magilla Gorilla Vs Yogi Bear for President, Gold Key #3, 1964,
    EX, T2 ....$12.00
Man From UNCLE, Gold Key, #10, 1966, VG+, T2..........$5.00
Man in Space, Dell Four-Color #716, VG+, T2 ....$8.00
Marvel Super Heroes Tales Annual, #1, 1964, EX, C1.....$65.00
Mary Poppins, Gold Key, 1964, EX, T2 ....$18.00
Maverick, Dell #16, 1960, VG+, T2 ....$16.00
Mickey & Donald in Vacationland, Dell Giant #47, EX, M14,
    from $30 to..$40.00
Mickey Mouse Birthday Party, Dell Giant #1, VG+, M14....$60.00
Mickey Mouse in Frontierland, Dell Giant #1, VG+, M14 ..$34.00
Mission Impossible, Dell #3, 1967, photo cover, NM.......$30.00
Moby Dick, Dell #717, 1956, G+, T2 ....$10.00
Munsters, Gold Key #1, VG+ $45.00
My Little Margie, Dell #27, EX, M14................................$11.00

Nancy & Sluggo, Dell #145, EX+, M14 ....$15.00
Old Ironsides w/Johnny Tremain, Dell #874, 1957, VG, T2..$8.00

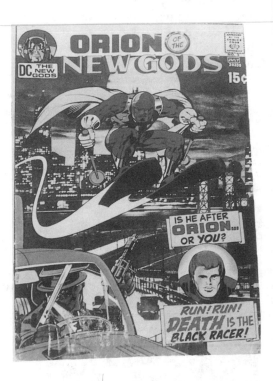

Orion of the New Gods, DC Comics #3, NM, $10.00.

Our Gang, Dell #20, G, M14..............................$15.00
Pat Boone, DC Comics #4, 1960, rare, EX......................$80.00
Peter Panda, Dell #31, 1958, M14..............................$16.00
Peter Potamus, Gold Key #1, 1964, G.............................$15.00
Picnic Party, Dell Giant #7, 1956, unused, EX, J5 ....$35.00
Pinocchio, Dell #252, 1949 movie version, VG, M14......$20.00
Pixie & Dixie, Dell #631, 1962, G+, T2 ....$5.00
Playful Little Audry, Dell #1, 1957, EX+, M14.................$60.00
Police Against Crime, Dell #3, 1954, VG, M14 ....$14.00
Queen of the West, Dale Evans, Dell #5, NM, M14........$50.00
Range Rider, Dell #13, 1955, VG, T2 ....$8.00

Rat Patrol, Dell #1, EX, M14..$17.00
Rawhide, Dell Four-Color #1097, 1960, photo cover, VG..$22.00
Rawhide Kid, Dell #34, VG, M14 ....$12.00
Real McCoys, Dell Four-Color #1134, 1960, photo cover, VG+ $18.00
Red Ryder, Dell #69, 1949, EX..$20.00
Rifleman, #20, G, J2..$12.00
Rin-Tin-Tin & Rusty, Dell Four-Color #523, 1953, G, T2...$10.00
Rootie Kazootie, Dell #4, 1954, G, T2 ....$5.00
Roy Rogers, Dell #139, 1950s, NM $35.00
Santa Claus Funnies, Dell #205, 1948, EX, J5 ....$35.00
Savage Sword of Conan, Marvel #1, NM, M14 ....$65.00
Sea Hunt, Dell Four-Color #994, 1959, photo cover, VG ..$15.00
Secret Agent, Gold Key #1, 1966, NM..........................$100.00
Sergeant Preston of the Yukon, Dell #28, VG+, M14 ......$14.00
Sir Lancelot & Brian, Dell Four-Color #775, 1957, photo cover, VG $20.00
Sir Walter Raleigh, Dell #644, 1955, G+, T2 ....$10.00
Snagglepuss, Gold Key #2, 1964, VG+, T2 ....$8.00
Snow White & the Seven Dwarfs, Dell Four-Color #382, 1944, EX+, M8...$45.00
Soldiers of Fortune, Dell #1, 1951, VG, M14...................$34.00
Spin & Marty & Annette, Dell Four-Color #826, 1957, photo cover, VG+ $35.00
Star Trek, Gold Key #19, 1969, EX, from $30 to.............$35.00
Strange Galaxy, Dell #8, NM, M14..................................$7.00
Super Duck in the Cockeyed Wonder, MLJ Comics #1, 1944, VG $80.00
Super Mouse, Dell #36, EX, M14 ....$12.00
Superboy, Dell #22, 1952, VG, M14................................$50.00
Superman's Girlfriend Lois Lane, Dell #13, NM, M14 .....$95.00
Superman's Pal Jimmy Olsen, Dell #32, EX, M14............$30.00
Tales From the Crypt, Dell #28, VG, M14, from $70 to...$80.00
Tales of Suspense, Dell #10, VG+, M14 ....$85.00
Tarzan, Dell #28, 1952, photo cover, EX $45.00
Tarzan, Dell #101, 1958, photo cover, EX, T2................$10.00

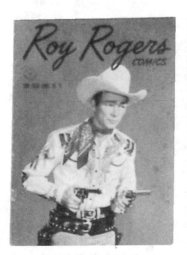
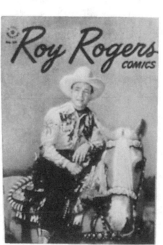

Roy Rogers, Dell Four-Color #95, 1945, NM, from $250.00 to $285.00; Roy Rogers, Dell Four-Color #124, 1946, NM, from $140.00 to $160.00.

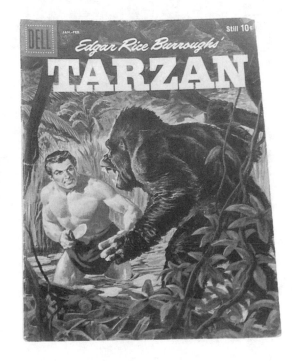

Tarzan, Dell #116, 1960, EX, from $7.00 to $10.00.

Tarzan's Jungle World, Dell Giant #25, VG, M14............**$22.00**
Tex Ritter Western, Fawcett/Charlton #33, EX, M14......**$20.00**
That Darn Cat, Movie Comics, NM, M14, from $40 to...**$50.00**

The Phantom, Gold Key, NM, $20.00.

Three Stooges, Dell #1170, 1961, VG **$20.00**
Three Stooges, Gold Key #32, 1967, photo cover, NM, C1..**$45.00**
Thunder Agents, Tower #12, EX, M14 ....**$8.00**
Tippy's Friends & Go-Go Animal, Tower #7, 1967, EX, F8 ..**$12.00**
Tom & Jerry Back to School, Dell Giant #1, 1956, EX+, M14..**$120.00**
Tom & Jerry Funhouse, Gold Key #213, 1962, 1st Funhouse issure, EX, F8..**$15.00**

Walt Disney's Treasure Island, Dell #624, 1955, EX, $22.00.

Tom & Jerry Summer Fun, Dell Giant #2, 1955, G, F8......**$5.00**
Tom Mix, Fawcett #10, 1948, VG, F8..............................**$35.00**
Top Cat, #8, VG+, J2...**$12.00**
Tweety & Sylvester, Dell #11, NM, M14.........................**$15.00**
Uncle Scrooge, Dell #13, EX, 1956, from $35 to **$40.00**
Underworld Crime, Dell #3, 1952, EX, M14....................**$35.00**
Untouchables, Dell #207, 1962, EX, M14........................**$25.00**
Vacation in Disneyland, Dell Giant #1, 1959, NM, M14..**$150.00**
Voyage to the Bottom of the Sea, Gold Key #2, 1965, EX, F8.**$10.00**
Wagon Train, Dell Four-Color #1019, 1959, 3rd issue, VG+..**$10.00**

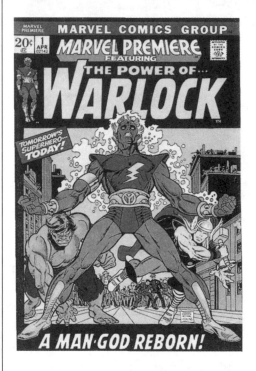

Warlock, Marvel Premiere #1, 1972, NM, $12.00.

Western Roundup, Dell Giant #14, 1956, VG+, from $15 to .**$18.00**
Wings of Eagles, Dell #790, VG, T2................................**$30.00**
Woody Woodpecker, Dell Four-Color #288, 1950, EX **$20.00**
Woody Woodpecker Back to School, Dell Giant #1, EX, M14...**$20.00**
X-Men, Marvel #60, 1969, EX..**$15.00**
Yak Yak, Dell #1186, EX **$30.00**
Young Men, Atlas #27, 1954, EX+ **$225.00**
Zorro, Dell #11, 1960, EX..**$20.00**
Zorro, Gold Key #1, 1957, EX, W6 ....**$14.00**
Zorro, Gold Key #3, 1966, EX+, W6 ....**$15.00**

Corgi

Corgi vehicles are among the favorites of the diecast collectors; they've been made in Great Britain since 1956, and they're still in production today. They were well detailed and ruggedly built to last. Some of the most expensive Corgi's on today's collector market are the character-related vehicles, for instance, James Bond (there are several variations), Batman, and U.N.C.L.E.

Values are for mint-in-the-box or mint-in-package examples.
Other Sources: G2, L1, N3, W1

#050, Massey-Ferguson 50B Tractor.................$40.00
#050, Massey-Ferguson 65 Tractor..................$110.00
#051, Massey-Ferguson Tipper Trailer $20.00
#053, Massey-Ferguson Tractor Shovel...............$100.00
#054, Fordson Half-Track Tractor $160.00
#054, Massey-Ferguson Tractor Shovel...............$50.00
#055, David Brown Tractor..........................$50.00
#055, Fordson Major Tractor........................$100.00
#056, Plough.......................................$25.00
#057, Massey-Ferguson Tractor & Fork $110.00
#058, Beast Carrier $30.00
#060, Fordson Power Major Tractor..................$100.00
#061, Four-Furrow Plough $15.00
#062, Ford Tipper Trailer $20.00
#064, Conveyor on Jeep.............................$75.00
#066, Massey-Ferguson Tractor $85.00
#067, Ford Super Major Tractor $90.00
#069, Massey-Ferguson Tractor Shovel...............$100.00
#071, Fordson Disc Harrow $20.00
#072, Ford 5000 Tractor & Trencher $125.00
#073, Massey-Ferguson Tractor & Saw $125.00
#074, Ford 5000 Tractor & Scoop $100.00
#100, Dropside Trailer $20.00
#101, Platform Trailer.............................$20.00
#102, Pony Trailer $25.00
#104, Dolphin Cabin Cruiser $30.00
#107, Batboat & Trailer $125.00
#109, Penny Burn Trailer $50.00
#112, Rice Horse Box $45.00
#150, Surtees TS9 ....$35.00
#150, Vanwall......................................$70.00
#151, Lotus XI $80.00
#151, McLaren Yardley M19A $30.00
#152, BRM Racer....................................$80.00
#152, Ferrari 312 B2...............................$35.00
#153, Bluebird Record Car $125.00
#153, Team Surtees.................................$35.00
#154, Ferrari Formula I $50.00
#154, Lotus John Player $40.00
#154, Lotus Texaco Special $40.00
#155, Shadow F1 Racer $40.00
#156, Shadow F1, Graham Hill $40.00
#158, Lotus Climax $50.00
#158, Tyrrell-Ford Elf $40.00
#159, Cooper Maserati $50.00
#159, Indianapolis Racer $40.00
#160, Hesketh Racer $40.00
#161, Elf-Tyrrel Project 34 ....$50.00
#161, Santa Pod Commuter...........................$40.00
#162, Quartermaster Dragster.......................$40.00
#163, Santa Pod Dragster...........................$50.00
#164, Wild Honey Dragster $50.00
#165, Adams Bros Dragster..........................$40.00
#166, Ford Mustang $45.00
#167, USA Racing Buggy $35.00
#169, Starfighter Jet Dragster $40.00
#170, John Wolfe's Dragster $40.00
#190, Lotus John Player Special $60.00

#191, McLaren Texaco-Marlboro......................$65.00
#200, BMC Mini 1000................................$50.00
#200, Ford Consul, dual colors $200.00
#200, Ford Consul, solid colors $175.00
#200m, Ford Consul, w/motor........................$200.00
#201, Austin Cambridge.............................$175.00
#201, Saint's Volvo................................$120.00
#201m, Austin Cambridge, w/motor...................$200.00
#202, Morris Cowley................................$175.00
#202, Renault R16..................................$40.00
#202m, Morris Cowley, w/motor......................$200.00
#203, Detomaso Mangust $40.00
#203, Vauxhall Velox, dual colors $200.00
#203, Vauxhall Velox, solid colors $175.00
#203m, Vauxhall Velox, w/motor, dual colors........$300.00
#203m, Vauxhall Velox, w/motor, red or yel $200.00
#204, Morris Mini-Minor, bl $150.00
#204, Morris Mini-Minor, metallic bl $100.00
#204, Rover 90, other colors $175.00
#204, Rover 90, wht & red, 2-tone $300.00
#204m, Rover 90, w/motor...........................$175.00
#205, Riley Pathfinder, bl $175.00
#205, Riley Pathfinder, red $130.00
#205m, Riley Pathfinder, w/motor, bl $175.00
#205m, Riley Pathfinder, w/motor, red $225.00
#206, Hillman Husky Estate, metallic bl & silver, 2-tone ...$175.00
#206, Hillman Husky Estate, solid colors...........$130.00
#206m, Hillman Husky Estate, w/motor $200.00
#207, Standard Vanguard............................$125.00
#207m, Standard Vanguard, w/motor $175.00
#208, Jaguar 2.4 Saloon $160.00
#208m, Jaguar 2.4 Saloon, w/motor $200.00
#208s, Jaguar 2.4 Saloon, w/suspension.............$100.00

#209, Riley Police Car, $120.00.

#210, Citroen DS19.................................$90.00
#210s, Citroen DS19, w/suspension $100.00
#211, Studebaker Golden Hawk $100.00

#211m, Studebaker Golden Hawk, w/motor...................$175.00
#211s, Studebaker Golden Hawk, w/suspension.............$125.00
#213, Jaguar Fire Chief...$150.00
#213s, Jaguar Fire Chief, w/suspension.........................$200.00
#214, Ford Thunderbird...$95.00
#214m, Ford Thunderbird, w/motor.............................$300.00
#214s, Ford Thunderbird, w/suspension.......................$100.00
#215, Ford Thunderbird Sport.....................................$100.00
#215s, Ford Thunderbird Sport, w/suspension...............$100.00
#216, Austin A-40, red & blk......................................$175.00
#216, Austin A-40, 2-tone bl.......................................$100.00
#216m, Austin A-40, w/motor.....................................$300.00
#217, Fiat 1800...$80.00
#218, Austin Martin DB4...$100.00
#219, Plymouth Suburban..$80.00
#220, Chevrolet Impala...$80.00
#221, Chevrolet Impala Cab.......................................$90.00
#222, Renault Floride..$80.00
#223, Chevrolet Police...$70.00
#224, Bentley Continental..$100.00
#225, Austin 7, red...$100.00
#225, Austin 7, yel...$300.00
#226, Morris Mini-Minor...$100.00
#227, Mini-Cooper Rally..$300.00
#228, Volvo P-1800..$80.00
#229, Chevrolet Corvair..$70.00
#230, Mercedes Benz 220..$75.00
#231, Triumph Herald...$100.00
#232, Fiat 2100...$75.00
#233, Heinkel Trojan..$100.00
#234, Ford Consul Classic..$75.00
#235, Oldsmobile Super 88...$75.00
#236, Motor School, right-hand drive...........................$90.00
#237, Oldsmobile Sheriff's Car....................................$100.00
#238, Jaguar MK10, gr or silver..................................$200.00
#238, Jaguar MK10, metallic gr, red or bl.....................$100.00
#239, VW Karman Ghia...$90.00
#240, Fiat 500 Jolly..$125.00
#241, Chrysler Ghia..$90.00
#242, Fiat 600 Jolly..$175.00
#245, Buick Riviera..$75.00

#246, Chrysler Imperial, metallic turq..........................$250.00
#246, Chrysler Imperial, red.......................................$100.00
#248, Chevrolet Impala...$70.00
#249, Morris Mini-Cooper, wicker................................$130.00
#251, Hillman Imp..$100.00
#252, Rover 2000, metallic bl......................................$80.00
#252, Rover 2000, metallic maroon..............................$150.00
#253, Mercedes Benz 220 SE......................................$90.00
#255, Motor School, left-hand drive.............................$225.00
#256, VW 1200 East Africa Safari................................$200.00
#258, Saint's Volvo P1800..$175.00
#259, Citroen Le Dandy, bl...$200.00
#259, Citroen Le Dandy, maroon..................................$120.00
#259, Penguin Mobile..$50.00
#260, Renault R16..$40.00
#261, James Bond's Aston Martin DBS..........................$200.00
#261, Spiderbuggy..$100.00
#262, Capt Marvel's Porsche.......................................$65.00
#262, Lincoln Continental Limo, bl...............................$200.00
#262, Lincoln Continental Limo, gold............................$100.00
#263, Capt America's Jetmobile...................................$50.00
#263, Rambler Marlin..$50.00
#264, Incredible Hulk..$75.00
#264, Oldsmobile Toronado..$65.00
#265, Supermobile..$65.00
#266, Chitty-Chitty Bang-Bang, original.......................$350.00
#266, Chitty-Chitty Bang-Bang, replica.........................$125.00
#266, Superbike...$50.00

#267, Batmobile, red 'Bat'-hubs, $400.00.

#267, Batmobile, w/red whizzwheels.............................$500.00
#267, Batmobile, w/whizzwheels..................................$150.00
#268, Batman's Bat Bike..$70.00
#269, James Bond's Lotus...$100.00
#270, James Bond's Aston Martin, w/tire slashers, 1/43 scale....$250.00
#270, James Bond's Aston Martin, w/whizzwheels, 1/43 scale...$100.00
#271, Ghia Mangusta De Tomaso..................................$50.00
#271, James Bond's Aston Martin..................................$90.00

#247, Mercedes Benz 600 Pullman, $65.00.

#272, James Bond's Citroen 2CV $60.00
#273, Honda Driving School...........................$40.00
#273, Rolls Royce Silver Shadow.....................$100.00
#274, Bentley Mulliner $80.00
#275, Mini Metro, colors other than gold $20.00
#275, Mini Metro, gold................................$75.00
#275, Rover 2000 TC, gr $75.00
#275, Rover 2000 TC, wht.............................$160.00
#275, Royal Wedding Mini Metro $25.00
#276, Oldsmobile Toronado $70.00
#276, Triumph Acclaim $15.00

#277, Monkeemobile, $300.00.

#277, Triumph Driving School $25.00
#279, Rolls Royce Corniche $30.00
#280, Rolls Royce Silver Shadow $50.00
#281, Metro Datapost $20.00
#281, Rover 2000 TC $150.00
#282, Mini Cooper Rally Car $90.00
#283, DAF City Car $40.00
#284, Citroen SM $40.00
#285, Mercedes Benz 240D...........................$20.00
#286, Jaguar XJ12C...................................$40.00
#287, Citroen Dyane $25.00

#288, Minissima $20.00
#289, VW Polo $25.00
#290, Kojak's Buick, no hat..........................$100.00
#290, Kojak's Buick, w/hat...........................$75.00
#291, AMC Pacer $20.00
#291, Mercedes Benz 240 Rally $35.00
#292, Starsky & Hutch's Ford Torino $60.00
#293, Renault 5TS.....................................$20.00
#294, Renault Alpine $20.00
#298, Magnum PI's Ferrari $50.00
#299, Ford Sierra 2.3 Ghia $20.00
#300, Austin Healey, red or cream $150.00
#300, Austin Healey Sports Car, bl...................$300.00
#300, Chevrolet Corvette.............................$70.00
#300, Ferrari Daytona $25.00
#301, Iso Grifo 7 Litre................................$50.00
#301, Lotus Elite $25.00
#301, Triumph TR2 Sports Car $150.00
#302, Hillman Hunter Rally, kangaroo.................$130.00
#302, MGA Sports Car $130.00
#302, VW Polo $20.00
#303, Mercedes Benz 300SL..........................$100.00
#303, Porsche 924 ....$20.00
#303, Roger Clark's Ford Capri $75.00
#303s, Mercedes Benz 300SL, w/suspension $100.00
#304, Chevrolet SS350 Camaro $65.00
#304, Mercedes Benz 300SL, yel $150.00
#304, Mercedes Benz 300SL, yel & red $100.00
#304s, Mercedes Benz 300SL, w/suspension $100.00
#305, Mini Marcos GT 850 ....$50.00
#305, Triumph TR3....................................$135.00
#306, Fiat X1/9.......................................$20.00
#306, Morris Marina $55.00
#307, Jaguar E Type $125.00
#307, Renault...$20.00
#308, BMW M1 Racer, gold plated....................$100.00
#308, BMW M1 Racer, yel...........................$25.00
#308, Monte Carlo Mini $100.00
#309, Aston Martin DB4..............................$125.00
#309, Aston Martin DB4, w/spoked hubs $200.00
#309, VW Turbo $20.00
#310, Chevrolet Corvette, bronze $175.00
#310, Chevrolet Corvette, red or silver...............$65.00
#310, Porsche 924 ....$20.00
#311, Ford Capri, orange $125.00
#311, Ford Capri, red $80.00
#311, Ford Capri, w/gold hubs $150.00
#312, Ford Capri S $35.00
#312, Jaguar E Type $100.00
#312, Marcos Mantis..................................$40.00
#313, Ford Cortina, bronze or bl $100.00
#313, Ford Cortina, yel...............................$300.00
#314, Ferrari Berlinetta Le Mans......................$65.00
#314, Supercat Jaguar $30.00
#315, Lotus Elite $25.00
#315, Simca Sports Car, metallic bl $200.00
#315, Simca Sports Car, silver........................$65.00
#316, Ford GT70......................................$50.00

#316, NSU Sport Prinz	$90.00
#317, Mini Cooper Monte Carlo	$200.00
#318, Jaguar XJS	$25.00
#318, Lotus Elan, copper	$300.00
#318, Lotus Elan, metallic bl	$90.00
#318, Lotus Elan, wht	$160.00
#319, Jaguar XJS	$35.00
#319, Lamborghini P400 GT Miura	$35.00
#319, Lotus Elan, gr or yel	$140.00
#319, Lotus Elan, red or bl	$100.00
#320, Saint's Jaguar XJS	$70.00
#321, Monte Carlo Mini Cooper, 1965	$300.00
#321, Monte Carlo Mini Cooper, 1966, w/autographs	$600.00
#321, Porsche 924, metallic gr	$70.00
#321, Porsche 924, red	$25.00
#322, Rover Monte Carlo	$200.00
#323, Citroen DS19 Monte Carlo	$200.00
#323, Ferrari Daytona 365 GTB4	$25.00
#324, Marcos Volvo 1800 GT	$70.00
#325, Chevrolet Caprice	$50.00
#325, Ford Mustang Competition	$80.00
#326, Chevrolet Police Car	$30.00
#327, Chevrolet Caprice Cab	$30.00
#327, MGB GT	$130.00
#328, Hillman Imp Monte Carlo	$125.00
#329, Ford Mustang Rally	$50.00
#329, Opel Senator, bl or bronze	$30.00
#329, Opel Senator, silver	$50.00
#330, Porsche Carrera 6, wht & bl	$120.00
#330, Porsche Carrera 6, wht & red	$50.00
#331, Ford Capri Rally	$90.00
#332, Lancia Fulvia Sport, red or bl	$50.00
#332, Lancia Fulvia Sport, yel & blk	$125.00
#332, Opel, Doctor's Car	$50.00
#333, Mini Cooper Sun/Rac	$400.00
#334, Ford Escort	$20.00
#334, Mini Magnifique	$100.00
#335, Jaguar 4.2 Litre E Type	$125.00
#336, James Bond's Toyota 2000 GT	$350.00
#337, Chevrolet Stingray	$65.00
#338, Chevrolet SS350 Camaro	$65.00
#338, Rover 3500	$30.00
#339, Rover 3500 Police Car	$30.00
#339, 1967 Mini Cooper Monte Carlo, w/roof rack	$300.00
#340, Rover Triplex	$25.00
#340, 1967 Sunbeam Imp Monte Carlo	$135.00
#341, Chevrolet Caprice Racer	$25.00
#341, Mini Marcos GT850	$60.00
#342, Lamborghini P400 GT Miura	$50.00
#342, Professionals Ford Capri	$80.00
#342, Professionals Ford Capri, w/chrome bumpers	$100.00
#343, Pontiac Firebird	$50.00
#344, Ferrari 206 Dino Sport	$50.00
#345, Honda Prelude	$25.00
#345, MGC GT, orange	$300.00
#345, MGC GT, yel	$125.00
#346, Citroen 2 CV	$20.00
#347, Chevrolet Astro 1	$50.00
#348, Pop Art Mustang Stock Car	$150.00
#348, Vegas Ford Thunderbird	$75.00
#349, Pop Art Morris Mini	$1,500.00
#350, Thunderbird Guided Missile	$125.00
#351, RAF Land Rover	$80.00
#352, RAF Vanguard Staff Car	$100.00
#353, Road Scanner	$50.00
#354, Commer Military Ambulance	$100.00
#355, Commer Military Police	$135.00
#356, VW Personnel Carrier	$135.00
#357, Land Rover Weapons Carrier	$200.00
#358, Oldsmobile Staff Car	$100.00
#359, Commer Army Field Kitchen	$165.00
#370, Ford Cobra Mustang	$20.00
#371, Porsche Carrera	$40.00
#373, Peugeot 505	$20.00
#374, Jaguar 4.2 Litre E Type	$70.00
#374, Jaguar 5.3 Litre	$70.00
#375, Toyota 2000 GT	$60.00
#376, Chevrolet Stingray Stock Car	$50.00
#377, Marcos 3 Litre, wht & gray	$100.00
#377, Marcos 3 Litre, yel or bl	$60.00
#378, Ferrari 308 GT	$25.00
#378, MGC GT	$140.00
#380, Alfa Romeo P33	$40.00
#380, Beach Buggy	$40.00
#381, Renault Turbo	$20.00
#382, Lotus Elite	$20.00
#382, Porsche Targa 911S	$50.00
#383, VW 1200, red or orange	$80.00
#383, VW 1200, Swiss PTT	$130.00
#383, VW 1200, yel ADAC	$200.00
#384, Adams Bros Probe 15	$40.00
#384, Renault 11 GTL, cream	$20.00
#384, Renault 11 GTL, maroon	$40.00
#384, VW 1200 Rally	$70.00
#385, Porsche 917	$40.00
#386, Bertone Runabout	$40.00
#387, Chevrolet Corvette Stingray	$100.00
#388, Mercedes Benz C111	$40.00
#389, Reliant Bond Bug 700, gr	$100.00
#389, Reliant Bond Bug 700 ES, orange	$60.00
#391, James Bond's 007 Mustang	$250.00
#392, Bertone Shake Buggy	$40.00
#393, Mercedes Benz 350 SL, metallic gr	$100.00
#393, Mercedes Benz 350 SL, wht or bl	$50.00
#394, Datsun 240Z, East African Safari	$45.00
#396, Datsun 240Z, US Rally	$45.00
#397, Can Am Porsche Audi	$35.00
#400, VW Driving School, bl	$65.00
#400, VW Driving School, red	$140.00
#401, VW 1200	$60.00
#402, Ford Cortina GXL, wht w/red stripe	$80.00
#402, Ford Cortina GXL Police, wht	$50.00
#402, Ford Cortina GXL Polizei	$150.00
#403, Bedford Daily Express	$200.00
#403, Thwaites Dumper	$45.00
#403m, Bedford KLG Plugs, w/motor	$230.00

#404, Bedford Dormobile, cream, maroon & turq	$110.00
#404, Bedford Dormobile, yel & 2-tone bl	$200.00
#404, Bedford Dormobile, yel w/bl roof	$125.00
#404m, Bedford Dormobile, w/motor	$160.00
#405, Bedford Utilicon Fire Department, red	$200.00
#405, Bedford Utilicon Fire Tender, gr	$160.00
#405, Chevrolet Superior Ambulance	$40.00
#405, Ford Milk Float	$25.00
#405m, Bedford Utilicon Fire Tender, w/motor	$200.00
#406, Land Rover	$80.00
#406, Mercedes Ambulance	$35.00
#406, Mercedes Benz Unimog	$50.00
#407, Karrier Mobile Grocers	$150.00
#408, Bedford AA Road Service	$150.00
#409, Allis Chalmers Fork Lift	$30.00
#409, Forward Control Jeep	$50.00
#409, Mercedes Dumper	$40.00
#411, Karrier Lucozade Van	$160.00
#411, Mercedes 240D, orange	$80.00
#411, Mercedes 240D Taxi, cream or blk	$60.00
#411, Mercedes 240D Taxi, orange w/blk roof	$30.00
#412, Bedford Ambulance, split windscreen	$130.00
#412, Bedford Ambulance, 1-pc windscreen	$250.00
#412, Mercedes Police Car, Police	$50.00
#412, Mercedes Police Car, Polizei	$40.00
#413, Karrier Bantam Butcher Shop	$150.00
#413, Mazda Maintenence Truck	$50.00
#413s, Karrier Bantam Butcher Shop, w/suspension	$200.00
#414, Bedford Military Ambulance	$120.00
#414, Coastguard Jaguar	$35.00
#415, Mazda Camper	$50.00
#416, Buick Police Car	$40.00
#416, Radio Rescue Rover, bl	$125.00
#416, Radio Rescue Rover, yel	$400.00
#416s, Radio Rescue Rover, w/suspension, bl	$100.00
#416s, Radio Rescue Rover, w/suspension, yel	$400.00
#417, Land Rover Breakdown	$80.00
#418, Austin Taxi	$40.00
#419, Ford Zephyr, Rijks Politei	$350.00
#419, Ford Zephyr Politei	$300.00
#419, Jeep	$30.00
#420, Airbone Caravan	$100.00
#421, Bedford Evening Standard	$200.00
#422, Bedford Van, Corgi Toys, bl w/yel roof	$500.00
#422, Bedford Van, Corgi Toys, yel w/bl roof	$200.00
#422, Riot Police Wagon	$30.00
#423, Rough Rider Van	$30.00
#424, Ford Zephyr Estate	$85.00
#424, Security Van	$20.00
#425, London Taxi	$25.00
#426, Chipperfield's Circus Booking Office	$300.00
#426, Pinder's Circus Booking Office	$50.00
#428, Mister Softee's Ice Cream Van	$175.00
#428, Renault Police Car	$25.00
#429, Jaguar Police Car	$40.00
#430, Bermuda Taxi, metallic bl & red	$400.00
#430, Bermuda Taxi, wht	$120.00
#430, Porsche 924 Polizei	$30.00
#431, Vanatic Van	$30.00
#431, VW Pickup, metallic gold	$300.00
#431, VW Pickup, yel	$100.00
#432, Vanatic Van	$30.00
#433, VW Delivery Van	$100.00
#434, VW Kombi	$100.00
#435, Karrier Dairy Van	$125.00
#435, Superman Van	$50.00
#436, Citroen Safari	$100.00
#436, Spider Van	$50.00
#437, Cadillac Ambulance	$100.00
#437, Coca-Cola Van	$40.00
#438, Land Rover, gr	$60.00
#438, Land Rover, Lepra	$400.00
#439, Chevrolet Fire Chief	$100.00
#440, Ford Cortina Estate, w/golfer & caddy	$170.00
#440, Mazda Pickup	$25.00
#441, Jeep	$25.00
#441, VW Toblerone Van	$135.00
#443, Plymouth US Mail	$100.00
#445, Plymouth Suburban	$90.00
#447, Walls Ice Cream Van	$250.00
#448, Police Mini Van, w/dog & handler	$200.00
#448, Renagade Jeep	$20.00
#450, Austin Mini Van	$100.00
#450, Austin Mini Van, w/pnt grille	$160.00
#450, Peugeot Taxi	$25.00
#452, Commer Lorry	$130.00
#453, Commer Walls Van	$200.00
#454, Commer Platform Lorry	$130.00
#455, Karrier Bantam 2-ton	$120.00
#456, ERF Dropside Lorry	$100.00
#457, ERF Platform Lorry	$100.00
#457, Talbot Matra Rancho, gr or red	$25.00
#457, Talbot Matra Rancho, wht or orange	$45.00
#458, ERF Tipper Dumper	$75.00
#459, ERF Moorhouse Van	$375.00
#459, Raygo Road Roller	$40.00
#460, ERF Cement Tipper	$90.00
#461, Police Vigilant Range Rover, Police	$35.00
#461, Police Viligant Range Rover, Politie	$80.00
#462, Commer Van, Co-op	$125.00
#462, Commer Van, Hammonds	$170.00
#463, Commer Ambulance	$100.00
#464, Commer Police Van, City Police	$300.00
#464, Commer Police Van, County Police, bl	$100.00
#464, Commer Police Van, Police , bl	$100.00
#464, Commer Police Van, Police, gr	$750.00
#464, Commer Police Van, Rijks Politie, bl	$300.00
#465, Commer Pickup Truck	$65.00
#466, Commer Milk Float, Co-op	$170.00
#466, Commer Milk Float, wht	$70.00
#467, London Routemaster Bus	$70.00
#468, London Transport Routemaster, Design Centre, red	$250.00
#468, London Transport Routemaster, Gamages, red	$200.00
#468, London Transport Routemaster Bus, Church's Shoes, red	$200.00
#468, London Transport Routemaster Bus, Corgi Toys, brn, gr or cream	$1,000.00

#468, London Transport Routemaster Bus, Corgi Toys, red ..$100.00
#468, London Transport Routemaster Bus, Madame Tussand's, red $200.00
#468, London Transport Routemaster Bus, Outspan, red ..$60.00
#470, Disneyland Bus......$40.00
#470, Forward Control Jeep......$60.00
#470, Greenline Bus $20.00
#471, Karrier Snack Bar, Joe's Diner......$125.00
#471, Karrier Snack Bar, Patates Frites......$300.00
#471, Silver Jubilee Bus $40.00
#471, Woolworth Silver Jubilee Bus......$40.00
#472, Public Address Land Rover $130.00
#474, Ford Musical Walls Ice Cream Van $250.00
#475, Citroen Ski Safari $150.00
#477, Land Rover Breakdown $60.00
#478, Forward Control Jeep, Tower Wagon......$50.00
#479, Mobile Camaro Van $150.00
#480, Chevrolet Impala Cab $80.00
#480, Chevrolet Police Car $80.00
#482, Chevrolet Fire Chief Car......$100.00
#482, Range Rover Ambulance $40.00
#483, Dodge Tipper $50.00
#483, Police Range Rover, Belgian $75.00
#484, AMC Pacer Rescue......$25.00
#484, AMC Pacer Secours......$40.00
#484, Livestock Transporter......$60.00
#484, Mini Countryman Surfer $175.00
#485, Mini Countryman Surfer, w/unpnt grille $225.00
#486, Chevrolet Kennel Service $100.00
#487, Chipperfield's Circus Parade $200.00
#489, VW Police Car......$30.00
#490, Caravan $25.00
#490, VW Breakdown Truck $80.00
#491, Ford Escort Estate $100.00
#492, VW Police Car, Polizei......$300.00

#492, VW Police Car, Polizei $80.00
#492, VW Police Car, w/gr mudguards $300.00
#493, Mazda Pickup $25.00
#494, Bedford Tipper, red & silver $175.00
#494, Bedford Tipper, red & yel $70.00
#495, Opel Open Truck $15.00
#497, Man From UNCLE, bl......$250.00
#497, Man From UNCLE, wht......$600.00
#499, Citroen, 1968 Olympics $175.00
#500, US Army Rover......$400.00
#506, Sunbeam Imp Police $100.00
#508, Holiday Minibus $100.00
#509, Porsche Police Car, Polizei $80.00
#509, Porsche Police Car, Rijks Politie......$125.00
#510, Citroen Tour De France $125.00
#511, Chipperfield's Circus Poodle Pickup $600.00
#513, Alpine Rescue Car......$350.00
#647, Buck Roger's Starfighter $75.00
#648, Space Shuttle $50.00
#649, James Bond's Space Shuttle $80.00
#650, BOAC Concorde, all others $25.00
#650, BOAC Concorde, gold logo on tail......$100.00
#651, Air France Concorde, all others $50.00
#651, Japan Air Line Concorde $400.00
#653, Air Canada Concorde $300.00
#681, Stunt Bike $250.00
#700, Motorway Ambulance $20.00
#701, Intercity Minibus $15.00
#703, Breakdown Truck $20.00
#703, Hi Speed Fire Engine $20.00
#801, Ford Thunderbird......$25.00

#503, Chipperfield Circus Giraffe Transporter, $125.00.

#801, Noddy's Car, $450.00.

#801, Noddy's Car, w/blk-face golly......$1,000.00
#802, Mercedes Benz 300SL $20.00
#802, Popeye's Paddle Wagon $500.00
#803, Beatle's Yellow Submarine $500.00
#803, Jaguar XK120 ......$20.00

#804, Jaguar XK120 Rally $20.00
#804, Jaguar XK120 Rally, w/spats $50.00
#804, Noddy's Car, Noddy only $275.00
#804, Noddy's Car, w/Mr Tubby $350.00

#805, Hardy Boys' Rolls Royce, $300.00.

#805, Mercedes Benz 300SC $20.00
#806, Lunar Bug...$150.00
#806, Mercedes Benz 300SC $20.00
#807, Basil Brush's Car $200.00
#807, Dougal's Car..$300.00
#809, Dick Dastardly's Racer $150.00
#810, Ford Thunderbird...$20.00
#811, James Bond's Moon Buggy.................................$500.00
#831, Mercedes Benz 300SL..$20.00
#851, Magic Roundabout Train $350.00
#852, Magic Roundabout Carousel $800.00
#853, Magic Roundabout Playground.........................$1,500.00
#859, Mr McHenry's Trike $250.00
#900, German Tank..$50.00
#901, British Centurion $50.00
#902, American Tank..$50.00
#903, British Chieftain Tank $50.00
#904, King Tiger Tank $50.00
#905, SU100 Tank Destroyer $50.00
#906, Saladin Armoured Car..$50.00
#907, German Rocket Launcher $60.00
#908, French Recovery Tank $75.00
#909, Quad Gun Tank, Trailer & Field Gun $60.00
#920, Bell Helicopter..$30.00
#921, Hughes Helicopter $30.00
#922, Sikorsky Helicopter $30.00
#923, Sikorsky Helicopter Military $30.00
#925, Batcopter...$60.00
#926, Stromberg Helicopter $60.00
#927, Chopper Squad Helicopter....................................$60.00
#928, Spidercopter...$90.00
#929, Daily Planet Helicopter $50.00
#930, DAAX Helicopter $60.00
#931, Jet Police Helicopter...$50.00

CORGITRONICS

#1001, Corgitronics Firestreak.......................................$80.00
#1002, Corgitronics Landtrain $50.00
#1003, Ford Torino $30.00
#1004, Corgitronics Beep Beep Bus................................$40.00

#1005, Police Land Rover..$30.00
#1006, Roadshow, Radio $50.00
#1007, Land Rover & Compressor $50.00
#1008, Chevrolet Fire Chief..$40.00
#1009, Maestro MG1600 ....$50.00
#1011, Firestreak $40.00

EXPLORATION MODELS

#2022, Scanotron...$60.00
#2023, Rocketron..$60.00
#2024, Lasertron...$60.00
#2025, Magnetron $600.00

GIFT SETS

#01, Car Transporter Set $900.00
#01, Ford Sierra & Caravan..$40.00
#01, Ford 500 Tractor & Beast Trailer $160.00
#02, Land Rover & Horsebox...$150.00
#02, Unimog Dumper $150.00
#03, Batmobile & Batboat, w/'Bat'-hubs.......................$400.00
#03, Batmobile & Batboat, w/whizzwheels $200.00
#03, RAF Land Rover & Missile....................................$250.00
#04, Country Farm Set..$75.00
#04, RAF Land Rover & Missile....................................$500.00
#05, Country Farm Set, w/no hay..................................$100.00
#05, Racing Car Set..$300.00
#06, Rocket Age Set..$1,000.00
#06, VW Transporter & Copper Maserati $175.00
#07, Daktari Set..$150.00
#07, Tractor & Trailer Set $130.00
#08, Combine Harvester Set $400.00
#08, Lions of Longleat $200.00
#09, Corporal Missile & Launcher $600.00
#09, Tractor w/Shovel & Trailer.....................................$200.00
#10, Centurion Tank & Transporter $120.00
#10, Rambler Marlin, w/kayaks $200.00
#11, ERF Truck & Trailer $200.00
#11, London Set, no Policeman $125.00
#11, London Set, w/Policeman.......................................$600.00

#12, Chipperfield's Circus Crane Truck and Cage, $300.00.

#12, Glider Set..$80.00
#12, Grand Prix Set...$450.00

#13, Fordson Tractor & Plough..............................$150.00
#13, Peugeot Tour De France $90.00
#13, Renault Tour De France $150.00
#14, Giant Daktari Set $500.00
#14, Tower Wagon $100.00
#15, Giant Daktari Set $500.00
#15, Land Rover & Horsebox $100.00
#15, Silverstone Set..$1,600.00
#16, Ecurie Ecosse Set $500.00
#17, Land Rover & Ferrari $200.00
#17, Military Set $90.00
#18, Emergency Set..$80.00
#18, Fordson Tractor & Plough.............................$135.00
#19, Chipperfield's Circus Rover & Elephant Trailer $350.00
#19, Emergency Set..$80.00
#19, Flying Club Set $85.00
#20, Car Transporter Set......................................$100.00
#20, Emergency Set..$80.00
#20, Golden Guinea Set..$300.00
#21, Chipperfield's Circus Crane & Trailer................$1,600.00
#21, ERF Milk Truck & Trailer..............................$400.00
#21, Superman Set...$250.00
#22, Farm Set...$1,100.00
#22, James Bond Set $300.00
#23, Chipperfield's Circus Set, w/Booking Office $1,000.00
#23, Spider-Man Set..$200.00
#24, Construction Set...$150.00
#24, Mercedes & Caravan $50.00
#25, Shell or BP Garage Set $50.00
#25, VW Transporter & Cooper Maserati $160.00
#26, Beach Buggy Set...$50.00
#26, Matra Rancho & Racer....................................$75.00
#27, Priestman Shovel Set.....................................$180.00
#28, Mazda & Dinghy...$50.00
#28, Transporter Set $800.00
#29, Ferrari Racing Set $80.00
#29, Tractor & Trailer...$140.00
#30, Grand Prix Set $250.00
#30, Pinder's Circus Rover & Trailer $100.00
#31, Buick Riviera & Boat $225.00
#31, Safari Set...$75.00

#32, Tractor & Trailer...$170.00
#35, Chopper Squad $60.00
#35, London Set $175.00
#36, Tornado Set $250.00
#37, Fiat & Boat..$60.00
#37, Lotus Racing Team..$500.00
#38, Jaguar & Powerboat $60.00
#38, Mini Camping Set $75.00
#38, Monte Carlo Set $800.00
#40, Avenger Set, w/Bentley, gr.............................$800.00
#40, Avenger Set, w/Bentley, red............................$650.00
#40, Batman Set $250.00
#41, Ford Transporter Set $800.00
#41, Silver Jubilee State Landau..............................$40.00
#42, Agricultural Set...$80.00
#43, Silo & Conveyor $70.00
#44, Police Rover Set..$70.00
#45, All Winners Set...$800.00
#46, All Winners Set...$600.00
#46, Super Karts..$30.00
#47, Ford Tractor & Conveyor................................$180.00
#47, Pony Club Set $50.00
#48, Ford Transporter Set......................................$600.00
#48, Jean Richard's Circus Set $200.00
#48, Scammell Transporter Set $900.00
#49, Flying Club Set $50.00

HUSKIES

Huskies were marketed exclusively through the Woolworth stores from 1965 to 1969. In 1970, Corgi Juniors were introduced. Both lines were sold in blister packs. Models produced up to 1975 (as dated on the package) are valued from $15.00 to $30.00 (MIP), except for the character-related examples listed below.

#1001A, James Bond Aston Martin, Husky on base.......$200.00
#1001B, James Bond Aston Martin, Junior on base........$175.00
#1002A, Batmobile, Husky on base $200.00
#1002B, Batmobile, Junior on base $175.00
#1003A, Bat Boat, Husky on base............................$125.00
#1003B, Bat Boat, Junior on base.............................$85.00
#1004A, Monkeemobile, Husky on base.....................$200.00
#1004B, Monkeemobile, Junior on base $175.00
#1005A, UNCLE Car, Husky on base $175.00
#1005B, UNCLE Car, Junior on base $1,500.00
#1006A, Chitty-Chitty Bang-Bang, Husky on base........$200.00
#1006B, Chitty-Chitty Bang-Bang, Junior on base $175.00
#1007, Ironsides Police Van $125.00
#1008, Popeye Paddle Wagon $250.00
#1011, James Bond Bobsleigh.................................$300.00
#1012, Spectre Bobsleigh $300.00
#1013, Tom's Go-Kart $75.00
#1014, Jerry's Banger..$75.00
#1017, Ford Holmes Wrecker.................................$175.00

MAJOR PACKS

#1100, Carrimore Low Loader, red cab $140.00

#36, Tarzan Set, $250.00.

#1100, Carrimore Low Loader, yel cab..........................$225.00
#1100, Mack Truck...$80.00
#1101, Carrimore Car Transporter, bl cab.....................$250.00
#1101, Carrimore Car Transporter, red cab...................$100.00
#1101, Hydraulic Crane...$50.00
#1102, Crane Fruehauf Dumper $50.00
#1102, Euclid Tractor, gr..$150.00
#1102, Euclid Tractor, yel..$200.00
#1103, Airport Crash Truck $75.00
#1103, Euclid Crawler Tractor...$125.00
#1104, Machinery Carrier $150.00
#1104, Racehorse Transporter...$100.00
#1105, Berliet Racehorse Transporter $60.00
#1106, Decca Mobile Radar Van $160.00
#1106, Mack Container Truck..$75.00
#1107, Berliet Container Truck $60.00
#1107, Euclid Tractor & Dozer, gr......................................$150.00
#1107, Euclid Tractor & Dozer, orange $300.00
#1107, Euclid Tractor & Dozer, red $375.00
#1108, Bristol Bloodhound & Launching Ramp............$125.00
#1108, Michelin Container Truck $50.00
#1109, Bristol Bloodhound & Loading Trolley..............$130.00
#1109, Michelin Truck...$50.00
#1110, JCB Crawler Loader $60.00
#1110, Mobilgas Tanker $300.00
#1110, Shell Tanker..$3,000.00
#1111, Massey-Ferguson Harvester $150.00
#1112, Corporal Missile on Launching Ramp.................$160.00
#1112, David Brown Combine...$120.00
#1113, Corporal Erector & Missile....................................$375.00
#1113, Hyster...$50.00
#1113, Hyster Sealink...$125.00
#1115, Bloodhound Missile $110.00
#1116, Bloodhound Missile Platform $100.00
#1116, Refuse Lorry..$30.00
#1117, Bloodhound Missile Trolley.....................................$65.00
#1117, Faun Street Sweeper $30.00
#1118, Airport Emergency Tender $70.00
#1118, International Truck, Dutch Army............................$300.00
#1118, International Truck, gr...$150.00

#1118, International Truck, US Army $275.00
#1119, HDL Hovercraft..$100.00
#1121, Chipperfield's Circus Crane $250.00
#1121, Corgimatic Ford Tipper.....................................$50.00
#1123, Chipperfield's Circus Animal Cage................$120.00
#1124, Corporal Missile Launching Ramp..................$80.00
#1126, Ecurie Ecosse Transporter...............................$200.00
#1126, Simon Snorkel Dennis Fire Engine $50.00
#1127, Simon Snorkel Bedford TK Fire Engine..........$100.00
#1128, Priestman Cub Shovel $50.00
#1129, Mercedes Truck...$25.00
#1129, Milk Tanker..$250.00

#1130, Chipperfield's Circus Horse Transporter, $275.00.

#1130, Mercedes Tanker, Corgi $25.00
#1131, Carrimore Machinery Carrier.......................$135.00
#1131, Mercedes Refrigerated Van...........................$20.00
#1132, Carrimore Low Loader...................................$250.00
#1132, Scania Truck..$20.00
#1133, Troop Transporter $250.00
#1134, Army Fuel Tanker $400.00
#1135, Heavy Equipment Transporter $400.00
#1137, Ford Tilt Cab w/Trailer $100.00
#1138, Carrimore Car Transporter, Corgi................$135.00
#1140, Bedford Mobilgas Tanker $300.00
#1140, Ford Transit Wrecker......................................$25.00
#1141, Milk Tanker...$250.00
#1142, Holmes Wrecker...$150.00
#1143, American LaFrance Rescue Truck $125.00
#1144, Berliet Wrecker..$80.00
#1144, Chipperfield's Circus Crane Truck................$600.00
#1145, Mercedes Unimog Dumper.............................$50.00
#1146, Tri-Deck Transporter $170.00
#1147, Ferrymaster Truck $100.00
#1148, Carrimore Car Transporter............................$160.00
#1150, Mercedes Unimog Snowplough......................$60.00
#1151, Scammell Co-op Set..$350.00
#1151, Scammell Co-op Truck $250.00
#1152, Mack Truck, Esso Tanker $75.00
#1152, Mack Truck, Exxon Tanker $140.00
#1153, Priestman Boom Crane....................................$80.00
#1154, Priestman Crane $85.00
#1154, Tower Crane...$75.00

#1120, Midland Coach, $250.00.

#1155, Skyscraper Tower Crane...$60.00
#1156, Volvo Cement Mixer...$60.00
#1157, Ford Esso Tanker..$50.00
#1158, Ford Exxon Tanker..$75.00
#1159, Ford Car Transporter..$60.00
#1160, Ford Gulf Tanker..$55.00
#1161, Ford Aral Tanker..$85.00
#1163, Circus Cannon Truck $70.00
#1164, Dolphinarium...$125.00
#1169, Ford Guiness Tanker..$60.00
#1170, Ford Car Transporter $60.00

Dakins

Dakin has been an importer of stuffed toys as far back as 1955, but it wasn't until 1959 that the name of this San Francisco-based company actually appeared on the toy labels. They produced three distinct lines: Dream Pets (1960 – early 1970s), Dream Dolls (1965 – mid-1970s), and licensed characters and advertising figures, starting in 1968. Of them all, the latter series was the most popular and the one that holds most interest for collectors. Originally there were seven Warner Brothers characters. Each was made with a hard plastic body and a soft vinyl head, and all were under 10" tall. All in all, more than fifty cartoon characters were produced, some with several variations. Advertising figures were made as well. Some were extensions of the three already existing lines; others were completely original.

Goofy Grams was a series featuring many of their character figures mounted on a base lettered with a 'goofy' message. They also utilized some of their large stock characters as banks in a series called Cash Catchers. A second bank series consisted of Warner Brothers characters molded in a squatting position and therefore smaller. Other figures made by Dakin include squeeze toys, PVCs, and water squirters.

Advisor: Jim Rash (R3).

Alice in Wonderland, set of 3 w/Alice, Mad Hatter & White
    Rabbit, artist Faith Wick, 18", MIB.........................$300.00
Baby Puss, Hanna-Barbera, 1971, EX+, R3.....................$100.00
Bambi, Disney, 1960s, MIP, R3 ....$35.00
Bamm-Bamm, Hanna-Barbera, w/club, 1970, EX, R3 ......$35.00
Barney Rubble, Hanna-Barbera, 1970, EX, R3/B10, from $35
    to..$40.00
Benji, 1978, cloth, VG...$30.00
Bozo the Clown, Larry Harmon, 1974, EX, R3 ....$35.00
Bugs Bunny, Warner Bros, 1971, MIP, R3 ....$30.00
Bugs Bunny, Warner Bros, 1976, MIB (TV Cartoon Theater
    box), R3 ....$40.00
Bugs Bunny, Warner Bros, 1978, MIP (Fun Farm bag), R3..$20.00
Bullwinkle, Jay Ward, 1976, MIB (TV Cartoon Theater box),
    R3...$60.00
Cool Cat, Warner Bros, w/beret, 1970, EX+, R3 ....$40.00
Daffy Duck, Warner Bros, 1968, EX, R3 ....$30.00
Daffy Duck, Warner Bros, 1976, MIB (TV Cartoon Theater
    box), R3 ....$40.00
Deputy Dawg, Terrytoons, 1977, EX, R3 ....$40.00

Charlie Brown and Linus, 1966, NM, $45.00 each.

Dewey Duck, Disney, straight or bent legs, EX, R3...........$40.00
Dino Dinosaur, Hanna-Barbera, 1970, EX, R3 ....$40.00
Donald Duck, Disney, 1960s, straight or bent legs, EX, R3..$20.00
Donald Duck, Disney, 1960s, straight or bent legs, NMIP..$30.00
Dream Pets, Bull Dog, EX....................................$15.00
Dream Pets, Hawaiian Hound, w/surfboard & orig tag, EX,
    H4 ....$30.00
Dream Pets, Kangaroo, w/camera, wearing beret, EX $15.00
Dream Pets, Midnight Mouse, w/orig tag, EX $15.00
Dudley Do-Right, Jay Ward, 1976, MIB (TV Cartoon Theater
    box), R3 ....$75.00
Dumbo, Disney, 1960s, cloth collar, MIB, R3...................$25.00
Elmer Fudd, Warner Bros, 1968, hunting outfit w/rifle, EX, R3...$125.00

Goofy, Disney, with original tag, EX, $20.00.

Elmer Fudd, Warner Bros, 1968, tuxedo, EX, R3 ....$30.00
Elmer Fudd, Warner Bros, 1978, MIP (Fun Farm bag), R3 ..$35.00
Foghorn Leghorn, Warner Bros, 1970, EX+, R3 ....$75.00
Fred Flintstone, Hanna-Barbera, 1970, EX, R3/B10, from $35 to...$40.00
Goofy Gram, Bloodhound, You Think You Feel Bad!, EX, R3...$20.00
Goofy Gram, Dog, You're Top Dog, EX, R3 ....$20.00
Goofy Gram, Fox, Wanna See My Etchings?, EX R3 ....$20.00
Goofy Gram, Kangaroo, World's Greatest Mom!, EX, R3 .$20.00
Goofy Gram, Lion, Sorry You're Feeling Beastly!, EX, R3.$20.00
Hokey Wolf, Hanna-Barbera, 1971, EX+, R3.................$250.00
Hoppy Hopperoo, Hanna-Barbera, 1971, EX+, R3 ....$100.00
Huckleberry Hound, Hanna-Barbera, 1970, EX+, R3 ......$75.00
Huey Duck, Disney, straight or bent legs, EX, R3.............$30.00
Jack-in-the Box, bank, 1971, EX, R3 ....$25.00
Lion in a Cage, bank, 1971, EX, R3 ....$25.00
Louie Duck, Disney, straight or bent legs, EX, R3 ....$30.00
Merlin the Magic Mouse, Warner Bros, 1970, EX+..........$25.00
Mickey Mouse, Disney, 1960s, cloth clothes, EX, R3 ....$20.00
Mighty Mouse, Terrytoons, 1978, EX, R3.....................$100.00
Minnie Mouse, Disney, 1960s, cloth clothes, EX, R3 ....$20.00
Monkey on a Barrel, bank, 1971, EX, R3 ....$25.00
Olive Oyl, King Features, 1974, cloth clothes, MIP, R3...$50.00
Olive Oyl, King Features, 1976, MIB (TV Cartoon Theater box), R3 ....$40.00
Oliver Hardy, Larry Harmon, 1974, EX+, R3 ....$30.00
Opus, 1982, cloth, w/tag, 12", EX, B10 ....$15.00
Pebbles Flintstone, Hanna-Barbera, 1970, EX, R3...........$35.00

Pink Panther, Mirisch-Freleng, 1971, EX+, R3 ....$50.00
Pink Panther, Mirisch-Freleng, 1976, MIB (TV Cartoon Theater box), R3 ....$50.00

Pinocchio, 1960s, EX, $20.00.

Popeye, King Features, 1974, cloth clothes, MIP, R3 ....$50.00
Popeye, King Features, 1976, MIB (TV Cartoon Theater box), R3..$50.00
Porky Pig, Warner Bros, 1968, EX+, R3..........................$30.00
Porky Pig, Warner Bros, 1976, MIB (TV Cartoon Theater box), R3..$40.00
Ren & Stimpy, water squirters, Nickelodeon, 1993, EX, R3 ..$10.00

Pepe Le Peu, 1971, You're a Real Stinker on base, EX, 55.00.

Road Runner, Warner Bros, 1976, MIB, $45.00.

Road Runner, Warner Bros, 1968, EX+, R3 ....$30.00

Rocky Squirrel, Jay Ward, 1976, MIB (TV Cartoon Theater box), $60.00.

Scooby Doo, Hanna-Barbera, 1980, EX, R3 ....$75.00
Scrappy Doo, Hanna-Barbera, 1982, EX+, R3 ....$75.00
Seal on a Box, bank, 1971, EX, R3..................................$25.00
Second Banana, Warner Bros, 1970, EX, R3 ....$35.00

Smokey Bear, 1970s, M, $30.00.

Smokey Bear, 1976, MIB (TV Cartoon Theater box), R3..$30.00
Snagglepuss, Hanna-Barbera, 1971, EX, R3...................$100.00
Speedy Gonzalez, Warner Bros, MIB (TV Cartoon Theater box), R3 ....$50.00
Stan Laurel, Larry Harmon, 1974, EX+, R3.....................$30.00

Swee' Pea, beanbag doll, King Features, 1974, VG, R3 ....$20.00
Sylvester, Warner Bros, 1968, EX+, R3 ....$20.00
Sylvester, Warner Bros, 1976, MIB (TV Cartoon Theater box) $40.00
Sylvester, Warner Bros, 1978, MIP (Fun Farm bag), R3...$20.00

Tasmanian Devil, Warner Bros, 1978, rare, EX (Fun Farm bag not shown) $400.00.

Tiger in a Cage, bank, 1971, EX, R3 ....$25.00
Top Banana, NM, C17 ....$25.00
Tweety Bird, Warner Bros, 1966, EX+, R3 ....$20.00
Tweety Bird, Warner Bros, 1975, EX+, R3 ....$50.00
Tweety Bird, Warner Bros, 1976, MIB (TV Cartoon Theater box), R3 ....$40.00
Underdog, Jay Ward, 1976, MIB (TV Cartoon Theater box), R3 ....$150.00

Yosemite Sam, Warner Bros, 1968, MIB (not shown), $40.00.

Wile E Coyote, bank, 1971, EX, C17..............................$230.00
Wile E Coyote, Warner Bros, 1968, MIB, R3 ....$30.00
Wile E Coyote, Warner Bros, 1976, MIB (TV Cartoon Theater box), R3 ....$40.00
Yogi Bear, Hanna-Barbera, 1970, EX, R3........................$60.00
Yosemite Sam, Warner Bros, 1976, MIP (Fun Farm bag), R3...$40.00

ADVERTISING

Bay View, bank, 1976, EX+, R3 ....$30.00
Big Foot Sasquatch Savings, bank, EX, H4 ....$65.00
Bob's Big Boy, missing hamburger o/w VG, H4 ....$80.00
Bob's Big Boy, 1974, w/hamburger, EX+, R3 ....$180.00
Christian Bros Brandy St Bernard, 1982, VG, M15..........$30.00
Crocker National Bank's Cocker Spaniel, 1979, 12", VG, M15 ....$20.00
Diaperene Baby, Sterling Drug Co, 1980, EX, R3.............$40.00
Freddie Fast, 1976, M, P12 ....$100.00
Glamour Kitty, 1977, EX, R3 ....$150.00
Kernal Renk, American Seeds, 1970, rare, EX+, R3 ......$350.00
Li'l Miss Just Rite, 1965, EX+, R3 ....$75.00
Miss Liberty Belle, 1975, MIP, R3....................................$75.00
Quasar Robot, bank, 1975, NM, R3...................................$150.00
Sambo's Boy, 1974, EX+, R3 ....$75.00
Sambo's Tiger, 1974, EX+, R3 ....$125.00
Woodsy Owl, 1974, MIP, R3..$60.00

Woodsy Owl, 1974, missing clothes, EX, $30.00.

Diecast

Diecast replicas of cars, trucks, planes, trains, etc., represent a huge corner of today's collector market, and their manufacturers see to it that there is no shortage. Back in the 1920s, Tootsietoy had the market virtually by themselves, but one by one other companies had a go at it, some with more success than others. Among them were the American companies of Barclay, Hubley, and Manoil, all of whom are much better known for other types of toys. After the war, Metal Masters, Smith-Miller, and Doepke Ohlsson-Rice (among others) tried the market with varying degrees of success. Some companies were phased out over the years, while many more entered the market with fervor. Today it's those fondly remembered models from the '50s and '60s that many collectors yearn to own. Solido produced well-modeled, detailed little cars; some had dome lights that actually came on when the doors were opened. Politoy's were cleanly molded with good detailing and finishes. Mebetoys, an Italian company that has been bought out by Mattel, produced several; and some of the finest come from Brooklyn, whose Shelby (signed) GT-350H Mustang can easily cost you from $900.00 to $1,000.00 when you can find one.

In 1968 the Topper Toy Company introduced its line of low-friction, high-speed Johnny Lightning cars to be in direct competition with Mattel's Hot Wheels. To gain attention, Topper sponsored Al Unser's winning race car, the 'Johnny Lightning,' in the 1970 Indianapolis 500. Despite the popularity of their cars, the Topper Toy Company went out of business in 1971. Today the Johnny Lightnings are highly sought after and a new company, Playing Mantis, is reproducing many of the original designs as well as several models that never made it into regular production.

If you're interested in Majorette Toys, we recommend *Collecting Majorette Toys* by Dana Johnson; ordering information is given with Dana's listing under Diecast, in the section called Categories of Special Interest in the back of the book. Dana is also the author of the book, *Collector's Guide to Diecast Toys & Scale Models*, published by Collector Books.

Advisor: Dan Wells (W1).

Other Sources: P3, N3, S5

See also Corgi; Dinky; Diecast Collector Banks; Farm Toys; Tootsietoys; Hot Wheels; Matchbox; Tekno.

Aurora Cigarbox, AC Cobra, purple w/tan interior, chrome detail, blk plastic tires, NM, W1 ....$50.00
Aurora Cigarbox, Chaparral, cream w/blk '3,' red interior, blk rubber tires, NM, W1 ....$12.00
Aurora Cigarbox, Charger, gold w/tan interior, chrome detail, blk plastic tires, loose chassis, NM, W1 ....$80.00
Aurora Cigarbox, Cobra, purple w/silver stripe, tan interior, chrome detail, blk plastic tires, NM, W1 ....$26.00
Aurora Cigarbox, Dino Ferrari, orange w/silver stripe, tan interior, blk plastic tires, NM, W1..................................$27.00
Aurora Cigarbox, Ferrari Berlinetta, orange w/silver stripe, tan interior, chrome detail, blk plastic tires, NM, W1.....$18.00
Aurora Cigarbox, Ford GT, lt bl w/gray interior, blk rubber tires, NM+, W1 ....$14.00
Aurora Cigarbox, Ford J Car, cream w/bl stripe, tan interior, silver headlights, blk rubber tires, M, W1....................$18.00
Aurora Cigarbox, Ford XL-500, dk bl w/tan interior, blk plastic tires, NM+, W1 ....$45.00
Aurora Cigarbox, Jaguar (E-type), silver w/red stripe, wht interior, blk plastic tires, M (Canadian blister pack), W1..$50.00

Aurora Cigarbox, Lola GT, gold w/silver stripe, tan interior, chrome detail, blk plastic tires, NM, W1 .... $16.00

Aurora Cigarbox, Mako Shark, lt bl w/tan interior, blk plastic tires, M, W1 .... $45.00

Aurora Cigarbox, Porsche 904, purple w/silver stripe, tan interior, chrome detail, blk plastic tires, NM, W1 .... $10.00

Aurora Cigarbox, Riviera, lt bl w/tan interior, blk rubber tires, M, W1 .... $50.00

Aurora Cigarbox, Stingray, cream w/tan interior, blk rubber tires, NM, W1 .... $40.00

Aurora Cigarbox, Thunderbird, lt bl w/tan interior, blk rubber tires, M, W1 .... $40.00

Aurora Cigarbox, Toronado, yel or lt cream w/tan interior, blk rubber tires, M, W1, ea $45.00

Aurora Cigarbox, Willys Gasser, purple w/tan interior, blk plastic tires, NM, W1 .... $40.00

Benbros, Land Rover, gr, gr metal tires, England, ca 1960, NM, W1 .... $12.00

Benbros, 1957 Chevy Nomad Station Wagon, red, silver plastic tires, England, ca 1957, NM+, W1 .... $40.00

Best Box, 1919 Ford Model T, gr & red, Holland, 1960s, EX, W1 .... $8.00

Budgie, #216 Renault Truck, red and yellow with canvas cover marked Fresh Fruit Daily, NM (EX box), M5, $70.00.

Budgie, AEC Routemaster Bus (London double-decker), red w/Esso decals, blk rubber tires, 1960s, NMIB, W1 ..... $26.00

Budgie, Austin London Taxi, blk, metal wheels, England, 1950s, M, W1 .... $24.00

Budgie, Packard Convertible, tan, blk plastic wheels, England, 1950s, NM+, W1 .... $40.00

Budgie, REA Express Parcel Delivery Van, gr, gr plastic wheels, England, 1960s, NM, W1 .... $16.00

Budgie, VW Micro Bus, tan, metal wheels, England, 1950s, NM, W1 .... $30.00

Budgie, Wolseley Police Car, blk, MIB, L1 .... $75.00

Conrad, #1015 Volkswagen Santana, bl, MIB, L1 .... $25.00

Conrad, #1034 Mercedes Race Car Carrier, bl, MIB, L1 ... $115.00

Diapet, Sunny Coupe 1200 GL, orange, blk rubber tires, 1960s, MIB, W1 .... $15.00

Eligor, #1026 Bugatti, bl, NMIB, L1 .... $60.00

Eligor, #1157 Peugeot 404 Lindt Pick-up, cream, MIB, L1 .. $20.00

Eligor, #1164 Peugeot 404 Fire Wrecker, red, MIB, L1 .... $20.00

Ertl, #2652 Pontiac Fiero GT, maroon, MIB, L1 .... $15.00

Ertl, #2653 Camaro GT, bl, MIB, L1 .... $15.00

Ertl, Campbell's Freightliner, 1/64 scale, MIB, S5 .... $24.00

Ertl, Deutz-Allis Parts Truck, 1/64 scale, MIB, S5 .... $14.00

Ertl, NFL Super Bowl XXVIII Freightliner, 1/64 scale, MIB, S5 .... $20.00

Ertl, True Value delivery truck, 1/25 scale, M, $30.00.

Ertl, 1980 Chevrolet Mountain Dew Nascar Stocker, wht, blk plastic tires, 1980s, M (creased card), W1 .... $64.00

Ertl, 50th Anniversary Freightliner, 1/64 scale, MIB, S5 .. $20.00

Gama, #0894 BMW 733 Sedan, gray, M, L1 .... $25.00

Gama, #0931 Mercedes Benz Truck & Trailer, orange & yel, blk rubber tires, Germany, 1960s, M (EX window box), W1 ...... $80.00

Gama, #0973 Porsche 911, ivory, blk rubber tires, Germany, 1966, broken windshield o/w VG+, W1 .... $14.00

Gama, #1130 Opel Omega Sedan, dk bl, M, L1 .... $20.00

Gama, #1135 Opel GSI Cabriolet, red, M, L1 .... $20.00

Gama, #1137 Mercedes Benz 500 SL Convertible, red, MIB, L1 .... $28.00

Gama, #9680 Mercedes Benz 350 SE, metallic gray, MIB, L1 .... $25.00

Impy, Chrysler Imperial, metallic bl w/tan interior, blk plastic tires, 1960s, NM+, W1 .... $32.00

Impy, Jaguar MK X, metallic tan w/gr interior, blk plastic tires, England, 1960s, NMIB, W1 .... $34.00

Johnny Lightning, Baja, red w/chrome detail, 1969, EX, A .. $90.00

Johnny Lightning, Big Rig, metallic orange, missing blower o/w NM, W1 .... $40.00

Johnny Lightning, Bubble, metallic orange w/wht interior, complete, EX+, W1 .... $32.00

Johnny Lightning, Custom '32 Ford, metallic purple w/wht interior, loose windshield, MBP, W1 .... $50.00

Johnny Lightning, Custom Dragster, metallic bl, no canopy version, M (NM+ card), W1 .... $50.00

Johnny Lightning, Custom El Camino, metallic purple w/wht interior, blk roof, open doors, prof rpt, NM+, W1 ... $100.00

Johnny Lightning, Custom Eldorado, metallic brn w/wht interior, open doors, scarce, NM, W1 .... $100.00

Johnny Lightning, Custom Eldorado, purple w/red interior, opening doors, 1969, NM, A $50.00

Johnny Lightning, Custom Ferrari, gold w/red interior, closed doors, poor pnt finish, EX+, W1 ....$40.00

Johnny Lightning, Custom Mako Shark, gold w/red interior, NM, W1 ....$44.00

Johnny Lightning, Custom Spoiler, metallic red, NM+, W1...$40.00

Johnny Lightning, Custom Thunderbird, metallic lime w/red interior, open doors, colored roof, scarce, EX, W1.....$90.00

Johnny Lightning, Custom Thunderbird, mirror purple w/red interior, 1969, NM, A $250.00

Johnny Lightning, Custom Turbine, metallic red, unpnt interior, missing top, EX, W1 ....$8.00

Johnny Lightning, Custom XKE, metallic gold w/red interior, closed doors, EX+, W1 ....$28.00

Johnny Lightning, Flame Out, metallic dk bl, missing pipes & ladder, VG+, W1 ....$6.00

Johnny Lightning, Frantic Ferrari, metallic dk aqua, engine missing 2 stacks o/w complete, NM+, W1 ....$40.00

Johnny Lightning, Hairy Hauler, metallic magenta, missing exhaust covers & stickers o/w EX+, W1 ....$14.00

Johnny Lightning, Jumpin' Jag, metallic orange, missing stacks o/w EX+, W1 ....$14.00

Johnny Lightning, Movin' Van, metallic gr, missing windshield o/w EX, W1 ....$14.00

Johnny Lightning, Nucleon, gold, complete, NM, W1 ....$40.00

Johnny Lightning, Parnelli Jones, metallic purple, complete, EX+, W1 ....$40.00

Johnny Lightning, Sand Stormer, metallic dk aqua, complete, NM+, W1 ....$44.00

Johnny Lightning, Screamer, metallic purple w/blk interior, complete, NM, W1 ....$40.00

Johnny Lightning, Sling Shot, metallic lime, dragster front wheels, complete, NM, W1 ....$38.00

Johnny Lightning, Smuggler, metallic purple, complete, NM, W1 ....$30.00

Johnny Lightning, Stiletto, metallic orange, complete, EX+, W1 ....$24.00

Johnny Lightning, TNT, gold, dragster front wheels, complete, NM, W1 ....$40.00

Johnny Lightning, Triple Threat, metallic orange, missing front engine o/w EX+, W1 ....$10.00

Johnny Lightning, Vicious Vette, metallic lt bl, complete, EX+, W1 ....$34.00

Johnny Lightning, Vulture, metallic dk bl, missing wing & 1 blower o/w EX, W1 ....$30.00

Johnny Lightning, Wasp, metallic purple, complete, NM, W1 .$48.00

Johnny Lightning, Wedge, metallic purple w/brn interior, scarce, missing nose cone o/w EX+, W1 ....$40.00

Johnny Lightning, Wild Winner, metallic red, missing both wings o/w VG+, W1 ....$12.00

Lonestar, Cadillac Coupe de Ville, bl & wht, NM, L1 .....$75.00

Lonestar, Chevrolet Corvair, coral, M, L1 ....$45.00

Lonestar, Ford Sunliner Convertible, lt bl, MIB, L1 ......$115.00

Majorette, BMW 3.0 CSI, metallic lime, blk plastic tires, 1970s, M, W1 ....$24.00

Marklin, #5524/18 Mercedes Benz 300SL, gray, blk rubber tires, Germany, 1953, EX, W1 ....$90.00

Mebetoys, #A22 Corvette Rondine, silver, blk rubber tires, Italy, 1967, M (NM+ box), W1.............................$70.00

Mebetoys, #A26 Rolls Royce Silver Shadow, bl, M, L1 ...$65.00

Mebetoys, #A29 Toyota 2000 GT, gr, M, L1 ....$65.00

Mebetoys, #A43 Fiat 124 Roman Taxi, gr, NM, L1 ....$30.00

Mercury, #029 Rolls Royce Silver Cloud, dk gray, M, L1 ..$195.00

Mercury, #031-2 Maserati, red, rare, NM, L1 ....$150.00

Mercury, #14 Lancia Appia Coupe, cream, M, L1 ....$150.00

Mercury, #30 Bentley S Sedan, gray, M, L1 ....$195.00

Mercury, #8 Willys Jeep, pale gr body w/tan doors, blk rubber tires, 1948, M, W1 ....$395.00

Minialuxe, Hotchkiss Gregoire, dk gray, rare, M, L1 ....$65.00

Minialuxe, Volvo 144 Sedan, butterscotch, M, L1 ....$35.00

Muscle Car Set, limited edition, set of 8, MBP, W1 ....$40.00

Penny, Fiat 124, metallic bl, blk rubber tires, Italy, ca 1970, M, W1 ....$30.00

Playart, Jaguar E-Type 2+2, dk gr, blk plastic tires, Hong Kong, 1970s, MBP, W1 ....$30.00

Playart, 1965 Mustang, orange w/blk roof, lt bl interior, blk plastic tires, 1970s, NM, W1 ....$18.00

Politoys, #111 1919 Ford Model T, metallic brn, added driver, blk rubber tires, Italy, 1963, EX (in container), W1 ..$18.00

Politoys, #502 Fiat 1500 Siata, bl, M, L1 ....$65.00

Politoys, #514 Alfa Romeo 2600 Sprint Bertone, red, MIB, L1 ....$85.00

Politoys, #518 Rolls Royce, silver, opening doors, hood & trunk, blk rubber tires, 1960s, M (EX+ box), W1.................$40.00

Politoys, #536 Fiat Dino Ferrari, gr, MIB, L1 ....$85.00

Politoys, #538 VW 1600 Fastback, metallic aqua, blk rubber tires, 1960s, M (EX box), W1....................$40.00

Politoys, #562 Ferarri 350 GTC Berlinetta, bl, M, L1 ......$65.00

Politoys, #567 Oldsmobile Toronado, bl, M, L1 ....$65.00

Politoys, #573 Jensen Vignale Coupe, silver, M, L1 ....$65.00

Politoys, #591 Maserati Ghibli, red, MIB, L1 ....$65.00

Schaback, #1018 Volkswagen Corrado, dk red, MIB, L1..$22.00

Schaback, #1030 Audi 90 Quattro, gr, NM, L1 ....$15.00

Schuco, #611 Audi 80GL, orange, M, L1 ....$25.00

Schuco, #613 BMW Turbo Coupe, orange, M, L1 ....$25.00

Schuco, #622 Audi 50 Coupe, pumpkin, M, L1................$25.00

Schuco, #629 BMW 630 Coupe, chestnut, NM, L1 ....$15.00

Schuco, Ford Taurus GT, red, blk plastic tires, 1960s, MIB, W1 ....$32.00

Siku, #2519 Unimog Mercedes w/Trailer, gray, MIB, L1..$35.00

Siku, #2921 Mercedes Fire Truck w/Water Cannon, red, MIB, L1 ....$25.00

Siku, Corvette Stingray, bl w/orange interior, blk plastic tires, Germany, 1960s, VG+, W1....................................$10.00

Siku, Ford F500 Pickup, dk gr w/red chassis, wht interior, blk plastic tires, 1960s, EX+, W1................................$20.00

Siku, Porsche 901, metallic bl, blk plastic tires, 1960s, M, W1 ....$20.00

Solido, #107 Vanwall Racer #10, dk gr, M, L1 ....$85.00

Solido, #165 Ferrari Daytona, red, M, L1 ....$55.00

Solido, #356 Volvo Dumpster, yel, M, L1 ....$65.00

Solido, #366 Saviem Fire Wrecker, red, M, L1 ....$22.00

Solido, #66 Landrover Fire Department, red, M, L1 ....$25.00

Speedy, Chaparral 2F, bl, blk rubber tires, Italy, 1960s, missing wing o/w EX+, W1......................................$8.00

Diecast Collector Banks

Thousands of banks have been produced since Ertl made its first model in 1981, the 1913 Model T Parcel Post Mail Service #9647. The Ertl company was founded by Fred Ertl, Sr., in Dubuque, Iowa, back in the mid-1940s. Until they made their first diecast banks, most of what they made were farm tractors. Today they specialize in vehicles made to specification and carrying logos of companies as large as Texaco and as small as your hometown bank. The size of each 'run' is dictated by the client and can vary from a few hundred up to several thousand. Some clients will later add a serial number to the vehicle; this is not done by Ertl. Other numbers that appear on the base of each bank are a 4-number dating code (the first three indicate the day of the year up to 365 and the fourth number is the last digit of the year, '5' for 1995, for instance). The stock number is shown only on the box, never on the bank, so it is extremely important that you keep them in their original boxes.

Other producers of these banks are Scale Models, incorporated in 1991, First Gear Inc., and Spec-Cast, whose founders at one time all worked for the Ertl company.

In the listings that follow, unless another condition is given, all values are for banks mint and in their original boxes. (#d) indicates a bank that was numbered by the client, not Ertl.

Advisors: Art and Judy Turner (H8), who provided us with all listings that do not include the codes of other dealers.

Other Sources: S5, T4

Key: JLE — Joseph L. Ertl

Ertl

AC Sparkplugs, 1950 Chevy, #2901 ....$34.00

Agway #3, 1905 Ford, #9743 ....$65.00

Air Rescue, DC3, #F493 ....$45.00

Alka Seltzer, 1917 Ford, #9791 ....$28.00

Amoco, 1929 International Tanker, JLE, #4032.............$22.00

Amoco Motor Club #4, 1920 International, JLE, #3102 ..$25.00

Amoco-Standard Oil Co, 1931 International, JLE, #5081..$12.00

Ace Hardware, 1955 Chevy Cameo Pickup, #B384, MIB, $24.00.

American Ambulance, 1917 Model T Van, $35.00.

Apics, 1913 Ford, #8202 ....$27.00

Atlas Van Lines #1, 1926 Mack, #9514 ....$40.00

Aunt Jemima Pancakes, 1923 Chevy, #2085 ....$95.00

Blain's Farm & Fleet, 1931 International, JLE, #5005......$15.00

Bobby Allison, 1940 Ford, JLE, #6014 ....$44.00

BP Gasoline, 1935 Mack, JLE, #3014...............................$30.00

County Post, 1905 Ford Delivery Car, MIB, $35.00.

Branson MO, Music City, 1920 International, JLE, #3044..$20.00
Cam-2 Motor Oil, 1931 International, JLE, #4103...........$14.00
CC of Tulsa, 1931 International, JLE, #5034.................$85.00
Chaplin Refining, 1931 International, JLE, #4088...........$20.00
Clearkote Protector, 1940 Ford, JLE, #6061 ....$15.00
Co-op, 1929 International, JLE, #4089 ....$24.00
Coca-Cola, 1920 International, JLE, #3015.....................$95.00
Coca-Cola/Ronald McDonald House, 1929 International, JLE, #5023 ....$48.00
Conoco Oil, 1929 International, JLE, #4003 ....$28.00
Coors Beer/Sussex County Fair, 1931 International, JLE, #5002 ....$27.00
Curtis Turner #26, 1920 International, JLE, #3062 ....$26.00
Custom Chrome #1, 1931 International, JLE, #5030 ....$95.00
Diamond Motor Oil, 1931 International, #4079 ....$20.00
Dyversville Fire Chief, 1940 Ford, #0005 ....$95.00
Eason Oil, 1931 International Tanker, JLE, #4033...........$15.00
Edelbrock (sampler), International, JLE, #5055..............$24.00
Ertl Air Express, Air Express Plane, #B270 ....$32.00
Ertl Collectibles, 1905 Ford, #F860 ....$20.00
Ertl Racing, 1937 Ford Tractor Trailer, #9066................$18.00
Eskimo Pie, 1948 Peterbilt Tractor Trailer, #H121 ....$22.00
Esso, 1939 Dodge Airflow, #B285 ....$35.00
Ethyl Gasoline, 1931 International, JLE, #4006 ....$20.00
Exxon, P51 Mustang, #47004..................................$38.00
Fannie Farmer Candies, 1913 Ford, #2104...................$30.00
Farm & Dairy, 1931 Hawkeye, #B075.........................$26.00
Farm Progress Show, 1931 International, JLE, #5008.......$20.00
Farm Safety for Kids, Orion Plane, #42510....................$38.00
Farmers Almanac, 1913 Ford, #1359..........................$24.00
FDR Associates, 1905 Ford, #9378.............................$28.00

Ford Tractor Trailer, 50th Anniversary, MIB, $25.00.

Football II, Atlanta Falcons, 1955 Cameo Pickup, #B341 ..$22.00
Football II, Indianapolis Colts, 1955 Cameo Pickup, #B345 ...$15.00
Football II, Pittsburgh Steelers, 1955 Cameo Pickup, #B330...$45.00
Football III, Buffalo Bills, 1951 GMC, #B843...................$20.00
Football III, Detroit Lions, 1951 GMC, #B834................$20.00
Football III, Los Angeles Raiders, 1951 GMC, #B818......$20.00
Football III, New York Jets, 1951 GMC, #B826 ....$20.00
Football III, St Louis Rams, 1951 GMC, #B833 ....$20.00
Football IV, Carolina Panthers, 1957 Chevy, #F639........$20.00
Football IV, Green Bay Packers, 1957 Chevy, #F643 ....$20.00
Football IV, Minnesota Vikings, 1957 Chevy, #F651.......$20.00
Football IV, San Fransisco 49ers, 1957 Chevy, #F642......$20.00
Forbes Magazine, 1950 Chevy, #9978.........................$34.00

Ford, 1918 Ford, #0870..$24.00
Ford Motor Co Seasons Greetings #2, 1937 Ford Tractor Trailer, #B724 ....$34.00
Ford Motorsports, F16, #0501..................................$32.00
Ford Motorsports, 1932 Ford, #9693..........................$45.00
Fordson #2, 1912 Ford, #0306 ....$20.00
Fram Filters, 1925 Kenworth, #B722..........................$75.00
Frame Mica, 1932 Ford, #B813.................................$95.00
GDS Fair, 1917 Ford, #2996.....................................$24.00
Giant Food Store, 1923 Chevy, #B627.........................$30.00
Gilmore Oil Co (sampler), 1931 International Tanker, JLE, #4009 ....$60.00
Global Van Lines, 1913 Ford, #1655...........................$45.00
GM Parts & Service, Chevy Tractor Trailer, #F801.........$20.00
Golden Flakes, Grumann Step Van, #9118 ....$65.00
Goldsboro Fire Co, 1926 Fire Truck, #9678...................$24.00
Goodyear, 1931 Hawkeye Wrecker, #3614....................$30.00
Goodyear, 1950 Chevy, #7538..................................$40.00
Graceton Store, 1913 Ford, #7566.............................$24.00
Graduation 1992, 1905 Ford, #9775............................$12.00
Grapette Soda, 1940 Ford, JLE, #6002........................$34.00
Great Train Store, 1950 Chevy, #7536........................$38.00
Green Spot Beverage, 1931 International, JLE, #4107.....$27.00
GTE, 1950 Chevy, #9661...$34.00
Gulf Oil, 1918 Ford Tanker, #1368.............................$28.00
Gulf Oil, 1938 Chevy, #B555....................................$22.00
Gulf Oil, 1951 GMC, #B613......................................$22.00
Gulf Power Co, Bucket Truck, #F335 ....$35.00
H&W Motor Express, 1931 International, JLE, #5073.....$15.00
Hamm's Beer, 1913 Ford, #2145................................$75.00
Hank Williams Jr, Vega Plane, #35045........................$34.00
Harbor Freight Tools, 1931 Hawkeye, #B730 ....$25.00
Harley-Davidson, 1927 Servicar, #99211.....................$75.00
Harley-Davidson, 1933 Motorcycle w/(gold) Sidecar, #99205 ....$395.00
Harley-Davidson of Baltimore, 1931 International, JLE, #5033 ....$115.00
Harleys-R-Us #3 Schott Enterprises, 1931 International, JLE, #5063 ....$48.00
Hart-Parr Tractors, 1913 Ford, #2296 ....$20.00
Hawkeye Tech, 1913 Ford, #9533..............................$25.00
Heartland Park, 1950 Chevy, #2087 ....$24.00
Heidt's Hot Rod Shop, 1955 Cameo Pickup, #B440 ....$35.00
Hemming's Motor News, DC3, #45014.........................$45.00
Hempstead Harley-Davidson #1, 1940 Ford, JLE, #6047..$50.00
Henderson Motorcycles, 1920 International, JLE, #3066.$22.00
Henny Penny, 1918 Ford, #9945................................$22.00
Henny Penny, 1931 Hawkeye, #9691 ....$25.00
Hershey's Antique Auto Club, 1918 Ford, #9084.............$65.00
Hershey's Antique Auto Club, 1931 Hawkeye Wrecker, #3270 ....$45.00
Hershey's Antique Auto Show, 1955 Cameo Pickup, #3815 ....$75.00
Hershey's Chocolate, 1931 Hawkeye, #9349 ....$30.00
Hershey's Syrup, 1931 Hawkeye Tanker, #F014.............$16.00
Highway Patrol, Air Express Plane, #B533 ....$30.00
Hills Bank & Trust, 1950 Chevy, #9109.......................$95.00
Hog Farm Motorcycle Specialists, 1923 Chevy, #3550.....$45.00

Holston Electric, Bucket Truck, #F056 ....$32.00
Holt Mfg Co (Caterpillar), 1905 Ford, #7709 ....$20.00
Home Hardware #8, 1917 Ford, #9011 ....$30.00
Home Savings & Loan, 1932 Ford, #9309 ....$34.00
Hormel Foods, 1917 Ford, #9451 ....$65.00
Hudson Bay Co, 1913 Ford, #9781 ....$35.00
Humble Oil Co, 1950 Chevy Pickup, #F855 ....$35.00
Hummelstown Fire Co #4, 1955 Cameo Pickup, #9425 ...$24.00
Husker Harvest, Indian Warrior Motorcycle, 1940 Ford, JLE, silver, #6023 ....$48.00
HWI Hardware, 1905 Ford, #9674 ....$25.00
HWI Hardware, 1923 Chevy, #1365 ....$18.00
I-70 Speedway, 1950 Chevy, #1319 ....$28.00
IBC, Step Van, #9610 ....$48.00
IGA, 1917 Ford, #F951 ....$20.00
IGA, 1925 Kenworth, #B449 ....$18.00
IGA, 1950 Chevy, #9015 ....$25.00
Imperial Oil #3, 1925 Kenworth Stakebed, #B414 ....$30.00
Indian Motorcycle, Hubley Plane, #4102 ....$45.00
Indian Motorcycle, 1931 International, JLE, #5028 ....$85.00
Indian Motorcycle #1 Chief, 1920 International, JLE, #3025..$135.00
International Harvester, 1959 Chevy El Camino, #4450 .$28.00
Iowa Gas, 1931 Hawkeye, #9589 ....$50.00
Iowa Hawkeyes #14, 1951 GMC, #B782 ....$25.00
Iowa Rural Electric Co, Bucket Truck, #F060 ....$32.00
Iowa Saftey Council, 1913 Ford, #9337 ....$34.00
Iowa 106th Fireman Association, 1913 Ford, #2137 ....$85.00
Iowa 80 Truck Stop Group, 1925 Kenworth, #F845 ....$30.00
J&P Cycles #1, 1938 Chevy, #3834 ....$35.00
Jack Daniels, 1931 Hawkeye, #9342 ....$65.00
James Jordan Boys/Girls Club, 1935 Mack, JLE, #8021 ....$25.00
Janesville, Iowa, 1913 Ford, #9344 ....$25.00
JC Penney, Horse & Wagon, #9445 ....$28.00
JC Penney, 1905 Ford, #1326 ....$35.00
JC Penney, 1925 Kenworth, #9636 ....$25.00
JC Penney, 1951 GMC, #F481 ....$28.00
JC Whitney, 1932 Ford, #3809 ....$30.00
Jericho Temple, 1950 Chevy, #9992 ....$40.00
JF Good Co, 1918 Ford, #9603 ....$35.00
JI Case, DC3, #0722 ....$34.00
Jim Beam, 1948 Peterbilt Tractor Trailer, #F957 ....$22.00
Jim Beam District 1, 1938 Chevy, #F324 ....$25.00
Jim Beam District 1, 1992, 1918 Ford, #9332 ....$24.00
Jim Beam District 10, 1989, 1926 Mack, #9989 ....$25.00
Jim Beam District 5, 1991, 1931 Hawkeye, #9319 ....$35.00
Jim Beam District 6, Chicago, Trolley Car, #B445 ....$50.00
Jim Beam Louisville Convention, 1959 Chevy El Camino, #F323 ....$25.00
Jim's Auto Sales, 1913 Ford, #9818 ....$24.00
John Deere #102, 1926 Mack, #5534 ....$115.00
John Deere #107, 1937 Ahrens-Fox Fire Truck, #5773 ....$25.00
John Deere #2, Vega Plane, #35024 ....$55.00
John Deere #5, DC3, #45007 ....$32.00
John Deere Serviceguard #102, 1938 Chevy, #F072 ....$95.00
Johnson Gasoline (sampler), 1920 International, JLE, #4046 .$34.00
Jolly Rogers Motorcycle Club, 1925 Kenworth, #B304 ....$50.00
Jolt Cola, 1931 Ford, #9232 ....$38.00
K-Mart, 1931 International, JLE, #5043 ....$32.00

Kauffman's Fruit Farm, 1918 Ford, #7560 ....$25.00
Kendall Oil, 1929 International Tanker, JLE, #4073 ....$15.00
Kerr-McGee, DC# Plane, #B538 ....$85.00
Kerr-McGee #3, 1932 Ford, #7662 ....$35.00
Key Aid Distributors, 1931 Hawkeye, #9648 ....$25.00
Kingsport Press, 1923 Chevy, #2933 ....$50.00
Kingway Realty, 1913 Ford, #F224 ....$30.00
Kodak #1, 1905 Ford, gold spokes, #9885 ....$225.00
Kodak Film Racing #4, 1923 Chevy, #B230 ....$30.00
Kwik Shop, 1918 Ford, #B226 ....$22.00
Kyle Petty, 1950 Chevy, #2880 ....$34.00
Lake Speed, 1931 International, JLE, #5056 ....$45.00
Lakeside Speedway, 1950 Chevy, #7522 ....$25.00
Lapp Electric, Bucket Truck, #B120 ....$32.00
Lennox #5, 1926 Mack, #7561 ....$35.00
Lepage Glue, 1913 Ford, #2120 ....$25.00
Lion Coffee, 1913 Ford, #9306 ....$50.00
Lionel Trains, Stearman Plane, #37525 ....$65.00
Lipton Tea Co, 1932 Ford, #9087 ....$35.00
Lone Star Beer, 1926 Mack, #9167 ....$42.00
Lone Star Beer, 1926 Mack, #9168 ....$55.00
Longview, Ill, 1917 Ford, #9704 ....$22.00
Loon Mountain, 1940 Ford, JLE, #6044 ....$48.00
Los Angeles Times, 1917 Ford, #7667 ....$25.00
Mace Brothers, 1913 Ford, #9391 ....$32.00
Magnolia Oil, 1931 Sterling, JLE, #4022 ....$32.00
Mailboxes Etc #1, 1950 Chevy, #9215 ....$80.00
Marathon Oil, 1931 Hawkeye Tanker, #9631 ....$24.00
Marathon Oil (sampler), 1929 International Tanker, JLE, #4045 ....$40.00
Marland Oil, 1929 International Tanker, JLE, #4001 ......$30.00
Marshall Fields, 1913 Ford, #1650 ....$40.00
Martel Brothers Racing, 1950 Chevy, #2783 ....$12.00
Martin, CF & Co, 1932 Ford, #F834 ....$35.00
Massey Ferguson, 1913 Ford, #1348 ....$22.00
Massey Ferguson, 1955 Chevy Cameo Pickup, #2305 ......$24.00
Maurice's, 1932 Ford, #9476 ....$34.00
Maytag #3, 1948 Diamond Rio Tractor Trailer, #F196 ....$45.00
McDonalds Racing #27, Vega Plane, #00327 ....$40.00
McGee Plumbing/Lennox Distributors, Grumman Step Van, #9161 ....$24.00
Mead Paper Co, 1923 Chevy, #B196 ....$65.00
Mechanics SFE, Waynesboro, PA, Horse & Wagon, #9410..$32.00
Meijer Foods, 1913 Ford, #9352 ....$20.00
Merit Oil Co, 1926 Mack Tanker, #9980 ....$75.00
Messick Farm Equipment, Grumman Step Van, #9235 ....$25.00
Michelin Tires, 1931 International, JLE, #5046 ....$30.00
Michigan Milk Producers Association, 1905 Ford, #9308 .$30.00
Michigan Milk Producers Association, 1913 Ford, #1325 .$55.00
Mike's Trainland #6, Trolley Car, #3557 ....$32.00
Miller Beer, 1905 Ford, #9276 ....$34.00
Miller Beer, 1913 Ford, #9277 ....$45.00
Miller High Life, 1950 Chevy, #9269 ....$30.00
Millers Paint & Wallpaper Store, 1917 Ford, #F044 ....$32.00
Mirabito Fuel Group, Propane Truck, #F883 ....$36.00
Mobil Oil, Stearman Plane, #37527 ....$40.00
Mobil Oil, 1913 Ford, #9743 ....$55.00
Mobil Oil, 1925 Kenworth, #B121 ....$35.00

Mobil Oil, 1930 Diamond T Tanker, #9459 ....$45.00
Mobil Oil, 1931 Hawkeye, #9742...$60.00
Mobil Oil, 1931 Hawkeye Tanker, Employment Issue, #7540..$125.00
Monogram, 1912 Ford, #F387...$45.00
Monogram, 1917 Ford, #F388...$45.00
Montgomery School District, School Bus, #F097 ....$26.00
Montgomery Wards #2, 1917 Ford, #9052 ....$60.00
Montgomery Wards #4, Horse & Wagon, #1367...............$50.00
Moorsman's Mfg Co #5, 1931 Hawkeye, #B491 ....$45.00
Mopar, Dodge Brothers #1, 1939 Dodge Airflow, #B507 .$30.00
Mounds Candy Bar, 1923 Chevy, #7652...........................$24.00
Mountain Dew, 1950 Chevy, #7670 ....$35.00
Mt Saint Helens, 1938 Chevy, #B685 ....$45.00
Mutual Savings & Loan, 1905 Ford, #9187.......................$25.00
NASCAR Racing, Vega Plane, #00312...............................$40.00
National Association of Auctioneers, 1918 Ford, #2875..$34.00
National City Bank, 1913 Ford, #F214 ....$30.00
National Farm Toy Show, 1913 Ford, #9711 ....$22.00
National Van Lines, 1913 Ford, #9505 ....$60.00
Neilson's Ice Cream, 1913 Ford, #2131 ....$22.00
Nestle's #2 Baby Ruth, 1926 Mack, #9096......................$25.00
New Hampshire International Speedway, 1929 Ford, #0233..$14.00
New Hobby, 1950 Chevy, #9104.......................................$25.00
New Holland, 1913 Ford, #9397 ....$75.00
Nintendo, Grumman Step Van, #2111..............................$48.00
Norand Data Systems, 1926 Mack, #9207 ....$25.00
Northern Electric, 1905 Ford, #9517................................$30.00
O'Dell Hardware, 1912 Ford, #3641 ....$25.00
Ocean Spray, 1918 Ford, #9977..$30.00
Oklahoma Oil Marketers, 1931 Hawkeye Tanker, #9592...$50.00
Old El Paso, 1905 Ford, #7636 ....$45.00
Old Milwaukee Beer, 1918 Ford, #9173 ....$35.00
Old Style Beer, Stearman Plane, #F579 ....$24.00
Oliver Tractors, Orion Plane, #42501 ....$32.00
Orchard Supply, 1932 Ford, #B081 ....$40.00
Owatonna Tool Co, 1932 Ford, #B198 ....$75.00
Pabst Beer, Vintage Plane, #40016...................................$28.00
Pabst Beer, 1938 Chevy, #F587 ....$20.00
Pacific Coast Oil, Horse & Wagon, #9244 ....$20.00
Pan American Air, 1931 International, JLE, #4081 ....$32.00
Pathmark #3, 1932 Ford, #2882.......................................$25.00
Pepsi-Cola, 1935 Mack, JLE, #8019 ....$34.00
Pepsi-Cola #1, 1957 Chevy Nomad, JLE, #2003...............$65.00
Phillips 66 Super Clean, 1920 International Tanker, JLE,
    #4020 ....$35.00
Phillips 66 75th Anniversary, 1929 International, JLE,
    #4030 ....$125.00
Pronto Oil Co, 1931 International Tanker, JLE, #4016 ...$25.00
PSI Energy, Bucket Truck, #3593......................................$32.00
Richard Petty, 1931 International, JLE, #4101 ....$30.00
Ronald McDonald House, 1920 International, JLE, #3083 .$24.00
Ryder Truck Rental, 1931 International, JLE, #5054 ....$30.00
Seacoast Harley Davidson #3, 1940 Ford, JLE, #6038 ......$40.00
Servistar #8, 1912 Ford, #F394 ....$24.00
Seven-Up, 1913 Ford, #1662..$125.00
Shell Oil Co, #3, Stearman Plane, #37505 ....$195.00
Shell Oil Co, DC3, #F926 ....$48.00
Shell Oil Co, 1925 Kenworth Stakebed, #9250................$30.00

Shell Oil Co, 1930 Diamond T Tanker, #7542 ....$35.00
Shell Oil Co, 1950 Chevy Pickup, #F854 ....$38.00
Sheridan Orion, Orion Plane, #42508 ....$28.00
Sico Independent Oil Co, 1925 Kenworth Stakebed,
    #9224 ....$25.00
Signal Oil Co, 1931 International, JLE, #4015 ....$30.00
Silver Springs Flea Market, 1918 Ford, #9619 ....$25.00
Silver Springs Speedway, 1926 Mack, #9172 ....$22.00
Simpson Racing Equipment #1, 1940 Ford, JLE, #6012 ...$54.00
Sinclair #2, 1926 Mack, #2120..$65.00
Skelly Oil Co, 1931 International Tanker, JLE, #3035 ....$30.00
Slice, Grumman Step Van, #9709......................................$25.00
Smith & Wesson, 1951 GMC, #B410................................$19.00
Smith Corona, 1932 Ford, #1355 ....$25.00
Smith Racing, 1938 Chevy, #3826....................................$14.00
Smokecraft, 1918 Ford, #9493 ....$30.00
Speedway Racing, 1940 Ford, JLE, #6006 ....$45.00
Steel City Beer, 1931 International, JLE, #5049 ....$30.00
Sturgis 53rd Annual Ralley, 1929 International, JLE,
    #5057 ....$22.00

Sun-Maid Raisins, 1905 Ford Delivery Car, MIB, $30.00.

Sunoco, 1926 Mack Tanker, #9796.....................................$50.00
Super Bowl XXVII, 1931 Hawkeye, #9346 ....$35.00
Super Valu, Air Express Plane, #B419 ....$30.00
Supertest Petroleum #3, 1938 Chevy, #9538 ....$32.00
Sweet & Low, 1950 Chevy, #7631 ....$60.00
Tabasco Sauce, 1938 Chevy, #3640 ....$28.00
Tennessee Highway Patrol, GMC Tractor Trailer, NB,
    #T580...$45.00
Texaco #11, 1934 Doodle Bug, #B195 ....$20.00
Texaco #12, 1910 Mack, #F122..$30.00
Texaco #2, 1926 Mack, #9238 ....$595.00
Texaco #4, 1905 Ford, #9321 ....$165.00
Texaco #6, 1926 Ford, #9040 ....$75.00
Texaco #8, Horse & Wagon, #9390 ....$40.00
Texaco Bruce's in Tulsa (sampler), 1931 International,
    #4101 ....$75.00

Texaco, Ford Model A Roadster, Liberty Classics, MIB, $60.00.

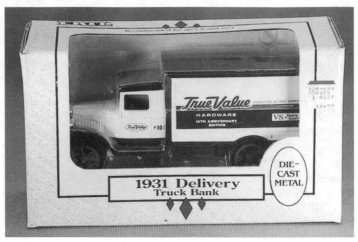

True Value Hardware, 1931 Delivery Truck, MIB, $20.00.

Texaco Fire Chief Gasoline, Ford Model A Tanker, Liberty Classics, MIB, $60.00.

Texas A&M University, 1931 Hawkeye, #F437 ....$30.00
Third Savings & Loan, 1923 Chevy, #B715 ....$26.00
Thunderhills Golf Classic, 1918 Ford, #7566 ....$150.00
TIC Inc, 1931 Hawkeye, #2954.....................................$28.00
Tiny Lund Fish Camp, 1955 Cameo Pickup, #3264 ....$55.00
Tisco, 1917 Ford, #9983 ....$55.00
Titlist Golf Balls, 1913 Ford, #9489 ....$55.00
Tom Mix Museum #1, Horse & Wagon, #3224................$48.00
Tom's Snack Foods, Grumman Step Van, #1337 ....$25.00
Tonka, 1913 Ford, #9739...$35.00
Tower City Ambulance, 1917 Ford, #9142 ....$25.00
Tower City Ambulance, 1950 Chevy, #9012.....................$30.00
Toy Collector & Prices, 1938 Chevy, #B001 ....$38.00
Toy House, 1925 Kenworth, #B279 ....$25.00
Toy Shop, 1926 Mack, #9442.......................................$22.00
Tractor Supply Co #15, 1925 Kenworth Stakebed, #3762..$32.00
Tractor Supply Co #3, 1926 Mack, #2121 ....$45.00
Tractor Supply Co #7, 1917 Ford, #9356 ....$25.00
Tremont Ambulance Association, 1932 Ford, #7665 ....$40.00
Tropicana Orange Juice, 1932 Ford, #9798.....................$35.00
Truckstops of America, 1925 Kenworth Wrecker, #B459...$35.00
True Value Hardware #10, 1931 Hawkeye, #9501............$18.00
True Value Hardware #4, 1932 Ford, #9232 ....$75.00

Trustworthy Hardware #2, 1905 Ford, #9395.....................$95.00
Trustworthy Hardware #7, 1918 Ford, #9377.....................$25.00
TRW #1, 1913 Ford, #2887...$95.00
Turkey Hills Market #3, 1923 Chevy, #B049 ....$20.00
Tydol Flying A, 1931 Hawkeye Tanker, #9123 ....$30.00
United Airlines, 1913 Ford, #9233....................................$40.00
United Hardware, 1940 Ford Pickup, #F528.....................$28.00
United Van Lines, 1917 Ford, #9715 ....$26.00
University of Alabama, 1918 Ford Barrel, #F902..............$45.00
University of Auburn Tigers, 1918 Ford, #F449 ....$40.00
University of North Carolina, Vintage Plane, #40039 .....$50.00
University of Northern Iowa, 1913 Ford, #9254.............$395.00
US Army Air Corps, Vega Plane, #12700.........................$22.00
US Mail, 1905 Ford, #1659 ....$75.00
US Mail, 1923 Chevy, #1352 ....$25.00
US Mail, 1938 Chevy, #B447...$35.00
US Navy, Air Express Plane, #F017 ....$25.00
USAF Thunderbirds, F16, #46002 ....$20.00
USAF Thunderbirds, Signature Series, F-16, #46003.......$48.00
V&S Variety Store, 1931 Hawkeye, #B632 ....$30.00
V&S Variety Store #4, 1932 Ford, #9755 ....$20.00
Valley Forge, 1926 Mack, #9616 ....$95.00
Valvoline, 1932 Ford, #9259 ....$25.00
Valvoline, 1937 Ford Tractor Trailer, #9260 ....$30.00
Vickers Oil, 1931 Hawkeye Tanker, #9942 ....$22.00
Vitalizer, 1932 Ford, #9602...$22.00
Wayne Towing, 1931 Hawkeye Wrecker, #9089.............$30.00
Weber's Supermarket, 1913 Ford, #9267........................$30.00
West Bend, 1913 Ford, #9237 ....$34.00
Westlake Hardware 90th Anniversary, 1912 Ford, #F567 ..$30.00
Wilwerts Harley-Davidson #1, 1920 International, JLE, #3031 ....$345.00
Winchester, Stearman Plane, #37540 ....$35.00
Wings & Things, 1932 Ford, #9634 ....$24.00
Winn Dixie, 1926 Mack, #9014 ....$25.00
Wireless, 1931 Hawkeye, #F080 ....$35.00
Wireless, 1950 Chevy, #2953 ....$20.00
Wix Filters, 1932 Ford, #9810 ....$165.00
Wolfgang Candy, 1913 Ford, #9440...............................$35.00
Wolf's Head Motor Oil, 1931 International, JLE, #4031..$35.00

Wonder Bread, 1913 Ford, #9161......................................$48.00
Wood Heat, 1905 Ford, #9498 ....$35.00
Wragtime Transportaion #1, 1932 Ford, #9226.............$195.00
Wrangler, 1913 Ford, #9171...$40.00
Wrigley's Juice Fruit, Stearman Plane, #37513 ....$35.00
Yeoman Co, 1931 Hawkeye, #B383 ....$45.00
Yuengling Beer, 1950 Ford, #9176 ....$125.00
Zenith Electronics, 1925 Kenworth, #F477.......................$40.00
Zinc Corporation, 1913 Ford, #9670 ....$65.00

FIRST GEAR

Akers Motor Lines, Mack B-61 Tractor Trailer, #19-1468.....$58.00
All American Plaza, 1957 International Wrecker, #19-1467.$40.00
All States Transmissions, Mack B-61 Tractor Trailer, #19-1469..$58.00
Alliance Racing, 1960 Mack Tractor Trailer, #19-1447...$75.00
American Flyer, 1951 Ford Stake, #19-0118.....................$50.00
Anheiser Busch Eagle Snacks #1, 1951 Ford Van, #19-1121...$75.00
Anheiser Busch Eagle Snacks #3, 1951 Ford Stake Truck, #19-1191 ....$65.00
Armstrong Tires, Mack B-61 Tractor Trailer, #19-1465 ..$74.00
Atlas Van Lines, 1957 International Harvester Moving Van, #19-1310 ....$90.00
Auto Value, 1951 Ford Van, #10-0102 ....$20.00
BASF Corp #3 R-M Diamont, 1951 Ford Stake, #19-1126 ..$175.00
Bennett's Towing, 1951 Ford Hauler w/56 Stock Car, #19-1644 ....$45.00
Boar's Head Meats, 1953 Ford C600, #18-1761 ....$40.00
BP Gasoline, Mack B-61 Tractor Trailer, #19-2006.........$65.00
Budweiser, 1953 White 3000 Tractor Trailer, #19-1912 ..$50.00
Burlington Truck Lines, 1956 White Tractor Trailer, #18-1545 ....$65.00
Campbell's Soup, Mack 61 Tractor Trailer, #19-1314......$65.00
Canadian Pacific Railroad, 1953 White 3000 Tractor Trailer, #18-1853 ....$70.00
Cape Cod Potato Chips, 1957 International Van, #19-1193...$32.00
Carlisle Collector Events, 1957 International Wrecker, #19-1732 ....$38.00
Chevrolet Motor Co, 1949 Chevy, #10-1328 ....$32.00
Chevrolet Solid Rock, 1949 Chevy, #10-1329 ....$30.00
Chevrolet-See the USA, 1949 Chevy Van, #19-1410 .....$28.00
Chevron Gasoline, 1951 Ford Tanker, #19-1021 ....$40.00
Citgo, 1957 International Tanker, #29-1248 ....$60.00
Coker Tire, 1951 Ford Stake, #19-1249 ....$45.00
Conrock Corporation, B-61 Mack Dump Truck, #19-1956 ....$50.00
CP Ward Construction, B-61 Mack Dump Truck, #19-1827..$75.00
Custom Chrome 25th Anniversary, 1952 GMC Box, #18-1361 ....$95.00
Daisy Air Rifles, 1952 GMC Van, #10-0126 ....$30.00
Dearborn Fire Pumper, 1951 Ford F7, #19-1900.............$45.00
Dr Pepper, 1951 Ford Bottle Truck, #19-1700 ....$40.00
Eastern Express, 1953 Ford Box, #19-1481......................$32.00
Eastwood Club #6, 1955 Diamond T Wrecker, #19-1918...$48.00
Eastwood Museum, 1951 Ford Van, #19-1010................$115.00
Erector (AC Gilbert), 1957 International Van, #19-0111..$30.00
Esso, Mack B-61 Tractor Trailer, #19-1670 ....$75.00
Exxon, Mack B-61 Tractor Trailer, #19-1708...................$44.00

Exxon Aviation, 1957 International Tanker, #19-1800...$35.00
Farmall M Tractors, 1957 International, #19-1577 ....$70.00

Firestone Gum-Dipped, 1957 International R-190 with Dry Goods Van, MIB, $38.00.

First Gear Inc, 1955 Diamond T Wrecker, #19-0009 ....$75.00
Ford Motorcraft, 1951 Ford Tanker, #20-1124 ....$12.00
Ford Quality Parts, 1951 Ford Box, #20-1123 ....$12.00
Frank Dibella Moving, 1957 International Moving Van, #19-1450 ....$45.00
Global Van Lines, Mack B-61 Tractor Trailer, #19-1810...$70.00
GMC Truck & Coach Division, 1952 GMC Stake, #10-1253 ....$30.00
Graham Trucking Co, 1952 GMC Box, #19-1066 ....$35.00
Grapette Soda, Mack B-61 Tractor Trailer, #19-1619......$75.00
Gulf Oil #1, 1957 International Wrecker, #19-1336 ....$80.00
Hamm's Beer, 1953 Ford, #29-1480 ....$35.00
Hershey's Chocolate, 1957 International Box, #19-1283.$36.00
Hooker Headers, 1957 International Van, #10-1283........$40.00
Hostess Cupcakes, 1949 Chevy, #19-1494.......................$58.00
Howard Johnson's, 1952 GMC Van, #18-1795 ....$35.00
Humble Oil Co, Mack B-61 Tractor Trailer, #19-1395..$175.00
Indian Motorcycle, Mack B-61 Tractor Trailer, #19-1462..$65.00
International Harvester 50th Anniversary, 1957 International Box, #10-1411...$38.00
Iowa Hawkeyes, 1952 GMC Van, #29-1268.....................$42.00
Jax Beer, 1953 Ford, #29-1461..$28.00
JC Whitney, 1957 International Wrecker, #10-1207 ....$45.00
Kazim Temple Shrine Circus, 1949 Chevy Panel, #29-1413 ...$35.00
Kelly-Springfield Tires, 1955 Diamond T Wrecker, #19-1884 ..$36.00
Leffler Inc Carlos R, B-61 Mack Dump Truck, #18-1899.$49.00
Lionel Trains #2, 1952 GMC Van, #19-0108 ....$50.00
Lionel Trains-Madison Hardware, 1953 Ford Van, #19-1396 ..$50.00
Lone Star Beer, 1952 GMC Van, #10-1258......................$32.00
Marathon Oil, 1953 Ford Tanker, #29-1588.....................$34.00

Marx Toys, 1957 International F/T, #19-0113.................$48.00

Mayflower Transit Co, 1953 Kenworth Tractor Trailer, #19-1803 ....$80.00

McLean Trucking, 1956 White Tractor Trailer, #18-1845..$65.00

Mercury Marine, 1957 International Box, #10-1649.......$36.00

Michelin Tires, Mack B-61 Tractor Trailer, #19-1502 .....$65.00

Mobil Oil, 1952 GMC Tanker, #29-1231.....................$45.00

Mobilgas, 1957 International Wrecker, #18-1381 ....$95.00

Moon Pie-Banana, 1951 Ford Box, #19-1267 ....$32.00

Morton Salt, 1952 GMC Sack Truck, #19-1130 ....$32.00

Mountain Dew, 1952 GMC Bottle Truck, #19-1730 ....$34.00

Moxie Cola, 1952 GMC Bottle Truck, #19-0119.............$55.00

National Motorcycle Museum, 1951 Ford Van, #29-1274..$48.00

New York Central System, 1957 International Box, #10-1188 ....$40.00

New York Fire Department, 1957 International Wrecker, #19-1401 ....$55.00

Northern Pacific Railroad, 1953 Ford Pickup, #19-1559..$20.00

O'Doul's Non-Alcohol Brew #1, 1952 GMC Van, #19-1352...$34.00

Olympia Beer, 1952 GMC Reefer, #29-1482 ....$30.00

Paul Arpin Moving, 1957 International Moving Van, #19-1382 ....$45.00

Pennsylvania Railroad, Mack B-61 Tractor Trailer, #19-1435 ....$50.00

Pennzoil, 1952 GMC Wrecker, #19-1062.....................$45.00

Pepsi-Cola Miss Pepsi, 1951 Ford Van, #19-1567.............$45.00

Pepsi-Cola Santa, 1951 Ford Bottle Truck, #19-1092 ......$95.00

Pepsi-Cola-Long Cool, 1953 Kenworth Tractor Trailer, #19-1733 ....$72.00

Philadelphia Fire Department, 1953 Ford Pickup, #18-1585.$45.00

Philadelphia Police Department, 1949 Chevy, #18-1442.$40.00

Phillips 66, 1951 Ford Tanker, #19-1034 ....$50.00

Phillips 66 Pipeline #2, 1949 Chevy Panel, #19-1831 ......$40.00

Police Department, 1957 International Wrecker, #19-1264 ..$35.00

Police Department Mounted Patrol, 1957 International Box, #19-1384 ....$42.00

Railway Express, Mack B-61 Tractor Trailer, #19-1654 ...$65.00

Ralph Moody, 1951 Ford w/stock car, #19-1512..............$50.00

RC Cola, 1951 Ford Bottle, #19-1131..............................$45.00

Reading Anthracite Co, Mack B-61 Dump Truck, #18-1872...$55.00

Red Crown Gasoline, 1951 Ford Stake/Barrel Truck, #19-1631 ....$35.00

Red Star Express, Mack B-61 Tractor Trailer, #19-1312 ..$200.00

Remington, Mack B-61 Tractor Trailer, #10-1292 ....$74.00

Remington I-Dove, 1951 Ford Van, #10-1098.................$30.00

Remington II-Deer, 1953 Ford Van, #10-1485 ....$28.00

Roadrunner Express, 1951 Ford Van, #19-1108...............$45.00

Roadway Express, 1953 Ford, #10-1379 ....$38.00

Rolling Thunder Cycles, 1951 Ford Box, #28-1141.........$32.00

Sante Fe Trail Trans, 1957 International Van, #10-1168...$85.00

Schultz Co Grand Pianos, 1957 International Box, #19-1332 ....$42.00

Shell Oil Co, Mack B-61 Tractor Trailer, #19-1392 ......$175.00

Smith & Wesson, 1952 GMC Stake Truck, #10-1326.....$30.00

Special Export, 1951 Ford Stake, #10-1259 ....$32.00

Spra' N Strip, 1952 GMC Wrecker, #19-1769 ....$38.00

State Highway Department, Mack B-61 Dump Truck, #19-1813........$59.00

Storey Wrecker, 1957 International Wrecker, #19-1665 .$38.00

Sunshine Biscuits, 1957 International, #10-1473 ....$32.00

Texaco (Star Enterprises), 1955 Diamond T Wrecker, #18-1941 ....$65.00

Texaco Pipeline #3, 1953 Ford Pickup, #19-1688.............$95.00

Texaco Star, 1955 Diamond T Tractor Trailer, #18-1941 ..$90.00

TNT Trucking, Mack B-61 Tractor Trailer, #10-1598.....$55.00

Tollway & Tunnel, 1957 International Wrecker, #19-1439 ..$55.00

True Value Hardware, 1953 Ford Van, #19-1490 ....$34.00

United Ice & Coal, Mack B-61 Dump Truck, #18-1850 ..$70.00

US Army, 1957 International Fire Truck, #19-1389 ....$28.00

US Army Ambulance, 1949 Chevy, #19-1388 ....$28.00

US Army Fuel, 1957 International Tanker, #29-1380 .....$34.00

US Mail, 1953 Ford Van, #19-1441 ....$40.00

US Navy, 1949 Chevy, #19-1552.....................................$35.00

Von Der Ahe Moving, 1957 International Moving Van, #19-1448 ....$45.00

West Coast Freight, 1952 GMC Box, #19-1007 ....$32.00

Winchester, 1957 International Box, #18-1319 ....$25.00

Winchester 100th Anniversary (w/knife), 1951 Ford Van, #10-1648 ....$68.00

Wonder Bread, 1949 Chevy, #19-1493 ....$24.00

Yellow Freight Lines, Mack B-61 Tractor Trailer, #10-1293 ...$95.00

Zephyr Petroleum, 1957 International Box, #19-1166 .....$24.00

RACING CHAMPIONS

Alliance Racing/Dennis Setzer, Lumina, #453, D13.........$40.00

Amoco/Bill Elliot #11, T-Bird, #488RC, D13...................$50.00

Atlanta Motor Speedway, Kenworth Tractor Trailer, #215, D13........$55.00

Bojangle/Derrike Cope #98, T-Bird, #424, D13...............$55.00

Buss Fuses/B Hillin, T-Bird, #2281, D13 ....$25.00

Citgo/M Shepard #21, T-Bird, #335, D13........................$30.00

Coca-Cola 600/Charlotte #2, Kenworth Tractor Trailer, #203, D13........$100.00

Coca-Cola 600/Charlotte #4, Chevy Lumina, #263, D13...$65.00

Dallas Cowboys/Super Bowl Champions 1994, #551, D13..$60.00

Daytona 500 by STP, Model A Roadster, #231, D13 ....$80.00

Dentyne/J Nemechek #87, Chevy Lumina, #372, D13.....$50.00

Dupont Racing/Jeff Gordon #24, Kenworth Tractor Trailer, #367, D13........$40.00

Family Channel/Ted Musgrave #16, T-Bird, #2208, D13.$30.00

Ford Motorsports, 1934 Biplane, #460, D13....................$60.00

Ford Motorsports/J Ridley #98, T-Bird, #472, D13 ....$35.00

Goodwrench Racing/Dale Earnhardt #3, Kenworth Tractor Trailer, #358, D13 ....$40.00

Goody's 500 Martinsville, Lumina, #510, D13 ....$40.00

Hardees/Mello Yello/W Burton, Chevy Lumina, #413, D13........$40.00

Havoline/D Allison #28, T-Bird, #446, D13.....................$75.00

Interstate Batteries/D Jarret, 1955 Chevy, #474, D13......$30.00

Kleenex/J Spencer #10, Chevy Lumina, #407, D13..........$65.00

Kyle Petty, 1955 Convertible, #473, D13 ....$25.00

Leo Jackson/Harry Gant, Lumina, #2284, D13................$30.00

Manheim Auction/H Gant #7, Chevy Lumina, #2270, D13 .$40.00

Mello Yello/Kyle Petty #42, Pontiac, #356, D13 ....$55.00

Motorcraft/G Bodine #15, T-Bird, #338, D13...................$25.00

NASCAR Racing #93, Kenworth Tractor Trailer, #313, D13.**$35.00**
New Hampshire, Model A Panel, #233, D13 ....**$35.00**
Petty Enterprises/Petty #42, 1934 Biplane, #449, D13......**$90.00**
Polaroid/S Robinson #35, Chevy Lumina, #2803, D13 ....**$35.00**
Pontiac/Rusty Wallace #2, Pontiac, #428, D13 ....**$160.00**
Quaker State/B Bodine #26, T-Bird, #339, D13 ....**$25.00**
Racing Champs Club #93, Chevy Lumina, #371, D13...**$100.00**
Raybestos/S Marlin #8, T-Bird, #337, D13 ....**$30.00**
Slim Jim/D Green #44, Lumina, #463, D13 ....**$40.00**
STP/R Petty #43, Pontiac, #346, D13 ....**$100.00**
STP/R Wilson #44, Pontiac, #360, D13 ....**$40.00**
Tide/D Waltrip #17, Lumina, #405, orange, D13 ....**$65.00**
US Air/G Sacks #77 Winston Cup, T-Bird, #2248, D13..**$40.00**
Valvoline/M Martin #6, T-Bird, #334, D13 ....**$50.00**

SPEC-CAST

Ace Hardware (Grand Island NE), 1937 Chevy, #15025.**$24.00**
Agway (Mill Hall), 1936 Dodge Panel, #74040 ....**$36.00**
Agway #11, 1936 Dodge Pickup, #72030 ....**$25.00**
Alabama, 1955 Chevy, #50029 ....**$24.00**
Allied Van Lines, 1929 Ford, #2551................................**$20.00**
Allis Chalmers, 1929 Ford Freight Truck, #2028..............**$25.00**
American Airlines, 1929 Ford Fire Pumper, #02053 ....**$22.00**
Amoco #1, Vintage Plane, #0805 ....**$110.00**
Bell System, 1931 Ford, #1004 ....**$24.00**
Big A Auto Parts #11, 1936 Dodge Panel, #74028 ....**$22.00**
Billy Ray Cyrus, 1929 Ford, #2588 ....**$24.00**
Brickyard 400, 1955 Chevy Convertible, #0459 ....**$60.00**
California Highway Patrol #2, 1937 Chevy, #15023 ....**$24.00**
Campbell's Soup, 1936 Dodge Convertible, #70002 ....**$24.00**
Canada Tire, 1940 Ford Pickup, #3888 ....**$28.00**
Central Tractor Farm & Family, 1940 Ford, #62506 ....**$34.00**
Cheerios, 1942 Chevy Box, #75005 ....**$28.00**
Chevrolet Factory Service, 1937 Chevy, #15011..............**$20.00**
Chevrolet License, 1955 Chevy Convertible, #55005......**$15.00**
Chevrolet Motor Co, 1937 Chevy Convertible, #0489 ......**$22.00**
Chevrolet Parts & Service, 1955 Chevy Sedan, #50020 ..**$22.00**
Chevron Employment Club of Houston #3, 1955 Chevy Convertible, #55015 ....**$28.00**
Chicago 10th Anniversary Bike Show, 1937 Chevy, #12504..**$34.00**
Christmas Happy Holidays, 1929 Ford, #2613 ....**$15.00**
Chrome Specialties, 1955 Chevy, #50045 ....**$45.00**
Citgo, 1940 Ford Tanker, #65501 ....**$25.00**
Classic Auto Series, 1955 Chevy Convertible, #55002 ....**$22.00**
Classic Street Rods, 1929 Ford, #2578 ....**$25.00**
Coca-Cola 600, Kenworth Tractor Trailer, #30001..........**$48.00**
Conoco Oil, 1929 Ford, #2002 ....**$30.00**
Cooper Tire #1, 1929 Ford, #1003 ....**$95.00**
Crown Petroleum #5, 1929 Ford Tanker, #2043 ....**$30.00**
Darlington Transouth 500, 1929 Ford Tanker, #0216......**$25.00**
Daytona 500, 1929 Ford, #0231......................................**$24.00**
Diamond Rio, 1940 Ford, #67503 ....**$24.00**
Drag Speciality's #3, 1937 Chevy, #12510 ....**$22.00**
Dubuque Country Club, 1929 Ford, #1079 ....**$20.00**
Ducks Unlimited, 1937 Chevy, #15014 ....**$45.00**
Eastwood Club #1, 1929 Ford, #1735............................**$65.00**
Eastwood Co #3, Stearman Plane, #21200.....................**$40.00**

Eastwood Co UK #2, 1937 Chevy Pickup, #1165.............**$24.00**
Essolube Motor Oil, 1936 Dodge, #74003 ....**$32.00**
Fina Oil, 1929 Ford, #2004...**$28.00**
Ford, NY World's Fair 1940, 1940 Ford, #2495................**$35.00**
Ford, 1929 Ford Fire Truck, #2025 ....**$20.00**
Ford Sales & Service, 1940 Ford, #67502 ....**$22.00**
GDS Fair, 1937 Chevy, #15029......................................**$30.00**
Gold Medal Flour, 1916 Studebaker, #25025..................**$22.00**
Goodyear, 1937 Chevy, #15001 ....**$20.00**
Gulf Oil, 1929 Ford Wrecker, #1005..............................**$35.00**
Gumout Carburetor Cleaner, 1942 Chevy Box, #75002 ..**$26.00**
Hamm's Beer, 1936 Dodge Panel, #74032 ....**$22.00**
Hank Williams Jr, 1916 Studebaker, #22516 ....**$24.00**
Harley-Davidson, Kenworth Tractor Trailer, #99197.......**$75.00**
Harry Gant #33, 1929 Ford, #0228.................................**$44.00**
Heinz 57, 1916 Studebaker, #22502 ....**$22.00**
Hershey's Milk Chocolate, 1936 Dodge, #74012 ....**$24.00**
Home Hardware #12 (prototype), 1937 Chevy, #0012.....**$65.00**
Hooter's Atlanta 500, 1929 Ford, #2709 ....**$75.00**
House of Kolor, 1937 Chevy, #15013..............................**$24.00**
Indian Ace Motorcycle, 1929 Ford, #1059......................**$35.00**
Indian Motorcycle, 1955 Chevy Convertible, #55014 .....**$22.00**
Iowa Hawkeyes, 1955 Chevy Convertible, #55012 ....**$25.00**
James Dean, 1955 Chevy, #50043 ....**$24.00**
JC Whitney, 1940 Ford, #62508.....................................**$32.00**
JC Whitney w/Santa, 1937 Chevy, #10023 ....**$32.00**
Jewel Tea, 1931 Ford, #2584 ....**$65.00**
Jim Beam Dist #2-Evergreen, 1929 Ford, #2586 ....**$30.00**
John Deere, 1936 Dodge Panel, #74042 ....**$24.00**
Joie Chitwood Auto Daredevils, 1955 Chevy, #245000 ...**$35.00**
Kentucky Fried Chicken, 1940 Ford Panel, #67519 ....**$22.00**
Laconia Motorcycle Rally, 1929 Ford, #2553...................**$20.00**
Lennox #2 100th Anniversary, 1940 Ford, #62525 ....**$55.00**
Lennox 100th Anniversary, 1916 Studebaker, #22510 ....**$95.00**
Lionel Trains, 1955 Chevy, #303500 ....**$32.00**
Louisville Slugger, 1931 Ford, #1036.............................**$25.00**
Mailboxes Etc #3, 1955 Chevy Sedan, #50053 ....**$28.00**
Mello Yello 500, 1929 Ford, #2710 ....**$20.00**
Miller Genuine Draft, 1940 Ford Tanker, #65507 ....**$22.00**
Mobil Oil, 1940 Ford Tanker, #65506 ....**$35.00**
Mobilgas, 1936 Dodge Tanker, #72007 ....**$30.00**
Model A Ford Club of America, 1929 Ford, #2542 ....**$25.00**
Moon Pie 75th Anniversary, 1957 Ford Sedan, #58009 ...**$35.00**
Mopar, 1936 Dodge Panel, #321000 ....**$34.00**
Motorcraft #15 Racing, 1929 Ford, #0307 ....**$20.00**
Neil Bonnett/Citgo #21, 1929 Ford, #0300......................**$65.00**
Olympia Beer, 1929 Ford, #2528 ....**$15.00**
Oreo Cookies, 1916 Studebaker, #25013 ....**$22.00**
Pabst Beer, 1929 Ford, #1512 ....**$30.00**
Pennzoil, 1929 Ford, #1062 ....**$28.00**
Pennzoil, 1936 Dodge Tanker, #72010 ....**$30.00**
Pepsi-Cola, 1936 Dodge Convertible, #70004 ....**$25.00**
Pepsi-Cola, 1957 Ford Ranchero, #57006 ....**$22.00**
Police Department, 1937 Chevy Convertible, #10008.....**$24.00**
Quaker State Racing, 1929 Ford, #0308..........................**$22.00**
Red Crown Gasoline, 1940 Ford Tanker, #65502.............**$25.00**
Richard Petty Hooters 500, Kenworth Tractor Trailer, #0316...**$40.00**

Richard Petty/Rick Wilson, 1937 Chevy, #0362 ....$40.00
Richmond Pontiac 400, 1929 Ford, #0212 ....$32.00
Rockingham Raceway, 1929 Ford, #0210 ....$65.00
Shell Oil #6, 1957 International Tanker, #29-1270 ....$40.00
Shell Oil Co, 1929 Ford, #2007 ....$175.00
Snap-On Tools, 1929 Ford, #2598 ....$40.00
State Highway Garage, 1940 Ford Convertible, #60004 ..$24.00
Sturgis 53rd Annual Rally, 1937 Chevy, #15004 ....$125.00
Sunsweet 75th Anniversary, 1929 Ford, #2520 ....$35.00
Sweet & Low, 1929 Ford Roadster, #1554 ....$30.00
Texaco, 1929 Ford, #2012 ....$40.00
Tootsie Roll, 1916 Studebaker, #22516 ....$45.00
Toy Farmer Zeke, 1929 Ford, #1532 ....$25.00
US Mail, 1916 Studebaker, #25019 ....$26.00
Wrigley's Spearmint Gum, 1929 Ford, #2572 ....$24.00

Dinky

Dinky diecasts were made by Meccano (Britain) as early as 1933, but high on the list of many of today's collectors are those from the decades of the '50s and '60s. They made commercial vehicles, firefighting equipment, farm toys, and heavy equipment as well as classic cars that were the epitome of high style, such as the #157 Jaguar XK120, produced from the mid-'50s through the early '60s. Some Dinkys were made in France; since 1979 no toys have been produced in Great Britain. Values are for examples mint and in the original packaging unless noted otherwise.

See also Soldiers.

#100, Lady Penelope's Fab 1, luminous pk $400.00
#100, Lady Penelope's Fab 1, pk $250.00
#101, Sunbeam Alpine $200.00
#101, Thunderbird II & IV, gr $300.00
#101, Thunderbird II & IV, metallic gr $400.00
#102, Joe's Car $170.00
#102, MG Midget $300.00
#103, Austin Healey 100 ....$350.00
#103, Spectrum Patrol Car $160.00
#104, Aston Martin DB3S $250.00
#105, Maximum Security Vehicle $170.00
#105, Triumph TR2 ....$250.00
#106, Austin Atlantic, bl or blk $200.00
#106, Austin Atlantic, pk $350.00
#106, Prisoner Mini Moke $300.00
#106, Thunderbird II & IV $150.00
#107, Stripey, The Magi Mini $400.00
#107, Sunbeam Alpine $150.00
#108, MG Midget $200.00
#108, Sam's Car, gold, red or bl $160.00
#108, Sam's Car, silver $120.00
#109, Austin Healey 100 ....$160.00
#109, Gabriel Model T Ford $150.00
#110, Aston Martin DB3S $150.00
#110, Aston Martin DB5 ....$125.00
#111, Cinderella's Coach $50.00
#111, Triumph TR2 ....$160.00

#112, Austin Healy Sprite, $125.00.

#112, Purdey's Triumph TR7 ....$75.00
#113, MGB $100.00
#114, Triumph Spitfire, gray, gold or red $125.00
#114, Triumph Spitfire, purple $170.00
#115, Plymouth Fury $125.00
#115, UB Taxi $85.00
#116, Volvo 1800S $100.00
#117, Four Berth Caravan $60.00
#118, Tow-Away Glider Set $250.00
#120, Happy Cab $75.00
#120, Jaguar E-Type $110.00
#121, Goodwood Racing Gift Set $2,000.00
#122, Touring Gift Set $2,000.00
#122, Volvo 265 Estate Car $50.00
#123, Mayfair Gift Set $3,000.00
#123, Princess 2200 HL $50.00
#124, Holiday Gift Set $1,000.00
#124, Rolls Royce Phantom V $90.00
#125, Fun A'Hoy Set $300.00
#126, Motor Show Set $2,000.00
#127, Rolls Royce Silver Cloud III $140.00
#128, Mercedes Benz 600 ....$8.00
#129, MG Midget $500.00
#129, VW 1200 Sedan $80.00
#130, Ford Consul Corsair $100.00
#131, Cadillac El Dorado $200.00
#131, Jaguar E-Type 2+2 ....$160.00
#132, Ford 40-RV $60.00
#132, Packard Convertible $200.00
#133, Cunningham C-5R $150.00
#133, Ford Cortina $110.00
#134, Triumph Vitesse $100.00
#135, Triumph 2000 ....$100.00
#136, Vauxhall Viva $80.00
#137, Plymouth Fury $150.00
#138, Hillman Imp $100.00
#139, Ford Cortina $130.00
#139a, Ford Fordor Sedan, cream & red or pk & bl $300.00
#139a, Ford Fordor Sedan, solid colors $160.00
#139a, US Army Staff Car $350.00
#139b, Hudson Commodore Sedan, dual colors $350.00
#139b, Hudson Commodore Sedan, solid colors $225.00

#140, Morris 1100	$60.00
#141, Vauxhall Victor	$80.00
#142, Jaguar Mark 10	$100.00
#143, Ford Capri	$125.00
#144, VW 1500	$100.00
#145, Singer Vogue	$100.00
#146, Daimler V8	$125.00
#147, Cadillac 62	$125.00
#148, Ford Fairlane, gr	$125.00
#148, Ford Fairlane, metallic gr	$225.00
#149, Citroen Dyane	$50.00
#149, Sports Car Gift Set	$1,800.00
#150, Rolls Royce Silver Wraith	$100.00
#150, Royal Tank Corps Personnel	$250.00
#151, Royal Tank Corps Med Tank Set	$600.00
#151, Triumph 1800 Saloon	$150.00
#151, Vauxhall Victor 101	$100.00
#151a, Med Tank	$250.00
#151b, 6-Wheeled Covered Wagon	$180.00
#151c, Cooker Trailer	$100.00
#151d, Water Tank Trailer	$100.00
#152, Rolls Royce Phantom V	$65.00
#152, Royal Tank Corps Light Tank Set	$600.00
#152a, Light Tank	$160.00
#152b, Reconnaissance Car	$175.00
#152c, Austin 7 Car	$250.00
#153, Aston Martin	$100.00
#153, Standard Vanguard-Spats	$160.00
#153a, Jeep	$160.00
#154, Ford Taunus 17m	$65.00
#155, Ford Anglia	$140.00
#156, Mechanized Army Set	$5,000.00
#156, Rover 75, dual colors	$300.00
#156, Rover 75, solid colors	$150.00
#156, Saab 96	$100.00
#157, BMW 2000 Tilux	$100.00
#157, Jaguar XK120, wht or dual colors	$400.00
#158, Riley	$160.00
#158, Rolls Royce Silver Shadow	$100.00
#159, Ford Cortina MKII	$100.00
#159, Morris Oxford, dual colors	$300.00
#159, Morris Oxford, solid colors	$170.00

#160, Austin A30	$150.00
#160, Mercedes Benz 250 SE	$80.00
#160, Royal Artillery Personnel	$300.00
#161, Austin Somerset, dual colors	$300.00
#161, Austin Somerset, solid colors	$150.00
#161, Ford Mustang	$70.00
#161, Mobile Antiaircraft Unit	$1,000.00
#161a, Lorry w/Searchlight	$500.00
#161b, Antiaircraft Gun on Trailer	$150.00
#162, Ford Zephyr	$150.00
#162, Triumph 1300	$75.00
#162a, Light Dragon Tractor	$150.00
#162b, Trailer	$40.00
#162c, 18-Pounder Gun	$50.00
#163, Bristol 450 Coupe	$100.00
#163, VW 1600 TL, metallic bl	$150.00
#163, VW 1600 TL, red	$75.00
#164, Ford Zodiac MKIV, bronze	$200.00
#164, Ford Zodiac MKIV, silver	$100.00
#164, Vauxhall Cresta	$150.00
#165, Ford Capri	$100.00
#165, Humber Hawk	$180.00
#166, Renault R16	$60.00
#166, Sunbeam Rapier	$150.00
#167, AC Aceca, all cream	$300.00
#167, AC Aceca, dual colors	$160.00
#168, Ford Escort	$100.00
#168, Singer Gazelle	$160.00
#169, Ford Corsair	$100.00
#169, Studebaker Golden Hawk	$170.00
#170, Ford Fordor, dual colors	$300.00
#170, Ford Fordor, solid colors	$100.00
#170, Lincoln Continental	$120.00
#170m, Ford Fordor US Army Staff Car	$350.00
#171, Austin 1800	$100.00
#171, Hudson Commodore, dual colors	$350.00
#172, Fiat 2300 Station Wagon	$80.00
#172, Studebaker Land Cruiser, dual colors	$300.00
#172, Studebaker Land Cruiser, solid colors	$180.00
#173, Nash Rambler	$110.00
#173, Pontiac Parisienne	$75.00

#174, Hudson Hornet, $160.00.

#174, Mercury Cougar $80.00
#175, Cadillac El Dorado.....................................$100.00
#175, Hillman Minx $150.00
#176, Austin A105, cream or gray $160.00
#176, Austin A105, cream w/bl roof, or gray w/red roof ...$250.00
#176, NSU R80, metallic bl $180.00
#176, NSU R80, metallic red $80.00
#177, Opel Kapitan..$100.00
#178, Mini Clubman..$60.00
#178, Plymouth Plaza, bl w/wht roof.................$400.00
#178, Plymouth Plaza, pk, gr or 2-tone bl $170.00
#179, Opel Commodore $70.00
#179, Studebaker President $170.00
#180, Packard Clipper $170.00
#180, Rover 3500 Sedan $30.00
#181, VW $100.00
#182, Porsche 356A Coupe, cream, red or bl.....$130.00
#182, Porsche 356A Coupe, dual colors............$325.00
#183, Fiat 600 ....$100.00
#183, Morris Mini Minor....................................$125.00
#184, Volvo 122S, red $130.00
#184, Volvo 122S, wht $375.00
#185, Alpha Romeo 1900......................................$125.00
#186, Mercedes Benz 200......................................$65.00
#187, De Tomaso Mangusta 5000 ....$65.00

#187, Volkswagen Karmann-Ghia Coupe, $120.00.

#188, Ford Berth Caravan $60.00
#188, Jensen FF...$75.00
#189, Lamborghini Marzal.................................$65.00
#189, Triumph Herald.......................................$130.00
#190, Caravan $60.00
#191, Dodge Royal Sedan, cream w/bl flash $300.00
#191, Dodge Royal Sedan, cream w/brn flash, or gr w/blk flash ...$170.00
#192, Desoto Fireflite $200.00
#192, Range Rover..$50.00
#193, Rambler Station Wagon............................$130.00
#194, Bentley S Coupe $140.00
#195, Jaguar 3.4 Litre MKII $150.00
#195, Range Rover Fire Chief $60.00
#196, Holden Special Sedan $100.00

#197, Morris Mini Traveller, dk gr & brn.....................$400.00
#197, Morris Mini Traveller, lime gr.............................$300.00
#197, Morris Mini Traveller, wht & brn.......................$130.00
#198, Austin Countryman, orange................................$325.00
#198, Rolls Royce Phantom V $125.00
#199, Austin Countryman, bl...$125.00
#200, Matra 630..$50.00
#201, Plymouth Stock Car..$85.00
#201, Racing Car Set..$750.00
#202, Customized Land Rover..................................$40.00
#202, Fiat Abarth 2000..$40.00
#203, Customized Range Rover................................$40.00
#204, Ferrari $40.00
#205, Lotus Cortina..$125.00
#205, Talbot Lago, in bubble pkg...........................$325.00
#206, Customized Corvette Stingray $50.00
#206, Maserati, in bubble pkg $360.00
#207, Alfa Romeo, in bubble pkg $300.00
#207, Triumph TR7 ....$40.00
#208, Cooper-Bristol, in bubble pkg $300.00
#208, VW Porsche 914 ....$50.00
#209, Ferrari, in bubble pkg $300.00
#210, Alfa Romeo 33 ....$50.00
#210, Vanwall, in bubble pkg.................................$200.00
#211, Triumph TR7 ....$80.00
#212, Ford Cortina Rally $135.00
#213, Ford Capri $75.00
#214, Hillman Imp Rally $100.00
#215, Ford GT Racing Car $70.00
#216, Ferrari Dino $50.00
#217, Alfa Romeo Scarabeo $40.00
#218, Lotus Europa $65.00
#219, Jaguar XJS Coupe..$65.00
#220, Ferrari P5..$50.00
#221, Corvette Stingray..$40.00
#222, Hesketh Racing Car, dk bl.............................$50.00
#222, Hesketh Racing Car, Olympus Camera $100.00
#223, McLaren M8A Can-Am....................................$40.00
#224, Mercedes Benz C111......................................$40.00
#225, Lotus Formula 1 Racer $40.00
#226, Ferrari 312/B2 ....$40.00
#227, Beach Bunny $40.00
#228, Super Sprinter..$40.00
#236, Connaught Racer...$125.00
#237, Mercedes Benz Racer.....................................$140.00
#238, Jaguar Type-D Racer.....................................$160.00
#239, Vanwall Racer...$100.00
#240, Cooper Racer $70.00
#240, Dinky Way Gift Set.......................................$100.00
#241, Lotus Racer $80.00
#241, Silver Jubilee Taxi $50.00
#242, Ferrari Racer..$90.00
#243, BRM Racer..$90.00
#243, Volvo Police Racer..$40.00
#244, Plymouth Police Racer...................................$40.00
#245, Superfast Gift Set..$200.00
#246, International GT Gift Set $200.00
#249, Racing Car Gift Set......................................$1,500.00

#249, Racing Car Gift Set, in bubble pkg...................$1,800.00
#250, Mini Coopers Police Car $75.00
#251, USA Police Car, Pontiac $80.00
#252, RCMP Car, Pontiac $100.00
#254, Austin Taxi, yel $120.00
#254, Police Range Rover $50.00
#255, Ford Zodiac Police Car $100.00
#255, Mersey Tunnel Police Van $100.00
#255, Police Mini Clubman...$50.00
#256, Humber Hawk Police Car..$150.00
#257, Nash Rambler Candian Fire Chief Car $100.00
#258, USA Police Car, Cadillac, Desoto, Dodge or Ford..$150.00
#259, Bedford Fire Engine $130.00
#260, Royal Mail Van...$160.00
#260, VW Deutsch Bundepost $185.00
#261, Ford Taunus Polizei $300.00
#261, Telephone Service Van...$170.00
#262, VW Swiss Post PTT Car, casting #129 ....$300.00
#262, VW Swiss Post PTT Car, casting #181 ....$500.00
#263, Airport Fire Rescue Tender $70.00
#263, Superior Criterion Ambulance...............................$100.00
#264, RCMP Patrol Car, Cadillac $175.00
#264, RCMP Patrol Car, Fairlane $150.00
#265, Plymouth Taxi $170.00
#266, ERF Fire Tender..$75.00
#266, ERF Fire Tender, Falck $100.00
#266, Plymouth Taxi, Metro Cab $200.00
#267, Paramedic Truck $50.00
#267, Superior Cadillac Ambulance $100.00
#268, Range Rover Ambulance...$40.00
#268, Renault Dauphine Mini Cab..................................$150.00
#269, Ford Transit Police Accident Unit, Faulk Zonen ...$60.00
#269, Jaguar Motorway Police Car $160.00
#270, AA Motorcycle Patrol $100.00
#270, Ford Panda Police Car $70.00
#271, Ford Transit Fire, Appliance $100.00
#271, Ford Transit Fire, Falck $150.00
#271, TS Motorcycle Patrol $300.00
#272, ANNB Motorcycle Patrol $350.00
#272, Police Accident Unit..$60.00
#273, RAC Patrol Mini Van...$200.00
#274, AA Patrol Mini Van..$250.00
#274, Ford Transit Ambulance..$50.00
#274, Mini Van, Joseph Mason Paints $750.00
#275, Brink's Armoured Car, no boullion $75.00
#275, Brink's Armoured Car, w/gold bullion $200.00
#275, Brink's Armoured Car, w/Mexican bullion........$1,000.00
#276, Airport Fire Tender $100.00
#276, Ford Transit Ambulance..$60.00
#277, Police Range Rover...$40.00
#277, Superior Criterion Ambulance...............................$100.00
#278, Plymouth Yellow Cab $40.00
#278, Vauxhall Victor Ambulance $100.00
#279, Aveling Barford Diesel Roller.................................$80.00
#280, Midland Mobile Bank...$140.00
#281, Fiat 2300 Pathe News Camera Car $200.00
#281, Military Hovercraft $50.00
#282, Austin 1800 Taxi..$100.00

#282, Land Rover Fire, Appliance.....................................$50.00
#282, Land Rover Fire, Falck..$80.00
#283, BOAC Coach $150.00
#283, Single-Decker Bus $80.00
#284, London Austin Taxi $60.00
#285, Merryweather Fire Engine $80.00
#285, Merryweather Fire Engine, Falck...........................$150.00
#286, Ford Transit Fire, Appliance $100.00
#286, Ford Transit Fire, Falck $160.00
#288, Superior Cadillac Ambulance $80.00
#288, Superior Cadillac Ambulance, Falck......................$150.00
#289, Routemaster Bus, Esso, purple $750.00
#289, Routemaster Bus, Esso, red $100.00
#289, Routemaster Bus, Festival of London Stores $200.00

#289, Routemaster Bus, Madame Tussaud's, $150.00.

#289, Routemaster Bus, Silver Jubilee.............................$40.00
#289, Routemaster Bus, Tern Shirts or Schweppes.........$150.00
#290, Double-Decker Bus $175.00
#290, SRN-6 Hovercraft...$40.00
#291, Atlantean City Bus $70.00
#292, Atlantean Bus, Regent or Ribble $150.00
#293, Swiss Postal Bus $50.00
#294, Police Vehicle Gift Set $200.00
#295, Atlantean Bus, Yellow Pages $70.00
#296, Duple Luxury Coach...$40.00
#296, Police Accident Unit...$100.00
#297, Police Vehicles Gift Set $200.00
#297, Silver Jubilee Bus, National or Woolworth............$40.00
#298, Emergency Services Gift Set $1,300.00
#299, Crash Squad Gift Set $70.00
#299, Motorway Services Gift Set $1,600.00
#299, Post Office Services Gift Set $650.00
#300, London Scene Gift Set $100.00
#302, Emergency Squad Gift Set......................................$100.00
#303, Commando Gift Set $120.00
#304, Fire Rescue Gift Set $120.00
#305, David Brown Tractor...$100.00
#308, Leyland 384 Tractor..$75.00
#309, Star Trek Gift Set $150.00

#319, Week's Tipping Farm Trailer..............................$40.00
#320, Halesowen Harvest Trailer $50.00
#321, Massey-Harris Manure Spreader........................$60.00
#322, Disc Harrow...$50.00
#323, Triple Gang Mower $50.00
#324, Hay Rake...$50.00
#325, David Brown Tractor & Harrow $150.00
#340, Land Rover $100.00
#341, Land Rover Trailer..$40.00
#342, Austin Mini Moke $70.00
#342, Moto-Cart...$75.00
#344, Estate Car..$80.00
#344, Land Rover Pickup..$40.00
#350, Tony's Mini Moke...$150.00
#351, UFO Interceptor..$90.00
#352, Ed Straker's Car, red...$100.00
#352, Ed Straker's Car, yel or gold-plated...................$140.00
#353, Shado 2 Mobile...$100.00
#354, Pink Panther $60.00
#355, Lunar Roving Vehicle..$60.00
#357, Klingon Battle Cruiser.......................................$80.00
#358, USS Enterprise...$75.00
#359, Eagle Transporter...$75.00
#360, Eagle Freighter...$75.00
#361, Galactic War Chariot...$75.00
#362, Trident Star Fighter...$75.00
#363, Cosmic Zygon Patroller, for Marks & Spencer.......$80.00
#364, NASA Space Shuttle, w/booster.........................$100.00
#366, NASA Space Shuttle, w/no booster.....................$50.00
#367, Space Battle Cruiser...$80.00
#368, Zygon Marauder..$80.00
#370, Dragster Set...$70.00
#371, USS Enterprise, sm version $50.00
#372, Klingon Battle Cruiser, sm version....................$50.00
#380, Convoy Skip Truck..$20.00
#381, Convoy Farm Truck...$20.00
#382, Convoy Dumper...$20.00
#382, Wheelbarrow..$25.00
#383, Convoy NCL Truck..$30.00
#384, Convoy Fire Rescue Truck $25.00
#384, Grass Cutter...$25.00
#385, Convoy Royal Mail Truck...................................$30.00
#385, Sack Truck...$25.00
#386, Lawn Mower $125.00
#390, Customized Transit Van $50.00
#398, Farm Equipment Gift Set...................................$2,000.00
#399, Farm Tractor & Trailer Set.................................$200.00
#400, BEV Electric Truck..$70.00
#401, Coventry-Climax Fork Lift, orange $70.00
#401, Coventry-Climax Fork Lift, red..........................$500.00
#402, Bedford Coca-Cola Truck $250.00
#404, Conveyancer Fork Lift..$50.00
#405, Universal Jeep..$50.00
#406, Commer Articulated Truck.................................$200.00
#407, Ford Transit, Kenworth or Hertz........................$120.00
#408, Big Ben Lorry, bl & yel, or bl & orange $350.00
#408, Big Ben Lorry, maroon & fawn $200.00
#408, Big Ben Lorry, pk & cream................................$2,000.00

#409, Bedford Articulated Lorry $175.00
#410, Bedford Van, Danish Post or Simpsons................$125.00
#410, Bedford Van, MJ Hire, Marley or Collectors Gazette..$50.00
#410, Bedford Van, Royal Mail....................................$30.00
#411, Bedford Truck..$160.00
#412, Austin Wagon...$500.00
#412, Bedford Van AA...$40.00
#413, Austin Covered Wagon, lt & dk bl, or red & tan ...$650.00
#413, Austin Covered Wagon, maroon & cream, or med bl & lt bl..$200.00
#413, Austin Covered Wagon, red & gray, or bl & cream ..$450.00
#414, Dodge Tipper, all colors other than Royal bl........$125.00
#414, Dodge Tipper, Royal bl.......................................$200.00
#415, Mechanical Horse & Wagon................................$200.00
#416, Ford Transit Van...$50.00
#416, Ford Transit Van, 1,000,000 Transits $200.00
#417, Ford Transit Van...$50.00
#417, Leyland Comet Lorry..$150.00
#418, Leyland Comet Lorry..$175.00
#419, Leyland Comet Cement Lorry.............................$200.00
#420, Leyland Forward Control Lorry...........................$100.00
#421, Hindle-Smart Electric Lorry...............................$100.00
#422, Thames Flat Truck, bright gr..............................$200.00
#422, Thames Flat Truck, dk gr or red.........................$100.00
#424, Commer Articulated Truck..................................$250.00
#425, Bedford TK Coal Lorry.......................................$200.00
#428, Trailer, lg...$50.00
#429, Trailer..$50.00
#430, Commer Breakdown Lorry, all colors other than tan & gr $1,000.00
#430, Commer Breakdown Lorry, tan & gr...................$200.00
#430, Johnson Dumper...$40.00
#431, Guy 4-Ton Lorry...$600.00
#432, Foden Tipper..$50.00
#432, Guy Warrior Flat Truck......................................$500.00
#433, Guy Flat Truck w/Tailboard................................$350.00
#434, Bedford Crash Truck $150.00
#435, Bedford TK Tipper, gray or yel cab $125.00
#435, Bedford TK Tipper, wht, silver & bl...................$250.00
#436, Atlas COPCO Compressor Lorry..........................$100.00

#440, Mobilgas Tanker, $200.00.

#437, Muir Hill Loader $40.00

#438, Ford D 800 Tipper, opening doors....................$50.00

#439, Ford D 800 Snow Plough & Tipper......................$75.00

#441, Petrol Tanker, Castrol.................................$200.00

#442, Land Rover Breakdown Crane $50.00

#442, Land Rover Breakdown Crane, Falck...................$70.00

#442, Petrol Tanker, Esso....................................$200.00

#443, Petrol Tanker, National Benzole........................$200.00

#448, Chevrolet El Camino w/Trailer........................$400.00

#449, Chevrolet El Camino Pickup $120.00

#449, Johnston Road Sweeper $70.00

#450, Bedford TK Box Van, Castrol $200.00

#450, Trojan Van, Esso......................................$200.00

#451, Johnston Road Sweeper, opening doors $70.00

#451, Trojan Van, Dunlop $200.00

#452, Trojan Van, Chivers...................................$200.00

#453, Trojan Van, Oxo $300.00

#454, Trojan Van, Cydrax....................................$200.00

#455, Trojan Van, Brooke Bond Tea $200.00

#465, Morris Van, Capstan...................................$325.00

#470, Austin Van, Shell-BP..................................$200.00

#471, Austin Van, Nestle's..................................$225.00

#472, Austin Van, Raleigh Cycles $225.00

#475, Ford Model T $100.00

#476, Morris Oxford $100.00

#477, Parsley's Car $100.00

#480, Bedford Van, Kodak $180.00

#481, Bedford Van, Ovaltine $180.00

#482, Bedford Van, Dinky Toys $200.00

#485, Ford Model T w/Santa Claus $200.00

#486, Morris Oxford, Dinky Beats...........................$200.00

#490, Electric Dairy Van, Express Dairy $100.00

#491, Electric Dairy Van, NCB or Job Dairies.................$150.00

#492, Electric Mini Van $350.00

#492, Loudspeaker Van $125.00

#501, Foden Diesel 8 Wheel, 1st cab......................$1,000.00

#501, Foden Diesel 8 Wheel, 2nd cab........................$600.00

#502, Foden Flat Truck, 1st or 2nd cab $1,000.00

#503, Foden Flat Truck, 1st cab $1,200.00

#503, Foden Flat Truck, 2nd cab, bl & orange $400.00

#503, Foden Flat Truck, 2nd cab, bl & yel $1,200.00

#503, Foden Flat Truck, 2nd cab, 2-tone gr................$3,000.00

#504, Foden Tanker, red.....................................$800.00

#504, Foden Tanker, 1st cab, 2-tone bl......................$500.00

#504, Foden Tanker, 2nd cab, red............................$600.00

#504, Foden Tanker, 2nd cab, 2-tone bl....................$3,500.00

#505, Foden Flat Truck w/Chains, 1st cab.................$3,000.00

#505, Foden Flat Truck w/Chains, 2nd cab...................$450.00

#511, Guy 4-Ton Lorry, red, gr or brn......................$900.00

#511, Guy 4-Ton Lorry, 2-tone bl...........................$350.00

#512, Guy Flat Truck, all colors other than bl or red $750.00

#512, Guy Flat Truck, bl or red............................$400.00

#513, Guy Flat Truck w/Tailboard...........................$400.00

#514, Guy Van, Lyons......................................$2,000.00

#514, Guy Van, Slumberland.................................$600.00

#514, Guy Van, Spratt's $600.00

#514, Guy Van, Weetabix...................................$3,500.00

#521, Bedford Articulated Lorry $200.00

#522, Big Bedford Lorry, bl & yel...........................$350.00

#522, Big Bedford Lorry, maroon & fawn $175.00

#531, Leyland Comet Lorry, all colors other than bl or brn...$300.00

#531, Leyland Comet Lorry, bl & brn........................$500.00

#532, Bedford Comet Lorry w/Tailboard......................$300.00

#533, Leyland Cement Wagon.................................$200.00

#551, Trailer...$60.00

#555, Fire Engine, w/extension ladder $100.00

#561, Blaw-Knox Bulldozer $100.00

#561, Blaw-Knox Bulldozer, plastic..........................$500.00

#562, Muir-Hill Dumper......................................$40.00

#563, Blaw-Knox Heavy Tractor, $100.00.

#564, Elevator Loader.......................................$100.00

#571, Coles Mobile Crane....................................$120.00

#581, Horse Box, British Railway............................$150.00

#581, Horse Box, Express Horse Van $800.00

#582, Pullman Car Transporter...............................$160.00

#591, AEC Tanker, Shell.....................................$225.00

#601, Austin Para Moke......................................$100.00

#602, Armoured Command Car..................................$50.00

#603, Army Personnel, box of 12.............................$100.00

#604, Land Rover Bomb Disposal Unit.........................$70.00

#604, Royal Tank Corps......................................$250.00

#609, 105mm Howitzer & Gun Crew $50.00

#612, Commando Jeep...$50.00

#615, US Jeep & 105mm Howitzer $60.00

#616, AEC Articulated Transporter & Tank....................$90.00

#617, VW KDF w/Antitank Gun................................$100.00

#618, AEC Articulated Transporter & Helicopter.........$100.00

#619, Bren Gun Carrier & Antitank Gun $50.00

#620, Berliet Missle Launcher...............................$170.00

#621, 3-Ton Army Wagon......................................$100.00

#622, Bren Gun Carrier $40.00

#622, 10-Ton Army Truck.....................................$140.00

#623, Army Covered Wagon....................................$80.00

#624, Daimler Military Ambulance $300.00

#625, Austin Covered Wagon..................................$500.00

#625, 6-Pounder Antitank Gun $40.00

#626, Military Ambulance $100.00

#640, Bedford Military Truck................................$400.00

#641, Army 1-Ton Cargo Truck	$75.00
#642, RAF Pressure Refueler	$150.00
#643, Army Water Carrier	$120.00
#650, Light Tank	$160.00
#651, Centurion Tank	$90.00
#654, Mobile Gun	$40.00
#656, 88mm Gun	$40.00
#660, Tank Transporter	$150.00
#661, Recovery Tractor	$150.00
#662, Static 88mm Gun & Crew	$40.00
#665, Honest John Missle Erector	$175.00
#666, Missle Erector Vehicle w/Corporal Missle & Launching Platform	$400.00
#667, Armoured Patrol Car	$40.00
#667, Missle Servicing Platform Vehicle	$250.00
#668, Foden Army Truck	$50.00
#669, US Army Jeep	$450.00
#670, Armoured Car	$45.00
#671, MKI Corvette (boat)	$25.00
#671, Reconnaissance Car	$175.00
#672, OSA Missle Boat	$25.00
#672, US Army Jeep	$160.00
#673, Scout Car	$45.00
#674, Austin Champ, olive drab	$60.00
#674, Austin Champ, wht, UN version	$500.00
#674, Coast Guard Missle Launch	$25.00
#675, Motor Patrol Boat	$20.00
#675, US Army Staff Car	$35.00
#676, Armoured Personnal Carrier	$60.00
#676, Daimler Armoured Car, w/speedwheels	$40.00
#677, Armoured Command Vehicle	$100.00
#677, Task Force Set	$70.00
#678, Air Sea Rescue	$30.00
#680, Ferret Armoured Car	$30.00
#681, DUKW	$30.00
#682, Stalwart Load Carrier	$30.00
#683, Chieftain Tank	$50.00
#686, 25-Pounder Field Gun	$25.00
#687, Convoy Army Truck	$25.00
#687, Trailer	$20.00
#688, Field Artillery Tractor	$50.00
#689, Med Artillery Tractor	$100.00
#690, Mobile Antiaircraft Gun	$100.00
#690, Scorpion Tank	$30.00
#691, Field Gun Unit	$350.00
#691, Striker Antitank Vehicle	$60.00
#692, Leopard Tank	$60.00
#692, 5.5 Med Gun	$60.00
#693, Howitzer & Tractor	$300.00
#693, 7.2 Howitzer	$60.00
#694, Hanomag Tank Destroyer	$60.00
#696, Leopard Antiaircraft Tank	$60.00
#697, 25-Pounder Field Gun Set	$150.00
#698, Tank Transporter & Tank	$250.00
#699, Leopard Recovery Tank	$70.00
#699, Military Gift Set	$500.00
#700, Seaplane	$200.00
#700, Spitfire MKII RAF Jubilee	$200.00
#701, Shetland Flying Boat	$650.00
#702, DH Comet Jet Airliner	$200.00
#704, Avro York Airliner	$200.00
#705, Viking Airliner	$100.00
#706, Vickers Viscount Airliner, Air France	$200.00
#708, Vickers Viscount Airliner, BEA	$200.00
#710, Beechcraft S35 Bonanza	$100.00
#712, US Army T-42A	$100.00
#715, Beechcraft C-55 Baron	$60.00
#715, Bristol 173 Helicopter	$70.00
#716, Westland Sikorsky Helicopter	$60.00
#717, Boeing 737	$100.00
#718, Hawker Hurricane	$100.00
#719, Spitfire MKII	$100.00
#721, Junkers Stuka	$100.00
#722, Hawker Harrier	$100.00
#723, Hawker Executive Jet	$60.00
#724, Sea King Helicopter	$75.00
#725, Phantom II	$135.00
#726, Messerschmitt, desert camouflage	$135.00
#726, Messerschmitt, gray & gr	$200.00
#727, US Air Force F-4 Phantom II	$350.00
#728, RAF Dominie	$80.00
#729, Multi-Role Combat Aircraft	$80.00
#730, US Navy Phantom	$130.00
#731, SEPECAT Jaguar	$80.00
#731, Twin-Engine Fighter	$50.00
#732, Bell Police Helicopter, M*A*S*H	$100.00
#732, Bell Police Helicopter, wht & bl	$60.00
#733, German Phantom II	$200.00
#733, Lockheed Shooting Star Jet Fighter	$50.00
#734, P47 Thunderbolt	$200.00
#734, Submarine Swift	$60.00
#735, Glouster Javelin	$60.00
#736, Bundesmarine Sea King	$100.00
#736, Hawker Hunter	$60.00
#737, P1B, Lightning Fighter	$100.00
#738, DH110 Sea Vixen Fighter	$60.00
#739, Zero-Sen	$120.00
#741, Spitfire MKII	$100.00
#749, RAF Avro Vulcan Bomber	$3,500.00
#750, Call Telephone Box	$50.00
#751, Lawn Mower	$100.00
#751, Police Box	$50.00
#752, Goods Yard Crane	$70.00
#753, Police Controlled Crossing	$120.00
#755-6, Standard Lamp, single or dbl arm	$30.00
#760, Pillar Box	$30.00
#766-7, British Road Signs, Country Set A or B	$100.00
#768-9, British Road Signs, Town Set A or B	$100.00
#770, Road Signs, set of 12	$200.00
#771, International Road Signs, set of 12	$160.00
#772, British Road Signs, set of 24	$300.00
#773, Traffic Signal	$25.00
#777, Belisha Beacon	$20.00
#778, Road Repair Warning Boards	$25.00
#781, Petrol Pumping Station, Esso	$100.00
#782, Petrol Pumping Station, Shell	$100.00

#784, Dinky Goods Train Set.................................$60.00
#785, Service Station $270.00
#786, Tyre Rack...$60.00
#787, Lighting Kit..$35.00
#796, Healy Sports Boat $40.00
#798, Express Passenger Train............................$170.00
#801, Mini USS Enterprise.................................$60.00
#802, Mini Klingon Cruiser................................$60.00
#815, Panhard Armoured Tank..............................$150.00
#816, Berliet Missle Launcher............................$275.00
#817, AMX 13-Ton Tank....................................$125.00
#822, M3 Half-Track......................................$125.00
#884, Brockway Bridge Truck..............................$300.00
#893, UNIC Boilot Car Transporter........................$175.00
#893, UNIC Pipe-Line Transporter.........................$175.00
#900, Building Site Gift Set...........................$1,500.00
#901, Guy 4-Ton Lorry, see #501
#902, Foden Flat Truck, see #502
#903, Foden Flat Truck w/Tailboard, see #503

#912, Guy Flat Truck, see #512
#913, Guy Flat Truck w/Tailboard, see #513
#914, AEC Articulated Lorry..............................$200.00
#915, AEC Flat Trailer....................................$80.00
#917, Mercedes Benz Truck & Trailer......................$120.00
#917, Mercedes Benz Truck & Trailer, Munsterland $300.00
#918, Guy Van, Ever Ready................................$350.00
#919, Guy Van, Golden Shred............................$1,000.00
#920, Guy Warrior Van, Heinz...........................$3,000.00
#921, Bedford Articulated Lorry $200.00
#922, Big Bedford Lorry..................................$200.00

#923, Big Bedford Van, Heinz Baked Beans can, $600.00.

#905, Foden Flat Truck with Chains, $450.00.

#908, Mighty Antar w/Transformer $750.00
#911, Guy 4-Ton Lorry, see #511

#923, Big Bedford Van, Heinz Ketchup bottle $2,000.00
#924, Aveling-Barford Dumper $75.00
#925, Leyland Dump Truck................................$250.00
#930, Bedford Pallet-Jekta Van, Dinky Toys $300.00
#931, Leyland Comet Lorry, all colors other than bl & brn...$300.00
#931, Leyland Comet Lorry, bl & brn......................$500.00
#932, Leyland Comet Wagon w/Tailboard $300.00
#933, Leyland Comet Wagon...............................$200.00

#917, Guy Van 'Spratts,' $350.00.

#941, Foden 14-Ton Tanker, Mobilgas, $750.00.

#934, Leyland Octopus Wagon, all colors other than bl & yel $400.00
#934, Leyland Octopus Wagon, bl & yel $2,000.00
#935, Leyland Octopus Flat Truck w/Chains, bl cab...$3,000.00
#935, Leyland Octopus Flat Truck w/Chains, gr & gray ...$2,000.00
#936, Leyland 8-Wheel Test Chassis $150.00
#940, Mercedes Benz Truck $60.00
#942, Foden Tanker, Regent $600.00
#943, Leyland Octopus Tanker, Esso $500.00
#944, Shell-BP Fuel Tanker $300.00
#944, Shell-BP Fuel Tanker, red wheels $500.00
#945, AEC Fuel Tanker, Esso $150.00
#945, AEC Fuel Tanker, Lucas $175.00
#948, Tractor-Trailer, McLean $300.00
#949, Wayne School Bus $350.00
#950, Foden S20 Fuel Tanker, Burmah $100.00
#950, Foden S20 Fuel Tanker, Shell $100.00
#951, Trailer $50.00
#952, Vega Major Luxury Coach $150.00
#953, Continental Touring Coach $400.00
#954, Fire Station $400.00
#954, Vega Major Luxury Coach, no lights $130.00
#955, Fire Engine $100.00
#956, Turntable Fire Escape, Bedford $150.00
#956, Turntable Fire Escape, Berliet $250.00
#957, Fire Services Gift Set $600.00
#958, Snow Plough $300.00

#959, Foden Dump Truck, $125.00.

#960, Lorry-Mounted Concrete Mixer $125.00
#961, Blaw-Knox Bulldozer, see #561
#961, Vega Major Luxury Coach $250.00
#962, Muir-Hill Dumper $40.00
#963, Blaw-Knox Heavy Tractor $100.00
#963, Road Grader $50.00
#964, Elevator Loader $100.00
#965, Euclid Rear Dump Truck $80.00
#965, Terex Dump Truck $275.00
#966, Marrel Multi-Bucket Unit $160.00

#967, BBC TV Mobile Control Room $200.00
#967, Muir-Hill Loader & Trencher $50.00
#968, BBC TV Roving Eye Vehicle $225.00
#969, BBC TV Extending Mast Vehicle $225.00
#970, Jones Cantilever Crane $100.00
#971, Coles Mobile Crane $120.00
#972, Coles 20-Ton Lorry, mounted crane, yel & blk $200.00
#972, Coles 20-Ton Lorry, mounted crane, yel & orange..$100.00
#973, Eaton Yale Tractor Shovel $50.00
#973, Goods Yard Crane $70.00
#974, AEC Hoyner Transporter $100.00
#975, Ruston Bucyrus Excavator $375.00
#976, Michigan Tractor Dozer $50.00

#977, Commercial Servicing Platform Vehicle, $250.00.

#977, Shovel Dozer $50.00
#978, Refuse Wagon $80.00
#979, Racehorse Transporter $450.00
#980, Coles Hydra Truck $60.00
#980, Horse Box Express $800.00
#981, Horse Box, British Railways $200.00
#982, Pullman Car Transporter $160.00
#983, Car Carrier & Trailer $350.00
#984, Atlas Digger $60.00
#984, Car Carrier $225.00
#985, Trailer for Car Carrier $80.00

#986, Mighty Antar Low Loader with Propeller, $400.00.

#987, ABC TV Control Room $375.00

#988, ABC TV Transmitter Van $375.00
#989, Car Carrier, Autotransporters $2,000.00

#990, Pullman Car Transporter with 4 Cars, $2,500.00.

#991, AEC Tanker, Shell Chemicals.............................$225.00
#992, Avro Vulcan Delta Wing Bomber $3,000.00
#994, Loading Ramp for #992 ....$30.00
#997, Caravelle, Air France $400.00
#998, Bristol Britannia Canadian Pacific.......................$350.00
#999, DH Comet Jet..$200.00

Disney

Through the magic of the silver screen, Walt Disney's characters have come to life, and it is virtually impossible to imagine a child growing up without the influence of his genius. As each classic film was introduced, toy manufacturers scurried to fill department store shelves with the dolls, games, battery-ops, and windups that carried the likeness of every member of its cast. Though today it is the toys of the 1930s and '40s that are bringing exorbitant prices, later toys are certainly collectible as well, as you'll see in our listings. Even characters as recently introduced as Roger Rabbit already have their own cult following.

For more information we recommend *Character Toys and Collectibles, First and Second Series*, and *Antique & Collectible Toys, 1870-1950*, by David Longest; *Stern's Guide to Disney Collectibles* by Michael Stern (there are three in the series); *The Collector's Encyclopedia of Disneyana* by Michael Stern and David Longest; *Disneyana* by Cecil Munsey (Hawthorne Books, 1974); *Disneyana* by Robert Heide and John Gilman; *Walt Disney's Mickey Mouse Memorabilia* by Hillier and Shine (Abrams Inc., 1986); *Tomart's Disneyana Update Magazine*; and *Elmer's Price Guide to Toys* by Elmer Duellman (L-W Books).

Advisors: Joel J. Cohen (C12); Don Hamm (H10), Rocketeer.

See also Battery-Operated; Books; Bubble Bath Containers; Character and Promotional Drinking Glasses; Character Clocks and Watches; Chein; Coloring, Activity, and Paint Books; Dakins; Fisher-Price; Games; Lunch Boxes; Marx; Paper Dolls; Pez Dispensers; Pin-Back Buttons; Plastic Figures; Puppets; Puzzles; Records; Toothbrush Holders; View-Master; Western; Windups, Friction, and Other Mechanicals.

Aladdin, figure set, Applause, 1993, PVC, set of 4, F1 .....$12.00
Aladdin, playset, Final Battle, unused, MIB, B10.............$12.00
Alice in Wonderland, figure, Alice, Shaw, 1950s, ceramic bust image, 4", scarce, EX, A $395.00
Alice in Wonderland, figure, Alice, United China & Glass/WDP, ceramic, 1970s, 5½", MIB, P6 ....$35.00
Alice in Wonderland, figure, Mad Hatter, Shaw, 1940s, ceramic, EX, P6 ....$400.00
Alice in Wonderland, figure, Tweedle Dum, Shaw, 1940s, ceramic, EX, P6 ....$300.00
Alice in Wonderland, figure set, Applause, 1993, PVC, set of 5, F1 ....$15.00
Alice in Wonderland, note paper, Whitman, 1951, w/16 sheets of paper & 11 envelopes, 9½x8", EX, P6 ....$95.00
Alice in Wonderland, stacking cans, Nursery Play Toy, WD, 1950s, 5 litho tin cans stack to 15", NMIB, A.........$400.00
Alice in Wonderland, tea set, WDP, 1960s, china, w/various images, 11-pc set, MIB, P6 ....$150.00
Alice in Wonderland, 3-D Plastic Cutouts, Aldon, 1950s, MIP, P6..$150.00
Aristocats, figure set, Berlioz, Marie & Toulouse, Enesco/WDP, furry forehead & straw whiskers, set of 3, 4¼", EX, P6 .$75.00

Aristocats, Marie the Cat, General Electric giveaway, plush, NM, $15.00.

Photo courtesy Jon Thurmond.

Aristocats, rug, mc images of characters in garden setting, fringed ends, dates from orig release of film, 4x5", EX, P6..$375.00

Babes in Toyland, doll, Toyland Soldier, Gundikins, 1961, plush body w/rubber head, red & blk, 9½", EX+, M8 ....$40.00

Babes in Toyland, printing set, Colorforms, 1960, complete, EX (EX box), T2...$20.00

Bambi, bank, Bambi, Leeds, 1940s, ceramic, airbrushed glazes, advertises a dairy on bottom, 7", EX, P6 ....$100.00

Bambi, bicycle ornament, Bambi, 1940s, celluloid figure on metal spring, M, P6...$125.00

Bambi, Colorforms, 1966, scarce, complete, NMIB..........$35.00

Bambi, doll, Bambi, Character Novelty/WDP, 1940s, plush velvet, 12½", EX, P6 ....$85.00

Bambi, figure, Bambi, Shaw, 1940s, ceramic, 7¾", M, P6..$145.00

Bambi, figure, Bambi, Steiff/WDP, 1950, velvet & mohair, orig chest tag, 5½", M..$175.00

Bambi, figure, Bambi w/Flower, Goebel/WDP #17214-72, ceramic, 5¼", M, P6 ....$125.00

Bambi, figure, Flower, Am Pottery, 1940s, ceramic, no label, 4½", NM...$125.00

Bambi, figure, Flower, Am Pottery, 1940s, ceramic, w/label, 3½", NM, M8...$115.00

Bambi, figure, Flower, Shaw Pottery, ceramic, 3¼", M, P6..$80.00

Bambi, figure, Thumper, Am Pottery, 1940s, ceramic, no label, 3", NM, M8..$100.00

Bambi, figure set, Bambi (3"), Flower (2") & Thumper (2"), WDP, 1960s, plastic, set of 3, EX+, M8 ....$35.00

Bambi, mirror, 1960s, molded plastic fr w/various characters, 20x24", EX...$175.00

Bambi, print, 1940s, felt image of Bambi by forest stream, 8x10", EX, A $25.00

Big Bad Wolf, see Three Little Pigs

Black Hole, Colorforms, 1970s, complete, NM (VG box), J5 ....$15.00

Casey Jr, pencil sharpener, WDP, 1940, Bakelite, 1¾", NM, A $90.00

Chip & Dale, figure, Chip as Rescue Ranger, Just Toy, bendable, 5", EX, B10..$6.00

Cinderella, dolls, Cinderella & Prince Charming, Effanbee, hard plastic, orig wrist tags, 14", EX, pr...........................$450.00

Cinderella, figure, Avon, bsk, w/stand, 10", MIB..............$20.00

Disney, binoculars, WDP, 1970s, Disney on Ice, blk & wht w/images of Mickey & Minnie, 6", M, A $10.00

Disney, Character Blox, New Enterprises, 1940s, 24 wooden blocks w/7 pgs of uncut stickers, EX+ (EX+ box), M8 ....$75.00

Disney, Cockamamies Skin Transfers, 1961, MIB............$20.00

Disney, comic books, Wheaties premiums, 1950s, stories w/different characters, pocket-sz, NM, M8, ea.....................$12.00

Disney, globe, Rand McNally, 1950s, characters lithoed on globe & base, EX..$150.00

Disney, luncheon set, Brechner/WDP, 1961, ceramic, Donald picnic plates, Mickey glasses, Ludwig bowls, 12-pc set, M, P6...$275.00

Disney, mold set, Model Craft, 1950s, EXIB.................$125.00

Disney, piano, Jaymar, 1960s, wooden w/decal of Mickey, Goofy & Donald, 9x16", EX, A.......................................$85.00

Disney, record player, 1950s, Bakelite, decaled characters, VG...$110.00

Disney, shovel, Ohio Art, 1930s, snow scene w/Mickey, Minnie & Donald, 26", VG $175.00

Disney, kaleidoscope, West Germany, 1970s-80s, EX, $50.00.

Disney, Mickey Mouse Shooting Gallery Game, Classic Toy, 1970s, MOC, $55.00.

Disney, Show Boat, Playworld Ltd, 1981, plastic, Mickey, Minnie & Pluto figures bob up & down as boat moves, MIB, A $50.00

Disney, stacking blocks, Art No 3401, Eichhorn/Germany, WDP, 1970s, paper litho on wood w/various characters, MIB, A $50.00

Disney, suitcase, vinyl w/allover character design, EX, T1 ..$12.00

Disney, top, WDP, 1973, Mickey, Donald, Goofy & Pluto on bl & wht striped top w/red plunger, 6", NM, A $50.00

Disney, tray, England, 1950s, various characters, 12½x16", VG, M8...$45.00

Disney, Walt Disney Characters Paint Set, WDE, 1938, EXIB, A...$250.00

Disney, WD TV Set, Automatic Toy, pull knob & strips revolve, plastic, complete w/4 film strips, 5", EX+ (EX box), A...$165.00

Disneyland, charm bracelet, Little Miss Disneyland, 1950s, souvenir, MIB, P6 ....$35.00

Disneyland, coin purse, WDP, 1960s, vinyl w/metal clasp & chain hdl, mk Disneyland w/image of Tinkerbell, M, P6........$30.00

Disneyland, Happy Birthday Carousel, cake topper, 1940s, litho tin, lighted candles cause bells to ring, 9", EXIB $150.00

Disneyland, metal tooling kit, NM, T1 ....$35.00

Disneyland, Monorail, Schuco, bl version, complete, NM (EX box), A...$325.00

Disneyland, pencil case, 1950s, rectangular cb box w/image of Mickey as train engineer, bl border, VG+, A.............$20.00

Disneyland, pennant, 1950s, w/Tinkerbell, gr w/bl & yel trim, EX...$40.00

Disneyland, pennant, 1950s, wht on red w/bl trim, EX, P6 ....$40.00

Disneyland, tea set, Chein, tin, Mickey, Minnie, Donald & Pluto, yel trim, 2 cups & saucers, teapot & plate, NMIB $275.00

Disneyland, tea set, Chein, tin, Mickey, Minnie, Donald & Pluto, yel trim, 4 cups & saucers, lg tray, NM, A $125.00

Disneyland, tray, litho tin, aerial view of an early Disneyland w/modes of transportation on rim, rectangular, EX, P6..$150.00

Disneyland, xylophone, Original Concert Grand, w/music stand, NMIB, P6...$135.00

Photo courtesy Joel Cohen.

Donald Duck, animation cel, from *Donald Gets Drafted*, with painted background, $5,500.00.

Donald Duck, bank, Donald camping out in tent, ceramic, NM, T1...$25.00

Donald Duck, bank, Donald lying atop gr van, ceramic, MIB, T1...$25.00

Donald Duck, bank, Donald w/arm reaching, looking up, compositon w/mc decor, 6", M, A.....................................$25.00

Donald Duck, bank, Leeds, 1940s, Donald sitting & looking up, ceramic w/cold-pnt, 7½", EX, P6 ....$110.00

Donald Duck, bank, Marx, 1950s, tin w/litho carnival scenes, trap door opens at $10, 4", NM, A...........................$550.00

Donald Duck, bicycle ornament, 1940s, jtd celluloid figure on metal spring, M, P6...$125.00

Donald Duck, blotter, Nu-Blue Sunoco, 1939, features Donald as Ben Franklin, NM, M8.....................................$25.00

Donald Duck, blotter, Nu-Blue Sunoco, 1940, features Donald in car at gas pump, EX+, M8 ....$25.00

Donald Duck, blotter, Nu-Blue Sunoco, 1941, features Donald w/boxing gloves & punching bag, EX, M8 ....$22.00

Donald Duck, bubble blower, 1950s, 8", MIB, H12 ....$45.00

Donald Duck, cake decoration, Marx/Disneyland, nodder figure, 1½", MIP, T1 ....$20.00

Donald Duck, camera, WDP/Herbert George, 3x5", M (VG box), A...$75.00

Donald Duck, charm, 1930s, enamel, long-billed figure, EX, P6 ....$65.00

Donald Duck, comic books, Cheerios premium, 1947, Donald & the Pirates or Donald Counter Spy, pocket-sz, NM, M8, ea $24.00

Donald Duck, doll, Dell, squeeze vinyl, 9", EX, J2 ....$35.00

Donald Duck, doll, Gund, plush over wood, 6", M $95.00

Donald Duck, doll, pop-apart, 9", MOC (sealed), J2 .... $45.00

Donald Duck, doll, Walking Donald Duck, Hasbro, 1960s, squeeze hands & he walks, MIB, A $75.00

Donald Duck, Donald the Bubble Duck, 1950s, plastic figure of Donald as soda jerk, blows bubbles, MIB, P6 .... $70.00

Donald Duck, figure, Dan Brechner/WD 26, 1961, ceramic, 5½", M, P6 .... $60.00

Donald Duck, figure, Japan, 1930s, bsk, Admiral Donald, 3¼", NM, A $100.00

Donald Duck, figure, Japan, 1930s, bsk, hands on hips, 1", M $75.00

Donald Duck, figure, Japan, 1930s, bsk, playing accordion, 5", EX $250.00

Donald Duck, figure, Japan, 1930s, bsk, proud pose w/head up, 3¼", NM, A $100.00

Donald Duck, figure, Japan, 1930s, bsk, standing on gr scooter, 3½", EX $125.00

Donald Duck, figure, Japan, 1930s, bsk, w/rifle, 3", EX .. $125.00

Donald Duck, figure, Japan, 1930s, bsk, w/trumpet, 3", M, A ... $125.00

Donald Duck, figure, Leeds, 1940s, ceramic, airbrushed pastels, Walt Disney incised on back, 6½", M, P6 .... $95.00

Donald Duck, figure, 1930s, chalkware, 14", EX, H12 ...... $95.00

Donald Duck, figure, 1940s, chalkware, standing figure w/arm up, silver glitter trim, 7", M, P6 .... $60.00

Donald Duck, flip book, EX $20.00

Donald Duck, Fun-Cycle, Empire, plastic figure scoots back & forth on high wire, 12", EX (worn box), A $75.00

Donald Duck, Funnee Movee Viewer, Irwin, 1960s, w/4 boxed films, EX, J5 .... $35.00

Donald Duck, L'Auto Di Paperino, Politoys/Italy, 1960s, Donald & nephews in car w/rumble seat, 3½", EXIB, A $150.00

Donald Duck, lamp, Glowies, Universal Lamp Co, 1969-71, vinyl figure on sq base, 9½", MIB, P6 .... $75.00

Donald Duck, Magic Slate, Whitman, 1970s, NM, $25.00.

Donald Duck, music box, 1960s, Donald as engineer on rnd base mk Donald Duck, plays Mickey Mouse Club song, EX $125.00

Donald Duck, nodder, WDP, hard plastic, Donald bent forward, 2", EX $70.00

Donald Duck, paint box, Page of London/WDP, 1970s, 5x9", EX, A $25.00

Donald Duck, pencil sharpener, 1930s, celluloid, long-billed figure w/sharpener under base, 2¾", rare, EX, M8 .... $400.00

Donald Duck, pencil sharpener, 1930s, red Bakelite w/decal, 1¼" dia, scarce, NM, A $85.00

Donald Duck, photo album, Spanish Donald strumming guitar on leather cover, 8x14", NM $75.00

Donald Duck, pull toy, Donald's Dairy, Salco/England, Donald in Pure Milk cart pulled by Pluto, pot metal, 4", EX+, A .. $275.00

Donald Duck, pull toy, Jaymar, 1950s, Donald sitting on wheeled cart w/bell, wood, 7" L, scarce, EX (G box), A $80.00

Donald Duck, ring, Living Toy, Kellogg's Pep Cereal premium, 1949, EX, M8 .... $145.00

Donald Duck, ring toss, Transogram, 1940s, single diecut pressed cb image of Donald & nephews, 3 rope rings, 15", EX, A $150.00

Donald Duck, Rocket Pops, MIP, T1 .... $25.00

Donald Duck, roly poly, celluloid jtd figure sitting atop, 4¼", EX+, A $325.00

Donald Duck, rug, 1950s, shows Donald & nephews as a band, bright colors, 43x60", EX, P6 .... $150.00

Donald Duck, soap, Cussons/England, molded figure, scarce, MIB, A $100.00

Donald Duck, tea set, Ohio Art, 1939, litho tin, features Donald serving, 27-pc set w/tray, EX, P6 .... $400.00

Donald Duck, transfer booklet, England, 1940s, upper half of cover is diecut shape of Donald, unused, NM, M8 .... $65.00

Donald Duck's Nephew, figure, baseball catcher, Shaw Pottery, 2⅞", EX $125.00

Duck Tales, figure, Bugsy Beagle, Just Toys, bendable, MOC, B10 .... $5.00

Dumbo, figure, Am Pottery, 1940s, ceramic, sitting w/yel bonnet atop head, 5", NM $125.00

Dumbo, figure, vinyl, M, T1 .... $20.00

Dumbo, pencil sharpener, WD, 1930s, Bakelite, 1¾", rare, NM, A $125.00

Elmer, figure, Japan, prewar, celluloid w/movable head, trunk & arms, 5½", M, A $325.00

Elmer, figure, Japan, 1930s, bsk, jtd arms, 5", NM, A $235.00

Elmer, figure, Japan, 1930s, bsk, string controls position of trunk, 4", M, A $235.00

Fantasia, figure, Ballerina Elephant, Vernon Kilns #26, 1940, M, P6 .... $800.00

Feivel Goes West, figures, Applause, 1993, PVC, set of 4, F1 .. $10.00

Ferdinand the Bull, figure, compo, jtd, VG, T1 .... $125.00

Ferdinand the Bull, figure, Seiberling, 1930s, rubber, 6", VG+, M8 .... $65.00

Ferdinand the Bull, figure, 1930s, bsk, blk w/tan head, 3", EX, M8 .... $45.00

Figaro, see Pinocchio

Goofy, bank, Playpals, 1971, vinyl head form, 12", NM, A .. $25.00

Goofy, blotter, Nu-Blue Sunoco, 1939, features Goofy w/igloo & polar bear, EX+, M8 .... $25.00

Goofy, doll, California Stuffed Dolls, 1960s, w/orange jacket, 18", EX, J5...$15.00

Goofy, doll, Merry Thoughts/England, stuffed cloth, 12", EX, A...$75.00

Goofy, figure, Crostallerie Antonia Imperatore/Italy, 1960s, frosted glass, MIB, P6..................................$45.00

Gremlins (Ronald Dahl's WWII story), doll, Disney, 1943, lt pk plush free-form body, 9", EX+, A.............................$400.00

Hook, knife & compass set, 1991, MIB, B10..................$8.00

Jiminy Cricket, see Pinocchio

Jungle Book, Action Arcade, 1970, litho tin, MIB, J8......$65.00

Jungle Book, charms, Shere Khan, Bagheera, Vulture or Mowgli, gold- or silver-tone metal, 1960s, ¾", NM, M8, ea......$5.00

Jungle Book, figure, Baloo, Japan, 1966, velvet & felt, 6", NM, G16...$45.00

Jungle Book, figure, Kaa the snake, stuffed cloth, 1967, M, P6..$40.00

Jungle Book, figure, Vulture, 1967, stuffed cloth, M, P6...$40.00

Jungle Book, pencil box, Empire Pencil, 1966, cb w/full-color litho of characters, snap-open lid, w/drawer, 4x8", NM, A...$25.00

Kanga, see Winnie the Pooh

Lady & the Tramp, Cartoon Kit, Colorforms, 1962, complete, NM (NM box)...$35.00

Lady & the Tramp, figure, Lady, Hagen-Renaker, 1950s, 1¼", NM...$65.00

Lady & the Tramp, figure, puppy, Hagen-Renaker, 1950s, stands upright w/front paws on chest, 1", NM.......................$65.00

Lady & the Tramp, figure, Tramp, 1950s, ceramic, seated pose, tan airbrushing, 4½", EX....................................$65.00

Lady & the Tramp, figure, Tramp, 1960s, plush, 12", EX, P6..$30.00

Lady & the Tramp, figure, Trusty, Hagen-Renaker, 1950s, 2", NM, M8...$75.00

Lady & the Tramp, figures, cereal premiums, 1950s, assorted characters in solid colors, 1½"-2", NM, M8, ea.........$12.00

Lady & the Tramp, figures, Cracker Jack premiums, 6 different characters, M, P6, ea.......................................$18.00

Lion King, figures, Applause, 1993, PVC, set of 5, F1......$15.00

Little Mermaid, figure, Ariel, Just Toys, bendable, MOC, B10..$5.00

Little Mermaid, figure, Ariel, Tyco, MOC, B10.................$6.00

Ludwig Von Drake, doll, vinyl, squeaks, 9", NM, J2.........$35.00

Ludwig Von Drake, gumball machine, WDC, Ludwig next to rnd gumball machine on gray base, plastic, NM, A...$25.00

Ludwig Von Drake, squeeze toy, Viceroy of Canada, 1960s, rubber, 7", EX+, M8..$25.00

Mary Poppins, doll, 1964, MIB, T1..............................$150.00

Mary Poppins, purse, vinyl, NM, J2..............................$80.00

Mary Poppins, tea set, 1964, plastic, MIB, P6................$100.00

Mickey Mouse, acrobat toy, WD, 1930s, Mickey figure w/hand-controlled acrobatic action on 2 wooden sticks, 9", EX+, A...$110.00

Mickey Mouse, banjo, mk Down South British Made, dated 1932, wood & litho tin, 22", EX, A.......................$435.00

Mickey Mouse, banjo, WDE, metal w/wooden neck, paper litho image of Mickey strumming, 18", NM, A................$650.00

Mickey Mouse, bank, Animals Plus, 1977, vinyl, Mickey as band leader in red car, 12", NM, A..............................$25.00

Mickey Mouse, bank, Crown, compo, Mickey beside trunk, 6", minor crazing o/w EX, A.......................................$75.00

Mickey Mouse, bank, Dime Register, WDP, 1959, litho tin, slide trap, 2½", VG, A...$415.00

Mickey Mouse, bank, Germany, 1932, litho tin, Mickey holding jar of honey, beehive background, 3", rare, EX, A...$350.00

Mickey Mouse, bank, Mickey Mouse Treasure Chest, Japan, 1930s, litho tin, 2x3", VG, A.............................$625.00

Mickey Mouse, bank, Reliable Toys/Canada, 1950s, vinyl head form w/red bow tie, 10", M, A................................$35.00

Mickey Mouse, bank, Zell Products, 1934, leatherette book shape, 4¼x3¼", EX+, M8......................................$175.00

Mickey Mouse, bank, 1960s, compo, integral figure of Mickey standing in front of clubhouse, EX, A.................$25.00

Mickey Mouse, banks/bookends, WDP, 1960s, CI, figure seated w/hands on tummy leaning against books, 5x4", M, P6, pr...$275.00

Mickey Mouse, belt, Pyramid Belt Co, 1978, commemorates Mickey's 50th birthday, MIB, A..............................$30.00

Mickey Mouse, bicycle bell, WDP, 1960s, chrome w/decal of Mickey, NM, A...$40.00

Mickey Mouse, Big Little Kit, Whitman/WDE, 1937, all pgs uncolored, missing crayons, VG, A...........................$175.00

Mickey Mouse, birthday candle holders, Cypress/WDE, 1930s, pk w/raised images of Mickey, set of 5, NMIB, A....$250.00

Mickey Mouse, blackboard easel, Pressman, 1950s, unused, MIB, A...$100.00

Mickey Mouse, blotter, Nu-Blue Sunoco, 1940, features Mickey in speeding car, EX+, M8.....................................$25.00

Mickey Mouse, blotter, Post O-Wheat Cereal, 1930s, Get My Swell Mickey Mouse Spoon, 3½x6¼", NM, M8.......$50.00

Mickey Mouse, Bubble Buster Bubblets, Kilgore, 1930s, for use w/Bubble Buster, VG (orig box), A...................$225.00

Mickey Mouse, bubble pipe, yel plastic pipe w/Mickey figure atop, NM, A...$25.00

Mickey Mouse, camera, Mick-A-Matic, plastic head figure w/flash cube on top, MIB, A.....................................$50.00

Mickey Mouse, camera, WDP, 1960s, blk & wht plastic head form w/strap, 7", NM, A.......................................$50.00

Mickey Mouse, Canasta Junior, 1950s, complete, EXIB...$45.00

Mickey Mouse, cane, 1930s, wood w/compo head figure, 32", EX...$225.00

Mickey Mouse, Choral Spinning Top, Borgefeldt/WDE, 1930s, red w/mc images, 10" dia, NMIB...........................$750.00

Mickey Mouse, comic book, Cheerios premium, 1947, Mickey Mouse & the Haunted House, pocket-sz, NM, M8....$24.00

Mickey Mouse, comic books, Cheerios 3-D Giveaway Series, 1954, #2, #6 or #8, pocket-sz, NM, M8, ea...............$30.00

Mickey Mouse, doll, Bigo Bello, Schuco, stuffed, EX, A...$100.00

Mickey Mouse, doll, Birthday Party Mickey Mouse, Remco, vinyl w/gr cloth suit, 2 party hats & favor, M (EX box), A...$40.00

Mickey Mouse, doll, Charlotte Clark, 1930s, stuffed cloth, 19", NM...$2,200.00

Mickey Mouse, doll, Dean, 1930s, stuffed velour w/red shorts, 8½", VG+...$600.00

Mickey Mouse, doll, Knickerbocker, stuffed cloth, 10", missing tail o/w EX...$250.00

Mickey Mouse, doll, Knickerbocker/WDE, 1930s, stuffed cloth w/compo shoes, 4-fingered, brn shorts, 12", VG......$425.00

Mickey Mouse, doll, Posie, Ideal, 1950s, EXIB, J2 ....$45.00

Mickey Mouse, doll, Rollo, Gund, 1950s, stuffed roly-poly body, orange & blk, NM, A...$50.00

Mickey Mouse, doll, Steiff, 1930s, button in ear, 7", EX..$1,200.00

Mickey Mouse, doll, Sun Rubber, 1950s, dressed in cloth sunsuit, 9", EX, A...$40.00

Mickey Mouse, drum, Ohio Art/WDE, features Mickey as band leader & playing the tuba, litho tin, 6" dia, NM, A...$195.00

Mickey Mouse, fan, Japan, prewar, heavy paper w/wood hdl, movable eyes, 5", NM, A...$100.00

Mickey Mouse, figure, English, celluloid, standing w/hands on hips, bl shorts w/yel shoes & pk scarf, 2½", NM, A..$585.00

Mickey Mouse, figure, Germany, 1933, porcelain, playing mandolin, saxophone or tuba, 3", rare, NM, A, ea.........$375.00

Mickey Mouse, figure, Japan, 1930s, bsk, hand on hip, other in front, gr shorts, gold hat, 4", EX+, A......................$80.00

Mickey Mouse, figure, Japan, 1930s, bsk, hands on hips, 2¾", EX, M8..$75.00

Mickey Mouse, figure, Japan, 1930s, bsk, hands on tummy, gr shorts & brn shoes, 1¾", EX, P6 ....$75.00

Mickey Mouse, figure, Japan, 1930s, bsk, in nightshirt, 4", EX, M8...$175.00

Mickey Mouse, figure, Japan, 1930s, bsk, jtd arms, 6", EX+, A...$445.00

Mickey Mouse, figure, Japan, 1930s, bsk, movable arms, name incised on back, 3", EX, A..$375.00

Mickey Mouse, figure, Japan, 1930s, bsk, movable arms, 4¾", EX, M8...$475.00

Mickey Mouse, figure, Japan, 1930s, bsk, musician, 3½", NM, A..$125.00

Mickey Mouse, figure, Japan, 1930s, bsk, playing French horn, 5", NM, A...$400.00

Mickey Mouse, figure, Japan, 1930s, bsk, w/hand on hip & cane wearing hat, from Two Pals set, 4¼", NM, A.........$150.00

Mickey Mouse, figure, Japan, 1930s, bsk, w/rifle, 3¼", EX, M8...$150.00

Mickey Mouse, figure, Japan, 1930s, bsk, waving right hand, 1½", EX, M8...$75.00

Mickey Mouse, figure, Japan, 1930s, celluloid, w/movable arms & legs, string attached to head, 4", EX, A $175.00

Mickey Mouse, figure, Leeds, 1940s, ceramic, airbrushed pastels, 7", M, P6...$100.00

Mickey Mouse, figure, Seiberling, 1930s, rubber, blk w/wht-pnt pie-eyes, red-pnt buttons, 3½", tail missing, EX, M8 ...$85.00

Mickey Mouse, figure, Seiberling, 1930s, rubber, movable head, arms down w/palms up, 6", EX+, A.........................$675.00

Mickey Mouse, figure, Sun Rubber, Mickey's Airmail, rubber, 6", missing propeller o/w EX $40.00

Mickey Mouse, figure, 1960s, porcelain, Chef Mickey in 3 different poses, set, 3", EX, M8 ....$65.00

Mickey Mouse, figure, 1960s, vinyl, bendable, bl shirt & shorts w/blk buttons & shoes, wht gloved hands up, 10", NM, A.........$50.00

Mickey Mouse, figure, 1965, rubber, 17", VG, $35.00.

Mickey Mouse, globe, tin, EX+, T1 ....$225.00

Mickey Mouse, guitar, Carnival, 1960s, Mousegetar, plastic, 30", EX, A $25.00

Mickey Mouse, guitar, Carnival, 1960s, Walt Disney's Mickey Mouse De Luxe Guitar, plastic, MIP, A....................$60.00

Mickey Mouse, gumball machine, Hasbro, 1968, head form on red base, M, A...$50.00

Mickey Mouse, figure, Mattel, pull-string talker, 6¾", EX, from $15.00 to $18.00.

Mickey Mouse, gumball machine, WDP, 1970s, Mickey w/hand on hip leans on rnd gumball machine, plastic, MIB, A $50.00

Mickey Mouse, kaleidoscope, VG, T1 ....$50.00

Mickey Mouse, lantern, WDP, 1977, figural, battery-op, MIB, P6 ....$90.00

Mickey Mouse, magic slate, Whitman/WDP, 1970s, NM, A .$20.00

Mickey Mouse, Magic Slate Blackboard, Strathmore, 1943, features Mickey & Donald on diecut top, 18½x12½", MIB, P6 ....$85.00

Mickey Mouse, magnifier, Monogram, 1980s, MOC, J8 .....$5.00

Mickey Mouse, Medical Kit, Hasbro, 1960s-70s, red molded plastic case w/decal, 12x16", M, A $100.00

Mickey Mouse, Mickey's Tricky Stunt Shooter, Funtoy, EXIB, A $25.00

Mickey Mouse, milk pitcher, 1930s, figural pottery, glazed-on colors, 7", EX, P6 ....$175.00

Mickey Mouse, Movie Jector, WDE, 1930s, working, G (worn box) $900.00

Mickey Mouse, music box, Schmidt, Mickey dressed western style playing guitar & wagon wheel on rnd base, M, P6 ....$75.00

Mickey Mouse, music box, Schmidt, 50th Birthday, Mickey as magician on rnd base, It's a Small World, M, P6 ....$75.00

Mickey Mouse, music box, Schmidt, 60th Birthday #2431, limited edition, plays Mickey Mouse Club song, EX, P6.$75.00

Mickey Mouse, MW Photo-Films, Holland, 1930s, complete, EX (EX box), A $95.00

Mickey Mouse, night light, 1950s, plastic TV shape w/image of Mickey reading to 2 tucked-in children, EX, P6 ....$90.00

Mickey Mouse, Nintendo video game, 1980s, hand-held, MIB, J8 ....$25.00

Mickey Mouse, ornament, blown glass, mc-pnt full figure in running pose w/wht face, 6", M, P6 ....$100.00

Mickey Mouse, ornament, bsk figure w/pie-eyes on string, early, 5½", EX+, A $275.00

Mickey Mouse, paint box, Page of London/WDP, 1970s, M, A $50.00

Mickey Mouse, paint set, Transogram, 1952, complete, NM (EX box), C1 ....$90.00

Mickey Mouse, pencil box, WDE, mk Dixon USA 2917, w/orig eraser & ruler, 5½x8½", EX, A $75.00

Mickey Mouse, pencil box, 1970s, plastic rocket-shape, EX, J8 ....$10.00

Mickey Mouse, pencil sharpener, WDE, 1930s, Bakelite, 1¾", NM, A $100.00

Mickey Mouse, piano, Gabriel, 1970s, Mickey pops up as crank is turned & music plays, plastic, yel w/decal, NM, A.$40.00

Mickey Mouse, piano, Marks Bros, red & gr wood & cb w/Mickey & Minnie dancing behind clear panel, 5", VG (orig box) $1,800.00

Mickey Mouse, pin, mc celluloid figure, EX, P6 ....$75.00

Mickey Mouse, plate, Schmidt, Bicentennial, patriotic image of Mickey in military uniform w/rifle, MIB $45.00

Mickey Mouse, playing cards, no Disney mk, 1930s, bl box, VG (VG box), A $30.00

Mickey Mouse, playing cards, Thomas De La Rue & Co Ltd, dbl deck in orig 4" case, complete, EX $350.00

Mickey Mouse, playing cards, WDE, 1930s, red, wht & bl box, VG (VG box), A $50.00

Mickey Mouse, porringer, Wm Rogers, 1930s, sterling silver, hdl w/pie-eyed Mickey & bowl w/Mickey on horse, EX, M8 .$125.00

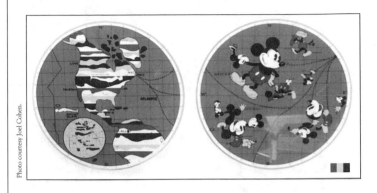

Photo courtesy Joel Cohen.

Mickey Mouse, print, limited edition serigraph by Ernest Trova, 1968, only 60 made with a blue background, 100 made with a white background, 23x29", estimate $1,200.00.

Mickey Mouse, pull toy, Japan, prewar, Mickey on scooter, swings foot for simulated action, 3", scarce, NM ..$2,500.00

Mickey Mouse, pull toy, Toy Kraft/WDE, 1935, pnt diecut dog pulling sleigh-type wagon w/image of Mickey, 15" L, EX, A $250.00

Mickey Mouse, pull toy, 1930s, paper-on-wood figure of Mickey pulling tin wagon, 11" L, VG, A $115.00

Mickey Mouse, purse, American, 1930s, mesh, NM, $550.00.

Photo courtesy Dunbar Gallery.

Mickey Mouse, recipe card, Bell Bread premium, 1934, Now I Lay Me Down To Sleep or Wrong Number, 3½x5", M, P6, ea $38.00

Mickey Mouse, record player, wht case w/bl hdl & interior base, Mickey's arm plays records, Hi Kids & image on lid, M..**$55.00**

Mickey Mouse, ring, Ostby & Barton Co, 1940s, sterling silver, sq face w/emb Mickey, non-adjustable child's sz, EX+, M8..**$45.00**

Mickey Mouse, roly poly, jtd celluloid figure sitting atop, 4½", EX+, A...**$350.00**

Mickey Mouse, Sew-Ons, Colorforms, 1960s, MIB, P6 ....**$45.00**

Mickey Mouse, Sketch-A-Graph, Toy Creation, 1955, unused old store stock, MIB, A..**$50.00**

Mickey Mouse, sled, pressed steel & wood, 30½", G, A ...**$115.00**

Mickey Mouse, spoon, Wm Rogers/Post Toasties premium, 1930s, silverplated, EX, M8 ....**$25.00**

Mickey Mouse, squeak toy, Japan/WD, straw-like body w/celluloid head, arms & legs, red gathered cloth shorts, 6", EX..**$1,800.00**

Mickey Mouse, swim mask, Ideal, 1970s, yel w/blk ears, face decal, M, A **$40.00**

Mickey Mouse, tea set, 1930s, lustreware, images of Mickey in various poses, 10-pc set, M, P6................................**$325.00**

Mickey Mouse, tea set, 1930s, lustreware, images of Mickey in various poses, rare divided grill plates, 17 pcs, M, P6 ....**$600.00**

Mickey Mouse, top, Chein/WDP, 1970s, various images of Mickey on alternating red & wht backgrounds, VG..**$25.00**

Mickey Mouse, toy chest, WDE, 1938, cb w/colorful scenes on all sides, 14x27", NM, A **$850.00**

Mickey Mouse, viewer & films, Craftsman/WDP, 1947, complete w/13 films, MIB, A **$250.00**

Mickey Mouse, wall plaque, Disneyland, 1970s, ceramic head as band leader, M, P6..**$100.00**

Mickey Mouse, whirligig, 1950s, Mickey on wheeled base w/balloons overhead, celluloid & plastic, 7", EX..............**$400.00**

Mickey Mouse & Donald Duck & Pluto, switch plate, 1950s, plastic w/mc characters, MIP....................................**$25.00**

Mickey Mouse & Minnie, bank, glass, rnd w/molded faces on sides, M, T1..**$10.00**

Mickey Mouse & Minnie, bookends, Determined, 1970, compo, seated figures, 6½", EX, P6, pr.............................**$95.00**

Mickey Mouse & Minnie, figure set, Japan, 1930s, celluloid, movable head & arms, emb names on front, 5", EX, A, pr **$750.00**

Mickey Mouse & Minnie, figure set, WDE/Japan, 1930s, bsk, 4", NM (VG box mk The Two Pals) **$375.00**

Mickey Mouse & Minnie, hairbrush, Hughes/WD, 1930s, wooden w/Mickey & Minnie standing, EX, P6..........**$50.00**

Mickey Mouse & Minnie, Magic Movie Palette, 1935 store giveaway, 8x5½", VG, A..**$85.00**

Mickey Mouse & Minnie, music box, 1970s, Love Story mk on base, plays Love Makes the World Go 'Round, M, P6..**$75.00**

Mickey Mouse & Minnie, party horn, Marks Bros/WDE, cb cone shape w/wooden mouthpiece & hdl, 7", NM, A......**$150.00**

Mickey Mouse & Minnie Mouse & Pluto, figures, Borgfeldt, bsk, NM (EX box mk The Three Pals), A **$765.00**

Mickey Mouse & Minnie Mouse & Pluto, tea set, Chein, 1940s, litho tin, images w/leaf-band trim, 12-pc set, EX, P6..**$200.00**

Mickey Mouse & Pluto, figure, Japan, 1930s, bsk, Mickey riding Pluto, 3", NM, from $150 to...................................**$200.00**

Mickey Mouse & Pluto, figure, Japan, 1930s, bsk, Mickey riding Pluto, 3", worn pnt, G, A **$50.00**

Mickey Mouse & Pluto, mirror, plastic, drum-shaped mirror w/drum major Mickey & Pluto figures, 24", NM, A ..**$150.00**

Mickey Mouse Club, bank, compo, clubhouse, MIB, T1..**$25.00**

Mickey Mouse Club, blanket, 1950s, cream w/lg repeated images embroidered in red, blk, wht & gr, 106x84",EX, J5 .**$175.00**

Mickey Mouse Club, doll, Mousketeer, Horsman, vinyl w/blond hair & orig clothes, M, P6 ....**$55.00**

Mickey Mouse Club, kaleidoscope, 1970s, wht w/character images, gr trim, 8", M, A **$25.00**

Mickey Mouse Club, Mickey's Roadster, Knickerbocker, WDP, cloth doll w/plastic car, MIB, P6 ....**$85.00**

Mickey Mouse Club, Mousegetar Jr, Mattel, 1950s, plastic w/4 strings & crank, EX, M8...**$200.00**

Mickey Mouse Club, Mousketeer Handbag kit, Connecticut Leather/WDP, complete, EX+ (EX box), A, $50.00.

Mickey Mouse Club, Newsreel, Mattel, 1950s, complete, EXIB **$150.00**

Mickey Mouse Club, pencil case, Hasbro, 1950s, cover w/Mickey & friends, w/2 wood & 2 plastic rulers, 4x8", EX, M8..**$30.00**

Mickey Mouse Club, projector, Stephens, 1950s, plastic, complete with 4 films, MIB, $125.00.

Mickey Mouse Club, Telescope, WDP, 1970s, 9", MIP, A ..**$25.00**

Photo courtesy Dunbar Gallery.

Mickey Mouse Club, See-Straw Magic Sippers display, NM, $150.00.

Photo courtesy Dunbar Gallery.

Mickey Mouse Club, wallet, features Donald Duck, NMIB, D10, $70.00.

Photo courtesy Dunbar Gallery.

Mickey Mouse Club, Western Wagon, 1950s, EX, D10, minimum value, $250.00.

Mickey Mouse Club, umbrella, clear plastic w/plastic head of Mickey atop & red feet as hdl, M, A $75.00

Minnie Mouse, brush & comb set, Reed & Burton, 1980s, emb silverplate, MIB, A $40.00

Minnie Mouse, doll, Dean, 1930s, velour plush w/red, wht & bl striped skirt, 9", VG+, A $370.00

Minnie Mouse, doll, Steiff, 1930s, open mouth, button in ear, 7", EX, A $1,500.00

Minnie Mouse, doll, 1970s, rag type, 6", MIB (sealed), J8 .$15.00

Minnie Mouse, figure, Am Pottery, 1940s, ceramic, w/broom in hand & bl bow on head, 7", M, M8 ....$265.00

Minnie Mouse, figure, Japan, 1930s, bsk, hands on hips looking up, 3½", NM $250.00

Minnie Mouse, figure, Japan, 1930s, bsk, in nightshirt, 4", EX $225.00

Minnie Mouse, figure, Japan, 1930s, bsk, standing wearing hat, jtd arms, 6", EX $250.00

Minnie Mouse, figure, Japan, 1930s, bsk, w/nurses kit, 3", EX, M8 ....$145.00

Minnie Mouse, gumball machine, WDP, Minnie in pk leans against rnd gumball machine on red base, NM, A $25.00

Minnie Mouse, music box, Schmidt, 1975, Minnie spins on top in bl dress, M, J8 ....$40.00

Minnie Mouse, ornament, late 1940s, blown glass, head on ball body, pk face, 4½", M, P6 ....$90.00

Minnie Mouse, soap dish, ceramic, EX, T1 ....$20.00

Minnie Mouse, wall plaque, Disneyland, 1970s, ceramic head, M, P6 ....$100.00

Mouseketeers, TV Story Teller, Cohn, 1956, phonograph combining pictures which move as records play, complete, NMIB, A...$150.00

Nightmare Before Christmas, doll, Santa Claus, plush, 9", M, D4 ....$25.00

Photo courtesy June Moon.

Nightmare Before Christmas, figures, Lock, Shock, and Barrel, Hasbro, 1993, with 3 masks, MIB, J6, $125.00.

Nightmare Before Christmas, pencil toppers, Lock, Shock & Barrel, set of 3, M, D4..$10.00

Nightmare Before Christmas, postcard book, unused, M, H4...$15.00

Peter Pan, bell, Tinkerbell, 1950s, souvenir, gold-tone metal w/Tinkerbell figural hdl, 3", EX, P6 ....$60.00

Peter Pan, figure, Tinkerbell, Goebel, stylized bee mk, ceramic, 5½", M, P6...$400.00

Peter Pan, figure, Tinkerbell, 1950s, ceramic, sitting on lily pad w/knees up, mc w/gold nylon wings, EX, P6 ....$60.00

Peter Pan, figure, Tinkerbell, 1980s, porcelain, w/gold string for hanging, 6", M, P6...$75.00

Peter Pan, outfit, Cadillac Toys, 1950s, w/parts to make belt, hat & sheath, EX, J5 ....$25.00

Peter Pan, pin, Captain Hook, 1950s, EX, P6 ....$35.00

Peter Pan, pin, Peter Pan, 1950s, full color on cast metal, EX, P6..$35.00

Peter Pan, towel set, Gildex, 1950s, M (worn pkg), P6 ....$65.00

Piglet, see Winnie the Pooh

Pinocchio, Adventure Theatre, Holland, 1940s, litho cb w/unpunched diecut figures, complete, 10x13", EX+, A.........................$160.00

Pinocchio, bank, compo, Pinocchio standing next to tree stump, Crown, 5", EXIB, A...$200.00

Pinocchio, charm, 1940s, silver-tone metal head shape, M...$10.00

Pinocchio, clicker, Jiminy Cricket, 1940s, metal, Jiminy pointing to You Help More the United Way, M, P6..........$45.00

Pinocchio, doll, Jiminy Cricket, stuffed body w/vinyl face, NM, T1..$35.00

Pinocchio, doll, Pinocchio, Ideal, 1940, wood & compo, complete w/rare chest ribbon & pin, 11", NM, A $275.00

Pinocchio, doll, Pinocchio, Knickerbocker, 1940, wood & compo w/jtd limbs, w/orig outfit & hat, 15", VG, A..............$175.00

Pinocchio, doll, Pinocchio, Knickerbocker, 1960, Bend 'Em, 7", MIP, F8 ....$50.00

Pinocchio, doll, Pinocchio, Knickerbocker, 1963, stuffed cloth w/vinyl head, 13", NM, F8.....................................$45.00

Pinocchio, figure, Figaro, Brayton, 1940s, ceramic, 3", M, P6..$100.00

Pinocchio, figure, Figaro, Japan, 1930s, bsk, 2½", VG+, A ..$100.00

Pinocchio, figure, Figaro, National, 1940, porcelain, pale bl tones, 2½", M, P6 ....$40.00

Pinocchio, figure, Pinocchio, Evan K Shaw, 1940s, ceramic, 3", M, P6 ....$300.00

Pinocchio, figure set, Geppetto, Lampwick, Giddy & Honest John, Syroco, Multi Products/WDP, 1940, set of 4, EX, A $375.00

Pinocchio, knife, fork & spoon set, 1940s, silverplated, EX, M8..$85.00

Pinocchio, mask, Figaro, Gillette Blue Blade, 1939, VG, M8...$8.00

Pinocchio, mask, Geppetto, Gillette Blue Blade, 1939, EX, M8..$15.00

Pinocchio, Meal Time Set, box only, 1939, 10x6¾x3½", EX, M8..$135.00

Pinocchio, medal, Jiminy Cricket, Official Conscience, premium, 1940s, brass w/Jiminy in center, 1¼", EX, J5 ..$95.00

Pinocchio, pencil case, NM, T1 ....$45.00

Pinocchio, pencil sharpener, Jiminy Cricket, w/flashing eyes, VG, T1 ....$35.00

Pinocchio, pencil sharpener, WDP, 1939, gr Bakelite w/decal, NM, A...$85.00

Pinocchio, shovel, Italy, 1940s, litho tin, wood hdl, shows Pinocchio w/donkey ears & tail & Jiminy Cricket, 16", EX, M8..$85.00

Pinocchio, shovel, 1940s, litho tin, pictures Pinocchio playing w/fire, 4", EX, J5..$25.00

Pinocchio, roly poly, celluloid, 5", EX, $175.00.

Photo courtesy Mike's General Store.

Pinocchio, stationery, Whitman, 1939, paper & envelopes in 3-way cb folder w/character illus inside & out, EX, M8 ...$85.00

Pinocchio, tablet, Jiminy Cricket, Wonderful World of Color, Westab, 1961, 5x3", unused, NM..............................$10.00

Pinocchio, tea set, ceramic trimmed in red, 8-pc set w/teapot, creamer & sugar, 2 cups & saucers & 1 plate, EX+, A ..$240.00

Pinocchio, toothbrush holder, Jiminy Cricket, 1949, emb hard plastic, made to hang on wall, mostly pk & blk, EX, P6.......$95.00

Pluto, bank, compo, figural, MIB, T1 ....$65.00

Pluto, doll, Deans, 1930s, stuffed yel velvet w/blk felt ears & blk trim, 7", VG+ $325.00

Pluto, figure, celluloid, England, yel w/blk ears & red collar, 3", EX+, A $130.00

Pluto, figure, rubber, Seiberling, 1930s, blk-pnt pie-eyes, 3½", VG $40.00

Pluto, figure, wood, Borgfeldt, 1930, w/twisted fiber legs & tail, felt ears, 5¾", EX (Pluto the Pup on VG box) $525.00

Pluto, figure & doghouse, Fun-E-Flex, 1930s, Pluto the Pup decal & picture of Pluto, 3½" figure, rare, VG $525.00

Pluto, pencil sharpener, WDP, 1940, Bakelite, 1½" dia, NM, A $65.00

Pluto, print, 1940s, felt image of Pluto eyeing bone, 8x10", EX, A $25.00

Robin Hood, Colorforms, 1970s, no booklet o/w complete & EX (EX box), A $15.00

Rocketeer, backpack, leather-like, promo for AMC Theatres, H10, from $75 to $125.00

Rocketeer, beach towel, 2 designs, promo for AMC Treatres, H10, ea...$25.00

Rocketeer, belt, turq or bl, H10, ea $30.00

Rocketeer, Fan Club Membership Card, H10 ....$10.00

Rocketeer, figure, Applause, vinyl, 9", H10 ....$20.00

Rocketeer, figure, prototype, water propelled, only 12 made, 6 w/blister packs, M (M blister pkg), H10, from $1,500 to......$2,000.00

Rocketeer, Gee Bee plane, Spectra Star, MIB, H10 ....$45.00

Rocketeer, jacket, made in Great Britian & sold only in France, red cloth w/image on back, M, H10, from $300 to ..$450.00

Rocketeer, notebook, Mead, 4 different, H10, ea................$4.00

Rocketeer, pin, Dave Stevens/Disney, 1991, enameled head design, 2", scarce, M, M8....................................$20.00

Rocketeer, poster, features Disney Channel, M, H10.......$50.00

Rocketeer, Poster Pen Set, Rose Art #1921, 1991, w/2 posters & 6 markers, MOC, from $20 to $30.00

Rocketeer, sleeping bag, H10 ....$45.00

Rocketeer, tape & book set, MIP (sealed), J8 ....$10.00

Rocketeer, umbrella, Pyramid Handbag Co, H10, from $75 to....$100.00

Rocketeer, wallet, Pyramid Handbag Co, H10 ....$40.00

Roger Rabbit, see Who Framed Roger Rabbit

Roo, see Winnie the Pooh

Scrooge McDuck, figure, Hagen-Renaker, 1950s, w/cane, 1⅝", NM, M8 ....$350.00

Scrooge McDuck & 3 Nephews, bank/squeeze toy, Dell, 1960s, rubber, 6", EX, M8 ....$35.00

Shaggy Dog, figure, ceramic, Enesco/WDE 192, 1960s, hitchhiking pose, driver pose or in pajamas, 5", M, P6, ea $75.00

Shaggy Dog, squeaker, Dell, 1960s, minor tear in back o/w EX, J8 ....$20.00

Sleeping Beauty, bubble wand, unused, MOC, J2 ....$25.00

Sleeping Beauty, Dress Designer Kit, Colorforms, 1959, MIB, P6..$65.00

Sleeping Beauty, figure, Flora (fairy), Hagen-Renaker, 1959, ceramic, EX, P6 ....$250.00

Sleeping Beauty, sewing set, Transogram, 1959, unused, scarce, EX+, M8..$65.00

Sleeping Beauty, wall plaques, 1950s, w/Sleeping Beauty, Prince, horse & 3 fairies, MIB, P6 ....$125.00

Snow White & the Seven Dwarfs, bagatelle game, bl-pnt wood, 7 slots w/figural paper-litho-on-wood dwarf, 10x20", VG+, A $120.00

Snow White & the Seven Dwarfs, bank, Dime Register, metal box w/canted corners, slide trap, 2½" sq, EX+.........$150.00

Snow White & the Seven Dwarfs, birthday card, WDE/White & Wycoff #8220, 1938, Happy on front w/Happy Birthday, EX..$35.00

Snow White & the Seven Dwarfs, birthday card w/33⅓ record, Buzza Cardozo/WDP, 1960s, 6" sq, M $40.00

Snow White & the Seven Dwarfs, board game, Tek Toothbrush premium, EX+ (orig envelope)..................................$350.00

Snow White & the Seven Dwarfs, brush, Grumpy & Dopey, Hughes, 1938, metal-clad wood, EX+, M8.................$85.00

Snow White & the Seven Dwarfs, charms, Japan, 1930s, hand-pnt celluloid, ea w/names on back, set of 8, NM, M8........$185.00

Snow White & the Seven Dwarfs, cup & saucer, Dopey & Grumpy, Marx/WD, ceramic, gold trim, EX+, A.......$45.00

Snow White & the Seven Dwarfs, desk set, 1937, printed cloth-covered set w/desk pad & accessories, EX+, A $135.00

Snow White & the Seven Dwarfs, doll, Snow White, Ideal, 1938, stuffed body w/cloth dress, 15½", EX+, A......$350.00

Snow White and the Seven Dwarfs, doll set, Knickerbocker, sold at McMasters 'Portraits' cataloged auction for $1,800.00 in November 1996.

Snow White & the Seven Dwarfs, figure, Doc, Enesco, 1960s, ceramic, 4½", M, M8..$50.00

Snow White & the Seven Dwarfs, figure, Sleepy, Enesco, ceramic, no label, 4½", NM, M8..............................$48.00

Snow White & the Seven Dwarfs, figure, Snow White, Japan, 1937, celluloid, standing w/hands behind back, 6", NM, A $90.00

Snow White & the Seven Dwarfs, figure, Snow White & Sleepy, Hagen-Renaker, 1950s, ceramic, 2¼" & 1½", M, P6, pr...$325.00

Snow White & the Seven Dwarfs, figure, Snow White kissing Dopey's head, bsk, 7", NM, A $125.00

Snow White and the Seven Dwarfs, figures, 1939, painted bisque, MIB, $1,200.00.

Snow White & the Seven Dwarfs, figure set, Applause, 1993, PVC, set of 8, F1 ....$30.00

Snow White & the Seven Dwarfs, figure set, 1930s, bsk, w/instruments, set of 8, 2½"-3", EX, M8 ....$550.00

Snow White & the Seven Dwarfs, figure set, dwarfs, 1938, bsk, ea emb w/name on cap, 2½", VG+ $250.00

Snow White & the Seven Dwarfs, figure set, Goebel, ceramic, 1st set w/full bee & crown mks, NM $975.00

Snow White & the Seven Dwarfs, figure set, Japan, celluloid, humorous positions, shades of pk, 7½"-5½", VG, A...$300.00

Snow White & the Seven Dwarfs, figure set, 1938, paper diecuts, Snow White leaning on hand w/bird & 7 dwarfs, EX, P6 ....$125.00

Snow White & the Seven Dwarfs, handkerchief, 1930s, images of the dwarfs, unused, 9x9", NM, M8.........................$23.00

Snow White & the Seven Dwarfs, handkerchief, 1930s, Snow White w/broom & animals, unused, 9x9", NM, M8 ..$23.00

Snow White & the Seven Dwarfs, movie, The Dwarfs' Dilemma, 1970s, blk & wht Super-8 film, EXIB, P6 ....$25.00

Snow White & the Seven Dwarfs, night light, Snow White, Hankscraft, 1959, plastic figure, musical, 8½", EX, M8 ....$75.00

Snow White & the Seven Dwarfs, pencil sharpener, Doc's Storage barrel, Enesco/WDP, 1960s, 4¼" $85.00

Snow White & the Seven Dwarfs, pencil sharpener, Snow White playing mandolin, Bakelite, 1930s, 1¾", M $110.00

Snow White & the Seven Dwarfs, perfume bottles, Sneezey & Grumpy, pnt glass on plastic base, 4", M $225.00

Snow White & the Seven Dwarfs, pin, WD, 1938, Snow White & Doc connected by chain, gold-tone w/enameled colors, EX $125.00

Snow White & the Seven Dwarfs, print, 1940s, glow-in-the-dark image of Snow White & Dopey, orig wooden fr, M, P6 ....$50.00

Snow White & the Seven Dwarfs, pull toy, Dopey, Dutch, 1938, gr-pnt wood figure on red wooden wheels, 10", EX+, A $225.00

Snow White & the Seven Dwarfs, pull toy, Dopey & Doc pull bell, NN Hill Brass Co, 1938, paper on wood & tin, EX $450.00

Snow White & the Seven Dwarfs, pull toy, WDE, 1938, 2 Dwarfs pull Snow White on 2 lg wheels, paper on wood, 14", EX, A $270.00

Snow White & the Seven Dwarfs, purse, 1930s, red silk-type fabric w/printed characters, cloth hdl w/metal fr, EX, P6 ....$125.00

Snow White & the Seven Dwarfs, purse, 1930s, silky fabric w/ various characters, cloth hdl w/Bakelite fr, EX, P6 ....$100.00

Snow White & the Seven Dwarfs, rattle, Bashful, 1938, celluloid figure in red & purple, 6", EX+, A $90.00

Snow White & the Seven Dwarfs, rattle, Snow White, figural image sitting inside ring, 4" dia, EX+, A..................$175.00

Snow White & the Seven Dwarfs, school tablet, Hilroy Series #3830, 1938, unused, EX, M8....................................$65.00

Snow White & the Seven Dwarfs, soap, dwarfs, Ben Rickert Inc, 1980, snap-apart heads, 5", unused, NM (NM box), M8 ..$45.00

Snow White & the Seven Dwarfs, soap, Snow White, Ben Rickert Inc, 1980, figural, 5", NM (NM Box), M8............$45.00

Snow White & the Seven Dwarfs, tea set, Japan, 1930s, lustreware, Snow White in forest scene, partial set, EX+, A.........$165.00

Snow White & the Seven Dwarfs, tea set, Marx, 1938, 9-pc set, EX, A $125.00

Snow White and the Seven Dwarfs, tea set, Marx/WDP, china, 23 pieces, EX (VG box), A, $370.00.

Snow White and the Seven Dwarfs, Talking Telephone, Hasbro, 1967, M (VG box), J6, $225.00.

Three Little Pigs, bank, Treasure Chest, 1934, EX, D10, $175.00.

Tail Spin, figures, Kellogg's premium, 1989, Baloo, Molly, Kit & villian Don Carnage, set of 4, NM, M8......................$20.00

Three Little Pigs, balancing toy, European, 1930s, diecut metal pig w/fiddle balances on metal stand, 11", EX+, A..$250.00

Three Little Pigs, bank, 1960s, Big Bad Wolf in front of house, compo, NM, A......................$50.00

Three Little Pigs, bank, 1960s, pig playing fiddle in front of yel straw house, compo, M, A......................$40.00

Three Little Pigs, dolls, Lars/Italy, playing instruments, stuffed felt, set of 3, 13", EX, A......................$1,100.00

Three Little Pigs, Ezechvele Lupo (car & trailer), Politoys/Italy, 1960s, wolf in car pulls pigs in trailer, 8", EXIB, A..$175.00

Three Little Pigs, figure, Big Bad Wolf, Japan, 1930s, bsk, in overalls & top hat, 3½", EX......................$75.00

Three Little Pigs, figure set, Borgfeldt/WD, bsk, Big Bad Wolf w/the 3 Pigs, 2 w/instruments & 1 w/trowel, 3", NMIB............$325.00

Three Little Pigs, figure set, Fun-E-Flex/WDP, pnt wood w/flexible paper arms & legs, set of 3, 3½", EX, A $135.00

Three Little Pigs, print, Silly Symphonies, WDP, glow-in-the-dark image of 3 pigs in front of house, fr, EX, P6.......$50.00

Three Little Pigs, pull toy, 2 pigs in 4-wheeled canoe, Wm Rogers, silverplated, 8x5", M (EX box), A...............$415.00

Three Little Pigs, switch plate, 1950s, plastic, MIP, P6....$35.00

Three Little Pigs, tea set, 1930s, lustreware, various images & name, creamer, covered sugar bowl & 3 plates, EX, P6.............$100.00

Three Little Pigs, tea set, 1930s, lustreware, 11 pcs, EX+, A...$360.00

Tigger, see Winnie the Pooh

Tinkerbell, see Disneyland & Peter Pan

Toy Story, doll, Buzz, Thinkway Toys, talker, 12", MIB...$45.00

Toy Story, doll, Woody, Thinkway Toys, talker, 14", MIB..$45.00

Toy Story, figures, Buzz & Woody, bendable, MOC, J8 ...$20.00

Toy Story, pin, Buzz Lightyear, Woody or Army Soldier, 2", MOC, M8, ea......................$25.00

Uncle Scrooge, bank, 1960s, Uncle Scrooge in bed, ceramic, G......................$35.00

Who Framed Roger Rabbit, Dip Flip, MIB, $25.00.

Who Framed Roger Rabbit, doll, Roger Rabbit, stuffed, 24", M......................$75.00

Who Framed Roger Rabbit, figure, Benny the Cab, plush, MIB......................$50.00

Who Framed Roger Rabbit, figure, Jessica, LJN, bendable, 6", MOC......................$30.00

Who Framed Roger Rabbit, figure, Judge Doom, LJN, bendable, 6", MOC......................$5.00

Who Framed Roger Rabbit, figure, Roger Rabbit on skateboard, battery-op, 10", EX, B10......................$14.00

Who Framed Roger Rabbit, figure, Smart Guy, LJN, bendable, 6", MOC......................$5.00

Who Framed Roger Rabbit, figure, window stick-on, 8", EX, J8......................$8.00

Who Framed Roger Rabbit, party favor bags, plastic, MIP...$20.00

Who Framed Roger Rabbit, pins, Roger, Jessica, Doom, Weasle, Baby Herman & Benny, cloisonne & enamel, set of 6, M......................$40.00

Who Framed Roger Rabbit, tray, Jessica figure, M............$70.00

Winnie the Pooh, doll, Winnie, Gund, 1967, plush w/hat & name on pullover sweater, 9", EX+......................$800.00

Winnie the Pooh, doll, Winnie, Knickerbocker, 1963, bl shirt, 13", VG+, J2......................$60.00

Winnie the Pooh, figure, Eeyore, 1960s, ceramic, curled-up position, EX, P6......................$55.00

Winnie the Pooh, figure, Kanga, Beswick, ceramic, P6....$75.00

Winnie the Pooh, figure, Piglet, Beswick, ceramic, M, P6..$75.00

Winnie the Pooh, figure, Piglet, PVC, 2", EX, B10 ....$3.00

Winnie the Pooh, figure, Tigger, Beswick, ceramic, M, P6..$75.00

Winnie the Pooh, figure, Winnie, Beswick, ceramic, EX, P6......................$55.00

Winnie the Pooh, figures, Beswick, England, set of 8 characters on stand, M, $1,000.00.

Winnie the Pooh, lamp, Dolly Toy Co, 1977, Winnie sitting on base w/various characters on shade, EX, P6 ....$75.00

Winnie the Pooh, lamp, plastic, Winnie in wagon mk Winnie the Pooh pulled by Eeyore on rnd base, EX, P6.........$55.00

Winnie the Pooh, night light, ceramic, various characters sleeping on grass under mushroom, EX, H4 ....$40.00

Winnie the Pooh, spoon rider set, 7 mc plastic Pooh characters, cereal premiums, 1960s, 2", EX, J5 ....$65.00

Winnie the Pooh, squeeze toy, Roo, NM, T1 ....$28.00

Winnie the Pooh, squeeze toy, Tigger, NM, T1...............$28.00

Winnie the Pooh, top, Ohio Art, 1960s, clear plastic cone-shaped dome w/wooden hdl & lithoed graphics, EX, P6.........$75.00

Zorro, charm bracelet, 1957, MIB, $125.00.

101 Dalmatians, cane, 1961, promotional, plastic figural head for hdl, 27", VG................................$30.00
101 Dalmatians, figure, Blot, Enesco, 1960s, ceramic, 4", M, P6................................$125.00
101 Dalmatians, figure, Penny, Enesco, 1960s, ceramic, seated, 4¾", M, P6................................$125.00
101 Dalmatians, figure, puppy, Japan/dbl-D mk, ceramic, sleeping pose, 3", M, P6................................$40.00

Dollhouse Furniture

Back in the '40s and '50s, little girls often spent hour after hour with their dollhouses, keeping house for their imaginary families, cooking on tiny stoves (that sometimes came with scaled-to-fit pots and pans), serving meals in lovely dining rooms, making beds, and rearranging furniture, most of which was plastic, much of which was made by Renwal, Ideal, Marx, Irwin, and Plasco. Jaydon made plastic furniture as well but sadly never marked it. Tootsietoy produced metal items, many in boxed sets.

Of all of these manufacturers, Renwal and Ideal are considered the most collectible. Renwal's furniture was usually detailed; some pieces had moving parts. Many were made in more than one color, often brightened with decals. Besides the furniture, they made accessory items as well as 'dollhouse' dolls of the whole family. Ideal's Petite Princess line was packaged in sets with wonderful detail, accessorized down to the perfume bottles on the top of the vanity. Ideal furniture and parts are numbered, always with an 'I' prefix. Most Renwal pieces are also numbered.

Advisor: Judith Mosholder (M7).

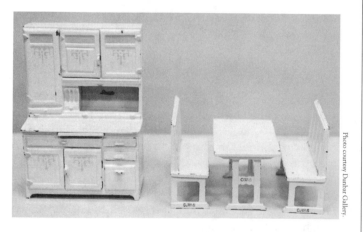

Arcade, kitchen set, painted cast iron, NM, D10, $750.00.

Acme/Thomas, dog sled, 2-seat, w/dog, M7......................$35.00
Acme/Thomas, hammock, bl w/red supports, M7............$12.00
Acme/Thomas, seesaw, red or bl w/horse head, M7, ea......$8.00
Acme/Thomas, shoofly rocker, red w/yel horse head, M7......................$8.00
Acme/Thomas, stroller, bl w/yel horse head, M7................$8.00
Acme/Thomas, swing, gr w/yel ropes & bl supports, M7..$15.00
Acme/Thomas, wagon, bl w/red hdl & wheels, M7..........$25.00
Allied, chair, kitchen; wht, M7......................$2.00
Allied, hutch, red, M7......................$4.00
Allied, toilet, wht & red, M7......................$4.00
Allied, tub, pk or wht, M7, ea......................$3.00
Allied, vanity, red, M7......................$3.00

Bliss, paper lithograph on wood, 12 pieces (not a matching set), NM, A, $900.00.

Bliss, 8-pc set w/table & 2 chairs, rocking chair, bed, lg & sm dresser & baby's cradle, paper litho on wood, EX+, A..............$775.00
Blue Box, chair, caramel w/red back & seat, M7................$3.00
Blue Box, chair, kitchen; avocado gr, M7......................$2.00
Blue Box, vanity, w/heart-shaped mirror, tan, M7..............$3.00
Commonwealth, wheelbarrow, red w/yel wheel, M7..........$8.00
Fisher-Price, baby's room, #257, baby crib, rocking horse & armoire, 1978, C13, ea......................$2.00
Fisher-Price, bathroom set #253, sink, toilet unit & shower stall, 1978, M, C13, ea......................$2.00
Fisher-Price, bedroom set #255, brass bed w/cover, dresser w/mirror & 3 drawers, 1978, M, C13, ea......................$2.00
Fisher-Price, desk set #261, roll-top desk w/swivel chair & spinning globe, 1980, M, C13, ea......................$2.00
Fisher-Price, dinette #251, pedestal table w/4 chairs, M, C13, ea......................$2.00
Fisher-Price, grandfather clock & rocker #262, 1980, M, C13, ea......................$2.00
Fisher-Price, kitchen appliance set #252, oven range w/exhaust, refrigerator & sink, M, C13, ea......................$2.00

Fisher-Price, living room set #256, sofa w/cushion & coffee table, 1978, M, C13, ea...$2.00

Fisher-Price, music room #258, grand piano w/stool & stereo center, 1978, M, C13, ea $2.00

Fisher-Price, patio set #259, redwood-type chair, chaise lounge, grill & collie dog, 1978, M, C13, ea $2.00

Grand Rapids, bed, wood w/stained finish, approximately 1½" scale, M7 ....$12.00

Grand Rapids, dresser w/mirror, wood w/stained finish, approximately 1½" scale, M7 ....$15.00

Ideal, buffet, dk brn or marbleized maroon, M7, ea..........$10.00

Ideal, chair, dining room; brn w/yel seat, armless, M7 ....$6.00

Ideal, chair, kitchen; ivory w/red or bl seats, M7.................$5.00

Ideal, china closet, dk marbleized maroon, M7 ....$15.00

Ideal, dbl seesaw, yel w/red base, MIB, M7.......................$75.00

Ideal, doll, baby, w/diaper, M7, ea $12.00

Ideal, hamper, ivory or bl, M7, ea.......................................$5.00

Ideal, highboy, ivory w/bl trim or dk marbleized maroon, M7, ea..$15.00

Ideal, mangle, wht or blk, M7, ea $15.00

Ideal, nightstand, brn, M7 ....$6.00

Ideal, nightstand, ivory, M7 ....$8.00

Ideal, nightstand, lt bl, M7...$10.00

Ideal, potty chair, pk, w/potty, M7....................................$15.00

Ideal, radio, floor; brn or dk marbleized maroon, M7, ea..$10.00

Ideal, refrigerator, ivory w/blk, M7 ....$15.00

Ideal, sewing machine, dk marbleized maroon, M7 ....$20.00

Ideal, sink, bathroom; ivory or bl, M7, ea...........................$8.00

Ideal, table, kitchen; ivory, M7..$6.00

Ideal, tub, corner; bl w/yel faucets, M7.............................$15.00

Ideal, vanity, brn or ivory, mirror wear, M7, ea $12.00

Ideal, vanity, dk maroon, M7 ....$15.00

Ideal Petite Princess, boudoir chaise lounge, #4408-1, bl, MIB, M7 ....$22.00

Ideal Petite Princess, chair, dining; guest, #4414-9, M7 ...$10.00

Ideal Petite Princess, chair, dining; host, #4413-1, M7.......$8.00

Ideal Petite Princess, chair, dining; hostess, #4415-6, MIB, M7...$24.00

Ideal Petite Princess, dressing table w/chair, bl, w/accessories, M7...$25.00

Ideal Petite Princess, Fantasy room, #4450-3, MIB (sealed), M7...$75.00

Ideal Petite Princess, Fantasy telephone set, #4432-1, complete, MIB, M7...$25.00

Ideal Petite Princess, grandfather clock, #4423-0, M7......$18.00

Ideal Petite Princess, hamper, M7 ....$20.00

Ideal Petite Princess, lyre table set, #4426-3, complete, M7..$25.00

Ideal Petite Princess, occasional table set, #4437-0, complete, M7...$20.00

Ideal Petite Princess, Palace chest, #4420-6, w/picture, MIB, M7...$18.00

Ideal Petite Princess, pedestal table set, #4427, complete, MIB, M7...$20.00

Ideal Petite Princess, Regency hearth place, #4422-2, w/accessories, M7...$20.00

Ideal Petite Princess, Royal buffet, #4419-8, MIB, M7 .....$25.00

Ideal Petite Princess, Royal candleabra, #4439-6, MIB (unopened), M7..$25.00

Ideal Petite Princess, Royal grand piano, #4425-5, complete, MIB, M7...$45.00

Ideal Petite Princess, Royal grand piano, #4425-5, no accessories, M7 ....$15.00

Ideal Petite Princess, Salon coffee table, #4433-9, M7 ....$5.00

Ideal Petite Princess, Salon drum chair, #4411-5, gold, MIB, M7...$18.00

Ideal Petite Princess, table, dining; #4421-4, MIB, M7 ....$15.00

Ideal Petite Princess, table, dining; #4421-4, w/picture, MIB, M7...$24.00

Ideal Petite Princess, tea cart, #4424-8, complete, MIB, M7 ..$25.00

Ideal Petite Princess, tier table set, #4429-7, complete, MIB, M7...$18.00

Ideal Young Decorator, sofa section, middle, rose, M7 .....$10.00

Imagination, chair, rnd or sq back in various color combinations, M7, ea...$2.00

Imagination, dresser, long, gr, M7 ....$2.00

Imagination, hutch top, gr, M7..$2.00

Imagination, TV, gr, M7...$2.00

Jaydon, bed, reddish brn swirl, no spread, M7...................$12.00

Jaydon, corner cupboard, reddish brn, M7...........................$4.00

Jaydon, piano w/bench, reddish brn swirl, M7...................$12.00

Jaydon, toilet, ivory w/red seat, M7.....................................$8.00

JP Co, chair, dining; brn, M7...$2.00

JP Co, hutch, brn, M7...$4.00

Lundby, kitchen set, sink w/upper cabinets & stove w/side & upper cabinets, MIB, M7 ....$24.00

Marklin, bed, bl tin w/scrolled headboard, footboard & side rails, gold trim, springs & canvas mattress, 8", EX, A $250.00

Marklin, bed, wht tin w/scrolled headboard, footboard & side rails, gold trim, springs & canvas mattress, 6", EX, A $200.00

Marklin, sink, bathroom; porcelain, mounted on floor against simulated tile wall w/rnd mirror, 8½", NM, A.........$470.00

Marklin, toilet, porcelain w/wood-look tank & lid, mounted on tin floor, 5", NM, A...$600.00

Marx, accessory, frying pan, metallic gold, sm, M7 ....$4.00

Ideal Petite Princess, Heirloom table set, #4428-9, complete, MIB, $30.00.

Marx, accessory, mixer & bowl, gray, M7............................$4.00

Marx, accessory, pitcher, tan or metallic gold, M7, ea........$4.00

Marx, accessory, pressure cooker, metallic gold, M7...........$4.00

Marx, accessory, toaster, gray, M7.....................................$4.00

Marx, bathroom set, corner tub, toilet, sink & hamper, dk ivory, hard plastic, ¾" scale, M7......................................$15.00

Marx, bed, bright yel, hard plastic, ¾" scale, M7.................$5.00

Marx, bedroom set, bed, chair/hassock, nightstand, highboy, lamp, vanity & bench, hard plastic, ¾" scale, M7.....$35.00

Marx, buffet, dk maroon swirl, hard plastic, ¾" scale, M7..$5.00

Marx, chair, armless; lt bl, soft plastic, ½" scale, M7..........$2.00

Marx, chair, bedroom; pale yel, soft plastic, ¾" scale, M7..$3.00

Marx, chair, boudoir; bright yel, hard plastic, ¾" scale, M7..$5.00

Marx, chair, captain's; bl, soft plastic, ½" scale, M7...........$3.00

Marx, chair, dining; dk maroon swirl, hard plastic, ¾" scale, M7...$5.00

Marx, chair, highback, bl, soft plastic, ¾" scale, M7...........$3.00

Marx, chair, highback, various colors, hard plastic, ¾" scale, M7, ea..$5.00

Marx, chair, kitchen; ivory or wht, hard plastic, ¾" scale, M7, ea..$2.00

Marx, chair, patio; bl, hard plastic w/molded wheels, ½" scale, M7...$4.00

Marx, chair, patio; yel, hard plastic, ¾" scale, M7..............$5.00

Marx, chair, tufted back, red, beige or yel, soft plastic, ¾" scale, M7, ea..$3.00

Marx, chest of drawers, pk, hard plastic, ¾" scale, M7........$5.00

Marx, china cupboard, dk brn or dk maroon swirl, hard plastic, ½" scale, M7, ea..$2.00

Marx, crib, lt bl, soft plastic, ½" scale, M7.........................$3.00

Marx, crib, pk, emb Mickey Mouse, hard plastic, ½" scale, M7...$8.00

Marx, dining room set, table, buffet, china cupboard & 1 chair, med maroon swirl, hard plastic, ¾" scale, M7............$15.00

Marx, dining room set, table, buffet, hutch & 3 chairs, marbleized maroon, hard plastic, ¾" scale, M7................$20.00

Marx, dining room set, table, hutch & 4 chairs (2 w/arms), brn, soft plastic, ¾" scale, M7..$18.00

Marx, doll, nurse, flesh, soft plastic, M7............................$5.00

Marx, doll, several variations, soft plastic, M7, ea..............$3.00

Marx, garbage can, ivory, hard plastic, ½" scale, M7..........$3.00

Marx, hamper, lt yel, soft plastic, ½" scale, M7..................$2.00

Marx, hamper, various colors, hard plastic, ¾" scale, M7, ea.$5.00

Marx, hassock, yel, hard plastic, ¾" scale, M7....................$4.00

Marx, hassock, yel, soft plastic, ¾" scale, M7.....................$3.00

Marx, highboy, yel or lt bl, hard plastic, ½" scale, M7, ea..$2.00

Marx, highchair, pk, hard plastic, ¾" scale, M7..................$8.00

Marx, hobby horse, lt bl, soft plastic, ½" scale, M7.............$3.00

Marx, hutch, maroon, hard plastic, ¾" scale, M7................$5.00

Marx, kitchen counter, wht, w/molded phone & hot plate, hard plastic, ½" scale, M7..$4.00

Marx, kitchen set, sink, stove, refrigerator, sm counter & 4 chairs, dk ivory, hard plastic, ¾" scale, M7.............$32.00

Marx, lamp, floor; lt yel, hard plastic, ¾" scale, M7.........$10.00

Marx, lamp, floor; lt yel, soft plastic, ¾" scale, M7............$8.00

Marx, lamp, table; lt bl, soft plastic, ½" scale, M7.............$2.00

Marx, mangle, wht or ivory, hard plastic, ½" scale, M7, ea..$4.00

Marx, nightstand, ivory or yel, hard plastic, ¾" scale, M7, ea..$5.00

Marx, nightstand, yel or lt bl, hard plastic, ½" scale, M7, ea...$2.00

Marx, patio set, red table w/bl umbrella, pole & 1 red chair, hard plastic, ½" scale, M7..$15.00

Marx, piano, yel, soft plastic, ½" scale, M7.........................$5.00

Marx, playground pail, bright yel, hard plastic, ¾" scale, M7...$6.00

Marx, playground slide, bright yel, hard plastic, ¾" scale, M7.$10.00

Marx, playpen, pk, emb Donald Duck, hard plastic, ½" scale, M7...$8.00

Marx, playpen, pk, hard plastic, ¾" scale, M7.....................$5.00

Marx, potty chair, pk, hard plastic, ¾", scale, M7...............$5.00

Marx, refrigerator, ivory, hard plastic, ¾" scale, M7...........$5.00

Marx, refrigerator, lt yel, soft plastic, ½" scale, M7............$2.00

Marx, refrigerator, wht, hard plastic, ½" scale, M7.............$2.00

Marx, sewing machine, wht, hard plastic, ½" scale, M7......$5.00

Marx, sink, bathroom; lt yel, soft pastic, ½" scale, M7........$2.00

Marx, sink, bathroom; various colors, hard plastic, ¾" scale, M7, ea..$5.00

Marx, sink, dbl bowl, wht, hard plastic, ½" scale, M7.........$4.00

Marx, sink, kitchen; lt ivory, soft plastic, ¾" scale, M7.......$3.00

Marx, sink, kitchen; wht or ivory, hard plastic, ¾" scale, M7, ea..$5.00

Marx, sofa, bl, curved, for game room, soft plastic, ½" scale, M7...$5.00

Marx, sofa, gr or yel, hard plastic, ½" scale, M7, ea............$2.00

Marx, sofa, red or yel, soft plastic, ¾" scale, M7, ea...........$3.00

Marx, sofa, red w/decal, hard plastic, ¾" scale, M7............$6.00

Marx, sofa, various colors, no decal, hard plastic, ¾" scale, M7, ea..$5.00

Marx, sofa, 3-pc, lt bl, soft plastic, ½" scale, M7................$5.00

Marx, stool, 4-legged, lt yel, soft plastic, ½" scale, M7.......$3.00

Marx, stool, 4-legged, various colors, hard plastic, ¾" scale, M7.$4.00

Marx, stove, ivory, soft plastic, ¾" scale, M7......................$3.00

Marx, stove, ivory or wht, hard plastic, ¾" scale, M7, ea....$5.00

Marx, stove, lt yel, soft plastic, ½" scale, M7......................$2.00

Marx, stove/sink combo, lt yel, soft plastic, ½" scale, M7...$2.00

Marx, table, coffee; curved, red, soft plastic, ¾" scale, M7.$5.00

Marx, table, dining; dk maroon swirl, hard plastic, ¾" scale, M7...$6.00

Marx, table, kitchen; ivory, hard plastic, ¾" scale, M7.......$5.00

Marx, table, kitchen; wht, hard plastic, ½" scale, M7.........$2.00

Marx, table, lawn; red, hard plastic w/molded wheels, ½" scale, M7...$4.00

Marx, table, step end; lt bl, hard plastic, ¾" scale, M7.......$4.00

Marx, toilet, ivory, hard plastic, ½" scale, M7....................$3.00

Marx, toilet, lt yel, soft plastic, ½" scale, M7.....................$2.00

Marx, toilet, various colors, hard plastic, ¾" scale, M7, ea.$5.00

Marx, tub, corner; ivory, hard plastic, ½" scale, M7...........$3.00

Marx, tub, corner; peach, bl or ivory, hard plastic, ¾" scale, M7, ea..$5.00

Marx, TV, floor model w/Marx insignia on front, tan, soft plastic, ½" scale, M7..$5.00

Marx, TV/phonograph, bright yel, bl or lt bl, hard plastic, ¾" scale, M7, ea..$5.00

Marx, TV/phonograph, red, soft plastic, ¾" scale, M7........$3.00

Marx, umbrella table, gr, hard plastic, ¾" scale, no umbrella, M7...$3.00

Marx, umbrella table, red w/yel umbrella, soft plastic, ½" scale, M7...$5.00

Marx, umbrella w/pole, gr, hard plastic, ¾" scale, M7 ....$8.00

Marx, vanity, yel, hard plastic, ¾" scale, M7 ....$5.00

Marx, vanity, yel or bl, hard plastic, ½" scale, M7, ea $2.00

Marx, vanity/sink, ivory, hard plastic, ½" scale, M7 ....$3.00

Marx, washer, front-load; ivory, hard plastic, ½" scale, M7 .$4.00

Mattel Littles, armoire, M7 ....$8.00

Mattel Littles, chair, living room; M7 ....$4.00

Mattel Littles, dresser, M7 ....$8.00

Mattel Littles, Hedy & sofa, MIB, M7 ....$15.00

Mattel Littles, sofa, M7 ....$8.00

Mattel Littles, table, tilt-top; M7 ....$6.00

Plasco, bathroom set, tub, toilet, sink, vanity, bench & hamper, w/paper floor plan, MIB, M7 ....$65.00

Plasco, bathroom set, tub, toilet, sink, vanity, bench & hamper, no floor plan, MIB, M7 ....$55.00

Plasco, bed, ivory, complete, M7 ....$8.00

Plasco, bed, yel w/spread & footboard, M7 ....$4.00

Plasco, birdbath/fountain, ivory, M7 ....$12.00

Plasco, buffet, various colors, M7, ea $4.00

Plasco, buffet, w/top, various colors, M7, ea $8.00

Plasco, chair, dining; tan w/paper seat cover, M7 ....$4.00

Plasco, chair, living room; lt gr, brn base, M7 ....$6.00

Plasco, chair, living room; yel, no-base style, M7 ....$3.00

Plasco, chair, patio; gr w/lt gr legs, M7 ....$4.00

Plasco, dining room set, table, buffet, 2 side tables & 4 chairs, MIB, M7..$55.00

Plasco, grandfather clock, brn, cb face, M7 ....$8.00

Plasco, hamper, pk or rose, opening lid, M7, ea $5.00

Plasco, highboy, med brn swirl, M7 ....$8.00

Plasco, kitchen counter, pk, no-base style, M7 ....$3.00

Plasco, kitchen counter, wht, bl base, rectangular, M7 ....$5.00

Plasco, lawn chaise, red w/dk ivory legs, M7 ....$12.00

Plasco, nightstand, ivory, stenciled, M7 ....$5.00

Plasco, nightstand, mauve, M7 ....$4.00

Plasco, refrigerator, wht, bl base, M7 ....$5.00

Plasco, refrigerator, wht or pk, no-base style, M7, ea $3.00

Plasco, sink, bathroom; pk or rose, M7, ea $4.00

Plasco, sink, kitchen; pk, no-base style, M7 ....$3.00

Plasco, sofa, lt bl, brn base, M7 ....$8.00

Plasco, sofa, lt bl, no-base style, M7 ....$3.00

Plasco, stove, pk, no-base style, M7 ....$3.00

Plasco, stove, wht, bl base, M7 ....$5.00

Plasco, table, coffee; brn, marbleized, M7 ....$3.00

Plasco, table, dining; lt tan, M7 ....$8.00

Plasco, table, kitchen; lt bl or royal bl, M7, ea $5.00

Plasco, toilet, pk w/gr marble or rose w/wht seat, M7, ea $8.00

Plasco, tub, various colors, M7, ea $4.00

Plasco, umbrella, lt gr, M7 ....$5.00

Plasco, umbrella table, bl w/dk ivory legs, table only, M7 ...$5.00

Plasco, vanity, dk brn, sq mirror, M7 ....$5.00

Plasco, vanity, w/bench, pk, no-mirror style, M7 ....$8.00

Pyro, floor radio, yel, M7 ....$10.00

Renwal, baby bath, #122, bl w/bear decal, M7 ....$15.00

Renwal, bathtub, #T95, pk w/bl or ivory w/blk, M7, ea $7.00

Renwal, bed, #81, brn w/ivory, M7..................................$8.00

Renwal, bed, #81, brn w/ivory, stenciled, M7 ....$12.00

Renwal, buffet, #D55, brn, opening drawer, M7 ....$8.00

Renwal, buffet, #D55, red, opening drawer, M7................$12.00

Renwal, carriage, #115, blanket insert, pk w/bl wheels, M7 ..$30.00

Renwal, carriage, #115, doll insert, bl, stenciled, M7 ....$35.00

Renwal, chair, barrel; #77, turq or bl w/brn base, stenciled, M7, ea..$10.00

Renwal, chair, club; #76, chartreuse or ivory w/brn base, stenciled, M7, ea..$10.00

Renwal, chair, folding; #109, red w/metallic gold seat, M7 ..$18.00

Renwal, chair, rocking; #65, pk w/bl, M7.......................$10.00

Renwal, chair, rocking; #65, red or yel, M7, ea $8.00

Renwal, chair, teacher's; #34, bl, M7 ....$20.00

Renwal, china closet, #D52, brn, M7 ....$5.00

Renwal, china closet, #D52, lt orange, opening door, M7 .$10.00

Renwal, china closet, #K52, brn, stenciled, M7 ....$15.00

Renwal, clock, kitchen; #11, red or ivory, M7, ea $20.00

Renwal, clock, mantel; #14, ivory or red, M7, ea $10.00

Renwal, cradle, #120, baby insert, bl, stenciled, M7 ....$35.00

Renwal, desk, student's; #33, red, brn or yel, M7, ea $12.00

Renwal, desk, teacher's; #34, bl, M7 ....$25.00

Renwal, desk, teacher's; #34, brn, M7 ....$20.00

Renwal, doll, baby, #8, w/pnt diaper, M7.......................$10.00

Renwal, doll, brother, #42, tan w/metal rivets or yel w/plastic rivets, M7, ea $25.00

Renwal, doll, father, #44, tan, plastic rivets, M7 ....$25.00

Renwal, doll, mother, #43, all pk, plastic rivets, M7........$25.00

Renwal, doll, mother, #43, lt pk dress, M7 ....$30.00

Renwal, doll, nurse, #43, no-cap style, VG, M7..............$20.00

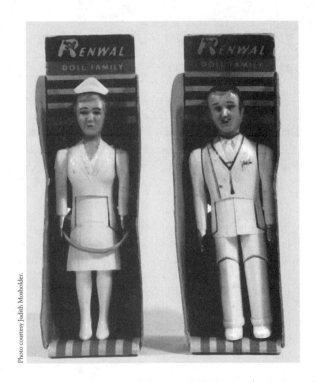

Renwal, dolls, nurse and doctor, MIB, M7, $75.00 each.

Renwal, doll, sister, #41, ivory, plastic rivets, M7 ....$25.00

Renwal, dresser, #83, simplified style, brn, stenciled, M7 .$15.00

Renwal, fireplace, #80, brn w/ivory, M7..........................$35.00

Renwal, garbage can, #64, red or yel, w/dustpan, M7, ea ..$22.00

Renwal, garbage can, #64, red w/yel lid, no decal, M7.......$8.00

Renwal, hamper, #T98, pk, opening lid, M7 ....$4.00
Renwal, highboy, #B85, brn, M7 ....$6.00
Renwal, highboy, #B85, brn, opening drawers, M7 ....$8.00
Renwal, highboy, #35, pk, M7 ....$15.00
Renwal, highboy, #85, brn, stenciled, M7 ....$12.00
Renwal, highchair, #30, pk, no decal, M7 ....$15.00
Renwal, highchair, #30, pk w/bear decal, M7 ....$30.00
Renwal, ironing board w/iron, #32, bl & pk, M7 ....$22.00

Photo courtesy Judith Mosholder.

Renwal, Jolly Twins dining room set, complete, MIB, M7, from $100.00 to $125.00.

Photo courtesy Judith Mosholder.

Renwal, kitchen set, complete with boxes, M7, $150.00 for the set.

Renwal, kiddie car, #27, yel w/red & bl, M7 ....$55.00
Renwal, lamp, table, #71, most colors, M7, ea $10.00
Renwal, lamp, table; #73, brn or reddish brn, stenciled, M7,
    ea $10.00
Renwal, nightstand/end table, #B84, lt bl, M7 ....$3.00
Renwal, nightstand/end table, #B84, pk, M7 ....$4.00
Renwal, piano, #74, brn, marbleized, M7 ....$30.00
Renwal, playground seesaw, #21, yel w/red & bl, M7 ....$25.00
Renwal, playground slide, #20, bl w/red stripes or yel w/bl stripes,
    M7, ea $20.00
Renwal, playpen, #118, bl & pk, M7 ....$15.00
Renwal, playpen, #118, pk, stenciled, M7 ....$25.00
Renwal, radio, floor; #79, brn, M7 ....$10.00
Renwal, radio, phono; #18, brn or red, M7, ea $15.00
Renwal, radio, table; #16, brn or red, M7, ea $15.00
Renwal, refrigerator, #66, ivory, 2 shelves, M7 ....$18.00
Renwal, refrigerator, #66, ivory w/blk, non-opening doors,
    M7 ....$10.00

Renwal, scale, #10, red, M7 ....$10.00

Photo courtesy Judith Mosholder.

Renwal, seesaw, #21, $25.00; slide, #20, $20.00; kiddie car, #27, $55.00; tricycle, #7, $25.00.

Renwal, server, #D54, red, opening drawer, M7 ....$12.00
Renwal, sink, #68, ivory w/bl, opening door, M7 ....$10.00
Renwal, sink, #68, ivory w/red, opening door, stenciled, M7 ...$17.00
Renwal, sink, bathroom; #T96, pk w/bl, M7 ....$5.00
Renwal, sink, bathroom; #T96, pk w/bl, stenciled, M7 ....$8.00
Renwal, smoking stand, #13, red w/ivory or ivory w/red, M7,
    ea $12.00
Renwal, sofa, #78, 2-tone colors, M7, ea $15.00
Renwal, sofa, #78, 2-tone colors, stenciled, M7, ea $17.00
Renwal, stool, #12, red w/ivory seat or ivory w/red seat, M7,
    ea $10.00
Renwal, stove, #K69, ivory w/red, opening door, M7 ....$15.00
Renwal, stove, #K69, ivory w/red, opening door, stenciled,
    M7 ....$17.00
Renwal, stroller, #87, pk w/bl wheels, M7 ....$35.00
Renwal, table, #67, brn, yel or caramel, #67, M7, ea $8.00
Renwal, table, #67, ivory, M7 ....$5.00
Renwal, table, cocktail; #72, reddish brn, M7 ....$8.00
Renwal, table, cocktail; #72, reddish brn swirl, stenciled, M7 ..$10.00
Renwal, table, dining; #D51, brn, stenciled, M7 ....$20.00
Renwal, table, dining; #D51, lt brn swirl, M7 ....$15.00
Renwal, table, folding; #108, metallic gold, M7 ....$15.00
Renwal, telephone, #28, yel w/red, M7 ....$22.00
Renwal, toilet, #T97, various colors, M7, ea $9.00
Renwal, toydee, #36, pk or matt pk, M7, ea $6.00
Renwal, toydee, #36, pk w/Little Bo-Peep decal, M7 ....$12.00
Renwal, tricycle, #7, red, bl & yel, M7 ....$25.00
Renwal, vacuum cleaner, #37, red or yel, no decal, M7, ea ..$15.00
Renwal, vacuum cleaner, #37, red or yel, w/decal, M7, ea ..$25.00
Renwal, vanity, #82, simplified style, brn, stenciled, M7 ..$10.00
Renwal, washing machine, #31, bl or pk w/decal, M7, ea.$30.00
Strombecker, armchair, blond-finished wood, 1950s, MIB,
    H12 ....$40.00
Strombecker, bathroom set, wood, ¾" scale, NRFB, H12..$150.00
Strombecker, bedroom set, pk-pnt wood, ¾" scale, NRFB,
    H12 ....$150.00
Strombecker, chair, kitchen; aqua, ¾" scale, M7 ....$8.00
Strombecker, chair, living room; aqua, ¾" scale, M7 ....$10.00
Strombecker, chair, rocking; for 8" or smaller dolls, 1950s, MIB,
    H12 ....$65.00
Strombecker, clock, table; rnd top, walnut, ¾" scale, M7 ..$8.00

Strombecker, dining room set, walnut, marked Strombecker Playthings, $50.00 for the set.

Strombecker, grandfather clock, walnut w/gold trim, ¾" scale, M7 ....$15.00

Strombecker, highchair, blond-finished wood, 1950s, MIB, H12 ....$40.00

Strombecker, lamp, table; aqua w/ivory shade, M7 ....$12.00

Strombecker, living room set, couch, lamp, chair, ottoman & coffee table, wood & velour, 1950s, MIB, H12........$135.00

Strombecker, living room set, unfinished wood, 1936, 6 pcs, MIB, M7..$75.00

Strombecker, piano bench, walnut, ¾" scale, M7.............$30.00

Strombecker, radio, floor; walnut w/circle of gold trim on front, ¾" scale, M7 ....$20.00

Strombecker, radio, floor; walnut w/etched details, ¾" scale, M7...$12.00

Strombecker, school room set, wood, complete, 1930s-40s, MIB, H12 ....$225.00

Strombecker, sink, bathroom; aqua, ¾" scale, M7 ....$8.00

Strombecker, table, coffee; blond-finished wood, 1950s, MIB, H12 ....$40.00

Strombecker, table, coffee; wood, for 8" dolls, 1950s, MIB, H12 ....$45.00

Strombecker, table, corner; blond-finished wood, 1950s, MIB, H12 ....$40.00

Strombecker, table, end; walnut, ¾" scale, M7 ....$6.00

Strombecker, table, kitchen; aqua, ¾" scale, M7.............$10.00

Strombecker, table, tilt-top; walnut, 1" scale, M7.............$40.00

Strombecker, tub, aqua, ¾" scale, M7 ....$8.00

Superior, bed, bright yel, ¾" scale, M7.................................$5.00

Superior, chair, living room; sq back, red, bl, pk or brn, ¾" scale, M7, ea..$4.00

Superior, chest of drawers, low, gr or yel, ¾" scale, M7, ea.$5.00

Superior, hutch, pk or red, ¾" scale, M7, ea $5.00

Superior, lamp, table; gr, soft plastic, M7 ....$3.00

Superior, piano, lt bl, soft plastic, M7..................................$4.00

Superior, refrigerator, wht, ¾" scale, M7.............................$5.00

Superior, toilet, wht, ¾" scale, M7 ....$4.00

Superior, tub, bl or yel, ¾" scale, M7, ea $5.00

Superior, vanity, bl, ¾" scale, M7...$5.00

Thomas, doll, baby w/diaper, 1⅛", M7..................................$2.00

Thomas, doll, baby w/diaper, 2" or 3", M7, ea.....................$4.00

Thomas, doll, boy w/raised hand, M7 ....$3.00

Tomy Smaller Homes, accessory, fork, spoon & knife, M7...$15.00

Tomy Smaller Homes, accessory, hamper, wht, M7...........$6.00

Tomy Smaller Homes, accessory, place mat, yel or orange, M7, ea $3.00

Tomy Smaller Homes, accessory, 4 napkins w/napkin rings, MIP, M7 ....$20.00

Tomy Smaller Homes, bar, M7...$6.00

Tomy Smaller Homes, bentwood rocker, M7......................$5.00

Tomy Smaller Homes, cabinet, living room; tall, M7 ....$8.00

Tomy Smaller Homes, cabinet, low, M7 ....$6.00

Tomy Smaller Homes, chair, kitchen; M7 ....$2.00

Tomy Smaller Homes, counter-top range w/hood, M7.....$12.00

Tomy Smaller Homes, crib, M7..$15.00

Tomy Smaller Homes, dresser, w/3 hangers, M7..............$13.00

Tomy Smaller Homes, refrigerator, 2 drawers, M7...........$10.00

Tomy Smaller Homes, refrigerator, 3 drawers, M7...........$12.00

Tomy Smaller Homes, rocker, nursery; M7.......................$12.00

Tomy Smaller Homes, sink w/dishwasher, dbl bowl, M7..$12.00

Tomy Smaller Homes, table, kitchen; M7..........................$8.00

Tomy Smaller Homes, tub, M7...$8.00

Tootsietoy, bathroom scale, lavender, no step-on plate, M7...$15.00

Tootsietoy, bathroom set, tub, sink, toilet, stool & medicine cabinet, ivory, M7 ....$110.00

Tootsietoy, bed, pk or gr w/slatted headboard & footboard, M7, ea..$18.00

Tootsietoy, bed, pk w/pk-flocked spread, M7...................$25.00

Tootsietoy, bedroom set, pink-painted cast metal, 6 pieces, EX+ (VG box), 125.00.

Tootsietoy, bench, vanity; pk w/pk-flocked seat, M7 ....$10.00

Tootsietoy, chair, kitchen; lavender, M7 ....$6.00

Tootsietoy, cupboard, ivory, M7......................................$20.00

Tootsietoy, dresser, w/mirror, gr, M7...............................$22.00

Tootsietoy, lamp, floor; goose-neck type, brn w/tan-flocked shade, M7..$25.00

Tootsietoy, lamp, table; ivory w/pk shade, M7.................$12.00

Tootsietoy, medicine cabinet, lavender, no mirror, M7 ...$15.00

Tootsietoy, medicine cabinet, lavender, w/mirror, M7.....$30.00

Tootsietoy, sink, kitchen; 2-legged, ivory, M7.................$12.00

Tootsietoy, stove, ivory, M7...$20.00

Tootsietoy, table, dining; brn, M7.....................................$8.00

Tootsietoy, table, living room; long w/bottom strut, gr w/ivory crackle, M7 ....$25.00

Tootsietoy, table, oval, brn w/crackled top, M7 ....$10.00

Tootsietoy, Victrola, gold, M7...$35.00

Wolverine, crib, M7 ....$8.00

Wolverine, dolls, mom, dad or baby, M7, ea $8.00

Wolverine, nursery set, #870, crib, playpen & dresser, MIB, M7...$30.00

Dollhouses

Dollhouses were first made commercially in America in the late 1700s. A century later, Bliss and Schoenhut were making wonderful dollhouses that even yet occasionally turn up on the market, and many were being imported from Germany. During the '40s and '50s, American toy makers made a variety of cottages; today they're all collectible.

Advisor: Bob and Marcie Tubbs (T5).

Other Sources: M15

Bliss, 1½-story, paper litho on wood, red slanted roof w/attic dormers, extensive front porch w/steps, 20x18", VG $1,800.00

Bliss, 2-story, front opening, curtained windows, wallpapered interior, front porch w/turned posts & banister, 18", G, A...$750.00

Bliss, 2-story, paper litho on wood, bay window & attic gable, front opens to upper & lower room, VG..................$375.00

Bliss, 2-story, paper litho on wood, opening face, wallpapered interior, 9", G $450.00

Bliss, 2-story, paper litho on wood, wht w/brn roof, sm porch, curtained windows, door opens to 2 rooms, 13x9x7", EX, A...$635.00

FAO Schwarz, house trailer, yel & red w/wooden interior compartments & furniture, metal wheels, 1930s, 16x30", EX, A..$175.00

Fisher-Price, #0250, 3-story w/5 rooms, spiral staircase, w/2 figures & instructions, 1978-79, M, C13 ....$40.00

German, 2-story, brick w/gables, railed porch over front door, basement windows, 1905, 25", EX $1,650.00

German, 2-story townhouse, wood, red & gold roof w/tower-type dormer, attached fence, 30", EX $7,700.00

German, 2½-story, paper lithograph on wood, cutout windows, red roof, front panel opens to reveal 3 rooms, ca 1900s, 19x13x7", EX, A, $900.00.

Grimm & Leeds, 2-story, cb, simulated brick w/gr roof, wht trim, EX (EX wood box), A...$450.00

Photo courtesy Brad Cassity.

Fisher-Price, 3-story light-up with 5 rooms, spiral staircase, battery-operated with 7 outlets, 1981, M, $30.00.

Photo courtesy Bob and Marcie Tubbs.

Jayline, 2-story with 5 rooms, lithographed tin, green siding over white with red bricks, purple roof, 1949, 14½x18½", VG, T5, $50.00.

Mansford, 3-story, 2 rooms on ea floor, front opening w/lift-off roof, orig wallpaper & floors, late 1800s, 29", VG, A...$2,185.00

Marx, red siding, gray roof, patio above garage, some rust on garage floor, M7...$60.00

Marx, split-level, wht roof, gray siding & yel brick, w/fireplace, set of steps & breakfast bar, EX, M7..........................$80.00

Marx, split-level, wht roof, gray siding & yel brick, w/pool, doorbell, light fixture & 60 pcs of furniture, EX, M7......$125.00

Marx, 2-story, litho tin, wht clapboard over mc stone, red roof, 14x38", VG, T5...$95.00

Marx, 2-story, red roof, patio above garage, ABC nursery, ½" scale, EX, M7...$50.00

Meritoy, Cape Cod, litho tin with ivory clapboard over gray stone, red roof, plastic window inserts, 1949, 14½x21x10¼", M, T5, $200.00.

Rich, bungalow, Arts & Crafts-style litho cb, wht w/red roof, 4 windows, 2 chimneys, 1930s, 32x21", VG, T5 ....$200.00

Rich, lithographed fiberboard with red roof, blue shutters, 1940s, 16x24x9", VG, T5, $135.00.

Schoenhut, 2-story, brick w/red roof, porch w/litho columns, 2 rooms, 16½x12½", G $650.00

Schoenhut, 2-story colonial style, wood, 4 rooms & attic, 4 shuttered windows, gr shingled roof, 1930, 17x17", VG, A............$735.00

Schoenhut, 2-story cottage style w/porch, pnt wood & cb, lift-off roof, ca 1920, 27x23x23", VG $1,100.00

T Cohn, lithographed tin with blue shutters and red roof, 1951, 16x24x9", VG, T5, $195.00.

Tootsietoy, 2-story, cb, cream w/red roof, bl shutters, fold-out attic windows, 2 chimneys, 1927, 17", EX $650.00

Unknown Maker, 1-story, wht simulated brick on wood w/brn trim, shingled roof, sm porch, roof lifts off, 13x16", EX, A...$125.00

Unknown Maker, 2-story, simulated red brick on wood, brn & wht trim, 2 front bay windows w/railed entry, 34", EX, A..$1,700.00

Unknown Maker, 3-story, wht clapboard w/brn trim, cedar shingles, lg railed front porch, glass windows, 26x24x17", EX, A...$400.00

Wolverine, Colonial Mansion, no garage, ½" scale, EX, M7..$45.00

Wolverine, Country Cottage #800, 1986, ½" scale, EX, M7..$45.00

SHOPS AND SINGLE ROOMS

Butcher's Shop, Germany, litho wood w/cut-out door & window, complete w/figure & accessories, 10x15", EX, A $3,500.00

Hometown Meat Market, Marx #181, 1930, litho tin w/3 walls & floor, NM (EX box), A.....................................$245.00

Hometown Your Favorite Store (FW Woolworth), Marx #182, 1930, EX+ (VG+ box), A $125.00

Kitchen, Germany, wood w/center stove alcove, papered walls, wood table, assorted tinware & accessories, 12x22", VG, A $700.00

Kitchen, pnt tin w/red hood over stove, gr walls, assorted tinware, 19x10x9", VG, A $650.00

Newlyweds Bathroom, Marx #192, 3-sided litho tin room complete w/furniture, 1925, 3x5x3", MIB $400.00

Newlyweds Dining Room, Marx #194, 3-sided litho tin room complete w/furniture, 1925, 3x5x3", MIB...............$300.00

Newlyweds Kitchen, Marx #190, 3-sided litho tin room complete w/furniture, 1925, 3x5x3", MIB $400.00

Newlyweds Parlor, Marx #193, 3-sided litho tin room complete w/furniture, 1925, 3x5x3", MIB $300.00

Retail Shop, faux tortoise-shell columns & fitted shelves, miscellaneous merchandise, 1800s, 15x21x11", VG, A .$1,950.00

Stable, pnt wood room w/roof, 3 compo & wood horses (2 on wheeled platforms), 2 wagons, 13x9", EX, A $385.00

Dolls and Accessories

Obviously the field of dolls cannot be covered in a price guide such as this, but we wanted to touch on some of the later plastic dolls from the '50s and '60s, since so much of the collector interest today is centered on those decades. For in-depth information on dolls of all types, we recommend the many lovely doll books written by authority Pat Smith; all are available from Collector Books. Other great publications by Collector Books are *Doll Values, Antique to Modern*, and *Modern Collectible Dolls* both by Patsy Moyer; *Madame Alexander Collector's Dolls Price Guide #22* by Linda Crowsey; *The World of Raggedy Ann Collectibles* by Kim Avery; and *Guide to Ideal Dolls* by Judith Izen.

See also Action Figures; Barbie and Friends; Character, TV, and Movie Collectibles; GI Joe; and other specific categories.

BABY DOLLS

Baby Big Eyes, Ideal, 1954-59, soft vinyl, rooted curly hair, orig blanket & nightie, 20", EX..........................$50.00
Baby Brother Tenderlove, Mattel, 1969, 16", MIB, M15 .$35.00
Baby Burps, Vogue, 1970s, MIB, J5 ....$25.00
Baby First Step, Mattel, 1964, 20", VG (orig box), M15 ..$85.00
Baby Go Bye-Bye & Her Bumpety Buggy, Mattel, VG (worn box), M15 ....$125.00
Baby Grows Up, Mattel, 1978, grows from 16" to 18", MIB, M15.$35.00
Baby Jumpsy, Remco, 1970, 15", MIB, M15 ....$75.00
Baby Luv, Eegee, 1973, rare dk hair version, all orig, 15", VG, M15...$25.00

Betty Big Girl, Ideal, 32", NM, S14, $200.00.

Baby Mine, Ideal, 10½", MIB, H12....................................$75.00
Baby Skates, Mattel, 1982, 15", MIB, M15 ....$35.00
Baby Soft Sounds, Fisher-Price, 1979, redressed, 16", VG, M15...$25.00
Baby Talk, Galoob, 1986, 18", NRFB, M15......................$60.00
Baby That Away, Mattel, 1974, all orig, 16", VG, M15 ...$25.00
Baby Walk & Play, Mattel, 1967, orig outfit, 11", VG, M15 ...$30.00
Baby Wet & Care, Kenner, complete w/accessories, 13", MIB, H12..$85.00
Baby's First Baby, Horsman, 1960s, complete w/accessories, MIB, H12..$95.00
Big Huggems', Madame Alexander, 1963, rare brunette hair, 25", VG, M15..$100.00
Bylo Baby, Horsman, 1972, issued for Montgomery Ward's 100th Anniversary, 14", MIB, M15...........................$60.00
Cabbage Patch, Ideal, 1983, red fuzzy hair, wearing jeans, MIB, H12...$125.00
Cabbage Patch (Black), Ideal, 1985, foreign issue, wht dress, MIB, H12...$100.00
Chatterbox, Madame Alexander, 1961, 23", MIB, M15...$275.00
Chew Suzy Chew, Black, Ideal, 1980, 15", NRFB, M15...$30.00
Cream Puff, Ideal, 1950s, blond hair, bl sleep eyes, 21", rare, MIB, H12...$175.00

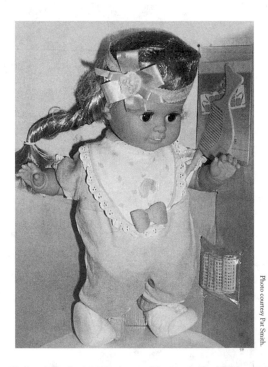

Crissy Baby, Ideal, 1989, rooted hair, 16", MIB, $35.00.

Crissy, Magic Hair; Ideal, 1977, w/5 hairpieces, MIB, M15 ...$100.00
Crissy, Magic Hair; Ideal, 1977, 18", missing wigs o/w NM (damaged box), J5 ....$25.00
Crissy, Moovin' Groovin'; Ideal, 1977, MIB, M15............$55.00
Crissy, Swirla Curla; Ideal, 1971, orig outfit, 19", VG, M15 .....$35.00
Crissy, Teeny Baby; Ideal, 1992, blond hair, 10", NRFB, M15...$30.00
Crissy, Twirly Bead; Ideal, 1971, 19", MIB, M15.............$45.00
Dancerella, Mattel, 1978, 17", NRFB, M15 ....$35.00
Dancerina, Mattel, 1968, orig outfit, 24", VG, M15.........$45.00

Dream Dancer, Tomy, 1984, 12", NRFB, M15 ....$30.00

Gabbigale, Kenner, 1972, 19", MIB, M15 ....$55.00

Jenny, Fisher-Price #209, 1984, aerobic outfit, 16", MIB, M15 ....$45.00

Lil Shaver, Madame Alexander, 1963, rooted blond hair, orig sunsuit, 11", VG, M15...................................$125.00

Little Miss Echo, Am Character, 1964, orig outfit & tape recorder, 30", VG (orig box), M15.......................$225.00

Little Miss No Name, Hasbro, 1965, all orig, 15", VG, M15 ...$65.00

Magic Baby Tenderlove, Mattel, 1978, complete w/accessories, 14", MIB, M15 ....$30.00

Mandy, Fisher-Price #211, 1979, 16", MIB, M15..............$45.00

My Beautiful Doll, Hasbro, 1989, Rachel, Brenda Marissa or Mary Beth, 18", NRFB, M15, ea $45.00

Oopsie Daisy, Irwin, 1988, orig outfit, 16", EX, M15........$40.00

Patty Playpal, Ideal, 1960s, redressed, 36", EX, M15 ......$225.00

Patty Playpal, reissue, Ideal, 1980s, platinum blond hair, 36", MIB, M15 ....$265.00

Rub-A-Dub Dolly, Blk, Ideal, 1979-80, 16", NRFB, M16...$50.00

Ruthie, Horsman, 1964, all orig, 16", VG, M15 ....$65.00

Shoppin' Sheryl, Mattel, 1970, orig outfit, 15", VG, M15 ..$20.00

Sleepy Doll, Knickerbocker, plush w/cloth face, 22", MIB, H12 ....$145.00

Suzie Snoozie, Am Character, 1960, orig outfit, 21", VG, M15 ....$70.00

Sweet Cookie, Hasbro, 1972, orig outfit, 18", VG, M15 ..$20.00

Talking Patty Playpal, Ideal, 1986, 27", MIB, M15 ....$225.00

Tearful Tenderlove, Mattel, 1971, all orig, 16", VG, M15..$25.00

Teeny Betsy Wetsy, Playmate, 1991, 10", NRFB, M15 ....$22.00

Teeny Tiny Tears, Playmate, 1991, rare red hair, 10", NRFB, M15...$25.00

Tender Love & Kisses, Mattel, 1976, 14", MIB, M15.......$25.00

Tiny Baby Tenderlove, Mattel, 1971, all orig, 11½", VG, M15..$25.00

Tiny Tears, Am Character, 1950s, orig outfit, 12", VG, M15..$45.00

Tippee Toes, Mattel, 1967, 16", MIB, M15....................$100.00

Tippy Tumbles, Ideal, 1970s, NMIB, J5 ....$30.00

BETSY MCCALL

The tiny 8" Betsy McCall doll was manufactured by the American Character Doll Co. from 1957 through 1963. She was made from high-quality hard plastic with a bisque-like finish and hand-painted features. Betsy came in four hair colors — tosca, red, blond, and brunette. She had blue sleep eyes, molded lashes, a winsome smile, and a fully jointed body with bendable knees. On her back there is an identification circle which reads McCall Corp. The basic doll wore a sheer chemise, white taffeta panties, nylon socks, and Maryjane-style shoes, and could be purchased for $2.25.

There were two different materials used for tiny Betsy's hair. The first was a soft mohair sewn into fine mesh. Later the rubber scullcap was rooted with saran which was more suitable for washing and combing.

Betsy McCall had an extensive wardrobe with nearly one hundred outfits, each of which could be purchased separately. They were made from wonderful fabrics such as velvet, taffeta, felt, and even real mink. Each ensemble came with the appropriate footwear and was priced under $3.00. Since none of Betsy's clothing was tagged, it is often difficult to identify other than by its square snap closures (although these were used by other companies as well).

Betsy McCall is a highly collectible doll today but is still fairly easy to find at doll shows. Prices remain reasonable for this beautiful clothes horse and her many accessories.

Advisor: Marci Van Ausdall (V2).

See also Clubs and Newsletters.

Toni, Ideal, 14", MIB, sold at McMasters 'Portraits' cataloged auction for $450.00 in November 1996.

Doll, American Character, in Playtime outfit, 14", $225.00.

Doll, School Girl outfit, 8", M, V2, minimum value $125.00

Doll, starter kit #9300, blond hair w/side part, complete, EX (worn card), minimum value..................................$175.00

Doll, Uneeda, all orig, 11½", V2.....................................$45.00

Doll, 1st year bridal outfit, complete, EX, V2 ....$150.00

Outfit, April Showers, complete, EX, V2.........................$35.00

Outfit, Cotillion #1, complete, for 8" doll, EX, V2 ....$75.00

Outfit, School Days, dress, jumper, tights & hat, 1959, for 14" Am Character doll, EX, V2, minimum value.............$65.00

Outfit, Sunday Best, complete, EX, V2 ....$50.00

Outfit, Sweet Dreams, for 8" doll, VG, V2......................$35.00

Outfit, Zoo Time, for 8" doll, VG, V2..............................$45.00

Record, Sing Along w/Betsy, 33⅓ rpm, EX, V2.............$25.00

CELEBRITY AND PERSONALITY DOLLS

Celebrity and character dolls have been widely collected for many years, but they've lately shown a significant increase in demand. Except for the rarer examples, most of these dolls are still fairly easy to find at doll shows, toy auctions, and flea markets, and the majority are priced under $100.00. These are the dolls that bring back memories of childhood TV shows, popular songs, favorite movies, and familiar characters. Mego, Mattel, Remco, and Hasbro are among the largest manufacturers.

Condition is a very important worth-assessing factor, and if the doll is still in the original box, so much the better! Should the box be unopened (NRFB), the value is further enhanced. Using mint as a standard, add 50% for the same doll mint in the box and 75% if it has never been taken out. On the other hand, dolls in only good or poorer condition drop at a rapid pace.

Advisor: Henri Yunes (Y1).

Al Lewis (Grandpa Munster), Remco #1821, 1964, 6", MIB .$200.00

Andy Gibb, Ideal, 1979, w/disco dancing stand, 7½", NRFB ...$50.00

Angie Dickinson (Police Woman), Horsman, 1976, 9", MIB ..$60.00

Barbara Eden (I Dream of Jeannie), Libby Majorette Doll Corp, 1966, 20", rare, NRFB $500.00

Barbara Eden (I Dream of Jeannie), Remco, 1972, 6½", NRFB...$100.00

Beatles, Remco, 1964, ea member w/instrument, MIB, ea from $150 to $200.00

Beverly Johnson, Real Models Collection, Matchbox, 1989, 11½", NRFB, M15 ....$35.00

Boy George, LJN, 1984, 11½", scarce, MIB, O1.............$125.00

Boy George LJN, soft plush body w/vinyl head, 14", NMIB..$50.00

Brooke Shields, LJN, 1982, 1st issue, bl or pk sweater, 11½", NRFB $50.00

Brooke Shields, LJN, 1983, 2nd issue, in swimsuit w/suntan body, 11½", rare, NRFB $95.00

Brooke Shields, LJN, 1983, 3rd issue, Prom Party outfit, 11½", rare, NRFB...$200.00

Charlie Chaplin, Presents, 9", M, J2 ....$30.00

Charlie Chaplin, World Doll, 1989, 100th Anniversary, 11½", NRFB $45.00

Cher, Mego, 1976, 1st issue, pk dress, 12¼", NRFB $70.00

Cher, Mego, 1977, 2nd issue, Growing Hair, 12¼", NRFB...$80.00

Cher, Mego, 1981, 3rd issue, red swimsuit, 12", rare, NRFB (photo on box)..$95.00

Cheryl Ladd, Mattel, 1978, red dress, 11½", NRFB..........$60.00

Cheryl Ladd (Kris from Charlie's Angels), Hasbro, 1977, in jumpsuit & scarf, 8½", MOC $40.00

Cheryl Tiegs, Matchbox, Real Models Collection, 1989, 11½", NRFB $35.00

Christy Brinkley, Matchbox, Real Models Collection, 1989, 11½", NRFB $35.00

Clark Gable (Rhett Butler), World Dolls, 1980, 1st edition, 12", NRFB $65.00

Carol Channing (Hello Dolly), Nasco Dolls, 1962, rare, MIB, $250.00.

Photo courtesy Henri Yunes.

Photo courtesy Henri Yunes.

Diahann Carroll (Julia), Mattel, 1969, in nurse uniform, NRFB, $150.00; Talking Julia in gold and silver jumpsuit, MIB, $200.00.

Diahann Carroll (Julia), Mattel, 1969, 1st edition, reddish brn hair, gold & silver jumpsuit, 11½", NRFB..............$300.00

Diahann Carroll (Julia), Mattel, 1970, 2nd edition, dk Afro hair, 1-pc outfit, 11½", NRFB...$200.00

Diahann Carroll (Julia), Mattel, 1971, dk Afro hair, talker, gold & silver jumpsuit, vinyl, 11½", NRFB.....................$200.00

Diana Ross, Mego, 1977, wht & silver dress, 12", NRFB..$125.00

Diana Ross (of the Supremes), Ideal, 1969, 19", NRFB..$150.00

Dolly Parton, Eegee, 1980, 1st issue, red jumpsuit, 11½", NRFB..$65.00

Dolly Parton, Eegee, 1987, 2nd issue, blk jumpsuit, 11½", NRFB..$50.00

Dolly Parton, Eegee, 1987, 2nd issue, cowgirl outfit, 11½", MIB, $45.00.

Dolly Parton, World Doll, 1987, red gown, 18", NRFB, M15...$90.00

Donny & Marie Osmond, Mattel, 1976, gift set, NRFB.$100.00

Donny Osmond, Mattel, 1976, 11½", MIB.......................$50.00

Dorothy Hamill, 1977, red olympic outfit w/medal, 11½", NRFB..$75.00

Elizabeth Taylor, Butterfield 8 or Cat on Hot Tin Roof, Tristar, 1982, 11½", MIB, ea..$125.00

Elizabeth Taylor, Father of the Bride, Butterfield 8 or Cat on Hot Tin Roof, World Doll, 1989, 11½", MIB, ea......$65.00

Elizabeth Taylor, The Bluebird, Horsman, 1976, w/3 outfits, 12", NRFB..$150.00

Elvis Presley, Burning Love, World Doll, 1984, 21", VG+.$110.00

Elvis Presley, Eugene, 1984, issued in 6 different outfits, 12", MIB, ea..$65.00

Elvis Presley, Teen Idol, Jail House Rock or '68 Special, Hasbro, 1993, ea from numbered edition, 12", MIB, ea..........$40.00

Farrah Fawcett (Jill from Charlie's Angels), Hasbro, 1977, in jumpsuit & scarf, 8½", MOC...................................$40.00

Farrah Fawcett (Jill from Charlie's Angels), Mego, 1976, 1st issue, wht jumpsuit, 12", NRFB.................................$60.00

Farrah Fawcett (Jill from Charlie's Angels), Mego, 1981, lavender swimsuit, 12", rare, NRFB (photo on box)..........$95.00

Flip Wilson/Geraldine, Shindana, 1976, talker, 16", MIB, M15...$65.00

Florence Griffith Joiner (Flo-Jo), LJN, 1989, pk & bl athletic outfit w/bag, 11½", MIB....................................$60.00

Fred Gwynne (Herman Munster), Remco #1820, 1964, MIB.$150.00

Grace Kelly, The Swan or Mogambo, Tristar, 1982, 11½", MIB...$125.00

Groucho Marx, Effanbee, 1983, 17", MIB, M15 ....$90.00

Jaclyn Smith (Kelly from Charlie's Angels), Hasbro, 1977, in jumpsuit & scarf, 8½", MOC...................................$40.00

Jaclyn Smith (Kelly from Charlie's Angels), Mego, 1977, bl dress, 12", rare, NRFB...$125.00

James Dean, DSI, 1994, Rebel Rouser or City Streets outfit, 12", NRFB, M15, ea...$75.00

John Travolta (On Stage...Superstar), Chemtoy, 1977, 12", MIB...$55.00

John Wayne, Effanbee, 1981, Great Legends series, Spirit of the West cowboy outfit, 17", MIB................................$125.00

John Wayne, Effanbee, 1982, Great Legends series, Guardian of the West cavalry outfit, 18", MIB $120.00

Judy Garland (Wizard of Oz), Effanbee, 1984, Great Legends series, w/basket & vinyl Toto, 14½", MIB..............$100.00

Julie Andrews (Mary Poppins), Horsman, 1964, w/Michael & Jane dolls, 3-pc set, 10", rare, NRFB.......................$250.00

Kate Jackson (Sabrina from Charlie's Angels), Hasbro, 1977, in jumpsuit & scarf, 8½", MOC...................................$40.00

Kate Jackson (Sabrina from Charlie's Angels), Mattel, 1978, red & wht dress, 11½", NRFB.......................................$60.00

KISS, Ace Frehley, Gene Simmons, Paul Stanley or Peter Criss, Mego, 1978, 12", NRFB, ea.....................................$125.00

Laurel & Hardy, Knickerbocker, 1960s, plastic bendable body w/vinyl head, cloth outfit, 9½", MIP, ea.....................$60.00

Laurel & Hardy (Music Box), Peggy Nisbet Dolls, 1970s, MIB, ea..$50.00

Laverne & Shirley (Penny Marshall as Laverne & Cindy Williams as Shirley), Mego, 1977, 12", NRFB, pr...$125.00

Lenny & Squiggy ((Michael McKean as Lenny & David Lander as Squiggy), Mego, 1977, 12", NRFB, pr..................$200.00

Lucy (I Love Lucy), ca 1952, stuffed cloth w/pnt features, yarn hair, w/scarf, pants, top & apron, 26", rare, NRFB..$800.00

Macaully Caulkin (Kevin from Home Alone), vinyl, screams, MIB, T1...$20.00

Madonna (Breathless Mahoney in Dick Tracy), Applause, 1990, blk evening gown w/gold trim & heels, 10", MIB......$40.00

Madonna (Breathless Mahoney in Dick Tracy), Playmates, 1990, plastic, bl dress, 19", NRFB $60.00

Mae West, Effanbee, 1982, Great Legends series, 18", vinyl, MIB...$120.00

Marie Osmond, Mattel, 1976, 11", MIB...........................$50.00

Marie Osmond, Mattel, 1976, 30", MIB $115.00

Marilyn Monroe, DSI, 1993, in 6 different outfits, 11½", NRFB, ea..$60.00

Marilyn Monroe, Tristar, 1982, in 4 different outfits, 16", NRFB, ea..$110.00

Marilyn Monroe, Tristar, 1982, in 8 different outfits, 11½", NRFB, ea..$100.00

Michael Jackson, LJN, 1984, issued in 4 different outfits, 11", NRFB, ea..$60.00

Mr T, Galoob, 1983, 1st issue, bib overalls, 12", MIB.......**$50.00**

Mr T, Galoob, 1983, 2nd issue, talker, vest & jeans outfit, 12", MIB...**$65.00**

New Kids on the Block, 1990, 1st issue, Hangin' Loose, vinyl, 5 different dolls, 12", MIB, ea.......................................**$35.00**

New Kids on the Block, 1990, 2nd issue, In Concert, vinyl, 5 different dolls, 12", MIB, ea.......................................**$45.00**

OJ Simpson, Shindana, Deluxe Set, 1975, w/several outfits & accessories, 9½", MIB...**$250.00**

OJ Simpson, Shindana, 1975, in football uniform, 9½", MIB...**$125.00**

Parker Stevenson (Hardy Boys), Kenner, 1978, 12", NRFB...**$50.00**

Patty Duke (Patty Duke Show), Horsman, 1967, w/phone, 12½", rare, NRFB...**$400.00**

Prince Charles, Goldberger, 1982, palace guard or military wedding outfit, 12", NRFB, ea.......................................**$125.00**

Prince Charles, Peggy Nesbit/England, 1984, wedding outfit, 8", MIB...**$100.00**

Princess Diana, Danbury Mint, 1985, pk dress, 15", MIB ..**$110.00**

Princess Diana, Goldberger, 1982, silver dress or wedding gown, 11½", NRFB, ea.......................................**$125.00**

Princess Diana, Peggy Nesbit/England, 1984, wedding gown, 8", M...**$100.00**

Redd Foxx, Shindana, 1976, 2-sided image, stuffed cloth, MIB...**$35.00**

Redd Foxx, Shindana, 1977, talker, stuffed cloth, MIB....**$45.00**

Rex Harrison (Dr Dolittle), Mattel, 1967, w/Polynesia parrot, 6", NRFB, ea.......................................**$65.00**

Rex Harrison (Dr Dolittle), Mattel, 1967, w/Pushmi-Pullyu & Polynesia, 6", MIB **$90.00**

Rex Harrison (Dr Dolittle), Mattel, 1969, talker, vinyl & cloth, 24", MIB **$130.00**

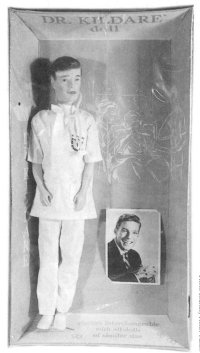

Richard Chamberlain (Dr Kildare), 1962, rare, MIB, $350.00.

Photo courtesy Henri Yunes.

Robert Vaughn (Man From UNCLE), Gilbert, 1965, 12½", MIB...**$215.00**

Robin Williams (Mork & Mindy), Mattel, 1979, pull-string talker, cloth, 16", MIB.......................................**$50.00**

Robin Williams (Mork & Mindy), Mattel, 1979, 4", in egg ship, MIB...**$35.00**

Robin Williams (Mork & Mindy), Mattel, 1979, 9", MIB..**$45.00**

Roger Moore (James Bond in Moonraker), Mego, 1979, 12", MIB, D8...**$100.00**

Roy Rogers & Dale Evans, Dutchess Doll Co (?), 1950s, jtd plastic, pnt hair, 7", EX, J5, ea, from $150 to.................**$200.00**

Sally Field (Flying Nun), Hasbro, 1967, 12", MIB..........**$200.00**

Sally Field (Flying Nun), Hasbro, 1967, 5", MIB.............**$80.00**

Sarah Stimson (Little Miss Marker), Ideal, 1980, 12", MIB..**$40.00**

Shaun Cassidy (Hardy Boys), Kenner, 1978, 12", NRFB..**$50.00**

Shirley Temple, Ideal, 1930s, compo w/orig mohair wig, sleep eyes, orig dress & shoes, 24", some crazing, A **$200.00**

Shirley Temple, Ideal, 1934, Stand Up & Cheer outfit, 15", EX, A...**$700.00**

Shirley Temple, Ideal, 1957, orig bl & pk flocked dress, 12", VG, M15...**$150.00**

Shirley Temple, Ideal, 1972, Stand Up & Cheer outfit, 16", MIB, M15 ....**$160.00**

Shirley Temple, Ideal, 1982, in 6 different outfits, 8", MIB, M15, ea...**$60.00**

Shirley Temple, Ideal, 1984, in Glad Rags to Riches outfit, 16", rare, MIB, M15 ....**$125.00**

Sonny Bono, Mego, 1976, 12", NRFB.............................**$70.00**

Soupy Sales, Sunshine Dolls, 1965, 6", MIB (sealed), J2 ...**$235.00**

Susan Dey (Laurie from Partridge Family), Remco, 1973, rare, MIB...**$250.00**

Suzanne Sommers (Three's Company), Mego, 1975, 12½", MIB...**$65.00**

Sylvester Stallone (Over the Top), Lewco Toys, 1986, 20", NRFB **$35.00**

Sylvester Stallone (Rocky), Phoenix Toys, 1986, 8", NRFB..**$15.00**

Three Stooges, Collins, 1982, set of 3, 13", MOC..........**$140.00**

Twiggy, Mattel, 1967, 11½", rare, MIB **$350.00**

Vanilla Ice, THQ (Toy Headquarters), 1991, issued in 3 different outfits, 12", NRFB, ea.......................................**$35.00**

Vanna White, Pacific Media/Home Shopping Network, 1990, issued in 20 different outfits, 11½", NRFB, ea...........**$50.00**

Vince Edwards (Ben Casey), Bing Crosby Prod, 1962, vinyl, 12", rare, MIB...**$400.00**

Vivian Leigh (Scarlett), World Dolls, 1980, 1st edition, 12", NRFB...**$65.00**

Wayne Gretsky, Mattel, 1982, The Great Gretsky/Le Magnifique, 11½", MIB...**$150.00**

Yvonne De Carlo (Lily Munster), Remco #1822, 1964, MIB ...**$150.00**

CHATTY CATHY

In their book, *Chatty Cathy Dolls, An Identification & Value Guide*, authorities Kathy and Don Lewis (L6) tell us that Chatty Cathy (made by Mattel) has been the second most popular doll ever made. She was introduced in the 1960s and came as either a blond or a brunette. For five years, she sold very well. Much of her success can be attributed to the fact that Chatty Cathy talked. By pulling the string on her back, she could respond with eleven different phrases. During her five years of fame, Mattel added to the line with Chatty Baby, Tiny Chatty Baby and Tiny Chatty Brother (the twins), Charmin' Chatty, and finally Singing' Chatty. Charmin' Chatty had sixteen interchangeable records. Her voice box was activated in the same manner as the above-mentioned dolls, by means of a pull string located at the base of her neck. The line was brought back in 1969, smaller and with a restyled face, but it was not well received.

Advisor: Kathy and Don Lewis (L6).

See Also Coloring, Activity, and Paint Books; Paper Dolls; Puzzles.

Armoire, Chatty Cathy, L6 ....$170.00
Bedspread, Chatty Baby, twin-sz, L6 ....$200.00
Carrying Case, Chatty Baby, pk or bl, L6.............$20.00
Carrying Case, Tiny Chatty Baby, bl or pk, L6 ......$20.00
Cover & Pillow Set, Tiny Chatty Baby, L6 ....$55.00
Crib, Tiny Chatty Baby, MIB, L6 ....$200.00
Doll, Black Chatty Baby, M, L6 ....$325.00
Doll, Black Chatty Baby, w/pigtails, M, L6............$700.00
Doll, Black Chatty Cathy, 1962, pageboy-style hair, M, L6 ....$600.00
Doll, Black Tiny Chatty Baby, M, L6 ....$300.00
Doll, Charmin' Chatty, auburn or blond hair, bl eyes, 1 record, M, L6...$95.00
Doll, Chatty Baby, brunette hair, red pinafore over wht romper, orig tag, MIB, L6 ....$200.00
Doll, Chatty Baby, open speaker, blond hair, bl eyes, M, L6 ..$75.00

Doll, Chatty Baby, open speaker, brunette hair, bl eyes, M, L6 ....$90.00
Doll, Chatty Baby, open speaker, brunette hair, brn eyes, M, L6 .$125.00
Doll, Chatty Cathy, brunette hair, brn eyes, M, L6........$150.00
Doll, Chatty Cathy, later issue, open speaker, blond hair, bl eyes, M, L6 ....$130.00
Doll, Chatty Cathy, later issue, open speaker, brunette hair, bl eyes, M, L6...$150.00
Doll, Chatty Cathy, later issue, open speaker, brunette hair, brn eyes, M, L6...$175.00
Doll, Chatty Cathy, mid-year or transitional, brunette hair, brn eyes, M, L6...$135.00
Doll, Chatty Cathy, mid-year or transitional, brunette hair, bl eyes, M, L6...$125.00
Doll, Chatty Cathy, mid-year or transitional, open speaker, blond hair, bl eyes, M, L6.............................$120.00
Doll, Chatty Cathy, patent pending, brunette hair, bl eyes, M, L6 ....$150.00
Doll, Chatty Cathy, patent pending, cloth over speaker or ring around speaker, blond hair, bl eyes, M, L6..............$150.00
Doll, Chatty Cathy, porcelain, 1980, MIB, L6 ....$700.00

Photo courtesy Kathy Lewis.

Doll, Chatty Cathy, reissue, blond hair, blue eyes, M, $55.00; MIB, $80.00.

Doll, Chatty Cathy, soft face, w/pigtails, blond, brunette or auburn hair, M, L6.............................$200.00
Doll, Chatty Cathy, unmk prototype, brunette hair, bl eyes, M, L6 ....$145.00
Doll, Chatty Cathy, unmk prototype, brunette hair, brn eyes, M, L6 ....$200.00
Doll, Chatty Cathy, unmk prototype, cloth over speaker, blond hair, bl eyes, M, L6 ....$150.00

Doll, early Chatty Baby, blond hair, bl eyes, ring around speaker, M, L6..$90.00

Doll, early Chatty Baby, brunette hair, bl eyes, M, L6......$85.00

Doll, early Chatty Baby, brunette hair, brn eyes, M, L6.$125.00

Doll, Singin' Chatty, blond hair, M, L6........................$100.00

Doll, Singin' Chatty, brunette hair, M, L6 ....$125.00

Doll, Timey Tell, blond hair, bl eyes, M, L6...................$55.00

Doll, Tiny Chatty Baby, blond hair, bl eyes, M, L6 ....$75.00

Doll, Tiny Chatty Baby, brunette hair, bl eyes, M, L6......$90.00

Doll, Tiny Chatty Baby, brunette hair, brn eyes, M, L6.$125.00

Jewelry Set, Chatty Cathy, MIP, L6...............................$150.00

Nursery Set, Chatty Baby, NRFB, L6.............................$150.00

Outfit, Charmin' Chatty, Cinderella, MIP, L6 ....$75.00

Outfit, Charmin' Chatty, Let's Go Shopping, MIP, L6 ....$75.00

Outfit, Charmin' Chatty, Let's Play Birthday Party, MIP, L6 ..$75.00

Outfit, Charmin' Chatty, Let's Play Nurse, MIP, L6 ....$75.00

Outfit, Charmin' Chatty, Let's Play Pajama Party, MIP, L6..$75.00

Outfit, Charmin' Chatty, Let's Play Tea Party, MIP, L6 ..$90.00

Outfit, Charmin' Chatty, Let's Play Together, MIP, L6 ...$75.00

Photo courtesy Kathy Lewis.

Outfit, Chatty Baby, Coverall Set, pink or blue, MIP, L6, $50.00.

Outfit, Chatty Baby, Dots-n-Dash, MIP, L6 ....$125.00

Outfit, Chatty Baby, Leotard set, MIP, L6 ....$75.00

Outfit, Chatty Baby, Outdoors, MIP, L6..........................$75.00

Outfit, Chatty Baby, Party Pink, MIP, L6.......................$100.00

Outfit, Chatty Baby, Playtime, MIP, L6...........................$40.00

Outfit, Chatty Baby, Sleeper set, MIP, L6.......................$50.00

Outfit, Chatty Cathy, Nursery School, MIP, L6 ....$85.00

Outfit, Chatty Cathy, Party Coat, MIP, L6......................$90.00

Outfit, Chatty Cathy, Party Dress, bl gingham, MIP, L6 ..$150.00

Outfit, Chatty Cathy, Pink Peppermint Stick, MIP, L6.$150.00

Outfit, Chatty Cathy, Sleepytime, MIP, L6 ....$80.00

Outfit, Chatty Cathy, Sunday Visit, MIP, L6 ....$150.00

Outfit, Chatty Cathy, Sunny Day, MIP, L6 ....$150.00

Outfit, Tiny Chatty Baby, Bye-Bye, MIP, L6 ....$60.00

Outfit, Tiny Chatty Baby, Fun Time, MIP, L6 ....$100.00

Outfit, Tiny Chatty Baby, Night-Night, MIP, L6............$60.00

Outfit, Tiny Chatty Baby, Party Dress, bl gingham, MIP, L6...$150.00

Outfit, Tiny Chatty Baby, Pink Frill, MIP, L6 ....$80.00

Pattern, Chatty Baby, uncut, L6.......................................$15.00

Pattern, Chatty Cathy, uncut, L6......................................$15.00

Pencil-Point Bed, Chatty Cathy, L6 ....$200.00

Play Hats, Charmin' Chatty, L6 ....$55.00

Play Table, Chatty Baby, L6...$150.00

Stroll-a-Buggy, Chatty Baby, 9-way, complete, L6 ....$225.00

Stroller, Chatty Cathy, 5-way, complete, L6 ....$175.00

Stroller, Chatty Walk'n Talk, L6 ....$175.00

Tea Cart, Chatty Cathy, w/2 trays, L6 ....$100.00

Teeter-Totter, Tiny Chatty Baby Twins, L6..................$250.00

DAWN

Dawn and her friends were made by Deluxe Topper, ca 1970s. They're becoming highly collectible, especially when mint in the box. Dawn was a 6" fashion doll, part of a series sold as the Dawn Model Agency. They were issued in boxes already dressed in clothes of the highest style, or you could buy additional outfits, many complete with matching shoes and accessories.

Advisor: Dawn Parrish (P2).

Case, Irwin Toy Ltd. 1970, vinyl, EX, $25.00.

Dawn's Apartment, complete w/furniture, MIB................$50.00

Doll, Dancing Angie, NRFB...$30.00

Doll, Dancing Dale, NRFB...$50.00

Doll, Dancing Gary, NRFB...$40.00

Doll, Dancing Glory, NRFB $30.00

Doll, Dancing Jessica, NRFB...$30.00

Doll, Dancing Van, NRFB..$50.00

Doll, Daphne, Dawn Model Agency, gr & silver dress, NRFB $75.00

Doll, Dawn Head to Toe, pk & silver dress, NRFB, P2 ....$90.00

Dolls, Dancing Dawn, NRFB, $30.00; Dancing Ron, NRFB, $40.00.

Doll, Dawn Majorette, NRFB...$75.00
Doll, Denise, NRFB $75.00
Doll, Dinah, NRFB $75.00
Doll, Gary, NRFB $30.00
Doll, Jessica, NRFB...$30.00
Doll, Kevin, EX...$15.00
Doll, Kip Majorette, NRFB $45.00

Doll, Longlocks, NRFB, $30.00.

Doll, Maureen, Dawn Model Agency, red & gold dress, MIB, P2...$75.00
Doll, Ron, NRFB $30.00
Outfit, Bell Bottom Bounce, #0717, pants & top, EX, P2 ..$8.00
Outfit, Blubelle, #0722, dress & wrap, G, P2 ....$5.00
Outfit, Bouffant Bubble, #0711, dress & wrap, M, P2.........$8.00
Outfit, Bride, MIP..$25.00

Outfit, City Slicker, #0720, coat, hat & boots, M, P2 ....$8.00
Outfit, Fuchsia Flash, #0612, NRFB, P2............................$30.00
Outfit, Gala Go-Go, #0621, NRFB, P2 ....$30.00
Outfit, Green Slink, dress only, EX, P2.............................$5.00
Outfit, Groovy Baby Groovy, #0620, NRFB, P2...............$30.00
Outfit, Neat Pleats, #0710, dress, M, P2 ....$6.00
Outfit, Pajama Drama, top & pants, P2 ....$10.00
Outfit, Party Puffery, #0712, dress, M, P2.........................$8.00
Outfit, Pink Slink, #8122, NRFB, P2................................$30.00
Outfit, Silver Sparkler, #8120, NRFB, P2 ....$25.00
Outfit, Silver Starlight, #0719, dress, M, P2......................$6.00
Outfit, Silverbeam Dream, #0714, dress & wrap, M, P2 .....$8.00
Outfit, Singin' in the Rain, #0724, coat, scarf & boots, M, P2...$8.00
Outfit, Wedding Belle Dream, NRFB, P2 ....$30.00

FLATSYS

Flatsy dolls were a product of the Ideal Novelty and Toy Company. They were produced from 1968 until 1970 in 2", 5", and 8" sizes. There was only one boy in the 5" line; all were dressed in '70s fashions, and not only clothing but accessory items such as bicycles were made as well.

In 1994 Justoys reissued Mini Flatsys. They were sold alone or with accessories such as bikes, rollerblades and jet skis.

Advisor: Dawn Parrish (P2).

Baby Flatsy, EX, P2 ....$10.00
Bonnie Flatsy, sailing, NRFB (tear in cellophane), P2 .....$55.00
Candy Mountain Flatsy, lavender ice cream truck w/pk wheels, P2 ....$15.00
Cory Flatsy, print mini-dress, NRFB, P2 ....$60.00
Dale Fashion Flatsy, hot pk maxi, NRFB, P2 ....$60.00
Dale Fashion Flatsy, 2-pc wet-look outfit, NRFB, P2 ....$60.00
Fall Mini Flatsy Collection, NRFB, P2.............................$65.00
Filly Flatsy, doll only, outfit slightly faded, P2 ....$10.00
Flatsy in Locket/Frame, 5", MIP $50.00

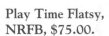

Play Time Flatsy, NRFB, $75.00.

Flatsy Townhouse, house only, P2.....................................$35.00

Gwen Fashion Flatsy, gr hair, peach poncho & boots, 9", NRFB, P2...$65.00

Munch-Time Flatsy Clock, NRFB, P2 ....$75.00

Munch-Time Flatsys, Lemonade Flatsys, boy or girl, ea....$10.00

Nancy Flatsy, nurse w/baby carriage, EX, P2 ....$15.00

Rally Flatsy, w/car in picture fr, VG, M15...........................$35.00

Sandy Flatsy, beach outfit, NRFB, P2 ....$50.00

Spinderella Flatsy, doll only, EX, P2 ....$20.00

Summer Mini Flatsy Collection, NRFB, P2 ....$65.00

GERBER BABIES

The first Gerber Baby dolls were manufactured in 1936. These dolls were made of cloth and produced by an unknown manufacturer. Since that time, six different companies working with leading artists, craftsmen, and designers have attempted to capture the charm of the winsome baby in the charcoal drawing done by Dorothy Hope Smith of her friend's baby, Ann Turner (Cook). This drawing became known as the Gerber Baby and was adopted as the trademark of the Gerber Products Company, located in Fremont, Michigan. For further information see *Gerber Baby Dolls and Advertising Collectibles* by Joan S. Grubaugh.

Advisor: Joan S. Grubaugh (G8).

Amsco, 1972-73, vinyl, pk & wht rosebud sleeper, 10", MIB, G8..$65.00

Amsco, 1972-73, vinyl, plastic pants & bib-type shirt, 14", EX, G8..$35.00

Amsco, 1972-73, vinyl, 2-pc dress w/shoes & socks, 14", EX, G8..$40.00

Arrow Rubber & Plastic Corp, 1965-67, footed clown pajamas, 14", VG, G8..$45.00

Atlanta Novelty, Bathtub Baby, 1985, vinyl, 12", complete with accessories, MIB, G8, $85.00.

Arrow Rubber & Plastic Corp, 1965-67, jeans & shirt, 14", VG, G8..$45.00

Atlanta Novelty, 1978, 50th Anniversary, stuffed body w/vinyl head, arms & legs, eyelet skirt & bib, 17", NRFB, G8 ..$95.00

Atlanta Novelty, 1979, flowered bed jacket w/matching pillow & coverlet, 17", NRFB, G8 ....$95.00

Atlanta Novelty, 1979, zipper snowsuit w/matching hood, 17", NRFB, G8..$95.00

Atlanta Novelty, 1979-81, w/'mama' voice, several different outfits, 17", NRFB, G8, ea...$100.00

Atlanta Novelty, 1981, porcelain w/soft body, wht eyelet christening gown, limited edition, 14", NRFB, G8 ....$350.00

Atlanta Novelty, 1981, stuffed body w/vinyl head, arms & legs, pk checked bodysuit w/lacy skirt & bib, 17", NRFB, G8..$90.00

Atlanta Novelty, 1985, foam-filled, several different outfits, complete w/tub & accessories, 12", EX, G8, ea..........$45.00

Lucky Ltd, 1989, Birthday Party Twins, 6", NRFB, G8 ....$40.00

Lucky Ltd, 1989, vinyl w/soft body, wht christening gown, 16", EX, G8 ....$30.00

Sun Rubber, 1955-58, red polka-dot dress, 12", VG, G8 ..$65.00

Sun Rubber, 1955-58, 2-pc pajamas, 12", VG, G8.............$65.00

Toy Biz, 1994, Potty Time Baby, vinyl, 15", NRFB, G8 ...$25.00

Toy Biz, 1995, Lullaby Baby, plays Brahms' Lullaby, vinyl w/soft body, 11", NRFB, G8..$25.00

HOLLY HOBBIE

Sometime around 1970 a young homemaker and mother, Holly Hobbie, approached the American Greeting Company with some charming country-styled drawings of children. Her concepts were well received by the company, and since that time over four hundred Holly Hobbie items have been produced, nearly all marked HH, H. Hobbie, or Holly Hobbie. See also Clubs and Newsletters.

Advisor: Helen McCale (M13).

Bake-a-Craft Kit, complete w/3 diecast molds, MIB $6.00

Bookcase/Toy Chest, Holly Hobbie & Heather decal, 1976, VG $35.00

Cash Register, Holly Hobbie, VG $12.00

Cast'n Paint Set, MIB..$10.00

Country Hutch Kit, MIB $8.00

Doll, Country Fun Holly Hobbie, 1989, 16", NRFB.........$20.00

Doll, Grandma Holly, Knickerbocker, cloth, 14", MIB $15.00

Doll, Grandma Holly, Knickerbocker, cloth, 24", MIB $25.00

Doll, Holiday Holly Hobbie, 1988, berry scented, w/clear ornament around neck, 18", NRFB $35.00

Doll, Holly Hobbie, Heather, Amy or Carrie, Knickerbocker, cloth, 27", MIB, ea...$30.00

Doll, Holly Hobbie, Heather, Amy or Carrie, Knickerbocker, cloth, 6", MIB, ea...$6.00

Doll, Holly Hobbie, Heather, Amy or Carrie, Knickerbocker, cloth, 9", MIB, ea...$10.00

Doll, Holly Hobbie, Heather, Amy or Carrie, Knickerbocker, cloth, 16", MIB, ea...$20.00

Doll, Holly Hobbie, Heather, Amy or Carrie, Knickerbocker, cloth, 33", MIB, ea...$40.00

Doll, Holly Hobbie Bicentennial, Knickerbocker, cloth, 12", MIB $25.00

Doll, Holly Hobbie Day 'N Night, Knickerbocker, cloth, 14", MIB $15.00

Doll, Holly Hobbie Talker, Knickerbocker, cloth, 4 sayings, 16", MIB $25.00

Doll, Little Girl Holly, Knickerbocker, 1980, cloth, 15", MIB..$25.00

Doll, Robby, Knickerbocker, cloth, 1981, 16", MIB $25.00

Doll, Robby, Knickerbocker, cloth, 9", MIB $15.00

Doll Making Kit, Heather, complete, EXIB, B10.............$10.00

Earrings, bl cameo, sterling silver $18.00

Gazebo Garden House, 1976, hinged cb sides open to 25" play area, VG..$25.00

Pendant, bl cameo, sterling silver.....................................$24.00

Pendant, lg bl girl, sterling silver......................................$22.00

Phonograph w/Gramophone Horn, Holly Hobbie decal, battery-op & electric, 1976, VG.......................................$30.00

Playset, Holly Hobbie doll w/house, rocker, hobbyhorse & doghouse, MIP $15.00

Radio, Holly Hobbie sitting in rocking chair, plastic base, VG $20.00

Radio, old style w/Holly Hobbie standing at side, VG......$20.00

Radio, Sing-A-Long, w/microphone, battery-op, 4¾x6¾x2", VG $20.00

Stickpin, Lang, sterling silver $14.00

Swiss Chalet Hutch Kit, MIB, from $8 to $10.00

Table & Chairs, Holly Hobbie decal, 1976, 3-pc set, VG...$50.00

Tote Bag, Heather, old-time print, VG..............................$6.00

Tote Bag, Holly Hobbie, patchwork print, VG..................$6.00

Trinket Box, porcelain, egg shape, various designs, sm, ea .$6.00

Typewriter, Hollie Hobbie, 1977, VG...............................$12.00

JEM

The glamorous life of Jem mesmerized little girls who watched her Saturday morning cartoons, and she was a natural as a fashion doll. Hasbro saw the potential in 1985 when they introduced the Jem line of 12" dolls representing her, the rock stars from Jem's musical group, the Holograms, and other members of the cast, including the only boy, Rio, Jem's road manager and Jerrica's boyfriend. Each doll was posable, jointed at the waist, head, and wrists, so that they could be positioned at will with their musical instruments and other accessory items. Their clothing, their makeup, and their hairdos were wonderfully exotic, and their faces were beautifully modeled. The Jem line was discontinued in 1987 after being on the market for only two years. Our values are given for mint-in-box dolls. All loose dolls are valued at about $8.00 each.

Accessory, Jem Roadster, AM/FM radio in trunk, scarce, EX.$150.00

Accessory, Jem Soundstage, Starlight House #17, from $40 to.$50.00

Aja, bl hair, complete, MIB..$40.00

Ashley, curly blond hair, w/stand, 11", MIB $25.00

Banee, waist-length straight blk hair, w/stand, 11", MIB..$25.00

Clash, straight purple hair, complete, MIB $40.00

Danse, pk & blond hair, invents dance routines, MIB......$40.00

Jem/Jerrica, Glitter & Gold, complete, MIB $50.00

Jetta, blk hair w/silver streaks, complete, MIB $40.00

Kimber, red hair, complete w/cassette, instrument & poster, MIB..$40.00

Krissie, dk skin w/brn curly hair, complete, 11", MIB.......$25.00

Pizzaz (Misfits), chartreuse hair, complete, MIB $40.00

Raya, pk hair, complete, MIB...$40.00

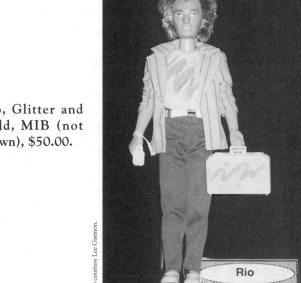

Rio, Glitter and Gold, MIB (not shown), $50.00.

Photo courtesy Lee Garmon.

Roxy, blond hair, complete, MIB $40.00

Shana, member of the Holograms Band, purple hair, complete, M, from $30 to $40.00

Stormer, curly bl hair, complete, MIB................................$40.00

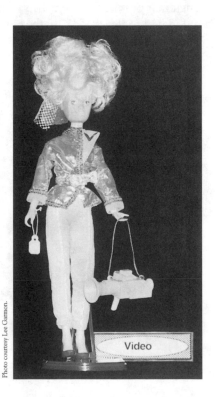

Video, MIB (not shown), from $30.00 to $40.00.

Photo courtesy Lee Garmon.

LIDDLE KIDDLES

From 1966 to 1971, Mattel produced Liddle Kiddle dolls and accessories, typical of the 'little kid next door.' They were made in sizes ranging from a tiny ¾" up to 4". They were all posable and had rooted hair that could be restyled. Eventually there were Animiddles and Zoolery Jewelry Kiddles, which were of course animals, and two other series that represented storybook and nursery-rhyme characters. There was a set of extraterrestrials, and lastly in 1979, Sweet Treets dolls were added to the assortment.

In the mid-1970s Mattel reissued Lucky Locket Kiddles. The dolls had names identical to the earlier lockets but were not of the same high quality.

In 1994-95 Tyco reissued Liddle Kiddles in strap-on, clip-on, Lovely Locket, Pretty Perfume, and baby bottle collections.

As a rule, loose dolls, if complete and with all their original accessories, are worth about 50% less than the same mint in the box. Dressed, loose dolls with no accessories are worth 75% less. For more information, refer to *Little Kiddles, Identification and Value Guide*, by Paris Langford (Collector Books).

Advisor: Dawn Parrish (P2).

Other Sources: S14

Anabelle Autodiddle, #3770, complete, M, P2.................$40.00
Apple Blossom Kologne, #3707, complete, P2..................$25.00
Apple Blossom Kologne, #3707, missing cap, P2 ....$15.00
Babe Biddle, #3505, missing windshield, P2 ....$45.00
Baby Din-Din, #3820, complete, M, P2 ....$60.00
Beddy-Bye Biddle, #3548, missing bedposts, P2................$40.00
Blue Beauty, #3585, MIP, P2......................................$35.00
Bunson Burnie, #3501, figure & fire truck only, M, P2 ....$30.00
Bunson Burnie, #3501, missing shoes, M, P2 ....$50.00
Calamity Jiddle, #3506, complete, M, P2.........................$65.00
Case, Kiddles Collector's Case, #3569, lt pk background, few
   melt mks & torn insert o/w EX, P2 ....$20.00
Case, Liddle Kiddles, #3531, hatbox style w/hdl, zipper closure,
   bl or purple, EX, P2, ea..$30.00

Case, Liddle Kiddles, #3567, rectangular w/zipper closure, gr or
   pk, EX, P2, ea...$35.00
Cook'n, outfit, #LK8, Totsy, MIP, P2 ....$35.00
Dainty Deer, #3637, complete, M, P2 ....$40.00
Florence Niddle, #3507, complete, M, P2.........................$65.00
Florence Niddle, #3507, missing baby, P2.........................$50.00

Flower Bracelet, #3747, MIP, $25.00.

Flower Pin, #3741, complete, P2 ....$20.00
Flower Pin Kiddle, #3741, MIP, P2 ....$45.00
Freezy Sliddle, #3516, complete, M, P2.............................$45.00
Goofy Skediddler, #3627, MIP, P2 ....$70.00
Greta Grape, #3728, complete, M, P2................................$45.00
Greta Griddle, #3508, missing few pcs, EX, P2 ....$40.00
Heart Bracelet, #3747, complete, P2 ....$15.00
Heart Charm Bracelet Jewelry Kiddle, #3747, MIP, P2....$25.00

Clown'n Play Outfit, #LK4, MIP, $35.00.

Liddle Middle Muffet and Her Spider, #3545, complete, M, $75.00.

Heart Ring, #3744, complete, P2 ....$15.00
Henrietta Horseless Carriage, #3641, doll only, P2 ....$15.00
Honeysuckle Kologne, #3704, complete, P2 ....$25.00
Howard Biff Boodle, #3502, complete, M, P2 ....$65.00
Kiddle Komedy Theatre, #3592, MIP, P2 ....$25.00
Kleo Kola, #3729, complete, M, P2 ....$45.00
Lady Silver, #A3840, NRFP, P2 ....$100.00
Laffy Lemon, #3732, complete, P2 ....$45.00
Larky Locket, #3539, P2 ....$25.00
Laverne Locket, #3678, gold frame, P2 ....$35.00
Liddle Diddle, #3503, complete, M, P2 ....$55.00
Liddle Kiddles Klub, #3521, torn flap o/w EX, P2 ....$20.00
Liddle Kiddles Kolony, #3571, M, P2 ....$25.00
Liddle Middle Muffet, #3545, doll & pillow, P2 ....$30.00
Liddle Red Riding Hiddle, #3546, doll only, G, P2 ....$45.00
Lilac Locket, #3540, P2 ....$25.00
Lily of the Valley Kologne, #3706, complete, P2 ....$25.00
Lola Liddle, #3504, complete, boat broken where sail goes in o/w
    EX, P2 ....$40.00
Lolli-Grape, #3656, complete, P2 ....$55.00
Lolli-Grape, #3656, doll only, P2 ....$15.00
Lolli-Mint, #3658, complete, P2 ....$45.00
Lorelei Locket, #3677, gold frame, P2 ....$35.00
Lorelei Locket, #3717, 1976 remake, MIP, P2 ....$25.00
Loretta Locket, #3722, 1976 remake, MIP, P2 ....$25.00
Lottie Locket, #3719, 1976 remake, MIP, P2 ....$25.00
Lou Locket, #3535, doll only, P2 ....$25.00
Lou Locket, #3537, MIP, P2 ....$75.00
Louise Locket, #3681, gold frame, P2 ....$35.00
Louise Locket, #3721, P2 ....$25.00
Luanna Locket, #3680, P2 ....$35.00
Luscious Lime, #3733, doll only, P2 ....$10.00
Miss Mouse, #3638, complete, M, P2 ....$40.00
Nappytime Baby, #3818, complete, M, P2 ....$75.00
Nurse'n, outfit, #LK7, Totsy, name sticker missing, MIP, P2 ...$30.00
Orange Ice Kone, #3654, complete, M, P2 ....$40.00

Out'n, outfit, #LK6, Totsy, MIP, P2 ....$35.00
Peter Paniddle, #3547, doll only, P2 ....$30.00
Pink Funny Bunny, #3532, complete, P2 ....$25.00
Pretty Priddle, #3549, doll, vanity & stool, M, P2 ....$55.00
Sheila Skediddle, #3765, missing shoes, P2 ....$20.00
Shirley Skediddle, #3766, complete, M, P2 ....$25.00
Shirley Strawberry, #3727, complete, M, P2 ....$40.00
Shop'N, outfit, #LK2, Totsy, MIP, P2 ....$35.00
Sizzly Friddle, #3515, missing spatula & polka-dot dress, P2 ...$50.00
Sleep'n, outfit, #LK5, Totsy, MIP, P2 ....$35.00
Sleeping Biddle, #3527, doll only, P2 ....$30.00
Slipsy Sliddle, #3754, doll & slide, M, P2 ....$50.00
Snap Happy Patio Furniture, #5171, complete, P2 ....$10.00
Snap Happy Patio Furniture, #5171, MIP, P2 ....$35.00
Suki Skediddle, #3767, complete, M, P2 ....$25.00
Suki Skediddler, #3767, MIP, P2 ....$50.00
Surfy Skiddle, #3517, complete, M, P2 ....$65.00
Sweet Pea Kologne, #3705, complete, P2 ....$25.00
Telly Viddle, #3751, complete, M, P2 ....$75.00
Teresa Touring Car, #3644, complete, M, P2 ....$65.00
Tiny Tiger, #3636, complete, M, P2 ....$40.00
Trikey Triddle, #3515, floral dress, missing seatbelt & shoes,
    P2 ....$45.00
Trikey Triddle, #3515, red dress, missing seatbelt, P2 ......$75.00
Tutti Frutti Kone, #3655, complete, P2 ....$45.00
Vanilly Lilly, #2819, MIP, P2 ....$25.00
Violet Kologne, #3703, complete, P2 ....$25.00
Windy Fliddle, #3514, missing goggles & map, P2 ....$40.00

LITTLECHAPS

In 1964 Remco Industries created a family of four fashion dolls that represented an upper-middle class American family. The Littlechaps family consisted of the father, Dr. John Littlechap, his wife, Lisa, and their two children, Judy and Libby. Their clothing and fashion accessories were made in Japan and are of the finest quality. Because these dolls are not as pretty as other fashion dolls of the era and their size and placement of arms and legs made them awkward to dress, children had little interest in them at the time. This lack of interest during the 1960s has created shortages of them for collectors of today. Mint and complete outfits or outfits never-removed-from-box are especially desirable to Littlechap collectors. Values listed for loose clothing are for ensembles complete with all their small accessories. If only the main pieces of the outfit are available, then the value could go down significantly.

Advisor: Cindy Sabulis (S14).

Doll, Doctor John, EX, S14 ....$25.00
Doll, Doctor John, NRFB, S14 ....$60.00
Doll, Judy, EX, S14 ....$25.00
Doll, Judy, NRFB, S14 ....$65.00
Doll, Libby, EX, S14 ....$20.00
Doll, Libby, NRFB, S14 ....$45.00
Doll, Lisa, EX, S14 ....$25.00
Doll, Lisa, NRFB, S14 ....$60.00
Family Room, Bedroom or Doctor John's Office, EX, S14, ea .$125.00
Outfit, Doctor John, complete, EX, S14, from $25 to $35.00

Orange Meringue, #3585, MIP, $25.00.

Outfit, Doctor John, NRFB, S14, from $30 to $50.00
Outfit, Judy, complete, EX, S14, from $20 to..................$40.00
Outfit, Judy, NRFB, S14, from $25 to $65.00
Outfit, Libby, complete, EX, S14, from $15 to..................$30.00
Outfit, Libby, NRFB, S14, from $30 to $50.00
Outfit, Lisa, complete, EX, S14, from $25 to $40.00
Outfit, Lisa, NRFB, S14, from $40 to..............................$75.00

MATTEL TALKING DOLLS

When a range is given, use the low side to evaluate dolls that have been played with and are non-working. The high side reflects the value of a doll still mint and in the original box.
Advisor: Kathy Lewis (L6).
See also Disney; Character, TV, and Movie Memorabilia.

Baby First Step, MIB, L6 ....$150.00
Baby Secret, 1965, vinyl w/foam body, red hair, pull-string talker, 18", EX...$45.00
Baby See 'N Say, MIB, L6 ....$125.00
Baby Small Talk, MIB, L6 ....$75.00
Matty-Mattel the Talking Boy, MIB, L6........................$200.00
Sister Belle, MIB, L6.......................................$200.00
Sister Small Talk, 1967, plastic & vinyl, rooted blond hair, 10", EX...$30.00
Teachy Keen, MIB, L6 ....$125.00
Timey Tell, MIB, L6...$100.00

ROCKFLOWERS BY MATTEL

Rockflowers were introduced in the early 1970s as Mattel's answer to Topper's Dawn Dolls. Rockflowers are 6½" tall and have wire articulated bodies that came with mod sunglasses attached to their heads. There were four girls and one boy in the series with eighteen groovy outfits that could be purchased separately. Each doll came with their own 45 rpm record, and the clothing packages were also in the shape of a 45 rpm record.
Advisor: Dawn Parrish (P2).

Doll, Heather, #1166, NRFB, P2......................................$35.00

Outfit, Jeans in Fringe, #4052, MOC, $12.00.

Doll, Lilac, #1167, NRFB, P2...$35.00
Doll, Rosemary, #1168, NRFB, P2 ....$45.00
Outfit, Flares 'N Lace, #4057, MOC, P2.............................$12.00
Outfit, Overall Orange, #4065, MOC, P2............................$12.00

STRAWBERRY SHORTCAKE

It was around 1980 when Strawberry Shortcake came on the market with a bang. The line included everything to attract small girls — swimsuits, bed linens, blankets, anklets, underclothing, coats, shoes, sleeping bags, dolls and accessories, games, and many other delightful items. Strawberry Shortcake and her friends were short lived, lasting only until middle of the decade.
Advisor: Geneva Addy (A5).

Bassinet, pk wicker on stand, 18x20", EX $50.00
Bicycle Basket, EX, A5 ....$15.00
Big Berry Trolley, 1982, EX..$35.00
Book Bag, EX, A5 ....$8.00
Cabinet, Wonderful World of Strawberry Shortcake, w/17 scented figures, sm, NM, J6.....................................$75.00
Christmas Tree Lights, MIB, A5 ....$35.00

Clock, 1984, M, $75.00.

Photo courtesy June Moon.

Coat Rack/Growth Chart, wood, reads Good Friends Grow on Each Other on diecut image, EX, A5........................$20.00
Doll, Raspberry Tart, MIB $25.00

Photo courtesy June Moon.

Dolls, Cafe Ole, Mint Tulip, or Almond Tea, MIB, $25.00 each.

Doll, Strawberry Shortcake, strawberry scented, 12", NRFB .$25.00
Doll, Strawberry Shortcake, 15", NM $35.00
Dollhouse $95.00
Figure, Merry Berry Worm, MIB $20.00
Figure, Purple Pieman w/Berry Bird, poseable, MIB.........$30.00
Figure, Sour Grapes w/Drego, MIB $30.00
Night Light, strawberry form, battery-op, EX..................$25.00
Record Cabinet, EX, A5 ....$55.00
Roller Skates, EX, A5 ....$40.00
School Desk, w/attached seat, A5 ....$65.00
School Desk, w/2 shelves, wood, Three Cheers For Fun & image
    on side, EX, A5 ....$65.00
Stroller, Berry Buggy, Coleco, 1981, M, J6......................$85.00

TAMMY

In 1962 the Ideal Novelty and Toy Company introduced their teenage Tammy doll. Slightly pudgy and not quite as sophisticated-looking as some of the teen fashion dolls on the market at the time, Tammy's innocent charm captivated consumers. Her extensive wardrobe and numerous accessories added to her popularity with children. Tammy had a car, a house, and her own catamaran. In addition, a large number of companies obtained licenses to issue products using the 'Tammy' name. Everything from paper dolls to nurse's kits were made with Tammy's image on them. Her success was not confined to the United States; she was also successful in Canada and several other European countries.

Interest in Tammy has risen quite a bit in the past year according to Cindy Sabulis, co-author of *Tammy, the Ideal Teen* (Collector Books). Values have gone up and supply for quality mint-in-box items is going down. Loose, played-with dolls are still readily available and can be found for as low as $10.00 at doll shows. Values are given for mint-in-box dolls. Loose dolls are worth considerably less.

Advisor: Cindy Sabulis (S14).

Doll, Black Grown Up Tammy, MIB, S14, minimum value ..$250.00
Doll, Bud, MIB, S14, minimum value............................$300.00
Doll, Dodi, MIB, S14 ....$75.00
Doll, Glamour Misty the Miss Clairol Doll, MIB, S14 ...$125.00

Doll, Grown Up Tammy, MIB, S14 ....$75.00
Doll, Misty, straight legs, MIB, S14 ....$100.00
Doll, Patti, MIB, S14...$200.00
Doll, Pepper (trimmer body w/smaller face), 1965, MIB, S14...$75.00
Doll, Pepper, MIB, S14...$55.00
Doll, Pepper w/'carrot'-colored hair, MIB, S14 ....$75.00
Doll, Pos'n Dodi, MIB, S14..$150.00
Doll, Pos'n Misty & Her Telephone Booth, MIB, S14...$125.00
Doll, Pos'n Pepper, MIB, S14 ....$75.00
Doll, Pos'n Pepper (trimmer body & smaller face w/poseable
    legs), 1965, MIB, S14..$75.00
Doll, Pos'n Pete, MIB, S14 ....$125.00
Doll, Pos'n Salty, MIB, S14 ....$100.00
Doll, Pos'n Tammy, MIB, S14.......................................$95.00
Doll, Pos'n Tammy & Her Telephone Booth, MIB, S14..$95.00
Doll, Pos'n Ted, MIB, S14..$100.00
Doll, Tammy, MIB, S14..$65.00
Doll, Tammy's Dad, MIB, S14 ....$65.00
Doll, Tammy's Mom, MIB, S14.....................................$65.00
Doll, Ted, MIB, S14..$65.00
Tammy Car, S14, minimum value...................................$75.00
Tammy Cases, S14, ea from $15 to $35.00
Tammy Records, S14, minimum value ea $25.00
Tammy's Ideal House, S14, minimum value...................$100.00

TONKA

The Aurora line of fashion dolls made by Tonka in 1987 are unique in that their Barbie-like bodies are metallic. There were four in the line, Aurora herself, Crysta, Lustra, and Mirra. Their costumes are futuristic, and their eyes are inset, faceted jewels. Their long tresses are shockingly bright — Aurora's is gold, Crysta's is pink, Mirra's blue, and Lustra's lavender. Mattel made a very similar line of dolls; the most notable difference is that they lacked the jewel eyes. Mattel's are dated 1975. Dolls from either series are valued at about $25.00 each, mint in box.

Mirra, MIB (not shown), $25.00.

Dolls, Misty with straight legs (2 on left), Pos'n Misty (2 on right), EX, from $20.00 to $30.00 each.

TRESSY

American Character's Tressy doll was produced in this country from 1963 to 1967. The unique thing about this 11½" fashion doll was that her hair 'grew' by pushing a button on her stomach. Tressy also had a 9" little sister named Cricket. These two dolls had numerous fashions and accessories produced for them. Never-removed-from-box Tressy and Cricket items are rare, so unless indicated, values listed are for loose, mint items. A never-removed-from-box item's worth is at least double the item's loose value.

Advisor: Cindy Sabulis (S14).

Apartment, M, S14...$150.00
Beauty Salon, M, S14 ....$125.00
Case, features Cricket, M, S14 ....$30.00
Case, features Tressy, M, S14 ....$25.00

Cricket, $30.00;
Tressy, $25.00.

Photo courtesy Cindy Sabulis.

Doll, Pre-Teen Tressy, M, S14 ....$75.00
Doll, Tressy in Miss America Character outfit, NM.........$50.00
Doll, Tressy w/Magic Makeup Face, M, S14 ....$20.00
Doll Clothes Pattern, M, S14..$10.00
Gift Paks w/Doll & Clothing, NRFB, S14, minimum value
   ea $100.00
Hair Accessory Paks, NRFB, S14, ea................................$20.00
Hair Dryer, M, S14 ....$40.00
Hair or Cosmetic Accessory Kits, M, S14, minimum value
   ea...$50.00
Millinery, M, S14..$150.00
Outfits, MOC, S14, ea..$25.00
Outfits, NRFB, S14, minimum value ea.............................$40.00

UPSY DOWNSYS BY MATTEL

The Upsy Downsy dolls were made by Mattel during the late 1960s. They were small, 2½" to 3½", made of vinyl and plastic. Some of the group were 'Upsies' that walked on their feet, while others were 'Downsies' that walked or rode fantasy animals while upsidedown.

Advisor: Dawn Parrish (P2).

Baby So-High, #3828, missing playland o/w complete, P4..$50.00
Baby So-High, #3828, playland board only, P2.................$16.00
Downy Dilly, #3832, NRFB, P2 ....$150.00
Downy Dilly, #3832, playland board only, P2 ....$15.00
Flossy Glossy, #3827, doll & playland, P2 ....$25.00
Flossy Glossy, #3827, playland board only, P2 ....$15.00
Miss Information, #3831, NRFB, P2.................................$150.00
Mother What Now, #3829, NRFB, P2.............................$150.00
Pocus Hocus, #3820, playland board only, P2 ....$16.00
Pocus Hocus, #3820, missing playland o/w complete, P2 .$50.00
Pudgy Fudgy, #3826, NRFB, P2.......................................$150.00
Tickle Pickle, #3825, complete w/accessories & board, P2 ...$65.00

Downy Dilly and
Foot Mobile, EX,
$30.00.

Photo courtesy Pat Smith.

Mother What Now
and Go Getter, EX,
$30.00.

Photo courtesy Pat Smith.

Farm Toys

It's entirely probable that more toy tractors have been sold than real ones. They've been made to represent all makes and models, of plastic, cast iron, diecast metal, and even wood. They've been made in at least 1/16th scale, 1/32nd, 1/43rd, and 1/64th. If you buy a 1/16th-scale replica, that small piece of equipment would have to be sixteen times larger to equal the size of the real item. Limited editions (meaning that a specific number will be made and no more) and commemorative editions (made for special events) are usually very popular with collectors. Many models on the market today are being made by the Ertl company.

Advisor: John Rammacher (S5).

See also Cast Iron, Farm.

Agco Allis 6670 Row Crop, Ertl, 1/64th scale, #1214, MIB, S5...$3.50
Agco Allis 6690 Tractor w/Duals, Ertl, 1/64th scale, #1286, MIB, S5 ....$3.50
Agco R-52 Combine, Ertl, 1/64th scale, #1282, MIB, S5 ...$10.00
Allis Chalmers D-19, Ertl, Collectors Edition, 1/16th scale, #2220, MIB, S5 ....$40.00
Allis Chalmers D-19 Tractor, Ertl, 1/43rd scale, #2566, MIB, S5 ....$5.50
Allis Chalmers 220, Ertl, 1/43rd scale, #2336, MIB, S5......$6.00
Big Bud 370 w/Duals, Ertl, 1/64th scale, #4187, MIB, S5.$12.00
Case IH Forage Harvester, Ertl, 1/64th scale, #201, MIB, S5..$2.50
Case IH Gravity Wagon, Ertl, 1/64th scale, #1864, MIB, S5..$2.50
Case IH Hay Rake, Ertl, 1/64th scale, #210, MIB, S5.........$3.00
Case IH Historical Set, Ertl, 1/64th scale, #238, 2 pcs, MIB, S5 ....$5.50
Case IH Milk Truck, Ertl, 1/64th scale, #648, MIB, S5 ......$6.00
Case IH Mixer Mill, Ertl, 1/64th scale, #480, MIB, S5 ....$2.50
Case IH Planter, Ertl, 1/64th scale, #478, MIB, S15...........$2.50
Case IH Round Baler, Ertl, 1/64th scale, #274, MIB, S5 ....$3.50
Case IH Self-Propelled Windrower, Ertl, 1/64th scale, #4405, MIB, S5 ....$8.00
Case IH Tractor w/End Loader, Ertl, 1/64th scale, #212, MIB, S5...$5.00
Case IH 12-Row Planter, Ertl, 900 Series, 1/64th scale, #656, MIB, S5 ....$5.00
Case IH 1586 w/Loader, Ertl, 1/16th scale, #416, MIB, S5 ..$25.00
Case IH 1660 Combine, Ertl, 1/64th scale, #655, MIB, S5..$10.50
Case IH 2188 Combine, Ertl, 1995 Farm Show Edition, 1/64th scale, #4607, MIB, S5 ....$15.00
Case IH 2594 Tractor, Ertl, 1/64th scale, #227, MIB, S5 ...$3.00
Case IH 496 Wing Disk, Ertl, 1/64th scale, #694, MIB, S5..$5.00
Case IH 5130 Row Crop, Ertl, 1991 Farm Show, 1/64th scale, #229, MIB, S5 ....$10.00
Case IH 5131 Row Crop, Ertl, 1/64th scale, #229, MIB, S5 .$3.00
Case IH 7130 Magnum Tractor, Ertl, 1/64th scale, #458, MIB, S5 ....$3.00
Case IH 7140 Mechanical Front Drive Tractor, Ertl, 1/64th scale, #616, MIB, S5 ....$3.50
Case IH 7150 Front Wheel Assist, Ertl, 1992 Farm Show, 1/64th scale, #285, MIB, S5 ....$10.00
Case IH 7220 w/Loader, Ertl, 1/64th scale, #460, MIB, S5.$5.00
Case IH 9260 4-Wheel Drive, Ertl, 1993 Farm Show, 1/64th scale, #231, MIB, S5 ....$10.00
Case L Tractor, Ertl, 1/43rd scale, #2554, MIB, S5 ....$5.50
Case L Tractor, Ertl, 150 Year Collectors Edition, 1/16th scale, #252, MIB, S5 ....$35.00

Case Uniloader, Ertl, 1/64th scale, #455, MIB, S5...............$4.50
Case 800, Ertl, Collectors Edition, 1/16th scale, #693, MIB, S5 ....$40.00
Caterpillar 2-Ton Tractor, Ertl, National Toy Truck Show, 1/16th scale, #2438, MIB, S5 ....$65.00
Caterpillar 32 Ford Panel Truck, Ertl, 1/43rd scale, #7707, MIB, S5 ....$5.50
Cockshut 1655 Tractor, Ertl, 1/16th scale, #4179, MIB, S5..$22.50
Deutz Allis Barge Wagon, Ertl, 1/64th scale, #2241, MIB, S5 ...$2.50
Deutz Allis Mixer Mill, Ertl, 1/64th scale, #2208, MIB, S5...$2.50
Deutz Allis R-50 Combine, Ertl, 1/64th scale, #1284, MIB, S5 ..$13.00
Deutz Allis 6260 Tractor, Ertl, 1/64th scale, #1241, MIB, S5........$2.50
Deutz Allis 7085 Tractor w/Duals, Ertl, 1/64th scale, #2234, MIB, S5 ....$3.50
Deutz Allis 7085 Tractor w/Loader, Ertl, 1/64th scale, #2233, MIB, S5 ....$4.00
Deutz Allis 9150 Orlando Show Tractor, Ertl, 1/16th scale, #1280, MIB, S5 ....$190.00
Farmall F-20, Ertl, 1/16th scale, #260, MIB, S5 ....$18.00
Farmall Super M-T-A Tractor, Ertl, 1/16th scale, #445, MIB, S5 ....$20.00
Farmall 140 Tractor, Ertl, 1995 Farm Show Edition, 1/16th scale, #4741, MIB, S5 ....$35.00
Farmall 650 Tractor, Ertl, 1/16th scale, #246, MIB, S5 ....$22.00
Ford F Tractor, Ertl, Collectors Edition, 1/16th scale, #872, MIB, S5 ....$45.00
Ford F-250 Pick-Up w/Livestock Trailer, Ertl, 1/64th scale, #311, MIB, S5 ....$5.00
Ford F-250 Pick-Up w/Trailer, Ertl, 1/64th scale, #328, MIB, S5 ....$5.00
Ford Harvest Heritage Cards w/Tractor, Ertl, 1/64th scale, #809, MIB, S5 ....$10.00
Ford New Holland Hay Rake, Ertl, 1/64th scale, #369, MIB, S5...$3.00
Ford New Holland TR-97 Combine, Ertl, 1/64th scale, #815, MIB, S5 ....$10.00
Ford Pick-Up, 1940, Ertl, 50th Anniversary, 1/25th scale, #F019, MIB, S5 ....$22.00
Ford Precision Classic 2N, Ertl, 1/16th scale, #354, MIB, S5...$95.00
Ford Precision Classic 8N, Ertl, 1/16th scale, #352, MIB, S5...$95.00
Ford Tractor w/Loader, Ertl, 1/64th scale, #897, MIB, S5 ..$5.00
Ford 5640 w/Loader, Ertl, 1/64th scale, #334, MIB, S5.......$4.00
Ford 6640 Row Crop, Ertl, 1/64th scale, #332, MIB, S5 .....$3.50
Ford 7740 Row Crop, Ertl, Collectors Edition, 1/16th scale, #873, MIB, S5 ....$50.00
Ford 7740 w/Loader, Ertl, 1/64th scale, #387, MIB, S5.......$4.50
Ford 7740 w/4-Wheel Drive, Ertl, 1/64th scale, #333, MIB, S5...$4.00
Ford 7840 w/Duals, Ertl, 1/64th scale, #335, MIB, S5.........$3.00
Ford 8N Tractor, Ertl, 1/16th scale, #843, MIB, S5 ....$20.00
Ford 8240 Tractor w/4-Wheel Drive, Ertl, 1/64th scale, #389, MIB, S5 ....$4.00
Ford 8340 w/Duals, Ertl, 1/64th scale, #388, MIB, S5.........$3.50
Ford 8340 w/4-Wheel Drive, Ertl, Collectors Edition, 1/16th scale, #877, MIB, S5 ....$50.00
Ford 8730 Tractor w/Loader, Ertl, 1/64th scale, #303, MIB, S5 .$4.50
Ford 8830 Tractor w/Front Wheel Drive Assist, Ertl, 1/64th scale, #854, MIB, S5 ....$3.00

Ford 9N, Ertl, 1/64th scale, #926, MIB, S5 ....$3.50

Ford 901 Dealer Demo Tractor, Ertl, Collectors Edition, 1/16th scale, #363, MIB, S5 ....$38.00

Ford 901 Power Master Tractor, Ertl, 1/64th scale, #927, MIB, S5 ....$3.50

Fordson Model F Tractor, Ertl, 1/16th scale, #301, MIB, S5..$18.00

Fordson Tractor, Ertl, 1/43rd scale, #2526, MIB, S5 ....$5.50

Genesis 8870 Tractor w/4-Wheel Drive, Ertl, 1/64th scale, #392, MIB, S5 ....$3.50

Hesston Forage Harvester, Ertl, 1/64th scale, #2262, MIB, S5..$2.50

Hesston Round Baler, Ertl, 1/64th scale, #2263, MIB, S5 ..$3.00

Hesston SL-30 Skidsteer Loader, Ertl, 1/64th scale, #2267, MIB, S5 ....$4.50

Heston 8400 Self-Propelled Windrower, Ertl, 1/64th scale, #2261, MIB, S5 ....$8.00

IH Anhydrous Ammonia Tank, Ertl, 1/64th scale, #1550, MIB, S5 ....$2.50

IH Cub, Ertl, 1976 Collectors Edition, yel, 1/16th scale, #653, MIB, S5 ....$36.00

International Cub Tractor, Ertl, 1964-76, 1/16th scale, MIB, $18.00.

International 1066 Rops, Ertl, MIB, $350.00.

IH Farmall Cub, 1964-76, Ertl, 1/16th scale, #653, MIB, S5..$18.00

IH Farmall M-T-A, Ertl, 1/43rd scale, #4263, MIB, S5 ......$5.50

IH I-D9 Tractor, Ertl, 1993 Farm Show Edition, 1/16th scale, #4611, MIB, S5 ....$36.00

IH Wing Disk, Ertl, 1/64th scale, #1862, MIB, S5 ....$2.50

IH 1568 V-8 Tractor w/Duals, Ertl, Collectors Edition, 1/16th scale, #4630, MIB, S5 ....$40.00

International 600 Diesel Tractor, Ertl, 1/16th scale, #282, MIB, S5 ....$20.00

John Deere Bale Processor, Ertl, 1/64th scale, #5568, MIB, S5 ....$2.50

John Deere Bale Throw Wagon, Ertl, 1/64th scale, #5755, MIB, S5 ....$3.50

John Deere Barge Wagon, Ertl, 1/64th scale, #5529, MIB, S5..$2.50

John Deere Combine, Ertl, 1/64th scale, #5604, MIB, S5...$10.00

John Deere Compact Utility Tractor, Ertl, 1/16th scale, #581, MIB, S5 ....$16.00

John Deere Cotton Picker, Ertl, 1/80th scale, #1000, MIB, S5 ....$6.50

John Deere Fertilizer Spreader, Ertl, 1/64th scale, #5558, MIB, S5 ....$3.00

John Deere Forage Harvester, Ertl, 1/64th scale, #566, MIB, S5 ....$3.00

John Deere GP Standard, Ertl, Collectors Edition, 1/16th scale, #5767, MIB, S5 ....$35.00

John Deere GP Wide Tread, Ertl, Collectors Edition, 1/16th scale, #5798, MIB, S5 ....$36.00

John Deere GP Wide Tread, Ertl, 1/16th scale, #5787, MIB, S5 ....$25.00

John Deere Grain Cart, Ertl, 1/64th scale, #5565, MIB, S5 ..$3.50

John Deere Grain Drill, Ertl, 1/64th scale, #5528, MIB, S5 ..$3.00

John Deere Gravity Wagon, Ertl, 1/64th scale, #5552, MIB, S5 ....$3.00

John Deere Hay Rake, Ertl, 1/64th scale, #5751, MIB, S5..$3.50

John Deere Historical Set, Ertl, 1/64th scale, #5523, 4 pcs, MIB, S5 ....$10.00

John Deere Historical Set, Ertl, 1/64th scale, #5665, 2 pcs, MIB, S5 ....$6.00

John Deere Hydra-Push Spreader, Ertl, 1/64th scale, #574, MIB, S5 ....$2.50

John Deere MC Crawler, Ertl, 1/16th scale, #JDM-076, MIB, S5 ....$45.00

John Deere Model A, Ertl, 1/43rd scale, #5598, MIB, S5 ...$5.50

John Deere Model A Tractor, Ertl, 1/16th scale, #539, MIB, S5 ....$18.00

John Deere Road Grater, Ertl, M, $25.00.

John Deere Model LI Tractor, Ertl, 1/16th scale, #21056, MIB, S5 ....$28.00

John Deere Model 70 Precision Classic, Ertl, 1/16th scale, #5788, MIB, S5 ....$100.00

John Deere Mower Conditioner, Ertl, 1/64th scale, #5657, MIB, S5 ....$3.00

John Deere Mulch Master Tillage Plow, Ertl, 1/64th scale, #5727, MIB, S5 ....$5.00

John Deere Mulch Tiller, Ertl, 1/64th scale, #578, MIB, S5 ..$3.50

John Deere Overtime Tractor, Ertl, 1/16th scale, #5811, MIB, S5 ....$24.00

John Deere Rotary Cutter, Ertl, 1/64th scale, #5600, MIB, S5........$3.50

John Deere Rotary Mower, Ertl, 1/16th scale, #20098, MIB, S5 ..$22.00

John Deere Row Crop, Ertl, 1/64th scale, #5571, MIB, S5 .$2.50

John Deere Skid Loader, Ertl, 1/64th scale, #5536, MIB, S5..$4.50

John Deere Skid Steer Loader, Ertl, 1/16th scale, #569, MIB, S5 ....$18.00

John Deere Skid Steer Loader, Ertl, 1/64th scale, #5622, MIB, S5 ....$4.50

John Deere Sprayer, Ertl, 1/64th scale, #5553, MIB, S5 .....$3.00

John Deere Tractor w/Duals, Ertl, 1/64th scale, #5606, MIB, S5 ....$3.50

John Deere Tractor w/Loader, Ertl, 1/64th scale, #5613, MIB, S5 ....$4.50

John Deere Utility Tractor, Ertl, 1/16th scale, #516, MIB, S5 ..$14.50

John Deere Utility Tractor w/Loader, Ertl, 1/16th scale, #517, MIB, S5 ....$20.00

John Deere Waterloo Engine, Ertl, 1/16th scale, #5645, MIB, S5 ....$20.00

John Deere 12-A Combine, Ertl, Collectors Edition, 1/16th scale, #5601, MIB, S5 ....$44.00

John Deere 12-A Combine, Ertl, 1/16th scale, #5601, MIB, S5 ....$24.00

John Deere 12-Row Planter, Ertl, 1/64th scale, #576, MIB, S5 ....$4.50

John Deere 1930 GP Tractor, Ertl, 1/16th scale, #5801, MIB, S5 ....$25.00

John Deere 1949 Model AR Tractor, Ertl, 1/16th scale, #5680, MIB, S5 ....$25.00

John Deere 2640, Ertl, Field of Dreams Collection, 1/16th scale, #516, MIB, S5 ....$40.00

John Deere 3010, Ertl, Collectors Edition, 1/16th scale, #5635, MIB, S5 ....$38.00

John Deere 3010 Tractor, Ertl, 1/16th scale, #5635, MIB, S5 ....$20.00

John Deere 348 Rectangular Baler, Ertl, 1/64th scale, #5646, MIB, S5 ....$3.50

John Deere 4010 Diesel, Ertl, 1994 National Toy Show, 1/43rd scale, #5725, MIB, S5 ....$25.00

John Deere 4010 Diesel Tractor, Ertl, 1/16th scale, #5716, MIB, S5 ....$24.00

John Deere 4010 Tractor, Ertl, 1/43rd scale, #5725, MIB, S5 .$6.00

John Deere 4020 Precision #3, Ertl, 1/16th scale, #5638, MIB, S5 ....$95.00

John Deere 494-A 4-Row Planter Precision Classic, Ertl, 1/16th scale, #5838, MIB, S5 ....$125.00

John Deere 535 Round Baler, Ertl, 1/64th scale, #577, MIB, S5...$3.00

John Deere 630 LP Tractor, Ertl, 1/43rd scale, #5599, MIB, S5...$5.50

John Deere 6400 Mechanical Front Wheel Drive, Ertl, Collectors Edition, 1/16th scale, #5667, MIB, S5 ....$36.00

John Deere 6400 Row Crop, Ertl, Collectors Edition, 1/16th scale, #5666, MIB, S5 ....$38.00

John Deere 6400 w/Duals, Ertl, 1/64th scale, #5734, MIB, S5 ....$4.00

John Deere 6400 w/Rops & Loader, Ertl, 1/64th scale, #5732, MIB, S5 ....$5.00

John Deere 6910 Self-Propelled Harvester, Ertl, 1/64th scale, #5658, MIB, S5 ....$9.00

John Deere 70 Tractor, Ertl, 1/16th scale, #5611, MIB, S5 ..$20.00

John Deere 7800 Row Crop, Ertl, 1/64th scale, #5538, MIB, S5 ....$4.00

John Deere 820 Diesel Tractor, Ertl, 1/16th scale, #5705, MIB, S5 ....$20.00

John Deere 8560 4-Wheel Drive Tractor, Ertl, 1/64th scale, #5603, MIB, S3 ....$4.50

John Deere 876 V-Tank Slurry Spreader, Ertl, 1/64th scale, #5928, MIB, S5 ....$4.50

John Deere 8870 4-Wheel Drive Tractor, Ertl, 1/64th scale, #5791, MIB, S5 ....$5.00

Knudson 4-Wheel Drive, Ertl, 1/64th scale, #TF4400, 1 of 5,000, MIB, S5 ....$35.00

Knudson 4-Wheel Drive Tractor w/Duals, Ertl, 1/64th scale, #TF4400, MIB, S5 ....$20.00

Massey-Ferguson Bale Processor, Ertl, 1/64th scale, #1093, MIB, S5 ....$2.50

Massey-Ferguson Challenger, Ertl, 1/16th scale, #1103, MIB, S5 ....$25.00

Massey-Ferguson 3070 Front Wheel Drive, Ertl, 1/64th scale, #1107, MIB, S5 ....$3.50

Massey-Ferguson 3070 Tractor, Ertl, 1/64th scale, #1177, MIB, S5 ....$3.00

Massey-Ferguson 3070 w/Loader, Ertl, 1/64th scale, #1109, MIB, S5 ....$5.00

Massey-Ferguson 3120 Tractor, Ertl, 1/64th scale, #1177, MIB, S5 ....$3.00

Massey-Ferguson 3140 Front Wheel Drive, Ertl, 1/64th scale, #1107, MIB, S5 ....$3.50

Massey-Ferguson 3140 w/Duals, Ertl, 1/64th scale, #1176, MIB, S5 ....$3.50

Massey-Ferguson 555 Tractor, Ertl, 1/16th scale, #1105, MIB, S5 ....$22.00

Massey-Ferguson 699 Tractor, Ertl, 1/64th scale, #1120, MIB, S5 ....$3.00

Massey-Ferguson 699 Tractor w/Loader, Ertl, 1/64th scale, #1125, MIB, S5 ....$5.00

Massey-Harris Challenger Tractor, Ertl, 1/43rd scale, #2511, MIB, S5 ....$5.50

Massey-Harris 44 Special Tractor, Ertl, 1/16th scale, #1115, MIB, S5 ....$18.00

Massey-Harris 55, Ertl, 1/43rd scale, #1131, MIB, S5 ....$5.50

Massey-Harris 55, Ertl, 1992 National Farm Toy Show, 1/43rd scale, #1131, MIB, S5 ....$25.00

Massey-Harris 55 Wide-Front, Ertl, 1/16th scale, #1292, MIB, S5 ....$20.00

McCormick Farmall 130 Tractor, Ertl, 1993 Lafayette Farm Toy Show Edition, 1/16th scale, MIB, $44.00.

McCormick-Deering Farmall Tractor, Ertl, Precision Series, 1/16th scale, MIB, $120.00.

McCormick-Deering WD-40 Tractor, Wheat Belt Works, dk gray w/red spoked wheels, 1/16th scale, 9", MIB, A..$265.00
McCormick-Deering WD-40 Tractor, Wheat Belt Works, red w/red spoked wheels, 1/16th scale, 9", MIB, A........$255.00
Minneapolis Moline G750, Ertl, 1/16th scale, #4375, MIB, S5 ....$24.00
Minneapolis Moline G750, Ertl, 1994 National Tractor Show, 1/16th scale, #4375, MIB, S5 ....$80.00
New Holland Baler, Ertl, 1/64th scale, #337, MIB, S5........$2.50
New Holland Box Spreader, Ertl, 1/64th scale, #308, MIB, S5 ....$3.00
New Holland Forage Harvester, Ertl, 1/64th scale, #372, MIB, S5 ....$3.00
New Holland Forage Wagon, Ertl, 1/64th scale, #373, MIB, S5 ....$2.50
New Holland Mower Conditioner, Ertl, 1/64th scale, #322, MIB, S5 ....$3.50
New Holland Skid Loader, Ertl, 1/64th scale, #381, MIB, S5 ....$4.00
Oliver 1555 Diesel Tractor, Ertl, 1/16th scale, #2223, MIB, S5 ....$22.00

Oliver 1655 w/Wide Front, Ertl, 1/16th scale, #4472, MIB, S5...$20.00
Precision Farmall M, 1939, Ertl, 1/16th scale, #4610, MIB, S5...$100.00
Tractor Set, Ertl, 50th Anniversary, 1/64th scale, #4496, 6 pcs, MIB, S5...$28.00

Tru Scale Wagon, red-painted tin, 7½", EX, $18.00.

Fast Food Collectibles

Fast food collectibles are attracting lots of attention right now — the hobby is fun and inexpensive (so far), and the little toys, games, buttons, and dolls originally meant for the kids are now being snatched up by adults who are much more likely to appreciate them. They were first included in kiddie meals in the late 1970s. They're often issued in series of up to eight or ten characters; the ones you'll want to watch for are Disney characters, popular kids' icons like Barbie dolls, Cabbage Patch Kids, My Little Pony, Star Trek, etc. But it's not just the toys that are collectible. So are the boxes, store signs and displays, and promotional items (like the Christmas ornaments you can buy for 99¢). Supply dictates price. For instance, a test market box might be worth $20.00, a box from a regional promotion might be $10.00, while one from a national promotion could be virtually worthless.

Toys don't have to be old to be collectible, but if you can find them still in their original package, so much the better. Though there are exceptions, a loose toy is worth one half to two thirds the value of one mint in package. For more information we recommend *McDonald's® Happy Meal® Toys — In the USA* and *McDonald's® Happy Meal® Toys — Around the World*, by Joyce and Terry Losonsky, *Tomart's Price Guide to Kid's Meal Collectibles (Non-McDonald's)* and *Kid's Meal Collectibles Update '94 - '95* by Ken Clee, and *McDonald's Collectibles®* by Gary Henriques and Audre Du Vall. The Losonskys and Clee are listed under Fast-Food Collectibles in the Categories of Special Interest section of this book.

Advisors: Bill and Pat Poe (P10); Scott Smiles (S10), Foreign.
Other Sources: C3, C11, I2, K1 (Simpsons), M8, P3

ARBY'S

Babar's World Tour, finger puppets, 1990, M, ea $2.00
Babar's World Tour, pull-back racers, 1992, ea $3.00

Babar's World Tour, squirters, 1992, ea $2.00
Babar's World Tour, stampers, 1991, ea $3.00
Babar's World Tour, vehicles, 1990, ea $3.00
Little Miss, 1981, ea $4.00
Looney Tunes Car Tunes, 1989, ea $3.00
Looney Tunes Characters, 1987, oval base, ea $5.00
Looney Tunes Characters, 1988, standing, ea $5.00
Looney Tunes Fun Fingers, 1989, ea $5.00
Mr Men, 1981, ea from $4 to $5.00
Snow Domes, 1995, Yogi or Snagglepuss, MIP, ea $5.00
Winter Wonderland Crazy Cruisers, 1995, ea $4.00
Yogi Bear Fun Squirters, 1994, MIP, ea $4.00

BURGER KING

Action Figures, MIP, ea $3.00
Aladdin Hidden Treasures, 1994, MIP, ea $2.00
Archies, 1991, MIP, ea $4.00

Beauty and the Beast, 1991, MIP, $4.00 each.

Beetlejuice, 1990, ea $2.00
Bone Age, 1989, ea $5.00
Bonkers, 1993, 6 different, MIP, ea $3.00
Capitol Critters, 1992, 4 different, MIP, ea.........................$2.00
Captain Planet Flipover Star Cruisers, 4 different, MIP, ea ..$2.00
Cool Stuff, 1995, MIP, ea from $2 to $3.00
Crayola Christmas Bears, 1986, plush, 4 different colors, ea ..$5.00
Dino Crawlers, 1994, 5 different, MIP, ea $2.00
Gargoyles (1st Set), 1995, MIP, ea from $2 to $3.00
Gargoyles (2nd Set), 1995, MIP, ea $3.00
Glo Force, 1996, 5 different, MIP, ea $3.00
Glow-in-the Dark Troll Patrol, 1993, 4 different, MIP, ea .$2.00
Go-Go Gadget Gizmos, 1991, 4 different, MIP, ea $3.00
Good Gobblin', 1989, 3 different, ea $3.00
Goof Troop Bowlers, 1992, 4 different, MIP, ea $3.00
Goofy & Max Adventures, 1995, any except yel runaway car,
    MIP, ea $3.00
Goofy & Max Adventures, 1995, yel runaway car, MIP $4.00
Hunchback of Notre Dame, 1995, hand puppets, 4 different,
    MIP, ea $10.00
Hunchback of Notre Dame, 1996, 8 different, MIP, P10, ea..$4.00
It's Magic, 1992, 4 different, MIP, ea...................................$2.00
Kid Transporters, 1990, 6 different, ea $2.00
Life Savers Freaky Fellas (No Life Savers), 4 different colors,
    ea $2.00
Lion King, 1994, 7 different, MIP, ea $3.00
Lion King, 1995, finger puppets, MIP, ea $3.00

Little Mermaid, 1993, Urchin squirt gun, Flounder squirter or
    Sebastian w/up, MIP, ea..$3.00
Mini Record Breakers, 1989, 6 different, ea $2.00
Mini Sports Games, 1993, 4 different, MIP, ea $3.00

Minnie Mouse, 1992, MIP, $6.00.

Miss Daisy's Trolley with Chip and Dale, MIP, $6.00.

Nerfuls, 1989, 3 different, ea...$4.00
Oliver & Co, 1996, 5 different, MIP, ea...............................$3.00
Pocahontas, 1995, 8 different, MIP, ea................................$3.00
Pocahontas, 1996, finger puppets, 6 different, MIP, ea $3.00
Pranksters, 1994, 5 different, MIP, ea..................................$3.00
Pumbaa & Timon, 1996, set of 4, MIP...............................$20.00
Purrtenders, 1988, Free Wheeling Cheese Rider or Flip Top Car,
    ea $2.00
Rodney Reindeer & Friends, 1986, 4 different, ea $5.00

Silverhawks, 1987, pencil topper.................................$5.00
Simpsons, 1990, 5 different, ea $2.00
Spacebase Racers, 1989, 4 different, ea $3.00
Super Powers, 1987, Aquaman tub toy....................$6.00
Super Powers, 1987, door shield...............................$8.00
Surprize Celebration Parade, 1992, 4 different, w/track, MIP,
    ea...$6.00
Toy Story, 1995, Action Wing Buzz, ea $6.00
Toy Story, 1995, Rex Dinosaur, RC Racer, Mr Potato Head or
    Army Recon Squadron, ea................................$3.00
Toy Story, 1995, Woody, MIP..................................$8.00
Trak-Pak Golden Jr Classic Books, 1988, 4 different, ea $4.00
Water Mates, 1991, any except Snaps/rowboat w/pk shirt or
    Wheels/hovercraft w/bl control panel, MIP, ea............$3.00
Water Mates, 1991, Snaps/rowboat w/pk shirt or Wheels/hover-
    craft w/bl control panel, MIP, ea.................$6.00
World Travel Adventure Kit, 1991, 4 different, MIP, ea....$5.00

DAIRY QUEEN

Alvin & the Chipmunks Music Makers, 4 different, MIP, ea .$5.00
Dennis the Menace, 1994, 4 different, MIP, ea..................$6.00
Rock-A-Doodle, 1991, 6 different, MIP, ea $7.00
Tom & Jerry, 1993, 4 different, MIP, ea.............................$6.00

DENNY'S

Dino-makers, 5 different, MIP, ea..................................$3.00
Flintstones, 1989, plush figures, Fred & Wilma or Barney &
    Betty, MIP, ea $8.00
Flintstones, 1989, plush figures, Pebbles & Bamm-Bamm, MIP,
    pr $12.00
Flintstones, 1990, vehicles, 3 different, ea.....................$4.00
Flintstones Dino-Racers, 1991, 3 different, MIP, ea $4.00
Flintstones Fun Squirters, 1991, 5 different, MIP, ea $4.00
Flintstones Glacier Gliders, 1990, Barney playing hockey,
    Bamm-Bamm on sled or Dino, ea...............$3.00

DOMINOS PIZZA

Avoid the Noid, 1988, 3 different, MIP, ea........................$5.00
Donnie Domino, 1989, figure, 4", M $6.00
Keep the Noid Out, 1987, 3 different, MIP, ea $5.00
Noid, 1989, bookmark $10.00

HARDEE'S

Apollo 13 Spaceship, 1995, 3-pc set, MIP $12.00
Balto, 1995, 6 different, MIP, ea......................................$3.00
Beach Bunnies, 1989, 4 different, ea $1.00
Bobby's World (At the Circus), 1996, 5 different, MIP, ea..$3.00
Dinosaur in My Pocket, 1993, 4 different, MIP, ea.............$3.00
Eureka Castle Stampers, 1994, 4 different, ea $3.00
Fender-Bender 500 Racers, 1990, 5 different, MIP, ea........$3.00
Flintstones First 30 Years, 1991, 4 different, MIP, ea..........$5.00
Gremlin Adventures Read Along Book & Record, 1984, 5 dif-
    ferent, MIP, ea $6.00
Halloween Hideaway, 1989, 4 different, ea..........................$2.00

Homeward Bound II, 1996, 5 different, MIP, ea $3.00
Marvel Super Heroes in Vehicles, 1990, 4 different, MIP, ea...$3.00
Mickey's Christmas Carol, 1984, plush figures, 4 different, ea..$6.00
Micro Super Soakers, 1994, 4 different, MIP, ea................$3.00
Mouth Figurines, 1989, 4 different, MIP, ea.......................$3.00
Nickelodeon School Tools, 1995, 6 different, MIP, ea $3.00
Pound Puppies, 1986, plush, 4 different, ea $5.00
Pound Puppies & Pur-R-Ries, 1987, plush, 5 different, ea..$5.00
Shirt Tales, 1990, plush figures, 5 different, 7", ea $5.00
Smurfs Funmeal Pack, 1990, 6 different, ea......................$3.00
Speed Bunnies, 1994, 4 different, MIP, ea........................$3.00
Tattoads, 1995, 4 different, MIP, ea..................................$3.00
Tune-A-Fish, 1994, 4 different, MIP, ea $3.00
Walt Disney Animated Film Classic, 1985, plush, 5 different,
    ea $6.00
X-Men, 1995, 6 different, MIP, ea.....................................$3.00

INTERNATIONAL HOUSE OF PANCAKES

Pancake Kids, 1992, 3 different, MIP, ea..........................$6.00
Pancake Kids Cruisers, 1993, 3 different, MIP, ea.............$5.00

JACK-IN-THE-BOX

Bendable Buddies, 1975, 4 different, G, ea $10.00
Bendable Buddies, 1991, 5 different, ea............................$3.00
Finger Puppets, 1994, 5 different, MIP, ea $10.00

LONG JOHN SILVER'S

Fish Car, 1989, 3 different, ea...$3.00
Map Activities, 1991, 3 different, MIP, ea $4.00
Once Upon a Forest, 1993, 2 different, MIP, ea.................$4.00
Sea Watchers, 1991, mini kaleidoscope, 3 different, MIP, ea..$5.00
Treasure Trolls, 1992, pencil toppers, 4 different, MIP, ea .$3.00
Water Blasters, 1990, 4 different, ea.................................$4.00

McDONALD'S

Airport, 1986, Fry Guy Flyer, Grimace Ace or Birdie Bent Wing
    Blazer, ea $4.00
Airport, 1986, Ronald McDonald seaplane.......................$5.00
Airport, 1986, under age 3, Fry Guy Flyer (floater) $5.00
Aladdin & the King of Thieves, 1996, any except under age 3,
    MIP, ea $3.00
Aladdin & the King of Thieves, 1996, under age 3, Abu, MIP...$4.00
Amazing Wildlife, 1995, MIP, ea $2.00
Animaniacs, 1995, any except under age 3, MIP, ea..........$3.00
Animaniacs, 1995, under age 3, MIP, ea $5.00
Babe, 1996, 7 different, MIP, ea $3.00
Bambi, 1988, 4 different, MIP, ea $5.00
Barbie/Hot Wheels, 1991, Barbie, any except under age 3, MIP,
    ea $5.00
Barbie/Hot Wheels, 1991, Barbie, under age 3, Costume Ball or
    Wedding Day Midge, MIP, ea $8.00
Barbie/Hot Wheels, 1991, Hot Wheels, MIP, ea $4.00
Barbie/Hot Wheels, 1993, Barbie, any except under age 3, MIP,
    ea $3.00

Barbie/Hot Wheels, 1993, Barbie, under age 3, Rose Bride, MIP $4.00

Barbie/Hot Wheels, 1993, Hot Wheels, any except under age 3, MIP, ea $3.00

Barbie/Hot Wheels, 1993, Hot Wheels, under age 3, Hammer & Wrench, MIP, ea...............................$4.00

Barbie/Hot Wheels, 1994, Barbie, any except Camp Teresa (variation) or under age 3, from $4 to $5.00

Barbie/Hot Wheels, 1994, Camp Teresa (variation), MIP .$8.00

Barbie/Hot Wheels, 1994, under age 3, Barbie Ball, MIP ...$5.00

Barbie/Hot Wheels, 1995, Barbie, any except Afro-American Life Guard Barbie & under age 3, MIP, ea $3.00

Barbie/Hot Wheels, 1995, Barbie, under age 3, Lil' Miss Candi Stripe, MIP..$4.00

Barbie/Hot Wheels, 1995, Hot Wheels, any except under age 3, MIP, ea $3.00

Barbie/Hot Wheels, 1995, Hot Wheels, under age 3, Key Force truck, MIP...$4.00

Barbie/Hot Wheels, 1996, Barbie, any except under age 3, MIP, ea $3.00

Barbie/Hot Wheels, 1996, Hot Wheels, under age 3, mini steering wheel, MIP $4.00

Barbie/Mini Streex, 1991, Barbie, any except under age 3, MIP, ea $3.00

Barbie/Mini Streex, 1992, Barbie, under age 3, Sparkle Eyes, MIP..$4.00

Barbie/Mini Streex, 1992, Mini Streex, any except under age 3, MIP, ea $2.00

Barbie/Mini Streex, 1992, Mini Streex, under age 3, Orange Arrow, MIP $4.00

Barnyard (Old McDonald's Farm), 1986, 6 different, ea.....$8.00

Batman, 1992, Bat-Mobile, Batman, Cat Woman or Penguin Umbrella Roto Roadster, MIP, ea $3.00

Batman (Animated), 1993, any except under age 3, MIP, ea..$3.00

Batman (Animated), 1993, under age 3, Batman, MIP $4.00

Bedtime, 1989, drinking cup, M $3.00

Bedtime, 1989, Ronald, set of 4 ....$3.00

Bedtime, 1989, wash mitt, bl foam, MIP $5.00

Berenstain Bears, 1987, any except under age 3, MIP, ea ...$5.00

Berenstain Bears, 1987, under age 3, Mama or Papa w/paper punchouts, MIP, ea $8.00

Boats & Floats, 1987, Fry Kids raft or McNuggets lifeboat, M (w/separate sticker sheet), ea......................$15.00

Cabbage Patch Kids/Tonka Trucks, 1992, Cabbage Patch Dolls, any except under age 3, ea $2.00

Cabbage Patch Kids/Tonka Trucks, 1992, Tonka Trucks, under age 3, dump truck, MIP......................$4.00

Changeables, 1987, Big Mac, Chicken McNuggets, Egg McMuffin, Quarter Pounder or French Fries, MIP, ea $5.00

Changeables, 1987, milk shake, MIP...................................$8.00

Chip 'N' Dale Rescue Rangers, 1989, 4 different, MIP, ea..$4.00

Circus Parade, 1991, MIP, ea $5.00

COSMc Crayola, 1988, under age 3, So Big, w/2 crayons & activity sheet, P10 ....$5.00

Crayola Stencils, 1987, any except under age 3, ea............$2.00

Crayola Stencils, 1987, under age 3, Ronald, cb $12.00

Crazy Creatures w/Popoids, 1985, 4 different, ea $5.00

Dinosaur Days, 1981, 6 different, ea $2.00

Disney Favorites, 1987, activity book, Sword & the Stone..$5.00

Disneyland — 40 Years of Adventures, 1995, MIP, ea $3.00

Ducktails II, 1988, launch pad in airport, MIP...................$5.00

Ducktails II, 1988, Scrooge McDuck in car or Huey, Louie & Dewey on surf ski, MIP, ea.........................$7.00

Ducktails II, 1988, Webby on tricycle, MIP $8.00

Fast Mac II, 1985, wht squad car, pk cruiser, red sports car or yel jeep, MOC, ea $5.00

Feeling Good, 1985, comb, Captain, red..............................$2.00

Feeling Good, 1985, Fry Guy on duck $4.00

Feeling Good, 1985, mirror, Birdie $3.00

Feeling Good, 1985, soap dish, Grimace $5.00

Feeling Good, 1985, under age 3, Grimace in tub, yel $4.00

Flintstone Kids, 1988, any except under age 3, ea..............$8.00

Flintstone Kids, 1988, under age 3, Dino $12.00

Friendly Skies, 1991, Ronald or Grimace, MIP, ea $8.00

Friendly Skies, 1993, Ronald or Grimace, MIP, ea $10.00

Friendly Skies, 1994, United hangar w/Ronald in plane, MIP..$10.00

Fun w/Food, 1989, MIP, ea..$10.00

Funny Fry Friends, 1989, any set except under age 3, ea.....$2.00

Funny Fry Friends, 1989, under age 3, Little Darling or Lil' Chief, ea..$6.00

Ghostbusters, 1987, pencil case, Containment Chamber...$5.00

Ghostbusters, 1987, pencil sharpener, ghost $3.00

Halloween, 1994, cookie cutter, M, ea $2.00

Halloween (What Am I Going To Be?), 1995, any except under age 3, MIP, ea...$3.00

Halloween (What Am I Going To Be?), 1995, under age 3, Grimace in Pumpkin, MIP $4.00

Halloween McNuggets, 1993, any except under age 3, MIP, ea..$3.00

Halloween McNuggets, 1993, under age 3, McBoo McNugget, MIP..$4.00

Happy Birthday 15 Years, 1994, any except Tonka or Muppet Babies, MIP, ea from $3 to..........................$5.00

Happy Birthday 15 Years, 1994, Muppet Babies #11 train pc, MIP...$8.00

Happy Birthday 15 Years, 1994, Tonka #7 train pc, MIP .$15.00

Happy Pail, 1986, 5 different, ea.......................................$5.00

Jungle Book, 1989, Baloo, King Louie, Kaa & Shere Khan w/ups, set of 4, NMIP, M8 ....$15.00

Jungle Book, 1990, under age 3, Junior or Mowgli, ea $9.00

Lego Building Set, 1986, helicopter or airplane, MIP, ea ...$3.00

Lego Building Set, 1986, race car or tanker boat, MIP, ea..$6.00

Looney Toons Quack-Up Cars, Daffy Splittin' Roadster and Taz Tornado Tracker, 1993, MIP, $2.00 each.

Lego Motion, 1989, any except under age 3, MIP, ea $5.00

Lego Motion, 1989, under age 3, Giddy Gator or Tuttle Turtle, MIP, ea...$6.00

Little Gardener, 1989, Birdie shovel, Fry Kids planter, Grimace rake or Ronald water can, ea $2.00

Little Mermaid, 1989, Ursula, Prince Eric & Sebastian w/boat or Ariel, MIP, ea...$5.00

Littlest Pet Shop/Transformers, 1996, any except under age 3, MIP, ea...$3.00

Littlest Pet Shop/Transformers, 1996, under age 3, MIP, ea ..$4.00

Mac Tonight, 1988, any except surf ski w/wheels, MIP, ea..$6.00

Mac Tonight, 1988, surf ski w/wheels, MIP $8.00

Mac Tonight, 1988, under age 3, skateboard, MIP $8.00

Marvel Super Heroes, 1996, any except under age 3, MIP, ea..$3.00

Marvel Super Heroes, 1996, under age 3, MIP....................$4.00

McDino Changeables, 1991, any except under age 3, MIP, ea..$3.00

McDino Changeables, 1991, under age 3, Bronto Cheeseburger or Small Fry Ceratops, MIP, ea.....................................$4.00

McDonaldland Band, 1986, Fry Kid Trumpet, Pan Pipes or Grimace Saxaphone, ea...$3.00

McDonaldland Band, 1986, Hamburglar siren whistle, Ronald train whistle or Fry Guy boat whistle, ea......................$1.00

McDonaldland Band, 1986, Ronald Harmonica.................$5.00

McDonaldland Dough, 1990, M, ea $5.00

McNugget Buddies, 1988, any except Corny w/red popcorn belt or Cowpoke w/scarf, ea $2.00

McNugget Buddies, 1988, Corny w/red popcorn belt $4.00

McNugget Buddies, 1988, Cowpoke w/scarf.......................$3.00

Mickey's Birthdayland, 1988, any except under age 3, MIP, ea..$2.00

Mickey's Birthdayland, 1988, under age 3, MIP..................$6.00

Mix 'Em Up Monsters, 1989, Bibble, Corkle, Gropple or Thugger, ea $3.00

Moveables, 1988, any except Ronald, ea..............................$8.00

Moveables, 1988, Ronald..$9.00

Muppet Treasure Island, 1996, book for bath, MIP.............$4.00

Muppet Treasure Island, 1996, tub toys, any except under age 3, MIP, ea...$3.00

Muppet Workshop, 1995, MIP, ea.......................................$2.00

Music — Mie, 1985, 4 different, ea $7.00

Mystery of the Lost Arches, 1992, Magic Lens Camera (recalled), MIP...$4.00

Mystery of the Lost Arches, 1992, micro-cassette/magnifier, phone/periscope or flashlight/telescope, MIP, ea $3.00

Mystery of the Lost Arches, 1992, under age 3, Magic Lens camera (recalled), MIP...$5.00

New Archies, 1988, 6 different characters, ea.....................$8.00

New Food Changeables, 1989, any except under age 3, ea..$2.00

New Food Changeables, 1989, under age 3, Pals Changeable Cube...$4.00

Oliver & Co, 1988, 4 different, ea.......................................$2.00

Peanuts, 1990, any except under age 3, MIP, ea $3.00

Peanuts, 1990, under age 3, Charlie Brown egg basket or Snoopy's potato sack, ea $5.00

Polly Pocket/Attack Pack, 1995, any except under age 3, MIP, ea $2.00

Polly Pocket/Attack Pack, 1995, under age 3, Polly Pocket or Attack Pack, MIP, ea..$3.00

Power Rangers, 1995, any except under age 3, MIP, ea $3.00

Power Rangers, 1995, under age 3, MIP $4.00

Rescuers Down Under, 1990, any except under age 3, ea...$1.00

Rescuers Down Under, 1990, under age 3, Bernard in cheese ..$3.00

Safari Adventure, 1980, cookie molds, Ronald or Grimace, red or yel, ea...$3.00

Safari Adventure, 1980, sponge, Ronald sitting cross-legged, M...$5.00

School Days, 1984, eraser, Birdie or Grimace, ea...............$7.00

School Days, 1984, pencil, Grimace, Hamburglar or Ronald, ea...$7.00

School Days, 1984, pencil case, clear $6.00

School Days, 1984, pencil sharpener, Grimace or Ronald, M, ea...$8.00

School Days, 1984, pencil sharpener, Ronald, MIP.........$10.00

School Days, 1984, ruler $4.00

Sea World of Texas, 1988, 4 different, ea $10.00

Snow White and the Seven Dwarfs, 1993, MIP, $3.00 each.

Snow White & the Seven Dwarfs, 1993, under age 3, Dopey or Sneezy, MIP, ea...$4.00

Space Rescue, 1995, any except under age 3, MIP, ea $3.00

Space Rescue, 1995, under age 3, Astro Viewer, MIP.........$4.00

Spider-Man, 1995, any except under age 3, MIP, ea..........$3.00

Spider-Man, 1995, under age 3, MIP..................................$4.00

Sports Ball, 1990, ea...$3.00

Stomper Mini 4x4, 1986, 15 different, ea..........................$8.00

Super Looney Tunes, 1991, any except under age 3, MIP, ea .$3.00

Super Looney Tunes, 1991, under age 3, Daffy Duck as Bat Duck, MIP, ea..$4.00

Super Mario Brothers, 1990, any except under age 3, MIP, ea .$3.00

Super Mario Brothers, 1990, under age 3, Super Mario, MIP ...$4.00

Tale Spin, 1990, any except under age 3, MIP, ea $3.00

Tale Spin, 1990, under age 3, Baloo's Seaplane or Wildcat's Flying Machine, MIP, ea $4.00

Totally Toy Holiday, 1995, any except under age 3, MIP, ea from $3 to...$4.00

Totally Toy Holiday, 1995, under age 3, MIP, ea from $4 to ..$5.00

Totally Toys, 1993, any except Magic Nursery (boy) or under age 3, MIP, ea...$2.00

Totally Toys, 1993, Magic Nursery (boy), MIP..................$3.00

Totally Toys, 1993, under age 3, Key Force car, MIP.........$3.00

Totally Toys, 1993, under age 3, Magic Nursery (boy), MIP..$6.00

Totally Toys, 1993, under age 3, Magic Nursery (girl), MIP ..$4.00

Turbo Macs, 1988, any except under age 3, ea...................$4.00

Turbo Macs, 1988, under age 3, Ronald in soft rubber car..**$6.00**

VR Troopers, 1996, any except under age 3, MIP, ea **$3.00**

VR Troopers, 1996, under age 3, MIP **$4.00**

Water Games, 1992, MIP, ea...**$4.00**

Winter Worlds, 1983, ornament, Birdie or Mayor McCheese, ea **$8.00**

Winter Worlds, 1983, ornament, Grimace or Hamburglar, ea **$6.00**

Winter Worlds, 1983, ornament, Ronald McDonald **$3.00**

Young Astronauts, 1992, any except under age 3, MIP, ea.**$2.00**

Young Astronauts, 1992, under age 3, Ronald in lunar rover, MIP...**$4.00**

Zoo Face, 1988, 4 different, MIP, ea...................................**$4.00**

PIZZA HUT

Air Garfield, kite, MIP...**$6.00**

Air Garfield, parachute, MIP...**$8.00**

Beauty & the Beast, hand puppets, 1992, Beast, Belle, Chip or Cogsworth, rubber, ea **$4.00**

Eureeka's Castle, 1990, hand puppets, Batley, Eureeka or Magellan, rubber, ea...**$5.00**

Land Before Time, 1988, hand puppet, Sharptooth............**$8.00**

Land Before Time, 1988, hand puppets, Cara, Littlefoot, Spike or Duckie, ea **$5.00**

Universal Monsters, 1991, hologram cards, 3 different, MIP, ea..**$5.00**

SONIC

Airtoads, 6 different, MIP, ea **$4.00**

Animal Straws, 1995, 4 different, MIP, ea **$3.00**

Bone-A-Fide Friends, 1994, 4 different, MIP, ea.................**$3.00**

Brown Bag Bowlers, 1994, 4 different, MIP, ea **$5.00**

Brown Bag Buddies, 1993, 3 different, ea **$4.00**

Brown Bag Juniors, 1989, 4 different, ea............................**$5.00**

Creepy Strawlers, 1995, 4 different, MIP, ea **$5.00**

Flippin' Food, 1995, 3 different, MIP, ea **$3.00**

Food Train, 1995, set of 7 cars w/engine, MIP **$22.00**

Go Wild Balls, 1995, 4 different, MIP, ea **$3.00**

Holiday Kids, 1994, 4 different, MIP, ea **$4.00**

Monster Peepers, 1994, 4 different, MIP, ea.......................**$3.00**

Shoe Biters, 1995, 4 different, MIP, ea...............................**$5.00**

Super Sonic Racers, set of 4, MIP......................................**$12.00**

Totem Pal Squirters, 1995, 4 different, MIP, ea **$5.00**

Very Fast Food, 1996, 4 different, MIP, ea **$4.00**

Wacky Sackers, 1994, set of 6, MIP **$20.00**

SUBWAY

Bobby's World, 1995, 4 different, MIP, ea..........................**$4.00**

Santa Claus, 1994, any except under age 3, MIP, ea..........**$4.00**

Santa Claus, 1994, under age 3, Comet the Reindeer, MIP ..**$5.00**

Save the Wildlife, 1995, 4 different, MIP, ea......................**$3.00**

Tale Tale, 1995, any except under age 3, MIP, ea **$4.00**

Tale Tale, 1995, under age 3, Bunyon & Babe the Blue Ox, MIP...**$5.00**

Tom & Jerry, 1994, 4 different, ea......................................**$3.00**

TACO BELL

Congo, 1995, watches, 3 different, MIB, ea **$5.00**

Mask, 1995, Its Party Time switch plate or Milo w/mask, MIP, ea **$4.00**

The Tick, 1995, finger puppet, Arthur Wall Climber or Thrakkorzog Squirter, MIP, ea **$4.00**

The Tick, 1996, Arthur w/wings or Sewer Urchin, MIP, ea ..**$4.00**

TARGET MARKETS

Olympic Sports Weiner Pack, 1996, figurines, 4 different, MIP, ea **$4.00**

Targeteers, 1992, 5 different, MIP, ea.................................**$5.00**

Targeteers, 1994, 5 different, rooted hair, MIP, ea.............**$4.00**

WENDY'S

Alf Tales, 1990, 6 different, ea..**$2.00**

All Dogs Go To Heaven, 1989, $2.00 each.

Animalinks, 1995, 6 different, ea **$2.00**

Cybercycles, 1994, 4 different, MIP, ea **$3.00**

Definitely Dinosaurs, 1988, 4 different, ea **$4.00**

Definitely Dinosaurs, 1989, 5 different, ea **$4.00**

Dino Games, 1993, 3 different, ea **$3.00**

Endangered Animal Games, 1993, any except under age 3, ea..**$2.00**

Endangered Animals Games, 1993, under age 3, elephant puzzle...**$3.00**

Fast Food Racers, 1990, 6 different, ea **$3.00**

Felix the Cat, 1990, plush figure..**$2.00**

Felix the Cat, 1990, Story Board, Zeotrope, Milk Cap set or Ask Felix toy, ea **$3.00**

Felix the Cat, 1990, under age 3, rub-on set......................**$4.00**

Furskins Bears, 1986, 4 different, plush, ea **$6.00**

Gear Up, 1992, handlebar streamers or Back-Off license plate, ea..**$2.00**

Glo-Ahead, 1993, any except under age 3, ea.....................**$2.00**

Glo-Ahead, 1993, under age 3, finger puppet **$3.00**

Glofriends, 1989, 9 different, ea **$2.00**

Gobots, 1986, Odd Ball/Monster.......................................**$8.00**

Good Stuff Gang, 1985, ea..**$3.00**

Jetsons Space Vehicles, 1989, 6 different, MIP, ea..............**$5.00**

Jetsons: The Movie, 1990, 5 different, MIP, ea **$3.00**

Kids 4 Parks, compass, magnifying glass or belt pouch, ea ..**$2.00**

Mega Wheels, any except under age 3, ea **$2.00**

Mega Wheels, under age 3, circus wagon **$3.00**

Mighty Mouse, 1989, 6 different, MIP, ea $4.00
Potato Head II, 1988, 5 different, ea..............................$4.00
Rocket Writers, 1992, 4 different, ea...............................$2.00
Speed Bumpers, 1992, any except under age 3, ea $2.00
Speed Bumpers, 1992, under age 3, Truck Speed Roller $3.00
Speed Writers, 1991, any except under age 3, ea $3.00
Speed Writers, 1991, under age 3, paint w/water book $4.00
Tecno Tows, 1995, any except under age 3, ea $2.00
Tecno Tows, 1995, under age 3, Diamond tow truck..........$3.00
Too Cool! For School, 1992, pencil bag or gr pickle pen, ea..$3.00

Wacky Windups, 1991, $2.00.

Wacky Windups, 1991, under age 3, Wacky Roller............$3.00
Weird Writers, 1991, 3 different, ea....................................$2.00
World of Teddy Ruxpin, 1987, 5 different, ea from $3 to...$4.00
World Wild Life, 1988, books, 4 different, ea $3.00
World Wild Life, 1988, plush figures, 4 different, ea $5.00
Write & Sniff, 1994, any except under age 3, ea $2.00
Write & Sniff, 1994, under age 3, set of stencils.................$3.00
Yogi Bear & Friends, 1990, 6 different, MIP, ea.................$3.00

WHITE CASTLE

Bow Biters, 1989, Blue Meany, MIP....................................$5.00
Camp White Castle, 1990, fork & spoon, MIP, ea $4.00
Castle Dude Squirters, 1994, 3 different, MIP, ea $3.00
Castleburger Dudes, 1991, 4 different, MIP, ea..................$6.00
Castleburger Friends, 1989, set of 6, MIP..........................$30.00

Fat Albert and the Cosby Kids, 1990, $10.00 each.

Holiday Huggables, 1990, 3 different, MIP, ea...................$6.00
Super Balls, 1994, 3 different, MIP, ea $5.00

BOXES AND BAGS

Burger King, Bone Age, 1989, ea.......................................$7.00
Burger King, Critter Carton/Punch-Out Paper Masks, 1985, ea ...$18.00
Burger King, Fairy Tales Cassettes, 1989, ea $6.00
Burger King, Trak-Pak, 1988, ea..$8.00
Hardee's, Cruisin' Back to School, 1993, ea.......................$1.00
Hardee's, Days of Thunder, 1990, ea $2.00
Hardee's, Eureka's Castle, 1994, ea....................................$1.00
Hardee's, Fender Bender 500 Racers, 1990, ea $2.00
Hardee's, Little Golden Books, 1987, ea $4.00
Hardee's, Marvel Super Heroes, 1990, ea...........................$2.00
Hardee's, Micro Soakers, 1994, ea $1.00
Hardee's, Muppet Christmas Carol, 1993, ea $2.00

Hardee's, Old MacDonald Had a Farm, Little Golden Book series, 1 from series of 4, $6.00.

Hardee's, Squirters, 1990, ea...$2.00
Hardee's, Swan Princess, 1994, ea $1.00
McDonald's, Amazing Wildlife, 1995, ea...........................$1.00
McDonald's, Animaniacs, 1994, ea $1.00
McDonald's, Back to the Future, 1992, ea..........................$2.00
McDonald's, Barbie/Hot Wheels, 1991, ea.........................$2.00
McDonald's, Barbie/Hot Wheels, 1995, ea.........................$1.00
McDonald's, Barbie/Mini Streex, 1992, ea.........................$1.00
McDonald's, Batman, 1992, ea $1.00
McDonald's, Batman, 1993, ea $1.00
McDonald's, Beach Toy, 1990, ea $3.00
McDonald's, Bobby's World, 1994, ea................................$1.00
McDonald's, Camp McDonaldland, 1990, ea......................$3.00
McDonald's, Carnival rides, 1990.......................................$2.00
McDonald's, Chip 'N' Dale Rescue Rangers, 1989, ea........$3.00
McDonald's, Crayon Squeeze Bottle, 1992, ea....................$3.00
McDonald's, Dink the Dinosaur, 1990.................................$10.00
McDonald's, Dino-Motion Dinosaurs, 1993, ea $1.00
McDonald's, Disneyland Adventures, ea..............................$1.00
McDonald's, Ducktails II, 1988, press-outs.........................$5.00

McDonald's, Field Trip, 1993, ea.............................$1.00
McDonald's, Fraggle Rock, 1988, ea.......................$3.00
McDonald's, Fry Benders, 1990, clubhouse $5.00
McDonald's, Garfield, 1989, ea...............................$3.00
McDonald's, Good Morning, 1991, ea $2.00
McDonald's, Gravedale High, 1991, ea....................$3.00
McDonald's, Halloween McNugget Buddies, 1993, ea $1.00
McDonald's, Happy Birthday 15 Years, 1994, ea $1.00
McDonald's, Happy Meal Workshop, 1996, Ronald or Grimace,
    M, ea...$1.00
McDonald's, Hook, 1991, ea....................................$3.00
McDonald's, Jungle Book, 1990, ea $3.00
McDonald's, Little Mermaid, 1989, ea.....................$4.00
McDonald's, Littlest Pet Shop Transformers, 1996, ea $1.00
McDonald's, Looney Tunes Quack-Up Cars, 1993, ea $1.00
McDonald's, M-Squad, 1993, ea...............................$1.00
McDonald's, Mac Tonight, 1988, ea $5.00
McDonald's, Making Movies, 1994, ea......................$1.00
McDonald's, Marvel, 1996, ea $1.00
McDonald's, Masterpiece Home Video Collection, 1996, ea..$1.00
McDonald's, McDonaldland Dough, 1990, Tic-Tac-Toe ...$3.00
McDonald's, McNugget Buddies, 1988, ea.................$4.00
McDonald's, Mickey & Friends/Epcot, 1994, ea $1.00
McDonald's, Mickey's Birthdayland, 1989, ea $4.00
McDonald's, Muppet Babies, 1991, ea.......................$3.00
McDonald's, Muppet Treasure Island, 1996, ea $1.00
McDonald's, Muppet Workshop, 1995, ea $1.00
McDonald's, Oliver & Co, 1988, ea $5.00
McDonald's, Out for Fun, 1993, ea...........................$1.00
McDonald's, Peanuts, 1990, ea.................................$2.00
McDonald's, Power Rangers, 1995, ea.......................$1.00
McDonald's, Raggedy Ann, 1989, schoolhouse $5.00
McDonald's, Rain or Shine, 1989, Bubbles or Umbrella (no toys
    produced to match boxes), ea $4.00
McDonald's, Real Ghostbusters, 1987, ea $5.00
McDonald's, Rescuers Down Under, 1990, ea...............$3.00
McDonald's, Snow White & the Seven Dwarfs, 1993, ea ..$2.00
McDonald's, Space Rescue, 1995, ea.........................$1.00
McDonald's, Sportsball, 1990, Ronald at bat $5.00
McDonald's, Super Mario, 1990, ea..........................$2.00
McDonald's, Tale Spin, 1990, ea..............................$3.00
McDonald's, Tiny Toon Adventures, 1992, ea $1.00
McDonald's, Tiny Toons, 1991, ea............................$2.00
McDonald's, Totally Toy Holiday, 1995, ea.................$1.00
McDonald's, Turbo Macs, 1988, Ronald/Red Race Car......$7.00
McDonald's, Valentine From the Heart, 1990, Play Match-
    maker $3.00
McDonald's, Wild Friends, 1992, ea.........................$3.00
McDonald's, Yo-Yogi, 1992, ea................................$2.00
McDonald's, Zoo Face, 1988, ea $5.00
McDonald's, 101 Dalmatians, 1991, ea $3.00
Wendy's, Carmen Sandiego Code Cracker, 1994, ea..........$2.00
Wendy's, Fast Food Racers, 1990, ea $4.00
Wendy's, Jetsons: The Movie, 1990, ea.....................$4.00
Wendy's, Micro Machines Super Sky Carrier, 1990, ea......$3.00
Wendy's, Rhyme Time, 1991, ea $2.00
Wendy's, Weather Watch, 1991, ea..........................$2.00
Wendy's, Wendy & the Good Stuff Gang, 1989, ea $3.00

Wendy's, Wizard of Wonders, 1991, ea $2.00
Wendy's, Yogi Bear & Friends, 1990, ea....................$4.00

FOREIGN

Burger King, Beauty & the Beast, 1992, set of 4, MIP, S10...$25.00
Burger King, Flintstones, 1994, set of 4, MIP, S10............$30.00
Burger King, Snow White, 1995, set of 4, MIP.................$25.00
Burger King, X-Men, 1996, set of 4, MIP, S10.................$30.00
Burger King (England), Peter Pan, 1993, set of 5, MIP $35.00
Burger King (England), Robin Hood, 1993, set of 5 ....$25.00
Burger King (England), Taz-Mania Crazies, 1994, set of 4,
    MIP..$20.00
Burger King (England), Tiny Toon Adventures, 1995, set of
    4..$25.00
Burger King (England), Tom & Jerry, 1995, set of 4.........$25.00
McDonald's, Aristocrats, 1993, set of 4, MIP, S10 ....$20.00
McDonald's, Dinosaurs, 1995, set of 4, MIP, S10 ....$25.00
McDonald's, Hunchback of Notre Dame, 1996, set of 4 w/boxes,
    MIP, S10 ....$35.00
McDonald's, Island Getaway, 1996, set of 4 w/boxes, MIP, S10...$30.00
McDonald's, McFarm, 1995, set of 4 w/boxes, MIP, S10..$30.00
McDonald's, McRodeo, 1995, set of 4 w/boxes, MIP, S10 .....$30.00
McDonald's, Pocahontas, 1996, set of 4 w/boxes, MIP, S10..$30.00
McDonald's, Toy Story, 1996, set of 4 w/boxes, MIP, S10..$35.00
McDonald's, Winter Sports, 1995, set of 4, MIP, S10 ......$25.00
McDonald's (Australia), Aladdin Straw Grippers, 1994, set of 4,
    MIP $20.00
McDonald's (Australia), Batman Flicker Badges, 1995, set of 4,
    MIP $20.00
McDonald's (Australia), Dark Wing Duck, 1994, set of 4,
    M...$20.00
McDonald's (Australia), Flintstone Stationary Series, 1994, set
    of 4, MIP $20.00
McDonald's (Australia), Lion King stampers, 1995, set of 4,
    MIP..$20.00
McDonald's (Australia), Pocahontas finger puppets, 1995, set of
    4, MIP $25.00
McDonald's (Australia), Summer Fun Toys, 1995, set of 4,
    MIP...$15.00
McDonald's (Australia), Winnie the Pooh cups, 1995, set of 4,
    M...$25.00
McDonald's (Australia), World Cup, 1994, set of 4, MIP...$20.00
McDonald's (Australia), Zoomballs, 1995, set of 4, MIP..$20.00
McDonald's (Australia), 101 Dalmatians, 1995, set of 4,
    MIP $25.00
McDonald's (Autralia), McSports, 1995, set of 4, MIP $25.00
McDonald's (European), Airport, 1995, set of 4 w/boxes,
    MIP $25.00
McDonald's (European), Aladdin, 1994, set of 4, MIP.....$25.00
McDonald's (European), Barbie, 1995, set of 4 w/boxes,
    MIP $30.00
McDonald's (European), Connect-A-Car, 1991, set of 4, M .$20.00
McDonald's (European), Disneyland Paris, 1996, set of 4,
    MIP $30.00
McDonald's (European), Draakjes (Dragonettes), 1993, set of 4,
    MIP $20.00
McDonald's (European), Euro Disney, 1992, set of 4, MIP...$30.00

McDonald's (European), Flintstones, 1994, set of 4 w/boxes, MIP $25.00

McDonald's (European), Fly & Drive, 1995, set of 4, MIP ..$25.00

McDonald's (European), garage/village, set of 4, MIP $25.00

McDonald's (European), I Like Bikes, 1991, set of 4, MIP ..$20.00

McDonald's (European), Kapt'n Baloo, 1993, set of 4, M...$20.00

McDonald's (European), Lion King, 1994, set of 4 puzzles, MIP $25.00

McDonald's (European), Lion King, 1994, set of 4 w/boxes, MIP $25.00

McDonald's (European), McDonald's Band, 1993, set of 4 w/ups w/boxes, MIP $25.00

McDonald's (Japan), Snoopy, 1996, set of 4, MIP, S10....$45.00

McDonald's (New Zealand), Batman Forever 3-D pop-up cards, 1995, set of 4, MIP...................................$20.00

McDonald's (New Zealand), Disney Fun Riders, 1994, set of 4, M $25.00

McDonald's (New Zealand), Mystery Riders, 1993, set of 4, M ..$20.00

McDonald's (Pacific Rim), Big Top, 1995, set of 4, MIP..$30.00

MISCELLANEOUS

This section lists items other than those that are free with kids' meals, for instance, store displays and memorabilia such as Christmas ornaments and plush dolls that can be purchased at the counter.

Burger King, puppet, Rex (Toy Story), M, B10...................$6.00

Burger King, puppets, Toy Story, set of 4, MIP, J8............$40.00

Chuck E Cheese, bank, 8", NM, B10 ....$6.00

Chuck E Cheese, doll, stuffed, 12", EX, B10 ....$10.00

Hardee's, rag doll, Gilbert Giddy Up, 15", EX, H4 ....$12.00

Kentucky Fried Chicken, bank, Colonel Sanders, plastic figure, yel, 12", EX, B10 ....$25.00

Long John Silver's, paint book, 1991, Adventure on Volcano Island, M $5.00

McDonald's, bank, Grimace, ceramic, purple, 9", P10......$12.00

McDonald's, bank, Happy Times, 1993, P10 ....$15.00

McDonald's, book, The World of Ronald McDonald, 1983, edited by Marshall Fishwick, paperback, M, A $40.00

McDonald's, Coloring Board, 1981, M, $4.00.

McDonald's, bop bag, Grimace, 1978, 8", MIP, P10...........$4.00

McDonald's, Bounce-A-Ball, 1981, ball on elastic attached to wooden paddle w/head image of Ronald, MIP, A......$20.00

McDonald's, cap, Sam the Olympic Eagle, P10 ....$5.00

McDonald's, cap, Season's Greetings, 1992, red, P10 ....$4.00

McDonald's, crayon set, Ronald McDonald, 1985, pkg of 4, M, L2 ....$4.00

McDonald's, Dinosaur birthday cup, 1992, P10 ....$2.00

McDonald's, display w/toys, Cabbage Patch Kids, 1994, P10...$20.00

McDonald's, display w/toys, Disney Masterpiece Video Collection, 1996, P10...$40.00

McDonald's, display w/toys, Spider-Man, 1995, P10 ....$40.00

McDonald's, doll, Ronald McDonald, cloth, 14", NM, $18.00.

McDonald's, doll, Ronald McDonald, inflatable, 14", EX, B10 ....$14.00

McDonald's, doll, Ronald McDonald, stuffed, w/whistle, 24", EX, T1 ....$35.00

McDonald's, eraser, Ronald w/book, 1991, P10 ....$2.00

McDonald's, Fun Tattoos, cactus & dinosaurs, 1995, P10..$2.00

McDonald's, glider, 1977, foam w/metal nosepc, Ronald in cockpit, 4x5", M, L2 ....$8.00

McDonald's, hand puppets, 1993, Ronald, Grimace & Hamburglar, set of 3, MIB, P10 ....$25.00

McDonald's, key chain, diecut w/full figure of Ronald, 3¾", MIP, L2 ....$4.00

McDonald's, NASCAR vehicles, 1/64 scale, MOC, P10, ea from $3 to $5.00

McDonald's, ornament, Christmas stocking w/Ronald, 1981, vinyl, P10 ....$5.00

McDonald's, ornament, Dodger, 1988, plush, MIB, P10.....$4.00

McDonald's, ornament, Holiday Seasoning, 1994, Enesco, miniature, MIB, P10 ....$12.00

McDonald's, ornament, Holiday Take Out, 1992, Enesco, MIB, P10 ....$25.00

McDonald's, Muppet Babies, Kermit and Gonzo, MIP, $3.00 each.

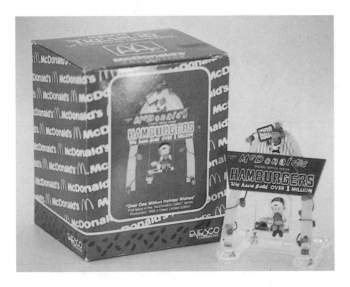

McDonald's, ornament, Enesco, 1990, 1st edition, MIB, $25.00.

McDonald's, ornament, Oliver, 1988, plush, MIP, P10 ......**$3.00**
McDonald's, plates, 1993, carnival scenes, melamine, 9½", M, P10, ea **$5.00**
McDonald's, playing cards, 1984 Store Manager's Convention, 'Hands on Hot 'N Hustle,' MIB, A **$30.00**
McDonald's, popsicle mold w/Ronald on hdl, 1980, P10....**$3.00**
McDonald's, puppet, Big Mac, Milton Bradley, 1972, 12", VG, A **$38.00**
McDonald's, record, Share a Song From Your Heart, 1980, P10 ....**$10.00**
McDonald's, stencil, 1973, Ronald waving, M, L2 ....**$15.00**
McDonald's, sunglasses, MIP, P10, ea from $4 to...............**$5.00**
McDonald's, Tic-Tac-Go slate, 1988, P10 ....**$2.00**
McDonald's, Tic-Tac-Mac game, 1981, P10 ....**$5.00**
McDonald's, translite, Barbie/Hot Wheels, 1991, P10 .....**$12.00**
McDonald's, translite, Changeables, 1987, P10...............**$25.00**
McDonald's, translite, Chip & Dale Rescue Rangers, 1989, P10 ....**$8.00**
McDonald's, translite, Halloween, 1989, P10 ....**$6.00**
McDonald's, translite, M-Squad, 1993, P10.....................**$6.00**
McDonald's, translite, Mickey & Friends, 1994, P10..........**$8.00**

McDonald's, translite, Super Mario, 1990, P10...................**$6.00**
McDonald's, translite, Yo-Yogi, 1992, P10......................**$8.00**
White Castle, magnet, Castleburger, M, P10 ....**$4.00**

Fisher-Price

Fisher-Price toys are becoming one of the hottest new trends in the collector's market place today. In 1930 Herman Fisher, backed by Irving Price, Elbert Hubbard, and Helen Schelle, formed one of the most successful toy companies ever to exist. Located in East Aurora, New York, the company has seen many changes since then, the most notable being the changes in ownership. From 1930 to 1968, it was owned by the individuals mentioned previously and a few stockholders. In 1969 it became an aquisition of Quaker Oats, and in June of 1991 it became independently owned. In November of 1993, one of the biggest sell-outs in the toy industry took place: Fisher-Price became a division of Mattel.

There are a few things to keep in mind when collecting Fisher-Price toys. You should count on a little edge wear as well as some wear and fading to the paint. Unless noted otherwise, the prices in the listings are for toys in very good condition. Pull toys found in mint condition are truly rare and command a much higher value, especially if you find one with its original box. This also applies to playsets, but to command the higher prices, they must also be complete, with all pieces present. Another very important rule to remember is there are no standard colors for pieces that came with a playset. Fisher-Price often substituted a piece of a different color when they ran short. Please note that dates on the toys indicate their copyright date and not the date they were manufactured.

The company put much time and thought into designing their toys. They took care to operate by their 5-point creed: to make toys with (1) intrinsic play value, (2) ingenuity, (3) strong construction, (4) good value for the money, and (5) action. Some of the most sought-after pull toys are those bearing the Walt Disney logo.

The ToyFest limited editions are a series of toys produced in conjunction with ToyFest, an annual weekend of festivities for young and old alike held in East Aurora, New York. It is sponsored by the 'Toy Town USA Museum' and is held every year in August. Fisher-Price produces a limited-edition toy for this event. (For more information on ToyFest and the museum, write to Toy Town Museum, P.O. Box 238, East Aurora, NY 14052.) For more information on Fisher-Price toys we recommend *Fisher-Price, A Historical Rarity Value Guide*, by John J. Murray and Bruce R. Fox, and *Modern Toys, American Toys, 1930-1980*, by Linda Baker.

Additional information may be obtained through the Fisher-Price Collectors' Club who publish a quarterly newsletter; their address may be found in the Directory under Clubs, Newsletters, and Other Publications.

Advisor: Brad Cassity (C13). (Brad asks that he be allowed to thank his wife and three daughters, his brother, Beau, Jeanne Kennedy, and Deanna Korth, all of whom he feels have been very instrumental in his life and hold a special place in his heart.)

Note: Prices are for examples that show only a little edge and paint wear and minimal fading (VG).

Other Sources: J2, J6, N2, O1, S20, T1

See also Dollhouse Furniture; Dollhouses.

#0005 Bunny Cart, 1948, C13..............................$75.00
#0007 Doggy Racer, 1942, C13 ....$200.00
#0007 Looky Fire Truck, 1950, C13......................$100.00
#0008 Bouncy Racer, 1960, C13 ....$40.00
#0010 Bunny Cart, 1940, C13..............................$75.00
#0012 Bunny Truck, 1941, C13 ....$75.00
#0015 Bunny Cart, 1946, C13..............................$75.00
#0020 Animal Cutouts, 1942, duck, elephant, pony or Scotty dog, C13, ea $50.00
#0028 Bunny Egg Cart, 1950, C13 ....$75.00
#0050 Bunny Chick Tandem Cart, C13 ....$100.00
#0075 Baby Duck Tandem Cart, 1953, no number on toy, C13 ....$100.00
#0100 Dr Doodle, 1931, C13................................$800.00
#0100 Dr Doodle, 1995, 1st Fisher-Price limited edition of 5,000, C13 ....$125.00
#0100 Musical Sweeper, 1950, plays Whistle While You Work, C13 ....$250.00
#0101 Granny Doodle, 1931, C13 ....$800.00
#0102 Drumming Bear, 1931, C13........................$700.00
#0102 Drumming Bear, 1932, fatter & taller version, C13 ..$700.00
#0103 Barky Puppy, 1931, C13 ....$700.00
#0104 Looky Monk, 1931, C13..............................$700.00
#0105 Bunny Scoot, 1931, C13.............................$700.00
#0107 Music Box Clock Radio, 1971, plays Hickory Dickory Dock $5.00
#0109 Lucky Monk, 1932, C13..............................$700.00
#0110 Chubby Chief, 1932, C13............................$700.00
#0111 Play Family Merry-Go-Round, 1972-76, plays Skater's Waltz, w/4 figures, C13..................................$40.00
#0112 Picture Disk Camera, 1968-71, w/5 picture disks, C13 .$40.00
#0114 Music Box TV, 1967, plays London Bridge & Row Row Row Your Boat as picture passes screen, C13.............$20.00
#0114 Sesame Street Music Box TV, 1984-87, plays People in Your Neighborhood, C13 ....$10.00
#0118 Tumble Tower Game, 1972-75, w/10 marbles, C13 .$15.00

#0125 Music Box Iron, 1967-69, $50.00.

#0120 Cackling Hen, 1958, wht, C13..............................$40.00
#0121 Happy Hopper, 1969-76, C13.................................$25.00
#0122 Bouncing Buggy, 1974-79, 6 wheels, C13 ....$10.00
#0123 Cackling Hen, 1967, red litho, C13 ....$40.00
#0125 Uncle Timmy Turtle, 1956, red shell, C13 ....$100.00
#0130 Wobbles, 1964-65, dog wobbles when pulled, C13 ..$50.00
#0131 Milk Wagon, 1964, truck w/bottle carrier, C13 .....$55.00
#0131 Toy Wagon, 1951 driver's head pops up & down when pulled by 2 musical horses, C13 ....$250.00
#0132 Dr Doodle, 1957, C13...$85.00
#0132 Molly Moo Cow, 1972-78, C13..............................$35.00
#0135 Play Animal Circus, 1974-76, complete, C13........$50.00
#0136 Play Family Lacing Shoe, 1966-69, complete, C13 ..$50.00
#0137 Pony Chime, 1962, pk plastic wheels, C13 ....$40.00
#0138 Jack-in-the-Box Puppet, 1970-73, C13 ....$30.00

#0139 Tuggy Tooter, 1967-73, $40.00.

#0139 Tuggy Turtle, 1959, C13 ....$100.00
#0140 Coaster Boy, 1941, C13.......................................$700.00
#0142 Three Men in a Tub, 1970-73, w/bell atop spring mast, C13..$20.00
#0145 Humpty Dumpty Truck, 1963, rnd heads w/wood nose, C13..$40.00
#0146 Play Pull-A-Long Lacing Shoe, 1970-75, w/6 figures, & 50" rnd lace, C13 ....$45.00
#0148 TV-Radio, 1959-67, Jack & Jill, wood & plastic, C13 ..$40.00
#0149 Dog Cart Donald, 1936, C13................................$700.00
#0150 Barky Bubby, 1934, C13......................................$600.00
#0150 Pop-Up-Pal Chime Phone, 1968-78, C13..............$40.00
#0150 Teddy Turtle, 1940, C13 ....$400.00
#0150 Timmy Turtle, 1953, gr shell, C13 ....$100.00
#0152 Road Roller, 1934, C13..$700.00
#0154 Frisky Frog, 1971-83, squeeze plastic bulb & frog jumps, C13..$20.00
#0154 TV-Radio, 1964-67, Pop Goes the Weasel, wood & plastic, C13 ....$25.00
#0155 Skippy Sam, 1934, C13 ....$850.00
#0155 TV Radio, 1968-70, Jack 'N Jill, wood & plastic w/see-through window on back, C13 ....$40.00

#0156 Circus Wagon, 1942, band leader in wagon, C13 ..**$400.00**

#0156 Jiffy Dump Truck, 1971-73, squeeze bulb & dump moves, C13...**$30.00**

#0156 TV-Radio, 1966-67, Baa-Baa Black Sheep, wood & plastic, C13 ....**$50.00**

#0158 Katie Kangaroo, 1976-77, squeeze bulb & she hops, C13 ....**$30.00**

#0158 TV-Radio, 1967, Little Boy Blue, wood & plastic, C13 ....**$50.00**

#0159 TV-Radio, 1961-65 & Easter 1966, Ten Little Indians, wood & plastic, C13 ....**$20.00**

#0160 Donald & Donna Duck, 1937, C13 ....**$850.00**

#0161 Creative Block Wagon, 1961-64, 18 building blocks & 6 wooden dowels fit into pull-along wagon, C13.........**$75.00**

#0161 Looky Chug-Chug, 1949, C13 ....**$250.00**

#0161 TV-Radio, 1968-70, Old Woman Who Lived in a Shoe, wood & plastic w/see-through window on back, C13.**$40.00**

#0162 Roly Poly Sailboats, 1968-69, C13 ....**$15.00**

#0164 Chubby Cub, 1969-72, C13..................................**$20.00**

#0164 Mother Goose, 1964-66, C13 ....**$40.00**

#0166 Bucky Burro, 1955, C13 ....**$250.00**

#0166 Piggy Bank, 1981-82, pk plastic, C13....................**$20.00**

#0166 TV-Radio, 1963-66, Farmer in the Dell, C13 ....**$20.00**

#0168 Magnetic Chug-Chug, 1964-69, C13 ....**$50.00**

#0168 Snorky Fire Engine, 1960, gr litho, 4 wooden firemen & dog, C13...**$150.00**

#0169 Snorky Fire Engine, 1961, red litho, 4 wht wooden firemen, C13 ....**$150.00**

#0170, American Airline Flagship, 1942, twin-engine plane w/plastic propellers, C13 ....**$700.00**

#0170 Change-A-Tune Carousel, 1981-83, music box w/crank hdl, 3 molded records & 3 child figures, C13.............**$40.00**

#0171 Toy Wagon, 1942, ponies move up & down, bell rings, C13 ....**$300.00**

#0172 Roly Raccoon, 1980-82, waddles side to side, tail bobs & weaves, C13 ....**$15.00**

#0175 Gold Star Stagecoach, 1954, w/2 litho wood mail pouches, C13 ....**$275.00**

#0175 Kicking Donkey, 1937, C13 ....**$450.00**

#0175 TV-Radio, 1971-73, Winnie the Pooh, Sears distribution only, C13 ....**$65.00**

#0177 Donald Duck Xylophone, 1946, 2nd version w/'Donald Duck' on hat, C13 ....**$300.00**

#0177 Oscar the Grouch, 1977-84, C13 ....**$30.00**

#0178 What's in My Pocket, 1972-73, 10-pg cloth book w/8 pockets & 8 plastic replicas of boy's pocket items, C13 ....**$20.00**

#0183 Play Family Fun Jet, 1970-80, 1st version, red plastic wings w/bl engines, 4 wooden figures, no hole for gas, C13 ....**$15.00**

#0185 Donald Duck Xylophone, 1938, mk WDE, C13 ..**$800.00**

#0189 Pull-a-Tune Blue Bird Music Box, 1968-79, hangs on crib, plays Children's Prayer, C13 ....**$15.00**

#0190 Gabby Duck, 1939, C13 ....**$350.00**

#0190 Molly Moo-Moo, 1956, C13.................................**$225.00**

#0190 Pull-A-Tune Pony Music Box, 1969-72, hangs on crib, plays Shubert's Cradle Song, C13 ....**$20.00**

#0191 Golden Gulch Express, 1961, C13 ....$100.00

#0192 Playland Express, 1962, C13..........................$100.00

#0194 Push Pullet, 1971-72, 16" push stick, C13..............$25.00

#0195 Double-Screen TV Music Box, 1965-69, Mary Had a Little Lamb, wood & plastic, C13, from $20 to $30.00

#0195 Teddy Bear Parade, 1938, C13 ....$600.00

#0196 Double-Screen TV Music Box, 1964-69, Hey Diddle Diddle, wood & plastic, C13 ....$30.00

#0200 Mary Doll, 1974-78, vinyl face & hands w/cloth body, removable apron & skirt, C13.................................$25.00

#0200 Mary Doll, 1974-78, vinyl face & hands w/cloth body, removable apron & skirt, MIB, C13..........................$50.00

#0200 Winky Blinky Fire Truck, 1954, C13...................$100.00

#0201 Jenny Doll, 1974-78, vinyl face & hands w/cloth body, removable skirt, C13.......................................$25.00

#0201 Jenny Doll, 1974-78, vinyl face & hands w/cloth body, removable skirt, MIB, C13 ....$50.00

#0201 Woodsy-Wee Circus, 1931, complete, C13 ....$700.00

#0202 Natalie Doll, 1974-78, vinyl face & hands w/cloth body, removable skirt & bonnet, C13.............................$25.00

#0202 Natalie Doll, 1974-78, vinyl face & hands w/cloth body, removable skirt & bonnet, MIB, C13 ....$50.00

#0203 Audrey Doll, 1974-78, vinyl face & hands w/cloth body, removable jeans, C13 ....$25.00

#0203 Audrey Doll, 1974-78, vinyl face & hands w/cloth body, removable jeans, MIB, C13 ....$50.00

#0204 Baby Ann Doll, 1974-78, vinyl face & hands w/cloth body, removable nightgown & diaper, C13 ....$25.00

#0204 Baby Ann Doll, 1974-78, vinyl face & hands w/cloth body, removable nightgown & diaper, MIB, C13 ......$50.00

#0205 Black Elizabeth Doll, 1974-78, vinyl face & hands w/cloth body, removable skirt, C13........................$30.00

#0205 Black Elizabeth Doll, 1974-78, vinyl face & hands w/cloth body, removable skirt, MIB, C13 ....$55.00

#0205 Woodsy-Wee Zoo, 1931, complete w/camel, giraffe, lion, bear & elephant, C13.....................................$700.00

#0206 Joey Doll, 1975, vinyl face & hands w/cloth body, w/jacket, lace & tie sneakers, C13........................$25.00

#0206 Joey Doll, 1975, vinyl face & hands w/cloth body, w/jacket, lace & tie sneakers, MIB, C13 ....$50.00

#0207 Woodsy-Wee Pets, 1931, complete w/goat, donkey, cow, pig & cart, C13 ....$700.00

#0208 Honey Doll, 1978, yel & wht print, C13...............$20.00

#0208 Honey Doll, 1978, yel & wht print, MIB, C13 ......$45.00

#0209 Woodsy-Wee Dog Show, 1932, complete w/5 dogs, C13 ....$700.00

#0215 Fisher-Price Choo-Choo, 1955, engine w/4 cars, C13 ....$85.00

#0234 Nifty Station Wagon, 1960, removable roof, 4 wooden family figures & dog, C13..............................$250.00

#0250 Big Performing Circus, 1932, complete w/figures, animals & accessories, C13..$950.00

#0302 Chick Basket Cart, 1957, C13............................$40.00

#0303 Adventure People Emergency Rescue Truck, 1975-78, complete, C13..$15.00

#0303 Bunny Push Cart, 1957, C13 ....$75.00

#0304 Adventure People Safari Set, 1975-78, complete, C13..$25.00

#0304 Running Bunny Cart, 1957, C13........................$75.00

#0306 Adventure People Sport Plane, 1975-80, orange & wht plane w/gold pilot, C13..$8.00

#0307 Adventure People & Their Wilderness Patrol, 1975-79, complete, C13..$20.00

#0309 Adventure People & Their TV Action Team, 1977-78, complete, C13..$25.00

#0310 Adventure People & Their Sea Explorer, 1975-80, complete, C13..$15.00

#0310 Mickey Mouse Puddle Jumper, 1953, C13 ....$140.00

#0312 Adventure People & Their North Woods Trailblazer, 1977-82, complete, C13 ....$15.00

#0318 Adventure People Daredevil Sports Van, 1978-82, complete, C13..$25.00

#0322 Adventure People Dune Buster, 1979-82, complete, C13 ....$12.00

#0323 Aero-Marine Search Team, 1978-83, complete, C13..$20.00

#0325 Adventure People Alpha Probe, 1980-84, complete, C13 ....$25.00

#0325 Buzzy Bee, 1950, 1st version, dk yel & blk litho, wooden wheels & antenna tips, C13 ....$40.00

#0333 Butch the Pup, 1951, C13 ....$75.00

#0334 Adventure People Sea Shark, 1981-84, complete, C13.$20.00

#0345 Penelope the Performing Penguin, 1935, w/up, C13 .$800.00

#0350 Adventure People Rescue Team, 1976-79, complete, C13..$18.00

#0350 Go 'N Back Mule, 1931, w/up, C13 ....$800.00

#0351 Adventure People Mountain Climbers, 1976-79, complete, C13..$20.00

#0352 Adventure People Construction Workers, 1976-79, complete, C13..$15.00

#0353 Adventure People Scuba Divers, 1976-81, complete, C13 ....$12.00

#0354 Adventure People Daredevil Skydiver, 1977-81, complete, C13..$12.00

#0355 Adventure People White Water Kayak, 1977-80, complete, C13..$15.00

#0355 Go 'N Back Bruno, 1931, C13 ....$800.00

#0356 Adventure People Cycle Racing Team, 1977-81, complete, C13..$10.00

#0357 Adventure People Fire Star 1, blk & silver rocket sled, life-support cable & pilot figure, C13.......................$15.00

#0358 Adventure People Deep Sea Diver, 1980-84, complete, C13..$10.00

#0358 Donald Duck Back-Up, 1936, w/up, C13............$800.00

#0360 Go 'N Back Jumbo, 1931, w/up, C13 ....$800.00

#0365 Puppy Back-Up, 1932, w/up, C13 ....$800.00

#0367 Adventure People Turbo Hawk, 1982-83, complete, C13 ....$15.00

#0368 Adventure People Alpha Interceptor, 1982-83, wht 2-stage space vehicle, astronaut & tether, C13 ....$15.00

#0375 Bruno Back-Up, 1932, w/up, C13 ....$800.00

#0377 Adventure People Astro Knight, 1979-80, foam plastic space glider & figure, C13 ....$15.00

#0400 Donald Duck Drum Major, 1946, C13.................$275.00

#0400 Donald Duck Drum Major Cart, 1946, C13 ....$275.00

#0404 Bunny Egg Cart, 1949, C13 ....$80.00

#0405 Lofty Lizzy, 1931, Giraffe Pop-Up Kritter, C13 ...$225.00

#0407 Chick Cart, 1950, C13 ....$50.00

#0407 Dizzy Dino, 1931, Dinosaur Pop-Up Kritter, C13 ..$225.00
#0410 Stoopy Stork, 1931, Pop-Up Kritter, C13............$225.00
#0415 Lop-Ear Looie, 1934, Mouse Pop-Up Kritter, C13 .$225.00
#0415 Super Jet, 1952, C13....................................$225.00
#0420 Sunny Fish, 1955, C13 ....$225.00
#0422 Jumbo Jitterbug, 1940, Elephant Pop-Up Kritter, C13...$225.00
#0425 Donald Duck Pop-Up, 1938, C13 ....$400.00
#0432 Mickey Mouse Choo-Choo, mk WDE, 1938, C13 .$600.00
#0432-532 Donald Duck Drum Major Cart, 1948, C13 .$300.00

#0445 Hot Dog Wagon, 1940, $225.00.

Photo courtesy Brad Cassity.

#0433 Dizzy Donkey, 1939, Pop-Up Kritter, C13...........$125.00
#0434 Ferdinand the Bull, 1939, C13 ....$600.00
#0435 Happy Apple, 1979, short stem, C13........................$3.00
#0440 Goofy Gertie, 1935, Stork Pop-Up Kritter, C13..$225.00
#0440 Pluto Pop-Up, 1936, mk WDE, oilcloth ears, C13 .$225.00
#0440 Pluto Pop-Up, 1936, mk WDP, C13 ....$125.00
#0444, Queen Buzzy Bee, 1959, red litho, C13 ....$40.00
#0445 Nosey Pup, 1956, C13..................................$75.00
#0448 Mini Copter, 1971-83, bl litho, C13 ....$25.00
#0450 Donald Duck Choo-Choo, 1941, 8½", C13.........$400.00
#0450 Donald Duck Choo-Choo, 1942, bl hat, C13 ......$200.00
#0450 Music Box Bear, 1981-83, plays Schubert's Cradle Song,
     plastic, C13 ....$15.00
#0454 Donald Duck Drummer, 1949, C13 ....$300.00
#0460 Dapper Donald Duck, 1936, C13 ....$600.00
#0460 Movie Viewer, 1973-90, crank hdl, C13 ....$5.00
#0460-499 Movie Viewer Cartridge's, 1973-90, color, C13 ...$6.00
#0469 Donald Cart, 1940, C13 ....$400.00
#0474 Bunny Racer, 1942, C13..................................$225.00
#0476 Cookie Pig, 1967, C13....................................$50.00
#0476 Mickey Mouse Drummer, 1941, C13 ....$300.00
#0477 Dr Doodle, 1940, C13....................................$225.00
#0478 Pudgy Pig, 1962, C13 ....$50.00
#0480 Leo the Drummer, 1952, C13............................$225.00
#0485 Mickey Mouse Choo-Choo, 1949, new litho version of
     #432, C13 ....$100.00
#0488 Popeye Spinach Eater, 1939, C13 ....$600.00
#0494 Pinocchio, 1939, C13 ....$600.00

#0499 Kitty Bell, 1950, C13 ....$125.00

#0500 Donald Duck Cart, 1937, no number on toy, 3 colors, C13 ....$700.00

#0500 Donald Duck Cart, 1951, no baton, gr litho background, C13 ....$350.00

#0500 Donald Duck Cart, 1953, w/baton, new litho w/yel background, C13 ....$350.00

#0500 Pick-Up & Peek Puzzles, 1972-86, C13 ....$10.00

#0510 Strutter Donald Duck, 1941, C13 ....$300.00

#0530 Mickey Mouse Band, 1935, C13 ....$900.00

#0533 Thumper Bunny, 1942, C13 ....$500.00

#0544 Donald Duck Cart, 1942, $300.00.

#0550 Toy Lunch Kit, 1957, red, wht & gr plastic barn shape, no litho, C13 ....$40.00

#0600 Tailspin Tabby Pop-Up, 1947, 5", NM, A $235.00

#0604 Bunny Bell Cart, 1954, C13 ....$100.00

#0605 Donald Duck Cart, 1954, C13 ....$300.00

#0605 Horse & Wagon, 1933, C13 ....$600.00

#0605 Woodsey Major Goodgrub Mole & Book, 1981, 32-pgs, C13 ....$20.00

#0606 Woodsey Bramble Beaver & Book, 1981, 32 pgs, C13 .$20.00

#0607 Woodsey Very Blue Bird & Book, 1981, 32 pgs, C13 ...$20.00

#0615 Tow Truck, 1960, C13 ....$75.00

#0616 Chuggy Pop-Up, 1955, C13 ....$100.00

#0616 Patch Pony, 1963, C13 ....$50.00

#0617 Prancing Pony, 1965-70, C13 ....$40.00

#0625 Playful Puppy, 1961, w/shoe, C13 ....$50.00

#0626 Playful Puppy, 1963, w/shoe, C13 ....$50.00

#0628 Tug-A-Dug, 1975-77, C13 ....$15.00

#0629 Fisher-Price Tractor, 1962, C13 ....$50.00

#0630 Fire Truck, 1959, C13 ....$50.00

#0634 Drummer Boy, 1967-69, drummer beats hollow drum w/spring-mounted mallets, plastic base, C13 ....$50.00

#0641 Toot-Toot Engine, 1962, bl litho, C13 ....$75.00

#0642 Dinky Engine, 1959, blk litho, C13 ....$75.00

#0642 Smokie Engine, 1960, blk litho, C13 ....$75.00

#0643 Toot-Toot Engine, 1964, plastic wheels, C13 ....$5.00

#0649 Stake Truck, 1960, C13 ....$50.00

#0653 Allie Gator, 1960, C13 ....$100.00

#0654 Tawny Tiger, 1962, C13 ....$125.00

#0656 Bossy Bell, 1960, w/bonnet, C13 ....$60.00

#0656 Bossy Bell, 1961, no bonnet, new litho design, C13 .$50.00

#0658 Lady Bug, 1961-62, C13 ....$55.00

#0659 Puzzle Puppy, 1976, 8-pc take-apart & put-together dog, C13 ....$15.00

#0662 Merry Mousewife, 1962, C13 ....$50.00

#0677 Picnic Basket, 1975-79, plastic w/accessories & cotton tablecloth, C13 ....$30.00

#0678 Kriss Krickey, 1955, C13 ....$100.00

#0684 Little Lamb, 1964-65, C13 ....$50.00

#0685 Car & Boat, 1968-69, wood & plastic, 5 pcs, C13 .$40.00

#0686 Car & Camper, 1968-70, wood & plastic, 5 pcs, C13 ...$50.00

#0686 Perky Pot, 1958, C13 ....$50.00

#0693 Little Snoopy, 1964-87, C13 ....$3.00

#0695 Pinky Pig, 1956, missing wooden eyes, C13 ....$100.00

#0695 Pinky Pig, 1958, litho eyes, C13 ....$100.00

#0698 Talky Parrot, 1963, C13 ....$100.00

#0700 Cowboy Chime, 1951, C13 ....$250.00

#0700 Popeye, 1935, hitting bell, C13 ....$700.00

#0700 Woofy Wowser, 1940, C13 ....$400.00

#0703 Bunny Engine, 1954, C13 ....$100.00

#0703 Popeye the Sailor, 1936, C13 ....$700.00

#0705 Mini Snowmobile, 1971-73, w/sled, 2 figures & dog, C13 ....$50.00

#0705 Popeye Cowboy, 1937, on horse, C13 ....$700.00

#0711 Cry Baby Bear, 1967-69, C13 ....$40.00

#0711 Huckleberry Hound, 1961, Sears only, C13 ....$300.00

#0711 Raggedy Ann & Andy, 1941, C13 ....$850.00

#0712 Fred Flintstone Xylophone, 1962, Sears only, C13 ..$250.00

#0712 Teddy Tooter, 1957, C13 ....$250.00

#0714 Mickey Mouse Xylophone, 1963, Sears only, C13..$275.00

#0715 Ducky Flip Flap, 1964-65, 21" push stick, C13 ......$50.00

#0715 Peter Bunny Engine, 1941, $225.00.

#0717 Ducky Flip Flap, 1937-40, Easter only, C13 ....$400.00

#0718 Tow Truck & Car, 1969-70, wood & plastic, C13.$30.00

#0719 Cuddly Cub, 1973-77, head turns & chimes when rocked, C13 ....$15.00

#0719 Fisher-Price Choo-Choo, 1963, engine, 3 cars, 3 figures & dog, C13 ....$40.00

#0720 Fisher-Price Fire Engine, 1969, w/wood driver & 2 firemen, C13 ....$20.00

#0720 Pinocchio, 1939, C13 ....$500.00

#0721 Peter Bunny Engine, 1949, C13 ....$200.00

#0724 Jolly Jalopy, 1965-78, circus clown's roadster, C13...$15.00

#0725 Play Family Bath/Utility Room Set, 1972, 4 wooden figures & accessories, C13..$20.00

#0726 Play Family Patio Set, 1970, 3 figures w/dog & accessories, C13 ....$20.00

#0728 Buddy Bullfrog, 1959, yel body w/red litho coat, C13 ...$75.00

#0728 Buddy Bullfrog, 1961, gr coat w/red & wht pants, C13 .$75.00

#0728 Play Family House Decorator Set, 1970, 4 figures w/accessories, C13 ....$20.00

#0729 Play Family Kitchen Set, 1970, w/4 figures & accessories, C13...$20.00

#0730 Racing Rowboat, 1952, C13 ....$350.00

#0732 Happy Hauler, 1968-70, wooden garden tractor w/plastic cart, C13 ....$40.00

#0733 Mickey Mouse Saftey Patrol, 1956, C13 ....$250.00

#0734 Teddy Zilo, 1964-66, C13 ....$45.00

#0735 Juggling Jumbo, 1958, C13 ....$250.00

#0736 Humpty Dumpty, 1972-79, plastic, C13 ....$8.00

#0737 Galloping Horse & Wagon, 1948, C13................$250.00

#0737 Ziggy Zilo, 1958, C13...$75.00

#0738 Dumbo Circus Racer, 1941, rubber arms, C13.....$700.00

#0738 Shaggy Zilo, 1960, C13 ....$75.00

#0739 Poodle Zilo, 1962, C13 ....$75.00

#0741 Teddy Zilo, 1967, C13 ....$40.00

#0741 Trotting Donald Duck, 1937, C13 ....$800.00

#0745 Elsie's Dairy Truck, 1948, w/2 bottles, C13 ....$550.00

#0746 Pocket Radio, 1977-78, It's a Small World, wood & plastic, C13 ....$25.00

#0750 Hot Dog Wagon, 1938, C13................................$400.00

#0750 Space Blazer, 1953, C13 ....$400.00

#0752 Teddy Zilo, 1948, 1st version, clown outfit w/red cheeks, C13 ....$350.00

#0752 Teddy Zilo, 1948, 2nd version, no outfit, C13.....$325.00

#0756 Pocket Radio, 1973, 12 Days of Christmas, wood & plastic, C13 ....$25.00

#0757 Humpty Dumpty, 1957, C13 ....$250.00

#0758 Pocket Radio, 1970-72, Mulberry Bush, wood & plastic, C13...$20.00

#0759 Pocket Radio, 1969-73, Do-Re-Me, wood & plastic, C13 ....$20.00

#0760 Peek-A-Boo Block, 1970-79, C13 ....$20.00

#0761 Play Family Nursery Set, 1973, family of 4 w/baby & accessories, C13...$20.00

#0762 Pocket Radio, 1972-77, Raindrops, wood & plastic, C13 ....$15.00

#0763 Music Box, 1962, Farmer in the Dell, yel litho, C13.$50.00

#0763 Pocket Radio, 1978, Whistle a Happy Tune, wood & plastic, C13 ....$20.00

#0764 Music Box, 1960-61 & Easter 1962, Farmer in the Dell, red litho, C13...$50.00

#0764 Pocket Radio, 1975-76, My Name Is Michael, C13 ..$15.00

#0765 Pocket Radio, 1976, Humpty Dumpty, wood & plastic, C13...$25.00

#0765 Talking Donald Duck, 1955, C13 ....$125.00

#0766 Pocket Radio, 1968-70, Where Has My Little Dog Gone?, wood & plastic, C13 ....$20.00

#0766 Pocket Radio, 1977-78, I'd Like To Teach the World To Sing, C13 ....$20.00

#0767 Pocket Radio, 1977, Twinkle Twinkle Little Star, C13...$20.00

#0767 Tiny Ding-Dong, 1940, C13................................$400.00

#0768 Pocket Radio, 1971-76, Happy Birthday, wood & plastic, C13...$15.00

#0770 Doc & Dopey Dwarfs, 1938, C13 ....$800.00

#0772 Pocket Radio, 1974-76, Jack & Jill, C13 ....$15.00

#0773 Tip-Toe Turtle, 1962, $20.00.

#0774 Pocket Radio, 1967-71, Twinkle Twinkle Little Star, wood & plastic, C13 ....$20.00

#0775 Pocket Radio, 1967-68, Sing a Song of Six Pence, C13...$25.00

#0775 Pocket Radio, 1973-75, Pop Goes the Weasel, wood & plastic, C13 ....$15.00

#0775 Teddy Drummer, 1936, C13................................$675.00

#0777 Pushy Bruno, 1934, C13 ....$725.00

#0777 Squeaky the Clown, 1958, C13 ....$250.00

#0778 Ice Cream Wagon, 1940, C13 ....$350.00

#0778 Pocket Radio, 1967-68, Frere Jacques, wood & plastic, C13...$20.00

#0779 Pocket Radio, 1976, Yankee Doodle, wood & plastic, C13...$20.00

#0780 Jumbo Xylophone, 1937, C13 ....$275.00

#0784 Mother Goose Music Cart, 1955, C13 ....$100.00

#0785 Blackie Drummer, 1939, C13 ....$550.00

#0785 Corn Popper, 1957, red base w/bl wood wheels, C13 ..$85.00

#0786 Perky Penguin, 1973-75, C13 ....$30.00

#0788 Rock-A-Bye Bunny Cart, 1940, C13 ....$300.00

#0791 Candy Man Tote-A-Tune Radio, 1979, Let's Go Fly a Kite, plastic, C13 ....$15.00

#0792 Music Box, 1980-81, Teddy Bear's Picnic, plastic, C13 ....$15.00

#0793 Jolly Jumper, 1963, C13......................................$50.00

#0793 Tote-A-Tune Radio, 1981, When You Wish Upon a Star, plastic, C13 ....$10.00

#0794 Big Bill Pelican, 1961, w/cb fish, C13 ....$85.00

#0794 Tote-A-Tune Radio, 1982-91, Over the Rainbow, plastic, C13 ....$5.00

#0795 Mickey Mouse Drummer, 1937, pie-eyed, C13 ....$700.00

#0795 Musical Duck, 1952, C13 ....$100.00

#0795 Tote-A-Tune Radio, 1984-91, Toyland, C13 ....$10.00

#0798 Chatter Monk, 1957, C13 ....$100.00

#0798 Mickey Mouse Xylophone, 1939, 1st version, w/hat, C13 ....$450.00

#0798 Mickey Mouse Xylophone, 1942, 2nd version, no hat, C13 ....$450.00

#0800 Hot Diggety, 1934, w/up, C13 ....$700.00

#0808 Pop'n Ring, 1956, C13 ....$85.00

#0810 Hot Mammy, 1934, w/up, C13 ....$700.00

#0909 Play Family Rooms, 1972, Sears only, 4 figures w/dog & accessories, C13, from $75 to $125.00

#0910 Change-A-Tune Piano, 1969-72, Pop Goes the Weasel, This Old Man & The Muffin Man, C13 ....$40.00

#0910 This Little Pig, 1963, C13 ....$40.00

#0915 Play Family Farm, 1968-91, 1st version, complete, $30.00.

#0916 Fisher-Price Zoo, 1984-87, 6 figures w/accessories, C13 ....$35.00

#0919 Music Box Movie Camera, 1968-70, plays This Old Man, w/5 picture disks, C13 ....$40.00

#0923 Play Family School, 1971-78, 1st version, roof & side hinge open, 5 figures & accessories, C13 ....$30.00

#0926 Concrete Mixer, 1959, C13 ....$250.00

#0928 Play Family Fire Station, 1980-82, w/3 figures, dog & accessories, C13 ....$75.00

#0929 Play Family Nursery School, 1978-79, 6 figures & accessories, removable roof, 13¾x10x5½", C13 ....$70.00

#0930 Play Family Action Garage, 1970-85, 1st version, w/elevator ramp, 4 cars & 4 figures, masonite & plastic, C13...$20.00

#0931 Play Family Hospital, 1976-78, w/figures & accessories, C13 ....$125.00

#0932 Amusement Park, 1963, park map, 5 wooden figures, musical merry-go-round & accessories, C13 ....$325.00

#0932 Ferry Boat, 1979-80, 3 figures, 2 cars & 2 life preservers, C13..$25.00

#0934 Play Family Western Town, 1982-84, 4 figures & accessories, C13..$75.00

#0937 Play Family Sesame Street Clubhouse, 1977-79, w/4 Sesame Street characters & accessories, C13 ....$75.00

#0938 Play Family Sesame Street, 1975-78, w/8 Sesame Street characters & accessories, C13....................$75.00

#0940 Sesame Street Characters, 1977, C13, ea $3.00

#0942 Play Family Lift & Load Depot, 1977-79, w/3 figures & accessories, C13 ....$50.00

#0945 Offshore Cargo Base, 1979-80, 3 platforms, 4 figures & accessories, C13 ....$50.00

#0952 Play Family House, 1969-79, 1st version, 2-story w/yel roof, figures & accessories (no cb delivery truck), C13.........$35.00

#0952 Play Family House, 1980-87, 2nd version, new-style litho & brn roof, no staircase, C13 ....$20.00

#0952 Play Family House, 1987-88, 2-story w/brn roof, gr plastic base, complete, C13 ....$20.00

#0960 Woodsey's Log House, 1979, w/figures, accessories & 32-pg book, C13 ....$40.00

#0961 Woodsey's Store, 1980, hollow tree w/figures, accessories & 32-pg book, C13 ....$40.00

#0962 Woodsey's Airport, 1980, airplane, hanger, 1 figure & 32-pg book, C13 ....$40.00

#0969 Musical Ferris Wheel, 1966-72, 1st version w/4 wooden straight-body figures, rods in seats, C13 ....$50.00

#0979 Dump Trucker Playset, 1965-70, w/3 figures & accessories, C13..$75.00

#0982 Hot Rod Roadster, 1983-84, riding toy w/4-pc take-apart engine, C13..$65.00

#0983 Safety School Bus, 1959, w/6 figures, Fisher-Price Club logo, C13 ....$250.00

#0985 Play Family Houseboat, 1972-76, w/2 deck lounges, figures & accessories, C13..$40.00

#0987 Creative Coaster, 1964-81, $75.00.

#0990 Play Family A-Frame, 1974-76, w/4 figures, dog & accessories, C13..$75.00

#0991 Music Box Lacing Shoe, 1964-67, w/3 wooden straight-body figures, red & wht shoelace, C13 ....$50.00

#0991 Play Family Circus Train, 1973-78, 1st version, w/figures, animals & gondola car, C13 ....$25.00

#0991 Play Family Circus Train, 1979-86, 2nd version, w/figures & animals, no gondola car, C13 ....$15.00

#0992 Play Family Car & Camper, 1980-84, camper unfolds into tent, 4 figures & accessories, C13................................$35.00

#0993 Play Family Castle, 1974-77, 1st version, w/6 figures & accessories, C13 ....$100.00

#0994 Play Family Camper, 1973-76, w/4 figures & accessories, C13...$75.00

#0996 Play Family Airport, 1972-76, 1st version, bl airport w/clear look-out tower, 6 figures & accessories, C13 .$70.00

#0997 Play Family Village, 1973-77, 2-pc village w/bridge, 8 figures, dog & accessories, C13.................................$75.00

#2500 Little People Main Street, 1986-90, 8 figures & accessories, C13..$50.00

#2525 Little People Playground, 1986-90, w/2 figures & accessories, C13...$15.00

#2526 Little People Pool, 1986-88, w/2 figures & accessories, C13...$15.00

#2551 Little People Neighborhood, 1988-90, 2-pc playset connects w/tree house, 4 figures & accessories, C13........$55.00

#2552 McDonald's Restaurant, 1990, 1st version, bl car trash can, fry coaster, arches & 5 figures, C13, from $75 to $75.00

#2552 McDonald's Restaurant, 1991-92, 2nd version, same pcs as 1st version but lg-sz figures, C13 ....$50.00

#6145 Jingle Elephant, 1993, ToyFest limited edition of 5,000, C13 ....$100.00

#6464 Grana'Pa Frog, 1994 ToyFest limited edition of 5,000, C13..$60.00

#6550 Buzzy Bee, 1987, ToyFest limited edition of 5,000, C13 ....$120.00

#6558 Snoopy Sniffer, 1988, ToyFest limited edition of 3,000, C13 ....$600.00

#6575 Toot-Toot, 1989, ToyFest limited edition of 5,000, C13..$100.00

#6588 Snoopy Sniffer, 1990, Fisher-Price Commemorative limited edition of 3,500, Ponderosa pine, C13..............$150.00

#6590 Prancing Horses, 1990, ToyFest limited edition of 5,000, C13 ....$100.00

#6592 Teddy Bear Parade, 1991, ToyFest limited edition of 5,000, C13...$70.00

#6593 Squeaky the Clown, 1995, ToyFest limited edition of 5,000, C13 ....$150.00

#6599 Molly Bell Cow, 1992, ToyFest limited edition of 5,000, C13 ....$175.00

#8121 My Friend Karen Doll, 1990, was never produced, C13 ....$125.00

Games

Early games (those from 1850 to 1910) are very often appreciated more for their wonderful lithographed boxes than their 'playability,' and you'll find collectors displaying them as they would any fine artwork. Many boxes and boards were designed by commercial artists of the day.

Though they were in a decline a few years ago, baby-boomer game prices have leveled off. Some science fiction and rare TV games are still in high demand. Games produced in the Art Deco era between the World Wars have gained in popularity —

especially those with great design. Victorian games have become harder to find; their prices have also grown steadily. Condition and rarity are the factors that most influence game prices.

When you buy a game, check to see that all pieces are there. Look on the instructions or in the box lid for a listing of contents. For further information we recommend *Baby Boomer Games* by Rick Polizzi (Collector Books) and *Board Games of the '50s, '60s and '70s* (L-W Book Sales). Note: In the listings that follow, assume that all are board games (unless specifically indicated card game, target game, bagatelle, etc.), and that each is complete as issued, unless missing components are mentioned.

Advisor: Paul Fink (F3).

See also Black Americana; specific categories.

$64,000 Question, Lowell, 1955, NMIB, F8 ....$50.00

Acme Bible Book Game, card game, Goodenough & Woglow, 1930s, VG (VG box), S16...............................$45.00

Across the Continent, Parker Bros, 1952, EX (EX box) ...$50.00

Addams Family, card game, Milton Bradley, 1964, incomplete, VG, S16...$45.00

Adventures of Lassie, Lisbeth Whiting, 1955, EX (NM box), A...$50.00

Aerial Contest, JW Spear & Sons, EX (EX box), A.......$450.00

Air Raid Defense Target, Wyandotte, 1940, NM (VG box), A...$175.00

Alphabet Board Game, Cress, 1916, 10" dia, G, A...........$50.00

Amazing Dunninger Mind Reading Game, Hasbro, MIB, $20.00.

Amazing Spider-Man & Fantastic Four, Milton Bradley, 1977, MIB (sealed), T2...$50.00

Annette's Secret Passage Game, Parker Bros, 1958, VG (VG box)...$50.00

Annie, Parker Bros, 1981, VG (VG box), S16 ....$22.00

Archie Bunker, card game, Milton Bradley, 1970s, MIB, J5.$15.00

Around the World With Nellie Bly, McLoughlin Bros, 1890, EXIB, F3..$325.00

Art Linkletter's House Party, Whitman, 1968, NM+ (NM box), P3, from $30 to $50.00

Astronaut Outer Space, card game, 1962, MIB, J2 ....$25.00

Auto Drome, skill game, Transogram, 1967, NMIB, F8..$45.00

Automobile Race, LH Mace, 1905, VG (orig box), A ...$625.00

Baretta, Milton Bradley, 1976, VG (VG box), S16..........$20.00

Barnabas Collins Dark Shadows, Milton Bradley, 1969, NM (NM box), F8...$40.00

Barney Google & Spark Plug, Milton Bradley, 1923, NM (EX box), A $175.00

Barney Miller, Parker Bros, 1977, VG (VG box), S16 .....$20.00

Baseball, McLoughlin Bros, 1886, VG (wooden box), A..$1,000.00

Baseball, Parker Bros, 1950, VG (VG box), S16 ....$35.00

Baseball & Checkers, Milton Bradley, ca 1900, EX (worn box), A...$225.00

Bat Masterson, Lowell, 1956, EXIB, S16..........................$90.00

Batman, card game, Ideal, 1966, NM (VG+ box), A $55.00

Batman, card game, Whitman, 1966, EX (clear plastic box), A $45.00

Batman, Milton Bradley, 1966, EX+ (EX+ box), A..........$65.00

Batman Adventures of the Caped Crusader, Hasbro, EXIB, T1 ....$30.00

Batman Game, University Games, 1989, 50th Anniversary edition, EXIB, S16...$40.00

Battle Cry, Milton Bradley, 1961, VG (G box), S16........$35.00

Battle of the Planets, Milton Bradley, 1979, VG (VG box)..$35.00

Battle Star Galactica, Parker Bros, 1978, French-Canadian version, name in English/French, EXIB, S16 ....$55.00

Battlestar Galactica, Parker Bros, 1978, VG (VG box), S16..$20.00

Beetle Bailey, Milton Bradley, 1964, EXIB, J2 ....$65.00

Ben Hur Chariot Race, Lowe, 1959, EXIB, P3 ....$50.00

Bicycle Race, McLoughlin Bros, VG+ (VG+ wooden box), A...$500.00

Billionaire, Parker Bros, 1973, VG (VG box)...................$25.00

Bionic Woman, Parker Bros, 1976, VG (VG box), S16...$30.00

Black Beauty, Transogram, 1958, EXIB, T1......................$25.00

Black Cat Fortune Telling Game, Parker Bros, 1930s, NMIB, F8...$45.00

Blackout, Today's Game of Thrills, Milton Bradley, 1939, MIB, F3, $85.00.

Blockade, Corey Games, 1941, early version w/metal pcs, VG (G box), S16...$75.00

Blondie, card game, Whitman, 1941, NM (EX box), A ...$50.00

Boy Scouts Progress Game, Parker Bros, 1924, VG+ (VG+ box), A...$225.00

Bozo TV Lotto, Ideal, 1961, NMIB, T2 ....$30.00

Branded, Milton Bradley, 1960s, EXIB, F3, $50.00.

Break the Bank, Bettye-B Prod, 1955, NM (EX box), A ..$50.00

Break-A-Plate Carnival Pitch, target game, Transogram, 1964, NM (EX box), F8...$55.00

Brownie Horseshoe Game, MH Miller, G, A $150.00

Buck Rogers Game of the 25th Century, Lutz/Slesinger, 1934, missing playing pcs, scarce, EX (VG box), A $500.00

Bugaloos, Milton Bradley, 1971, VG (VG box), S16 ....$25.00

Buster Brown Bag Toss, Bliss, ca 1900, target only, paper litho on wood, some wear, A $250.00

Buying & Selling, Milton Bradley, EXIB, A $250.00

Calling All Cars, Parker Bros, 1938, EXIB, S16...............$30.00

Camelot, John Waddington Ltd/Great Britain, 1960s, EX (G box), S16...$25.00

Candid Camera, Lowell, 1963, NM (EX box), F8 ....$70.00

Captain Kangaroo, Milton Bradley, 1956, EX (VG box), A ..$35.00

Captive Princess & Pathfinders Tournament, McLoughlin Bros, EX (G slip case), A...$150.00

Careers, Parker Bros, 1957, VG (VG box), S16................$30.00

Catching Mice, McLoughlin Bros, 1888, EXIB, A $275.00

Cats & Mice, Gantlope & Lost Diamond, McLoughlin Bros, EX (EX slip case), A...$200.00

Champion Bowling Alley, Gotham, 1930s, EX (partial box), A $85.00

Charlie Chaplin Ball Toss, European, paper on wood, diecut image w/pendulum causing target eyes to move, 22", VG+, A...$1,000.00

Charlie McCarthy Game of Topper, Whitman, 1938, EX (EX box), F8...$60.00

Charlie's Angels, Milton Bradley, 1978, NM (EX box), F8 ..$35.00

Checkered Game of Life, Milton Bradley, ca 1911, early reissue, EX (VG box), A...$225.00

Checkered Game of Life (New England Series), Milton Bradley, Pat 1866, VG (G implement box only), A.............$200.00

Checkers, Backgammon & Tousel, McLoughlin Bros, incomplete, (G- slip cover), A...$50.00

Chester Gump Game, Milton Bradley, 1938, NM (EX+ box), A.$145.00

Chiromagica, McLoughlin Bros, 1870s, VG (VG box), A...$350.00

Chopper Strike, Milton Bradley, 1975, VG (VG box), S16...$22.00

Christmas Jewel, McLoughlin Bros, 1899, EX (EX box), A .$650.00

Chuggedy Chug, Milton Bradley, 1955, VG (VG box) $75.00

Chutes & Ladders, Milton Bradley, 1956, early version, G (G box), S16...$30.00

Chutes & Ladders, Parker Bros, 1977, VG (VG box), S16..$20.00

Classic Major League Baseball, Game Time, 1987, incomplete, VG (VG box), S16...$65.00

Columbo Detective Game, Milton Bradley, 1973, EXIB, J2 ..$15.00

Combat, Ideal, 1963, G (G box), S16...............................$25.00

Combination Board Games — 7 Games in One, Wilder Mfg, EXIB, A $125.00

Comical Conversation Cards, Parker Bros, 1890s, EXIB, F3 ..$45.00

Comical Tivoli, Spear, EXIB, A.......................................$250.00

Concentration, Milton Bradley, 1959, 1st edition, VG (VG box), S16...$40.00

Photo courtesy June Moon.

Cootie, W.H. Schaper Mfg. Co. Inc., 1950s, MIB, J6, $45.00.

Countdown Space Game, Transogram, 1959, rare, VG (VG box)...$50.00

Course a Anes — The Donkey Race, EXIB, A...............$600.00

Cover 'Em Up, Parker Bros, 1891, VG (VG box), S16 ..$210.00

Crazy Clock, Ideal, 1964, NM (EX box), F8 ....$80.00

Creature Features, Athol Research, 1975, VG (VG box), S16...$145.00

Cross Country Race by Land, Air & Sea, Chicago Game Co, 1922, incomplete, G (orig box), A $575.00

Crow Hunt, Parker Bros, 1930, EX (G box), S16 ....$75.00

Dark Shadows Mysterious Maze, Whitman, 1968, EX (EX box), F8...$30.00

Dave Garroway's Today Game, Quality, 1960s, NMIB, F8 ..$90.00

Davy Crockett Rescue Race, Gabriel, 1955, NMIB, F8....$95.00

Deck Derby, Wolverine, 1937, litho tin, rare, NM (VG box), A...$95.00

Detectives, Transogram, 1961, EXIB, J5 ....$50.00

Dice Ball, Milton Bradley, 1934, VG (VG box), S16.......$70.00

Dick Tracy Bagatelle Pinball, Marx, 1960s, NMIB, D11 ..$75.00

Dick Tracy Mystery, card game, Whitman, 1937, complete, EXIB, T1 ....$45.00

Dick Tracy Sunday Funnies, Ideal, 1972, MIB, D11.........$50.00

Dino the Dinosaur, Transogram, 1961, VG (VG box), S16 ..$60.00

Disneyland, card game, Whitman, 1964, old store stock, MIP (sealed), A $25.00

Disneyland, pinball game, Wolverine, 1970s, 25", EX, A.$75.00

District Messenger Boy, McLoughlin Bros, 1886, VG+ (VG box)...$250.00

Donald Duck, card game, Whitman, 1941, NM (EX box), A ..$60.00

Donald Duck Bean Bag Party, Parker Bros, 1939, EXIB, M8 ...$65.00

Dondi Potato Race, Hassenfeld Bros, 1950s, G (G box), S16..$28.00

Donkey Party, McLoughlin Bros, 1890, VG+ (VG+ box) .$100.00

Double Board Game of Football, Baseball & Checkers, Parker Bros, EX (EX box), A $175.00

Down You Go, Selchow & Righter, 1954, VG (VG box), S16...$25.00

Dr Dolittle, card game, Whitman #4851, NMIB, A7 ....$25.00

Dr Dolittle, Mattel #5451, 3-D w/floating island, NMIB, A7..$60.00

Dr Dolittle Animal Electric Picture Quiz, Remco #890, NMIB, A7...$30.00

Dragnet TV, Transogram, 1955, incomplete, VG (VG box), T1...$45.00

Drew Pearson's Predict-A-Word, Dee-Jay, 1949, VG (VG box)...$25.00

Duck Shooting, Parker Bros, 1901, VG (VG box), S16 ...$75.00

Easy Money, Milton Bradley, 1936, VG (VG box), S16 ..$22.00

Electric Bunny Run, Prentice, 1951, NM (EX box), T2..$50.00

Electronic Radar Search, Ideal, 1969, NMIB, M17 ....$65.00

Ella Cinders, Milton Bradley, 1944, NM (EX box), A $85.00

Elliot Ness & the Untouchables, Transogram, 1961, NMIB, A.$100.00

Eroi Del Futuro (Rockets Away Space Game) Italy, 1950s, EX (VG+ box), A...$250.00

Errand Boy, McLoughlin Bros, 1891, EX (EX wooden box), A...$300.00

Escape From Colditz, Parker Bros/British, 1960s, VG (VG box)...$100.00

Everest, skill game, J&L Randall Ltd/England, 1961, incomplete, VG (VG box), S16 ....$60.00

F-Troop, Ideal, 1965, NM (NM box), A.........................$165.00

Fall Guy, Milton Bradley, 1982, EXIB, S16 ....$20.00

Fang Bang, Milton Bradley, 1967, NMIB, F8.................$50.00

Fantasy Island, Ideal, 1978, NM (EX box), P3.................$20.00

FBI Game, Transogram, MIB (sealed), A $150.00

Felix the Cat, Milton Bradley, 1960, NM (EX box), F8 ...$35.00

Finance & Fortune, Parker Bros, 1936, NM (NM box), F8..$25.00

Fish Pond, McLoughlin Bros, 1890, EX (2 children in boat on EX box), A...$300.00

Fish Pond, McLoughlin Bros, 1890, VG (2 fish on VG box), A...$150.00

Flag Game, card game, McLoughlin Bros, 1887, incomplete, G (G wooden box), S16 ....$55.00

Flash Gordon Adventure on the Moons of Mongo, Wadding-ton's House of Games/King Features, 1977, MIB, P4.$55.00

Flintstones Present...Dino the Dinosaur Game, Transogram, 1961, NM (NM box), F8 ....$55.00

Flintstones' Big Game Hunt, Whitman, 1962, NMIB, C1 ..$100.00

Flintstones' Stone Age Game, Transogram, 1961, NM (EX box), from $55 to...$65.00

Flip Your Lid, Ideal, 1976, MIB (sealed), J5......................$15.00

Flivver Game, Milton Bradley, 1923-24, VG (VG box), A........$150.00

Floating Satellite, target game, 1960s, battery-op, MIB, L4.........$200.00

Flying Nun, Milton Bradley, 1968, contents sealed (NM box) $85.00

Foolish Questions, card game, Rube Goldberg, 1925, EXIB, A ..$145.00

Fortress America, Milton Bradley, 1986, EX (G box), S16 ....$35.00

Foto-Electric Football, Cadaco, 1965, VG+ (VG box), P3 .$25.00

Frank Buck's Wild Cargo, 1934, EX+, A $145.00

Frosty the Snowman, Parker Bros, 1979, VG (VG box), S16..$25.00

Fun on the Farm, Milton Bradley, 1940s, rare, NMIB, T2 ..$45.00

Game of Alice in Wonderland, S&E, NM (EX box), A...$125.00

Game of Assembly Line, Selchow & Righter, 1953, NM (EX box), T2 ....$80.00

Game of Bagatelle, McLoughlin Bros, 1898, NMIB $400.00

Game of Colors, McLoughlin Bros, 1888, EXIB, A $125.00

Game of Dracula, Waddington, 1978, Canadian issue, NM (EX box), F8 ....$145.00

Game of Fox & Cheese, Milton Bradley, EX (EX box), A..$75.00

Game of High Spirits w/Calvin & the Colonel, Milton Bradley, 1962, NMIB, F8 ....$45.00

Game of Li'l Abner, Milton Bradley, 1944, NM (EX box), F8 ....$70.00

Game of Moon Tag, Parker Bros, 1957, G+ (G+ box), S16 .$95.00

Game of Politics, Parker Bros, 1952, VG (VG box), S16.$45.00

Game of Politics (The Race for the Presidency), WS Reed, 1889, incomplete, VG, A $250.00

Game of Puss in the Corner, Gabriel & Sons, 1940s, EXIB, S16 ....$80.00

Game of the Crusaders, McLoughlin Bros, 1888, EXIB, A ..$350.00

Game of the States, Milton Bradley, 1940, 2nd edition, VG (VG box) $35.00

Game of Tortoise & the Hare, Russell Mfg Co, 1922, VG (VG box), S16 ....$120.00

Game of Uncle Sam's Mail, McLoughlin Bros, ca 1893, EX (EX wooden box), A $580.00

Game of Uncle Sam's Mail, McLoughlin Bros, ca 1893, G- (orig wooden box), A $125.00

Games of Gong, Fox & Geese & Tivoli, McLoughlin Bros, 1878, VG+ (G slip case), A..$50.00

Games You Like To Play, Parker Bros, 1920s, VG (VG box), A $30.00

Get Smart, Ideal, 1960, missing few pcs, VG (orig box), J5 ..$45.00

Go Bang, Milton Bradley, EX (EX box) $125.00

Go to the Head of the Class, Milton Bradley, 1955, 8th edition, NMIB, F8 ....$25.00

Godfather, Family Games, 1971, VG (VG box), S16.......$30.00

Godzilla, Mattel, 1978, VG (VG box), S16...................$120.00

Gomer Pyle, Transogram, 1966, NM (EX box), F8 ....$50.00

Gracie Allen Murder Case, Milton Bradley, 1939, rare, M (EX+ box), A..$600.00

Grand Bicycle Race Game, unmk, VG+ (VG+ box), A ..$400.00

Grand Prix Merry-Go-Round Race Game, mk Made in France, litho cb horses circle wood & metal pole, EXIB, A .$350.00

Great American Game — Baseball, Hustler Toy Corp, tin & wood, 13x9", VG, A $135.00

Green Ghost, Transogram, 1965, NMIB, F8 ....$85.00

Halma, El Horsman, 1888, VG (VG box for pcs).............$50.00

Hardy Boys Treasure Game, Parker Bros, 1957, NMIB, F8..$75.00

Hare & Hounds, McLoughlin Bros, 1891, VG+ (VG+ box), A $550.00

Harold Teen Game, Milton Bradley/FAS, EXIB, A $65.00

Have Gun Will Travel, Parker Bros, 1959, EX (EX box), A ..$75.00

Hawaiian Eye, Lowell, 1963, rare, NM (EX box), F8 .....$150.00

Hector Heathcote, Transogram, 1963, NM (EX box), F8...$60.00

Hi-Ho! Cherry-O, Whitman, 1960, incomplete, VG (VG box), S16 ....$35.00

Hialeah, Milton Bradley, 1940, VG (VG box), S16.........$60.00

Hippety Hop, Corey Games, 1940, VG (VG box), S16 ...$75.00

Hippopotamus Electronic Puzzle, Remco, 1971, EXIB, J2...$20.00

Hokum, card game, Parker Bros, 1927, VG (VG box), S16..$50.00

Hold the Fort, Parker Bros, 1895, G (G box), A $200.00

Home Baseball Game, McLoughlin Bros, 1897, VG (VG box), A $2,000.00

Hopalong Cassidy, Milton Bradley, 1950, MIB, $150.00.

Hopalong Cassidy Bar Twenty Shooting Game, British, 1953, NMIB..$400.00

Hopalong Cassidy Lasso Game, Transogram, 1950, NM (EX box), A...$230.00

Hopalong Cassidy Shooting Gallery, Automatic Toy, 1950, NM (G box), A $375.00

How Silias Popped the Question, Parker Bros, 1915, VG (VG box), S16..$40.00

Howdy Doody Bean Bag Game, Parker Bros, 1950s, EXIB, J5 ..$165.00

Howdy Doody Card Game, Russell, 1950s, NM (EX box), F8/J5...$25.00

Howdy Doody's Adventure Game, Milton Bradley, unused, MIB, A...$225.00

Howdy Doody's Bowling Game, Parker Bros, 1949, NM (EX box), F8...$85.00

Huckleberry Hound, card game, Ed-U, 1961, MIB (sealed), F8...$20.00

Huckleberry Hound, Milton Bradley, 1981, VG (VG box), S16...$20.00

Huckleberry Hound Bumps, Transogram, 1961, NMIB, M17..$65.00

Huckleberry Hound Juggle-Roll, Transogram, 1960, EX, C17..$35.00

Huggin' the Rail, Selchow and Righter, 1948, complete, NMIB, $65.00.

Hunting the Grizzly, Spear, EXIB, A $475.00
I Dream of Jeannie, Milton Bradley, 1960s, EX (VG box), J5..$45.00

I Spy, Ideal, 1965, EX (EX box), P3, $65.00.

Improved & Illustrated Game of Dr Busby, Ives, 1843, set of 20 hand-colored engraved cards in slip case, EX, A $175.00
Improved Historical Cards, McLoughlin Bros, EXIB, A ...$150.00
India, McLoughlin Bros, 1895, VG+ (VG+ wooden box mk An Oriental Game), A $75.00
India, Milton Bradley, 1910, EX (VG+ box), P3 ....$40.00
Inspector Gadget, Milton Bradley, 1983, VG (VG box), S16 ..$20.00
Intrigue, Milton Bradley, 1954, VG (VG box), S16 ....$45.00
Ironside, Ideal, 1967, scarce, EX+ (VG box), A $185.00
Jack & the Beanstalk, Parker Bros, 1890s, VG (orig box), F3 ..$65.00
James Bond 007 Tarot, US Games System, 1973, VG $45.00

James Bond 007 Thunderball, Milton Bradley, 1965, EX (EX box), F3, $85.00.

Jarts Missile Game, lawn game, Jarts, 1960s, NMIB, F8 ...$30.00
Jeanette Express Automobile Race, Jeanette Toy & Novelty, 9½", G, A $260.00
Jeu De Loto Bus, G&B Paris, complete, EX (EX box), A ..$135.00
John Drake Secret Agent, Milton Bradley, 1966, NM (EX box), A $40.00
Junior Aeroplane Race, Wolverine, NM (EX box), A ...$140.00
Junior Bicycle Game, Parker Bros, 1897, VG+ (VG+ box), A $200.00
Justice League of America/Wonder Woman, Hasbro, 1967, NMIB, A $565.00
Ker Plunk, Ideal, 1967, NMIB, P4.....................................$30.00
King Kong, Ideal, 1976, VG (VG box), S16.....................$40.00
Knight Rider, Parker Bros, 1983, VG (VG box), S16.......$20.00
Kojak, Milton Bradley, 1975, unused, NM (VG box), S16..$35.00

Kooky Carnival, skill game, Milton Bradley, 1969, NMIB, F8 ....$45.00

Kukla and Ollie, Parker Bros, 1962, NMIB, $35.00.

L'Astro Guerre Des Galactica (Battlestar Galactica), Parker Bros, 1978, Canadian, no instructions, VG (VG box), S16 ....$55.00
Laurel & Hardy, card game, Ed-U, 1972, NMIB, J2 ....$20.00
Laverne & Shirley, Parker Bros, 1977, VG (VG box), S16 .$20.00
Leap Frog, McLoughlin Bros, EXIB, A............................$225.00

Leave It to Beaver Money Maker, Hasbro, VG (VG box), F3, $40.00.

Les Jackos Sings Savants — Jeu Magnetique, EX (EX wooden box), A...$900.00
Letter Carrier, McLoughlin Bros, EXIB, A $450.00
Li'l Abner, Parker Bros, 1969, NMIB, F8..........................$50.00
Life's Mishaps a Merry Game & Domino Rex, McLoughlin Bros, 1875, G (G slip case), A.......................................$200.00
Little America Admiral Byrd's South Pole Game, Parker Bros, EXIB, A $600.00
Little Cowboy, Parker Bros, 1890s, EXIB, F3.................$525.00
Little House on the Prairie, Parker Bros, 1978, VG (VG box), S16 ....$20.00
Little Orphan Annie, Milton Bradley, 1927, NM (EX box), A $225.00
Little Red Riding Hood, McLoughlin Bros, 1900, EX+ (VG wooden box), A $550.00
Lone Ranger, card game, Parker Bros, 1938, EXIB, from $75 to $100.00
Lone Ranger, Parker Bros, 1938, VG (VG box for pcs)....$65.00
Lone Ranger, target game, Marx, NM, A $275.00

Lone Ranger (The New), Parker Bros, 1956, EXIB, A $40.00

Lost Diamond, Gem Series, McLoughlin Bros, EXIB $300.00

Lost in Space, Milton Bradley, 1965, EXIB, J2 ....$135.00

Lucky Stars, Ideal, 1960s, EXIB, J2 ....$30.00

Luno Rocket Race to the Moon, magnetic, EX (EX box), A...$125.00

M*A*S*H Trivia, 1984, EXIB, J2.......................................$25.00

Mad Magazine Game, Parker Bros, 1979, MIB $20.00

Magic Dots for Little Tots, Milton Bradley, 1907, EX (taped box), P3...$25.00

Magic Kingdom Pinball Machine, Wolverine, 25", EX, A ..$75.00

Magnetic Fish Pond, McLoughlin Bros, 1891, incomplete, EX (EX box) $275.00

Magnetic Fish Pond, Parker Bros, 1920s, EXIB, F3 ....$125.00

Mail Express & Accommodation, McLoughlin Bros, 1895, G+ (G+ box), A $525.00

Make-A-Million, card game, Parker Bros, 1945, VG (VG box), S16 ....$32.00

Man From UNCLE, card game, Milton Bradley, 1965, VG (VG box), T1 ....$25.00

Man From UNCLE Thrush Ray-Gun Affair Game, Ideal, 1966, rare, P3, EX (EX box), $125.00.

Mandrake the Magician, Transogram, 1966, NM (NM box), F8 ....$50.00

Mansion of Happiness, board only, Ives, 1864, G, F3.....$250.00

Mansion of Happiness, McLoughlin Bros, 1895, VG (VG wooden box), A..$400.00

Marathon, Sports Games, 1978, VG (orig box), S16 ....$20.00

Margie, Milton Bradley, 1961, VG (VG box), S16 ....$28.00

Marlin Perkins' Zoo Parade, Cadaco, 1955, NM (EX box), F8 ....$55.00

Men in Space, Milton Bradley, 1960, rare, EXIB, S16 ...$100.00

Merry Hunt, Singer, VG+ (VG+ box), A $400.00

Miami Vice, Pepper Lane, 1984, EXIB, S16 ....$20.00

Mickey Mouse Action Target Set, Lido, 1950s, NM (EX box), A..$100.00

Mickey Mouse Bean Bag Game, Marks Bros/WDE, 1930s, NMIB, A..$400.00

Mickey Mouse Canasta Junior, 1950s, EXIB, A................$60.00

Mickey Mouse Coming Home, Marx/WDE, 1930s, EXIB, A..$100.00

Mickey Mouse Don't Wake the Dragons, Whitman, 1970s, MIB, A $25.00

Mickey Mouse Hoop-La, Marks Bros, 1930s, G+, A $260.00

Mickey Mouse Party Game, Marks Bros/WDE, 1930s, EX (EX box), A $125.00

Mickey Mouse Shooting Gallery, Chad Valley, NMIB, A ..$175.00

Mickey Mouse Slugaroo, WDP, 1950s, MIB, T1 ....$35.00

Mickey Mouse Spin-N-Win, Northwestern Products, 1957, litho tin, incomplete, EXIB, M8 ....$80.00

Mickey Mouse Tidleywinks, Chad Valley, 1935, EXIB, A...$425.00

Mighty Mouse Playhouse Rescue, Harett Gilman, 1956, EXIB, S16 ....$95.00

Milton the Monster, Milton Bradley, 1966, NM (EX box), F8 ....$35.00

Miss Popularity, Transogram, 1960s, EXIB, J5 ....$25.00

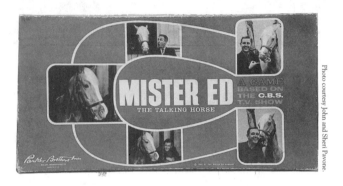

Mister Ed, Parker Bros, 1962, EX (EX box), P3, $55.00.

Mod Squad, Remco, 1968, rare, EX (EX box), A $200.00

Monopoly, John Waddington/England, 1961, VG (G box)..$30.00

Monopoly, Parker Bros, 1937, VG (VG box), S16 ....$40.00

Moon Mullins, Milton Bradley, 1927, scarce, NM (EX box), A..$250.00

Moon Mullins Automobile Race Game, Milton Bradley, EXIB, A..$100.00

Moon Mullins Gets the Run Around, Milton Bradley, 1930s, VG (orig box), F3 ....$95.00

Mostly Ghostly, Cadaco, 1975, EX (VG+ box), P3..........$20.00

Mother Goose's Christmas Party, McLoughlin Bros, 1898, VG (VG box), A $475.00

Motorcycle Game, Milton Bradley, EXIB, A.................$475.00

Mouse Trap, Ideal, 1963, NM (EX box), T2 ....$80.00

Movie Millions, Transogram, 1938, incomplete, VG (VG box), S16 ....$125.00

Movie Moguls, Research Games, 1970, scarce, NM (NM box), A..$200.00

Moving Picture Game, Milton Bradley, 1920s, NM (EX box), A..$90.00

Munsters Masquerade Party, board game, Hasbro, 1965, complete, EX (EX box), from $150.00 to $300.00.

Mr Doodles Dog, Selchow & Righter, 1940, Jr edition, VG (VG box), S16......$28.00

Munsters, card game, Milton Bradley, 1964, VG (VG box), T1 ......$20.00

My First Game, Gabriel, 1956, DeLuxe Model, MIB, P6 .$50.00

Mystery Date, Milton Bradley, 1965, NM (EX box)......**$95.00**

Name That Tune, Milton Bradley, 1959, sealed contents (VG box), A......$25.00

Nancy Drew Mystery, Parker Bros, 1957, NM (NM box)...$85.00

NBC Peacock, Selchow & Righter, 1966, rare, MIB (sealed), A......$200.00

NBC-TV News, Dadan, 1960, NM (EX box), F8......$125.00

New Adventures of Gilligan, Milton Bradley, 1974, NM (NM box), F8......**$55.00**

New Pilgrim's Progress, McLoughlin Bros, 1893, VG (VG wooden box), A......$250.00

Newlywed Game, Hasbro, 1969, NMIB, T2 ......$15.00

Newport Yacht Race, McLoughlin Bros, 1891, VG (VG box), A......**$485.00**

Photo courtesy Paul Fink.

Night Before Christmas, Parker Bros, 1896, missing few pieces, G (worn box), F3, $1,200.00.

No Time for Sergeants, Ideal, 1964, EX (G box), T1 ......$40.00

North Pole by Airship, Milton Bradley, EX (VG box), A ..$475.00

Northwest Passage, Impact, 1969, G, S16......$20.00

Nutty Mad Pinball, Marx, G, J2 ......$30.00

Off To See the Wizard, Milton Bradley, 1968, EXIB, J5 ..$50.00

Office Boy the Good Old Game, Parker Bros, 1889, VG (VG box), A $230.00

Old Maid, card game, Parker Bros, 1940s-50s, NMIB, F8.$25.00

Old Witch, card game, Whitman/WDP, 1970s, features Mickey Mouse, MIP (sealed), A......$15.00

Operation, Milton Bradley, 1965, EX+ (EX+ box), P3 ....$20.00

Our Game of Authors, Selchow & Righter, EX (VG+ box), P3 ......$30.00

Outdraw the Outlaw, target game, Mattel, 1959, M (EX box), A......$350.00

Owl & the Pussy Cat, Edger Clark, Tokalon Series, VG (VG box), A $400.00

Photo courtesy June Moon.

Orbit, Parker Bros, NMIB, J6, $85.00.

Park & Shop, Milton Bradley, 1960s, EXIB......$50.00

Park & Shop, Traffic Game Co, 1952, rare, VG (VG box)......$100.00

Parlor Foot-Ball, McLoughlin Bros, 1891, VG (VG box), A ..**$1,380.00**

Partridge Family, Milton Bradley, 1970, EX (EX box), J5 ...$25.00

Patty Duke, Milton Bradley, 1963, EXIB, J2 ......$35.00

Peg Baseball, Parker Bros, 1930s, EXIB, A......$100.00

Perry Mason, Transogram, 1959, VG (VG box), S16......$60.00

Peter Pan, Hunts premium, 1960, unused, M, J2 ......$45.00

Philip Marlow, Transogram, 1960, NM (NM box), F8.....$65.00

Physogs, card game, Waddy/England, ca 1935, EXIB, A...$130.00

Pike's Peak or Bust, Parker Bros, 1890s, VG (orig box), F3 ..$100.00

Pinball, Somerville Toys/Canada, wood & tin w/sports theme, 23", EX, A......$25.00

Pinocchio, card game, Ed-U, 1960s, MIB (sealed), F8......$18.00

Pirate & the Traveler, Milton Bradley, 1940s, G (orig box), A.**$35.00**

Pit, card game, Parker Bros, 1919, VG (orig box)......$15.00

Planet of the Apes, Milton Bradley, 1974, VG (VG box), S16...$20.00

Play Football, Whitman, 1934, NM (EX box), A......$100.00

Playing Department Store, Milton Bradley, VG (McLoughlin cover on VG box), A $325.00

Polyanna: The Glad Game, Parker Bros, 1916, 2nd edition, missing 1 disk, VG (VG box) $50.00

Popeye Pipe Toss, Rosebud Art Co, 1935, EX+, A......$80.00

Popeye Skooz-It Pick-A-Picture, puzzle game, Ideal, 1963, NM (NM canister), C1 ......$65.00

Premium Game of Logomachy, Milton Bradley, 1930s, G, S16......$20.00

Popeye's Sliding Boards and Ladders Game, Built Rite, 1958, NMIB, $35.00.

Prince Valiant Game of Valor, Transogram, 1957, NM (EX box), F8 ....$55.00

Pro-Quarterback, Championship Games, 1965, incomplete, G (G box), S16 ....$22.00

Put the Tail on Ferdinand the Bull, Whitman, 1938, G (worn box), M8 ....$15.00

Quick-Draw McGraw, card game, 1961, NMIB, J2 ....$25.00

Quick Draw McGraw Moving Target, Knickerbocker, 1960, complete, scarce, EX+ (EX box), A, $200.00.

Quick-Draw McGraw Private Eye, Milton Bradley, 1960s, EXIB, J5 ....$45.00

Quilly Willy, Eldon, 1970, M (EX box), F8 ....$70.00

Quiz Kids Radio Question Bee, card game, Whitman, 1941, VG, S16 ....$20.00

Race Trap, Multiple, 1960s, EXIB, J5 ....$25.00

Radar Search Game, Ideal, 1969, EXIB, J2 ....$25.00

Radion Amateur Hour Game, Milton Bradley, 1930s, VG (VG box), S16 ....$85.00

Red Riding Hood, Adventure Series, Parker Bros, EX (EX wooden box), A $475.00

Red Ryder Whirli-Crow Game, Daisy, ca 1950, complete and unused, MIB, A, $200.00.

Rex Mar's Space Target Game, Marx, battery-op, EX+ (EX box), A $425.00

Rex Morgan MD, Ideal, 1972, NM (EX box), F8 ....$45.00

Rich Uncle, Parker Bros, 1955, VG (VG box), S16 ....$60.00

Ring My Nose, Milton Bradley, 1920s, MIB $75.00

Ring My Nose, Spear, EXIB $75.00

Rival Armies, McLoughlin Bros, VG (orig box), F3 ....$750.00

Road Runner, Milton Bradley, 1968, VG (VG box), S16 ...$35.00

Road Runner & Wile E Coyote, Whitman, 1969, NMIB, J2 ..$25.00

Road Runner Pop-Up Game, 1982, EXIB, J2 ....$20.00

Robin Hood, Parker Bros, 1973, VG (VG box), S16 ....$35.00

Rock, Paper & Scissors, Ideal, 1967, NMIB, F8 ....$25.00

Rocket-Socket Dart Game, Kenner, 1955, EXIB, J2 ....$35.00

Route 66 Travel Game, Transogram, 1962, scarce, NM (EX box), A $225.00

Roy Rogers Horseshoe Set, Ohio Art, 1950s, EX+ (EX box), J5 ....$250.00

Sandlot Slugger, Milton Bradley, 1968, EXIB, J2 ....$45.00

Satellite Target Game, battery-op, rare, MIB, A $325.00

Say When!, Parker Bros, 1961, NM (EX box), A $30.00

Scooby-Doo & Scrappy-Doo, Milton Bradley, 1983, EXIB, S16 ....$20.00

Screwball: The Mad Mad Mad Game, Transogram, 1960, G (G box), S16 ....$40.00

Sergeant Preston, Milton Bradley, 1956, rare Canadian version w/instructions in French, EXIB $65.00

Sherlock Holmes, Cadaco, 1982, VG (VG box), S16 ......$38.00

Shindig Teen, Remco, 1965, M (NM box), A $100.00

Skipper, Mattel, 1964, NM (NM box), F8 ....$70.00

Skirmish, Milton Bradley, 1975, Am Heritage Series, VG (VG box), S16 ....$40.00

Skittle Score Ball, Aurora, 1971, EXIB (Get Smart's Don Adams on box), P3 ....$40.00

Sleeping Beauty, Whitman, 1958, NMIB, F8 ....$70.00

Slugger, Northwestern Products, 1950s, EX (G box), J6, $75.00.

Photo courtesy June Moon.

Smurf Game, Milton Bradley, 1981, VG (VG box), S16 .$30.00

Snagglepuss, Transogram, 1961, no instructions, VG (VG box), S16 ....$65.00

Snake's Alive!, Ideal, 1966, NM (EX box), F8 ....$45.00

Snow White & the Seven Dwarfs, Cadaco, 1977, VG (VG box), S16 ....$20.00

Snow White & the Seven Dwarfs, Milton Bradley, 1937, EXIB, M8 ....$135.00

Snuffy Smith, Milton Bradley, 1963, NMIB, T1 ....$45.00

Solarquest, Western Publishing, 1986, EXIB, S16...........$30.00

Soldiers Five w/Pistol, target game, Milton Bradley, EX (EX box), A $100.00

Soldiers on Guard, target game, McLoughlin Bros, EXIB, A..$350.00

Space Game, Parker Bros, 1953, VG (G box), P4..........$125.00

Space Shuttle 101, Media, 1978, VG (VG box), S16 ......$20.00

Space: 1999, Milton Bradley, 1976, VG (VG box), S16 ..$35.00

Speed Boat Race, Parker Bros, 1930s, EXIB, F3...............$90.00

Spider's Web, McLoughlin Bros, 1895, VG (VG box), A ..$200.00

Stampede! Cowboy Marble Game, Cadaco, 1945, NM (NM box), F8..$50.00

Steve Canyon, Lowell, 1959, VG (VG box), S16 ....$70.00

Steve Scott Space Scout Game of Adventure, Transogram, 1952, EX+ (VG box), A...$100.00

Stock Market, Avalon Hill, 1970, MIB (sealed), S16 ......$28.00

Stock Market, Whitman, 1968, NMIB $40.00

Straight Arrow, Selchow & Righter, 1950, missing 2 arrows, NM (EX box), A...$85.00

Strategic Command, Transogram, 1960s, NM (damaged box), J5..$15.00

Stubborn Pig, Milton Bradley, EXIB, A.........................$200.00

Summit, Milton Bradley, 1960, G (G box), S16.............$35.00

Superboy, Hasbro, 1965, EXIB, A $100.00

Supercar to the Rescue, Milton Bradley, 1962, board only, VG (VG box), S16 ....$40.00

Superman, Hasbro, 1965, EXIB, A.................................$110.00

Superman Electronic Question & Answer Quiz Machine, Lisbeth & Whiting, 1966, scarce, NMIB, A $135.00

Superman III, Parker Bros, 1982, EX (EX box), S16 ....$20.00

Susceptibles, McLoughlin Bros, 1891, complete, EX (EX box), A, $500.00.

Swayze, Milton Bradley, 1955, VG (G box), S16 ....$35.00

Tabit, John Norton, 1954, VG (G box), S16....................$32.00

Table Croquet, Bradley, VG (VG wooden box), A $50.00

Telepathy, Cadaco-Ellis, 1939, incomplete, S16 ....$75.00

Ten-To-Tal, Selchow & Righter, EX (EX box), P3..........$45.00

Terry & the Pirates, Whitman, 1937, rare, NM (EX box), A $275.00

Three Chipmunks Big Record, Hasbro, 1960, NMIB, T2..$40.00

Thunderbirds, Parker Bros, 1967, NMIB, F8 ....$125.00

Ticker the Wall St Game, Glow Productions, EXIB $100.00

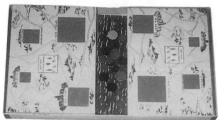

Tiddly Winks Barrage Game, Corey Games, WWII, EX (EX box), F3, $125.00.

Time Tunnel, Ideal, 1966, rare, NMIB, $250.00.

Tin Can Alley Electronic Rifle & Target, Ideal, 1976, MIB, J5 ....$45.00

Tobogganing at Christmas, McLoughlin Bros, 1899, G (G box) $1,650.00

Tom & Jerry, Milton Bradley, 1977, VG (VG box), S16 .$20.00

Tom Swift, Parker Bros, 1966, rare, NM (EX box).........$250.00

Toonerville Trolley, Milton Bradley, 1927, rare, NM (EX box) $350.00

Top of the Town, Cadaco, 1937, EX (EX box), F8...........$70.00

Trans-World Flyer, Biller, EX (EX box), A $325.00

Travel With Woody Woodpecker, Walter Lantz/Cadaco, 1956, NM (NM box)..$150.00

Troublesome Pigs, McLoughlin Bros, EXIB, F3 ....$225.00

TV Guide TV Game, Trivia Inc, 1984, VG+ (orig box)..$20.00

Twilight Zone, Ideal, 1964, rare, NM (EX box), F8 ....$175.00

Two-Game Combination of Baseball & Checkers, Milton Bradley, EXIB, A $200.00

Two-Game Combination of Messenger Boy & Checkers, Milton Bradley, no checkers o/w EXIB $125.00

Uncle Sam's Postman, Milton Bradley, 1890, incomplete o/w EXIB, A $375.00

Uncle Wiggily, Parker Bros, 1967, NMIB.......................$15.00

Underdog Saves Aunt Polly, Whitman, 1975, unused, MIB, J5 ....$35.00

Underdog Saves Sweet Molly, Whitman, 1975, NMIB, J5..$25.00

Undersea World of Jacques Cousteau, Parker Bros, 1968, NMIB, from $35 to..$55.00

Untouchables, Transogram, 1961, NM (EX box), F8 ....$85.00

Untouchables Target Game, Marx, NMIB, A $235.00

Vest Pocket Checkers, Embossing Co, 1929, VG+ (VG+ box), P3 ....$25.00

Voodoo, action game, Schaper, 1967, NM (EX box), F8 .$50.00

Vox Pop, Milton Bradley, 1939, VG (VG box), S16........$35.00

Wacky Races, Milton Bradley, 1968, NM (EX box), F8...$45.00

Wagon Train, Milton Bradley, 1960, VG (VG box), P4 ..$55.00

Walt & Skeezix Gasoline Alley Game, Milton Bradley, 1930s, EX (NM box), A $150.00

Walt Disney's Big Track Meet, Ontex/Canada, 1940s, EXIB, M8..$75.00

Walt Disney's Ski-Jump Target Game, American Toy Works, 1938, complete, NM (EX box), A, $725.00.

Walt Disney's Three Little Pigs, Einson-Freeman, 1933, NMIB, M8..$85.00

Waltons, Milton Bradley, 1974, VG (VG box), S16........$20.00

What Shall I Be?, Selchow & Righter, 1968, VG (VG box)...$20.00

What's My Line?, Lowell, 1955, NM (EX box), F8 ....$40.00

White Shadow, skill game, Cadaco, 1970s, very rare, VG (VG box), S16 ....$110.00

Who Am I?, Ed-U-Cards, 1954, based on Pinky Lee TV Show, VG (VG box), S16..$125.00

Why Presented by Alfred Hitchcock, 1958, VG (VG box), S16 .$40.00

Wide World Travel, Parker Bros, 1957, NM (EX box), F8 ..$40.00

Wild Kingdom, Teaching Concepts, 1977, VG (VG box), S16 ....$25.00

Wildlife, ES Lowe, 1971, VG (VG box), S16...................$45.00

Winnie the Pooh Old Maid, Jaymar, 1965, EXIB, P6.......$50.00

Wizard of Oz, Cadaco, 1974, VG (VG box) $30.00

Wonderful Game of Oz, Parker Bros, 1922, w/implement box, VG $350.00

Yacht Race, McLoughlin Bros, 1887, EX (Game lettered on VG box), A $475.00

Yacht Race, McLoughlin Bros, 1900, EXIB (Game not lettered on box), A $150.00

Yankee Doodle Game of American History, Parker Bros, 1895, VG (VG wood-fr box), A...$225.00

Yogi Bear, Milton Bradley, 1971, VG (VG box), S16 ......$30.00

Yogi Bear, Milton Bradley, 1980, VG (VG box), S16 ......$20.00

You Don't Say, Milton Bradley, 1963, unused, NM (VG box), S16 ....$20.00

Zoo Game, Milton Bradley, 1920s, VG (orig box), F3 .....$55.00

Zorro, Whitman/WD, 1958, EXIB, W6 ....$50.00

Zorro, Whitman/WD, 1965, EXIB, W6 ....$30.00

Zorro Target, Knickerbocker, 1958, EX+ (EX+ box), F8...$175.00

101 Dalmatians, Whitman, 1960, rare, NMIB, F8...........$70.00

Gasoline-Powered Toys

Two of the largest companies to manufacture gas-powered models are Cox and Wen Mac. Since the late '50s they have been making faithfully detailed models of airplanes as well as some automobiles and boats. Condition of used models will vary greatly because of the nature of the miniature gas engine and damage resulting from the fuel that has been used. Because of this, 'new in box' gas toys command a premium.

Advisor: Danny Bynum (B7).

Cox, AA Fuel Dragster, 1968-70, bl & red, M $125.00

Cox, Baja Bug, 1968-73, yel & orange, M.........................$65.00

Cox, Chopper, MIB $95.00

Cox, Delta F-15, Wings Series, 1981-86, gray, M $25.00

Cox, E-Z Flyer Commanche, wht, NMIB $35.00

Cox, Golden Bee, .049 engine, M $30.00

Cox, Kitty Hawk Spitfire, gr w/yel tail & lettering, EX $60.00

Cox, Mercedes Benz W196 Race Car, 1963-65, red, EX ..$85.00

Cox, Navy Helldiver, 1963-66, lt bl & dk bl, EX..............$65.00

Cox, PT-19 Flight Trainer, yellow and blue, EX, from $35.00 to $45.00.

Photo courtesy Danny Bynum.

Cox, Sandblaster, 1968-72, brn & tan, M $65.00
Cox, Shrike, 1968, yel, M $65.00
Cox, Shrike, 1974, red, M $50.00
Cox, Sky Raider, gray, EX (EX box) $125.00
Cox, Snowmobile, 1968, silver, M $95.00
Cox, Super Chipmunk, 1975-82, red, wht & bl, M $40.00
Cox, Super Cub 150, 1961-62, red & cream, upright engine
    w/metal tank, EX $45.00
Cox, Thimble Drome Champion Racer, red & bl, no engine,
    10", EX..$125.00
Cox, Thimble Drome Prop Rod, red plastic body w/metal chas-
    sis, EX...$75.00
Cox, Thimble Drome Prop Rod, yel plastic body w/metal chassis,
    EX...$85.00
Cox, UFO Flying Saucer, Wings Series, 1990-91, wht, M ..$25.00

Photo courtesy Dunbar Gallery.

Dooling Bros., Racer #4, orange, restored, McCoy motor, articulating front end, original tires, EX, $1,500.00.

Testors, OD P-51 Mustang, VG $30.00
Testors, Sprite Indy Car, 1966-68, wht, M.......................$75.00
Testors Cosmic Wind, orange, MIB $50.00
Testors Cosmic Wind, Spirit of '76, M..............................$60.00
Testors Fly 'Em, Red Albatross, NM $35.00
Testors Fly 'Em, Zero, M $40.00
Testors Fly'Em, Sopwith Camel, NM...............................$30.00
Wen-Mac, A-24 Army Attack Bomber, 1962-64, olive drab,
    EX $45.00
Wen-Mac, Albatross, Flying Wings Series, red, wht & bl,
    EX $40.00
Wen-Mac, Eagle, Flying Wings Series, 1963-64, red, wht & bl,
    EX..$40.00
Wen-Mac, Marine Corsair, 1958-64, red, EX $40.00
Wen-Mac, Mustang Fast-Back, 1968, bl, EX $125.00
Wen-Mac, P-39 Air Cobra, 1962-64, olive drab, M $70.00
Wen-Mac, P-63 King Cobra, 1962-64, chrome, EX $45.00
Wen-Mac, Yellow Jacket Corsair, 1959-64, yel, EX $40.00

GI Joe

GI Joe, the most famous action figure of them all, has been made in hundreds of variations since Hasbro introduced him in 1964. The first of these jointed figures was 12" tall; they can be identified today by the mark each carried on his back: GI Joe T.M. (trademark), Copyright 1964. They came with four differ-

ent hair colors: blond, auburn, black, and brown, each with a scar on his right cheek. They were sold in four basic packages: Action Soldier, Action Sailor, Action Marine, and Action Pilot. A Black figure was also included in the line, and there were representatives of many nations as well — France, Germany, Japan, Russia, etc. These figures did not have scars and are more valuable. Talking GI Joes were issued in 1967 when the only female (the nurse) was introduced. Besides the figures, uniforms, vehicles, guns, and accessories of many varieties were produced. The Adventure Team series, made from 1970 to 1976, included Black Adventurer, Air Adventurer, Talking Astronaut, Sea Adventurer, Talking Team Commander, Land Adventurer, and several variations. Joe's hard plastic hands were replaced with kung fu grips, so that he could better grasp his weapons. Assorted playsets allowed young imaginations to run wild, and besides the doll-size items, there were wristwatches, foot lockers, toys, walkie-talkies, etc., made for the kids themselves. Due to increased production costs, the large GI Joe was discontinued in 1976.

In 1982, Hasbro brought out the 'little' 3¾" GI Joe figures, each with its own descriptive name. Of the first series, some characters were produced with either a swivel or straight arm. Vehicles, weapons, and playsets were available, and some characters could only be had by redeeming flag points from the backs of packages. This small version proved to be the most successful action figure line ever made. Loose items are common; collectors value those still mint in the original packages at two to four times higher.

In 1993 Hasbro reintroduced the 12" line while retaining the 3¾" size. The highlights of the comeback are the 30th anniversary collection of six figures which are already selling in the collector's market at well above retail ($29.00): Soldier, $100.00; Sailor, $140.00; Marine, $75.00; Pilot, $140.00; Black Soldier, $180.00; and Green Beret, $285.00.

Production of the 3¾" figures came to an end in December 1994. For more information we recommend *Collectible Male Action Figures* by Paris and Susan Manos (Collector Books); *Encyclopedia to GI Joe* and *The 30th Anniversary Salute to GI Joe* both by Vincent Santelmo; *Official Collector's Guide to Collecting and Completing, Official Guide to Completing 3¾" Series and Hall of Fame: Vol II*, and *Official Guide To GI Joe: '64-'78*, all by James DeSimone. There is also a section on GI Joe in *Dolls in Uniform*, a publication by Joseph Bourgeois (Collector Books). Note: all items are American issue unless indicated otherwise. (Action Man was made in England by Hasbro circa 1960 into the 1970s.)

Advisor: Cotswold Collectibles (C6).

Other Sources: D4, D8, M15, O1, P3, S17, T1, T2

See also Games; Lunch Boxes; Windups, Friction, and Other Mechanicals.

Key: A/M — Action Man

12" GI JOE FIGURES AND FIGURE SETS

Action Marine, complete w/accessories, 1964, M (EX box),
    A $225.00
Action Pilot, complete w/accessories, MIB, H4..............$450.00
Action Pilot, 30th Anniversary, 1994, NRFB, H4 ....$140.00

Action Sailor, complete w/accessories, EX (VG box), H4 ..$250.00

Action Sailor, 30th Anniversary, 1994, NRFB, H4 ....$140.00

Action Soldier, complete w/accessories, EX (G- box), H4...$175.00

Action Soldier, complete w/accessories, 1964, NM (EX box), A $325.00

Action Soldier, 30th Anniversary, 1994, NRFB, H4 .....$100.00

Adventure Team Black Adventurer, complete w/accessories, NM (VG box), H4 ....$250.00

Adventure Team Intruder Soldier, orig outfit, VG, H4....$30.00

Adventure Team Man of Action, orig outfit, no beard, EX, H4 ....$60.00

Adventure Team Talking Commander, orig outfit, EX, H4 ..$90.00

Air Security, complete w/accessories, rare, NM, H4 ...$1,000.00

Astronaut, complete w/accessories, EX, H4 ....$185.00

Australian Jungle Fighter, complete w/accessories, #8205, M (VG resealed narrow box) $800.00

British Commando, w/helmet, jackets, trousers & boots, #8204, M (EX narrow box) $1,100.00

British Commando w/Chevrons, complete w/accessories, VG $295.00

British Infantry Major, A/M, complete, MIP $65.00

Combat Soldier, A/M, complete w/Army gear, M (VG box) ..$95.00

Crash Crew, complete w/accessories, EX $180.00

Deep Freeze, complete w/accessories, NM, H4 ....$225.00

Deep Sea Diver, complete w/accessories, M (G box) $885.00

Deep Sea Diver, complete w/accessories, VG, H4 ....$160.00

Fighter Pilot, complete w/accessories, EX, H4 ....$365.00

French Resistance Fighter, complete w/accessories, #8103, M (M repro box) $525.00

French Resistance Fighter, complete w/accessories, NM ..$275.00

German Soldier, complete w/accessories, #8100, M (G box)...$1,750.00

German Stormtrooper, complete w/accessories (rpl sling), VG $295.00

Green Beret, missing scarf o/w complete & EX+, H4.....$200.00

Heavy Weapons Deluxe Soldier, missing few pcs o/w EX, H4 ....$350.00

Russian Infantryman, no accessories, NM, $170.00.

Japanese Imperial Soldier, complete w/accessories, M....$625.00

Joseph Colton Artic Explorer, 30th Anniversary, mail-in, complete w/display stand, MIP, H4 ....$130.00

Landing Signal Officer, complete w/accessories, VG.....$230.00

LSO, complete w/accessories, EX, H4............................$225.00

Man of Action, complete w/accessories, 1970, NM (VG box), A $175.00

Marine Demolition, complete w/accessories, EX $150.00

Military Police, brn outfit, complete w/accessories, VG, H4...$160.00

Military Police, complete w/accessories, rpl strap in helmet, VG $225.00

Mountain Troops, complete w/accessories, VG, H4.......$165.00

Navy Attack, complete w/accessories, EX.......................$225.00

Race Car Driver, rpl strap on goggles, VG $150.00

Russian Infantryman, complete w/accessories, #8102, M (EX window box)..$2,700.00

Sabotage Set w/Action Marine, complete, EX, H4 ....$250.00

Scramble Pilot, complete w/accessories, EX+, H4 ....$300.00

Sea Adventurer, hard hands, complete w/accessories, EX (EX box)...$190.00

Shore Patrol, complete w/accessories, VG $265.00

Ski Patrol, complete w/accessories, VG, H4 ....$175.00

Space Ranger Captain, A/M, complete w/accessories, M (G box)...$90.00

Space Ranger Patroller, A/M, complete w/accessories, M (VG box)...$50.00

Special Forces, complete w/accessories, #7532, M (NM+ box), C6 ....$975.00

Special Talking GI Joe Adventure Pack, French Resistance Fighter outfit, #9083, M (G box).........................$1,350.00

Talking Action Soldier, complete w/accessories, #7590, NM (VG box) $350.00

Talking Astronaut, complete w/accessories, EX, H4 ......$200.00

Tank Commander, complete w/accessories, EX, H4.......$450.00

West Point Cadet, complete w/accessories, EX, H4 ....$185.00

West Point Cadet, complete w/accessories, M (EX window box) $1,000.00

Accessories for 12" GI Joe

.45 Pistol, blk revolver-type, EX, H4 ....$6.00

Action Marine Shirt & Pants, camouflage, VG, H4...........$8.00

Action Pilot Coveralls, G, H4 ....$4.00

Action Soldier Camouflage Netting, w/helmet sticker, MOC, H4 ....$45.00

Action Soldier Flame Thrower, A/M, gr, w/helmet sticker, 1960s, M (EX card)...$60.00

Adventure Team Coveralls, bl or gr, EX, H4, ea................$4.00

Adventure Team Infiltration Equipment, complete, 1973, NMIB, A $65.00

Adventure Team Mouth of Doom Jacket, EX, H4...........$12.00

Adventure Team Poncho, camouflage, EX, H4 ....$6.00

Adventure Team Training Center, missing few pcs o/w VG, H4 ....$70.00

Air Cadet, #7822, complete, M (EX box) $1,450.00

Air Cadet Hat, EX, H4 ....$25.00

Air Force Dress Jacket, no helmet sticker, MOC............$200.00

Air Force Dress Uniform, #7803, complete, M (EX box)...$1,450.00

Air Police Helmet, no strap o/w EX, H4 ....$25.00
Airborne Military Police Pants, tan, EX, H4 ....$25.00
Annapolis Cadet, complete, #7264, MIB (sealed) $1,250.00
Annapolis Cadet Belt, EX, H4 ....$40.00
Annapolis Cadet Hat, EX, H4 ....$25.00
Annapolis Cadet Jacket, G, H4..$25.00
Army Communications Radio, gr, EX, H4..........................$15.00
Army Field Jacket, zipper needs re-sewn o/w EX, H4 ....$20.00
Army Poncho, gr, EX, H4...$10.00
Army Tent, gr, complete w/accessories, EX, H4 ....$35.00
Astro Locker, EX, H4 ....$190.00
Australian Hat, EX, H4 ....$25.00
Australian Jacket, EX, H4...$35.00
Binoculars, red, EX, H4...$4.00
Bivouac Machine Gun Set, #7514, MOC.............................$60.00
Bivouac Sleeping Bag, #7515, MOC....................................$55.00
Breeches Buoy Sling, w/pulley mechanism, 2 ropes broken o/w
     EX, H4..$35.00
British Commando Equipment, #8304, MOC $245.00
British Greatcoat, A/M, knit cap, MOC $30.00
British Helmet, EX, H4...$40.00
British Pants, EX, H4..$32.00
Capture of the Pygmy Gorilla Set, complete, EX, H4.......$45.00
Carbine, A/M, w/.45 & 6 grenades, MIP...........................$12.00
Combat Camouflage Netting Set, #7511, MOC..............$25.00
Combat Set, #7502, complete, MIB, H4............................$150.00
Command Post Poncho, gr, #7519, MOC...........................$55.00
Communications Field Set, #7703, MOC............................$85.00
Convention Outfit, complete, 1990, rare, M, H4...........$185.00
Crash Crew Jacket & Pants, EX, H4 ....$30.00
Crash Crew Set, #7820, M (VG box) $260.00
Danger of the Depths Sea Adventurer Equipment, complete,
     1973, NMIB, A..$100.00
Deep Sea Diver, complete, VG, H4 ....$100.00
Deep Sea Diver Sledge Hammer, EX, H4 ....$12.00
Deep Sea Diver Weight Belt, EX, H4 ....$14.00
Demolition Set, complete, M (EX box) $85.00
Detonator Gun, A/M, MIP..$5.00
Dog Tag, VG, H4...$20.00
El Alamein Weapons Arsenal, Lewis machine gun, Sten sub
     machine gun, Mausser, Ger & Brit grenades, M (VG
     box)..$70.00
Field Phone, brn vinyl, VG, H4...$5.00
Fighter Pilot Helmet, EX, H4 ....$80.00
Fire Fighter Accessories, A/M, complete, M (VG card)...$18.00
Footlocker, w/tray, EX, H4 ....$30.00
French Greatcoat, French Foreign Legion, A/M, MOC...$30.00
French Medal, EX, H4 ....$18.00
French 7.65 Lt Machine Gun, A/M, MIP $15.00
German Field Pack, EX, H4...$25.00
German Helmet, no decals o/w VG, H4 ....$30.00
German Lugar Pistol, EX, H4 ....$20.00
German Stormtrooper Equipment, complete w/accessories,
     #8300, MOC...$265.00
Gravity Boots, A/M, dk gray boots w/canteen & tan pouch that
     attaches to belt, MOC $8.00
Green Beret Bazooka, w/2 shells, EX, H4..........................$32.00
Green Beret French Radio, EX, H4.....................................$14.00

Green Beret Hat, w/emblem, EX, H4................................$45.00
Green Beret M-16 Rifle, w/strap, EX, H4.........................$40.00
Green Beret Pants, VG, H4...$20.00
Grenade Launcher, w/lugar, silencer & removable stock,
     MOC...$30.00
Grenade Launcher Rifle, w/strap, EX, H4 ....$45.00
Highway Hazard Accessories, A/M, w/jack, axe, bolt cutters &
     fire extinguisher, M (VG card)..$20.00
Highway Hazard Uniform, A/M, w/bl coveralls & visibility vest,
     MOC...$20.00
HK-MP5, A/M, w/.45 & holster, MIP................................$10.00
Indian Brave, A/M, complete, M (EX box) $60.00
Indian Chief, A/M, complete, M (VG box)........................$60.00
Japanese Backyard Patrol Uniform, complete, MIP, H4 ...$50.00
Japanese Jacket, EX, H4 ....$10.00
Jeep Searchlight, EX, H4 ....$15.00
Jettison to Safety, Canadian, complete, M (VG box) $110.00
Life Ring, MOC..$45.00
M-1 Carbine, brn plastic, no strap o/w EX, H4.................$10.00
M-60 Machine Gun, no bipod o/w EX, H4 ....$30.00

Panzer Captain Outfit, Action Man, MIP, $125.00.

Paratrooper Accessory Set, 1964, MIP, $275.00.

Mae West Life Vest, orange cloth, EX, H4 ....$12.00
Map Case, w/map, EX, H4 ....$4.00
Marine Flame Thrower, EX, H4 ....$25.00
Marine Flame Thrower, MOC...$80.00
Marine Parachute Pack, no helmet sticker, MOC $75.00
Marine Parachute Set, complete, #7705, M (NM box) ..$225.00
Marine Tent Camouflage Set, #7708, MOC.....................$55.00
Medic Arm Band, EX, H4 ....$15.00
Medic Flag, EX, H4 ....$12.00
Medic Shoulder Bag, EX, H4..$15.00
Mess Kit, EX, H4..$10.00
Military Police, #7521, complete, M (NM box)..........$1,025.00
Military Police Duffle Bag, #7523, MOC.........................$40.00
Military Police Helmet, EX, H4 ....$20.00
Military Police Jacket, brn, MOC $115.00
Military Police Jacket, brn, VG, H4 ....$15.00
Military Police Trousers, brn, MOC................................$70.00
Mine Detection Set, A/M, complete, MIB $145.00
Mortar, A/M, complete w/3 shells, M (G+ card) $65.00
Mortar Launcher, no shells, EX, H4 ....$50.00
Mountain & Artic Set, A/M, complete, M (VG box)......$55.00
Mountain Troops, #7530, complete, M (EX+ box) $175.00
NATO Night Maneuvers Arsenal, A/M, complete, MOC ..$70.00
Navy Attack Helmet, bl, missing strap o/w VG, H4.........$30.00
Navy Basics, no sticker, #7628, MOC.............................$100.00
Navy Frogman Scuba Tanks, #7606, MOC $45.00
Navy Frogman Set, #7602, complete, MIB (sealed) $765.00
Parachute, wht cloth w/strings, EX, H4...........................$25.00
Parachute Regiments, A/M, complete, M (VG+ pkg)......$75.00
Pilot Survival Set, #7801, complete, MIB.......................$950.00
Polar Explorer, A/M, complete, MIP...............................$55.00
Pursuit Craft Pilot, A/M, complete, M (VG+ pkg)...........$70.00
Radioactive Satellite, EX, H4 ....$5.00
Raft Anchor, no rope o/w EX, H4 ....$18.00
Rescue Raft Backpack, complete, G (VG box), H4..........$25.00
Royal Air Force, A/M, complete, M (EX box)..................$70.00
Russian Ammo Disk, EX, H4..$20.00
Russian Grenade, EX, H4 ....$10.00
Russian Infantryman Equipment, #8302, MOC $290.00
Russian Lt Machine Gun, A/M, MOC...............................$45.00
Russian Soldier Equipment, #8302B, MIP......................$250.00
Sabotage Set, #7516, complete, EX (VG photo box) $725.00
Sabotage Set, A/M, complete, M (VG pkg)......................$50.00
SAS Secret Mission, A/M, complete, M (EX box) $85.00
Scramble Pilot Air Vest & Accessories, MOC $90.00
Scramble Pilot Coveralls, gray, G, H4.............................$20.00
Scramble Pilot Parachute Pack, cloth, EX, H4 ....$30.00
Scramble Pilot Parachute Pack, MOC $70.00
Scramble Pilot Set, #7807, complete, M (NM box) $645.00
Scuba Bottom, #7604, MOC...$60.00
Scuba Tank, orange, EX, H4...$8.00
Scuba Wrist Gauge, EX, H4 ....$16.00
Sea Rescue Set, #7601, complete, MIB...........................$650.00
Search for the Abominable Snowman, complete, MIB
   (sealed)...$295.00
Searchlight, A/M, battery-op, MIB $20.00
Secret Agent Set, missing few pcs o/w EX, H4 ....$25.00
Secret Mountain Outpost, complete, M (G box) $125.00

Secret of Mummy's Tomb Set, complete, EX (EX box), H4...$175.00
Shore Patrol Dress Pants, no sticker, #7641, MOC $65.00
Shore Patrol Jumper, VG, H4..$20.00
Shore Patrol Pants, VG, H4 ....$15.00
Shore Patrol Sea Bag, #7615, MOC $40.00
Shore Patrol Set, #7612, M (EX box) $1,000.00
Ski Patrol Bear Helmet, w/strap, part of emblem worn off o/w
   EX, H4...$20.00
Ski Patrol Boots, EX, H4 ....$15.00
Ski Patrol Gloves, EX, H4 ....$12.00
Ski Patrol Goggles, no elastic o/w EX, H4 ....$10.00
Ski Patrol Ice Pick, w/rope, EX, H4...................................$16.00
Ski Patrol Jacket & Pants, wht, EX, H4.............................$40.00
Ski Patrol Skis & Poles, EX, H4 ....$60.00
Sleeping Bag, EX, H4 ....$10.00
Space Coveralls, wht, EX, H4...$30.00
Space Rifle, A/M, MIP $10.00
Special Operations Kit, A/M, complete, M (VG card).....$40.00
Stethoscope, EX, H4..$8.00
Treasure Chest, gold, EX, H4 ....$8.00
US Air Force Dress Uniform, #7803, complete, M (EX
   box) $1,450.00
Weapons Rack, no weapons, EX, H4 ....$30.00
West Point Cadet Hat, no plume o/w EX, H4 ....$12.00
White Tiger Set, complete, EX, H4 ....$50.00
Workshop Accessories, A/M, M (VG+ card) $20.00
Wrist Camera, EX, H4..$10.00
2.30 Caliber Machine Gun & Tripod, w/ammo, EX, H4..$30.00

1964-1969 PAPERWORK

Air Manual for Action Pilot, narrow, EX............................$10.00
Air Manual for Action Pilot, wide, EX................................$7.00
Army Manual, lg, EX, H4 ....$3.00
Army Manual, sm, EX, H4...$4.00
Army Manual for Action Soldier, narrow, VG $7.00
Counter Intelligence Manual, EX, H4 ....$20.00
Instructions, Cave $3.00
Instructions, Danger of the Depths....................................$4.00
Instructions, Signal Flasher, in color $4.00
Intelligence Manual, A/M (same as GI Joe's), 1960s, EX.$25.00
Marine Manual, narrow, VG $10.00
Marine Manual, wide, EX+ $8.00
Navy Manual for Action Sailor, narrow, EX+ $10.00
Navy Manual for Action Sailor, wide, EX+ $8.00
Official Gear & Equipment Manual, EX, H4....................$15.00
Pamphlet, Join the GI Joe Club...$5.00

VEHICLES FOR 12" GI JOE

Action Pack Turbo Copter, MIB (sealed), H4..................$50.00
Action Pilot Space Capsule, complete, M (EX box) $245.00
Action Pilot Space Capsule, missing few pcs & has been rpt o/w
   VG (VG box), H4 ....$100.00
Adventure Team Sandstorm Adventure Jeep, gr, EX (EX box),
   H4 ....$185.00
Adventure Team Skyhawk, 1975, MIB (sealed), A........$110.00
Amphibious Duck, complete, EX (EX box), H4.............$750.00

Armoured Jeep, Browning MG, A/M, camo net, shovel, wire cutters & jerry cans, EX (G box)................................$90.00

Big Trapper, VG, H4 ....$75.00

British Armored Car, Irwin, EX, H4 ....$275.00

Crash Crew Truck, VG (orig box w/minor damage from moisture), H4..$1,300.00

Fire Engine, A/M, holds 1 figure, extension ladder, operating pump & hose, MIP..$75.00

German Staff Car, blk plastic, #5652, no spare tire, EX (worn illus box) $695.00

Iron Knight Tank, #9031, EX (EX box)...................$245.00

Iron Knight Tank, A/M, M (NM box) $175.00

Jeep Trailer, A/M, missing canopy o/w MIB $55.00

Jet Helicopter, complete, EX (EX box), H4.................$400.00

Official Jeep Combat Set, complete, EX (EX box), $350.00.

Sea Wolf Submarine, EX (VG box), H4............................$80.00

Skyhawk, EX (EX box), H4..$80.00

Space Speeder, A/M, spacecraft converts to 4 vehicles, M (EX box)..$65.00

Survival Raft, A/M, complete w/accessories, MIB............$45.00

Team Vehicle, yel ATV, winch, hook, rope, VG+ (G+ box) ..$85.00

Windboat, Canadian issue, bl w/yel mast & sail, M (NM box)..$60.00

3¾" GI JOE FIGURES

Ace, complete w/accessories, 1983, MIP......................$25.00

Airborne, complete w/accessories, 1983, EX, H4..............$16.00

Airborne, complete w/accessories, 1983, MIP..................$48.00

Airtight, complete w/accessories & ID card, 1985, EX, H4...$10.00

Alley Viper, complete w/accessories, 1989, EX..................$6.00

Alpine, complete w/accessories, 1985, EX, H4 ....$8.00

Alpine, complete w/accessories, 1986, MIP $30.00

Annihilator, complete w/accessories, 1989, EX, H4 ....$4.00

Annihilator, complete w/accessories, 1989, MIP $14.00

Astro Viper, complete w/accessories & ID card, 1988, EX, H4...$6.00

Astro Viper, 1988, MIP $12.00

Barbecue, 1983-85, MOC, H4......................................$25.00

Baroness, complete w/accessories, 1984, EX, H4 ....$30.00

Bazooka, 1983-85, MIP...$35.00

Beachhead, 1983-85, MIP, H4.....................................$30.00

Big Boa, 1987, MIP..$25.00

Blizzard, complete w/accessories, 1988, EX......................$8.00

Budo, complete w/accessories & ID card, 1988, EX, H4 .....$6.00

Buzzer, 1985, MIP $35.00

Capt Grid Iron, 1990, MIP $11.00

Charbroil, complete w/accessories, 1988, EX, H4 ....$4.00

Charbroil, red eyes, 1988, M (pkg faults) $14.00

Chuckles, complete w/accessories, 1986, EX, H4................$5.00

Chuckles, 1987, M (pkg faults) $18.00

Clutch, complete w/accessories, 1988, MIP $18.00

Cobra, complete w/accessories, 1983, EX, H4..................$16.00

Cobra Commander, Chinese pkg, 1983, MIP $25.00

Cobra Commander, complete w/accessories & ID card, 1983, EX, H4 ....$14.00

Cobra Commander, 1983, MIP....................................$125.00

Cobra HISS Driver, complete w/accessories & ID card, 1983, EX, H4 ....$12.00

Cobra Soldier, 1983, MIP...$62.00

Cobra Stinger Driver, w/ID card, 1982, MIP (factory bag), H4...$15.00

Countdown, 1989, MIP...$18.00

Cover Girl, complete w/accessories, 1983, MIP................$25.00

Crazylegs, 1986, MIP (dented bubble), H4 ....$15.00

Crimson Guard, complete w/accessories, 1984, EX, H4......$7.00

Croc Master, 1987, M (pkg faults) $22.00

Crystal Ball, complete w/accessories & ID card, 1986, EX, H4 ..$7.00

Crystal Ball, 1986, MIP, H4 ....$15.00

Cutter, complete w/accessories, 1984, MIP.....................$15.00

D-Day, 1995, MIP..$7.00

Darklon, complete w/accessories & ID card, 1989, EX, H4 .$10.00

Dee-Jay, complete w/accessories & ID card, 1988, EX, H4.$6.00

Dee-Jay, 1989, MIP, $13.00.

Deep Six, 1989, MIP...$14.00

Deep Six w/Finback, 1992, MIP $15.00

Dial Tone, Chinese pkg, 1988, MIP............................$16.00

Dial Tone, complete w/accessories, 1986, EX, H4 ....$5.00

Dial Tone, complete w/accessories & ID card, 1987, EX, H4..$7.00

Doc, complete w/accessories, 1983, EX..........................$16.00

Dojo, 1992, MIP...$9.00

Dr Mindbender, complete w/accessories, 1986, EX............$9.00

Dr Mindbender, 1983-85, MIP, H4.................................$25.00

Duke, 1984, MIP..$105.00

Dusty, 1985, MIP $40.00

Dynomite, 1995, MIP..$7.00
Eels, 1985, MIP..$52.00
Eels, 1992, MIP..$10.00
Fast Draw, complete w/accessories, 1987, EX.........$8.00
Firefly, complete w/accessories, 1984, EX............$18.00
Flash, complete w/accessories, 1982, EX, H4 ....$20.00
Flint, 1985, MIP...$55.00
Footloose, 1985, M (pkg faults) $30.00
Frag Viper, 1989, MIP $14.00
Fridge, complete w/accessories & ID card, 1987, EX, H4 .$25.00
Fridge, no accessories, 1987, EX, H4 ....$20.00
Fridge, w/ID card, 1986, MIP (factory bag), H4....$30.00
Frostbite, complete w/accessories, 1985, EX, H4 ....$10.00
Gen Flagg, 1992, MIP $6.00
Gnawgahyde, 1989, MIP $20.00
Green Beret, limited edition made for NY convention, 1 of
    5,000, MIB, H4..$50.00
Grunt, complete w/accessories, 1982, EX, H4 ....$20.00
Gung Ho, complete w/accessories, 1983, EX $16.00
Hardball, 1988, MIP $18.00
Hardtop, complete w/accessories, 1987, EX $18.00
Hawk, complete w/accessories, 1987, EX $13.00

Hawk, 1987, missing helmet, NM, $10.00.

Heavy Duty, 1991, MIP......................................$8.00
Ice Viper, w/1993 convention sticker, MIP $20.00
Iceberg, complete w/accessories, 1986, EX, H4 ....$8.00
Iceberg, 1983-85, MOC.....................................$32.00
Iceberg, 1986, MIP...$32.00
Interrogator, complete w/accessories, 1991, EX $6.00
Iron Grenadiers, 1988, MIP $18.00
Jinx, complete w/accessories & ID card, 1987, EX, H4.......$6.00
Jinx, mail-in, 1986, MIP $12.00
Jinx, w/ID card, 1987, MIP (factory bag), H4 ......$10.00
Keel Haul, mail-in, complete w/accessories, 1989, M (pkg
    faults) $10.00
Lady Jaye, 1985, MIP..$75.00

Lamprey, complete w/accessories, 1985, EX.........$10.00
Leatherneck, complete w/accessories, 1986, EX, H4..........$8.00
Leatherneck, 1983-85, MIP, H4..........................$25.00
Lifeline, Chinese pkg, 1986, MIP $18.00
Lift Ticket, incomplete, 1986 ....$10.00
Low-Light, complete w/accessories, 1986, EX, H4 ....$8.00
Low-Light, 1983-85, MIP, H4.............................$25.00

Low-Light Night Spotter, MIP, from $10.00 to $15.00.

Mainframe, 1986, MIP.......................................$32.00
Major Bludd, complete w/accessories & ID card, 1983, EX, H4..$12.00
Maverick, 1988, MIP $27.00
Mega Marine Blast-Off, 1993, MIP $12.00
Mega Marine Cyber-Viper, 1993, MIP..................$12.00
Mega Marine Mega-Viper, 1993, MIP...................$12.00
Mega Marine Mirage, 1993, MIP..........................$12.00
Mega Monster Bio-Viper, 1993, MIP $15.00
Mega Monster Monstro-Viper, 1993, MIP $15.00
Mercer, complete w/accessories, 1987, EX, H4 ....$4.00
Metal-Head, 1990, MIP......................................$15.00
Monkey Wrench, 1983-85, MOC, H4 ....$20.00
Motor Viper, 1986, MIP.....................................$22.00
Mutt & Junkyard, 1984, M (pkg faults)................$35.00
Night Creeper, complete w/accessories, 1990, EX..............$6.00
Night Force Outback, complete w/accessories, 1988, EX .$14.00
Night Viper, complete w/accessories, 1989, EX $8.00
Ninja Force Bushido, 1993, MIP $5.00
Ninja Force Lt Falcon, complete w/accessories, 1988, EX ..$6.00
Ninja Force Night Creeper, 1993, MIP $5.00
Ninja Force Snake Eyes, 1993, MIP $6.00
Ninja Force Zartan, 1993, MIP............................$6.00
Outback, complete w/accessories & ID card, 1987, EX, H4 ...$8.00
Outback, 1987, M (pkg faults)............................$18.00
Ozone, 1993, M (pkg faults) $5.00
Payload, complete w/accessories, 1987, EX $24.00
Phyche-Out, 1987, MIP......................................$22.00
Quick Kick, 1985, MIP.......................................$35.00
Range-Viper, 1990, MIP.....................................$12.00

Raptor, complete w/accessories & ID card, 1987, EX, H4 ..$8.00
Raptor, 1987, MIP $20.00
Recoil, 1989, MIP $15.00
Recondo, complete w/accessories & ID card, 1984, EX, H4 ..$12.00
Recondo, 1989, MIP $40.00

Red Star Okto-ber Guard, MIP, $10.00.

Repeater, complete w/accessories, 1988, EX $8.00
Rip Cord, 1984, MIP $45.00
Ripper, complete w/accessories, 1985, EX, H4..................$10.00
Ripper, 1985, MIP...$36.00
Road Pig, complete w/accessories & ID card, 1988, EX, H4 ....$10.00
Road Pig, 1988, MIP...$20.00
Roadblock, complete w/accessories, 1984, EX $16.00
Roadblock, 1986, MIP...$36.00
Rock 'N Roll, complete w/accessories, 1983, EX $18.00
Rock Viper, Chinese pkg, MIP $8.00
Rolling Thunder, English pkg, 1988, M (pkg faults) $30.00
Salvo, complete w/accessories, 1990, EX............................$8.00
Scarlett, complete w/accessories, 1982, EX $25.00
Sci-Fi, 1991, MIP...$10.00
Scoop, 1989, MIP $15.00

Scrap Iron, complete w/accessories, 1984, EX..................$14.00
Sergeant Savage, 1995, MIP $6.00
Sgt Slaughter, complete w/accessories & ID card, 1985 mail-in, EX, H4 ....$20.00
Shipwreck, w/parrot, 1985, MIP.......................................$60.00
Shockwave, 1988, MIP $22.00
Short Fuse, complete w/accessories, 1982, EX, H4 ....$20.00
Short Fuse, complete w/accessories, 1983, EX..................$18.00
Skidmark, complete w/accessories & ID card, 1988, EX, H4 ..$6.00
Sky Patrol Drop Zone w/Parachute Pack, brn, 1990, MIP ..$18.00
Slaughter's Marauders Footloose, MIP $18.00
Slaughter's Renegades Mercer/Taurus/Red Dog, 1987, MIP...$30.00
Slip Stream, complete w/accessories, 1986, EX $10.00
Slip Stream, complete w/accessories & ID card, 1987, EX, H4 ...$8.00
Snake Eyes, complete w/accessories & ID card, 1982, EX, H4..$45.00
Snake Eyes, 1985, M (pkg faults) $95.00
Snake Eyes, 1988, MOC (torn open & resealed), H4.......$15.00
Snake Eyes, 1989, MIP $30.00
Snow Job, complete w/accessories, 1984, EX, H4 ....$7.00
Snow Serpent, 1985, MIP...$45.00
Sonic Fighter Dial-Tone, 1990, MIP.................................$18.00
Stalker, complete w/accessories, 1983, MIP $18.00
Stalker, complete w/accessories & ID card, 1989, EX, H4 ..$8.00
Stalker, Japan pkg, 1983, MIP $20.00
Steeler, 1983, MIP $35.00
Strato Viper, w/ID card, 1982, MIP (factory bag), H4......$10.00
Street Fighter Blanka, 1993, M (pkg faults) $5.00
Street Fighter Guile, 1993, M (pkg faults) $5.00
Street Fighter Ken, 1993, M (pkg faults) $6.00
Street Fighter Ryu, 1993, M (pkg faults) $6.00
Stretcher, 1990, MIP $15.00
Sub-Zero, 1990, MIP..$10.00
Super Trooper, mail-in, complete w/accessories, 1988, EX ...$20.00
T'Jbang, 1992, MIP $10.00
Talking Battle Commander Cobra Commander, 1991, MIP .$12.00
Talking Battle Commander Stalker, 1991, MIP $12.00
TARGAT, 1989, MIP $18.00

Vipers Cobra Infantry, 1983-85, MIP, $24.00.

Taurus, complete w/accessories, 1987, EX, H4.................$4.00
Techno-Viper, complete w/accessories, 1987......................$8.00
Tele-Viper, 1985, MIP...$42.00
Tele-Viper, 1989, MIP...$14.00
Thrasher, complete w/accessories, 1986, EX $8.00
Tiger Force Duke, complete w/accessories, 1988, EX........$12.00
Tiger Force Roadblock, complete w/accessories, 1988 ....$8.00
Tiger Force Tiger Shark, 1988, MIP................................$18.00
Tiger Force Tripwire, complete w/accessories, 1988, EX ..$10.00
Topside, 1990, MIP...$10.00
Torch, 1985, M (pkg faults)..$32.00
Torpedo, 1983, MIP..$48.00
Toxo Viper, 1988, M (pkg faults) $14.00
Tripwire, complete w/accessories, 1983, EX, H4.............$10.00
Tunnel Rat, 1987, MIP..$25.00
Vapor, 1990, MIP...$15.00
Viper, complete w/accessories, 1985, EX, H4....................$8.00
Wet Suit, 1986, MIP...$45.00
Wild Bill, complete w/accessories & ID card, 1983, EX, H4..$12.00
Wild Bill, 1992, MIP...$5.00
Wild Weasel, complete w/accessories, 1984, EX...............$15.00
Wolverine w/Cover Girl, tow hook, complete w/accessories ..$42.00
Zandar, complete w/accessories, 1986, EX........................$6.00
Zandar, 1983-85, MIP, H4...$18.00
Zap, olive drab gr, India pkg, M (pkg faults) $15.00
Zarana, complete w/accessories, 1985, EX, H4.................$10.00
Zartan, complete w/accessories, 1984, EX........................$35.00
Zartan w/Swamp Skier, 1984, M (pkg faults)....................$85.00

ACCESSORIES FOR 3¾" GI JOE

Air Defense Battle Station, 1985, EXIP............................$12.00
Ammo Dump Unit, 1985, EXIP.......................................$10.00
Armadillo Mini Tank, 1984, EX..$8.00
Artic Blast, w/instructions, 1988, EX, H4.........................$12.00
Attack Vehicle Vamp, w/Clutch, 1982, EX, H4.................$40.00
Battle Gear Accessory Pack #1, 1983, MIP.......................$16.00
Battlefield Robot Devastator, 1986, missing 1 rocket o/w EX, H4..$5.00
Bomb Disposal Unit, 1985, MIP.......................................$8.00
Cobra Claw, 1984, EX, H4...$10.00
Cobra Ferret, 1984, EX, H4..$12.00
Cobra HISS, complete w/driver & ID card, 1983, EX, H4...$35.00
Cobra HISS, w/driver, 1984, EX, H4 ....$20.00
Cobra Pom Pom Gun, 1983, EX, H4................................$12.00
Cobra Rifle Range Set, complete, EX, H4...........................$6.00
Cobra Sea Ray, w/Sea Slug, 1987, missing several rockets o/w EX, H4..$8.00
Cobra Thunder Machine, complete w/Thrasher & ID card, 1985, EX, H4 ....$20.00
Cobra Wolf w/Ice Viper, 1985, EX, H4.............................$18.00
Condor Z25, 1989, w/instructions, decals worn o/w EX, H4 ..$25.00
Crusader Space Shuttle, 1988, NRFB, H4 ....$140.00
Desert Fox, w/Skidmark, complete, 1988, front wheel axle broken o/w EX, H4...$15.00
Dictator, 1989, w/instructions, EX, H4 ....$10.00
Dragonfly Helicopter, w/Wild Bill, complete, 1983, EX, H4..$40.00
Evader, w/Darklon, complete w/instructions, 1989, EX, H4...$25.00

Falcon Glider w/Grunt, complete w/ID card, EX (G glider), H4...$60.00
Fang II, complete w/instructions, 1989, EX, H4 ....$10.00
Flame Thrower, 1983, EX, H4...$5.00
Forward Observer Unit, 1985, complete w/accessories, EX...$8.00
Heavy Artillery Laser w/Grand Slam, 1982, NRFB........$110.00
Hovercraft, mail-in, 1984, M (pkg faults) $40.00
Jet Pack JUMP & Platform, Canadian pkg, 1982, MIP $50.00
LCV Recon Sled, complete, 1983, EX, H4 ....$5.00
Locust, 1989, complete w/instructions, EX, H4 ....$10.00
Machine Gun, 1983, EX, H4...$5.00
Manta Windsurfer, mail-in, MIB.....................................$18.00
Mauler MBT Tank, 1985, NRFB, H4 ....$80.00
Missile Defense Unit, 1984, MIP.....................................$20.00
Missile Launcher, 1983, EX, H4..$5.00
Mobile Missile System, complete w/Hawk, EX.................$45.00
Mobile Support Vehicle, no accessories, VG, H4..............$40.00
Motorized Battle Wagon, 1991, MIP................................$35.00
Mountain Climber Motorized Action Pack, 1986, EX, H4.$4.00
Mountain Howitzer, 1984, complete w/accessories, EX......$8.00
P-40 Warhawk w/Pilot Savage, 1995, MIP $34.00
Pac/Rat Machine Gun Mini Vehicle, M (orig mailer), H4 ..$10.00
Pac/Rat Missile Launcher Mini Vehicle, M (orig mailer), H4..$10.00
Parasite, 1991, Cobra personnel carrier, EX, H4 ....$8.00
Persuader, w/Backstop, 1987, EX, H4.............................$18.00
Pogo, complete w/instructions, 1987, EX, H4 ....$8.00
Polar Battle Bear, mail-in, 1983, M (pkg faults) $10.00
Python Conquest, 1988, complete w/instructions, EX, H4...$15.00
Python Stun, complete w/instructions, 1988, EX, H4 ......$10.00
Q Force Battle Gear, Action Force, MIP...........................$4.00
Rope Crosser Action Pack, 1987, MOC...........................$5.00
SAS Parachutist Attack, Action Force, MIP $25.00
Sea Ray w/Sea Slug, complete w/instructions, EX, H4 .....$15.00
Shark w/Deep Six, complete w/ID card, EX, H4..............$25.00
Sky Patrol Airwave, w/parachute pack, 1990, MIP..........$18.00
Sky Patrol Drop Zone, 1990, brn, w/parachute pack, MIP...$18.00
Skyhawk, complete w/accessories, EX (G box)................$18.00
Snow Cat, w/Frostbite, 1984, EX, H4..............................$25.00
Space Force Battle Gear, Action Force, MIP $3.00
Swamp Skier, w/Zartan, complete w/ID card, 1983, EX, H4..$45.00
Tiger Cat, w/Frostbite, complete, 1988, front wheel broken off o/w EX, H4...$18.00
Tiger Fish, 1988, complete w/instructions, EX, H4..........$10.00
Tiger Shark, 1988, complete w/instructions, EX, H4........$12.00
Transportable Tactical Battle Platform, 1985, complete w/accessories, EX..$22.00
Weapons Transport, 1984, EX, H4..................................$12.00
Whirlwind Twin Battle Gun, 1983, EX, H4 ....$20.00

MISCELLANEOUS

Activity Box, Whitman, 1965, complete, MIB $125.00
Combat Watch, Gilbert, 1965, shows standard & military time, w/compass & sighting lens, MIB $265.00
Dog Tag, GI Joe Club, w/chain, child sz, EX, H4 ....$40.00
Footlocker, 1964, gr wood carrying case w/plastic compartment, complete w/layout guide & display wrapper, 13" L, NM, A $200.00

Electric Drawing Set, 1965, with desk, lamp and 22 guide sheets, complete, MIB, $80.00.

Magic Slate, Whitman, 1966, cb w/erasable lift-up film sheet, missing pencil, VG $15.00

Official GI Joe Fan Club Kit, 1964, complete, NMIP, H4..$125.00

Official GI Joe Field Belt Playset, Nasta, 1982, NRFB, H4...$30.00

Official GI Joe Inter-Com Telephone Set, Hasbro, 1982, NRFB, H4 ....$30.00

Official Space Capsule & Astronaut Set, made for 1995 convention, complete w/3¾" figure, CD & raft, MIB, H4..$175.00

Official Space Capsule & Authentic Space Suit, 1966, missing record o/w complete & NM (NM box), A $150.00

Radio Command Unit, NM, $100.00.

Record & Book Set, Secret Spy Mission to Spy Island.....$25.00

Walkie-Talkies, Hasbro, 1983, MIB (taped), J5 ....$25.00

Guns

Until WWI, most cap guns were made of cast iron. Some from the 1930s were nickel-plated, had fancy plastic grips, and were designed with realistic details like revolving cylinders. After the war, a trend developed toward using cast metal, a less expensive material. These diecast guns were made for two decades, during which time the TV western was born. Kids were offered a dazzling array of weapons, endorsed by stars like the Lone Ranger, Gene, Roy, and Hoppy. Sales of space guns, made popular by Flash Gordon and Tom Corbett, kept pace with the robots coming in from Japan. Some of these early tin lithographed guns were fantastic futuristic styles that spat out rays of sparks when you pulled the trigger. But gradually the space race lost its fervor, westerns were phased out, and guns began to be looked upon with disfavor by the public in general and parents in particular. Since guns were meant to see lots of action, most will show wear. Learn to be realistic when you assess condition; it's critical when evaluating the value of a gun.

Advisor: Bill Hamburg (H1).

Other Sources: C10, I2, H7, K4, M16

Actoy Restless Gun, 1950s, diecast w/NP finish, brn plastic grips & secret trap door, 10", VG $150.00

BCM Space Outlaw Cap Firing Ray Gun, 1960s, diecast w/silver finish, red plastic windows, 10", M (NM box).........$200.00

Chad Valley Astro Ray Target Set, 1969, shoots darts, plastic & litho tin, complete, NM (EX box) $125.00

Chein Atomic Flash Ray Gun, 1950s, fires sparks, pressed steel w/red plastic windows, 7¼", G $75.00

Crescent Rustler Texan Six Shooter Cap Pistol, 1960, diecast w/blk-pnt finish, plastic woodgrain grips, 10", NMIB $150.00

Daisy Marshal of the West, complete w/2 cap guns, holster, dbl-barrel cork gun & corks in pouch, MIB $125.00

Daisy Trail Scout Rifle, pop-gun w/plastic stock & metal barrel, leather scabbard mk Daisy, 28", EX............................$75.00

Daisy Water Pistol No 80, EX $65.00

Daisy Zooka Pop Pistol, 1950s, litho tin, 7½", minor scratches on finish o/w VG..$125.00

Elvin Atomic Sparking Ray Gun, 1960s, litho tin, 4", NMIP..$25.00

Hiller Atom Ray Water Pistol, 1948, diecast w/orig silver finish, 6", rare, EX...$250.00

Hiller Atom Ray Water Pistol, 1948, diecast w/red-pnt finish, 6", rare, tip of trigger missing o/w VG......................$125.00

Hubley Army .45 Cap Pistol, 1940, nickel-plated cast iron with Colt logo, NM, P4, $125.00.

Hubley Atomic Disintegrator Cap Pistol, 1954-55, diecast with red plastic grip, MIB, $350.00.

Hubley Automatic No 290, 1957, diecast w/NP finish, brn checkered grips, 6½", MIB $150.00

Hubley Buck Cap Gun, CI w/NP finish, 3¼", VG $25.00

Hubley Civil War Centennial Set, 1963, complete w/2 8" Remington .36 guns, rare, M (EX box) $400.00

Hubley Colt .45 Cap Pistol No 281, 1958, diecast w/NP finish, revolving gold cylinder, wht plastic grips, 13", VG ...$95.00

Hubley Cowboy Cap Gun, 1940, CI w/NP finish, brn plastic colt grips, friction break, 8", VG, P4 ....$100.00

Hubley Cowboy Jr Cap Pistol, emb longhorns on wht plastic inset grips, 9", M (G- box), A $85.00

Hubley Dagger Derringer, rotating dbl barrel, push button & dagger extends from middle, 7", NMOC, A $145.00

Hubley Deputy Pistol, metal w/ribbed barrel, inset cowboy on hdl, 10½", w/plastic badge, NM (EX box) $175.00

Hubley Flintlock Jr Cap Gun, metal & plastic, 7½", M (EX box) $45.00

Hubley Padlock Pistol, metal, fires caps when opened w/key, 4½", M (G box), A..$100.00

Hubley Panther Pistol, derringer on spring-loaded wrist cuff, M (EX display box w/cb arm), A $150.00

Hubley Patrol Cap Pistol, NP CI w/brn plastic inset grips, 6", NM (VG box), A...$85.00

Hubley Pioneer Cap Pistol, diecast with red grip, MIB, $175.00.

Hubley Pirate Cap Pistol, 1950, diecast frame with cast double hammers and trigger, flintlock style, unfired, NMIB, $225.00.

Hubley Ric-O-Shay .45, blk plastic inset grips, complete w/cartridges & comic book, 12", MIB.............................$225.00

Hubley Ruff 'N Ready Holster Set, 1950, blk & tan leather holster w/studs & jewels, 9" cap guns, M (EX box).......$150.00

Hubley Savage Cap Gun, CI w/NP finish, 7", VG+, A $40.00

Hubley Shoulder Holster w/Colt .38 Detective Special & Badge, 4½", M (EX card) $45.00

Hubley Texan .38 Cap Pistol, 1958, diecast w/NP finish, wht plastic grips w/blk steer head, 10½", VG $75.00

Hubley Texan Gold-Plated Deluxe Cap Gun, emb longhorns on blk plastic grips, 9", MIB $275.00

Hubley Texan Jr Cap Pistol, gold-plated metal w/wht plastic inset grips, 9", M (EX box) $165.00

Ideal Clip Fire .223 Autopistol & Holster, 1966, blk plastic gun w/gr holster, 7", MOC $50.00

Irwin Flashing Rocket Ship Space Pistol, flashes & clicks interplanetary signals, battery-op, 7", NM (EX box).......$175.00

Ives Bulldog Cap Gun, CI w/japan finish, 4½", G..........$250.00

Ives Butting Match Cap Gun, CI w/traces of dk finish, 5", VG+...$425.00

Ives Cadet Cap Gun, CI w/blk finish, 3", VG+ $150.00

Ives Climax Cap Gun, CI w/japan finish, 5", VG+ $250.00

Ives Clown & Mule Cap Gun, CI w/japan finish, 5", VG .$650.00

Ives Crack Double-Barrel Cap Gun, CI w/japan finish, 4½", G+ $225.00

Ives Frontier Cap Gun, CI w/japan finish, 5¼", G+.......$350.00

Ives Hunter Cap Gun, CI w/japan finish, 5½", G+ $200.00

Ives Just Out Cap Gun, CI w/japan finish, 5¾", VG+ ...$750.00

Ives Liberty Cap Gun, CI w/japan finish, 7", G+, A.........$50.00

Ives Man-on-Alligator Cap Gun, CI w/japan finish, 5", G+ ..$700.00

Ives Sambo & Bear Cap Strike, pnt CI, VG+.................$450.00

Ives Sambo Cap Gun, CI w/blk finish, 4½", VG...........$400.00

Ives Sambo Cap Gun, CI w/blk finish, 6¼", VG...........$650.00

Kenton Custer Cap Gun, CI w/NP finish, 10", EX........$150.00

Kenton Lightening Express, CI w/NP finish, 5", VG+ ...$275.00

Kenton Locomotive Cap Gun, CI w/blk finish, 5", VG+......$450.00

Kenton Sheik Cap Gun, CI w/japan finish, 10½", VG+, A..$125.00

Kilgore American, CI w/emb bear, moose & elk, emb eagle on plastic grips, 9½", MIB $450.00

Kilgore Border Patrol Cap Gun, CI w/NP finish, 4½", G+, A..$50.00

Kilgore Buster Cap Gun, CI w/NP finish, 6", G, A $140.00

Kilgore Dough Boy Cap Gun, CI w/NP finish, 5", VG+, A..$75.00

Kilgore Eagle Cap Gun, gold-plated w/emb eagle on wht plastic inset grips, 8", EX, A $150.00

Kilgore Federal No 1 Cap Gun, heavy metal w/emb lettering, 5¼", EX, A...$50.00

Kilgore Long Boy Cap Gun, CI, 11", VG+, A $125.00

Kilgore Mountie Cap Pistol, 1950, diecast w/blk fr & silver highlights, lever release w/pop-up magazine, MIB, P4 ......$45.00

Kilgore Oh Boy Cap Gun, CI, 4¼", G, A $55.00

Kilgore President Cap Gun, CI w/japan finish, 8¾", VG+, A $40.00

Kilgore Ra-Ta-Tat Machine Gun, CI w/NP finish, 5", EX...$175.00

Kilgore Ranger Cap Gun, CI w/silver-pnt trigger & hammer, 8", VG+, A $100.00

Kilgore Star Ranger Holster Set, emb cowboy on wht plastic inset grips, gun mk Ranger, 9", EX (EX box), A........$80.00

Kilgore Tophand Twins, gold Mustang cap guns w/emb horse heads on wht plastic inset grips, 9", MIB $275.00

Kilgore Western Water Pistol, red plastic, unused, 8", NMIB...$50.00

KO Super Jet Gun, 1957, litho tin & plastic, sparking action, reciprocating bullet in barrel, unused, MIB, A $150.00

Lockwood Echo Cap Gun, CI w/japan finish, 4¾", VG+ ..$350.00

Lockwood Novelty Cap Gun, CI w/traces of dk finish, 5", G+ .$300.00

Lockwood Peerless Continual Shot Cap Gun, CI, 4¾", G....$425.00

Lone Star .45 Cork Gun, 1960s, diecast w/bl-pnt finish, wht plastic horse head grips, 6½", M, P4 ....$25.00

Lone Star Luger 9mm Cap Pistol, 1960, diecast w/blk-pnt finish, brn plastic grips, pop-up magazine, 8", MIB, P4.........$65.00

Lone Star Rebel Cap Pistol, 1960, diecast w/silver finish, star on blk plastic grips, lever release, 11", G......................$125.00

Lone Star Sawed-Off Shot Gun, 1960, diecast body w/brn plastic stocks & blk barrel, mk Pony Express, 16½", MIB, P4...$135.00

Lone Star Scout Cap Pistol, 1960s, diecast w/chrome finish, brn plastic diamond grips, friction break, 7", MIB, P4 .....$35.00

Lockwood Monkeys, cast iron with no finish, 4¼", G, $350.00.

Lone Star Westerner Cap Pistol, 1960, diecast w/silver finish, reddish brn grips, 10", MIB, P4...........................$55.00

Marx Anti-Aircraft Defense Gun, 1930, litho tin w/up, 17", scarce, NM (G box)...$175.00

Marx Pump Action Shotgun, 1950s, plastic w/diecast works, chambers & ejects shells, 33", VG (worn box), P4....$85.00

Marx Tommy Gun, 24", EX, J2 ....$55.00

Marx Wild West Cap Rifle, 30", NM, J2 ....$70.00

Mattel Air Cooled Machine Gun, 1950s, shoots caps, complete w/tripod, 15", NM (EX box), A................................$75.00

Mattel Fanner Frontier Holster Set, 1958, complete w/smoking cap gun & leather holster, 9", MIB $300.00

Mattel Fanner-50 Smoking Cap Pistol, plastic inset grips, revolving cylinder, 11", w/comic book, M (EX box) $225.00

Mattel Indian Scout Rolling Block Rifle, 1958, plastic & steel w/diecast works, 29½", EX, P4 ....$125.00

Mattel Shootin' Shell .45, simulated stag plastic grips, 11½", w/6 cartridges, rare, NM, A...$275.00

Mattel Shootin' Shell .45 Vigilante Holster Set, complete, 11½" pistol, rare, M (EX+ box) $650.00

Mattel Shootin' Shell Buckle Gun, 1959, derringer pops out of belt buckle, complete, MOC, P4...............................$125.00

Mattel Shootin' Shell Fanner Cap Pistol, complete w/bullets & shells, 9", MIB...$250.00

Mattel Shootin' Shell Fanner Frontier Double Holster Set, 1958, complete, 9" cap guns, rare, MIB $400.00

Mattel Shootin' Shell Indian Scout Rifle & Bandolier, plastic & metal, rolling block carbine, leather bandolier, MIB...$250.00

Mattel Shootin' Shell Snub-Nose .38 & Holster, 1959, diecast w/brn plastic grips, blk vinyl holster, EX (EX box)..$125.00

Mattel Swivel Shot Fanner 50 Trick Holster, push down holster & gun fires, 10", EX (EX box), A...........................$175.00

Mattel Winchester Saddle Gun, plastic & metal w/bl steel barrel, fires caps w/smoking action, 33", MIB, A..........$350.00

Mattel-O-Matic Air Cooled Machine Gun, 1957, plastic & diecast, mounted on tripod, crank hdl for action, 16", MIB, P4 ....$95.00

Mecklenburg King Size Bubble Shooter, 1950s, plastic & pressed steel, remote dip arm, MIB, P4 ....$55.00

National Automatic Cap Gun, bl-pnt CI, 6", EX, J2......$100.00

Newell Atomic 5 Pistol, 1950s, plastic, spring-fired, 10", EX (VG box), P4 ....$75.00

Nichols Detective Shooting Bullet Pistol, 1960, gray-pnt finish w/wht plastic grips, revolving cylinder, 6", NM, P4...$125.00

Nichols Dynamite Derringer Cap Pistol, EXIB, J2............$65.00

Nichols Mustang 500, gold trigger & hammer w/wht plastic inset grips, 12", rare, M (EX box) $350.00

Nichols Silver Mustang Repeating Cap Pistol, 1948, diecast w/NP finish, faux pearl grips w/red jewels, 9", NMIB...........$250.00

Nichols Spitfire Hip Gun, 1950s, diecast w/silver finish, brn plastic holster, 9", M (NM box), P4.........................$60.00

Nichols Stallion .32 Six Shooter Cap Pistol, 1950s, diecast w/NP finish, blk plastic grips, 8", MIB.....................$125.00

Nichols Stallion .38 Six Shooter Cap Pistol, 1950s, diecast w/NP finish, wht plastic grips, 9½", MIB.................$175.00

Nichols Stallion .45 Mark I Cap Pistol, rearing horse emb on simulated pearl grips, 12", rare, M (VG box)...........$300.00

Nichols Stallion .45 Mark II Cap Gun, CI w/blk & wht plastic interchangeable grips, 12", M (EX box)...................$300.00

Nichols Stallion 300 Saddle Gun, plastic & metal, lever action, 27", rare, MIB...$300.00

Nichols Stallion 41-40, highly emb, wht plastic inset grips, 10½", M (EX box) $250.00

Nichols Tophand 250 Cap Gun & Holster, 1960, diecast w/brn & wht stag grips, blk holster, 9½", NM $125.00

Ohio Art Astro Ray Target Set, 1969, litho tin & plastic flashlight gun fires darts, 10", VG, P4.............................$100.00

Palmer Plastics Jet Ace Cap Gun, 1950s, blk plastic w/diecast mechanism, lift-up magazine door, M (NM card), P4..$35.00

Park Plastics Squirt Ray Automatic Repeater Water Gun, 1950s-60s, blk w/brass nozzle, 5½", M, P4 ....$25.00

Park Plastics Watermatic Machine Gun, 1960s, blk plastic, 4-way action, metal crank fires rapid shots, 25", NMIB, P4 ...$45.00

Randall Space Pilot Super-Sonic Gun, 1953, plastic, Interplanet Space Fleet emb on hdl, battery-op, 9", M (EX box).$150.00

Ranger Steel Cosmic Ray Gun, plastic w/emb detail, 7", needs new flint o/w NM (EX box) $200.00

Ranger Steel Cosmic Ray Gun, 1954, litho pressed steel w/bl plastic barrel, friction, 9", VG, P4 ....$75.00

Remco Jupiter 4-Color Signal Gun No 600, 1950s, red plastic w/blk trim, complete w/lenses, 9", M (NM box), P4...$90.00

Renwal Western Shootin' Set, complete w/2 western-style pellet pistols, pellets & target, scarce, NM (EX box), A ...$125.00

Schmidt Buck 'N Bronc-Cowhand Dummy Cap Gun, 1950s, NP w/diamond-textured grips, poppy design on cylinder, 10", NM, P4 ....$125.00

Stevens .25 Repeating Cap Pistol, NP CI, 4½", NM (EX box), A...$50.00

Stevens Acorn Cap Gun, CI w/blk finish, 3½", G, A $125.00

Stevens Big Scout Cap Pistol, NP CI w/wht plastic inset grips, 7½", M (EX box), A..$150.00

Stevens Buddy Cap Gun, CI w/NP finish, 6¼", G+.......$150.00

Stevens Columbia Cap Gun, CI w/bl finish, 8¾", G+ ...$275.00

Stevens Comet Cap Gun, CI w/blk finish, 5½", G+, A ...$45.00

Stevens Dead Shot Cap Gun, CI w/japan finish, 8¾", VG, A $85.00

Stevens Firecracker Gun, CI w/japan finish, 4½", G+, A..$130.00

Stevens Jet Jr Cap Gun, 1949, diecast w/silver finish, sliding door in grip, 6", NMIB $200.00

Stevens Jumbo Cap Gun, CI, 9½", G+, A......................$150.00

Stevens Knight Cap Gun, CI, 5", G+, A........................$225.00

Stevens Lion Cap Gun, CI w/japan finish, 5½", EX......$275.00

Stevens Look Out Cap Gun, CI w/NP finish, 4½", G+ .$350.00

Stevens Monkey & Coconut Cap Gun, CI w/traces of dk finish, 4¼", VG+ $600.00

Stevens Our Navy Forever Double-Barrel Cap Gun, CI w/japan finish, 4", G+ $275.00

Stevens Perfection Cap Gun, CI w/japan finish, 3¾", EX+, A $85.00

Stevens Pioneer Cap Gun, metal, 7¾", M (EX box), A...$75.00

Stevens Ranger Cap Gun, CI w/silver-pnt trigger & hammer, 8", VG+, A $95.00

Stevens Sea Serpent Cap Gun, CI w/brn, gold & red finish, 3½", VG+ $850.00

Stevens Star Cap Gun, CI w/blk finish, 4½", EX $125.00

Stevens Victor Cap Gun, CI w/blk finish, 4¾", G, A $85.00

Stevens Western Boy Holster Set, copper-colored cap guns w/blk plastic grips mk Cowboy King, leather holster, MIB, A $200.00

Stevens 1880 Cap Gun, CI w/traces of orig finish, 4", G+, A..$150.00

Remco Electronic Space Gun, 1950s, gray plastic with red trim, battery-operated light with 4-color wheel, MIB, $175.00.

Stevens 6-Shot Cap Gun, cast iron, 6¾", VG+, A, $275.00.

Stevens 49-ER, gold-tone CI w/wht plastic inset grips, cowboy on 1 grip, oxen-drawn conestoga on the other, 9", EX.....$300.00

Strauss Ball Shooter, CI w/blk finish, 8½", G, A............$110.00

Thomas Western Water Rifle, 1960s, gray plastic, telescopic sight, 27", M (NM box), P4..$65.00

Tigrett Atom Flash Zoomeray Pistol, 1950s, fires paper roll-up into the air, 7", EX (VG box), A................................$80.00

TN Space Gun, 1950s, litho tin, battery-op, 8", MIB, A..$125.00

Unknown Maker, Army No 55 Cap Gun, CI w/blk finish, 4½", G, A $65.00

Unknown Maker, Cat Cap Gun, CI w/japan finish, 4¾", EX .$850.00

Unknown Maker, Dewey Cap Gun, CI w/traces of orig finish, 2¼", G+ $250.00

Unknown Maker, Dragon Cap Gun, CI, 4", VG+, A $110.00

Unknown Maker, Modoc Cap Gun, CI w/NP finish, 4¼", G+ $500.00

Unknown Maker, Our Boy Cap Gun, CI w/bl finish, 3", EX, A $80.00

Unknown Maker, Perfect 2-Shot Monitor Pistol, CI w/blk finish, 4¾", VG+ $225.00

Unknown Maker, Royal Pistol Cap Gun, CI w/lt japan finish, 5", G...$175.00

Unknown Maker, Shoofly Cap Gun, CI, 4", VG+ $800.00

Unknown Maker, Shoot the Hat Cap Gun, CI w/lt japan finish, 4¾", VG+ $600.00

Unknown Maker, Squirrel Cap Gun, brass, 5", G, A $325.00

US Plastic Space Patrol Dart Gun, 1951, blk w/wht trim, 9½", EX, P4 ....$165.00

Wes-Ko Thompson Automatic Sub-Machine Gun Jr, 1950s, plastic (Styron 475), fires plastic balls, 26", NMIB....$65.00

Woodsman Luger Cap Pistol, CI, 5", EX, J2 ....$100.00

Wyandotte Dart Pistol, 1950s, MIB, J2 ....$65.00

Wyandotte Pop Ray Gun, 1937, red-pnt pressed steel, internal cork, 7", VG...$100.00

CHARACTER

Bat Masterson Holster Set w/Cane & Vest, ZIV TV, 1958, complete, scarce, NM (EX box)..$350.00

Batman Bat-Ray Gun, Remco, 1977, plastic, projects images w/sound, EX $85.00

Battlestar Galactica Laser Gun, EX, B10 ....$25.00

Billy the Kid Cap Gun, Stevens, NP CI, red star on ivory plastic grips, 7", NM..$125.00

Buck Rogers Atomic Pistol, Daisy, 1930s, 9½", VG+, A..$185.00

Buck Rogers Pop Gun, Daisy, 1930s, 10", VG+, J2 ....$215.00

Buck Rogers XZ-31 Rocket Pistol Pop Gun, Daisy, 1934, pressed steel w/bl finish & chrome detail, 9½", VG $250.00

Buck Rogers XZ-44 Liquid Helium Water Pistol, Daisy, pressed steel w/red & yel finish, plunger action, 7½", VG...$200.00

Buffalo Bill Cap Gun, Kenton, CI w/NP finish, 13½", EX+..$275.00

Buffalo Bill Cap Gun, Stevens, CI w/japan finish, 11½", VG+..$150.00

Buffalo Bill Gun & Holster Set, Leslie-Henry, silverplated w/wht plastic inset grips, brn & blk cowhide holster, MIB, A ..$175.00

Captain Buck Flash Buzz Ray Gun, Remco, 1965, plastic space gun w/revolving turret flashes 3 colors, 9", NM (EX box), A..$125.00

Captain Space Solar Scout Atomic Ray Gun, Marx, 1950s, red plastic, flashes red, green, or clear light, 27", NMIB, $200.00.

Cheyenne Singin' Saddle Gun, Daisy, 1959, plastic & metal, 32", NM (EX box) $100.00

Dan Dare Planet Gun, Merit, 1969, plastic, MIB $150.00

Dan Dare Planet Gun, Randall, 1953, plastic, shoots propeller missiles, 4½", MIB..$175.00

Daniel Boone Cork/Flint Gun, Japan (?), 1950s, litho tin, 10", sparks not working o/w VG $65.00

Davy Crockett Gun & Holster Set, Betty Leach Inc, diecast pistol, imitation leather holster w/fringe, 7", NMIB $250.00

Davy Crockett Texas Rifle, AVC/Spain, plastic & metal, 23", NM (EX box w/Davy at the Alamo) $75.00

Davy Crockett Water Gun, Knickerbocker, plastic w/emb image on grips, mk Davy Crockett, 8", NMOC...................$75.00

Dick Tracy .45 Water Pistol, Tops, 1950s, sticker on barrel shows Tracy & Sam, scarce, EX, D11 ....$40.00

Dick Tracy Click Pistol, Marx, 1935, pressed steel w/Dick Tracy decal, 8", MIB...$175.00

Dick Tracy Crimestopper Machine Gun, Larami, 1973, plastic, EXIB $35.00

Dick Tracy Power Jet Squad Gun, Mattel, plastic, shoots water & caps, 31", M (EX box) $100.00

Dick Tracy Sparking Pop Pistol, Marx, 1940s, EX+ (VG box)...$250.00

Flash Gordon Radio Repeater Click Pistol, Marx, 1935, red and silver, 10", MIB, $450.00.

Dick Tracy Special Agent Dart Gun, Larami, 1972, w/handcuffs & badge, NMIP..$35.00

Dick Tracy Water Gun, Larami, 1971, red plastic sub-machine gun, 6", MOC $35.00

Dragnet Detective Special Repeating Revolver, Knickerbocker, 1955, metal w/badge inset on plastic grips, M (EX box)...........$125.00

Dragnet 2 in 1 Combination, Carnell, complete w/Hubley cap gun, M (EX box)..$175.00

Dune Fremen Target Gun, LJN, 1984, plastic, w/flashing lights & sound, battery-op, 8", MIB $35.00

Flash Gordon Air Ray Gun, Budson, red & silver tin w/Flash Gordon emb on ea side, 10½", EX+ (G- box) $300.00

G-Man Automatic Gun, Marx, 1930, pressed steel w/G-Man decal, w/up, 4", EX (EX+ box), A $125.00

G-Man Cap Gun, Kilgore, 9", EX $125.00

G-Man Machine Gun, Exelo, battery-operated, 10", EX (EX box), A, $175.00.

Gene Autry Gun & Holster Set, CI w/name on plastic simulated pearl hdl, brn holster w/decal & belt, 8", VG+, A ..$300.00

Gene Autry Gun & Holster Set, metal gun w/Gene Autry emb on plastic grips, wht leather holster w/jewels & studs, EX $350.00

Gene Autry Pistol, Leslie-Henry, 1950s, diecast with embossed horse head on white plastic grip, 9", MIB, P4, $275.00.

Godzilla Water Pistol, Japan, transparent bl plastic w/decals, 4x4", M, M17..$60.00

Hawaii Five-O Periscope Dart Gun, unused, M (worn card), J2 ....$20.00

Hopalong Cassidy Buck 'N Bronc Cap Gun, Schmidt, 1950s, NP w/blk plastic grips, poppies on barrel & cylinder, 9", VG $225.00

Hopalong Cassidy Cap Gun, Buzz Henry, gold-tone w/blk plastic inset grips, 7½", rare, EX+ $300.00

Hopalong Cassidy Gun & Holster, Schmidt, bust-pc of Hoppy on wht grips, w/left-handed blk leather holster only, NM, A $325.00

Hopalong Cassidy Holster Set, Wyandotte, wht plastic inset grips, blk leather holster w/studs, M (EX box).........$850.00

I Spy Official Shoulder Holster Set, Ray-Line, 1966, M (EX card), A..$50.00

James Bond Goldfinger 100-Shot Repeater Cap Pistol, Lone Star, 1960s, w/silencer, NMIB................................$150.00

James Bond 007 Attache Case, MPC, 1965, blk plastic case complete w/shell-firing pistol & accessories, scarce, NMIB...$400.00

James Bond 007 Gun & Holster Set, Pilen, plastic, w/handcuffs, badge & star, 9", NM (EX box)................................$250.00

Johnny West Ranch Rifle, Marx, 1960, built-in noisemaker & speaker, 26", EX..$75.00

Kit Carson Cap Gun, Kilgore, gold-plated w/emb image of Kit on wht plastic inset grips, 8", NM............................$125.00

Lone Ranger Cap Gun, Kilgore, CI, sm hammer, 8½", NM..$350.00

Lone Ranger Carbine Rifle, Marx, plastic, inscr Lone Ranger TLR, shoots caps w/smoking action, 26", NM (G box).........$175.00

Lone Ranger Rifle, Hubley, 1970s, 35", EX.......................$75.00

Lone Ranger Victory Corps Gun Set, papier-mache, w/holster & bullets, M...$200.00

Lost in Space Roto Jet Gun, Mattel, 1966, changes into 4 different weapons, 15" w/10" attachment, rare, MIB (sealed) $350.00

Magnum PI Cap Gun, Ja-Ru, brn & blk plastic, 5", MOC, M17 .$30.00

Man From UNCLE Napoleon Solo Gun, Ideal, 1965, blk plastic cap-firing pistol w/orange decal, scarce, M (EX box)..$300.00

Matt Dillon Cap Pistol, Leslie-Henry, 1950, diecast w/NP finish, emb steer on copper grips, 10"................................$175.00

Mickey Mouse Pop Shot Rifle, Durham, 1977, automation pump action w/balls, MIB, C1 ....$30.00

Overland Trail Holster Set, Hubley, 1960, 2 cap guns w/blk simulated leather grips, dbl holster, MIB......................$300.00

Planet of the Apes Fanner 50, Mattel, Ibis emb on wht plastic grips, 10½", VG $50.00

Popeye Cap Guns & Holster, metal guns, leather holster w/image of Popeye, 5¼" guns, EX, A $100.00

Popeye Pirate Pistol, Marx, 1935, litho tin click pistol, 10", NM (VG box) $400.00

Punch & Judy Cap Gun, Ives, CI w/japan finish, 5¼", VG...$700.00

Range Rider Cap Gun, unmk, all metal, 10", scarce, EX, A ..$125.00

Red Ranger Engraved Gold Repeating Cap Pistol, gold-plated diecast w/blk plastic grips, 8", NM (EX box) $175.00

Red Ranger Six-Shooter Repeater Pistol, Wyandotte, pressed steel, plastic grips w/emb bust images, 10", rare, MIB............$175.00

Red Ryder Carbine BB Gun, Daisy No 111, Model 40, 1940s, pressed steel w/brn wood stock, 36", VG (VG box), P4.............$200.00

Rex Mars Planet Patrol Gun, Marx, litho tin & plastic w/up, 21", needs new flint o/w NM (VG box)...................$200.00

Rifleman Flip Special, Hubley, 1959, diecast & plastic, ring-lever action, brn stock, 32½", EX $200.00

Rin-Tin-Tin Cap Pistol & Holster, Actoy, 1956, diecast w/copper finish, plastic grips, blk & yel holster, 9", EX $250.00

Roy Rogers Cap Pistol, Kilgore, gold w/horse head emb on plastic inset grips, inscr Roy, 8", MOC $250.00

Roy Rogers Gun & Holster Set, Schmidt, metal cap guns, brn leather holster w/studs, mk Roy Rogers, EX, A........$500.00

Roy Rogers Mini Cap Gun, w/holster, NM.....................$65.00

Roy Rogers Tuck-A-Way Gun, metal cap-firing derringer, 2½", NMOC...$75.00

Roy Rogers Western Set Cap Gun, Classy Products, metal, complete w/holster, 6", MIP, A..$155.00

Smoky Joe Cap Pistol & Holster, Leslie-Henry, 1950s, diecast w/NP finish, amber plastic horse head grips, 9", EX...$125.00

Star Trek Tracer Gun, Ray Line, 1967, fires jet disks, bl plastic w/brn grips, 6½", M (EX card), P4 ....$75.00

Superman Cinematic Pistol, Daisy, raised figure on barrel, EX $250.00

Superman Krypto Ray Gun, Daisy, 1939, Superman emb on barrel, battery-op, 7", NMIB $400.00

Texas Ranger Gun & Holster, Leslie-Henry, 1946, gold-plated metal w/plastic grip, emb leather holster, MIB........$200.00

T.H.E. CAT Hide-A-Way Gun Set, Ideal, 1966, complete, scarce, MIB, $150.00.

Tom Corbett Sparking Space Gun, Marx, 1950, tin & plastic w/up, 22", needs new flint o/w NM (box missing end flaps) $200.00

V (TV Show) Gundam Beam Rifle, Bandai, fires w/lights & sound, EX $75.00

V (TV Show) P.38 Pistol Dart Gun, Arco, 1975, MOC ..$75.00

Wagon Train Cap Pistol, Leslie-Henry, 1950s, NP finish w/scroll design, wht plastic horse head grips, 9", M, P4 ....$110.00

Wagon Train 5-in-1 Rifle, Leslie-Henry, complete, NM (M box) $400.00

Wild Bill Hickok Cap Gun, Leslie-Henry, metal w/emb longhorn & Marshall... on copper grips, 10", EX+, A................$135.00

Wyatt Earp Frontier Marshall Set, Service Mfg, 2 Hubley Coyote cap guns, Wyatt Earp emb on holster, NM (EX box) $350.00

Zorro Flintlock Cap Pistol, Marx, 1950s, plastic, 11", NMOC..$75.00

BB Guns

Values are suggested for BB guns that are in excellent condition. Advisor: Jim Buskirk.

Daisy (Early), break action, wire stock, B6 ....$450.00

Daisy (Early), top lever, wire stock, B6 ....$600.00

Daisy '1000' Shot Daisy,' lever action, wood stock, B6 ..$250.00

Daisy '500 Shot Daisy,' lever action, wood stock, B6 .....$250.00

Daisy Model A, break action, wood stock, B6 ....$200.00

Daisy Model B, lever action, wood stock, B6 ....$80.00

Daisy Model C, break action, wood stock, B6.................$200.00

Daisy Model H, lever action, wood stock, B6 ....$80.00

Daisy Model 1938B, Christmas Story/Red Ryder, B6 ....$65.00

Daisy Model 21, 1968, dbl barrel, plastic stock, B6 ....$350.00

Daisy No 100, Model 38, break action, wood stock, B6....$25.00

Daisy No 101, Model 33, lever action, wood stock, B6 ....$40.00

Daisy No 101, Model 36, lever action, wood stock, B6 ....$35.00

Photo courtesy Jim Buskirk.

Daisy No 103, Model 33, Buzz Barton, B6, $200.00; Daisy No 195, Buzz Barton, lever action, wood stock, B6, $65.00.

Daisy No 103, Model 33, lever action, wood stock, B6 ..$150.00

Daisy No 104, dbl barrel, wood stock, B6 ....$550.00

Daisy No 105, 'Junior Pump Gun,' wood stock, B6 ....$150.00

Daisy No 106, break action, wood stock, B6.....................$25.00

Daisy No 107, 'Buck Jones Special,' pump action, wood stock, B6..$100.00

Daisy No 107, pump action, plastic stock, B6 ....$20.00

Daisy No 108, Model 39, 'Carbine,' lever action, wood stock, B6..$65.00

Daisy No 11, lever action, wood stock, B6 ....$65.00

Daisy No 111, Model 40, Red Ryder, aluminum lever, B6..$50.00

Daisy No 111, Model 40, Red Ryder, iron lever, B6 ....$80.00

Daisy No 111, Model 40, Red Ryder, plastic stock, B6.....$30.00

Daisy No 12, break action, wood stock, B6 ....$50.00

Daisy No 140, 'Defender,' lever action, wood stock, B6....$200.00

Daisy No 195, Model 36, Buzz Barton, lever action, wood stock, B6..$70.00

Daisy No 25, pump action, pistol-grip wood stock, B6 .....$45.00

Daisy No 25, pump action, straight wood stock, B6..........$50.00

Daisy No 30, lever action, wood stock, B6 ....$80.00

Daisy No 40, 'Military,' lever action, wood stock, B6.....$175.00

Daisy No 40, 'Military,' w/bayonet, lever action, wood stock, B6..$400.00

Daisy No 50, copper-plated, lever action, blk wood stock, B6..$80.00

King Model 5533, lever action, wood stock, B6...............$35.00

King No 1, break action, wood stock, B6 ....$50.00
King No 10, break action, wood stock, B6 ....$30.00
King No 17, break action, wood stock, B6 ....$125.00
King No 2, break action, wood stock, B6 ....$45.00
King No 21, lever action, wood stock, B6 ....$55.00
King No 2136, lever action, wood stock, B6 ....$20.00
King No 22, lever action, wood stock, B6 ....$55.00
King No 2236, lever action, wood stock, B6 ....$20.00
King No 24, break action, wood stock, B6 ....$175.00
King No 24, lever action, wood stock, B6 ....$65.00
King No 4, lever action, wood stock, B6 ....$150.00
King No 5, 'Pump Gun,' wood stock, B6 ....$125.00
King No 5, lever action, wood stock, B6 ....$150.00
King No 55, lever action, wood stock, B6 ....$70.00
Markham/King 'Chicago,' break action, all wood, B6 ....$200.00
New King, repeater, break action, wood stock, B6 ....$125.00
New King, single shot, break action, wood stock, B6 .....$100.00

Related Items and Accessories

Box, Buck Rogers Atomic Pistol, EX $200.00
Box, Lone Ranger holster set, Leslie-Henry, EX, J2 ....$40.00
Box, Red Ryder Rifle Model 111, 1940s, EX, C10 ....$165.00
Box, Texas Holster, Halco, early, VG+, J2 ....$40.00
Buckle, Roy Rogers, from holster set, EX $50.00
Bullets, Hubley Texan .38, 1957, 6 brass-colored bullets in wht
    plastic belt, M, P4 ....$20.00
Bullets, Nichols Stallion, 1950s, 2-part w/brass casing, 6 in wht
    plastic strip belt, M, P4 ....$20.00
Caps, Hubley Texan .38 Six Shooters, 1950s, 100 per box, M, P4 .$5.00
Caps, Marx Thundercaps, 1950s, 5 rolls per box, M, P4 .....$5.00
Caps, Mattel Bullet Pak No 637, 1958, w/8 play bullets, MOC,
    P4 ....$25.00
Caps, Mattel Greenie Stick-M-Caps, 1958, 2 sheets of 60 per
    box, M, P4 ....$5.00
Caps, Nichols Tophand 250 Shot Roll Caps, 1 roll per box, M,
    P4 ....$5.00
Cartridge Clips, Hubley Colt .45, 1958, store display complete
    w/6 cartridge clips, rare, NM, A $375.00
Holster, Buck Rogers, 1930s, red & yel leather w/metal studs &
    rocketship, rare, EX $300.00
Holster, Dick Tracy, 1950s, leather w/cartoon graphics, EX...$50.00
Holster, Kilgore Fast Draw, vinyl, no belt, NMIB, T1 ......$35.00
Holster, Lone Ranger, early, leather, 8", VG, J2 ....$55.00
Holster, Maverick, Carnell, wht & blk leather w/jewels & studs,
    unused, NMIB $175.00
Holster, Roy Rogers, leather, dbl, EX, J2 ....$240.00
Holster, Roy Rogers, 1950s, RR studs w/etched images of Roy &
    Trigger, no belt, VG, J5 ....$45.00
Holster, Texas Ranger, w/jewels & studs, EX, J2 ....$90.00
Holster, Wyatt Earp, Hubley, EX, J2 ....$50.00

Halloween

Halloween is a uniquely American holiday melded from the
traditions of superstitions brought to the new world from Ger-

many and Scotland. St. Matrimony was reportedly the patron
saint of this holiday, as it was at this time of the year when the
harvest was safely in that betrothals and weddings took place.
Most activity for the holiday focused on getting young eligible
people married. Trick or Treat was a way of getting rid of both-
ersome younger siblings. Robert Burns, the poet of Scotland was
a major influence on the folklore of the holiday. In this country
today, Halloween is a holiday with little or no association with
earlier religious rites of any group. It's an evening of fun, frolic,
and fantasy filled with lots of sugar and calories!

Note: Our values are prices realized at a high-profile, spe-
cialty auction and should be considered high retail, though certainly valid.

Advisor: Pamela E. Apkarian-Russell, The Halloween
Queen (H9).

See also Halloween Costumes.

Accordion Toy, moon & cat, push & pull action, 1950s, 6x4",
    EX, A $115.00
Balancing Toy, witch on broom, wood, 1950s, 12", MIB .$35.00
Bell, 4-sided w/various images, tin w/wood hdl, American,
    1930s, 6", EX, A $300.00
Book, Dennison's Bogie Book, 1919, 32 pgs, rare, EX $95.00
Bowl, glass, orange w/blk bats & flying witches, 1960s, 5x7" dia,
    NM, A $100.00

**Candy Bag, 1940s,
features Popeye and
Olive Oyl, 9", EX,
D10, $85.00.**

Photo courtesy Dunbar Gallery.

Candy Box, jack-o'-lantern w/Halloween band, Japan, 1930s, 3"
    dia, NM, A..$175.00
Candy Box, striped jack-o'-lantern w/lg grin, cb & crepe paper,
    Japan, 1930s, 3", EX, A $160.00
Candy Container, blk cat atop jack-o'-lantern w/toothy grin,
    compo, German, 1910, 2½", M, A............................$325.00
Candy Container, blk cat in Halloween suit on candy box,
    compo, German, 1920, 7", NM, A...........................$700.00
Candy Container, blk cat w/orange hood, compo, German,
    1920, 2½", NM, A...$400.00

Candy Container, candle face, striped box w/cb & crepe-paper candle, Japan, 1930s, 3", EX, A..................................$100.00

Candy Container, jack-o'-lantern, pulp w/molded bow, ATCO, 1940s, 5", NM, A...$85.00

Candy Container, jack-o'-lantern w/stem, compo w/pull-out base, German, 1910, 2½", EX, A.............................$325.00

Candy Container, owl, compo, Japan, 1930, 3", scarce, NM $200.00

Candy Container, skull head, compo w/mesh clothing, German, 1920s, 4½", NM, A...$350.00

Candy Container, vegetable girl in apron, compo, head pulls off, German, 1910, 4", scarce, EX, A.............................$350.00

Candy Container, watermelon, cb, Austrian, 1920s, 4" L, EX, A...$265.00

Candy Container, witch hat on box, cb & crepe paper, mk Nippon, 1930s, 2½", EX, A..$110.00

Candy Container, witch w/broom, molded compo w/crepe-paper clothes, German, 1920s, 7", M, A.........................$400.00

Centerpiece, blk cat, crepe paper & cb w/accordion body, 1930s-40s, 10", M, A..$55.00

Chocolate Mold, silverplated metal, 1930s, 5", EX, A ...$225.00

Diecut, black cat, German, 1920s, 20", EX+, $110.00.

Diecut, blk cat & quarter moon, American, 1930s, 9x8", NM, A..$55.00

Diecut, flapper girl jack-o'-lantern, German, 1920s, 5x5½", M, A $60.00

Diecut, jack-o'-lantern, German, 1920s, 13x14", scarce, NM, A $80.00

Diecut, kitty w/banjo, German, 1920s, 25x11", EX $150.00

Diecut, pirate owl, 1930s, 18", NM, A $45.00

Diecut, pumpkin man in clown costume, German, 1920s, 16x6", EX, A $135.00

Diecut, scarecrow, crows & pumpkin patch, American, 1930s, 9x8", NM, A..$125.00

Diecut, skeleton musicians, It's a Hot Time in the Pumpkin Patch Tonight, American, 1930, 9x9", EX, A.........$185.00

Diecut, witch, German, 15", EX+, $95.00.

Doll, jack-o'-lantern face w/sunflower hat, cb body w/crepe-paper limbs, German, 1920s, 16", scarce, EX, A......$185.00

Drum, dbl-face jack-o'-lantern, cb, orig inserts, German, 1930, 4x2½", M, A..$550.00

Figure, blk cat w/red neck ribbon, papier-mache w/twine tail, German, 1920s, 4", EX, A $255.00

Figure, owl, orange pulp w/glass eyes, American, 1930s, 10", NM, A $300.00

Figures, black cats, German, composition, 1¾", EX, D10, $45.00 each.

Figures, devil, witch & jack-o'-lantern w/hat, compo, German, 1920s, 4", NM, A...$925.00

Game, Spear's Halloween Ring Toss, lg jack-o'-lantern w/2 pipes & cb rings, NMIB..$350.00

Horn, devil figure, molded compo, red, German, 10" L, NM, A..$700.00

Horn, devil head, pulp, German, 1920s-30s, 5x8", scarce, NM, A $255.00

Horn, jack-o'-lantern w/horn nose, night scene w/owls & bats on back, US Metal Co, 1950s, 6x6" dia, EX, A.......$125.00

Horn, jack-o'-lantern, German, 1920s, EX, $75.00.

Jack-in-the-Box, compo skeleton in blk box, Japan, 1930s, 5", NM, A $325.00

Jack-o'-Lantern, cb w/papier-mache wash, bright red lips, orig insert, German, 1920s, 6", NM, A $425.00

Jack-o'-Lantern, cb w/papier-mache wash, gr stripes around top, mk DRGM Germany, 1920s, 6", NM, A $550.00

Jack-o'-Lantern, cb w/papier-mache wash, wht skull face, orig insert, mk DRGM Germany, 1920s, 5", rare, NM, A ..$700.00

Jack-o'-Lantern, compo w/molded skull face, orig insert, German, 1910, 3½", EX $450.00

Jack-o'-Lantern, fire face w/horned ears, orig insert, German, 1920, 6", scarce, NM $500.00

Jack-o'-Lantern, pressed cb goblin, wht, orig insert, German, 1920s, 4", EX, A $700.00

Jack-o'-Lantern, pressed cb goblin w/horned ears, red & gr, orig insert, German, 1920s, 4½", scarce, NM, A $400.00

Jack-o'-Lantern, pulp, monster head, orange, yel & gr, orig insert, American, 1930s, 9", scarce, EX, A $640.00

Jack-o'-Lantern, pulp, orange w/gr detail, American, 1940s, 6", EX, A $215.00

Jack-o'-Lantern, pulp, pumpkin man w/bow tie, orig insert, American, 1940s, 7", NM..$200.00

Jack-o'-Lantern, pulp, smiling face, orig insert, FN Burt Co, 1940s, 5½", EX, A $550.00

Jack-o'-Lantern, pulp, smiling face, w/stem & orig insert, FN Burt & Co, 1940s, 7", rare, EX, A...........................$585.00

Jack-o'-Lantern, pulp light-up, full-figure man, American, 1940s, 9½", scarce, EX, A...$425.00

Jack-o'-Lantern, 8 panels w/smiling faces on 2 sides, orange w/orig inserts, 1940s, 5", M, A $145.00

Jack-o'-Lantern w/Candle Holder Hat, pulp w/molded face, American, 1940s, 3", NM, A $200.00

Lantern, blk cat, pressed cb w/papier-mache wash, orig insert, German, 1920s, 3½", EX, A............................$425.00

Lantern, dbl-face pulp w/stem, mouth wide open, orig inserts, American, 1940s, 7", NM, A $250.00

Lantern, devil, compo w/molded features, springy horns, orig insert, German, 1917, 4", rare, NM, A $1,000.00

Lantern, devil, pressed cb, orig insert, German, 1920s, 5", EX, A $500.00

Lantern, devil head, pulp, American, 8", EX, $175.00.

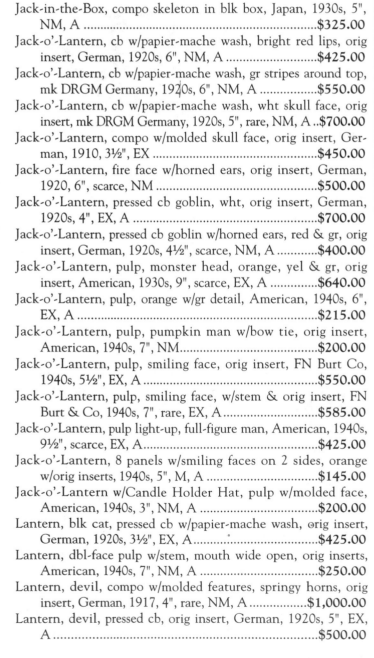

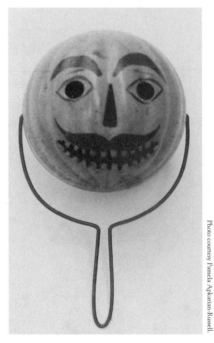

Lantern, jack-o'-lantern, tin, Toledo, OH, 1908, EX, $650.00.

Nodder, jack-o'-lantern in top hat w/feather, German, 1920s, 7", NM, A $200.00

Nodder/Nut Basket, jack-o'-lantern in top hat w/feather & gr basket on rnd orange base, Germany, 1920s, 6", rare, EX, A $195.00

Noisemaker, witch, wooden w/pnt compo head, Germany, 6", EX, A $230.00

Panel, pumpkin girl & jack-o'-lantern, crepe paper, 1920s, 18½x19", NM, A...$85.00

Panel, witches, bats & stars, crepe paper, 1920, 20x36", rare, EX, A $100.00

Pin, dancing skeleton, pull string for arm & leg movement, German, 1920s, scarce, EX, A $160.00

Pin, jack-o'-lantern violinist, compo, German, 1920s, 2¼", M, A $200.00

Pin, jack-o'-lantern w/toothy grin, leafy arms & squash-style ft, compo, German, 1920, 1¾", NM, A $240.00

Pin, vegetable man w/toothy grin, compo, German, 1920s, 2", scarce, NM, A..$200.00

Pipe, jack-o'-lantern w/red molded ball nose, hand-pnt, German, 1920s, 6" L, scarce, EX, A $225.00

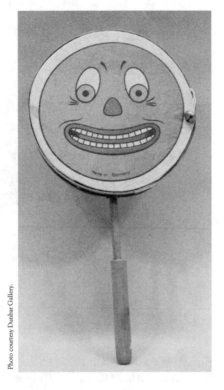

Rattle/Whistle, jack-o'-lantern, German, 1920s, EX, from $175.00 to $275.00.

Photo courtesy Dunbar Gallery.

Seals, blk cat faces, Gibson, 1920s, set of 4, MIP, A $125.00

Tambourine, orange & gr w/jack-o'-lantern face, litho tin, 1920s, 7" dia, scarce, EX $75.00

Tambourine, orange w/blk cat face, litho tin, T Cohn, 1940s, 7" dia, EX..$75.00

Whirligig, witch w/broom arms & stovepipe hat, wood, 1920s, 13", NM...$225.00

Halloween Costumes

During the '50s and '60s Ben Cooper and Collegeville made Halloween costumes representing the popular TV and movie characters of the day. If you can find one in excellent to mint condition and still in its original box, some of the better ones can go for over $100.00. MAD's Alfred E. Neuman (Collegeville, 1959-60) usually carries an asking price of $150.00 to $175.00, and The Green Hornet (Ben Cooper, 1966), $200.00. Earlier handmade costumes are especially valuable if they are 'Dennison-Made.'

Advisor: Pamela E. Apkarian-Russell, The Halloween Queen (H9).

Addams Family, Lurch, Ben Cooper, 1965, blk 1-pc suit w/silver glitter illus, scarce, M, A...$50.00

Alfred E Neuman, mask only, 1960s, M, P12.....................$50.00

Andromeda Lady Space Fighter, EX (EX box), J2 ....$35.00

Aquaman, Ben Cooper, 1967, suit only, synthetic fabric w/colorful image, M, T2 ....$40.00

Banana Splits, Ben Cooper, 1969, suit only, yel & red fabric w/colorful image, M, T2 ....$30.00

Bart Simpson, Ben Cooper/Canadian, 1989, MIB, K1 .....$15.00

Batgirl, Ben Cooper, 1973, EX (EX box) $45.00

Batman, Ben Cooper, 1966, costume & mask, NMIB, T2..$90.00

Beatles, Paul McCartney, Ben Cooper, NMIB $300.00

Beatles, Ringo Starr, mask only, G....................................$40.00

Bullwinkle, Ben Cooper, 1971, EX (EX box), F8.............$45.00

Captain America, Ben Cooper, 1967, MIB, $100.00.

Cryptkeeper, Ace Novelty, 1994, mask only, latex, EX....$45.00

Daffy Duck, Collegeville, 1960s, EX (EX box).................$40.00

Dick Tracy, 1960s, mask only, plastic w/movable jaw, EX+, D11 ....$25.00

Donald Duck, Collegeville, NMIB, $40.00.

Dr Doom, Ben Cooper, 1967, MIB, A $115.00

Dukes of Hazzard, Bo, Ben Cooper, 1979, EX (EX box), J2 .$30.00

Fantastic Four, Ben Cooper, 1967, EX+ (EX box), A.......$50.00
Farrah Fawcett, Collegeville, 1977, EX (EX box), A........$60.00
Fred Flintstone, 1973, NMIB..$50.00
Freddy Krueger, Don Post, 1986, mask & hat, latex, EX, F1 ..$40.00
Garrison's Gorillas, Ben Cooper, 1967, red, yel & tan fabric
    w/plastic mask, scarce, MIP, T2 ....$70.00
GI Joe, 1989, NMIB...$35.00
Grandpa Munster, Illusive Concepts, mask only, latex, EX ..$30.00
Green Lantern, Ben Cooper, 1967, EX (EX box) $80.00
Herman (Herman & Katnip), Collegeville, 1960s, VG (EX
    box), F8..$35.00
HR Pufnstuf, Witchie Poo, 1970, NMIB.........................$50.00
I Dream of Jeannie, Ben Cooper, 1970s, NMIB..............$125.00
Incredible Hulk, Ben Cooper, 1977, MIB $45.00
Iron Man, Ben Cooper, 1966, M, A $50.00
Jolly Green Giant, Halco, 1950s-60s, complete, VG (EX box),
    F8...$55.00
King Kong, Ben Cooper, 1976, MIB $40.00
KISS, Gene Simmons, Collegeville, 1978, MIB $95.00
Kung Fu, Ben Cooper, 1970s, EX (VG box), J5................$25.00

Little Orphan Annie, 1930s, marked Leapin'
Lizards! Its Little Orphan Annie, complete with bag
and party favors, EX+ (EX box), A, $175.00.

Max Headroom,
1986, M, J6,
$12.00.

Man From UNCLE, Halco, EX (EX box) $45.00
Mandrake the Magician, Collegeville, 1950s, NMIB, F8..$120.00
Mr Ed, Brown, 1962, gown only, EX, J5 ....$25.00
Mr Fantastic, Ben Cooper, 1967, EX (EX box), A...........$50.00
Mummy, Ben Cooper, 1963, M, T2 ....$60.00

Raggedy Ann, Ben Cooper, TV-Comic series,
1973, MIB, $38.00.

Ratfink, 1990, MIB, B10..$8.00
Scooby Doo, 1970s, MIB, from $30 to $40.00
Sour Grapes (Strawberry Shortcake), MIB, A5 ....$30.00
Spider-Man, Ben Cooper, 1950s, NMIB, M17 ....$135.00
Spider-Man, Ben Cooper, 1972, MIB, J7 ....$35.00
Spider-Woman, Ben Cooper, 1970s, NM (EX+ box).....$110.00
Spock, Ben Cooper, 1970s, EXIB, J5 ....$25.00
Strawberry Shortcake, MIB, A5 ....$30.00
Superman, Ben Cooper, 1976, EX (EX box) $95.00
Tarzan, 1975, NMIB...$75.00
Tonto, 1950s, gr & yel, EX, J5..$25.00
Top Cat, Ben Cooper, EX, J2 ....$20.00
Underdog, Collegeville, 1974, NM (VG box), F8 ....$35.00
Wonder Woman, Ben Cooper, 1976, EX (EX box).........$75.00
Wonder Woman, Ben Cooper, 1987, MIB, C17..............$12.00
Yogi Bear Glitter-Glo, Ben Cooper, 1960s, NM (VG box),
    M17..$55.00
Zorro, Ben Cooper, EX, W6 ....$75.00

Hartland Plastics, Inc.

Originally known as the Electro Forming Co., Hartland
Plastics Ind. was founded in 1941 by Ed and Iola Walters. They
first produced heels for military shoes, birdhouses and ornamen-
tal wall decor. It wasn't until the late 1940s that Hartland produced their first horse and rider. Figures were hand painted with
an eye for detail. The Western and Historic Horsemen, Minia-

ture Western Series, Authentic Scale Model Horses, Famous Gunfighter Series, and the Hartland Sports Series of Famous Baseball Stars were a symbol of the fine workmanship of the '40s, '50s, and '60s. The plastic used was a virgin acetate. Paint was formulated by Bee Chemical Co., Chicago, Illinois, and Wolverine Finishes Corp., Grand Rapids, Michigan. Hartland figures are best known for their uncanny resemblance to the TV Western stars who portrayed characters like the Lone Ranger, Matt Dillon, and Roy Rogers. For more information we recommend *Hartland Horses and Riders* by Gail Fitch. See Also Clubs, Newsletters, and Other Publications.

Advisor: Judy and Kerry Irvin (K5).

Alkine Ike, NM, K5 ....$150.00
Annie Oakley, NM, K5 ....$275.00
Bill Longley, NM, K5 ....$600.00
Brave Eagle, NM, K5 ....$200.00
Brave Eagle, NMIB, K5 ....$300.00
Bret Maverick, miniature series, NM, K5 ....$75.00
Bret Maverick, NMIB, K5 ....$750.00
Bret Maverick, w/coffeedunn horse, NM, K5 ....$650.00
Bret Maverick, w/gray horse, rare, NM, K5 ....$700.00
Buffalo Bill, NM, K5 ....$300.00
Bullet, NM, K5 ....$45.00
Bullet, w/tag, NM, K5 ....$75.00
Cactus Pete, NM, K5 ....$150.00
Champ Cowgirl, NM, K5 ....$150.00
Cheyenne, miniature series, NM, K5 ....$75.00
Cheyenne, w/tag, NM, K5 ....$190.00
Chief Thunderbird, rare shield, NM, K5 ....$150.00

Cochise, NM, K5, $150.00.

Commanche Kid, NM, K5 ....$150.00
Dale Evans, gr, NM, K5 ....$125.00
Dale Evans, purple, NM, K5 ....$300.00

Dale Evans, rare bl version, NM, K5 ....$400.00
Davy Crockett, NM, K5 ....$550.00
General Custer, NMIB, K5 ....$200.00
General Custer, repro flag, NM, K5 ....$150.00
General George Washington, NMIB, K5 ....$175.00
General Robert E Lee, NMIB, K5 ....$175.00
Gil Favor, prancing, NM, K5 ....$80.00
Gil Favor, semi-rearing, NM, K5 ....$600.00
Hoby Gillman, NM, K5 ....$225.00
Jim Bowie, w/tag, NM, K5 ....$250.00
Jim Hardy, NMIB, K5 ....$275.00
Jockey, NM, K5 ....$150.00
Jockey, repro crop, NM, K5 ....$100.00
Josh Randle, NM, K5 ....$650.00
Lone Ranger, champ, blk breast collar, NM, K5 ......$125.00
Lone Ranger, miniature series, NM, K5 ....$75.00
Lone Ranger, NM, K5 ....$150.00
Lone Ranger, rearing, NMIB, K5 ....$300.00
Matt Dillon, w/tag, NMIB, K5 ....$275.00

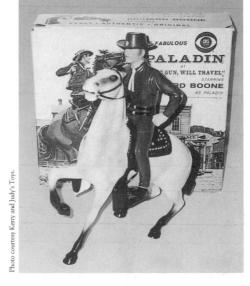

Paladin, NMIB, K5, $350.00.

Photo courtesy Kerry and Judy's Toys.

Rebel, miniature series, repro hat, NM, K5 ....$100.00
Rebel, NMIB, K5 ....$1,200.00

Photo courtesy Ellen and Jerry Harnish.

Rifleman, NMIB, $350.00.

Rifleman, miniature series, repro rifle, EX, K5 ....$75.00
Ronald MacKenzie, NM, K5 ....$1,200.00
Roy Rogers, semi-rearing, NMIB, K5 ....$350.00
Roy Rogers, walking, NMIB, K5 ....$250.00
Seth Adams, NM, K5 ....$275.00
Sgt Lance O'Rourke, NMIB, K5 ....$250.00
Sgt Preston, repro flag, NM, K5 ....$750.00
Tom Jeffords, NM, K5 ....$175.00
Tonto, miniature series, NM, K5.....................................$75.00
Tonto, NM, K5...$150.00
Tonto, rare semi-rearing, NM, K5 ....$650.00
Warpaint Thunderbird, w/shield, NMIB, K5.................$350.00
Wyatt Earp, w/tag, NMIB, K5 ....$275.00

STANDING GUNFIGHTERS

Bat Masterson, NMIB, K5 ....$500.00

Bret Maverick, NM, $150.00.

Photo courtesy Ellen and Jerry Harnish.

Chris Colt, NM, K5...$150.00
Clay Holister, NM, K5..$225.00
Dan Troop, NM, K5...$400.00
Jim Hardy, NM, K5..$150.00
Johnny McKay, NM, K5...$800.00
Paladin, NM, K5...$400.00
Vint Bonner, w/tag, NMIB, K5 ....$650.00
Wyatt Earp, NM, K5...$200.00

Horses

Horse riding being the order of the day, many children of the 19th century had their own horses to ride indoors; some were wooden while others were stuffed, and many had glass eyes

and real horsehair tails. There were several ways to construct these horses so as to achieve a galloping action. The most common types had rocker bases or were mounted with a spring on each leg.

Gliding Horse, glass eyes, hair mane & tail, leather tack, 1900s, 32½", pnt & leather wear..$575.00
Platform Horse, blk cloth-covered & stuffed, hair mane & tail, 4-wheeled wooden platform, 20", VG.....................$235.00
Platform Horse, stuffed brn burlap w/hair mane & tail, glass eyes, wooden platform w/CI wheels, 25", EX...................$525.00

Photo courtesy Allan Licht.

Riding Horse, Hi-Prancer hobby horse, early 1950s, white with black detail, red saddle, wooden stand, VG, from $150.00 to $200.00.

Rocking Horse, carved & pnt wood body w/applied legs on 48" red wood runners, leatherette saddle, 32", crazing, G $425.00
Rocking Horse, cream w/dapple effect, glass eyes, blk hooves, leatherette saddle, 4-legged platform, 34", VG........$400.00
Rocking Horse, cvd wood w/dapple gray pnt, pnt eyes, hair mane & tail, red rockers, 51", VG $525.00
Rocking Horse, Gibbs, paper litho on wood w/tin legs, wood rockers, 9", scratches on litho & split on chest, VG $250.00
Rocking Horse, pnt pine w/hair mane & tail, leatherette saddle on cloth blanket w/gold fringe, 36", eyes missing, G+ ...$1,000.00
Rocking Horse, W Reed, wood w/dapple gray pnt, hair mane & tail, oilcloth saddle, leather tackle, 47", VG $2,900.00

Hot Wheels

When they were introduced in 1968, Hot Wheels were an instant success. Sure, their racy style and flashy custom paint jobs were instant attention-getters, but what the kids loved most was the fact that they were fast! The fastest on the market! It's estimated that more than two billion Hot Wheels have been sold to date — every model with a little variation, keeping up with new trends in the big car industry. The line has included futuristic vehicles, muscle cars, trucks, hot rods, racers, and some military vehicles. Lots of these can still be found for very little, but if you want to buy the older models (collectors call them 'Red Lines' because of their red sidewall tires), it's going to cost you a little more, though many can still be found for under $25.00. By 1971, earlier on some models, black-wall tires had become the standard.

A line of cars with Goodyear tires called Real Riders were made from 1983 until about 1987. (In 1983 the tires had gray hubs with white lettering; in 1984 the hubs were white.) California Customs were made in 1989 and 1990. These had the Real Rider tires, but they were not lettered 'Good Year' (and some had different wheels entirely).

Chopcycles are similar to Sizzlers in that they have rechargable batteries. The first series was issued in 1973 in these models: Mighty Zork, Blown Torch, Speed Steed, and Bruiser Cruiser. Generally speaking, these are valued at $35.00 (loose) to $75.00 (MIB). A second series issued in 1974 was made up of Ghost Rider, Rage Coach, Riptide, Sourkraut, and Triking Viking. This series is considerably harder to find and much more expensive today; expect to pay as much as $250.00 to $350.00 for a mint-in-box example.

Though recent re-releases have dampened the collector market somewhat, cars mint and in the original packages are holding their values and are still moving well. Near mint examples (no package) are worth about 50% to 60% less than those mint and still in their original package, excellent condition about 65% to 75% less.

Advisor: Steve Stephenson.

'31 Doozie, wht walls, maroon, M, W1 ....$5.00
'32 Classic Vicky, red line tires, metallic gr, tan interior, smooth blk roof, unlisted color, 1969, NM $16.00
'32 Ford Delivery, blk walls, wht, mc tampo, 1991, NM+, W1 ....$4.00
'34 Ford 3-Window Coupe, blk walls, red, blk interior, yel flame tampo, 1980, NM+, W1 ....$6.00
'35 Classic Caddy, wht walls, metal-flake silver, beige interior, pk fenders, 1989, NM+ $15.00
'36 Classic Coupe, red line tires, metallic magenta, blk interior, smooth blk roof, 1969, M $30.00

'37 Bugatti, wht walls, blk, red hood/side tampo, metal fenders, M (EX+ card) $8.00
'40s Woodie, blk walls, yel, lt brn wood panels, hi-raker, M (NM+ card) $8.00
'55 Chevy, blk walls, blk, wht/orange '3' tampo, 1992, M (NM+ card, opened blister pack), W1 ....$13.50

'56 Hi-Tail Hauler, basic wheels, blue with red and yellow flames, 1977, NM, $50.00.

'57 Chevy, blk walls, red, clear bl interior, yel/wht stripe, '57 Chevy tampo, NM+, W1 ....$9.00
'57 Classic Bird, red line tires, metallic purple, med interior, 1969, NM $20.00
'57 T-Bird, blk walls, red, blk interior, bl/yel tampo, M (EX+ card) $12.00
'59 Caddy, wht walls, pk, mc tampo, blk California Custom on windshield, 1991, M $20.00
'63 Split Window Corvette, blk walls, blk, yel/red/bl tampo, 1984, M (NM card) $15.00
'65 Mustang Convertible, wht walls, wht, Park 'N Plates, 1989, M (EX+) $8.00
'80 Corvette, gold wheels, red, yel/brn interior, blk top, M (NM card), W1 ....$7.50
Alien, blk walls, dk bl, no tampo, 1988, M (NM card) $15.00
Alive '55, red line tires, dk gr, blk interior, 1974, NM, W1 ..$49.00
Ambulance, red line tires, metallic purple, lt interior, M (NM card) $75.00
American Hauler, red line tires, dk bl, blk windshield, 1976, NM $20.00
American Tipper, red line tires, red, 1976, M $20.00
American Victory, red line tires, lt bl, red/wht '9' tampo, 1975, NM+ $15.00
AMX/2, red line tires, metallic lt gr, blk interior, 1971, M ..$40.00
Assault Crawler, blk walls, olive, 1987, M (NM+ card), W1 ....$8.00
Backwoods Bomb, red line tires, lt bl, clear bl interior/windshield, complete, 1975, NM+, W1 ....$49.00
Baja Breaker, blk walls, motorcycle tampo, silver construction tires, 1989, M (NM+ card), W1 ....$5.00
Baja Bruiser, red line tires, orange, blk interior, red/wht/bl tampo, 1974, NM, W1 ....$44.00
Beach Bomb, red line tires, metallic gr, cream interior, orig boards, few cracks, M (EX European Series card), W1 ....$130.00

Beach Patrol, blk walls, wht, bl interior, red/bl tampo, 1 cracked surfboard support, 1985, EX, W1 ....$4.50

Beatnik Bandits, red line tires, metallic aqua, med interior, 1968, M (VG card), W1 ....$40.00

Blazer 4x4, blk walls, silver construction tires, bl, gray interior, mc tampo, M, W1 ....$3.50

Blown Camaro Z-28, gold wheels, blk, yel/red/orange tampo, 1984, M (NM+ card), W1 ....$15.00

Brabham Repco F1, red line tires, metallic aqua, blk interior, orig decal, 1969, NM+ $12.00

Bronco 4-Wheeler, blk walls, red, yel/blk/wht '21' tampo, 1982, NM $5.00

Bugeye, California Custom Miniatures, red, 1971, MIP ...$95.00

Photo courtesy June Moon.

Bugeye, designed by Larry Wood, red line tires, metallic magenta, blue-tinted windows, 1971, NM, J6, $35.00.

Buzz Off, blk walls, gold chrome, red/dk red/blk The Gold One tampo, 1977, NM+ $15.00

Buzz Off, red line tires, fluorescent lime, blk interior, 1973, NM, W1 ....$100.00

Bye-Focal, red line tires, metallic magenta, dk interior, complete, 1971, NM+ $80.00

Camaro Z-28, gold wheels, red, bl/blk/yel tampo, M (NM card) $10.00

Carabo, red line tires, metallic magenta, blk interior, 1970, NM+ $25.00

CAT Dump Truck, yel, blk interior, yel construction tires, M (EX card), W1 ....$4.50

CAT Earth Mover, blk walls, yel, yel construction tires, 1987, M (NM+ card), W1 ....$12.00

Cement Mixer, red line tires, metallic lt gr, blk interior, orig bed/barrel, 1970, NM+, W1 ....$26.00

Chapparal 2G, red line tires, wht, blk interior, orig wing/stickers, headlights pnt silver, 1969, NM+ $20.00

Chevy Citation, gold wheels, metal-flake brn, red interior, wht/blk/dk red tampo, 1983, M (EX+ card), W1 ....$7.00

Chevy Monza 2+2, red line tires, lt gr, rare color, blk/wht tampo, 1975, NM+ $350.00

Chevy Stocker, blk walls, blk, yel/red/wht '3' tampo, lg red wheels, union-V stickers, 1989, M (NM+ card), W1 ..$7.00

Classic '57 T-Bird, red line tires, hot pk, wht interior, 1969, NM $100.00

Classic Cord, red line tires, gold, 1971, VG $100.00

Classic Cord, red line tires, ice bl, 1971, rare, EX $300.00

Classic Cord, red line tires, magenta, 1971, NM, A $200.00

Classic Nomad, red line tires, hot pk, 1970, EX $80.00

Classic Nomad, red line tires, metallic gr, lt interior, some rub on car, 1970, M (EX+ card) $120.00

Cockney Cab, red line tires, metallic yel, blk interior, orig stickers, 1971, M $45.00

Combat Medic, blk walls, gold chrome, 20th Anniversary, w/lines, 1988, EX, W1 ....$12.00

Command Tank, blk walls, olive, 1985, M (EX card) $6.00

Cool One, red line tires, plum, 1976, NM, W1 ....$34.00

Corvette Stingray, red line tires, red, bl/yel/wht ribbon tampo, 1976, NM, W1 ....$35.00

Custom AMX, red line tires, metallic magenta, cream interior, 1969, M (NM cracked card), W1 ....$70.00

Custom Barracuda, red line tires, ice bl, 1968, NM $100.00

Custom Barracuda, red line tires, metallic orange, med interior, 1968, NM+, W1 ....$55.00

Custom Camaro, red line tires, bl, 1968, MOC, A $225.00

Custom Camaro, red line tires, lime gr w/blk top, 1968, EX .$45.00

Custom Camaro, red line tires, orange, 1968, VG $30.00

Custom Corvette, red line tires, purple, 1968, NM $75.00

Custom Cougar, red line tires, metallic orange, med interior, lt toning, 1968, NM+ $60.00

Custom Dodge Charger, red line tires, lime gr, 1969, NM ...$70.00

Custom Dodge Charger, red line tires, metallic red, cream interior, 1969, M (NM card) $130.00

Custom Dodge Charger, red line tires, orange, 1968, VG ...$45.00

Custom Dodge Charger, red line tires, purple, 1969, NM ...$75.00

Custom Eldorado, red line tires, creamy pk, wht interior, 1968, NM $175.00

Custom Eldorado, red line tires, purple, 1968, rare, VG ...$30.00

Custom Firebird, red line tires, metallic orange, med interior, lt toning, 1968, M (EX+ card), W1 ....$200.00

Custom Fleetside, red line tires, aqua, 1968, M $50.00

Custom Fleetside, red line tires, metallic aqua, blk interior, smooth blk roof, 1968, NM, W1 ....$33.00

Custom Fleetside, red line tires, purple, 1968, MOC, A ...$140.00

Custom Mustang, red line tires, metallic red, scarce red interior, blk windshield, rare open scoops, 1968, VG, W1 ....$152.00

Custom Mustang, red line tires, red, 1968, MOC (unpunched) $300.00

Custom Police Cruiser, red line tires, blk & wht, 1969, VG ..$30.00

Custom T-Bird, red line tires, aqua, 1968, MOC, A $120.00

Custom T-Bird, red line tires, purple w/blk top, 1968, NM...$50.00

Custom VW, red line tires, metallic aqua, cream interior, 1968, M $25.00

Custom VW, red line tires, orange w/striped tampo, 1975, EX .$125.00

Datsun 200SX, gold wheels, yel, blk interior, blk/purple/bl tampo, 1982, NM, W1 ....$9.00

Delivery Truck, blk walls, wht, Air France International box, 1990, M (NM+ box), W1 ....$9.00

Demon, red line tires, metallic bl, dk interior, smooth blk roof, 1970, MOC, W1 ....$39.00

Deora, red line tires, metallic aqua, lt interior, cracks around button, 1968, M (EX+ card) $250.00

Dodge D-50, blk walls, red, blk/orange/yel tampo, 1980, NM+, W1 ....$7.00

Dodge Rampage, gray hub Goodyear tires, red, yel interior, yel/blk/wht tampo, 1984, NM+ $15.00

Double Vision, red line tires, red, cream interior, 1973, NM, W1 ....$90.00

Dream Van XGW, gray hub Goodyear tires, lt gr, yel interior, bl/red/yel tampo, 1985, EX, W1 ....$8.00

Dump Truck, red line tires, metallic brn, cream interior, 1970, M..$25.00

Dune Daddy, Flying Colors, red line tires, lt gr, 1975, MOC...$80.00

Emergency Squad, red line tires, red, gray windshield, 1976, NM $15.00

Evil Weevil, red line tires, metallic red, blk interior, 1971, M $50.00

Ferrari F40, Ultra Wheels, red, yel 'F40' tampo, 1989, M (EX+ card), W1 ....$4.00

Ferrari 312P, red line tires, fluorescent lime, blk interior, orig stickers, 1973, NM, W1.............................$150.00

Ferrari 512 S, red line tires, lt gr, 1972, NM, A $55.00

Fiero 2M4, gold wheels, red, red/wht/bl stars & stripes tampo, 1987, M (NM card) $6.00

Fire Chief Cruiser, red line tires, metallic red, cream interior, 1970, NM+ $15.00

Fire Eater, blk walls, red, 1982, M (EX card), W1..............$6.00

Fire Engine, red line tires, metallic red, wht interior, sm crack in windshield, 1970, NM+, W1 ....$30.00

Firebird Funny Car, blk walls, wht, Fireball tampo, 1982, M (EX+ card) $15.00

Flame Stopper, blk walls, red, yel/wht tampo, silver construction tires, 1988, M (NM card), W1 ....$6.00

Flat Out 442, gold wheels, yel, bl/maroon/orange tampo, no pentagon, 1982, NM+, W1 ....$7.00

Ford Aerostar, blk walls, Qantas, 1991, M (NM+ International box), W1 ....$10.00

Ford Escort, blk walls, blk, orange tampo, 1986, M (EX+ card), W1 ....$8.00

Ford Stake Bed Truck, blk walls, metal-flake red, Rapid Delivery tampo, M (NM card), W1 ....$20.00

Formula 5000, red line tires, wht, bl/red '76' tampo, 1976, NM+ $15.00

Front Runnin' Fairmont, gold wheels, red, yel/wht/blk '27' tampo, 1982, NM...$5.00

Fuel Tanker, red line tires, wht, med interior, complete, 1971, M, W1 ....$80.00

Funny Money, red line tires, gray, complete, 1972, M, W1...$60.00

GMC Motorhome, blk walls, orange, bl/wht/yel tampo, 1977, NM, W1 ....$8.00

Greased Gremlin, blk walls, red, 1982, M (NM card) $25.00

Gremlin Grinder, red line tires, gr, orange/yel/blk tampo, 1975, NM $15.00

Gulch Stepper, blk walls, yel, tan roof, orange/red/purple tampo, 8-spoke construction tires, 1985, M (EX+ card), W1 ..$13.00

Gun Bucket, red line tires, olive, wht Army tampo, 1976, NM..$15.00

Gun Slinger, red line tires, olive, w/gun clip, 1976, M $22.00

Hairy Hauler, red line tires, metallic magenta, cream interior, 1971, M, W1 ....$29.00

Hare Splitter, blk walls, yel, orig tire rack, 1982, M (EX- card), W1 ....$8.00

Heavy Chevy, red line tires, yel, blk interior, '7' tampo, 1974, NM, W1 ....$60.00

Highway Patrol, blk walls, wht, blk/yel '12' tampo on roof, 1979, NM+, W1 ....$7.00

Hiway Robber, red line tires, lt gr, blk interior, 1973, EX+.$75.00

Holden Commodore, blk walls, wht, 1991, M (NM+ International card), W1...$7.00

Hot Bird, blk walls, bl, orange/yel tampo, yel bird on hood, trim pnt added, scarce color, 1980, NM, W1 ....$44.00

Hot Heap, red line tires, metallic brn, med interior, 1968, NM+ $25.00

Ice 'T', red line tires, yel, blk interior, complete, 1971, M, W1 ....$59.00

Incredible Hulk, blk walls, yel, gr/blk/wht tampo, 2 rear windows, 1979, NM+, W1 ....$14.00

Incredible Hulk Scene Machine, blk walls, wht, gr/blk/red tampo, 1979, EX+ $15.00

Indy Eagle, Grand Prix Series, gold chrome, 1969, MOC...$200.00

Indy Eagle, red line tires, metallic purple, blk interior, orig decal, 1969, NM+, W1 ....$19.00

Inferno, red line tires, yel, 1976, NM+.............................$35.00

Inside Story, blk walls, gray, red/yel/bl tampo, 1979, M (NM-card) $15.00

Jack Rabbit Special, red line tires, wht, blk interior, 1970, M, W1 ....$26.00

Jaguar XJS, blk walls, gray, red/yel/blk tampo, 1978, NM+, W1 ....$4.50

Jeep CJ-7, blk walls, wht, blk interior, orange/red/blk bird tampo, wht windshield fr, 1982, M (EX card)............$15.00

Jeep Scrambler, blk walls, metal-flake bl, gray interior, yel/blk/wht '13/Jeep' tampo, 1987, M (NM card), W1 ....$9.00

Jet Sweep X5, Ultra Wheels, metallic yel, 1985, blister cracks, M (VG card), W1 ....$5.00

Jet Threat, red line tires, lt gr, '15' decals, 1971, NM $20.00

Jet Threat, red line tires, metallic lt gr, complete, lt toning, 1971, NM, W1...$34.00

Khaki Kooler, red line tires, olive, wht Army tampo, plastic base, 1976, M...$25.00

King Kuda, red line tires, metallic red, dk interior, complete, sm crack in rear deck, 1970, NM $25.00

Land Lord, blk walls, orange, 1982, M (NM card), W1 ......$7.00

Large Charge, red line tires, gr, blk/yel/orange tampo, 1975, NM+, W1 ....$31.00

Large Charge, Super Chrome, chrome, blk/yel/orange tampo, 1977, NM+, W1 ....$8.00

Lickety Six, blk walls, dk bl, red/wht '6' tampo, 1978, EX-, W1 ....$4.50

Light My Firebird, red line tires, metallic aqua, dk interior, toning, 1970, M (EX card) $50.00

Lola GT70, red line tires, metallic red, blk interior, M (NM-Grand Prix Series card) $35.00

Lotus Turbine, red line tires, metallic aqua, blk interior, orig decal, few cracks, M (EX+ Grand Prix Series card)...$25.00

Lowdown, red line tires, lt bl, blk interior, plum/yel/wht tampo, 1976, M, W1 ....$49.00

Maserati Mistral, red line tires, metallic orange, cream interior, 1969, NM+ $55.00

Maserati Mistral, red line tires, purple, wht interior, 1969, NM...$55.00

Maxi Taxi, red line tires, yel, 1976, NM+.........................$20.00

Mercedes C-111, blk walls, red, yel/wht/bl tampo, 1977, EX, W1 ....$4.50

Mercedes 280SL, red line tires, metallic purple, med interior, 1969, NM+ $20.00

Mercedes 380 SEL, Ultra Wheels, wht, wht metal base, 1989, M (NM+ card) $8.00

Mercedes 540K, blk walls, blk, tan interior/top, 1988, M (NM- card), W1 ....$5.00

Mirada Stocker, blk walls, yel, tan interior, blk/yel/wht '10' tampo, 1981, EX, W1 ....$4.50

Mod Squad, red line tires, gold, blk interior, nicely toned, 1970, M $25.00

Mongoose, red line tires, red, complete, stickers faded, 1970, NM, W1 ....$40.00

Mongoose II, red line tires, metallic bl, complete, sm dk spots, 1971, EX $70.00

Mongoose Rear Engine Dragster, red line tires, dk bl, clear front wheels, complete, 1972, NM+, W1 ....$200.00

Monster Vette, blk walls, yel, flame tampo, 8-spoke silver construction tires, 1987, M (NM card) $10.00

Monte Carlo Stocker, blk walls, yel, bl/red/wht '38' tampo, 1977, EX+, W1 ....$16.00

Moving Van, red line tires, metallic aqua, cream interior, wht trailer, complete, 1970, NM+, W1 ....$30.00

Mustang Stocker, blk walls, Speed Machine, blk, yel stripe tampo, 1983, M (NM card) $20.00

Mustang SVO, gold wheeels, blk, 1985, M (NM card), W1 ..$14.00

Mutt Mobile, red line tires, metallic aqua, blk interior, complete, 1971, NM+ $45.00

Neet Streeter, blk walls, lt bl, blk interior, red/wht/bl tampo, 1977, NM+, W1 ....$9.50

Nissan 300ZX, gold wheels, Park 'N Plates, wht, blk interior, 1989, M (EX card) $10.00

Nitty Gritty Kitty, red line tires, metallic red, cream interior, complete, toning, 1970, NM, W1 ....$35.00

Noodle Head, California Custom Miniatures, bl, 1971, MOC $100.00

Odd Job, red line tires, fluorescent lime, blk interior, complete, 1973, M, W1 ....$150.00

Odd Rod, blk walls, plum, flame tampo, rare color, 1977, M..$300.00

Old Number 5, blk walls, red, blk/yel tampo, 1982, M (NM card), W1 ....$6.00

Omni 024, blk walls, gray, orange/blk tampo, 1981, NM+, W1 ....$4.50

Oshkosh Snowplow, blk walls, orange plastic cab/construction tires, 1991, M, W1 ....$4.50

P-911, Super Chrome, red/orange/yel tampo, 1976, VG+, W1 ..$5.00

Paddy Wagon, blk walls, bl, gold letters, plastic base, 1977, NM+, W1 ....$4.50

Paddy Wagon, red line tires, bl, gold letters, 1970, M, W1 ...$14.00

Paramedic, blk walls, yel, red/wht tampo, metal base, 1977, NM, W1 ....$11.50

Paramedic, red line tires, yel, red/wht 'Paramedic Ambulance' tampo, gray windshield, 1977, NM+, W1 ....$30.00

Path Beater, blk walls, blk, yel/red/wht '10' tampo, 1989, M (EX International card), W1 ....$10.50

Pepsi Challenger, blk walls, yel, red/wht/bl Don Prudhomme tampo, 1982, VG, W1 ....$4.50

Peterbilt Cement Truck, blk walls, red, M (EX card), W1...$7.00

Peterbilt Dump Truck, blk walls, metal-flake bl, wht dumper, #15 in circle on card, M (EX card), W1 ....$5.00

Peterbilt Tank Truck, blk walls, red, Railroad, 1986, M (EX card), W1 ....$8.00

Peugeot 205 Rallye, blk walls, wht, gray interior, red/bl/yel/blk '2' tampo, 1989, NM+, W1 ....$5.00

Peugeot 405, blk walls, blk, no tampo, 1991, M (NM+ International card), W1 ....$6.00

Phantomachine, Ultra Hot Wheels, dk bl, 1987, M (NM card), W1 ....$8.00

Poison Pinto, red line tires, lt gr, yel/blk/wht tampo, 1976, NM+, W1 ....$40.00

Police Cruiser, Flying Colors, wht, opening hood, 1974, MOC, A $155.00

Poppa Vette, blk walls, wht, M (NM- card), W1.............$34.00

Porsche 917, red line tires, gray, cream interior, 1970, M (EX+ card w/several cracks) $35.00

Power Pad, red line tires, metallic pk, blk interior, missing top, 1970, VG+ $10.00

Power Plower, blk walls, blk, Midnight Removal, silver construction tires, 1990, M (EX+ card), W1 ....$8.00

Python, red line tires, gold, cream interior, smooth blk roof, 1968, NM+, W1 ....$20.00

Racer Rig, red line tires, wht, med interior, complete, 1971, NM, W1 ....$90.00

Ramblin' Wrecker, red line tires, wht, bl windshield, w/phone #, 1975, NM+, W1 ....$30.00

Ranger Rig, red line tires, gr, yel tampo, gray windshield, 1975, NM..$25.00

Rash 1, red line tires, gr, blk interior, yel/wht/red tampo, 1974, NM+, W1 ....$60.00

Photo courtesy Mike's General Store.

Red Baron, red line tires, metallic red, 1970, designed by Tom Daniels for Monogram, MBP, $40.00.

Renault 5 Turbo, blk walls, bl, yel/orange/wht tampo, 1991, M (NM International card) $5.00

Rescue Ranger, blk walls, red, blk/yel/wht tampo, 1988, M (NM card), W1 ....$7.00

Rig Wrecker, blk walls, wht, red/bl tampo, metal base, 1983, M (EX- card), W1 ....$9.00

Rock Buster, blk walls, yel, red/wht/bl '10' tampo, 1977, M (EX card) $25.00

Rock Buster, red line tires, yel, red/wht/bl '10' tampo, 1976, NM+, W1 ....$30.00

Rocket Bye Baby, red line tires, metallic aqua, cream interior, lt toning, 1971, NM+ $50.00

Rodger Dodger, blk walls, gold chrome, magenta/wht/red tampo, 1977, VG, W1 ....$4.50

Rodger Dodger, red line tires, plum, blk interior, orange/yel flame tampo, metal base, 1974, EX+ $25.00

Rolls Royce Silver Shadow, metallic red, cream interior, blk roof, 1969, NM+ $35.00

Sand Crab, red line tires, metallic pk, blk interior, 1 flower decal, 1970, NM+ $25.00

Sand Drifter, red line tires, yel, blk interior, orange/magenta flame tampo, 1975, M, W1 ....$44.00

Sand Witch, red line tires, yel, blk interior, prof rpt, 1973, NM $50.00

Scooper, red line tires, metallic yel (greenish color), blk interior, complete, 1971, NM $75.00

Scooper, red line tires, purple & yel, wht interior, 1971, EX ..$25.00

Shelby Turbine, red line tires, metallic gr, blk interior, orig decal, 1969, M $20.00

Sheriff Patrol, blk walls, blk, wht/yel tampo, 1982, M (EX+ card), W1 ....$5.00

Short Order, California Custom Miniatures, teal, 1971, MIP, A $135.00

Show Off, red line tires, yel, dk interior, 1973, EX+, W1 ..$100.00

Silhouette, red line tires, metallic lt gr, cream interior, 1968, NM+, W1 ....$14.00

Silver Bullet, Ultra Hot Wheels, metal-flake silver, M (NM card), W1 ....$6.00

Sir Rodney Roadster, red line tires, yel, red flame tampo, complete, 1974, NM+, W1 ....$54.00

Six Shooter, red line tires, ice bl, 1971, M $90.00

Snake, red line tires, yel, complete, 1970, NM+, W1 ....$70.00

Snake Rear Engine Dragster, red line tires, yel, clear front wheels, complete, 1972, NM+, W1 ....$200.00

Special Delivery, red line tires, metallic bl, wht interior, orig stickers, 1971, NM+, W1 ....$50.00

Speed Seeker, Ultra Hot Wheels, metallic red, 1984, M (EX card), W1 ....$8.00

Spider-Man, blk walls, blk, 1979, M (NM card), W1 ....$40.00

Spoiler Sport, blk walls, wht, bl/yel/magenta flame tampo, 1982, M (EX card), W1 ....$20.00

Staff Car, red line tires, olive, blk interior, wht tampo, rare, 1976, NM $450.00

Stagefright, blk walls, brn, yel/orange tampo, 1978, NM+, W1 ..$8.00

Steam Roller, red line tires, wht, red/bl '3' tampo w/3 stars, 1974, M, W1 ....$40.00

Sting Rod, blk walls, tan, blk 8-spoke construction tires, 1988, M (EX+ card), W1 ....$12.50

Street Beast, gold wheels, metal-flake silver, blk/yel/red tampo, 1988, M (EX+ card), W1 ....$5.00

Street Eater, red line tires, yel, red/orange flame tampo, 1975, M, W1 ....$70.00

Street Rodder, red line tires, blk, red/yel flame tampo, 1976, NM+, W1 ....$30.00

Street Snorter, red line tires, red, dk interior, 1973, NM+, W1 ....$200.00

Strip Teaser, red line tires, metallic aqua, orig blk interior/stickers, toning, 1971, NM $40.00

Sugar Caddy, red line tires, hot pk, 1971, VG $60.00

Sugar Daddy, red line tires, metallic lt gr, dk interior, orig stickers, plastic button, 1971, M (EX Spoilers card), W1 .$90.00

Super Van, blk walls, blk, red/yel flame tampo, 1977, NM, W1 ....$6.00

Photo courtesy June Moon.

Super Van, red line tires, plum, 1975, NM, J6, $75.00.

Suzuki Quad Racer, blk walls, yel, no tampo, yel construction tires, 1987, M (EX card), W1 ....$5.00

SWAT Van Scene Machine, blk walls, bl, orange/wht tampo, 1979, EX+, W1 ....$23.00

Swingin' Wing, red line tires, metallic lt gr, cream interior, orig wing, 1970, NM+, W1 ....$22.00

T-Bucket, blk walls, yel, red/bl flame tampo, 1989, M (NM+ card), W1 ....$5.00

T-Totaller, blk walls, blk, orange/wht/bl tampo, 1977, EX, W1 ..$4.50

T-4-2, red line tires, metallic red, med interior, complete, dk spots, 1971, NM $20.00

Team Bus, blk walls, Rapid Transit, yel, 1984, M (NM card), W1 ....$8.00

Team Trailer, red line tires, metallic red, blk interior, complete, 1971, NM $75.00

Thor Van, blk walls, yel, 1979, M (VG card, blister crack), W1 ....$15.00

Thrill Driver's Torino, blk walls, wht, bl/yel/red tampo, G+, W1 ....$15.00

Thunder Roller, blk walls, yel, 1983, M (NM card), W1 ....$6.00

Thunderstreak, blk walls, maroon, purple sides, wht/red/yel '8' tampo, 1988, M (NM card), W1 ....$8.00

TNT Bird, red line tires, aqua, wht interior, 1970, MIP ...$65.00

TNT Bird, red line tires, metallic aqua, cream interior, smooth blk roof, complete, 1970, NM+ $35.00

Top Eliminator, blk walls, gold chrome, red/bl/magenta 'Ancel' tampo, 1977, NM, W1 ....$26.00

Top Eliminator, red line tires, dk bl, orange/gr/yel tampo, 1974, NM, W1 ....$50.00

Torero, red line tires, metallic yel, cream interior, toning, 1969, NM, W1 ....$10.50

Torino Stocker, red line tires, red, yel/bl/wht '23' tampo, NM-, W1 ....$34.00

Tough Customer, red line tires, olive, wht Army tampo, complete, 1975, M $20.00

Tow Truck, red line tires, metallic yel, blk interior, complete, 1970, M, W1 ....$30.00

Toyota MR2 Rally, Ultra Hot Wheels, wht, red/yel/orange tampo, 1991, NM+, W1 ....$6.00

Tri-Baby, California Custom Miniatures, hot pk, 1970, EX, A..$85.00

Tri-Baby, red line tires, metallic red, cream interior, 1970, M ...$40.00

Turbo Mustang, gold wheels, red, 1982, M (NM- card), W1 ....$8.00

Turbofire, red line tires, metallic purple, cream interior, 1969, M, W1 ....$20.00

Twinmill, red line tires, metallic aqua, cream interior, 1969, NM+, W1 ....$14.00

Upfront 924, blk walls, yel, red/orange/blk tampo, 1979, NM+, W1 ....$5.00

Vega Bomb, red line tires, orange, red/yel/bl tampo, complete, 1975, NM, W1 ....$60.00

Vette Van, blk walls, red, yel/wht/bl tampo, 1982, NM, W1 ..$7.00

Vetty Funny, blk walls, wht, red/yel/purple tampo, 1983, VG+, W1 ....$6.00

VW, red line tires, orange, blk interior, bug tampo, 1974, NM.$20.00

VW Bug, blk walls, turq, pk/lt gr/bl tampo, 1991, NM $10.00

Whip Creamer, red line tires, metallic pk, blk interior, complete, NM $20.00

RUMBLERS

Bold Eagle, yel, missing driver/front tire (wheel ok), damaged right wing, 1972, EX, W1 ....$35.00

Choppin' Chariot, yel, orig driver, 1972, NM, W1 ....$32.00

Mean Machine, orange, 1971, missing driver, NM, W1 ...$20.00

Revolution, yel, orig driver/top, 1972, NM, W1 ....$44.00

Rip Code, bl, orig driver/top, 1973, NM+, W1................$134.00

Rip Snorter, red, orig driver, 1971, NM, W1 ....$24.00

Road Hog, orange, orig driver, 1971, NM, W1 ....$15.00

Roamin' Cradle, bronze, orig driver, 1972, NM, W1 ....$32.00

Torque Chop, orange, orig driver/arrowhead, 1971, EX+, W1 ....$14.00

3 Squealer, orange, orig driver, 1971, NM, W1 ....$24.00

SIZZLERS

Angeleno M-70, metallic pk, chip off wing, NMIB, W1 ..$30.00

Anteater, metallic bl, EX+, W1 ....$22.00

Backfire, metallic rose, loose chassis, EX+, W1 ....$24.00

Co-Motion, metallic gr, chrome rpt silver, NM+, W1 .....$40.00

Corvette 4 Rotor, yel, orig headlight bulbs, scarce, NM...$75.00

Dark Shadow, yel, orig headlight bulbs, loose chassis, scarce, NM, W1 ....$70.00

Double Boiler, metallic yel, chrome rpt silver, scarce, EX+, W1 ....$44.00

Ferrari 512S, red, orig top, German cross decal, NM, W1 .$30.00

Flat Out, metallic red, orig wing, scarce, NM+, W1 ....$44.00

Ford Mark IV, metallic gr, clear tape on car, NMIB.........$40.00

Hot Head, metallic gr, chrome rpt silver, NM+, W1........$36.00

Indy Eagle, metallic bl, orig stickers, EX+, W1 ....$22.00

Long Count, bl, orig headlight bulbs/wing, unlisted color, scarce, NM+, W1 ....$90.00

Firebird Trans-Am, white, MIB, from $80.00 to $120.00; Ford Mark IV, metallic red, MIB, from $55.00 to $75.00.

March F-1, metallic brn, orig wing, clear tape on car, EX (orig box), W1 ....$30.00

Moon Ghost, wht, missing headlight bulbs, scarce, EX $45.00

Mustang Boss 302, metallic orange, orig wing, EX (orig box), W1 ....$50.00

Revvin' Heaven, metallic orange, NMIB, W1 ....$40.00

Short Fuse, lt gr, orig headlight bulbs, scarce, NM, W1 ...$70.00

Side Burn, blk, chrome mostly gone, EX+, W1 ....$22.00

Straight Scoop, metallic pk, front grille chipped, NMIB, W1...$40.00

Trans-Am Camaro, prof rechromed, no stickers, scarce, NM+, W1 ....$60.00

Trans-Am Cuda, metallic bl, loose chassis, sticker residue, EX.$25.00

Trans-Am Cuda, red line tires, hot pk, 1971, EX $75.00

Trans-Am Firebird, metallic brn, NM+ $40.00

Up Roar, metallic yel, orig top, chrome rpt silver, NM, W1 ....$26.00

Vantom, prof rechromed, scarce, NM+, W1 ....$50.00

ACCESSORIES

Belt Buckle, 15th Anniversary, 3-pack, '67 Camaro, P-928, Long Shot, MBP $75.00

Burger Stand Stop & Go Set #9512, w/Minitruck, MIB, W1..$10.00

Case, Collector's, Snake & Mongoose, 1970, 72-car, NM, A..$35.00

Case, Collector's Race, 24-car, 1970, EX, W1 ....$18.50

Case, Collector's Race, 48-car, 1970, VG+, W1................$20.00

Case, Show Case, Mattel, 1966 (pre-Hot Wheels), EX, W1 ...$9.00

Case, Super Rally, 24-car, plastic wheel insert, EX, W1 ...$10.00

Club Kit, MIB, $200.00; Automatic Lap Counter, MIB, $45.00.

Flip Out Drag Flip, red, M (NM card), W1 ....$8.00

Hot Wheels Showcase Carry Case, brn, plastic, orig stickers, wall hanging type, EX+, W1 ....$9.00

Micro Park 'N Plates Firebird, metal-flake red, yel license plate, M (EX+ card), W1 ....$7.00

Photo courtesy Mike's General Store.

Hot Line Great Freight Set, MIB, $150.00; Sizzlers Laguna Oval Set, MIB, $160.00; Chopcycles Hairy Hurdle Set, M5, MIB, $210.00.

Mongoose vs Snake Drag Race Set, complete, decals on sheet, M (EX box), W1 ....$450.00
Pop-Up Service Station, 1967, self-contained plastic w/pop-up service station, NM, A $35.00
Revvers Bug Bomb, red, VG, W1 ....$12.00
Revvers Draggin' Dagger, yel, VG $20.00
Revvers Haulin' Horses, dk bl, EX+ $35.00
Revvers Stingin' Thing, yel, EX+, W1 ....$24.00
Service Station w/Foldaway Garage, 1979, MIB, J5..........$25.00
Sizzlers Fat Track California 500 Layout, 1969, molded plastic, complete, 10-ft track, NMIB, A $45.00
Sizzlers Juice Machine, 1969, gas pump-shaped charging unit w/detachable hose & nozzle, M (EX box), A $40.00
Sizzlers Pacific/8 Race Set, 1969, figure-8 track w/dual-lane lap counter, complete, NM (EX box), A $100.00
Sizzlers U-Turn Pak, 1970, 2 plastic loop-designed tracks for non-stop & circle-back action, 16", M (VG box), A...$25.00
Sky Show Set, Sky Show Fleetside w/decals, 6 planes, all plastic pcs, missing collector's catalogue, NM (EX box), W1 .$650.00
Speedometer, 1969, plastic building design w/front & rear exits, MIB, A $20.00
Strip Action Set, 1969, MIB (sealed), A $90.00
Tune-Up Tower, 1970, complete, MIB (sealed contents) ..$250.00
Ultra Hots Stomper, 3-pack, Sol-Aire, Speed Seeker, Flame Runner, M (EX card)...$45.00

Housewares

Back in the dark ages before women's lib and career-minded mothers, little girls emulated mommy's lifestyle, not realizing that by the time they grew up, total evolution would have taken place before their very eyes. They'd sew and bake, sweep, do laundry and iron (gasp!), and imagine what fun it would be when *they* were big like mommy. Those little gadgets they played with are precious collectibles today, and any child-size houseware item is treasured, especially those from the '40s and '50s. Values are suggested for items in excellent condition unless noted otherwise. If you're interested in learning about toy sewing machines, we recommend *Toy and Miniature Sewing Machines* by Glenda Thomas (Collector Books).

Advisor: Lorraine Punchard (P13) author of *Playtime Kitchen Items and Table Accessories.*

CLEANING AND LAUNDRY

Boiler, 1910s, tin, w/lid, 6", NM, G16 ....$135.00
Broom, Arcade, salesman's sample, red-pnt CI w/straw bristles, M, A..$135.00
Cleaning Set, Little Homemaker, 1950s, litho metal, 4 pcs, MIP, H12 ....$45.00

Photo courtesy June Moon.

Clothes Presser, 1930s, yellow and green tin with wooden roller, windup and electric, EX, J6, $85.00.

Ironing Set, Wolverine, 1940s, complete, MIB, H12 ....$35.00
Kitchenette Set, Johnny & Mary, 1950s, complete, MIB, H12 ....$55.00
Washing Machine, Maytag, Ertl, 1993, mk 100 Year Anniversary, M...$50.00
Washing Machine, Maytag, Hubley, late 1920s, 8,000 made in red or bl, 7½", VG..$750.00
Washing Machine, Wolverine, glass & tin, 9¾", EX $55.00
Washing Machine Set, Sunny Suzy, 6-pc w/washtub & board, wash rack & clothespins, tin & wood, G-EX, A........$95.00

COOKING

Baking Set, Mother's Little Helper, complete, MIB, H12..$145.00
Boiler, late 1800s, tin, 5½" L, M, G16 ....$135.00
Canister Set, Wolverine, tin, MIB, G16 ....$130.00
Cooking Set, Mirro, 1940s, aluminum, 16 pcs, MIB, H12 ..$150.00
Cooking Utensils, Wagner Mfg, CI frying pan, teakettle w/lid & pot w/bail hdl, EXIB...$300.00

Stove, Favorite Stove & Range Co, Dolly's Favorite, CI
w/NP door, heavily scrolled & emb, 4-ftd, 14x11x18½",
VG, A $400.00

**Stove, Graniteware, cream and green, 8½x9½x5¾",
EX, $65.00.**

Stove, Home, CI, emb & scrolled, 4-ftd, 10x11", EX, A ..$135.00
Stove, Hoosier, 15x15", VG, P3..$75.00

**Stove, Ideal, cast-iron flat-top with stovepipe and 6 burn-
ers, Baby lettered on oven door, 8x16", EX, A, $525.00.**

Stove, Kenton, Eagle, CI, heavily scrolled, 4-ftd, 11½x10", G,
A...$120.00
Stove, Kenton, Eva, CI, heavily scrolled & emb, 4-ftd,
11½x10½", VG, A..$475.00
Stove, Kenton, Favorite, pnt CI, bl w/NP trim, 9½x7½", EX,
A $965.00

**Stove, Marklin, tin with brass doors and claw feet,
ornate smoke pipe, 11½x9½", EX, A, $800.00.**

Stove, NP CI & tin w/XX on oven door, 4-ftd, 3 removable
stove lids, w/1 pan, 4⅜x3¼", EX, A $475.00
Stove, Ore Painter & Co/USA, Dainty, CI, 4-ftd, w/2 pots &
coal bucket, 18½x12", EX, A $580.00
Stove, Qualified Range Co, aluminum & tin w/latch front door
& temperature dial, 4-ftd, 21½x13", EX, A.............$880.00
Stove, Royal, NP CI w/heavy scrollwork, 2 removable side pan-
els, 7 stove lids, 4-ftd, 12x11", EX, A......................$165.00
Stove, Royal, ornate NP CI, w/removable side rack, ftd, 10½",
G, A $275.00
Stove, Superior Gas Range, CI, heavily scrolled front doors, low-
ftd, 8½x6", missing side panels, A..............................$25.00
Stove, Wolverine, electric style w/2 working doors, 15x15",
EX+, P3...$65.00

Toaster, EX, $40.00.

Utensil Set, rolling pin, slotted spoon, spatula, masher, wire soap
holder, etc, wht-pnt wood hdls, 9 pcs, VG................$60.00

Waffle Iron, Little Deb, suction-cup plug, 6" dia, VG, $65.00.

NURSERY

Carriage, att Joel Ellis, red-pnt wood horizontal seat w/striping & decor, orig upholstery, spoked wheels, 47", EX....**$325.00**

Carriage, ca 1870, blk & red-pnt wood, cloth convertible top w/fringe, spoke wheels, 35", G..................................**$225.00**

Carriage, horse-drawn; hide-covered horse pulling wooden 2-wheeled seat, bl w/yel trim, 21", VG, A...................**$550.00**

Carriage, Joel Ellis type, aqua-pnt wood w/fringed canopy, leather cushioned seat, wooden spoke wheels, 38", EX **$385.00**

Carriage, wicker automobile with black cloth top, 2 headlights, running boards over spoked wheels, 36", EX, A, $855.00.

Carriage, Kelly Bros, wicker w/side compartments & cloth parasol, metal spoke wheels, upholstered interior, rstr, VG, A **$700.00**

Carriage, orange-pnt wood w/railed sides, collapsible fringed top, wooden spoke wheels, orig pnt, 22", EX **$275.00**

Carriage, 1880s, pnt wood w/iron canopy fr, orig bl cloth canopy, pnt-wood spoke wheels, 34", EX................**$260.00**

Cradle, American, gr-pnt tin w/floral design, hooded w/cut-out spindle sides, curved bottom, 8¼", EX, A...............**$385.00**

Cradle, France, blk scrolled wrought iron w/wht lace covering & head drape, 27x19", VG **$200.00**

Stroller, Loeminster, 1920s, blk-pnt wicker, 26", rpt, A ..**$115.00**

SEWING

Cutting Machine, Singer, wht plastic w/suction-cup ft, 5x6½", EX, from $35 to..**$50.00**

Sewing Basket, sq wicker basket w/lid on 4 tall legs w/bottom shelf, 17x9", EX..**$55.00**

Sewing Machine, Betsy Ross, metal, NM, H12.................**$75.00**

Sewing Machine, Casige, mk Made in Germany, metal w/yel flowers & gr leaves, 7½x8", from $75 to **$95.00**

Sewing Machine, Casige, mk Made in Germany, sheet metal w/gold & red geometric designs, missing base, 5x5", from $100 to..**$135.00**

Sewing Machine, Foley & Williams, CI, working, EX (orig wood box), from $200 to...**$300.00**

Sewing Machine, Hoge, 1920s-30s, sheet metal w/enclosed mechanism, metal eye on bottom for table clamp, 6½x8¼", EX..**$55.00**

Photo courtesy June Moon.

Sewing Machine, Kay and EE Sew Master, US Zone Germany, red, NM, J6, $85.00.

Sewing Machine, Little Princess, Frankonia/Hong Kong, plastic, manual-op, 5x8", EX, from $25 to **$50.00**

Sewing Machine, Olympia, Japan, bl metal, manual or battery-op w/ft pedal, 5½x7", EX, from $25 to **$35.00**

Sewing Machine, Playskool, 1989, uses markers to to make designs on paper & fabric, 9¼x11¼", EX $25.00

Sewing Machine, Romance, Japan, red metal mtd on wood base, plastic hand wheel, manual or battery-op, 6x7", from $45 to..$65.00

Sewing Machine, Sears Kenmore, 1930s-40s, red-pnt metal on wood base, chain-driven mechanism, 6½x9", EX....$100.00

Sewing Machine, Sew-Ette, mk Made in Japan, 2-tone bl crinkle-finished metal, battery-op, 6½x8", EX, from $35 to.....$50.00

Sewing Machine, Sew-Mate, CK w/diamond & Japan mk on bottom, red-pnt metal, battery-op, 5x6", EX, from $35 to..$50.00

Sewing Machine, Singer Lockstitch, Model No T 6406, 1987-90, plastic & metal w/red metal carrying case, EX, from $30 to..$50.00

Sewing Machine, Singer No 20, 1922, metal w/oval base, blk spiral hand wheel w/NP rim, 6x7", EX, from $125 to ...$150.00

Sewing Machine, Singer Sewhandy No 20, 1940s, pressed steel & CI, MIB, from $75 to $100.00

Sewing Machine, Unitoys Ltd/Hong Kong, orange & wht plastic mk Universal, manual-op, 5½x7½", EX, from $20 to..$30.00

TABLE SERVICE

Decanter Set, brass, service for 6, MIB, H12......................$40.00

Dinner & Tea Set, 1920s, wht porcelain trimmed w/lustre & floral ribbon design, service for 6, MIB, H12 ....$300.00

Lemonade Set, Mirro, 1930s, service for 6, MIB, H12....$125.00

Percolator Set, Tootsietoy, 1920s, complete w/samovar, sugar bowl & creamer on tray, MIB, H12 ....$185.00

Platter, Blue Willow, oval, 6", M, H12 ....$45.00

Silverware Set, Banner Metaltone Tableware, service for 4, MIB, H12 ....$55.00

Tea Set, Blue Willow, service for 6, MIB, H12...............$275.00

Tea Set, early 1900s, gold leaves on wht porcelain w/jet blk hdls, service for 6, MIB, H12 ....$325.00

Tea Set, German, cranberry w/hand-pnt flowers, gold trim, 12 pcs, M, H12..$70.00

Tea Set, Ideal, 1950s, tin & plastic, service for 4, rare, MIB, H12 ....$165.00

Tea Set, Japan, 1940s, red, bl & yel flowers w/leaf design & silver trim, service for 4, MIB, H12 ....$95.00

Tea Set, Morimura Bros, 1917, Moss Rose pattern w/blk, gr & gold trim, service for 6, MIB, H12 ....$225.00

Tea Set, Noritake, hand-pnt yel & blk Art Deco design w/gold trim, service for 4, MIB, from $350 to......................$450.00

Tea Set, 1880s, persimmon & coral flowers w/gold trim, service for 6, MIB, H12 ....$425.00

Tea Set, 1920s, golden lustreware w/pk roses & gr leaves, service for 3, MIB, H12 ....$125.00

Tea Set, 1930s, autumn flowers on lt gr, service for 5, MIB, H12 ....$165.00

Tea Set, 1930s, hand-pnt gladiolas w/lt bl trim, service for 3, MIB, H12..$175.00

Teapot, Blue Willow, 3", M, H12..$45.00

Tureen, Blue Willow, M, H12 ....$65.00

Vegetable Server, Blue Willow, 6", H12 ....$55.00

MISCELLANEOUS

Cruet Set, late 1800s, Victorian style w/pewter holder & filigree top, orig glass bottles, 6½", M, G16 ....$275.00

Crumb Set, aluminum, Little Miss Muffet... emb on crumb catcher, Little Jack Horner... on scraper, 1920s, NM, G16 ....$100.00

Dresser Set, 1930s, celluloid mirror, brush, comb & hair receiver, doll sz, MIB, H12 ....$200.00

Kitchen Scale, mk Germany, early 1900s, litho tin, 3½", EX, G16 ....$125.00

Lawn Mower, Arcade, push-type w/wooden hdl, CI cutter, 22", VG $55.00

Picnic Set, Strombecker, early, ¾" scale, complete, MIB, H12.$125.00

Salt Box, wood & metal w/blk stenciled letters, 1920, 4½", M, G16 ....$85.00

Jack-in-the Boxes

Very early jack-in-the-box toys were often made of papier-mache and cloth, fragile material to withstand the everyday wear and tear to which they were subjected, so these vintage German examples are scarce today and very expensive. But even those from the '50s and '60s are collectible, especially when they represent well-known TV or storybook characters. Examples with lithographed space themes are popular as well.

See also Character, TV, and Movie Collectibles; Disney.

Boy, ca 1910, compo head of boy in box with images of children and St. Bernard, 8", EX, A, $325.00.

Chimney Sweep, wood & wire figure w/blk paper clothes & papier-mache head, brick paper-covered wood box, 6", VG+, A..$300.00

Leprechaun, German, papier-mache & cloth figure, paper-covered box, 3½" sq, G, A $115.00

Man in Red Top Hat, German, papier-mache head w/gray furry hair, paper-covered wood box, enclosed squeaker, 5" sq, EX, A $440.00

Policeman, German, papier-mache head w/bl hat, brn mustache, paper-covered box, w/squeaker, 4" sq, VG, A..........$245.00

Santa Claus, ca 1910, Santa in cloth suit & fur beard in chimney box, 9½", EX, A...$350.00

Keystone

Though this Massachusetts company produced a variety of toys during their years of operation (ca 1920-late '50s), their pressed-steel vehicles are the most collectible, and that's what we've listed here. As a rule they were very large, with some of the riders being 30" in length.

Aerial Ladder Truck, w/side ladders & extension ladder, 31", rstr, A...$700.00

Aerial Ladder Truck, 12", G, A.............................$550.00

Aerial Ladder Truck #1, w/up, spring-loaded ladder, 18", broken lever o/w VG, A $200.00

Aerial Ladder Truck #2, w/climbing fireman figure, 16", VG, A...$200.00

Aerial Ladder Truck #79, crank-op siren w/battery-op headlights & searchlight, 30", G, A $315.00

Airmail Single-Engine Plane #NX-265, 23", VG, A......$550.00

Ambulance, 1929, khaki w/canvas sides & curtains, 28", rstr, A..$575.00

American Railway Express Truck, Packard, black and green with enclosed screen bed, red hubs, 26½", EX, from $1,000.00 to $1,400.00.

Bluebird Racer, w/up, 19", rpt, G, A $400.00

Cargo Truck, open cab, tall canvas cover over bed, 26½", poor rpt, new cover, A $150.00

Circus Truck, w/animals in 3 removable cages, 26½", repro cages, G, A $2,750.00

Coast-To-Coast Bus, lt bl w/gray roof, 32", rstr, A $1,400.00

Dugan Bros Bakery Truck, ride-on, doorless cab, enclosed bed w/rear doors, 26", VG, A............................$3,300.00

Dump Truck, 1920s, w/crank, 26", rpt, A $250.00

Dump Truck, 1920s, w/hydraulic lift, 28", VG, A.......$1,250.00

Dump Truck, 1938, gr cab w/red dump, 25", G, A $300.00

Fire Chemical Pump Engine, w/tank, ladders, siren & bell, 28", G, A...$875.00

Fire Tower Truck, ca late 1920s, 32", G+, A..............$1,150.00

Fire Department Combination Truck #49 with Ladders and Bell, T-type steering wheel, 28", G, A, $325.00.

Fire Truck, combination hose reel w/2 side ladders, 28", G, hose missing, pnt wear, A $350.00

Fire Truck, 1930s, red w/NP grille & bell, battery-op headlights, orig hose, 30", G+, A $750.00

Inter-City Bus, bl w/red wheels, 24", G, A....................$200.00

Koaster Truck, blk open bed w/red flat bed for riding, 26", front-end rpt, G, A $450.00

Locomotive, 1930s, battery-op headlights, 28", VG, A..$225.00

Moving Van, blk cab w/red body & chassis, 26", G, A...$900.00

Packard Flatbed Truck, w/winch, 26", rstr, A $500.00

Police Patrol Truck, w/caged bed, 27", G, A.................$700.00

Pullman Car, 1930s, 25", EX, A $700.00

Railroad Wrecking Car #6000, 1929, 20¾", G-, A $115.00

Steam Roller #60, 1931, blk & red w/corrugated roof, brass bell, spoke wheels, 20", EX, A...........................$750.00

Steam Shovel, open sides w/corrugated roof, G, A.........$250.00

Tank Department Truck, 24", rstr, A............................$800.00

US Army Truck, open cab w/canvas cover, 26", rstr, A .$450.00

US Mail Truck, 1923, battery-op headlights, 27", rstr, A ..$650.00

Wrecker, 27", rstr, A...$700.00

Lehmann

Lehmann toys were made in Germany as early as 1881. Early on they were sometimes animated by means of an inertia-generated flywheel; later, clockwork mechanisms were used. Some of their best-known turn-of-the-century toys were actually very racist and unflattering to certain ethnic groups. But the wonderful antics they perform and the imagination that went into their conception have made them and all the other Lehmann toys favorites with collectors today. Though the company faltered with the onset of WWI, they were quick to recover and during the war years produced some of their best toys, several of which were copied by their competitors. Business declined after WWI. Lehmann died in 1934, but the company continued for awhile under the direction of Lehmann's partner and cousin, Johannes Richter.

Advisor: Scott Smiles (S10).

Adam the Porter, man pushing trunk on hand cart, litho tin, 8", EX+, A $1,500.00

AHA Delivery Van, 8", NMIB, A $1,000.00
Airplane Model #817 Construction Kit, single prop, MIB..$400.00
Airplane Model #833 Construction Kit, 2-prop, EX, A .$500.00
Ajax, acrobat, litho tin figure w/cloth costume, 9½", EX, A ...$1,600.00
Ajax, acrobat, litho tin figure w/cloth costume, 9½", G, A $850.00

Alabama Coon Jigger, 1910, lithographed tin, rare version with yellow and black checked pants, NM, D10, $650.00.

Photo courtesy Dunbar Gallery.

ALSO Automobile, yel & red open auto w/driver, 4", NM, A.$600.00
AM POL, Hensley w/globe umbrella over explorer Robt E Peary in 3-wheeled vehicle, 5¾", EX, A $1,700.00
Autin Delivery Cart, 1914-35, Am boy & pedal car, 4", VG, A $325.00
Auto Post, driver in red mail van, litho tin, 5", VG, A ..$1,100.00
Autobus, red & wht dbl-decker bus w/driver, litho tin, 7", VG (EX box), A...$2,300.00
Autobus, yel & wht dbl-decker bus w/driver, litho tin, 7", EX, A $1,650.00

Beetle, Pat April 23, 1895, 4", EX, $250.00.

Photo courtesy Dunbar Gallery.

Autohutte, gr sedan parked in wht garage w/lithoed scenes & red roof, 6", NM...$650.00
Autohutte (Two Car), Sedan EPL #760 & the Gallop parked in wht dbl-car garage w/red roof, 6¼", MIB, A.........$3,300.00
Baker & Chimney Sweep, 1900-35, baker on front of 3-wheeled car w/chimney sweep on back, 5½", EX+ $4,500.00
Baldur Limousine, 1920-35, yel w/blk top, open cab, litho tin, 10", EX..$2,000.00
Balky Mule, 1910, clown bounces as cart advances w/crazy action, litho tin, 8", EX $475.00
Berolina Convertible, w/driver, litho tin, 7¼", NM, A ..$2,800.00
Buster Brown, seated in open auto, litho & pnt tin, 4", NM, A $1,850.00
Captain of Kopenivk, soldier figure in long brn cloth coat, EX $1,500.00
Cat & Mouse, blk & wht cat chases mouse, tin, NM..$1,400.00
Climbing Monkey, 1903, plain vest, hand-pnt face, 7½", MIB, A $275.00
Climbing Monkey, 1903, polka-dot vest, litho face, 7½", M, A .$200.00
Crocodile, advances w/jaw movement, litho tin, 9½", NM...$400.00
Dancing Sailor, litho tin figure in cloth outfit, cap reads SMS Bradenburg, 7", MIB $1,250.00
Deutsche Reichpost (Mail Truck), w/swastika emblems on sides, 7", MIB, A $6,100.00
DUO Rooster & Rabbit, rabbit atop 2-wheeled cart pulled by rooster, litho tin, 6½", NM, A............................$1,100.00
EPL-1 Dirigible, yel litho tin w/celluloid props, 2 observation decks, 7½", EX...$400.00
EPL-11 Zeppelin, gold tin w/celluloid props, 9½", EX, A...$1,000.00
Express, porter pulling trunk on 2-wheeled cart, litho & pnt tin, 6", NM, A $650.00
Galop Racer #1, w/driver, yel w/bl stripe, 5½", NM, A..$550.00
Gnome Series Racer #808, red w/#1 on wht door, EX, A .$175.00
Gnome Series Shell Truck, red & yel, NM, A.................$350.00
Gnome Top, rnd globe that whistles when spun, 2x3", VG..$75.00
Going to the Fair, man pushing lady in promenade chair, pnt & litho tin, 5", NM, A $5,000.00
Gustav the Miller, pull string & figure climbs pole to mill, litho tin, 18", EX $250.00
Halloh Rider on Cycle, flywheel mechanism, 8", EX, A..$2,100.00
IHI Meat Delivery Van, driver in open van w/cloth curtains, 6½", EX, A $2,300.00
Irakus Airplane, litho tin body & tail wings, wire-supported paper wings, pilot in open seat, 10½", NM, A $6,200.00
Kadi, 2 Chinese men carrying tea chest, litho tin, 7" L, EX..$1,250.00
Lehmann Family (Walking Down Broadway), couple w/dog on leash, litho tin, 6½", EX, A $5,700.00
Lila Hansom Cab, w/driver, 2 lady passengers & dog, pnt & litho tin, 5½", EX+ $2,500.00
Lo & Li, seated clown plays accordion for jigger on platform, scarce, EX, A $6,000.00
Lolo Automobile, w/driver, wht & gr litho tin, 4", EX...$700.00
Luxus Sedan, driver in red & wht auto w/running boards, battery-op lights, 12½", NM, A...............................$5,100.00
Magic Ball Dancer, ballerina w/arms extended on gyroscope stabilizer, pnt & litho tin, 6", EX, A $3,300.00
Mandarin, Chinese man in sedan chair carried by 2 other Chinese men, pnt & litho tin, 7', EX+, A $2,750.00

Mars Tank, gray litho & pnt tin w/rubber treads, 5⅝", EX, A $400.00

Mikado Family, man pulling female passenger in rickshaw, hand-pnt & litho tin, 7", NMIB, A..............................$4,400.00

Military Combat Plane Assembly Kit, camouflage w/iron cross markings, 5¾" W, MIB $600.00

Miss Blondin, lady tightrope walker, litho tin, 10½", NMIB, A $6,200.00

Motor Kutsche Car #420, 5", EX (worn box), A $750.00

NA-OB, donkey cart w/driver, litho tin, 6½", EX..........$400.00

Naughty Boy, 1903, wht & bl auto w/driver & boy facing each other at center wheel, 5", NMIB, A $2,000.00

New Century Cycle, man holding umbrella over driver of 3-wheeled vehicle, litho tin, 5", NMIB $1,500.00

Nu-Nu, Chinese man pulling tea chest, pnt & litho tin, 5", VG, A...$800.00

OHO, 1903, open auto w/driver, litho tin, 3¾", NM.....$750.00

Paak-Paak (Quack-Quack) Duck Cart, mother duck pulling 3 ducklings in 2-wheeled cart, litho tin, 7", EX..........$600.00

Paddy the Pig, man on pig, litho tin, 5", NMIB, A $3,000.00

Playing Mice, 2 mice revolve on spiral rod when turned upside down, hand-pnt & litho tin, EX, A $125.00

Primus Roller Skater, boy on skates, litho tin, 8½", rare, NM, A $9,900.00

Shenandoah Dirigible, litho tin w/celluloid props, 7½", EXIB, A...$1,700.00

Skirolf, man in gray brimless hat & bl suit on skis, pnt & litho tin, 7", EX+, A $3,300.00

Snik-Snak, man walking 2 dogs, litho tin, 8", EX $7,500.00

Susi the Turtle, 4", MIB, A $250.00

Swing Doll, china doll in cloth dress seated in tin swing, 7¼", EX+, A $2,300.00

Taku Torpedo Boat, litho tin floor toy, EX, A $350.00

Tap-Tap Man w/Wheelbarrow, litho tin, 6½", MIB, A .$1,600.00

Terra Towing Co. Vehicle, EPL-720, missing cloth flag and post otherwise EX, A, $875.00.

Titiania Sedan, driver in red & bl auto w/electric headlights, litho tin, 10", VG, A..............................$2,500.00

Toy Balloon Luna, hot-air balloon w/rider holding flag in gondola, litho tin, 5¼", NMIB, A $8,800.00

Tut-Tut, driver in open auto, litho & pnt tin, 6½", EX...$1,200.00

Tut-Tut, driver in open auto, litho & pnt tin, 6½", NMIB, A...$1,700.00

UHU Amphibious Car, w/driver, litho & pnt tin, 9", VG, A...$1,150.00

Velleda Touring Car, driver in orange open touring car w/folding seats, litho tin, 10", EX, A $4,300.00

Vineta, monorail car w/gyroscope stabilizer, litho tin, 9½", NM, A...$1,450.00

Waltzing Doll, mk EPL, celluloid head w/pnt-tin body & hands, floral cloth dress, wheeled platform, 8½", EX+, A ...$1,100.00

Wild-West Bucking Bronco, 7", EX............................$1,000.00

Wild-West Bucking Bronco, lithographed tin, 7", NMIB, $1,500.00.

Zebra Cart, advances as cowboy bounces up & down in seat, 7½", M (EX box), A.................................$350.00

Photo courtesy Dunbar Gallery.

Zig-Zag, lithographed tin, NM, $2,200.00.

Zirka-Dare Devil, driver on zebra cart, litho tin, 7¼", NMIB, A...$1,100.00

Zulu Ostrich Mail, driver on ostrich-driven 2-wheeled cart, yel litho tin w/red trim, 6½", VG, A $600.00

Lunch Boxes

When the lunch box craze began in the mid-1980s, it was only the metal boxes that so quickly soared to sometimes astronomical prices. But today, even the plastic and vinyl ones are collectible. Though most lunch box dealers agree that with few exceptions, prices have become much more reasonable than they were at first, they're still holding their own and values seem to be stabilizing. So pick a genre and have fun. There are literally hundreds to choose from, and just as is true in other areas of character-related collectibles, the more desirable lunch boxes are those with easily recognized, well-known subjects — western heroes, TV, Disney and other cartoon characters, and famous entertainers. Thermoses are collectible as well. In our listings, values are just for the box unless a thermos is mentioned in the description. If you'd like to learn more about them, we recommend *A Pictorial Price Guide to Metal Lunch Boxes and Thermoses* and a companion book *A Pictorial Price Guide to Vinyl and Plastic Lunch Boxes* by Larry Aikins. For more pricing information, Philip R. Norman (Norman's Olde Store) has prepared a listing of hundreds of boxes, thermoses, and their variations. He is listed in the Categories of Special Interest under Lunch Boxes.

Advisor: Terri Ivers (I2).

Other Sources: C1, C10, G7, J6, J7, M15, T1, T2

METAL

A-Team, 1983, EX, N2	$25.00
Adam-12, 1972, G+, N2	$28.00
Addams Family, 1974, w/thermos, EX	$100.00
America on Parade, 1976, VG, N2	$15.00
Animal Friends (blk letters), 1975, VG+, N2	$28.00
Animal Friends (yel letters), 1975, VG+, N2	$25.00
Annie, 1981, VG+, N2	$15.00
Annie, 1981, w/thermos, M, N2	$45.00
Apple's Way, 1975, VG, N2	$65.00
Archies, 1969, VG+, N2	$65.00
Atom Ant, Thermos, 1966, w/thermos, EX	$170.00
Auto Race, 1967, VG+, N2	$55.00
Back in 1976, VG+	$30.00
Barbie Campus Queen, 1967, EX, N2	$30.00
Batman & Robin, 1966, VG+, N2	$100.00
Battle Kit, 1965, VG, N2	$50.00
Battle of the Planets, 1979, VG+, N2	$40.00
Battlestar Galactica, 1978, w/thermos, EX, N2	$65.00
Beatles, Aladdin, head shots on bl, VG+, B3	$285.00
Beatles, Thermos, yel & pk, edge wear & scratches, G+, B3	$180.00
Bee Gees, 1978, Maurice, w/thermos, EX, N2	$40.00
Berenstain Bears, 1983, VG+, N2	$22.00
Betsy Clark, 1975, beige, VG, N2	$10.00
Black Hole, 1979, EX+, I2	$70.00
Bonanza, 1965, brn, EX+, I2	$145.00
Bond XX Secret Agent, 1966, VG+, N2	$150.00
Brady Bunch, 1970, EX, I2	$200.00
Brave Eagle, 1957, VG, N2	$135.00
Buccaneer, 1957, dome top, VG+, N2	$195.00

Buck Rogers, 1979, VG, N2	$18.00
Buck Rogers, 1979, w/thermos, M	$100.00

Photo courtesy June Moon.

Bugaloos, Aladdin, 1971, VG, J6, $85.00.

Bugaloos, 1971, EX+, I2	$100.00
Cabbage Patch Kids, 1983, VG+, N2	$10.00
Care Bears, 1983, VG, I2	$15.00
Cartoon Zoo Lunch Chest, 1961, VG, N2	$250.00
Chan Clan, 1973, w/thermos, EX, I2	$100.00
Chavo, 1979, M, N2	$300.00
Children at Play, 1930s, gr, 2 hdls, VG+, N2	$60.00
Children on Picnic, 1970s, 2 hdls, EX, N2	$35.00
Children w/Cat, 1930s, red & gr, 2 hdls, VG+, N2	$75.00
Chitty-Chitty Bang-Bang, 1968, EX, N2	$100.00
Clash of the Titans, 1980, VG+, N2	$24.00
Corsage, 1964, G+, I2	$24.00
Cowboy Lassoing Steer, 1950s, decal, VG+, N2	$250.00
Cracker Jack, 1980, 2 hdls, NM+, N2	$75.00
Curiosity Shop, 1972, EX, N2	$50.00
Cyclist, 1979, w/thermos, M, N2	$125.00
Daniel Boone (same front & back), 1955, VG+, N2	$165.00
Dark Crystal, 1982, EX, N2	$15.00
Dark Crystal, 1982, w/thermos, NM+, N2	$35.00
Davy Crockett, Holtemp, 1955, w/thermos, EX, I2	$190.00
Davy Crockett/Kit Carson, 1955, VG+, N2	$250.00
Denim Diner, 1975, dome top, EX, N2	$50.00
Dick Tracy, 1967, EX, N2	$145.00
Disco, 1980, EX, N2	$28.00
Disney Express, 1979, VG+, N2	$20.00
Disney Firefighter, 1969, dome top, VG+, N2	$135.00
Disney on Parade, 1970, VG, N2	$25.00
Disney School Bus, 1969, dome top, orange, NM+, N2	$125.00
Disneyland Castle, 1957, VG, N2	$75.00
Doctor Dolittle, 1967, VG+, N2	$85.00
Dragon's Lair, 1983, VG+, N2	$18.00
Duchess, 1960, w/thermos, EX, N2	$150.00
Dukes of Hazzard, 1983, new boys, w/thermos, EX, N2	$45.00
Dynomutt, 1976, EX, I2	$44.00

Empire Strikes Back, 1980, G, N2..................................$14.00
Evel Knievel, 1974, w/thermos, EX, N2...........................$65.00
Exciting World of Metrics, 1976, VG+, N2.....................$35.00
Fall Guy, 1981, w/thermos, VG+, N2...............................$25.00
Family Affair, 1969, EX, N2...$75.00
Fireball XJ-5, 1964, VG+, N2...$85.00
Flag, 1973, VG+, N2..$45.00
Flintstones, Wonderful World of Hanna-Barbera, 1977, w/thermos, VG+, N2..$35.00
Fonz, 1976, VG+, N2...$35.00
Fox & the Hound, 1982, VG+, N2...................................$15.00
Fozzie (Muppets), 1979, w/thermos, M, N2.....................$50.00
Fraggle Rock, 1984, VG, N2..$15.00
Frontier Days, 1957, VG, N2...$90.00
Fruit Basket, 1975, EX, N2..$45.00
Gentle Ben, 1968, VG+, N2...$65.00
Ghostland, 1977, VG+, N2..$48.00
GI Joe, 1967, VG+, N2...$85.00
GI Joe, 1982, w/thermos, VG, I2.....................................$15.00
Goober & the Ghost Chasers, 1974, VG+, N2.................$65.00
Great Wild West, 1959, VG+, N2.....................................$400.00
Gremlins, 1984, VG, I2..$16.00
Gremlins, 1984, w/thermos, M, N2..................................$50.00
Grizzly Adams, 1977, dome top, EX, N2.........................$80.00
Grizzly Adams, 1977, dome top, w/thermos, EX+, N2...$125.00
Guns of Will Sonnett, 1968, EX, N2................................$175.00

Gunsmoke, Aladdin, 1959, orange rim, VG, $70.00.

Gunsmoke, 1972, VG, N2...$70.00
Hair Bear Bunch, 1971, EX, N2.......................................$75.00
Hansel & Gretel, 1982, EX, N2...$80.00
Happy Days, 1976, VG+, N2...$45.00
Happy Easter, 1980s, 2 hdls, EX, N2...............................$15.00
Hardy Boys, 1977, EX, I2...$48.00
He-Man & the Master of the Universe, 1983, w/thermos, VG+, N2...$15.00
Heathcliff, 1982, M, N2...$45.00
Hi-My Lunch, 1977, VG+, N2...$15.00

Highway Markers, 1968, 1st design, VG, N2...................$50.00

Holly Hobbie, Aladdin, 1972, blue rim, VG, $12.00.

Hong Kong Phooey, 1975, VG+, N2.................................$35.00
How the West Was Won, 1978, VG+, N2..........................$40.00
Huckleberry Hound, 1961, VG, N2..................................$80.00
Incredible Hulk, 1978, EX+, I2..$28.00
Indiana Jones, 1984, VG, N2...$10.00
Jetsons, Aladdin, 1963, dome top, EX.............................$550.00
Jungle Book, 1966, rusty on bottom, G-..........................$20.00
Junior Miss, 1970, 3 girls w/duck, EX, N2......................$50.00
Junior Miss, 1978, basset hound, VG+, N2.....................$25.00
Kermit (Muppets), 1979, w/thermos, EX, N2..................$20.00
Kid Power (Wee Pals), 1973, VG+, N2............................$20.00

KISS, 1977, NM, $100.00.

Korg, 1975, VG+..$30.00
Krofft Supershow, 1976, w/thermos (G), VG+, I2...........$68.00
Kung Fu, 1974, VG+...$30.00
Lassie, 1978, G-, N2...$10.00
Legend of the Lone Ranger, 1980, VG+, N2....................$30.00

Little Dutch Miss, 1959, w/thermos, EX+, N2................$250.00
Little House on the Prairie, 1978, VG+.........................$50.00
Little Red Riding Hood, 1982, EX+ $65.00
Lost in Space, Thermos, 1967, dome top, w/thermos, NM....$500.00
Luggage Tweed, Am Thermos, 1957, tan, VG, I2 ....$22.00
Magic Kingdom, 1980, w/thermos, EX, N2.....................$25.00
Magic of Lassie, 1978, VG+, N2 ....$35.00
Marvel Comics Super Heroes, 1976, VG+, N2................$20.00
Mary Poppins, 1964, VG+, N2.....................................$68.00
Masters of the Universe, 1983, EX, I2 ....$20.00
Mickey Mouse Club, 1977, red, VG+, N2 ....$35.00
Mod Floral, 1975, EX+, N2 ....$250.00
Monroes, 1967, VG+..$120.00
Mork & Mindy, 1978, VG+, N2 ....$35.00
Mr Merlin, 1981, VG, N2 ....$14.00
Mr Merlin, 1981, w/thermos, M, N2 ....$95.00
Muppet Babies, 1985, EX+, I2 ....$18.00
Muppet Show, 1978, EX, I2..$18.00
National Airlines, 1968, EX $40.00
NFL, 1976, VG+, N2 ....$25.00
NFL, 1978, VG+, N2 ....$15.00
NFL Quarterback, 1964, EX, N2 ....$175.00
Pac-Man, 1980, w/thermos, EX, N2 ....$30.00
Partridge Family, Aladdin, 1970, blk rim, w/thermos, EX, T2 ..$30.00
Pathfinder, 1959, VG+, N2 ....$350.00
Peanuts, 1973, red, VG, I2 ....$10.00
Peanuts, 1980, yel, w/thermos, M, N2.........................$45.00
Pebbles & Bamm-Bamm, 1971, lt wear, EX, I2...............$65.00
Pennants, 1950s, oval, 2 hdls, VG+, N2 ....$40.00
Pete's Dragon, 1978, VG+, N2 ....$30.00
Peter Pan, 1969, VG+ $65.00
Pigs in Space, 1977, VG, N2 ....$16.00
Pink Panther & Sons, 1984, VG+, N2 ....$25.00

Popples, 1986, EX, I2...$15.00
Popples, 1986, w/thermos, EX, N2 ....$20.00
Pro Sports, 1962, EX, N2..$75.00
Psychedelic, 1968, dome top, EX, N2 ....$250.00
Racing Wheels, 1977, back has lt pnt wear, EX, I2 ....$45.00

Raggedy Ann and Andy, blue rim, with thermos, EX, $35.00.

Rambo, 1985, w/thermos, EX+, I2................................$30.00
Red Barn, 1957, closed doors, VG+, N2 ....$75.00
Return of the Jedi, 1983, VG+, I2 ....$34.00
Road Runner, 1970, VG, N2 ....$16.00
Robin Hood, Disney, 1974, VG+, N2.............................$30.00
Ronald McDonald, 1982, VG+, N2 ....$20.00
Rose Petal Place, 1983, EX, N2 ....$30.00
Rough Rider, 1972, G, N2..$14.00
Roy Rogers, 1955, w/thermos, EX, N2 ....$175.00
Roy Rogers & Dale Evans Chow Wagon, Thermos, 1950s, dome
     top, w/thermos, NM, A $300.00

Pit Stop, 1968, white rim, NM, $115.00.

Plaid McPherson, 1964, VG, I2.....................................$14.00
Planet of the Apes, 1974, EX, N2 ....$80.00
Polly Pal, 1974, w/thermos, VG+, N2 ....$25.00
Pony Express, 1957, G, N2 ....$75.00
Popeye, 1964, VG+, N2...$100.00
Popeye, 1980, VG+, N2..$35.00

Roy Rogers and Dale Evans Double R Bar Ranch, with thermos, VG, J6, $155.00.

Saddlebags, 1977, NM, N2..$140.00
Satellite, 1958, VG+, N2..$75.00
Satellite, 1958, w/thermos, VG+ $100.00
School Days, 1960, VG...$50.00

Secret of the Nymh, 1982, VG+, N2 ....$15.00
Secret Wars, 1984, EX, N2 ....$35.00
See America, 1972, VG+ $40.00
Sesame Street, 1979, w/thermos, yel, VG+, N2.............$20.00
Skateboarder, 1978, w/thermos, VG+, N2 ....$30.00
Snoopy, 1968, dome top, VG, N2 ....$35.00
Space, 1940s, bl, 2 hdls, VG, N2 ....$68.00
Speed Buggy, 1973, lt wear & scratches, dent on back, G+, I2 ...$30.00
Spider-Man/Hulk, 1980, VG+, N2 ....$25.00
Sport Goofy, 1984, VG+, N2 ....$20.00
Sport Skwirts, 1972, basketball, w/generic thermos, M, N2 ..$75.00
Star Trek, 1979, w/cracked thermos, VG+, N2 ....$50.00
Steve Canyon, 1959, VG+, N2 ....$250.00
Strawberry Shortcake, 1981, w/thermos, EX, N2.............$25.00
Strawberryland, 1985, w/thermos, EX, N2 ....$35.00
Submarine, 1960, VG, N2..$75.00
Sunnie Miss Cosmetics Case, 1972, VG+, N2 ....$75.00
Super Heroes, 1976, EX, I2....................................$45.00
Super Powers, 1983, VG+, N2 ....$22.00
Superman, 1978, w/thermos, VG+, N2........................$38.00
Tapestry, 1963, VG+, N2 ....$40.00
Teenager, 1957, dome top, EX+, I2 ....$125.00
Three Little Pigs, 1982, EX, N2 ....$80.00
Thundercats, 1985, EX, I2......................................$20.00
Tom Corbett (red decal), 1952, VG+, N2....................$200.00

Tom Corbett Space Cadet, 1952, decal on blue, with thermos, EX, $225.00.

Train (CP Rail), 1970, M, N2..................................$35.00
Transformers, 1986, VG+, N2..................................$20.00
Traveler, 1962, red trim, VG, N2..............................$48.00
Valentine, 1980s, 2 hdls, EX, N2 ....$18.00
Varsity Football, 1930s, oval, 2 hdls, VG+, N2 ....$80.00
Wags 'N Whiskers, 1978, VG+, N2 ....$25.00
Walt Disney World, 1970, w/thermos (NM), EX, I2 ....$38.00
Washington Redskins, 1970, VG+.............................$170.00
Weave Pattern, 1972, VG, N2 ....$8.00
Wild Bill Hickok, 1955, no hdl, G+, N2 ....$60.00
Wild Frontier, 1977, VG+, N2 ....$45.00
Woody Woodpecker, 1972, VG, N2 ....$50.00

Universal's Movie Monsters, Aladdin, 1980, green rim, EX, J6, $85.00.

Yankee Doodle, 1975, w/thermos, VG+, N2 ....$35.00
Yogi Bear, 1974, G-, N2 ....$20.00
Zorro, 1958, blk rim, VG+, N2 ....$150.00
18 Wheeler, 1978, EX, N2.......................................$60.00

PLASTIC

A-Team, 1985, red, w/thermos, EX, I2........................$25.00
ABC Dog, w/thermos, VG+, N2 ....$10.00
ABC Rabbit, w/thermos, VG+, N2 ....$10.00
Alf, Thermos, 1987, red, w/thermos, EX, I2..................$16.00
American Gladiators, 1987, w/thermos, EX, N2..............$15.00
Atari Missile Command, 1983, dome top, VG+, N2........$25.00
Back to the Future, 1989, w/thermos, M, N2 ....$25.00
Barbie, 1990, w/thermos, VG+, N2............................$12.00
Barbie in Hollywood, 1988, w/thermos, VG+, N2...........$15.00
Barbie Rockers, 1987, w/thermos, VG+, N2 ....$12.00
Barn, Fisher-Price #549, mini-lunch box, VG, N2 ....$4.00
Batman, 1982, gray, no glove, VG+, N2.....................$30.00
Batman, 1982, lt bl, w/thermos, M, N2.......................$40.00
Baywatch Barbie, 1995, w/thermos, M, N2 ....$20.00
Beauty & the Beast, 1991, w/thermos, EX, N2 ....$16.00
Bozostuffs, 1988, yel, w/thermos, M, N2 ....$35.00
Cabbage Patch, 1983, yel, w/thermos, VG+, I2 ....$10.00
California Raisins, 1988, yel, w/thermos, M, N2 ....$20.00
Captain Planet, 1990, w/thermos, M, N2.....................$25.00
Carolina Mud Cats (baseball team), red, EX, N2 ....$20.00
Cherry Merry Muffin, 1988, w/thermos, EX, N2............$15.00
Chiclets Chewing Gum, 1987, w/thermos, M, N2...........$50.00
Chip 'N Dale, 1989, VG+.......................................$8.00
Cinderella, Aladdin, pk, EX, I2 ....$5.00
Days of Thunder, 1988, w/thermos, M, N2 ....$25.00
Dick Tracy, 1989, red, w/thermos, EX, I2 ....$10.00
Dinosaurs, 1990, purple, w/thermos, NM, N2 ....$20.00
Double Dare, 1988, w/thermos, M, N2.......................$25.00
Dr Pepper, 1982, VG+, N2......................................$25.00

Dukes of Hazzard, 1981, dome top, EX, N2......................$35.00
Ecology, 1980, dome top, w/thermos, EX, N2.................$50.00
Elephant, Hippo & Lion, 1986, EX, N2...........................$20.00
Empire Strikes Back, 1980, VG+, N2 ....$25.00

Ewoks, Thermos, 1983, decal on red, with thermos, NM, $20.00.

Fame, 1983, w/thermos, M, N2 ....$25.00
Fievel Goes West, 1991, w/thermos, EX, N2 ....$15.00
Flash Gordon, 1979, dome top, w/thermos, NM, N2........$95.00
Flintstones (John Goodman), w/thermos, M, N2 ....$15.00
Food for Thought, 1991, w/thermos, M, N2 ....$25.00
Garfield, 1978, red or yel, w/thermos, EX, N2 ....$12.00
Ghostbusters, 1986, red, w/thermos, EX, N2 ....$20.00

GI Joe, Aladdin, 1987, with thermos, NM, $25.00.

GI Joe, 1990, w/thermos, NM, N2 ....$20.00
Go Bots, 1984, VG+, N2..$10.00
Golden Girl, 1984, w/thermos, EX, N2 ....$20.00
Here's Boomer, 1980, yel, EX, N2 ....$25.00
Herself the Elf, 1982, VG+, N2..$10.00
Home Alone, 1991, w/thermos, EX, N2..............................$12.00

Hot Wheels, Thermos, 1984, red, EX, I2 ....$30.00
Hulk Hogan, 1989, EX, N2...$20.00
Incredible Hulk, 1980, dome top, w/thermos, EX, N2 ......$85.00
Jabberjaw, 1977, EX, N2...$45.00
Jems, 1986, purple, w/thermos, EX, I2 ....$15.00
Jurassic Park, 1992, w/thermos, M, N2...............................$25.00
Keebler Cookie, 1978, w/thermos, M, N2 ....$60.00
Kellogg's Corn Flakes, 1985, w/thermos, NM, N2 ....$60.00
Kermit the Frog, 1988, dome top, w/thermos, VG+, N2 ..$30.00
Kissyfur (Bears), 1985, w/thermos, EX, N2 ....$20.00
Laser Tag, 1986, w/thermos, EX, N2 ....$25.00
Little Orphan Annie, 1973, dome top, w/thermos, NM, N2 ...$95.00
Looney Tunes, 1977, w/thermos, VG+, N2 ....$40.00
Looney Tunes, 1989, w/thermos, VG+, N2 ....$12.00
Lunch 'N Tunes, 1986, beach scene, EX, N2......................$45.00
Marvel Super Heroes, 1990, w/thermos, EX, N2................$20.00
Mask, 1985, w/thermos, VG+, N2.......................................$15.00
Masters of the Universe, 1983, w/thermos, EX, N2 ....$20.00
Merle Norman, Lolly's New Look, 1985, w/thermos, M, I2....$25.00
Mickey & Minnie, in school, w/thermos, EX, N2.............$12.00
Mickey at the Zoo, 1985, w/thermos, EX, N2 ....$15.00
Mickey Mouse Fights Dragon, w/thermos, EX, N2 ....$10.00
Mighty Mouse, 1979, VG+, N2...$45.00
Miss Piggy, 1980, EX, N2...$20.00
Monster (Creature Feature), roars when opened, M, N2..$25.00
Moon Dreamers, 1987, EX, N2..$10.00
Muppet School Bus, 1989, VG, N2 ....$12.00
My Child, 1986, w/thermos, VG+, N2 ....$20.00
New Kids on the Block, 1990, orange, w/thermos, EX, I2...$20.00
Ninja Turtles, red, w/thermos, EX, N2................................$14.00
Odie Kissing Garfield, 1978, w/thermos, EX, N2 ....$15.00
Oreo Cookies, 1980s, EX, N2...$25.00
Peanuts, 1980, picnic scene, w/thermos, VG, N2 ....$10.00
Popeye, 1979, dome top, EX..$50.00
Popeye, 1987, 3-D, yel, w/thermos, M, N2.........................$75.00
Rainbow Brite, 1983, w/thermos, VG+, N2........................$10.00
Rambo, 1985, red, VG+, N2 ....$15.00
Real Ghostbusters, 1986, orange, w/thermos, EX, N2 ......$18.00
Rocketeer, 1990, w/thermos, M, N2....................................$25.00
Roger Rabbit, 1987, w/thermos, VG+, N2..........................$10.00
Sesame Street, 1979, red, w/thermos, M, N2 ....$28.00
Sesame Street, 1985, w/thermos, EX, N2 ....$15.00
Shadow, 1994, w/thermos, M, N2 ....$35.00
Shirt Tales, 1981, w/thermos, EX, N2 ....$15.00
Silverhawks, 1986, VG+, N2...$15.00
Slow, Genius at Work, 1986, VG+, N2 ....$25.00
Smurfette, 1984, VG+, N2 ....$10.00
Smurfs, 1983, dome top, EX, N2 ....$25.00
Smurfs, 1984, bl, EX, I2 ....$8.00
Snoopy, 1978, dome top, bl, EX, I2.....................................$20.00
Snoopy & Woodstock, 1970, dome top, w/thermos, VG+, N2...$25.00
Snow White, 1988, w/thermos, EX, N2...............................$25.00
Sport Billy, 1982, w/thermos, VG+, N2..............................$20.00
Star Trek, The Next Generation, 1989, w/thermos, M, N2..$25.00
StarCom US Space Force, 1987, w/thermos, M, N2.........$25.00
Super Mario Bros, 1988, w/thermos, EX, N2......................$15.00
Superman, 1980, dome top, NM, N2 ....$60.00
Superman, 1986, phone booth scene, VG+, N2 ....$20.00

Star Wars, Return of the Jedi, 1983, red, EX, $20.00.

Teenage Mutant Ninja Turtles, 1990, bl, w/thermos, EX, I2...$8.00
Tidewater Tides (Virginia baseball team), 1990, EX, N2 .$20.00
Tom & Jerry, 1992, w/thermos, VG+, N2.........................$20.00
Transformers, 1986, red, VG, I2.....................................$10.00
Tyrannosaurus Rex, dome top, EX, N2 ....$20.00
Up, Up & Away, 1986, w/thermos, M, N2 ....$25.00
Wayne Gretsky, 1980, w/thermos, VG+, N2 ....$60.00
Where's Waldo, 1990, w/thermos, VG+, N2 ....$8.00
Wuzzles, 1985, w/thermos, EX, I2....................................$15.00
101 Dalmatians, bl, w/thermos, EX, I2.............................$10.00

Vinyl

Alvin & the Chipmunks, Thermos, 1963, dk gr, EX, I2..$285.00
Annie, 1981, VG, N2 ....$20.00
Annie, 1981, w/thermos, M, N2......................................$75.00
Ballerina, 1960s, on lily pads, pk, VG+, N2 ....$135.00
Barbarino, 1977, bl, brunch bag, w/thermos, EX+, I2.....$220.00
Barbie & Francie, 1965, w/metal thermos, EX, N2.........$125.00
Boston Red Sox, 1960, EX, N2 ....$100.00
Captain Kangaroo, 1964, EX, N2 ....$375.00
Challenger, 1986, gr, M, N2..$250.00
Corsage, 1970, VG+, N2 ....$100.00
Denim, 1970s, VG+, N2..$35.00
Denim w/Strawberries, 1970, brunch bag, w/thermos, EX, N2....$65.00
Don't Bug Me Ladybug, 1978, drawstring closure, EX, N2 .$65.00
Donny & Marie (long hair), 1976, EX, N2 ....$100.00
Donny & Marie (short hair), 1978, brunch bag, EX, N2..$95.00
Fire Department, 1974, softee, EX, N2............................$95.00
First Union Bank, 1980s, zipper closure, EX, N2 ....$20.00
Hawaiian Islanders, 1980s, zipper closure, VG+, N2 ....$20.00
Holly Hobbie, 1972, w/thermos, EX, N2.........................$50.00
Ice Cream Cone, 1975, pk gingham, VG+.......................$40.00
Kaboodle Kit, 1960, bl, VG+ $130.00
Leo Lion, 1978, brunch bag, drawstring closure, NM, N2...$145.00
Lil Jodie, 1978, softee, M, N2......................................$125.00
Lion in the Cart, 1985, puffy, VG+, N2.........................$65.00
Lion in the Van, 1978, M, N2.......................................$150.00
Little Old Schoolhouse, 1974, softee, EX, N2...................$95.00
Mardi Gras, 1971, w/thermos, VG+, N2.......................$100.00

Oscar Mayer Into Sausage, zipper closure, EX, N2.............$25.00
Peanuts, 1969, red, Snoopy at mailbox, NM, N2 ....$100.00
Peanuts, 1977, Snoopy, brunch bag, EX, N2.....................$85.00
Pepsi-Cola, 1980, wht, softee, EX, N2...............................$30.00
Picadilly, 1971, VG+, N2..$75.00
Pink Panther, 1980, VG+, N2...$65.00
Pinocchio, Mexican, 1970s, rare, EX, J8 ....$85.00
Psychedelic Blue, 1970, w/metal thermos, NM...............$100.00
Pussycats, 1968, VG+ $120.00
Sabrina, 1972, EX, N2..$200.00
Sesame Street, 1979, checkerboard, w/thermos, VG+, N2 ..$45.00
Sesame Street, 1979, orange, w/thermos, EX, N2 ....$95.00
Sophisticates, 1969, brn, brunch bag, w/thermos, EX, N2 ..$95.00
Speedy Turtle, 1978, drawstring closure, EX, N2.............$65.00
Strawberry Shortcake, 1980, w/thermos, EX, N2.............$45.00
Swan Lake, 1960s, bl, VG+, N2......................................$125.00
Tic Tac Toe, 1977, red, VG+, N2.....................................$50.00
Tropical Swim Club, red, EX, N2....................................$60.00
White Polka Dots, 1969, brunch bag, w/thermos, EX, N2 ..$75.00
Wise Guy Owl, 1977, brunch bag, drawstring closure, NM, N2 ....$145.00
Wizard in the Van, 1978, VG, N2 ....$60.00
1910 Ford, 1974, VG+, N2...$60.00

Thermoses

Action Jackson, Okay Industries, metal, 1973.................$140.00
Addams Family, 1974, plastic, NM, J2.............................$25.00
Aladdin Cable Car, 1982, metal, NM, N2.......................$150.00
Alvin, King Seeley, 1963, plastic, NM, N2 ....$125.00
Annie Oakley & Tagg, Aladdin, 1955, metal, NM $95.00
Barbie Lunch Kit, King Seeley, metal, 1962, NM.............$85.00
Battle Kit, King Seeley Thermos, metal, 1965, NM $55.00
Black Hole, Aladdin, 1979, plastic, NM $30.00
Boating, 1959, metal, NM, N2..$100.00
Bozo the Clown, Aladdin, 1963, EX $50.00
Brave Eagle (red band), Am Thermos, 1957, metal, NM ..$120.00
Bullwinkle & Rocky, unknown maker, 1962, metal, NM..$220.00
Carousel, Aladdin, 1962, metal & glass, NM $135.00
Chan Clan, King Seeley, 1973, plastic, NM $35.00
Cowboy in Africa, King Seeley, 1968, metal, NM...........$75.00
Cowboy in Africa, King Seeley, 1968, metal, EX, N2 ......$60.00
Daniel Boone, Aladdin, 1965, metal, NM $90.00
Dick Tracy, Aladdin, 1967, metal, NM $80.00
Disneyland, 1959, metal, w/Riverboat, NM, I2................$80.00
Doctor Dolittle, Aladdin, 1968, metal, NM.....................$45.00
Dr Seuss, Aladdin, 1970, plastic, NM $50.00
Dudley Do-Right, Universal, 1962, metal, NM $260.00
Dukes of Hazzard, 1968, plastic, EX+, N2......................$12.00
Evil Knievel, Aladdin, 1974, plastic, NM $30.00
Family Affair, 1969, metal, EX, N2 ....$45.00
Fireball XL5, King Seeley, 1964, metal, NM....................$80.00
Firehouse, 1959, metal, EX+, I2.....................................$110.00
Flintstones, 1964, metal, EX, N2 ....$75.00
Garfield, 1978, plastic, yel, VG+, I2.................................$2.50
Gene Autry, Universal, 1954, metal, NM $120.00
Get Smart, King Seeley, 1966, metal, NM......................$80.00
Go-Go, Aladdin, metal, 1966, NM $65.00

Green Hornet, King Seeley, 1967, metal, NM $130.00
Hair Bear Bunch, 1971, metal, NM, N2 ....$45.00
Have Gun Will Travel, Aladdin, 1950s, metal, NM......$150.00
Hector Heathcote, Aladdin, 1964, metal, NM $95.00
Hopalong Cassidy, Aladdin, 1952, metal, NM $75.00
James Bond, Aladdin, 1966, metal, NM $125.00
Jet Patrol, Aladdin, 1957, metal, NM $145.00
Jetsons, Aladdin, 1963, NM..$140.00
Junior Nurse, 1963, metal, EX+, I2 ....$75.00
Kellogg's Breakfast, Aladdin, 1969, plastic, NM.............$65.00
Land of the Giants, Aladdin, 1968, plastic, NM, T2........$35.00
Lassie, 1978, plastic, w/dk bl cup, EX, I2.........................$22.00
Lawman, King Seeley, 1961, metal, NM..........................$65.00
Life & Times of Grizzly Adams, 1977, plastic, EX, I2.......$40.00

Secret Agent, King Seeley Thermos, NM, $30.00.

Ludwig Von Drake, Aladdin, 1962, metal, NM, $95.00.

Snoopy Doghouse, 1968, plastic, EX+, N2.......................$20.00
Space Shuttle, King Seeley, 1977, plastic, NM.................$45.00
Speed Buggy, 1973, plastic, EX, N2................................$20.00
Steve Canyon, Aladdin, 1959, metal, NM $120.00
Super Friends, Aladdin, 1976, plastic, NM $25.00
Superman, King Seeley, metal, 1967, EX $75.00
Tammy & Pepper, Aladdin, 1965, metal, NM.................$90.00
Tom Corbett Space Cadet, Aladdin, 1952, metal, EX, A...$90.00
US Mail, 1969, plastic w/glass liner, EX, N2....................$20.00
Wonder Woman, Thermos, 1976, NM, C17 ....$30.00
Woody Woodpecker, 1972, plastic w/glass liner, some litho
    wear, VG, I2..$30.00

Man From Uncle, King Seeley, 1966, metal, NM............$95.00
Mary Poppins, Aladdin, 1973, plastic, NM......................$55.00
Mickey Mouse & Donald, Adco Liberty, 1954, metal, NM .$200.00
Mighty Mouse, 1979, plastic, bl w/wht cup, EX+, I2 ....$24.00
Munsters, King Seeley, 1965, metal, NM........................$120.00
NFL Quarterback, Aladdin, 1964, metal, NM $60.00
Orbit, 1963, metal, EX+, N2 ....$50.00
Pebbles & Bamm-Bamm, Aladdin, 1971, plastic, NM $50.00
Peter Pan, Aladdin, 1969, plastic, NM...........................$35.00
Pets & Pals, King Seeley, 1961, metal, NM $30.00
Pit Stop, Ohio Art, 1968, metal, NM $25.00
Police Patrol, Aladdin, 1978, plastic, NM $50.00
Racing Wheels, 1977, plastic, EX+, N2..........................$12.00
Rat Patrol, Aladdin, 1967, metal, NM $60.00
Robot Man & Friends, 1984, plastic, yel, EX+, I2 ....$12.00
Roy Rogers, Am Thermos, 1953, metal, NM...................$80.00
Satellite, King Seeley, 1960, metal, NM $75.00
Scooby Doo, 1973, plastic, gr, EX+ $15.00
Sesame Street, 1985, plastic, 4 characters in a circle, EX, I2..$2.50
Six Million Dollar Man, 1974, plastic, NM, I2.................$20.00
Sizzlers, King Seeley, 1971, metal, NM $35.00
Smokey Bear, Okay Industries, 1975, plastic & metal, NM .$185.00

Marbles

Antique marbles are divided into several classifications: 1) Transparent Swirl (Solid Core, Latticinio Core, Divided Core, Ribbon Core, Lobed Core, and Coreless); 2) Lutz or Lutz-type (with bands having copper flecks which alternate with colored or clear bands); 3) Peppermint Swirl (made of red, white, and blue opaque glass); 4) Indian Swirl (black with multicolored surface swirls); 5) Banded Swirl (wide swirling bands on opaque or transparent glass); 6) Onionskin (having an overall mottled appearance due to its spotted, swirling lines or lobes); 7) End-of-Day (single pontil, allover spots, either 2-colored or multicolored); 8) Clambroth (evenly spaced, swirled lines on opaque glass); 9) Mica (transparent color with mica flakes added); 10) Sulphide (nearly always clear, colored examples are rare, containing figures). Besides glass marbles, some were made of clay, pottery, china, steel, and even semiprecious stones.

Most machine-made marbles are still very reasonable, but some of the better examples may sell for $50.00 and up, depending on the colors that were used and how they are defined. Guineas (Christensen agates with small multicolored specks instead of swirls) sometime go for as much as $200.00.

Mt. Peltier comic character marbles often bring prices of $100.00 and more with Betty Boop, Moon Mullins, and Kayo being the rarest and most valuable.

From the nature of their use, mint-condition marbles are extremely rare and may be worth as much as three to five times more than one that is near-mint, while chipped and cracked marbles may be worth half or less. The same is true of one that has been polished, regardless of how successful the polishing was. If you'd like to learn more, Everett Grist has written three books on the subject that you will find helpful: *Antique and Collectible Marbles, Machine Made and Contemporary Marbles,* and *Everett Grist's Big Book of Marbles.* Also refer to MCSA's *Marble Identification and Price Guide,* recently re-written by Robert Block (Schiffer Publishing). See Clubs, Newsletters, and Other Publications for club information.

Akro Agate, 1930s, boxed set of 100 tri-color agates, M (EX box), A **$500.00**

Akro Agate, 1930s, unopened mesh bag w/27 high-grade marbles, NM, A **$85.00**

Artist-made, angelfish or sea horse, David Salazar, 1⅜", M, B8, ea...**$100.00**

Artist-made, crown filigree & peppermints, Bill Burchfield, 1", M, B8 ....**$40.00**

Artist-made, end-of-day, Bill Burchfield, 1", M, B8.........**$40.00**

Artist-made, end-of-day or swirl, Jody Fine, 1½", M, B8, ea .**$50.00**

Artist-made, end-of-day or swirl, Jody Fine, 1¼", M, B8, ea .**$25.00**

Artist-made, end-of-day or swirl, Mark Matthews, 1½", M, B8, ea...**$75.00**

Artist-made, end-of-day w/lutz, aventurine or mica, Rolf & Genie Wald, 1½", M, B8, ea **$50.00**

Artist-made, end-of-day w/lutz or mica, Bill Burchfield, 1½", M, B8, ea **$75.00**

Artist-made, lutz-type, Harry Boyer, 1⅝", M, B8..............**$50.00**

Artist-made, millefiori w/aventurine, Harry Boyer, 2", M, B8 ....**$200.00**

Artist-made, peppermint w/mica, Mark Matthews, ⅝" to ¾", M, B8 ....**$50.00**

Artist-made, single flower or 3 flowers, Harry Boyer, 1½", M, B8, ea **$50.00**

Artist-made, swirl, Bill Burchfield, 1", M, B8 ....**$40.00**

Artist-made, swirl w/lutz, aventurine or mica, Rolf & Genie Wald, 1⅛", M, B8, ea **$25.00**

Artist-made, swirl w/lutz or mica, Bill Burchfield, 1½", M, B8, ea **$75.00**

Artist-made, swirls & ribbons, Harry Boyer, 1¼", M, B8 .**$25.00**

Artist-made, swirls & ribbons, Harry Boyer, 1⅝", M, B8 .**$50.00**

Clambroth Swirl, any color variation, ½" to ⅞", M, B8, ea .**$250.00**

Comic, Andy Gump, Peltier Glass, M, B8.....................**$125.00**

Comic, Annie, Peltier Glass, M, B8.............................**$150.00**

Comic, Betty Boop, Peltier Glass, M, B8 ....**$200.00**

Comic, Emma, Peltier Glass, M, B8 ....**$75.00**

Comic, Herbie, Peltier Glass, M, B8............................**$150.00**

Comic, Kayo, Peltier Glass, M, B8 ....**$450.00**

Comic, Koko, Peltier Glass, M, B8..............................**$125.00**

Comic, Moon Mullins, Peltier Glass, M, B8 ....**$300.00**

Comic, Skeezix, Peltier Glass, M, B8 ....**$150.00**

Comic, Smitty, Peltier Glass, M, B8 ....**$125.00**

Divided Core Swirl, bl-tinted glass w/3 sets of wht outer bands, 3 red, wht & bl inner bands, 1¼", NM, B8...................**$80.00**

Divided Core Swirl, gray-tinted glass w/4 sets of wht outer bands, 4 3-color inner bands, 1⅝", NM, B8 ....**$175.00**

Divided Core Swirl, peewee, any color variation, ⅜" to ½", M, B8, ea **$25.00**

Divided Core Swirl, tinted glass w/3 sets of yel outer bands, 4 mc inner bands, 1¾", NM, B8...............................**$175.00**

End-of-Day, cloud-type w/mica, wht w/red & bl blend, 1⅝", NM, B8 ....**$300.00**

End-of-Day, onionskin w/mica, wht base w/2 red & 2 bl panels, some turq, 1⅜", NM, B8 ....**$150.00**

End-of-Day, paneled submarine, bright blue, green, and red inner core, outer layer is 7 white bands, 1 green and 1 blue, 1½", rare, few small chips and light pitting, G, A, $170.00.

End-of-Day, peewee, any color variation, ⅜" to ½", M, B8, ea.**$50.00**

End-of-Day, red, wht & bl, 1¼", M, B8 ....**$125.00**

End-of-Day, red & wht, 1½", NM, B8 ....**$225.00**

End-of-Day, single pontil cloud w/mica, mc, 1⅝", NM, B8..**$550.00**

End-of-Day, wht base w/bl, red & gr splotches, 1⅜", NM, B8 ....**$150.00**

Banded Lutz, transparent clear base with 4 light green bands, lutz bands edged in white, shooter-size, NM, A, $120.00.

End-of-Day, wht base w/red & emerald gr splotches, 2", minor dings & chips, G+, B8 ....$225.00

End-of-Day, wht w/2 bl & 2 red panels, 1⅞", NM, B8 ...$250.00

Indian Swirl, any color variation, ½" to ⅞", M, B8, ea ..$125.00

Joseph's Coat, 4 layers (extremely rare), multicolored swirl, 1⁵⁄₁₆", NM, A, $300.00.

Latticinio Swirl, bl-tinted glass w/6 2-color outer bands, wht core, 1⅝", NM, B8 ....$150.00

Latticinio Swirl, peewee, any color variation, ⅜" to ½", M, B8, ea $25.00

Latticinio Swirl, 2 pr of 3-color outer bands, wht core, 1¾", G, B8..............................$100.00

Latticinio Swirl, 3 translucent turq & 3 red & wht outer bands, wht core, 1⅞", NM, B8 ....$150.00

Latticinio Swirl, 4 3-color outer bands, yel core, 1½", M, B8..$175.00

Latticinio Swirl, 6 red & wht outer bands, yel core, 1⅝", NM, B8..............................$150.00

Latticinio Swirl, 7 alternating red & wht outer bands, yel core, 2", G, B8 ....$125.00

Photo courtesy Dunbar Gallery.

Lucky Boy Pouch (no marbles), 1930s, black and orange, EX, D10, from $75.00 to $125.00.

Lutz, banded colored glass, any color, ½" to ⅞", M, B8, ea $200.00

Lutz, banded opaque, any color, ½" to ⅞", M, B8, ea.....$400.00

Machine-made, aqua or clear slag, Akro Agate, ⁹⁄₁₆" to ¹¹⁄₁₆", M, B8, ea..............................$8.00

Machine-made, aventurine, Akro Agate, ⁹⁄₁₆" to ¹¹⁄₁₆", M, B8..$25.00

Machine-made, bl oxblood, Akro Agate, ⁹⁄₁₆" to ¹¹⁄₁₆", M, B8 .$65.00

Machine-made, brick, MF Christensen, ⁹⁄₁₆" to ¹¹⁄₁₆", M, B8....$60.00

Machine-made, brn slag, MF Christensen, 1³⁄₁₆", NM, B8 ....$75.00

Machine-made, carnelian, Akro Agate, ⁹⁄₁₆" to ¹¹⁄₁₆", M, B8.$12.50

Machine-made, carnelian oxblood, Akro Agate, ⁹⁄₁₆" to ¹¹⁄₁₆", M, B8..............................$80.00

Machine-made, clear rainbow, Peltier Glass, ⁹⁄₁₆" to ¹¹⁄₁₆", M, B8..............................$40.00

Machine-made, corkscrew, Akro Agate, 3-color, ⁹⁄₁₆" to ¹¹⁄₁₆", M, B8..............................$15.00

Machine-made, corkscrew, Akro Agate, 4-color, ⁹⁄₁₆" to ¹¹⁄₁₆", M, B8..............................$30.00

Machine-made, corkscrew, Akro Agate, 5-color, ⁹⁄₁₆" to ¹¹⁄₁₆", M, B8..............................$60.00

Machine-made, egg yolk oxblood, Akro Agate, ⁹⁄₁₆" to ¹¹⁄₁₆", M, B8..............................$100.00

Machine-made, guinea, Christensen Agate, transparent base w/melted flecks of color, ¹¹⁄₁₆", M, B8 ....$475.00

Machine-made, honey onyx, Peltier Glass, ⁹⁄₁₆" to ¹¹⁄₁₆", M, B8.$20.00

Machine-made, lemonade corkscrew or swirl, Akro Agate, ⁹⁄₁₆" to ¹¹⁄₁₆", M, B8, ea..............................$12.50

Machine-made, lemonade oxblood, Akro Agate, ⁹⁄₁₆" to ¹¹⁄₁₆", M, B8..............................$50.00

Machine-made, limeade corkscrew or swirl, Akro Agate, ⁹⁄₁₆" to ¹¹⁄₁₆", M, B8, ea $20.00

Machine-made, limeade oxblood, Akro Agate, ⁹⁄₁₆" to ¹¹⁄₁₆", M, B8..............................$100.00

Machine-made, milky oxblood, Akro Agate, ⁹⁄₁₆" to ¹¹⁄₁₆", M, B8..............................$20.00

Machine-made, National Line Rainbo, bumblebee, Peltier Glass, ⁹⁄₁₆" to ¹¹⁄₁₆", M, B8..............................$12.50

Machine-made, National Line Rainbo, Christmas tree, Peltier Glass, ⁹⁄₁₆" to ¹¹⁄₁₆", M, B8..............................$85.00

Machine-made, National Line Rainbo, Liberty, Peltier Glass, ⁹⁄₁₆" to ¹¹⁄₁₆", M, B8..............................$75.00

Machine-made, National Line Rainbo, Superman, Peltier Glass, ⁹⁄₁₆" to ¹¹⁄₁₆", M, B8..............................$125.00

Machine-made, National Line Rainbo, tiger, Peltier Glass, ⁹⁄₁₆" to ¹¹⁄₁₆", M, B8..............................$20.00

Machine-made, National Line Rainbo, wasp, Peltier Glass, ⁹⁄₁₆" to ¹¹⁄₁₆", M, B8..............................$20.00

Machine-made, National Line Rainbo, zebra, Peltier Glass, ⁹⁄₁₆" to ¹¹⁄₁₆", M, B8..............................$10.00

Machine-made, opaque swirl, Christensen Agate, 2-color, ⁹⁄₁₆" to ¹¹⁄₁₆", M, B8..............................$15.00

Machine-made, opaque swirl, Christensen Agate, 3-color, ⁹⁄₁₆" to ¹¹⁄₁₆", M, B8..............................$35.00

Machine-made, orangeade corkscrew or swirl, Akro Agate, ⁹⁄₁₆" to ¹¹⁄₁₆", M, B8, ea..............................$30.00

Machine-made, oxblood patch, Vitro Agate, ⁹⁄₁₆" to ¹¹⁄₁₆", M, B8..............................$10.00

Machine-made, oxblood slag, MF Christensen, ⁹⁄₁₆" to ¹¹⁄₁₆", M, B8..............................$110.00

Machine-made, Popeye corkscrew, Akro Agate, bl & yel, ⁹⁄₁₆" to ¹¹⁄₁₆", M, B8..............................$25.00

Machine-made, Popeye corkscrew, Akro Agate, purple & yel or red & bl, 9/16" to 11/16", M, B8, ea $65.00

Machine-made, Popeye corkscrew, Akro Agate, red & gr, 9/16" to 11/16", M, B8 ....$18.00

Machine-made, Popeye corkscrew, Akro Agate, red & yel or gr & yel, 9/16" to 11/16", M, B8, ea....................$12.00

Machine-made, Popeye patch, Akro Agate, red, gr, wht & clear, ¾", rare, NM, B8 ....$150.00

Machine-made, red slag, Akro Agate, 9/16" to 11/16", M, B8 .$5.00

Machine-made, silver oxblood, Akro Agate, 9/16" to 11/16", M, B8................$40.00

Machine-made, slag, Peltier Glass, 9/16" to 11/16", M, B8....$12.00

Machine-made, striped opaque, Christensen Agate, 9/16" to 11/16", M, B8 ....$45.00

Machine-made, striped transparent, Christensen Agate, 9/16" to 11/16", M, B8................$35.00

Machine-made, sunburst, Master Marble, clear, 9/16" to 11/16", M, B8................$10.00

Machine-made, sunburst, Master Marble, opaque, 9/16" to 11/16", M, B8................$5.00

Machine-made, swirl, Ravenswood Novelty Works, mc, 9/16" to 11/16", M, B8 ....$10.00

Machine-made, swirl, Ravenswood Novelty Works, 2-color, 9/16" to 11/16", M, B8 ....$3.00

Machine-made, swirl oxblood, Akro Agate, 9/16" to 11/16", M, B8................$20.00

Machine-made, tiger eye, Master Marble, 9/16" to 11/16", M, B8 ....$20.00

Machine-made, turkey swirl, Christensen Agate, 2-color, 9/16" to 11/16", M, B8 ....$50.00

Machine-made, yel slag, Akro Agate, 9/16" to 11/16", M, B8 ..$12.00

Peppermint Swirl, any color variation, ½" to ⅞", M, B8, ea.$125.00

Ribbon Core Swirl, any color variation, ½" to ⅞", M, B8, ea.$150.00

Solid Core Swirl, bl-tinted glass w/4 sets of orange outer bands, red, wht & bl core, 1⅝", M, B8................$250.00

Solid Core Swirl, peewee, any color variation, ⅜" to ½", M, B8, ea................$40.00

Solid Core Swirl, 12 yel outer bands w/red, gr & bl middle bands, wht 3-layer solid core, 1¼", NM, B8 ....$75.00

Solid Core Swirl, 4 sets of gr-yel outer bands w/mc core, 1⅜", M, B8................$100.00

Solid Core Swirl, 8 yel outer bands, red, gr & bl bands on wht core, 1½", NM, B8 ....$125.00

Sulfide, bear, standing on grass mound, 1⅞", NM, B8 ...$150.00

Sulfide, bird, pecking on grass mound, 1⅞", NM, B8.....$150.00

Sulfide, boar, 1⅞", NM................$165.00

Sulfide, camel (1 hump), standing on grass mound, 1½", NM, B8................$200.00

Sulfide, cat, 1¼", NM................$100.00

Sulfide, child w/hammer, 1¾", M $600.00

Sulfide, child w/sailboat, 1¾", M $650.00

Sulfide, circus bear, 2", NM................$140.00

Sulfide, crucifix, 1¾", M................$600.00

Sulfide, dog, 1¾", NM................$125.00

Sulfide, dove, 1⅝", M................$165.00

Sulfide, fish, 1½", NM................$170.00

Sulfide, goat, standing, 2¼", EX................$165.00

Sulfide, hen, 1⅛", M................$100.00

Sulfide, hog, standing on grass mound, 1⅜", NM, B8 ....$150.00

Sulfide, Jenny Lind, 1½", NM, B8 ....$750.00

Sulfide, lion, standing on mound of grass, 2", NM, B8 ...$125.00

Sulfide, monkey, seated on drum, 1⅜", M $200.00

Sulfide, owl, standing, 2", M................$135.00

Sulfide, papoose, 1¾", M................$700.00

Sulfide, peasant boy, on stump w/legs crossed, 1½", NM, B8..$400.00

Sulfide, pony, 1¾", M................$200.00

Sulfide, rabbit, sprinting over grass, 1⅞", NM $150.00

Sulfide, raccoon, 2", M $200.00

Sulfide, Santa Claus, 1¾", M................$1,200.00

Sulfide, sheep, standing on grass mound, 1¼", NM, B8 ..$150.00

Sulfide, squirrel w/nut, 2", EX $200.00

Sulfide, woman (Kate Greenaway), 1½", NM, B8..........$450.00

Marx

Louis Marx founded his company in New York in the 1920s. He was a genius not only at designing toys but also marketing them. His business grew until it became one of the largest toy companies ever to exist, eventually expanding to include several factories in the United States as well as other countries. Marx sold his company in the early 1970s; he died in 1982. Though toys of every description were produced, collectors today admire his mechanical toys above all others.

Advisor: Scott Smiles (S10), windups; Tom Lastrapes (L4), battery-ops.

See also Advertising; Banks; Character, TV, and Movie Collectibles; Dollhouse Furniture; Games; Guns; Plastic Figures; Playsets; and other categories. For toys made by Linemar (Marx's subsidiary in Japan), see Battery-Operated Toys; Windups, Friction, and Other Mechanicals.

BATTERY-OPERATED

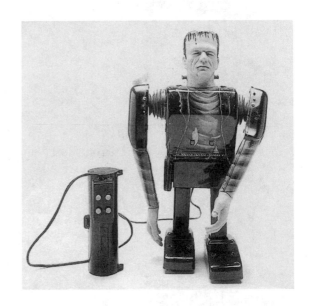

Frankenstein, 1950s, lithographed tin, remote control, 12½", EX, $875.00.

Aircraft Carrier, 20", EX, L4 ....$375.00

Alley the Roaring Stalking Alligator, MIB, L4...............$475.00

Amphibious Military Vehicle w/Soldiers, forward & reverse action, plastic, 9", EX (EX box), A $150.00

Big Parade, soldiers march together w/drum in front, 15" L, MIB.$300.00

Brewster the Rooster, advances, lifts head, opens beak & crows, 10", MIB $225.00

Clang-Clang Locomotive, early 1960s, advances w/lights & sound, 13", MIB $85.00

Colonel Hap Hazard, advances w/swinging arms & spinning antenna, tin & plastic, 12", NMIB $1,500.00

Electric Robot & Son, advances & lifts baby robot, light-up eyes & buzzer, plastic, 16", EX (EX box), A $500.00

Flashy Flickers, plastic picture gun shows 16 comic characters on flat surface, 16", MIB, A $125.00

Fred Flintstone on Dino, 1961, bump-&-go w/several actions, litho tin & plush, 12", NM (VG box).....................$775.00

Fred Flintstone on Dino, 1961, 12", VG, L4...................$350.00

Futuristic Airport, plane circles airport, remote control, 16x16" base, EX (EX box), A $400.00

Great Garloo, w/orig medallion, NM $500.00

Hootin' Hollerin' Haunted House, litho tin, NM, T1.$1,150.00

International Agent Car, MIB, L4 ....$200.00

Marx-A-Serve Table Tennis, rare, MIB, L4 ....$200.00

Mickey Mouse Krazy Kar, Mickey in high-wheel cart advances w/bump-&-go action, plastic, 6" dia, EX (EX box), A ..$75.00

Mickey the Musician, 1950s, Mickey plays xylophone on sq base, plastic & tin, 12", EX, A $275.00

Mighty Kong, advances in chains w/several actions, plush & plastic, remote control, 11", NM (VG box), A $600.00

Moon Scout Helicopter, MIB, L4 ....$150.00

Motorcycle Delivery, 1929, w/driver, litho tin, rare, EX (EX box), A...$925.00

Mr Mercury, advances, bends over & grasps objects, tin & plastic, remote control, 13", EX, A $350.00

Nutty Mad Car, advances on rear wheels, stops & shakes w/monster sound, litho tin, 9", EX, A $200.00

Nutty Mad Indian, 1960s, rocks while beating drum, tongue moves & makes war hoop sounds, tin & vinyl, 12", MIB $175.00

Nutty Mad Indian, 1960s, 12", EX, L4 ....$125.00

Space-Mobile, litho tin, 4½", NM (EX+ box), A...........$725.00

Teddy Bear Swing, TN, 1950s, 3 actions, NMIB, L4......$425.00

Tower Aeroplane, 2 litho tin planes w/celluloid props fly around Sky-hawk tower on rods, litho tin, 8", EX (VG box), A.........$250.00

Walking 'Esso' Tiger, 1950s, 4 actions, 11½", M, L4......$500.00

Whistling Spooky Kooky Tree, 1960s, bump-&-go w/several other actions, litho tin, 14", NM (EX box), A $2,000.00

Whistling Spooky Kooky Tree, 1960s, 14", VG, A $525.00

Yeti the Abominable Snowman, advances w/several actions & grunts, plush, tin & vinyl, remote control, 11", NMIB, A...........$735.00

PRESSED STEEL

Ambulance, 1930s, VG $400.00

Auto Transport, red, wht & bl, complete w/loading ramp & 3 plastic vehicles, 21", NM (EX box), A $230.00

Caterpiller Tractor w/Snow Blade & Wagon, 1930s, w/driver, 20", VG...$200.00

Crescent Ice Co Delivery Truck, w/metal tongs & glass ice cube, 11", NM (EX+ box), A..$485.00

Emergency Searchlight Truck, #448, Emergency Searchlight Unit decal on door, complete w/accessories, NM (EX box), A $275.00

Fire Hose & Ladder Truck, w/up w/electric lights, red open body w/railed platform, wht ladders, 14¾", EX, A $315.00

Fire Patrol Truck, 1935, travels w/siren sound, red w/yel extension ladders, 14½", rare, NM (EX box), A $1,100.00

First National Stores Delivery Truck, red & silver, 19", EX+ (EX+ box), A..$550.00

Guided Missile Truck, red, wht & bl, complete w/accessories, 18", NM (EX box), A $500.00

Highway Emergency Truck w/Blinker Lights, mk Day-Night Service, blk & wht w/blk Lumar tires, 18", NMIB........$400.00

Loblaws Tractor-Trailer, ...Your Finest Food Store lettered on sides of trailer, yel & red, 30", MIB, A....................$550.00

Log Trailer Truck, mk Northland Logging Co, complete w/chains & 5 logs, 19", NM (EX box), A $315.00

Pete the Talking Parrot, plush, tin and plastic, several actions, NM, $275.00.

Lumar Utility Service Truck and Accessories, complete with plastic accessories, NM (EX box), A, $435.00.

Lumar Dump Truck w/Front Loader, 1930s, 20½", G+, A .$150.00

Magnetic Crane Truck, 1950, bright yel, 18", EX (EX box), A...$350.00

Nellybelle Jeep, complete w/figures & decals, 11", MIB, A..$400.00

Stake Bed Truck with Advertising Cartons and Banks, #1008, black with red plastic stake bed, Lumar tires, 19", NM (NM box), A, $300.00.

US Air Force Jeep & Trailer w/Radar Unit, 1950, radar spins as jeep advances, plastic figures, 24", rare, NM (EX box), A $365.00

US Army Jeep w/Trailer, 1950, plastic driver, Radar decal on hood, 21", NM (EX box), A.......................................$265.00

US Army Truck w/Soldiers, mk 5th Division, bl & yel w/canvas top, complete w/5 plastic figures, 16", NM (EX box), A $275.00

Willys Jeep & Trailer, tin tires mk Louis Marx, 22", EX (EX box), A $250.00

WINDUPS, FRICTIONS AND OTHER MECHANICALS

Aero Oil Co Truck, friction, litho tin, 5½", EX+, A $485.00

American Tractor, w/driver, litho tin, 8", VG, A...........$200.00

Amos 'N Andy Fresh Air Taxi, Amos 'N Andy w/dog in taxi, crazy action, litho tin, 8½", NM, A.....................$1,100.00

Amos 'N Andy Fresh Air Taxi, 8", G, A $525.00

Amos 'N Andy in Person, 1930, 2 figures rock & walk around, litho tin, 11", G (EX box), A.................................$2,700.00

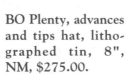

BO Plenty, advances and tips hat, lithographed tin, 8", NM, $275.00.

Photo courtesy Dunbar Gallery.

Archie Jalopy, Mexico, litho tin w/comical sayings in Spanish, 7", EX, A..$300.00

Archie Jalopy, 1975, plastic, MIB $125.00

Army Staff Car, early 1950s, EX, J6 ....$85.00

Army Tank #12, 1930s, litho tin, 9½", VG+, A $100.00

Astronaut, see Walking Astronaut

Automatic Car Wash Garage, mk Mid Town, car goes in & out of car wash, litho tin & plastic, EX (VG box) $350.00

Balky Mule, 1948, man in 2-wheeled wood-grain cart tries to control mule, litho tin, 8", NM, from $225 to $250.00

Barney Rubble's Wreck, 1962, litho tin w/vinyl-headed figure, friction, 7¼", NM, A...$450.00

Bedrock Express Train, 1962, litho tin, 12", EX, A $250.00

BO Plenty, advances while holding baby Sparkles, tips hat, litho tin, 8", MIB...$350.00

Boat-Tail Racer, 1930s, rare purplish color w/balloon tires, litho tin, w/driver, 13½", EX, A $300.00

Buck Rogers Rocket Police Patrol, 1934, advances w/sparks & sound, litho tin, 11½", VG, from $850 to................$900.00

Bulldozer Tractor, orange & red tin w/chrome hubs, plastic driver, 11", needs new flint o/w MIB, A $300.00

Busy Bridge, vehicles travel bridge w/tunnel at ea end, litho tin, 24", VG, A...$200.00

Busy Miners, 1930s, coal cart w/2 miners travels track from station house to coal mine, litho tin, 16", NM (EX box).........$350.00

Busy Miners, 1930s, 16", EX, A....................................$175.00

Cannonball Keller Roadster & Racer, 1950, tin roadster pulls plastic Indy-style racer, rare, NM (EX box), A........$375.00

Car Transporter, Mack-type cab, complete w/3 racers, 12", EX, A $825.00

Carcacha (Ganster Car), Plasti Marx/Mexico, 7", M (EX box), A $575.00

Careful Johnnie, Johnnie drives car w/non-fall action, plastic & tin, 6½", EX...$100.00

Champion Skater, 1930s, lady ice skater spins around, pull rod for action, litho tin, 6", M (G box), A.....................$275.00

Charleston Trio, 1921, jigger dances, boy plays violin & dog w/cane jumps atop cabin w/litho audience, 10", EX ...$900.00

Charlie McCarthy & Mortimer Snerd Private Car, 1930s, travels w/actuated bumpers, heads turn, litho tin, 15", VG .$1,500.00

Charlie McCarthy in His Benzine Buggy, 1938, Charlie's head spins as crazy car advances, 7", EX+, A....................$700.00

Charlie McCarthy Parade Drummer, Charlie in parade dress wheeling lg bass drum, red, wht & bl litho tin, 8", EX+.....$1,275.00

Charlie McCarthy Walker, moves side to side as jaws open & close, litho tin, 8", EX, A $350.00

Civilian Ambulance, red & wht litho pressed steel w/blk tires, 14", rare, NM, A..$750.00

Climbing Fireman, all-tin version, G.............................$300.00

Climbing Fireman, plastic & tin, VG $200.00

Coast Defense, plane circles above defense station, litho tin, 8½" dia, EX (VG rare box) $1,000.00

Combat Tank, advances as turret moves in & out w/firing sound, litho tin, 10", NM, A..$125.00

Comicoche, Plasti Marx/Mexico, w/driver, travels w/non-fall action, 7", NM (EX box), A.......................................$150.00

Coo-Coo Car, 1931, advances in circular motion w/full-figure driver bouncing up & down, 8", EX, from $650 to ..$750.00

Cowboy Rider, ca 1939, rearing horse vibrates as cowboy spins lariat overhead & aims gun, 8¼", MIB, A $400.00

Dagwood Aeroplane, 1935, travels w/crazy action as Dagwood's head bobs, litho tin, 9", NMIB, from $1,000 to....**$1,100.00**

Dagwood the Driver, Dagwood in crazy action car, litho tin, 8", NMIB, from $1,200 to...**$1,300.00**

Dapper Dan Coon Jigger, 1925, w/up & insert coin & figure dances on stage, litho tin, 10", VG $550.00

Dick Tracy Police Station, litho tin, complete w/car, 9" L, NM (EX box), A...**$1,300.00**

Dick Tracy Siren Squad Car, metallic gr w/various characters lithoed in windows, battery-op light, 11", scarce, NMIB $500.00

Dick Tracy Sparkling Riot Car, mk Squad Car No 1, various characters in window, litho tin, friction, 6", NM (NM box), A $335.00

Dippy Dumper, 1930s, travels in circles as driver gets thrown out & dumpster lifts, tin & celluloid, 9", EX (G box)...**$1,800.00**

Disney Express, 1950s, Mickey as engineer pulling 3 cars w/Disney characters, litho tin, 12½", EX+ (EX box), A ..$250.00

Disney Parade Roadster, litho tin w/plastic Donald, Mickey, Goofy & Nephew seated in car, 11½", NM (G box), A.........$725.00

Disney Turnover Tank, WDP/Mexico, 1950s, Goofy creates turnover action, Daisy litho on turret, 4", rare, EX .$750.00

Disneyland Jeep, litho tin w/fold-down windshield, friction, 9", EX (EX box) $250.00

Disneyland Train, ca 1956, happy-faced locomotive w/3 passenger cars lithoed w/host of Disney characters, 11", EX, A $50.00

Donald Duck Dipsy Car, litho tin car w/plastic figure, EXIB, A...$500.00

Donald Duck Drummer, 1950s, lithographed tin, NM (NM box), D10, $1,250.00.

Donald Duck Duet, 1946, Goofy dances while Donald plays drums, litho tin, 10½", VG+, from $650 to.............$700.00

Donald Duck Twirly Tail, 1950s, vibrates around as tail spins, plastic, 6", NM (EX box)...$300.00

Donald Duck Twirly Tail, 1950s, 6", EX........................$150.00

Donald the Driver, advances in erratic motion as Donald's head bobs, litho tin w/plastic figure, 6", EX (EX box), A.$800.00

Donkey Cart, man seated on 2-wheeled cart pulled by 2 donkeys, litho tin, 9½", NMIB, A..................................$255.00

Dopey Walker, 1938, advances in vibrating motion as his eyes move up & down, litho tin, 8", EX $350.00

Doughboy Tank, 1930s, advances w/erratic motion, guns move & soldier pops out, litho tin, 9", EX (EX box).........$550.00

Doughboy Tank, 1930s, 9", G, A.....................................$150.00

Driv-Ur-Self Car, 1935, cord attached to hood controls direction, red litho tin, 14", NM (VG box), A................$125.00

Drummer Boy, advances & plays bass drum, litho tin, 8½", VG, A...$325.00

Dumbo, WDP, 1941, performs somersaults, litho tin, 4", VG+ $225.00

El Dulcero Velocin (Happy Gardener), Mexico, man moves legs rapidly & pushes wheelbarrow, tin & plastic, 8", NMIB, A...**$165.00**

Expreso Disneylandia, Mexico, litho tin w/plastic engine, 12", M (EX box), A..$400.00

Ferdinand & Matador, WDE, 1939, advances as bull simulates attacking matador's cape, litho tin, 7", EX (EX+ box), A...$875.00

Ferdinand the Bull, 1938, vibrates around w/spinning tail, tin, 6", EXIB, A...$300.00

Ferdinand the Bull, 1938, 6", EX, A...............................$225.00

Figaro, see Rollover Figaro

Fire Water Boat, w/driver, red racer-type boat w/yel & red canopy, litho tin, 9¼", VG, A.....................................$525.00

Flash Gordon Rocket Fighter, 1939, litho tin, 12", VG+, A ..$450.00

Flintstone Flivver, 1962, Fred as driver, litho tin w/vinyl figure, 4", EX, A...$200.00

Flintstone Pals, Barney riding Dino, litho tin & vinyl, 8½", VG...$325.00

Flintstone Pals, Fred riding Dino, litho tin & vinyl, 8½", NMIB..$750.00

Fred Flintstone Tricycle, litho tin, 4", NMIB $500.00

Funny Face Walker, advances w/animated face change, litho tin, 10½", VG, A...$600.00

Funny Flivver, 1926, eccentric car w/comical driver advances in erratic motion, 7", EX (EX box)..............................$900.00

Funny Tiger, advances & plays drum, litho tin, 7", VG (VG box), A...$200.00

George the Drummer Boy, 1930s, drum major advances & plays drum, litho tin, 9", NM (EX box) $350.00

Goofy the Walking Gardener, Goofy pushes cart, litho tin, 9x8", EX $450.00

Gorilla, advances in chains w/several actions, plush & tin, 8", NM (EX box), A...$375.00

Harold Lloyd Funny Face Walker, 1929, sways as facial expressions change, litho tin, 10½", EX+ (G- box), A $935.00

Hee-Haw the Balky Mule, mk England, litho tin, NM (EX box), H7 ....$350.00

Hey Hey Chicken Snatcher, 1927, Black man advances w/chicken as dog bites his pants, tin, 8½", VG, from $1,100 to...**$1,200.00**

Highboy Climbing Tractor, 1950s, plastic blade version, w/driver, MIB, A $200.00

Highboy Climbing Tractor, 1950s, tin blade version, w/driver, 11", MIB, A..$250.00

Hop-A-Long Cassidy, rider w/lariat on rocking base, arms move depicting bucking horse, 10", VG $400.00

Hi-Yo Silver the Lone Ranger, lithographed tin, MIB, $450.00.

Hopping Dino, litho tin, 4", G, M5....................................$80.00

Hopping Elroy, 1963, litho tin, 4", MIB......................$1,000.00

Hopping Fred Flintstone, 1962, litho tin, 3½", NM.......$325.00

Hopping Rosie the Robot, 1963, litho tin, 4", rare, EX, A .$400.00

Huckleberry Hound Car, 1962, litho tin w/vinyl figure, friction, 4", NM (EX box) $300.00

International Agent Car, litho tin w/vinyl-headed figure, friction, 4", NM (NM box), A..$200.00

Jetson Express, tin train w/George & family lithoed in windows of engine & cars, 13", EX+ $375.00

Jetsons, see also Hopping Elroy and Hopping Rosie the Robot

Joe Penner & His Duck Goo Goo, 1934, advances w/shuffling feet & tips hat, litho tin, 8½", NM (EX box), A.....$900.00

Joe Penner & His Duck Goo Goo, 1934, 8", EX, A........$425.00

Joy Rider, 1930, advances in erratic motion as driver's head spins, litho tin, 7½", EX, A $450.00

Jumpin' Jeep, 1939, advances in erratic motion, litho tin, 6", NM (EX box), A $400.00

Jumpin' Jeep, 1939, 6", EX...$150.00

King Racer, 1925, w/driver, litho tin, 9¼", G, A............$500.00

Knockout Champs, 2 boy boxers on revolving disk in boxing ring, celluloid & litho tin, 7x7", NMIB...................$700.00

Limping Lizzie, advances in swaying motion w/rattling sound, litho tin, 7", VG (EX box) $450.00

Little Orphan Annie Skipping Rope, 1930s, litho tin, 6", EX..$600.00

Little Orphan Annie's Dog Sandy, dog w/suitcase in mouth, litho tin, 5½", EX (box missing side flaps), A $500.00

Lizzie of the Valley Jalopy, blk litho tin w/allover wht lettering, 7", VG, A...$275.00

Machine Gun & Soldier, 1920s, soldier turns crank & gun fires sparks, litho tin, 5½", NM (EX box), A $400.00

Mack Dump Truck, 1930, mk Coke & Coal, City Coal Co, bl & silver w/gr hubs, tin, 13", NM (G box), A............$1,150.00

Magic Car & Garage (Dick Tracy version), 1950, litho tin, friction, 10", rare, M (EX box) $400.00

Magic Garage & Car, garage door flies open upon impact of car, litho tin, 10" garage, VG $150.00

Mammy's Boy, ca 1925, Black man w/cane sways as eyes shift, litho tin, 11", EX, A $600.00

Mary Poppins, 1964, whirls around, plastic, 8", NM (EX box), M8..$225.00

Merry Makers, 1930, 9½", EX, $1,100.00.

Merry Makers, 1930, 3 mice band members w/band leader atop piano, w/marquee, 9½", NM (EX box).................$1,350.00

Mickey Mouse, see also Whirling Tail Mickey Mouse

Mickey Mouse & Donald Duck Handcar, 1950s, Mickey & Donald navigate track, litho tin & plastic, 22" base, EX (VG box)..$600.00

Mickey Mouse Dipsy Car, 1949, head bobs while crazy car advances, litho tin w/plastic figure, 6", MIB, from $700 to $800.00

Mickey Mouse Express, 1950s, Mickey flies above track w/Disneyville station in center, tin, 9" dia, NMIB, from $900 to $1,000.00

Mickey the Driver, 1948, advances & turns around, litho tin w/plastic figure, 6½", NM (EX box), A $725.00

Mickey the Musician, 1950s, Mickey plays xylophone on sq tin base, 12", EXIB..$350.00

Midget Climbing Fighting Tank, 1920s, advances w/sparks & sound, litho tin, 5", scarce, NM (EX box), A $225.00

Milton Berle Car, tractor-type vehicle w/figure advances in erratic motion, litho tin, 6", NM (EX box) $575.00

Monarch of the Sky, 1930, advances w/spinning prop, tin (no graphics), friction, 6", scarce, NM (EX box), A $525.00

Moon Mullins & Kayo Handcar, 1930s, flat litho tin figures work handlebars, 6", NM (NM box), A $1,225.00

Moon Mullins & Kayo Handcar, 1930s, flat litho tin figures work handlebars, 6", w/7 pcs of track, VG, A $400.00

Mortimer Snerd, 1939, sways as hat bounces up & down, litho tin, 8½", NM $450.00

Mortimer Snerd, 1939, 8½", VG, A $325.00

Mortimer Snerd Tricky Auto, 1939, advances w/erratic motion, head swivels in complete circle, 7", EX, A...............$500.00

Mortimer Snerd's Hometown Band, Mortimer w/lg bass drum, red, wht & bl litho tin, 8½", VG, A $850.00

Motorcycle Delivery, 1935, mk Speed Boy, driver on cycle pulling wagon, litho tin, 10", VG, A $350.00

Mountain Climber, futuristic bus travels along track & up mountain, litho tin, 33" base, NM (VG box), A.....$125.00

Moving Van, mk Am Trucking Co #65, friction, 5", VG, A...$325.00

Mysterious Pluto, 1939, press tail for action, litho tin, 9", NM (EX box), A $650.00

Mystic Motorcycle, 1930s, non-fall action, w/driver, litho tin, 4", NM (VG box), A $250.00

New York Honeymoon Express, 1928, train travels track as plane flies above base w/skyscrapers, tin, 9" dia base, NMIB $1,000.00

Old Jalopy, litho tin, 7", EX, S10 ....$200.00

Old Mother Goose, 1930, lithographed tin, 9", NM (VG rare box), A, $1,925.00.

PD Police Cycle, 1930s, litho tin w/wood wheels, 3¾", NM, A .$325.00

Pebbles on Dino, advances as Pebbles bounces up & down, plastic, friction, 4", rare, NM, A $1,850.00

Pecos Bill Ridin' Widowmaker, WDP, 1950s, vibrates around as cowboy spins lasso, plastic, 10", NM (EX box), A...$300.00

Penny the Poodle, NMIB, T1 ....$65.00

Pinocchio, see Walking Pinocchio

Pluto, see also Mysterious Pluto, Rollover Pluto and Wise Pluto

Pluto the Drum Major, 1940s, rocks & shakes bell, litho tin w/rubbers ears & tail, 6½", NM (EX box), A $575.00

Pluto the Drum Major, 1940s, 6½", NM $275.00

Pluto Twirling Tail, advances in vibrating motion w/twirling tail, plastic w/metal tail, 6x6", EX (EX box), A.......$225.00

Police Motorcycle, early orange version w/driver in bl uniform, 8", litho tin, VG, A $300.00

Police Tip-Over Motorcycle, 1933, travels in circle, tips over & gets up, 8", EX, A $400.00

Popeye, see also Walking Popeye

Popeye & Olive Oyl Jiggers, 1934, Olive Oyl plays accordion & sways while Popeye dances on roof, 10", NMIB, A .$1,700.00

Popeye & Olive Oyl Jiggers, 1934, 10", VG, A $950.00

Popeye Express, 1935, train travels under bridges as Popeye circles in plane overhead, EX (EX box), from $1,750 to ...$1,850.00

Popeye the Champ, lithographed tin with celluloid figures, 7x7", NMIB, $3,000.00; Popeye the Pilot (Popeye Eccentric Airplane), 1930s, lithographed tin, 7", NMIB, $1,800.00.

Popeye Express, 1935, 9½" dia, VG $1,000.00

Popeye Express w/Parrot, parrot pops out of crate & wheelbarrow pushed by Popeye, 8½", EX, from $650 to $750.00

Popeye Handcar, Olive Oyl standing & Popeye sitting on spinach crate, tin w/rubber figures, 7", EX (VG box) $525.00

Popeye the Champ, 7x7" ring, EX $1,500.00

Popeye the Pilot (Popeye Eccentric Airplane), 1930s, 7", EX, A $900.00

Porky Pig, 1939, Porky dressed as cowboy twirls lasso & vibrates around, litho tin, NM (EX rare box), A $1,150.00

Racer #1, w/driver, litho tin w/balloon tires, 6", EX+, A ..$125.00

Racer #12, w/driver & passenger, litho tin, 17", scarce, EX, A $300.00

Racer #3, w/driver, litho tin w/balloon tires, 5", NM, A ...$200.00

Racer #5, w/driver, litho tin w/balloon tires, 5", EX, A ..$225.00

Range Rider, 1938, Lone Ranger on Silver swings lasso on rocking base, litho tin, M (EX box), A $1,225.00

Red Cap Porter, 1930, Black man w/toothy grin & fast moving legs carrying 2 bags, litho tin, 8", VG, from $650 to..$750.00

Red the Iceman, 1930s, litho tin, complete w/ice tongs & wooden block of ice, 8½", scarce, NM (VG box)................$3,400.00

Reversible Coupe, 1936, bump-&-go action, red tin w/aluminum plating, 16", VG, A $425.00

Rex Mars Space Tank, mk Planet Patrol, w/pop-up soldier, litho tin, 10", NM, A $250.00

Ring-A-Ling Circus, 1925, ringmaster w/elephant & monkey on gr base, several actions, litho tin, 7" dia, EX.........$1,750.00

Ring-A-Ling Circus, 1925, lithographed tin, pink base, 7" dia, scarce, EX, $2,000.00.

Rocket Fighter, advances w/sound, litho tin w/pilot in open cockpit, 12", VG, A $275.00

Rocket Racer, futuristic vehicle w/driver, litho tin, 16½", not working o/w NM, A..$400.00

Rollover Figaro, 1941, litho tin, EX, M8 ....$250.00

Rollover Plane, 1939, advances & flips over, litho tin, 6" wingspan, EX (EX box), A $600.00

Rollover Plane, 1939, 6" wingspan, VG+, A $225.00

Rollover Pluto, 1939, Pluto advances & rolls over, litho tin, 9",
NM (EX box), A $500.00

Rollover Pluto, 1939, 9", EX $300.00

Rookie Pilot, 1940, advances in erratic motion, red & yel litho
tin, 7", EX+, A...$550.00

Rookie Pilot, 1940, 7", G, A $250.00

Royal Bus Lines, red & yel w/blk tires, 10", MIB, A $750.00

Royal Van Co Delivery Truck, w/driver, litho tin, 9½", EX,
A $500.00

Running Scottie, 1939, mk Wee Scottie, advances as front legs
move, litho tin, 5", NM (M box), A $200.00

Sam the City Gardener, 1940, dapper man pulling wheelbarrow,
plastic & litho tin, 8", EXIB, A..............................$200.00

Sand & Gravel Truck, red & bl, 11", EX, A $475.00

Scottie the Guid-A-Dog, 1930s, advances w/guided leash control, 10", EX (VG box), A....................................$265.00

Sheriff Sam Whoopee Car, advances w/crazy action, tin & plastic, 6", M (worn box), A..$200.00

Skybird Flyer, 2 airplanes circle tower, litho tin, 9", EX (VG
box), A...$400.00

Smokey Joe the Climbing Fireman, 1930s, fireman climbs ladder
attached to base, 11½", EX (EX box), from $350 to.$375.00

Snoopy Gus Wild Fireman, 1927, travels in erratic motion as
fireman spins on ladder, litho tin, 8", rare, NM (EX box),
A $2,750.00

Somstepa, 1926, Black man performs jig on stage, litho tin, 8",
EX $650.00

Sonic Jet Plane, advances w/sparks & revolving rotors, plastic,
friction, 15", NM (EX box), A $200.00

Sparkling Climbing Tractor, 1950, litho tin w/blk rubber treads, plastic driver, 8", needs new flint o/w NM (EX box), A.......$200.00

Sparkling Soldier Motorcycle, 1930s, advances w/sparks, camouflage cycle w/driver, litho tin, 8", EX (EX box), A ..$400.00

Sparkling Super Power Combat Tank, 1950s, advances as cannon
moves, litho tin, needs new flint o/w NM (EX box), A .$250.00

Sparkling Tank No 3, 1930s, advances as dbl-guns fire sparks,
litho tin, 8", NM (G box), A $275.00

Spic & Span, 1924, 2 Black minstrels on stage mk The Hams
What Am, litho tin, 10½", EX, A $1,650.00

Stake Truck, mk Merchants Transfer on side, litho tin, 10½",
EX, A $500.00

Steam Roller, red & blk litho tin w/flat figure, 8½", EX+, A..$250.00

Streamlined Speedway, 1930s, w/figure-8 track & 3 autos, EX (G
box)..$350.00

Superman Rollover Plane, 1940, advances as Superman causes plane
to roll over, tin, 5", NM (EX box), from $2,500 to $2,750.00

Thor (Marvel Super-Heroes), 1968, figure rolls across floor in
various patterns, mc plastic, 4", NMIB, A $125.00

Tom Corbett Space Cadet Rocket Ship, 1930s, advances
w/sparks & sound, litho tin, 12", EX $600.00

Toyland Milk Wagon, horse-drawn wagon w/disk wheels, 10½",
MIB...$450.00

Tractor, 1939, advances w/sound, litho tin w/driver, 5½", M (EX
box), A..$175.00

Tractor-Trailer Set, 1940, farmer on tractor pulls Marbrook
trailer, litho tin, 21", NM (G box), A......................$300.00

Trans Atlantic Zeppelin, 1930, advances in circular motion, tin
(no graphics), 10", NM (EX box), A $525.00

Tricky Motorcycle, 1930s, mystery action, litho tin, 4¼", MIB,
A $300.00

Tricky Taxi, 1940, travels to end of table & turns around, litho
tin, 5", scarce, NM (EX box), from $300 to.............$350.00

Trumpton Climbing Fireman, European-style fireman climbs
ladder, plastic, 9", NM (NM box), A.......................$250.00

Tumbling Monkey, 1942, circus monkey flips between 2 chairs,
litho tin, 6", NM (EX box), A..................................$300.00

Turnover Military Tank, soldier on underside forces tank to turn
over, litho tin, 4", EX (VG box) $200.00

Uncle Wiggily Car, 1935, travels w/crazy action as Uncle Wiggily's
head turns, litho tin w/Easter motif, 8", EX, A $1,000.00

US Army Command Car, litho tin, friction w/battery-op lights
& siren, 19", EX (VG box).....................................$350.00

US Army Fighter Plane, (non-sparking version), dbl guns on ea
wing, tin w/balloon tires, 7", EX.............................$175.00

US Army Fighter Plane, (sparking version), dbl guns on ea wing,
tin w/balloon tires, 7", EX $225.00

Wacky Taxi #77, litho tin w/driver & passengers in windows,
friction, 7", NM, A $150.00

Walking Astronaut, VG, T1...................................$45.00

Walking Pinocchio, WDE, 1939, moving eyes, litho tin,
MIB...$750.00

Walking Pinocchio, WDE, 1939, stationary eyes, litho tin,
MIB...$600.00

Walking Popeye, King Features, 1935, carries 2 cages w/lithoed
parrots, 8½", NM (G box), A $785.00

Walking Popeye, King Features, 1935, 8½", EX, from $450
to..$500.00

Walking Tiger, advances w/several actions & roars, plush & celluloid, 8", MIB, A $125.00

Walt Disney's Television Car, litho tin, friction, 7½",
EX $450.00

Whirling Tail Mickey Mouse, tail spins when activated, plastic,
7", NMIB $300.00

Winnie the Pooh, plastic, VG, T1 ....$100.00

Wise Pluto, 1939, advances w/non-fall action & simulates sniffing,
litho tin w/rubber ears & tail, 8", EX (VG box), A.......$350.00

Photo courtesy Jacquie and Bob Henry.

Whoopee Cowboy, 1932, lithographed tin, EX, $400.00.

WWI Tank, 1930, flag version, advances as soldier & flag pop out, litho tin, 9", scarce, EX+, A..............................$250.00

MISCELLANEOUS

Army Transport Truck, litho tin w/canvas top, complete w/soldiers & cannon, 13", NM (VG box), A....................$225.00

Blue Bird Garage, litho tin, 12x6½", EX, A $350.00

Brightlite Filling Station, 1940s, litho tin, 9", EXIB, A..$1,650.00

Bungalow w/Garage & Car, litho tin, 17x11", EXIB, A.$750.00

Bus Terminal, litho tin, complete, 12x6½", EX, A $325.00

Day & Night Service Station, litho tin, complete, 12", NM, A $440.00

Delivery Truck, red & yel plastic w/opening rear doors, 10", NM (EX box), A $125.00

General Alarm Fire House, litho tin, clockwork ejects vehicles, complete, 17x11", EX+, A $550.00

Glenside Depot, battery-op lights & gate, 13½x10", EX, A ..$225.00

Grand Central Station, litho tin, battery-op lights, 17x11", EX+, A $475.00

Greyhound Bus Station, litho tin, 17x11", EX, A $400.00

Hometown Fire House, #186, 1930, litho tin, EX+ (EX box), A $155.00

Hometown Meat Market, #181, 1930, litho tin, complete, EX (VG box), A $245.00

Hometown Police Station, #185, 1930, litho tin, complete, rare, MIB, A..$425.00

Hometown Your Favorite Store (FW Woolworth), #182, 1930, EX+ (VG+ box), A $125.00

Lincoln Highway, 1930s, complete, rare, MIB, A $2,400.00

Magic Garage, 1935, litho-tin garage w/pressed-steel Airflow car, 4x6½x8", VG (G box), A $350.00

Mammoth Zeppelin, tin, clicker in wheel assembly, 27½", G, A...$275.00

Motor Delivery Market Truck, red & bl tin & plastic, complete w/cb food boxes, 15", M (M box), H12....................$265.00

Roadside Rest Service Station, litho tin, complete, 14x10", MIB, A..$2,975.00

Roadside Rest Service Station, litho tin, incomplete, 14x10", EX, A $700.00

Sign, Caution High Speed Trains, wht sign w/red lettering on blk post, 7½", MIB, A $50.00

Sunny Side Service Station, 1930s, litho tin, complete, 13½x10", M, A...$935.00

Telephone Truck, 1950s, red, bl & yel plastic, complete w/side ladders & poles, 10", NM (EX box), A $150.00

Matchbox

The Matchbox series of English and American-made autos, trucks, taxis, Pepsi-Cola trucks, steamrollers, Greyhound buses, etc., was very extensive. By the late 1970s, the company was cranking out more than five million cars every week, and while those days may be over, Matchbox still produces about seventy-five million vehicles on a yearly basis.

Introduced in 1953, the Matchbox Miniatures series has always been the mainstay of the company. There were seventy-five models in all but with enough variations to make collecting them a real challenge. Larger, more detailed models were introduced in 1957; this series, called Major Pack, was replaced a few years later by a similar line called King Size. To compete with Hot Wheels, Matchbox converted most models over to a line called SuperFast that sported thinner, low-friction axles and wheels. (These are much more readily available than the original 'regular wheels,' the last of which were made in 1969.) At about the same time, the King Size series became known as Speed Kings; in 1977 the line was reintroduced under the name Super Kings.

In the early '70s, Lesney started to put dates on the baseplates of their toy cars. The name 'Lesney' was coined from the first names of the company's founders. The last Matchboxes that carried the Lesney mark were made in 1982. Today many models can be bought for less than $10.00, though a few are priced much higher.

In 1988, to celebrate the company's 40th anniversary, Matchbox issued a limited set of five models that except for minor variations were exact replicas of the originals. These five were repackaged in 1991 and sold under the name Matchbox Originals. In 1993 a second series expanded the line of reproductions.

Another line that's become very popular is their Models of Yesteryear. These are slightly larger replicas of antique and vintage vehicles. Values of $20.00 to $60.00 for mint-in-box examples are average, though a few sell for even more.

Sky Busters are small-scale aircraft measuring an average of 3½" in length. They were introduced in 1973. Models currently being produced sell for about $4.00 each.

To learn more, we recommend *Matchbox Toys, 1948 to 1993*, and *Matchbox Toys, 1947-1996*, by Dana Johnson; and a series of books by Charlie Mack: *Lesney's Matchbox Toys* (there are two: *Regular Wheel Years* and *Super Fast Years*) and *Universal Years*.

To determine values of examples in conditions other than given in our listings, based on MIB or MOC prices, deduct a minimum of 10% if the original container is missing, 30% if the condition is excellent, and as much as 70% for a toy graded only very good. In the following listings, we have added zeroes ahead of the numbers to avoid the idiosyncrasies of computer sorting.

Advisors: Mark Giles (G2) 1-75 Series; Dan Wells (W1) King Size, Speed Kings, and Super Kings; Matchbox Originals; Models of Yesteryear; Skybusters.

Other Sources: C18, N3

Key:
LW — Laser Wheels (introduced in 1987)
reg — regular wheels (Matchbox Miniatures)
SF — SuperFast

1-75 SERIES

II, Sleet-N-Snow, SF, bl, wht base/top, silver hubs, US Mail tampo, M, W1...$9.00

IX, Flamin' Manta, SF, yel, M (top of card cut off), W1.....$7.00

VI, Lady Bug, SF, blk, purple windows, yel interior, flame/beetle tampo, EX...$7.00

01-A, Diesel Road Roller, reg, dk gr, 1953, NM, W1.......$43.00

01-C, Road Roller, reg, driver rpt to look more lifelike, 1958, partial pnt fading o/w NM, W1 ....$37.50

01-D, Aveling Barford Road Roller, reg, 1962, NM+, W1 ..$18.00

Photo courtesy Dana Johnson.

01-I, Revin' Rebel Dodge Challenger, red, white, and blue, 1982, M, $6.00.

02-A, Dumper, reg, rare gr metal wheels, missing driver, VG................................$30.00

02-C, Muir Hill Dumper, reg, blk wheels, Laing decal, 1961, M $16.00

02-D, Mercedes Trailer, reg, blk wheels, orange canopy, 1968, M (VG+ box), W1 ....$8.00

02-F, Jeep Hot Rod, SF, pk, lt gr base, cream interior, spoke wheels, 1971, missing exhaust pipe o/w EX+ $5.00

03-B, Bedford Tipper, reg, blk wheels, red dumper, 1961, M (NM+ box) $22.00

03-C, Mercedes Ambulance, reg, blk wheels, labels, orig patient, 1968, M (EX box).....................$14.00

03-F, Porsche Turbo, SF, brn, cream interior, blk base, 1978, M (EX box), W1.................................$7.00

04-A, Massey Harris Tractor, reg, metal wheels, rear fenders, 1954, broken tow hook o/w EX, W1 ....$23.00

04-C, Triumph Motorcycle & Sidecar, reg, blk wheels, 1960, NM+, W1 ....$39.00

04-D, Dodge Stake Truck, reg, blk wheels, gr stakes, 1967, M (EX+ box), W1 ....$12.00

04-F, Gruesome Twosome, SF, gold, unpnt base, purple windshield, cream interior, 1971, M $13.00

05-A, London Bus, reg, metal wheels, 1954, NM, W1 .....$51.00

05-B, London Bus, reg, gray wheels, Buy Matchbox Series decals, 1957, EX, W1....................................$35.00

05-C, London Bus, reg, blk wheels, Visco Static, 1961, EX+...$20.00

05-D, London Bus, reg, blk wheels, Longlife decals, 1965, M, W1 ....$13.00

05-E, Lotus Europa, SF, pk, unpnt base, 1969, MBP, W1.$12.00

06-B, Quarry Truck, reg, blk wheels, 1957, NM+, W1.....$40.00

06-C, Euclid Quarry Truck, reg, blk wheels, solid tires, 1964, M, W1 ....$19.00

06-D, Ford Pickup Truck, reg, blk wheels, wht grille, 1968, M (EX box) $17.00

06-F, Mercedes 350SL, SF, yel, 1973, M (VG- box), W1.$11.00

07-A, Milk Float, reg, metal wheels, wht letters/driver/bottles, 1954, NM..$70.00

07-B, Ford Anglia, reg, blk wheels, 1961, M.....................$18.00

07-C, Ford Refuse Truck, reg, blk wheels, straight side pipes, 1966, M, W1 ....$10.00

07-E, Hairy Hustler, SF, bronze, blk base, amber windshield, #5 labels, 1971, NMIB..................................$17.00

08-C, Caterpillar Tractor, reg, scarce silver plastic rollers, orig treads, yel, 1961, NM..............................$70.00

08-E, Ford Mustang, reg, blk wheels, wht, 1966, NM+.....$15.00

08-F, Ford Mustang, SF, orange, ivory interior, 1970, EX+..$33.00

09-C, Merryweather Marquis Fire Engine, reg, blk wheels, tan ladder, 1959, NM, W1...................................$22.00

09-D, Boat & Trailer, reg, blk wheels, 1966, NM+, W1 ..$10.00-

10-B, Mechanical Horse & Trailer, reg, gray wheels, 1958, VG..$18.00

10-C, Sugar Container Truck, reg, blk wheels, no crown decal, 1961, EX+, W1 ....$28.00

10-D, Pipe Truck, reg, blk wheels, silver grille, 7 orig pipes on tree, 1966, M (NM+ box) $14.00

11-C, Jumbo Crane, reg, blk wheels, yel weight box, 1965, M (NM box), W1.......................................$17.00

11-D, Scaffolding Truck, reg, blk wheels, complete, 1969, M (VG+ box)..$13.00

11-F, Flying Bug, SF, metallic red, unpnt base, gray windows, heart label, 5-spoke wheels, 1972, NM $18.00

12-A, Land Rover, reg, metal wheels, missing driver, 1955, EX, W1 ....$18.00

12-B, Land Rover, reg, blk wheels, 1959, M $21.00

12-C, Safari Land Rover, reg, blk wheels, gr, brn luggage, 1965, M, W1 ....$16.00

12-D, Safari Land Rover, SF, gold, tan luggage, 1970, NM+ .$22.00

12-E, Setra Coach, SF, burgundy, wht roof, gr window, 1970, MBP (partially loose), W1...............................$14.00

12-H, Pontiac Firebird, SF, red, tan interior, clear window, arch wheels, 1982, MBP, W1.................................$7.00

13-D, Dodge BP Wreck Truck, yel cab, gr bed, blk wheels, 1965, MIB $20.00

14-A, Daimler Ambulance, reg, metal wheels, no-cross version, 1956, VG+, W1 ....$14.00

14-B, Daimler Ambulance, reg, metal wheels, no-cross version, 1958, EX+, W1 ....$22.00

14-C, Bedford Ambulance, reg, blk wheels, 1962, M $19.00

14-D, Iso Grifo, reg, blk wheels, 1968, M..........................$8.00

14-E, Iso Grifo, SF, bl, unpnt base, bl interior, 5-spoke wheels, 1969, EX+ $14.00

14-F, Mini Ha Ha, SF, red, lt pk driver, brn helmet, 4 labels, Maltese cross front wheels, 1975, M...........................$13.00

15-A, Prime Mover, reg, metal wheels, orange, 1956, M, W1 ....$35.00

15-B, Atlantic Prime Mover, reg, blk wheels, 1959, M (EX box) $29.00

15-C, Tippax Refuse Truck, reg, blk wheels, peep holes, decals, 1963, M..$18.00

15-F, Fork Lift Truck, SF, red, blk steering wheel, yel hoist, gray forks, Lansing labels, 1972, NM+.................$10.00

16-A, Atlantic Trailer, reg, metal wheels, 1956, NM+ $34.00

16-B, Atlantic Trailer, reg, blk wheels, orange, blk tow bar, 1957, M..$20.00

16-C, Scammell Mountaineer Snow Plow, reg, blk wheels, orange/wht decal, 1964, NM+.....................$28.00

16-D, Case Bulldozer, reg, complete, 1969, M (NM box)...$18.00

17-A, Bedford Removals Van, reg, metal wheels, gr, solid letters, 1956, VG+ $31.00

17-C, Austin Taxi, reg, gray wheels, complete, 1960, EX+.$35.00

17-D, Hoveringham Tipper, reg, blk wheels, red base, 1963, M (EX+) $15.00

17-E, Horse Box, reg, blk wheels, complete, 1969, M (EX box)..$8.00

17-E, Horse Box, SF, red, no horses, 1970, M (NM+ box), W1 ....$23.00

17-F, Londoner Bus, SF, silver, chartreuse base, Silver Jubilee labels, 1972, MBP (few wrinkles), W1 ....$15.00

18-C, Caterpillar Bulldozer, reg, metal rollers, orig tread, 1961, M..$32.00

18-D, CAT D8 Bulldozer, reg, blk plastic rollers, orig treads (1 broken), 1964, NM+ $16.00

18-E, Field Car, reg, blk wheels, unpnt base, red hubs, orig top, 1969, M (EX+ box) $13.00

18-F, Field Car, SF, yel, red-brn roof, unpnt base, no labels, 5-spoke wheels, 1970, NM+ $14.00

19-B, MGA Sports Car, reg, metal wheels, missing driver, 1958, NM...$52.50

19-C, Aston Martin Racing Car, reg, blk wheels, gray driver, #19 decal, 1961, NM+..$30.00

19-D, Lotus Racing Car, reg, blk wheels, scarce orange, labels, 1966, M..$30.00

19-F, Road Dragster, SF, red-orange, #8 labels, 1970, NM..$14.00

20-A, Stake Truck, reg, metal wheels, silver grille & tanks, 1956, VG+ $12.00

20-C, Chevrolet Impala Taxi, reg, blk wheels, orange, ivory interior, decal, unpnt base, 1965, M (EX+ box), W1........$24.00

Photo courtesy Dana Johnson.

20-D, Lamborghini Marzal, SuperFast, red, 1969, M, $12.00.

21-B, Long Distance Coach, reg, metal wheels, missing decals, 1958, M, W1...$42.00

21-C, Commer Milk Float, reg, blk wheels, gr windows, cow decals, 1961, M (NM+ box), W1 ....$29.00

21-D, Foden Concrete Truck, reg, blk wheels, 1968, NM+ ..$11.00

22-C, Pontiac Grand Prix Sports Coupe, reg, blk wheels, 1964, M..$17.00

22-E, Freeman Intercity Commuter, SF, metallic magenta, unpnt base, ivory interior, w/labels, 1970, NM+ $16.00

23-B, Berkely Cavalier Trailer, reg, metal wheels, pale bl, #23 cast, bit of red pnt on base, 1958, EX, W1 ....$24.00

23-C, Bluebird Dauphine Trailer, reg, silver wheels, tan, 1960, NM+ $52.00

23-D, House Trailer Caravan, reg, blk wheels, pk, 1965, M, W1 ....$17.00

24-A, Weatherhill Hydraulic Excavator, red, metal wheels, yel, 1956, NM+, W1 ....$43.00

24-B, Weatherhill Hydraulic Excavator, red, blk wheels, 1959, M...$32.00

24-C, Rolls Royce Silver Shadow, reg, blk wheels, 1967, M, W1 ....$12.00

24-E, Team Matchbox, SF, scarce gr, wht driver, Maltese cross rear wheels, no trailer, 1973, NM.........................$42.00

24-F, Shunter, SF, gr, red undercarriage/base, tan panel, Rail Freight label, 1978, M (NM+ box) $10.00

25-A, Dunlop Van, reg, metal wheels, decals 100%, 1956, M, W1 ....$59.00

25-C, BP Petrol Tanker, reg, blk wheels, gr, complete, 1964, M (EX box), W1 ....$25.00

25-D, Ford Cortina, reg, blk wheels, no-rack version, 1968, M (EX+ box) $12.00

26-A, Concrete Truck, reg, metal wheels, silver grille, 1956, NM+ $48.00

26-C, GMC Tipper Truck, reg, blk wheels, 1968, M (EX+ box), W1 ....$15.00

27-C, Cadillac Sixty Special, reg, silver wheels, lilac, pk roof, red base, 1960, missing tip of axle o/w EX+ $33.00

27-D, Mercedes 230SL, reg, blk wheels, 1966, M, W1 .....$15.00

28-B, Thames Compressor Truck, reg, blk wheels, 1959, EX+...$31.00

28-D, Mack Dump Truck, reg, blk wheels, red hubs, 1968, M (NM+ box) $16.00

28-G, Lincoln Continental Mk V, SF, red, unpnt base, tan interior, wht roof, 1979, NM, W1...............................$6.00

29-A, Bedford Milk Delivery Van, reg, metal wheels, 1956, NM+, W1 ....$44.00

29-B, Austin A55 Cambridge Sedan, reg, silver wheels, 1961, NM...$29.00

29-C, Fire Pumper, reg, blk wheels, Denver decals, 1966, M, W1 ....$15.00

30-A, Ford Perfect, reg, metal wheels, 1956, M, W1 ....$49.00

30-B, Magirux-Deutz 6-Wheel Crane, reg, blk wheels, silver, orange boom, gray plastic hook, 1961, NM $36.00

30-C, 8-Wheel Crane Truck, reg, blk wheels, yel hook, 1965, M (EX box), W1 ....$10.00

30-E, Beach Buggy, SF, lavender, 1970, EX+....................$11.00

31-A, Ford Station Wagon, reg, metal wheels, yel, no-window version, 1957, NM+..$46.00

31-B, Ford Fairlane Station Wagon, reg, silver wheels, gr, pk roof, red base, gr windows, 1960, NM+.....................$45.00

31-C, Lincoln Continental, reg, blk wheels, aqua, 1964, M..$12.00

31-D, Lincoln Continental, SF, gr-gold, 1970, NM+, W1..**$26.00**

32-A, Jaguar XK140, reg, metal wheels, cream, 1957, EX+..**$46.00**

32-B, E-Type Jaguar, reg, blk wheels, clear windows, wire wheels, 1962, NM **$22.00**

32-C, Leyland Petrol Tanker, reg, blk wheels, gr, silver grille, labels, 1968, NM+, W1 ....**$10.00**

32-E, Maserati Bora, SF, burgundy, dk gr base, #8 labels, no tow hook, 1972, M (NM card) **$12.00**

33-A, Ford Zodiac Mk II Sedan, reg, metal wheels, dk gr, no-window version, 1957, NM+, W1 ....**$42.00**

33-B, Ford Zephyr Mk III, reg, blk wheels, aqua, 1963, M (NM box) **$18.00**

33-C, Lamborghini Miura, reg, blk wheels, yel, red interior, 1969, M (NM box) **$12.00**

33-D, Lamborghini Miura, SF, gold, unpnt base, ivory interior, 1969, M, W1 ....**$14.00**

33-F, Police Motorcycle, SF, blk, wht seat, lt bl driver, silver motor, mag wheels, LAPD labels, 1977, MBP, W1......**$7.00**

34-C, VW Camper, reg, blk wheels, silver, raised roof, 1967, M..**$22.00**

35-A, Marshall Horse Box, reg, metal wheels, 1957, missing ramp, G+, W1 ....**$12.00**

35-B, Snowtrac Tractor, reg, cast letters, orig tread, 1964, M **$13.00**

35-C, Merryweather Fire Engine, SF, red, gray base, 2 clips, 5-spoke wheels, 1969, MBP **$15.00**

35-D, Fandango, SF, red, unpnt base, clear windows, ivory interior, bl prop, #35 label, 1975, NM+ **$10.00**

36-A, Austin A50, reg, gold wheels, 1957, M, W1 ....**$39.00**

36-B, Lambretta Scooter & Sidecar, reg, blk wheels, 1961, EX .**$37.00**

36-C, Opel Diplomat, reg, blk wheels, gold/silver motor, 1966, M (EX+ box), W1 ....**$15.00**

36-E, Hot Rod Draguar, metallic red, unpnt base, ivory interior, trunk label, 1970, NM **$16.00**

37-A, Coca-Cola Lorry, reg, metal wheels, no base, sm letters, even load, 1956, VG+, W1 ....**$26.00**

37-B, Coca-Cola Lorry, reg, blk wheels, w/base, sm letters, even load, 1960, NM..**$54.00**

37-C, Dodge Cattle Truck, reg, blk wheels, metal base, orig cattle on tree, 1966, M (NM+ box) **$8.00**

37-E, Cattle Truck, SF, orange, orig cattle on tree, 1970, M, W1 ....**$16.00**

37-F, Soopa Coopa, SF, metallic pk, unpnt base, flower label, Maltese cross wheels, 1972, EX+................................**$11.00**

38-A, Karrier Refuse Collector, reg, metal wheels, gray, 1957, NM, W1 ....**$38.00**

38-B, Vauxhall Victor Estate Car, reg, blk wheels, gr interior, 1963, M, W1 ....**$34.00**

38-C, Honda Motorcycle & Trailer, reg, blk wheels, yel trailer, labels, 1967, NM+ **$11.00**

38-D, Honda Motorcycle & Trailer, SF, bl bike, yel trailer, 5-spoke wheels, 1970, NM..**$13.00**

38-E, Stingeroo Motorcycle, SF, metallic purple, purple handle-bars, 1972, NM+ **$16.00**

38-F, Jeep, SF, olive, blk base, star label, no gun, blk hubs, 1976, NM+ **$15.00**

39-A, Ford Zodiac Convertible, reg, metal wheels, turq interior, 1957, missing tow hook o/w VG+ **$15.00**

39-B, Pontiac Convertible, reg, blk wheels, yel, ivory steering wheel, blk base, 1962, sm windshield crack o/w NM, W1 ....**$30.00**

39-C, Ford Tractor, reg, blk wheels, bl & yel, 1967, M **$16.00**

39-D, Clipper, SF, metallic magenta, gr base, yel interior, amber windshield, silver pipes, 1973, NM+ **$12.00**

40-A, Bedford Tipper Truck, reg, metal wheels, 1957, NM ..**$36.00**

40-B, Leyland Royal Tiger Coach, reg, blk wheels, 1961, M.**$29.00**

40-C, Hay Trailer, reg, blk wheels, orig rails, 1967, M (NM box), W1 ....**$12.00**

40-D, Vauxhall Guildsman, SF, pk, unpnt base, gr window, flames label, 5-spoke wheels, 1971, M......................**$14.00**

41-B, D-Type Jaguar, reg, blk spoked wheels, #41 decals, 1960, NM+ **$38.00**

41-C, Ford GT Race Car, reg, blk wheels, wht, yel hubs, #9 label, 1965, NM+..**$12.00**

41-D, Ford GT, SF, wht, lt gr base, #6 labels, 5-spoke wheels, 1970, MBP **$15.00**

41-E, Siva Spyder, SF, metallic red, no tampo, cream interior, blk strap, 5-spoke wheels, 1972, M............................**$16.00**

41-F, Ambulance, SF, wht, unpnt base, gray interior, EMS labels, 1978, M, W1 ....**$4.00**

42-A, Bedford Evening News, reg, metal wheels, 1957, NM+..**$48.00**

42-B, Studebaker Lark Wagon, reg, blk wheels, orig hunter/dog, 1965, NM+, W1 ....**$18.00**

42-C, Iron Fairy Crane, reg, blk wheels, 1969, M **$14.00**

42-E, Tyre Fryer, SF, metallic bl, blk base, yel interior, no labels, 5-spoke wheels, 1972, NM+ **$15.00**

43-A, Hillman Minx, reg, metal wheels, bl-gray, gray roof, 1958, M (NM box), W1 ....**$54.00**

43-B, Aveling Barford Tractor Shovel, reg, blk wheels, yel body/shovel, red driver/base, 1962, NM+ **$28.00**

37-G, Atlas Skip Truck, red and yellow, 1976, M, $12.00.

43-F, Steam Locomotive, 1978, M, $10.00; 44-F, Railway Passenger Car, 1978, M, $10.00.

43-C, Pony Trailer, reg, blk wheels, gr base, orig horses, 1968, M (EX box), W1 ....$12.00

43-D, Pony Trailer, SF, yel, dk gr base, orig horses, 1970, M, W1 ....$17.00

43-E, VW Bug Dragon Wheels, SF, gr, 1972, NM............$17.00

44-A, Rolls Royce Silver Cloud, reg, metal wheels, 1958, M (NM box)............................$39.00

44-C, GMC Refrigerator Truck, reg, blk wheels, 1967, M, W1............................$8.00

45-A, Vauxhall Victor, reg, gray wheels, yel, gr windows, 1958, M............................$40.00

45-B, Ford Corsair, reg, blk wheels, complete, unpnt base, rack/boat on tree, 1965, M, W1 ....$19.00

45-C, Ford Group 6, SF, metallic gr, unpnt base, clear windows, silver motor, rnd #7 label, 1970, M, W1 ....$14.00

46-B, Pickford's Removal Van, reg, blk wheels, gr, 3-line decal, 1960, NM+ $25.00

46-C, Mercedes Benz 300 SE, reg, blk wheels, metallic bl, 1968, M............................$15.00

46-D, Mercedes 300 SE, SF, gold, unpnt base, cast doors, no labels, 5-spoke wheels, 1970, NM+ (NM box), W1 ..$20.00

46-E, Stretcha Fetcha, SF, wht, red base, bl window, Ambulance label, lt yel interior, Maltese cross wheels, 1972, M...$15.00

46-F, Ford Tractor, SF, metallic lime, unpnt base, lt yel interior, yel harrow/hubs, 1978, M $10.00

47-A, 1-Ton Trojan Van, reg, metal wheels, 1958, NM+ ..$45.00

47-B, Commer Ice Cream Canteen, reg, blk wheels, cream, oval roof, plain side decal, 1963, NM+, W1 ....$40.00

47-C, DAF Tipper Truck, reg, blk wheels, silver/yel, lt gray top, 1968, M (NM+ box), W1............................$14.00

47-D, DAF Tipper Truck, SF, silver/yel, 1970, M............$24.00

47-E, Beach Hopper, SF, dk bl, windscreen, pk base, orange interior, tan driver, 1974, M $16.00

48-A, Meteor Sports Boat & Trailer, reg, metal wheels, 1958, NM+ $41.00

48-B, Sports Boat & Trailer, reg, blk wheels, red deck, wht hull, dk bl trailer, gold motor, 1961, M, W1 ....$39.00

48-C, Dodge Dump Truck, reg, blk wheels, full-length base, 1966, M, W1............................$12.00

49-A, M3 Personnel Carrier, reg, blk wheels, blk plastic rollers, new tread, 1958, M $35.00

49-C, Unimog, SF, metallic bl/gr, plain grille, red base, spiro wheels, no label, 1970, M............................$19.00

49-D, Chop Suey, SF, metallic magenta, red handlebars, 1973, M............................$16.00

49-E, Crane Truck, SF, yel, yel boom, gr windows, no labels, 5-arch wheels, 1976, M, W1 ....$5.00

50-A, Commer Pickup Truck, reg, tan, metal wheels, 1958, NM............................$47.00

50-B, John Deere Tractor, reg, blk wheels, 1964, M.........$25.00

50-D, Kennel Truck, SF, metallic gr, gray base, silver grille, orig top/dogs, 1970, NM+............................$12.00

51-A, Albion Chieftain, reg, gray wheels, Blue Circle Portland Cement decals, 1958, M (NM box), W1 ....$54.00

51-B, John Deere Trailer, reg, blk wheels, complete, 1964, M (G+ box)............................$18.00

51-C, 8-Wheel Tipper Truck, reg, blk wheels, orange/silver, Douglas, 1969, M............................$20.00

51-D, 8-Wheel Tipper, SF, yel, silver-gray dump, silver base, Pointer labels, 1970, NM+, W1 ....$17.00

51-E, Citroen SM, SF, bronze, cream interior, unpnt base, no labels, 5-spoke wheels, 1972, NM+ $10.00

52-A, Maserati 4CLT Racer, reg, blk wheels, yel, #52 decal, complete, 1958, NM............................$40.00

52-B, BRM Racing Car, reg, blk wheels, bl, #5 labels, 1965, M (EX box), W1 ....$19.00

53-A, Aston Martin, reg, metal wheels, metallic gr, 1958, NM+, W1 ....$42.00

53-B, Mercedes Benz 220 SE, reg, blk wheels, red, 1963, M............................$24.00

53-C, Ford Zodiac Mk IV, reg, blk wheels, bl, 1968, M (NM+ box), W1............................$16.00

53-D, Ford Zodiac, SF, metallic gr, unpnt base, 1970, M, W1 ....$20.00

53-E, Tanzara, SF, orange, unpnt base, silver interior, bl-gr windows, no tampo, 1972, M $14.00

54-A, Saracen Personnel Carrier, reg, blk wheels, 1958, M, W1 ....$29.00

54-B, S&S Cadillac Ambulance, reg, blk wheels, labels, 1965, M (NM box)............................$20.00

54-C, Cadillac Ambulance, SF, wht, blk base, silver grille, 1970, NM+ $22.00

54-D, Ford Capri, SF, metallic purple, ivory interior, unpnt base, 5-spoke wheels, 1971, M............................$15.00

55-A, DUKW, reg, metal wheels, 1958, NM+............$32.00

55-B, Ford Fairlane Police Car, reg, blk wheels, metallic bl, poor decals, 1963, EX, W1............................$22.00

55-C, Ford Galaxie Police Car, reg, blk wheels, decals, red dome, 1966, NM............................$17.00

55-D, Mercury Police Car, reg, blk wheels, bl dome light, NM+ $9.00

55-E, Mercury Police Car, SF, wht, bl dome light, 1970, NMIB............................$14.00

55-G, Hellraiser, SF, wht, unpnt base, red interior, clear windows, stars/stripes label, 1975, NM............................$14.00

55-H, Ford Cortina, SF, beige, London Holiday Sweepstakes card, 1979, MBP, W1............................$7.00

56-A, London Trolley Bus, reg, blk wheels, red poles, decals 95%, 1958, NM $49.00

56-B, Fiat 1500 Sedan, reg, blk wheels, aqua, brn luggage, 1965, M (NM+ box), W1............................$15.00

56-C, BMC 1800 Pininfarina, SF, gold, no labels, 1969, M (NM box)............................$18.00

57-A, Wolseley 1500, reg, gray wheels, pale gr, silver grille, 1958, M............................$37.00

57-B, Chevrolet Impala, reg, blk wheels, blk base, 1961, M...$29.00

57-C, Land Rover Fire Truck, reg, blk wheels, decals, orig ladder, 1966, M............................$13.00

58-B, Drott Excavator, reg, orange, blk plastic rollers, orig tread, 1962, M............................$38.00

58-C, DAF Girder Truck, reg, blk wheels, complete, girders on tree, 1968, M (NM+ box), W1............................$17.00

58-E, Whoosh 'N Push, SF, yel, red interior, #2 label, Maltese cross wheels, 1972, M (EX box) $13.00

59-A, Ford Thames Singer Van, reg, gray wheels, rare Kelly gr, 1958, EX+............................$85.00

59-B, Ford Fairlane Fire Chief Car, reg, blk wheels, 1963, EX, W1 ....$22.00

59-C, Ford Galaxie Fire Chief Car, reg, blk wheels, decals, 1966, M, W1 ....$20.00

59-F, Planet Scout, SF, metallic gr, lime chassis, amber windows, 1975, MBP $15.00

59-G, Porsche 959, SF, metallic tan, charcoal base, brn interior, orange windows, no tampo, 1980, M $8.00

60-A, Morris J-2 Pickup, reg, blk wheels, red/wht decals, no window, 1958, M (EX+ box) $42.00

60-B, Site Hut Truck, reg, blk wheels, 1966, M (EX box) ..$19.00

60-D, Lotus Super Seven, SF, orange, flame label, 1971, missing steering wheel o/w EX $14.00

61-A, Ferret Scout Car, reg, blk wheels, 1959, NM+ $27.00

61-B, Alvis Stalwart, reg, blk wheels, gr hubs, labels, 1966, M (NM box) $15.00

61-C, Blue Shark, SF, dk bl, clear window, unpnt base, #86 label, 1971, EX+ $10.00

62-A, General Service Lorry, reg, blk wheels, 1959, M, W1 ....$49.00

62-C, Mercury Cougar, reg, blk wheels, metallic lime, 1968, M .$14.00

63-A, Ford Service Ambulance, reg, blk wheels, 1959, EX $35.00

63-B, Foamite Airport Crash Tender, reg, blk wheels, gold nozzle, complete, orig pcs on tree, 1964, M (NM box) ...$23.00

63-C, Dodge Crane Truck, reg, blk wheels, red hook, 1968, M (NM+ box) $14.00

63-D, Dodge Crane Truck, SF, yel, blk axle covers, 1970, M (NM box), W1 ....$24.00

Photo courtesy Dana Johnson.

63-I, Dunes 4x4 Truck, red, white and blue, 1987, NM, $5.00.

64-A, Scammel Breakdown Truck, reg, blk wheels, gray plastic hook, 1959, NM+ $37.00

64-B, MG 1100 Sedan, reg, blk wheels, 1966, M (EX+ box)...$18.00

64-C, MG 1100, SF, rare gr, 1970, NMIB......................$150.00

64-D, Slingshot Dragster, SF, metallic bl, blk base/pipes, #9/flame tampo, 1971, missing some pipes o/w EX $8.00

64-E, Fire Chief Car, SF, red, plain shield label, 1976, MBP...$12.00

65-B, Jaguar 3.4 Litre Saloon, reg, blk wheels, red, 1962, NM+ $29.00

66-C, Greyhound Bus, red, blk wheels, amber windows, labels, 1967, M (EX+ box) $16.00

66-E, Mazda RX 500, SF, dk gr, #66 tampo, 1971, M (EX taped box)..$11.00

67-A, Saladin Armoured Car, reg, blk wheels, 1959, M...$30.00

67-B, VW 1600 TL, reg, blk wheels, red, scarce roof-rack version, 1967, M $14.00

67-D, Hot Rocker, SF, orange-red, unpnt base, 5-spoke wheels, 1973, M (EX+ card)..$14.00

68-B, Mercedes Coach, reg, blk wheels, orange, 1965, M (EX box), W1 ....$15.00

68-E, Chevy Van, SF, wht, unpnt base, bl windows, USA-1 tampo, 1979, NM..$9.00

69-A, Commer 30 CWT Nestle's Van, reg, gold wheels, 1959, M $47.00

69-B, Hatra Tractor Shovel, reg, blk wheels, all yel, 1965, M (NM box) $16.00

69-C, Rolls Royce Silver Shadow Coupe, SF, metallic bl, orange-brn interior, tan tonneau, lt yel base, 1969, NM..........$19.00

69-D, Turbo Fury, SF, metallic red, blk base, clear window, #69 label, 5-spoke wheels, 1973, NM..............................$15.00

70-A, Ford Thames Estate Car, reg, silver wheels, 1959, NM+ .$32.00

70-B, Ford Grit Spreader, reg, blk wheels, gray pull, 1966, M (NM box), W1 ....$15.00

71-A, Austin 200 Gallon Water Truck, reg, blk wheels, 1959, NM+ $35.00

71-B, Jeep Gladiator Pickup, reg, blk wheels, wht interior, 1964, NM $20.00

71-G, 1962 Corvette, SF, red, Heinz 57 promo, silver wheels, 1982, M (NM+ box), W1 ....$24.00

72-A, Fordson Tractor, reg, blk wheels, orange hubs, 1959, M $38.00

72-B, Standard Jeep, reg, blk wheels, 1966, M (NM box)...$20.00

73-A, 10-Ton Pressure Refueler, reg, gray wheels, decals 98%, 1959, M $19.00

73-B, Ferrari F1 Racer, reg, blk wheels, gray driver, 1962, NM+ $26.00

73-B, Ferrari F1 Racer, reg, blk wheels, wht driver, 1962, NM+..$32.00

73-C, Mercury Station Wagon, reg, blk wheels, 1968, M, W1 ....$15.00

73-D, Mercury Station Wagon, SF, metallic lime, NMIB...$18.00

74-A, Mobile Refreshment Canteen, reg, gray wheels, silver, bl base/interior, 1959, NM+ $40.00

74-B, Damier Bus, reg, blk wheels, gr, labels, 1966, M $17.00

75-A, Ford Thunderbird, reg, silver wheels, cream/pk, dk bl base, 1960, EX..$45.00

75-B, Ferrari Berlinetta, reg, blk wheels, gr, wire wheels, unpnt base, 1965, M, W1 ....$14.00

KING SIZE, SPEED KINGS, AND SUPER KINGS

K-O8B, Guy Warrior Car Transporter, aqua cab, orange trailer/hubs, EX+, W1 ....$25.00

K-04D, Big Tipper, metallic red body, yel dump, M (EX+ window box), W1 ....$13.00

K-05C, Muir Hill Tractor & Trailer, yel body, red chassis, bl driver, NM+ (VG+ window box), W1....................$15.00

K-07B, Refuse Truck, 1967, NM, W1 ....$13.50

K-1B, Hoveringham Tipper Truck, 1964, NM+ (EX box), W1 ....$43.00

K-10C, Car Transporter, clear windows, NM, W1 ....$8.50

K-11C, Breakdown Truck, yel, blk base, wht booms, red hooks, AA labels, NM+, W1 ....$6.50

K-12A, Heavy Breakdown Truck, red hubs, roof light, orig hook, M (VG+ box), W1 ....$59.00

K-14A, Taylor Jumbo Crane, red weight box, 1964, M (EX+ box), W1........................$38.00

K-14C, Heavy Breakdown Truck, amber windows, NM, W1 ..$6.50

Photo courtesy June Moon.

K-15, Londoner, red with yellow interior, 1973, MIB, $45.00.

K-15A, Merryweather Fire Engine, decals, M, W1 ....$38.00

K-15C, The Londoner, Berlin labels, 1982, M (EX+ window box), W1........................$12.00

K-17A, Lowloader w/Bulldozer, Taylor Woodrow decals, dozer missing roof o/w VG+, W1........................$19.00

K-17B, Articulated Container Truck, metallic red cab, red trailer chassis, Gentransco labels, NM, W1 ....$12.00

K-20C, Peterbilt Wrecker, dk gr, unpnt roof mount/base, red lights, M (NM window box), W1........................$22.00

K-21A, Mercury Cougar, red interior, NMIB, W1 ....$29.00

K-31A, Bertone Runabout, gr windows, M (NM+ window box), W1........................$9.00

K-31B, Peterbilt Refrigerator Truck, Burger King decals, M (NM+ box), W1........................$49.00

K-34A, Thunderclap, yel background, #34 labels, NM (NM box), W1........................$8.00

K-35A, Lightning, red #35 Team Matchbox hood label, Firestone wing label, #35 side label, M (NM box), W1...$10.00

K-40A, Blaze Trailer, red body, yel base/interior, amber windows, blk antenna, bl lights, EX+, W1........................$8.00

K-41A, Fuzz Buggy, wht body, blk base, clear windows, yel interior, amber lights, wht steering wheel, EX+, W1.........$8.00

K-48A, Mercedes 350 SLC, bronze, silver-gray base, yel interior, amber windows, M (EX+ box), W1........................$10.00

K-49A, Ambulance, wht body, red roof/interior, blk base, clear windows, bl lights, orig stretcher/blanket, NM, W1..$10.00

K-51A, Barracuda, bl body, yel interior/spoiler, clear windshield, wht driver, #5 labels, NM+, W1........................$6.00

K-53A, Hot Fire Engine, blk driver w/gold helmet, missing rider, NM, W1........................$9.00

K-62A, Doctor's Emergency Car, silver-gray base, NM, W1..$9.00

K-66A, Jaguar XJ12 Police Patrol, brn interior, bl lights, Maltese cross wheels, 2 bl/1 orange stripe tampo, NM+, W1....$9.00

K-78A, Gran Fury Police Car, bl & wht body, bl interior, red lights, Polizei decals, orig key, M (NM window box), W1 ....$12.00

Photo courtesy Dana Johnson.

K-95A, Audi Quattro, metallic blue, black wheels, 1982, MIB, $6.00.

MODELS OF YESTERYEAR

Y-01A, 1925 Allchin Traction Engine, diagonal unpnt treads, gold boiler door, 1956, NM, W1 ....$48.00

Y-01B, 1911 Ford Model T, red, smooth blk roof, brass 12-spoke wheels, NMIB, W1........................$14.00

Y-02A, 1911 B-Type London Bus, red, unpnt wheels, bl driver, rare 4-over-4 windows, 1956, EX, W1........................$150.00

Y-02B, 1911 Renault 2-Seater, gr, 3-prong spare, gr metal steering wheel, M (VG+ box), W1........................$16.00

Y-02C, 1914 Prince Henry Vauxhall, red, blk chassis, silver hood, wht seats, spoke wheels, wht-walls, 1970, NM+, W1 ....$17.00

Y-03A, 1907 London E Class Tramcar, wht roof, new decals, 1956, M, W1 ....$69.00

Y-03B, 1910 Benz Limo, cream, gr roof/seats/grille, metal steering wheel, low lights, 1966, NM+, W1........................$16.00

Y-04A, 1928 Sentinel Steam Wagon, bl, 1956, NM, W1...$59.00

Y-04B, 1905 Shand Mason Horse-Drawn Fire Engine, red, blk horses, gold London decals/boiler, 1960, NM, W1....$95.00

Y-04C, 1909 Opel Coupe, wht, smooth tan roof, bright red seats/radiator, M, W1........................$12.00

Y-04D, 1930 Duesenberg, red, blk roof/seats, 24-spoke wheels, 1976, NM+, W1........................$14.00

Y-05A, 1929 LeMans Bentley, gold radiator, gr grille/tonneau, silver steering wheel, 1958, NM, W1........................$49.00

Y-05B, 1929 4½ Litre Bentley, gr, unpnt radiator, red seats/tonneau, M (EX+ box), W1........................$35.00

Y-05C, 1907 Peugeot, yel, blk roof, red seats/grille, amber windows, 1969, M, W1........................$13.00

Y-06A, 1916 AEC Y-Type Lorry, dk gray, 1957, decals 98%, 1957, NM+, W1........................$89.00

Y-06B, 1926 Type 35 Bugatti, bl, red dash/floor, #6 decal, 1961, NM, W1........................$26.00

Y-06C, 1913 Cadillac, gold, maroon roof/grille/seats, rare version w/no side body cutouts for seat pins, 1967, NM+, W1........................$79.00

Y-07A, 1918 4-Ton Leyland Van, red-brn, cream roof, full decal, 1957, EX+........................$52.00

Y-07B, 1913 Mercer Raceabout, lilac, short spotlight, fine tread, NM+, W1........................$38.00

Y-07C, 1912 Rolls Royce, silver, red base/seats, smooth gray roof, 1968, NM+, W1 ....**$10.00**

Y-08A, 1926 Morris Cowley Bullnose, unplated wheels, 1958, M, W1 ....**$84.00**

Y-08B, 1914 Sunbeam Motorcycle & Sidecar, dk gr seat, 1962, NM, W1 ....**$23.00**

Y-08C, 1914 Stutz Roadster, metallic red, smooth tan roof, copper gas tank, 1969, NM+, W1 ....**$15.00**

Y-09A, 1924 Fowler Big Lion Showman Engine, red, wht roof, gold boiler/supports, 1958, NM, W1 ....**$42.00**

Y-09B, 1912 Simplex, yel-gr, smooth tan roof, red seats, 1968, EX+, W1 ....**$13.00**

Y-10A, 1908 GP Mercedes, cream, lt gr seats, gold trim, 1958, NM, W1 ....**$35.00**

Y-10B, 1928 Mercedes Benz 36/200, wht, single spare, 1963, NM, W1 ....**$10.00**

Y-11A, 1920 Aveling Porter Steam Roller, gr body, blk supports/flywheels, 1958, M, W1 ....**$89.00**

Y-11B, 1912 Packard Landaulet, dk red, blk seats, brass wheels/radiator/steering wheel, 3-prong spare, 1964, NM+, W1 ......**$10.00**

Y-11C, 1938 Lagonda Drophead Coupe, copper, gold chassis, blk seats/radiator, silver 24-spoke wheels, 1972, NM+, W1 ..**$9.00**

Y-12, 1899 London Horse-Drawn Bus, 1957, MIB, $100.00.

Y-12A, 1899 London Horse-Drawn Bus, beige driver/seats, brn horses, 1959, NM+, W1 ....**$72.00**

Y-12B, 1909 Thomas Flyabout, bl, smooth tan top, red seats, seat pins, B base, M, W1 ....**$14.00**

Y-13A, 1868 Santa Fe Locomotive, gr, 1959, NM+, W1 .**$79.00**

Y-13B, 1911 Daimler, yel, dk red seats, 4-spoke steering wheel, open spare recess, D base, missing radiator, EX+, W1 .**$9.00**

Y-13C, 1918 Crossley, bl-gray, cream seat, tan roof/grille/top, RAF/cross label, 24-spoke wheels, 1974, NM+, W1 ..**$48.00**

Y-14A, 1903 Duke of Connaught Locomotive, gold boiler, 1959, NM, W1 ....**$75.00**

Y-14B, 1914 Maxwell Roadster, turq, blk roof/grille, maroon seats, copper gas tank, 1965, NM+, W1 ....**$12.00**

Y-15A, 1907 Rolls Royce Silver Ghost, metallic lt gr, blk seats, brass C wheels, M (NM box), W1 ....**$34.00**

Y-16A, 1904 Spyker, mustard yel, yel radiator/seats, fine tread, M (EX- box), W1 ....**$25.00**

Y-21A, 1930 Model A Ford Woody Wagon, bronze hood, brn chassis, cream interior, 1981, NM+, W1 ....**$12.00**

SKYBUSTERS

SB-01, Learjet, US Air Force, MBP..............................**$4.00**

SB-04, Mirage F1, thick axles, bull's-eye labels, NM, W1 ..**$5.00**

SB-10, Boeing 747, Pan Am, wht, pearly silver underside, Macau, M, W1 ....**$9.00**

SB-10, Boeing 747, wht & gray, Lufthansa, VG+, W1 ....**$3.00**

SB-13, DC-10, United, wht & gray, NM+, W1 ....**$8.00**

SB-15, Boeing 747, bl & wht, MIB..............................**$5.00**

SB-22, Tornado, lt gray, wht base, F132 ornate design, Thailand, NM, W1 ....**$3.00**

SB-23, Supersonic Transport, Air France, wht, fuselage tampo, NM, W1 ....**$5.00**

SB-28, Airbus A300, Lufthansa, NM, W1 ....**$5.00**

SB-36, F-117 Stealth Fighter, blk, MBP.............................**$4.00**

SB-38, BAE 146, wht, MIB..............................**$5.00**

Model Kits

While values for military kits seem to have leveled off and others may have actually gone down, this is certainly not the case with the Aurora monster and character kits which are continuing to increase in value.

Though model kits were popular with kids of the '50s who enjoyed the challenge of assembling a classic car or two or a Musketeer figure now and then, when the monster series hit in the early 1960s, sales shot through the ceiling. Made popular by all the monster movies of that decade, ghouls like Vampirella, Frankenstein, and the Wolfman were eagerly built up by kids everywhere. They could (if their parents didn't object too strongly) even construct an actual working guillotine. Aurora had other successful series of figure kits, too, based on characters from comic strips and TV shows as well as a line of sports stars.

But the vast majority of model kits were vehicles. They varied in complexity, some requiring much more dexterity on the part of the model builder than others, and they came in several scales, from 1/8 (which might be as large as 20" to 24") down to 1/43 (generally about 3" to 4"), but the most popular scale was 1/25 (usually between 6" to 8"). Some of the largest producers of vehicle kits were AMT, MPC, and IMC. Though production obviously waned during the late 1970s and early '80s, with the intensity of today's collector market, companies like Ertl (who now is producing 1/25 scale vehicles using some of the old AMT dies) are proving that model kits still sell very well.

As a rule of thumb, assembled kits (built-ups) are priced at about 25% to 50% of the price range for a boxed kit, but this is not always true on the higher-priced kits. One mint in the box with the factory seal intact will often sell for up to 15% more than if the seal were broken, though depending on the kit, a sealed perfect box may add as much $100.00. Condition of the box is crucial. For more information, we recommend *Aurora History and Price Guide* by Bill Bruegman and *Collectible Figure Kits of the '50s, '60s & '70s*, by Gordy Dutt.

Advisors: Mike and Kurt Fredericks (F4); John and Sheri Pavone (P3).
Other Sources: B10, J7, T1, P4
See also Plasticville.

Action Kits International, Dark Shadows, Barnabas Collins, 1993, resin, 1/8, MIB, G5 ....**$100.00**

Adams, Around the World in Eighty Days (TV), Balloon w/Figures #80, 1959, 1/40, MIB, G5 ....$150.00

Adams, Vanguard #161, 1958, 1/80, MIB, G5 ....$170.00

Addar, Evel Knievel #152, 1974, 1/12, MIB (sealed), G5..$120.00

Addar, Jaws, Diorama #S31, 1975, MIB (sealed), G5 ....$70.00

Addar, Planet of the Apes, Caesar #106, 1974, 1/11, MIB, G5 ....$85.00

Addar, Planet of the Apes, Cornelius #101, 1973, 1/11, MIB, G5 ....$75.00

Addar, Planet of the Apes, Dr. Zaius, 1973, MIB, $70.00.

Photo courtesy John and Sheri Pavone.

Addar, Planet of the Apes, Dr Zira #105, 1974, 1/11, MIB, G5 ....$70.00

Addar, Planet of the Apes, General Ursus #103, 1974, 1/11, MIB (sealed), G5 ....$80.00

Addar, Planet of the Apes, Tree House Diorama #215, 1975, 1/32, MIB (sealed), G5 ....$50.00

AEF Designs, Aliens, Bishop #AC-3, 1980s, 1/35, MIB, G5 ...$35.00

AEF Designs, Aliens, Burke #AC-4, 1980s, 1/35, MIB, G5..$24.00

AEF Designs, Aliens, Corp Hicks #AM-1, 1980s, 1/35, MIB, G5 ....$26.00

AEF Designs, Aliens, Crowe #AM-9, Ferro #AM-11, Frost #AM-3, Gorman #AM-10 or Sgt Apone #AM-5, 1980s, 1/35, MIB, G5, ea $26.00

AEF Designs, Aliens, Egg Assortment #AX-5 or Egg Assortment #AX5-b (closed), 1980s, 1/35, MIB, G5, ea..............$35.00

AEF Designs, Aliens, Ripley #AC-1 (combat), 1980s, 1/35, MIB, G5 ....$30.00

AEF Designs, Aliens, Spunkmeyer #AM-12, 1980s, 1/35, MIB, G5 ....$25.00

AEF Designs, Aliens, Vasquez #AM-6a, 1980s, 1/35, MIB, G5 ....$28.00

AEF Designs, Aliens, Warrior Alien A #AX-1 (inverted) or Warrior Alien #AX-3 (kneeling), 1980s, 1/35, MIB, G5, ea..$45.00

AEF Designs, Aliens, Wiergbowski #AM-8, 1980s, 1/35, MIB, G5 ....$32.00

AHM, Mighty American Buffalo (reissue of Precision's Buffalo Head), late 1960s-early 1970s, EXIB, D9 ....$25.00

Airfix, Bristol Bloodhound #M01703, 1/75, MIB, G5 ......$15.00

Airfix, Captain Scarlet, Angel Interceptor #2026, 1975, 1/72, MIB, G5 ....$16.00

Airfix, Captain Scarlet, Angel Interceptor #2070, 1981, 1/72, MIB (sealed), G5 ....$12.00

Airfix, Captain Scarlet, Angel Interceptor #256, 1967, 1/72, MIB, G5 ....$30.00

Airfix, Coldstream Guardsman #205, 1960s, 1/12, MIB, G5...$16.00

Airfix, Corythosaurus #3804, 1979, MIB (sealed), G5 .....$14.00

Airfix, George Washington #2554, 1980, 1/32, MIB (sealed), G5 ....$20.00

Airfix, Henry VIII #2501, 1979, 1/12, MIB, G5 ....$20.00

Airfix, High Chaparral #38, 1/75, MIB, G5 ....$8.00

Airfix, Lunar Module #3013, 1975, 1/72, MIB, G5 ....$20.00

Airfix, Lunar Module #3013, 1981, 1/72, MIB, G5 ....$16.00

Airfix, Mounted Bengal Lancer #07501, 1991, 1/12, MIB (sealed), G5 ....$40.00

Airfix, Russian Vostok #5172, 1991, 1/144, MIB (sealed), G5..$20.00

Airfix, Space Shuttle w/Boosters #9172, 1978, 1/144, MIB, G5 ....$40.00

Airfix, Space Warriors #51577, 1982, MIB, G5................$15.00

Airfix, Space: 1999, Hawk Spaceship #05173, 1977, 1/72, MIB, G5 ....$70.00

Airfix, Wildlife Series, Bullfinches #3830, 1976, 1/1, MIB, G5 ....$26.00

Airfix, Yeoman of the Guard, #2507, 1978, 1/12, MIB (sealed), G5 ....$25.00

Airfix, Zoo Playset #1686, 1960s, 1/75, MIB, G5 ....$30.00

Airfix, 2001: A Space Odyssey, Orion #05175, 1980, 1/144, MIB, G5 ....$40.00

Airfix, 2001: A Space Odyssey, Orion #701, 1970, orig issue, Pan Am decals, 1/144, MIB, G5................................$90.00

Aishima, APEX-Russia, Carrier Rocket Sputnik, 1993, 1/144, MIB, G5 ....$20.00

Alabe, Neanderthal Man #2963 or Stegosaurus #2962, 1976, MIB, G5, ea..$40.00

Amaquest, Star Trek: The Next Generation, Romulan Spaceship #200, 1/200, MIB, G5 ....$48.00

AMT, Airwolf Helicopter #6680, 1984, 1/48, MIB, G5...$40.00

AMT, Apollo Spacecraft #955, 1970, 1/200, MIB, G5.....$15.00

AMT, BJ & the Bear, KW Aerodyne Cabover #5025 or Trailer #7705, 1980, MIB (sealed), G5, ea............................$50.00

AMT, Bonnie & Clyde, 1932 Ford Roadster #219, 1970, 1/25, MIB, G5 ....$80.00

AMT, Budweiser Clydesdale 8-Horse Hitch #7702, 30", MIB (sealed), G5 ....$50.00

AMT, Farrah's Foxy Vette #3101, 1970s, 1/25, MIB (sealed), G5 ....$30.00

AMT, Flintstones, Sportscar #495, 1974, MIB, G5 ....$40.00

AMT, Get Smart, Sunbeam Car #925, 1967, 1/25, MIB, G5..$120.00

AMT, Hang-Outs, Baseball #615, 1970s, MIB (sealed), G5 ......$24.00

AMT, Hang-Outs, Football #614, 1970s, MIB, G5 ....$20.00

AMT, Interplanetary UFO #960, 1970s, 1/635, MIB, G5...$140.00

AMT, Intrepid Civil War Balloon #571, 1970s, 11", MIB, G5 ....$20.00

AMT, Laurel & Hardy, 1925 T Roadster w/Figure #462 or 1927 T Touring Car w/Figure #461, 1976, 1/25, MIB (sealed), G5, ea..$60.00

AMT, Leonardo Da Vinci Inventions, Movable Crane #100, 1973, 13", MIB (sealed), G5..................................$24.00

AMT, Leonardo Da Vinci Inventions, Steam Cannon #101, 1973, 12", MIB (sealed), G5..................................$26.00

AMT, Man in Space Set #953, 1/200, MIB, G5.............$220.00

AMT, Movin' On, Kenworth Tractor-Trailer #650, 1970s, MIB, G5 ....$40.00

AMT, Munster Koach #901, 1964, orig issue, 1/25, MIB, G5 ....$190.00

AMT, My Mother the Car #904, 1965, 1/25, MIB, G5....$70.00

AMT, Star Trek, Exploration Set #958, 1974, orig issue, assembled, G5 ....$30.00

AMT, Star Trek, Exploration Set #958, 1974, orig issue, MIB (sealed), G5 ....$100.00

AMT, Star Trek, Klingon Cruiser #971, 1979, 1/600, MIB, G5 ....$40.00

AMT, Star Trek, Romulan Bird of Prey, 1975, MIB (sealed), T2 ....$20.00

AMT, Star Trek, Spock, 1968, complete, NM (EX+ box), T2 .$160.00

AMT, Star Trek, Spock #956, 1973, 1/12, MIB (sealed), G5..$100.00

AMT, Star Trek, Spock #973, 1979, 1/12, MIB (sealed), G5....$40.00

AMT, Star Trek, USS Enterprise #921, 1967, orig issue, 1/635, MIB, G5 ....$190.00

AMT, Star Trek, USS Enterprise #970, 1979, 1/535, w/lights, MIB, G5 ....$60.00

AMT, Star Trek, Vulcan Shuttle #972, 1979, 1/220, MIB, G5 ....$40.00

AMT, UFO #960, 1970s, 1/635, assembled, no stand, w/box, G5 ....$35.00

AMT, Vegas, Thunderbird #3105, 1979, 1/25, MIB, G5..$24.00

AMT/Ertl, A-Team Van #6616, 1983, 1/25, MIB, G5 .....$26.00

AMT/Ertl, Age of the Dinosaurs, Stegosaurus #8738, 1993, MIB, G5 ....$5.00

AMT/Ertl, Back to the Future, Delorian (1st movie) #6122, 1991, 1/24, MIB (sealed), G5 ....$26.00

AMT/Ertl, Batman (movie), Batmobile #6877, 1989, 1/25, MIB, G5 ....$26.00

AMT/Ertl, Batman (movie), Batmobile Cocoon #6772, 1989, 1/25, MIB, G5 ....$30.00

AMT/Ertl, Batman (movie), Batwing #6970, 1990, 1/25, MIB (sealed), G5 ....$50.00

AMT/Ertl, Batman (movie), Joker Goon Car #6826, 1989, 1/25, MIB (sealed), G5 ....$20.00

AMT/Ertl, Batman Returns, Batmissile #6614, 1992, 1/25 scale, MIB (sealed) $16.00

AMT/Ertl, Batman Returns, Batmobile #6650, 1992, 1/25, MIB (sealed), G5 ....$10.00

AMT/Ertl, Batman Returns, Batskimobile #6615, 1992, 1/25, MIB, G5 ....$8.00

AMT/Ertl, Ghostbusters II, Ecto 1-A #6017, 1989, 1/25, MIB, G5 ....$30.00

AMT/Ertl, Knight Rider, KITT 4000 #8084, 1991, 1/25, MIB (sealed), G5 ....$12.00

AMT/Ertl, Monkeemobile #6058, 1990, 1/24, MIB, G5 ..$50.00

AMT/Ertl, Munsters Koach & Dragula Cars #8059, 1991, 1/25, MIB, G5 ....$80.00

AMT/Ertl, Rescue 911, Rescue Ambulance #6416 or Police Car #6417, 1993, 1/25, MIB (sealed), ea..........................$15.00

AMT/Ertl, Rescue 911, Rescue Helicopter #6400, 1993, 1/48, MIB (sealed), G5 ....$16.00

AMT/Ertl, Riptide, 1960 Corvette #6621, 1984, 1/25, MIB (sealed), G5 ....$20.00

AMT/Ertl, RoboCop 2, Robo 1 Police Car #6059, 1990, 1/25, MIB (sealed), G5 ....$10.00

AMT/Ertl, Star Trek, Captain Kirk #8773, 1994, 12", MIB, G5 ....$16.00

AMT/Ertl, Star Trek, Dr McCoy #8774, 1994, 12", MIB (sealed), G5 ....$12.00

AMT/Ertl, Star Trek, Galileo II Shuttlecraft #6006, 1991, 1/48, MIB, G5 ....$6.00

AMT/Ertl, Star Trek, Klingon Cruiser #6743, 1991, 1/600, MIB, G5 ....$6.00

AMT/Ertl, Star Trek, USS Enterprise, 1983, M (EX sealed box), D9...$15.00

AMT/Ertl, Star Trek, USS Enterprise Bridge #6007, 1991, 1/32, MIB (sealed), G5 ....$10.00

AMT/Ertl, Star Trek III: The Search for Spock, USS Enterprise #6675, 1984, 1/535, MIB (sealed), G5 ....$50.00

AMT/Ertl, Star Trek IV: The Voyage Home, USS Enterprise #6693, 1986, 1/535, MIB, G5..$16.00

AMT/Ertl, Star Trek VI: Undiscovered Country, Enterprise/Shuttlecraft #8617, 1991, 1/535, MIB (sealed), G5 ....$10.00

AMT/Ertl, Star Trek: Generations, Klingon Bird of Prey #8230, 1995, 1/650, MIB, G5..$14.00

AMT/Ertl, Star Trek: Generations, USS Enterprise B #8762, 1995, 1/1000, MIB, G5 ....$14.00

AMT/Ertl, Star Trek: The Motion Picture, Klingon Cruiser #6682, 1984, 1/600, MIB, G5 ....$20.00

Aoshima, Eagle 5-Apollo LEM #SS01, 1975, 1/40, MIB, G5 ....$80.00

Aoshima, Ideon: Space Runaway, Zanza-Lubu Robot #TS11, 1/600, MIB, G5 ....$20.00

Aoshima, SS-6 Sapwood ICBM & Trailer #0021, 1970s, 1/175, MIB, G5 ....$270.00

Aoshima, Technopolice 21C, Roadranger #TP04, 1/48, MIB, G5 ....$15.00

Aoshima, Vostok w/Launcher #AS-4, 1/96, MIB, G5 ....$190.00

Apollo, Golden Palomino Horse #1921, 1963, 1/10, MIB, G5 ..$35.00

Arii, Barugon #26011, 1/450, MIB, G5 ....$10.00

Arii, Gyoas #26010, 1/450, MIB, G5 ....$10.00

Arii, Macross, Fighter VF-1A #325, 1/100, MIB, G5 ....$10.00

Arii, Macross, Fighter VF-1D #365 (metalized), 1/100, no instructions, MIB, G5 ....$6.00

Arii, Macross, Gerwalk Valkyrie VF-1A #808, 1/100, MIB, G5 ....$12.00

Arii, Macross, Gerwalk Valkyrie VF-1J #805, 1/100, MIB, G5 ....$20.00

Arii, Macross, Thurverl-Salan Starship #333, MIB, G5 ...$16.00

Arii, Macross, Valkyrie VF-1D #324, 1/100, MIB, G5 .....$16.00

Arii, Macross, Valkyrie VF-1J #318, 1/100, MIB, G5 ....$16.00

Arii, Macross, Valkyrie VF-1S #319, 1/100, MIB, G5 ......$14.00

Arii, Orguss, M-Lover Lieea #506, 1/42, MIB, G5.............$16.00

Articles & Objects, Babylon 5, Station #BF-01 or Narn Fighter #BF-02, MIB, G5, ea..$70.00

Articles & Objects, Firefox Jet #FF-01, 5", MIB, G5 ....$20.00

Articles & Objects, Man From Planet-X Ship #PX-01, 3", MIB, G5 ....$10.00

Articles & Objects, Star Trek, Nomad #SRC-02, 9", MIB, G5 ....$30.00

Articles & Objects, Star Trek III: The Search for Spock, Spacedock #STM-01, 6", MIB, G5 ....$45.00

Articles & Objects, Star Trek: Deep Space 9, Bajoran Fighter #DSN-04, 4", MIB, G5 ....$20.00

Articles & Objects, Star Trek: Deep Space 9, Cardassian Shuttle #DSN-05, 8", MIB, G5 ....$35.00

Articles & Objects, Star Trek: The Next Generation, USS Jenilan #STN-05, 4", MIB, G5 ....$20.00

Articles & Objects, Star Wars, Deathstar #SW-01, 5", MIB, G5 ....$40.00

Articles & Objects, Star Wars, T-16 Skyhopper #SW-02, 9", MIB, G5 ....$35.00

Articles & Objects, Starman Ship #SM-01, 4", MIB, G5.$10.00

Articles & Objects, V, Fighter Craft #VS-01, 3½", MIB, G5 ....$20.00

Articles & Objects, V, Transport Ship, #VS-02, 5½", MIB, G5..$30.00

ATL/PAM Murray, Beauty & the Beast (French movie), Beast, 1/10, MIB, G5 ....$45.00

ATL/PAM Murray, RoboCop, 1/6, MIB, G5....................$60.00

ATL/PAM Murray, Seven Faces of Dr Lao, Giant Serpent, MIB, G5 ....$60.00

ATL/PAM Murray, Star Trek, Dreadnaught, 1/2000, MIB, G5 ....$60.00

ATL/PAM Murray, Star Trek, USS Excelsior, 1/1000, MIB, G5 ....$42.00

ATL/PAM Murray, Vampirella-Frazetta, 7", MIB, G5 .....$50.00

ATL/PAM Murray, X-Files, Agent X (Fox Mulder), 1/6, MIB, G5 ....$100.00

Atlantic, Atlantis (Alcadia) #153, 37cm, MIB, G5 ....$50.00

Aurora, Addams Family House #805, 1965, 1/64, minor assembly, NMIB, G5 ....$500.00

Aurora, Adventure Series, Gladiator #406, 1964, 1/8, MIB, G5 ....$200.00

Aurora, Adventure Series, Spartacus #405, 1964, 1/8, MIB, G5 ....$270.00

Aurora, Alfred E Neuman #802, 1965, M (NM box), D9...$360.00

Aurora, American Astronaut #409, 1967, 1/12, MIB, G5 ..$100.00

Aurora, American Buffalo #402, 1964, orig issue, 1/16, assembled, G5 ....$15.00

Aurora, American Buffalo #402, 1969, 1/16, MIB, G5.....$55.00

Aurora, American Buffalo #402, 1972, 1/16, MIB, G5.....$35.00

Aurora, Astronaut #409, 1967, 1/12, partially assembled, few pcs missing, G5 ....$60.00

Aurora, Batman #467, orig issue, 1964, 1/8, NM (EX+ box), D9 ....$275.00

Aurora, Batmobile #486, 1966, 1/32, MIB, G5...............$540.00

Aurora, Birds of the World, Red-Headed Woodpecker #9004, 1/1, MIB, G5 ....$30.00

Aurora, Black Bear & Cubs #407, 1962, orig issue, 1/12, assembled, G5 ....$25.00

Aurora, Black Bear & Cubs #407, 1972, 1/12, MIB (sealed), G5 ....$70.00

Aurora, Black Falcon Pirate Ship #210, 1972, 1/100, MIB, G5 ....$45.00

Aurora, Black Falcon Pirate Ship #765, 1972, 1/100, MIB (club box), G5 ....$30.00

Aurora, Bloodthirsty Pirates, Blackbeard #463, 1965, 1/8, MIB, G5 ....$400.00

Aurora, Bloodthirsty Pirates, Captain Kidd #464, 1965, 1/8, MIB, G5 ....$90.00

Aurora, Blue Knight of Milan, 2nd issue, MIB (sealed), T1..$25.00

Aurora, Bride of Frankenstein #482, 1964, 1/12, partially assembled, MIB, G5 ....$480.00

Aurora, British Centurion Tank #330, 1969, 1/48, MIB, G5.$30.00

Aurora, Buccaneer, Pirate Ship #429, 1959, MIB, G5 ...$100.00

Aurora, Buffalo #445, 1969, 1/16, MIB, G5 ....$40.00

Aurora, Butterflies of the World #561, 1959, 1/1, MIB, G5 .$70.00

Aurora, C-199 Flying Boxcar #393, 1960, 1/77, MIB (sealed), G5 ....$30.00

Aurora, Chitty-Chitty Bang-Bang, Flying Car #828, 1968, 1/25, MIB, G5 ....$160.00

Aurora, Comic Scenes, Batman #187, 1974, 1/8, MIB (sealed), G5 ....$130.00

Aurora, Comic Scenes, Captain America #192, 1974, 1/12, MIB, G5 ....$130.00

Aurora, Comic Scenes, Incredible Hulk #184, 1974, 1/12, MIB, G5 ....$110.00

Aurora, Comic Scenes, Lone Ranger #188, 1974, 1/12, MIB (sealed), G5 ....$100.00

Aurora, Comic Scenes, Robin the Teen Wonder #193, 1974, 1/8, MIB, G5 ....$140.00

Aurora, Comic Scenes, Spider-Man #182, 1974, 1/12, MIB, G5 ....$170.00

Aurora, Comic Scenes, Superboy #186, 1974, 1/8, MIB (sealed), G5 ....$150.00

Aurora, Comic Scenes, Superman #185, 1974, 1/8, MIB (sealed), G5 ....$90.00

Aurora, Comic Scenes, Tarzan #181, 1974, 1/11, MIB (sealed), G5 ....$80.00

Aurora, Comic Scenes, Tonto #183, 1974, 1/12, MIB (sealed), G5 ....$40.00

Aurora, Cougar #453, 1963, 1/8, MIB, G5 ....$50.00

Aurora, Creature From the Black Lagoon, 1963, original issue, MIB, $450.00.

Aurora, Creature From the Black Lagoon #483, 1969, 1/8, MIB, G5 ....$350.00

Aurora, Customizing Monster Kit, Skull/Lizard/Bat #463, 1963, 1/8, MIB, G5...$170.00

Aurora, Customizing Monster Kit, Vulture & Mad Dog #464, 1963, 1/8, MIB, G5...$280.00

Aurora, Cutty Sark, 1993, NM (EX box), D9 ....$18.00

Aurora, Dick Tracy #818, 1968, 1/16, MIB, G5 ....$290.00

Aurora, Dick Tracy Space Coupe, 1968, MIB, C1 ....$300.00

Aurora, Dr Dolittle, Pushmi-Pullyu #814, 1968, 1/15, MIB, G5...$140.00

Aurora, Dr Jekyll & Mr Hyde #460, 1964, orig issue, 1/8, assembled, G5 ....$90.00

Aurora, Dracula #424, 1962, orig issue, 1/8, MIB, G5 ....$290.00

Aurora, Dracula #454, 1972, 1/8, partially assembled, G5 ..$110.00

Aurora, Famous Fighters, Black Falcon Pirate Ship #H210, 1957, 1/100, MIB, G5...$50.00

Aurora, Famous Fighters, Black Fury #H400, 1958, 1/8, MIB, G5...$50.00

Aurora, Famous Fighters, Black Knight (Crown) #KC3, 1956, 1/8, MIB, G5...$70.00

Aurora, Famous Fighters, Black Knight #H473, 1956, 1/8, MIB, G5...$50.00

Aurora, Famous Fighters, Confederate Raider #H402, 1958, 1/8, M (worn box), G5 ....$470.00

Aurora, Famous Fighters, Crusader #KH7, 1958, 1/8, MIB, G5...$300.00

Aurora, Famous Fighters, Gladiator w/Trident #H406, 1958, 1/8, MIB, G5...$200.00

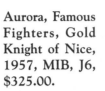

Aurora, Famous Fighters, Gold Knight of Nice, 1957, MIB, J6, $325.00.

Aurora, Famous Fighters, Steve Canyon #H404, 1958, 1/8, MIB, G5...$300.00

Aurora, Famous Fighters, US Marine #HD412, 1956, 1/8, MIB, G5...$120.00

Aurora, Famous Fighters, US Marshall #408, 1958, 1/8, MIB, G5...$60.00

Aurora, Famous Fighters, US Sailor #H410, 1957, 1/8, MIB, G5...$60.00

Aurora, Famous Fighters, Viking #K6, 1958, 1/8, MIB, G5...$400.00

Aurora, Famous Fighters, Viking Ship #H320, 1957, 1/80, MIB, G5...$60.00

Aurora, Famous Fighters, 3 Musketeers (Aramis) #KH10, 1958, 1/8, MIB, G5...$175.00

Aurora, Ferrari Tiger Shark Customizing Car Kit #543-79, 1960, M (NM sealed box), D9 ....$44.00

Aurora, Ford T Dragster 'Spyder' #535, 1963, 1/32, MIB, G5...$25.00

Aurora, Forgotten Prisoner #453, 1972, 1/8, assembled, G5...$50.00

Aurora, Forgotten Prisoner #453, 1972, 1/8, MIB (sealed), G5...$250.00

Aurora, Frankenstein #449, 1972, 1/8, MIB, G5 ....$150.00

Aurora, Frankenstein's Flivver #465, 1964, assembled, missing yo-yo, G5 ....$200.00

Aurora, Frightening Lightning, Frankenstein #449, 1969, 1/8, MIB, G5...$380.00

Aurora, Frightening Lightning, Phantom of the Opera #451, 1969, 1/8, MIB, G5...$460.00

Aurora, Gigantic Frankenstein #470, 1964-65, partially assembled (color repro box), G5 ....$200.00

Aurora, Godzilla #466, 1969, 1/600, MIB, G5..............$320.00

Aurora, Great Moments in Sports, Babe Ruth, 1965, MIB, A...$340.00

Aurora, Great Moments in Sports, Dempsey vs Firpo #861, 1965, 1/8, MIB (sealed), G5....................................$150.00

Aurora, Green Beret #413, 1966, foreign issue, 1/18, MIB, G5...$135.00

Aurora, Green Hornet, Black Beauty #489, 1967, 1/32, assembled, G5..$150.00

Aurora, Green Hornet, Black Beauty #489, 1967, 1/32, MIB, G5...$500.00

Aurora, Guys & Gals of All Nations, Chinese Girl #416, 1957, 1/8, MIB, G5..$60.00

Aurora, Guys & Gals of All Nations, Chinese Mandarin #415, 1957, 1/8, MIB, G5..$45.00

Aurora, Guys & Gals of All Nations, Dutch Boy #413 (red letters), 1957, 1/8, MIB, G5..................................$45.00

Aurora, Guys & Gals of All Nations, Dutch Boy #413 (yel letters), 1957, 1/8, MIB, G5..................................$35.00

Aurora, Guys & Gals of All Nations, Dutch Girl #414 (red letters), 1957, 1/8, MIB, G5..................................$55.00

Aurora, Guys & Gals of All Nations, Indian Chief #417, 1957, 1/8, MIB, G5..$150.00

Aurora, Guys and Gals of All Nations, Scotch Lassie, 1957, MIB, $40.00.

Photo courtesy June Moon.

Aurora, Hunchback of Notre Dame #460, orig issue, 1964, NM (VG+ Anthony Quinn box), D9 ....$365.00

Aurora, Hunchback of Notre Dame #481, 1969, 1/6, MIB, G5...$190.00

Aurora, Hunchback of Notre Dame #481, 1972, 1/8, assembled, G5..$60.00

Aurora, Invaders, UFO #813, 1968, orig issue, 1/72, MIB, G5.$220.00

Aurora, James Bond #414, 1966, 1/8, MIB, G5 ....$470.00

Aurora, John F Kennedy #851, 1965, 1/12, no decals, NMIB, G5...$170.00

Aurora, King Kong #468, 1969, 1/25, MIB, G5.............$320.00

Aurora, Knights in Shining Armour, Sir Galahad #881, 1973, 1/8, MIB, G5..$60.00

Aurora, Knights in Shining Armour, Sir Kay #882 or Sir Percival #884, 1973, 1/8, MIB, G5, ea $55.00

Aurora, Land of the Giants, Snake Scene #816, 1968, NM (EX+ box), P3 ....$425.00

Aurora, Land of the Giants, Spindrift #255, 1975, 1/64, MIB, G5...$370.00

Aurora, Lost in Space, Cyclops Diorama #419, 1967, 1/32, assembled, G5...$260.00

Aurora, Lost in Space, Robot #418, 1968, 1/11, partially assembled, (VG box), G5...$400.00

Aurora, Mad Barber, 1960s, 1/7 scale, assembled & pnt, complete, scarce, NM, A...$400.00

Aurora, Man From UNCLE, Gruesome Goodies #634, 1971, 1/13, MIB, G5...$140.00

Aurora, Man From UNCLE, Hanging Cage #637, 1971, 1/13, MIB, G5..$145.00

Aurora, Man From UNCLE, Illya Kuryakin #412, 1966, 1/12, MIB, G5..$250.00

Aurora, Man From UNCLE, Napoleon Solo #411, 1966, 1/12, MIB, G5..$300.00

Aurora, Man From UNCLE, Vampirella #638 or Victim #632, 1971, 1/13, MIB, G5, ea $200.00

Aurora, Monster Scenes, Dr Deadly #631, 1971, 1/13, MIB, G5...$180.00

Aurora, Monster Scenes, Dr Deadly's Daughter #632, 1971, foreign issue, 1/13, MIB, G5 ....$180.00

Aurora, Monsters of the Movies, Creature From the Black Lagoon #653, 1975, 1/12, MIB, G5.........................$280.00

Aurora, Monsters of the Movies, Creature From the Black Lagoon #653, 1975, 1/12, partially assembled (orig box), G5 .$180.00

Aurora, Monsters of the Movies, Dr Jekyll #654, 1975, 1/12, MIB (sealed), G5 ....$75.00

Aurora, Monsters of the Movies, Dracula #656, 1975, 1/12, MIB, G5..$285.00

Aurora, Monsters of the Movies, Frankenstein #651, 1975, 1/12, assembled, no nameplate, G5 ....$80.00

Aurora, Monsters of the Movies, Ghidrah #658, 1975, assembled, few pcs missing, G5..................................$70.00

Aurora, Monsters of the Movies, Mr Hyde #655, 1975, 1/12, MIB (sealed), G5 ....$110.00

Aurora, Monsters of the Movies, Rodan #657, 1975, MIB, G5...$480.00

Aurora, Monsters of the Movies, Wolfman #652, 1975, 1/12, assembled, G5...$80.00

Aurora, Mummy #427, 1963, orig issue, partially assembled & pnt, complete, D9 ....$14.00

Aurora, Mummy #452, 1972, 1/8, MIB (sealed), G5......$110.00

Aurora, Mummy's Chariot, 1964, assembled, complete, NM, A...$200.00

Aurora, Munsters' Living Room, 1964, 1/16 scale, assembled, NM, A $500.00

Aurora, Phantom of the Opera #428, 1963, orig issue, 1/8, MIB, G5..$300.00

Aurora, Phantom of the Opera #451, 1972, 1/8, MIB, G5..$130.00

Aurora, Prehistoric Scenes, Allosaurus #736, 1971, orig issue, 1/13, MIB, G5..$145.00

Aurora, Prehistoric Scenes, Armored Dinosaur #744, 1974, 1/13, MIB, G5..$120.00

Aurora, Prehistoric Scenes, Cave, EXIB, T1 .... $45.00

Aurora, Prehistoric Scenes, Cave Bear #738, 1972, 1/13, MIB, G5 .... $60.00

Aurora, Prehistoric Scenes, Cro-Magnon Man #730, EXIB, T1 .... $40.00

Aurora, Prehistoric Scenes, Cro-Magnon Woman #731, 1971, orig issue, 1/12, MIB (sealed), G5 .... $55.00

Aurora, Prehistoric Scenes, Flying Reptile #734, EXIB, T1 .. $50.00

Aurora, Prehistoric Scenes, Giant Bird #739, 1/13, EXIB, T1 .... $40.00

Aurora, Prehistoric Scenes, Jungle Swamp #740, 1972, 1/13, EXIB, T1 .... $40.00

Aurora, Prehistoric Scenes, Neanderthal Man, EXIB, T1 . $40.00

Aurora, Prehistoric Scenes, Sabertooth Tiger #733, 1971, orig foreign issue, 1/13, MIB, G5 .... $65.00

Aurora, Prehistoric Scenes, Sailback Reptile #745, 1974, 1/13, MIB (sealed), G5 .... $140.00

Aurora, Prehistoric Scenes, Spiked Dinosaur #742, 1972, 1/13, G5 .... $80.00

Aurora, Prehistoric Scenes, Tar Pit, M (NM box), $95.00.

Photo courtesy John and Sheri Pavone.

Aurora, Prehistoric Scenes, Tyrannosaurus #746, 1974, 1/13, M (EX box), G5 .... $300.00

Aurora, Prehistoric Scenes, Wooly Mammoth #743, 1972, 1/13, assembled, G5 .... $35.00

Aurora, Ragnarok Interceptor #251, 1975, 1/200, MIB, G5 ... $100.00

Aurora, Robin the Boy Wonder #488, 1966, 1/18, MIB, G5 .. $140.00

Aurora, Silver Knight of Augsburg #1560, 1956, orig issue, NM (VG+ box), D9 .... $65.00

Aurora, Sovereign of the Seas Ship #434, 1967, 1/260, MIB, G5 .... $50.00

Aurora, Spider-Man #477, 1966, orig foreign issue, partially assembled (orig box), G5 .... $150.00

Aurora, SSN Sea Wolf, 1962, M (NM sealed box), D9 .... $24.00

Aurora, Superboy #478, 1964, orig issue, 1/8, MIB (sealed), G5 .... $350.00

Aurora, Tarzan #820, 1967, orig issue, 1/11, assembled, G5.. $60.00

Aurora, Thoroughbred Race Horse, 1972, EX (VG+ box), D9 .... $24.00

Aurora, USS Bainbridge #717, 1964, 1/209, MIB, G5 ..... $25.00

Aurora, USS Constitution 'Old Ironsides,' 1967, M (NM sealed box), D9 .... $34.00

Aurora, Viking Ship #320, 1972, 1/80, MIB (sealed), G5... $40.00

Aurora, White Stallion #401, 1967, orig issue, 1/12, MIB, G5 .... $50.00

Aurora, White-Tail Deer #403, 1962, 1/18, MIB, G5 ...... $45.00

Aurora, Witch #470, 1969, orig issue, 1/12, MIB, G5 .... $250.00

Aurora, Witch #470, 1972, 1/12, MIB, G5 .... $210.00

Aurora, Witch #483, 1965, 1/12, assembled, G5 .... $150.00

Aurora, Witch #483, 1965, 1/12, MIB, G5 .... $500.00

Aurora, Wolfman #425, 1962, orig issue, 1/8, assembled, G5 .... $65.00

Aurora, Wolfman #450, 1969, 1/8, MIB, G5 .... $140.00

Aurora, Wolfman's Wagon #458, 1964, assembled, G5 . $300.00

Aurora, Zorro #801, 1965, 1/12, MIB, G5 .... $375.00

Aurora, 1921 Ford 'T for Two' #527, 1962, 1/32, MIB, G5... $30.00

Aurora, 2001: Space Odyssey, Moon Bus, 1969, Canadian issue, M (EX box), A $135.00

Bachmann, Americana, Bowlers #6001, 1962, 1/15, MIB, G5 .... $70.00

Bachmann, Animals of the World, Lion #7101, 1/12, MIB, G5 .... $40.00

Bachmann, Birds of the World, Baltimore Oriole #9000, 1/1, MIB, G5 .... $30.00

Bachmann, Birds of the World, Barn Swallow #9009, Bohemian Waxwing #9011 or Painted Bunting #9012, 1/1, MIB, G5, ea $20.00

Bachmann, Birds of the World, Bluebird #9002, Canary #9010, Goldfinch #9001 or Parakeet #9006, 1/1, MIB, G5, ea $25.00

Bachmann, Birds of the World, Robin #9005, 1/1, MIB, G5 .. $15.00

Bachmann, Birds of the World, Rose-Breasted Grosbeak #9019, 1/1, MIB, G5 .... $40.00

Bachmann, Birds of the World, Scarlet Tanager #9003, 1/1, MIB, G5 .... $16.00

Bachmann, Dogs of the World, Cocker Spaniel #8003, 1/16, MIB, G5 .... $16.00

Bachmann, Dogs of the World, Dalmatian #8008, 1/16, assembled, G5 .... $10.00

Bachmann, Dogs of the World, Pointer #8006, 1/5, MIB, G5 .... $16.00

Bachmann, Dogs of the World, St Bernard #8009, 1/6, MIB, G5 .... $25.00

Bachmann, Dogs of the World, Standard Poodle #8007, 1/16, MIB, G5 .... $25.00

Bandai, Avatar's Flagship 19 #36125, MIB, G5 .... $20.00

Bandai, Baltanseizin #3524, 1990, 1/350, MIB, G5 .... $15.00

Bandai, Battleship Andromeda 4 #536044, MIB, G5 .... $25.00

Bandai, Captain Harlock Space Pirate, Arcadia #14019, 1/1600, MIB, G5 .... $40.00

Bandai, Cosmo Zero (Super Star) #36132, 1980, MIB, G5... $12.00

Bandai, Dark Nebula Battleship 17 #36122, MIB, G5 ...... $20.00

Bandai, Dark Nebula Tri-Leg Tank #36146, MIB, G5 ..... $50.00

Bandai, Desslock's Command Cruiser #11577, 1989, MIB, G5 .... $25.00

Bandai, Dunbine, Aura Battler Dunbine #501101, 1/72, MIB, G5 .... $16.00

Bandai, EDF Cruiser 22 #36128, MIB, G5 .... $20.00

Bandai, EDF Patrol Cruiser 13 #36090, MIB, G5 .... $20.00

Bandai, EDF Unmanned Battleship #36135, 1/1220, MIB, G5 .. $40.00

Bandai, Galamon #3529, 1990, 1/350, MIB, G5 .... $16.00

Bandai, Gamera #3543, 1990, 1/350, MIB, G5 ....$35.00

Bandai, Gamera #503543, 1984, 1/350, MIB, G5 ....$50.00

Bandai, Garuman/Gamilon 3 Deck 27 #536286, MIB, G5 ..$20.00

Bandai, Godzilla #3526, 1990, 1/350, MIB, G5 ....$70.00

Bandai, Godzilla #503526, 1984, 1/350, MIB, G5 ....$60.00

Bandai, Gomola #3527, 1990, 1/350, MIB, G5 ....$15.00

Bandai, Gundam, MS-06R Zaku II Variation #501326, 1/100, MIB, G5 ....$20.00

Bandai, Kinggidrah #503533, 1984, 1/350, MIB, G5 ....$70.00

Bandai, Macross, VF-1J Battroid Valkyrie #30550, 1990, 1/72, MIB, G5 ....$26.00

Bandai, Mecha-Godzilla #3525, 1990, 1/350, MIB, G5 ....$30.00

Bandai, Mecha-Godzilla #503525, 1984, 1/350, MIB, G5 ..$40.00

Bandai, Pegila #3528, 1990, 1/350, MIB, G5 ....$20.00

Bandai, Prehistoric Animals, Stegosaurus #8332 or Triceratops #8335, 1973, MIB, G5, ea $65.00

Bandai, Rhinoceros Beetle #8700R, 1974, MIB, G5 ....$30.00

Bandai, Silly Gamera & Rodan #503866, 1985, MIB, G5 ..$18.00

Bandai, Silly Samurai #503565, MIB, G5 ....$6.00

Bandai, Thunderbird 1 #35755, 1992, MIB, G5 ....$26.00

Bandai, Thunderbird 2 #38602, 1971, MIB, G5 ....$40.00

Bandai, Thunderbird 4 #36188, 1980, MIB, G5 ....$20.00

Bandai, UFO, SHADO Interceptor #36120, MIB, G5 .....$80.00

Bandai, Ultraman #3523 or Ultraseven #3563, 1990, 1/350, MIB, G5, ea $20.00

Bandai, Wildstar's Destroyer 20 #536126, MIB, G5 ....$20.00

Bandai, Z-Ton #3564, 1990, 1/350, MIB, G5 ....$15.00

Bandai, Zordar's Dreadnaught #36035, 1980, MIB, G5 ....$40.00

Billiken, Alien Vs Predator, 1995, vinyl, MIB, G5 ....$180.00

Billiken, Beast From 20,000 Fathoms (Movie), Rhedosaurus, 1984, vinyl, MIB, G5 ....$310.00

Billiken, Creature From the Black Lagoon, 1989, 13", partially assembled (orig box), G5 ....$60.00

Billiken, Dracula, 1989, MIB, G5 ....$290.00

Billiken, Exotic Fairy Edina, 1994, MIB, G5 ....$60.00

Billiken, Frankenstein, 1988, MIB, G5 ....$240.00

Billiken, Gamera, vinyl, MIB, G5 ....$80.00

Billiken, Godzilla (Against Mothra), 1992, MIB, G5 .....$100.00

Billiken, Gorilla I (King Kong), vinyl, MIB, G5 ....$160.00

Billiken, Gyaos, vinyl, MIB, G5 ....$80.00

Billiken, Invasion of the Saucermen (Movie), Saucer Man, vinyl, MIB, G5 ....$130.00

Billiken, It Conquered the World, It Alien, 1985, vinyl, MIB, G5 ....$140.00

Billiken, Joker (Batman), 1989, vinyl, 1/16, MIB, G5 ....$200.00

Billiken, Kanegon, 1991, vinyl, partially assembled, MIB, G5 ..$40.00

Billiken, Kemur-Jin, 1990, vinyl, MIB, G5 ....$80.00

Billiken, King Kong, 1987, vinyl, MIB, G5 ....$180.00

Billiken, King Kong Vs Godzilla, Godzilla, 1986, vinyl, MIB, G5 ....$160.00

Billiken, Laser Blast Alien (Movie), 1988, MIB, G5 ......$100.00

Billiken, Mechanic Kong, 1987, vinyl, MIB, G5 ....$180.00

Billiken, Nana Iro Kamen, 1992, vinyl, partially assembled, MIB, G5 ....$40.00

Billiken, Phantom of the Opera, 1982, 1/8, complete, rare, MIB, A $125.00

Billiken, Predator, 1991, vinyl, MIB, G5 ....$90.00

Billiken, Scared to Death, Sygenor, 1984, vinyl, MIB, G5 .$200.00

Billiken, She Creature (Movie), 1989, vinyl, partially assembled, MIB, G5 ....$60.00

Billiken, Thing, 1984, vinyl, MIB, G5 ....$200.00

Billiken, This Island Earth, Metalunan Mutant, vinyl, MIB, G5 ....$180.00

Billiken, Ultra Man, 1987, partially assembled, VG, D9 ..$20.00

Billiken, Ultra Seven, 1993, vinyl, partially assembled, MIB, G5 ....$40.00

Billiken, Ultra Zone, Antlar, 1987, vinyl, MIB, G5 ....$60.00

Billiken, Ultra Zone, Baltan Seljin, 1986, vinyl, MIB, G5 ..$90.00

Billiken, Ultra Zone, Gomess, vinyl, MIB, G5 ....$70.00

Billiken, Ultra Zone, Namegon, vinyl, MIB, G5 ....$90.00

Billiken, Ultra Zone, Pagos, 1990, vinyl, MIB, G5 ....$40.00

Billiken, Ultra Zone, Peguila, 1989, vinyl, MIB, G5 ......$100.00

Billiken, Ultra Zone, Red King, 1988, vinyl, MIB, G5 ...$110.00

Billiken, Ultra Zone, Ultraman, 1986, vinyl, MIB, G5 ....$60.00

Billiken, War of the Colossal Beast, 1986, vinyl, MIB, G5 ...$70.00

Billiken, 7th Voyage of Sinbad, 1984, vinyl, MIB, G5 ...$140.00

CHiPs, Ponch's Firebird #6226, 1981, 1/25, MIB, G5 ......$30.00

Dark Horse, Frankenstein #D22, 1991, 1/18, MIB, G5 ..$100.00

Dark Horse, King Kong #K22, 1/48, MIB, G5 ....$150.00

Dark Horse, Mask #23-552, MIB, G5 ....$150.00

Dark Horse, Mummy #22-391, 1995, 1/8, MIB, G5 ....$150.00

Dimensional Designs, Bowen Werewolf, MIB, G5 ....$140.00

Dimensional Designs, Obit-Obit Monster, MIB, G5 ....$80.00

Dimensional Designs, Outer Limits, Bellaro Shield-Bifrost Allen or Cold Hands-Venusian, MIB, G5, ea $60.00

Dimensional Designs, The Day the Earth Stood Still, Gort & Klaatu set, MIB, G5 ....$130.00

Doyusha, Goldfinger, 007's Aston Martin w/Bond & Odd Job #07-1, 1990s, 1/24, MIB, G5 ....$70.00

Doyusha, Kochi Castle #JC-4, 1/5000, MIB, G5 ....$15.00

Doyusha, Voyage to the Bottom of the Sea, Big Seaview #2, 1992, MIB, G5 ....$100.00

Eidai, Cicada #1004, 1965, MIB, G5 ....$30.00

Entex, Battle of the Planets, G-1 Spaceship #8403 or G-1SP Spaceship #8402, 1978, MIB (sealed), G5, ea $40.00

Entex, Space Station #8411, 1978, MIB, G5 ....$55.00

Fun Dimensions, Ape Man, glow-in-the-dark, MIB, T1 ...$45.00

Glencoe, Lunar Lander #5003, 1993, 1/96, MIB (sealed), G5 ..$15.00

Glencoe, Neanderthal Man #5912, 1993, 1/8, MIB (sealed), G5 ....$16.00

Glencoe, Retriever Rocket (RM-1) #5002, 1993, 1/72, MIB (sealed), G5 ....$30.00

Glencoe, US Paratrooper #5902, 1991, 1/10, MIB (sealed), G5 .$15.00

Glencoe, 1940s Space Men & Women #5907, 1991, 1/20, MIB, G5 ....$30.00

Golden Era, Outer Limits, Sixth Finger #901, 1988, 1/8, G5 ...$140.00

Halcyon, Alien, Alien Face Hugger #V02, 1991, 1/1, MIB, G5 ....$100.00

Halcyon, Alien, Chest Buster #20, 1992, 1/1, MIB, G5 ....$70.00

Halcyon, Alien, Space Jockey #HT04, 1992, 1/60, MIB, G5 ..$60.00

Halcyon, Alien 3, Dog Buster #07, 1992, 1/1, MIB, G5 ....$80.00

Halcyon, Alien 3, Face Hugger & Queen Fetus #06, 1992, 1/1, MIB, G5 ....$110.00

Halcyon, Predator 2 #13, 1994, MIB, G5 ....$20.00

Hasegawa, Boeing F4B-4 Biplane, 1970s, 1/32, M (NM sealed box), P3 ....$30.00

Hasegawa, Curtis Soc-3 Seagull Biplane, 1970s, 1/72, M (NM sealed box), P3 ....$20.00

Hawk, Frantics, Frantic Banana #548, 1965, MIB, G5...$170.00

Hawk, Frantics, Frantic Cats #550, 1965, MIB, G5........$120.00

Hawk, Frantics, Steel Pluckers #546, 1965, MIB, G5.......$85.00

Hawk, Frantics, Totally Fab #549, 1965, MIB, G5.........$140.00

Hawk, German V-1 Terror Weapon #615, 1958, 1/48, MIB, G5 ....$60.00

Hawk, Indian Totem Poles, Thunderbird #555, 1966, MIB, G5 ....$50.00

Hawk, Saturn Interplanetary Ship #200, 1967, 1/87, MIB, G5 ....$200.00

Hawk, Weird-Ohs, Drag Hag, 1963, MIB, J6, $95.00.

Hawk, Weird-Ohs, Francis the Foul, 1963, complete, NMIB, T2..$60.00

Horizon, Batman Returns, Penguin #33, 1992, 1/6, MIB, G5 ....$50.00

Horizon, Bride of Frankenstein #3, 1988, assembled, G5 .$25.00

Horizon, DC Comics, Joker #56, 1993, 1/6, MIB, G5 ......$50.00

Horizon, DC Comics, Steel #66, 1994, 1/6, MIB, G5.......$25.00

Horizon, Dinosaur Series, Apatosaurus #60, 1993, 1/30, MIB, G5 ....$25.00

Horizon, Dinosaur Series, Elasmosaurus #65, 1993, 1/30, MIB, G5 ....$15.00

Horizon, Dinosaur Series, Stegosaurus #28, 1992, 1/30, MIB, G5 ....$16.00

Horizon, Dr Jones, 1993, NM (EX box), D9 ....$20.00

Horizon, Dracula #4, 1988, MIB, G5 ....$25.00

Horizon, Marvel Universe, Dr Doom #25, 1993, 1/6, MIB, G5..$45.00

Horizon, Marvel Universe, Punisher #7, 1988, MIB, G5..$50.00

Horizon, Marvel Universe, She Hulk #54, 1994, 1/6, MIB, G5 ....$55.00

Horizon, Marvel Universe, Silver Surfer #8, 1989, MIB, G5 .$60.00

Horizon, Marvel Universe, Spider-Man #6, 1988, MIB, G5 ..$35.00

Horizon, Phantom of the Opera #1, 1988, MIB, G5.........$80.00

Imai, Captain Scarlet, Spectrum Helicopter #2015, 1992, MIB, G5 ....$70.00

Imai, Captain Scarlet, Spectrum Pursuit Vehicle #1713, 1988, MIB, G5 ....$30.00

Imai, Captain Scarlet, Supersonic Transport Jet #1205, 1982, MIB, G5 ....$10.00

Imai, Gemini Pick-Up Boat w/Two Astronauts #712, 1966, 1/24, MIB, G5 ....$70.00

Inteleg Int, Cthukhu, 1990s, EX (G+ box), D9 ....$45.00

ITC, Neanderthal Man #3808, 1959, 1/8, MIB, G5 ....$80.00

ITC, US Navy Blimp #3723, 1950s, 1/336, MIB, G5 ....$60.00

ITC Model Craft, Boxer Dog, 1959-60, NM (EX+ box), D9 ..$25.00

ITC Model Craft, Marvel Metal Giraffe, 1960, EX (EX box), D9 ....$30.00

Lifelike, American Wildlife, Bald Eagle (reissue of Pyro's eagle kit), 1970s, M (EX+ sealed box), D9..........................$20.00

Lifelike, American Wildlife, Mallard Duck, 1970s, M (EX+ sealed box), D9 ....$15.00

Lifelike, American Wildlife, Ring Neck Pheasant (reissue of Pyro's pheasant kit), 1970s, M (EX+ sealed box), D9..$15.00

Lifelike, Circle H Chuck Wagon #9680, 1970s, 1/48, MIB, G5 ....$30.00

Lifelike, Civil War Navy '36' Pistol, NM (VG+ box), D9..$15.00

Lifelike, Corythosaurus #9280, 1970s, 1/37, MIB (sealed), G5 ....$20.00

Lifelike, Cro-Magnon Man #383, 1973, 1/8, MIB (sealed), G5 ....$25.00

Lifelike, Honest John w/Launcher #9656, 1974, 1/40, MIB, G5 ....$85.00

Lifelike, 1860 Western Army '44' Pistol, 1970, 1/1, EX (G box), D9 ....$15.00

Lindberg, Baywatch, Beach Patrol Pick-Up #72588, 1995, 1/20, MIB (sealed), G5 ....$20.00

Lindberg, Jumpin' Jeans, Slick Slacks or Thrill Threads, 1975, M (EX+ box), D9, ea...$12.00

Lindberg, Jurassic Park, Dilphosaurus Spitter or Velociraptor Raptor, MIB (sealed), G5, ea $20.00

Lindberg, Jurassic Park, Hadrosaurus Corythosaurus or Stegosaurus, MIB (sealed), T1, ea $15.00

Lindberg, Mars Probe, Space Station, #1148, 1969, 1/350, MIB, G5 ....$80.00

Lindberg, Nothrop Snark Missile #687, 1988, 1/48, MIB, G5 ..$16.00

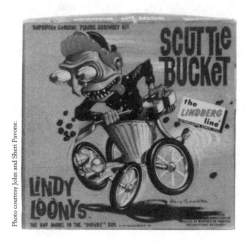

Lindberg, Scuttle Bucket, Lindy Loonys, 1964, NM (EX box), $110.00.

Lindberg, Star Probe, Space Shuttle, 1976, M (NM sealed box), D9...$50.00

Lindberg, Star Probe, USS Explorer, 1976, M (EX+ sealed box), D9...$45.00

Lindberg, 13th Century Clock #339, 1969, 16", MIB, G5 ..$28.00

Lunar Models, Batmobile #SF039, 1/25, MIB, G5 ....$90.00

Lunar Models, Beauty & the Beast (TV), Vincent #FG14, 9½", MIB, G5 ....$40.00

Lunar Models, Crawling Eye #FG44, 13", MIB, G5 ....$110.00

Lunar Models, Return of the Fly #FG09, 9", MIB, G5......$70.00

Lunar Models, Time Machine, Morlock w/Lights #FG01, 9", MIB, G5 ....$65.00

Marusan, Ben Casey MD, Visible Man #510, 1968, 1/5, MIB, G5 ....$70.00

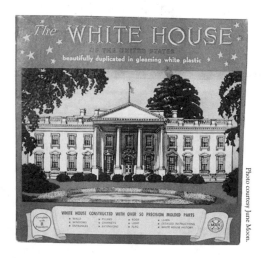

Marx, White House, 1950s, complete with 8 figures, MIB, J6, $75.00.

Max Factory, Guyver Bio Fighter Collection, Atom 5 Version, 1990s, M (EX+ box), D9 ....$35.00

Max Factory, Guyver Bio Fighter Collection, Gaster, 1990s, M (EX+ box), D9 ....$35.00

Max Factory, Guyver Bio Fighter Collection, Ramotith, 1990s, M (EX+ box), D9 ....$40.00

Monogram, A-10 Warthog Jet, MIB, T1 ....$15.00

Monogram, AH-1S Cobra Attack Helicopter, MIB, T1 ..$10.00

Monogram, Aircobra, 1973, 1/48, M (NM sealed box), P3 ......$22.00

Monogram, Allosaurus #6078, 1987, 1/13, MIB (sealed), G5...$20.00

Monogram, Apollo Saturn #193, 1968, 1/144, MIB (sealed), G5 ....$50.00

Monogram, Barbie's Silver 'Vette #1408, 1984, 1/24, MIB, G5 ....$25.00

Monogram, Battlestar Galactica, Cylon Raider #6026, 1979, orig issue, 1/48, MIB (sealed), G5 ....$130.00

Monogram, Battlestar Galactica, Space Fighter #6026, 1978, orig issue, 1/48, MIB (sealed), G5 ....$140.00

Monogram, Battlestar Galactica, Space Fighter Viper #6027, 1978, orig issue, 1/24, MIB, G5 ....$160.00

Monogram, Beer Wagon, 1995, M (NM sealed box), P3 .$25.00

Monogram, Buck Rogers Draconian Marauder, 1979, MIB, C1 ....$45.00

Monogram, Call to Glory, F-4 Phantom II #5814, 1984, 1/48, MIB (sealed), G5 ....$15.00

Monogram, Days of Thunder, City Chevy Lumina Stock Car #2920, 1990, 1/24, MIB (sealed), G5 ....$14.00

Monogram, Days of Thunder, Mello Yello Stock Car #2921, 1990, 1/24, MIB (sealed), G5 ....$18.00

Monogram, De Havilland Mosquito, NMIB, T1.............$12.00

Monogram, Elvira Mobile #2783, 1/24, MIB (sealed), G5.$30.00

Monogram, Flip Out! The Beachcomber, 1965, complete, scarce, NMIB, A..$375.00

Monogram, Garbage Truck, reissue, 1/24, MIB (sealed), P3 ..$20.00

Monogram, Hawker Harrier Jet, MIB, T1 ....$15.00

Monogram, Kingfisher Navy Catapult Plane, 1966, M (NM box), P3...$20.00

Monogram, Lion Diorama #102, 1961, MIB, G5 ....$40.00

Monogram, Luminators, Frankenstein #1619 or Wolfman #1621, 1991, 1/8, MIB (sealed), G5, ea $25.00

Monogram, Luminators, King Kong #1623, 1992, 1/25, MIB (sealed), G5/T1, from $50 to....................................$60.00

Monogram, Lunar Landing 10th Anniversary #5503, 1979, 1/48, MIB, G5 ....$30.00

Monogram, Masters of the Universe, Attack Trak #6014, 1983, 13", MIB (sealed), G5....................................$10.00

Monogram, Masters of the Universe, Talon Fighter #6015, 1983, 13", MIB (sealed), G5....................................$15.00

Monogram, Mork and Mindy Jeep, 1979, MIB, $35.00.

Monogram, Mummy (reissue of 1960s Aurora kit), glow-in-the-dark, 1991, M (EX+ sealed box), D9.........................$15.00

Monogram, Mummy #6010, 1983, 1/8, MIB (sealed), G5 ..$50.00

Monogram, Orbital Rocket, #46, 1959, 1/192, partially assembled, NMIB, G5...$190.00

Monogram, Rambo, Chopper & Riverboat #6039, 1985, 1/48, MIB (sealed), G5 ....$35.00

Monogram, Shogun Warriors, Dragun #6020, 1977, 1/10, MIB, G5 ....$26.00

Monogram, Shogun Warriors, Raider #6023, 1978, MIB (sealed), G5 ....$28.00

Monogram, Snark Guided Missile #27, 1957, 1/80, MIB, G5.$160.00

Monogram, Space Buggy #194, 1969, 1/48, MIB, G5.....$110.00

Monogram, Space Taxi #45, 1959, 1/48, MIB, G5.........$155.00

Monogram, TBF Avenger, 1966, M (NM+ sealed box), P3...$25.00

Monogram, Universal Monsters, Dracula, Mummy or Frankenstein, Luminator Series, 1/8, 1991, MIB, F1, ea........$15.00

Monogram, Voyage to the Bottom of the Sea, Flying Sub #6011, 1979, 1/60, MIB (sealed), G5 ....$65.00

Monogram, Wolfman #6009, 1983, 1/8, MIB (sealed), G5...$70.00

Monogram, Young Astronauts, First Lunar Landing #5901, 1986, 1/48, MIB (sealed), G5 ....$25.00

Monogram, Young Astronauts, Mercury 7 Altas Boosters #5910, 1987, 1/112, MIB (sealed), G5 ....$40.00

MPC, Alien, 1979, MIB (sealed), C1 ....$145.00

MPC, Batman #1702, 1984, 1/8, MIB (sealed), G5..........$60.00

MPC, Beatles Yellow Submarine, MIB (sealed), B3.......$425.00

MPC, Bionic Woman Repair Lab #610, 1/12, M (NM sealed box), D9...$32.00

MPC, Black Hole, Cygnus Spaceship, 1983, 1979, 1/4225, MIB, G5 ....$120.00

MPC, Black Hole, Maximilian Robot #1982, 1979, 1/12, MIB (sealed), G5 ....$70.00

MPC, Black Hole, Vincent Robot #1981, 1979, 1/12, MIB (sealed), G5 ....$85.00

MPC, Columbia Space Shuttle, 1982, missing few pcs & decals, VG (EX box), D9..$5.00

MPC, Dark Shadows, Barnabas Collins #550, 1969, assembled, 2 pcs missing, G5 ....$100.00

MPC, Dark Shadows, Vampire Van #626, 1969, partially assembled, G5 ....$120.00

MPC, Dark Shadows, Werewolf #552, 1970, 1/8, no glow parts, G5 ....$240.00

MPC, Disney's Haunted Mansion, Escape From the Crypt #5053, 1974, 1/12, MIB (sealed), G5 ....$190.00

MPC, Disney's Haunted Mansion, Vampire's Midnight Madness #5051, 1974, 1/12, MIB, G5...........................$120.00

MPC, Disney's Pirates of the Caribbean, Dead Men Tell No Tales #5001, 1972, 1/12, MIB, G5 ....$110.00

MPC, Disney's Pirates of the Caribbean, Fate of the Mutineers #5004, 1972, 1/12, MIB (sealed), G5 ....$100.00

MPC, Disney's Pirates of the Caribbean, Hoist High the Roger #5002, 1972, 1/12, MIB (sealed), G5 ....$90.00

MPC, Dukes of Hazzard, Cooter's Tow Truck #441 or Rosco's Police Car #663, 1981-82, MIB (sealed), G5, ea $45.00

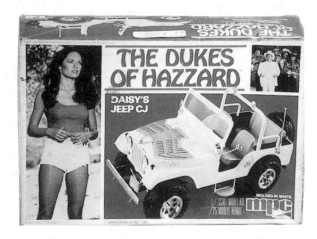

MPC, Dukes of Hazzard, Daisy's Jeep CJ #0662, 1980, 1/25 scale, MIB, $50.00.

MPC, Empire Strikes Back, Encounter w/Yoda on Dagobah, 1981, M (EX sealed box), D9 ....$30.00

MPC, Good Guys Taxi #616, 1968, 1/25, MIB, G5..........$90.00

MPC, Happy Days, Fonz on His Bike #634, 1976, 1/12, MIB, G5 ....$50.00

MPC, Hogan's Heroes Jeep #402, 1968, 1/25, MIB, G5 ...$60.00

MPC, Incredible Hulk #1932, 1979, 1/9, MIB (sealed), G5..$75.00

MPC, Ironside Van #3012, 1970, 1/20, MIB, G5 ....$100.00

MPC, Knight Rider, KITT 2000 #675, 1983, 1/25, MIB (sealed), G5 ....$50.00

MPC, Pilgrim Observer Space Station #9001, 1970, MIB (sealed), D9...$28.00

MPC, Schwinn 5-Speed Ray Bicycle, late 1970s-early 1980s, 1/8, M (EX+ sealed box), D9....................................$24.00

MPC, Six Million Dollar Man, Bionic Bustout #601, 1975, 1/12, MIB (sealed), G5 ....$35.00

MPC, Six Million Dollar Man, Fight for Survival #602, 1975, 1/12, MIB (sealed), G5 ....$40.00

MPC, Six Million Dollar Man, Jaws of Doom #603, 1975, 1/12, MIB (sealed), G5 ....$50.00

MPC, Space: 1999, Eagle Transporter #1901, 1975, 1/72, MIB (sealed), G5 ....$170.00

MPC, Space: 1999, Hawk Spaceship #1904, 1977, 1/72, MIB, G5 ....$115.00

MPC, Star Wars, C-3PO, 1977, M (EX+ sealed larger box), D9...$20.00

MPC, Star Wars, Darth Vader, action kit, battery-op, 1978, M (NM sealed box), D9...$55.00

MPC, Star Wars, Darth Vader Tie-Fighter, 1978, MIB (sealed), D9...$25.00

MPC, Star Wars, Encounter w/Yoda #1923, 1981, 1/12, MIB (sealed), G5 ....$70.00

MPC, Star Wars, Luke Skywalker's X-Wing Fighter #1914, 1978, 1/48, MIB (sealed), G5 ....$15.00

MPC, Star Wars, Millennium Falcon #1925, 1978, illuminated version, NMIB, D9 ....$25.00

MPC, Star Wars, R2-D2 #1912, 1977, orig issue, 1/8, MIB, G5...$45.00

MPC, Star Wars, Y-Wing Fighter #1975, 1984, 1/72, MIB (sealed), G5 ....$60.00

MPC, Strange Changing, Vampire #901, 1974, 1/12, MIB, G5 ....$120.00

MPC, Street Hawk, Jesse Hawk's Mustang Coupe #687, 1984, 1/25, MIB, G5 ....$25.00

MPC, Titan IIIC #1902, 1970, 1/100, MIB, G5 ....$180.00

MPC/Ertl, Hardcastle & McCormick, Coyote Super Sportscar #6379, 1983, 1/25, MIB (sealed), G5 ....$30.00

Multiple, Flying Floogle, MIB, T1 ....$75.00

Nikken, Eagle Apollo Lunar Module #1, 1969, 1/80, MIB, G5 ....$20.00

Nitto, MS Cargo Liner Trinidad #987, 1/450, MIB, G5 ...$30.00

Nitto, Psycho Armor, Duguros Death Gander #23058, 1/100, MIB, G5 ....$30.00

Palmer, Animals of the World, African Lion #21, 1950s, MIB, G5 ....$30.00

Palmer, Animals of the World, Atlantic Shellfish #23, 1950s, MIB, G5 ....$35.00

Palmer, Animals of the World, Kodiak Bear, 1950s, EX (VG box), D9...$10.00

Palmer, Animals of the World, Shoveler Duck, 1950s, EX (EX box), D9...$15.00

Palmer, Revolutionary War Cannon #34, 1950s, 1/24, MIB, G5 ....$20.00

Palmer, Scout Award Trophies, African Lion #21, 1950s, MIB, G5 ....$25.00

Palmer, Spirit of '76 Diorama #76, 1950s, 1/12, MIB, G5 ...$95.00

Palmer, US Navy Vanguard Missile #106, 1958, 1/48, MIB, G5 ....$250.00

Plastic Age Concepts, Giant Insect (Aurora recast), 1/13, MIB, G5 ....$60.00

Plastic Age Concepts, Munster Family (Aurora recast), 1/16, MIB, G5 ....$90.00

Plastic Age Concepts, Willy Wonka, 12", MIB, G5 ....$70.00

Pyro, American President Liner, 1967, MIB (sealed), D9 ...$25.00

Pyro, Indian Chief #281, 1960s, 1/8, MIB, G5 ....$85.00

Pyro, Indian Medicine Man #282, 1960s, 1/8, MIB, G5 ..$100.00

Pyro, Italian Miquelet Pistol #226, 1967, 1/1, MIB, G5 ...$20.00

Pyro, Protoceratops #279, 1968, 1/8, MIB (sealed), G5 ....$30.00

Pyro, Texas Cowboy #284, 1960s, 1/8, MIB, G5 ....$65.00

Pyro, Vintage Brass Car, Stevens-Duryea Tourer, 1967, 1/32, M (EX+ sealed box), D9 ....$10.00

Pyro, Vintage Brass Car, 1911 Packard Touring Car, 1967, 1/32, M (EX sealed box), D9 ....$10.00

Remco, Action Stallions, Circus Liberty Horse, MIB (sealed)...$40.00

Remco, Flintstones Motorized Car & Trailer, 1961, complete, MIB, T2 ....$170.00

Renwal, Botany Science, 1964, M (NM sealed box), D9 .$35.00

Renwal, Family Coat-of-Arms #950, 1960s, 1/1, MIB, G5....$50.00

Renwal, Hawk Guided Missiles #558, 1974, 1/32, MIB, G5.$45.00

Renwal, Human Skeleton, 1950s-1960s, EXIB, D9 ....$25.00

Renwal, Human Skull #821, 1960s, 1/1, glows, MIB, G5 .$50.00

Renwal, Leopard Frog, 1960s, partially assembled, unpnt, EX (EX box), D9...$35.00

Renwal, Nike-Ajax Missile #550, 1958, orig issue, 1/32, MIB, G5 ....$75.00

Renwal, Reptile Science, NM (VG+ box), D9 ....$38.00

Renwal, Sculpt-A-Form Mannikin #920, 1964, MIB, G5 ..$70.00

Renwal, Teracruzer/Mace Missile #561, 1959, 1/32, MIB, G5 ....$450.00

Renwal, Visible Automobile Chassis #813, 1963, 1/4, minor assembly, NMIB, G5 ....$100.00

Renwal, Visible Man #800, 1959, orig issue, 1/5, MIB, G5 ..$40.00

Revell, American Space Pioneers #1847, 1969, 1/48, MIB, G5...$230.00

Revell, Apollo Lunar Module #1861, 1975, 1/48, MIB (sealed), G5 ....$50.00

Revell, Apollo Saturn-5 Rocket #1843, 1969, 1/96, MIB, G5 ..$225.00

Revell, Apollo-Soyuz Link-Up #1800, 1975, 1/96, MIB (sealed), G5 ....$100.00

Revell, Astronaut in Space (smaller reissue of Gemini Astronaut kit), 1969, M (NM sealed box), D9 ....$35.00

Revell, Atomic Power Plant #1550, 1959, 1/192, MIB, G5...$600.00

Revell, Beatles, George Harrison, assembled, missing few minor pcs, B3 ....$80.00

Revell, Beatles, John Lennon, assembled, complete, EX, B3 .$100.00

Revell, Beatles, Paul McCartney, MIB (sealed contents), B3 ...$335.00

Revell, Beatles, Ringo Starr, MIB (sealed contents), B3...$230.00

Revell, Billy Carter's Redneck Power Pick-Up, 1978, M (NM sealed box), D9 ....$32.00

Revell, Blaze King #1920, 1962, 1/10, MIB, G5 ....$50.00

Revell, Bonanza, Ben, Hoss & Little Joe #1931, 1966, 1/7, MIB, G5 ....$210.00

Revell, Charlie's Angels, Mobile Unit Van, 1977, NM (VG+ sealed box), D9 ....$25.00

Revell, Charlie's Angels Van #1130, 1977, 1/32, MIB (sealed), G5 ....$35.00

Revell, CHiPs, Helicopter #6102, 1980, 1/32, MIB, G5...$20.00

Revell, Code Red, Emergency Van #6029, 1981, 1/32, MIB (sealed), G5 ....$25.00

Revell, Code Red, Fire Chief's Car #6030, 1981, 1/32, MIB, G5 ....$30.00

Revell, Cowboys Cheerleader's Van #6405, 1979, 1/20, MIB (sealed), G5 ....$40.00

Revell, Deal's Wheels, Go-Mad Nomad #1364, 1971, 1/25, MIB, G5 ....$65.00

Revell, Deal's Wheels, Stinky Ray #3403, 1970, 1/25, MIB (sealed), G5 ....$60.00

Revell, Deal's Wheels, ZZZZZZZZ-28 #3402, 1970, 1/25, MIB (sealed), G5 ....$40.00

Revell, Discovery Boosters #4544, 1988, 1/144, MIB, G5...$30.00

Revell, Discovery Shuttle #4543, 1988, 1/144, MIB (sealed), G5 ....$15.00

Revell, Disney's Robin Hood Set 1 #945, 1974, MIB (sealed), G5 ....$130.00

Revell, Disney's Robin Hood Set 2 #946, 1974, MIB (sealed), G5 ....$110.00

Revell, Douglas United DC-7, 1974, M (NM sealed box), P3 ...$25.00

Revell, Dr Seuss, Game of the Yertle #2100, 1960, EXIB, G5.$125.00

Revell, Dr Seuss, Norval the Bashful Blinket #2003, 1959, MIB, G5 ....$220.00

Revell, Ed 'Big Daddy' Roth, Fink Eliminator #6196, 1990, MIB, G5 ....$40.00

Revell, Ed 'Big Daddy' Roth, Mother's Worry #1302, 1963, MIB, G5 ....$140.00

Revell, Eiffel Tower #8876, 1985, 1/385, MIB, G5..........$20.00

Revell, Endangered Animals, Komodo Dragon #6461, 1991, 10", MIB (sealed), G5 ....$50.00

Revell, Endangered Species, California Condor #702, 1974, M (NM box), D9...$25.00

Revell, Endangered Species, Polar Bear #704, 1974, MIB (sealed), G5 ....$40.00

Revell, Flipper & Sandy #1930, 1965, 1/12, MIB, G5....$170.00

Revell, Gemini Astronaut #1837, 1967, NM (EX box), D9 .$65.00

Revell, Gemini Space Capsule #1835, 1965, 1/24, MIB, G5..$60.00

Revell, Gemini Space Capsule #8618, 1982, 1/24, MIB, G5..$50.00

Revell, German V-2 Rocket, #560, 1973, 1/54, MIB (sealed), G5 ....$20.00

Revell, GI Joe, Attack Vehicle #8901, 1982, 7½", MIB (sealed), G5 ....$25.00

Revell, GI Joe, Rapid Fire Motorcycle #8900, 1982, 5", MIB, G5 ....$35.00

Revell, Grease II, '53 Chevy #7341 or '56 Ford F-100 Pick-Up #7375, 1982, 1/25, MIB, G5, ea $30.00

Revell, Hardy Boys Van #1398, 1977, 1/25, MIB (sealed), G5 ....$35.00

Revell, Jupiter C #1819, 1958, 1/96, MIB, G5...............$270.00

Revell, Launch Tower & Shuttle #4911, 1986, 1/144, MIB (sealed), G5 ....$130.00

Revell, M*A*S*H 4077th Bell H-13H Helicopter, MIB (sealed), T1 ....$20.00

Revell, Magnum PI, Island Hopper's Vanagon #7328 or TC's Helicopter #4416, MIB (sealed), G5, ea $70.00

Revell, Mercury/Gemini #1834, 1964, 1/48, MIB, G5 ...**$120.00**
Revell, Moon Ship #1825, 1957, 1/96, MIB, G5 ....**$200.00**
Revell, New Avengers Gambit's Jaguar XJS, 1979, complete, M (NM box), F8..**$50.00**
Revell, Phantom w/Witch Doctor #1451, 1965, 1/8, MIB, G5 ..**$150.00**
Revell, Quarter Horse #1922, 1963, 1/10, MIB, G5 ....**$40.00**
Revell, Robotech, Commando #1199, 1984, 1/48, MIB (sealed), G5 ....**$70.00**
Revell, Robotech, Space Fortress SDF1 #1144, 1985, 1/5000, MIB (sealed), G5 ....**$60.00**
Revell, Robotech, Thoren #1150, 1984, 1/72, MIB (sealed), G5...**$40.00**
Revell, Robotech, Zoltek #1151, 1984, 1/72, MIB (sealed), G5...**$50.00**
Revell, Saint's Jaguar XJS #6402, 1979, 1/25, MIB (sealed), G5...**$35.00**
Revell, Space Explorer Solaris #1851, 1969, 1/160, MIB, G5..**$190.00**
Revell, Space Pursuit #1850, 1969, MIB (sealed), G5....**$310.00**
Revell, Space Station, 1950s, complete, scarce, EX (VG box), A...**$575.00**

Photo courtesy Jane Moon.

Revell, Stage Coach of England, Miniature Masterpieces, MIB, J6, $45.00.

Revell, Tranquility Base #8604, 1982, 1/48, MIB, G5......**$25.00**
Revell, US Army Nike Hercules #1804, 1958, 1/40, MIB, G5 ....**$90.00**
Revell, US Frigate Constitution 'Old Ironsides,' 1966, NM (EX+ box), D9..**$12.00**
Revell, USN Bendix Talos Missile #1808, 1957, 1/40, MIB, G5 ....**$90.00**
Revell, Vostok #1844, 1969, 1/24, MIB, G5 ....**$130.00**
Screamin', Army of Darkness, Ash #1100, 1993, 1/4, MIB, G5 ....**$60.00**
Screamin', Bram Stoker's Dracula #1500, 1995, 1/4, MIB, G5 ....**$50.00**
Screamin', Flash Gordon, 1993, 1/4, G (EX box), D9 ......**$32.00**
Screamin', Freddy Krueger #1, 1987, 1/4, MIB, G5 ....**$50.00**
Screamin', Hellraiser, Pinhead Cenobite #500, 1989, 1/4, MIB, G5 ....**$70.00**
Screamin', Mary Shelly's Frankenstein #1400, 1994, 1/4, MIB, G5 ....**$35.00**
Screamin', Star Wars, C-3PO #3550, 1995, 1/6, MIB, G5..**$45.00**
Screamin', Star Wars, Chewbacca #3700, 1994, 1/4, MIB, G5 ...**$45.00**
Screamin', Star Wars, Darth Vader #3250, 1993, 1/6, MIB, G5..**$35.00**
Screamin', Star Wars, Han Solo #3400, 1993, 1/4, MIB, G5.......**$35.00**
Screamin', Star Wars, Yoda #3300, 1992, 1/4, MIB, G5...**$40.00**

Screamin', Suburban Commando, General Suitor Mutant #3100, 1991, 1/4, MIB, G5...**$55.00**
Screamin', Werewolf #400, 1989, MIB, G5 ....**$40.00**
Strombecker, Lunar Recon Vehicle #M37, 1958, 1/91, MIB, G5 ....**$90.00**
Strombecker, Man in Space, Satellite Launcher #D35, 1957, 1/262, MIB, G5..**$210.00**
Strombecker, Regulus I #M1, 1950s, 1/80, MIB, G5.........**$60.00**
Superior Plastics, Giant American Bull Frog #4600, 1960, 1/1, MIB, G5 ....**$40.00**
Superior Plastics, Transparent Breathing Man #4100, 1964, MIB, G5 ....**$25.00**
Takara, Eastland Groundsearch #40025, 1/48, MIB, G5 ..**$10.00**
Takara, Hunter Diskhound #443006, 1/25, MIB, G5 ....**$25.00**
Tamiya, Space Shuttle Orbiter #SO-001, 1/100, MIB, G5 ..**$70.00**
Testors, Area S4 UFO Revealed #576, 1994, 1/48, MIB (sealed), G5 ....**$30.00**
Testors, Grey ET Life Form #761, 1995, 1/6, MIB (sealed), P3.**$12.00**
Testors, Grodies, Davey #531, Flameout Freddie #533 or Huey's Hut Rod #538, 1983, MIB, ea, from $10 to...............**$20.00**
Testors, Weird-Ohs, Davey the Cyclist #731, 1993, MIB, G5 ....**$15.00**
Testors, Weird-Ohs, Leaky Boat Louie #734, 1993-94, MIB, G5...**$20.00**
Tomy, Disney, Goofy #4, 1980s, MIB, G5 ....**$50.00**
Tsukuda, Creature From the Black Lagoon #19, 1984, 1/5, MIB, G5...**$95.00**
Tsukuda, King Kong #JF-49, 1986, 16", MIB, G5 ....**$90.00**
Tsukuda, King Kong #49, 1986, 16", MIB, G5..................**$70.00**
Tsukuda, Mummy #39, 1985, 1/5, MIB, G5 ....**$70.00**
Tsukuda, Star Wars, Wicket #R1500, MIB, G5................**$50.00**
Tsukuda, Terminator (Arnold) #44B, 1985, 1/12, MIB, G5....**$75.00**
Tsukuda, Terminator Skeleton #44A, 1985, 1/6, MIB, G5 ...**$100.00**
Tsukuda, Terminator 2, T800 Endoskeleton #N012, 1991, 1/9, MIB, G5 ....**$60.00**
Tsukuda, Wolfman #40, 1985, 1/5, MIB, G5 ....**$40.00**
Union, Columbia Boosters #13, 1981, 1/288, MIB (sealed), G5...**$15.00**
Union, Stingray (TV show), 1983, MIB, G5 ....**$70.00**

Movie Posters and Lobby Cards

This field is a natural extension of the interest in character collectibles, and one where there is a great deal of activity. There are tradepapers that deal exclusively with movie memorabilia, and some of the larger auction galleries hold cataloged sales on a regular basis. The hottest genre right now is the monster movies, but westerns and Disney films are close behind.

Advisors: John and Sheri Pavone (P3).

Alice in Wonderland, 1974, lobby cards, set of 8, 11x14", EX, F8..**$45.00**
Amityville Horror, 1979, lobby cards, set of 8, 11x14", NM, P3..**$22.00**
And Now the Screaming Starts, 1973, Peter Cushing, 1-sheet, 41x27", EX+, P3 ....**$50.00**
Battle for the Planet of the Apes, Belgium, 21x14", rolled, EX, P3..**$35.00**

Battle for the Planet of the Apes, 1973, 1-sheet, 41x27", EX, P3..$50.00

Bedknobs & Broomsticks, 1971, 1-sheet, 41x27", NM, P3 ..$30.00

Ben, 1972, shows Ben leading his buddies, ½-sheet, 22x28", EX, P3..$20.00

Beneath the Planet of the Apes, 1970, 1-sheet, 41x27", EX, P3..$50.00

Big Top Pee Wee, 1988, 1-sheet, 41x27", rolled, NM, P3 ..$20.00

Billy the Kid Meets Dracula/Jesse James Meets Frankenstein's Daughter, 1965, 1-sheet, 41x27", EX, P3 ....$55.00

Burnt Offerings, 1976, Bette Davis, style A, 1-sheet, 41x27", EX+, P3..$25.00

Captain & the Kids in Old Smokey, 1930s, linen, 1-sheet, 41x27", rare, EX..$875.00

Captain Kronos, 1972, Hammer Productions, 1-sheet, 41x27", EX+, P3..$55.00

Chitty-Chitty Bang-Bang, 1968, Dick Van Dyke, ½-sheet, 22x28", folded, EX, P3.....................................$35.00

Chitty-Chitty Bang-Bang, 1968, lobby card, 11x14", EX, F8.....$5.00

Christine, 1983, John Carpenter, 1-sheet, 41x27", EX+, P3....$30.00

Coast of Skeletons, 1965, Sevens Arts Productions, 1-sheet, 41x27", EX, P3...$20.00

Cold Turkey, 1971, Dick Van Dyke & Bob Newhart, 1-sheet, 41x27", VG+, P3 ....$12.00

Conquest of the Planet of the Apes, 1972, lobby cards, set of 8, NM+, P3..$65.00

Conquest of the Planet of the Apes, 1972, style B, 40x30", rolled, EX+, P3..$60.00

Conquest of the Planet of the Apes, 1972, 1-sheet, 41x27", EX+, P3..$55.00

Conquest of the Planet of the Apes, 1972, 60x40", rolled, EX+, P3..$85.00

Cry of the Banshee, 1970, Vincent Price, lobby cards, set of 8, 11x14", NM, P3...$35.00

Curse of the Fly, 1965, lobby cards, set of 8, 11x14", VG+, P3..$50.00

Curse of the Mummy's Tomb, 1964, 1-sheet, 41x27", VG+, P3..$25.00

Daniel Boone, 1966, Fess Parker & Ed James, ½-sheet, 22x28", rolled, EX+, P3..$20.00

Day Mars Invaded Earth, 1963, 1-sheet, NM, P3..............$25.00

Day of the Triffids, Allied Artists, 1962, lobby cards, set of 8, EX, P3..$85.00

Day of the Triffids, 1962, 1-sheet, 41x27", VG+, P3......$155.00

Diary of a Madman, 1963, Vincent Price, 1-sheet, 41x27", EX, P3..$55.00

Dick Tracy, Disney, 1990, I'm on My Way, D11 ....$75.00

Dick Tracy, Disney, 1990, June 15th Everywhere, Tracy w/machine gun, D11...$50.00

Dick Tracy, Disney, 1990, Mind if I Call You Dick?, Breathless Mahoney, D11 ....$75.00

Dick Tracy, Disney, 1990, Next Summer They're Out To Get Him, D11 ....$75.00

Dick Tracy's G-Men, 1955, lobby card, 11x14", M, D11...$40.00

Disorderly Orderly, 1964, Jerry Lewis, lobby cards, set of 8, 11x14", EX, P3...$25.00

Dr Blood's Coffin, 1961, 1-sheet, 41x27", EX, P3.............$45.00

Dr Phibes Rises Again, 1972, 1-sheet, 41x27", EX+, P3...$45.00

Dracula AD/Cresenco, 1972, Hammer Productions, 1-sheet, 41x27", EX+, P3 ....$45.00

Dumb-Hounded, 1951, 1-sheet, 41x27", EX, from $700.00 to $1,000.00.

Empire of the Ants, 1977, Joan Collins, 1-sheet, 41x27", EX, P3..$17.00

Escape From the Planet of the Apes, 1971, lobby cards, complete set, 11x14", EX, P3 ....$50.00

Escape From the Planet of the Apes, 1971, 1-sheet, 41x27", EX+, P3..$55.00

Flipper, 1963, 1-sheet, 41x27", EX, P3.............................$28.00

Flipper, 1963, ½-sheet, 22x28", rolled, EX+, P3..............$35.00

Fog, 1980, 1-sheet, 41x27", EX, P3..................................$45.00

For Your Eyes Only, 1981, James Bond, Roger Moore, 1-sheet, 41x27", EX, P3...$45.00

Forbidden Planet, 1956, 36x14", NM, $1,200.00.

Frankenstein & the Monster From Hell, 1964, lobby card #7, 11x14", EX+, P3 ....$15.00

Frankenstein & the Monster From Hell, 1973, Peter Cushing, 1-sheet, 41x27", EX+, P3 ....$65.00

Frankenstein Created Woman/Mummy's Shroud, 1967, 1-sheet, 41x27", EX, P3 ....$45.00

Frankenstein Meets the Space Monster/Curse of the Voodoo, 1965, 1-sheet, 41x27", EX, P3 ....$45.00

From Beyond the Grave, 1974, Peter Cushing, 1-sheet, 41x27", EX+, P3 ....$35.00

G-Men River of Fire, G-Men Vs Phantom Legion, lobby card, 11x14", rare, M, A $50.00

Golden Eye, James Bond, 1-sheet, rolled, NM, P3 ....$15.00

Grease, 1978, John Travolta & Olivia Newton-John, 1-sheet, 41x27", EX+, P3 ....$45.00

Halloween, 1978, 1-sheet, 41x27", EX, P3 ....$45.00

Halloween II, 1981, 1-sheet, 41x27", EX+, P3 ....$45.00

Hold On, 1966, Hermans Hermits, 1-sheet, 41x27", VG+, P3 ....$45.00

Horror House, 1970, Frankie Avalon, lobby cards, complete set, 11x14", EX, P3 ....$30.00

House of Frankenstein, Universal Pictures, 1944, lobby card, 11x14", scarce, EX, minimum value........................$255.00

Invasion of the Body Snatchers, 1978, 1-sheet, 41x27", EX+, P3 ....$20.00

Island of Terror/Projected Man, 1966, 1-sheet, 41x27", VG+, P3 ....$35.00

It, 1966, Roddy McDowall & Jill Hatworth, ½-sheet, 22x28", VG+, P3 ....$25.00

It's Alive, 1974, 1-sheet, 41x27", EX, P3 ....$20.00

Jewel of the Nile, 1985, 1-sheet, 41x27", EX+, P3............$15.00

King Kong, 1976, 1-sheet, 41x27", EX+, P3 ....$40.00

King Kong Escapes, 1968, 1-sheet, 41x27", EX+, P3 ......$110.00

King Rat, 1965, 1-sheet, 41x27", EX+, P3 ....$35.00

Lion King, 1995, 1-sheet, 41x27", rolled, M, P3 ....$45.00

Macabro, 1966, 1-sheet, 41x27", EX, P3 ....$35.00

Mad Max, 1979, 1-sheet, 41x27", EX+, P3 ....$65.00

McHale's Navy, 1964, 1-sheet, 41x27", EX, P3 ....$55.00

McHale's Navy Joins the Air Force, 1965, 1-sheet, 41x27", VG+, P3 ....$30.00

Munsters Go Home, 1-sheet, 41x27", EX+, P3 ....$65.00

Never Say Never Again, 1983, James Bond, 1-sheet, 41x27", rolled, NM+, P3 ....$40.00

Nightmare, 1964, Hammer Productions, 1-sheet, 41x27", EX, P3 ....$40.00

Octopussy, 1983, James Bond, Roger Moore & Maude Adams, 1-sheet, 41x27", EX+, P3 ....$35.00

Old Yeller, 1974, re-release, 1-sheet, 41x27", EX, M8......$35.00

Operation Bikini, 1963, Tab Hunter, Frankie Avalon & Jim Backus, 1-sheet, 41x27", EX+, P3 ....$40.00

Poseidon Adventure, 1974, style B, 1-sheet, 41x27", EX+, P3 ....$25.00

Red Dawn, 1984, image of cast, 1-sheet, 41x27", EX+, P3..$20.00

Return From Witch Mountain, 1978, Disney, 1-sheet, 41x27", EX+, P3 ....$25.00

Return of Count Yorga, 1971, 1-sheet, 41x27", EX+, P3..$45.00

Return of Count Yorga, 1971, ½-sheet, 22x28", rolled, NM+, P3 ....$35.00

Shirley Temple in Captain January, 1936, 1-sheet, linen backed, 41x27", NM, $2,000.00.

Lady and the Tramp, 1-sheet, 1st animated feature to be made in CinemaScope, 41x17", VG, $350.00.

Smurfs & the Magic Flute, 1983, 1-sheet, 41x27", EX+, P3 ....$25.00

Snow White & the Seven Dwarfs, 1975, re-release, 1-sheet, 40x28", VG+, M8...$30.00

Star Wars Return of the Jedi, 1983, 1-sheet, 41x27", NM, P3 ..$50.00

Ten Little Indians, 1966, 1-sheet, 41x27", EX, P3............$25.00

Terror in the Wax Museum, 1973, lobby cards, set of 8, 11x14", NM, P3 ....$40.00

The Fog, 1980, ½-sheet, 22x28", EX, P3 ....$25.00

The Nanny, 1965, Bette Davis, 1-sheet, 41x27", EX, P3..$40.00

The Oblong Box, 1969, 1-sheet, 41x27", EX, P3 ....$40.00

Last Action Hero, 1993, 1-sheet, 41x27", rolled, NM, P3 ..$10.00

Latitude Zero, 1970, 1-sheet, 41x27", EX+, P3 ....$30.00

The Skull, 1965, Peter Cushing & Janet Lee, ½-sheet, 22x28", VG+, P3 ....$40.00

Thirteen Ghosts, 1960, 1-sheet, 41x27", EX, P3 ....$80.00

Tomb of Ligeia, 1965, Vincent Price, lobby cards, set of 8, 11x14", EX, P3 ....$45.00

Toy Story, 1995, backside is reverse of front print, 1-sheet, 41x27", NM, minimum value $25.00

Who Slew Auntie Roo?, 1971, Shelley Winters, 1-sheet, 41x27", EX, P3 ....$28.00

Witchcraft, 1964, Lon Chaney, 1-sheet, 41x27", NM+, P3 ...$25.00

Yours, Mine & Ours, 1968, Lucille Ball & Henry Fonda, 1-sheet, 41x27", EX, P3 ....$45.00

101 Dalmatians, 1961, 3-sheet, 41x82", EX, A $625.00

Musical Toys

Whether meant to soothe, entertain, or inspire, musical toys were part of our growing-up years. Some were as simple as a windup music box, others as elaborate as a lacquered French baby grand piano.
See also Disney; Character, TV, and Movie Collectibles.

Accordion, Emenee, 1957, plastic w/18 keys & 52 tuned reeds, cb case, complete w/song book & harness strap, NM....$50.00

Accordion, Hohner, 2-octave, leatherette case, 10", EX....$235.00

Blippy-in-the-Music Box, 1968, litho tin, NM, I2 ....$175.00

Blow-a-Tune, Kenner, 1949, crank hdl & blow to turn Happy Birthday disk, MIB.................................$30.00

Drum, tin w/wood rims, Canadian flags w/crest on maple leaf background, mc metallic, 8" dia, VG $165.00

Drum, tin w/wood rims, Converse/USA, portrait of Admiral Dewey flanked by Am flags, 11" dia, VG $715.00

Drum, tin w/wood rims, Santa leading an animal orchestra, gold on red, 6" dia, VG.................................$255.00

Drum, tin w/wood rims, Union soldiers in battle, 13" dia, VG ...$500.00

Drum, wood veneer shell w/wood rims, images of various battleships, 10" dia, VG $550.00

Guitar, Mattel, Mother Goose graphics, NM...................$60.00

Nodders

Nodders representing comic characters of the day were made in Germany in the 1930s. These were small doll-like figures approximately 3" to 4" tall, and the popular ones often came in boxed sets. But the lesser-known characters were sold separately, making them rarer and harder to find today. While the more common nodders go for $125.00 and under, The Old Timer, Widow Zander, and Ma and Pa Winkle often bring about $350.00 — Happy Hooligan even more, about $625.00. (We've listed the more valuable ones here; any German bisque nodder not listed is worth $125.00 or under.)
    Advisor: Doug Dezso (D6).
    See also Character Bobbin' Heads; Sports Collectibles.

Ambrose Potts, NM...$300.00

Auntie Blossom, NM...$150.00
Auntie Mamie, NM...$350.00
Avery, NM...$200.00
Bill, NM...$200.00
Buttercup, NM...$175.00
Chubby Chaney, NM...$200.00
Corky, NM...$475.00
Dock, NM...$200.00
Fanny Nebbs, NM...$250.00
Ferina, NM...$350.00
Grandpa Teen, NM...$350.00
Happy Hooligan, NM...$625.00
Harold Teen, NM...$150.00
Josie, NM...$425.00

Junior Nebbs, German, painted bisque, NM, $575.00.

Photo courtesy Doug Dezso.

Lilacs, NM $425.00
Lillums, NM...$150.00
Little Annie Rooney, movable arms, NM.................$250.00
Little Egypt, NM...$350.00
Lord Plushbottom, NM...$150.00
Ma & Pa Winkle, NM, ea $350.00
Marjorie, NM...$425.00
Mary Ann Jackson, NM...$250.00
Max, NM...$200.00
Min Gump, NM...$150.00
Mr Bailey, NM...$150.00
Mr Bibb, NM...$350.00
Mr Wicker, NM...$250.00
Mushmouth, NM...$200.00
Mutt or Jeff, med or lg, NM, ea $250.00
Mutt or Jeff, sm, NM...$175.00
Nicodemus, NM...$350.00
Old Timer, NM...$350.00
Our Gang, 6-pc set, MIB.................................$1,200.00
Pat Finnegan, NM $400.00
Patsy, NM...$425.00
Pete the Dog, NM...$150.00
Pop Jenks, NM...$200.00

Rudy Nebbs, NM $250.00
Scraps, NM $250.00
Uncle Willie, NM..$350.00
Widow Zander, NM...$400.00
Winnie Winkle, NM $150.00

Optical Toys

Compared to the bulky viewers of years ago, contrary to the usual course of advancement, optical toys of more recent years have tended to become more simplified in concept.

See also View-Master and Tru-View.

Anamorphoses, Julien/France, 1850s, 24 mc cards w/distorted images transform under viewing glass, EX (orig case), B12..$4,500.00
Batman Pick-A-Go-Go, 1960s, turn knob for moving pictures, rare, MIB, H12...$85.00

Bionic Video Center, Six Million Dollar Man, Kenner, 1976, shows color movie with hand-crank cassette, MIB, J6, $125.00.

Cinderella Pixie Viewer, Stori-Views, 1950s, plastic viewer w/3-D slides, NM (EX box), T2...$15.00
Flashy Flickers Magic Picture Gun, Marx/King Features, displays Phantom, Dagwood & others, EX (EX box), A.......$125.00
Flintstones Magic Movies, Embree, 1965, complete, 9x13", scarce, NMIB, A..$250.00
Give-A-Show Projector, Kenner, 1963, complete, NM (VG box), P3...$55.00
Jean Schoenner Lanterna Magica (Magic Lantern), late 1800s, w/glass slides, VG, A $375.00
Jeu de Thaumatrope, Academie Arts Graphiques, 1890s, complete set of 12 disks, spin to merge images, NMIB, B12..$2,850.00
Kaleidoscope, brass, mounted on rnd wooden base, 11", VG, A $175.00

Kaleidoscope, Space Scope w/snap-on heads, TN, MIB, J2 ..$55.00
Kaleidoscope, Walt Disney Epcot Center/Figment, 1980s, 7¼", EX, M8...$25.00
Kaleidoscope Wonder Wheel, Steven Manufacturing, 1975, NM..$15.00
Magic Lantern, Bing, 1907, tin, complete w/lantern, 30 slides & accessories, unused, NM (VG box), A....................$250.00
Magic Lantern, Plank, pnt tin, w/11 slides, lamp & glass chimney, 6", EX (EX wood box) $250.00
Magic Lantern #7, Plank, w/12 slides, G (orig litho paper-covered box w/hinged lid)...............................$125.00
Mickey Mouse Club Newsreel, Mattel, 1950s, complete, MIB, M17...$265.00

Movieland Drive-In Theater, Remco, battery-operated screen, complete, EX, T1, $135.00.

Promenade de Longchamp (Walk to Longchamp), France, 1830s-40s, peep show w/3 holes, 5 levels, EX (cover forms box), B12 ....$2,250.00
Telescopic View of the Great Exhibition, C Moody, Holborn (London), 1851, peep show, 10-level litho on cb, EX, B12.$850.00

Paper Dolls

Turn-of-the-century paper dolls are seldom found today and when they are, they're very expensive. Advertising companies used them to promote their products, and some were printed on the pages of leading ladies' magazines. By the late 1920s most paper dolls were being made in book form — the doll on the cover, the clothes on the inside pages. Because they were so inexpensive, paper dolls survived the Depression and went on to peak in the 1940s. Though the advent of television caused sales to decline, paper doll companies were able to hang on by making paper dolls representing Hollywood celebrities and TV stars. These are some of the most collectible today. Even celebrity dolls from more recent years like the Brady Bunch or the Waltons are popular. Remember, condition is very important; if they've been cut out, even when they're still in fine condition and have all their original accessories, they're worth only about half as much as an uncut book or box set.

For more information, refer to *Price Guide to Lowe and Whitman Paper Dolls* by Mary Young, *Collecting Toys* by Richard O'Brien, and *Toys, Antique and Collectible*, by David Longest.

Advisor: Mary Young (Y2).

Alice in Wonderland, Whitman #993, 1933, uncut, M .$150.00
Ann Sheridan, Whitman #986, 1944, uncut, M.............$200.00
Annie Laurie, Lowe #1030, 1941, uncut, M $75.00
Archies Girls, Lowe #2764, 1964, uncut, M.....................$50.00
Ava Gardner, Whitman #965, 1949, uncut, M $125.00
Bab & Her Doll Furniture, Lowe #523, 1943, uncut, M ...$25.00
Baby Show, Lowe #1021, 25 dolls, 1940, uncut, M $100.00

Baby-Sitter, Saalfield #2747, 1956, uncut, M, $35.00.

Photo courtesy Mary Young.

Baby Sparkle Plenty, Saalfield #2500, 1948, uncut, NM, D11..$50.00
Beauty Contest, Lowe #1026, 1941, uncut, M................$100.00
Betty Bo-Peep, Lowe #1043, 1942, uncut, M....................$85.00
Betty Grable, Whitman #962, 1946, uncut, M..............$175.00
Betty Grable, Whitman #989, 1941, uncut, M..............$200.00
Beverly Hillbillies, Whitman #1955, 1964, cut, complete, EX .$30.00
Blondie, Whitman #967, 1948, uncut, M......................$125.00
Blondie, Whitman #982, 1940, uncut, M......................$150.00
Blondie at the Movies, Whitman #979, 1941, uncut, M ..$175.00
Blue Feather Indian, Lowe #1044, 1944, uncut, M...........$65.00
Bob Cummings Fashion Models, Lowe #2407, 1957, uncut,
    M...$75.00
Bob Hope & Dorothy Lamour, Whitman #976, 1942, uncut,
    M $250.00
Bobbsey Twins, Lowe #1254, 1952, uncut, M..................$75.00
Brady Bunch, Whitman #1976, 1973, uncut, EX, J5 ....$35.00
Brenda Lee, Lowe #2785, 1961, uncut, M.......................$60.00
Bride Doll, Lowe #1043, 1946, uncut, M $55.00
Buffy & Jody, Whitman #4764, 1970, cut, EX (EX box)..$20.00
Career Girls, Lowe #1045, 1942, uncut, M $75.00
Carmen Miranda, Whitman #995, 1942, uncut, M........$160.00
Cinderella Steps Out, Lowe #1242, 1948, uncut, M.........$60.00
Claudette Colbert, Saalfield #2451, 1943, uncut, M $200.00
Clothes Crazy, Lowe #1046, 1945, uncut, M $35.00
Clothes Make a Lady, Lowe #1029, 1942, uncut, M.......$100.00
Cowboys & Cowgirls, Lowe #1286, 1950, uncut, M.........$25.00
Cuddles & Rags, Lowe #1283, 1950, uncut, M $55.00

Dinah Shore, Whitman #977, 1943, uncut, M..............$200.00
Dinah Shore & George Montgomery, Whitman #1970, 1959,
    cut, EX $35.00
Dionne Quints, Whitman #998, 1935, uncut, M $125.00
Dodie (My Three Sons), Artcraft #5115, 1971, unpunched, EX,
    J5 ....$35.00
Down on the Farm, Lowe #1056, uncut, M....................$30.00
Dr Kildare & Nurse Susan, Lowe #2740, 1962, uncut, M.$50.00
Dr Kildare Play Book, Lowe, #955, uncut, M..................$20.00
Dude Ranch, Lowe #1026, 1943, uncut, M....................$35.00
Edgar Bergman's Charlie McCarthy, Whitman #995, 1938,
    uncut, M $250.00
Elizabeth Taylor, Whitman #968, 1949, uncut, M $135.00
Elly May (Beverly Hillbillies), Watkins/Strathmore #1819-A,
    1963, uncut, NM $50.00
Farmer Fred, Lowe #523, 1943, uncut, M.....................$25.00
Fashion Previews, Lowe #1246, 1949, uncut, M $45.00
Faye Emerson, Saalfield #2722, 1952, uncut, M $125.00
Five Little Peppers, Lowe #1030, 1941, uncut, M.............$75.00
Gabby Hayes, Lowe #4171, 1954, turn pg to give doll a new out-
    fit, M $50.00
Gene Autry's Melody Ranch, Whitman #990, 1950, uncut,
    M..$100.00
Gene Tierney, Whitman #992, 1947, uncut, M $200.00
Gigi Perreau, Saalfield #2605, 1951, uncut, M $65.00
Girls in the War, Lowe #1028, 1943, turnabout doll book,
    uncut, M $125.00
Girls in Uniform, Lowe #1048, 1942, uncut, M.............$100.00
Glenn Miller-Marion Hutton, Lowe #1041, 1942, uncut, M .$400.00
Goldilocks & the Three Bears, Lowe #2561, 1955, uncut, M...$35.00

Green Acres, Whitman #4773, 1968, uncut, M, $55.00.

Photo courtesy John and Sheri Pavone.

Haley Mills in That Darn Cat!, Whitman #1955, 1965, cut, EX,
    F8 ....$16.00
Hedy Lamarr, Saalfield #2600, 1951, uncut, M $100.00
Here Comes the Bride, Lowe #2562, 1955, uncut, M $30.00

Hollywood Personalities, Lowe #1049, 1941, uncut, M..$400.00
Honeymooners, Lowe #2560, 1956, uncut, M $300.00
In Our Backyard, Lowe #1027, 1941, uncut, M $60.00
Jane Withers, Whitman #989, 1940, uncut, M.............$150.00
Janet Leigh, Lowe #2405, 1957, uncut, M $85.00
Janie & Her Doll, Lowe #523, 1943, uncut, M $25.00
Joanne Woodward, Saalfield #4436, 1958, fold-out book, uncut,
    EX $85.00
Judy & Jack, Peg & Bill, Lowe #1024, 1940, uncut, M...$100.00
Judy Garland, Whitman #996, 1945, uncut, M $225.00
Julia, Saalfield #6055, 1970, complete, uncut, MIB.........$50.00
June Allyson, Whitman #970, 1950, uncut, M $100.00
Junior Prom, Lowe #1042, 1942, uncut, M $50.00
King of Swing & Queen of Song, Lowe #1040, 1942, uncut,
    M...$400.00
Lana Turner, Whitman #988, 1942, uncut, M $200.00
Laugh-In, Saalfield #1325, 1969, complete & unused, NM,
    C1 ....$50.00
Let's Play House, Lowe #1248, 1949, uncut, M $25.00
Linda Darnell, Saalfield #2733, 1953, uncut, M.............$100.00
Little Cousins, Lowe #521, uncut, 1940, M $50.00
Little Orphan Annie, Whitman #938, 1934, uncut, M..$250.00
Little Pet Paper Dolls, McLoughlin Bros, ca 1861-70, 1 doll
    w/extra head, 3 outfits, EX (EX orig folder), A........$150.00

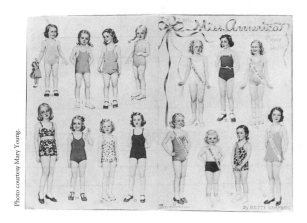

Photo courtesy Mary Young.

Little Miss America, Saalfield #2358, 1941, uncut, M, $75.00.

Little Women, Lowe #1030, 1941, uncut, M $75.00
Lola Talley, Whitman #971, 1942, uncut, M $125.00
Lollypop Crowd, Lowe #1049, 1945, uncut, M $45.00
Malibu Skipper, Whitman #1952, 1973, uncut, M $10.00
Margaret O'Brien, Whitman #970, 1944, uncut, M $150.00
Mary Martin, Saalfield #2492, 1944, uncut, M.............$125.00
Mary Poppins, Whitman #1982, 1964, complete w/press-out car-
    pet bag, uncut, NM, F8...$45.00
Me & Mimi, Lowe #1044, 1942, uncut, M......................$60.00
Mother Goose, Whitman #987, 1937, uncut, M..............$25.00
Movie Stars Paper Dolls, Whitman #905, 1931, uncut, M .$250.00
My Fair Lady, Ottenheimer #2961-0, 1965, uncut, EX.....$35.00
New Toni Hair-Do Dress-Up Dolls, Lowe #1251, 1951, uncut,
    M $75.00
Old Lady Who Lived in a Shoe, Whitman #985, 1940, uncut,
    M $125.00

Our Dollies & How To Dress Them, McLoughlin Bros, 1903,
    EXIB, A $250.00
Our Gang, Whitman #900, 1931, uncut, M $200.00
Ozzie & Harriet, Saalfield #4319, 1954, uncut, M..........$100.00

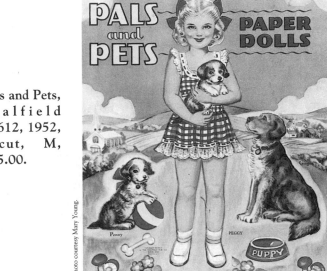

Photo courtesy Mary Young.

Pals and Pets, Saalfield #2612, 1952, uncut, M, $35.00.

Partridge Family, Artcraft #5137, 1971, uncut, NM $40.00
Pat Boone, Whitman #1968, 1959, uncut, EX, F5............$45.00
Pat the Stand-Up Doll, Lowe #1042, 1946, uncut, M $35.00
Patti Page, Lowe #2488, 1958, uncut, M...........................$75.00
Peter Rabbit, Whitman #955, ca 1939, uncut, M $90.00
Playhouse Paper Dolls, Lowe #1057, 1947, uncut, M $20.00
Playtime Pals, Lowe #1045, 1946, uncut, M $25.00
Polly Patchwork & Her Friends, Lowe #1024, 1941, uncut,
    M...$50.00
Popeye, Whitman #980, 1937, uncut, M $350.00
Prom Home Permanent, Lowe #1253, 1952, uncut, M.....$40.00
Raggedy Ann & Andy, Saalfield #2497, 1944, uncut, M...$100.00
Raggedy Ann & Andy, Whitman #946, 1935, uncut, M...$150.00
Rosemary Clooney, Lowe #2569, 1956, uncut, M $125.00
Roy Rogers, Dale Evans & Dusty, Whitman #1950, 1957, uncut,
    EX $125.00
Roy Rogers, Whitman #995, 1948, uncut, M $135.00
Sally & Dick, Bob & Jean, Lowe #1023, 1940, uncut, M .$50.00
Sandra Dee, Saalfield #4413, 1959, uncut, M...................$75.00
Shirley Temple, Saalfield #2112, 1934, uncut, M...........$200.00
Sparkle Plenty (Dick Tracy), Saalfield #5160, 1948, unused,
    NMIB..$65.00
Square Dance, Lowe #968, 1950, uncut, M.....................$25.00
Tap Stars, Lowe #990, 1952, uncut, M............................$25.00
Tina & Tony, Lowe #1022, 1940, uncut, M $50.00
Turnabouts Doll Book, Lowe #1048, 1943, uncut, M.......$35.00
Twinkle Twins, Lowe #521, 1944, uncut, M.....................$25.00
Walt Disney's Donald Duck & Clara Cluck, Whitman #969,
    1937, uncut, M $550.00
Walt Disney's Pinocchio, Whitman #935, 1939, uncut, M...$250.00
Walt Disney's Snow White & the Seven Dwarfs, Whitman
    #970, 1938, bl background, uncut, M $200.00

Wee Wee Baby, Lowe #1045, 1945, uncut, M $50.00
Winnie the Pooh, Whitman #947, 1935, uncut, M........$100.00

Paper-Lithographed Toys

Following the development of color lithography, early toy makers soon recognized the possibility of using this technology in their own field. Both here and abroad, by the 1880s toys ranging from soldiers to involved dioramas of entire villages were being produced of wood with colorful and well-detailed paper lithographed surfaces. Some of the best known manufacturers were Crandall, Bliss, Reed, and McLoughlin. This style of toy remained popular until well after the turn of the century.

Advisors: Mark and Lynda Suozzi (S24).

See Also Black Americana; Boats; Circus Toys; Dollhouses; Games; Pull Toys; Puzzles.

Alphabet Blocks, Hill, 1870, set of 18, G (orig box), A ...$55.00
Baby's Rattle Blocks, Germany, set of 4, 4" sq, EXIB, A ...$300.00
Band Chariot w/Musicians & Driver, Reed, ca 1895, 27½" L,
   EX...$2,000.00
Boy Scouts in Camp, McLoughlin Bros, 22 Scouts on wooden
   stands, 9x16", NM (EX box), A $225.00
Brownie Blocks, McLoughlin/Palmer Cox, 1891, shows Brownies
   in various activities, set of 20, 11x13", EX, S24.......$1,050.00
Castle, ca 1900, mounted on wooden green w/added side walls,
   10x16x17", G, A...$100.00
Clock Blocks, Strauss, 1904, learning clock reverses to months
   & seasons, 8½" sq, EX (EX cb box), A $165.00
Converse Circus Acrobat Toy, ca 1885, stenciled paper & wood
   pull toy, 12", EX, S24 ....$825.00
Crandall's District School, ca 1876, pnt wood, 10 articulated
   students, teacher, desk & books, VG (orig hinged box),
   S24 ....$1,100.00

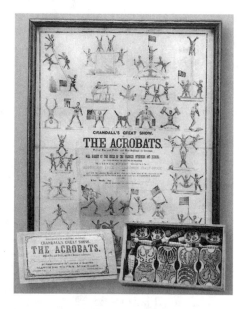

Crandall's Great Show, The Acrobats, 1875, complete, EX (EX box), from $900.00 to $1,150.00.

Crandall's Menagerie, 1875, pnt & jtd wood pcs form 6 different
   figures, 7½x13", EX (EX wooden box) $1,100.00
Easy Spelling Board for Little Ones & Improved ABC Blocks,
   Parker Bros, 40 blocks, EX (EX 5-sectioned wooden box),
   A...$225.00
Embossing Co's Cube Spelling Blocks, #18, animals w/letters &
   numbers, emb, 8x9", EXIB, A $125.00
Embossing Co's Cube Spelling Blocks, #88, 18 cubes w/animals,
   letters & numbers, emb, 6x11", VG (VG box), A...$200.00
Golden Letter Blocks, McLoughlin Bros, 18 blocks w/alphabet
   & images, 15x8x3", VG (VG wooden box), A........$525.00
Main 6500 Yellow Cab, blk & yel litho paper over wood
   w/wooden wheels, 5", VG, A $130.00
Nesting Blocks, McLoughlin, ABC blocks w/animals & birds, set
   of 7 (2 missing), paper damage, A $800.00
Nesting Blocks, McLoughlin, ca 1890, alphabet letters w/pictorial nursery rhymes, stacks to 36", EX, S24...........$1,850.00

Obleisk Alphabet Blocks, Pat. 1882, letters over hieroglyphics and various animal scenes, set of 8, VG, A, $700.00.

Old Guard Soldiers, Ives, w/cannon, EX, S24 ....$1,100.00
Panorama Nursery Alphabet, McLoughlin Bros, 5½" sq, EX
   (edge wear to box), A...$525.00
Play & Learn Block Set, McLoughlin, 2-sided, set of 16, 7½" sq,
   EX (damaged box), A...$715.00
Pretty Village, Boathouse Set, McLoughlin Bros, ca 1898, paper litho
   on cb, w/4 buildings & figures, complete, EXIB, A..........$100.00
Pretty Village, Church Set, McLoughlin Bros, ca 1898, EX+ (EX
   box), A...$140.00
Pretty Village, Colonial Park, McLoughlin Bros, 1897 & 1900,
   20x14", EXIB, A...$275.00
Pretty Village, Engine House Set, McLoughlin Bros, 1897,
   12x8", no figures o/w EXIB, A................................$100.00
Pretty Village, Small Set No 2, McLoughlin Bros, 1890, 8x11",
   EXIB, A $250.00
Punch & Judy Theatre Bell Toy, bell rings as paper & wood theatre w/curved base rocks side to side, 9", VG, A......$250.00
Read & Learn Block Set, Bliss, 8 cylindrical blocks w/letters &
   other graphics, 4", G (G box), A $2,200.00

Soldiers, McLoughlin Bros, 16 cavalrymen on wooden bases, 13x17", G (G box), A $165.00

Soldiers on Parade, Set #2, McLoughlin Bros, 50 soldiers on wood stands, 9x22", NM (VG+ box), A $250.00

Spelling Blocks, Hill, numbers on reverse, set of 20, G (G box w/Victorian image of children at play), A $85.00

Train, Bliss, ca 1885, 'US Grant' engine, tender & passenger coach, Columbian Expo Chicago Floor Train, 36", EX, S24 ....$4,750.00

Train, Bliss, 1890, NY Central RR, w/engine, baggage car, Pawtucket car & 7 flat blocks, 28", VG, A $1,250.00

Train, Milton Bradley, ca 1880, Hercules engine, tender & Atlantic-Pacific Coach, 34", VG+, S24 ....$3,750.00

Transformation Block Set, German, 3 blocks make up people of different ethnic backgrounds, 24 blocks in all, EXIB, A ...$475.00

Pedal Cars and Other Wheeled Goods

Just like Daddy, all little boys (and girls as well) are thrilled and happy to drive a brand new shiny car. Today both generations search through flea markets and auto swap meets for cars, boats, fire engines, tractors, and trains that run not on gas but pedal power. Some of the largest manufacturers of wheeled goods were AMF (American Machine and Foundry Company), Murray, and Garton. Values depend to a very large extent on condition, and those that have been restored sell for upwards of $1,000.00, depending on year and model.

Advisor: Nate Stoller (S7).

Airplane, Murray-Otto, silver w/bl & red trim, US decals on sides w/wings, 45", EX $3,500.00

Bearcat, Bartholomew, 1984, wood w/high-gloss maroon pnt, wht trim, banded rear tank, rubber tires w/hubs, 31", NM, A...$500.00

BMC Special Race Car #8, rubber tires, 41", pnt wear, G, A .$700.00

Car, Am National, early fenderless model w/winged hood ornament, 34", orig pnt, G, A $1,600.00

Caterpillar Diesel Tractor, New London Metal Products, 1950s, yellow with black trim and treads, restored, S7, from $3,000.00 to $6,000.00.

Car, Austin Motor Co, ca 1940, lt bl w/chrome detail & hubs, upholstered seat, electric horn, opening hood, 60", rstr, A...$1,700.00

Car, Gendron, wood & pressed steel, w/fenders & running boards, open seat, scalloped hood w/windshield, 39", G, A $2,100.00

Car, Kirk-Latty, ca 1915, red w/blk louvered hood, yel trim, thin rubber tires w/wire spoke wheels, 37", VG $3,000.00

Casey Jones Locomotive, Garland, orig pnt, 40", no steering wheel, 40", G $580.00

Chrysler, Steelcraft, 1941, deep bl w/wht radiator grille & hubs, chrome steering wheel, windshield & trim, S7 ....$2,500.00

Chrysler, 1938, gray w/wht wheels, chrome-plated windshield, plunger-type horn, 45", rstr, A..............................$2,000.00

Chrysler Airflow Fire Engine, modeled after 1936 vehicle, red with white detail, 2 wooden ladders, 50", restored, A, $1,150.00.

Diamond T Dump Truck, Am National, 1930, red w/blk & yel striping, NP radiator, running boards, 58", G, A..$2,550.00

Dodge, Am National, 1920, red w/orange trim, lg blk spoke wheels, winged hood ornament, 37", VG $3,500.00

Epoch, Tri-ang/England, ca 1937, red & blk w/NP trim, adjustable windshield, lithoed dash, balloon wheels, 43", EX, A $3,750.00

Fire Chief Car, Gendron, orig pnt, decals & bell, 35", EX...$2,500.00

Fire Department Ladder Truck, Murray, 1940s, 47", missing bell & ladders, G finish, A $460.00

Ford Convertible, Garton, 1937, teal gr, wht interior, chrome steering, windshield, wht-walls, rstr, from $1,000 to $1,800.00

Garford Dump Truck, Am National, maker's plate & decal, crank horn & electric headlights, 49", VG+, A ...$7,900.00

Irish Mail Racer, Frank Taylor Mfg Co, ca 1930, alternate backrest, 60", EX, A $400.00

Jeep Town & Country, Steger, wood body w/pressed steel hood & fenders, covered storage, 43", no steering wheel, EX, A $440.00

Limousine Convertible, Steelcraft, dk gr & beige w/dk gr upholstered 2-seat interior, chrome trim, hub wheels, rstr, A.........$2,550.00

Locomotive, Pioneer, early, pressed steel & wood, wire wheels, 54", rare, rpt, G, A...$935.00

Mack Dump Truck, Steelcraft (?), front fenders & running boards, extended front bumper, rubber tires, 54", rstr, G, A...$2,050.00

Mustang, w/rear wire luggage rack, 40", EX.................$1,750.00

Packard Coupe, Am National, enclosed w/opening doors, 60", rstr, A...$5,500.00

Packard Twin-Six Fire Chief's Car, Gendron, ca 1925, opening doors, 14" disk wheels, 64", rstr, A.........................$6,800.00

Playload Dump Truck, Murray, 1961, yel, blk trim, wht-walls w/blk & chrome hubs, Earth Mover logo on sides, rstr, S7 ....$1,500.00

Racer, BMC, 1950s, yel w/wht hubs, chrome steering & side pipes, Gilmore Speedway Special & logo on sides, rstr, S7...$2,500.00

Racer, Garton, gr metal w/simulated yel side vents & trim, fenders & running boards over spoked tires, 33½", G+, A $650.00

Racer #7, Am National, 1910, tin seat & nose w/side vents on wooden platform, thin metal spoke wheels, 42", EX, A..............$2,500.00

Racer #7, white with red flame design, red interior, 60", M, A, $1,200.00.

Racer #9, Am National, metal body, wooden spoke wheels, bell & noisemaker, 42", VG+, A.................................$2,550.00

Soap Box Derby Racer, 1934, St Paul Daily News, exterior exhaust pipe, EX, A..$330.00

Special Race Car #8, BMC, 41x19½", pnt wear, G, A...$695.00

Sterns Pedal Car, Gendron, 1920, blue metal body with white stripes on steel and wood frame, wood dash and seat, spoke wheels, G, $2,500.00.

Torpedo Convertible, Murray, 1949, wht w/red interior & hubs, chrome trim w/4 side vents, rstr, S7, from $2,250 to...$2,500.00

Touring Car, Mors, 1907, red wooden body w/gr plush-tufted seat, wire spoke wheels, center steering, 45", EX, A.......$1,600.00

Tractor, no markings, 38", rpt, VG, A..............................$75.00

Wagons

Badger Coaster, wood, wooden spoke wheels w/steel bands, 42", VG, A...$350.00

Buckboard, Old West style w/wood body, wood wheels w/steel bands, 48", VG, A..$775.00

Overland, wood w/metal pull hdl, rubber tires, VG, A...$135.00

Staley's Special, ca 1905-1915, natural wood w/red disk wheels, name stenciled on sides, VG, A...............................$200.00

Penny Toys

Penny toys were around as early as the late 1800s and as late as the 1920s. Many were made in Germany, but some were made in France as well. With few exceptions, they ranged in size from 5" on down; some had moving parts, and a few had clockwork mechanisms. Though many were unmarked, you'll sometimes find them signed 'Kellermann,' 'Meier,' 'Fischer,' or 'Distler,' or carrying an embossed company logo such as the 'dog and cart' emblem. They were made of lithographed tin with exquisite detailing — imagine an entire carousel less than 2½" tall. Because of a recent surge in collector interest, many have been crossing the auction block of some of the country's large galleries. Our values are prices realized at several of these auctions.

Advisor: Jane Anderson (A2).

Airmail Biplane, Levy/Germany, gray w/red trim, single prop, 3½", EX, A $525.00

Airplane, Kellermann/Germany, yel, single bl prop, 2 spoke wheels, w/pilot, 5¼", EX, A $440.00

Airplane, Kellermann/Germany, yel w/red trim, single bl prop, blk rubber tires, EX, A..$690.00

Airplane #2, Kellermann/Germany, single prop w/pilot in cockpit, yel w/gr trim & red numbers on wings, 2½", EX, A....$475.00

Airplane #592, Distler/Germany, single prop w/pilot in open cockpit, gr body w/yel wings, 2¾", EX, A................$450.00

Airplane in Hangar, Germany, early monocoupe plane w/pilot, 3", EX, A...$550.00

Airplane Spiral Toy, Einfalt/Germany, gr & maroon, 2 planes on rod spiral up & down by spring mechanism, 6½", EX+ $250.00

Airplane String Toy, Germany, orange prop spins as gray plane w/red wheels climbs string, 5¼", EX, A $550.00

Airplane Whistle, paper label on wing reads Kauffmann & Bear Co Pittsburg's Greatest Store, 4¼", EX, A $500.00

Alligator on Wheels, Einfalt/Germany, realistic w/articulated head & tail, 4 red disk wheels, 4½", EX, A..............$250.00

Auto Garage w/Sedan & Racer, Kellermann/Germany, 3½", EX, A $330.00

Auto Gyro Horn #1, France, pnt tin, blowing makes sound & rotates props, 5½", EX, A..$300.00

Auto Gyro Horn #2, France, pnt tin, blowing makes sound & rotates props, 5½", NM, A $400.00

Baby Buggy, Fischer/Germany, diecut figure in brn & blk buggy w/4 spoke wheels, 3½", EX, A...............................$230.00

Baby Carriage, Fischer/Germany, yel 4-wheeled buggy w/folded hood showing baby covered w/blanket, 3½", EX, A..$385.00

Baby in Highchair w/Table, Fischer/Germany, mc baby in yel chair w/animal pictures on table, 2¾", EX, A $250.00

Ballerina Horn, air-operated, 5½", EX, A.......................$150.00

Biplane Horn, France, pnt tin, blowing makes sound & rotates props, 4", EX, A $225.00

Bird in Cage, Meier/Germany, bird on swing in gr cage w/gold finial & base, 3½", EX...$225.00

Bird in Cage, Meier/Germany, mc w/slotted roof & sides, gold-tone loop hdl on roof, lever action, 3", EX+, A.......$150.00

Boat w/Sailor at Helm, gr w/bl cabin, w/flag, 4⅝", EX+, A..$600.00

Boy Holding Rabbit in Bentwood Rocker, Meier/Germany, boy in bl in red-fr rocker, 2¾", VG, A $445.00

Boy on Sled, Germany, boy in red top & pants that read Chicago Ill, 2⅜", EX, A $230.00

Boy on Sled, Levy/Germany, mc boy lying on yel sled w/wht wheels, 2½", VG+, A $275.00

Boy on Sled, Meier/Germany, mc boy on yel sleigh w/inner wheels, 3", VG+, A $525.00

Bullfighter, bull charges as matador raises red cape, lever action, 6", EX, A...$150.00

Camel w/Backpack Candy Container, Meier/Germany, realistic camel on silver-toned irregular base, 3", EX, A $330.00

CAMPSA Oil Truck, RSA/Spain, 4¼", VG, A.............$275.00

Carousel, Germany, complete w/3 children in swings, 3", EX, A...$275.00

Carousel, Meier/Germany, complete w/4 horses & riders, lever action, 2¾", EX, A $475.00

Chickens Feeding on Platform, Meier/Germany, 2 chickens pecking at center basket on 4-wheeled platform, 4¾", VG, A..$110.00

Chinese Man on Cart w/Parasol, Distler/Germany, parasol rotates as 4-wheeled cart is pulled, 2¾", EX, A $475.00

Clown, Germany, squeezing action allows articulated clown to bounce erratically, 6½", EX, A $415.00

Clown Riding Pig on Platform, pig rocks as toy is pulled, 3¼", VG, A $400.00

Clowns Clubbing Ball Back & Forth on Rails, Germany, lever action, 4½", extremely rare, EX, A........................$1,100.00

Couple in Swing, Meier/Germany, couple in double swing on platform, 3¼", EX, A..$300.00

Cow on Platform, Meier/Germany, bell around neck, w/horns, disk wheels, 3", EX, A $225.00

Dancing Dog Horn, dog twirls on pipe organ, 4", G, A..$175.00

Delivery Truck, RAS/Germany, simulated wood-finished body w/red open bed, blk roof, spoke wheels, 4½", EX, A...$165.00

Delivery Van, Germany, red body w/bl undercarriage, yel top, driver in open cab, 3⅝", EX, A $300.00

Dirigible, Distler/Germany, mc w/side-mounted props, passenger car & pull cord, 3", EX, A $880.00

Dog Cab, Meier/Germany, gold dog, blk & red open wagon w/gold side seats, stake rails, spoke wheels, 5½", EX, A...........$135.00

Dog on Platform, Meier/Germany, dog w/pointed tail & collar on platform w/4 disk wheels, 2½", VG, A $275.00

Donkey on Platform, Germany, gray donkey w/red blanket on platform w/4 disk wheels, 2½", EX+, A $250.00

Double-Decker Bus, Distler/Germany, red & gold w/long-nose cab, spoke wheels, litho tin, 4¼", EX......................$275.00

Dump Truck w/Driver, sgn GF, yel & red w/spoked wheels, push-down action activates dump, 4½", EX, A $275.00

Elephant on Platform, Distler/Germany, gray elephant on gr platform w/4 spoke wheels, 4", EX+, A....................$360.00

Express Parcels Delivery Truck, Distler/Germany, w/up, w/driver, 4½", EX+, A...$250.00

Ferris Wheel Whistle, Germany, revolves, 4", VG, A....$175.00

Fire Hose Truck, Meier/Germany, red chassis w/gold nose, yel back-to-back seats, silver wheels, 2 firemen, 3½", NM, A..$250.00

Fire Ladder Truck, Germany, w/up, red w/chrome-like grille, fenders & ladder, lithoed tires, w/5 firemen, 4¼", NM, A $300.00

Fire Pumper Truck, Meier/Germany, red chassis w/gold-tone nose & vertical tank, silver wheels, w/driver, 3½", EX+, A $275.00

Flying Hollander, Kellermann/Germany, boy holding lever on cart w/4 spoke wheels, 3", EX+, A $1,100.00

Garage & 2 Limousines, cars mk CKO Germany, gr & bl version, 3x4" garage, EX, A...$300.00

Gas Station & Car, JDN, station mk Gas & Oil, 3" car, EX, A...$165.00

Gas Station & Sedan, Distler, ca 1930, yel building w/red roof, bl & yel sedan w/red wheels, rare, 2¾", EX, A $500.00

Geese Pecking in Shed, Meier/Germany, 2 geese protruding from slant-roof shed pecking for food, 2¼", EX, A..$200.00

Globe, Germany, revolves on tin base, 3½", VG, A $150.00

Gnomes, Meier/Germany, 2 gnomes cutting wood on beveled platform, 4", EX, A...$415.00

Gnomes, Meier/Germany, 2 gnomes opposite each other on gr platform, each hammering, 4", EX, A.....................$250.00

Goat Cart w/Girl, tan & blk goat pulling bl cart w/2 gold spoked wheels, 4¼", EX, A...$165.00

Goat on Base, Meier/Germany, wht & blk goat in stride w/red bell collar on silver-tone irregular base, 3", EX, A...$275.00

Goose on Platform, Distler/Germany, w/bobbing neck, gr platform w/red spoked wheels, 3½", EX, A $350.00

Horse and Jockey on Platform, Germany, spoke wheels, 5", EX, $495.00.

Highchair w/Child, Meier/Germany, top folds into tray table w/litho castle scene, 3¾", EX, A $250.00

Horn Boat w/Sailor, spirit-pnt tin w/lead figure, blowing sounds horn & spins prop, red w/blk stack (horn), 4", EX, A..$700.00

Horse & Jockey on Platform, Germany, brn horse w/blk mane & tail on gr platform, spoke wheels, 4¼", EX+, A.......$415.00

Horse & Jockey on Platform, Germany, brn horse w/blk mane & tail on gr platform, bl disk wheels, 3", EX, A...........$200.00

Horse-Drawn Cab, Fischer/Germany, dapple gray horse, gray & blk cab, red spoke wheels, gold driver, 4½", VG+, A $175.00

Horse-Drawn Caisson, Meier/Germany, 4 horses w/2 riders, bl caisson w/red spoked wheels, gold gun, 7½", VG+, A $225.00

Horse-Drawn Carriage, Germany, driver on carriage w/4 spoke wheels & single horse, lithoed lady passenger, 4¼", EX, A $165.00

Horse-Drawn Cart, Italy, dapple gray horse w/blk mane, 2-wheeled stake cart w/open ends, 5", NM $100.00

Horse-Drawn Dray Wagon, Fischer/Germany, orange wagon w/wht spoke wheels & horse, w/driver, 5", EX, A ...$175.00

Horse-Drawn Fire Patrol Wagon, Meier/Germany, gr wagon w/red bench & gold spoke wheels, 5 firemen, 5½", EX, A $575.00

Horse-Drawn Hansom Cab, Meier/Germany, dappled horse, gr & blk cab w/gold trim, red spoke wheels, 3¾", EX+, A ..$200.00

Horse-Drawn Landau, Meier/Germany, spoke wheels, w/driver & 1 horse, 5", EX, A...$175.00

Horse-Drawn Lorry, Meier/Germany, dapple gray horse, red wagon w/gold trim & spoke wheels, 5½", EX, A $150.00

Horse-Drawn Military Ambulance, Meier/Germany, 2 horses w/1 rider, wht w/red roof, bl trim, spoke wheels, 4¼", VG+, A $100.00

Horse-Drawn Military Cart w/Boat, Meier/Germany, 2 horses w/1 rider, spoke wheels, 4¾", EX, A $200.00

Horse-Drawn Military Supply Cart, Meier/Germany, 4 horses w/2 riders, bl & yel cart w/red spoke wheels, 6¾", EX, A..$275.00

Horse-Drawn Military Wagon, Italy, red ammo container on platform w/2 spoke wheels, 1 horse, 4¼", EX, A $75.00

Horse-Drawn Postal Van, Meier/Germany, dappled horse, metallic gold van, no driver, 5½", EX, A.................$250.00

Horse-Drawn Water Wagon, Meier/Germany, dappled horse, red tank w/gold trim on gr platform, 4¾", VG, A ...$180.00

Jigger Horn, Distler/Germany, figure twirls on rnd slotted base, 5", A...$225.00

Jigger on Base, Distler/Germany, crank-operated, 3½", EX, A $400.00

Lamb on Platform, Meier/Germany, lamb w/red bell collar on platform w/red disk wheels, 3", VG, A....................$360.00

Launch w/Sailor, Meier/Germany, gr boat w/bl house, gold flags & 2 wheels, sailor stands behind compass, 4½", EX, A....$1,050.00

Limousine, Distler/Germany, bl & wht w/gold trim, luggage rail on roof, spoke wheels, 4¼", EX...............................$400.00

Limousine, Fischer/Germany, brn w/dk brn grille, wht spoke wheels, w/driver, 4", EX, A...................................$175.00

Lion on Platform, Meier/Germany, lion on gr platform w/red spoke wheels, 3½", EX+, A.......................................$600.00

Lizard on Wheels, Germany, realistic lizard w/articulated jaw & tail, 4 spoke wheels, 7½", NM, A $200.00

Locomotive, Meier/Germany, w/cowl & smoking stack, 4", EX, A $200.00

Locomotive/Road Roller, Germany, blk w/bl, red & gold striped trim, 3", EX, A $130.00

Man Smoking Pipe & Pushing Wheelbarrow, Germany, 2¾", EX, A $165.00

Mantel Clock, blk face w/gold-tone case & trim, pendulum & hands move, 2¼", EX, A..$200.00

Military Motorcycle, Meier/Germany, soldier w/knapsack seated on cycle w/spoke wheels, 4", missing hdls o/w EX, A..$300.00

Mobile Gas Station, Japan, complete w/Mobile station, gas pump & race car, 2½x2" base, NM (EX box), A.....$135.00

Monkey & Chicken on Beveled Platform, Meier/Germany, mc figures on cream platform, 4½", G, A $440.00

Motorcycle, Kellermann/Germany, #187, mk CKO, 2¾", EX $1,050.00

Motorcycle w/Driver, Japan, red cycle w/gr & yel driver, blk rubber tires, friction, 3½", EX+, A $150.00

Motorcycle w/Driver, Paya, prewar, gr w/balloon tires, 3½", NM, A $280.00

Motorcycle w/Sidecar, Germany, civilian driver w/lady passenger, 3¼", EX, A...$455.00

Mouse in Trap, Meier/Germany, lever action opens door for mouse to enter, door closes, yel & red, 4¾", EX, A..$200.00

Mule & Clown on Platform, Germany, mule rears up to kick clown, 4", EX, A...$300.00

Ocean Liner, Meier/Germany, red, wht & bl w/2 stacks, flags fore & aft, w/lifeboat graphics, 4¾", EX+, A...........$300.00

Peanut Roaster, Meier/Germany, spirit-pnt tin, crank-operated drum w/sliding door on gold-tone stand, 2¾", VG+, A...........$250.00

Phonograph, Meier/Germany, side lever activates 2-note musical sound, 3½", EX, A..$145.00

Photo courtesy Dunbar Gallery.

Pool Player, Kellermann, 4", EX, A, $245.00.

Porter Pushing Trunk on Dolly, Fischer/Germany, 3½", EX+, A $385.00

Porter Pushing Trunk on Dolly, Fischer/Germany, 3½", G, A...$155.00

Rabbit on Platform, disk wheels, 2½", EX, A $225.00

Racer, GF/Germany, boat-tail style w/driver, spoked wheels, 4½", EX, A $200.00

Racer, Meier/Germany, yel w/red detail, NP hubs, w/driver, 3", EX $350.00

Robin Perched on Base, Germany, makes chirping sound w/motion, 4½", EX, A...................................$255.00

Roller Coaster Wagon, w/up, highly detailed w/emb passengers, 2¾", VG+, A...$425.00

Roosters Feeding, Meier/Germany, lever action, 2 roosters on platform peck at feeding box (not emb), 4", EX, A.$225.00

Roosters Feeding, Meier/Germany, lever action, 2 roosters on platform peck at feeding box (emb), 4", VG, A $100.00

Service Station, mk Japan, bright litho tin w/diecut pumps, 2½x4", NM, A...$160.00

Sewing Machine, Distler/Germany, floral decor on blk machine w/spool of thread, yel table top, 4", VG, A..............$230.00

Sewing Machine, Meier/Germany, bl machine w/red hdl, yel table w/gold decorative brace, red treadle, 3¼", EX, A.......$135.00

Side-Wheeler, Meier/Germany, gr w/stack atop red & wht striped canopy, operative wheel, 3¼", EX, A..........$600.00

Speedboat w/Lady Driver, Meier/Germany, inertia wheel, flag mk #5, 4½", EX, A.......................................$950.00

Squirrel in Cage w/Horn, France, horn activates spinning cage, 4½", NM..$150.00

Steam Engine, Distler/Germany, pnt tin, operating piston & wheel, 4", EX, A...$385.00

Swan on Platform, Meier/Germany, gray swan on platform w/silver-tone spoke wheels, 2¾", EX+, A........................$745.00

Sword Fighters Squeeze Toy, Distler/Germany, hand-held squeezer executes action between 2 swordsmen, 5¾", EX, A...$100.00

Three-Wheeler w/Driver, Kellermann/Germany, olive gr driver w/red detail, spoke wheels, 3½", VG, A $475.00

Tiger on Platform, Germany, realistic tiger on platform w/lg gold-tone spoke wheels, 4", EX+, A......................$415.00

Touring car, Fischer/Germany, brn closed cab, spoke wheels, 4", EX $250.00

Touring car, Fischer/Germany, open, yel w/red detail & bl interior, spoke wheels, 4¼", driver missing o/w VG, A ...$75.00

Touring car, Meier/Germany, open, gray w/red interior, red spoke wheels, w/driver, 4¼", VG+, A.....................$200.00

Tractor w/Driver, Distler/Germany, 3¾", VG, A...........$125.00

Tractor w/Driver, Distler/Germany, 4¼", EX, A...........$300.00

Traffic Policeman, Levy/Germany, lever action, arm raises & lowers, 5", EX, A...$175.00

Train, CK, engine mk #150, 2 red passenger cars & 1 bl, 12", EX (EX box), A $450.00

Train, Distler/Germany, red, bl & gr locomotive & passenger car, 3⅞", EX+, A..$120.00

Train, Hess/Germany, locomotive & tender w/3 passenger cars, 9¼", EX, A $275.00

Train, Meier/Germany, all-in-one locomotive & passenger car on 4-wheeled base, 4", missing blk smokestack o/w EX, A..$85.00

Train, Paya/Spain, locomotive, tender & 2 passenger cars on single yel base w/2 disk wheels, 5½", EX+, A.............$175.00

Truck, Kellermann/Germany, open bed, 3¼", NM, A ...$175.00

Trunk, mk GMS, images of children at play, spring-loaded dome lid, 2¼", EX, A...$330.00

Watering Can, Meier/Germany, images of children at play, spring-loaded lid, 3", VG, A...............................$225.00

Wheelbarrow, gr w/animal decoration & gold trim, 4", VG, A $250.00

Windmill, emb & spirit-pnt tin, pedestal base, 3½", VG, A....$100.00

Zeppelin, Germany, mk Ges Gesch, passengers in 2 open gondolas, yel w/4 red props, 4", EX, A $950.00

Zeppelin Horn, France, 4", EX, A $225.00

Zeppelin String Toy, Distler/Germany, detailed zeppelin w/passengers in open compartment descends string, 6", EX, A...$950.00

Pez Dispensers

Pez was originally designed as a breath mint for smokers, but by the '50s kids were the target market, and the candies were packaged in the dispensers that we all know and love today. There is already more than three hundred variations to collect, and more arrive on the supermarket shelves every day. Though early on collectors seemed to prefer the dispensers without feet, that attitude has changed, and now it's the character head they concentrate on. Feet were added in 1987, so if you were to limit yourself to only 'feetless' dispensers, your collection would be far from complete. Some dispensers have variations in color and design that can influence their values. Don't buy any that are damaged, incomplete, or that have been tampered with in any way; those are nearly worthless. For more information refer to *A Pictorial Guide to Plastic Candy Dispensers Featuring Pez* by David Welch and *Collecting Toys* #6 by Richard O'Brien. Values are for mint-condition dispensers unless noted otherwise.

Advisor: Richard Belyski (B1).

Other Sources: B10, O1, P10, T1

Angel, no ft, B1...$45.00

Arlene, w/ft, pk, from $1 to $3.00

Baloo, w/ft $20.00

Bambi, no ft...$35.00

Barney Bear, no ft, H4..$35.00

Barney Bear, w/ft..$20.00

Baseball Glove, no ft $150.00

Batgirl, no ft, soft head, MIP, H4.........................$110.00

Batman, no ft, H4..$15.00

Batman, no ft, w/cape, B1......................................$150.00

Batman, w/ft, bl or blk, ea, from $3 to.....................$5.00

Betsy Ross, no ft, J6...$100.00

Bouncer Beagle, w/ft, M, B1....................................$6.00

Boy, w/ft, brn hair, from $1 to..................................$3.00

Bozo, no ft, diecut, B1..$125.00

Bubble Man, w/ft, B1..$15.00

Bugs Bunny, no ft, H4...$20.00

Bugs Bunny, w/ft, from $1 to....................................$3.00

Bullwinkle, no ft $175.00

Candy Shooter, red & wht, w/candy & gun license, unused..$95.00

Captain America, no ft...$45.00

Captain Hook, no ft...$35.00

Casper, no ft...$70.00

Charlie Brown, w/ft, from $1 to.................................$3.00

Charlie Brown, w/ft & tongue $6.00

Chick, w/ft, from $1 to..$3.00

Chick (no hat), B1...$50.00

Chick in Egg, no ft, H4...$25.00

Chick in Egg, no ft, w/hair..$50.00

Chip, w/ft, B1 ....$95.00
Clown, w/ft, whistle head, P10 ....$6.00
Clown w/Collar, no ft $65.00
Cockatoo, no ft, bl face, red beak $35.00
Cool Cat, w/ft $35.00
Cow (A or B), no ft, bl, ea $45.00
Creature From the Black Lagoon, no ft........$225.00
Crocodile, no ft $65.00
Daffy Duck, no ft...$10.00
Daffy Duck, w/ft, from $1 to $3.00
Dalmatian Pup, w/ft, B1 ....$35.00

Daniel Boone, no feet, $110.00; Indian Maiden, no feet, $95.00.

Dino, w/ft, purple, from $1 to $3.00
Dinosaur, w/ft, 4 different, ea, from $1 to.....$3.00
Doctor, M $100.00
Donald Duck, no ft $15.00
Donald Duck, no ft, diecut............................$115.00
Donald Duck's Nephew, no ft $20.00
Donald Duck's Nephew, w/ft, gr or bl hat, B1, ea $6.00
Donald Duck's Nephew, w/ft, red hat, B1 ....$10.00

Eerie Spectres, Diabolic and Zombie, $125.00 each.

Donkey, w/ft, whistle head, P10 ....$6.00
Droopy Dog (A), no ft, plastic swivel ears, MIP, B1 ....$15.00
Droopy Dog (B), w/ft, pnt ears, B1 ....$6.00
Dumbo, w/ft, bl head.....................................$25.00
Elephant, no ft, orange & bl, flat hat $45.00
Fat-Ears Rabbit, no ft, pk head......................$15.00
Fat-Ears Rabbit, no ft, yel head......................$10.00
Fishman, no ft, gr $150.00
Foghorn Leghorn, w/ft $55.00
Fozzie Bear, w/ft, from $1 to $3.00
Frankenstein, no ft..$200.00
Fred Flintstone, w/ft, B1, from $1 to..............$3.00
Frog, w/ft, whistle head, B1...........................$30.00
Garfield, w/ft, orange w/gr hat, from $1 to $3.00
Garfield, w/ft, teeth, B1, from $1 to $10.00
Garfield, w/ft, visor, from $1 to.....................$3.00
Girl, w/ft, blond hair, B1...............................$15.00
Gonzo, w/ft, from $1 to $3.00
Goofy, no ft, old $10.00
Gorilla, no ft, blk head..................................$45.00
Green Hornet, 1960s, from $200 to $250.00
Gyro Gearloose, w/ft, B1 ....$6.00
Henry Hawk, no ft $65.00
Hulk, no ft, dk gr $30.00
Hulk, no ft, lt gr, remake, P10 ....$3.00
Indian, w/ft, whistle head, B1 ....$12.00
Indian Brave, no ft, reddish $150.00
Indian Chief, no ft, yel headdress $95.00
Jerry Mouse, w/ft, plastic face, B1 ....$15.00
Jerry Mouse, w/ft, pnt face $6.00
Jiminy Cricket, no ft $175.00
Joker (Batman), no ft, soft head $125.00
Kermit the Frog, w/ft, red, from $1 to $3.00
Knight, no ft $225.00
Koala, w/ft, whistle head...............................$25.00
Lamb, no ft $10.00
Lamb, w/ft, from $1 to $3.00
Lamb, w/ft, whistle head, from $15 to $25.00
Li'l Bad Wolf, w/ft..$15.00
Lion w/Crown, no ft......................................$55.00
Lion's Club Lion, minimum value $2,000.00
Lucy, w/ft, from $1 to $3.00
Make-A-Face, works like Mr Potato Head, minimum value ...$1,500.00
Mary Poppins, no ft, B1 ....$750.00
Merlin Mouse, w/ft..$15.00
Mexican, no ft, B1 ....$125.00
Mickey Mouse, no ft, removable nose or cast nose, ea, from $10 to $15.00
Mickey Mouse, w/ft, from $1 to $3.00
Mimic Monkey (monkey w/ball cap), no ft, several colors, ea, from $25 to........$35.00
Miss Piggy, w/ft, ea, from $1 to $3.00
Miss Piggy, w/ft, eyelashes, B1 ....$10.00
Monkey Sailor, no ft, w/wht cap, M, J2...........$25.00
Mowgli, w/ft $20.00
Mr Ugly, no ft $20.00
Muscle Mouse (gray Jerry), w/ft, plastic nose ...$15.00
Nermal, w/ft, gray, from $1 to........................$3.00

Nurse, no ft, brn hair, B1	$100.00
Octopus, no ft, blk	$60.00
Olive Oyl, no ft, B1, minimum value	$150.00
Olympic Wolf	$750.00
Orange, no ft	$165.00
Panda, no ft, diecut eyes	$20.00
Panda, w/ft, remake, from $1 to	$3.00
Panda, w/ft, whistle head	$6.00

Pinocchio, no feet, $125.00; Snow White, no feet, $125.00.

Papa Smurf, w/ft, red, P10	$5.00
Parrot, w/ft, whistle head, B1	$6.00
Pebbles Flintstone, w/ft, B1, from $1 to	$3.00
Penguin, w/ft, whistle head, B1	$6.00
Penguin (Batman), no ft, soft head, NM	$125.00
Peter Pez (A), no ft	$65.00
Peter Pez (B), w/ft, from $1 to	$3.00
Pilgrim, no ft, J6	$100.00
Pirate, no ft	$40.00
Pluto, no ft, red	$10.00
Pluto, w/ft, from $1 to	$3.00
Popeye (B), no ft	$60.00
Popeye (C), no ft, w/removable pipe	$65.00
Practical Pig (B), no ft	$30.00
Psychedelic Eye, no ft	$450.00
Psychedelic Flower, no ft, B1	$400.00
Pumpkin (A), no ft, from $10 to	$15.00
Pumpkin (B), w/ft, from $1 to	$3.00
Raven, no ft, yel beak	$30.00
Rhino, w/ft, whistle head, P10	$6.00
Ringmaster, no ft	$225.00
Road Runner, w/ft, B1	$10.00
Rooster, w/ft, whistle head, B1	$25.00
Rooster, w/ft, wht or yel head, ea	$25.00
Rudolph, no ft	$35.00
Santa Claus (A), no ft, steel pin, from $95 to	$125.00
Santa Claus (B), no ft, B1	$85.00
Santa Claus (C), no ft, from $5 to	$15.00
Santa Claus (C), w/ft, B1, from $1 to	$3.00
Scrooge McDuck (A), no ft, B1	$25.00
Scrooge McDuck (B), w/ft, B1	$6.00
Sheik, no ft	$30.00
Skull (A), no ft, from $5 to	$10.00
Skull (B), w/ft, from $1 to	$3.00
Smurf, w/ft	$5.00
Smurfette, w/ft, bl, P10	$5.00
Snoopy, w/ft, from $1 to	$5.00
Snowman (A), no ft, from $5 to	$10.00

Spaceman, no feet, $125.00

Snowman (B), w/ft, from $1 to $5.00
Space Trooper Robot, no ft, full body $325.00
Speedy Gonzales (A), w/ft $10.00
Speedy Gonzales (B), no ft, from $1 to $3.00
Spider-Man, no ft, from $10 to $15.00
Spider-Man, w/ft, from $1 to $3.00
Spike, w/ft, B1 ....$6.00
Star Wars, Darth Vader, C3P0, Storm Trooper or Chewbacca,
    B1, ea, from $1 to $2.00
Sylvester (A), w/ft, cream or wht whiskers, B1, ea..............$5.00
Sylvester (B), w/ft, from $1 to $3.00
Teenage Mutant Ninja Turtles, w/ft, 8 variations, ea, from $1 to.$3.00
Thor, no ft...$175.00
Thumper, w/ft, no copyright, D8 ....$30.00
Tiger, w/ft, whistle head, P10 ....$6.00
Tinkerbell, no ft..$150.00
Tom, no ft $35.00
Tom, w/ft, plastic face $15.00
Tom, w/ft, pnt face $6.00
Truck, many variations, B1, ea, minimum value................$1.00
Tweety Bird, no ft, H4 ....$10.00
Tweety Bird, w/ft, from $1 to $3.00
Tyke, w/ft, B1 ....$6.00
Valentine Heart, B1, from $1 to $2.00
Whistle, w/ft, from $1 to $3.00
Wile E Coyote, w/ft, B1 ....$35.00
Winnie the Pooh, w/ft, B1..$50.00
Witch, 3-pc, no ft $10.00
Wolfman, no ft $225.00
Wonder Woman, no ft, soft head..$125.00
Wonder Woman, w/ft, from $1 to $3.00
Woodstock, w/ft, from $1 to $3.00
Woodstock, w/ft, pk feathers $10.00
Yappy Dog, no ft, orange or gr, ea $45.00
Yosemite Sam, w/ft, from $1 to $2.00

Miscellaneous

Bank, truck #1, metal $200.00
Bank, truck #2, metal..$40.00
Body Parts, fit over stem of dispenser & make it look like a per-
    son, many variations, B1, ea $5.00
Bracelet, pk, P10 ....$5.00
Clicker, US Zone Germany, 1950, litho tin, 3½", NM ..$300.00
Coloring Book, Safety #2, non-English, B1......................$15.00
Power Pez, rnd mechanical dispenser, B1 ....$5.00
Puzzle, Springbok/Hallmark, 500 pcs, B1, minimum value.....$10.00
Tin, Pez Specials, stars & lines on checked background, gold
    colors, 2½x4½", rare, EX, A $225.00
Watch, pk face w/yel band or yel face w/bl band, ea.........$10.00

Pin-Back Buttons

Pin-back buttons produced up to the early 1920s were made
with a celluloid covering. After that time, a large number of buttons were lithographed on tin; these are referred to as tin 'lithos.'

Character and toy-related buttons represent a popular collecting field. There are countless categories to base a collection
on. Buttons were given out at stores and theatres, offered as premiums, attached to dolls, or received with a club membership.

In the late '40s and into the '50s, some cereal companies
packed one in each box of their product. Quaker Puffed Oats
offered a series of movie star pin-backs, but probably the best
known are Kellogg's Pep Pins. There were eighty-six in all, so
theoretically if you wanted the whole series as Kellogg hoped
you would, you'd have to buy at least that many boxes of their
cereal. Pep pins came in five sets, the first in 1945, three more in
1946, and the last in 1947. They were printed with full-color
lithographs of comic characters licensed by King Features and
Famous Artists — Maggie and Jiggs, the Winkles, and Dagwood
and Blondie, for instance. Superman, the only D.C. Comics
character, was included in each set. Most Pep pins range in
value from $10.00 to $15.00 in NM/M condition; any not mentioned in our listings fall into this range. There are exceptions,
and we've made sure they're evaluated below.

Nearly all pin-backs are collectible today with these possible
exceptions: common buttons picturing flags of various nations,
general labor union buttons denoting the payment of dues, and
common buttons with clever sayings. Be sure that you buy only
buttons with well-centered designs, well-alligned colors, no fading or yellowing, no spots or stains, and no cracks, splits, or
dents. In the listings that follow, sizes are approximate.

Advisor: Doug Dezso (D6), Kellogg's Pep Pins only.
Other Sources: C10, D11, S20

Archie, Club Member, red, wht & bl w/face image, 1960s, 1½",
    M (w/membership card, letter & envelope)..............$75.00
Batman, This Is the Year of the Batman, red, wht & bl w/image
    & logo, 1966, 1½", EX, J5 ....$40.00
Batman, WXYZ Radio Club/TV Batman Club, wht w/blk Bat-
    man logo, 1966, 2" $15.00
Batman & Robin, Charter Member/Batman & Robin Society,
    lettering around image of Batman & Robin, 1966, 3½",
    NM...$30.00
Batman & Robin, I'm a Batman Crime Fighter, red, wht & bl
    litho, 1⅜", EX $20.00
Beatles, blk & wht photo w/gr border, 3", EX, B3.............$25.00
Beatles, I Like the Beatles & faces, flasher, bl, 2½", EX, B3..$25.00
Beatles, I Love Paul, red, wht & bl, 1960s, 3½", EX.........$25.00
Beatles, I Love the Beatles, red, wht & bl w/music notes, 3½",
    EX...$20.00
Beatles, I Still Love the Beatles, red, wht & bl, 3½", EX..$25.00
Beatles, I'm an Official Beatles Fan, red, wht & blk w/images &
    names, 1960s, 3½", EX $20.00
Beauty & the Beast, heart shape, 1991, M8 ....$5.00
Betty Boop, A Paramount Star Created by Fleischer Studios,
    head image, ⅞", M..$150.00
Betty Boop, Max Fleischer's Talkatoons, image of Betty holding
    parasol, ¾", EX+ $40.00
Bullwinkle, Charge, Bring Back the Bullmoose Party!..., image of
    Bullwinkle yelling, 2¼", EX, J5 ....$35.00
Captain Marvel Club, Shazam!, litho, EX........................$50.00
Cat in the Hat, Happy 30th Anniversary, blk, wht & orange,
    1987, 2½", EX..$25.00

Chip 'N Dale Rescue Rangers, 1990s, 3", M8 ....$5.00

Cisco Kid/Butter-Nut Bread, I Eat Cisco Kid's Butter-Nut Bread, wht w/red lettering, 1950s, 1", VG.............................$25.00

Cisco Kid/Triple S Club, red, wht & yel, 1⅜", EX $65.00

Daisy Air Rifles, boy w/rifles, ⅞", EX...............................$125.00

Darkwing Duck, mc, 1990s, 3", NM, M8 ....$3.00

Davy Crockett Indian Fighter, yel & red image of Davy w/rifle on the frontier, 1950s, 1½", EX, J5 ....$15.00

Dick Tracy, Authorized Guide to Dick Tracy/50th Anniversary, 2¼", M, D11 ....$25.00

Dick Tracy, Home of Dick Tracy — Woodstock Illinois, shows Tracy in profile talking on wrist radio, 2¼", M, D11..$20.00

Dick Tracy Detective, shows Tracy in profile w/gun, 1930s, EX+...$50.00

Disneyana Convention, flasher, 1994, 4", NM, M8..........$10.00

Donald Duck, Happy Birthday..., 1934-84, 2½", M8..........$8.00

Dumbo D-X, red & gray on wht, 1¼", NM, A...................$35.00

Elvis, Love Me Tender, blk & wht image on gold record, 1956, ⅞", EX...$25.00

Hank Aaron, Thanks Milwaukee, 1954-1976, full color w/blk lettering, 2¼", EX, J5...$15.00

Hawkman, Official Member Hawkman Super Hero Club, lettering surrounds image, 1966, 3½", EX+ $25.00

Honey I Blew Up the Kids, 1992, rectangular, M8 ....$5.00

Hopalong Cassidy, Best Wishes From Hoppy, gray & blk, 1¾", rare, C10 ....$125.00

Hopalong Cassidy, In the Daily News, 2", C10.................$45.00

Hopalong Cassidy, Savings Rodeo, Bronc Buster, 1950s ..$45.00

Hopalong Cassidy, Savings Rodeo, Tenderfoot, 1950s.....$45.00

Hopalong Cassidy, Savings Rodeo, Wrangler, 1950s, C10 ..$25.00

Howdy Doody, It's Howdy Doody Time, 1980s, 2¼", M $5.00

Ideal Fun & Games Day, gr, bl, red & wht, 4", EX $25.00

Ideal's Blessed Event, Doll Just Born, red, wht & bl, 1950s, 1¾", EX, J5 ....$15.00

Ink Spots, photo on yellow background, 3½", $15.00.

Jackie Gleason the Loud-Mouth, VIP Corp, 1955, 1¾", VG, P4 ....$25.00

KISS, Madison Square Garden, WPLJ Radio, NYC, Dec, 1977, M $18.00

Lion King, features all characters, 1993, 3", NM, M8.........$5.00

Little Mermaid, 1980s, 3", M8...$5.00

Lone Ranger on Silver, mc, ca 1959, 1¼", EX $30.00

Lone Ranger, black and white on yellow background, 1¾", $65.00.

Mad, What Me Worry? I'm Voting Mad — Alfred E Neuman for President, color image of Alfred, 1960s, 2½", NM ..$125.00

Marvel Comics Convention '75, various characters surround lettering, red, yel & wht, 3", NM $30.00

Mickey Mantle/Lee Jeans, 1960s, 3", NM $15.00

Mickey Mouse, Emerson Radio, lettering surrounds image of Mickey waving, 1¼", EX+, A $100.00

Mickey Mouse, Mod Mickey, Beny-Albee, late 1960s, 3½", NM..$20.00

Mickey Mouse, Penney's for Back to School Needs around image of Mickey waving, 1930s, ¾", EX+ $95.00

Mickey Mouse, Sixty Years w/Mickey, 1988, 2¼", NM, M8...$3.00

Mummy, Universal Studios, red, wht & bl, 1960s, 3½", EX .$25.00

Oliver & Co, 1988, 3", M8 ....$5.00

Peanuts, Let's See Eye to Eye, Snoopy & Woodstock face off, 2¼", EX $8.00

Peanuts, Snoopy Come Home, yel background, 1972, 6", EX, H11 ....$15.00

Peanuts, We Love You Charlie Brown, no graphics, 1¼", M, H11..$5.00

Peanuts, You're a Good Man Charlie Brown, Charlie Brown on the mound, orange background, 1¼", VG, H11 ....$12.00

Peter Pan, Beny-Albee/WD, bust image, red & wht, 1950s, 3½", NM, A...$20.00

Pocahontas, I Was There, Wang Center, Boston, 1995, rectangular, NM, M8 ....$8.00

Pocahontas, Sing Along Songs video button, 1995, rectangular, NM, M8 ....$8.00

Popeye the Sailor, 1980s, 1¼", M.......................................$5.00

Rin-Tin-Tin, Every Kid Needs a Super Dog, blk & wht, 2¼", EX..$5.00

Rocketeer, 1990, oval, rectangular or sq, NM, M8, ea........$5.00

Roy Rogers My Pal, blk, wht & red, 1950s, 1¾", EX......$150.00

Snow White, Jungle Club Member, w/orig Kay Kamen paper, 1930s, 1¼", NM, M8 ....$45.00

Superman, Official Member Superman Club, wht w/mc image of Superman, 3½", NM, A $22.00

Tom & Jerry, Stroehmann's Bread, red, wht & blk, 1⅛", EX ..$25.00

Toy Story, Buzz Lightyear, rare, theatre employee button, 3", NM, M8 ....$15.00

Toy Story, features all characters, available at theatres only, 1995, rectangular, NM, M8 ....$10.00

Toy Story, Pick Up Your Toys, features Buzz, Hamm, Woody or Rex, Burger King promotion, 1995, set of 4, 3", M8..$35.00

Toy Story, video release, 1995, rectangular, NM, M8 ......$10.00

Yogi Bear for President, red, wht & bl, 1964, 3", EX $50.00
Zorro/7-Up, logo & image of Zorro on rearing horse, blk, red & wht, 1957, 1⅜", M, A..$25.00

KELLOGG'S PEP PINS

BO Plenty, NM..$30.00
Corky, NM..$16.00
Dagwood, NM...$30.00
Dick Tracy, NM...$30.00
Fat Stuff, NM...$15.00
Felix the Cat, NM..$85.00
Flash Gordon, NM...$30.00
Flat Top, NM..$30.00
Goofy, NM..$10.00
Gravel Gertie, NM $15.00
Harold Teen, NM...$15.00
Inspector, NM...$12.50
Jiggs, NM...$25.00
Judy, NM...$10.00
Kayo, NM...$20.00
Little King, NM...$15.00
Little Moose, NM $15.00
Maggie, NM $25.00
Mama De Stross, NM...$30.00
Mama Katzenjammer, NM $25.00
Mamie, NM...$15.00
Moon Mullins, NM...$10.00
Olive Oyl, NM...$30.00
Orphan Annie, NM...$25.00
Pat Patton, NM..$10.00
Perry Winkle, NM $15.00
Phantom, NM...$80.00
Pop Jenks, NM...$15.00
Popeye, NM $30.00
Rip Winkle, NM...$20.00
Skeezix, NM..$15.00
Superman, NM...$42.00
Toots, NM...$15.00
Uncle Walt, NM...$20.00
Uncle Willie, NM..$12.50
Winkles Twins, NM $90.00
Winnie Winkle, NM $15.00

Pipsqueaks

Pipsqueak toys were popular among the Pennsylvania Germans. Many featured animals made of painted papier-mache; some were on spring legs. All had bellows that produced a squeaking sound, hence the name. Early toys had bellows made from sheepskin. Cloth bellows followed, and on later examples, the bellows were made of paper.

Baby at School Desk, Germany, ca 1850, compo baby w/nodding head, wooden platform & desk w/opening front door, 7", EX, A $880.00

Cat w/Kitten, pnt papier-mache, cloth bellows, late 1800s, 6", EX $325.00
Chicken Coop, papier-mache & wood, person standing in front of polychrome coop feeding chickens, 6x4x5", some rstr..$650.00
Dancer, articulated figure on wire pole dances on rnd squeak box, 5½", G, A $100.00
Dog Sitting, papier-mache, wht w/blk spots on body & around eyes & ears, mouth opens & closes, kid bellows, EX, A..$750.00
Hen, papier-mache, off-wht w/blk accents, fabric bellows, 6", A...$150.00

Horse, papier-mache, white with black mane and tail, 5", VG, A, $175.00.

Horse in Cage, dapple-gray flannel coat, glass eyes, 9", EX ..$475.00
Moon Face, dbl-sided, pnt papier-mache, cloth bellows, 3x2¾", EX $725.00
Panther, papier-mache, crouching pose, 3¾", rpl bellows & some rpt, A $115.00

Parrot, felt with glass eyes and papier-mache beak, coiled wire legs, wooden perch, fabric bellows, 7⅜", VG, A, $145.00.

Parrot on Stump, papier-mache, dk bl w/metallic red wing accents, beak opens & closes w/working bellows, 8⅜x6", A $200.00

Sheep in Cage, wood & paper, silent, EX, 5¾" $165.00

Spaniel, golden-flocked papier-mache, 4⅞", rpl bellows, A ..$85.00

Plastic Figures

Plastic figures were made by many toy companies. They were first boxed with playsets, but in the early '50s, some became available individually. Marx was the first company to offer single figures (at 10¢ each), and even some cereal companies included one in boxes of their product. (Kellogg offered a series of sixteen 54mm Historic Warriors, and Nabisco had a line of ten dinosaurs in marbleized, primary colors.) Virtually every type of man and beast has been modeled in plastic; today some have become very collectible and expensive. There are lots of factors you'll need to be aware of to be a wise buyer. For instance, Marx made cowboys during the mid-'60s in a flat finish, and these are much harder to find and more valuable than the later figures with a waxy finish. Marvel Super Heroes in the fluorescent hues are worth about half as much as the earlier, light gray issue. Because of limited space, it isn't possible to evaluate more than a representative few of these plastic figures in a general price guide, so if you'd like to learn more about them, we recommend *Geppert's Guide* by Tim Geppert. See the Clubs and Newsletters section for information on how to order the *Plastic Figure & Playset Collector* magazine.

Advisors: Mike and Kurt Fredericks (F4).

See also Playsets.

ACTION AND ADVENTURE

Ajax, Spacemen, glow-in-the-dark, M, ea.........................$10.00

Ajax, Spacemen, M, ea $8.00

Ajax, Spacemen, w/helmets, MIB, ea................................$15.00

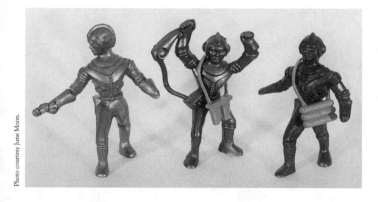

Archer, Spacemen, 1950s, vinyl accessories, 4", M, J6, $55.00 each.

Archer, Space People, man, woman holding baby, child, 3-pc set, NM (NM box), A $225.00

Archer, Spaceman, GI, metallic gr, M $8.00

Archer, Spaceman, robot, hard plastic, M, from $15 to....

Ideal, Arctic, penguin, wht, M.................................

Ideal, Captain Action, 70mm, Batman, w/10 accessory pcs, ... F5 ....$130.0

Ideal, DC Villian, 60mm, Keyman, soft plastic, fluorescent gr, NM, from $35 to...$50.00

Ideal, Underwater Adventure, diver, red, M $5.00

Ideal, Untouchables, gangster w/tommy gun or satchel, red, M, ea $6.00

Lido, Captain Video Interplanetary Spacemen set, complete, NM (EX box), A $345.00

Lido, Spacemen, M, ea $8.00

Marx, Aliens, 35mm, P11, ea...$6.00

Marx, Aliens, 45mm, crawling, gray, P11 ....$22.00

Marx, Arctic Explorer, 54mm, various poses, lt gray, M, P11, ea..$5.00

Marx, Astronauts, 35mm, P11, ea $3.00

Marx, Astronauts, 54mm, Moon Base, floating w/wrench, silver, NM, F5 ....$6.00

Marx, Astronauts, 54mm, Moon Base, standing & pointing, silver, EX+, F5 ....$4.00

Marx, Astronauts, 54mm, Moon Base, tan, P11.................$6.00

Marx, Ben Hur, 54mm, chariot driver w/spear, dk gray-brn, EX, F5...$4.00

Marx, Ben Hur, 54mm, coliseum spectator, seated, tan, NM, F5 ....$8.50

Marx, Ben Hur, 54mm, herald w/trumpet, cream, NM, F5......$10.00

Marx, Ben Hur, 54mm, merchant w/money box, gray, NM, F5.$8.50

Marx, Ben Hur, 54mm, slave in chains, cream, EX+, F5 ....$6.00

Marx, Ben Hur, 54mm, woman walking w/vase, gray, NM, F5 ....$7.50

Marx, Cape Canaveral Personnel, 54mm, beige, set of 15 in 10 poses, NM, F5 ....$35.00

Marx, Cape Canaveral Personnel, 54mm, bl, set of 10 in 8 poses, NM, F5 ....$28.00

Marx, Cave Man, 45mm, reddish brn, P11, ea...................$2.00

Marx, Cave Man, 45mm, 6 poses, caramel, P11, ea $1.00

Marx, Cave Man, 6", advancing w/club, stone knife in left hand, soft plastic, rust, EX+, F5 ....$8.00

Marx, Cave Man, 6", holding rock overhead, soft plastic, rust, NM, F5 ....$13.00

Marx, Cop on Motorcycle, 35mm, P11 ....$5.00

Marx, Eskimos, dog sled w/harness & pack, M, from $18 to..$25.00

Marx, Eskimos, igloo, M $14.00

Marx, Jungle Jim or Daktari, chief w/top hat & cigar, M..$20.00

Marx, Jungle Jim or Daktari, climbing monkey, M $5.00

Marx, Jungle Jim or Daktari, hunter w/rifle, M $10.00

Marx, Jungle Jim or Daktari, jeep driver, M.....................$10.00

Marx, Jungle Jim or Daktari, ostrich or lion, M, ea...........$8.00

Marx, Jungle Jim or Daktari, Paula, M $35.00

Marx, Jungle Jim or Daktari, witch doctor, M...................$10.00

Marx, Lassie & Jeff, 1955, lt yel, Lassie 1"/Jeff 2", NM, A, pr ..$55.00

Marx, Lost in Space, Will Robinson, M.............................$45.00

Marx, Monsters, 6", Frankenstein, bl, 1960s, NM $10.00

Marx, Monsters, 6", Frankenstein, lt orange, 1960s, M $25.00

Marx, Phantom of the Opera, orange, NM $20.00

Marx, Pirates, 60mm, bl, M, ea..$12.00

Marx, Pirates, 60mm, cream, M, ea $20.00

Marx, Robin Hood, 54mm, Friar Tuck or Little John, cream, M, ea $12.00

Marx, Robin Hood, 54mm, minstrel, red or yel, M, ea $4.00

Marx, Robin Hood, 60mm, Little John, M $15.00

Marx, Robin Hood, 60mm, Maid Marian, M $10.00

Marx, Robin Hood, 60mm, Richard Green, NM $65.00

Marx, Space Cadets, 45mm, P11, ea..................................$4.00

Marx, Space Patrol, 45mm, P11, ea $8.00

Marx, Super Heroes, 6", Captain America, gr, NM $14.00

Marx, Tom Corbett Space Cadet, 45mm, cadet, bl, M.....$10.00

Marx, Tom Corbett Space Cadet, 45mm, female cadet, gray, M...$10.00

Marx, Tom Corbett Space Cadet, 45mm, space car, M....$65.00

Marx, Untouchables, Elliot Ness, NM $13.00

MPC, Monsters, Grim Reaper, M.......................................$8.00

MPC, Monsters, Hangman, M...$8.00

Superior, Captain Video, GIs, M, ea..................................$5.00

Superior, Captain Video, spaceman, M.............................$15.00

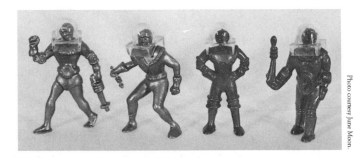

Superior, spacemen, 1950s, various colors and poses, clear removable helmets, 2½", M, J6, $45.00 each.

CAMPUS CUTIES AND AMERICAN BEAUTIES

Marx, American Beauties, ballerina, hula dancer & reclining nude, set of 3, NM $90.00

Marx, Campus Cuties, Dinner for Two, M.........................$8.00

Marx, Campus Cuties, Lazy Afternoon, M.........................$8.00

Marx, Campus Cuties, Lodge Party, M...............................$8.00

Marx, Campus Cuties, Nighty Night, M $8.00

Marx, Campus Cuties, On the Beach, M $8.00

Marx, Campus Cuties, On the Town, M..............................$8.00

Marx, Campus Cuties, Shopping Alone, M $8.00

Marx, Campus Cuties, Shopping Anyone, M $8.00

Marx, Campus Cuties, Stormy Weather, M........................$8.00

CIRCUS AND ACCESSORIES

Marx, Animal Kingdom, elephant, jaguar or panther, NMIB, F5, ea.$12.00

Marx, Circus Animals, 45mm, gray, set of 16 in 13 poses, NM, F5 ....$68.00

Marx, Circus Performers, 48mm, salmon, set of 17 in different poses, NM, F5 ....$70.00

Marx, Circus Performers, 48mm, yel, set of 18 in different poses, NM, F5...$75.00

Marx, Dinosaur #PL-0750, lt gr, set of 6 in different poses, NM, F5 ....$12.50

Marx, Dinosaur #PL-0750, matt gray, set of 6 in different poses, NM, F5 ....$25.00

Marx, Dinosaurs, Allosaurus, 1st issue, gray, NM, F5..........$4.00

Marx, Dinosaurs, Allosaurus, 1st issue, lt gr, NM, F5..........$5.00

Marx, Dinosaurs, Ankylosaurus, 1st issue, gray, NM, F5.....$5.00

Marx, Dinosaurs, Dimetrodon, 1st issue, dk marbled gray, NM, F5 ....$5.00

Marx, Dinosaurs, Dimetrodon, 1st issue, mint gr, NM, F5..$4.00

Marx, Dinosaurs, Hadrosaurus, gray, NM, F5 ....$6.00

Marx, Dinosaurs, Trachodon, 1st issue, foreleg down, lt gr, NM, F5 ....$5.00

Marx, Fox Hunt Animals, brn, set of 7 in 5 poses, NMIP, F5..$70.00

Marx, Fox Hunt Animals, cream, set of 7 in 5 poses, NMIB, F5 ....$75.00

Marx, Ice-Age Mammals, Smilodon, gray, NM, F5 ....$5.00

Marx, Ice-Age Mammals, Wooly Mammoth, dk brn, NM, F5.$22.50

Marx, Super Circus, 45mm, balloon vendor, P11 ....$10.00

Marx, Wild Animals, 5", elephant & Indian, gray, NM, F5...$20.00

Marx, Wild Animals, 5", grizzly bear, brn, NM, F5...........$10.00

Marx, Wild Animals, 60mm, ostrich, tan, flat, NM, F5......$6.00

Marx, Wild Animals, 60mm, seal, wht or gray, NM, F5, ea..$2.00

COMIC, DISNEY AND NURSERY CHARACTERS

Ideal, Comic Strip, Batman, w/accessories, M $35.00

Ideal, Comic Strip, Brainstorm, M $40.00

Ideal, Comic Strip, Joker, NM..$35.00

Lido, Disney, Zorro, MIP $18.00

Marx, Comic Strip, BO Plenty, M......................................$8.00

Marx, Comic Strip, Boltar, P11..$12.00

Marx, Comic Strip, Jiggs, gr, M..$10.00

Marx, Comic Strip, Li'l Abner, M.......................................$7.00

Marx, Comic Strip, Prince Valiant, P11 ....$22.00

Marx, Comic Strip, Snuffy Smith, M $9.00

Marx, Disney, Rolykins; Dopey, 1960s, NMIB, M8..........$25.00

Marx, Disney, Rolykins; Pinocchio, 1960s, NMIB, M8....$25.00

Marx, Disney, 6", Bambi, M, from $10 to.........................$12.00

Marx, Disney, 6", Goofy, fluorescent orange, M, J6, $12.00.

Marx, Disney, 6", Donald Duck, fluorescent gr, M, from $6 to....$10.00

Marx, Disney, 6", Donald Duck, fluorescent red, M, from $6 to..$10.00

Marx, Disney, 6", Mickey Mouse, fluorescent red, M, from $6 to..$10.00

Marx, Disney, 6", Peter Pan, bl, no feather, 1970s, M, from $6 to..$10.00

Marx, Disney, 6", Pluto, fluorescent red, M, from $6 to ...$10.00

Marx, Disney, 60mm, Dumbo Singing Clown, beige, NM, F5...$6.50

Marx, Disney, 60mm, Goofy, pk, NM, F5 ....$12.50

Marx, Disney, 60mm, Happy Dwarf, NM, F5 ....$7.50

Marx, Disney, 60mm, Huey, Louie or Dewey, beige, NM, F5, ea..$7.50

Marx, Disney, 60mm, Monty Mouse (Mickey's Nephew), beige, NM, F5 ....$5.50

Marx, Disneykids, Peter Pan; Wendy, 1960s, scarce, EX, M8....$50.00

Photo courtesy June Moon.

Marx, Disneykings, Donald Duck, Goofy, and Pluto, 1960s, MIB, $25.00 each.

Marx, Disneykings, Pecos Bill, 1960s, NMIB, M8 ....$22.00

Marx, Disneykings, Peter Pan; Blue Fairy, 1960s, NMIB, M8..$22.00

Marx, Disneykings, Peter Pan; Captain Hook, 1960s, NMIB, M8..$22.00

Marx, Disneykings, Pinocchio; Figaro, 1960s, NMIB, M8 ..$22.00

Marx, Disneykins, Cinderella, 2nd series; Gus the Mouse, 1960s, NM, M8 ....$95.00

Marx, Disneykins, Jungle Book, 2nd series; Bagheera, 1960s, NM, M8 ....$45.00

Marx, Disneykins, Jungle Book, 2nd series; Baloo, 1960s, NM, M8..$45.00

Marx, Disneykins, Jungle Book, 2nd series; Colonel Haithi, 1960s, NM, M8...$45.00

Marx, Disneykins, Jungle Book, 2nd series; King Louie, 1960s, NM, M8 ....$45.00

Marx, Disneykins, Jungle Book, 2nd series; Mowgli, 1960s, NM, M8..$45.00

Marx, Disneykins, Jungle Book, 2nd series; Shere Khan, 1960s, NM, M8 ....$45.00

Marx, Disneykins, Lady & the Tramp, 2nd series; Am, 1960s, NM, M8 ....$75.00

Marx, Disneykins, Lady & the Tramp, 2nd series; Boris, 1960s, NM, M8 ....$75.00

Marx, Disneykins, Lady & the Tramp, 2nd series; Bull, 1960s, NM, M8 ....$85.00

Marx, Disneykins, Lady & the Tramp, 2nd series; Lady sitting, 1960s, NM, M8...$85.00

Marx, Disneykins, Lady & the Tramp, 2nd series; Si, NM, M8 ....$75.00

Marx, Disneykins, Peter Pan, 2nd series; lost boy w/club, 1960s, EX, M8 ....$75.00

Marx, Disneykins, Pinocchio, 2nd series; Lampwick, 1960s, NM, M8 ....$75.00

Marx, Disneykins, 101 Dalmatians, 2nd series; Colonel, 1960s, NM, M8 ....$85.00

Marx, Disneykins, 101 Dalmatians, 2nd series; Hungry w/slipper, 1960s, NM, M8 ....$75.00

Marx, Disneykins, 101 Dalmatians, 2nd series; Inky, 1960s, NM, M8 ....$65.00

Marx, Disneykins, 101 Dalmatians, 2nd series; Lucky w/book, 1960s, NM, M8 ....$75.00

Marx, Disneykins, 101 Dalmatians, 2nd series; Patch, 1960s, NM, M8 ....$65.00

Marx, Disneykins, 101 Dalmatians, 2nd series; Perdita lying down, 1960s, NM, M8 ....$60.00

Marx, Disneykins, 101 Dalmatians, 2nd series; Pongo lying down, 1960s, NM, M8 ....$60.00

Marx, Disneykins, 101 Dalmatians, 2nd series; Sleepy w/dog bed, 1960s, NM, M8 ....$75.00

Marx, Disneykins, 101 Dalmatians, 2nd series; Sniff, 1960s, NM, M8 ....$65.00

Marx, Fairytales, 60mm, Goldilocks, bl, NM, F5 ....$12.50

Marx, Fairytales, 60mm, Little Red Riding Hood, pk, NM, F5 ....$10.00

Marx, Fun-Pals, Jungle Book, Colonel Haithi, 1960s, NM, M8..$30.00

Marx, Hanna-Barbera, Flintstones, 54mm, Townspeople, P11, ea...$2.00

Marx, Hanna-Barbera, Flintstones, 60mm, Barney Rubble, cream, NM, F5 ....$4.00

Marx, King Features, 60mm, Blondie, Alexander or Daisy the Dog, lt bl, NM, F5, ea.....................................$30.00

Marx, Nursery Rhymes, 60mm, Humpty Dumpty, gr, NM, F5 .$12.50

Marx, Nursery Rhymes, 60mm, Humpty Dumpty, pk, NM, F5 ....$10.00

Marx, Nursery Rhymes, 60mm, Jack & Jill, pk, NM, F5, ea......$10.00

Marx, Nursery Rhymes, 60mm, Jack Be Nimble, pk, NM, F5 ..$10.00

Marx, Nursery Rhymes, 60mm, Little Bo Peep, gr or pk, NM, F5, ea...$10.00

Marx, Nursery Rhymes, 60mm, Little Bo Peep, sheep, pk, NM, F5 ....$10.00

Marx, Nursery Rhymes, 60mm, Little Boy Blue, pk, NM, F5 ....$8.50

Marx, Nursery Rhymes, 60mm, Little Jack Horner, pk, NM, F5 ..$10.00

Marx, Nursery Rhymes, 60mm, Little Miss Muffet, pk, NM, F5 ...$12.50

Marx, Nursery Rhymes, 60mm, Little Miss Muffet, wht, EX, F5 .....$5.00

Marx, TV Fairykins, Goldilocks & the 3 Bears, M $75.00

Marx, TV Fairykins, Hansel & Gretel, MIB, J5 ....$25.00

Marx, TV Fairykins, Mary Had a Little Lamb, MIB, J5 ....$25.00

Marx, TV Tinykins, 35mm, Flintstones; fire chief, MIB, J5.....$25.00

Marx, TV Tinykins, 35mm, Flintstones; traffic cop, MIB, J5 ..$25.00

Marx, TV Tinykins, 35mm, Flintstones; Wilma, P11, ea .$30.00

Marx, TV Tinykins, 35mm, Huckleberry Hound; Dixie, NMIB, F5 ....$22.00

Marx, TV Tinykins, 35mm, Huckleberry Hound; Huckleberry Hound, NMIB, F5..$22.00

Marx, TV Tinykins, 35mm, Quick Draw McGraw; Blabber, EX+, F5 ....$10.00

Marx, TV Tinykins, 35mm, Quick Draw McGraw; Snooper, NM, F5 ....$16.50

Marx, TV Tinykins, 35mm, Top Cat, NMIB...............$30.00

Marx, TV Tinykins, 35mm, Yogi Bear or Fibber Fox, NMIB, F5, ea...$25.00

FAMOUS PEOPLE AND CIVILIANS

Marx, Canadian VIPs, 60mm, Sir William Alexander, NM, F5 ....$18.00

Marx, Civilians & Workmen, 35mm, fire chief yelling orders, cream, NM, from $6 to $8.00

Marx, Civilians & Workmen, 35mm, fireman running w/axe, cream, NM, from $6 to $8.00

Marx, International VIPs, 60mm, Duke of Edinburgh, wht, sq base, NM, F5 ....$30.00

Marx, International VIPs, 60mm, Prince Charles, wht, sq base, NM, F5 ....$20.00

Marx, International VIPs, 60mm, Princess Margaret, wht, sq base, NM, F5 ....$20.00

Marx, International VIPs, 60mm, Queen Elizabeth II, wht, sq base, NM, F5 ....$25.00

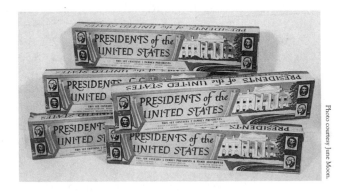

Marx, Presidents of the United States, 1950s, series 1 through 5, MIB, J6, $25.00 each.

Marx, Religious, 60mm, Andrew the Apostle, ivory, sq base, NM, F5..$10.00

Marx, Religious, 60mm, Bartholomew, ivory, sq base, NM, F5 ....$10.00

Marx, Religious, 60mm, Cardinal Spellman, ivory, sq base, NM, F5 ....$15.00

Marx, Skyscraper Civilians, 54mm, cream, set of 16, NMIP, F5 ....$130.00

Marx, US Presidents, 40mm, President Eisenhower, wht, sq base, NM, from $4 to $6.00

Marx, US Presidents, 60mm, President FD Roosevelt, Yalta cape, wht, sq base, NM, from $4 to $6.00

MILITARY AND WARRIORS

Marx, Civil War, Confederate; General Lee, P11...............$6.00

Marx, Civil War, Confederate; Jeff Davis, P11 ....$6.00

Marx, Civil War, Union; Centennial series, set of 16 in 13 poses, dk bl, P11..$65.00

Marx, Civil War, Union; General Grant, P11 ....$6.00

Marx, English Guard, 60mm, P11 ....$15.00

Marx, Goldmarx Ancient Warriors, 6", Egyptian w/spear & shield, NM, F5 ....$30.00

Marx, Goldmarx Ancient Warriors, 6", Maximus w/sword raised, NM, F5 ....$30.00

Marx, Goldmarx Ancient Warriors, 6", Roman Warrior w/whip & sword, NM, F5 ....$30.00

Marx, Goldmarx Ancient Warriors, 6", Viking Warrior w/sword & shield, NM, F5 ....$30.00

Marx, Legionaire, 60mm, firing, bl, P11....................$10.00

Marx, Legionaire, 60mm, firing, silver, P11 ....$8.00

Marx, Mexican War, 60mm, US soldier aiming rifle, metallic bl, NM, F5 ....$16.00

Marx, Mexican War, 60mm, US soldier reading orders, metallic bl, NM, F5 ....$16.00

Marx, Warriors of the World, 60mm, Civil War; Bill Mason blowing bugle, NMIB $15.00

Marx, Warriors of the World, 60mm, Civil War; Harry Dugan w/pistol, NMIB $15.00

Marx, Warriors of the World, 60mm, Civil War; Mike Burns aiming rifle, NMIB $15.00

Marx, Warriors of the World, 60mm, Cowboys, NMIB, ea...$15.00

Marx, Warriors of the World, 60mm, Indians, NMIB, ea.$15.00

Marx, Warriors of the World, 60mm, Pirates; Captain Cobham standing w/hands on pistol & sword, NMIB $15.00

Marx, Warriors of the World, 60mm, Revolutionary War; American soldier E Bray marching w/rifle, NMIB $15.00

Marx, Warriors of the World, 60mm, Revolutionary War; American soldier Richard Travis w/sword, NMIB $15.00

Marx, Warriors of the World, 60mm, Revolutionary War; British soldier Henry Knox at attention, NMIB $15.00

Marx, Warriors of the World, 60mm, Revolutionary War; British soldier D Dickson w/rifle at waist, NMIB.......$15.00

Marx, Warriors of the World, 60mm, Roman Warriors; Flacius Stilecho, NMIB $15.00

Marx, Warriors of the World, 60mm, Roman Warriors; Laelius standing guard w/spear, NMIB $15.00

Marx, Warriors of the World, 60mm, Roman Warriors; Marcus Gaius w/sword & shield, NMIB.............................$15.00

Marx, Warriors of the World, 60mm, Roman Warriors; Marius w/sword & shield, NMIB.............................$15.00

Marx, Warriors of the World, 60mm, Roman Warriors; Maximus w/sword raised, NMIB.............................$15.00

Marx, Warriors of the World, 60mm, Union Soldiers; Harry Dugan, NMIB $15.00

Marx, Warriors of the World, 60mm, Union Soldiers; Herb Tanner, NMIB...$15.00

Marx, Warriors of the World, 60mm, Union Soldiers; Mike Burns, NMIB...$15.00

Marx, Warriors of the World, 60mm, US Combat Soldiers; Bill James, NMIB...$15.00

Marx, Warriors of the World, 60mm, US Combat Soldiers; Dan Warner, NMIB...$15.00

Marx, Warriors of the World, 60mm, US Combat Soldiers; Hank Myers, NMIB...$15.00

Marx, Warriors of the World, 60mm, US Combat Soldiers; Joe Dixon, NMIB..$15.00

Marx, Warriors of the World, 60mm, Viking Warriors; Eric the Red, NMIB..$20.00

Marx, Warriors of the World, 60mm, Viking Warriors; Haakon aiming bow & arrow, NMIB...$20.00

Marx, Warriors of the World, 60mm, Viking Warriors; Ketil, NMIB...$20.00

Marx, Warriors of the World, 60mm, Viking Warriors; Olaf, NMIB...$20.00

Marx, Warriors of the World, 60mm, Viking Warriors; Thorfinn, NMIB...$20.00

Marx, Warriors of the World, 60mm, West Point Cadets, NMIB, F5, ea..$20.00

Marx, Warriors of the World, 60mm, WWI; Canadian Soldiers, NMIB, ea...$20.00

Marx, Warriors of the World, 60mm, WWI; French Soldiers, NMIB, ea...$20.00

Marx, Warriors of the World, 60mm, WWI; German Soldiers, NMIB, ea...$20.00

Marx, Warriors of the World, 60mm, WWII; German Soldiers, NMIB, ea..$20.00

Marx, WWII, 54mm, Americans; combat soldiers, gr, set of 32, NM, F5..$65.00

Marx, WWII, 54mm, Americans; GIs marching, matt gr, set of 8 in 3 poses, NM, F5..$32.00

Marx, WWII, 54mm, Germans; soldiers, gray, set of 16 in 13 poses, NM, F5...$25.00

Marx, WWII, 54mm, Japanese; soldiers, matt tan, set of 16 in 12 poses, NM, F5..$65.00

Marx, WWII, 60mm, Americans; combat soldier carrying ammo case, gr, NM, F5..$4.50

Marx, WWII, 60mm, Americans; GIs in crouched position, set of 5, NM, F5..$15.00

Marx, WWII, 60mm, Americans; Naval officer w/binoculars, matt wht, NM, F5..$10.00

Marx, WWII, 60mm, Americans; sailor pulling rope, matt wht, NM, F5...$14.50

Marx, WWII, 60mm, Americans; sailor standing at attention, lt bl, EX+, F5...$4.00

Marx, WWII, 60mm, Americans; shore patrolman, matt royal bl, NM, F5..$10.00

Tim-Mee Toys, soldier launching grenade, 4¼", $2.00; Marx, soldier running, green with orange face and hand, $2.00.

NUTTY MADS

Roddy the Hotrod, green, $30.00.

Marx, All-Heart Hogan, dk gr, NM, F5 ....$26.00
Marx, All-Heart Hogan, maroon, NM, F5 ....$35.00
Marx, Bull Pen Boo Boo, maroon, NM, F5 ....$35.00
Marx, Bull Pen Boo Boo, sand, NM, F5 ....$28.00
Marx, Dippy the Deep Diver, lt gr, NM, F5 ....$32.00
Marx, Donald the Demon, dk gr, EX, F5..........................$20.00
Marx, Lost Teepee, maroon, NM, F5 ....$35.00
Marx, Lost Teepee, pk, NM, F5.......................................$22.50
Marx, Manny the Reckless Mariner, lime gr, NM, F5 ......$20.00
Marx, Suburban Sidney, dk gr, NM, F5............................$32.00
Marx, Suburban Sidney, lime gr, NM, F5 ....$22.50
Marx, The Thinker, fluorescent red, EX+, F5.................$20.00
Marx, The Thinker, gr, EX, J5..$15.00

WESTERN AND FRONTIER HEROES

Airfix, Wagon Train, 1st series, HO scale, MIB $30.00
Britains, Cowboys & Indians, Apache, standing, M $6.00
Ideal, Famous Frontier Americans, 5", Pat Brady, M $10.00
Ideal, Famous Frontier Americans, 5", Roy Rogers, M $10.00
Marx, Cavalry, 54mm, soldier in long coat, no sword, turq, NM, P11 ....$12.00
Marx, Cavalry, 54mm, soldier in long coat, w/sword, turq, NM, P11 .$15.00
Marx, Cavalry, 54mm, soldier in long coat w/arms at side, sky bl, NM, P11..$12.00
Marx, Cavalry, 54mm, 7th Cavalry foot soldiers, steel bl, set of 16, NMIP, F5 ....$60.00
Marx, Cavalry, 6", buglar w/rifle at side, steel bl, NM, F5..$12.50
Marx, Cavalry, 6", captain advancing w/sword raised, steel bl, NM, F5...$12.50
Marx, Cavalry, 60mm, soldier firing, NM, P11 ....$12.00
Marx, Cavalry, 60mm, soldier kneeling w/carbine, NM, P11 ..$20.00
Marx, Cavalry, 60mm, soldier kneeling w/pistol, bl, NM, F5 ..$10.00
Marx, Cavalry, 60mm, soldier w/sword raised, tan, EX, F5 ...$12.50
Marx, Cowboy, 6", fanning pistol, rust brn, NM, F5..........$5.00
Marx, Famous Frontier Americans, 54mm, Dale Evans, cream, M..$12.00

Marx, Famous Frontier Americans, 54mm, Zorro, NM, F5 .$40.00

Marx, Famous Frontier Americans, 60mm, General Custer, M $25.00

Marx, Famous Frontier Americans, 60mm, Lone Ranger mounted w/pistol, cream, NM, F5 ....$30.00

Marx, Famous Frontier Americans, 60mm, Roy Rogers standing or mounted, cream, M, ea........................$20.00

Marx, Famous Frontier Americans, 60mm, Tonto, cream, NM, F5 ....$20.00

Marx, Fort Apache Frontiersmen, 54mm, dk bl, set of 10, NMIP, F5 ....$30.00

Marx, Indian Brave, 6", aiming bow, pumpkin, NM, F5...$10.00

Marx, Indian Brave, 6", throwing spear, pumpkin, NM, F5 ..$5.00

Marx, Indian Chief on Horse, 54mm, reddish brn or yel, NM, F5, ea..$10.00

Marx, Mining Town, 54mm, cowboy drawing pistol, matt gray, NM, F5 ....$8.50

Marx, Mining Town, 54mm, cowboy w/rifle & lantern, matt gray, NM, F5 ....$12.50

Marx, Pioneers, 45mm, silver or tan, M, ea.......................$5.00

Marx, Pioneers, 54mm, wounded, M...............................$10.00

Marx, Pioneers, 60mm, standing shooting rifle, cream, M..$8.00

Marx, Pioneers, 60mm, woman loading rifle, cream, M ...$10.00

Marx, Rin-Tin-Tin, 60mm, Corporal Rusty, cream, NM, F5 ..$46.00

Marx, Rin-Tin-Tin, 60mm, Lt Rip Masters, cream, NM, F5 ...$38.00

Plasticville

From the 1940s through the '60s, Bachmann Brothers produced plastic accessories for train layouts such as buildings, fences, trees, and animals. Buildings often included several smaller pieces — for instance, ladders, railings, windsocks, etc. — everything you could ever need to play out just about any scenario. Beware of reissues.

Advisor: Gary Mosholder, Gary's Trains (G1).

#AD-4, Airport Administration Building, wht sides, bl roof .$45.00

#AP-1 Airport Hangar..$25.00

#BB-9 Billboard, gr or wht, ea...$1.00

#BK-1 Bank, gray sides, gr roof.......................................$30.00

#BL-2 Bridge & Pond...$9.00

#BN-1 Barn, red sides, wht roof......................................$12.00

#BR-2 Trestle Bridge $18.00

#BY-4 Barnyard Animals $12.00

#C-18 Cathedral, wht sides, dk gray roof $25.00

#CC-7 Church, wht sides, gray roof $12.00

#CC-8 Country Church, wht sides, gray roof, lg door $12.00

#CC-9 Church, wht sides, lt gray roof..............................$15.00

#CS-5 Chain Store/5 & 10¢...$18.00

#DE-7 Diner, gray sides, red roof....................................$18.00

#DH-2 Hardware/Pharmacy $18.00

#FB-1 Frosty Bar, yel sides, wht roof..............................$15.00

#FB-4 Fire House, wht sides, red roof $15.00

#FP-5 Fireplace, gray...$3.00

#FP-5 Flagpole...$3.00

#GO-2 Gas Station (sm), wht sides, red roof, wht insert..$15.00

#GO-3 Gas Station (lg), w/Plasticville logo & pumps......$25.00

#HP-9 Cape Cod House, wht sides, red roof & trim.........$10.00

#HS-6 Hospital, no furniture...$20.00

#HS-6 Hospital, w/furniture $30.00

#LC-2 Log Cabin, w/fence..$15.00

#LH-4 Two-Story Colonial House, wht sides, gray roof & trim $18.00

#LM-3 Freight Station Kit..$15.00

#LM-3 Station Platform...$8.00

#LP-9 Lamppost $1.00

#MH-2 New England Ranch House, tan sides, brn roof ...$18.00

#ON-5 Outdoor Necessities..$15.00

#PB-5 Footbridge...$7.00

#PD-3 Police Station, dk gray..$25.00

#PD-3 Police Station, lt gray $20.00

#PF-4 Citizens, w/pnts...$15.00

#PH-1 Town Hall, tan sides, red roof...............................$35.00

#PO-1 Post Office, gray front & roof................................$18.00

#RH-1 Ranch House, wht sides, bl roof & trim................$10.00

#RS-7 Suburban Station, gr roof & trim, brn platform.......$8.00

#SA-7 Outhouse, red sides, wht roof $4.00

#SC-4 School, red sides, gray roof...................................$20.00

#SG-2 Signal Bridge, blk $8.00

#SL-1 Boulevard Light $1.00

#SM-6 Supermarket, sm $15.00

#SW-2 Switch Tower, brn sides, gray roof $6.00

#WG-2 Crossing Gate, blk & wht.......................................$1.00

#WW-3 Wishing Well, brn $3.00

#YW-4, Yard Pump, brn..$3.00

#0012-A Railroad & Street Signs $8.00

#1090 Telephone Booth, wht sides, bl roof......................$15.00

#1302 Farm Implement Set, yel vehicles w/red trim.........$40.00

#1304 Crossing Signal $10.00

#1305 Block Signal $10.00

#1406 Playground Equipment, yel accessories & pool $25.00

#1407 Watchman Shanty, brn sides, gray roof.................$11.00

#1408 Windmill, lt gray..$40.00

#1502 Cape Cod House, pk $35.00

#1503 Add-A-Floor $30.00

#1504 Mobile Home, wht sides, turq roof & trim $55.00

#1603 Ranch House..$28.00

#1608 School $20.00

#1615 Water Tower, gray sides, brn roof.........................$10.00

#1616 Suburban Station $15.00

#1617 Farm Buildings & Animals $25.00

#1618 TV Station, wht sides, red roof & antenna $40.00

#1620 Loading Platform, brn shack, gray roof & platform..$8.00

#1621 Motel, w/3 autos, paper flowers $18.00

#1622 Dairy Barn, wht sides, red roof.............................$22.00

#1623 Loading Pen $45.00

#1624 House, under construction, lt gray........................$45.00

#1625 Railroad Work Car...$18.00

#1626 Corner Store $45.00

#1627 Hobo Shack, gray sides, brn roof........................$135.00

#1629 Bungalow, wht sides, gray roof.............................$28.00

#1700 Two-Story Colonial House $22.00

#1703 Colonial Mansion, wht sides, red roof..................$30.00

#1803 Colonial Church $20.00

#1804 Greenhouse, w/flowers.................................$75.00
#1805 Covered Bridge $18.00
#1806 Roadside Stand, w/pnt................................$30.00
#1853 Drug Store...$25.00
#1900 Turnpike..$45.00
#1901 Union Station..$25.00
#1906 Factory, tan sides, gray roof........................$35.00
#1907 Apartment House $65.00
#1908 Split-Level House $25.00
#1912 New England Ranch $28.00
#1918 Park Assortment $15.00
#1922 Two-Story House $20.00
#1957 Coaling Station...$35.00

Playsets

Louis Marx is given credit for developing the modern-age playset and during the '50s and '60s produced hundreds of boxed sets, each with the buildings, figures, and accessories that when combined with a child's imagination could bring any scenario alive, from the days of Ben Hur to medieval battles, through the cowboy and Indian era, and on up to Cape Canaveral. Marx's prices were kept low by mass marketing (through retail giants such as Sears and Montgomery Wards) and overseas production. But on today's market, playsets are anything but low-priced;

some mint-in-box examples sell for upwards of $1,000.00. Just remember that a set that shows wear or has even a few minor pieces missing quickly drops in value.

Advisors: Bob Wilson, Phoenix Toy Soldier Co. (P11); Mike and Kurt Fredericks (F4).

Airmail Pilot for Boys & Girls, Advance Games, w/hat, stamps, war bonds, money orders, etc, EXIB, A....................$550.00
Airport, Superior, 1930s, litho tin, 23½x17", VG, A.....$175.00
Alaska Playset #3708, Marx, 1959, complete, MIB........$950.00

Photo courtesy Bob Wilson.

American Airlines International Jetport, box only, Marx, Series 1000, P11, $35.00.

Armed Forces Training Center #4152, Marx, complete, MIB..$275.00
Army Battleground Maneuvers, T Cohn, complete, MIB, P11..$150.00
Army Combat #6017, Marx, complete, EXIB..............$200.00
Artic Explorer #3702, Marx, complete, MIB..................$850.00
Barzso Rogers Rangers #B1000, Marx, MIB (sealed) $250.00
Bat Masterson Indian Fighter, Multiple Toys, complete w/6 figures, unused, NM (EX box), A................................$185.00
Batman Batcave, Ideal/Sears, 1966, complete, NMIB, A $300.00
Battle of the Alamo, Marx/Sears Heritage, 1972, MIB, P11..$400.00
Battleground, Lido, complete, NMIB............................$100.00
Battleground #4754, Marx, 1962, box only, G+, P11.......$25.00
Battleground #4754, Marx, 1962, complete, MIB $300.00
Battleground #4756, Marx, 1967, complete, NM (EX box), F5.$225.00
Ben Hur Series 2000, Marx, box only, EX, P11 ....$200.00
Ben Hur Series 2000, Marx, complete, MIB, P11........$2,000.00
Beyond Tomorrow, Multiple Toys, 1975, complete, NMIB, T1...$100.00
Big Top Circus, Marx, complete, NMIB........................$650.00
Blue & the Gray, Sears Heritage, 1972, complete, MIB, P11..$300.00
Bradley's Toy Town Post Office, post office window, stamps, envelopes, paper mask, etc, VG (VG box), A.........$100.00
Bradley's Toy Village, Milton Bradley #4422, 1909, complete, EX (worn box), A...$150.00
British Soldier & Battle Props Set, Elastolin, military tower & church w/soldiers, wagons & many accessories, NM, A..............$650.00
Buddy L Roundup, GMC pressed-steel truck mk Buddy L Cattle Ranch, w/plastic cowboys, animals & fences, unused, NMIB, A..$450.00
Cape Canaveral #2656, Marx, complete, MIB, P11 ....$900.00

Cape Canaveral #4521, Marx, box only, EX, P11.............$60.00

Cape Canaveral #4521, Marx, complete, MIB, P11 ....$250.00

Cape Canaveral #4524, Marx, 1963, complete, MIB, F5 ..$600.00

Cape Canaveral Missile Set #4526, Marx, box only, G+, P11 ....$30.00

Cape Canaveral Missile Set #4526, Marx, complete, MIB, P11 ....$900.00

Captain Gallant of the Foreign Legion #4729, Marx, complete, MIB...$1,500.00

Captain Space Solar Port, box only, Marx, 1954, P11, $60.00.

Casey's Car Wash, Remco, complete, NMIB, P11 ....$125.00

Civil War Centennial #5929, Marx/Sears, few pcs missing o/w VG (G box)...$400.00

Comanche Pass #3416, Marx, missing few minor pcs, NM (VG box)...$225.00

Combat Landing Force #2646, Marx, complete, MIB, F5 ..$350.00

Construction Camp #4440, Marx, 1954, complete, MIB, F5 .$300.00

Cowboys & Indians, Payton, MIP (sealed), P11 ....$25.00

Cowboys & Indians Fort & Campsite Set, Elastolin, w/log buildings, fence, lithoed Indian village & figures, NM, A $1,265.00

Crop Duster Plane Set #0796, Marx, complete, NM (EX box), A $125.00

Daktari, Marx, 1967, w/figures, tiger, village pcs & accessories, EXIB, from $150 to..$200.00

Davy Crockett at the Alamo #3544, Marx, complete, MIB...$1,000.00

Davy Crockett Covered Wagon Kit & Armed Escort, Lido, unused, NM (VG+ box), A.......................................$200.00

Davy Crockett Far West Story, Atlantic, 17 pcs, MIB, P11 ..$16.00

Disaster Rescue Squad, MPC, complete, M (VG box) $80.00

Dow Service Center w/Sky-View Parking, Marx, complete, NM, A $265.00

Farm Irrigated Garden Set #6021, Marx, 1963, complete, M (Sears-Allstate box), F5..$90.00

Farm Set #6050, Marx, complete, M (NM Sears mail-order box), F5 ....$250.00

Fighting Knights Carry-All Set #4635, Marx, 1968, complete, EX (EX metal case), F5..$175.00

Filling Station, Gibbs, 1930, litho tin & wood, 6½x8½x15½", no accessories, G+, A $600.00

Flintstones #4672, Marx, 1961, orig issue, complete, MIB, F5 ....$395.00

Flintstones #5948, Marx, complete, MIB, P11 ....$50.00

Flying Devils, Lakeside Toys, 1985, EXIB, J2...................$30.00

Fort Apache #3681, Marx, 1973, box only, EX, P11 ....$20.00

Fort Apache #3681, Marx, 1973, complete, EX (EX box), F5...$185.00

Fort Apache #3692, Marx, 1963, Deluxe edition, 196 pcs, M (Sears/Allstate box)...$800.00

Fort Apache #3698-6063, Marx/Sears Exclusive, 1964, Deluxe edition, 335 pcs, M (EX box)..............................$1,200.00

Fort Apache Carry-All Set #4685, Marx, 1968, complete, NM (NM metal case), F5...$200.00

Fort Boone, MPC, complete, unused, MIB $225.00

Fort Cheyenne, Ideal, opens to playset with vacuform pieces, P11, $20.00.

Fort Courage, Dimensions for Children, 1981, complete, MIB, P11 ....$30.00

Fort Dearborn #3510, Marx, box only, VG, P11...............$60.00

Fort Dearborn #3514, Marx, complete, NM (EX box) ...$325.00

Fort Geronimo, Empire Toys, 1978, complete, MIB, P11.$50.00

Fort Laramie #4876, Ideal, 1957, complete, VG (VG box) ..$500.00

Fort Set w/Cavalry & Indians, Elastolin, complete, EX..$550.00

Freight Terminal #5420, Marx, complete, MIB, P11......$700.00

French Grenadiers Imperial Guard, Airfix, 29 pcs, MIB, P11..$35.00

Galaxy Command, Marx, complete, NMIB....................$150.00

Gallant Gladiator Warship, Remco, missing few pcs, EXIB, P11 ....$235.00

Guid-a-Traffic, Marx/Sears, 1952, missing few pcs, EX, P11...$180.00

Gunsmoke Dodge City #4628, Marx, Series 2000, 1960, complete, rare, MIB $2,500.00

Happy Time DeLuxe Farm Set #3949, Marx, Series 2000, complete, rare, VG (EX box) $500.00

Hauler & Livestock Trailer, Marx, 1950, complete w/13 farm animals, NM (G box), A...$225.00

Jungle Battle Front #3005, MPC, complete, VG (VG box) ..$130.00

Knights & Vikings Castle #4743, Marx, complete, EX (NM box) $250.00

Little Red School House #3382, Marx, complete, NM (NM box), A..$300.00

Masterbuilder Kit, Capitol of the US, Marx, w/35 miniature presidents, MIB, P11 ....$130.00

Medieval Castle #4700, Marx, complete, MIB, P11 ....$850.00

Medieval Castle Fort #4709, Marx, complete, NMIB $400.00

Missile Attack Force #4500, MPC, complete, NMIB.....$250.00

Missiles to the Moon, MPC, Deluxe issue, NMIB $350.00

Modern Farm, Marx/Sears, complete, EXIB....................$250.00

Pet Shop #4210, Marx, 1952, complete, M (G box), F5...$395.00

Post Office #183, Wolverine, 1930s, litho tin, complete, rare, NM (G box), A $400.00

Prehistoric Playset #3398, Marx, 1971, complete, MIB..$125.00

Prehistoric Times #3390, Marx, box only, EX, P11 ....$50.00

Prehistoric Times #3390, Marx, missing 1 caveman, NM (NM box), A...$200.00

Presidents of the US, Marx, complete, MIB, P11 ....$55.00

Revolutionary War #3401, Marx, Series 500, missing few cannon parts, EX (NM box), P11..............................$1,100.00

Rin Tin Tin Fort Apache, box only, Marx, Series 500, P11, $65.00.

Rex Mars #7040, Marx, complete, MIB (tin box), P11..$1,200.00

Rifleman Ranch, Marx, complete, P11 ....$750.00

Rin Tin Tin #3627, Marx, complete, EXIB $450.00

Robin Hood Castle Set #4719, Marx, 1956, complete, MIB.$300.00

Rocket Missile Base #5046, MPC, complete, NMIB $100.00

Roy Rogers Fix-It Chuck Wagon & Jeep, Ideal, 1950s, complete w/figures & accessories, EX+ (NM+ box), A...........$400.00

Roy Rogers Rodeo Ranch #3990, Marx, 1950s, box only, VG, J2...$95.00

Roy Rogers Rodeo Ranch #3990, Marx, 1950s, complete, NM (EX box), from $200 to $300.00

Roy Rogers Rodeo Ranch #3992, Marx, complete, NMIB..$275.00

Roy Rogers Western Town #4229, Marx, complete, MIB, P11...$1,200.00

Sears Automotive Center, Marx, battery-op elevator, complete, NM, A $445.00

Silver City Frontier Town #4220, Marx, 1955, complete, M (VG box), F5 ....$500.00

Skyscraper Building w/Electric Elevator #5450, Marx, complete, EX (EX+ box), A...$950.00

Super Circus #4320, Marx, 1952, complete, MIB...........$600.00

Super Service Center, Marx/Montgomery Wards, complete, EX, A $175.00

Tank Attack #4501, MPC, complete, EXIB $100.00

Tom Corbett Space Academy #7010, Marx, complete, EX (EX box)..$375.00

Toy-Town Telegraph Office, Parker Bros, w/wooden telegraph key, telegram blanks, etc, VG (VG box), A $100.00

Tricky Action Construction Set, Marx, complete, MIB, P11..$140.00

Troll Village Mini Playset #48-24396, Marx, 1969, complete, M (NM box), F5 ....$425.00

Trucking Terminal #5424, Marx, complete, NM (EX box), A $200.00

Turnpike Construction Set #1505, MPC, complete, MIB ...$350.00

US Air Force Missile Rocket Command #3007, MPC, complete, NMIB......................$175.00

US Army Front Line Command #5033, MPC, complete, NMIB......................$200.00

US Army Training Center #4133, Marx, complete, NM (EX box)......................$155.00

US Naval Base #888, complete, MIB, P11 ....$375.00

Viking Ship, Renwal, complete, NMIB, P11 ....$250.00

Photo courtesy Jon Thurmond.

Wagon Train, Marx, Series 2000, complete, NMIB, from $1,500.00 to $2,000.00.

Waltons, Amsco, cb, NMIB, T1......................$85.00

Waterloo Highland Infantry, Airfix, complete, MIB, P11 ..$35.00

Wild West Train Set #2873, Marx, complete, MIB, P11..$275.00

Wizard of Oz Munchkinland, Mego, 1976, complete, MIB, J6 ....$450.00

Zorro #3753, Marx, complete, NMIB $1,100.00

Political

As far back as the 19th century, children's toys with a political message were on the market. One of the most familiar was the 'Tammany Bank' patented by J. & E. Stevens in 1873. The message was obvious — a coin placed in the man's hand was deposited in his pocket, representing the kickbacks William Tweed was suspected of pocketing when he was the head of Tammany Hall in New York during the 1860s.

Advisors: Michael and Polly McQuillen (M11).

Agnew, Spiro; wristwatch, All American Time Co, caricature face, non-working, M11............................$40.00

Agnew, Spiro; wristwatch, Swiss made, sq face, expandable metal band, non-working, M11 ....$50.00

Bush, George; figure for car window, New Waves, bobbing hand under 9" face, NM, M11 ....$10.00

Bush, George; monkey toy, plush monkey w/hat, gripping arms, Bush for President '88 on back, 4", NM, M11 ....$5.00

Bush, George; squeeze doll, Santa w/Bush's face, rubber, EX, M11 ....$18.00

Carter, Amy; figure, Amy Peanut, baby Amy in peanut shell case, 3", MOC, H4......................$12.00

Carter, Jimmy; bank, plastic peanut with teeth, 12½", EX, $15.00.

Carter, Jimmy; mug, 1977, porcelain, MIB, N2 ....$15.00

Carter, Jimmy; peanut ring, C10 ....$25.00

Carter, Jimmy; walking peanut, plastic w/up, MIB, T1.....$18.00

Carter, Jimmy; wristwatch, 1977, From Peanuts to President, caricature face, flexible metal band, M11 ....$35.00

Cleveland/Harrison, wooden block game, VG, M11......$240.00

Clinton, Bill; alarm clock, Whitewater William, alligator snapping at Clinton ea second, 7", NM, M11 ....$40.00

Clinton, Bill; game, Barrel of Clintons, NM, M11 ....$12.00

Clinton/Dole, squeeze toy, The Great Debate, candidates pointing into ea other's face, metal, EX, M11 ....$15.00

Democrat, bank, 1950s, pnt compo donkey w/bobbing head, VG, M11......................$40.00

Dukakis, Michael; monkey toy, plush monkey w/hat, gripping arms, Win in '88 on back, 4", NM, M11 ....$5.00

Eisenhower, Dwight D; harmonica, red, wht & bl plastic w/I Like Ike on both sides, 6", VG, M11 ....$25.00

Eisenhower, Dwight D; nodder, 1950s, pnt compo elephant w/I'm for Ike, 6½", NM, M11................................$100.00

Eisenhower, Dwight D; Presidential Campaign Car, Lionel, 12", EX, M11......................$150.00

Eisenhower, Dwight D; walking elephant, plush, battery-op, EX, M11......................$125.00

Goldwater, Barry; board game, 1964 Presidential Election Game, MOC, M11 ....$30.00

Goldwater, Barry; figure, Remco, 1964, NMIB................$35.00

Goldwater, Barry; sunglasses, blk cb, NM, M11 ....$12.00

Hoover, Herbert; hat, gr felt, Hoover for President on band, 5", VG, M11......................$48.00

Johnson, Lyndon B; bubble gum cigar, 1964, MIP, M11 ....$6.00

Johnson, Lyndon B; doll, Remco, plastic, 5", MIB, M11 ..$30.00

Johnson, Lyndon B; flasher ring, Vari-Vue, LBJ for the USA, NM...$12.50

Kennedy, Jackie; mask, 1960, thin plastic, EX+, M11 ......$40.00

Kennedy, John F; balloon, Vote Kennedy, wht on bl, unused, M11.$10.00

Kennedy, John F; board game, The Kennedys, Mt Rushmore caricatures on box, NM, M11..$55.00

Kennedy, John F; charm bracelet, 1963, MOC.................$50.00

Kennedy, John F; coloring book, 1960, NM, M11 ....$25.00

Kennedy, John F; mask, 1960, thin plastic, EX+, M11 .....$40.00

Kennedy, John F; toy boat, Empire, 1960s, soft plastic, 7", EX, M11 ....$75.00

Kennedy, Ted; doll, 1980, cloth caricature, 5½", M11.....$15.00

Landon, Alf; bank, Land of Roosevelt emb on gr CI elephant, 6", EX, M11 ....$500.00

Lindsay, John; comb, bl plastic gun form w/Aim for Lindsay, NM, M11 ....$20.00

MacArthur, General Douglas; writing pad & candy, EX (EX mc portrait tin), M11 ....$55.00

McGovern, George; top, plastic, McGovern Is Tops for America, EX...$18.00

McKinley/Hobart, top, wood w/photos on paper label, G, M11 .$175.00

Mondale/Reagan, Politicards, 1984, MIP, M11 ....$10.00

Nixon, Richard; clicker, photo & Click w/Dick, NM, M11 ...$10.00

Nixon, Richard; dart board, Stick Dick, 11½" sq, NM, M11 .$25.00

Nixon, Richard; doll, Tricky Dick, rubber, 5", MOC, M11....$20.00

Nixon, Richard; hand puppet, 1968, plastic head w/cloth body, NM, M11 ....$32.00

Nixon, Richard; music box, 1972, w/up dancer, plays Ta Ra Ra Boom De Yea, NM, M11...$175.00

Nixon, Richard; wristwatch, Honest Time Co, I Am Not a Crook, caricature face, M11 ....$75.00

Reagan, Ronald; voodoo doll, MIP, M11 ....$25.00

Reagan, Ronald; wristwatch, caricature in garbage can, digital, leather band, MOC, M11 ....$30.00

Republican, bank, 1950s, pnt compo elephant w/bobbing head, VG, M11..$40.00

Roosevelt, Franklin D; bank, Happy Days, barrel shape, 5", EX, M11 ....$15.00

Roosevelt, Teddy; bank, bear figure w/'Teddy' on side, CI, 4", VG, M11..$250.00

Roosevelt, Teddy; board game, Rough Riders, Parker Bros, 1900, scarce, EX (VG box), M11 ....$125.00

Roosevelt, Teddy; game, Germany, 1904, drop balls into Teddy's mouth, mirror back w/glass cover, 2¼" dia, VG, M11 ..$850.00

Uncle Sam, bank, Roseville, ceramic, brn w/bl shading, 4½", EX, from $100 to $175.00

Uncle Sam, mask, Sloan & Woodward, 1904, litho cb, 13", rare, EX, A $75.00

Wilson, Woodrow; puzzle, diecut profile, w/envelope, VG, M11..$70.00

Premiums

Those of us from the pre-boomer era remember waiting in anticipation for our silver bullet ring, secret membership kit,

decoder pin, coloring book, or whatever other wonderful item we'd seen advertised in our favorite comic book or heard about on the Tom Mix show. Tom wasn't the only one to have these exciting premiums, though, just about any top character-oriented show from the 1930s through the '40s made similar offers, and even through the '50s some were still being distributed. Often they could be had free for a cereal boxtop or an Ovaltine inner seal, and if any money was involved, it was usually only a dime. Not especially durable and often made in somewhat limited amounts, few have survived to the present. Today some of these are bringing fantastic prices, but the market at present is very volatile.

Condition is very important in assessing value; items in pristine condition bring premium prices.

Advisor: Bill Campbell (C10).

See also Advertising; Cereal Boxes and Premiums; Pinback Buttons.

Amos & Andy, jigsaw puzzle, Pepsodent, 1930s, features characters at the OK Hotel, 8x10", EX+, A $85.00

Batman, comic book, Kellogg's Pop-Tarts, 1966, The Catwoman's Catnapping Caper, 3x5", EX+, A...............$60.00

Batman, stamp set, Kellogg's Corn Flakes, 1966, complete w/6 stamps, NM, A...$60.00

Buck Rogers, badge, Satellite Pioneer, w/membership card & 3 bulletins, C10 ....$300.00

Buck Rogers, badge, Solar Scouts, NM, C10 ....$125.00

Buck Rogers, Big Little Book, Buck Rogers of the 25th Century AD, Cocomalt, 1933, EX+, A $65.00

Buck Rogers, helmet & rocket pistol, Cocomalt, 1930s, cb, EX (NM envelope), A...$350.00

Buck Rogers, ring, Saturn, EX+, C10............................$650.00

Buck Rogers, ring, Saturn, G+, C10..............................$300.00

Photo courtesy Jon Thurmond.

Buck Rogers, Strato-Kite, 1940s, jet propelled, EX (original envelope), T1, $95.00.

Buffalo Bill Jr, ring, 1950s, VG, S20................................$45.00

Buster Brown, Moon Mission Agent wrist decoder w/secret compartment, 1950s, complete w/decoder book, EX, H4.$50.00

Buster Brown, wrist compass, Moon Mission Agent, EX, J2..$25.00

Captain Action, card game, Kool-Pops mail-in, 1967, EX+ (EX box), A...$135.00

Captain Action, flicker ring, Phantom, NM, C10............$65.00
Captain Action, flicker ring, Superman, NM, C10........$200.00
Captain Marvel, comic book, Wheaties, VG+, C10.........$65.00
Captain Marvel, iron-on transfer, Supersize, NM, C10..$150.00
Captain Marvel, Magic Flute, NM, C10.........................$125.00
Captain Marvel, Magic Lightning Box, NM, C10..........$100.00
Captain Marvel, pennant, NM, C10...............................$150.00
Captain Marvel, race car, bl, NM, C10...........................$210.00
Captain Marvel, race car, gr, NM, C10...........................$210.00
Captain Marvel, race car, yel, G+, C10 ....$75.00
Captain Marvel, race car, yel, NM, C10, from $180 to ..$210.00
Captain Marvel, stamps, Marvel Family Super Heroes, lick &
     stick, set of 6, NM, C10...$150.00
Captain Marvel, tattoo envelope, G, C10 ....$100.00
Captain Marvel, toss bag, EX, C10 ....$105.00
Captain Marvel, toss bag, Mary Marvel, G, C10 ....$50.00
Captain Midnight, badge, Flight Patrol Weather, NM, C10..$52.00
Captain Midnight, Certificate of Commission for Flight Com-
     mander of the Secret Squadron, 1950s, 8x6", NM ..$175.00
Captain Midnight, decoder, 1940, NM (orig mailer), C10 ..$175.00
Captain Midnight, decoder, 1940-41, NM, C10..............$75.00
Captain Midnight, decoder, 1942, w/orig photo, NM, C10..$175.00
Captain Midnight, decoder, 1945, NM, C10..................$100.00
Captain Midnight, decoder, 1946, NM, C10..................$135.00
Captain Midnight, decoder, 1947, EX, C10.....................$65.00
Captain Midnight, decoder, 1948, NM, C10..................$185.00
Captain Midnight, decoder, 1955, NM, C10..................$425.00
Captain Midnight, decoder, 1957, NM, C10..................$425.00
Captain Midnight, Detect-O-Scope, Ovaltine, 1940-41, red cb
     tube w/attached metal pc & mirror, 5", NM (NM mailer),
     A...$200.00
Captain Midnight, Flight Commander Handbook, NM,
     C10...$195.00
Captain Midnight, Flight Commander of the Secret Squadron
     Certificate of Commission, NM, C10......................$265.00
Captain Midnight, Key-O-Matic Code-O-Graph, 1949, gold-
     colored tin & plastic, missing key, VG.....................$50.00
Captain Midnight, manual, 1940-41, NM, C10 ....$185.00
Captain Midnight, manual, 1945, EX, C10 ....$125.00
Captain Midnight, manual, 1955, w/letter, NM, C10....$300.00
Captain Midnight, manual, 1957, w/letter, NM, C10....$200.00
Captain Midnight, membership card, 1955-56, NM, C10..$100.00
Captain Midnight, membership card, 1957, NM, C10.....$75.00
Captain Midnight, pin, American Flag, NM, C10 ....$125.00
Captain Midnight, pin, American Flag, w/pledge sheet, NM,
     C10...$325.00
Captain Midnight, ring, Flight Commander, NM, C10 .$450.00
Captain Midnight, ring, Mystic Eye, EX, C10 ....$195.00
Captain Midnight, ring, Seal, NM, C10 ....$400.00
Captain Midnight, ring, Seal, no top, EX $250.00
Captain Midnight, ring, Secret Compartment, NM, C10..$150.00
Captain Midnight, ring, Whirlwind Whistle, NM, C10...$400.00
Captain Midnight, Secret Squadron 1947 Official Manual,
     Ovaltine, 16 pgs, VG, P4...$90.00
Captain Midnight, Spy Scope, NM (orig mailer), C10 ..$100.00
Captain Midnight, Spy Scope instruction sheet, NM, C10...$100.00
Captain Midnight, token, VG, S20................................$20.00
Captain Midnight, trick & riddle book, G, J2.............$38.00

Captain Midnight, Weather Wings, NM, C10.................$50.00
Captain Video, ring, Flying Saucer, 1951, EX, S20........$150.00

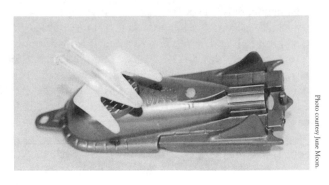

Photo courtesy June Moon.

Captain Video, spaceship, 1950s, hard plastic, missing 1 gun, EX, J6, $12.00.

Cisco Kid, masks, Cisco Kid or Poncho, Harvest Bread, 1949,
     paper, EX, J5, ea from $25 to $50.00
Dick Tracy, badge, Detective Club Shield, G, S20...........$45.00
Dick Tracy, badge, WGN TV, 1960s, Official Channel 9 Dick
     Tracy Crimestopper TV, metal 6-pointed star w/tab, EX+,
     D11..$75.00
Dick Tracy, book, Dick Tracy & the Crook Without a Face, Pan-
     Am Oil Co, 1938, softcover, 64 pgs, rare, VG+, D11.$150.00
Dick Tracy, book, Dick Tracy — Ghost Ship, Quaker, 1939,
     softcover, EX, D11 ....$75.00
Dick Tracy, book, Dick Tracy the Detective & Dick Tracy Jr,
     Perkins, 1933, softcover, 48 pgs, scarce, NM, D11 ..$200.00
Dick Tracy, book, Dick Tracy's Detective Methods Magic
     Tricks, Quaker, 1939, EX+, D11 ....$75.00
Dick Tracy, book, Secret Code Book, Quaker, 1938, 12 pgs,
     6x3", G, D11..$15.00
Dick Tracy, decoder card, Post Cereal, 1950s, NM, D11..$40.00
Dick Tracy, Flagship Airplane, Quaker, 1930s, balsa wood,
     NMIB, D11 ....$250.00
Dick Tracy, flashlight, gr, VG, S20................................$100.00
Dick Tracy, Jr Dick Tracy Crime Detection Folio, 1942, w/vari-
     ous items, complete, MIP (unopened), D11 ....$400.00
Dick Tracy, magnifying glass, EX, J2............................$30.00
Dick Tracy, mask & vest, Motorola, 1952, w/comic premium &
     brochure, M (orig envelope), D11..............................$80.00
Dick Tracy, ring, Hat, NM, C10 ....$265.00
Dick Tracy, Secret Service Patrol Official Dispatch, Quaker, 1939,
     letter confirming promotion to sergeant, EX, D11 ....$25.00
Disney Characters, comic books, Wheaties, 1950, pocket-sz,
     NM, M8, ea..$12.00
Donald Duck, comic books, Cheerios, 1947, Donald Duck & the
     Pirates or Donald Duck Counter Spy, pocket-sz, NM, M8,
     ea...$24.00
Flying Family, jigsaw puzzle, Cocomalt, 1932, EX (orig enve-
     lope), J2..$60.00
Frank Buck, Adventurers Club Handbook, Pepsodent, 1934, EX,
     J5..$45.00
Frank Buck, Adventures Club Handbook, Pepsodent, 1934, pre-
     mium offers & secret codes w/map on cover, NM (EX
     mailer), A $200.00

G-Man, see Melvin Pervis

Gabby Hayes, Chuckwagon set, EXIB (2 boxes), J2 ....$110.00

Gabby Hayes, ring, Cannon, NM, C10...........................$290.00

Gene Autry, ring, Flag, NM, C10....................................$95.00

Green Hornet, flicker rings, 7 different, NM, C10, ea......$35.00

Green Hornet, ring, Seal, General Mills, 1947, EX+, C10...$950.00

Green Hornet, ring, Seal, top only, General Mills, 1947, EX, A...$200.00

Gulliver's Travels, mask set, Hecker's Flour, 1939, David, Glory, King Bimbo, Snitch & Gabby, diecut paper, rare, EX+, A...$175.00

Hopalong Cassidy, badge, Ranch Boss, w/tab, Post Raisin Bran, NM, C10..$35.00

Hopalong Cassidy, picture, Mary Jane Bread, color, M, J2..$25.00

Hopalong Cassidy, poster, Compliments of Spunny Spread, 1950s, blk & wht, 23x17", EX, J5................................$45.00

Hopalong Cassidy, ring, compass/hat, EX+, C10............$285.00

Hopalong Cassidy, ring, face, NM, C10 ....$50.00

Hopalong Cassidy, ring, photo, EX+, C10 ....$25.00

Hopalong Cassidy, Savings Rodeo Club Membership Kit, complete, EX+ (orig mailer), C10...................................$300.00

Howdy Doody, flip-up paper badge, Princess Winterspring Summerfall, Wonder Bread, NM, J2 ....$35.00

Howdy Doody, mug, Wonder/Ovaltine, orange plastic w/colorful decal, complete w/pamphlet, NM (NM mailer), A ...$285.00

Howdy Doody, puppet, paper, Wonder Bread, 11", EX, J2..$75.00

Jack Armstrong, hike-o-meter, bl, G, S20.......................$20.00

Jack Armstrong, ring, baseball, EX+ $1,200.00

Jack Armstrong, ring, crocodile, glow-in-the-dark, EX, C10..$400.00

Jack Armstrong, Secret Whistle Code Card, VG, S20 .....$25.00

Jack Armstrong, telescope, EX, J2 ....$50.00

Jack Armstrong, torpedo flashlight, blk, VG, S20 ....$50.00

Jimmy Allen, ring, Flying Club, 1930, VG, S20 ....$95.00

Jr G-Man, see Melvin Pervis

Jr Rocket Rangers, membership card, EX+, C10 ....$100.00

Jr Rocket Rangers, membership card, M (orig mailer)....$195.00

Little Orphan Annie, see Radio Orphan Annie

Lone Ranger, badge, Lone Ranger Deputy, gray metal star, EX, S20 ....$35.00

Lone Ranger, book, How the Lone Ranger Captured Silver, Silvercup Bread, 1930s, EX, J5 ....$95.00

Lone Ranger, mechanical pencil, Merita Bread, NM $300.00

Lone Ranger, pedometer, VG, S20...................................$20.00

Lone Ranger, pedometer, w/ankle strap, EX+ $65.00

Lone Ranger, pencil sharpener, silver bullet, no label, G, S20 ....$20.00

Lone Ranger, ring, atomic bomb, NM $125.00

Lone Ranger, ring, defender, 1941, G, S20.....................$100.00

Lone Ranger, ring, filmstrip, NM $65.00

Lone Ranger, ring, filmstrip saddle, EX+, J2 ....$150.00

Lone Ranger, ring, flashlight, NM....................................$65.00

Lone Ranger, ring, secret compartment, w/1 photo, EX+, C10.$300.00

Lone Ranger, ring, secret compartment, w/2 photos, EX+, C10...$500.00

Lone Ranger, ring, weather, EX+ $125.00

Lone Ranger, star, Bond Bread, EX+..............................$50.00

Melvin Pervis, badge, G-Man, emb brass shield w/eagle atop, bl enamel trim, 2", NM+, A...$45.00

Lone Ranger, ring, Six-Shooter, NM, $165.00.

Melvin Pervis, badge, Junior G-Man Corps, enameled shield w/eagle atop, blk & gold lettering, 1½", NM, A........$65.00

Melvin Pervis, badge, Lieutenant Secret Operator, EX+, J2 .$48.00

Melvin Pervis, mask, 1930s, lithoed cb head w/G-Man lettered across band of hat, 9x8", scarce, EX, A $125.00

Melvin Pervis, Official Junior G-Man Equipment Manual, 2-sided foldout, NM, A..$75.00

Melvin Pervis, pencil sharpener, prewar, Bakelite gun-shape w/gold decal, NM+, A..$75.00

Melvin Pervis, ring, Jr G-Man, VG $75.00

Melvin Pervis, Signal Light (flashlight), 1940s, litho tin w/image of light shining on Wanted poster, 7", VG+, A $200.00

Melvin Purvis, hairbrush, G-Man, EX+ $135.00

Melvin Purvis, ring, Scarab, EX+...............................$1,100.00

Melvin Purvis, ring, Scarab, G $800.00

Mickey Mouse, comic book, Cheerios, 1947, Mickey Mouse & the Haunted House, pocket-sz, NM, M8.................$24.00

Mickey Mouse, comic books, Cheerios 3-D Giveaway Series 1, 1954, #2, #6 or #8, pocket-sz, NM, M8, ea $30.00

Phantom, Voodoo Pendant, 2-pc brass w/the Phantom skull & crossbones & secret built-in mirror, 1x1½", NM, A..$325.00

Radio Orphan Annie, book, Radio Orphan Annie Book on Dogs, EX, J2 ....$40.00

Radio Orphan Annie, book & signs, Secret Society, 1937, EX, J2...$115.00

Radio Orphan Annie, decoder, Slidomatic, EX+ $225.00

Radio Orphan Annie, decoder, 1935, VG, S20 ....$30.00

Radio Orphan Annie, decoder, 1937, VG, S20 ....$50.00

Radio Orphan Annie, decoder booklet, Secret Squadron, 1940, EX, S20 ....$120.00

Radio Orphan Annie, manual, 1935, EX+ $150.00

Radio Orphan Annie, manual, 1936, EX+......................$75.00

Radio Orphan Annie, Orphan Annie Circus, radio premium, early 1930s, complete, VG+ (EX+ mailing envelope), A $90.00

Radio Orphan Annie, pin, Secret Society, Ovaltine, 1934, bronze-colored tin, VG, P4.....................................$80.00

Radio Orphan Annie, ring, Magnifying, no magnifier, EX+ ...$1,200.00

Radio Orphan Annie, ring, Post Cereal, MIP, S20...........$50.00

Radio Orphan Annie, ring, Signet, 2-initial, EX+ $150.00

Radio Orphan Annie, ring, Silver Star, 1936, EX $300.00

Range Rider, clicker gun, Tip Top Bread, 1950s, cb, 8", EX, J5...$35.00

Red Ryder, key chain w/lucky coin, EX, C10...................$30.00

Rin-Tin-Tin, compass/mirror, VG, S20 ....$50.00

Rin-Tin-Tin, flag, Fighting Blue Devils, 1950s, bl & yel w/crossed swords & B Company, 8x11", VG, J5 ....$45.00

Robin Hood, playset, Kraft, 1950s, w/3-D castle & punch-out figures, unpunched, M (orig mailer), from $75 to ...$100.00

Space Patrol, membership badge, red and blue under clear plastic, EX, J6, $350.00.

Photo courtesy June Moon.

Roy Rogers, badge, copper, NM, $35.00.

Photo courtesy June Moon.

Roy Rogers, pencil case w/pencil & Rider's Club membership card, Sears premium, plastic, 8", EX, A.....................$140.00

Roy Rogers, ring, Branding Iron, EX $225.00

Roy Rogers, ring, Microscope, EX $115.00

Sgt Preston, Distance Finder, EX $125.00

Sgt Preston, Distance Finder, w/instructions, EX+ (orig mailer) $200.00

Sgt Preston, map, Yukon Territory, EX $60.00

Sgt Preston, pedometer, w/instructions, EX (orig mailer), EX...$175.00

Shadow, ring, Blue Coal, NM $650.00

Shadow, ring, Secret Agent, unused, MIB.....................$125.00

Sky King, Detecto Microscope, w/treasure map, NM (orig mailer) $225.00

Sky King, figure, Clipper or Sheriff, gr or yel, NM, ea $35.00

Sky King, figure, Penny, yel or gr, NM, ea $40.00

Sky King, figure, yel or red, NM, ea $45.00

Sky King, ring, Aztec, EX+...$880.00

Sky King, ring, Magni-Glo, EX, J2 ....$100.00

Sky King, ring, Mystery Picture, NM $500.00

Sky King, ring, Navajo Treasure, VG, A............................$75.00

Sky King, ring, Radar, EX+ $195.00

Sky King, ring, Teleblinker, NM.......................................$150.00

Sky King, ring, TV, w/all 4 photos, NM $195.00

Sky King, Secret Signal Scope, EX....................................$195.00

Sky King, Sky Detecto Writer, 1949, heavy brass, raised image of Sky King on underside, 2", EX, A $100.00

Space Patrol, binoculars, Ralston Purina, plastic rocket shape, NM (NM mailer), A $135.00

Space Patrol, catalog, ca 1950, EX, C10 ....$175.00

Space Patrol, Cosmic Rocket Launcher, w/instructions, EX (orig mailer) $500.00

Space Patrol, decoder belt buckle, EX+ $175.00

Space Patrol, decoder belt buckle & belt, w/instructions, EX (orig mailer), C10..$500.00

Space Patrol, Emergency Kit, complete, NM (worn box) ..$1,200.00

Space Patrol, flashlight, rocketship, MIB........................$650.00

Space Patrol, Flying Saucer Gun, EX+..............................$200.00

Space Patrol, membership card, w/plastic pin & chart of the universe, EX+ $1,300.00

Space Patrol, microscope, w/slides & instructions, NM (orig mailer) $200.00

Space Patrol, Outer Space Helmet, w/Mystic Stratoviewer, NM (orig mailer)..$500.00

Space Patrol, periscope, NM (orig mailer).....................$500.00

Space Patrol, ring, Hydrogen Ray Gun, M.....................$290.00

Space Patrol, ring, Hydrogen Ray Gun, w/instructions, EX (orig mailer), M $800.00

Space Patrol, Space Phones, w/string, NM (orig mailer) ..$150.00

Space Patrol, Stori-Viewer, w/4 sets of film, MIB...........$300.00

Space Patrol, Viewer Picture Gun, w/theatre & film, NMIB...$400.00

Straight Arrow, bracelet, Mystic, NM, J2 ....$160.00

Straight Arrow, headdress, no papers, M (orig mailer)...$125.00

Straight Arrow, headdress, w/papers, M (orig mailer) $250.00

Straight Arrow, Mystic Wrist Kit, w/bracelet, arrowhead & cowry shell, EX+...$400.00

Straight Arrow, ring, Cave Nugget, w/photo, NM $250.00

Straight Arrow, ring, Face, EX+ $65.00

Straight Arrow, ring, Golden Nugget, 1940s, no photo, EX $45.00

Straight Arrow, Rite-A-Lite Arrowhead, shell only, G, S20 ...$20.00

Superman, belt w/buckle, Kellogg's, 1950s, red plastic w/yel diecast metal buckle in 'S' crest shape, NM, A........$200.00

Superman, ring, Airplane, Kellogg's Pep, EX+ $265.00

Superman, ring, Airplane, Kellogg's Pep, VG+ $250.00

Superman, ring, Crusader, EX+.......................................$300.00

Superman of America, membership diploma, secret code manual & pin, #497509, 1958, EX, A $100.00

Tarzan, flicker ring, full-figure shooting arrow, red letters, VG, S20 ....$40.00

Tarzan, print, drawing by Rex Maxon, 1935, full-color, gift premium, EX+...$400.00

Terry & the Pirates, ring, Gold Ore Detector, EX+........$115.00

Three Stooges, Moving Picture Machine, Pillsbury Farina, 1937, assembled cb picturing Larry, Moe & Curly, 6½", NM, A $475.00

Tom Corbett Space Cadet, hat & glasses, EX+................$75.00

Tom Corbett Space Cadet, membership card, Rocket-Lite Squadron, 1950s, bl & wht, 2x4", unused, EX, J5......$30.00

Tom Corbett Space Cadet, membership certificate, NM .$100.00

Tom Corbett Space Cadet, membership patch, EX+......$100.00

Tom Corbett Space Cadet, ring, Dress Uniform, Kellogg's, EX, B10 ....$20.00

Tom Corbett Space Cadet, ring, Face, EX+ $85.00

Tom Mix, badge, Captain Ralston Straight Shooter, 1941, silver-tone, spurs hang from top of badge, EX, J5 ....$175.00

Tom Mix, belt buckle, secret compartment, EX, S20 ....$95.00

Tom Mix, comic books, #3, #4, #5, #6, #7 or #8, Ralston, 1930s, VG+, J5, ea $125.00

Tom Mix, compass, VG, S20.......................................$90.00

Tom Mix, compass/magnifier, brass, Ralston, 1940, G+...$35.00

Tom Mix, compass/magnifier, glow-in-the-dark, 1947, EX........$85.00

Tom Mix, decoder, 6-gun, 1941, EX, J2 ....$80.00

Tom Mix, decoder pin-back buttons, Mike Shaw, Jane, Tony, Washington, EX, J2, ea..$20.00

Tom Mix, ID bracelet, VG, S20....................................$50.00

Tom Mix, neckerchief, Ralston, 1940s, red, wht & bl checks, 20x20", EX, J5 ....$35.00

Tom Mix, photo, set A, Ralston, w/orig mailer, C10 .....$265.00

Tom Mix, pocketknife, EX+..$125.00

Tom Mix, ring, Circus, 1930s, VG, S20.........................$100.00

Tom Mix, ring, Look Around, EX+, C10/J2, from $110 to ..$125.00

Tom Mix, ring, Magnet, EX, C10..................................$60.00

Tom Mix, ring, Signature, NM, C10 ....$200.00

Tom Mix, ring, Siren, NM, C10 ....$125.00

Tom Mix, ring, Straight Shooters, NM, C10..................$115.00

Tom Mix, ring, Whistle, NM, C10 ....$130.00

Tom Mix, rocket parachute, Ralston Purina, 1936, complete w/diecut metal figure, 9" parachute, EX (EX box), A ..$110.00

Tom Mix, rocket parachute, unused, MIB, J2.................$130.00

Tom Mix, Signal Arrowhead, C10/S20...........................$85.00

Tom Mix, sliding whistle, EX, B10................................$80.00

Zorro, ring, 1960s, VG, S20...$75.00

Pressed Steel

Many companies were involved in the manufacture of pressed steel automotive toys which were often faithfully modeled after actual vehicles in production at the time they were made. Because they were so sturdy, some from as early as the 1920s have survived to the present, and those that are still in good condition are bringing very respectable prices at toy auctions around the country. Some of the better-known manufacturers are listed in other sections.

See also Aeronautical; Buddy L; Keystone; Marx; Pedal Cars and Other Wheeled Goods; Structo; Tonka; Wyandotte.

CARS AND BUSSES

American Deluxe Coast-to-Coast Bus, Dayton, friction, yel & blk, 26", G, A $850.00

Bus #788, Kingsbury, 1925, 16", G, A............................$500.00

Chrysler Airflow, Kingsbury, w/up, electric lights, 14", EX, A $575.00

Coupe, Converse, ca 1908, w/up, tan w/red trim, upholstered seat, spoke wheels, 15", EX, A $5,250.00

Coupe w/Rumble Seat, Kingsbury, w/up, electric lights, 2-tone gr, 13½", EX, A $900.00

Deluxe Coupe, Girard, 1934, w/up, electric lights, 14", G, A ..$125.00

Deluxe Coupe, Girard, 1934, w/up, electric lights, 14", NM (EX box), A $1,350.00

Golden Arrow Racer, Kingsbury, 1930, w/up, 20", EX, A .$925.00

Greyhound Bus #228, Kingsbury, 1930s, w/up, bl & cream, 18", G, A $225.00

Lincoln Sedan, Turner, orig emb tires, 26", total rpt, G, A ..$1,750.00

Lincoln Zephyr Coupe & Camper Trailer, Kingsbury, 1936, gr, 22½", EX, A $450.00

Moon Town Car, Neff, 1920s, orange w/blk hood & fenders, 12", G, A $150.00

Napier-Campbell Blue Bird Racer #335, Kingsbury, 1927, w/up, 10", G, A $700.00

Napier-Campbell Blue Bird Racer #335, Kingsbury, 1927, w/up, 18", rpt, A $775.00

Napier-Campbell Blue Bird Racer #335, Kingsbury, 1927, w/up, 18", VG+, A $925.00

Nylint Stables #650, gr open Blazer-type vehicle w/yel interior, gr & yel horse trailer, 20", NMIB, A.......................$150.00

Packard Sedan, Turner, red w/brn top & gold striping, 26", EX, A $2,400.00

Roadster, Dayton, late 1920s, friction, red w/orange tones, 12½", G, A $300.00

Roadster, Kingsbury, red, w/CI driver, disk wheels, 10½", G, A $275.00

Roadster, Kingsbury, windup, electric lights, white rubber tires with green hubs, 13", EX, A, $850.00.

Sedan, Turner, friction, bl w/blk top & fenders, rear spare, 18", G, A $400.00

Sight-Seeing Bus, Cor-Cor, 1929, electric lights, bl w/orange trim, 24", non-working headlights o/w VG, A $500.00

Sight-Seeing Bus, Cor-Cor, 1929, electric lights, 24", G, A ..$400.00

Sky Roof Sedan, Kingsbury, 1937, w/up, orange w/NP trim, 14", G, A $225.00

Sports Car, Meccano/England, w/up, 2-seater, bl & yel w/red seats, 8½", EXIB, A..$1,300.00

Streetcar #781, Kingsbury, orange w/passenger seats, cut-out windows, 9", EX, A $200.00

FIREFIGHTING

Aerial Ladder Truck, Kingsbury, open cab w/CI simulated upholstered seat, 35", ladders missing, pnt wear, VG, A $750.00

Aerial Ladder Truck, Kingsbury, open cab w/CI simulated upholstered seat, 35", pnt partially stripped, G, A...$500.00

Aerial Ladder Truck, Model Toys, later model open cab w/aluminum extension ladder, 34", EX, A $200.00

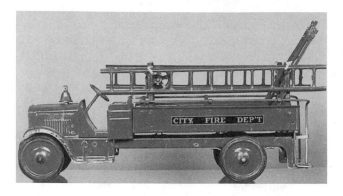

Aerial Ladder Truck, Steelcraft, lever action, all red with City Fire Dept. decal, 26", EX, A, $1,500.00.

Aerial Ladder Truck (Big Boy), Kelmet, 1927, wht rubber slip-on tires, 2 extinguishers, wooden ladders, 29", VG+, A .$1,950.00

American La France Water Tower Truck, Sturditoy, 1920s, 34", EX, A...$1,800.00

American La France Water Tower Truck, Sturditoy, 1920s, 34", G, A...$800.00

Chemical Fire Truck, Gendron/Sampson, open cab, rare, 28½", rstr, VG, A $1,700.00

Chemical Fire Truck, Kelmet, open cab, 26", missing ladders & equipment, rstr, VG, A $450.00

Chemical Fire Truck, Sturditoy #7, ca 1929, 27", VG+, A ..$3,100.00

Fire Chief's Car, w/up, electric lights, early red model w/yel stenciled letters, NP trim, blk rubber tires, 14", VG, A .$350.00

Ladder Truck, Hillclimber, w/flywheel mechanism, 19", pnt wear on ladders o/w G+, A...$200.00

Ladder Truck, Kingsbury, w/up, red w/wooden ladders, rubber tires, w/driver, 10", EX, A.....................................$385.00

Ladder Truck, Kingsbury, w/up, red w/wooden ladders, rubber tires, w/driver, 10", G, A..$225.00

Ladder Truck, Schieble, wht w/red ladders & supports, red trim, spoke wheels, 21", VG, A......................................$300.00

Ladder Truck, Victor Bonnet/France, w/up, electric lights, red w/gray ladder on rnd base, 15", EX, A.....................$925.00

Mack Aerial Ladder Truck, Turner, enclosed cab, crank-op ladder, 32", pnt loss, G, A...$150.00

Pumper Truck, marked Dayton Hillclimber, red with gold tank, 12", VG, $300.00.

Pumper Truck, Kingsbury, w/up, open cab w/CI simulated upholstered seat, 23½", hose missing, G, A $1,025.00

Pumper Truck, Schieble, red w/gold-pnt wood boiler, gold spoke wheels & trim, 14", G, A $400.00

Pumper Truck, Turner, open cab, 28½", rstr, VG, A $475.00

Pumper Truck, Wilkins, w/up, red open truck w/bench seat, silver trim, gold boiler, wht rubber tires, 9½", EX, A..$225.00

Tower Truck, Sturditoy, 34", rpt, G, A............................$550.00

TRUCKS AND VANS

American Railway Express Truck, Sturditoy #2, 1926, 26", rpt, G, A..$750.00

Antiaircraft Military Truck, Sonny, 24", G, A $450.00

Banner Wrecking Service Truck, gr & red w/yel & red advertising, 17", MIB, A $350.00

Bulldog Mack Dump Truck, Steelcraft, red w/blk chassis, 27", G, A..$900.00

Citreon Tanker Truck (Les Jouets), France, red cab & chassis w/silver tank, red trim & hubs, rubber tires, MIB, A.........$1,980.00

Coal Truck, Sturditoy, blk doorless enclosed cab w/orange hopper, rubber tires w/orange hubs, 27½", G, A.............$900.00

CW Brand Coffee Dump Truck, Metalcraft, blk enclosed cab w/yel bed, metal disk wheels, 10", VG, A................$350.00

Delivery Truck, Kingsbury, w/up, C-style cab w/canvas roll-up sides on open bed, rubber tires, 10", G, A................$450.00

Delivery Truck, Turner, friction, C-style cab w/long nose & running boards, open slats on sides of bed, 22", G-, A..$175.00

Delivery Truck, Turner, inertia drive, open cab w/long nose & running boards, open slats on sides of bed, 16", G, A........$100.00

Dredger Truck, Kelmet, open cab w/rear boiler under corrugated roof w/wench, spoke wheels, red & blk, 24", G, A ..$775.00

Dump Truck, Cor-Cor, blk cab & chassis w/red dump bed, 23½", G, A..$300.00

Dump Truck, JEP/France, red cab & chassis w/silver dump bed, chrome radiator, rubber tires, 17", M, A $500.00

Dump Truck, Kelmet, enclosed doorless cab, spoke wheels, 26", VG+, A...$600.00

Dump Truck, Kelmet, 1920s, Big Boy, 25", G-, A $350.00

Dump Truck, Kingsbury, w/up, bl cab & chassis w/yel dump bed, front bell clapper, rubber tires, 11", G, A $450.00

Dump Truck, Sturditoy #1, 1929, gr w/blk fenders, red chassis & wheels, 27", G, A..$750.00

Dump Truck, Sturditoy #6, 1927, 25", G-, A..................$625.00

Dump Truck, Turner, C-style cab, lever-action dump, 30", total rpt, G, A $330.00

Heinz Truck, Metalcraft, 1933, electric lights, wht w/logo, 12", G, A..$150.00

Hood's Ice Cream Truck, Steelcraft, 1930s, red w/gold decal, 21¾", G, A $400.00

Leslie Vacuum Packed Coffee Delivery Truck, Metalcraft, blk enclosed cab w/gr van, metal disk wheels, 11", EX, A .$775.00

Little Jim Tanker Truck, Steelcraft, open cab, 26", rstr, A...$475.00

Little Jim/JC Penney Mack Dump Truck, Steelcraft, 1930s, red cab w/khaki bed, 22", G-, A.......................................$300.00

Lumar Van Lines Delivery Truck, 1950s, mk Coast to Coast, red, yel & bl w/blk rubber tires, 19", EX, A.............$225.00

Mack Army Truck, Steelcraft, brn cab & chassis w/canvas top, 25", G, A $450.00

Mack Dump Truck, Steelcraft, C-style cab w/open doors, red w/blk chassis & fenders, 26", rstr, A $450.00

Mack Dump Truck, Steelcraft, open cab w/lever-action dump, 22½", pnt wear, missing steering wheel, G, A $200.00

Photo courtesy Dunbar Gallery.

Mack Dump Truck, Turner, late 1920s, red and green, 26", from $400.00 to $700.00.

Mack Police Patrol Van, Steelcraft, C-style doorless cab w/enclosed van, 22", rpt, missing steering wheel, G, A $600.00

Meadow Brook Dairy Stake Truck, wht w/red wooden barrels & bl metal cart, 10", VG, A $85.00

Photo courtesy Dunbar Gallery.

Morey-La Rue Laundry Delivery Truck, 1930s, yellow with red lettering, 19", EX, $950.00.

Parcel Post Truck, Sonny, open cab w/extended roof, screened van, orig decals, 26", rear doors missing, some rpt, G, A $600.00

Popeye Evening Ledger Truck, 21", VG+, A $1,425.00

Renault Stake Truck, JEP/France, bright bl w/chrome-plated radiator, blk rubber tires, stationary bed, 17", M, A .$440.00

Roadster, Kingsbury, w/up, electric lights, red & brn, 13", VG, A $450.00

Shell Tanker Truck, Mini-Toys/Canada, yel & red w/decals on sides & back, 28", rare, NM, A $650.00

Sonny Parcel Post Truck, blk cab & chassis w/gr body, 26", rstr, A $500.00

Stake Truck, Kingsbury, w/up, enclosed cab, dk olive gr, wht rubber tires w/red hubs, decals on sides, 10½", VG, A $385.00

Stake Truck, Kingsbury, w/up, open cab w/bench seat, bl, wht rubber tires w/red hubs, w/driver, 9", VG, A............$400.00

Stake Truck, Turner, 1930, friction, bl w/red & gold striping, 22", G, A $225.00

Sunshine Biscuit Truck, Metalcraft, 1933, red cab w/bl body, 11½", G, A $250.00

Tanker Truck, Kelmet, enclosed doorless cab, 27", rstr, EX, A **$1,325.00**

Tanker Truck, Kelmet, open cab, 27", rstr, EX, A **$1,325.00**

Tanker Truck, Sturditoy, doorless cab pulling tank on trailer, red, 33", EX, A **$4,700.00**

Tanker Truck, Sturditoy, doorless cab w/banded tank, 26", total rpt, G, A $1,200.00

Tow Truck, Kingsbury, w/up, electric lights, 9", EX, A ..$400.00

Traveling Store Truck, Sturditoy, 1926, orange body w/red chassis & wheels, 26", missing back doors, G, A $750.00

US Army Truck, Sonny, C-style cab w/canvas-covered bed, 26", VG, A $350.00

US Army Truck, Steelcraft, open cab w/canvas-covered bed, 22", G..$680.00

US Army Truck, Sturditoy #20, 1928, khaki w/orig canvas cover, 27", G, A $925.00

US Mail Truck, Sturditoy, blk cab w/red chassis, gr van w/screened sides, 26", rstr, A $700.00

Weston's English Quality Biscuits, Metalcraft, 1933, red cab w/bl stake body, NP grille, bumpers & wheels, 12", G, A..$300.00

White Dump Truck, Kelmet, blk & red w/doorless enclosed cab, wht rubber tires w/red hubs, 26", NM, A.............$2,650.00

Wolf & Dessauer Delivery Truck, Steelcraft, 1930s, electric lights, maroon w/wht lettering on side of van, 19", VG, A $700.00

Wrecker, Schieble, friction, enclosed cab w/long nose & running boards, 20", G, A................................$550.00

Wrecker, Sturditoy, doorless cab, 30½", EX, A...........$1,050.00

MISCELLANEOUS

Barber Greene Sand Loader, Doepke, 1950s, 24", EX, A..$275.00

Caterpiller Tractor, 1920, w/up, CI driver, 8½", VG, A..$350.00

Duck, Hillclimber, duck on flywheel mechanism, 8½", some pnt wear o/w VG+, A $275.00

Farm Tractor w/Trailer, Kingsbury, tractor w/wht rubber tires & driver, trailer w/4 spoke wheels, 23½", G, A $300.00

Rapid Transit Trolley, Dayton, 1920, flywheel mechanism, doors open & close, 21", G, A $175.00

Steam Shovel, Sturditoy, 22", G, A $200.00

Steam Shovel, Tri-ang/England, red & bl, 48½", EX, A ..$250.00

Steam Shovel, 1930, electric lights, red cab w/gr shovel, 28", G, A $450.00

Trolley Car, Hillclimber, w/geared inertia mechanism, 19", VG, A $165.00

Unit Crane, Doepke, 1950, orange, 19x22", VG+, A $150.00

Promotional Vehicles

Miniature Model T Fords were made by Tootsietoy during the 1920s, and though they were not actually licensed by Ford, a few of these were handed out by Ford dealers to promote the new models. In 1932 Tootsietoy was contacted by Graham-Paige to produce a model of their car. These 4" Grahams were sold in boxes as sales promotions by car dealerships, and some were sold through the toy company's catalog. But it wasn't until after WWII that distribution of 1/25 scale promotional models and kits became commonplace. Early models were of cast metal, but during the 1950s, manufacturers turned to plastic. Not only was the material less costly to use, but it could be molded in the color desired, thereby saving the time and expense previously involved in painting the metal. Though the early plastic cars were prone to warp easily when exposed to heat, by the mid-'50s, they had become more durable. Some were friction powered, and others held a battery-operated radio. Advertising extolling some of the model's features was often embossed on the underside. Among the toy manufacturers involved in making promotionals were National Products, Product Miniatures, AMT, MPC, and Jo-Han. Interest in '50s and '60s models is intense, and the muscle cars from the '60s and early '70s are especially collectible. The more popularity the life-size model attained, the more popular the promotional is with collectors.

Check the model for damage, warping, and amateur alterations. The original box can increase the value by as much as 30%. Jo-Han has reissued some of their 1950s and 1960s Mopar and Cadillac models as well as Chrysler's Turbine Car. These are usually priced between $20.00 and $30.00.

Advisor: Nancy and Jim Schaut (S15).

Key: u/c — undercarriage

1953 Chevy Bel Air, bank, brn, 2-door hardtop, plastic, EX+ $90.00
1955 Ford T-Bird Coupe, red, chrome hubs & wht-wall stickers, some warp, EX+ $135.00

1956 Cadillac, AMT, 2-tone blue, M, $175.00.

1960 Chevy Nova, lt metallic tan, 2-door hardtop, 2 minor roof scratches, EX+ $130.00
1961 Ford Hubley Wagon, wht & yel, NM $65.00
1961 Ford Squaretop, chrome-plated, 2-door hardtop, NM ..$75.00
1961 Ford T-Bird, beige, 2-door hardtop, replated bumpers, NM..$65.00
1961 Pontiac Bonneville Coupe, off-wht, EX $195.00
1963 Ford Galaxie Convertible, beige, molded u/c, 8½", EX, A $50.00
1963 Ford Galaxie XL Coupe, lt tan, NM.......................$95.00
1964 Chevy Chevelle, metallic tan, 2-door hardtop, NM $165.00
1964 Ford Fairlane, AMT, bl, molded u/c, friction, 8", EX, A ...$45.00
1964 Ford Falcon, wht, 2-door hardtop, EX+ $115.00

1964 Ford Galaxie, metallic champagne, 2-door hardtop, chrome foggy o/w EX+ $80.00

1960 Ford Starliner, AMT, 2-tone green, M, $125.00.

1964 Ford T-Bird Convertible, AMT, wht, molded u/c, friction, EX, A $45.00
1964 Ford T-Bird Convertible, AMT, yel, molded u/c, friction, 8½", EX, A...$45.00
1964 Pontiac Grand Prix, AMT, gray w/blk top, friction, 8¾", EX, A $60.00
1965 Chevy Impala SS, Artesian Turq, 2-door hardtop, EX..$125.00
1965 Ford Mustang Fastback, red, lt wear, EX+ $115.00
1965 Ford T-Bird Convertible, AMT, yel, molded u/c, friction, 8½", EX, A...$70.00
1965 Plymouth Baracuda, AMT, bl, molded u/c, friction, 7¾", EX, A $60.00
1966 Buick Riviera, tan, molded u/c, 8½", EX.............$95.00
1966 Ford Fairlane, antique bronze, 2-door hardtop, NMIB..$135.00
1966 Ford Galaxie, AMT, lt bl, molded u/c, friction, 8½", VG, A $40.00
1966 Ford Mustang Coupe, AMT, brn, molded u/c, 7½", EX..$95.00
1966 Ford Mustang Coupe, AMT, red, molded u/c, 7½", VG..$95.00
1966 Ford T-Bird, dk red, 2-door hardtop, EX+ $70.00
1966 Mercury Cyclone, wht, 2-door hardtop, MIB $165.00
1966 Plymouth Baracuda, AMT, yel, molded u/c, friction, 7¾", EX..$95.00
1966 Pontiac GTO, silver, 2-door hardtop, NM $440.00
1967 Buick Riviera, AMT, bl-gr, molded u/c, friction, 8½", VG $95.00
1967 Chevy Firebird, red, 2-door hardtop, M $160.00
1967 Chevy Impala SS, AMT, bl, molded u/c, friction, 9", EX $125.00
1968 Chevy Imperial, metallic Meadow Gr, 2-door hardtop, new chrome, NMIB...$70.00
1968 Chrysler, metallic olive, 2-door hardtop, NM.........$55.00
1968 Lincoln Continental, red-orange, 4-door sedan, MIB ..$65.00
1968 Olds 442, red w/wht interior, 2-door hardtop, MIB....$115.00
1969 AMC Javelin, tan, 2-door hardtop, MIB.................$95.00
1969 Buick Wildcat, crystal bl, 2-door hardtop, MIB.....$130.00
1969 Pontiac GTO, red, 2-door hardtop, hood tack rpl o/w M $260.00
1970 AMC AMX, bright bl, 2-door hardtop, MIB.........$120.00
1970 Chevy Monte Carlo, med metallic bl, 2-door hardtop, NM..$100.00
1970 Ford LTD, dk bl, 4-door hardtop, lt wear, EX+........$85.00
1972 Chevy Fleetside Pickup, med bl, MIB..................$165.00

1972 Chevy Vega Fastback, wht, MIB $44.00
1972 Dodge Challenger, red, 2-door hardtop, M $165.00
1972 Plymouth Roadrunner, metallic gr, 2-door hardtop, MIB..$165.00
1973 Chevy Camaro, Buccaneer Red, 2-door hardtop, MIB $120.00
1973 Chevy Corvette, bright metallic bl, 2-door hardtop, MIB..$420.00
1974 Olds Cutlass, Colonial Gr, 2-door hardtop, MIB $35.00
1975 Chevy Caprice, dk metallic bl, 2-door hardtop, MIB..$55.00
1975 Ford Mustang, silver, 2-door hardtop, MIB $35.00
1976 Dodge Dart, Vintage Red, 2-door sedan, MIB $50.00
1977 Cadillac Coupe DeVille, metallic gr, 2-door hardtop, M......$20.00
1978 Chevy Monza, dk camel, 2-door hardtop, MIB........$14.00
1984 Chevy Corvette, silver, 2-door hardtop, MIB $20.00
1991 Chevy Camaro, blk or teal, 2-door hardtop, MIB, ea ..$14.00
1993 Chevy Dually, blk, MIB.....................................$65.00
1993 Chevy Suburban, blk & silver, Dale Earnhardt edition, MIB......$85.00
1993 Ford F-150, blk, MIB $20.00
1994 Dodge Viper Coupe, yel, MIB $24.00
1995 Chevy Blazer, metallic bl or red, MIB, ea................$22.00
1995 Ford Explorer, blk, MIB.....................................$24.00
1995 Jeep Cherokee, red, wht or blk, MIB, ea $25.00
1996 GMC Jimmy, blk, MIB $24.00

Pull and Push Toys

Pull and push toys from the 1800s often were made of cast iron with bells that were activated as they moved along on wheeled platforms or frames. Hide and cloth animals with glass or shoe-button eyes were also popular, and some were made of wood.

See also specific companies such as Fisher-Price.

Buffalo Bill on Platform, Fallows, 1880s, EX, D10, $8,500.00.

Cow on Platform, German, hide-covered w/glass eyes, carved wood horns & hooves, wood platform w/metal wheels, 14", VG, A $225.00
Duck on Wheels, USA, 1912, mohair duck on CI spoke wheels, beak moves & makes quacking sound, 9", VG, A ...$125.00

Felix the Cat, Nifty/c Pat Sullivan, litho tin, Felix & 2 red mice on yel platform w/4 red disk wheels, EX, A $700.00
Girl & Goat on Platform, pnt tin, girl in wht dress holding grass for goat, 4 spoke wheels, squeaker on base, 6", EX, A $2,100.00
Goat Bell Toy, Gong Bell, 1890s, goat pulls bell between 2 wheels, EX, D10...$550.00

Goat on Platform, 1880s, 5", EX, D10, $450.00.

Horse & Jockey on Platform, Althof-Bergmann, pnt tin, 4", EX, D10 ....$650.00
Horse & Jockey on Platform, Fallows, 1880, pnt tin, 9½", EX, D10, from $1,200 to $1,800.00
Horse & Jockey Push Toy, Fallows, 1880s, pnt tin w/wood stick, 18", EX, D10, from $500 to.................................$1,250.00
Horse & Jockey w/Pony on Platform, Geo Brown, 1870s, pnt tin, 9", EX, D10..$4,500.00
Horse & Rider Jumping on Platform, Gibbs, 1915, paper-litho-on-wood rider & horse on tin platform, 10", EX, A...$500.00
Horse-Drawn Back-to-Back Trap, Bucher/Germany, tin trap w/2 spoke wheels pulled by papier-mache & wood horse, 10", EX, A $900.00
Horse-Drawn Bakery Wagon, tin, Pies & Cakes stenciled on blk wagon pulled by wht trotting horse, 8½", EX, A $600.00
Horse-Drawn Carriage, Merriam, 1860s, bl-pnt tin, 2 brn horses, 14", EX, D10...$3,200.00
Horse-Drawn Cart, Althof-Bergmann, 1870s, pnt tin, yel cart w/2 spoked wheels, 1 horse, 9", VG, D10, from $200 to $400.00
Horse-Drawn Cart, Geo Brown, 1870s, pnt tin, 1 horse, 14", EX, D10, from $200 to $400.00
Horse-Drawn Cart, wood cart w/scalloped ends, pinstriped trim, hide-covered horse on platform, 33", EX, A............$330.00
Horse-Drawn Cart, wooden 2-wheeled cart w/decorative arched side rails, cloth-covered horse on platform, 23", G+, A.........$275.00
Horse-Drawn Cart, wooden 2-wheeled cradle-type cart, hide-covered horse w/glass eyes on platform, 17", VG, A........$175.00
Horse-Drawn Circus Wagon, Arcade, wood wagon w/stamped steel cage, CI lion & pnt driver, 2 blk horses, 14", G, A $385.00
Horse-Drawn Coal Dump Cart, wooden 3-wheeled cart w/Coal stenciled on sides, blk mohair-covered horse, EX, A .$275.00
Horse-Drawn Coal Wagon, Hou & Stafford, 1860s, pnt tin, w/driver & wht horse, 14", D10...........................$5,500.00

Horse-Drawn Covered Wagon, Overland Trail 1849 printed on muslin top, 2 wht horses on cojoined platforms, 31", EX, A $600.00

Horse-Drawn Doctor's Buggy, Geo Brown, pnt tin, bl cart w/2 spoke wheels pulled by wht trotting horse, 13", G, A .$855.00

Horse-Drawn Dump Wagon, Contractors Supplies No 7 w/Landon-Knox Presidential Race sign on tailgate, 2 horses, 18", EX, A $650.00

Horse-Drawn Express Wagon, ca 1890, painted wood, 36", EX, D10, from $2,000.00 to $3,000.00.

Horse-Drawn Express Wagon, Geo Brown, 1870s, pnt tin, red & gr w/wht horse, 11", EX, D10, from $1,000 to $1,500.00

Horse-Drawn Fire Pumper, Fallows, 1880s, pnt tin, w/driver & 2 wht horses, 7½", VG, D10 ....$1,850.00

Horse-Drawn Freight Wagon, wood wagon w/folk-art style articulated wood figure, mohair horse on platform, 52", VG+, A $450.00

Horse-Drawn Goods Wagon, St Claus Dealer in Good Things, arched slats, brn mohair horse on platform, 22", VG+, A $385.00

Horse-Drawn Hansom Cab, European, pnt tin, yel, red & blk carriage w/bl interior, CI spoke wheels, 9", VG+, A $575.00

Horse-Drawn Hay Wagon, wood wagon outfitted w/chains, 2 compo horses in different poses, 27", VG+, A $300.00

Horse-Drawn Jackson Park Trolley, Bliss, paper on wood, 'Smoking on 3 Rear Seats Only' lettered on seat backs, 31", G, A $400.00

Horse-Drawn Milk Wagon, City Dairy, litho tin & wood, red & blk w/yel trim, blk cloth-covered horse, 20", EX, A...$385.00

Horse-Drawn Milk Wagon, Fallows, 1880s, Pure Milk stenciled on red wagon w/driver, brn horse, 13", D10, from $2,000 to $3,000.00

Horse-Drawn Milk Wagon, Rich Toys, Borden's, red & wht w/blk & wht lithoed horse, 20", NM, A $300.00

Horse-Drawn Milk Wagon, Rich Toys, Borden's Farm Products, litho tin & wood, articulated horse, 18", EX, A $350.00

Horse-Drawn Milk Wagon, Rich Toys, Borden's Farm Products, pnt wood, 9½", EX, A $200.00

Horse-Drawn Milk Wagon, Rich Toys, Rich's Little Milk Man, wht & red w/closed door, 20", NM, A $330.00

Horse-Drawn Milk Wagon, Rich Toys, Sealtest Dairy Products, litho-tin wagon w/wooden horse, 20", NM, A.........$330.00

Horse-Drawn Milk Wagon, Sheffield Farms Co, wood, blk & red w/gold lettering, blk & wht articulated horse, 20", EX, A...$580.00

Horse-Drawn Omnibus, wood w/German destinations listed, 2 hide-covered horses on single platform, 32", EX, A $2,200.00

Horse-Drawn Railroad Omnibus, Merriam, 1870s, pnt tin, w/driver & 2 horses, 12", EX, D10, from $4,500 to $6,500.00

Horse-Drawn Stake Wagon, wood w/arched side slats, spoke wheels, 2 wht dappled horses on dbl platform, 29", EX, A.........$475.00

Horse-Drawn Trolley, Althof-Bergmann, 1870s, pnt tin, red & bl w/2 wht horses, 10", EX, D10............................$1,850.00

Horse-Drawn Trolley, ca 1880, tin w/ornate window cutouts & 4 spoked wheels, 2 wht galloping horses, 9", EX, A....$650.00

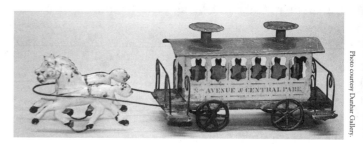

Horse-Drawn Trolley, George Brown, trolley marked 8th Ave. & Central Park, red, yellow, and green, white horses, 12", D10, from $2,500.00 to $3,500.00.

Horse-Drawn Trolley, Rich Toys, litho-tin trolley, front & back wooden figures, 2 blk & wht wooden horses, 20", MIB, A..$935.00

Landing of Columbus Bell Toy, CI, figures in ship w/lg bell, spoke wheels, 7", VG, A..$385.00

Mule Bell Ringer, Gong Bell, pnt CI, mule on platform kicks bell, 8", EX+, A $880.00

Old Dutch Girl, Hubley, 1932, girl in bl & wht dress w/wht bonnet & red shoes on wht base, 9", EX, A................$5,725.00

Pony Bell Ringer, Gong Bell, pnt CI, pony on platform kicks bell, 8", EX, A...$700.00

Pony Cart, Gibbs, red wood wagon w/horizontal stake sides, 2 wooden ponies w/paper litho graphics, jtd legs, 18", EX+, A...$385.00

Pony Circus, Gibbs, 2 ponies pulling circus wagon, litho tin & wood w/CI spoke wheels, 13", G, A $300.00

Rooster Pulling Cart, Gibbs, wooden rooster w/paper litho detail, red wood-slatted cart w/2 spoke wheels, 16", EX, A .$650.00

Sled, orange-pnt wood w/stenciled design, gr bent-wire frame, 15", EX, A...$580.00

Steer on Platform, cowhide-covered, wooden platform w/wheels, moos when head is turned, 17", VG, A $775.00

Sunny Andy Street Railway, orange w/lithoed passengers in windows, bell sounds when pulled, 14", VG, A.............$220.00

US Mail Train, Fallows, 1880s, engine mk Juno, pnt tin, 22", EX, D10...$3,800.00

Wild Mule Jack, Gong Bell, pnt CI, rider & mule on 2-wheeled base, 8", VG, A..$470.00

Puppets

Though many collectible puppets and the smaller scale marionettes were made commercially, others were handmade and are today considered fine examples of folk art which sometimes sell for several hundred dollars. Some of the most collectible today are character-related puppets representing well-known television stars.

Advisor: Bill Bruegman (T2), finger puppets, hand puppets, and push-button puppets; Steven Meltzer (M9), marionettes and ventriloquist dolls.

See also Advertising; Black Americana; Political.

FINGER PUPPETS

Crypt Keeper, rubber, M, H4, set of 3 ....$12.00
Lamb Chop, 1960, VG, N2 ....$35.00
Monkees, Davy & Mickey, Clever Finger Dolls by Remco, MOC (sealed), B3 ....$90.00
Monkees, Mickey, MIB (Sears box), B3........................$35.00
Pebbles & Bamm-Bamm, Knickerbocker, 1972, VG, pr...$10.00
Ricky Jr (Little Ricky from I Love Lucy), Zany Toys, 1952, vinyl w/cloth outfit, fleece blanket, 8", EXIB, from $400 to ..$500.00
Spider-Man, 1970s, NM, D8 ....$12.00
Three Stooges, MIP, T1, set of 3 ....$15.00

HAND PUPPETS

Alf, 1988, w/tag, EX, B10 ....$15.00
Archimedes the Owl (Sword & the Stone), EX, T1.........$35.00
Baby Huey, Gund, 1960, cloth w/vinyl head, 10", EX+, T2 ...$30.00
Bamm-Bamm, Ideal, 1964, cloth w/vinyl head, 10", EX, J8/T2, from $20 to..$25.00
Batman, Ideal, 1966, cloth w/vinyl head, unused, EX+ (EX card), A..$45.00
Bozo the Clown, Knickerbocker, 1962, cloth w/vinyl head, 9", NM, T2 ....$20.00
Bugs Bunny, Mattel, talker, non-working, EX, B10..........$30.00
Captain America, Ideal, 1966, plastic & vinyl, 11", EX+, A..$100.00
Charlie McCarthy, American, compo head w/blk cloth attire & hat, w/monocle, 12", EX, from $50 to $75.00

Dean Martin and Jerry Lewis Puppet Show, 1950s, complete, MIB, from $300.00 to $500.00.

Dennis the Menace, Gund, 1960, cloth w/vinyl head, 10", EX, T2..$30.00
Dick Tracy, Ideal, 1961, cloth w/vinyl head, 10", VG+, from $40 to..$50.00
Dilly-Dally (Howdy Doody), 1950s, cloth & vinyl, EX, J6 ..$25.00
Donald Duck, Gund, 1960s, cloth w/vinyl head, squeaker, MIP..$50.00
Dopey (Snow White), Gund, 1960s, cloth w/vinyl head, squeaker, MIP $50.00
Dumbo, Gund, 1950s, cloth w/vinyl head, squeaker, MIP ..$50.00
Fred Flintstone, Knickerbocker, 1960s, VG, C17 ....$25.00
Green Hornet, Ideal, 1966, plastic & vinyl, removable hat, 10", EX+, A...$85.00
Herman Munster, cloth & vinyl, missing talking box o/w EX, T1..$65.00

Hopalong Cassidy, 1950s, scarce, NM, $200.00.

Jiminy Cricket, Knickerbocker/Video Craft Ltd, 1962, cloth w/gr vinyl head & yel hat, EX, J5...$50.00
Laurel & Hardy, Knickerbocker, 1965, cloth w/vinyl heads, NM, F8, pr...$70.00
Little Audrey, 1950s, cloth & vinyl, hands missing o/w VG+, J5..$15.00
Lucy (Peanuts), Ideal, M...$45.00
Mean Moe (Inkwell Cartoon Character), Gund, 1962, cloth w/vinyl head & felt hands, EX, J5 ....$50.00
Mickey & Minnie, 1970s, cloth w/soft plastic heads, VG, M8, pr..$12.00
Mickey Mouse, Gund, 1960s, cloth w/vinyl head, squeaker, MIP $60.00
Miss Piggy, Fisher-Price, 1979, EX, B10...........................$25.00
Mister Ed, Mattel, 1962, plush w/vinyl head, pull-string talker, wht yarn mane, 12", NMIB, from $150 to $200.00
Mr Magoo, 1962, cloth & vinyl, NM, J6..........................$35.00
Olive Oyl, Gund, 1950s, cloth w/vinyl head, 10", EX, T2.$25.00
Papa Smurf, EX, B10...$18.00
Pinocchio, early 1930s, EX, J2..$115.00
Pinocchio, Gund, 1960s, cloth w/vinyl head, squeaker, MIP .$50.00

Pinocchio, Knickerbocker, 1962, cloth w/vinyl head, NM, F8 ....$35.00

Pluto, Gund, 1950s, cloth w/vinyl head, squeaker, MIP ...$50.00

Porky Pig, Mattel, 1964, talker, non-working, EX, B10....$30.00

Raggedy Ann & Andy, Knickerbocker, 1970s, MIP, H12 ..$15.00

Robin, Ideal, 1966, cloth & vinyl, P12/T2, from $185 to ...$195.00

Romper Room, Mr Do Bee & Happy Jack, Hasbro, 1970, cloth w/plastic heads, 11", EX+ (EX+ box), A.....................$50.00

Rosie the Robot, Knickerbocker, 1960s, cloth w/rubber head, NM, A $100.00

Sherman (Sesame Street), cloth & vinyl, NM, B10.........$15.00

Spike (Tom & Jerry), Multitoy, 1989, MOC, B10............$16.00

Swee' Pea, Gund, 1950s, cloth w/vinyl head, 10", EX, T2 ..$25.00

Sylvester, 1990, cloth, EX, B10 ....$12.00

Troupe, Germany, ca 1900, set of 8 Punch-type figures w/carved heads, limp cloth bodies w/wooden legs, 12", VG-NM, A $935.00

Wendy (Peter Pan), Gund, 1960s, cloth w/soft plastic head, non-working squeaker, VG, M8 ....$12.00

Wizard of Oz, Glinda, Toto or Tin Man, Proctor & Gamble premium, 1960s, EX, H4, ea $15.00

Wonder Woman, Ideal, 1966, cloth w/vinyl head, 11", MIP, A...$215.00

Yogi Bear, 1961, slight wear, B10 ....$25.00

MARIONETTES

Alice in Wonderland, Peter Puppet, 1950s, compo head, hands & feet, 14", VG, J5 ....$75.00

Alice in Wonderland (unlicensed), Hazelle's, talker, M, M9 ....$125.00

Angel, Pelham, MIB, M9 ....$125.00

Batman, Hazelle's, 1966, cloth & felt costume, 15", EX+, A ...$400.00

Bengo the Dog, Pelham, MIB, M9 ....$100.00

Bimbo the Clown, Hazelle's, 800 series, EX, M9 ....$75.00

Bimbo the Clown, Pelham, M, M9 ....$135.00

Buckaroo Bill, Hazelle's, talker, EX, M9 ....$175.00

Clippo the Clown, Curtis Craft, MIB, M9.....................$100.00

Clippo the Clown, Effanbee, WWII, MIB, M9..............$250.00

Clown, Pelham, talker, MIB, M9 ....$125.00

Cop, Pelham, talker, MIB, M9 ....$125.00

Donald Duck, Pelham, wood w/cloth clothes, 10", MIB, A ..$165.00

Emily Ann (Clippo's Girlfriend), Effanbee, M, M9........$160.00

Father, Mother & Son, Effanbee, EX, M9......................$425.00

Flub-A-Dub (Howdy Doody's Pal), Peter Puppet, compo, 12", MIB..$375.00

Freddy MC, Hazelle's, M, M9..$125.00

Gepetto (Pinocchio), Pelham, MIB, M9 ....$160.00

Girl, Pelham, talker, MIB, M9 ....$125.00

Hansel & Gretel, Hazelle's, M, M9, pr...........................$175.00

Hillbilly, Hazelle's, 800 series, M, M9 ....$95.00

Horse, Pelham, EX (EX box), M9 ....$125.00

Howdy Doody, 1950s, compo w/cloth clothes, 16", EX, A .$175.00

Jim-Bob & Susy Pigtail, Curtis Craft, 1950, M, M9, pr..$525.00

Little Boy Blue, Hazelle's, 800 series, compo, M, M9 .....$135.00

Mad Hatter (Alice in Wonderland), Peter Puppet, 1950s, compo head & hands w/wooden feet, 14", EX, J5 ....$125.00

Marie Osmond, Madison Ltd, 1978, 8", MIB.................$85.00

Marilyn, Hazelle's, talker, EX, M9.................................$225.00

Mickey Mouse, Pelham, wood, plastic & compo w/cloth clothing, 11", EX, P6...$150.00

Minnie Mouse, Pelham, wood w/cloth clothes, 13", MIB, A...$165.00

Nurse, Pelham, M, M9..$95.00

Old Lady, Pelham, MIB, M9 ....$125.00

Peter Pan, Peter Puppet, 1950s, EX+, J2 ....$130.00

Pinocchio, Pelham, MIB, T1, $135.00.

Planet Flyer (Tom Corbett Look-Alike), Hazelle's, 1950s, NMIB, J2 ....$210.00

Pop Singer, Pelham, gray suit, MIB, M9 ....$300.00

Pop Singer, Pelham, Hawaiian shirt, M, M9...................$145.00

Prince Charming, Pelham, MIB, M9 ....$125.00

Sailor, Hazelle's, talker, EX, M9.....................................$125.00

Small Fry, Peter Puppet, 1949, compo, NM, T1 ....$165.00

Snow White, Peter Puppet, wood w/compo head, cloth costume, articulated mouth, 15", EX....................................$185.00

Wolf, Pelham, G, M9 ....$250.00

Dagwood, Hazelle's, 1950s, MIB, M9, $250.00.

Wombles (Furry Creatures from English TV Show), Pelham, MIB, M9, ea..$85.00
Wonder Woman, Madison Ltd, 1977, vinyl w/pnt-on top & cloth shorts, 11½", EX..................................$100.00

PUSH-BUTTON PUPPETS

Atom Ant, Kohner, NM, C17..................................$40.00
Bamm-Bamm, Kohner, 1960s, missing club, VG, C17.....$20.00

Dino, Kohner, 1960s, M, J6, $65.00.

Photo courtesy June Moon.

Disney Pop Pals, Kohner/Hong Kong, Mickey, Donald, Pluto & Goofy, 3", EX, D9.......................................$35.00
Donald Duck Tricky Trapeze, EX, B10.....................$10.00
Felix the Cat, FTCP Inc, wood, EX, B10, from $25 to.....$30.00
Flub-a-Dub, Kohner, 1950s, wood w/felt ears, EX, J5.....$175.00
Fred Flintstone, Kohner, 1960s, EX, C1/F8.................$30.00
Fred Flintstone & Dino, Kohner, 1962, NMIB, A..........$455.00
Howdy Doody, Kohner, 1950s, wood w/plastic head, EX, J5..$150.00
Howdy Doody, Kohner, 1950s, wood w/plastic head, NM (EX box), A...$225.00
Huckleberry Hound, EX, B10................................$45.00
Lone Ranger on Silver, Kohner, EX+, T1.....................$100.00
Mickey Mouse, Gabriel, EX, B10............................$25.00
Paulette the Poodle, M, J2..................................$24.00
Pebbles, Kohner, scarce, NM (EX card), from $35 to.......$45.00
Princess Summerfall Winterspring, Kohner, 1950s, jtd wood, VG, J5..$150.00
Wilma Flintstone, Kohner, 1960s, NM, J6.................$35.00

VENTRILOQUIST DOLLS

Boy, Pelham, M, M9..$125.00
Charlie McCarthy, blk jacket w/blk & wht checked lapels & pants, wht shirt w/orange tie, no monocle, 30", EX, A.............$575.00
Charlie McCarthy, blk tux w/wht shirt & blk bow tie, pk rose on lapel, w/top hat, no monocle, 21", EX, A................$110.00
Charlie McCarthy, Effanbee, blk tux w/wht vest, shirt & bow tie, blk top hat, w/monocle & pin-back on lapel, 18", EX, A.....$385.00

Charlie McCarthy, Effanbee, tan jacket w/wht shirt & orange print bow tie, wht pants & hat, w/monocle, 15½", EX, A...$475.00
Girl, Pelham, M, M9..$125.00
Howdy Doody, Beehler Arts, molded head w/shirt & blue jeans, 8", EXIB, A...$190.00

Jerry Mahoney, 24", NM, D10, $550.00.

Photo courtesy Dunbar Gallery.

Knucklehead, 1950s, MIB, M9.............................$950.00
Mickey Mouse, Horsman, 1973, hard plastic head w/soft vinyl hands, blk tux w/red bow tie, 30", EX.....................$175.00
Monk, Pelham, M, M9......................................$225.00
Mortimer Snerd, molded plastic body w/orange hair, blk pants & vest w/wht shirt, red cummerbund, 26", EX.............$65.00
Rover, Pelham, M, M9......................................$95.00

Puzzles and Picture Blocks

Jigsaw puzzles have been around almost as long as games. The first examples were handcrafted from wood, and they are extremely difficult to find. Most of the early examples featured moral subjects and offered insight into the social atmosphere of their time. By the 1890s jigsaw puzzles had become a major form of home entertainment. Cube puzzles or blocks were often made by the same companies as board games. Early examples display lithography of the finest quality. While all subjects are collectible, some (such as Santa blocks) often command prices higher than games of the same period.

Because TV and personality-related puzzles have become so popular, they're now regarded as a field all their own apart from character collectibles in general, and these are listed here as well, under the subtitle 'Character.'

Advisors: Bob Armstrong (A4); Norm Vigue (V1), character.
See also Advertising.

Animal Picture Cubes, McLoughlin Bros, 1898, paper on wood, set of 12, 11x8", EX (EX wood-fr box), A...............$225.00
Arabian Chiefs (hunting), artist Schreyer, 1930s, plywood, 500 curve-knob semi-interlocking pcs, EX (rpl box), A4 ..$90.00

Arrival, 1909, solid wood, 91 push-to-fit pcs, color-line cutting, EX (orig box), A4 ....$18.00

At Edenbridge Kent (fishing), artist A Bowers, 1910-20, plywood, 166 crooked-line push-to-fit pcs, EX (rpl box), A4 ....$18.00

Au Boulevard, Hayter/Victory Artistic, 1930s, plywood, 800 rnd-knob interlocking pcs, semistrip-cut, EX (orig box), A4 ....$100.00

Aunt Louisa's Yankee Doodle Cube Puzzles, 30 paper-covered wooden cubes w/6 images of Uncle Sam, 10x12", EXIB, A $900.00

Autumn Sunset, Ernest Dower/Leisure Hour, 1930s, plywood, 163 interlocking pcs, 4 rpl pcs, EX (orig box), A4 .....$32.00

Band at the Tower, J Salmon/Academy, 1930s, plywood, 250 1-by-1 interlocking pcs, semistrip-cut, EX (orig box), A4 ......$32.00

Battle of Manila/Asiatic Squadron, McLoughlin Bros, 1898, 11x15", EX (EX wood box), A $600.00

Breaking Camp (untitled), artist P Goodwin, 1930s, 495 random-knob interlocking pcs, color-line cut, EX (orig box), A4 ....$90.00

Brownie Blocks, McLoughlin Bros, 6 Palmer Cox Brownie images, 11x13", G+ (G+ wooden box), A $525.00

Brownie Scroll Puzzles, Blind Man's Bluff & The Dance, McLoughlin Bros, 1891, 11x13", EX (EX wood box), A $250.00

Buffalo, Holabird, 1909, plywood, 39 push-to-fit pcs, color-line cut, silhouette, EX (orig envelope), A4 ....$35.00

Captive (animals), artist R Ernst-Parie, 1930s, plywood, 384 interlocking pcs, strip-cut, 9 rpl pcs, EX (rpl box), A4 ....$40.00

Chance Shot (hunt scene), JV, 1930s, jigsaw, 302 push-to-fit rnd-knob edge interlocking pcs, EX (orig box), A4...$55.00

Chicago Fair, Machinery Hall & US Government Building, McLoughlin Bros, 1892, 9x11", EX (VG box), A....$275.00

City of Worcester, McLoughlin Bros, nautical image, 7x19", EX (EX wooden box), A $700.00

Coaching Scene at Inn in Winter, Parker Bros/Pastime, 1910, plywood, 119 random semi-interlocking pcs, EX (rpl box), A4 ....$28.00

Cottage Scene, 1909, solid wood, 200 angular push-to-fit pcs, color-line cut, EX (orig box), A4 ....$40.00

Crossing the Brook (family & dogs), Skilton, 1910s, plywood, 314 push-to-fit pcs, color-line cut, EX (orig box), A4.........$55.00

Dancing Couple (courtship scene), 1909, solid wood, 155 push-to-fit pcs, 2 rpl pcs, EX (rpl box), A4 ....$25.00

Declaration of Independence, C Russell/Currier & Ives, 1976, plywood, 332 rnd-knob interlocking pcs, EX (orig box), A4 ....$50.00

Dissected Map of the World w/Picture Puzzle of the Capitol, McLoughlin Bros, 1888, VG+ (VG+ wood box), A..$350.00

Dutch Interior (family), 1910-20, masonite, 586 push-to-fit & semi-interlocking pcs, color-line cut, EX (orig box), A4 ....$100.00

Eiffel Tower (scenery), Condor/Craftsman, photo image, 1950-60, plywood, 630 interlocking pcs, EX (orig envelope), A4 ....$40.00

Excitement on the Range, J Straus/artist WH Hinton, 1940s, plywood, 300 rnd-knob interlocking pcs, EX (orig box), A4 ....$30.00

Farm (countryside), artist A Blake, 1930s, plywood, 430 interlocking pcs, color-line cut, EX (orig box), A4 ....$60.00

Farming in Toscan, J Straus, 1940s, plywood, 500 rnd-knob interlocking pcs, EX (orig box), A4 ....$50.00

Fire Engine Scroll Puzzle, McLoughlin Bros, 2 puzzles, horse-drawn fire pumper/train, 10x17", EXIB, A...............$525.00

Fishing Fleet (harbor & boats), 1930s, plywood, 172 interlocking pcs, EX (orig box), A4 ....$28.00

Garden in June, Parker Bros/Pastime, artist P Jun, 1930, plywood, 205 curled-knob interlocking pcs, EX (orig box), A4 ....$55.00

Gen Allenby Entering Jerusalem, Parker Bros/Pastime, 1919, plywood, 205 random-knob interlocking pcs, G+ (rpl box), A4 ....$50.00

Good Dose, artist Nosworthy, 1910s, plywood, 131 push-to-fit pcs, color-line cutting, 13x9", 1 rpl pc, EX (orig box), A4....$28.00

Grouse in Winter Scene (untitled), L Hart/artist AL Ripley, 1940s, cb, 1,000 diecut pcs, 1 rpl pc, EX (orig box), A4............$15.00

Harvest Scene, artist E Kenseler, 1910s, plywood, 210 push-to-fit pcs, 2 rpl pcs, EX (rpl box), A4 ....$30.00

Hearty Welcome (drawing room), Parker Bros/Pastime, 1933, plywood, 171 jagged semi-interlocking pcs, EX (orig box), A4 ....$48.00

Home Scroll Puzzle, McLoughlin Bros, 1897, boy on rocking horse, 9x7", VG+ (VG box), A $200.00

Home Sweet Home (cottages), Detroit Gasket, 1930s, cork, 300 push-to-fit edge-interlocking pcs, EX (orig box), A4...$55.00

Houses of Parliament & Westminster, Hayrer/Victory Topical, 1950-60, 288 rnd-knob interlocking pcs, EX (orig box), A4 ....$28.00

Indian Camp, MacDonald, 1920-30, plywood, 460 rnd-knob interlocking pcs, 3 rpl pcs, EX (orig box), A4............$85.00

Judenborge (town scene), R Chesley/artist E Niese, 1973, plywood, 206 rnd-knob interlocking pcs, EX (orig box), A4 ....$22.00

Just in Time (fox hunt), Chad Valley, 1930s, plywood, 100 curve-knob interlocking pcs, strip-cut, EX (orig box), A4......$20.00

Kentucky Girl, Parker Bros, 1910-20, plywood, jigsaw, 200 crooked-line strip-cut pcs, 1 rpl pc, EX (orig box), A4 .$32.00

Dog Eyeing Stuffed Pheasant (untitled), 1930s, plywood, 260 pieces, EX, A4, $45.00.

Photo courtesy Bob Armstrong.

Kentucky Lady (women & horses), Milton Bradley, 1930s, cb, 250 rnd-knob semi-interlocking pcs, EX (orig box), A4 ....$8.00

Lake Supreme (scenery), Ryther Novelty, photo image, 1940s, plywood, 14 rnd-knob interlocking pcs, EX (orig box), A4 ....$4.00

Leaving the Haven (harbor scene), 1930s, plywood, 202 rnd-knob interlocking pcs, EX (orig box), A4 ....$22.00

Leaving the Inn (fox hunt), J Straus/artist Slaughter, 1930s, plywood, 200 curved-knob interlocking pcs, EXIB, A4 ..$25.00

Little Folks Cubes/Puss in Boots, McLoughlin Bros, 12 paper-on-wood cubes, 8x11", EX (EX paper-covered wood-fr box), A $500.00

Little Nurse (children & dogs), Tuco, 1930s, cb, 180 diecut pcs, EX (orig box), A4 ....$10.00

Lower Glacier Grindelwald (mountains), photo image, 1970s, plywood, 396 rnd-knob interlocking pcs, EX (rpl box), A4 .$30.00

Mammy Tells a Fortune (An Anxious Moment), 1910s, masonite, 306 random pcs, color-line cut, EX (orig box), A4 ....$55.00

Market Street in India, 1930s, plywood, 70 rnd-knob interlocking pcs, strip-cut, 1 rpl pc, EX (orig box), A4 ....$10.00

Medicine Man, Parker Bros/Pastime, 1928, plywood, 100 push-to-fit pcs, color-line cut, 2 rpl pcs, EX (orig box), A4.......$25.00

Mediterranean Shores, J Straus/artist Arnegg, 1950s, plywood, 500 rnd-knob interlocking pcs, 1 rpl pc, EX (orig box), A4 ....$45.00

Memories (women), Ullman, 1909, solid wood, 75 crooked-line semistrip-cut pcs, EX (orig box), A4 ....$20.00

Men Around Punch Bowl, 1930s, plywood, 250 curved-knob semistrip-cut interlocking pcs, fragile (rpl box), A4 ..$25.00

Merchant Ship, artist A Siullue, 1930s, pressed board, 284 push-to-fit pcs, EX (orig box), A4 ....$35.00

Moonlight (lake scene), Jumbo Jigsaw Puzzles, 1930s, plywood, 319 random-knob interlocking pcs, EX (orig box), A4 ....$45.00

Mother's Garden, Parker Bros/Pastime, 1930s, plywood, 103 random-knob interlocking pcs, color-line cut, EX (rpl box), A4...$28.00

Motherhood (family scene), Price, 1909, solid wood, 112 push-to-fit pcs, 1 rpl pc, EX (orig box), A4..........................$25.00

Mountain Stream (Dutch), Hamlen/artist S Stone, 1930s, plywood, 120 random-knob interlocking pcs, EX (orig box), A4 ....$18.00

Napoleon on the Way to St Helena, University, 1930s, plywood, 150 push-to-fit pcs, EX (orig box), A4 ....$25.00

Nativity Scene, 1909, solid wood, 159 push-to-fit pcs, color-line cut, 1 rpl pc, EX (rpl box), A4..........................$28.00

New England Winter Day, Parker Bros/Pastime, 1910s, plywood, 170 curled-earlets interlocking pcs, EX (orig box), A4 .$45.00

New Judgement of Paris, Huvanco, 1930s, plywood, 200 rnd-knob interlocking pcs, semicolor-line cut, EX (orig box), A4 ....$35.00

Old Farm Home (horse in countryside), FL Gibbs/Bewitching, 1930s, 215 rnd-knob interlocking pcs, EX (orig box), A4 ....$40.00

Old Maine Harbor, Bliss, 1930s, plywood, 525 push-to-fit pcs, 4 rpl pcs, EX (rpl box), A4 ....$75.00

Old Mill, Madmar, 1930s, plywood, 96 crooked-line semi-interlocking pcs, EX (orig box), A4 ....$20.00

On the Range, Geo P Merrill/artist HW Amick, 1920-40, plywood, 473 push-to-fit pcs, 1 rpl pc, EX (orig box), A4 ....$80.00

On Venetian Waters, Tilden-Thurber, 1930s, plywood, 200 random-knob interlocking pcs, EX (orig box), A4..........$40.00

One Sunday Morning (winter church scene), Milton Bradley, 1930s, cb, 465 rnd-knob interlocking pcs, EX (orig box), A4 ....$12.00

Our Battleship New York, McLoughlin Bros., 1895, complete, 10½x12½", EX (EX box), A, $525.00.

Outside the Wall (eastern monuments), Parker Bros/Pastime, 1940-50, plywood, 151 interlocking pcs, EX (orig box), A4 ...$45.00

Picture Puzzle of the World, Parker Bros, 1893, litho paper on board, complete, 12¾x20¾", EX (EX box), A $230.00

Pleasant Flirtation, 1920s, plywood, 527 semi-interlocking pcs, 1 rpl pc, EX (orig box), A4...$90.00

Post Mortem, Parker Bros/Pastime, artist Razjam, 1930, plywood, 175 curved-knob, earlets & jagged pcs, EX (rpl box), A4...$45.00

Purest in Dewy Morning (flower garden), B Nowell, 1930s, 388 semi-interlocking pcs, EX (orig box), A4...................$60.00

Ready for Action (dogs in landscape), Milton Bradley, 1930s, plywood, 67 random-knob interlocking pcs, EX (orig box), A4 ....$15.00

Rehearsal (children), Barnard-Clogton, 1930s, plywood, 150 rnd-knob interlocking pcs, semistrip-cut, EX (orig box), A4.$30.00

Riders Going on Hunt, Playtime House/Fine Arts, 1950, cb, 1,000 sq-knob interlocking pcs, EX (orig box), A4 ...$10.00

Robber Kitten & Three Little Kittens Picture Cubes, McLoughlin Bros, 1898, paper on wood, set of 12, EX (wood-fr box), A $250.00

Roses (woman w/roses), 1909, solid wood, 185 push-to-fit pcs, color-line cut, 7 rpl pcs, EX (orig box), A4................$32.00

Rounding the Light Ship, R Chesly/artist Currier & Ives, 1971, plywood, 208 rnd-knob interlocking pcs, EX (orig box), A4..$22.00

Royal Family (dogs), Milton Bradley/artist A Hiebel, 1930s, plywood, 206 jagged semi-interlocking pcs, EX (orig box), A4........$40.00

Sagamore (buildings), W Harms/Aptus, photo image, 1980s, plywood, 120 rnd-knob interlocking pcs, EX (orig box), A4...$14.00

Scene in Brussels, 1910s, plywood, 174 push-to-fit pcs, color-line cut, EX (orig box), A4 ....$35.00

Scene in Venice (boats), JF Norton/Jimjig, 1930s, plywood, 436 interlocking pcs, semistrip-cut, EX (orig box), A4 ....**$55.00**

Searching the Files (18th C English scene), Cotswood, 1930s, plywood, 500 rnd-knob interlocking pcs, EX (orig box), A4 ....**$65.00**

Serious Case (children), artist Norman Rockwell, 1930s, plywood, 360 interlocking pcs, EX (rpl box), A4 ....**$50.00**

Shadowland, 1920s, plywood, 320 pieces, 16x12", EX (original box), A4, $25.00.

Photo courtesy Bob Armstrong.

Ship Pilgrim Fall River Line (side-wheeler passing under Brooklyn Bridge), McLoughlin Bros, 9x12", EX (EX wooden box), A..**$525.00**

Small Beginning of a Great Navy, artist Relyea, 1930s, plywood, 1930s, 425 long-rnd interlocking pcs, EX (orig box), A4 ....**$65.00**

Son of Erin (people in countryside), Hodges & Son, 1930s, plywood, 150 1-by-1 lg-knob interlocking pcs, EX (rpl box), A4 ....**$30.00**

Spring Unlocks Her Flowers (garden), B Nowell, 1930s, 401 semi-interlocking pcs, EX (orig box), A4 ....**$65.00**

Springtime (river town), Leisure Moment, 1930s, masonite, 1930s, 387 1-by-1 rnd-knob interlocking pcs, EX (orig box), A4 ....**$45.00**

Statecoach in the Mountains, Parker Bros/Pastime, 1930, plywood, 454 earlets semi-interlocking pcs, EX (rpl box), A4 ....**$125.00**

Stitch in Time Saves Nine, Ryther Novelty, 1930s, pressed board, 66 rnd-knob interlocking pcs, EX (orig box), A4..**$15.00**

Storyland Picture Cubes, McLoughlin Bros, 20 cubes w/6 guide sheets, 11x13", VG (VG paper-covered wooden box), A **$450.00**

Sunset on Lake (untitled), 1930s, cb, 205 rnd-knob push-to-fit semi-interlocking pcs, diecut, EX (rpl box), A4...........**$3.00**

Sunshine & Shadows, FN Burt/artist R Weber, 1930s, cb, 220 crooked-line strip-cut pcs, 2 rpl pcs, EX (orig box), A4 ..**$6.00**

Surrender of Cornwallis, Cape Cod, 1930s, plywood, 153 interlocking pcs, EX (orig box), A4 ....**$25.00**

Surrender of General Burgoyne, R Chesley/Currier & Ives, 1972, 184 rnd-knob interlocking pcs, EX (orig box), A4 ....**$24.00**

Tea Party (humorous scene w/children), artist CG Phillips, 1930s, plywood, 114 push-to-fit pcs, EX (orig box), A4..**$20.00**

The House That Jack Built, CS Shepard, paper on wood w/overlays that illus various characters, 11x13", G+ (G+ box), A..**$200.00**

The Kill (fox hunt), Chad Valley, 1930s, plywood, 100 curve-knob interlocking pcs, strip-cut, EX (orig box), A4 ..**$20.00**

Their Son's Letter, Gold Seal Toy/Locklite, 1930s, 300 interlocking pcs, semistrip-cut, EX (orig box), A4 ....**$40.00**

Three for Dinner (English drawing room), R Chesley, 1972, plywood, 323 rnd-knob interlocking pcs, EX (orig box), A4 ....**$45.00**

To Pleasant Valley (forest), Parker Bros/Pastime, 1928, plywood, 154 foot-knob interlocking pcs, EX (orig box), A4 ...**$35.00**

Toasting (17th C drawing room), Hammond, 1930s, plywood, 600 random curve-knob interlocking pcs, EX (orig box), A4..**$100.00**

Train Pulling Into Busy Station, McLoughlin Bros, 1895, smoke billowing from close-up of locomotive, fr, 18x24", EX, A..**$300.00**

Tyrolian Waters, Cape Cod, 1930s, plywood, 200 long-knob interlocking pcs, EX (orig box), A4 ....**$40.00**

United States Map Puzzle, Parker Bros, paper-on-wood pcs, 8x13", VG (VG box), A..**$35.00**

Venetian Scene, B Nowell, 1930s, pressed board, 1930s, 691 semi-interlocking pcs, 1 rpl pc, EX (orig box), A4 ..**$110.00**

Welcome Guest (campsite w/bears), 1930s, plywood, 390 1-by-1 rnd-knob curved pcs, 1 rpl pc, EX (rpl box), A4........**$60.00**

Western Sunrise, J Straus, 1950-60, plywood, 300 rnd-knob interlocking pcs, EX (orig box), A4 ....**$30.00**

Ye Olde Tavern, Milton Bradley/artist F Wagner, 1940s, cb, 1,000 interlocking pcs, EX (orig box), A4 ....**$7.00**

Yosemite Valley, Joseph Straus, 1930s, plywood, 175 pieces, MIB, A4, $20.00.

CHARACTER

Alf, fr-tray, Milton Bradley, Alf watering flower garden, EX+, I2 ....**$5.00**

Alien, jigsaw, HG Toys, 1979, complete in egg-shaped container, MOC $15.00

Aquaman, jigsaw, Whitman, 1968, Aquaman & Mera battling a giant squid, VG+ (VG+ box), A.................................$30.00

Batman, fr-tray, Watkins/Strathmore, 1966, Batman & Robin on rocky terrain w/giant eagle swooping down, EX+, A $20.00

Batman, fr-tray, Whitman, 1979, image from comics, EX, A4...$3.00

Batman, jigsaw, Whitman, 1966, 150 pcs, MIB, T2 ....$30.00

Bee Gees, jigsaw, 1979, MIB (sealed), B3 ....$20.00

Beetle Bailey, Snuffy Smith & Krazy Kat, fr-tray, Milton Bradley, 1964, set of 3, complete, 12x9", NM (NM box), F8 ....$45.00

Black Hole, jigsaw, Whitman/WDP, 1979, 500 pcs, MIB (sealed)...$12.00

Bonanza, jigsaw, Milton Bradley, 1964, Expecting Trouble, 600 pcs, NM (EX box)...$25.00

Broken Arrow, Built-Rite, set of 4, MIB, $65.00.

Bugs Bunny, fr-tray, Jaymar, 1950s, Bugs Bunny selling carrot burgers, complete, 11x14", EX+, T2 ....$15.00

Bullwinkle & Rocky, fr-tray, Jaymar, 1960s, complete, 10x13", NM, F8...$28.00

Buzzy the Crow, jigsaw, Built-Rite, 1961, complete, MIB...$18.00

Captain Kangaroo, jigsaw, Fairchild, 1956, scene inside the Treasure House, 75 pcs, EXIB, T2.............................$15.00

Captain Kangaroo, jigsaw, Fairchild, 1971, complete, NM (NM box) $10.00

Cat in the Hat, fr-tray, set of 3, MIP (sealed), P12...........$35.00

Children of All Nations, jigsaw, Cons Paper Box Co, set of 3 featuring Eskimo, Scotland & Japan, EX+ (VG+ box) $18.00

Columbia Space Shuttle, jigsaw, Jaymar, ca 1980, photo image of shuttle taking off, 800 pcs, NM (EX+ box), P3 .....$10.00

Creepy Magazine Puzzle, jigsaw, Milton Bradley, 1977, M (EX sealed box), P3...$75.00

Dick Tracy, jigsaw, Jaymar, 1950s-60s, Bank Holdup, complete, NMIB, C1 ....$65.00

Dick Tracy, jigsaw, Jaymar, 1950s-60s, Manhunt for Mumbles, complete, NMIB, C1 ....$65.00

Dino, fr-tray, shows Dino running the sweeper, complete, 10x8", NM, T2..$12.00

Disneyland, jigsaw, Jaymar, 1962, shows Disneyland castle w/fireworks & characters, 100 pcs, EX, P6.................$25.00

Donald Duck, fr-tray, 1960, NM $15.00

Donald Duck, jigsaw, Whitman, 1965, Donald & Nephews climbing, complete, NMIB.......................................$15.00

Dondi, fr-tray, Jaymar, 1961, Camping Trip, complete, 11x14", NM, T2 ....$15.00

Dr Dolittle, fit-in puzzle blocks, Lido #5015, plastic, NM...$15.00

Dr Dolittle, jigsaw, Whitman #4568, Dr Dolittle & Polynesia steering ship, NMIB...$12.00

Dracula, fr-tray, Jaymar, 1963, Dracula putting woman in casket beside Frankenstein, complete, 11x14", scarce, NM, A ..$55.00

Dumbo, jigsaw, Ontex/Canada, 1940s, set of 3, EX, M8...$60.00

Fall Guy, jigsaw, Craft Master, 1983, 170 pcs, MIB (sealed) ..$12.00

Family Affair, jigsaw, Whitman, 1970, Jody & Buffy covering Mr French w/sand, 125 pcs, 20" dia, EX (EX box), T2 ....$15.00

Fantastic Four, fr-tray, Whitman, 1968, Fantastic Four battling the Black Panther in front of cityscape, EX $30.00

Fat Albert, jigsaw, Whitman, 1975, picnic scene, 100 pcs, NM (EX box), F8 ....$18.00

Felix the Cat, fr-tray, Built-Rite, 1949, complete, 9x12", EX, F8 ....$35.00

Flash Gordon, fr-tray, Milton Bradley, 1951, shows Flash & Dale in cockpit of spacecraft, 14½x10¼", EX $60.00

Flintstones, fr-tray, Whitman, 1960, Betty & Barney getting in car, NMIB, C1 ....$35.00

Flintstones, fr-tray, Whitman, 1966, Man Called Flintstone, complete, 11x14", NM, F8 ....$30.00

Flintstones, jigsaw, Whitman, 1971, 125 pcs, 20" dia, NM (NM box), F8...$30.00

Flipper, jigsaw, Whitman, 1965, complete, NMIB, F8 .....$15.00

Frankenstein, jigsaw, Golden, 1990, 200 pcs, MIB, B10.....$6.00

Funky Phantom, jigsaw, Whitman, 1974, 100 pcs, NM (EX box)..$20.00

Gene Autry & Champion, fr-tray, Whitman, 1957, complete, NM..$35.00

Get Smart, jigsaw, Jaymar, 1965, Agent Maxwell holding fire hydrant for his canine partner, complete, EX (VG box), T2..$40.00

Hair Bear Bunch, jigsaw, Whitman, 1974, $5.00.

Photo courtesy Bob Armstrong.

GI Joe, jigsaw, Whitman, 1965, complete, NMIB, F8 ......$25.00

Gulliver's Travels, fr-tray, 1950s, complete, 10x13", NM, T2 ....$15.00

Gunsmoke, jigsaw, Whitman, 1969, NMIB, J2..................$25.00

Happy Days, jigsaw, HG Toys, 1970s, complete, EX (EX box), M17..........$20.00

Huckleberry Hound, fr-tray, 1961, EX, J2 ....$25.00

James Bond in Goldfinger, jigsaw, Milton Bradley, 1965, over 1,000 pcs, complete, NM (NM box), F8 ....$65.00

Jetsons, fr-tray, Whitman, 1962, EX, J2 ....$32.00

Kaptain Kool & the Kongs, fr-tray, 1978, M (sealed), J2..$18.00

KISS, jigsaw, Paul Stanley, MIB (sealed) $50.00

Krazy Ikes, fr-tray, Whitman, 1969, 11x14", NM (sealed), F8 ....$15.00

Lady & the Tramp, jigsaw, Jaymar, 1960s, Chicken Capers, complete, NM (EX box), F8..........................$20.00

Lassie & Timmy, fr-tray, Whitman, EX, J2 ....$25.00

Laverne & Shirley, jigsaw, HG Toys, 1970s, complete, MIB, M17..........................$20.00

Little Lulu, fr-tray, Whitman, 1959, 11x14", EX $25.00

Lone Ranger, fr-tray, 1958, EX, J2.....................................$35.00

Lone Ranger, jigsaw, Parker Bros, 1938, Story Puzzle, set of 4, 1 pc missing, EX (NM box), F8 ....$70.00

Ludwig Von Drake, fr-tray, 1960s, set of 4, MIB (sealed), J8..........................$45.00

Mickey Mouse, jigsaw, Whitman, 1967, Mickey & Minnie running from beehive, 100 pcs, NMIB, T2....................$10.00

Mickey Mouse Club, jigsaw, Jaymar, 1950s, birthday party scene, complete, NMIB, T2 ....$12.00

Mickey Mouse Club, jigsaw, Jaymar, 1950s, characters dressed as pirates, complete, NMIB, T2..........................$12.00

Mighty Heroes, fr-tray, Whitman, 1967, heroes fighting bad guys on roof, complete, 14x11", EX+, F8/J2..........................$25.00

Mighty Mouse, jigsaw, Fairchild, 1956, Playhouse, complete, NMIB, T2 ....$20.00

Mighty Mouse, jigsaw, Whitman, 1967, Mighty Mouse holding up bridge, 100 pcs, NMIB, T2 ....$12.00

Mr I Magination, jigsaw, Jaymar Television Stars series, 1951, 400 pcs, scarce, NMIB, T2 ....$50.00

Mr Magoo, fr-tray, Jaymar, 1967, complete, 10x13", EX, F8 ..$18.00

Mr Magoo, fr-tray, Warren, 1978, boxed set of 4, MIB.....$28.00

Nancy & Sluggo, jigsaw, Whitman, 1973, complete, NMIB..$12.00

Pinky Lee, fr-tray, Gabriel, 1955, Funny Picture Puzzles, set of 4, 12x10", NM (EX box), T2..........................$20.00

Pinocchio, jigsaw, Ontex/Canada 1940s, set of 2, EX+ (EX box), M8..........................$60.00

Planet of the Apes, jigsaw, HG Toys, 1967, General Aldo, complete, EX (EX canister)..........................$18.00

Popeye, fr-tray, Jaymar, 1961, set of 4, complete, 11x14", NMIB $35.00

Porky Pig, fr-tray, Connor, 1971, Troubador, 12 pcs, EX .$15.00

Punch & Judy, jigsaw, Peter G Thomson, late 1800s, depicts 4 stage scenes, VG (orig box & illus sheet), A $175.00

Quick Draw McGraw, fr-tray, 1963, EX $25.00

Raggedy Ann & Andy, fr-tray, Milton Bradley, 1955, picnic scene, complete, EX, F8..........................$16.00

Range Rider, fr-tray, Gabriel, 1955, set of 4, 10x12", 1 missing few pcs, EXIB, T2 ....$30.00

Return of the Jedi, fr-tray, 1983, gr fat creature w/horns & tusks, EX, I2 ....$8.00

Rin-Tin-Tin, jigsaw, Whitman, 1950s, complete, NMIB.$22.00

Rocky & Bullwinkle, fr-tray, Whitman, 1960, Rocky & Bullwinkle posing for Martians, complete, EX, H4 ....$25.00

Roger Ramjet, fr-tray, Whitman, 1966, complete, 14x11", EX, F8 ....$45.00

Roy Rogers, fr-tray, 1950s, 10x12", VG+, J5.....................$15.00

Ruff & Reddy, fr-tray, Whitman, 1950s, complete, 11x14", EX+, F8 ....$25.00

Silver Surfer (Marvel Super-Hero), jigsaw, Third Eye, 1971, I'm Changing, 500 pcs, MIB (sealed) $18.00

Silver Surfer (Marvel Super-Hero), jigsaw, Third Eye, 1971, At Last I'm Free, 500 pcs, unused, MIB (sealed) $18.00

Sleeping Beauty, fr-tray, 1958, M, J2.................................$25.00

Smedley, fr-tray, EX, J2 ....$15.00

Snow White & the Seven Dwarfs, jigsaw, Jaymar, 1940s, 300 pcs, EXIB..........................$45.00

Snow White and the Seven Dwarfs, Whitman, set of 2, VG (original box), $125.00.

Space Kidettes, fr-tray, Whitman, 1967, complete, 14x11", EX $25.00

Space Travel, fr-tray, 1959, EX+, J2................................$30.00

Superman, fr-tray, Whitman, 1965, Superman stopping scientist from launching missiles, EX, A $20.00

Superman, jigsaw, Saalfield #1516, 1940, Superman Springs Into Action, 500 pcs, EX (VG+ box), from $275 to $300.00

Sylvester & Tweety, fr-tray, Connor Toy, 1971, Cageman, 12 pcs, EX $15.00

Tarzan, jigsaw, Movie Cut-Ups, A Weekly Puzzle of Your Favorite Movie Stars, Buster Crabbe as Tarzan w/lion, EXIB, A $130.00

Tarzan, jigsaw, Whitman, 1968, Tarzan on lion, complete, NM (EX box) $20.00

Tennessee Tuxedo, fr-tray, Whitman, 1966, complete, 11x14", EX+, F8 ....$35.00

Terrytoons, fr-tray, Fairchild, 1950s, set of 4, complete, 9x11", NMIB, F8 ....$50.00

Terrytoons, fr-tray, Jaymar, 1956, complete, 11x14", EX, T2 ..$30.00

Tom & Jerry, fr-tray, Whitman, 1953, Tom & Jerry as sultans in India, complete, 14x11", VG+, T2..........................$20.00

Tom & Jerry, jigsaw, Whitman, 1969, Tom & Jerry as sheriff & deputy, complete, NMIB, F8 ....$15.00

Tom Corbett Jr, jigsaw, Saalfield, 1952, complete, NM (EX box), A..$75.00

Tommy Tortoise & Moe Hare, jigsaw, Built-Rite, 1961, 70 pcs, MIB, T2 ....$25.00

Topcat, fr-tray, Whitman, 1961, complete, 14x11", 1 pc torn o/w EX+, T2 ....$15.00

Uncle Wiggly, jigsaw, Rache, set of 3, 10¼x13½", very scarce, NMIB, A..$135.00

Underdog, jigsaw, Whitman, 1975, Underdog & Polly flying away from bad guy, MIB (sealed) $25.00

Underdog, Polly & Simon, fr-tray, 1965, EX, B10............$25.00

Universal Monsters, fr-tray, Dracula or Frankenstein, Jaymar, 1963, complete, EX, H4, ea...............$140.00

Universal Monsters, fr-tray, Mummy, Jaymar, 1963, complete, NM, H4 ....$145.00

Voyage to the Bottom of the Sea, fr-tray, Milton Bradley, 1964, set of 4, 11x14", scarce, NM (VG box), from $85 to.........$125.00

Walt Disney's World of Color, jigsaw, Jaymar, 1961, extra lg pcs, complete, NMIB, T2 ....$14.00

Wendy (Casper the Ghost), fr-tray, EX, J2 ....$15.00

Winky Dink, fr-tray, Jaymar, 1950s, complete, 10x12", VG .$30.00

Wolfman, jigsaw, American Publishing, 1974, EX (w/canister), B10/H4, from $20 to...............................$25.00

Woody Woodpecker, fr-tray, Whitman, 1954, complete, 14x11", EX+, T2 ....$22.00

Woody Woodpecker, jigsaw, Whitman, 1960, Woody being attacked by swordfish, complete, MIB, J8 ....$12.00

Wyatt Earp, fr-tray, Whitman, 1958, complete, NM, C1 .$50.00

Yogi Bear, fr-tray, 1960s, NM, J2......................................$28.00

Zorro, fr-tray, Jaymar #2311, EX, W6.............................$20.00

Zorro, fr-tray, Jaymar #2710-29, EX, W6 ....$22.00

Zorro, fr-tray, Whitman #4417, 1957, Zorro leaning on tree, 11x14", VG+..$22.00

Zorro, fr-tray, Whitman #4419, 1965, Zorro w/sword, 11x14", VG+ $20.00

Zorro, fr-tray, Whitman #4521, 1965, Zorro on horse, 11x14", VG+ $20.00

101 Dalmatians, fr-tray, Jaymar, 1960s, 3 different scenes, EX, P6, ea..$18.00

Radios, Novelty

Many novelty radios are made to resemble a commercial product box or can, and with the crossover interest into the advertising field, some of the more collectible, even though of recent vintage, are often seen carrying very respectible price tags. Likenesses of famous personalities such as Elvis or characters like Charlie Tuna house transistors in cases made of plastic that scarcely hint at their actual function. Others represent items ranging from baseball caps to Cadillacs. To learn more about this subject, we recommend *Collector's Guide to Transistor Radios* by Sue and Marty Bunis and *Collector's Guide to Novelty Radios* by Marty Bunis and Robert Breed.

Advisors: Sue and Marty Bunis (B11).

Avon Skin-So-Soft Bottle, NMIB, J2 ....$35.00

Big Bird, 2-dimensional figure, NM, T1 ....$15.00

Blabber Mouse on Cheese, VG, T1 ....$25.00

Bubble Tape, MIB...$20.00

Bugs Bunny w/Carrot, EX $40.00

Campbell's Tomato Soup Can, NM, from $35 to $50.00

Champion Spark Plug, MIB $100.00

Charlie McCarthy, Majestic, NM...............................$2,000.00

Coca-Cola Bottle, EX, T1..$35.00

Coca-Cola Can, EX, T1..$25.00

Coca-Cola Vending Machine, China, 1989, MIB, J6.......$65.00

Crest Man, M..$30.00

Delco Battery, MIB, $35.00.

Donald Duck, 1970s, plastic 2-dimensional head w/open mouth, NMIB, A..$70.00

Elvis on Stage, M, T1...$75.00

Fred Flintstone, Sutton, 1972, molded plastic head, NMIB...$75.00

Gulden's Mustard, shaped like mustard jar, rare, MIB $50.00

Gumby, Lewco, 1970s, NM..$150.00

Heinz Ketchup Bottle, NM...$50.00

Hershey Syrup Bottle, MIB...$75.00

Hot Dog, Hong Kong, plastic, M..$65.00

**KISS, M, $60.00.**

Manwich Can, EX, T1 ....$45.00

Mickey Mouse, Walt Disney Productions, blue background, NM, $15.00.

Mickey Mouse Clock Radio!, GE/WDP, 1970s (?), 12x5", MIB, A $80.00
Mr Tom Candy Bar, British, M, P12 ....$85.00
On the Air Microphone, MIB, T1 ....$35.00
Oscar the Grouch in Trash Can, MIB, T1 ....$35.00
Pepsi-Cola Can, EX, J2 ....$25.00
Pepsi-Cola Fountain Dispenser, say 'Pepsi Please' on front, 7", EX, A $225.00
Planters Cocktail Nuts Can, MIB $55.00
Popeye, Dist Development, 1972, molded plastic head, EX+ ..$60.00
Pound Puppy, MIB, T1 ....$15.00

Raggedy Ann and Andy, Philgee International, 1973, NM, $22.00.

Raid Bug, clock radio, M, P12 ....$225.00
RC Cola Can, EX, J6 ....$25.00
Red Goose Shoe, VG+ $50.00
Santa Maria Ship, EX, T1 ....$45.00
Shell Petroleum Gas Pump, early style w/rnd globe atop cylindrical tank w/hose, plastic, 10", new old stock $25.00
Sinclair Gas Pump, EX...$25.00
Six Million Dollar Man Backpack, MIB $25.00
Smurf, NM $10.00
Snoopy on Doghouse, Determined, 1970s, 7", EX $40.00

Snow White & the Seven Dwarfs, Emerson, 1939, pressed-wood front emb w/Snow White & Dwarfs, 7¾", VG $2,500.00
Sunoco Gas Pump, yel & bl, 4", EX $25.00
Tropicana Orange Juice, EX $10.00
Welch's Grape Juice Can, M $50.00

Ramp Walkers

Ramp walkers date back to at least 1873 when Ives produced two versions of a cast-iron elephant walker. Wood and composition ramp walkers were made in Czechoslovakia and the U.S.A. from the 1930s through the 1950s. The most common were made by John Wilson of Pennsylvania and were sold worldwide. These became known as 'Wilson Walkies.' Most are two-legged and stand approximately 4½" tall. While some of the Wilson Walkies were made of a composite material with wood legs (for instance, Donald, Wimpy, Popeye, and Olive Oyl), most are made with cardboard thread-cone bodies with wood legs and head. The walkers made in Czechoslovakia are similar but they are generally made of wood.

Plastic ramp walkers were primarily manufactured by the Louis Marx Co. and were made from the early 1950s through the mid-1960s. The majority were produced in Hong Kong, but some were made in the United States and sold under the Marx logo or by the Charmore Co., which was a subsidiary of the Marx Co. Some walkers are still being produced today as fast-food premiums.

The three common sizes are (1) small, about 1½"x2"; (2) medium, about 2¾"x3"; and (3) large, about 4"x5". Most of the small walkers are unpainted while the medium or large sizes were either spray painted or painted by hand. Several of the walking toys were sold with wooden, plastic, or colorful lithographed tin ramps.

Advisor: Randy Welch (W4).

ADVERTISING

Captain Flint, Long John Silvers, 1989, w/plastic coin weight...$15.00
Choo-Choo Cherry, Funny Face Kool-Aid, w/plastic coin weight..$60.00
Flash Turtle, Long John Silvers, 1989, w/plastic coin weight .$15.00
Goofy Grape, Funny Face Kool-Aid, w/plastic coin weight....$60.00
Jolly Ollie Orange, Funny Face Kool-Aid, w/plastic coin weight..$60.00
Quinn Penguin, Long John Silvers, 1989, blk & wht, w/plastic coin weight $15.00
Root'n Toot'n Raspberry, Funny Face Kool-Aid, w/plastic coin weight..$60.00
Sydney Dinosaur, Long John Silvers, 1989, yel & purple, w/plastic coin weight $15.00
Sylvia Dinosaur, Long John Silvers, 1989, lavender & pk, w/plastic coin weight $15.00

CZECHOSLOVAKIAN

Dog..$20.00
Man w/Carved Wood Hat $30.00

Monkey $30.00
Pig $20.00
Policeman $40.00

DISNEY CHARACTERS BY MARX

Big Bad Wolf & Mason Pig $40.00
Big Bad Wolf & Three Little Pigs $125.00
Donald Duck, pulling nephews in wagon...........$35.00
Donald Duck, pushing wheelbarrow, all plastic $25.00
Donald Duck, pushing wheelbarrow, plastic w/metal legs, sm ..$30.00
Donald Duck & Goofy, riding go-cart..................$40.00
Fiddler & Fifer Pigs $40.00
Figaro the Cat, w/ball $30.00
Goofy, riding hippo..$45.00
Jiminy Cricket, w/cello $30.00
Mad Hatter w/March Hare $50.00
Mickey Mouse, pushing lawn roller.....................$35.00

Mickey and Donald Riding Alligator, $40.00.

Mickey Mouse & Minnie, plastic w/metal wheels, sm $40.00
Mickey Mouse & Pluto, hunting $40.00
Minnie Mouse, pushing baby stroller $35.00
Pluto, plastic w/metal legs, sm $30.00
Wiggly Walkers, complete set of 4 w/Mickey, Minnie, Pluto & Donald, EX (VG scarce box), A $400.00

HANNA-BARBERA, KING FEATURES & OTHER CHARACTERS BY MARX

Astro, Hanna-Barbera $150.00
Astro & George Jetson, Hanna-Barbera............$90.00
Astro & Rosey, Hanna-Barbera...........................$95.00
Chilly Willy, penguin on sled pulled by parent, Walter Lantz..$25.00
Fred & Wilma Flintstone on Dino, Hanna-Barbera $60.00
Fred Flintstone on Dino, Hanna-Barbera............$70.00
Hap & Hop Soldiers $20.00
Little King & Guards, King Features $70.00
Pebbles on Dino, Hanna-Barbera $70.00
Popeye, Erwin, celluloid, lg.................................$60.00
Santa, w/gold sack..$45.00
Santa, w/wht sack $40.00
Santa, w/yel sack $35.00

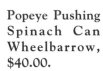

Popeye Pushing Spinach Can Wheelbarrow, $40.00.

Photo courtesy June Moon.

Santa & Mrs Claus, faces on both sides............................$40.00
Santa & Snowman, faces on both sides............................$40.00
Spark Plug..$200.00
Top Cat & Benny $65.00
Yogi Bear & Huckleberry Hound, Hanna-Barbera $50.00

MARX ANIMALS WITH RIDERS SERIES

Ankylosaurus w/Clown $25.00
Bison w/Native..$25.00
Brontosaurus w/Monkey $25.00
Hippo w/Native...$25.00
Lion w/Clown $25.00
Stegosaurus w/Black Caveman $25.00
Triceratops w/Native $25.00
Zebra w/Native..$25.00

PLASTIC

Baby Walk-A-Way, lg...$40.00
Baseball Player w/Bat & Ball $40.00
Bear $15.00
Boy & Girl Dancing...$60.00
Bull $15.00
Bunnies Carrying Carrot..$30.00
Bunny Pushing Cart...$45.00
Camel w/2 Humps, head bobs................................$20.00
Chicks Carrying Easter Egg....................................$30.00
Chinese Men w/Duck in Basket $30.00
Chipmunks Carrying Acorns...................................$30.00
Chipmunks Marching Band w/Drum & Horn $30.00
Cow, w/metal legs, sm..$15.00
Cowboy on Horse, w/metal legs, sm $20.00
Dachshund $15.00
Dairy Cow $15.00
Dog, Pluto look-alike w/metal legs, sm..................$15.00
Double Walking Doll, boy behind girl, lg $45.00
Duck...$15.00
Dutch Boy & Girl $30.00
Elephant...$20.00
Elephant, w/metal legs, sm....................................$20.00
Farmer Pushing Wheelbarrow $20.00

Frontiersman w/Dog...$95.00
Goat $20.00
Horse, circus style $15.00
Horse, lg $30.00
Horse, yel w/rubber ears & string tail, lg $30.00
Horse w/English rider, lg, MIB.....................................$40.00
Indian Woman Pulling Baby on Travois $95.00
Kangaroo w/Baby in Pouch...$25.00
Mama Duck w/3 Ducklings...$25.00
Marty's Market Lady Pushing Shopping Cart $45.00
Mexican Cowboy on Horse, w/metal legs, sm $20.00
Milking Cow, lg, MIB..$40.00
Monkeys Carrying Bananas $60.00
Nursemaid Pushing Baby Stroller..................................$15.00
Pig $15.00
Pigs, 2 carrying 1 in basket...$40.00
Popeye & Wimpy, heads on springs, lg, MIB $65.00
Pumpkin Head Man & Woman, faces both sides $45.00
Reindeer...$40.00

Sailors SS Shoreleave, $20.00.

Sheriff Facing Outlaw $65.00
Teeny Toddler, walking baby girl, Dolls Inc, lg $40.00
Tin Man Robot Pushing Cart...$125.00
Walking Baby, in Canadian Mountie uniform, lg............$50.00
Walking Baby, w/moving eyes & cloth dress, lg $40.00
Wiz Walker Milking Cow, Charmore, lg $40.00

WILSON

Photo courtesy Randy and Adrienne Welch.

Indian Chief, $45.00; Black Mammy, $35.00; Soldier, $25.00.

Donald Duck..$175.00
Eskimo..$75.00
Nurse...$30.00
Olive Oyl...$175.00
Penguin...$25.00
Pinocchio...$175.00
Popeye...$175.00
Rabbit...$40.00
Sailor...$30.00
Santa Claus $60.00
Wimpy $175.00

Records

Most of the records listed here are related to TV shows and movies, and all are specifically geared toward children. The more successful the show, the more collectible the record. But condition is critical as well, and unless the record is excellent or better, its value is lowered very dramatically.

33⅓ RPM RECORDS

Andy Griffith Show, Capitol, 1962, contains theme song & 11 other songs, scarce, NM (NM cover), A $65.00
Archies Greatest Hits, Kirshner, 1970, EX (NM sleeve), F8...$14.00
Banana Splits, Decca, 1969, VG (EX sleeve), J5 ....$35.00
Brer Rabbit, #3907, 1970, w/storybook, EX, P6 ....$25.00
Dennis the Menace Soundtrack, Colpix, 1960, EX (EX sleeve), T2...$15.00
Dr Seuss, How the Grinch Stole Christmas, Random House, 1975, M (sealed), F8..................................$20.00
Everything's Archie, Kirshner, 1969, NM (NM sleeve), J5 ..$50.00
Flipper, King of the Sea, Leo, 1966, features theme song & story, NM (EX sleeve), A.............................$25.00
Hogan's Heroes Sing the Best of World War II, Sunset, 1960s, M (NM sleeve), J5 ....$40.00
Howl Along With Huckleberry Hound & Yogi Bear, Golden, 1960, NM (NM sleeve), F8 ....$25.00
Let's All Sing With the Chipmunks, Liberty, 1960, EX (EX sleeve), F8 ....$8.00
Let's Get Together With Hayley Mills, Vista, 1962, NM (NM sleeve), F8 ....$35.00
Marvel Age Comic Spectaculars, Golden Records/Marvel, 1966, Journey Into Mystery #83, w/comic book, NM (EX sleeve), A $45.00
Mary Poppins, #3922, w/storybook, EX, P6.....................$25.00
Meet the Brady Bunch, Paramount, 1960s, EX (EX sleeve), J5 ....$40.00
Mr Jinks, Pixie & Dixie, Colpix, 1960s, tells 4 stories, rare, EX (EX+ sleeve), F8 ....$30.00
New Adventures of Pinocchio, FTP, 1961, soundtrack w/stories & songs from Animagic TV series, M (NM sealed sleeve), J5 ....$100.00
Peter & the Wolf Narrated by Captain Kangaroo, Everest, 1960, jacket shows Captain & puppets, EX (EX sleeve), T2....$10.00

Roger Ramjet & the American Eagles, RCA, 1966, narration of Amazing Adventures..., VG+ (EX sleeve), A............$25.00

Ruff & Reddy Adventures in Space, Colpix, 1958, NM (NM sleeve), F8..$48.00

Snow White & the Seven Dwarfs, #3906, 1969, w/storybook, EX, P6...$25.00

Snow White & the Seven Dwarfs, Decca #5015, 1949, VG (VG sleeve), P6..$45.00

Bugs Bunny in Storyland, Capitol, 1949, 2-record set w/booklet, EX (EX sleeve), J5...$25.00

Captain Kangaroo, Golden, 1960s, EX, C17.....................$10.00

Casper the Ghost, Golden, 1962, EX, C17......................$12.00

CHiPs, 1979, EX (EX photo sleeve), J7..........................$20.00

Dennis the Menace, Golden, 1960, EX, C17.....................$12.00

Flying Nun, 1967, EX (EX sleeve), J7.............................$25.00

Snow White and the Seven Dwarfs, See, Hear and Read record and book set, Disneyland records #310, 1982, from $10.00 to $12.00.

Songs From Annette, Disney, 1960, EX (EX sleeve), T2 .$20.00

Spider-Man Adventures, Power Records, 1970s, Abominable Snowman, M (sealed sleeve), A...................................$5.00

Story of Star Wars, 1977, M (shrink-wrapped sleeve), P6...$45.00

Superman, Leo the Lion Records, 1966, adventures of Superman as told by Bob Holiday, EX+ (VG+ sleeve), A..........$10.00

Three Stooges Nonsense Song Book, Coral, 1960, EX+ (VG sleeve), T2...$15.00

Walt Disney's Parent Trap!, 1961, NM (NM sleeve), F8 .$35.00

Wild Bill Hickok & Jingles, London, 1954, stories & songs from On the Santa Fe Trail, VG (VG sleeve).....................$20.00

Winnie the Pooh, #3953, 1967, w/storybook, EX, P6.......$25.00

Wizard of Oz, MGM, 1960s, orig soundtrack album, EX (EX+ sleeve), T2...$10.00

Wonder Woman Book & Record Set, Peter Pan Records, 1977, EX (orig box), T2...$12.00

Woody the Woodchuck Christmas Sing Songs, 1960s, NM (NM sleeve), F8...$15.00

45 RPM RECORDS

Addams Family, Dot, 1965, theme song by Lawrence Welk & his orchestra, rare, M, T2..$25.00

Batman Meets Man Bat, 1976, w/20-pg book, EX, F1 ......$10.00

Batman Theme, by Neal Hefti, w/11 other Batman songs, used for jukeboxes, NM (plastic-wrapped sleeve), A.......$375.00

Fred Flintstone and Good Old Unreliable Dino, Peter Pan, 1976, from $8.00 to $10.00.

Gene Autry at the Rodeo, Columbia Records, 1950s, story & song, EX+ (VG+ sleeve), T2.......................................$8.00

Gunsmoke, RCA Victor, 1960s, EX (EX sleeve), F8........$12.00

Heckle & Jeckle, Little Golden, 1958, NM (EX sleeve), from $10 to..$15.00

Howdy Doody Laughing Circus, RCA Victor, 1950s, 2-record set w/booklet, EX (EX sleeve), J5..............................$45.00

Huckleberry Hound & Yogi Bear, Little Golden Record, 1959, EX, from $10 to...$15.00

Laurel & Hardy, Golden, 1963, theme to cartoon, EX (EX sleeve), F8..$12.00

Leave It to Beaver, Golden, 1958, EX (EX sleeve), A......$15.00

Mickey Mouse Club March, 1955, VG (EX sleeve), F8....$12.00

Mr Jinx & Boo Boo Bear, Golden, 1959, EX, C17............$15.00

Partridge Family, I Think I Love You, Bell, 1970, EX (EX photo sleeve), F8...$6.00

Ronald McDonald & Friends, Casablanca, 1980, features Friends & Share a Song From Your Heart, NM (NM sleeve), F8.....$5.00

Scarecrow of Oz, Happy Glow, Disneyland Record, 1965, rare, NM (NM sleeve), S6...$35.00

Songs from Walt Disney's Lady & the Tramp, Decca, 1950s, 2-record set w/Peggy Lee, EX (EX book sleeve), from $20 to..$25.00

Superman Song/Tarzan Song, Golden #723, 1960s, NM (VG sleeve), from $10 to...$15.00

Tex Ritter's Sunday School Songs, Capitol, 1960s, 2-record set w/6 songs, EX (EX sleeves), F8................................$18.00

Tom Corbett Space Cadet Song & March, 1951, scarce, EX, from $35 to..$45.00

Wonder Woman Theme Song, Shadybrook, 1977, New World Symphony, M (VG+ sleeve), A $80.00

Woody Woodpecker March & Andy Panda Polka, Golden, 1962, NM (NM sleeve), F8 ....$10.00

Wyatt Earp/Jesse James, RCA, 1950s, NM (NM sleeve), F8...$8.00

78 RPM PICTURE AND NON-PICTURE RECORDS

Alice in Wonderland, I'm Late, Little Golden, 1951, NM (NM sleeve), F8 ....$12.00

Bubble Book, Harper-Columbia, 1917, set of 3 in book, from $20 to $30.00

Bugs Bunny, Rabbit Seasoning, Capitol, 1953, EX (EX sleeve), F8, from $12 to $15.00

Captain Kangaroo, When a Bunny Wants a Carrot/Treasure House on Parade, 1962, EX (EX sleeve), from $15 to..$18.00

Champion the Wonder Horse, Little Golden, 1955, NM (NM sleeve), F8, from $12 to $15.00

Deputy Dawg, Peter Pan, 1962, EX, C17, from $10 to $12.00

Donald Duck & Uncle Milty, RCA, 1950s, Animated Cartoon/Little Nipper Series, EX (EX sleeve), from $40 to $50.00

Flipper, Golden, 1960s, EX (EX sleeve), F8, from $10 to ..$12.00

Genie the Magic Record, Decca CV102, 1946, from $10 to..$15.00

Gossamer Wump, Capitol EAS 3012, 1948, from $20.00 to $25.00.

Gulliver's Travels, Bluebird BC23, 1939, from orig soundtrack, set of 3, very rare, from $150 to................................$200.00

Hap-Hap-Happy Christmas Yogi Bear, Little Golden, 1961, NM (NM sleeve), F8, from $8 to $10.00

Howdy Doody & the Air-O-Doodle, RCA Victor, Little Nipper Series Y-397, 1949, EX (EX sleeve), from $40 to.......$50.00

I Saw Mommy Kissing Santa Claus, Peter Pan, VG (VG sleeve), P3 ....$3.00

Laurel & Hardy Chiller Diller Thriller, 1963, EX (NM sleeve), from $15 to..$20.00

Little Red Riding Hood, Listen Look Picture Book, 1941, from $8 to $10.00

Lone Ranger: He Finds Silver, Decca K-30, 1951, from $25 to..$35.00

Magic Land of Alla-Kazam, Peter Pan, 1962, includes television theme song, NM (EX sleeve), T2, from $8 to............$10.00

Melodyland Record Book, Billy Bee, Old King Cole, Silver Nutcracker, and Wicked Old Witch, 1942, complete set of 4 in spiral-bound book, from $45.00 to $55.00.

Merry Christmas From Dennis the Menace, Little Golden, 1961, NM (NM sleeve), F8, from $8 to $10.00

Mickey & the Beanstalk, Capitol CCX67, 1948, 1 from series of 3, from $35 to...$45.00

Mighty Mouse Saves Dinky, RCA, 1953, NM (EX sleeve), from $15 to $20.00

Myrtle the Turtle, Listen Look Picture Book, 1941, from $8 to.$10.00

Peter & the Wolf, Disney, 1949, w/booklet, EX, from $20 to $30.00

Pinocchio, Little Nipper Story Book Album, RCA, 1949, 2 records w/24-pg book, EX+, M8, from $45 to $50.00

Popeye, Peter Pan, 1962, EX, C17, from $12 to................$15.00

Roy Rogers Calling Cowboy Square Dances, Decca, 1950s, 3-record set, EX (EX folding sleeve), P6, from $50 to...$60.00

Roy Rogers in the Television Ambush, RCA, 1950s, NM (EX sleeve), from $50 to $60.00

Singing Mother Goose Book, Magic Talking Books T-1, 1955, EX (EX cover), from $12 to...$15.00

Sparkle Plenty Birthday Party, Mercury, 1947, NM (EX sleeve), from $40 to...$50.00

Superman/Tarzan Songs, Little Golden, 1950s, NM (EX+ sleeve), from $18 to $22.00

Tweety Bird, I Taut I Taw a Puddy Tat/Yosemite Sam, Capitol, 1950s, EX (EX sleeve), F8, from $12 to......................$15.00

Uncle Remus Stories, Youth Series, RCA Victor, 1940s, 2-record set, EX (EX sleeve), from $40 to $50.00

Walt Disney's Pinocchio, Victor P18, 1941, from orig soundtrack, set of 3, rare, from $75 to $100.00

William Tell, Toytime Record & Picture Books, 1941, complete w/book, from $10 to...$12.00

Zorro, Golden, 1950s, features Adventures of Zorro part 1 & 2, NM (EX sleeve), from $12 to $15.00

KIDDIE PICTURE DISKS

Listed here is a representative sampling of kiddie picture disks that were produced through the 1940s. Most are 6" to 7" in diameter and are made of cardboard with plastic-laminated grooves. They are very colorful and seldom came with original sleeves. Value ranges are for items in very good to near-mint condition. Ultimately, the value of any collectible is what a buyer is willing to pay, and prices tend to fluctuate. Our values are for records only (no sleeves) — note that unlike other records, the value of a picture disk is not diminished if there is no original sleeve.

Advisor: Peter Muldavin (M21).

Alice in Wonderland, Toy Toon Records, 1952, from $10 to .**$15.00**
Birthday Song to You, Voco 35215, 1948, 5" sq, from $15 to..**$20.00**

Photo courtesy Peter Muldavin.

Bunny Easter Party, Voco EB ½, 1948, diecut, from $25.00 to $30.00.

Camptown Races: Little Brown Jug, Record Guild of America 2004P, 1949, rare picture sleeve, from $10 to **$15.00**
Cinderella, Toy Toon Records, 1952, from $10 to **$15.00**
Goldilocks & the Three Bears, Toy Toon Records, 1952, from $10 to **$15.00**
I'm Called Little Buttercup, PicturTone, Gilbert & Sullivan series, 1948, from $15 to **$20.00**
Jack & the Bean Stalk, Toy Toon Records, 1952, from $10 to..**$15.00**
Jacob's Dreams, Bible Storytime, 1948, from $10 to **$15.00**
Jesus Loves Me, Bible Storytime, 1948, from $10 to **$15.00**
Laugh Laugh Phonograph, Voco, 1948, rare 6" size, from $15 to...**$20.00**
Laugh Laugh Phonograph, Voco, 1948, 7", from $10 to...**$15.00**
Little Jack Horner, Pix 104, 1941, 10", from $60 to **$80.00**
Little White Duck, Red Raven Movie Records M ¾, 1956, from $30 to **$40.00**
Lord High Executioner, PicturTone, Gilbert & Sullivan series, 1948, from $15 to...**$20.00**
Old McDonald Had a Farm, Voco, 1948, rare 6" size, from $15 to...**$20.00**
Old McDonald Had a Farm, Voco, 1948, 7", from $10 to...**$15.00**
Red River Valley, Record Guild of America 2002P, 1949, rare picture sleeve, from $10 to **$15.00**
Robin Hood, Toy Toon Records, 1952, from $10 to **$15.00**
Rover the Strong Man, Voco, 1948, diecut, 7", from $25 to ..**$30.00**
Shepherd Boy, Bible Storytime, 1948, from $10 to...........**$15.00**
Singing Mother Goose, Magic Talking Books T-1, 1955, EX (EX cover), from $15 to **$20.00**

Songs From Mother Goose, Toy Toon Records, 1952, from $10 to **$15.00**

Photo courtesy Peter Muldavin.

Superman: The Magic Ring, Musette (Picturetone), 1947, from $60.00 to $80.00.

Swing Your Partner, Record Guild of America, Picture-Play Records PR11A, 1948, 10½", from $80 to...............**$100.00**
Ten Little Indians, Toy Toon Records, 1952, from $10 to..**$15.00**
Terry & the Pirates, Record Guild of America F501, 1948, from $35 to **$45.00**
The Fox, Talking Book Corp, 1919, record mounted on diecut figure, 4", from $60 to **$80.00**
The Three Bears With Uncle Henry, Kidisks KD-77A, 1948, 4", from $10 to...**$15.00**
Tom Cat the Tightrope Walker, Voco, 1948, diecut, from $25 to...**$30.00**
Tom Tom the Piper's Son, Kiddie-Rekord, 1925, rare, from $50 to...**$60.00**
Trial of Bumble, The Bee Part 1, Vogue R745, 1947, 10", from $50 to **$60.00**
Wandering Minstrel, PicturTone, Gilbert & Sullivan series, 1948, from $15 to...**$20.00**
When Jesus Was Born, Bible Storytime, 1948, from $10 to.**$15.00**
Winnie-The-Pooh-Songs, RCA, 1931-33, very rare, set of 3 w/orig folder, from $300 to **$500.00**

Reynolds Toys

Reynolds Toys began production in 1964, at first making large copies of early tin toys for window displays, though some were sold to collectors as well. These toys included trains, horse-drawn vehicles, boats, a steam toy, and several sizes of Toonerville trolleys. In the early 1970s, they designed and produced six animated cap guns. Finding the market limited, by 1971 they had switched to a line of banks they call 'New Original Limited Numbered Editions (10-50) of Mechanical Penny Banks.' Still banks were added to their line in 1980 and figural bottle openers in 1988. Each bank design is original; no reproductions are produced. Reynolds' banks are in the White House and the Smithsonian as well as many of the country's major private collections. *The Penny Bank Book* by Andy and Susan Moore (Schiffer Publishing, 1984) shows and describes the first twelve still banks Reynolds produced. Values are given for mint-condition banks.

Advisor: Charlie Reynolds (R5).

MECHANICAL BANKS

1M, Train Man Bank, 1971, edition of 30 ....$350.00
2M, Trolley Bank, 1971, edition of 30 ....$350.00
3M, Drive-In Bank, 1971, edition of 10 ....$1,000.00
4M, Pirate Bank, 1972, edition of 10 ....$725.00
5M, Blackbeard Bank, 1972, edition of 10......................$650.00
6M, Frog & Fly Bank, 1972, edition of 10 ....$1,200.00
7M, Toy Collector Bank, 1972, unlimited edition $550.00
8M, Balancing Bank, 1972, edition of 10........................$725.00
9M, Save the Girl Bank, 1972, edition of 10...............$2,000.00
10M, Father Christmas Bank, 1972, 1 made ea year at Christmas..$750.00
11M, Gump on a Stump Bank, 1973, edition of 10.....$1,100.00
12M, Trick Bank, 1973, edition of 10...........................:..$1,000.00
13M, Kid Savings Bank, 1973, edition of 10 ....$1,200.00
14M, Christmas Tree Bank, 1973, edition of 10............$725.00
15M, Foxy Grandpa Bank, 1974, edition of 10...............$975.00
16M, Happy Hooligan Bank, 1974, edition of 10........$1,075.00
17M, Chester's Fishing Bank, 1974, edition of 10 ....$900.00
18M, Gloomy Gus Bank, 1874, edition of 10..............$1,200.00
19M, Kids' Prank Bank, 1974, edition of 10................$1,100.00
20M, Mary & the Little Lamb, 1974, edition of 20 ....$850.00
21M, Spook Bank, 1974, edition of 10...........................$800.00
22M, Decoy Bank, 1974, edition of 10...........................$600.00
23M, Decoy Hen Bank, 1974, edition of 10 ....$600.00
24M, Comedy Bank, 1974, edition of 10 ....$975.00
25M, Bozo Bank, 1974, edition of 10 ....$825.00
26M, Reynolds Foundry Bank, 1974, edition of 15 .....$2,000.00
27M, Toonerville Bank, 1974, edition of 10...................$950.00
28M, Bank of Reynolds Toys, 1974, edition of 10 ....$425.00
29M, Simple Simon Bank, 1975, edition of 10...............$925.00
30M, Humpty Dumpty Bank, 1975, edition of 20.......$1,250.00
31M, Three Blind Mice, 1975, edition of 15 ....$1,100.00
32M, Clubhouse Bank, 1975, edition of 10 ....$1,100.00
33M, Boat Bank, 1975, edition of 10...........................$1,500.00
34M, St Nicholas Bank, 1975, edition of 50...................$775.00
35M, Forging America, 1976, edition of 13 ....$1,200.00
36M, Suitcase Bank, 1979, edition of 22 ....$725.00
37M, North Wind Bank, 1980, edition of 23 ....$675.00
40M, Columbia Bank, 1984, edition of 25 ....$1,350.00
41M, Whirligig Bank, edition of 30 ....$800.00
42M, Miss Liberty, 1986, edition of 36 ....$950.00
42M, Miss Liberty on a Pedestal, 1986, edition of 4....$1,400.00
43M, Auto Giant Bank, 1987, edition of 2000 ....$2,250.00
45M, Campaign '88 Bank, 1988, edition of 50............$2,750.00
46M, Hollywood, 1989, edition of 35 ....$750.00
47M, Buffalos Revenge, 1990, edition of 35 ....$900.00
48M, Williamsburg Bank, 1991, edition of 35 ....$725.00
49M, Duel at the Dome Bank, 1992, edition of 50.........$850.00

50M, '92 Voting Bank, 1992, edition of 50 ....$1,800.00
51M, Oregon Trail Bank, 1993, edition of 50.................$800.00
52M, Norway Bank (Lillehammer), 1994, edition of 50...$825.00
53M, Shoe House Bank, 1994, edition of 50 ....$950.00

54M, J&E Stevens Co., 1995, edition of 50, $1,300.00.

55M, Hyakutake Bank (The Comet), 1996, edition of 50..$395.00
56M, '96 Political Wish Bank, 1996, edition of 50.........$800.00

STILL BANKS

1S, Amish Man Bank, 1980, edition of 50......................$135.00
2S, Santa, 1980, edition of 50 ....$80.00
3S, Deco Dog, 1981, edition of 50....................................$70.00

4S, Jelly Bean King, 1981, edition of 100, $250.00.

5S, Hag Bank, 1981, edition of 50 ....$125.00
6S, Snowman, 1981, edition of 50....................................$90.00
7S, Mark Twain, 1982, edition of 50 ....$110.00
8S, Santa, 1982, edition of 50 ....$125.00
10S, Redskins Hog Bank, 1983, edition of 50..................$125.00
11S, Lock-up Savings Bank, 1983, edition of 50..............$45.00

12S, Miniature Bank Building, 1983, edition of 50 ....$125.00

13S, Santa in Chimney, 1983, edition of 50 ....$80.00

14S, Santa w/Tree (bank & doorstop), 1983, edition of 25 .$325.00

15S, Redskins NFC Champs, 1983, edition of 35...........$185.00

16S, Chick Bank, 1984, edition of 50 ....$50.00

17S, Ty-Up Bank, 1984, edition of 35 ....$225.00

18S, Tiniest Elephant Bank, 1984, edition of 50 ....$90.00

19S, Baltimore Town Crier, 1984, edition of 50...............$55.00

20S, Father Christmas Comes to America, July 4th, 1984, edition of 25 ....$310.00

21S, Campaign '84 bank, 1984, edition of 100...............$160.00

22S, Santa, 1984, edition of 50 ....$100.00

23S, Reagan '85 Bank, 1985, edition of 100 ....$275.00

24S, Columbus Ohio, 1985, edition of 50..........................$55.00

25S, Austrian Santa (bank & doorstop), 1985, edition of 25 ..$350.00

26S, Halloween Bank, 1985, edition of 50.........................$90.00

27S, 1893 Kriss Kringle Bank (w/tree & candle decorations), 1985, edition of 20 ....$1,400.00

28S, Santa Coming to a Child, 1985, edition of 50........$165.00

29S, Halley's Comet, 1986, edition of 50 ....$190.00

30S, 20th Anniversary Bank, 1986, edition of 86 ....$155.00

31S, Father Christmas (bank & doorstop), gr, 1986, edition of 25 ....$280.00

32S, Santa & the Reindeer, 1986, edition of 50.............$160.00

33S, Charlie O'Conner Bank, 1987, edition of 50...........$65.00

34S, Chocolate Rabbit Bank, 1987, edition of 50 ....$85.00

35S, St Louis River Boat, 1987, edition of 60 ....$55.00

36S, German Santa (bank & doorstop), 1987, edition of 25 ...$275.00

38S, Old Stump Halloween, 1987, edition of 50 ....$75.00

39S, Santa in Race Car, 1987, edition of 100 ....$95.00

40S, Technology Education Bank, edition of 88 ....$50.00

41S, Super Bowl XXII Redskins, 1988, edition of 50........$80.00

42S, Easter Rabbit Bank, 1988, edition of 50...................$45.00

43S, Florida Souvenir Bank, 1988, edition of 75 ....$90.00

44S, Father Christmas w/Lantern (bank & doorstop), 1988, edition of 35 ....$260.00

47S, Santa on Polar Bear, 1988, edition of 75 ....$90.00

48S, Bush-Quayle, 1989, edition of 100...........................$250.00

49S, Shuffle Off to Buffalo, 1989, edition of 75 ....$65.00

50S, Pocket Pigs, 1989, edition of 75..............................$125.00

51S, Regal Santa (bank & doorstop), 1989, edition of 35 ..$250.00

52S, Tiniest Snowman, 1989, edition of 75 ....$50.00

53S, Santa on Motorcycle, 1989, edition of 75.................$85.00

54S, Rabbit w/Mammy, 1990, edition of 75.....................$160.00

55S, Antique Row Sign Post, 1990, edition of 75.............$65.00

56S, Duck w/Puppy & Bee Bank, 1990, edition of 75.......$90.00

57S, 1895 Santa w/Wreath, 1990, edition of 35 ....$250.00

58S, Santa Coming on a Pig, 1990, edition of 75 ....$65.00

59S, St Louis Sally Bank, 1991, edition of 55 ....$60.00

60S, Santa w/Wassail Bowl, 1991, edition of 35.............$250.00

61S, Santa Express Bank, 1991, edition of 55..................$125.00

62S, Pig on Sled Bank, 1992, edition of 55......................$65.00

63S, Santa About To Leave, 1992, edition of 25............$290.00

64S, Jack-O-Lantern, 1992, edition of 60 ....$65.00

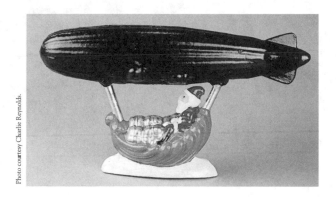

65S, Santa in Zeppelin, 1992, edition of 100, $300.00.

66S, Clinton Bank, 1993, edition of 100 ....$300.00

67S, Windy City Bank (Chicago Convention), 1993, edition of 60 ....$85.00

68S, Santa & the Bad Boy (Summer Santa), 1993, edition of 50 ....$225.00

69S, Arkansas President, 1994, edition of 100................$150.00

70S, Santa & the Good Kids, 1994, edition of 35 ....$200.00

71S, Penny Santa, 1994, edition of 60 ....$75.00

72S, School Days Bank, 1995, edition of 100 ....$75.00

73S, 1880 Snow Santa, 1995, edition of 50 ....$200.00

74S, Santa on Donkey, 1995, edition of 50......................$95.00

75S, Clinton/Dole '96 (SBCCA '96), 1996, edition of 100....$150.00

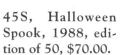

45S, Halloween Spook, 1988, edition of 50, $70.00.

46S, NCRPBC (National Capitol Region Club), 1988, edition of 20 ....$300.00

Robots and Space Toys

Space is a genre that anyone who grew up in the '60s can relate to, but whether you're from that generation or not, chances are the fantastic robots, space vehicles, and rocket launchers from that era are fascinating to you as well. Some emitted beams of colored light and eerie sounds and suggested technology the secrets of which were still locked away in the future. To a collector, the stranger, the better. Some were made of lithographed tin, but even plastic toys (Atom Robot, for example) are high on the want list of many serious buyers. Condition is extremely important, both in general appearance and internal workings. Mint-in-box examples may be worth twice as much as one mint-no-box, since the package art was often just as awesome as the toy itself.

Because of the high prices these toys now command, many have been reproduced. Beware!

Other Sources: 01

See also Marx; Guns, Miscellaneous.

Apollo Module, Japan, mystery action w/lights & sound, litho tin & plastic, battery-op, 8", scarce, MIB, A **$200.00**
Apollo Moon Flights Globe, Bonus Enterprises, 1970, litho tin globe on plastic stand, 6", NM (NM box), A **$100.00**
Apollo Space Patrol w/Satellite Ship, TPS, battery-op, EXIB, L4...**$175.00**

Apollo-X Moon Challenger, TN, plastic, battery-operated, 16", EX, $185.00.

Astro Captain, Daiya, advances w/sparks & engine sound, litho tin w/plastic arms, w/up, 6½", MIB, A.....................**$325.00**
Astro-Scout, Yonezawa, chest plate mk #3, litho tin, friction, 9", NMIB, A **$2,300.00**
Astronaut, Daiya, advances, stops & fires machine gun w/lights & sound, litho tin, battery-op, 14", NM (EX box), A ..**$1,800.00**
Astronaut, Rosko, bl version, advances w/lights & sound, litho tin, battery-op, 13", NM (EX box), A **$1,900.00**
Atlas ICBM Missile Launcher, battery-op, NMIB, L4....**$675.00**
Atom Robot, KO, 1960s, bump-&-go action, battery-op, 6½", EX **$375.00**
Atomic Robot, Y, advances in waddling motion as facial expressions change, litho tin & plastic, w/up, 6", EX (EX box), A **$675.00**
Change Man, SH, advances as head opens & boy's head pops up, tin & plastic, remote control, 14", approx 12 made, M, A **$5,500.00**
Chief Robot Man, KO, bump-&-go w/lights & sound, litho tin, battery-op, 12", NM (EX box), A **$2,100.00**
Chief Robot Man, KO, 12", EX, A..................................**$850.00**
Cone Head Robot, Yonezawa, advances w/sparking action behind plastic eyes, litho tin, w/up, NMIB...........**$4,000.00**
Cragstan Astronaut, Y, 10", EX, A................................**$650.00**
Cragstan Launching Pad w/Rocket & Satellite, battery-op, EXIB, L4 ....**$375.00**
Cragstan Space Tank, Y, mk Mars Patrol, advances & driver spins in ball in cockpit, litho tin, 6", NM (EX box), A **$300.00**

Dino the Robot, SH, head splits open to reveal dinosaur w/growling sound, head lights up, EX (EX box), A **$1,000.00**
Dr Who Giant Robot, Denys-Fisher, 1976, plastic w/jointed arms, legs & torso, 10", NM (EX box), A **$245.00**
Earth Man, TN, advances & raises rifle w/flashing lights & sound, remote control, 9", NM **$800.00**
Engine Robot, SH, advances w/swinging arms & spinning gears in chest, plastic, battery-op, 9", NMIB **$200.00**
Fighting Robot, advances w/swinging arms, spinning gears atop head & light-up chest, 12", EX **$150.00**
Flash Space Patrol, TPS, 1950s, bump-&-go action w/lights & sound, litho tin, battery-op, 8", scarce, NMIB, A....**$250.00**

Flashy Jim, SNK, 1950s, scissors walking action, light-up eyes, tin, battery-operated, 7½", EX (worn box), A, $1,250.00.

Flying Saucer w/Space Pilot, KO, litho tin & plastic, battery-op, 7½" dia, non-working, G (G box), A **$125.00**
Flying Saucer Z-106, MT, litho tin, friction, 5", EX, A..**$150.00**
Friendship Rocket #7, battery-op, NMIB, L4 ....**$375.00**
Gama Zooming Satellite, German, 1958, w/up litho tin globe on tripod joined to sm plastic satellite, 12", EXIB, A ...**$160.00**
Giant Robot, late 1950s, battery-op, blk w/red trim, 16", NM, A..**$550.00**
High Wheel Robot, KO, blk w/red hands & feet, walks w/engine noise & sparks, gears spin in chest, 10½", M, A......**$250.00**
King Ding Robot, battery-op, EX, L4............................**$325.00**
King Flying Saucer, battery-op, tin, EXIB, J2 ....**$140.00**
Laughing Robot, Waco/Japan, laughs hysterically & advances w/swinging arms, lights flash, battery-op, 13", EXIB, A...**$350.00**
Lavender Robot, Modern Toys, rolls forward w/blinking eyes & mouth, battery-op, 15", VG, A............................**$2,000.00**
Lighted Space Vehicle w/Floating Satellite, MT, bump-&-go action, litho tin, battery-op, 8", EX+ (EX box), A ..**$300.00**
Looping Space Tank, Daiya, 1960s, battery-op, 8" L, NMIB, L4..**$500.00**
Lost in Space Robot, Remco, 1966, plastic, all red, 12", EX+ (EX box), A..**$500.00**
Lost in Space Robot, Remco, 1966, plastic, metallic bl w/red arms, battery-op, 12", NM (EX box), A..................**$850.00**
Luna Hovercraft, TPS, rises & hovers, litho tin, remote control, 8", rare, MIB, A **$500.00**

Machine Robot, SH, advances w/several actions & visible gears in chest, battery-op, 11½", EXIB, A $250.00

Man From Mars, Irwin, man in red space suit w/clear bubble helmet walks as gun moves, plastic, w/up, 11", EX+ (G box), A $300.00

Mars Patrol Spacemobile, YM, 1950s, litho tin w/pilot under spinning dome, friction, 6", NM, A $185.00

Matt Mason Space Station, Mattel, 1966, plastic, battery-op, complete w/accessories, NM (EX box), A $475.00

Mercury 1 Space Saucer, mystery action w/radar, revolving engine, lights & sound, litho tin, battery-op, NMIB, A...........$235.00

Mighty Robot, advances w/sparks, litho tin, w/up, 5½", NM, H12 ....$135.00

Mighty Robot Carrying Apollo, Y, bl & red litho tin robot w/red plastic feet pulling bl plastic capsule, 7", EXIB, A ...$450.00

Mobile Satellite Tracking Station, Y, 1950s, advances w/space scenes on screen, battery-op, litho tin, 9", MIB, A..$1,200.00

Mobile Space TV Unit w/Trailer, TN, bump-&-go w/light-up screen, litho tin, battery-op, 10½", MIB, A $2,800.00

Moon City, Cragstan, 1970, battery-op, MIB, J2 ....$250.00

Moon Detector, battery-op, MIB, L4 ....$975.00

Moon Explorer, KO, advances w/spinning antenna, red & blk tin w/clear plastic helmet, lever action, 8", MIB, A $900.00

Moon Explorer Robot, Yoshiya, flywheel bump-&-go action, red w/blk trim, spinner atop, 7", EX, A...........................$265.00

Moon Explorer Vehicle, Gakken, 1960s, battery-op, 11", MIB, L4 ....$500.00

Moon Patrol, Japan, mystery action w/lights & sound, litho tin, battery-op, 12", scarce, NMIB, A $2,000.00

Moon Rocket, MT, advances w/non-fall action as astronaut revolves above, litho tin, battery-op, 9", NM (NM box), A..$350.00

Moon Rocket, Y, 1950s, battery-op, 15", MIB, L4..........$325.00

Moon Spaceship, TN, bump-&-go w/lights & several other actions, litho tin, battery-op, 13", EX (VG box mk Space Car), A $2,000.00

Moon Traveler Apollo-Z, TN, stop-&-go action w/lights & sound, litho tin, battery-op, MIB, A $175.00

Mr Rembrandt, Ideal, 1970, robot holds pens in base & draws on paper, complete w/6 disks, NMIB..............................$55.00

Mystery Moon Man, KO, rare variation of Chief Robot Man, bump-&-go w/lights & sound, battery-op, 12", NM (EX box), A $1,550.00

NASA Space Patrol, MT, advances w/sound, litho tin, friction, 6", EX, A...$125.00

Orbit Explorer w/Airborne Satellite, KO, advances as figure in bubble rotates, ball floats above, 5", NM (EX box) .$650.00

Outer Space Ape Man, Illco, 1970, MIB $50.00

Outer Space Spider, Taiwan, plastic figure, battery-op, 11", MIB, A $125.00

Pioneer PX-3 Robot Dog, litho tin, friction, 9", EX $475.00

Pioneer 3-Stage Rocket w/Launcher, Kraemer, litho tin, 11", rare, EX (G box) $400.00

Piston Action Robot, TN, advances w/lights & sound, red & silver w/plastic helmet, remote control, 8", rare, NMIB, A ..$1,600.00

Piston Action Robot, TN, 8", EX, A $1,000.00

Planet Patrol Tank, Japan, advances w/sound, litho tin w/full-figure astronaut, friction, 6", NM (EX box), A........$300.00

Planet Robot, KO, tin, blue with red hands and feet, battery-operated, 9", MIB, A, $2,700.00.

Planet Robot, KO, advances w/spinning antenna & lights, bl w/red hands & feet, remote control, 9", rare, NM (EX box), A...$1,500.00

Planet Special Rocket, Great Britain, litho tin, friction, 6½", EX, A $265.00

Planet-Y Space Station, TN, spins w/lights & sound, pilot under dome, litho tin, battery-op, 8½" dia, NM (G box), A ..$175.00

Rachet Robot, TN, advances w/sparks in chest, litho tin w/coil head, w/up, 8", EX (NM box), A $1,060.00

Rachet Robot, TN, 8", EX, A.......................................$550.00

Radar Robot, SH, TV-type screen in chest captures scenes of the moon, w/human paper face, battery-op, 12½", EXIB, A ..$350.00

Radicon Space Pathfinder, battery-op, MIB, L4..........$1,275.00

Red Rosko Astronaut, TN, advances with flashing lights in helmet, battery-operated, 13", EX, $1,400.00.

Robbie the Robot, Japan, rare Army gr color w/red features, tin, w/up, 9", NM, A $925.00

Robert the Robot, Ideal, talker, gray & red plastic, remote control, 14", NM (EX box), from $400.00 to $500.00

Robot, Y, easel-back robot advances w/swinging arms, litho tin, remote control, 7", scarce, NM (EX box), A........$1,200.00

Robot Commando, battery-op, EXIB, L4......................$500.00

Robot Shepard, Jyesa/Spain, advances w/spinning & light-up gears, plastic, 9", EX (EX box), A $625.00

Robot Tractor w/Lighted Pistons, Showa/Japan, battery-op, MIB, L4...$575.00

Robot w/Buzzer, Yonezawa, advances w/several actions, lights & sound, litho tin, battery-op, 11", rare, NM (EX box), A $4,100.00

Robotank TR-2, TN, 1960s, battery-op, 5", MIB, L4.....$325.00

Robotank-Z, TN, advances w/swinging arms, head turns & lights up, litho tin, battery-op, 10", NM (NM box), A $600.00

Rocket Express, Linemar, spacecraft circles moon through space station & mountain, rare, M (EX box) $800.00

Rocket Ranger, Marusan, 2 full-figure soldiers in vehicle control gun w/attached airplane, litho tin, 6", NM (NM box), A ...$400.00

Rocket Ship Kit w/Launcher, Archer, plastic assembly kit, unused, 12", NM (NM box w/cut-out launching pad on back), A $130.00

Rocket X-6, MT, 1950s, litho tin, friction, 4", NM, A...$155.00

Rocket XB-115, SH, advances w/revolving head, sparks & sound, tin w/plastic accessories, friction, 11", NM (EX box), A $155.00

Rotate-O-Matic Super Astronaut, SH, advances w/several actions, lights & sounds, litho tin, battery-op, 12", MIB, H12 ....$225.00

Rotate-O-Matic Super Astronaut, SH, 12", EX, A.........$100.00

Roto Robot, SH, advances & rotates as guns fire w/lights, tin & plastic, battery-op, 9", EX (EX box), A....................$160.00

Satellite-Rotaryo, Gescha/Germany, 1958, wire-fr track centered on tin globe w/rotating satellite, 8", EXIB, A $200.00

Smoking Robot, Y (unauthorized reissue), several actions, litho tin, battery-op, 12", MIB, A..................................$1,100.00

Smoking Spaceman, Linemar, advances & puffs smoke, light-up eyes & dome top, battery-op, 12", EX, A..............$1,800.00

Solar-X Space Rocket, TN, rocket rises & wings extend w/lights & sound, tin & plastic, battery-op, 16", NM (EX box), A .$185.00

Sonar Space Patrol, Electro-Toy, blow whistle & spaceship changes direction, tin & plastic, 14", EX (VG box) ..$600.00

Space Bus, Bandai, battery-op, NMIB, L4 ....$850.00

Space Capsule w/Floating Astronaut, MT, 1960s, battery-op, 10", MIB, L4..$250.00

Space Cruiser, Japan, litho tin w/pilot under clear plastic dome, friction, 8½", NM, A..$125.00

Space Explorer, SH, metallic bl version, advances & chest opens, battery-op, 11½", EX, A $100.00

Space Explorer, SH, silver version, advances & chest opens to reveal Apollo flight, battery-op, 11½", NM (EX box), A $345.00

Space Patrol XII Tank, battery-op, VG+, L4................$185.00

Space Rocket Patrol Car, Courtland, 1950, advances w/sparks, litho tin w/red plastic roof, friction, 7", NM (EX box), A $250.00

Space Rocket Solar X, TN, 1960s, battery-op, 16", MIB, L4..$200.00

Space Saucer, Japan, 1950s, lithographed tin with astronaut under plastic dome, battery-operated, 7½" dia, NM, J6, $185.00.

Space Saucer Mercury X-1, Yonezawa, bump-&-go w/lights & sound, litho tin & plastic, battery-op, 8" dia, EX (G- box), A ..$165.00

Space Tank M-18, battery-op, EXIB, L4.........................$125.00

Space Traveler, 1950s, w/moving head, unused, 8", MIB, J2 ..$250.00

Space Whale Ship, KO, space whale undulates along w/several actions, litho tin, w/up, 9", NM (VG box), A......$1,650.00

Spaceship SS-18, S&E, litho tin w/astronaut under clear plastic dome, friction, 9", EX (EX box), A $250.00

Spaceship XY-07, advances w/spinning rotor, litho tin, friction, 8", MIB, A $145.00

Sparkling Space Ranger, Elvin, advances w/sparks, litho tin, friction, 7", NM (EX box) $400.00

Star Strider Robot, SH, 1980s, battery-op, MIB, L4.......$225.00

Strange Explorer, DSK, 1960s, battery-op, 7½", MIB, L4 .$300.00

Super Sonic Speedster Rocket, MT, advances w/sound, litho tin, friction, 6", NM (NM box), A $400.00

Super Space Capsule, SH, 1960s, battery-op, 9", MIB, L4 .$375.00

SX-10 Space Car, MT, advances in erratic motion, bl & red, battery-op, 9½", NM (EX+ box), A.........................$200.00

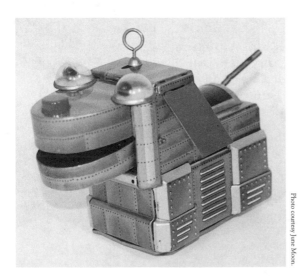

Space Dog, Yoshiya, 1950s, silver with red detail, clockwork mechanism, EX, J6, $235.00.

Target Set, Rocket Patrol, 1950, litho tin w/magnetic darts, scarce, MIB, A...$155.00

Television Spaceman, Alps, advances w/light-up space scenes in chest, battery-op, litho tin, 14", NM (EX box), A ..$525.00

Television Spaceman, Alps, advances w/light-up space scenes in chest, battery-op, litho tin, 14", EX (VG box), A ...$455.00

Television Spaceman, Alps, advances w/revolving antenna & space scenes in chest, tin & plastic, w/up, 7", NM (NM box), A...$400.00

Thunder Robot, Asakusa Toys, advances w/light-up features & shoots weapon, plastic, battery-op, 11", scarce, NMIB.............$2,000.00

Two-Stage Rocket Launching Pad, TN, rocket propels after several actions, litho tin, battery-op, 8", MIB, A..........$500.00

UFO-X05, MT, 1970s, battery-op, 7½" dia, MIB, L4.....$175.00

USA-NASA Apollo, MT, advances w/non-fall action as astronaut revolves above, lights & sound, tin, w/up, 9", NMIB, A...$200.00

V-1 Rocket, Japan, advances w/siren sound, litho tin w/rubber nose, friction, 12", NM (NM box), A $550.00

Venus Robot, KO, plastic, remote control, 5½", MIB....$175.00

Walking Robot, NBK, made as science kit w/opening head panel for battery, pnt plywood-type material, 8", VG (VG box), A...$1,700.00

Walking Spaceman, Tomiyama, advances w/swinging arms, tin & plastic, w/up, 5", NM (NM box), A $1,500.00

Wheel-A-Gear Robot, Taiyo, advances w/spinning gears, flashing lights & eyes roll, litho tin, battery-op, 15", NMIB, A $1,300.00

Winner Rocket, runs on adjustable rubber track, battery-op, mc litho tin, 5½", MIB, A.....................................$175.00

X-16 Space Patrol w/Floating Satellite, non-fall action w/styrofoam ball suspended above, battery-op, 8" dia, NMIB, A........$200.00

X-1800 Atomic Rocket, MT, 1950s, rare red & gr version, battery-op, litho tin, 9", EXIB, A $450.00

X-20 Space Tank w/Satellite, Y, astronaut under clear plastic dome, 6", EX, A...$400.00

X-70 Space Robot w/TV Camera & Screen, several actions, tin & plastic w/tulip-shaped head, battery-op, 12", NMIB, A.$2,250.00

X-80 Planet Explorer, Modern Toys, litho tin, battery-op, 8", NMIB, A...$100.00

XZ-7 Space Helicopter, ST, litho tin w/pilot in clear plastic cockpit, friction, unused, 7", MIB, A $200.00

Zoomer Robot, Japan, 1950s, blk & bl, holds wrench, w/up, EX, A $200.00

Zooming Satellite, GAMA, globe spins on tripod as satellite rotates, litho tin & plastic, w/up, 12", NM (EX box), A $165.00

MISCELLANEOUS

Bank, Astro Mfg, mk Berzac Creation, rocket shape w/chrome finish, 13", missing rubber nose o/w VG, P4 ....$45.00

Bank, Saturn Guided Missile Savings Bank, shoots coins into rocket top, 11", NMIB..$20.00

Bank, 1960s, plaster moon-shape mk Save Now for Your Trip to the Moon, 4½", VG, P4 ....$50.00

Cap, Jr Astronaut, 1950s, NM, J2.....................................$45.00

Drink Shaker, Space Patrol, United Plastics, 1950, red rocket ship w/orig straw, 8", MIB, A $65.00

Drum, Outer Space, 1950s, futuristic scene, litho tin, 8" dia, EX, A...$85.00

Eraser, Japan, 1960, gray plastic rocketship comes apart to reveal eraser, 3", M, P4 ....$5.00

Flasher Ring, Apollo II, flashes from Neil Armstrong to moon, NM..$35.00

Frisbee, Eureka U1 Flying Saucer, unused, M $55.00

Game, Mr Brain the Electronic Answer Man, Jacmar, Vacuform plastic, NM (VG box), A $145.00

Game, Spaceman Jiggle Puzzle, 1957, try to balance satellites in outer space, litho paper, MIB $60.00

Goggles, Magic Space, 1950s, unused, MOC, J2...............$50.00

Helmet, Space Patrol, 1950s, cb, EX, J2.........................$225.00

Helmet, Zenith Space Commander, 1950s, NMIP, J2....$125.00

Kaleidoscope, Space Scope, TN, w/snap-on heads, MIB, J2...$55.00

Lamp Shade, 1950s, red, yel & bl artwork on tan shade w/space station, rocket ships, etc, 9", EX, J5 ....$100.00

Morse Code Set, battery-op, scarce, NMIB, A $125.00

Musical Space Scope, TN, 12", EX, J2 ....$50.00

Pencil Case, ICBM missile, 1960s, vinyl, NM, T1...........$35.00

Pencil Sharpener, 1950s, plastic ray gun w/removable sharpener, dk gr or red, 3⅜", M, P4, ea.......................................$65.00

Projector, Zoom Outer Space, unused, M, J2 ....$28.00

Rocket Chalk, 1950s, NMIB, J2 ....$20.00

Walkie-Talkies, QX-2 Space Model, Remco, 1950s, electromagnetic 2-way phones, MIB..$250.00

Walkie-Talkies, Space Patrol, Randall/England, 1955, plastic, 5", M (EX box), A $200.00

Whistle, Pyro, 1950s, plastic spaceship w/spacemen in open cockpit, 4", chip on nose & tail, G, P4 ....$30.00

Rock 'n Roll

From the '50s on, rock 'n roll music has been an enjoyable part of many of our lives, and the performers themselves have often been venerated as icons. Today some of the all-time great artists such as Elvis, the Beatles, KISS, and the Monkees, for instance, have fans that not only continue to appreciate their music but actively search for the ticket stubs, concert posters, photographs, and autographs of their favorites. More easily found, through, are the items that sold through retail stores at the height of their careers — dolls, games, toys, books, magazines, etc. In recent years, some of the larger auction galleries have sold personal items such as guitars, jewelry, costumes, automobiles, contracts, and other one-of-a-kind items that realized astronomical prices. If you're an Elvis fan, we recommend *Elvis Collectibles* and *Best of Elvis Collectibles* by Rosalind Cranor (Overmountain Press).

Advisors: Bob Gottuso (B3), Beatles, KISS, Monkees; Rosalind Cranor (C15), Elvis.

See also Action Figures; Bubble Bath Containers; Coloring, Activity, and Paint Books; Dolls, Celebrity; Model Kits; Paper Dolls; Pin-Back Buttons; Puppets.

Beatles, beach hat, bl & wht or red & wht printed w/blk faces & autographs, NM, B3, ea $130.00

Beatles, beach towel, Cannon, 1964, VG, R2....................$90.00

Beatles, bedspread, 1964, United Kingdom, wht chenille w/mc appliques, EX, B3...$250.00

Beatles, belt buckle, gold-tone metal w/blk & wht photo under plastic, EX, B3/R2, from $35 to..................$40.00

Beatles, binder, Vernon, Yellow Submarine, 3-ring, EX+, A..$325.00

Beatles, birth certificates, 1964, 5x11", set of 4, VG (orig envelope), R2..$65.00

Beatles, blanket, United Kingdom, Whitney, tan w/red & blk photos & instruments, minor fading o/w EX, B3.....$250.00

Beatles, book, Beatles in Tokyo, JAM Pub, paperback, EX, B3...$25.00

Beatles, book, Beatles Up to Date, 1964, paperback, VG, R2...$8.00

Beatles, book, Forever Beatles, hardcover, full-color & blk & wht photos, EX, B3...................................$15.00

Beatles, book, Hard Day's Night, Australian edition, paperback, G, R2...$10.00

Beatles, book, Lennon: In His Own Write, 1968, hardbound, EX, R2...$65.00

Beatles, book, The Real Story, by Julius Fast, 1968, hardbound, w/dust jacket, VG, R2..................................$40.00

Beatles, book, The Writing Beatle, John Lennon, 1967, paperback, VG, R2...$10.00

Beatles, book, Yellow Submarine Press 'n Play, 1993, hardcover, w/words & music to sing along, EX, B3...............$20.00

Beatles, booklet, Official Fan Club, 1971, gr cover, 20 pgs, EX, B3...$20.00

Beatles, bookmarks, John, Ringo or Apple Bonker (Yellow Submarine), 9½x3", ea..$10.00

Beatles, bracelet, ceramic-type group photo on scalloped brass mounting, Yeh, Yeh, Yeh on back, EX (VG card), B3.$100.00

Beatles, brooch, blk & wht group photo on gold-tone metal, 2" dia, EX, B3...$75.00

Beatles, brooch, gold-tone banjo w/mop-top figures, movable beaded eyes, pnt hair & strings, EX, B3.............$60.00

Beatles, brooch, guitar shape w/blk & wht group photo, gold trim, 4¼", EX, B3...$45.00

Beatles, brooch, United Kingdom, plastic guitar w/blk & wht group photo, 3½", EX, B3................................$75.00

Beatles, bulletin board, Yellow Submarine, group photo, 17½x23", EX (orig shrink-wrap & sticker), B3.......$140.00

Beatles, cake topper, bl plastic figures of group playing instruments, mk Made in Hong Kong, 2½", NM...............$15.00

Beatles, Carefree Nylons, MIP (sealed), R2....................$120.00

Beatles, charms, from gumball machine, blk plastic records w/face on 1 side & label on the other, set of 4, EX, B3...........$30.00

Beatles, cup, United Kingdom, Broadhurst Bros, ceramic w/bl, gray & blk fired-on decal, EX, B3.............................$130.00

Beatles, Disk-Go-Case, record carrier, plastic w/group photo, various colors, rnd, EX, B3......................................$160.00

Beatles, doll, George Harrison w/instrument, inflatable vinyl, purple, 13", EX, B3...$35.00

Beatles, dolls, Beatles Forever by Applause, Raggedy Ann style, set of 4 w/stands & cb stage, 22", M, B3..................$440.00

Beatles, dolls, inflatable cartoon image of ea member, set of 4, EX, B3/R2, from $100 to...$125.00

Beatles, dolls, Remco, soft bodies, set of 4, NM, B3.......$355.00

Beatles, drumstick, 1964, wood, mk 13A Ringo Starr Ludwig USA in bl, EX, B3...$175.00

Beatles, figures, cartoon series, 1985, HP resin, set of 4, 6", NM, B3...$150.00

Beatles, figures, lead, set of 4 in blk leathers w/instruments, litho cb backdrop, NM, B3...............................$100.00

Beatles, figures, lead, set of 4 in outdoor snow scene pose from the movie Help!, EX, B3...$90.00

Beatles, figures, Remco, vinyl, set of 4, 4", NM, J6, $385.00.

Beatles, figures, Sabuteo, United Kingdom, 1965, set of 4, MIB, R2...$180.00

Beatles, film, Beatle Medal Story, 8mm, blk & wht, EX, R2......$40.00

Beatles, film, Live at Shea Stadium, 8mm, blk & wht, EX, R2..$30.00

Beatles, flasher rings, set of 4, EX, B3.........................$60.00

Beatles, guitar, Big Beat by Selcol, red plastic w/facsimile signatures, 20", VG, A...$770.00

Beatles, guitar, Big Six, box only, triangular w/paper label of group, EX, A...$165.00

Beatles, guitar, Big Six, rare 6-string version, EX (VG box), B3...$765.00

Beatles, guitar, Four Pop by Mastro, red and pink 4-string with faces and autographs, complete, 21", EX, B3, $325.00.

Beatles, guitar, Junior, Selco, red plastic w/name & image of group, 14", rare, EX+ $900.00

Beatles, guitar, New Beat by Selcol, 4-string w/paper group photo & autographs, 32", EX (EX box), B3 ....$800.00

Beatles, guitar, New Sound by Selcol, orange & cream 4-string w/blk & red faces & autographs, complete, 23", EX, B3...........$455.00

Beatles, guitar, New Sound by Selcol, 23", minor crack & rpl pegs, G+, B3 ....$300.00

Beatles, guitar strings, Hofner, NMIP, B3 ....$80.00

Beatles, hairbrush, Genco, MIP, B3 ....$50.00

Beatles, handkerchief, United Kingdom, With Love From Me to You, 8½", VG, R2 ....$35.00

Beatles, hat, brn corduroy w/image of Ringo, EX, R2 .....$100.00

Beatles, headband, Better Wear USA, Love the Beatles, w/photos & autographs, various colors, MIP, B3, from $50 to $70.00

Beatles, headband, Dame, 1964, allover head shots & signatures in blk on bl, EX, B3 ....$85.00

Beatles, headband, no mfg label, 1960s, I Love the Beatles w/music notes & clefs on red w/sparkles, EX, B3 ....$90.00

Beatles, hummer, cb w/yel plastic tip & mouthpiece, colorful faces & signatures on tube, 11", EX, B3 ....$160.00

Beatles, Kaboodle Kit, yel vinyl w/group photo & signatures, VG+, B3 ....$700.00

Beatles, key chain, brass w/group photo insert, Yeh, Yeh, Yeh on back, 1" dia, EX, B3 ....$90.00

Beatles, key chain, Yellow Submarine by Pride Creations, plastic, EX, B3 ....$60.00

Beatles, mobile, Sunshine Art Studios, cb pop-outs, unused, MIP, B3..$140.00

Beatles, necklace, mop-haired figures w/guitars on chain, EX, B3..$60.00

Beatles, necklace, silver-colored metal w/blk & wht photo under plastic on oval pendant, EX, B3 ....$100.00

Beatles, nesting dolls, Russian, HP wood, in Sgt Pepper suits, EX, B3 ....$40.00

Beatles, nodders, Carmascots, 1964, compo, signatures on gold bases, set of 4, 8", EX (EX box), B3.........................$850.00

Beatles, nodders, plastic w/signatures on base, set of 4, 4", M (sealed on Swingers card), B3................................$90.00

Beatles, notebook, group photo in Palladium doorway, unused, EX, B3 ....$60.00

Beatles, pencil, United Kingdom, head shots & signatures, EX, B3..$160.00

Beatles, pencil case, wht vinyl w/head shots & signatures in blk, 4x7", rare, VG, B3 ....$330.00

Beatles, pennant, felt, Beatles lettered next to image of Ringo & signature on wht background, red trim, 23", NM, A .$155.00

Beatles, pennant, felt, Canadian, Yeh, Yeh, Yeh, faces inside music notes, red, bl & yel on off-wht, 19½", EX, B3 ....$220.00

Beatles, pennant, felt, I Love the Beatles & hearts in wht on red, 29", VG, B3 ....$120.00

Beatles, pillow, bust portraits on bl, 12x12", EX, B3.......$150.00

Beatles, pillow, red guitars & photos on bl, 12x12", rare, EX+, B3..$250.00

Beatles, plate, Bamboo Tray Specialist, bamboo w/picture from Hard Days Night film, 12" dia, NM, A $100.00

Beatles, playing cards, photos in collarless suits on orange background, single deck, complete, MIB, B3 ....$385.00

Beatles, pop-out art decorations, Yellow Submarine, 9½x15" thin cb backings, set of 20, EX, B3 ....$45.00

Beatles, punch-out portraits, Whitman, 1964, cb, complete, EX, B3..$150.00

Beatles, purse, Canadian issue, 1970s, colorful image of John Lennon on silky material, gold metal clasp, EX, B3...$35.00

Beatles, purse, Dame, wht cloth clutch-style w/leather strap, blk faces & autographs, orig hang tag, unused, B3.........$300.00

Beatles, purse, Wako Plastics/Japan, vinyl w/photographed faces & cartoon bodies, 13x14", NM, B3..........................$220.00

Beatles, purse, wht cloth w/allover blk & wht photos, brass hdl, zipper closure, 14x14", M, B3.................................$325.00

Beatles, record box, Airflite, cb w/paper covering, gr w/wht top & blk hdl, 8½x8½", rare, G+, B3 ....$315.00

Beatles, record carrier, PYX, bl vinyl w/group photo insert, 7x7", NM..$150.00

Beatles, scarf, colorful photos & records on wht w/silky fringe, NM, B3..$45.00

Beatles, scarf, United Kingdom by Blackpool, brn & pk photos & designs on wht, 26x26", rare, NM, B3 ....$220.00

Beatles, scarf, 1960s, allover photos & signatures in blk on red, leatherette cord, triangular, EX, B3..........................$70.00

Beatles, scrapbook, Whitman, color photos on front & back, unused, 11x13", EX, B3 ....$70.00

Beatles, shirt, NEMS, 1960s, wht knit w/blk head shots & piping, orig photo hang tag, unused, NM, A $155.00

Beatles, spatter toy, Twirl w/the Beatles, NM (EX pkg), B3 ...$330.00

Beatles, stationery, 1968, Yellow Submarine, 4 sheets (1 w/ea member) & matching envelopes, EX, R2...................$18.00

Beatles, stick-ons, Yellow Submarine, colorful peel-off figures on 9x12" backing, set of 4, MIP (sealed), B3 ....$25.00

Beatles, sticker, from gumball machine, gold & blk w/faces & names, EX, B3..$25.00

Beatles, stickpin, Yellow Submarine, 1968, HP diecut tin, 1", EX, B3..$35.00

Beatles, switch plate, Yellow Submarine Snapping Turk, MIP (sealed), R2..$25.00

Beatles, talcum tin, Margo of Mayfair, 1964, EX, B3......$490.00

Beatles, tote bag, Japan, 1966, heavy gauge plastic w/hdl, orig hang tag, 14x13", VG, R2 ....$80.00

Beatles, tie tac, MOC, $125.00.

Beatles, wallet, plastic w/group photo on front, New Jersey tourist map on bk, gold trim, snap-open, NM $150.00

Beatles, wallpaper, 1964, single panel, 21x21", VG, R2 ...$30.00

Beatles, wastebasket, Gold Stars Series, Let It Be, litho tin, 17", EX, A $75.00

Beatles, wig, Lowell Toys, MIP (sealed), B3 ....$110.00

Blondie, International Fan Club Book, 1981, EX, B3.......$10.00

Bon Jovi, backstage pass, Kemper Arena 2/26/87, EX, B3 ..$4.00

Bruce Springsteen, key chain, metal ticket shape, MOC, J8..$8.00

Cheap Trick, bow tie, wht print on blk, EX, B3 ....$28.00

Crosby, Stills & Nash, whistle, ABC Records promotion, Whistling Down the Wire, EX, B3 ....$12.00

Dave Clark Five, dolls, Remco, NMIB, B3 ....$400.00

Dave Clark Five, tour book, 1964, lg format, EX, B3........$38.00

Donny and Marie Osmond, record carrier, Peerless Vidtronic Corp., 1977, yellow version, EX, small from $20.00 to $25.00; large $40.00 to $50.00.

Elvis, balloon toy, California Toytime, image of Elvis as boxer (Kid Galahad) on red balloon w/cb feet, 4", EX, A ...$65.00

Elvis, beach hat, 1956, w/orig photo hang tag, EX, B3 ...$125.00

Elvis, belt, EPE, 1956, vinyl w/full-color image of Elvis w/guitar against record & musical notes, 30", EX+, A...........$975.00

Elvis, bracelet, Elvis Presley Enterprises, 1977, full-color head shot, EX, B3 ....$15.00

Elvis, feather pen, 1956 Tickle Me promotion, EX, B3 ....$20.00

Elvis, guitar, Lapin, 1984, MOC (sealed), B3 ....$75.00

Elvis, guitar, Selcol, 1959, rare, EX, B3.........................$700.00

Elvis, hat, GI Blues, RCA Victor/Paramount, brn paper w/bl & red lettering & photo, EX, B3 ....$100.00

Elvis, key chain, Elvis Presley Boulevard, 1980s, EX, B3 ....$5.00

Elvis, key chain, flasher, full figure w/yel background, 2½x2", EX, B3 ....$20.00

Elvis, lipstick, Hound Dog Orange, 1956, rare, MOC, B3 ..$335.00

Elvis, pencil, 1956, Sincerely Yours, Elvis Presley, unused, B3 ....$18.00

Elvis, pennant, 1970s, King of Rock 'n Roll, The One & Only Elvis, bl & wht on red w/yel stripe, 31", EX $40.00

Elvis, picture frame, EPE, 1956, Love Me Tender/Sincerely Elvis Presley, plastic w/gold letters & musical images, NM ..$300.00

Elvis, playing cards, concert scene, MIB, T1 ....$12.00

Elvis, playing cards, in karate suit, MIB, T1 ....$12.00

Elvis, poster, Coloring Contest, 1962, M $20.00

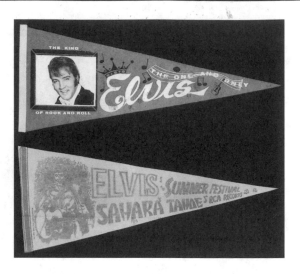

Elvis, pennant, early 1970s, red felt, NM, $40.00; Elvis Summer Festival pennant, 1971, NM, $75.00.

Elvis, sideburns sticker from vending machine, 1950s, EX...$55.00

Elvis, Teddy Bear perfume, 1960s photo on front, gold cap, 3", EX, B3 ....$45.00

Elvis, tray, 1977, early photo on front & part of his eulogy on back, 13", EX, B3 ....$20.00

Fleetwood Mac, backstage pass, 1982, EX, B3 ....$5.00

Grateful Dead, key chain, metal ticket shape, MOC, J8.....$8.00

Gregg Allman, slingshot, Epic promotion, I'm No Angel, EX, B3 ....$35.00

KD Lang, Good Luck horseshoe, metal, rare, NM, J8.......$18.00

KISS, backstage pass, Japan tour, laminated, EX, B3 ....$15.00

KISS, backstage pass, Return of KISS, 1979, laminated, EX, B3 ....$15.00

KISS, backstage pass, Revenge World Tour, 1992, laminated, EX, B3 ....$15.00

KISS, bracelet, gold chain & logo w/red inset, MOC, B3 ...$35.00

KISS, combs, Lady Jane/Australian, 1980, rare, set of 35, MIP (sealed), B3 ....$170.00

KISS, figures, lead, complete set of 4 w/instruments & make-up, MIB, B3..$90.00

KISS, guitar pick, wht w/Gene Simmons' autograph & logo in blk, EX, B3 ....$15.00

KISS, guitar pick, wht w/Paul Stanley's autograph & logo in gold, EX, B3 ....$15.00

KISS, jacket, colorful flame design w/photos & logo, child-sz, EX, B3 ....$90.00

KISS, necklace, 1980, lightning bolt w/silver logo, EX, B3...$25.00

KISS, necklace, 3-D logo in silver or gold finish, B3, ea...$10.00

KISS, pendant, features Gene Simmons, silver-colored metal w/head & logo, V-shape, EX, B3 ....$35.00

KISS, program, World Tour 1977-78, EX, B3...................$50.00

KISS, program, World Tour 1984, 24 pgs, EX, B3 ....$45.00

KISS, solo picture discs, 12", B3, ea $50.00

Michael Jackson, puffy stickers, 1980s, MIP, P3 ....$3.00

Michael Jackson, scarf, MJ License, 1983, 21x22", EX, P3..$13.00

Monkees, ankle bracelet, MOC, T1 ....$35.00

Monkees, backstage pass, 20th Anniversary Tour, EX, B3 .$8.00

Monkees, beach ball, says Pool It!, 1980s, inflatable, EX, R2 ....$25.00

Photo courtesy Greg Davis and Bill Morgan.

Monkees, blotter, Japan, 1981, plastic w/color photo, 7x10", NM, R2 ....$6.00

Monkees, book, Love Letters to the Monkees, 1967, paperback, VG, R2 ....$12.00

Monkees, book, Monkees Go Mod, 1967, paperback, VG, R2.$10.00

Monkees, bracelet, raised guitar logo on brass disk, rare, MOC, B3 ....$35.00

Monkees, bracelet, 4 head shots on brass disk, MOC, B3/R2 ..$30.00

Monkees, flasher ring, flashes from 2 members to the other 2, VG, B3 ....$20.00

Monkees, hat, Circus Boy, red & yel plastic w/Mickey riding elephant, VG, R2 ....$45.00

Monkees, mobile, United Kingdom, Corgi, complete, C10...$125.00

Monkees, oil paint set, Monkee Beat #2001, MIB (sealed), B3 ....$250.00

Monkees, paint-by-number set, Swingin', complete and unused, EX, B3, $140.00.

Monkees, pennant, Chicago Chapter 170, 1960s, felt, 10", VG, R2 ....$30.00

Monkees, program, Summer '87 Tour, EX, B3 ....$8.00

Monkees, Show Biz Babies, complete set of 4, EX, B3....$380.00

Monkees, sunglasses, w/orig hang tag, EX, B3 ....$45.00

Monkees, sweatshirt, 1967, pk w/logo, faces & autographs, short sleeves, VG, R2 ....$75.00

Monkees, tablet, photo cover, 11x8½", unused, B3..........$40.00

Monkees, tambourine, complete, EX, B3 ....$85.00

New Kids on the Block, key chain, metal ticket shape, MOC, J8..$6.00

New Kids on the Block, party banner, MIP, J8 ....$5.00

New Kids on the Block, rag dolls, Hasbro, MIB, J8, ea $20.00

Rolling Stones, photo stickers, 1987, plastic, several styles, MOC, J8, ea $5.00

Van Halen, binoculars, VH logo, EX, B3 ....$15.00

Van Halen, concert tour program, 1980, w/orig concert ticket on back pg, unused, EX, H4...$35.00

Rubber Toys

Toys listed here are made of rubber or a rubber-like vinyl. Some of the largest producers of this type of toy were Auburn Rubber (Indiana), Sun Rubber (Ohio), Rempel (also Ohio), and Seiberling. Because of the very nature of the material, most rubber toys soon cracked, collapsed, or otherwise disintegrated, so they're scarce today.

See also Character, TV, and Movie Collectibles; Soldiers.

Army Truck, Made in USA, gr w/canvas-look top, 5½", EX, I2 ....$14.00

Bobtail Racer, Sun Rubber, gr & wht, 4", VG, T1............$15.00

Boy on Tricycle, Auburn, NM, J6 ....$24.00

Catcher, Auburn, bl uniform, scarce, A1 ....$46.00

Circus Clown, Auburn, scarce, A1...................................$165.00

City Traffic Set, Auburn, 1950, complete, M (VG box), A ..$175.00

Collie, Auburn, lg, A1 ....$14.00

Colt, Auburn, brn, A1 ....$7.00

Cow, Auburn, blk & wht, slight warp to base, A1 ....$8.00

De Soto Airflow, Auburn Rubber, 1937, red with white tires, 5", VG, $35.00.

Football Player, Auburn, bl jersey, scarce, A1...................$44.00

Froggy the Gremlin, Rempel, EX, T1 ....$125.00

Indy Racer, Arcor Safe Toys/Auburn, red w/wht tires, 5¼", EX, S15 ....$45.00

Jet Plane, Auburn, XR 577 on wings, red & silver mks, very scarce, A1...$65.00

Krazy Tow Set, Auburn, 1950s, 8" truck pulls 7" hot rod car, NM (EX box)..$75.00

Lincoln 2-Door Convertible, Auburn, 1946 model, red, EX, I2 ....$30.00

Oldsmobile Sedan, Auburn, 1937 or 1938 models, red w/blk tires, 4¾", scarce, A1 ....$45.00

Sedan, Auburn, 4-door w/blk tires, scarce, A1.................$45.00

Telephone Truck, Auburn, turq w/yel tires, 7", EX $35.00

Turkey, Auburn, M, A1 ....$8.00

Russian Toys

Many types of collectible toys continue to be made in Russia. Some are typical novelty windups such as walking turtles and pecking birds, but they have also made robots, wooden puzzles, and trains. In addition they've produced cars, trucks, and military vehicles that are exact copies of those once used in Russia and its Republics, formerly known as the Soviet Union. These replicas were made prior to June 1991 and are marked Made in the USSR/CCCP. They're constructed of metal and are very detailed, often with doors, hoods, and trunks that open.

Because of the terrific rate of inflation in Russia, production costs have risen to the point that some of these toys are no longer being made.

Advisors: Natural Way (N1); David Riddle (R6).
Other Sources: O1

REPLICAS OF CIVILIAN VEHICLES

Aeroflot (Russian Airline) Service Station Wagon, 1/43 scale, MIB $18.00
Belarus Farm Tractor, 1/43 scale, MIB $20.00
Gorbi Limo, 1/43 scale, metal, MIB, R6..........................$25.00
KamA3 Model #5320 Flat Bed Truck, cab tilts forward, 1/43 scale, MIB, R6..$35.00
KamA3 Model #53213 Airport Fire Truck, 1/43 scale, MIB, R6..$40.00
KamA3 Model #5410 Truck Cab, 1/43 scale, MIP, R6 ....$40.00
KamA3-53212 Oil Truck, 1/43 scale, MIB, R6................$40.00
Lada #2121 4x4, trunk, doors & hood open, 1/43 scale, MIB, R6..$15.00
Lada #2121 4x4 w/Trailer, trunk, doors & hood opens, 1/43 scale, MIB, R6..$18.00

Lada Auto Service Station Wagon, 1/43 scale, MIB, $15.00.

Lada Sedan, trunk & hood opens, 1/43 scale, MIB, R6 ....$15.00
Lada Station Wagon, trunk & hood opens, 1/43 scale, MIB, R6..$15.00
Moksvitch Medical Services Sedan, 1/43 scale, MIB, R6.$15.00
Moskvitch Aeroflot (Soviet Airline) Station Wagon, hood opens, 1/43 scale, MIB, R6 ....$15.00
Moskvitch Auto Service Station Wagon, hood opens, 1/43 scale, MIB, R6...$15.00
Moskvitch Panel Station Wagon, hood opens, 1/43 scale, MIB, R6..$15.00
Moskvitch Sedan, hood opens, 1/43 scale, MIB, R6.........$15.00
Moskvitch Slant-Back Sedan, 1/43 scale, MIB, R6 ....$15.00
Moskvitch Soviet Traffic Sedan, hood opens, 1/43 scale, MIB, R6..$15.00

Moskvitch Station Wagon, hood opens, 1/43 scale, MIB, R6...$15.00
Moskvitch Taxi Sedan, hood opens, 1/43 scale, MIB, R6....$15.00
OMO 1937 Fire Truck, #1 in series of 6, 1/43 scale, MIB, R6...$40.00
OMO 1937 Fire Truck, #2 in series of 6, 1/43 scale, MIB, R6...$40.00
RAF Ambulance Van, back & 3 doors open, 1/43 scale, MIB, R6..$20.00
RAF Traffic Police Van, 1/43 scale, MIB, R6 ....$20.00
Volga Ambulance Station Wagon, back & 3 doors open, 1/43 scale, MIB, R6..$22.00
Volga Sedan, trunk, hood & doors open, 1/43 scale, MIB, R6...$20.00
Volga Taxi Sedan, trunk, hood & doors open, 1/43 scale, MIB, R6..$20.00
Volga Taxi Station Wagon, trunk, hood & doors open, 1/43 scale, MIB, R6..$20.00

Volga Traffic Police Sedan, 1/43 scale, MIB, $22.00.

REPLICAS OF MILITARY VEHICLES

Armored Car, 1/43 scale, MIB, R6 ....$15.00
Armored Personnel Carrier, 1/43 scale, MIB, R6.............$15.00
Armored Troop Carrier, 1/86 scale, MIB, R6...................$15.00
Cannon, 1/86 scale, MIB, R6 ....$15.00
Command Car, 1/86 scale, MIB, R6..................................$15.00
N-153 Biplane Fighter, 1/72 scale, MIB, R6 ....$40.00
N-16 Fighter, 1/72 scale, MIB, R6...................................$40.00
Rocket Launcher Armored Truck, 1/86 scale, MIB, R6 ...$15.00
Self-Propelled Cannon, 1/86 scale, MIB, R6....................$15.00
SU-100 Self-Propelled Cannon, 1/43 scale, MIB, R6.......$15.00
Tank, battery-op, 1/72 scale, MIB, R6 ....$45.00
Tank, 1/86 scale, MIB, R6 ....$12.00
Troop Truck, 1/86 scale, MIB, R6 ....$15.00
100mm Cannon, 1/43 scale, MIB, R6 ....$15.00
76mm Cannon, 1/43 scale, MIB, R6 ....$15.00

MISCELLANEOUS

Bird, metal, w/up, MIB, N1..$5.00
Car on Garage Lift, MIB, N1 ....$8.00
Car Set, metal, 6-pc, MIB, N1 ....$12.00
Car Track, metal, w/up, MIB, N1......................................$30.00
Chicken, metal, MIB, N1 ....$5.00
Chicken Inside Egg, w/up, MIB, N1 ....$5.00

Doll, Maytryoshki, metal, w/up, MIB, N1 ....$18.00

Doll Set, Lenin, Stalin, Kruschev, Brezhnev & Gorbechev, Maytryoshki, wood, made in China, MIB, N1 ....$30.00

Fighter Jet, plastic, bl, MIB, N1 ....$5.00

Hen, metal, w/up, MIB, N1 ....$8.00

Monster Beetle, metal, MIB, N1..$8.00

Moon Buggy w/2 Cosmonauts, plastic & metal, w/up, MIB, N1 ....$15.00

Parking Garage, metal, MIB, N1 ....$30.00

Rooster, metal, w/up, MIB, N1 ....$8.00

Tank, plastic, MIB, N1 ....$5.00

Train Track, metal, w/up, MIB, N1......................................$30.00

WWII Soldiers w/Rifles, cast metal, set of 10, MIB, N1 ...$25.00

Sand Toys and Pails

In the Victorian era a sand toy was a boxed wooden or cardboard scene with a glass front and a mechanism involving a hopper and/or chute leading to a paddle, then to various rods and levers attached to cardboard or tin figures or animals with loosely jointed limbs at the front of the scene. When the sand was poured, the mechanism was activated, and the figures went through a series of movements. These were imported mostly from Germany with a few coming from France and England.

By 1900, having seen the popularity of the European models, American companies were developing all sorts of sand toys, including free-standing models. The Sand Toy Company of Pittsburgh patented and made 'Sandy Andy' from 1909 onward. The company was later bought by the Wolverine Supply & Manufacturing Co. and continued to produce variations of the toy until the 1970s.

Today if you mention sand toys, people think of pails, spades, sifters, and molds, as the boxed scenes have all but disappeared due to their being quite fragile and not surviving use.

We have a rich heritage of lithographed tin pails with such wonderful manufacturers as J. Chein & Co., T. Cohn Inc., Morton Converse, Kirchoff Patent Co., Marx Toy Co., Ohio Art Co., etc, plus the small jobbing companies who neglected to sign their wares. Sand pails have really come into their own and are now recognized for their beautiful graphics and designs. A new book, *Pails by Comparison, Sand Pails and Other Sand Toys, A Study and Price Guide*, by Carole and Richard Smyth (our advisors for this category) is now available from the authors (S22 in Dealer Codes).

Busy Mike, Chein, ca 1935, boy & girl on seesaw, litho tin, 7", EX $275.00

Capt Sandy Andy Loader, Wolverine, tower w/chute & sand car that goes up & down, 13½", EX (orig box), minimum value $300.00

Dutch Mill, litho tin, McDowell Mfg Co, Pittsburg PA, ca 1927, 12", EX, from $225 to..$350.00

Leotard Acrobat, Brown, Blondin & Co/London, late 1800s, 8x10x3½", EX, minimum value...........................$1,000.00

Pail, emb tin, beach scenes w/children, images of birds & animals decorate sides, lobster on bottom, 5", VG, A ..$770.00

Pail, emb tin, boy & girl in boat, flock of geese on back, 3½", G, A..$120.00

Pail, emb tin, boy & girl w/teddy bear, children building castles on back, 7", G, A..$635.00

Pail, emb tin, boy & girl w/teddy bear, children building castles on back, 5", A..$415.00

Pail, emb tin, boy carries rope & walks w/girl, boy w/basket of fish on back, floral trim, 5", VG, A.....................$275.00

Pail, emb tin, boy carries rope & walks w/girl, boy w/basket of fish on back, floral trim, 4½", VG.......................$300.00

Pail, emb tin, boy on horse & girl on goat, mc on red & bl w/gold trim, wood hdl grip, 5½", G+, A $470.00

Pail, emb tin, cats in uniform marching in band, red & gold on bl, wood hdl grip, 5¾", VG, A $385.00

Pail, emb tin, children & goat cart on beach, floral border, emb lobsters on bottom, 5", VG, A $385.00

Pail, emb tin, dog w/puppies, red w/gold, emb eagle on bottom, wood hdl grip, 6", VG, A $340.00

Pail, emb tin, girl on dog, gr w/bl & gold trim, dog & puppies on back, wood hdl grip, 6", VG, A................................$470.00

Pail, emb tin, late 1800s, flowers & leaves fr rescue scene of lifeboat w/American flag & ship in distress, 3", EX.$400.00

Pail, emb tin, Little Red Riding Hood w/the Big Bad Wolf, emb eagle on bottom, wood hdl grip, 6", VG, A $470.00

Pail, litho tin, Chein, fish in the sun, EX+, J2 ....$35.00

Pail, litho tin, Chein, 4-sided w/nursery rhyme ea side, EX .$185.00

Pail, lithographed tin, safari scene with elephant, zebra, and tiger, unsigned, 5¼", EX, $100.00.

Pail, litho tin, nursery rhyme, w/matching sifter that fits inside, unsigned, 4", EX $175.00

Pail, litho tin, Ohio Art, Farmer in the Dell, 5", EX, J2 ...$30.00

Pail, litho tin, Ohio Art, Mickey & friends skating & doing magic tricks, w/swing hdl, 5", EX+, A....................$600.00

Pail, litho tin, Ohio Art, 1939, Donald Duck, 6", NM, A ..$240.00

Pail, litho tin, Ohio Art #6F175, Lil' Red Riding Hood, 7½", EX $150.00

Pail, litho tin, T Cohn, prewar, 3 pigs dressed as Indians dance around wolf tied to stake, unused, 8", M, A.............$185.00

Pail, litho tin, Wright Bros-type plane & hot air balloon, 4", rare, G, minimum value $300.00

Pail, litho tin, 1900-20, fisher boy & girl walking by shore 1 side, boy w/basket of fish on other, 5¼", EX....................$300.00

Pail, litho tin, 1940s, dressed farm animals, 8", EX, G16 ..$110.00

Pail, tin, Happynak #715, 1940s, features Mickey & Minnie, 4½", NM, minimum value $200.00

Pail, tin, Kiddies Metal Toys, early 1900s, boy & girl on swing & eagle perched on ball, wood hdl grip, 5½", G..........$350.00

Pail, tin, signed J Bros, 1890s, children at shore w/toys, border of lilies, wood hdl grip, 6½", NM.................................$600.00

Pail, tin, signed LS Co, Made in USA, red, gold & blk, Jack & Jill scenes w/flowers & vines, wood hdl grip, 6½", EX.......$450.00

Pail, tin, T Cohn, 1940s, children w/horns, drums & flags, Three Cheers for the Red, White & Blue, 7", EX $350.00

Pail, tin, US Metal Toy Mfg, Treasure Island, 7½", EX .$185.00

Pail & Shovel, litho tin, dressed cats, NM, G16.............$100.00

Pull Toy, 1890s, rectangular base on 4 wheels w/lift-out boat-shaped pail, hand-pnt tin, 4-pc, 11", EX.................$650.00

Pump, Ohio Art #77, children dressed as firemen, 10¼", EX ..$150.00

Sand Crane, Wolverine, 1916, mc litho, NM.................$375.00

Sand Lift, Ohio Art, M..$120.00

Sand Mill, Chein, sand causes cups to twirl, 11½", M (EX box), A $175.00

Sand Picture, drummer boy, mc image w/patriotic shield & cannon, paper-covered box w/sand-driven mechanism, 8x6", EX, A $225.00

Sand Picture, 3 musicians in front of fireplace w/dog, paper-covered box w/sand-driven mechanism, 7x9", EX, A ..$1,200.00

Sand Set, Ohio Art, 1940s-50s, litho tin shovel, sifter & 2 molds, MOC, from $80 to $120.00

Sand Sifter, litho tin, Ohio Art #187, children playing in sea, artist signed by Elaine Ends Hileman, 7½" dia, EX ...$80.00

Sand Sifter, litho tin, T Cohn, Flying Spray, shape of speed boat, red, wht & bl, window hole in cabin forms hdl, EX $185.00

Sand Sifter, litho tin w/wire mesh bottom, Ohio Art, 1930s, Mickey & Minnie in beach scene, 8" dia, EX, A.....$250.00

Shovel, Chein, mc pirates, 14", EX $70.00

Soldiers in Battle, Imagerie Pellerind/France, paper litho on wood, pour sand & soldiers attack, 9½", minimum value...$1,000.00

Spade, early 1900s, 6 kids in boat w/doll & horn, Seaside Pictures & Stories, litho tin, 11", G.............................$100.00

Spade, mk RN Made in USA on hdl, 1920s, 2 girls at beach, 11½", EX..$150.00

Spade, Ohio Art #184, boy in lg sea waders shows girl his fish, wood hdl, 28", EX...$125.00

Sunny Andy Merry Miller, Wolverine, elf moves & wheel spins, comes w/can of sand, 12", NM (G- box), from $200 to...$325.00

Windmill, T Cohn, pour sand in top & blades spin, litho tin w/rnd flowered base, 9", MIB, A $135.00

Santa Claus

Christmas is a magical time for young children; visions of Santa and his sleigh are mirrored in their faces, and their eyes are wide with the wonder of the Santa fantasy. There are many who collect ornaments, bulbs, trees, etc., but the focus of our listings is Santa himself.

Among the more valuable Santas are the German-made papier-mache figures and candy containers, especially the larger examples and those wearing costumes in colors other than the traditional red.

See also Battery Operated; Books; Reynolds Toys; Windups, Friction, and Other Mechanicals; and other specific categories.

Candy Container, 5", compo & papier-mache, wht beard, red cloth robe & hood, seated on wood pile, EX, A $125.00

Candy Container, 6½", Bakelite head w/molded glass body, red cap, 1940s, EX, H12..$55.00

Candy Container, 6½", compo head w/red cb robe, bl trim, wht beard, tree in hand, VG, A..$55.00

Candy Container, 7", compo & papier-mache, wht beard, red cloth hooded robe, wht trim, sprig tree, EX, A........$550.00

Candy Container, 7½", compo, wht cotton beard, red felt robe w/gray trim, pointed hat, twig tree in hand, VG, A...$130.00

Candy Container, 7¼", compo & papier-mache, gray beard, gr snow-flecked robe, basket on back, w/tree, VG, A..$550.00

Candy Container, 8½", compo & papier-mache, wht fur beard, red felt robe w/wht trim, feather tree, EX, A $700.00

Candy Container, 9", compo & papier-mache, wht beard, red cloth robe w/wht trim & gold belt, w/bag & tree, 1950s, G, A $45.00

Candy Container, 9½", compo head & hands w/cb body, wht beard, red cloth robe w/wht trim, rope belt, EX, A .$385.00

Candy Container, 9¾", papier-mache, wht beard, red cloth hooded robe w/wht trim, wht rope belt, tree in hand, EX, A $660.00

Candy Container, 10", compo, gray fur beard, red felt robe w/gray trim, basket on rope belt, feather tree, EX, A $1,000.00

Candy Container, 10", compo & cb, wht fur beard, red felt robe w/wht trim, rope belt, blk boots, G, A $700.00

Candy Container, 11", Belsnickle, molded & pnt figure, purple hooded coat w/bl trim, blk pants, w/tree, EX, A......$385.00

Candy Container, 12½", compo, wht beard, plush brn & wht hooded robe w/wht rope belt, blk boots, tree in hand, EX, A $1,650.00

Candy Container, 18", papier-mache, wht beard, red-pnt snow-flecked hooded robe, rope belt, sprig tree in hand, VG, A...$1,760.00

Candy Container, 18", papier-mache, wht fur beard, gray fur hooded robe w/metal buttons, tree in hand, EX, A ..$3,850.00

Candy Container, 21", compo, wht fur beard, red felt robe w/bl shoulders, wht trim, basket on belt, feather tree, EX, A.........$3,850.00

Candy Container, 22", compo & papier-mache, wht fur beard, red cloth robe w/wht trim, basket on belt, w/tree, EX, A..$1,375.00

Candy Container, 24", papier-mache, wht-pnt beard, silver-pnt hooded robe w/red trim, blk boots, feather tree, rpt, A .$1,320.00

Candy Container, 27", composition and papier-mache, red cloth robe, electrified candles on tree, tin lantern, EX, A, $1,925.00.

Candy Container, 27", compo & papier-mache, wht beard, red cloth hooded robe w/wht trim, rope belt, w/tree, VG, A $900.00

Candy Container, 32", compo & papier-mache, w/up, wht beard, red robe w/blk-dotted collar, rope belt, w/twigs, EX, A $2,750.00

Doll, stuffed cloth, w/bag & adjustable hat, 12", EX, A....$35.00

Doll, 1950s, stuffed cloth, 21", EX, H12...........................$35.00

Lantern, hand-pnt glass Santa face on tin base, steady wht or flashing pk lights, 5", MIB, A...................................$100.00

Lantern, pnt milk glass Santa w/lantern & sack on rnd base, battery-op, 6", MIB, A..$150.00

Marionette, USA (?), 1930s, wood & compo w/cloth suit & hat, 14", scarce, NM, A $175.00

Mask, Sloan & Woodward, 1904, cb, 14", scarce, MOC, A..$125.00

Nodder, compo & papier-mache w/up, red hooded robe, wht fur beard, w/toy basket, 26", VG, A...............................$880.00

Nodder, compo & papier-mache w/up, red robe w/blk-dotted collar & hat, wht fur beard, w/lantern, 32", VG, A.$935.00

Nodder, papier-mache w/sheepskin hair & beard, red fleece coat w/wht fur trim, 25½", EX, A..................................$1,250.00

Pull Toy, Santa on horse-drawn wagon, 2 leather hide horses on wheeled platform, 36", VG, A, $935.00.

Santa, papier-mache, red felt suit w/wht trim, 1920s, 6", H12 ..$65.00

Santa Driving Truck, German, papier-mache & felt Santa, w/feather tree, 20", EX (orig carton), A $1,250.00

Santa in Sleigh, bsk Santa w/toy sack on mica sleigh, 1930s, 3½", EX, H12...$65.00

Santa on Skis, 1930s, bsk w/mica skis, 4", H12 ....$75.00

Santa on Sleigh, wood sleigh w/8 felt-covered reindeer, 12", EX, A..$1,650.00

Santa Pulling Sleigh w/Toys, compo & papier-mache, fur beard, snow-flecked brn coat w/bl pants, 13½", EX, A $700.00

Santa w/Feather Tree, Electric Lights; papier-mache w/snow-flecked red cloth robe, wht trim, 9¼", EX, A $960.00

Santa w/Feather Tree, papier-mache & compo, wht fur beard, gray plush hooded coat w/bl pants, 8", EX, A $935.00

Santa w/Feather Tree, papier-mache body w/compo head & hands, wht fur beard, red hooded coat, gr pants, 7½", VG, A.$745.00

Santa w/Lantern, papier-mache body w/compo head & hands, red cloth robe w/wht trim & beard, 14½", VG, A........$1,265.00

Santa w/Toy Bag, papier-mache face w/molded felt body & plush detail, mica shoes, 1940s, 4", EX, H12 ....$25.00

Santa w/Toy Bag, pnt compo, red suit w/wht trim, blk belt, wht gloves, 9", G, A...$130.00

Santa w/Tree & Toy Bag, compo & papier-mache, gray beard, gr felt hooded robe w/red pants, 9", G, A $1,155.00

Wind-up Toy, Santa on skis, compo face w/wht beard, yel fur jacket w/bl pants, wood skis, basket on back, 7", EX, A $660.00

Wind-up Toy, Santa walker, compo face & beard, wooden legs, cast metal feet, red & wht cloth suit, tree & bag, 9", EX, A $850.00

Wind-up Toy, Santas on seesaw rocker, red felt jackets w/bl pants, baskets on backs, feather trees in hand, 8", EX, A ..$1,100.00

Schoenhut

Albert Schoenhut & Co. was located in Philadelphia, Pennsylvania. From as early as 1872 they produced toys of many types including dolls, pianos and other musical instruments, games, and a good assortment of roly polys (which they called Rolly Dollys). Around the turn of the century, they designed a line they called the Humpty Dumpty Circus. It was made up of circus animals, ringmasters, acrobats, lion tamers, and the like, and the concept proved to be so successful that it continued in production until the company closed in 1935. During the nearly thirty-five years they were made, the figures were continually altered either in size or by construction methods, and these variations can greatly affect their values today. Besides the figures themselves, many accessories were produced to go along with the circus theme — tents, cages, tubs, ladders, and wagons, just to mention a few. Teddy Roosevelt's African hunting adventures inspired the company to design a line that included not only Teddy and the animals he was apt to encounter in Africa but native tribesmen as well. A third line featured comic characters of the day, all with the same type of jointed wood construction, many dressed in cotton and felt clothing. There were several, among them were Felix the Cat, Maggie and Jiggs, Barney Google and Spark Plug, and Happy Hooligan.

Several factors come into play when evaluating Schoenhut figures. Foremost is condition. Since most found on the market today show signs of heavy wear, anything above a very good rating commands a premium price. Missing parts and retouched paint sharply reduce a figure's value, though a well-done restoration is usually acceptable. The earlier examples had glass eyes; by 1920 eyes were painted on. Soon after that, the company began to make their animals in a reduced size. While some of the earlier figures had bisque heads or carved wooden heads, by the '20s, pressed wood heads were the norm. Full-size examples with glass eyes and bisque or carved heads are generally more desirable and more valuable, though rarity must be considered as well.

Value ranges represent items in only fair condition (by the low end) up to those in good to very good condition, i.e., very minor scratches and wear, good original finish, no splits or chips, no excessive paint wear or cracked eyes, and, of course completeness. Animals with painted eyes in fair condition are represented by the low side of the range; use the high side to evaluate glass-eyed animals in very good condition.

During the 1950s, some of the figures and animals were produced by the Delvan Company, who had purchased the manufacturing rights.

Consult the index for Schoenhut toys that may be listed in other categories.

Advisor: Keith and Donna Kaonis (K6).

HUMPTY DUMPTY CIRCUS ANIMALS

Humpty Dumpty Circus animals with glass eyes, ca. 1903-1914, are more desirable and can demand much higher prices than the later painted-eye versions. As a general rule, a glass-eye version is 30% to 40% more than a painted-eye version. (There are exceptions.) The following list suggests values for both glass eye and painted eye versions and reflects a low painted eye price to a high glass eye price.

There are other variations and nuances of certain figures: Bulldog — white with black spots or brindle (brown); open-and closed-mouth zebras and giraffes; ball necks and hemispherical necks on some animals such as the pig, leopard, and tiger, to name a few. These points can affect the price and should be judged individually.

Alligator, glass or pnt eyes, $200 to....................................$650.00
Arabian Camel, 1 hump, glass or pnt eyes, $250 to........$750.00
Brown Bear, glass or pnt eyes, $200 to............................$900.00
Buffalo, carved mane, glass or pnt eyes, $200 to..........$1,200.00
Buffalo, cloth mane, glass or pnt eyes, $300 to $700.00
Bulldog, glass or pnt eyes, $400 to $1,600.00
Burro (made to go w/chariot & clown), glass or pnt eyes, $200 to..$700.00
Cat, glass or pnt eyes, rare, $600 to............................$3,000.00
Cow, glass or pnt eyes, $250 to $1,000.00
Deer, glass or pnt eyes, $300 to $1,000.00
Donkey, glass or pnt eyes, $75 to...................................$200.00
Donkey, w/blanket, glass or pnt eyes, $90 to...................$300.00
Elephant, glass or pnt eyes, $90 to.................................$300.00
Elephant, w/blanket, glass or pnt eyes, $200 to...............$500.00
Gazelle, glass or pnt eyes, rare, $700 to......................$3,000.00

Giraffe, glass or painted eyes, $200.00 to $700.00.

Goat, glass or pnt eyes, $150 to $400.00
Goose, pnt eyes, $200 to..$600.00
Gorilla, pnt eyes, $1,200 to $2,500.00
Hippo, glass or pnt eyes, $300 to................................$1,000.00
Horse, brn, w/saddle & stirrups, glass or pnt eyes, $150 to...$400.00
Horse, wht, platform, glass or pnt eyes, $125 to..............$400.00
Hyena, glass or pnt eyes, very rare, $1,000 to $3,700.00
Kangaroo, glass or pnt eyes, $400 to $1,400.00
Leopard, glass or pnt eyes, $350 to $800.00
Lion, carved mane, glass or pnt eyes, $250 to.............$2,000.00
Lion, cloth mane, glass eyes, $500 to...........................$1,200.00
Monkey, 1-part head, pnt eyes, $250 to $450.00
Monkey, 2-part head, wht face, $300 to..........................$900.00
Ostrich, glass or pnt eyes, $200 to $850.00
Pig, 5 versions, glass or pnt eyes, $200 to $900.00
Polar Bear, glass or pnt eyes, $500 to $1,800.00
Poodle, cloth mane, glass eyes, $300 to.........................$600.00
Poodle, glass or pnt eyes, $125 to $300.00
Rabbit, glass or pnt eyes, very rare, $1,000 to.............$4,000.00
Rhino, glass or pnt eyes, $250 to................................$1,200.00
Sea Lion, glass or pnt eyes, $400 to............................$1,000.00
Sheep (lamb), w/bell, glass or pnt eyes, $200 to $750.00

Zebra, glass or painted eyes, $250.00 to $1,000.00; Bactrian Camel, 2 humps, glass or painted eyes, $200.00 to $1,500.00.

Tiger, glass or pnt eyes, $250 to.......................................$900.00
Wolf, glass or pnt eyes, very rare, $600 to..................$4,000.00
Zebu, glass or pnt eyes, rare, $1,000 to.........................$3,000.00

HUMPTY DUMPTY CIRCUS CLOWNS AND OTHER PERSONNEL

Clowns with two-part heads (a cast face applied to a wooden head) were made from 1903 to 1915 and are most desirable — condition is always important. There have been nine distinct styles in fourteen different costumes recorded. Only eight costume styles apply to the two-part headed clowns. The later clowns, ca. 1920, had one-part heads whose features were pressed, and they were no longer tied at the wrists and ankles.

Black Dude, reduced sz, $300 to $600.00
Black Dude, 1-part head, purple coat, $250 to...............$800.00
Black Dude, 2-part head, blk coat, $500 to......................$800.00
Chinese Acrobat, 1-part head, $300 to $600.00
Chinese Acrobat, 2-part head, rare, $500 to $1,000.00
Clown, early, $150 to $500.00
Clown, reduced sz, 1926-35, $75 to...................................$150.00
Gent Acrobat, 1-part head, $500 to $900.00
Gent Acrobat, 2-part head, very rare, $800 to $1,200.00
Gent Arcobat, bsk head, rare, $300 to $600.00
Hobo, reduced sz, $300 to...$600.00
Hobo, 1-part head, $200 to $500.00
Hobo, 2-part head, curved-up toes, $700 to $1,200.00
Hobo, 2-part head, facet toe ft, $400 to $800.00
Lady Acrobat, bsk head, $300 to...$500.00
Lady Acrobat, 1-part head, $200 to $400.00
Lady Rider, bsk head, $250 to $500.00
Lady Rider, 1-part head, $200 to..$400.00
Lady Rider, 2-part head, very rare, $700 to $1,200.00
Lion Trainer, bsk head, rare, $350 to $600.00
Lion Trainer, 1-part head, $250 to.....................................$500.00
Lion Trainer, 2-part head, early, very rare, $600 to.....$1,200.00
Ringmaster, bsk, 1912-14, $450 to $650.00
Ringmaster, 1-part head, $200 to $450.00
Ringmaster, 2-part head, early, very rare, $500 to.......$1,200.00

HUMPTY DUMPTY CIRCUS ACCESSORIES

There are many accessories: wagons, tents, ladders, chairs, pedestals, tight ropes, weights, and various other items.

Menagerie Tent, ca 1904, $1,800 to $2,500.00
Menagerie Tent, 1914-20, $1,200 to $2,000.00
Oval Lithographed Tent, 1926, $3,000 to $4,000.00
Side Show Panels, 1926, pr, $3,000 to...........................$4,000.00

Schuco

A German company noted for both mechanical toys as well as the teddy bears and stuffed animals we've listed here, Schuco operated from the 1930s well into the '50s. Items were either marked Germany or US Zone, Germany.

Advisor: Candace Gunther, Candelaine (G16).
See also Battery-Operated; Windups, Friction, and Other Mechanicals.

Bear, bright gold, orig red ribbon, 1950, 3½", M, G16...$245.00
Bear, caramel, 1950s, 3½", G, G16 ....$85.00
Bear, champagne, orig red ribbon, 1950, 3½", M, G16 ..$245.00
Bear, champagne, 1950, 2½", NM, G16 ....$225.00
Bear, dk brn, 1950s, no ribbon, 3½", M, G16..................$195.00
Bear, in soccer outfit, 1960, 3½", M, G16 ....$250.00
Bear, in soccer outfit, 1960, 3½", MIB, G16....................$325.00
Bear, lavender, 1950, 3½", EX, G16 ....$500.00
Bear, pale gold, orig ribbon, 1950, 3½", NM, G16.........$235.00

Bear, peach-colored mohair with red floss nose, original green ribbon, 3½", minimum value, $225.00.

Photo courtesy Cynthia Powell.

Bear, tan, orig ribbon, 1950, 3½", M, G16 ....$225.00
Bigo-Bello Dog, orig clothes, 14", NM, G16...................$175.00
Bigo-Bello Tiger, cloth label, 1960s, 9½", EX, G16 ....$165.00
Black Scottie, Noah's Ark, 3" L, MIB, G16.....................$225.00
Blackbird, Noah's Ark, 3", MIB, G16 ....$225.00
Dog Mascott, felt clothes, MIB, G16 ....$175.00
Duck Mascott (Girl), bl & wht striped outfit w/red shoes, 1950, 3½", MIB, G16...$115.00
Elephant, Noah's Ark, 3" L, MIB, G16.............................$200.00
Fox, Noah's Ark, 1950, 2½", M (M box), G16.............$285.00
Hedgehog, Noah's Ark, 2", MIB, G16 ....$135.00
Janus Bear, 2 faces (googly & bear), cinnamon, 1950s, 3½", M, G16 ....$850.00
Janus Bear, 2 faces (googly & bear), tan, 1950s, 3½", EX, G16 ....$750.00
Ladybug, Noah's Ark, 1950, 2½", MIB, G16...................$150.00
Monkey, cinnamon w/felt hands & ft, mk Germany on ft, 2½", NM, G16 ....$200.00
Monkey, Noah's Ark, felt face, pipe-cleaner arms & legs, MIB, G16 ....$185.00
Orangutan, Noah's Ark, 3", very rare, MIB, G16...........$325.00
Owl, Noah's Ark, 3", MIB, G16...$150.00

Panda, on all fours, Noah's Ark, 1950, 3", rare, MIB, G16 ....$550.00

Panda, orig pk ribbon, 1950, 3½", M, G16 ....$325.00

Penguin, Noah's Ark, felt & mohair, 1950, 2½", NM, G16 ...$95.00

Penguin, Noah's Ark, 3", MIB, G16 ....$175.00

Perfume Bear, gold, 1930, 5", M, G16...........................$650.00

Perfume Monkey, cinnamon color, 5", EX, G16.............$250.00

Perfume Monkey, red, 5", rpl bottle o/w EX, G16 ....$445.00

Pig, Noah's Ark, pk, orig ribbon, 3", MIB, G16..............$300.00

Rabbit, Noah's Ark, caramel mohair, 1950, 3½", VG, G16..$100.00

Raccoon, Noah's Ark, 1950, 2½", M, G16 ....$275.00

Siamese Cat, Noah's Ark, orig ribbon, 1950s, 3", M, G16...$295.00

Tabby Cat, Noah's Ark, orig ribbon, 1950s, 3", M, G16....$265.00

Teddy Bear Compact, 1920s, dark golden mohair over metal frame, metal eyes, removable head, 3½", G, $650.00; Rabbit, 1920s, ivory mohair, brown metal eyes and red floss nose, swivel head, 4", VG, $85.00.

Tiger, Noah's Ark, 1950, 3", rare, NM, G16 ....$225.00

Tumbling Bear, bellhop, 1930s, 3½", M, G16 ....$975.00

Tumbling Bear, gold mohair, 1950s, 5", NM, G16 ....$850.00

Turtle, Noah's Ark, 3", MIB, G16..................................$175.00

Yes/No Bear, blk mohair, 1950, 5", NM, G16 ....$900.00

Yes/No Bear, tan mohair, 1950s, 5", NM, G16...............$600.00

Yes/No Bear, US Zone, 1948, 8", NM, G16....................$750.00

Yes/No Bellhop Monkey, 1920s, 14", NM, G16 ....$900.00

Yes/No Cat, 5", M, G16...$650.00

Yes/No Donkey, mohair w/felt ears, orig felt collar & ribbon, 1950, 5", NM, G16...$485.00

Yes/No Elephant, mohair w/felt tusks & ears, cloth US Zone tag, 1948, 5", EX, G16..$400.00

Yes/No Gnome, w/glasses, mohair & felt w/velvet pants & felt jacket, 1948, 12", EX, G16....................................$800.00

Yes/No Monkey, 1950s, 5", M, G16...............................$450.00

Yes/No Panda, orig pk bow, 1950, 5", rpl tail cover o/w MIB, G16...$1,250.00

Yes/No Panda, 1940-50, 8", rare, EX, G16 ....$1,300.00

Yes/No Rabbit, 5", M, G16..$650.00

Yes/No Tricky Elephant, orig ribbon & tag, 1948, 9", EX, G16...$500.00

Yes/No Tricky Monkey, US Zone tag & orig ribbon, 13", NM, G16...$450.00

Slot Cars

Slot cars first became popular in the early 1960s. Electric raceways set up in retail storefront windows were commonplace. Huge commercial tracks with eight and ten lanes were located in hobby store and raceways throughout the United States. Large corporations such as Aurora, Revell, Monogram, and Cox, many of which were already manufacturing toys and hobby items, jumped on the bandwagon to produce slot cars and race sets. By the end of the early 1970s, people were loosing interest in slot racing, and its popularity diminished. Today the same baby boomers that raced slot cars in earlier days are revitalizing the sport. Vintage slot cars are making a comeback as one of the hottest automobile collectibles of the 1990s. Want ads for slot cars appear more and more frequently in newspapers and publications geared toward the collector. As you would expect from their popularity, slot cars were generally well used, so finding vintage cars and race sets in like-new or mint condition is difficult. Slot cars replicating the 'muscle' cars from the '60s and '70s are extremely sought after, and clubs and organizations devoted to these collectibles are becoming more and more commonplace. Large toy companies such as Tomy and Tyco still produce some slots today, but not in the quality, quantity, or variety of years past.

Aurora produced several types of slots: Screachers (5700 and 5800 number series, valued at $5.00 to $20.00); the AC-powered Vibrators (1500 number series, valued at $20.00 to $150.00); DC-powered Thunderjets (1300 and 1400 number series, valued at $20.00 to $150.00); and the last-made AFX SP1000 (1900 number series, valued at $15.00 to $75.00).

Advisor: Gary Pollastro (P5).

COMPLETE SETS

AMT, Cobra Racing Set, NMIB......................................$185.00

Atlas, Racing Set #1000, HO scale, G (orig box), P5 ....$100.00

Aurora, Jackie Stewart Oval 8, VG (orig box)..................$85.00

Aurora, Mario Andretti GP International Challenge, G (orig box)...$55.00

Aurora, Stirling Moss 4-Lane Racing Set, EX (EX box), J2...$150.00

Aurora AFX, Jackie Stewart Winner's Circle Set, complete, B10..$50.00

Cox, Ontario 8, #3070, w/Eagle & McLaren, G (orig box), P5 ....$75.00

Eldon, Deluxe Road Race Set #9805-1800, G- (orig box), P5 ....$50.00

Eldon, Power 8 Road Racer Set, 1960s, EX (EX box).......$70.00

Eldon, Sky High Triple Road Race, w/Ferrari, Lotus, Stingray & Porsche, G (orig box), P5 ....$75.00

Ideal, Alcan Highway Torture Track, 1968, w/extra car & motor, M (EX box), D9 ....$50.00

Ideal, Dukes of Hazzard, MIB, J6 ....$85.00

Ideal, Mini-Motorific Set, #4939-5, EX, P5 ....$85.00

Ideal, Motorific Giant Detroit Race Track, w/Corvette, EX (EX box), T1 ....$85.00

Marx, Grand Prix Set, G (orig box) $65.00

Remco, Mighty Mike Action Track, NMIB, T1.............$100.00

Revell, HiBank Raceway Set #49-9503, 1/32 scale Cougar GTE & Pontiac Firebird, EX (orig box), P5 ....$125.00

Photo courtesy Gary Pollastro.

Scalextric, Electric Motor Racing Set, Officially Approved by Jim Clark, made in England, NMIB, $400.00.

Strombecker, Highway Patrol, VG (orig box) $200.00

Strombecker, Thunderbolt Monza, Montgomery Wards, 1/32 scale, VG (orig box), P5......................$150.00

Strombecker, 4 Lane Mark IV Race Set, VG (orig box) .$250.00

Tyco, International Pro Racing Set, #930086, EX, P5 ...$125.00

Tyco, Skyclimbers Cliffhanger Set, complete, B10...........$40.00

Tyco TCR, Jam Car 500, #6330, 1991, MIB, P5 ....$60.00

Slot Cars Only

AMT, Cobra Roadster, 1/25 scale, light blue, complete, NMIB, A, $185.00.

Aurora, International Semi Tractor, #1580, gray, M, P5 ...$150.00

Aurora AFX, Autoworld Beamer, #5, wht w/bl stripes, EX, B10...........................$12.00

Aurora AFX, Autoworld McLaren XLR, #1752, orange & gray, EX, B10......................$14.00

Aurora AFX, Autoworld Porsche Can Am, wht w/bl, yel & red stripes, VG, B10.......................$12.00

Aurora AFX, Aztec Dragster, #1963, red, B10..................$20.00

Aurora AFX, Blazer Flamethrower, #1984, wht w/red, orange & yel, NM, B10........................$18.00

Aurora AFX, BMW MI, #1957, wht w/red & bl, EX, B10..$20.00

Aurora AFX, BMW 3201 Turbo, #6201, yel & orange, EX, B10.$15.00

Aurora AFX, Camaro Z-28, #1901, red, wht & bl, EX, B10 .$15.00

Aurora AFX, Capri, #13, wht, orange & red, EX, B10 .....$15.00

Aurora AFX, Capri Trans Am, wht w/bl & lime stripes, EX, B10...........................$16.00

Aurora AFX, Chevelle Stock Car, #1704, yel, red & blk, EX, B10...........................$16.00

Aurora AFX, Chevy Nomad, #1760, bl, EX, B10 ....$20.00

Aurora AFX, Chevy Nomad, #1760, chrome, EX, B10 ....$25.00

Aurora AFX, Chevy Nomad, #1760, orange, EX, B10 .....$20.00

Aurora AFX, Dodge Charger, #1773, lime & bl, NM, B10 ..$35.00

Aurora AFX, Dodge Charger Daytona, #1753, yel & blk, EX, B10...........................$20.00

Aurora AFX, Dodge Charger Daytona, #1900, bl & blk, EX, B10...........................$24.00

Aurora AFX, Dodge Charger Daytona, #1900, orange & blk, no wing, VG, B10 ....$10.00

Aurora AFX, Dodge Charger Stock Car, #11, wht w/blk hood, EX, B10...........................$15.00

Aurora AFX, Dodge Fever Dragster, wht & yel, no wheelie bar, EX, B10...........................$15.00

Aurora AFX, Dodge Police Van, wht w/blk stripe, VG, B10..$15.00

Aurora AFX, Ferrari, #1763, red & wht, EX, B10............$10.00

Aurora AFX, Ferrari 512M, #1763, wht & bl, EX, B10 ....$12.00

Aurora AFX, Firebird, #31965, blk & gold, EX+, B10......$15.00

Aurora AFX, Ford Baja Bronco, #1909, red, EX, B10.......$14.00

Aurora AFX, Ford Baja Bronco, #1969, yel & wht, NM, B10...........................$16.00

Aurora AFX, Ford Escort, #1944, charcoal, bl & red, EX, B10...........................$14.00

Aurora AFX, Furious Fueler Dragster, #1774, wht & yel, EX, B10...........................$15.00

Aurora AFX, Grand Am Funny Car, #1702, red, wht & bl, EX, B10...........................$12.00

Aurora AFX, Javelin AMX, #1906, bl & blk, EX, B10.....$16.00

Aurora AFX, Javelin AMX, #1906, chrome & red, EX, B10...$40.00

Aurora AFX, Jeep CJ-7 Flamethrower, #1987, orange & red, NM, B10 ....$20.00

Aurora AFX, Matador Police Car, bl, wht & blk, VG, B10..$12.00

Aurora AFX, Matador Stock Car, #1930, orange, blk & red, EX, B10...........................$18.00

Aurora AFX, Matador Taxi, wht, EX, B10 ....$16.00

Aurora AFX, Peace Tank, #1782, gr, NM, B10 ....$18.00

Aurora AFX, Peterbilt Lighted Rig, #1156, red & yel, EX, B10 ....$25.00

Aurora AFX, Peterbilt Sleeper Tanker (Shell), #1155, red, orange & wht, EX, B10.............................$25.00

Aurora AFX, Plymouth Roadrunner Stock Car, #1762, bl & wht, EX, B10.............................$30.00

Aurora AFX, Plymouth Roadrunner Stock Car, #1762, yel & orange, EX, B10 ....$18.00

Aurora AFX, Pontiac Grand Am, #10-191, red, wht & bl, EX, B10...........................$15.00

Aurora AFX, Porsche 510K, #1786, gold chrome w/orange stripe, EX, B10 ....$16.00

Aurora AFX, Porsche 917, #1757, wht & purple, EX, B10 ..$14.00

Aurora AFX, Porsche 917-10, #1747, wht, red & bl, EX, B10 .$12.00

Aurora AFX, Roarin' Rolls, wht & blk, EX, B10 ....$15.00

Aurora AFX, Shadow Can Am, #1908, blk, MIB.............$25.00

Aurora AFX, Thunderbird, #8752, red, wht & bl, NM, B10...$12.00

Aurora AFX, Turbo Turn On, #1755, orange, yel & purple, EX, B10..$15.00

Aurora AFX, Turbo Turn On, #1755, red, wht & bl, EX, B10..$14.00

Aurora AFX, Ultra 5 Shadow, #3007, type A, wht, red, orange & yel, MIB, P5..$25.00

Aurora AFX, Vega Van Gasser, #1754, yel & red, EX, B10 ....$15.00

Aurora AFX, 1929 Model A Woodie, blk, no grille, EX, B10 .$10.00

Aurora AFX, 1929 Model A Woodie, yel & brn, MIB, B10....$15.00

Aurora AFX, 1931 Model A Ford, #1791, lime & blk, EX, B10...$20.00

Aurora AFX, 1957 Chevy Nomad, bl, EX, B10 ....$22.00

Aurora AFX, 1957 Chevy Nomad, bl, G, B10 ....$10.00

Aurora G-Plus, Camaro (NASCAR), #76, wht, orange & gold, EX, B10..$12.00

Aurora G-Plus, Capri, #1935, wht, orange & maroon, EX, B10..$12.00

Aurora G-Plus, Capri, wht w/gr & bl stripe, EX, B10 ....$12.00

Aurora G-Plus, Corvette, #1011, red, orange & wht, EX, B10..$15.00

Aurora G-Plus, Ferrari F1, #1734, red & wht, EX, B10 ....$25.00

Aurora G-Plus, Foyt Indy Special, #1789, orange, EX, B10 ..$25.00

Aurora G-Plus, Indy Special, #1735, blk, red & orange, EX, B10..$18.00

Aurora G-Plus, Indy Valvoline, blk, VG, B10 ....$12.00

Aurora G-Plus, Lotus F1, #1783, blk & gold, EX, B10 .....$20.00

Aurora G-Plus, Lotus F1, blk & yel, EX, B10.................$14.00

Aurora G-Plus, Rallye Ford Escort, #1737, gr & bl, EX, B10 ..$15.00

Aurora G-Plus, Six Wheel Elf, #1738, bl & yel, EX, B10.$25.00

Aurora Screacher, Flaming Cuda, wht, red & orange, EX, B10..$12.00

Aurora Screacher, Pinto Thunderbolt, wht w/orange & red flames, EX, B10..$12.00

Aurora Thunderjet, Alfa Romeo Type 33, #1409, yel, EX, B10..$25.00

Aurora Thunderjet, Chaparral II, #1377, tan, no rear pipes, VG, B10..$20.00

Aurora Thunderjet, Chaparral 2F, #1410, lime & bl, EX, B10..$20.00

Aurora Thunderjet, Chaparral 2F, #1410, wht & bl, no wing, EX, B10..$24.00

Aurora Thunderjet, Cheetah, #1403, gr, EX, B10 ....$25.00

Aurora Thunderjet, Cheetah, #1403, orange, EX, B10 ....$25.00

Aurora Thunderjet, Chevy Baja Blazer #4, wht w/bl & red flames, EX, B10..$30.00

Aurora Thunderjet, Chevy Blazer, #2747, wht, red & blk, EX, B10..$30.00

Aurora Thunderjet, Cobra GT, #1375, yel w/blk stripe, VG...$35.00

Aurora Thunderjet, Cobra GT, #1396, bl & silver, EX, B10...$45.00

Aurora Thunderjet, Cobra GT Flamethrower, #1495, bl & wht, EX...$25.00

Aurora Thunderjet, Cougar, #1389, gr, EX, B10 ....$30.00

Aurora Thunderjet, Cougar, #1389, wht, NM, B10.........$35.00

Aurora Thunderjet, Dino Ferrari, #1381, turq w/blk stripe, EX, B10..$24.00

Aurora Thunderjet, Dino Ferrari, #1381, yel w/red stripe, EX, B10..$28.00

Aurora Thunderjet, Dune Buggy, red, no roof, EX, B10...$20.00

Aurora Thunderjet, Dune Buggy, wht w/red striped roof, EX, B10..$30.00

Aurora Thunderjet, Dune Buggy Coupe, #1399, red, EX, B10..$30.00

Aurora Thunderjet, Dune Buggy Roadster, #1398, bl & blk, EX, B10..$32.00

Aurora Thunderjet, Ferrari GTO Flamethrower, #1493, lt bl & wht, NM, B10..$25.00

Aurora Thunderjet, Ferrari GTO 250, #1368, red w/wht stripes, EX, B10..$25.00

Aurora Thunderjet, Ferrari GTO 250, #1368, tan w/blk stripes, EX, B10..$25.00

Aurora Thunderjet, Ford GT, #1374, bl w/wht stripe, G, B10..$14.00

Aurora Thunderjet, Ford GT, #1374, red w/wht stripe, VG (orig box), B10..$30.00

Aurora Thunderjet, Ford GT, #1374, turq w/blk stripe, EX, B10..$25.00

Aurora Thunderjet, Ford GT, bl w/wht stripe, EX, B10 ...$25.00

Aurora Thunderjet, Ford GT Flamethrower, #1494, lt bl, EX, B10..$25.00

Aurora Thunderjet, Ford GT 40, #1374, red w/blk stripe, EX, B10..$25.00

Aurora Thunderjet, Ford GT 40, #1374, tan w/blk stripe, EX, B10..$20.00

Aurora Thunderjet, Ford GT 40, #1374, wht w/blk stripe, EX, B10..$18.00

Aurora Thunderjet, Ford J Car, #1382, bl w/blk stripe, EX, B10..$20.00

Aurora Thunderjet, Ford J Car, #1430, red & blk, EX, B10..$20.00

Aurora Thunderjet, Ford J Car Flamethrower, wht w/bl stripe, EX, B10..$15.00

Aurora Thunderjet, Ford Lola GT, #1378, turq w/blk & wht stripe, VG, B10..$25.00

Aurora Thunderjet, HO Dune Buggy, wht w/red & wht striped top, EX, B10..$30.00

Aurora Thunderjet, Hot Rod Coupe, #1366, wht & red, NM, B10..$40.00

Aurora Thunderjet, Indianapolis Racer, #1359, red, no chassis, EX, B10..$25.00

Aurora Thunderjet, International Tow Truck, #1364, wht, red & blk, EX...$65.00

Aurora Thunderjet, Jaguar, red, VG, B10 ....$30.00

Aurora Thunderjet, Jaguar XKE, #1358, turq, EX, B10 ....$34.00

Aurora Thunderjet, Lola GT, #1378, blk w/red & wht stripe, EX, B10..$35.00

Aurora Thunderjet, Lola GT, #1378, gr w/wht stripe, EX, B10..$20.00

Aurora Thunderjet, Lola GT, #1378, tan w/blk & wht stripe, EX, B10..$24.00

Aurora Thunderjet, Mack Dump Truck, #1362, yel & gray, EX, B10..$48.00

Aurora Thunderjet, Mako Shark, #1380, turq, EX, B10...$24.00

Aurora Thunderjet, Mako Shark Corvette, #1380, red, VG, B10..$28.00

Aurora Thunderjet, Mangusta Mongoose, #1400, gr, EX, B10..$34.00

Aurora Thunderjet, McLaren Elva, #1397, wht, red & blk, EX, B10 ....$24.00

Aurora Thunderjet, McLaren Elva, #1431, wht w/red stripe, VG, B10 ....$22.00

Aurora Thunderjet, McLaren Elva Flamethrower, #1431, blk w/wht stripe, VG, B10 ....$20.00

Aurora Thunderjet, Mustang 2+2 Fastback, #1373, yel w/red stripe, EX, B10 ....$42.00

Aurora Thunderjet, Pontiac Firebird, #1402, wht, EX, B10....$35.00

Aurora Thunderjet, Porsche 904, #1376, bl w/wht stripes, EX, B10 ....$24.00

Aurora Thunderjet, Porsche 904, #1376, turq, VG, B10..$18.00

Aurora Thunderjet, Porsche 904, #1376, wht w/red stripe, VG, B10 ....$20.00

Aurora Thunderjet, Porsche 906GT, red w/wht stripe, VG, B10 ....$22.00

Aurora Thunderjet, Repco Bradham F1, #1406, gr & gold, EX, B10 ....$32.00

Aurora Thunderjet, Sand Van Dune Buggy, #1483, pk & wht, EX, B10 ....$25.00

Aurora Thunderjet, Snowmobile, #1485, bl & yel, EX, B10..$28.00

Aurora Thunderjet, Willie Gasser, #1401, dk gr, VG, B10 ....$25.00

Aurora Thunderjet, 1932 Ford Pickup, #1421, bl & blk, EX, B10 ....$85.00

Aurora Thunderjet, 1963 Corvette, #1356, red, no rear bumper, VG, B10 ....$25.00

Bachman, Chapparal 2F, lime, VG, B10 ....$20.00

Bachman, James Bond Corvette, silver & bl stripe, VG, B10..$40.00

Bachman, Toyota 2000GT, red & yel stripe, wht roof, VG, B10 ....$20.00

Bachman, Toyota 2000GT, wht, EX, B10 ....$25.00

Cox, Ferrari, #9400, red, EX, $75.00.

Lionel, Corvette, bl, EX, B10 ....$28.00

Lionel, Corvette, tan, w/spare tire, EX, B10......................$30.00

Monogram, Cooper Ford, #SR3204-598, VG (orig box), P5..$60.00

Revell, Carroll Shelby's Cobra Ford, #R3100-600, VG (orig box), P5 ....$60.00

Strombecker, Jaguar SKE, #9620/595, red, MIB, P5 ....$50.00

Strombecker, Willard Special (authentic model of Agajanian Williard Battery Special #98 driven by Parnelli Jones), MIB..................................$150.00

TCR, Blazer, blk & yel w/orange flames, EX, B10 ....$14.00

TCR, Jam Car, yel & blk, EX, B10..................................$14.00

TCR, Maintenance Van, wht & red, EX, B10......................$14.00

TCR, Mercury Stock Car, purple chrome, VG, B10.........$14.00

Tyco, A-Team Van, blk w/red stripe, EX, B10..................$38.00

Tyco, Autoworld Carrera, wht w/red, wht & bl stripe, G, B10..................................$10.00

Tyco, Bandit Pickup, blk & red, EX, B10........................$12.00

Tyco, Blackbird Firebird, Tyco, #6914, blk & gold, EX, B10..................................$12.00

Tyco, Blazer, red & blk, VG, B10..................................$10.00

Tyco, Camaro Z-28, bl w/wht & red stripe, EX, B10 ....$10.00

Tyco, Chaparral 2G, #8504, wht, no wing o/w VG, B10..$14.00

Tyco, Corvette, fluorescent yel w/blk stripes, EX, B10 .....$10.00

Tyco, Corvette, glow-in-the-dark, any color, EX, B10, ea ..$10.00

Tyco, Corvette, red w/blk & orange stripe, EX, B10.........$10.00

Tyco, Corvette, wht w/red & bl stripes, EX, B10..............$10.00

Tyco, Corvette Cliffhanger, wht w/red stripe, EX, B10 ....$10.00

Tyco, Corvette Curvehanger, silver chrome w/flames, no driver, EX, B10 ....$15.00

Tyco, Dominoes Pizza, red, wht & bl, no driver, EX, B10...$15.00

Tyco, Ferrari F-40, #8697, red, VG, B10........................$12.00

Tyco, Fiero #23, yel w/wht & orange stripe, EX, B10.......$12.00

Tyco, Firebird, #6914, cream & red, VG, B10 ....$12.00

Tyco, Firebird, #6944, blk & gold w/bird on hood, EX, B10...$10.00

Tyco, Firebird, blk & gold w/emblem on hood, EX, B10..$10.00

Tyco, Firebird #15, #7113, red & blk, EX, B10..............$10.00

Tyco, Firebird Stock Car #35, red & silver lettering, EX, B10..................................$10.00

Tyco, Firebird Turbo, red, wht & blk, EX, B10................$10.00

Tyco, Firebird Turbo #12, blk & gold, EX, B10 ....$10.00

Tyco, Ford 7-Eleven NASCAR, red, wht & bl, EX, B10 .$12.00

Tyco, Funny Mustang, orange & yel flames, EX, B10.......$25.00

Tyco, GMC Pickup Truck, cream w/fluorescent pk & orange stripe, EX, B10 ....$15.00

Tyco, Hardee's Car, orange & bl, EX, B10......................$14.00

Tyco, Hardee's Ford #28, red & wht, G, B10..................$12.00

Tyco, Highway Patrol #56, blk & wht, w/sound, NM, B10..$16.00

Tyco, HP7, blk w/flames, NM, B10..................................$15.00

Tyco, Indy Diehard, blk & gold, EX, B10 ....$12.00

Tyco, Indy Lotus 440X2 #12, butterscotch, NM, B10 ......$15.00

Tyco, Indy Pennzoil, yel, no front spoilers, EX, B10.........$15.00

Tyco, Javelin, red, wht & bl, VG+, B10 ....$15.00

Tyco, Jeep CJ7, red & lt bl, VG, B10..................................$12.00

Tyco, Jeep Renegade, silver w/blk roof, EX, B10 ....$14.00

Tyco, Lamborghini, red, VG, B10..................................$12.00

Tyco, Lamborghini, wht w/blk lettering, EX, B10 ....$10.00

Tyco, Lighted Porsche #2, silver w/red nose, EX, B10 ......$20.00

Tyco, Lighted Silverstreak Porsche 908, silver & red, EX, B10..................................$15.00

Tyco, Lighted Silverstreak Porsche 908 #3, silver & gr, VG, B10..................................$15.00

Tyco, Lighted Super America, #8525, red, wht & bl, EX, B10..................................$20.00

Tyco, Lola 260, #8514, red, wht & bl, EX, B10 ....$14.00

Tyco, Mack Truck, dk bl & blk, EX, B10........................$22.00

Tyco, McLaren M8F, #8503, blk & red stripe, EX, B10 ...$25.00

Tyco, Mustang #1, orange & yel flames, VG, B10............$20.00

Tyco, Porsche Carrera, #8527, yel w/blk hood, VG, B10 .$14.00

Tyco, Porsche Carrera Turbo #3, yel w/orange & red stripe, EX, B10 ....$14.00

Tyco, Porsche 908 #3, gr & silver, EX, B10 ....$16.00

Tyco, Rokar 240Z #7, blk, EX, B10 ....$10.00

Tyco, Silverstreak Carrera #18, silver & blk, G, B10 ....$12.00

Tyco, Silverstreak Pickup, silver w/pk & orange stripes, EX, B10 ....$15.00

Tyco, Silverstreak Porsche #917, #8544, silver & lime, VG, B10 ....$15.00

Tyco, Silverstreak Racing Corvette, #8556, silver w/pk & orange stripe, VG, B10 ....$15.00

Tyco, Superbird, #8533, red, wht & bl, crack in wing o/w VG+, B10 ....$15.00

Tyco, Thunderbird #15, red & yel VG, B10 ....$10.00

Tyco, Turbo Hopper #27, red, EX, B10 ....$12.00

Tyco, Turbo Hopper #49, blk, VG, B10 ....$10.00

Tyco, Turbo Porsche #3, yel w/orange & red stripe, EX, B10 ..$12.00

Tyco, Van-Tastic, #8539, bl & wht, VG, B10 ....$20.00

Tyco, 1940, Ford Coupe, #8534, blk w/flames, EX, B10 ...$20.00

Tyco, 1957 Chevy, red w/orange & yel stripes, missing side pipes o/w VG, B10 ....$14.00

Accessories

AFX Pit Kit, blk, G, P5 ....$15.00

Aurora AFX, Speed Steer Intersection Overpass, #6055, 1979, MIB, B10 ....$20.00

Aurora AFX Carrying Case, blk, 2-level, EX, B10 ....$12.00

Aurora AFX Speed Steer Breakout Wall, #6056, MIB, B10 ...$18.00

Aurora AFX Wall Power Pack, plug or wire style, EX, B10, ea ...$8.00

Aurora Loop the Loop Track, #1504, VG (orig box), P5 .$20.00

Aurora Model Motoring Auto Starter, #1507, 1960, EX (EX box), B10 ....$15.00

Aurora Model Motoring Monza Banked Curve, #1467, EX (EX box), B10 ....$15.00

Aurora Model Motoring Power Pack, 18 or 20 volt, EX, B10, ea $8.00

Aurora Model Motoring Start & Finish Pylons, MIB $15.00

Aurora Model Motoring Steering Wheel Controller, EX, B10 ....$10.00

Aurora Model Motoring 4-Way Stop Track, EX, B10 ......$15.00

Aurora Thunderjet Carrying Case, butterscotch, VG, B10 .....$8.00

Aurora Trestle Posts, #1530, boxed set of 12, VG, P5 ......$10.00

Aurora Wide Track Adapter, #1505, 0 gauge to HO, EX (orig box), P5 ....$20.00

Gilbert Autorama Automatic Lap Counter, #19339, MIB, B10 .$35.00

Strombecker Grandstand, #9399, EX $20.00

Strombecker Lane-Changing Track, #9388, EX $15.00

Strombecker Pagoda Control Tower, #9290, EX $20.00

Strombecker Pit Garage, #9798, EX $15.00

Strombecker Track Customizer, #9150, EX $2.00

Strombecker Utility Building, #9199, EX $15.00

Tyco Stick Shift 4-Speed Controller, EX, B10 ....$10.00

Smith-Miller

Smith-Miller (Los Angeles, California) made toy trucks from 1944 until 1955. During that time they used four basic cab designs, and most of their trucks sold for about $15.00 each.

Over the past several years, these toys have become very popular, especially the Mack trucks which today sell at premium prices. The company made a few other types of toys as well, such as the train toy box and the 'Long, Long Trailer.'

Advisor: Doug Dezso (D6).

Army Materials Truck, G $325.00

Bank of America Brinks Truck, 1950s, diecast cab w/pressed-steel body, 14", G+ $250.00

Camper, 1950s, aluminum w/steel roof, wood interior, 27", VG+, A $225.00

Camper, 1950s, aluminum w/steel roof, wood interior, 27", G, A $100.00

GMC Bekins Truck, VG $400.00

GMC Dump Truck, VG $250.00

GMC Low Boy Truck, EX $575.00

GMC Lyons Truck, G $250.00

GMC Searchlight Truck, no lens, VG $850.00

GMC Wrecker, rstr $275.00

Lyon Van Lines Mack Truck, silver w/bl fenders, 21, G, A ...$475.00

Mack Aerial Ladder Truck, 34", G, A $300.00

Mack PIE Truck, EX $650.00

Mobiloil Tanker Truck, red w/name & Pegasus logo, 14", VG, A $450.00

SMFD Aerial Ladder Truck, red with aluminum extension ladders, black tires, G, $500.00.

Transcontinental Freight Truck, EX $650.00

Snow Domes

Snow domes are water-filled paperweights that come in several different styles. The earliest type was made in two pieces and consisted of a glass globe on a separate base. First made in the middle of the 19th century, they were revived during the '30s and '40s by companies in America, Italy, and Germany. Similar weights are now being imported into the country from the Orient. The most common snow dome on today's market are the plastic half-moon shapes made as souvenirs or Christmas toys, a style that originated in West Germany during the 1950s. Other shapes were made as well, including round and square bottles, short and tall rectangles, cubes, and other simple shapes.

During the 1970s, figural plastic snow domes were especially popular. There are two types — large animate shapes themselves containing the snow scene, or dome shapes that have figures draped over the top. Today's collectors buy them all, old or new. For further information we recommend *Collector's Guide to Snow Domes* by Helene Guarnaccia, published by Collector Books.

Advisor: Nancy McMichael (M18).

ADVERTISING

Coca-Cola, Santa w/bottle, music box in base, MIB, T1 ..$30.00

Days Inn, Catch Some Rays at Days, w/2 Flintstone characters, sm oval plastic dome, M18 ....$10.00

Days Inn, The Whole Family Stays at Days, yel & turq, sm oval plastic dome, M18...$10.00

Jubileum Vodka, Forget Vodka With a Twist..., bottle inside, blk base, bullet-shaped plastic dome, 3½", M18 ....$15.00

Michelin Man, Mr Bib in mountains, European issue, MIB ...$30.00

Michelin Tires, Mr Bib in mountains, European promo, MIB, P12 ....$45.00

FIGURES

Bear, atop sm dome, Great Smoky Mountains on plaque, old, M18...$12.00

Bear, in Christmas hat & gr neck ribbon, no plaque, M18 .$9.00

Boot, Santa in sled w/pine trees & red church inside, plastic, old, M18 ....$7.00

Bugs Bunny, wood w/glass dome, VG...............................$95.00

Cat Playing Drum, drum as water compartment, M18........$9.00

Christmas Tree, w/lights & balls, old, M18......................$10.00

Coffeepot, clear plastic, girl & snowman inside, old, M18..$10.00

Creature From the Black Lagoon, MIB, J2 ....$15.00

Crucifiction, Montenero emb on flat panel, Madonna & Child before monastery, plastic ball, elongated base, M18 ..$25.00

Dog w/Christmas Gift, gift is water compartment, M18 .....$9.00

Fish, yel Florida or orange Canada, M18, ea $10.00

Frog, Puerto Rico, frog family inside, no seesaw, M18 ....$7.00

Gift Box, lg red bow at top, clear cube w/waving snowman inside, old, rare, M18..$15.00

Ice Mountain, 2 deer inside, sm, M18 ....$7.00

Photo courtesy Helene Guarnaccia.

Mickey Mouse in Space Suit, Monogram Products, EX, $45.00.

Orange, w/gr leaves...$15.00

Santa, climbing out of chimney, plastic, M18.....................$8.00

Santa on Lamppost, M18 ....$8.00

Santa w/Gift, atop lg oval dome, angel & deer inside, old, rare, M18...$12.00

Snowman, w/tall blk hat, red ear muffs & lg red smile, carrot nose broken off, tall, old, M18...................................$12.00

HOLIDAYS AND SPECIAL OCCASIONS

Christmas Carol, Tiny Tim on Bob Cratchit's shoulder w/Scrooge nearby, no plaque, wood base, lg glass dome, M18...$15.00

Merry Christmas to All, Enesco, 1987, Santa in sleigh flying around roof, EX, I2 ....$6.00

Rabbit, full-scale model w/Easter eggs at front, stands next to pine tree, Austrian, glass dome, new, M18 ....$10.00

Santa, 1950s, glass dome, EX, $40.00.

Photo courtesy Nancy McMichael.

Santa on Rocket, Marx, 1965, plastic dome, 2¼x3", M, P4 ..$55.00

Saturday Evening Post, Norman Rockwell Christmas, December 4, 1926, on brass plaque on wood base, lg glass dome, M18...$30.00

SOUVENIR AND COMMEMORATIVES

Alaska Bear, lg wht bear bending over stream, sm oval plastic dome, M18 ....$6.00

Artis Zoo, Amsterdam, penguins marching in a row, sm oval plastic dome, M18...$10.00

Atlanta, blk skyline in front of puffy bl & wht clouds, orange sun & plane, M18...$4.00

Bahamas 500th Anniversary, on Lucite panel, sailing ship w/1942-1992 on yel banner across sails, lg, M18 ....$10.00

Berlin Blelbt Doch Berlin (Berlin Will Always Be Berlin), West Germany, mc city scene, sm oval plastic dome, M18...$8.00

Big Merino Goulburn, NSW, Australia, huge sheep w/national flag at front, sm oval plastic dome, M18 ....$18.00

Blue Ridge Parkway, 2 blk bears on seesaw, gr hills & rainbow at back, sm oval plastic dome, M18................................$9.00

Buffalo, New York, buffalo before Niagara Falls & rainbow, sm oval plastic dome, M18.......................................$8.00

Cancun, Cozumel, Mexico, on outside at top, fish on string inside, lg plastic dome, M18 ....$8.00

Cancun, Mexico, in blk script on outside lip of lg dome, 2 pk dolphins inside, M18......................................$6.00

Cape Cod, 2 sailboats, sm oval plastic dome, old, M18 ......$7.00

Capri Grotta Azzurra, Blue Grotto in brilliant bl, lg plastic dome, M18 ....$10.00

Carcassonne, word on plaque, French town w/red roofs, sm oval plastic dome, M18 ....$8.00

Connoaut Lake Park, in Gothic letters on plaque, 2 Lucite panels of amusement park rides, sm plastic dome, M18.....$6.00

Cooper Union (NYC Building), detailed replica, clear all around, broad blk base w/gold decal, rnd, lg, M18.....$18.00

Cozumel, Mexico, script letters on outside of base at bottom, fish on string inside, sm plastic dome, M18 ....$6.00

Devon, England, lg letters on plaque, Lucite panel w/elf, owl & mushrooms, rainbow panel at back, plastic dome, M18..$8.00

Enchanted Forest, lg fairy tale character w/forest & castle on back panel, sm plastic dome, late 1980s, M18..............$7.00

Florida Snowman, w/top hat, cane & pipe, plaque on ea side, clear oval plastic dome, orig version, 1980, M18.........$6.00

General Jackson, letters on lg plaque at base of lg bottle, panel w/drawing of paddle-wheeler, M18..............................$8.00

Gillette Castle, Hadlyme, Connecticut, w/castle & trees, low rectangle form, old, M18 ....$10.00

Gillette Castle State Park, Connecticut, w/castle inside, 3 peg-leg style, old, M18..$10.00

Howe Caverns, New York, lg letters w/caverns & boat tour, lg plastic dome, M18 ....$8.00

Kansas City, written on wavy band over star & diamond on Lucite panel, flat rectangular dome, early, M18............$6.00

Lake George, sailboat on lake scene, lg plastic dome, M18...$6.00

Library of Congress, on Lucite panel w/building, mc panel of DC monuments, Washington DC at outside, lg blk dome, M18..$6.00

Louisville Zoo, wht letters on base, bears on Lucite panel, seals at front, turq, toaster-shaped dome, M18 ....$5.00

Maritime Lobster on Plaque, fishing village & lobster, sm oval plastic dome, M18..$8.00

Mayflower II, emb in gold on base, ship scale model inside, cube dome, old, M18..$10.00

Mayflower II, lg blk letters on plaque, lg sailing ship inside, sm oval plastic dome, M18..................................$12.00

Melbourne, Australia, wht letters on back of base, trolley moves on groove, buildings inside, blk plastic dome, M18 .....$7.00

Minnesota Common Loon, State Bird, lg loon & rainbow inside lg plastic dome, old, M18..$8.00

Myrtle Beach, South Carolina, blk letters on band at bottom across sailing scene inside, plastic dome, old, sm chip, M18..$8.00

Nashua, Iowa, Little Brown Church in Vale scene, flat-back plastic dome, old, M18..$9.00

Niagara Falls, Canada, lg red letters on plaque at bottle neck, sm boat & shore at back, plastic dome, M18....................$5.00

Oberammergau Passion Theatre on curved band at base of detailed town w/red-domed church, Germany, plastic dome, M18...$12.00

Oregon Coast, fish inside, treasure-chest form, M18 ....$7.00

Outer Banks, North Carolina, fish on string w/seaweed, low flat rectangular dome, words slightly faded, M18 ....$5.00

Paris, w/Eiffel Tower, Notre Dame & Sacre Coeur at back, glitter, lg plastic dome, M18 ....$7.00

Pittsburgh Post Extra! Feeney & Hirsh Marry, written newspaper pg, wedding couple & May 15, 1993, lg plastic dome, M18 .$12.00

Roman S Pietro, peasant woman & Swiss guard in front of St Peter's Cathedral, sm plastic dome, M18......................$7.00

San Francisco, California, red trolley moves on groove, city scene at back, sm plastic dome, old, M18....................$6.00

San Gimignano (Italy), medieval town w/7 towers & red roofs, lg plastic dome, M18...$10.00

San Gimignano (Italy), medieval town w/7 towers & red roofs, sm plastic dome, M18..$8.00

Save the Earth, birds on Lucite, lg blk dome, M18 ....$5.00

Save the Earth, forest animals, sm oval plastic dome, M18...$5.00

Sea World, San Diego, lg red letters on plaque at bottle neck, dolphin w/penguins against tree panel, old, M18 ......$10.00

Sears Tower, Chicago, lg blk letters, fat bullet-shaped dome, M18..$10.00

Six Flags Magic Mountain, calendar dome $15.00

Six Flags Over Georgia, calendar dome............................$15.00

Snowy Mountains, Australia, skier in orange suit, snow scene at back, M18 ....$10.00

Space Needle, Seattle, Washington, salt & pepper shakers, pk & bl plastic, tall popsicle shape, M18, pr $18.00

Squire Boone Caverns & Village, Squire Boone w/whiskey still & geological formation, flat rectangular dome, M18 ...$8.00

SS Admiral River Boat, 2 plaques inside bottle, St Louis plaque at neck, Arch & Stadium at back, water loss, rare, M18....$18.00

St Augustine, Florida, fish on string, glitter, low rectangular dome w/blk rim, old, M18................................$7.00

St Francis Indian Mission, Stone Lake, Wisconsin, Mission School building on panel, lg plastic dome, M18........$12.00

St Thomas, Virgin Islands, parrot inside, sm oval plastic dome, M18..$10.00

Ste Anne de Beaupre (Canada), church & Sainte Anne, lg plastic dome, late 1980s, M18..$8.00

Sunsphere, Knoxville, Tennessee, w/Tower from World's Fair, tall popsicle form, old, rare version, M18..................$13.00

Taronga Zoo, tigers inside w/1 on lg dome, Australia, M18 ..$10.00

United Nations, written on blk base, UN building inside, heart-shaped dome, M18..$10.00

Nautilus Atomic Sub, glass dome, EX, $50.00; War Between the States, plastic dome, $15.00.

US Constitution, open-work ship inside, plastic dome, old, M18..**$12.00**

USS Massachusettes, Fall River, Massachusetts, lg gray battle-ship, sky panel at back, glitter, 1960s, G-, M18.........**$10.00**

Venice, Florida, script on outside of base, 2 pk dolphins & sea-weed, sm oval plastic dome, M18 ....**$6.00**

Williamsburg, Virginia, scene w/house, carriage & church in front, bottle form, minor water loss, M18.....................**$9.00**

Wisconsin, blk w/state name in wht script letters outside, Lucite cow panel before barn scene, sm plastic dome, M18....**$3.00**

Wisconsin, deer in center of seesaw, pine trees on ends, barn & cows at back, sm oval plastic dome, M18 ....**$5.00**

Wonderful World of Disney, 1960s, plastic, shows Mickey & Minnie w/castle in background, EX, P6 ....**$50.00**

Soldiers

'Dimestore soldiers' were made from the 1920s until some-time in the 1960s. Some of the better-known companies who made these small-scale figures and accessories were Barclay, Manoil, and Jones (hollow cast lead); Gray Iron (cast iron); and Auburn (rubber). They're about 3" to 3½" high. They were sold in Woolworth's and Kresge's 5 & 10 stores (most for just five cents), hence the name 'Dimestore.' Marx made tin soldiers for use in target gun games; these sell for about $8.00. Condition is most important as these soldiers saw a lot of action. They're most often found with much of the paint worn off and with some serious 'battle wounds' such as missing arms or legs. Nearly two thousand different figures were made by the major manufactur-ers, plus a number of others by minor makers such as Tommy Toy and All-Nu. Serious collectors should refer to *Collecting Toys* (1993) or *Toy Soldiers* (1992), both by Richard O'Brien, Books Americana.

Another very popular line of toy soldiers has been made by Britains of England since 1893. They are smaller and usually more detailed than 'Dimestores,' and variants number in the thousands. O'Brien's book has over two hundred pages devoted to Britains and other foreign makers.

You'll notice that in addition to the soldiers, many of our descriptions and values are for the vehicles, cannons, animals, and cowboys and Indians made and sold by the same manufacturers. Note: Percentages in the description lines refer to the amount of original paint remaining, a most important evaluation factor.

Advisors: Sally and Stan Alekna (A1).

See also Dinky; Plastic Figures.

Auburn Rubber, Marmon-Harrington tank, 3¼", NM, A1 ..**$38.00**

Auburn Rubber, soldier, crawling, rifle over shoulder, very scarce, 99%, A1 ....**$84.00**

Auburn Rubber, soldier, machine gunner, charging, early sm version, scarce, 99%, A1 ....**$49.00**

Auburn Rubber, soldier, marching, pot arms, early version, NM, A1 ....**$19.00**

Auburn Rubber, soldier, observer w/binoculars, 97%, A1 .**$20.00**

Auburn Rubber, stretcher bearer, scarce, 95%, A1 ....**$37.00**

Barclay, AA gun truck, 4", 97%, A1 ....**$53.00**

Barclay, aircraft carrier, no planes, very scarce, 97%, A1 .**$93.00**

Barclay, airplane, 1930s, very scarce, NM, $95.00.

Barclay, aviator, khaki, 98%, A1 ....**$22.00**

Barclay, boy, gray, 99%, A1 ....**$15.00**

Barclay, cannon, silver, open hitch, sm, 99%, A1 ....**$20.00**

Barclay, cavalryman, gray horse, 1930, sm, 98%, A..........**$34.00**

Barclay, coach w/driver & footman, gold w/red wheels, team of gray horses, scarce, 95%, A1....................................**$85.00**

Barclay, cook w/roast, 96%, A1 ....**$34.00**

Barclay, cowboy w/lasso, in wht, partial lasso, 98%, A1 ...**$17.00**

Barclay, cowboy w/rifle, 96%, A1 ....**$18.00**

Barclay, doctor, wht w/bl cross, brn bag, 98%, A1 ....**$29.00**

Barclay, fireman w/axe, flat base, scarce, 97%, A1 ....**$32.00**

Barclay, fireman w/axe, 97%, A1 ....**$28.00**

Barclay, grenade throwers, #738, extremely rare, from $550.00 to $625.00 each.

Barclay, horse, blk work-type, 98%, A1 ....**$15.00**

Barclay, horse-drawn sleigh w/couple, 99%, A1 ....**$70.00**

Barclay, Indian on horse firing rifle, scarce, 97%, A1.......**$48.00**

Barclay, Indian on rearing horse, scarce, 96%, A1...........**$51.00**

Barclay, Indian w/bow & arrow, 99%, A1 ....**$19.00**

Barclay, Indian w/spear, 99%, A1 ....**$19.00**

Barclay, knight w/pennant, 99%, A1 ....**$24.00**

Barclay, mailman, NM, A1 ....**$19.00**

Barclay, man on sled, 98%, A1 ....**$20.00**

Barclay, man passenger, 98%, A1 ....**$14.00**

Barclay, man skier, 99%, A1 ....**$26.00**

Barclay, marine, pod foot, 98%, A1 ....**$19.00**

Barclay, mechanic w/plane engine, scarce, 98%, A1 ....**$68.00**

Barclay, medical truck, w/Red Cross decal, ca 1960s, 97%, A1..**$19.00**

Barclay, motor unit, khaki w/wht tires, wire hitch, 97%, A1 ..**$29.00**

Barclay, motorcycle cop, EX, $65.00; Manoil, bicycle dispatch rider, EX, $48.00.

Britains Farm, complete, MIB, D10, from $175.00 to $275.00.

Barclay, naval officer, long stride, 98%, A1 ....$22.00
Barclay, nurse, bl cross, blond hair, 98%, A1 ....$25.00
Barclay, officer, gr, 99%, A1 ....$20.00
Barclay, officer, khaki, 98%, A1 ....$16.00
Barclay, officer w/sword, short stride, tin helmet, early version, 98%, A $27.00
Barclay, sailor, flag bearer, 97%, A1 ....$39.00
Barclay, sailor in bl, brn hair, 98%, A1 ....$22.00
Barclay, soldier, AA gunner, cast helmet, 99%, A1 ....$31.00
Barclay, soldier, at attention w/right shoulder arms, 93%, A1 ....$15.00
Barclay, soldier, at port arms, tin helmet, 99%, A1 ....$26.00
Barclay, soldier, bayonetting, scarce, rusty helmet, 94%, A1..$64.00
Barclay, soldier, bomb thrower, khaki, 98%, A1 ....$22.00
Barclay, soldier, bugler, khaki, 97%, A1 ....$18.00
Barclay, soldier, charging, gr, M, A1 ....$23.00
Barclay, soldier, charging, short stride, tin helmet, 97%, A1 .$27.00
Barclay, soldier, charging w/tommy gun, 98%, A1 ....$22.00
Barclay, soldier, clubbing w/rifle, cast helmet, very scarce, 95%, A1 ....$195.00
Barclay, soldier, crawling w/rifle, 99%, A1.......................$30.00
Barclay, soldier, dispatcher w/dog, scarce, 95%, A1..........$74.00
Barclay, soldier, flag bearer, flag on right, scarce, 95%, A1 ..$20.00
Barclay, soldier, flame thrower, gr, M, A1........................$22.00
Barclay, soldier, grenade thrower, 94%, A1 ....$16.00
Barclay, soldier, machine gunner, gr, 99%, A1 ....$21.00
Barclay, soldier, machine gunner, kneeling, short stride, 98%, A1 ....$24.00
Barclay, soldier, machine gunner, lying flat, M, A1..........$25.00
Barclay, soldier, marching w/pack, cast helmet, scarce, NM, A1 ....$43.00
Barclay, soldier, marching w/rifle, cast helmet, 99%, A1 .$39.00
Barclay, soldier, marching w/rifle, khaki, 98%, A1 ....$15.00
Barclay, soldier, on parade, long stride, 98%, A1 ....$22.00
Barclay, soldier, pigeon dispatcher, M, A1 ....$20.00
Barclay, soldier, pod foot; w/bazooka, khaki, bl barrel, 99%, A1 ....$19.00
Barclay, soldier, running, tin helmet, 97%, A1................$32.00
Barclay, soldier, seated w/rifle, tin helmet, scarce, 98%, A1 .$38.00
Barclay, soldier, sharpshooter, cast helmet, 99%, A1 ....$22.00
Barclay, soldier, sniper kneeling, gr, scarce, M, A............$28.00
Barclay, soldier, telephone operator, 95%, A1.................$25.00
Barclay, soldier, under marching orders, khaki, 99%, A1 .$26.00
Barclay, soldier, w/shell, 98%, A1 ....$20.00
Barclay, train conductor, HO scale, 98%, A1 ....$9.00

Britains, #1, Life Guards, 13-pc, EX+, A $175.00
Britains, #2, Royal Guardsmen, 16-pc, EX-M, A............$200.00
Britains, #7, Royal Fusiliers (City of London Regiment), 1930, 8-pc, EX (VG box), A..$300.00
Britains, #9, Rifle Brigade, 1900, 8-pc, G, A $300.00
Britains, #15, Argyll & Sutherland Highlanders, 8-pc, G (G box), A..$150.00
Britains, #16, East Kent Regiment (The Buffs), 9-pc, 1937, G-EX (VG Whisstock box), A $225.00
Britains, #24, 9th Queen's Royal Lancers, 5-pc, VG, A $150.00
Britains, #27, US Infantry, 1935, 8-pc, G-EX (Whisstock box), A..$160.00
Britains, #28, Mountain Gun of the Royal Artillery, 1930, 12-pc, G-EX (G Whisstock box), A..............................$425.00
Britains, #29, Royal Guardsmen, 16-pc, EX-M, A..........$200.00
Britains, #31, 1st Dragoons (The Royals), 1930, 5-pc, G (G box), A..$275.00
Britains, #33, 16th Lancers, 1900, 4-pc (partial set), G, A $200.00
Britains, #35, Royal Marine Artillery, 1925, 8-pc, G, A $350.00
Britains, #36, Royal Sussex Regiment, 7-pc, EX-M (EX box), A..$150.00
Britains, #39, Royal Horse Artillery, 13-pc, M (G- box), A.$285.00
Britains, #45, 3rd Madras Light Cavalry, 1920, 5-pc, G-EX (VG Soldiers box), A..$400.00
Britains, #46, 10th Duke of Cambridge's Own Bengal Lancers, 1920, 5-pc, G-EX (EX Sons of the Empire box), A ..$425.00
Britains, #48, Egyptian Camel Corps, 3-pc, EX-M (EX box), A..$225.00
Britains, #66, 13th Duke of Conaught's Own Lancers, 6-pc, M (EX box), A..$135.00
Britains, #68, 2nd Bombay Native Infantry, 1930, 8-pc, G-EX (VG Soldiers box), A..$650.00
Britains, #74, Royal Welch Fusiliers, 8-pc, M (EX Soldiers box), A..$150.00
Britains, #75, Scots Guards, 7-pc, EX-M (EX box), A $170.00
Britains, #77, Gordon Highlanders, 6-pc, G-EX (EX box), A..$170.00
Britains, #79, Royal Navy Landing Party, 1940, 11-pc, G-EX (G Regiments of All Nations box), A $325.00
Britains, #81, 17th Lancers, dtd 1902, 8-pc, G, A $350.00
Britains, #82, Colours & Pioneers of the Scots Guards, ca 1930, 8-pc, G (G box), A..$250.00
Britains, #88, Seaforth Highlanders Charging, 16-pc, VG (G Whisstock box), A..$375.00

Britains, #90, Coldstream Guards, 30-pc, EX (Whisstock box), A $450.00

Britains, #98, King's Royal Rifle Corps, 8-pc, G-EX (VG Whisstock box), A $250.00

Britains, #100, 21st Lancers (Empress of India's), 1930, 5-pc, G-EX (VG box), A $325.00

Britains, #101, Band of the Life Guards Mounted, 12-pc, G (G box), A $325.00

Britains, #112, Seaforth Highlanders, 1930, 8-pc, G-EX (G Whisstock box), A $250.00

Britains, #113, East Yorkshire Regiment, 1930, 8-pc, G-, A $225.00

Britains, #115, Egyptian Cavalry, 1960, 4-pc, EX (VG box), A $100.00

Britains, #116, Soudanese Infantry, 1930, 8-pc, EX (VG box), A $500.00

Britains, #117, Egyptian Infantry, 1957-59, 8-pc, EX-M (EX box), A $250.00

Britains, #123, Bikanir Camel Corps, 3-pc, G (G Types of the Indian Army box), A $475.00

Britains, #124, Irish Guard, 1940, 8-pc, EX (VG Whisstock box), A $300.00

Britains, #127, 7th Dragoon Guards, 1925, 5-pc, G, A $200.00

Britains, #142, French Army Zouaves Charging, 7-pc, EX+ (VG box), A $150.00

Britains, #143, French Navy Matelots, 8-pc, rare, EX-M (VG Armies of the World box), A $1,000.00

Britains, #147, Zulus of Africa, 8-pc, EX (EX box), A $275.00

Britains, #152, North American Indians, 4-pc, M (M Wild West box), A $200.00

Britains, #159, British Expeditionary Force Cavalry, 1920, 5-pc, G (G box), A $325.00

Britains, #164, Bedouin Arabs, 5-pc, EX (EX Whisstock box), A $325.00

Britains, #165, Italian Cavalry, 1935, 5-pc, EX (G Whisstock box), A $1,200.00

Britains, #167, Turkish Infantry Standing on Guard in Review Order, 1935, 8-pc, EX (G Whisstock box), A $350.00

Britains, #170, Greek Cavalry Mounted at the Trot in Review Order, 1925, 5-pc, G (G Types of the Greek Army box), A $700.00

Britains, #186, Mexican Infantry (Los Rurales de la Federacion), 1937-41, 8-pc, EX (G Whisstock box), A $600.00

Britains, #189, Belgian Infantry, 1930, 8-pc, EX (EX Types of the Belgian Army box), A $325.00

Britains, #194, British Army Machine Gun Section, 1925, 6-pc, G (VG box), A $150.00

Britains, #196, Greek Evzones, 8-pc, G-EX (G box), A $185.00

Britains, #198, British Infantry in Action w/Gas Masks, 1930, 4-pc, G-EX (VG Whisstock box), A $225.00

Britains, #199, Motor Machine Gun Corps, 3-pc, EX (G Whisstock box), A $425.00

Britains, #201, Officers of the General Staff, 1930, 4-pc, EX (VG box), A $225.00

Britains, #206, Royal Warwickshire Regiment, early version, 8-pc, G (VG Whisstock box), A $700.00

Britains, #208, North American Indians Mounted & on Foot, 11-pc, M (VG box), A $325.00

Britains, #212, Royal Scots, 1940, 5-pc, M (EX box), A $250.00

Britains, #216, Argentine Infantry, 1948-49, 6-pc, EX (G- box), A $300.00

Britains, #217, Argentine Cavalry, 1940, 5-pc, EX (EX Types of the Argentine Army box), A $350.00

Britains, #220, Uruguayan Cavalry (Artgas Lancers), postwar version, 4-pc, EX (EX box), A $350.00

Britains, #221, Uruguayan Military School Cadets, 1950, 8-pc, EX (VG box), A $400.00

Britains, #222, Uruguayan Infantry, 1935, 8-pc, EX (VG Types of Uruguayan Army box), A $900.00

Britains, #226, West Point Cadets, 1925, 8-pc, G, A $60.00

Britains, #226, West Point Cadets, 1930, 8-pc, G-EX (EX Whisstock box), A $150.00

Britains, #227, US Infantry, 8-pc, G, A $130.00

Britains, #228, US Marines, 1925, 8-pc, EX (EX box), A $260.00

Britains, #228, US Marines, 1925, 8-pc, G, A $50.00

Britains, #229, US Cavalry, 5-pc, G-EX (VG Whisstock box), A $200.00

Britains, #232, US Infantry, Marines & West Point Cadets, 24-pc, EX-M (EX box), A $375.00

Britains, #240, Royal Air Force, 1925, 8-pc, G-EX (G Whisstock box), A $300.00

Britains, #241, Chinese Infantry, 1930, 8-pc, EX (VG box), A $375.00

Britains, #242, US Infantry w/Mounted Officer, 1930, 7-pc, EX (G Types of USA Forces box), A $250.00

Britains, #258, British Infantry, 1930, 8-pc, G-EX (G- Whisstock box), A $160.00

Britains, #273, Imperial Russian Cosacks, 4-pc, M (M box), A $120.00

Britains, #312, Grenadier Guards, 8-pc, M (EX Soldiers box), A $200.00

Britains, #320, Royal Army Medical Corps Doctors & Nurses, 1935, 8-pc, G (G box), A $170.00

Britains, #359, US Army Machine Gunners, 1930, 6-pc, G (G Whisstock box), A $275.00

Britains, #396, 11th Hussars, 1940, 6-pc, G-EX (G Armies of the World box), A $700.00

Britains, #400, Life Guards, 5-pc, G-EX (VG box), A ...$110.00

Britains, #429, Scots Guards & The Life Guards in Winter Dress, 13-pc, EX-M (VG box), A $350.00

Britains, #437, Officers of the Gordon Highlanders, ca 1925, 5-pc, EX (VG Types of the British Army box), A $750.00

Britains, #1253, US Navy (White Jackets), 8-pc, G (VG box), A $120.00

Britains, #1260, British Infantry in Service Dress, 1935, 15-pc (partial set), G-EX, A $225.00

Britains, #1265, Howitzer, 1920, 18", G (G box), A $160.00

Britains, #1283, Grenadier Guards, 8-pc, M (EX Soldiers box), A $125.00

Britains, #1284, Royal Marines, 16-pc, G-EX (G box), A ..$275.00

Britains, #1290, British Infantry Band of the Line, 1930, 11-pc, G-EX, A $180.00

Britains, #1291, Band of the Royal Marines, 12-pc, G-EX (G box), A $225.00

Britains, #1294, British Infantry in Tropical Dress, 1935, 8-pc, G (G Armies of the World box), A $300.00

Britains, #1320, British Infantry, 1935, 9-pc, G-EX (G box), A $200.00

Britains, #1327, Grenadier Guards, 14-pc, M (EX box), A ..$200.00

Britains, #1329, Royal Army Service Corps General Service Limered Wagon, 1935, 4-pc, G-EX (G box), A $600.00

Britains, #1335, British Army 6-Wheel Lorry, postwar, 2-pc, EX (EX box), A $225.00

Britains, #1343, Royal Horse Guards, 5-pc, EX (VG box), A ..$275.00

Britains, #1383, Belgian Infantry of the Line, 14-pc, EX (G box), A $250.00

Britains, #1389, Belgian Infantry, 1940, 8-pc, G-EX (VG Armies of the World box), A $250.00

Britains, #1424, Bodyguard of the Emperor of Abyssinia, 1935, 8-pc, G-EX (G Armies of the World box), A $300.00

Britains, #1425, Abyssinian Tribesmen, 8-pc, G-EX (EX box), A $180.00

Britains, #1432, British 10-Wheeled Army Covered Tender, pre-war version, 2-pc, G (G box), A $225.00

Britains, #1433, British Army Covered Tender (Caterpiller Type), postwar version, 2-pc, EX (EX box), A $250.00

Britains, #1436, Italian Infantry in Foreign Service Dress, 1940, 8-pc, G (G Armies of the World box), A $375.00

Britains, #1437, Italian Carabinieri, 1939-41, 7-pc, G-EX (G box), A $200.00

Britains, #1462, Royal Artillery Caterpillar Covered Lorry w/Gun, 1935, 5-pc, G-EX (VG box), A $450.00

Britains, #1470, Her Majesty's State Coach, 11-pc, M (G Historical box), A $285.00

Britains, #1473, King George VI in Coronation Robes, pnt version, lg scale, VG (VG box), A................................$200.00

Britains, #1475, Attendants to the State Coach, 18-pc, EX (VG box), A..$425.00

Britains, #1477, State Coach & Procession, 44-pc, G (G- box), A $630.00

Britains, #1510, Royal Navy (Blue Jackets), 8-pc, M (VG box), A $150.00

Britains, #1512, British Army Ambulance, 4-pc, M (EX box), A $200.00

Britains, #1519, Waterloo Period Highlanders, 9-pc, EX (VG box), A $250.00

Britains, #1527, Royal Air Force Band, 1938, 12-pc, G, A....$200.00

Britains, #1527, Royal Air Force Band, 1938, 12-pc, M (G box), A $500.00

Britains, #1537, Territorial Infantry, 1940, 8-pc, rare, EX (VG Types of the Territorial Army box), A $1,500.00

Britains, #1543, New Zealand Infantry, 1937-41, 8-pc, rare, EX (VG Types of the Colonial Army box), A $900.00

Britains, #1544, Australian Infantry, 1940, 8-pc, G-EX (VG Types of the Colonial Army box), A $275.00

Britains, #1554, Royal Canadian Mounted Police, 1960, 6-pc, EX, A $60.00

Britains, #1554, Royal Canadian Mounted Police, 1960, 7-pc, EX (G Whisstock box), A $185.00

Britains, #1555, Changing of the Guard at Buckingham Palace, 83-pc, G-EX (VG box), A $1,600.00

Britains, #1598, Trooping of the Color, 11-pc, M (M box), A .$80.00

Britains, #1603, Irish Free State Infantry, EX (VG Armies of the World box), A $450.00

Britains, #1612, British Infantry, 1938-40, 8-pc, EX (VG box), A $160.00

Britains, #1614, British Infantry in Action w/Gas Masks, 1940, 21-pc, EX-M (VG box), A $250.00

Britains, #1620, Royal Marine Light Infantry, 1940, 10-pc, G-EX, A $200.00

Britains, #1630, Royal Canadian Dragoons, 5-pc, rare, G, A $350.00

Britains, #1631, Canadian Govenor General's Horse Guards, 5-pc, EX (M box), A $160.00

Britains, #1634, Canadian Governor General's Foot Guards, 8-pc, G-EX (VG box), A $160.00

Britains, #1640, Anti-Aircraft Searchlight, prewar version, EX (VG box), A $150.00

Britains, #1641, Heavy Duty Underslung Lorry, 1938, 2-pc, G-, A $120.00

Britains, #1662, Knight of Agincourt Mounted w/Standard, VG+, A $180.00

Britains, #1663, Knight of Agincourt Mounted w/Lance, VG, A $150.00

Britains, #1711, French Foreign Legion, 7-pc, EX (EX Whisstock box), A $300.00

Britains, #1720, Mounted Band of the Scots Greys, 7-pc, G ..$200.00

Britains, #1722, Pipe Band of Scots, 22-pc, EX-M, A $350.00

Britains, #1723, Royal Army Medical Corps Stretcher Bearer's Unit, 9-pc, EX-M (VG box), A $325.00

Britains, #1730, Royal Artillery Team of Gunners, 1939-41, 7-pc, EX (VG Whisstock box), A $160.00

Britains, #1749, Barrage Balloon w/Winch, 2-pc, rare, G (G box), A $1,200.00

Britains, #1759, Air Raid Precautions Stretcher Party Squad & Gas Detector, 9-pc, G (G box), A $900.00

Britains, #1791, Royal Corps of Signals Motorcycle Dispatch Riders, 4-pc, EX (VG box), A $300.00

Britains, #1793, British Army Motor Machine Gun Corps, 1940, 2-pc, EX (VG box), A $170.00

Britains, #1795, Life Guards at the Gallop, 1940, 6-pc, EX $425.00

Britains, #1850, Netherlands Infantry, 1939-41, 8-pc, rare, EX (G box), A $1,200.00

Britains, #1856, Polish Infantry, 1940, 8-pc, EX (VG Armies of the World box), A $700.00

Britains, #1877, Beetle Lorry Light Troop Transport, 2-pc, EX (EX box), A $160.00

Britains, #1892, Indian Army Infantry, 8-pc, EX (G Types of the Colonial Army box), A $400.00

Britains, #1893, Indian Army Service Corps, 1940, 7-pc, G-EX (VG Types of the Colonial Army box), A $160.00

Britains, #1895, Pilots of the German Luftwaffe, 8-pc, rare, G- (G Armies of the World box), A $750.00

Britains, #1898, British Infantry in Battledress, 1940, 8-pc, EX (G box), A $100.00

Britains, #1901, Capetown Highlanders, 8-pc, EX-M (G Regiments box), A $100.00

Britains, #1902, Union of the South Africa Defense Forces (Infantry), 8-pc, rare, EX (G Armies of the World box), A $1,900.00

Britains, #1907, British Army Staff Officers, khaki service dress, 5-pc, EX (G box), A $275.00

Britains, #1911, Officers & Petty Officers of the Royal Navy, EX (EX box), A $225.00

Britains, #1918, Home Guard, 8-pc, EX (EX #1854 box), A ..$300.00

Britains, #1980, US Infantry Marching, 7-pc, M (M box), A...$60.00

Britains, #2008, Royal Artillery Gun & Limber, 2-pc, M (VG box), A $100.00

Britains, #2009, Belgian Grenadiers, 8-pc, EX (EX box), A ..$150.00

Britains, #2018, Danish Guard Hussar Regiment (Display Set), 8-pc, EX-M (G box), A $700.00

Britains, #2019, Danish Life Guards, 7-pc, EX-M (VG box), A $325.00

Britains, #2021, US Snowdrops' MP, 8-pc, M (G Regiments box), A $260.00

Britains, #2022, Papal Swiss Guards, 9-pc, G-EX (VG box), A $275.00

Britains, #2027, Soviet Army Red Guards, 8-pc, EX-M (EX box), A $180.00

Britains, #2028, Red Army Cavalry, 5-pc, G-EX (VG box), A $150.00

Britains, #2030, Australian Infantry, 8-pc, EX-M (EX box), A $200.00

Britains, #2033, US Infantry, 8-pc, EX (VG box), A $100.00

Britains, #2044, US Air Corps, 1949, 7-pc, EX-M, A $125.00

Britains, #2046, Arabs of the Desert Mounted & on Foot, 12-pc, EX (G box), A $475.00

Britains, #2051, Uruguayan Military School Cadets, 1953-59, 8-pc, G-EX (G box), A $150.00

Britains, #2055, Confederate Cavalry, 5-pc, G (VG box), A ..$130.00

Britains, #2057, Union Artillery Gun w/Gunners, 3-pc, EX (EX box), A $110.00

Britains, #2058, Confederate Artillery Gun w/Gunners, 3-pc, EX (EX box), A $120.00

Britains, #2059, Union Infantry in Action, 7-pc, EX (EX box), A $100.00

Britains, #2060, Confederate Infantry in Action, 7-pc, EX-M (VG box), A $140.00

Britains, #2063, Argyll & Sutherland Highlanders, 6-pc, EX-M (VG box), A $130.00

Britains, #2065, Queen Elizabeth on horse, EX, A, $50.00.

Britains, #2067, Sovereign Standard of the Life Guards & Escort, 7-pc, EX (NM box), A $325.00

Britains, #2071, Royal Marines, 7-pc, EX (VG box), A .$170.00

Britains, #2072, King's Royal Rifle Corps, 1953-59, 8-pc, EX (G box), A...$250.00

Britains, #2073, Royal Air Force, 8-pc, EX-M (EX box), A ..$140.00

Britains, #2074, 1st King's Dragoon Guards, 5-pc, EX (VG box), A...$140.00

Britains, #2075, 7th Queen's Own Hussars, 4-pc, EX-M (G Nations box), A...$115.00

Britains, #2076, 12th Royal Lancers, 5-pc, EX (VG box), A..$100.00

Britains, #2079, Royal Co of Archers (The Queen's Bodyguard for Scotland), 13-pc, M (VG box), A $375.00

Britains, #2080, Royal Navy Sailors, 8-pc, M (EX box), A....$200.00

Britains, #2082, Coldstream Guards, 8-pc, EX (EX box), A..$250.00

Britains, #2083, Welsh Guards, 7-pc, G-EX (EX box), A......$140.00

Britains, #2084, Colour Party of the Scots Guards, 6-pc, EX-M, (G Regiments box), A...$375.00

Britains, #2088, Duke of Cornwall's Light Infantry, 1954-59, 8-pc, G-EX (G box), A...$350.00

Britains, #2089, Gloucestershire Regiment, 8-pc, M, A ..$150.00

Britains, #2095, French Foreign Legion in Action, 1960, 12-pc, G-EX (G box), A...$300.00

Britains, #2104, Venezuelan Infantry, 7-pc, EX-M (EX box), A...$325.00

Britains, #2110, US Military Band, yellow and black uniforms, rare, EX (G box), A, $4,500.00.

Britains, #2117, Band of the US Army, 12-pc, EX (G Britains box), A...$500.00

Britains, #2118, Life Guards, 11-pc, M (EX box), A $150.00

Britains, #2148, Fort Henry Guard, 7-pc, EX-M (VG box), A...$100.00

Britains, #2175, Self-Propelled Gun, 155mm, EX+ (VG box), A...$450.00

Britains, #2185, Bahamas Police Band, 15-pc, G, A.......$500.00

Britains, #4434, Confederate Forces w/Gun, 10-pc, M (G boxes), A $100.00

Britains, #5188, Seaforth Highlanders, limited issue, 11-pc, M (M boxes), A $285.00

Britains, #5290, Royal Scots Dragoon Guards, limited issue, 8-pc, M (M boxes), A...$150.00

Britains, #5400, Life Guards, 5-pc, EX (VG box), A......$110.00

Britains, #8825, Gun Team of the Royal Horse Artillery, new collector series, 8-pc, M (EX box), A.......................$170.00

Britains, #8912, Premier Series, 6-pc, M (EX box), A....$180.00

Britains, #9104, Attendants to the State Coach, 6-pc, M (M see-through box), A..$140.00

Britains, #9105, Life Guards, 5-pc, M (M box), A..........$100.00

Britains, #9121, Grenadier Guards Marching, 7-pc, M (EX box), A...$100.00

Britains, #9127, Welch Guards at Ease, 6-pc, M (EX box), A..$95.00

Britains, #9131, Gordon Highlanders, 5-pc, M (M box), A...$200.00

Britains, #9133, Argyll & Sutherland Highlanders, 5-pc, M (M box), A...$125.00

Britains, #9135, Black Watch Charging w/Piper, 5-pc, M (M box), A...$165.00

Britains, #9143, Somerset Light Infantry, 7-pc, M (G box), A.$100.00

Britains, #9144, Royal Welch Fusiliers, 7-pc, M (EX box), A.$80.00

Britains, #9145, Royal Scots Guards, 5-pc, M (M box), A.$140.00

Britains, #9146, British Infantry, 6-pc, M (M box), A......$80.00

Britains, #9149, British Machine Gunners, 5-pc, M (M box), A...$140.00

Britains, #9155, Fort Henry Guards 49th Foot (1812), 8-pc, G-EX, A...$125.00

Britains, #9156, Royal Canadian Mounted Police, 6-pc, M (M box), A...$115.00

Britains, #9157, Princess Patricia's Light Infantry, 7-pc, M (M box), A...$180.00

Britains, #9158, Fort Henry Guards, 7-pc, M (M box), A...$125.00

Britains, #9160, Fort Henry Guards 89th Foot (1812), 8-pc, G-EX, A...$120.00

Britains, #9162, King's African Rifles, prototype set, 7-pc, M (M box), A...$150.00

Britains, #9163, Italian Bersagliere, prototype set, 7-pc, M (G box), A...$100.00

Britains, #9166, French Zouaves Charging, 6-pc, M (EX box), A...$80.00

Britains, #9167, French Foreign Legion Marching, 6-pc, M (M box), A...$80.00

Britains, #9170, Greek Evzones, 6-pc, M (M box), A $150.00

Britains, #9175, Svea Life Guards, 7-pc, M (M box), A.$175.00

Britains, #9178, West Point Cadets, 7-pc, M (M box), A.$50.00

Britains, #9184, US Sailors Marching, 7-pc, M (M box), A...$100.00

Britains, #9190, Zulu Warriors of Africa, prototype set, 7-pc, M (M box), A...$135.00

Britains, #9192, Knights of Agincourt, 4-pc, M (M box), A....$175.00

Britains, #9209, Royal Horse Guards Mounted, 4-pc, M (M box), A...$100.00

Britains, #9210, Mounted Royal Grays, 4-pc, M (M box), A...$135.00

Britains, #9212, 1st Kings Dragoon Guards, 4-pc, M (M box), A...$100.00

Britains, #9214, 7th Queen's Own Hussars, 4-pc, M (M box), A...$100.00

Britains, #9256, Royal Canadian Mounted Police, 4-pc, M (M box), A...$100.00

Britains, #9261, Skinners Horse, 4-pc, M (M box), A....$100.00

Britains, #9264, Egyptian Cavalry, 4-pc, M (M box), A...$80.00

Britains, #9265, Egyptian Camel Corps, postwar version w/molded tails, 3-pc, M, A.................................$200.00

Britains, #9266, French Cuirassiers, 4-pc, M (M box), A.....$100.00

Britains, #9286, Confederate Cavalry, 4-pc, M (M box), A.$160.00

Britains, #9288, Cowboys Mounted, 4-pc, M (EX box), A..$115.00

Britains, #9289, Indians Mounted, 4-pc, M (G box), A.$100.00

Britains, #9291, Arabs Mounted & Charging, 4-pc, M (G box), A...$85.00

Britains, #9301, Royal Co of Archers, Queen's Bodyguard of Scotland, 14-pc, M (G box), A.............................$350.00

Britains, #9310, Royal Scots Grays & Grenadier Guards, 12-pc, M (G- box), A...$200.00

Britains, #9332, Seaforth Highlanders Charging, 12-pc, M (G box), A...$150.00

Britains, #9339, Queen's Royals Regiment, 15-pc, M (M box), A...$115.00

Britains, #9346, British Infantry, 17-pc, M (EX box), A..$220.00

Britains, #9371, Papal Swiss Guards, 11-pc, M (M box), A.$315.00

Britains, #9381, US Marines & West Point Cadets, 16-pc, M (G box), A...$100.00

Britains, #9386, Confederate Cavalry & Infantry, 11-pc, M (EX box), A...$500.00

Britains, #9387, Union Cavalry & Infantry, 11-pc, M (M box), A...$460.00

Britains, #9390, Cowboys & Indians Mounted & on Foot, 10-pc, M (M box), A...$230.00

Britains, #9391, Arabs, 12-pc, M (M box), A.................$350.00

Britains, #9392, Knights of Agincourt, 9-pc, M (M box), A ..$500.00

Britains, #9401, Her Majesty's State Coach, 9-pc, M (M box), A...$460.00

Britains, #9402, Landau, 11-pc, M (M box), A $285.00

Britains, #9419 (Formerly Set #39), Royal Horse Artillery Gun Team, 13-pc, EX (G- box), A $425.00

Britains, #9482, US Marines Corps Colour Guard, 4-pc, M (M box), A...$175.00

Britains, #9494, Knight of Agincourt w/Lance, 1-pc, M (M box), A...$175.00

Britains, #9497, Tournament Knights (Formerly #1258), 6-pc, EX (VG box), A $275.00

Britains, #9650, The Meet, 11-pc, M (M box), A $230.00

Britains, #9655, The Meet, 16-pc, M (M box), A $460.00

Britains, #9656, Full Cry, 16-pc, M (EX box), A............$575.00

Courtenay, Andre, Lord of Chauvigny, falling backward w/arrow in side on base, VG, A $750.00

Courtenay, Archbishop of Sens, position 4, falling wounded w/mace in right hand, VG, A..................................$225.00

Courtenay, Duke of Bourbon, position 12, falling back wounded w/arrow in side, sword falling from right hand, EX, A .$600.00

Courtenay, English Archer Livery of the Black Prince, standing shooting bow, EX, A...$550.00

Courtenay, Erle of Nassau, position Z-1, lying wounded, EX, A...$500.00

Courtenay, Guy, Sieur de Rochefort, position 2, advancing w/battleaxe in movable right arm, shield in left, EX, A.............$375.00

Courtenay, King George V & Queen Mary, in royal robes, 2-pc, EX, A $850.00

Courtenay, King John of France, modified position 1, tin-strip surcoat w/shield fighting w/knife & broken sword, VG, A $350.00

Courtenay, King of Castile, position 6, standing w/sword in right hand, VG, A..$550.00

Courtenay, Lord John of Clermont, Marshal of France, mounted on Joan of Arc horse falling back w/arrow in chest, VG, A $1,100.00

Courtenay, Louis, King of Fortunate Isles, position 7, advancing on foot w/battleaxe in extended right arm, VG, A..$400.00

Courtenay, Man-at-Arms Livery of the Black Prince, standing w/long-pole bill, EX, A..$300.00

Courtenay, Man-at-Arms Talbot Livery, in stride carrying long-poll bill in movable right arm, blk base, VG, A $400.00

Courtenay, Queen Cleopatra & Slave Girl Carrying Fan, 2-pc, VG, A $200.00

Courtenay, Queen Phillipa, in kirtle & mantle, EX, A ..$250.00

Courtenay, Sir Eustace de Ribeaumont, modified position 7, carrying banner of King John, VG, A.........................$1,300.00

Courtenay, Sir John de Vienne, position H-6, mounted w/battleaxe in right hand, detachable great helm, EX, A..$650.00

Courtenay, Sir John Mohun, position 17, advancing on foot w/battleaxe in movable right arm, shield in left, G, A $275.00

Courtenay, Tournament Knight of Capital de Buch, mounted w/lance in movable right arm, detachable great helm, EX, A $1,100.00

Courtenay, Tournament Knight of John Lord Beaumont, KG, mounted, EX, A...$700.00

Courtenay, Yeoman of the Guard (Beefeater), standing w/partisan, VG, A $225.00

Courtenay-Greenhill, Barthelemi de Burnes, position 22, attacking w/mace, EX+, A $325.00

Courtenay-Greenhill, Black Prince, position H-6, mounted w/mace in right hand, 1979, EX, A..........................$550.00

Courtenay-Greenhill, Jean de Bahuchet, modified position 4, falling wounded, EX, A $425.00

Courtenay-Greenhill, Michael de Pole, modified position 4, falling back w/mace in extended right arm, EX, A..$475.00

Courtenay-Greenhill, Sir Simon Burley, modified position 19, standing on base swinging sword, EX, A..................$550.00

Grey Iron, aviator, scarce, 98%, A1 ....$68.00

Grey Iron, baseball players, nickel-plated, only 3 sets known to exist, from $375.00 to $400.00 for the set.

Grey Iron, Black man, digging, scarce, 95%, A1 ....$29.00

Grey Iron, boy in cowboy suit, very scarce, 95%, A1........$53.00

Grey Iron, bucking bronco, for ranch set, blk, gr base, very scarce, 98%, A $58.00

Grey Iron, calf, blk, very scarce, 97%, A1 ....$70.00

Grey Iron, clown, straight back, wht w/red trim, scarce, 80%, A1 ....$20.00

Grey Iron, conductor, 98%, A1..$12.00

Grey Iron, cowboy on bucking horse, prewar, scarce, 97%, A1 ....$69.00

Grey Iron, cowboy w/lasso, old store stock, no lasso, M, A1..$65.00

Grey Iron, doctor in wht, Red Cross, scarce, 97%, A1 .....$42.00

Grey Iron, Ethiopian, charging w/rifle, scarce, 92%, A1 ..$60.00

Grey Iron, Ethiopian chief, stain area on back, scarce, 95%, A1 ....$65.00

Grey Iron, Ethiopian officer, very scarce, 90%, A1 ....$61.00

Grey Iron, garage man, gr or wht, scarce, 99%, A1..........$21.00

Grey Iron, girl in riding suit, for ranch set, very scarce, 96%, A1 ....$56.00

Grey Iron, Greek Evzone soldier, very scarce, 95%, A1 .$127.00

Grey Iron, hired man, digging, 98%, A1 ....$22.00

Grey Iron, Indian chief, attacking, very scarce, 97%, A1 .$115.00

Grey Iron, Indian chief w/knife, 98%, A1........................$32.00

Grey Iron, Indian on horse, red figure on black horse, 95%, $65.00.

Grey Iron, Indian on horse, scarce, 88%, A1 ....$41.00

Grey Iron, knight in armor, red plume, gr base, NM, A1 .$26.00

Grey Iron, Legion bugler, 97%, A1 ....$24.00

Grey Iron, Legion colour bearer, 98%, A1 ....$35.00

Grey Iron, milkman, scarce, 98%, A1 ....$24.00

Grey Iron, old man, sitting, M, A1....................................$15.00

Grey Iron, pirate w/sword, gr outfit, 99%, A1 ....$35.00

Grey Iron, signalman w/flags, 98%, A1 ....$40.00

Grey Iron, ski trooper w/new skis, scarce, 98%, A1 ....$58.00

Grey Iron, soldier, wounded, on crutches, shiny pnt, scarce, 98%, A1 ....$71.00

Grey Iron, soldier, wounded, on stretcher, 97%, A1.........$44.00

Grey Iron, train conductor, 98%, A1 ....$12.00

Grey Iron, train porter, aluminum, scarce, 98%, A1.........$19.00

Grey Iron, train porter, scarce, 99%, A1 ....$19.00

Grey Iron, trooper, mounted, EX, A1................................$9.00

Grey Iron, US Doughboy, bomber, crawling, postwar, 95%, A1 ....$28.00

Grey Iron, US Doughboy, bomber, crawling, 98%, A1 ....$31.00

Grey Iron, US Doughboy, charging, early version, 98%, A1..$22.00

Grey Iron, US Doughboy, grenade thrower, 97%, A1 ......$39.00

Grey Iron, US Doughboy, port arms, blk leggings & rifle, early version, 97%, A1 ....$21.00

Grey Iron, US Doughboy, port arms, orange leggings w/brn rifle, early version, 95%, A1 ....$19.00

Grey Iron, US Doughboy, sharpshooter, prewar, scarce, 98%, A1 ....$30.00

Grey Iron, US Doughboy, shoulder arms, 98%, A1 ....$21.00

Grey Iron, US Infantry, officer, 98%, A1....................$17.00

Grey Iron, US Infantry, w/shoulder arms, blk leggings & rifle, pre-war, early version, 99%, A1 ....$20.00

Grey Iron, US machine gunner, 97%, A1.......................$20.00

Jones, calf, #236, 93%, A1...$10.00

Jones, cow, standing, 99%, A1 ....$10.00

Jones, dog, brn, scarce, 96%, A1.................................$15.00

Jones, farmer, 99%, A1 ....$19.00

Jones, farmer's wife, 98%, A1 ....$18.00

Jones, German soldier, kneeling, firing long rifle, scarce, 99%, A1 ....$195.00

Jones, Hession soldier on guard, 54mm, scarce, 98%, A1 ..$28.00

Jones, marine, shoulder arms, 54mm, scarce, 98%, A1 .....$21.00

Jones, marine (early 18th C), w/pigtail, very scarce, 97%, A1.$39.00

Jones, pig, brn, 99%, A1 ....$12.00

Jones, reindeer, rare, from $50.00 to $75.00.

Photo courtesy Sally and Sean Alekna.

Jones, Scot Highlander (1814), 54mm, scarce, 98%, A1..$28.00

Jones, sheep, grazing, 99%, A1 ....$12.00

Jones, soldier, AA gunner, kneeling, brn, scarce, NM, A1 ....$115.00

Jones, soldier, kneeling at searchlight, brn, scarce, 99%, A1 .$105.00

Jones, soldier, machine gunner, prone, firing dbl machine gun, brn, scarce, 94%, A1 ....$105.00

Jones, soldier, standing, firing rifle, brn, scarce, 97%, A1 .$120.00

Jones, soldier, wounded, prone, scarce, 98%, A1 ....$145.00

Jones, tank, flame not touching hull, very scarce, 97%, A1...$135.00

Jones, Waynes Legion soldier on guard, no bayonet, scarce, 93%, A1 ....$15.00

Jones, Waynes Legion soldier on guard w/bayonet, 54mm, very scarce, M, A1 ....$32.00

Jones, 1775 officer, w/sword at side, scarce, 95%, A1 ....$28.00

Jones, 1775 soldier, port arms, metallic bl uniform, scarce, 98%, A1 ....$28.00

Manoil, anti-aircraft gunner, 99%, A1...........................$32.00

Manoil, aviator, holding bomb, 94%, A1.......................$34.00

Manoil, bench, 98%, A1 ....$15.00

Manoil, cactus, lg, scarce, 96%, A1..............................$35.00

Manoil, cannon, M 69 USA, gray w/wooden wheels, NM, A1 .$24.00

Manoil, carpenter, carrying door, sm dent in back, scarce, 98%, A1 ....$67.00

Manoil, colt, brn, scarce, 96%, A1................................$26.00

Manoil, cook's helper w/ladle, scarce, 96%, A1 ....$52.00

Manoil, cowboy on blk horse, 97%, A1.........................$55.00

Manoil, cowgirl on horse, in yel & red, 98%, A1 ....$56.00

Manoil, dispatcher on bicycle, scarce, 99%, A1 ....$48.00

Manoil, doctor in wht, Red Cross emblem on cap, NM, A1...$32.00

Manoil, farmer, cutting corn, 98%, A1 ....$25.00

Manoil, gas truck, 99%, A1 ....$32.00

Manoil, hostess in gr, scarce, 98%, A1 ....$72.00

Manoil, hound, 94%, A1 ....$20.00

Manoil, man & woman sitting on park bench, 97%, A1..$33.00

Manoil, man chopping wood, 97%, A1............................$22.00

Manoil, man planting tree, very scarce, 98%, A1 ....$44.00

Manoil, marine, 2nd version, 99%, A1 ....$36.00

Manoil, mechanic, w/orange prop against head, scarce, 92%, A1 ....$92.00

Manoil, nurse, 97%, A1...$24.00

Manoil, officer, 2nd version, 98%, A1 ....$28.00

Manoil, oil tanker, red, scarce, 95%, A1........................$39.00

Manoil, parachute jumper, scarce, 95%, A1 ....$50.00

Manoil, sailor in wht, hollow base, scarce, 94%, A1 ....$51.00

Manoil, soldier, AA gunner, barrel below arm, head glued back on, 98%, A1 ....$10.00

Manoil, soldier, AA gunner, w/range finder, 97%, A1 .....$24.00

Manoil, soldier, bomb thrower, 2 grenades in pouch, 94%, A1 ....$27.00

Manoil, soldier, bugler, 2nd version, 96%, A1 ....$24.00

Manoil, soldier, charging, w/rifle, scarce, 97%, A1...........$59.00

Manoil, soldier, combat, scarce, 98%, A1 ....$40.00

Manoil, soldier, flag bearer, scarce, 98%, A1 ....$41.00

Manoil, soldier, flag bearer, 3rd version, NM, A1.............$33.00

Manoil, soldier, fusing shell, scarce, 98%, A1 ....$43.00

Manoil, soldier, grenade thrower, crouching, scarce, 97%, A1 ....$79.00

Manoil, soldier, in gas mask w/flare pistol, scarce, 98%, A1..$47.00

Manoil, soldier, in poncho, scarce, 99%, A1 ....$59.00

Manoil, soldier, juggling barrel, scarce, 98%, A1.............$79.00

Manoil, soldier, machine gunner, Finn, prone, scarce, 94%, A1 ....$85.00

Manoil, soldier, machine gunner, no aperture, 99%, A1 ..$29.00

Manoil, soldier, machine gunner, sitting, 2 casting flaws on left & near base, 97%, A1....................................$14.00

Manoil, soldier, marching, thin, 98%, A1........................$41.00

Manoil, soldier, on parade, 99%, A1 ....$22.00

Manoil, soldier, running w/cannon on wooden wheels, 97%, A1 ....$69.00

Manoil, soldier, shell loader, 98%, A1 ....$27.00

Manoil, soldier, sniper, kneeling, 97%, A1 ....$28.00

Manoil, soldier, sniper, standing, 99%, A1 ....$31.00

Manoil, soldier, tommy gunner, 2nd version, 96%, A1 ....$27.00

Manoil, soldier w/gas mask & flare pistol, 95%, A1.........$31.00

Manoil, stretcher bearer w/medical kit, 99%, A1 ....$29.00

Manoil, woman w/pie, 97%, A1 ....$30.00

Mignot, Ancient Frank Cavalry, 6-pc, M (EX box), A ..$200.00

Mignot, Austrian Infantry, 16-pc, EX, A $550.00

Mignot, Band of the Imperial Guard (1812), 12-pc, EX-M (EX box), A...$400.00

Mignot, Chasse, #0031, 31-pc, EX (EX box), A $350.00

Mignot, Dahomean (African) Warriors, standing firing, 12-pc, EX-M (EX box), A $200.00

Mignot, Diorama of French Army Kitchen Scene (1890-1914), 9-pc, EX (VG box), A $425.00

Mignot, Diorama of Tennis Match, 5-pc, EX-M (EX box), A ..$180.00

Mignot, Dutch Grenadiers of the Imperial Guard (1812), marching at the slope, 12-pc, EX-M (EX box), A $375.00

Mignot, Egyptian War Chariot w/Pharaoh Ramses II, 10-pc, EX, A $425.00

Mignot, English Life Guards Cavalry, #0246, 5-pc, M (G Soldats de Plomb box), A $300.00

Mignot, French Army Field Artillery Caisson (1914), 1950, 4-horse team w/2 drivers, 6-pc, G-EX (VG box), A ...$225.00

Mignot, French Army Horse-Drawn Ambulance (1914), 4-horse team w/2 drivers, EX (VG box), A $375.00

Mignot, French Army Machine Gun Unit (1914), 14-pc, EX, A $200.00

Mignot, French Boy Scouts Marching, 12-pc, M (EX box), A..$275.00

Mignot, French Colonial Infantry (1890-1910), assaulting w/bayonets, w/1 officer, standard bearer, 12-pc, M (EX box), A $225.00

Mignot, French Cuirassiers (1914), 4 mounted, trumpeter & officer carrying standard, 6-pc, M (EX box), A $250.00

Mignot, French Imperial Grenadiers of the Guard (1812), marching at the slope, 12-pc, G-EX (EX box), A....$250.00

Mignot, French Infantry of the Line (1914), attacking, bl uniforms, winter coats, 12-pc, EX (EX box), A.............$250.00

Mignot, French Infantry of the Line (1914), marching at the slope, 12-pc, EX (EX box), A...................................$350.00

Mignot, French Military Aviation Reconnaissance Monoplane (1914), tinplate plane, mechanic, officer w/map, M (EX box), A...$850.00

Mignot, French Napoleonic Artillery & Infantry, 14-pc, M, A..$350.00

Mignot, French Napoleonic Camel Corps Regiment (Egyptian Campaign), 5-pc, M (EX box), A $325.00

Mignot, French Napoleonic Grenadiers of the Guard, 17 marching at the slope, 4 w/flags, 5 officers, 1 side drummer, M, A......$400.00

Mignot, French Napoleonic Infantry of the Line (1810), 1950, marching at the slope, 12-pc, EX-M (VG box), A ..$350.00

Mignot, French Napoleonic Marching Infantry, Coach w/Escort & Artillery Unit, 50-pc, G-EX (VG 3-tier Diorama box), A...$500.00

Mignot, French Napoleonic Marines of the Guard, (1812), marching, 12-pc, M (EX box), A $300.00

Mignot, French Napoleonic 1st Regiment of Light Cavalry (1812), w/officer, trumpeter & standard bearer, EX (EX box), A...$225.00

Mignot, French North African Goumiers (1890-1910), mounted w/slung rifles, 1950, 6-pc, EX-M (G box), A $225.00

Mignot, French World War I 75mm Cannon w/4 Gunners (1914), 5-pc, EX-M (EX box), A $170.00

Mignot, French 17th Dragoon Regiment (1812), dismounted, marching, 12-pc, M (EX box), A $250.00

Mignot, Horse Guards Cavalry, #0247, 5-pc, M (M box), A..$260.00

Mignot, Indian Army Infantry (1900), 12-pc, G-EX (EX box), A..$250.00

Mignot, Italian Dragoons, 16-pc, M (EX box), A...........$460.00

Mignot, Italian Infantry (1914), marching at the slope, 12-pc, M (EX box), A $275.00

Mignot, Mamelukes, w/1 bugler & 1 flag bearer, 5-pc, M, A..$315.00

Mignot, Napoleon & His General Staff (1810), mounted, 6-pc, EX-M (VG box), A $450.00

Mignot, Napoleonic English Grenadiers 1st Regiment, #0122, 12-pc, M (M box), A..$300.00

Mignot, Polish Lancers, #0229, 6-pc, M (M box), A......$115.00

Mignot, Polish Lancers (1812), 12-pc, EX (VG box), A ..$425.00

Mignot, Prussian Hussars (1890-1914), mounted w/lances, officer, drummer & standard bearer, 6-pc, G-EX (G box), A..$180.00

Mignot, Prussian Infantry (1914-1916), marching at slope, 12-pc, EX-M (EX box), A...$200.00

Mignot, Rumanian Hussars, (1910-1914), mounted w/sabers in review order, 6-pc, M (EX box), A $275.00

Mignot, Russian Imperial Guard (1900), #0235, 5-pc, M (G-box), A...$315.00

Mignot, Standard Bearers of Various Regiments, 6-pc, EX-M, A..$300.00

Mignot, Turkish Infantry (1910-1914), marching in review, 12-pc, EX (EX box), A $300.00

Mignot, Vistula Lancers (1808), 12-pc, EX-M (EX box), A...$275.00

Mignot, Vistula Lancers (1808), 6-pc, EX (EX box), A .$180.00

Mignot, Vistula Legion (1808), 12-pc, EX (EX box), A.$250.00

Mignot, 8th Bavarian Regiment (1812), 8-pc, M, A......$300.00

Ping, Dauphin of France, mounted w/lance in right hand (Britains #1663), EX, A $325.00

Ping, Sir Thomas Erpingham, KG, mounted w/lance in right hand (Britains #1663), VG, A $170.00

Stadden, Austrian Officer w/Sword & Private Firing Bayonet, wooden base, sgn, G, A $145.00

Stadden, French Cuirassier (1815), British artillerymen, guns & wounded horse on landscape base, G, A $115.00

Stadden, Scots Grays Trooper, mounted & charging w/sword raised on landscape base, M, A $210.00

Wippler, Austro Hungarian Empire Officer, in leotard pelisse on cobblestone base, sgn, EX, A $230.00

Wippler, Count Platov, full dress & medals on landscape base, EX, A $100.00

Wippler, Grenadier a Pied de la Garde (1906), drummer on wooden base, pnt in artist oils, sgn, EX, A...............$185.00

Wollner, #4015, Royal Hungarian Mounted Leibgarde, 12-pc, G, A..$120.00

Wollner Kober, Imperial Austrian Navy, 10-pc marching band, 1 mounted admiral, G-, A $125.00

Sporting Collectibles

Baseball — the great American pastime — has given us hundreds of real-life sports heroes plus a great amount of collectible memorabilia. Baseball gloves, bats, game-worn uniforms, ephemera of many types, even games and character watches are among the many items being sought out today. And there are fans of basketball, football, and hockey that are just as avid in their collecting.

As you can see, many of our listings describe Kenner's Starting Lineup figures. These small plastic likenesses of famous sports greats were first produced in 1988. New they can be purchased for $5.00 to $8.00 (though some may go a little higher), but they have wonderful potential to appreciate. As the sports stars fluctuate in popularity, so do their Starting Lineup figures. Some may occasionally sell for several hundred dollars, but on the average most from 1988 run from $25.00 to $50.00. Football and basketball series have been made as well, and in 1993 Kenner added hockey. If you're going to collect them, be critical of the condition of the packaging.

Bobbin' head dolls made of papier-mache were manufactured in Japan during the 1960s until about 1972 and were sold at ball parks, stadiums, and through the mail for about $2.98. They were about 7" high or so, hand painted and then varnished. Some of them represent sports teams and their mascots. Depending on scarcity and condition, they'll run from as low as $35.00 up to $100.00, though there are some that sell for $300.00 or so. A few were modeled in the likeness of a particular sports star; these are rare and when they can be found sell in the $500.00 to $1,000.00 range. Base colors indicate when the doll was made. During 1961 and '62, white bases were used; today these are very scarce. Green bases are from 1962 until '66, and gold bases were used from 1967 until 1972. Mascot-heads are favored by collectors, and football figures are becoming very collectible as well. Our advisor has prepared a *Bobbin' Head Guide,* with a rarity scale and current values. See Dealer Codes for his address.

Advisor: Tim Hunter (H13).

See also Cereal Boxes; Character Clocks and Watches; Games; Pin-Back Buttons.

Babe Ruth, autographed baseball, Reach, Official American League, NMIB, $1,200.00.

Babe Ruth, medallion, Sportsman Award, 1940s-50s, w/figure, EX..$30.00
Babe Ruth, record, The Legend Comes to Life, Fleetwood, 1970s, 33 rpm, M (sealed), M17................................$20.00
Babe Ruth, rule book, Babe Ruth League, 1973, EX...........$8.00
Bo Jackson, autographed football, M..............................$175.00
Bob Feller, book, How To Pitch, Ronald Press, 1948, hardcover, EX (w/dust jacket), J5..$15.00

Brett Hull, hockey stick, signed, EX................................$125.00
Brooks Robinson, record, Theory of Fielding, Sports Stars, 1972, 33 rpm, M (NM jacket), J5...$25.00
Dave Justice, poster, signed, EX.....................................$26.00
Dave McNally, record, Theory of Pitching, Sports Stars, 1972, 33 rpm, M (NM jacket), J5...$25.00
Detroit Tigers, doll, 1977, stuffed cloth, 12", EX..............$35.00
Enos Slaughter, autographed baseball, w/certificate of authenticity, M...$25.00
Ernie Banks, autographed baseball, EX............................$32.00
Hakeem Olajuwon, Houston Rockets jersey, replica, EX .$175.00
Harry Carey, book, Holy Cow! 1989, EX..........................$20.00
Jackie Robinson, bank, US, Save & Win w/Jackie Robinson Daily Dime Register, metal box w/canted corners, 2⅝", VG, A...$465.00
Joe Dimaggio, baseball shoes, NMIB, D10......................$400.00
Joe Garagiola, book, Baseball Is a Funny Game, 1960, w/autograph, EX..$25.00
Johnny Bench, bat, signed, EX.......................................$135.00
Johnny Unitas, football, facsimile signature, NM.............$80.00

L.A. Dodgers vs N.Y. Yankees, pennant, 1963 World Series, red, white, and blue, NM, from $45.00 to $55.00.

Los Angeles Dodgers, doll, 1960s, stuffed cloth, 12", VG.$25.00
Michael Jordan, Chicago Bulls cap, signed on bill, M....$120.00
Michael Jordan, poster, life-size, signed, EX...................$65.00
Mickey Mantle, Life Magazine, 1956, cover pictures Mickey batting, EX, J5..$35.00
Mickey Mantle, pen, 1960s, bat form, MIP (sealed), I2....$26.00
New York Jets, banner, 1970s, wht helmet on gr background, EX, J5..$15.00
New York Knicks, bear, Good Stuff, 1991, stuffed plush w/uniform & ball, 6", NM, P3..$20.00
Nolan Ryan, game, Arcade Strike Zone, electronic baseball w/autograph, EX...$55.00
Roberto Clemente, key chain, pictures 1960 Topps card, NM.$10.00
Sandy Koufax, autographed baseball, w/certificate of authenticity, M...$65.00
Shaquille O'Neal, poster, signed, EX...............................$50.00
Sid Luckman, autographed football, NM.........................$450.00
St Louis Cardinals, doll, 1960s, stuffed cloth w/vinyl head & hands, EX, T1...$65.00
Ted Williams, fishing reel, 1950s, facsimile autograph, NM.$100.00
Willie Mosconi, cue stick, signed, EX.............................$100.00
Yogi Berra, book, Sports Library, Grosett & Dunlap, 1965, photo cover, EX, J5...$15.00

BOBBIN' HEAD DOLLS

Photo courtesy Tim Hunter.

Houston Oilers, 1966-67, molded ear pads, round gold base, $55.00; Chicago Bears, 1967, round gold base, $75.00; Atlanta Falcons, 1967, round gold base, $75.00.

Atlanta Braves, team mascot, 1967-72, gold base...........$130.00
Baltimore Bullets, Little Dribblers.................................$125.00
Baltimore Colts, 1966-68, realistic face, rnd gold base ...$145.00
Baltimore Orioles, team mascot, 1961-62, wht base, rare, minimum value $350.00
Boston Patriots, Type VI, lg shoulder pads, from $300 to ..$400.00
Chicago Bears, Black player, 1965, gold base.................$350.00
Cincinnati Reds, Black Player, 1962-66, gr base $1,500.00
Cleveland Indians, team mascot, 1961-62, emb team name, sq wht base, rare $485.00
Dallas Cowboys, 1965, rnd base $200.00
Detroit Tigers, team mascot, 1962-66, gr base, minimum value .$180.00
Green Bay Packers, 1967, gold base, NM.......................$120.00
Harlem Globetrotters, 1962 ....$250.00
Los Angeles Dodgers, Black player, 1962-66, gr base $800.00
Los Angeles Lakers, 1962 ....$225.00
Los Angeles Rams, 1966-68, rnd gold base $70.00
Mickey Mantle, 1961-62, sq or rnd wht base, ea $600.00
New York Mets, 1960-61, sq bl base $200.00
New York Yankees, 1961-62, wht base, minimum value .$225.00
Philadelphia Eagles, 1961-62, 1960 Champions emb on gr base, scarce $135.00
Roger Maris, 1961-62, sq wht base $485.00
Seattle Sonics, 1967, yel uniform.................................$220.00
St Louis Cardinals, team mascot, 1961-62, wht base, minimum value...$400.00
Washington Redskins, Merger series, rnd gold base $200.00
Willie Mays, 1961-62, lt face, rnd wht base...................$300.00

KENNER STARTING LINEUP FIGURES

Andre Dawson, 1988, EX, B10.....................................$12.00
Andre Dawson, 1988, MIP, O1 ....$15.00
Charles Barkley, 1995, MIP, O1....................................$12.00
Darryl Strawberry, 1988, MIP, O1.................................$10.00

Dave Winfield, 1988, MIP, B10 ....$40.00
Dominique Wilkins, 1994, MIP, O1 ....$12.00
Don Mattingly, 1988, M, B10..$15.00
Don Mattingly, 1988, MIP, B10.....................................$30.00
Dwight Gooden, 1990, MIP, O1 ....$12.00
Gale Sayers, MIP, B10..$25.00
Jack Clark, 1988, MIP, B10 ....$20.00
Jerome Walton, 1990, MIP, O1.......................................$8.00
Jim McMahon, 1988, M, B10 ....$12.00
Johnny Unitas, MIP, B10 ....$35.00
Jose Canseco, 1989, M, B10 ....,,$12.00
Jose Canseco, 1989, MIP, B10......................................$18.00
Juan Gonzalez, 1992, MIP, O1 ....$12.00
Julius Irving, MIP, B10 ....$30.00
Kareem Abdul-Jabbar, 1988, MIP, O1 ....$85.00
Larry Bird, 1988, MIP, O1..$110.00
Magic Johnson, 1988, M, B10 ....$25.00
Mark McGwire, 1989, MIP, B10 ....$20.00
Mike Greenwell, 1989, MIP, B10...................................$15.00
Mike Mussina, 1994, MIP, B10 ....$10.00
Mike Piazza, 1995, MIP, O1 ....$12.00
Mike Richter, 1994, MIP, O1...$30.00
Patrick Ewing, 1988, MIP, B10......................................$35.00
Pete Rose, 1988, M, B10..$18.00
Phil Simms, 1994, MIP, O1...$10.00
Reggie Miller, 1995, MIP, O1..$35.00
Ricky Henderson, 1991, MIP, O1 ....$12.00
Roger Clemens, 1988, MIP, O1 ....$12.00
Steve Young, 1994, MIP, B10..$12.00
Troy Aikman, 1994, MIP, O1 ....$40.00
Wade Boggs, 1988, MIP, O1 ....$18.00
Wilt Chamberlin, MIP, B10...$40.00

Star Trek

The Star Trek concept was introduced to the public in the mid-1960s via a TV series which continued for many years in syndication. The impact it had on American culture has spanned two generations of loyal fans through its animated TV cartoon series (1977), six major motion pictures, Fox network's 1987 TV show, 'Star Trek, The Next Generation,' and two other television series, 'Deep Space 9,' and 'Voyager.' As a result of its success, vast amounts of merchandise (both licensed and unlicensed) have been marketed in a wide variety of items including jewelry, clothing, calendars, collector plates, comics, costumes, games, greeting and gum cards, party goods, magazines, model kits, posters, puzzles, records and tapes, school supplies, and toys. Packaging is very important; an item mint and in its original box is generally worth 75% to 100% more than one rated excellent.

Other Sources: P3

See also Character and Promotional Drinking Glasses; Fast-Food Collectibles; Halloween Costumes; Lunch Boxes; Model Kits.

FIGURES

Applause, Deep Space 9, 1994, Sisko, Odo, Quark, Kira Nerys, 10", MIP, H4, ea $10.00

Applause, Generations (movie), 1994, Kirk, Picard, Riker, Data, LaForge, Worf, 10", MIP, H4, ea...................$10.00
Ertl, Star Trek III, Kirk, 3¾", MOC, H4...................$25.00
Ertl, Star Trek III, Klingon Leader, 3¾", MOC, H4.........$30.00
Ertl, Star Trek III, Scotty, 3¾", MOC, H4 ....$25.00
Ertl, Star Trek III, Spock, 3¾", MOC, H4...................$30.00
Galoob, Final Frontier, Kirk, McCoy, Spock, Klaa or Sybok, 3¾", MOC, H4, ea $45.00
Galoob, STNG, Data, 1st Series, bl face, 3¾", MOC, H4..$125.00
Galoob, STNG, Data, 2nd series, 3¾", MOC, H4 ....$40.00
Galoob, STNG, Data, 3rd Series, 3¾", M, H4...................$7.00
Galoob, STNG, Data, 3rd Series, 3¾", MOC, H4 ....$20.00
Galoob, STNG, Data, 4th Series, 3¾", MOC (open bubble), H4 ....$8.00
Galoob, STNG, LaForge, 3¾", MOC, H4...................$12.00
Galoob, STNG, Picard, 3¾", MOC, H4...................$12.00
Galoob, STNG, Riker, 3¾", MOC, H4 ....$12.00
Galoob, STNG, Tasha Yar, 3¾", MOC, H4...................$20.00
Galoob, STNG, Worf, 3¾", MOC, H4...................$12.00

Mego, Arcturian, 1979, 12", MIB, $95.00.

Mego, Motion Picture, Decker, 3¾", EX, H4 ....$12.00
Mego, Motion Picture, Decker, 3¾", M (VG+ unpunched card), from $30 to...................$35.00
Mego, Motion Picture, Ilia, 12", EX (VG box), B10.........$40.00
Mego, Motion Picture, Ilia, 3¾", MOC, from $25 to.......$30.00
Mego, Motion Picture, Kirk, 12", NRFB, H4...................$80.00
Mego, Motion Picture, Kirk, 3¾", M (VG+ card), from $25 to...................$30.00
Mego, Motion Picture, McCoy, 3¾", NM, H4 ....$15.00
Mego, Motion Picture, Scotty, 3¾", EX, H4...................$12.00
Mego, Motion Picture, Spock, 3¾", MOC, from $30 to...$35.00
Mego, 1974, Kirk, 8", MIP, B3, from $45 to...................$55.00
Mego, 1974, Klingon, 8", MIP, B3, from $45 to.................$55.00
Mego, 1974, Spock, 8", MIP, B3, from $45 to...................$55.00
Playmates, Deep Space 9, 1st Series, O'Brien, Quark, Morn, Gil Dukat, Kira, MOC, F1, ea $15.00
Playmates, Generations (movie), Admiral Kirk, MOC, F1..$25.00

Playmates, Generations (movie), Bev Crusher, Data, Dr Soran, Guinan, LaForge, Picard, Riker, Troi, Worf, MOC, F1, ea $15.00
Playmates, Space Talk Series, Riker, 8", MOC, B10 ....$15.00
Playmates, STNG, 1st Series, Borg, Data, Gowron, LaForge, Picard, Troi, 5", MOC, F1, ea...................$20.00
Playmates, STNG, 7th Series, Picard, Spock, Riker, LaForge, Borg, Sela, Data, Barclay, Worf, MOC, F1, ea...........$15.00
Presents, Classic Star Trek, 1992, Kirk, Spock, Andorian or Talosian, vinyl, 11", M, F1, ea...................$15.00
Presents, Classic Star Trek, 1992, set of 13 w/Enterprise, PVC, 4", M, F1 ....$50.00
Presents, STNG, 1992, Data, Deanna Troi, Ferrengi, LaForge, Riker or Worf, vinyl, 11", M, F1, ea...................$15.00
Presents, STNG, 1992, set of 11 w/Enterprise, PVC, 4", M, F1 ....$45.00

PLAYSETS AND ACCESSORIES

Command Communication Console, Mego, 1976, MIB..$80.00
Mission to Gamma VI, Mego, MIB, rare, from $700 to..$950.00
USS Enterprise Bridge, Mego, 1975, MIB, B10 ....$125.00
USS Enterprise Bridge, Mego, 1975, complete, NM.........$75.00
USS Enterprise Bridge, Mego, 1980, Motion Picture, NRFB....$135.00

VEHICLES

Ferengi Fighter, Galoob, STNG, 1989, NRFB, H4...........$55.00
Klingon Warship, Corgi #149, Star Trek II, MOC...........$25.00
Klingon Warship, Dinky, MIB, from $75 to...................$85.00
Shuttlecraft Galileo, Galoob, STNG, NRFB, H4.............$50.00
USS Enterprise, Corgi, 1982, Star Trek II, MOC, from $18 to $25.00
USS Enterprise, Dinky #803, 1979, Motion Picture, 4", MOC...................$30.00
USS Enterprise, Ertl, 1984, Star Trek III, MOC, from $18 to $25.00
USS Enterprise, Galoob, 1988, STNG, NMOC, from $25 to..$35.00

MISCELLANEOUS

Bank, Ferengi, Applause, 1992, bust image, MIB, H4 ......$15.00
Bank, Klingon, Applause, 1992, bust image, MIB, H4 .....$15.00
Belt Buckle, 1979, copper color w/3-D bust of Kirk & Spock, EX $20.00
Book, Mission to Horatius, Whitman, 1968, illus, hardbound, NM, F8...................$25.00
Book, Star Trek III, The Search for Spock, Simon & Schuster, 1984, illus, hardcover, EX, F8...................$10.00
Book & Record Set, from 1st movie, Peter Pan, 1979, MIP, H4 ....$10.00
Colorforms Set, 1975, MIB...................$35.00
Coloring Book, Rescue at Raylo, Whitman, 1978, Kirk on cover, EX+ $10.00
Coloring Book, Star Trek Planet Ecnal's Dilemma, Whitman, 1979, NM...................$10.00
Communicators, 1974, unused (w/orig styrofoam but no box), B3 ....$75.00

Decanter, Mr Spock bust, ceramic, MIB $60.00
Diorama, Amok Time, Applause, 1996, M, F1 ....$60.00
Doll, Kirk, Knickerbocker, stuffed cloth w/vinyl head, 12",
 MIB...$50.00
Doll, Spock, Knickerbocker, stuffed cloth w/vinyl head, 12",
 MIB...$50.00
Finger Puppets, Borg, Ferengi & Klingon, STNG, set of 3, M
 (old store stock), H4..$15.00
Game, Star Trek, Ideal, 1967, complete, EX (EX box), from $50
 to $70.00
Game, Star Trek: The Motion Picture, Milton Bradley, 1979,
 NMIB...$40.00
Game, Super Phaser II Target, 1976, battery-op, unused, M (VG
 box), B3 ....$45.00
Movie Viewer w/Filmstrips, 1960s, MOC $35.00
Ornament, Galileo, Hallmark, NRFB, from $25 to $35.00
Ornament, Klingon Bird of Prey, Hallmark, w/flickering lights,
 MIB, B3...$30.00
Paint-By-Number Set #2109, Hasbro, 1974, MIB.............$60.00

Puzzle, fr-tray, Whitman, 1978, MIP (sealed) $12.00
Puzzle Cube, Applause, STNG, turn cube to reveal 9 photos, M,
 F1...$5.00
Silly Putty, Motion Picture, 1979, MOC $20.00
Tablet, 1967, Kirk w/phaser rifle & Enterprise orbiting planet,
 unused, NM, T2...$20.00
Vulcan Ears, 1976, MIP $20.00
Water Pistol, Aviva, 1979, gray phaser, 7", MOC $35.00
Yo-Yo, Data, Spectra Star, MOC $5.00
Yo-Yo, Picard, Spectra Star, MOC $5.00

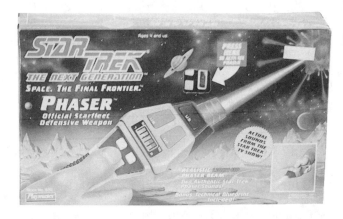

Phaser Weapon, Star Trek, The Next Generation, Playmates, MIB, $25.00.

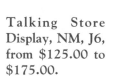

Talking Store Display, NM, J6, from $125.00 to $175.00.

Star Wars

The original 'Star Wars' movie was a phenomenal box office hit of the late 1970s, no doubt due to its ever-popular space travel theme and fantastic special effects. A sequel called 'Empire Strikes Back' (1980) and a third hit called 'Return of the Jedi' (1983) did just as well. As a result, an enormous amount of related merchandise was released — most of which was made by the Kenner Company. Palitoy of London supplied England and other overseas countries with Kenner's products and also made some toys that were never distributed in America. Until 1980 the logo of the 20th Century Fox studios (under whom the toys were licensed) appeared on each item; just before the second movie, 'Star Wars' creator, George Lucas, regained control of the merchandise rights, and items inspired by the last two films can be identified by his own Lucasfilm logo. Since 1987 Lucasfilm, Ltd., has operated shops in conjunction with the Star Tours at Disneyland theme parks.

The first action figures to be introduced were Luke Skywalker, Princess Leia, R2-D2, and Chewbacca. Because of delays in production that prevented Kenner from getting them on the market in time for Christmas, the company issued 'early bird' certificates so that they could be ordered by mail when they became available. In all, more than ninety action figures were designed. The last figures to be issued were the 'Power of the Force' series (1985), which though of more recent vintage are steadily climbing in value. A collector coin was included on each 'Power of the Force' card.

Original packaging is very important in assessing a toy's worth. As each movie was released, packaging was updated, making approximate dating relatively simple. A figure on an original 'Star Wars' card is worth more than the same character on an 'Empire Strikes Back' card, etc.; and the same 'Star Wars' figure valued at $50.00 in mint-on-card condition might be worth as little as $5.00 'loose.'

Especially prized are the original 12-back Star Wars cards (meaning twelve figures were shown on the back). Second issue cards showed eight more, and so on. Unpunched cards tend to be valued at about 15% to 20% more than punched cards, and naturally if the proof of purchase has been removed, the value of the card is less. (These could be mailed in to receive newly introduced figures before they appeared on the market.) A figure in a factory (Kenner) bag is valued at $2.00 to $3.00 more than it is worth loose, and an original backing card adds about $1.00 to $2.00. In our listings, you'll find many of these variations noted. These have been included for the information of potential buyers; remember, pricing is not a science — it hinges on many factors. For more information we recommend *Modern Toys, American Toys, 1930 to 1980*, by Linda Baker.

Advisor: George Downes (D8).

Other Sources: B3, B10, D4, D9, J2, J8, O1, P3

See also Character and Promotional Drinking Glasses; Coloring, Activity, and Paint Books; Fast-Food Collectibles; Halloween Costumes; Model Kits; Trading Cards.

Key:
ESB — Empire Strikes Back
POTF — Power of the Force
ROTJ — Return of the Jedi
* — proof of purchase removed

FIGURES

A-Wing Pilot, POTF, 3¾", MOC.................................$115.00
Admiral Ackbar, ROTJ, 3¾", MOC.............................$22.00
Admiral Ackbar, ROTJ, 3¾", w/accessories, NM, H4........$6.00
Amanaman, POTF, 3¾", MOC (dented bubble & corner dings), H4...$100.00
Amanaman, POTF, 3¾", no accessories, NM, H4...........$40.00
Anakin Skywalker, POTF, 3¾", from $30 to...................$40.00
Anakin Skywalker, SW, 3¾", w/accessories, NM, H4......$30.00
Anakin Skywalker, Tri-Logo, 3¾", MOC, H4..................$40.00
AT-AT Commander, ESB, 3¾", NM (EX card), H4.......$30.00
AT-AT Commander, ESB, 3¾", w/accessories, NM, H4.$10.00
AT-AT Commander, ROTJ, 3¾", MOC, H4..................$20.00
AT-AT Driver, ESB, 3¾", M (worn unpunched card), H4..$25.00
AT-AT Driver, ESB, 3¾", w/accessories, NM, H4...........$10.00
AT-AT Driver, ROTJ, 3¾", EX, I2..................................$9.00
AT-ST Driver, POTF, 3¾", MOC, H4...........................$70.00
AT-ST Driver, ROTJ, 3¾", MOC, H4...........................$20.00
AT-ST Driver, Tri-Logo, 3¾", MOC, H4.......................$16.00
B-Wing Pilot, POTF, 3¾", MOC (unpunched), H4........$20.00

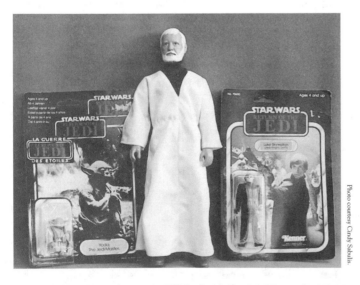

Ben Obi-Wan Kenobi, 12", NM, from $100.00 to $125.00; Yoda, tri-logo, 3¾", MOC, $50.00; Luke Skywalker, Return of the Jedi, Jedi Knight outfit, 3¾", MOC, $65.00.

B-Wing Pilot, ROTJ, 3¾", MOC, H4............................$15.00
B-Wing Pilot, ROTJ, 3¾", w/accessories, NM, H4.............$5.00
Barada, POTF, 3¾", MOC, H4.....................................$60.00
Barada, POTF, 3¾", w/coin, complete, NM, H4 ....$40.00
Ben Obi-Wan Kenobi, POTF, 3¾", MOC (unpunched), H4...$130.00
Ben Obi-Wan Kenobi, ROTJ, 3¾", gray hair, MOC, H4...$125.00
Ben Obi-Wan Kenobi, 12", MIB, from $350 to.............$375.00
Bespin Security Guard, ESB, 3¾", Black or Caucasian, MOC (unpunched), H4..$40.00
Bespin Security Guard, ESB, 3¾", Black or Caucasian, w/accessories, NM, H4..$8.00
Bespin Security Guard, ROTJ, 3¾", Black or Caucasian, MOC (unpunched), H4..$30.00
Bib Fortuna, ROTJ, 3¾", EX, I2.................................$10.00
Bib Fortuna, ROTJ, 3¾", MOC*.................................$22.00
Biker Scout, ROTJ, 3¾", MOC, H4.............................$18.00
Boba Fett, ROTJ, 3¾", MOC*....................................$40.00
Boba Fett, SW, 3¾", MOC (unpunched), H4...............$165.00
Boba Fett, 12", NM (VG box*), H4.............................$265.00
Bossk, ESB, 3¾", Bounty Hunter outfit, NM, H4..........$10.00
Bossk, ESB, 3¾", MOC (unpunched), H4......................$45.00
C-3PO, ROTJ, 3¾", removable limbs, complete, NM, H4...$10.00
C-3PO, SW, 3¾", w/accessories, NM, H4 ....$8.00
C-3PO, 12", EX...$35.00
C-3PO, 12", EX (VG box*), H4...................................$130.00
Chewbacca, ESB, 3¾", MOC (unpunched), H4.............$40.00
Chewbacca, POTF, 3¾", MOC, from $120 to...............$135.00
Chewbacca, ROTJ, 3¾", MOC, A................................$35.00
Chewbacca, SW, 3¾", w/accessories, NM, H4...............$10.00
Chief Chirpa, ROTJ, 3¾", MOC, H4............................$15.00
Chief Chirpa, ROTJ, 3¾", w/accessories, NM, H4...........$6.00
Cloud Car Pilot, ESB, 3¾", w/accessories, NM, H4..........$8.00
Cloud Car Pilot, ROTJ, 3¾", MOC*............................$35.00
Darth Vader, ESB, 3¾", M (EX card), H4.....................$40.00
Darth Vader, ROTJ, 3¾", MOC, H4.............................$30.00
Darth Vader, SW, 3¾", w/accessories, NM, H4.............$15.00
Darth Vader, 12", VG (worn box*), H4........................$100.00
Death Squad Commander, ESB, 3¾", MOC $75.00
Death Star Droid, ESB, 3¾", MOC $125.00
Death Star Droid, ROTJ, 3¾", MOC............................$80.00
Death Star Droid, SW, 3¾", w/accessories, NM, H4..........$8.00
Dengar, ESB, 3¾", NMOC (41-back), H4......................$55.00
Dengar, ESB, 3¾", w/accessories, NM, H4.....................$8.00
Dengar, ROTJ, 3¾", MOC (unpunched), H4..................$30.00
Dulok Scout, Ewoks, 3¾", MOC..................................$15.00
Emperor, ROTJ, 3¾", M (mail-order box), H4, from $8 to.$15.00
Emperor, ROTJ, 3¾", MOC...$35.00
Emperor, Tri-Logo, 3¾", MOC.....................................$25.00
Emperor's Royal Guard, ROTJ, 3¾", MOC, H4..............$25.00
EV-9D9, POTF, 3¾", MOC (dented bubble, unpunched), H4...$100.00
FX-7, ESB, 3¾", M (worn unpunched card), H4.............$40.00
FX-7, ESB, 3¾", w/accessories, NM, H4 ....$10.00
Gammorean Guard, ROTJ, 3¾", M (EX card w/open bubble), H4..$8.00
Gammorean Guard, ROTJ, 3¾", MOC, H4....................$20.00
Gammorean Guard, ROTJ, 3¾", w/accessories, NM, H4...$5.00

General Madine, ROTJ, 3¾", M (EX card w/open bubble), H4 ....$8.00

General Madine, ROTJ, 3¾", MOC, H4.....................$12.00

General Madine, ROTJ, 3¾", w/accessories, NM, H4........$6.00

General Madine & Ree-Yees (2-Pack), ROTJ, 3¾", MOC (dented bubble), H4 ....$50.00

Greedo, ESB, 3¾", MOC, from $85 to $100.00

Greedo, SW, 3¾", MOC (21-back).................................$150.00

Greedo, SW, 3¾", w/accessories, NM, H4.....................$10.00

Hammerhead, ESB, 3¾", MOC (unpunched), H4 ....$70.00

Hammerhead, SW, 3¾", EX, I2.......................................$8.00

Hammerhead, SW, 3¾", w/accessories, NM, H4.............$10.00

Han Solo, ESB, 3¾", Bespin outfit, MOC (unpunched), H4 ..$140.00

Han Solo, ESB, 3¾", Bespin outfit, NM, H4 ....$15.00

Han Solo, ESB, 3¾", Hoth gear, complete, NM, H4........$14.00

Han Solo, ESB, 3¾", Hoth gear, MOC (unpunched), H4, from $45 to...$55.00

Han Solo, POTF, 3¾", Carbonite Chamber outfit, MOC, from $100 to..$125.00

Han Solo, ROTJ, sm head, w/accessories, M.................$20.00

Han Solo, ROTJ, 3¾", Bespin outfit, MOC (unpunched, dented bubble), H4 ....$60.00

Han Solo, ROTJ, 3¾", lg head, MOC $125.00

Han Solo, ROTJ, 3¾", trench coat, MOC.......................$30.00

Han Solo, 12", NM (VG box*), H4.................................$375.00

Han Solo & Klaatu (2-Pack), ROTJ, 3¾", MOC (dented bubble), H4 ....$60.00

IG-88, ESB, 3¾", MOC (unpunched), H4 ....$55.00

IG-88, ESB, 3¾", w/accessories, NM, H4 ....$14.00

IG-88, 12", NM (EX box), H4 ....$400.00

IG-88, 15", M...$425.00

Imperial Commander, ESB, 3¾", MOC (unpunched), H4...$35.00

Imperial Commander, ESB, 3¾", MOC (41-back), H4....$55.00

Imperial Commander, ESB, 3¾", MOC (47-back), H4....$30.00

Imperial Commander, ESB, 3¾", w/accessories, NM, H4...$8.00

Imperial Commander, ROTJ, 3¾", MOC, H4, from $22 to..$28.00

Imperial Dignitary, POTF, 3¾", MOC, H4, from $50 to .$65.00

Imperial Gunner, POTF, 3¾", MOC, A.........................$100.00

Imperial Gunner, POTF, 3¾", no accessories, NM, H4 ...$35.00

Imperial Gunner, POTF, 3¾", w/accessories, NM, H4.....$45.00

Imperial Stormtrooper, ESB, 3¾", Hoth gear, complete, NM, H4 ....$12.00

Imperial Stormtrooper, ESB, 3¾", Hoth gear, MOC (unpunched), H4..$40.00

Imperial Stormtrooper, ESB, 3¾", M (VG 41-back card), H4 ....$30.00

Imperial Stormtrooper, ESB, 3¾", VG, I2.......................$8.00

Imperial Stormtrooper, ROTJ, 3¾", Hoth gear, MOC (unpunched) $30.00

Imperial TIE Fighter Pilot, ESB, 3¾", w/accessories, NM, H4..$12.00

Imperial TIE Fighter Pilot, ROTJ, 3¾", MOC (unpunched), H4 ....$45.00

Imperial TIE Fighter Pilot, ROTJ, 3¾", NMOC, H4 ....$30.00

Jawa, ESB, 3¾", MOC, from $70 to $80.00

Jawa, POTF, 3¾", MOC, from $65 to............................$75.00

Jawa, ROTJ, 3¾", MOC, A...$65.00

Jawa, SW, 3¾", MOC (12-back) $175.00

Jawa, SW, 3¾", w/cloth cape, NM, H4...........................$14.00

Jawa, 12", MIB..$225.00

King Gorneesh, Ewoks, 3¾", MOC................................$15.00

Klaatu, ROTJ, 3¾", M (EX card w/open bubble), H4 ......$10.00

Klaatu, ROTJ, 3¾", MOC (unpunched), H4 ....$20.00

Klaatu, ROTJ, 3¾", w/accessories, NM, H4....................$6.00

Lando Calrissian, ESB, 3¾", MOC* (31-back), H4 ....$35.00

Lando Calrissian, POTF, 3¾", MOC (unpunched), H4...$80.00

Lando Calrissian, POTF, 3¾", w/coin, complete, NM, H4..$45.00

Lando Calrissian, ROTJ, 3¾", Skiff Guard outfit, complete, NM, H4..$10.00

Lando Calrissian, Return of the Jedi, Skiff Guard Disguise, 3¾", MOC, 25.00.

Lando Calrissian, ROTJ, 3¾", Skiff Guard outfit, MOC, H4 ..$25.00

Lando Calrissian, ROTJ, 3¾", VG+, I2 ....$8.00

Lando Calrissian, SW, 3¾", w/accessories, NM, H4.........$12.00

Lobot, ESB, 3¾", MOC (unpunched), H4 ....$30.00

Lobot, ESB, 3¾", w/accessories, NM, H4........................$6.00

Logray, ROTJ, 3¾", M (EX card w/open bubble), H4 ....$8.00

Logray, ROTJ, 3¾", MOC...$22.00

Logray, ROTJ, 3¾", w/accessories, NM, H4....................$6.00

Luke Skywalker, ESB, 3¾", Bespin fatiques, MOC (unpunched), H4 ....$90.00

Luke Skywalker, ESB, 3¾", blond hair, MOC (unpunched), H4 ....$125.00

Luke Skywalker, ESB, 3¾", Hoth battle gear, complete, NM, H4 ....$15.00

Luke Skywalker, ESB, 3¾", X-Wing Pilot outfit, M (VG card), H4 ....$65.00

Luke Skywalker, POTF, 3¾", Battle Poncho, MOC (unpunched), H4 ....$80.00

Luke Skywalker, POTF, 3¾", Imperial Stormtrooper outfit, complete, NM, H4 ....$130.00

Luke Skywalker, POTF, 3¾", Jedi Knight outfit, MOC, from $150 to..$175.00

Luke Skywalker, ROTJ, 3¾", Bespin outfit, MOC (unpunched) $60.00

Luke Skywalker, ROTJ, 3¾", Hoth battle gear, MOC (unpunched), H4..$48.00

Luke Skywalker, ROTJ, 3¾", Jedi Knight outfit, M (EX card w/open bubble), H4 ....$45.00

Luke Skywalker, ROTJ, 3¾", X-Wing Pilot outfit, MOC...$50.00
Luke Skywalker, SW, 3¾", w/accessories, NM, H4..........$20.00
Luke Skywalker, 12", EX (VG box*), H4.......................$285.00
Luke Skywalker, 12", VG...$85.00
Lumat, POTF, 3¾", MOC, from $40 to............................$50.00
Lumat, ROTJ, 3¾", MOC*..$22.00
Nein Numb, ROTJ, 3¾", w/accessories, NM (orig Kenner bag),
    H4..$8.00
Nikto, ROTJ, 3¾", MOC, H4...$15.00
Nikto, SW, 3¾", w/accessories, NM, H4..........................$6.00
Paploo, POTF, 3¾", MOC..$45.00
Paploo, ROTJ, 3¾", MOC..$28.00
Power Droid, SW, 3¾", w/accessories, NM, H4..................$8.00
Princess Leia Organa, ESB, 3¾", Bespin fatiques, M (EX 31-back
    card), H4...$35.00
Princess Leia Organa, ESB, 3¾", Bespin fatiques, MOC
    (unpunched), H4..$70.00
Princess Leia Organa, ESB, 3¾", Bespin gown, MOC
    (unpunched), H4..$115.00
Princess Leia Organa, ESB, 3¾", Bespin gown w/regular collar,
    NM, H4...$18.00
Princess Leia Organa, ESB, 3¾", Hoth outfit, MOC
    (unpunched), H4..$50.00
Princess Leia Organa, ESB, 3¾", Hoth outfit, NM, H4....$15.00
Princess Leia Organa, POTF, 3¾", combat poncho, MOC, H4,
    from $45 to..$65.00
Princess Leia Organa, ROTJ, 3¾", Boushh disguise, MOC
    (dented bubble), H4..$30.00
Princess Leia Organa, ROTJ, 3¾", combat poncho, MOC, H4.$40.00
Princess Leia Organa, SW, 3¾", missing weapon, NM, H4.$18.00
Princess Leia Organa, 12", M (EX box), J5.....................$185.00
Princess Leia Organa, 12", NM....................................$100.00
Prune Face, ROTJ, 3¾", MOC, H4.................................$12.00
Rancor Keeper, ROTJ, 3¾", M (worn card), H4..............$10.00
Rancor Monster, ROTJ, arms & jaw move, 19x7", EX+..$35.00
Rebel Commander, ESB, 3¾", M (VG unpunched card),
    H4...$30.00
Rebel Commander, ESB, 3¾", w/accessories, NM, H4.......$6.00
Rebel Commando, ROTJ, 3¾", M (EX card w/open bubble),
    H4...$12.00
Rebel Commando, ROTJ, 3¾", w/accessories, NM, H4.....$6.00
Rebel Soldier, ESB, 3¾", MOC (unpunched), H4...........$40.00
Rebel Soldier, ESB, 3¾", w/accessories, NM, H4.............$8.00
Rebel Soldier, ROTJ, 3¾", Hoth outfit, MOC, H4..........$30.00
Ree-Yees, ROTJ, 3¾", M (EX card w/open bubble), H4..$10.00
Ree-Yees, ROTJ, 3¾", MOC, H4....................................$15.00
Ree-Yees, ROTJ, 3¾", w/accessories, NM, H4..................$6.00
Ree-Yees, Tri-Logo, 3¾", MOC, H4...............................$15.00
Romba, POTF, 3¾", MOC (unpunched), H4...................$40.00
R2-D2, ESB, 3¾", MOC (unpunched), H4......................$45.00
R2-D2, ESB, 3¾", w/sensorscope, NM, H4.....................$10.00
R2-D2, POTF, 3¾", MOC (unpunched), H4.....................$70.00
R2-D2, ROTJ, 3¾", w/sensorscope, MOC (unpunched), H4..$45.00
R2-D2, SW, 3¾", w/accessories, NM, H4..........................$8.00
R2-D2, 12", complete w/blueprints, NM........................$50.00
R2-D2, 12", remote control, MIB.................................$125.00
R5-D4, ESB, 3¾", MOC, A..$65.00
R5-D4, SW, 3¾", w/accessories, NM, H4..........................$8.00

Sand People, ESB, 3¾", MOC, from $65 to.....................$70.00
Sand People, SW, 3¾", MOC (12-back).........................$185.00
Sand People, SW, 3¾", no weapon o/w EX, I2..................$8.00
Security Guard, ROTJ, 3¾", wht, MOC.........................$30.00
Snaggletooth, ESB, 3¾", MOC (unpunched), H4...........$65.00
Snaggletooth, ROTJ, 3¾", MOC, from $50 to.................$60.00
Snaggletooth, SW, 3¾", MOC (21-back)........................$125.00
Snaggletooth, SW, 3¾", w/accessories, NM, H4...............$8.00
Squid Head, ROTJ, 3¾", EX, I2.......................................$9.00
Squid Head, ROTJ, 3¾", MOC, H4................................$18.00
Star Destroyer Commander, ESB, 3¾", MOC (unpunched),
    H4...$40.00
Star Destroyer Commander, ROTJ, 3¾", MOC (dented bubble),
    H4...$30.00
Star Destroyer Commander, SW, 3¾", w/accessories, NM,
    H4...$12.00
Stormtrooper, ESB, 3¾", MOC (unpunched), H4, from $50
    to...$60.00
Stormtrooper, ROTJ, 3¾", MOC, H4.............................$35.00
Stormtrooper, SW, 3¾", EX, I2.....................................$10.00
Stormtrooper, 12", EX (VG box*), H4..........................$200.00
Stormtrooper, 12", VG..$70.00
Teebo, ROTJ, 3¾", MOC (unpunched), H4, from $20 to..$25.00
Teebo, ROTJ, 3¾", w/accessories, NM, H4.......................$6.00
Teebo, Tri-Logo, 3¾", MOC, H4....................................$10.00
Tusken Raider, SW, 3¾", w/accessories, NM, H4...........$10.00
Ugnaught, ESB, 3¾", MOC (unpunched), H4.................$40.00
Ugnaught, ESB, 3¾", w/accessories, NM, H4...................$8.00
Walrus Man, ESB, 3¾", MOC (unpunched), H4.............$70.00
Walrus Man, SW, 3¾", MOC (21-back)..........................$125.00
Walrus Man, SW, 3¾", w/accessories, NM, H4...............$10.00
Warok, POTF, 3¾", MOC (unpunched), H4....................$35.00
Weequay, ROTJ, 3¾", M (EX card w/open bubble), H4..$10.00
Weequay, ROTJ, 3¾", MOC...$18.00
Weequay, ROTJ, 3¾", w/accessories, NM, H4..................$6.00
Wicket W Warrick, ROTJ, 3¾", MOC (unpunched), H4..$30.00
Wicket W Warrick, Tri-Logo, 3¾", MOC.......................$15.00
Yak Face, POTF, 3¾", MOC...$750.00
Yoda, ESB, 3¾", EX, I2...$12.00
Yoda, ESB, 3¾", orange snake, MOC.............................$50.00
Zuckuss, ESB, 3¾", w/accessories, NM, H4.....................$8.00
Zuckuss ROTJ, 3¾", MOC...$45.00
2-1B, ESB, 3¾", w/accessories, NM, H4.........................$10.00
2-1B, ROTJ, 3¾", MOC...$35.00
4-Lom, ROTJ, 3¾", MOC..$50.00
4-Lom, ROTJ, 3¾", w/accessories, M..............................$6.00
8D8, ROTJ, 3¾", MOC..$25.00
8D8, SW, 3¾", w/accessories, NM, H4............................$6.00

PLAYSETS AND ACCESSORIES

Bespin Control Room, Micro Collection, NRFB, H4.......$55.00
Bespin Gantry, Micro Collection, w/4 figures, NM.........$28.00
Cantina Adventure, Sears promo, EX...........................$200.00
Cloud City, EX (EX box)..$300.00
Creature Cantina, EX (EX box)....................................$75.00
Creature Cantina Adventure, SW, w/4 figures, EX (VG+
    box)..$170.00

Creature Cantina, MIB, J6, $85.00.

Death Star Compactor, SW, Micro Collection, MIB $85.00
Droid Factory, SW, EXIB $100.00
Ewok Assult Catapult, ROTJ, MIB $25.00
Ewok Village, ROTJ, MIB, H4...$100.00
Hoth Generator Attack, Micro Collection, NRFB (minor wear),
     H4 ....$55.00
Hoth Ice Planet, complete, EX, H4 ....$30.00
Hoth Ion Cannon, Micro Collection, NRFB (minor wear),
     H4 ....$70.00
Hoth Turret Defense, Micro Collection, crack in base o/w EX,
     H4 ....$25.00
Hoth Wampa Cave, Micro Collection, MIB, from $25 to..$35.00
Imperial Attack Base, EX...$32.00
Imperial Attack Base, EX (EX box), from $55 to.............$65.00
Jabba the Hutt, MIB, from $45 to $50.00
Jabba the Hutt, NRFB (Canadian/French), H4 ....$85.00
Jabba the Hutt Dungeon, Sears Exclusive, NRFB, H4 ...$100.00
Land of the Jawas, EX $50.00
Radar Laser Cannon, ROTJ, NMIB, H4 ....$20.00
Sy Snootles & the Rebo Band, NRFB, H4, from $75 to..$100.00
Tauntaun, ESB, EX (VG box missing insert*), H4...........$30.00
Tripod Laser Cannon, ESB, MIB (no insert), H4 ....$20.00
Turret & Probot, complete, EX, H4 ....$30.00
Vehicle Maintenance Energizer, M (VG box)...................$15.00

VEHICLES

Armored Sentinel Transport (AST-5), ROTJ, w/insert &
     instructions, NM (EX box)..$20.00
AT-AT, ESB, VG (VG box), H4 ....$140.00
B-Wing Fighter, ROTJ, MIB...$185.00
Boba Fett's Slave I, diecast, EX, H4 ....$25.00
Boba Fett's Slave I, ESB, complete, decals worn o/w VG, H4..$60.00
Boba Fett's Slave I, ESB, NM (EX box), H4....................$140.00
Darth Vader TIE Fighter, diecast, MOC...........................$60.00
Darth Vader TIE Fighter, SW, NMIB................................$75.00
Desert Snail Skiff, Mini-Rigs, EX (EX box), from $25 to .$30.00
Endor Forest Ranger, NRFB, H4 ....$25.00
Ewok Assault Catapult, NRFB, H4 ....$25.00
Ewok Combat Glider, ROTJ, w/instructions, MIB (no insert),
     H4 ....$30.00
Imperial Shuttle, ROTJ, NRFB, H4..................................$250.00
Imperial TIE Fighter, Micro Collection, NM....................$30.00

Imperial TIE Fighter (Battle Damaged), ROTJ, NM (EX box)...$80.00
Imperial Troop Transport, EX, H4 ....$35.00
Imperial Troop Transport, EX (EX box) $65.00
Interceptor (INT-4), Mini-Rigs, EX.................................$10.00

Jawa Sandcrawler, Star Wars, complete, NM, J6, from $300.00 to $350.00.

Landspeeder, diecast, NM..$35.00
Landspeeder, SW, VG (worn box, no insert), H4 ....$30.00
Millennium Falcon, diecast, M (NM box), H4...............$100.00
Millennium Falcon, Micro Collection, Sears Exclusive, MIB..$600.00
Millennium Falcon, SW, NMIB, H4 ....$130.00
Mobile Laser Cannon (MLC-3), EX $10.00
Multi-Terrain (MTV-7), EXIB...$18.00
One-Man Sand Skimmer, POTF, rare, MOC, H4............$85.00
Personnel Deployment Transport, EX...............................$10.00
Rebel Armored Snow Speeder, ESB, M (EX box) $70.00
Scout Walker, ROTJ, w/instructions, no insert o/w NM (EX
     box)...$50.00
Side-Gunner, Droids, M (EX+ box) $40.00
Slave I, diecast, EX, from $35 to....................................$50.00
Speeder Bike, ROTJ, NRFB, H4 ....$40.00
Star Destroyer, diecast, missing shuttle o/w VG, H4 ....$30.00
TIE Bomber, diecast, EX, H4 ....$250.00
TIE Interceptor, ROTJ, M (NM box), H4.........................$150.00
Twin-Pod Cloud Car, diecast, EX, H4 ....$25.00
Twin-Pod Cloud Car, NMIB, from $60 to $75.00
X-Wing Fighter, diecast, EX, from $30 to $45.00
X-Wing Fighter, Micro Collection, G, H4........................$15.00
X-Wing Fighter (Battle Damaged), ROTJ, NMIB, H4.....$75.00
Y-Wing Fighter, diecast, MOC, from $175 to $200.00
Y-Wing Fighter, ROTJ, M (VG box missing insert), H4..$100.00

MISCELLANEOUS

Album, SW, 1977, w/insert, EX, I2 ....$13.00
Bank, Chewbacca figure, Sigma, M, T1 ....$25.00
Belt, Darth Vader, leather, w/price tag, NM, G7..............$30.00
Belt, ROTJ, elastic w/Darth Vader buckle, EX, H4 ....$12.00
Birthday Candles, Wilton, 1980, any character, MIP, F1, ea..$5.00
Book, Empire Strikes Back, pop-up, M, T1 ....$15.00
Book, Han Solo & the Lost Legacy, 1st edition, Sept, 1980, VG,
     I2 ....$5.00
Book, Han Solo's Revenge, 1981, VG, I2 ....$5.00

Book, ROTJ Star Wars Book of Masks, M, T1..................$45.00
Book & Cassette, ROTJ, EX, H4.....................................$5.00
Bowl, ESB, G, G7..$8.00
Case, C-3PO, EX, G7 ....$30.00
Case, Darth Vader, complete w/orig cb header card, NM, H4..$35.00
Case, Darth Vader, EX+ $15.00
Case, ESB, EX $12.00
Case, Laser Rifle, NM (EX box) $45.00
Case, SW, vinyl, complete w/orig cb insert, EX, H4........$15.00
Centerpiece, ROTJ, Ewoks, MOC, G7 ....$10.00
Chewbacca Bandolier Strap, ROTJ, MIB, from $20 to.....$25.00
Clock, talking alarm, rnd dial next to figures of R2-D2 & C-3PO on base w/name & head image of Darth Vader, 8", EXIB, A $175.00
Doll, Chewbacca, stuffed, M, T1 ....$25.00
Eraser, ROTJ, Darth Vader, EX, G7 ....$4.00
Figure, Ewok, plastic, bl coat, 2¼", EX, I2........................$5.00
Folder, Ben Kenobi, NM, G7...$5.00
Folder, Darth Vader, NM, G7...$4.00
Fun Poncho, C-3PO, M, G7...$20.00
Fun Poncho, Darth Vader, MIP (sealed), G7....................$25.00
Game, Destroy Death Star, G, G7....................................$15.00
Invitations, R2-D2, 1977, set of 8, MIP, F1......................$5.00
Mask (Ben Cooper), C-3PO, NM, G7 ....$3.00
Mask (Don Post), Admiral Ackbar, Wicket W Warrick or C-3PO, hard plastic, EX, F1, ea.....................................$50.00
Mask (Don Post), Boba Fett, hard plastic, EX, F1 ....$100.00
Mask (Don Post), Cantina Band Member, hard plastic, EX, F1 ....$60.00
Mask (Don Post), Chewbacca, hard plastic, EX, F1.........$80.00
Mask (Don Post), Darth Vader, hard plastic, EX, F1 ....$65.00
Mask (Don Post), Emperor's Royal Guard, hard plastic, F1..$75.00
Mask (Don Post), Klaatu, hard plastic, EX, F1................$40.00
Mask (Don Post), Stormtrooper, hard plastic w/smoked eyes, EX, F1 ....$100.00
Mask (Don Post), Tusken Raider, Nein Numb or Gammorean Guard, hard plastic, EX, F1, ea..................................$35.00
Mask (Don Post), Yoda, hard plastic, EX, F1 ....$45.00
Movie Viewer, MIB, T1..$45.00
Mug, any character, Applause, 1995, 1st or 2nd series, ceramic, 14-oz, M, F1, ea..$16.00
Mug, Yoda figure, Sigma, M, T1......................................$25.00

Night Light, C-3PO, NM (VG card), G7 ....$5.00
Notebook, ESB, Luke & troopers, NM+, G7 ....$5.00
Paint Kit, Craft Master, Luke Skywalker or Han Solo, MOC (minor wear), H4, ea...$10.00
Paint Set, Ewok, watercolor, unused, NM, G7...................$5.00
Paper Plate, Chewbacca, MIP (sealed), G7.......................$5.00
Pencil Case, ROTJ, Luke & Darth Vader fighting, bl, NM (sealed), G7 ....$30.00
Photos, ESB, full-color, 1980, set of 4, 11x8", M, F1 ....$10.00
Pillow Case, box only, Glow-in-the Dark, 1983, EX, G7....$5.00
Pillow Case, 1970s, colorful image of main characters on space design background, EX, M17................................$25.00
Plate & Cup, Ewok, Deka, NM, G7 ....$18.00
Postcards, ESB, set of 10 w/different images, 4x6", M, F1.$10.00
Posters, Proctor & Gamble mail-in premium, 1978, various scenes, EX, H4, ea...$6.00
Puppet, Yoda, Kenner, 1981, hollow vinyl, 10", EX, I2 ....$25.00
Puzzle, Return of the Jedi, fr-tray, 1983, fat gr creature w/horns & tusks, EX, I2 ....$8.00
Record, Droid World, 45 rpm, w/booklet, M (sealed), G7..$9.00
Record, ESB, 45 rpm, w/booklet, M (sealed), G7 ....$9.00
Record, Ewoks Join the Fight, 45 rpm, w/booklet, M (sealed), G7..$9.00
Record, Planet of the Hoojibs, 45 rpm, w/booklet, M (sealed), G7..$9.00
Record, ROTJ, dialogue & music from orig motion picture, 33⅓ rpm, 1983, EX, F1 ....$15.00
Record, ROTJ, 33⅓ rpm, dialogue & music, w/souvenir photo booklet, M (sealed sleeve), G7 ....$40.00
Record, ROTJ, 45 rpm, w/booklet, M (sealed), G7.............$9.00
Record, Star Wars, 33⅓ rpm, w/cassette & souvenir booklet, M (sealed), G7 ....$35.00
Record, Star Wars, 45 rpm, w/book, M (sealed), G7 ....$9.00
Record, Story of Star Wars, 1977, orig soundtrack, M (shrink-wrapped sleeve), P6 ....$45.00
Record, Story of Star Wars, 1978, dialogue & music from orig movie, 33⅓ rpm, H4...$12.00
Record, Story of Star Wars, 33⅓ rpm, w/souvenir photo booklet, M (sealed), G7 ....$40.00
Record Tote, images of Yoda, C-3PO & R2-D2, M, G7...$30.00

Plate, Wicket and R2-D2, Hamilton, limited edition, late 1980s, MIB, J6, $85.00; Plate, Han Solo, Hamilton, limited edition, late 1980s, MIB, J6, $125.00.

Photo courtesy June Moon.

Speeder Bike, Huffy, pedal vehicle won through a sweepstakes, very rare, EX, J6, $1,250.00.

Stamp Collecting Set, Harris, 1977, set of 6 w/various Cantina scenes, EX, F1 ....$15.00

Tote Bag, ROTJ, bl canvas, MIP, T1 ....$15.00
Video Game Cartridge, ROTJ Death Star Battle, Atari 2600,
     EX, F1..$15.00
Wastebasket, ROTJ, litho tin, EX, T1 ....$25.00

Steam Powered

During the early part of the century until about 1930, though not employed to any great extent, live steam power was used to activate toys such as large boats, novelty toys, and model engines.
     See also Boats.

Accessory, butcher, Carette, articulated figure standing at rnd butcher's block, rectangular base, mc tin, 5", VG....**$200.00**
Accessory, clown in barrel w/hoop, pnt tin, hand-crank causes clown to spin, sq base, 6", EX, A.............................**$475.00**
Accessory, hypnotic wheel, Doll, ca 1910, dial w/spiral design fitted w/light bulbs, rectangular base, 8", EX, A **$250.00**
Accessory, swing ride, Doll, compo figures in 2 swings attached to rnd carousel, pnt tin, 6½", VG **$475.00**
Accessory, 2 zeppelins & 2 airplanes rotate under canopy on tower, hand-op drive wheel, tin, 11½", EX, A **$3,525.00**
Boiler, Weeden #3, ca 1910, stamped metal, 8½x10" dia, VG, A..**$250.00**

Carousel With Airplane, Zeppelin, and Hot Air Balloon, painted tin, beveled base, 32", restored, A, $17,000.00.

Ferris Wheel, Doll, tin, 6 gondolas w/4 compo figures on wheels between 2 towers w/flags, 22", rstr, A **$1,100.00**
Fire Pumper, Marklin, ca 1900, tinplate & CI, ornate brass steam dome, w/fire hose & orig burner, 9½x11", EX, A..**$11,000.00**
Fire Pumper, Weeden, Pat 1885, pnt CI w/brass boiler, engine w/dbl cylinders on wrist pins, 17¼", EX **$2,000.00**
Pickup Truck, Doll, blk & yel tin, rubber tires w/red spokes, chain-driven live steam mechanism, 19", rpt, EX, A **$3,300.00**
Speed Boat, ca 1920, pressed steel, gray hull w/brn deck, 26", VG, A **$425.00**

Steam Engine, Bing, brass & tin, mounted on CI base, 17", G, A..**$360.00**
Steam Engine, Frisbee/Am, Pat Aug 15, 1871, pnt CI water tank w/flywheel & other mechanisms, 3 legs, 8", EX ...**$1,600.00**
Steam Engine, Weeden, pnt tin & brass, w/orig instructions, 10¼", G, A...**$100.00**
Steam Engine #7, Weeden (?), 5½x4½", G (orig wooden box), A..**$250.00**
Steam Plant, Doll, gr base w/yel & red trim, 13x12x2", EX, A..**$250.00**
Steam Plant, Doll, oscillating cylinder engine w/2 flywheels, horizontal boiler, stairs, catwalk, 7½", G, A...........**$300.00**
Steam Plant, Ernest Plank, tin upright boiler w/NP gauges, levers & crank, 4-ftd CI base, 11", EX, A **$300.00**
Steam Plant, Weeden, w/5 workshop accessories mounted on 16x12" board, G plant/EX accessories, A.................**$250.00**
Tractor, Mamod, brass boiler, tall front stack, spoked wheels, 9", VG, A **$225.00**
76 Wonder Boat, Union, late 1800s, G (wood box), A..**$575.00**

Steiff

Margaret Steiff made the first of her felt toys in 1880, stuffing them with lamb's wool. Later followed toys of velvet, plush, and wool, and in addition to the lamb's wool stuffing, she used felt scraps, excelsior, and kapok as well. In 1897 and '98 her trademark was a paper label printed with an elephant; from 1900 to 1905 her toys carried a circular tag with an elephant logo that was different than the one she had previously used. The most famous 'button in ear' trademark was registered on December 20, 1904. 1904 and '05 saw the use of the button with an elephant (extremely rare) and the blank button (which is also rare). The button with Steiff and the underscored or trailing 'F' was used until 1948, and the raised script button is from the 1950s.

Steiff teddy bears, perhaps the favorite of collectors everywhere, are characterized by their long thin arms with curved wrists and paws that extend below their hips. Buyer beware: the Steiff company is now making many replicas of their old bears. For more information about Steiff's buttons, chest tags, and stock tags as well as the inspirational life of Margaret Steiff and the fascinating history of Steiff toys, we recommend *Button in Ear Book* and *The Steiff Book of Teddy Bears*, both by Jurgen and Marianne Cieslik; *Teddy Bears and Steiff Animals* 2nd and 3rd series by Margaret Fox Mandel; *4th Teddy Bear and Friends Price Guide* by Linda Mullins; *Collectible German Animals Value Guide* by Dee Hockenberry; and *Steiff Sortiment 1947-1995* by Gunther Pefiffer. (This book is in German; however, the reader can discern the size of the item, year of production, and price estimation.) See also Clubs, Newsletters, and Other Publications for Cynthia's Country Store.

Advisor: Cynthia's Country Store, Cynthia Brintnall (C14).
See also Disney; Santa.

Adebar Stork, felt, chest tag, 1950, 24", rare, NM, G16..**$1,275.00**
Arco German Shepherd, raised script button, remnant stock tag, 1950, 6", worn, G16 ....**$110.00**

Basset Hound, reddish brn & tan mohair, all ID, 1961, 5½", EX, G16 ....$125.00

Bazi Dachshund, orig collar, chest tag, 1940, 5½", NM, G16 ..$110.00

Bazi Dachshund, seated, orig collar & bell, raised script button & stock tag, 3¾", NM, G16 ....$95.00

Bear, caramel mohair, raised script button, 1950, 3½", EX, G16 ....$265.00

Bear, gold mohair w/glass eyes, raised script button, 1950s, 13", NM, G16 ....$675.00

Bear, on all fours, mohair, orig collar & bell, all ID, 1960s, 8", NM, G16 ....$250.00

Bear, on all fours, mohair, orig collar & bell, chest tag, 1950, 5½", M, G16..$175.00

Bear, shaved muzzle, orig red ribbon, raised script button & stock tag, 1960, 9", M, G16 ....$150.00

Bear, tan mohair, raised script button, 1950, 3¼", NM, G16....$285.00

Bear on Scooter, reddish-brown mohair with glass eyes, wire scooter with wood wheels, 9", VG, A, $3,200.00.

Bendy Bear, caramel, bear's-head chest tag, 1960, 3", M, G16 .$125.00

Bendy Bear, dk brn, all ID, 1970, 3½", M, G16................$55.00

Bendy Bear, reddish brn, bear's-head chest tag, 1950s, 3", M, G16 ....$125.00

Bendy Bear, tan, all ID, 1970, 3½", M, G16 ....$55.00

Bendy Bear, wht, all ID, 1970, 3½", M, G16 ....$55.00

Bendy Panda, all ID, 1960, M, G16 ....$275.00

Biggie Dog, seated, blk, brn & wht, orig collar, incised button & stock tag, 1960, 4", M, G16..$125.00

Bison, mohair w/felt horns, chest tag, 1950, 14", rare, NM, from $325 to $425.00

Bison, mohair w/felt horns, chest tag, 1950, 8", M, G16 .$225.00

Boar, blk w/brn face, all ID, 1950s, 11", M, G16 ....$175.00

Boar, blk w/brn face, all ID, 1960s, 8", NM, G16 ....$125.00

Boar, velvet, raised script button & stock tag, 1950, 4", NM, G16 ....$85.00

Brummbar Bear, inset muzzle, blank brass button, 1990, 13", EX, G16 ....$100.00

Bully Dog, tan & blk mohair, orig red leather collar, raised script button & stock tag, 1950, 4", EX, G16 ....$100.00

Bully Dog, tan & blk mohair, orig red leather collar, US Zone tag & all ID, 1948, 6½", M, G16 ....$365.00

Camel, all ID, 1950s, 6", NM, G16................................$125.00

Cat, blk & wht mohair w/glass eyes, velcro-type pads for wheels, orig pk ribbon & chest tag, 1967, 9", rare, NM, G16..$175.00

Cat, blk w/wht stripes, red claws & pk nose, no ID, 1940s, 7", VG, G16 ....$80.00

Coco Baboon, gray mohair, orig red leather collar, no ID, 1950, 6½", EX, G16 ....$85.00

Collie, laying down, all ID, 1960, 9", M, G16 ....$225.00

Cosy Fuzzy Fox, Dralon, all ID, 1968, 8½", NM, G16......$45.00

Cosy Camel, Dralon, all ID, 1968, 10½", M, G16..........$125.00

Cosy Teddy, Dralon, felt pads, orig ribbon, all ID, 1950s, 7", M, G16 ....$235.00

Crabby Lobster, mohair & felt, all ID, 1963, 7", M, G16..$365.00

Dormy Dormouse, mohair w/Dralon face, all ID, 1966, 7", M, G16 ....$165.00

Duck, chest tag, 1950, 4", NM, G16 ....$75.00

Easter Bunny w/Basket, all ID, 1967, 9", rare, NM, G16 ..$465.00

Elephant, mohair w/red felt blanket, orig bells, no ID, 1950s, 8", NM, G16 ....$95.00

Elephant, w/anniversary blanket, raised script button & stock tag, 1950, 2¾", M, G16 ....$85.00

Fawn, velvet, all ID, 1950, 5", M, G16 ....$100.00

Floppy Cockie, sleeping puppy, tan & brn, orig ribbon, no ID, 1950, 8", VG, G16..$45.00

Floppy Kitty, sleeping kitten, tan w/blk stripes, orig ribbon & chest tag, 8", VG, G16..$55.00

Flossy Fish, all ID, 1968, 4", EX, G16............................$65.00

Foxy Dog, tan w/brn ears, orig ribbon & bell, all ID, 4", EX, G16 ....$125.00

Froggy Frog, seated, velvet, all ID, 1968, 4½", M, G16..$135.00

Froggy Frog, swimming, mohair, chest tag, 1960s, 11", NM, G16 ....$175.00

Giraffe, printed mohair w/felt ears & mouth, glass eyes, ear button & tag, 98", EX..$2,500.00

Grizzly Donkey, Dralon, all ID, 1968, 9½", M, from $75 to...$100.00

Halloween Cat, blk velvet & mohair, orig ribbon, 1950, 3", EX, G16 ....$125.00

Hedgehog, raised script button & stock tag, 1950, 2¼", M, G16 ....$55.00

Hen, mohair w/felt tail, feet & face, raised script button & stock tag, 1953, 7", M, G16 ....$235.00

Hexie Dachshund, all ID, 1950, 5½", M, G16................$85.00

Hide-A-Gift Cocker Spaniel, blk & wht, all ID, 1950, 5½", NM, from $175 to $195.00

Hide-A-Gift Rabbit, all ID, 1950, 5½", NM, from $175 to..$195.00

Hucky Raven, mohair w/felt beak & metal legs, no ID, 1950s, 4", G, G16 ....$65.00

Jackie Bear, tan, 1950s, raised script button, remnant stock tag, 9½", rare, EX, G16..$1,250.00

Jocko Monkey, brn, all ID, 1948, 5¾", NM, G16...........$195.00

Jocko Monkey, on wheels, raised script button & stock tag, rpl ribbon, 1950s, 10", EX, G16................................$265.00

Jocko Monkey, wht, chest tag, 1950, 6", NM, G16 ......$165.00

Kangaroo & Joey, mohair w/velvet joey, raised script button, 1950s, 18", EX, G16 ....$495.00

Kangoo Kangaroo, mohair, w/joey, all ID, 1950, 6½", M, G16 ....$125.00

Kite, Roloplan #150, red & yel cotton on triangular form w/bamboo sticks, pewter button, 37", VG, A $175.00

Kitty, striped mohair w/velvet muzzle & felt ears, fully jointed, chest tag, 1940s, 4½", NM, G16 ....$245.00

Koala, tan, chest tag, 1950, 5", NM, G16 ....$300.00

Lamby Lamb, orig ribbon, bell & chest tag, 4", EX, G16..$85.00

Leo Lion, standing, raised script button & stock tag, 1968, 4½", M, G16.......................................$100.00

Leo Lion & Lea Lioness, chest tags, 1950, 4", NM, G16, pr ..$195.00

Lixie Cat, gray w/red & gr cloth outfit, chest tag, 1954, 4¼", EX, G16 ....$225.00

Lora Parrot, mohair & felt, chest tag, 1968, 5", EX, G16 .$85.00

Lora Parrot, mohair & felt, incised button & stock tag, 1968, 9", NM, G16 ....$145.00

Mama & Baby Bear, ltd edition gift set, 1981, mama: 13", baby: 6", MIB $700.00

Maxi Mole, w/orig shovel, all ID, 1950, 4", M, G16.........$85.00

Mockie Hippopotamus, chest tag, 1950, 5½", M, G16.....$85.00

Molly Dog, brn & wht, orig ribbon & bell, all ID, 1949, 4", EX.$200.00

Molly Dog, tan & brn, 1930, nose & mouth prof rstr, 2½", scarce, EX.................................$450.00

Mucki and Macki, 10", EX, from $145.00 to $165.00 each.

Murmy, all ID, 1950, 5", M, G16 ....$100.00

Nagy Beaver, stiff mohair, all ID, 1950, 4", NM, G16......$85.00

Nagy Beaver, stiff mohair, all ID, 1950, 7", M, G16.......$140.00

Navy Goat, no ID, 1950s, 5", M, G16.............................$225.00

Nellie Snail, bl, raised script button & chest tag, 1950s, 6½", NM, G16 ....$395.00

Nosy Rhinoceros, gray mohair w/felt horn & ears, chest tag, raised script button & stock tag, 1954, 5", M, G16 .$110.00

Original Teddy, caramel, chest tag, 1950, 6", EX, G16 ..$275.00

Original Teddy, caramel, orig ribbon & chest tag, 1950, 13½", NM, G16 ....$600.00

Original Teddy, champagne, orig ribbon, raised script button & stock tag, 1960, 9", M, G16.........................$150.00

Original Teddy, gold mohair, glass eyes, no ID, 1950s, 8", EX, G16 ....$250.00

Original Teddy, gold mohair, no ID, 1950s, 3½", NM, G16 ..$225.00

Ossi Rabbit, reddish brn & wht mohair, orig red ribbon, incised button & stock tag, 1960, 5½", M, G16 ....$85.00

Paddy Walrus, mohair, chest tag, 1950s, 4½", NM, G16..$100.00

Panda, raised script button, 1950, 8", wht fur yellowed o/w EX, G16 ....$695.00

Peggy Penguin, all ID, 1959, 5", M, G16 ....$125.00

Peggy Penguin, rare version w/velvet wings & orange feet, orig ribbon & all ID, 1952, 4½", EX, G16 ....$165.00

Peky Dog, plush & felt, orig ribbon & chest tag, 1950, 3½", NM, G16 ....$85.00

Polar Bear, 1960s, tan, orig collar & bell, all ID, 8", NM, G16 ....$275.00

Possy Squirrel, all ID, 1950s, 5", EX, G16 ....$95.00

Rabbit, wht Dralon w/brn airbrushing, orig ribbon, all ID, 9½", M, G16 ....$100.00

Raccy Raccoon, tan & brn mohair, chest tag, 1950, 3½", M, G16 ....$125.00

Renny Reindeer, all ID, 1959, 4½", NM, G16 ....$185.00

Robby Seal, chest tag, 1950, 5", M, G16........................$85.00

Rooster, mohair w/felt face, tail & feet, raised script button & stock tag, 1959, 6", EX, G16 ....$115.00

Slo Turtle, chest tag, 1950, 5", M, G16...........................$50.00

Snobby Poodle, gray mohair w/glass eyes, chest tag, 1950s, 5½", NM, G16 ....$125.00

Snobby Poodle, puppet, blk, orig ribbon, no ID, 1950s, EX, G16 ....$65.00

Snucki Ram, tan mohair w/blk face & feet, chest tag, 1950s, 6", NM, G16 ....$125.00

Sonny Rabbit, caramel mohair, raised script button & stock tag, 1950s, 5", NM, G16.....................................$100.00

Squirrel, mohair w/velvet nut, vivid airbrushing, raised script button, stock tag & US Zone tag, 1948, 8", M, G16.......$265.00

Stork, all ID, 1991, 7", M, G16 ....$45.00

Stork, felt, no ID, 1950, 6½", NM, G16 ....$110.00

Swinny Hamster, chest tag, 1950, 5", M, G16 ....$75.00

Tabby Cat, wht w/blk stripes, orig ribbon & bell, chest tag, 4½", NM, G16 ....$155.00

Tabby Cat on Wheels, wht w/blk stripes, orig bell, rpl ribbon, raised script button, US Zone tag, 1948, 8" L, EX, G16 ....$335.00

Tapsy Cat, tan w/striped tail, orig ribbon, chest tag, 1950, 7", EX, G16 ....$145.00

Teddy Baby, miniature replica, all ID, 1992, 6", M, G16 .$85.00

Terry Terrier, blk & tan mohair, orig red leather collar, US Zone tag & all ID, 1948, 9", M, G16.........................$325.00

Tiger, running, raised script button & chest tag, 1950, 6½", M, G16 ....$85.00

Tiger Cub, chest tag, 1950, 4", NM $125.00

Tucky Turkey, raised script button & stock tag, 1950, 6½", M, G16 ....$400.00

Tulla Goose, mohair w/felt feet & beak, bl glass eyes, airbrushed wings & tail, chest tag, 1950s, 11", EX, G16 ....$485.00

Turkey, raised script button, 1950s, 4¼", M, G16..........$285.00

Turtle, footstool, airbrushed mohair, all ID, 1950, 21" L, NM, G16 ....$500.00

Unicorn, split chest tag, brass button & stock tag, 1983, 7", M, G16 ....$125.00

Walrus, raised script button & stock tag, 1950, 5", M, G16..$75.00

Wittie Owl, raised script button & chest tag, 1970, 4½", NM, G16 ....$50.00

Woolie Angel Fish, incised button & stock tag, 1960, 4", M, G16 ....$35.00

Woolie Bear, tan, no ID (came on bag instead of bear), 1977, 1¾", M, G16...$55.00

Woolie Bird, mc, metal feet, raised script button & stock tag, 1950, 2½", EX, G16...$65.00

Woolie Cat, blk & wht, orig ribbon, raised script button & stock tag, 1950, 3", M, G16.................................$110.00

Woolie Cat, gray & wht, orig ribbon, raised script button & stock tag, 3", M, G16..$110.00

Woolie Chick, plastic feet, raised script button (brass), stock tag, 2", M, G16...$45.00

Woolie Crow, metal feet, raised script button & stock tag, 1950, 3", NM, G16...$65.00

Woolie Duck, metal feet, no ID, 1950, 2½", EX, G16......$55.00

Woolie Fantail Bird, plastic feet, incised button & stock tag, 1960, NM, G16...$45.00

Woolie Hen, metal feet, raised script button & stock tag, 1950, 2½", NM, G16...$85.00

Woolie Lady Bug, no ID, 1950, 1½", NM, G16.............$15.00

Woolie Penguin, no ID, 1950, 2", M, G16....................$65.00

Woolie Rabbit, blk & wht, raised script button & stock tag, 1950s, 4½", NM, G16.......................................$45.00

Woolie Raven, mohair w/felt beak & metal legs, raised script button & stock tag, 1959, 2½", M, G16...................$65.00

Woolie Rooster, metal feet, no ID, 1950, 3", NM, G16...$65.00

Xorry Desert Fox, all ID, 1950, 4½", M, G16................$100.00

Zicky Goat, caramel, orig ribbon & bell, all ID, US Zone, 1948, 7½", M, G16...$285.00

Zicky Goat, caramel, orig ribbon & bell, chest tag, 5½", EX, G16..$100.00

Zotty Bear, reddish mohair, orig ribbon, split chest tag, incised button & stock tag, 6", M...............................$300.00

Zotty Bear, tan mohair, orig red ribbon, raised script button, remnant stock tag, 1950, 8", NM, from $350 to......$400.00

Strauss

Imaginative, high-quality, tin windup toys were made by Ferdinand Strauss (New York, later New Jersey) from the onset of World War I until the 1940s. For about fifteen years prior to his becoming a toymaker, he was a distributor of toys he imported from Germany. Though hard to find in good working order, his toys are highly prized by today's collectors, and when found in even very good to excellent condition, many are in the $500.00 and up range.

Advisor: Scott Smiles (S10).

Air Devil, airplane w/pilot, 1926, 8½", EX, from $500 to..$600.00

All Aboard Limited Train, #46 loco & tender w/passenger car, gr & red, 17", EX, A...$220.00

Boob McNutt, man in red polka-dot pants & blk jacket, rnd flat hat, 8¾", VG, A..$450.00

Bus De Luxe, 1927, curtains lithoed in windows, 14", rare, EX (EX box), A...$3,200.00

Chek-A-Cab #69, yel & blk w/checked trim, 8½", VG.$650.00

Dandy Jim Clown Dancer, 1921, does the jig & plays cymbals atop circus tent, 10", EX...................................$600.00

Emergency Tow Cab, lithographed tin, 10", VG, from $200.00 to $250.00.

Flying Zeppelin, 1920, hung from string, propelled by spinning prop, aluminum, mk Graf...GZ-2017, 16", NM (EX box).....$1,100.00

Ham & Sam, 1921, Black banjo player standing by piano player, litho tin, 5½", VG...$625.00

Handcar, workmen pump yel handcar w/2 yel wheels, EX+ ..$300.00

Jackie the Hornpipe Dancer, boat advances as sailor dances on deck, 9", EXIB, A..$775.00

Jazzbo Jim, 1920s, figure plays banjo & dances atop cabin roof, 10", G, from $350 to....................................$400.00

Jitney Bus #66, 1920s, gr w/yel name & trim, metal tires w/gr hubs, w/driver, 9¼", EX...................................$650.00

Leaping Lena Car, 1930, blk w/wht lettering, w/driver, VG, from $400 to...$450.00

Man Pushing Wheelbarrow, man in red cap, bl coat & yel pants pushes yel & bl wheelbarrow w/Tip Top decal, 5½", VG...$175.00

Play Golf, lithographed tin, MIB, from $750.00 to $850.00.

Red Flash Racer #31, w/driver, red & yel, 9½", scarce, EX, A...$650.00

Rollo-Chair, G, from $650 to...................................$750.00

Santee Claus in Sleigh, 1923, Santa bounces up & down as sleigh advances, litho tin, 11", EX.......................$1,200.00

Speedboat Ferdinand, red tin floor toy w/driver, 10", G, from $200 to...$250.00

Spirit of St Louis Airplane, silver-tone w/pilot in open cockpit, 8", EX...$450.00

Tom Twist the Funny Clown, 8½", EX (orig box), from $1,100 to...$1,200.00

Tourist Car, 33 on front grille, full-figure chauffer, raised designs on doors & louvers, 10", VG+.........................$580.00

Travelchiks, 4 chicks atop railroad car bend & peck for food, litho tin chick passengers, 8", VG (G box), from $400 to....$450.00

Wildfire Trotter, driver jumps up & down in seat as donkey cart advances, 8½", EX..$250.00

Yell-O-Taxi #59, yel & blk w/driver, 8", VG, A.............$425.00

Zeppelin, mk Los Angeles 47, 10", propeller blades missing o/w VG, A $250.00

Structo

Pressed steel vehicles were made by Structo (Illinois) as early as 1920. They continued in business well into the 1960s, producing several army toys, trucks of all types, and firefighting and construction equipment.

Cattle Truck #708, red & wht, MIB $225.00

Cement Mixer Truck, bronze w/wht mixer tank, VG $100.00

Delivery Truck, red cab w/bl body, cast aluminum chassis, 12½", G, A..$100.00

Deluxe Roadster, orange w/blk convertible top, running boards & fenders, wht tin tire w/spoke wheels, 14", EX, A.$825.00

Dump Truck, hydraulic dump action, 21", VG+, A $85.00

Dump Truck, Loader & Ramp, 1930s, red, 16" truck, G, D10 ....$350.00

Earth Mover, red, 20", smoke stack missing o/w EX, A $75.00

Fire Pumper Truck, electric lights, brass pump, 22", G, A ..$275.00

Fire Truck, 1930s-40s, red with black rubber tires, 18", EX, D10, $650.00.

Missile Launcher Truck, gr, 13", G, A $50.00

Mobile Crane #810, gr & yel w/blk plastic tires, 19", NM (EX box), A $225.00

Ready Mix Cement Mixer #700, metallic enamel w/blk tires, NM (NM box)...$250.00

Rigger and Hauler, late 1940s, green with black rubber tires, chain pull mechanism, 20", EX, D10, from $175.00 to $250.00.

Roadster, 1920, orange body w/blk fenders, iron spoke wheels, w/up, 16", missing convertible top, G, A $350.00

Stationary Bed Truck, 1930, bl, battery-op lights, 21", VG, A ...$175.00

Steam Shovel, 1950s, gr w/yel decals, 16", from $75 to ..$125.00

Taxicab, early 2-tone 4-door w/spoke wheels, w/driver, 11", G.$250.00

Transport Tractor-Trailer, 1950s, bl cab w/red trailer, blk rubber tires, 21", EX, D10 ....$200.00

Truck Fleet Set #725, NMIB..$550.00

Teddy Bears

The history of old teddy bears goes way back to about 1902-1903. Today's collectors often find it difficult to determine exactly what company produced many of these early bears, but fortunately for them, there are many excellent books now available that contain a wealth of information on those early makers.

Interest in teddy bears has been increasing at a fast pace, and there are more and more collectors entering the market. This has lead to an escalation in the values of the early bears. Because most teddies were cherished childhood toys and were

usually very well loved, many that survive are well worn, so an early bear in mint condition can be very valuable.

We would like to direct your attention to the books on the market that are the most helpful on the detailed history and identification of teddies. *A Collectors History of the Teddy Bear* by Patricia Schoonmaker; *Teddy Bears Past and Present (Volumes I and II)* and *American Teddy Bear Encyclopedia* by Linda Mullins; *Teddy Bears — A Complete Guide to History, Collecting, and Care*, by Sue Pearson and Dottie Ayers; *Teddy Bear Encyclopedia* and *Ultimate Teddy Bear Book* by Pauline Cockrill; and *Big Bear Book* by Dee Hockenberry. The reader can easily see that a wealth of information exists and that it is impossible in a short column such as this to give any kind of a definitive background. If you intend to be a knowledgeable teddy bear collector, it is essential that you spend time in study. Many of these books will be available at your local library or through dealers who specialize in bears.

Advisor: Cynthia's Country Store, Cynthia Brintnall (C14). **See also Schuco; Steiff.**

2½", gold mohair w/glass eyes, straw-stuffed, orig collar, 1930, M, G16..$65.00
8½", mohair w/shoe-button eyes, jtd at shoulders & hips, excelsior stuffing, long thin arms, Steiff-like, 1905, VG..$900.00
10", gray mohair w/cotton print body, glass eyes, EX......$250.00
11", bottle warmer, wht plush w/glass eyes, zipper closure, rare, VG..$400.00
12", blond mohair w/beige felt pads, shoe-button eyes, tan embroidered nose, mouth & claws, fully jtd, Am, 1905, VG, A.$460.00
12½", gold mohair w/glass eyes & embroidered nose, long arms, felt pads, Steiff-like, 1920s, 50% fur loss...............$1,150.00
13", blond mohair w/shoe-button eyes, gr overalls w/checked shirt, jtd, early 1920s, rpl pads, fiber & fur loss........$230.00
15", brn mohair w/glass eyes, pnt details, German, 1927, EX..$350.00
16", burnished gold long-pile mohair, straw-stuffed, embroidered nose & mouth, music box in tummy, VG, minimum value..$325.00
16", yel mohair w/blk shoe-button eyes, embroidered snout, curved arms & straight legs, checked clown suit, 1920s, VG...$145.00

21", riding toy, brown plush with glass eyes, floss nose and mouth, straw stuffed, red metal frame with green metal wheels, ca 1950, VG, A, $350.00.

16½", orange mohair Roosevelt-type w/glass eyes, mouth opens to expose teeth, oval body, jtd, VG......................$460.00
17", Max, blond mohair w/beige felt pads, glass eyes, blk embroidered face, jtd, musical, 1920s, EX...................$2,185.00
17½", beige mohair w/short legs on football-shaped body, wide head w/steel eyes, fully jtd, worn, A................$230.00
18", lt brn mohair w/glass eyes, modified hump, straw-stuffed, fully jtd, Am, 1920s, rpl nose........................$485.00
18½", beige curly mohair w/glass eyes, embroidered snout & printed claws, fat body w/short fat limbs, 1940s, VG..$145.00
19", yel mohair w/glass eyes, embroidered snout, curved arms & straight legs, excelsior stuffing, jtd, Am, 1920s, VG..$315.00
20", gold mohair w/button eyes, twill nose, Ideal, 1910, M.$400.00
20½", deep honey gold fur w/embroidered snout, pk pads, fully jtd, wearing watch, Am, early, EX..................$200.00
21", frosted mohair w/glass eyes, open mouth, 1940s, NM..$265.00
24", lt gold short-hair fur w/embroidered snout, fully jtd, lg padded paws, VG..$275.00
25", blond mohair w/hump on football-shaped body, beige felt pads, embroidered face w/glass eyes, jtd, Am, 1915, worn, A..$260.00

Tekno

The Tekno company was formed in Denmark during the late 1920s. The toy vehicles they made were of the highest quality, fully able to compete with the German-made Marklin toys then dominating the market. The earliest Tekno vehicles were made of tinplate, and though some were not marked at all, others were stamped with a number. The factory continued to expand until WWII broke out and restrictions made further building impossible. In 1940 the government prohibited the use of tinplate for toy production, and the company began instead to manufacture diecast vehicles in a smaller (1/43) scale. These were exported worldwide in great volume. Collectors regard them as the finest diecasts ever made. Due to climbing production costs and the resulting increases in retail prices that inevitably hurt their sales, the company closed in 1972. Tekno dies were purchased by Mercury Kirk Joal who used them to produce toys identical to the originals except for the mark.

#142 Scania Truck & Long Wheel Base Trailer, bl & red w/silver trailer cover, NM...............................$50.00
#321 Falck Utility Truck, red, tinplate, G....................$195.00
#401 Flying Fortress, silver, US, VG..........................$75.00
#423 Ford VB Garbage Truck, gr & red, G....................$45.00
#428 V8 Wrecking Truck, red & blk, metal tires, rare, G..$175.00
#434 Scania-Vebis Esso Tank Truck, 1965, cream & gray, NM, W...$50.00
#445 Scania Vebis Ladder Truck, red, EX....................$100.00
#727 DKW Junior Coupe, metallic bl, M......................$85.00
#739 Dodge Truck, w/topper, yel & red, VG..................$125.00
#740 Dodge Milk & Cream Truck, bl & wht, NM........$175.00
#775 Small Utility Trailer, MIB...............................$30.00
#812 Cooper Norton #1, silver, EX............................$60.00
#824 MGA Coupe 1600, lt bl, EXIB............................$170.00
#833 Ford Mustang, 1967, wht & blk w/Rallye Monte Carlo #169 decals, EX.......................................$70.00

#834GCB Ford Mustang Convertible, metallic gold w/blk interior, MIB $70.00
#837 SAAB 99, wht, MIB $40.00
#914 Ford D800 Tipping Truck, red side panels, MIB......$45.00
#915 Ford D-Truck, red & silver, MIB..............................$85.00
#927 E-Type Jaguar, 1960s, red w/blk top, NMIB, W1...$100.00
#928 Mercedes 230SL Convertible, 1965, wht, EXIB, W1.$30.00
#930S Corvair Monza Coupe, chrome, M..........................$45.00
#931 Monza Spider, wht, MIB...$65.00
#933 Oldsmobile Toronado, 1965, brn & blk, MIB, W1.$180.00
#934TM Toyota 2000 GT, mustard body, MIB.................$40.00

Telephones

Novelty phones representing a well-known advertising or cartoon character are proving to be the focus of a lot of collector activity — the more recognizable the character the better. Telephones modeled after a product container are collectible too, and with the intense interest currently being shown in anything advertising related, competition is sometimes stiff and values are rising.

Advisor: Jon Thurmond (T1).

Bart Simpson, MIB, T1..$35.00
Batman Forever, Batmobile, MIB, J8, from $35 to...........$50.00
Bozo the Clown, 1980s, MIB, from $65 to $75.00
Bugs Bunny, Warner Exclusive, MIB, P12.......................$95.00
Cabbage Patch Girl, 1980s, EX, T1..................................$85.00
Charlie Tuna, 1987, MIB, P12, from $50 to $65.00
Crest Sparkle, NMIB, J2 ....$50.00
Keebler Elf, NM, T1 ....$100.00
Kermit the Frog, candlestick type, MIB, P12 ....$85.00
Lazy Pig, MIB, P12...$65.00
Little Green Sprout, EX, T1 ....$75.00
Mario Brothers, 1980s, MIB, T1..$45.00
Mickey Mouse, 1988, MIB, A...$50.00
Oscar Mayer Weiner, EX, P12..$65.00
Snoopy & Woodstock, Am Telephone, rotary dial, EX, from $100 to...$125.00
Snoopy as Joe Cool, 1980s, MIB, T1 ....$55.00

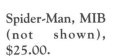

Spider-Man, MIB (not shown), $25.00.

Tang Lips, rnd red base, 9", MIB, from $125 to $150.00
Tetley Tea, man in wht coat on rnd bl base, 9", EX, A ..$100.00
Winnie the Pooh, sq base, M, from $225 to....................$250.00
Ziggy, 1989, MIB, T1 ....$75.00

Tonka

Since the mid-'40s, the Tonka Company (Minnesota) has produced an extensive variety of high-quality painted metal trucks, heavy equipment, tractors, and vans.

Advisor: Doug Dezso (D6).

Aerial Ladder Truck, 1957, w/alumium ladders, 34", EX..$200.00
Aerial Sand Loader, EX $275.00
Allied Van Lines, 1953, G...$150.00
Army Truck w/Topper, 1965, VG $75.00
Boat Transport Semi #41, 1959, 5-pc set, EX $550.00
Carnation Milk Delivery Van, #750, 1955, EX $475.00
CAT Cement Mixer, yel, M..$40.00
Cement Mixer, 1960, EX+ $300.00
COE Low Boy & Shovel, M..$300.00
Deluxe Fisherman Truck w/Trailer & Boat, 1960, VG ..$250.00
Dune Buggy, 1970, VG..$50.00
Farm Set, 1961, NMIB $525.00
Farm Truck, 1957, w/stock rack, EX $375.00
Farm Truck w/Horse Trailer, 1959, EX $300.00
Fire Pumper, #926, 1963, red metal w/working hose, 18", missing fire hydrant o/w complete & NM (VG+ box) $275.00
Fire Pumper Truck, 1958, VG...$175.00
Fisherman Pickup, #110, 1960, 14", M............................$150.00
Gambles Semi, 1956, EX $325.00
Grain Truck, 1956, G+..$150.00
Green Giant Semi, 1953, wht w/gr & wht decals, 24", EX, A $250.00
Hi-Way Custom Mixer, 1957, VG+ $185.00
Hi-Way Dump Truck, 1956, rstr $95.00
Hi-Way Road Grader, 1960, yel, 17", VG.........................$35.00
Jeep Pumper, #425, 1963, EX $150.00
Jeep Surrey, blk & wht, NMIB...$200.00
Jeep w/Tonka Clipper Boat, 1964, EX $225.00
Ladder Truck #5, 1962, w/extension ladder, 32", G+ $100.00
Low Boy & Shovel, 1955, red & bl, EX $300.00
Luggage Service Tractor, #2100, metal w/2 detachable trailers & plastic suitcases, aqua, 8", EX $100.00
Lumber Changeable Flatbed Truck, 1955, EX $325.00
Lumber Truck #998, 1956, M..$300.00
Minute Maid Delivery Truck, 1956, EX............................$550.00
Parcel Delivery Van, 1954, EX $350.00
Pickup Truck, 1957, bl, EX...$200.00
Pickup w/Camper, 1963, wht-wall tires, VG...................$125.00
Ramp Hoist Truck, 1963, red w/wht trim, EX $450.00
Ser-Vi-Car, 1963, VG $125.00
Service Truck, 1959, bl, EX...$185.00
Standard Oil Tanker Semi, 1961, G $350.00
Steam Shovel, #50, 1947, M $125.00
Suburban Pumper #46, 1958, NMIB.................................$275.00

Surrey Jeep, pk, NMIB..$190.00
Terminex Van, 1961, EX...$400.00
Transport Truck #140, ca 1950, w/trailer, EX+ $360.00
Wheaton Van Lines Truck, 1956, G..............................$450.00
Winnebago Camper, 1968, VG..$100.00

Photo courtesy Bill Bruegman.

Wrecker, #2518, 1963, white metal with heavy-duty winch, 12", NM, from $100.00 to $150.00.

Wrecker, 1954, EX $300.00

Toothbrush Holders

Figural ceramic toothbrush holders have become very popular collectibles, especially those modeled after well-known cartoon characters. Disney's Mickey Mouse, Donald Duck, and the Three Little Pigs are among the most desirable, and some of the harder-to-find examples in mint condition sell for upwards of $200.00. Many were made in Japan before WWII. Because the paint was not fired on, it is often beginning to flake off. Be sure to consider the condition of the paint as well as the bisque when evaluating your holdings. For more information we recommend *Pictorial Guide to Toothbrush Holders* by Marilyn Cooper. Plate numbers in the following listings refer to Marilyn's book.

Advisor Marilyn Cooper (C9).

Annie Oakley, Japan, hanger w/2 holes, plate #11, 5¾", from $90 to..$125.00
Bear w/Scarf & Hat, Japan, hanger w/2 holes, plate #16, 5½", from $70 to $90.00
Bonzo, Japan, hanger w/2 holes, lustre, w/1 red paw & red tongue, plate #22, 5¾", from $80 to.........................$90.00
Boy in Knickers, Japan, free-standing w/2 holes, red top, gr pants, plate #223, 4¾", from $65 to $80.00
Boy Seated w/Umbrella, Japan, hanger w/2 holes, plate #46, 4¾", from $65 to...$80.00
Boy w/Dog, Japan, hanger w/3 holes, plate #26, 6", from $70 to...$90.00
Bulldog Seated w/Tongue Out, bsk, free-standing w/1 hole, wht w/blk ears, feet & collar, plate #264, 3½", from $50 to.$70.00
Cat, Goldcastle/Japan, hanger w/2 holes, yel w/blk & wht trim, plate #36, 5¾", from $70 to......................................$90.00
Cat Winking on Pedestal, Diamond T/Japan, free-standing w/2 holes, plate #225, 5⅞", from $125 to $165.00

Clown Head w/Bug on Nose, Japan, hanger w/3 holes, plate #59, 5⅛", from $125 to...$170.00
Clown Juggling, Japan, hanger w/3 holes, plate #60, 5", from $75 to $90.00
Cow w/Bell, Japan, hanger w/3 holes, plate #69, 6", from $80 to $100.00
Crow on Pedestal, Diamond T/Japan, free-standing w/2 holes, plate #226, 6", from $125 to $170.00

Photo courtesy Marilyn Cooper.

Dog with Pup and Basket, Japan, 6¼", from $70.00 to $80.00.

Ducky Dandy, Japan, hanger w/2 holes, plate #84, 4¼", from $150 to..$175.00
Dutch Boy & Girl Kissing, Japan, hanger w/2 holes, plate #88, 6¼", from $55 to...$65.00
Dutch Girl w/Flowers, Japan, hanger w/1 hole, plate #86, 5⅞", from $75 to..$85.00
Elephant Seated w/Trunk Curled Down, Japan, free-standing, trunk holds toothbrush, lustre, plate #282, 3", from $85 to..$110.00
Girl w/Basket, Japan, hanger w/2 holes, plate #44, 4½" ...$80.00
Indian Chief, Japan, hanger w/2 holes, plate #115, 4½", from $225 to..$275.00
Little Red Riding Hood w/Wolf, Germany, free-standing w/shaker top, plate #2, 6¼", from $350 to $375.00
Mexican Boy, Japan, hanger w/2 holes, plate #120, 5½", from $80 to..$95.00

Mickey Mouse, Donald Duck & Minnie, prewar Japan/WDE, hanger w/2 holes, plate #121, 4½", from $325 to **$350.00**

Mickey Mouse, 1949, plastic, image of Mickey standing w/hands clasped to hold toothbrush, red & blk, EX, P6 ....**$125.00**

Orphan Annie & Sandy Seated on Couch, Japan, bsk, free-standing w/2 holes, plate #267, 3¾", from $110 to..**$135.00**

Penguin, Japan, hanger w/3 holes, plate #128, 5½", from $85 to..**$100.00**

Peter Rabbit, Germany, free-standing w/shaker top, plate #4, 6¼", from $350 to.....................**$400.00**

Pinocchio w/Big Ears & Figaro, Shafford, free-standing w/1 hole, plate #242, 5¼", from $450 to...............**$500.00**

Pirate w/Large Boots, Japan, hanger w/2 holes, plate #131, 5¼", from $80 to.........................**$90.00**

Pluto, Japan, hanger w/1 hole, plate #133, 4⅝", from $300 to.**$350.00**

Popeye, Japan, bsk, free-standing w/1 hole, plate #244, 5", from $475 to....................**$500.00**

Rabbit w/Large Eyes, Norwood/Germany, hanger w/1 hole, gr w/red muzzle & ears, plate #137, 5½", from $80 to....**$95.00**

Three Bears w/Bowls, Japan, free-standing w/3 holes, brn w/wht bowls, gold trim, plate #248, 4", from $85 to..........**$100.00**

Traffic Cop, Germany, Don't Forget the Teeth, free-standing w/1 hole, plate #243, 5¼", from $325 to.................**$375.00**

Tootsietoys

The first diecast Tootsietoys were made by the Samuel Dowst Company in 1906 when they reproduced the Model T Ford in miniature. Dowst merged with Cosmo Manufacturing in 1926 to form the Dowst Manufacturing Company and continued to turn out replicas of the full-scale vehicles in actual use at the time. After another merger in 1961, the company became known as the Stombecker Corporation. Over the years, many types of wheels and hubs were utilized, varying in both style and material. The last all-metal car was made in 1969; recent Tootsietoys mix plastic components with the metal and have soft plastic wheels. Early prewar mint-in-box toys are scarce and command high prices on today's market. For more information we recommend *Collector's Guide to Tootsietoys* by our advisor, David E. Richter. The recently released second edition features Tootsietoys from 1910-79 and contains nearly seven hundred color photos.

Advisor: David E. Richter (R1).

A&P Tractor-Trailer, 1929-32, EX, A............................**$135.00**

Aero-Dawn, #4660, 1928, silver, purple wheels, NM **$70.00**

Airplane Set, #5698, complete, MIB, A **$400.00**

Airplane Set, #7500, complete set of 8, EXIB, A **$1,025.00**

Airport, includes tin hangar & pylon w/trimotor, biplane & UX 214, G+ (G+ box), A.................................**$775.00**

Andy Gump Car, #5101X, 1932-33, articulated, w/figure, VG, A..............................**$300.00**

Auburn Roadster, #1016, 1942-46, red w/blk rubber tires, 6", VG+ **$25.00**

Battleship, #1034, 1940s, silver & red, complete, 6", NM.**$30.00**

Bild-A-Truck, #7600, Tootsietoys Coast to Coast emb on van, complete, M (EX box), A...........................**$650.00**

Biplane, #4650, 1926, red & yel, new prop, NM+..........**$140.00**

Box Truck, #234, 1940-41, silver, blk tires, 3", NM **$25.00**

Buck Rogers Battlecruiser, 1937, 5", EX, J2 ....**$150.00**

Buck Rogers Flash Blast Attack Ship, 1937, red & wht, 5", VG (EX box) **$200.00**

Buck Rogers Venus Duo-Destroyer, red & yel, 1937, 5", VG (VG box) **$175.00**

Buick Coupe, #4636, 1924-33, bl, 3", NM+.....................**$70.00**

Buick Sedan (General Motors Series), #6004, 1927-33, interchangeable, 3", NM+...............................**$70.00**

Camping Set, #4335, 1960, complete, NM (NM box) ...**$325.00**

Cannon, #4642, 1931-40, gr, M.....................**$30.00**

Chevy Cameo Pickup (1956), 1959-69, teal, plastic tires, 4", NM+ **$25.00**

Chevy Fastback, 1947-49, red, blk rubber tires, 4", EX.....**$35.00**

Chevy Panel Truck (1950), 1950-59, bl, 3", NM+ **$25.00**

Chrysler Convertible (1960), 1961-64, lt bl, 4", EX........**$20.00**

Chrysler Experimental Roadster, 1947-49, red, 6", VG **$30.00**

Coast to Coast Van, red & silver w/blk tires, 8½", M (EX box), A.........................**$200.00**

Coupe (1932), #101, red-orange, 2", NM+.....................**$42.00**

De Luxe Motors Set (Graham Paige), box only, 1933-39, EX ..**$300.00**

De Luxe Motors Set (Graham Paige), 1933-39, complete, EX+ (EX box), A...........................**$2,200.00**

De Luxe Truck Set, #05310, complete, NMIB, $2,350.00.

Dodge Pickup (1950), 1950-60, gr & silver, sm open windows, 4", EX.............................**$25.00**

Domaco Tanker Truck, wht rubber tires, EX.................**$175.00**

Doodlebug, #716, 1935-37, red, 4", rstr, NM+...............**$125.00**

EAL Lockheed Electra Airplane, #125, 1937, silver, NM+ .**$70.00**

F-86 Sabre Jet, red & silver, 1950, 2-pc body, NM+.........**$30.00**

Fageol Bus, #4651, 1927-33, lt bl, 3½", NM.....................**$70.00**

Fire Department Set, #411, 1937, complete, rare, NM (EX box), A **$750.00**

Ford Convertible (1949), 1949-54, red, 3", NM **$25.00**

Ford F6 Truck (1949), 1950-69, red w/silver bed, 4", NM+ ..**$25.00**

Ford Model A Coupe (1928), #4655, olive gr, 2½", NM+ .**$65.00**

Ford Sedan (1935), #0111, red, 3", NM+........................**$60.00**

Ford Station Wagon (1959), 1959-67, red & cream, 6", EX+...**$30.00**

Ford Station Wagon (1962), 1964-68, red, orange & wht, 6", NM+ **$35.00**

Ford Texaco Oil Truck (1949), 1949-52, red, 6", NM+ ...**$65.00**

Ford V-8 Hot Rod (1960), yel, no tow hook, 6", NM.......**$30.00**

Ford Wrecker (1935), #0133, 1935-41, pewter, 3", NM+..**$85.00**

Freight Train, #5550, complete set of 6, EX+ (NM box), A...**$400.00**

Photo courtesy David Richter.

Funnies Set, #5091, 1932, complete, NM (G box), $3,200.00; Aerial Offense Set, #5051, 1932, complete, NMIB, $2,800.00.

GMC Bus, #3571, 1948-55, bl & silver, 6", NM+ $65.00

Gravel Truck, 1976-79, red & yel, 6¼", NM+ $12.00

Hook & Ladder Truck, #4652, 1927-33, wine & bl, new ladders, 3½", NM+ $100.00

Hose Wagon, #238, 1947-48, red, blk rubber tires, 3", VG, from $25 to $30.00

International K11 Standard Oil, 1949-55, red, 6", NM+ .$75.00

International K5 Dump Truck (1947), 1948-53, red & orange, 6", NM+ $50.00

International K5 Stake Truck (1947), 1953, orange, ribbed bed (rare), 6", M $65.00

International K5 Tow Truck (1947), 1948-52, yel, 6", NM+ $42.00

KO Ice Truck, #5105X, 1932-33, olive gr w/red driver, 3", VG $265.00

La Salle Sedan, #713, 1935-39, blk & silver, wht rubber tires, 4", NM+ $240.00

Mack L-Line Oil Tanker, 1954-59, red, blk rubber tires, 9", NM (EX box) $175.00

Mack L-Line Oil Tanker, 1954-59, red, w/ladder rear of trailer, rubber tires, 9", NM+ $70.00

Mack Stake Truck (1925), #4638, 1925-28, orange & wine, 3", NM+ $80.00

Mack Stake Truck (1928), #4638, 1928-33, orange & bl, 3", NM+ $70.00

Mack Transport, #0190, 1931-33, red w/3 mc Buicks, 8½", NM+ $210.00

Photo courtesy David E. Richter.

MG TF Roadster, 1954, red, 6", M, $45.00.

Midget Set, #0510, 1935-41, complete w/8 vehicles & 2 sm planes, VG (EX box) $200.00

Moon Mullins Police Patrol, 1932, bl w/tan figures, 2¼", VG $275.00

P-38 Fighter Plane, 1950, EX, from $90 to.....................$95.00

P-80 Shooting Star Jet, 1948, red & silver, NM+ $30.00

Pan American Airport Set, #6500, rare, missing 1 badge, EX (EX box)..$550.00

Pan American Boeing Stratocruiser, 1951-54, silver, NM+ $100.00

Playtime Set, #5031, 1920s, complete, M (EX box), A $1,450.00

Rambler Wagon (1960), 1961-63, dk bl, 4", NM $30.00

Road Construction Set, #4330, complete, NM (M box), A..$400.00

Road Construction Set, #6000, complete, MIB, H12.....$450.00

Sedan, #103, 1932, dk orange, 2", NM+ $42.00

Semi Truck (Little Toughs), 1970-79, red cab w/bl trailer, 4¼", NM+ $12.00

Semi Truck (Tiny Toughs), 1976-79, bl & silver tractor, wht trailer w/stickers, 6¼", NM+ $12.00

Smitty on Motorcycle w/Herbie on Sidecar, 1932, diecast, red w/yel figures, 3", M $475.00

Stock Car, #1091, tan, orange & red, wht tires, 5", NM+ ..$25.00

Studebaker Coupe (1947), 1949, bl, 3", rstr, NM+..........$55.00

Tootsietoy Dairy (Milk Trailers), #1092, 1933-41, tractor w/3 trailers, G (G box) $175.00

Uncle Walt Roadster, #5102X, 1932-33, gr w/lt brn driver, 3", G..$240.00

US Army Armored Car, #4635, 1946-48, tan & gr, blk tires, 4", M...$55.00

US Army Mack Antiaircraft Gun, #4643, 1931, tan & gr, 3", M...$60.00

US Army RC 180 Rocket Launcher Truck, 1958-60, army gr, 9", rpr rocket o/w NM+.....................................$140.00

US Army Set, #5220, 1930, rare, complete, NM (EX box), A..$1,250.00

US Navy Set, #5750, complete, NM (EX box)..............$350.00

Watertower, #4653, 1927-33, bl, yel & red, 3½", NM+..$110.00

Yellow Cab Sedan, #4629, 1921-33, dk gr, 3", M $45.00

Yellow Cab Sedan, #4629, 1921-33, orange, 3", NM+ $40.00

Tops and Other Spinning Toys

Tops are among the oldest toys in human history. Homer in *The Iliad*, Plato in the *Republic,* and Virgil in *The Aeneid* mention tops. They are found in nearly all cultures, ancient and modern.

There are seven major categories: 1) The twirler — spun by the twisting action of fingers upon the axis. Examples are Teetotums, Dreidels, advertising spinners, and Tippe Tops. 2) The supported top — started with a string while the top is supported upright. These include 'recuperative,' having a string that automatically rewinds (Namurs); 'seperative,' with a top that detaches from the launcher; 'spring launched,' which is spun using a wound spring; 'pump' or 'helix,' whereby a twisted rod is pumped to spin the top; and 'flywheel-' or 'inertia wheel-powered.' 3) The peg top — spun by winding a string around the peg of the top which is then thrown. 4) The whip top — which is kept spinning by the use of a whip. 5) The yo-yo or return top. 6) The gyroscope. 7) The Diavuolo or Diabolo.

Advisor: Bruce Middleton (M20).

See also Yo-Yos.

Air Powered, Cracker Jack, Dowsy, Chicago, red, wht & bl, M, M20..$12.00

Air Powered, Poll Parrot Shoes, yel, NM, M20 ....$12.00

Photo courtesy Bruce Middleton.

Aladdin Ball and Top, early 1900s, helix rod powered, EX (EX box), M20, $550.00.

Autogyro Horse Race, Britians, lead & wire, flywheel mechanism, w/4 jockeys on horses, 11" L, EX, A............$1,000.00

Circus Horse & Rider, lead w/wire & tin, horse & female rider on rods attached to base, 7", VG+, A $375.00

Competition Award Patches, top shape, 1st, 2nd & 3rd, M, M20, ea $50.00

Dancing Couple, Ives, japanned & polychromed CI figures w/arms entwined, she in lead bell-shaped skirt, 3½", EX, A..$135.00

Disk, maroon & red wood flat-top w/natural wood holder, 3½" dia, EX..$45.00

Disk, red & natural wood w/gr stripes, w/hdl, 4" dia, EX ..$75.00

Game, Big Top, Marx, plastic, battery-op, MIB, M20 ......$35.00

Game, Brownie Kick-In, MH Miller, litho tin w/Brownies, top kicks balls into indentations for score, VG (G box), M20 ....$50.00

Game, Double Diabolos, Parker Bros, 1930s, EX (orig box), M20..$60.00

Gyro-Cycle Top, British Invention and Manufacture, boy rides circular track, EX (EX box), M20 ....$600.00

Hummer, German, litho tin, clown-head knob w/wooden hat, 8", VG..$580.00

Hummer, inverted wood beehive-shape w/mc stripes, 2½" dia, VG $415.00

Hummer, wht celluloid ball w/mc stripes, tall hdl, 7", EX..$415.00

Namur, wooden ball w/brass string housing, EX, M20......$20.00

Peg Top, Duncan Chicago Twister #329, wood, MIP, M20..$20.00

Peg Top, Duncan Tournament #349, wood, MIP, M20....$20.00

Peg Top, Duncan Twin Spin #310, wood, MIP, M20.......$20.00

Peg Top, Duncan Whistler #320, wood, MIP, M20..........$20.00

Peg Top, Helix Rod Launcher, advertising Kinney Shoes, VG, M20..$15.00

Recuperative, wood, 6-sided string housing over ovoid body, G, M20..$85.00

Spinner, Alemite Motor Oil, Bakelite, Keeps Your Car Humming Like a Top, NM, M20 ....$15.00

Photo courtesy Bruce Middleton.

Recuperative, natural wood with painted stripes, wood string housing, EX, from $50.00 to $100.00; Namur, wood with brass string housing, $20.00.

Spinner, Brown-Bilt Shoes, Buster Brown, blk & red letters on yel background w/red trim, EX, M20.........................$45.00

Spinner, Cracker Jack, M, M20, from $20 to $75.00

Spinner, Derby Petroleum Products, M, M20, from $20 to ...$75.00

Spinner, man w/mug of beer, Hvem Betaler on hat, litho metal, foreign, spin to see who pays, NM, M20 ....$85.00

Spinner, Nolde's American Maid Breads & Cakes, red & wht, NM, M20 ....$30.00

Spinner, OTC Trenton Oyster Crackers, bl letters on wht, M, M20..$50.00

Spinner, Poll Parrot Shoes, red parrot w/blk shoes on yel background, M, M20 ....$30.00

Spinner, Robin Hood Shoes, M, M20, from $20 to $75.00

Spinner, shaped like pointing spaniel, flat, Heads I Win, Tails You Lose, NM, M20 ....$25.00

Spinner, Tastykake Cakes & Pies, M, M20, from $20 to..$75.00

Spinner, Tip Top Bread, plastic, NM, M20 ....$10.00

Supported, pressed board disk w/graphics of boy shooting a toy gun, M, M20 ....$60.00

Supported, Rainbow, Seneca, pnt metal 4-tooth disks inside lg disk rotating around shaft, changes color, NM, M20.$65.00

Tip Tray, Canada Dry, red, gr, wht & yel, dimple in center to spin on, G, M20..$20.00

Tip Tray, SS Pierce, Wine & Spirit Merchants..., dimple in center to spin on, M, M20...$60.00

Trading Cards

Modern collector cards are really just an extension of a hobby that began well before the turn of the century. Advertising cards put out by the food and tobacco companies of that era sometimes featured cute children, their pets, stage stars, battle scenes, presidential candidates, and so forth. Collectors gathered them up and pasted them in scrapbooks.

In the 20th century, candy and bubble gum companies came to the forefront. The cards they issue with their products carry the likenesses of sports figures, fictional heroes, TV and movie stars, Disney characters, Barbie dolls, and country singers!

Distinguishing a collectible trading card from other cards may be a bit confusing. Remember, trading cards are released in only two ways: 1) in a wax or foil pack, generally in multiples of twelve — twenty-four, thirty-six, or forty-eight); or 2) as a premium with another product. The only exception to this rule are sets issued as limited editions, with each set individually numbered. Cards issued as factory sets are not trading cards and have no collector value unless they cross over into another collecting area, for example, the Tuff Stuff Norma Jean (Marilyn Monroe) series. In general, from 1980 to the present, wrappers tend to fall into the 50¢ to $2.00 range, though there are some exceptions. For more information we recommend *Collector's Guide to Trading Cards* by Robert Reed.

Advisors: Mark and Val Macaluso (M1).

Other Sources: C1, C10, D11, F1, F8, H4, H11, H12, J6, J7, M8, M17, T2

A-Team, Monty Gum, 1983, set of 100 ....$15.00
A-Team, Topps, 1983, 2 different packs, set of 66 w/12 stickers $9.50

Addams Family, Donruss, 1964, set of 66, from $5.00 to $8.00 each.

Aladdin, Panini, 1993, set of 100 w/10 stickers $25.00
Alf, Topps, 1987, 1st series, set of 47 w/11 stickers...........$12.00
Alien, Topps, 1979, set of 84 w/22 stickers......................$35.00
Alien Nation, FTCC, 1990, set of 60................................$15.00
Andy Griffith, Pacific, 1990, 1st series, set of 110 ....$25.00
Antique Autos, Bowman, 1950s, 3-D card set w/yel & gr waxed wrapper, J5 ....$45.00
Avengers, Cornerstone, 1993, set of 81.............................$35.00
Baby (Dinosaur Movie), Topps, 1984, set of 66 w/11 stickers $8.00
Babysitter's Club, Topps, 1992, set of 55..........................$15.00
Barbie, Dart/Panini, 1991, 1st series, set of 196 ....$30.00
Batman (Movie), Topps, 1989, 1st series, set of 132 w/22 stickers...$18.00
Batman Dark Knight, Skybox, 1994, set of 100 ....$15.00
Batman Returns, Topps, 1992, set of 88 w/10 stickers $12.50
Batman Returns, Topps, 1992, stadium, set of 100 ....$30.00
Battlestar Galactica, Topps, 1978, set of 132 w/22 stickers, M17...$40.00

Batman (Riddler back card), Topps, 1966, set of 38, from $3.00 to $5.00 each.

Beauty & the Beast, Pro Set, 1992, set of 75 w/10 stickers & 10 mirror cards $18.00
Beauty & the Beast, Upper Deck, 1993, set of 198...........$30.00
Bernard & Bianca, Panini, set of 360 ....$35.00
Betty Boop, Eclipse, 1993, set of 110................................$25.00
Beverly Hillbillies, Eclipse, 1993, set of 110......................$15.00
Beverly Hills 90210, Topps, 1991, set of 77 w/11 stickers...$17.50
Beyond Bizarre, Comic Images, 1993, set of 90.................$12.00
Bionic Woman, Donruss, 1976, set of 44 ....$22.00
Black Hole, Panini, complete set.....................................$45.00
Black Hole, Topps, 1979, set of 88 w/22 stickers $15.00
Boris, Comic Images, 1991, set of 90...............................$20.00
Bozo, Lime Rock, 1994, set of 54....................................$10.00
Buck Rogers, Topps, 1979, set of 88 w/22 stickers $25.00
Cabbage Patch Kids (Astronauts), Coleco, 1989, set of 6 (1 came w/ea doll) $90.00
Cabbage Patch Kids (Circus Clowns), Coleco, 1989, set of 6 (1 came w/ea doll) $60.00
California Raisins, Diamond, 1988, set of 35 ....$6.00
Captain America, Comic Images, 1990, set of 45 ....$25.00
Charlie's Angels, Topps, 1977, 1st series, set of 55 ....$35.00
Charlie's Angels, Topps, 1978, 4th series, set of 66 w/11 stickers $28.00
CHiPs, Donruss, 1979, set of 66 ....$50.00
Cinderella, Panini, 1987, set of 225 ....$40.00
Cinderella, Skybox, 1995, set of 90 ....$18.00
Close Encounters, Topps, 1978, set of 66 w/11 stickers $18.00
Comic Ball Looney Tunes, Upper Deck, 1990, set of 549...$20.00
Coneheads, Topps, 1993, set of 66 ....$8.50
Crazy Labels, Fleer, 1979, set of 64.................................$35.00
Creature Feature, Topps, 1980, 4 different packs, set of 88 w/22 stickers $40.00
Dark Crystal, Donruss, 1982, set of 78 ....$12.00
Dark Shadows, Image, 1993, set of 62 ....$18.00
DC Comic 3-Pack Cards, DC Comics, 1990, set of 72...$115.00
DC Legends, Skybox, 1995, set of 150 ....$55.00
DC Master Series, Skybox, 1994, set of 90.......................$35.00
Deep Space 9, Skybox, 1993, set of 50 ....$20.00
Desert Shield, Pacific, 1991, set of 110............................$7.50
Dinosaurs, Nu-Card, 1962, set of 80 ....$400.00

Dinosaurs (TV Show), Pro Set, 1992, set of 50 w/10 stickers & 5 puzzles..$15.00

Donkey Kong, Topps, 1982, set of 16 w/32 stickers..........$12.50

Dr Who, Cornerstone, 1994, 1st series, set of 110 ....$30.00

Dragon's Lair, Fleer, 1984, set of 30 w/63 stickers.............$54.00

Dream Machines, Champs, 1991, 1st series, set of 100.....$25.00

Duck Tails, Panini, 1988, 6 different packs, ea.................$40.00

Dukes of Hazzard, Donruss, 1981, 3rd series, set of 44 ......$16.00

Dune, Fleer, 1984, set of 44 stickers only, scarce $65.00

Dune, Fleer, 1984, 3 different packs, set of 132, ea...........$25.00

Elvis, Donruss, 1978, set of 66 ....$25.00

Empire Strikes Back, Topps, 1980, 1st series, set of 132 ...$40.00

Empire Strikes Back, Topps, 1980, 3rd series, set of 88 w/22 stickers $27.00

ET, Reeses, 1982, set of 9...$35.00

ET, Topps, 1982, set of 87...$12.00

ET, Topps, 1982, 12 stickers...$20.00

Fantastic Odd Rods, Donruss, 1973, 1st series, set of 66...$45.00

Fievel Goes West, Impel, 1991, set of 150 ....$15.00

Fire Engines, Bon Air, 1993, 1st series, set of 100.............$15.00

Flaming Carrot, Comic Images, 1988, set of 50 ....$60.00

Flying Things, Topps, set of 8...$24.00

Football Superfreaks, Donruss, 1974, set of 44 ....$20.00

Freddie & the Dreamers, Donruss, 1965, set of 66 ....$95.00

Garbage Pail Kids, Topps, 1985, 1st series, 88 stickers ...$150.00

Garfield, Skybox, 1992, set of 100.....................................$20.00

Ghostbusters II, Topps, 1989...$10.00

GI Joe, Diamond, 1987, set of 225 ....$20.00

GI Joe, Milton Bradley, 1986, set of 192 w/12 stickers $55.00

Gong Show, Fleer, 1979, set of 66.....................................$25.00

Grease, Topps, 1978, 1st series, set of 66 w/11 stickers.....$18.00

Gremlins, Topps, 1984, set of 82 w/11 stickers $16.00

Gunsmoke, Pacific, 1991, set of 110..................................$15.00

Happy Days, OPC, 1976, complete set................................$25.00

Harley-Davidson, Collect-A-Card, 1992, set of 100.........$35.00

Harry & the Hendersons, Topps, 1987, set of 77 w/22 stickers...$12.00

Here's Bo, Fleer, 1981, set of 72 ....$15.00

High Chaparral, Monty Gum, 1970, set of 124.................$75.00

Honeymooners, Comic Images, 1988, set of 50 ....$75.00

Howard the Duck, Topps, 1986, set of 77 w/22 stickers ...$18.00

I Love Lucy, Pacific, 1991, set of 110................................$18.00

Incredible Hulk, Drakes Cakes, 1978, set of 24 ....$175.00

Incredible Hulk, Topps, 1979, set of 88 w/22 stickers.......$16.00

James Bond, Philadelphia, 1965, set of 66, NM.............$200.00

James Bond (13 Movies), Monty Gum, 1986, set of 100 ..$150.00

Jaws II, Topps, 1978, set of 59 w/11 stickers........................$9.50

Jurassic Park, Topps, 1993, set of 88 w/11 stickers............$15.00

Jurassic Park Gold, Topps, 1993, set of 88 w/10 stickers...$45.00

King Kong, Eclipse, 1993, set of 110 ....$20.00

King Kong, Topps, 1976, set of 55 w/11 stickers...............$35.00

KISS I, Donruss, 1978, set of 66 ....$60.00

KISS II, Donruss, 1978, set of 66.......................................$75.00

Knight Rider, Donruss, 1985, set of 66 (11 puzzle variations)...$18.00

Kung Fu, Topps, 1973, set of 55 ....$100.00

Lady Death, Krome Prod, 1994, set of 100.......................$50.00

Leave It to Beaver, Pacific, 1984, set of 60.......................$75.00

Lion King, Skybox, 1994, 1st series, set of 90 ....$20.00

Little Mermaid, Pro Set, 1991, set of 90............................$10.00

Little Shop of Horrors, Topps, 1987, set of 44 ....$6.00

M*A*S*H, Donruss, 1982, set of 66.................................$30.00

M*A*S*H, Topps, 1982, set of 6, T2.................................$8.00

Magnum PI, Donruss, 1983, set of 66...............................$12.00

Man From UNCLE, Topps, 1965, set of 55, A $150.00

Marvel Super Heroes, Topps, 1975, set of 9 w/40 stickers .$75.00

Marvel Universe, Comic Images, 1987, series 1, set of 90..$125.00

Marvel Universe, Impel, 1990, series 1, 3 different packs, set of 162, ea $45.00

Masters of the Universe (Animated), Panini, 1987, complete set...$30.00

Masters of the Universe (Movie), Panini, 1987, set of 240 ..$32.00

Max Headroom, Topps, 1988, set of 33 stickers w/11 foils, scarce $75.00

McHale's Navy, Fleer, 1965, set of 66 ....$25.00

Menudo, Topps, 1983, set of 66 w/22 stickers..................$12.00

Mickey Mouse, Americana, set of 360 ....$150.00

Minnie & Me, Impel, 1991, 1st series, set of 160.............$15.00

Monster in My Pocket, Source Group, 1991, set of 48 w/24 stickers $22.00

Moonraker, Topps, 1979, set of 99 w/22 stickers $24.00

Mork & Mindy, Topps, 1978, set of 99 w/22 stickers.......$22.00

Muppets, Cardz, 1994, set of 60..$15.00

Musclecards Big Engine Cars, Performance, 1991, set of 102 ..$25.00

Nightmare Before Christmas, Skybox, 1993, set of 90......$23.00

Pepsi, Dart Flipcards, 1994, 1st series, set of 100.............$16.00

Pete's Dragon, Panini, 1980, complete set $45.00

Planet of the Apes (TV Show), Topps, 1975, set of 66 ....$65.00

Popeye, Card Creations, 1995, set of 100..........................$15.00

Popeye, Parker Bros, 1982, game cards, set of 72.................$6.00

Power Rangers, Collect-A-Card, 1994, set of 72 w/10 stickers..$18.00

Precious Moments, Enesco, 1992, set of 16 (1 given out w/purchase of ceramic figure) $35.00

Raiders of the Lost Ark, Topps, 1981, set of 88 ....$20.00

Rambo, Topps, 1985, set of 66 w/11 stickers....................$18.00

Ren & Stempy, Topps, 1994, set of 50...............................$15.00

Return of the Jedi, Monty Gum, 1983, set of 100 ....$60.00

Rock Superstars, Pro Set, 1991, 2nd series, set of 340 ......$20.00

Rocketship X-M, FTCC, 1979, set of 50...........................$35.00

Roger Rabbit, Topps, 1988, set of 132 w/22 stickers.........$18.00

Saturday Serials, Epic Cards, 1988, 1st series, set of 40 ....$25.00

Saturday Serials, Epic Cards, 1988, 2nd series, set of 40...$12.00

Savage Dragon, Comic Images, 1992, set of 90................$12.00

Saved By the Bell, Pacific, 1992, set of 110 ....$18.00

Seaquest, Skybox, 1994, set of 100 foils $25.00

Sesame Street, Idolmaker, 1992, set of 100......................$15.00

Sgt Pepper's Lonely Hearts Club, Donruss, 1978, set of 66 ..$14.00

She-Ra, Panini, 1987, set of 216 ....$35.00

Six Million Dollar Man, Donruss, 1975, set of 66.............$75.00

Space: 1999, Donruss, 1976, set of 66 ....$20.00

Space: 1999, Panini, 1976, set of 400................................$65.00

Spider-Man, Comic Images, 1988, set of 50 stickers.........$40.00

Spider-Man, Comic Images, 1992, 1st series, set of 90 .....$20.00

Star Trek, Morris National, 1975, set of 30 puzzle cards...$35.00

Star Trek, Topps, 1976, set of 22 stickers $175.00

Star Trek, Topps, 1976, set of 88 cards $395.00

Star Wars, Panini, 1978, set of 256 ....$150.00
Star Wars, Topps, 1977, 1st series, set of 11 stickers.........$27.00
Star Wars, Topps, 1977, 1st series, set of 66 cards $60.00
Star Wars, Topps, 1977, 5th series, set of 11 stickers.......$10.00
Star Wars, Topps, 1977, 5th series, set of 66 cards............$22.00
Star Wars, Vending, 1978, set of 8 ....$20.00
Superman III, Topps, 1983, set of 99 w/22 stickers...........$15.00
Superman the Movie, Topps, 1978, 1st series, set of 12
    stickers...$25.00
Superman the Movie, Topps, 1978, 1st series, set of 77
    cards $18.00
Tarzan, Panini, set of 400 ....$60.00
Teenage Mutant Ninja Turtles, Diamond, 1989, set of 180 ..$17.50
Teenage Mutant Ninja Turtles (Movie), Topps, 1990, set of 132
    w/11 stickers...$10.00
Terminator 2, Impel, 1991, set of 192 ....$15.00
Terminator 2, Topps, 1991, set of 44 stickers....................$6.00
Three Stooges, FTCC, 1985, 1st series, set of 60 ....$75.00
Three Stooges, FTCC, 1989, 2nd series, set of 60.............$24.00
Three's Company, Topps, 1978, set of 16 w/44 stickers....$22.00
Todd McFarlane Super Heroes, Comic Images, 1989, set of
    45 ....$40.00
Total Recall, Pacific, 1990, set of 110 ....$20.00
Trivia Battle, Topps, 1984, set of 132 w/11 stickers..........$18.00
Trolls (Trash Can), Topps, 1992, set of 66 w/11 stickers .$12.00
TV Smelly Awards, Fleer, 1970s, set of 64 ....$25.00
Uranus Strikes, Bob Ting, 1987, set of 36 ....$35.00
Wacko-Saurs, Diamond, 1987, set of 48 ....$10.00
Weird-Ohs, Fleer, 1963, set of 66.................................$175.00
Zorro, Topps, 1958, set of 88, W6 ....$300.00

BOXES

A-Team, Topps, 1983 ....$6.00
Achilleos (90), FPG, 1993 ....$4.00
Addams Family, Topps, 1991 ....$6.00
Akira, Cornerstone, 1994 ....$4.00
Alf, Topps, 1987, 1st series $6.00
Alien, Topps, 1979...$5.00
Alien 3, Star Pics, 1992 ....$4.00
American Bandstand, Collect-A-Card, 1993 ....$4.00
Andy Griffith, Pacific, 1990 ....$5.00
Avengers, Cornerstone, 1994, 2nd series $4.00
Babysitter's Club, Topps, 1992 ....$8.00
Baseball Superfreaks, Donruss, 1st series $20.00
Batman Returns, Topps, 1992..$6.00
Battlestar Galactica, Topps, 1978......................................$20.00
Beauty & the Beast, Upper Deck, 1993..............................$6.00
Berenstain Bears, Kenwis, 1992 ....$5.00
Beverly Hills 90210, Topps, 1991 ....$4.00
Beyond Bizarre, Comic Images, 1994................................$4.00
Bingo, Pacific, 1991 ....$4.00
Black Hole, Topps, 1979...$4.00
California Raisins, Diamond, 1988.....................................$4.00
Charlie's Angels, Topps, 1977, 2nd series $25.00
Charlie's Angels, Topps, 1978, 4th series............................$15.00
Cinderella, Skybox, 1995..$4.00
Comic Ball Looney Toons, Upper Deck, 1990...................$5.00

Conan, Comic Images, 1993 ....$8.00
Dark Crystal, Donruss, 1982 ....$5.00
Dark Shadows, Image, 1993 ....$4.00
Detective Comics, Active Marketing, 1991 ....$4.00
Dick Tracy, Topps, 1993...$7.00
Dinosaurs (TV Show), Pro Set, 1992 ....$4.00
Elvis, Donruss, 1978 ....$8.00
ET, Topps, 1982 ....$6.00
Golden Age of Comics, Comic Images, 1995....................$6.00
Grease, Topps, 1978...$6.00
Gremlins, Skybox, 1992 ....$4.00
Gremlins, Topps, 1984 ....$6.00
Growing Pains, Topps $6.00
Home Alone, Topps, 1992 ....$4.00
Hulk, Comic Images, 1991 ....$5.00
Indiana Jones, Topps, 1984...$6.00
Jurassic Park, Topps, 1993...$4.00
King Kong, Eclipse, 1993 ....$5.00
KISS, Donruss, 1978, A $20.00
Last Action Hero, Topps, 1993 ....$4.00
Lion King, Skybox, 1994, 2nd series $4.00
Little Mermaid, Pro Set, 1991 ....$4.00
Magnum PI, Donruss, 1983 ....$5.00
Marvel Universe, Comic Images, 1st series $10.00
Moonraker, Topps, 1979 ....$4.00
Pac-Man, Fleer, 1980, 1st print, yel wrapper...................$10.00
Planet of the Apes, Topps, 1967, bright yel w/full-color photo,
    scarce, A $100.00
Power Rangers, Collect-A-Card, 1994 ....$5.00
Rambo, Topps, 1985 ....$6.00
Robot Wars, Fleer, 1985 ....$4.00
Roger Rabbit, Topps, 1988 ....$4.00
Sgt Pepper's Lonely Hearts Club, Donruss, 1978 ....$8.00
Space: 1999, Donruss, 1976 ....$4.00
Spider-Man, Comic Images, 1992....................................$5.00
Star Wars, Topps, 1977, 1st series $50.00
Star Wars, Topps, 1977, 5th series $15.00
Superman III, Topps, 1983 ....$6.00
Teenage Mutant Ninja Turtles (Movie), Topps, 1990 ....$6.00
Toxic Crusader, Topps, 1992 ....$6.00
Uranus Strikes, Bob Ting, 1987.....................................$15.00
Where's Waldo?, Mattel, 1991 ....$4.00
Wizard of Oz, Pacific, 1990...$4.00
X-Men, Comic Image, 3rd series......................................$5.00
Zero Heroes, Donruss, 1984 ....$5.00

WRAPPERS

Aeroplanes, Morris National, 1981 ....$1.50
Alien, Topps, 1979..$1.00
Bad Channels, Full Moon, 1991 ....$2.50
Baseball Superfreaks, Donruss, 1973, 1st series $3.00
Batman Dark Knight, Skybox, 1994..................................$1.25
Batman Returns, Dynamic Marketing, 1992 ....$1.75
Battle of the Planets, Costa Rican, 1981 ....$2.00
Bay City Rollers, Topps, 1977 ....$7.50
Bionic Woman, Donruss, 1976 ....$3.00
Buck Rogers, Scanlens, 1979 ....$4.00

Charlie's Angels, Topps, 1977, 1st series	$3.00
Comic Book Foldees, Topps, 1966	$15.00
Creature Feature, Topps, 1973	$7.00
Dinosaurs, Nu-Card, 1962	$20.00
Dukes of Hazzard, Donruss, 1980, 1st series	$1.75
Empire Strikes Back, Topps, 1980	$2.00
Evel Kneivel, Topps, 1974	$8.00
Fantastic Odd Rods, Donruss, 1973	$4.00
Flying Nun, Donruss, 1968	$8.00
Football Superfreaks, Donruss, 1974	$2.00
Freddie & the Dreamers, Donruss, 1965	$30.00
Garbage Pail Kids, Topps, 1985, 1st series	$6.00
Gong Show, Fleer, 1979	$2.00
Happy Days, OPC, 1976	$1.50
Honeymooners, Comic Images, 1988	$2.00
James Bond (13 Movies), Monty Gum, 1986	$3.00
Jiggley's, Action Card, 1950	$9.50
Jurassic Park (Gold), Topps, 1993	$1.50
KISS I, Donruss, 1978	$2.00
Leave It to Beaver, Pacific, 1984	$3.00
Mad Magazine, stickers, Fleer, 1983	$4.00
Marvel Super Heroes, Topps, 1975	$4.00
Pac-Man, Fleer, 1980, 1st print, yel	$4.00
Planet of the Apes, Topps, 1975	$4.00
Return of the Jedi, Monty Gum, 1983	$2.00
Rocketship X-M, FTCC, 1979	$2.50
Six Million Dollar Man, Donruss, 1975	$4.00
Sky Birds, Goudey, 1930s, red w/yel & bl, VG+, J5	$95.00
Star Trek III, FTCC, 1984	$2.00
Star Wars, OPC, 1978, 1st series	$8.00
Star Wars, OPC, 1978, 2nd series	$5.00
Three Stooges, FTCC, 1985	$1.50
TV Cartoon Tattoos (Hanna-Barbera), Topps, 1976	$5.00

Trains

Some of the earliest trains (from ca 1860) were made of tin or cast iron, smaller versions of the full-scale steam-powered trains that transversed America from the east to the west. Most were made to simply be pushed or pulled along, though some had clockwork motors. Electric trains were produced as early as the late 19th century. Three of the largest manufacturers were Lionel, Ives, and American Flyer.

Lionel trains have been made since 1900. Until 1915 they produced only standard gauge models (measuring 2½" between the rails). The smaller O gauge (1¼") they introduced at that time proved to be highly successful, and the company grew until by 1955 it had become the largest producer of toys in the world. Until discontinued in 1940, standard gauge trains were produced on a limited scale, but O and 027 gauge models dominated the market. Production dwindled and nearly stopped in the mid-1960s, but the company was purchased by General Mills in 1969, and they continue to produce a very limited number of trains today.

The Ives company had been a major producer of toys since 1896. They were the first to initiate manufacture of the O gauge train and at first used only clockwork motors to propel them. Their first electric trains (in both O and #1 gauge) were made in 1910, but because electricity was not yet a common commodity in many areas, clockwork production continued for several years. By 1920, #1 gauge was phased out in favor of standard gauge. The company continued to prosper until the late 1920s when it floundered and was bought jointly by American Flyer and Lionel. American Flyer soon turned their interest over to Lionel, who continued to make Ives trains until 1933.

The American Flyer company had produced trains for several years, but it wasn't until it was bought by AC Gilbert in 1937 that it became successful enough to be considered a competitor of Lionel. They're best noted for their conversion from the standard (wide gauge) 3-rail system to the 2-rail S gauge (⅞") and the high-quality locomotives, passenger, and freight cars they produced in the 1950s. Interest in toy trains waned during the space-age decade of the 1960s. As a result, sales declined, and in 1966 the company was purchased by Lionel. Today both American Flyer and Lionel trains are being made from the original dies by Lionel Trains Inc., privately owned.

For more information we recommend *Collecting Toy Trains, An Identification and Value Guide*, by Richard O'Brien.

Advisors: Bill Mekalian (M4) and Gary Mosholder, Gary's Trains (G1).

See also Buddy L (for that company's Outdoor Railroad); **Paper-Lithographed Toys**.

Key:
acces — accessories	obv/c — observation car
b/c — boxcar	pass — passenger
bg/c — baggage car	st/c — stock car
fl/c — flat bed car	tk/c — tank car
loco — locomotive	/c — car
OB — original box	

AMERICAN FLYER

Acces, #2 transformer, 75 watts, 1947-52, EX	$12.00
Acces, #4B transformer, 100 watts, 1949-56, EX (OB)	$15.00
Acces, #12B transformer, 250 watts, 1946-52, EX (OB)	$75.00
Car, #779 oil drum loader, 1955-56, NM	$150.00
Car, #974 operating b/c, red, EX+	$150.00
Car, #24222 Domino Sugar hopper, 1963-64, VG+	$400.00
Car, #25515 USAF Rocket Sled, fl/c, EX	$200.00
Cars, #4332 obv/c (1), #4331 pullmans (2), red w/brass trim, EX (OBs), A	$1,150.00
Loco, #342 DC Switcher, MIB	$575.00
Loco, #481 Silver Flash, diesel, MIB, A	$750.00
Loco, #21551 Northern Pacific A-unit, NM, A	$375.00
Loco, #21573 NH EP5, 1958-59, EX	$600.00
Loco & tender, #21004 loco, #21404 tender, Gilbert, EX, A	$690.00
Locos, #370 GP-7 diesels (3), G, A	$260.00
Set, #23830 Piggyback Unloader & Car, NM (OB w/insert)	$150.00
Set, freight; 2-4-2 loco, tender, b/c, gondola, tk/c, fl/c w/load, all lg 8-wheeled, 1930-35, VG (OB), A	$690.00
Set, freight; 2-4-2 loco, tender, crane, gondola, fl/c, b/c, caboose, all lg 8-wheeled, 1930-35, G, A	$345.00

Set, freight; 2-6-4 loco, 8-wheeled tender; fl/c & b/c (OBs) derrick/c, tk/c, gondola, caboose, VG, 1930s, A...........$430.00

Set, K771 operating stockyard & car, NMIB, A.............$140.00

Set, pass; #360 & #364 locos, #660, #661, #662 & #663, VG, A..$260.00

Set, pass; #466, #960, #962, #963, 1954, G, A $290.00

Set, pass; #21927 loco, diesel; #24773, #24813 & #24833, VG A..$430.00

Set, The Comet, AA loco, coaches (2), end/c, turq litho, VG+, A..$510.00

LIONEL LTI 1987-96

Acces, #12723 microwave tower, NMIB...........................$25.00

Acces, #82008 auto-switch, left hand, NMIB...................$42.00

Car, #700 Pennsylvania caboose, NMIB..........................$35.00

Car, #701 Denver & Rio Grand caboose, NMIB.............$35.00

Car, #5733 Lionel bunk/c, NMIB......................................$30.00

Car, #9413 Naperville b/c, NMIB......................................$15.00

Car, #16303 Pennsylvania fl/c w/vans, NMIB.................$25.00

Car, #16640 Rutland b/c w/Diesel Railsounds, NMIB....$165.00

Car, #17605 Reading Woodside caboose, NMIB.............$38.00

Car, #19709 Pennsylvania caboose, working smoke, NMIB.$60.00

Car, #87000, New York Central b/c, NMIB......................$42.00

Car, #87002 ATSF/c, NMIB $38.00

Car, #87200 operating hand/c, lg gauge, EX, NMIB........$55.00

Car, #87204 Northern Pacific hopper/c, NMIB...............$32.00

Car, #87205 Pennsylvania hopper/c, NMIB $32.00

Car, #87405 PRR gondola, NMIB.....................................$25.00

Car, #87407 Baltimore & Ohio gondola, NMIB..............$32.00

Car, #87504 Union Pacific fl/c, NMIB.............................$30.00

Car, #87505 Soo Line-Logs, NMIB...................................$32.00

Car, #87600 Alaska tk/c, NMIB..$40.00

Car, #87602 Gulf tk/c, NMIB..$40.00

Car, #87603 Borden tk/c, NMIB.......................................$40.00

Car, #87705 Great Northern caboose, NMIB...................$45.00

Loco, #8602 Pennsylvania 4-4-2, steam, NMIB $120.00

Loco, #18001 Rhode Island 4-8-4, SOS whistle, NMIB.$445.00

Loco, #18303 Amtrak GG1, diesel, NMIB.......................$400.00

Loco, #18601 Great Northern, steam, NMIB..................$100.00

Loco, #18610 Rock Island 0-4-0, steam, NMIB.............$175.00

Loco, #18615 Grand Trunk West, steam, NMIB.............$90.00

Loco, #18804 Soo RS8, diesel, NMIB $90.00

Loco, #18901 Pennsylvania Alco AA, diesel, NMIB.....$125.00

Loco, #87004 Southern/c, NMIB $42.00

Loco, #87005 Northern Pacific b/c, NMIB $42.00

Loco, #87104 Gerber b/c, NMIB $48.00

Loco & Caboose, #18011 & #17608 Chessie, steam, NMIB..$900.00

Loco & Tender, #18004 Reading, NMIB, A $220.00

Set, #11745 Navy Set, NMIB..$190.00

Set, #11758 1989 SSS Desert King, NMIB.....................$240.00

Set, #81002 Frontier Freight, lg gauge, NMIB.............$140.00

Set, #81006 Union Pacific Limited, lg gauge, NMIB.....$220.00

Set, #85000 Seaboard GP9, lg gauge, NMIB..................$320.00

Set, #85001 Conrail GP9, lg gauge, NMIB.....................$320.00

Set, #85100 Pennsylvania 0-6-0, lg gauge, NMIB..........$110.00

Set, #85101 Rio Grande, lg gauge, NMIB.......................$110.00

Set, #85102 New York Central 4-4-2, lg gauge, NMIB..$200.00

Set, #85107 Great Northern 4-4-2, lg gauge, NMIB $200.00

Set, #85108 B&O 0-4-0, lg gauge, NMIB.......................$120.00

Set, Railscope, MIB, A $175.00

LIONEL MPC 1970-86

Acces, #115 station, red & cream, missing skylight o/w NMIB $190.00

Car, #5730 Strasburg Railroad reefer, NMIB $28.00

Car, #5735 New York Central bunk/c, NMIB $32.00

Car, #6126 Canadian National ore hopper/c, NMIB........$25.00

Car, #6127 Northern Pacific ore hopper/c, NMIB...........$25.00

Car, #6260 New York Central long gondola w/canisters, NMIB $15.00

Car, #6917 Jersey Central caboose, NMIB......................$65.00

Car, #7206 Norfolk & Western dining/c, MIB, A..........$320.00

Car, #7211 SP Daylight Vista Dome, MIB, A $430.00

Car, #7404 Jersey Central b/c, NMIB..............................$50.00

Car, #7509 Kentucky Fried Chicken reefer, NMIB $30.00

Car, #7513 Bonanza reefer, NMIB $30.00

Car, #8307 Southern Pacific Daylight, MIB, A $920.00

Car, #8850 Penn Central, GG1, MIB, A $375.00

Car, #9162 Pennsylvania Port Hole caboose, NMIB........$35.00

Car, #9186 Conrail caboose, lighted, NMIB....................$50.00

Car, #9726 Erie Lackawanna b/c, NMIB.........................$25.00

Car, #9802 Miller High Life reefer, std O ga, NMIB $40.00

Cars, #19105 Amtrak full vista dome (3), MIB, A $290.00

Loco, #6-8477 NY Central GP-9 diesel (4), uncataloged, MIB, A..$1,265.00

Loco, #8056 Chicago North Western Trainmaster, MIB, A..$375.00

Loco, #8104 Union Pacific 4-4-0, w/display case, MIB, A......$635.00

Loco, #8160 Burger King GP20, diesel, NMIB $120.00

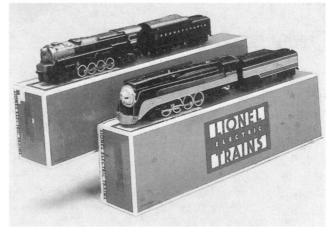

Locomotive, #8307, Southern Pacific daylight steam, MIB, A, $865.00; Locomotive, #8404, Pennsylvania S-2 6-8-6 turbine, MIB, A, $550.00.

Loco, #8406 NYC Hudson, MIB, A $750.00

Loco, #8466/67 Amtrak F3 AA, diesel, NMIB..............$425.00

Loco, #8850 Penn Central GG-1, NM, A $460.00

Loco, #18003 Delaware, Lackawanna & Western 4-8-4, NMIB, A $550.00

Loco, #18301 Southern FM diesel, NMIB, A $460.00
Loco, #18303 Amtrak GG1 diesel, NMIB, A.................$520.00
Loco, GP-7S (2), rpt as South Pacific power units, MIB, A ..$260.00
Loco, Reading T-1 4-8-4, NMIB..............................$920.00
Loco & Tender, #8606 B&A Hudson & #6907 NYC woodside
 caboose, NMIB, A...................................$1,050.00
Set, #1450 SS, Rio Grande #8764/#8465/#8474 ABA,
 NMIB $595.00
Set, #1970 Southern Pacific Limited, MIB, A $490.00
Set, #5-2587 American Freedom Train, MIB, A $80.00
Set, #6-11707 Silver Spike, MIB, A........................$230.00
Set, Mickey Mouse Express, #6-8773 U36B Diesel (1), #6-9183
 tender (1), assorted b/cs, NMIB, A $520.00
Set, Mid-Atlantic Limited, MIB, A $260.00
Set, pass; Chessie Steam Special, #8008 loco & tender, #9581,
 #9582, #9583, #9584 & #9585, 1980, NMIB, A $320.00
Set, TCA Anniversary GG1, NMIB..............................$345.00

LIONEL POSTWAR

Acces, #020 crossing, O ga, EXIB..............................$5.00
Acces, #020X 45" crossing, EXIB $6.00
Acces, #26 bumper, EX.......................................$15.00
Acces, #54 ballast tamper, test run, EX+, A $210.00
Acces, #58 rotary snowplow, EX, A $575.00
Acces, #97 coal elevator, EX................................$275.00
Acces, #97 coal elevator, NMIB $375.00
Acces, #110 trestle set, VG (OB)............................$15.00
Acces, #112 super switches, O ga, EX.........................$90.00
Acces, #125 whistling station, MIB, A......................$280.00
Acces, #128 animated newsstand, EX+, A $180.00
Acces, #147 whistle control, EX.............................$10.00
Acces, #164 lumber loader, EX $300.00
Acces, #167 whistle controller, EXIB........................$10.00
Acces, #195 floodlight tower, NMIB, A $190.00
Acces, #264 forklift, operating, no insert, EX+, A $550.00
Acces, #310 billboard set, EXIB $30.00
Acces, #350 engine transfer table, M (NM box), A $450.00
Acces, #352 icehouse & car, EXIB............................$295.00
Acces, #364 lumber loader, MIB, A $300.00
Acces, #3656 operating cattle set, EXIB $75.00
Acces, #375 turntable, motorized, NMIB, A $350.00
Acces, #415 diesel fueling station, MIB, A $350.00
Acces, #455 oil derrick & pumper, MIB, A $650.00
Acces, #462 derrick platform, NMIB (w/insert), A $550.00
Acces, #464 lumber mill, NMIB, A $300.00
Acces, #494 rotating beacon, red, EXIB......................$45.00
Acces, #497 coaling station, lt gr roof & base, EX.........$250.00
Acces, #497 coaling station, MIB, A.........................$500.00
Acces, #927 lubricating kit, EXIB...........................$50.00
Acces, #943 ammo dump, EX.................................$100.00
Acces, #970 Lionel ticket booth, MIB........................$250.00
Acces, #1025 bumper, EX.....................................$15.00
Acces, #1033 transformer, 90 watts, EXIB $55.00
Acces, #1043 transformer, 50 watts, EXIB $25.00
Acces, #1044 transformer, 90 watts, EX......................$60.00
Acces, #3472 operating milk set, EXIB $55.00
Car, #50 gang/c, gray bumpers, rare, EX (OB) $400.00

Car, #52 fire/c, EX, A.......................................$190.00
Car, #55 Tie Jector/c, test run, w/insert & peripherals, NMIB,
 A..$240.00
Car, #60 trolley, blk letters, no insert, NMIB, A $200.00
Car, #65 hand/c, screw crack, 2 broken hdl nibs, no melting, VG
 (worn OB), A...$200.00
Car, #68 Inspection/c, EX...................................$300.00
Car, #68 Inspection/c, NMIB (factory sealed), A........$1,100.00
Car, #69 maintenance/c, no insert, EX+ (OB), A $280.00
Car, #175 rocket launcher, M (NM box), A..................$900.00
Car, #182 remote control crane, G, A $115.00
Car, #623 SF switcher, NMIB $600.00
Car, #2452X PRR gondola, EX................................$20.00
Car, #2458X PRR b/c, dbl metal door, EX $85.00
Car, #3359 twin coal dump gondola, EX......................$45.00
Car, #3360 burro crane, EX, A $140.00
Car, #3360 burro crane, NMIB $600.00
Car, #3361X operating log dump/c, EX.......................$35.00
Car, #3366 operating circus/c & corral, 9 wht horses, EX ..$350.00
Car, #3419 dbl-prop copter, VG+ $95.00
Car, #3444D cop & hobo gondola, EX (OB) $85.00
Car, #3454 PRR Auto Merchant/c, VG+ $75.00
Car, #3461 log dump/c, blk, EX..............................$40.00
Car, #3494 operating NYC b/c, NMIB, A $200.00
Car, #3530 operating generator/c, short stripe, blk tanks & base
 pole, NM+ (worn box), A.............................$220.00
Car, #3619 helicopter recon, rpr roof, EX $95.00
Car, #3665 Minuteman missile launch, EX $115.00
Car, #6024 Shredded Wheat b/c, EX $25.00
Car, #6112 gondola, bl, EX...................................$8.00
Car, #6346 Alcoa, quad hopper, EX (OB) $55.00
Car, #6361 Timber/c, MIB, A $135.00

O Gauge, auto loader, #6414, 1960s, complete, EX, J6, $125.00.

Car, #6464-125 Pacemaker b/c, metal trucks, EX+ (OB rough &
 incomplete), A......................................$110.00
Car, #6464-225 SP b/c, NMIB, A $200.00
Car, #6464-250 WP b/c, Timken trucks, EX+, A $360.00
Car, #6464-300 Rutland b/c, unpnt door, metal trucks, EX+,
 A...$100.00
Car, #6464-325 Sentinel b/c, VG (worn OB), A $270.00
Car, #6464-450 GN b/c, metal trucks, NMIB, A...........$180.00
Car, #6464-825 Alaska b/c, EX+, A.........................$330.00
Car, #6517-75 Erie Bay-Window caboose, NM, A $375.00
Car, #6557 smoking caboose, NMIB...........................$400.00

Car, #6656 stock/c, yel, EX (OB) $25.00
Car, #6800 fl/c w/airplane, blk over yel, test run, NMIB, A ..$190.00
Car, #6803 fl/c w/military units, NMIB, A $400.00
Car, #6806 fl/c w/radar & hospital trucks, NMIB, A......$290.00
Car, #6807 fl/c w/DUWK, NMIB, A $200.00
Car, #6816 fl/c w/bulldozer, for set #1617S, lt orange dozer, red
    fl/c, EX+ (OB worn), A..$500.00
Car, #6817 fl/c w/earth scraper, EX+ $400.00
Car, #6822 searchlight/c, EX $60.00

Cars, #6823 flat with missile, #6463 rocket fuel car (not shown), #161 mail pick-up set, #3474 WP box car and #6517 caboose (not shown), all MIB, $575.00 for the set; Cars, #3545 TV monitor car and #3662 milk car, MIB, $550.00 for both.

Loco, #50 gang/c, EX (OB)...$60.00
Loco, #51 Navy switcher, unrun, NM+, A $260.00
Loco, #60 trolley, bl letters, EX $145.00
Loco, #209 NH Alco AA, EX, A....................................$625.00
Loco, #212 USMC, EX...$125.00
Loco, #218 & 212T Santa Fe Alco AA, VG $85.00
Loco, #218 SF AA, MIB...$400.00
Loco, #221 Rio Grande Alco A, EX................................$95.00
Loco, #400 powered Bud/c, VG+ $230.00
Loco, #600 Missouri, Kansas & Texas NW2, VG+ $155.00
Loco, #611 Jersey Central NW2, VG+ $165.00
Loco, #613 UP NW2 switcher, hairline screw crack, EX+ (OB
    taped & rough), A..$450.00
Loco, #626 B&O 44-tonner, minor chips in skirt, VG+, A ..$170.00
Loco, #632 NW2 switcher, NM, A $310.00
Loco, #1055 Texas Special Alco, EX $40.00
Loco, #1065 Union Pacific Alco, VG $65.00
Loco, #2028 Pennsylvania GP-7, gold lettering, EX (OB), A ...$635.00
Loco, #2242 NH F3 AB, EX, A $725.00
Loco, #2243 AB Sante Fe, VG, A..................................$275.00
Loco, #2245 MKT B-unit, MIB, A.................................$575.00
Loco, #228P Canadian National Alco, MIB..................$300.00
Loco, #2322 Virginia FM, diesel, EX (OB), A $920.00
Loco, #2322 Virginia Trainmaster, diesel, NMIB (factory
    sealed), A..$1,725.00
Loco, #2328 Burlington GP7, rstr, A $270.00
Loco, #2330 PRR GG1, stripes 30%, missing 1 insulator, VG,
    A...$260.00

Locomotives, O gauge, #2023, Union Pacific Alco diesel, yellow, and #2033, Union Pacific diesel, silver, NMIB, $800.00 for both.

Loco, #2331 Virginia FM, bl cab, 1 minor screw crack, NM,
    A...$500.00
Loco, #2331 Virginia FM, blk stripe, minor screw crack, EX+,
    A...$200.00
Loco, #2332 PA GG1, blk, 5 stripes (60%), VG+, A.....$675.00
Loco, #2333 AA, diesel, 2-pcs, G, A $220.00
Loco, #2333 Sante Fe F3 AA, rubber stamped, red GM decal on
    door, dummy A has rpl porthole lens, VG+, A $250.00
Loco, #2337 Wabash GP7, screw crack, VG+, A...........$200.00
Loco, #2339 Wabash GP7, diesel, MIB, A $1,035.00
Loco, #2340 Pennsylvania GG-1, EX $920.00
Loco, #2343 powered & dummy (2), diesels, G, A.........$400.00
Loco, #2343 Sante Fe B-unit, louver top, MIB, A..........$690.00
Loco, #2344 NYC F3 AA, missing 5 porthole lenses, EX (worn
    OB), A...$400.00
Loco, #2344 NYC F3 ABA, missing 9 porthole lenses & nose
    decal on dummy A, EX, A $510.00
Loco, #2344C NYC B unit, screen top, EX....................$425.00
Loco, #2346 B&M GP9, NMIB, A $570.00
Loco, #2348 M&StL GP9, VG+, A.................................$280.00
Loco, #2349 Northern Pacific GP-9, diesel, NMIB (sealed),
    A..$1,495.00
Loco, #2350 NH EP5, decal version, EX (OB) $450.00
Loco, #2350 NH EP5, NM, A $370.00
Loco, #2354 NYC AA unit, some chipping, EX, A........$270.00
Loco, #2355 WP F3 AA, silver, power unit has decal chips
    (OB), dummy has sm nicks in roof, EX, A..............$850.00
Loco, #2356 Southern ABA, NM, A...........................$1,200.00
Loco, #2358 Great Northern EP-5, electric, MIB, A ..$4,890.00
Loco, #2360 GG-1, gr w/5 stripes, NMIB (sealed), from $3,000
    to...$3,450.00
Loco, #2360 GG-1, solid gold stripe, EX, A $1,265.00
Loco, #2365 C&O GP7, EX..$325.00
Loco, #2367C Wabash B-unit, VG, A $175.00
Loco, #2378 Milwaukee Road F3 AB, yel stripe on both, nose
    decal chips, EX, A $775.00
Loco, #2378C Milwaukee F-3 B-unit, MIB, A $1,150.00

Loco, #2379 Rio Grande B-unit, repro box, EX, A.........$750.00

Loco, #2379 Rio Grande F3 AB, EX (OB), A $510.00

Loco, #2383 Sante Fe F3 AA, minor decal chipping on dummy, EX+, A $300.00

Loco, #3927 track cleaner, EX (OB) $110.00

Loco, #6220 NW2 switcher, missing bell, VG+, A $150.00

Loco, #6220 Sante Fe bell ringer, NW2, VG+ $295.00

Loco, #623 Sante Fe switcher, NMIB, A $300.00

Loco, #6250 Seaboard NW2 switcher, minor touchup on cab roof, VG+, A $190.00

Loco, dummy; #2344C NYC A unit, screen top, sm scratch on side o/w EX, A $230.00

Loco, 32351 Milwaukee Road EP5, rivet cracked on 1 side o/w EX, A $220.00

Loco & Tender, #665 loco, #736W tender, unrun, NMIB, A.$600.00

Loco & Tender, #736 & #736W, Berkshire, steam, NM, A $500.00

Loco & Tender, #773 LTS loco (factory sealed), #736W NYC tender, NMIB (w/master carton), A $1,900.00

Set, #1649, Sante Fe Alco, 1961, MIB, A $1,955.00

Set, #2293W GGI FRT, MIB, A $5,175.00

Set, #2295WS Super 'O,' MIB, A $9,775.00

Set, #2527, #44, #3419, #6844, #6823 (no missiles), #6814, #443 & #197, all military/cs, 1960s, G, A $435.00

Set, #11288, M&StL Alco, 1962, MIB, A...................$3,740.00

Set, #11600 Hagerstown, MIB, A $1,150.00

Set, cars; Congressional, #2530, #2542, #2543, #2544, #2541, EX (OB)..$750.00

Set, freight; #2573 736 Berkshire Freight, 1961, MIB, A..$3,450.00

Set, pass; #2533 coach, #2532 vista dome, #2534 coach, #2531 obv/c, all hex nut plates, EX, A $280.00

LIONEL PREWAR

Acces, #61 lampposts (2), dk gr, VG+, A $160.00

Acces, #63 lamppost, aluminum, EX, A..........................$310.00

Acces, #76 warning bell shack, VG+, A $180.00

Acces, #103 bridge, VG+ $230.00

Acces, #107 direct current reducers (2), MIB, A............$280.00

Acces, #115 station, late colors, EX $400.00

Acces, #118 tunnel, early, w/insert, VG+, A $95.00

Acces, #123 landscaped tunnel, pnt papier-mache, cb base, EX+ (OB), A $400.00

Acces, #124 station, early colors, NMIB, A...................$650.00

Acces, #124 station, Mojave, pea gr & red, EX, A $310.00

Acces, #126 station, mustard, pea gr base, red roof, EX, A .$210.00

Acces, #155 freight shed, early colors, VG+, A..............$280.00

Acces, #155 freight station, late colors, VG+, A............$210.00

Acces, #165 magnetic crane, gray, w/controller, VG+, A...$210.00

Acces, #189 villa, cream, gr base, gray roof, no dormer version, missing 1 tab off chimney top, EX+, A $500.00

Acces, #191 estate, brick litho, pea gr roof & dormers, pnt flaked off doorway, VG, A $270.00

Acces, #313 bascule bridge, complete, EX (OB & 1 insert), A $750.00

Acces, #436 power station, terra cotta, cream & gray, VG+, A .$425.00

Acces, #441 weigh scale, NM, A $2,300.00

Acces, #911 estate, yel, red roof & dormers, plot is clean, NMIB, A..$1,100.00

Acces, #912 Suburban Landscape Villa, EX, A $510.00

Acces, #914 landscaped park, EX (OB) $425.00

Acces, #927 landscaped flag plot, missing 2 bushes, EX+, A ...$220.00

Acces, Hellgate Bridge, G, A $865.00

Car, #217 caboose, peacock & red, EX (OB), A.............$300.00

Car, #219 derrick, early colors, missing 1 handrail & journal, EX (worn box), A...$250.00

Car, #422 Blue Comet obv/c, MIB, A $1,725.00

Car, #455 oil derrick, red top, EX (OB) $325.00

Car, #715 Shell tk/c, EX+, A $310.00

Car, #814R reefer, ivory & peacock, brass trim, VG+, A .$90.00

Car, #1107 Donald Duck & Pluto hand/c, clockwork, VG..$350.00

Car, #2814R reefer, wht, bl roof, VG+, A $180.00

Car, #2954 Pennsylvania semiscale b/c, 1941 HB couplers, EX+ $250.00

Car, #2955 semiscale shell tk/c, 1941 HB couplers, EX+, A...$275.00

Car, #3814 merchandise/c, operating, blk trim, heat stamped, 1941 HB couplers, VG $125.00

Car, pass; #421 West Phal Pullman Comet coach, bl w/nickel trim, VG, A $750.00

Cars, Standard Gauge, #512 gondola, green; #515 Sunoco tank car; #810 crane car, cream, all VG (original boxes), $525.00 for the set.

Loco, #318, electric, gray, EX, A.................................$345.00

Loco, #700E Hudson, VG+....................................$3,000.00

Loco, #763E Hudson, G $800.00

Loco & tender, #385E & #385W, gunmetal, EX (worn & taped OB), A..$1,000.00

Set, #33 loco, #35 coach & #36 obv/c, all olive gr, 1920, VG, A..$210.00

Set, #1835 loco (electric), #1835W tender, #310 bg/c, #309 pullman, #312 obv/c, bl w/silver roofs, EX, A..........$700.00

Set, Flying Yankee, #616W loco, #617 coaches (2), #618 obv/c, VG (OB)...$480.00

Set, freight; #8E loco (OB), olive gr; #511 fl/c, #515 tk/c, terra cotta; #3517 caboose, VG, A $635.00

Set, freight; #224E loco, #2666W tender, both blk; #3651, #654 & #2757, VG, A $195.00

Set, freight; #225E loco, #2235W tender, both blk; #2755 tk/c (2), #2758 b/c, #2757 caboose, VG, A $490.00

Set, freight; #249E loco, #265W tender, both blk; #1717 gondola & #1717 b/c, #1722 caboose, VG $450.00

Set, freight; #1666 loco, #2666 tender, both blk; #1679, #1680 & #1682, VG, A $140.00

Set, freight; #1688 loco, #2689 tender, both gray; #1679, #1680 & #1682, VG, A $160.00

Set, pass; #224 loco, #2224W tender, both blk in OB; #2640 (2), #2641 obv/c, all 2-tone gr w/cream inserts, VG, A ..$290.00

Set, pass; #253 loco, #610 pullman, #612 obv/c, dk gr, G, A $230.00

Set, pass; #253 loco, dk gr; #610 pullman (2), #612 obv/c, dk gr w/maroon inserts, G, A $260.00

Set, pass; #418 pullman & #419 combine, Mojave w/maroon trim, 6-wheeled trucks, VG, A $490.00

Tender, #400E, gray, VG $1,300.00

MISCELLANEOUS MANUFACTURERS

Car, #217 caboose, orange & maroon, EX (OB).............$970.00

Con-Cor, set, Special Edition 'The Cardinals Train,' MIB, A $140.00

Con-Cor, set, Special Edition Grand Trunk Western, MIB, A $140.00

Dayton, Hillclimber loco & tender, friction, red w/gold trim, cowl front, 26", EX, A $245.00

Dorfan, acces, bridge w/2 approaches, 1926-28, VG, A .$320.00

Dorfan, set, #921, loco & 4 cars, G, A.......................$1,495.00

Eliot Welz, pass set, Amtrak Metroliners (5), MIB, A ...$320.00

Eliot Welz, set, Amtrak Metroliner/cs, 1 powered, 3 coaches, MIB, A $230.00

Fleischman, set, STU #320/26 Clockwork Train, 1 loco, 2 cars & track, MIB, A $320.00

Hornby, cars, #6104 Stephenson Rocket Coaches (2), MIB, A $345.00

Hornby, set, Stephenson's Rocket Live Steam, MIB, A .$185.00

Ives, set, pass; #3242 loco, #184, #185 & #186, 1925-26, VG, A $545.00

Japan, pre-WWII, loco & tender w/4 pass/c mk 1st, 2nd, 3rd Class & Post Car, litho tin, 9½", NMIB, A $550.00

K-Line, Heavyweights, pass/c, B&O, MIB, A $230.00

K-Line, pass/c, SP Daylight/c (6), MIB, A $260.00

K-Line, set, Coca-Cola Train, MIB, A.........................$125.00

KTM, loco & tender, 4-8-4 brass loco w/matching 12-wheel tender, M, A $1,725.00

MAMOD, loco, steam, MIB, A.....................................$375.00

Marklin, #8189 MiniClub California Zephyr, MIB, A ...$550.00

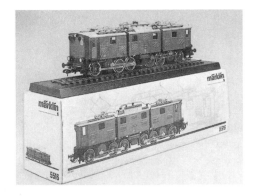

Marklin, #5516, 1 Gauge, class E-91 articulated electric in brown (limited edition), MIB, $800.00.

Marklin, loco, #3024, bl w/silver roof, NMIB, A $300.00

Marklin, loco, #3356 Crocodile, NMIB, A $170.00

Marklin, loco, CCS800 Crocodile, 1957, NMIB, A....$1,050.00

Marklin, loco, G800, blk & red, VG+, A $160.00

Marklin, loco & tender, #3094, test run, NMIB, A.........$150.00

Marklin, set, #R122880/19/2X, #R12880 loco, #889/0 tender, #17190 coaches (2), track, EX+ (OB), A $360.00

Marklin, set, #3036 loco, #4026, #4027, #4029, #4050, #4078, NMIB, A..$290.00

Marklin, set, #3073 loco, #4634, #4654, #4644, #4645, #4631, #4513, NMIB, A...$320.00

MTH, #840 powerhouse, NMIB, A $410.00

MTH, acces, #444 Roundhouse Section, Lionel repro, MIB, A $400.00

MTH, car, #219 crane, cream & red, MIB, A.................$260.00

MTH, loco, #263, steam, blk w/nickel trim, MIB, A......$320.00

MTH, loco, #263, steam, gray w/nickel trim, MIB, A $320.00

MTH, loco, #385, steam, gray w/brass trim, MIB, A $480.00

MTH, loco, #385, steam, gray w/nickel trim, MIB, A $490.00

MTH, loco, #392, steam, 2-tone bl, MIB, A...................$865.00

MTH, loco & tender, #385, MIB, A $490.00

MTH, loco & tender, #400E & #400T Blue Comet, 2-tone bl w/nickel trim, MIB, A $980.00

MTH, set, pass/c; #424-#427 Stephen Girard (4), MIB .$800.00

MTH, set, pass/c; Mojave #431, #419, #490 & #418, M...$575.00

Prideline, acces, station platform, tan & red, M, A $435.00

Prideline, Trolley, MIB, A..$140.00

Right-of-Way, loco & tender, PA TI, 3-rail, NMIB, A..$420.00

Schuco, set, Disneyland monorail, MIB, A....................$635.00

Weaver, loco, #6048 & #6050 SP EMD E-8 ABA, NMIB, A..$270.00

Weaver, loco, SP Daylight EMD E-8 ABA, 3-rail, test run, NMIB, A..$250.00

Williams, loco, #5010 PRR K45 Streamlined Pacific, NM, A $490.00

Williams, loco, #5200 PRR B6SB 0-6-0, steam, MIB, A .$375.00

Williams, loco, #5300 PRR E6S 4-4-2, steam, MIB, A ..$430.00

Williams, loco, #5602 NY Central 4-8-4 Niagara, steam, NM, A $635.00

Williams, loco, #6013 Southern PS-4 4-6-2, NM, A......$460.00

Williams, loco, #8000 Union Pacific 4-6-6-4 Challenger, MIB, A $865.00

Williams, loco, Amtrak F-7 A-units, 1 powered & 1 dummy, diesels, MIB, A $280.00

Williams, loco, Camelback 4-6-0, 3-rail, MIB, A...........$550.00

Williams, loco, Canadian Pacific Trainmaster, diesel, MIB, A...$220.00

Williams, loco, Jersey Central Trainmaster, diesel, MIB, A $220.00

Williams, loco, Lackawanna Trainmaster, MIB, A $290.00

Williams, loco, Pennsylvania GG-1, Brunswick gr w/gold stripes, MIB, A $200.00

Williams, loco, Pennsylvania GG-7, Brunswick gr w/gold stripes, MIB, A $220.00

Williams, loco, Pennsylvania Trainmaster, diesel, gr, MIB, A $220.00

Williams, loco, Pennsylvania Tucsan Trainmaster diesel, MIB, A $115.00

Williams, loco, Sante Fe Trainmaster, diesel, MIB, A ...$260.00

Williams, loco, Southern Pacific Black Widow Trainmaster, diesel, top of cab is scratched o/w MIB, A $175.00

Williams, loco, Southern Pacific Trainmaster, diesel, MIB, A...$290.00

Williams, loco, Tucsan SD-45 diesel, MIB, A $175.00

Williams, loco, Union Pacific SD-45, MIB, A $195.00

Williams, loco, Virginia Trainmaster, diesel, blk & yel, MIB, A...$195.00

Williams, loco, Virginia Trainmaster diesel, bl & yel, MIB, A...$130.00

Williams, loco, 4-6-0 Camelback, steam, MIB, A $430.00

Williams, loco & tender, Lackawanna 3-Rail Camelback, MIB, A $405.00

Williams, loco & tender, PRR E6S 4-4-2, MIB, A $345.00

Williams, loco & tender, USRA 4-6-2, MIB, A.............$375.00

Williams, locos, Amtrak F-7 A-unit, 1 powered & 1 dummy, MIB, A...$230.00

Williams, Pennsylvania Sharknose Baldwin, M, A $290.00

Williams, set, F-3 A-unit powered diesel, F-3 A-unit dummy diesel, Pennsylvania RR pass/c (4), MIB, A $375.00

Williams, set, NASA Space Shuttle Transporter, MIB, A .$190.00

Williams, set, pass; #2515 Southern Cresent Madison, bg/c, combine, obv/c & 2 pullmans, MIB, A $345.00

Williams, set, pass; #2519 Southern Pacific Madison/c, MIB, A...$290.00

Williams, set, pass; Amtrak Amfleet, 4 cars, MIB, A $210.00

Williams, set, pass; Great Northern Madison/c (5), MIB, A ..$230.00

Williams, set, pass; NY Central bg/c, NYC coaches (2), NYC obv/c, aluminum, MIB, A $185.00

Williams, set, pass; Pennsylvania (5), gr-pnt aluminum, MIB, A $210.00

Williams, set, pass; Pennsylvania Madison/c (5), gr, MIB, A...$260.00

Williams, set, pass; Pennsylvania RR, pnt aluminum, MIB, A...$345.00

Williams, set, Presidential; McKinley obv/c, Lincoln pullman & bg/c, Harrison Vista Dome, Garfield pullman, MIB, A...$230.00

Williams, set, Southern Cresent Madison, MIB, A $260.00

Wolverine, #163 loco & pullman, bl & red tin w/wooden wheels, orig pull-string, 32", NM (VG box), A $250.00

Transformers

Made by the Hasbro Company, Transformers were introduced in the United States in 1984. Originally there were twenty-eight figures — eighteen cars known as Autobots and ten Decepticons, evil robots capable of becoming such things as a jet or a handgun. Eventually the line was expanded to more than two hundred different models. Some were remakes of earlier Japanese robots that had been produced by Takara in the 1970s. (These can be identified through color differences and in the case of the Diaclone series, the absence of the small driver or pilot figures.)

The story of the Transformers and their epic adventures were told through several different comic books and animated

series as well as a highly successful movie. Their popularity was reflected internationally and eventually made its way back to Japan. There the American Transformer animated series was translated into Japanese and soon inspired several parallel series of the toys which were again produced by Takara. These new Transformers were sold in the U.S. until the line was discontinued in 1990.

A few years ago, Hasbro announced their plans to reintroduce the line with Transformers: Generation 2. Transformers once again had their own comic book, and the old animated series was brought back in a revamped format. So far, several new Transformers as well as recolored versions of the older ones have been released by Hasbro, and the size of the series continues to grow. Sustained interest in them has spawned a number of fan clubs with chapters worldwide.

Because Transformers came in a number of sizes, you'll find a wide range of pricing. Our values are for Transformers in unopened original boxes. One that has been opened or used is worth much less — about 25% to 75%, depending on whether it has all its parts (weapons, instruction book, tech specs, etc.) and what its condition is — whether decals are applied well or if it is worn.

Advisor: David Kolodny-Nagy (K2).

Other Sources: H4, O1, P3

SERIES 1, 1984

Autobot Car, #TF1023, Sunstreak, yel Countach, MIP ...$80.00

Autobot Car, #TF1025, Bluestreak, bl Datsun Z, MIP ...$120.00

Autobot Car, #TF1025, Bluestreak, silver Datsun Z, MIP ..$80.00

Autobot Car, #TF1027, Jazz, Porsche, MIP.....................$80.00

Autobot Car, #TF1029, Ratchet, ambulance, MIP..........$70.00

Autobot Car, #TF1031, Trailbreaker, camper, MIP $70.00

Autobot Car, #TF1033, Sideswipe, red Countach, MIP...$80.00

Autobot Car, #TF1035, Hound, jeep, MIP $70.00

Autobot Car, #TF1037, Mirage, Indy car, MIP...............$70.00

Autobot Car, #TF1039, Prowl, police car, MIP $80.00

Autobot Car, #TF1041, Wheeljack, Mazzerati, MIP $70.00

Autobot Car, #TF1055, Camshaft, silver car, mail-in, MIP ..$30.00

Autobot Car, #TF1057, Downshift, wht car, mail-in, MIP ...$30.00

Autobot Car, #TF1059, Overdrive, red car, mail-in, MIP $30.00

Autobot Car, #TF1063, Powerdasher #2, car, mail-in, MIP $15.00

Autobot Car, #TF1063, Powerdasher #3, drill, mail-in, MIP...$30.00

Autobot Car #TF1061, Powerdasher #1, jet, mail-in, MIP $15.00

Autobot Commander, #TF1053, Optimus Prime w/Roller, tractor trailer, MIP...$170.00

Case, #TF1069, Collector's Case, MIB...........................$15.00

Case, #TF1071, Collector's Case, red 3-D version, MIB ..$25.00

Cassette, #TF1017, Ravage & Rumble, MIP....................$20.00

Cassette, #TF1019, Frenzy & Lazerbeak, MIP..................$20.00

Decepticon Communicator, #TF1049, Soundwave & Buzzsaw, tape player & gold condor, MIB................................$50.00

Decepticon Jet, #TF1043, Starscream, gray jet, MIP......$100.00

Decepticon Jet, #TF1045, Thundercracker, bl jet, MIP ...$70.00

Decepticon Jet, #TF1047, Skywarp, blk jet, MIP..............$70.00

Decepticon Leader, #TF1051, Megatron, Walther P-38, MIP..$170.00

Minicar, #TF1000, Bumblejumper, M (Bumblebee card).$40.00

Minicar, #TF1000, Bumblejumper, M (Cliffjumper card) .$40.00

Minicar, #TF1001, Bumblebee, yel VW Bug, MIP $35.00
Minicar, #TF1003, Bumblebee, red VW Bug, MIP...........$25.00
Minicar, #TF1005, Cliffjumper, red race car, MIP............$25.00
Minicar, #TF1007, Cliffjumper, yel race car, MIP $25.00
Minicar, #TF1009, Huffer, orange semi cab, MIP.............$20.00
Minicar, #TF1011, Windcharger, red Firebird, MIP $20.00
Minicar, #TF1013, Brawn, gr jeep, MIP.......................$20.00
Minicar, #TF1015, Gears, bl truck, MIP $20.00
Watch, #TF1067, Time Warrior, transforming watch w/Autobot
    insignia, mail-in, MIP...$80.00

SERIES 2, 1985

Autobot Air Guardian, #TF1201, Jetfire, F-14 jet, MIP.$125.00
Autobot Car, #TF1163, Skids, Le Car, MIP $70.00
Autobot Car, #TF1165, Red Alert, fire chief, MIP...........$60.00
Autobot Car, #TF1167, Grapple, crane, MIP $60.00
Autobot Car, #TF1169, Hoist, tow truck, MIP.................$40.00
Autobot Car, #TF1171, Smokescreen, red, wht & bl Datsun Z,
    MIP $60.00
Autobot Car, #TF1173, Inferno, fire engine, MIP............$60.00
Autobot Car, #TF1175, Tracks, Corvette, MIP.................$70.00
Autobot Communicator, #TF1199, Blaster, radio/tape player,
    MIP $45.00
Autobot Scientist, #TF1197, Perceptor, microscope, MIP....$50.00
Constructicon, #TF1127, Bonecrusher (1), bulldozer, MIP ..$20.00
Constructicon, #TF1129, Scavenger (2), steam shovel, MIP.....$20.00
Constructicon, #TF1131, Scrapper (3), front-end loader, MIP..$20.00
Constructicon, #TF1133, Hook (4), crane, MIP $20.00
Constructicon, #TF1135, Long Haul (5), dump truck, MIP .$20.00
Constructicon, #TF1137, Mixmaster (6), cement mixer,
    MIP $25.00
Constructicon, #TF1139, Devastator, construction gift set,
    MIP $100.00
Decepticon Jet, #TF1187, Ramjet, MIP...........................$40.00

Decepticon Jet, #TF1189, Dirge, $40.00.

Decepticon Jet, #TF1191, Thrust, maroon jet, MIP $30.00
Decepticon Military Operations Commander, #TF1203, Shock-
    wave, lazer gun, MIP..$70.00

Deluxe Insecticon, #TF1155, Chop Shop, beetle, MIP $65.00
Deluxe Insecticon, #TF1157, Barrage, MIP $65.00
Deluxe Insecticon, #TF1159, Benom, bee, MIP $65.00
Deluxe Insecticon, #TF1161, Ransack, grasshopper, MIP...$65.00
Deluxe Vehicle, #TF1193, Whirl, lt bl helicopter, MIP...$70.00
Deluxe Vehicle, #TF1195, Roadster, off-road vehicle, MIP..$60.00
Dinobot, #TF1177, Grimlock, Tyrannosaurus, MIP.........$40.00
Dinobot, #TF1179, Slag, Triceratops, MIP $35.00
Dinobot, #TF1181, Sludge, Brontosaurus, MIP $35.00
Dinobot, #TF1183, Snarl, Stegosaurus, MIP...................$35.00
Insecticon, #TF1141, Kickback, grasshopper, MIP $20.00
Insecticon, #TF1143, Shrapnel, beetle, MIP...................$20.00
Insecticon, #TF1145, Bombshell, boll weevil, MIP $20.00
Jumpstarter, #TF1147, Twin Twist, Drill tank, MIP.........$15.00
Jumpstarter, #TF1149, Topspin, spaceship, MIP..............$15.00
Minicar, #TF1101, Bumblebee, yel VW bug, MIP...........$25.00
Minicar, #TF1102, Bumblebee, yel w/minispy, MIP.........$35.00
Minicar, #TF1103, Bumblebee, red VW bug, MIP...........$15.00
Minicar, #TF1104, Bumblebee, red w/minispy, MIP.........$25.00
Minicar, #TF1105, Cliffjumper, red race car, MIP............$15.00
Minicar, #TF1106, Cliffjumper, red w/minispy, MIP.........$25.00
Minicar, #TF1107, Cliffjumper, yel race car, MIP............$15.00
Minicar, #TF1108, Cliffjumper, yel w/minispy, MIP $25.00
Minicar, #TF1109, Huffer, orange semi cab, MIP............$15.00
Minicar, #TF1110, Huffer, w/minispy, MIP $25.00
Minicar, #TF1111, Windcharger, red Firebird, MIP.........$15.00
Minicar, #TF1112, Windcharger, w/minispy, MIP $25.00
Minicar, #TF1113, Brawn, gr jeep, MIP.........................$15.00
Minicar, #TF1115, Gears, bl truck, MIP $15.00
Minicar, #TF1116, Gears, w/minispy, MIP $25.00
Minicar, #TF1117, Seaspray, hovercraft, MIP $10.00
Minicar, #TF1119, Powerglide, plane, MIP $15.00
Minicar, #TF1121, Warpath, tank, MIP $15.00
Minicar, #TF1123, Beachcomber, dune buggy, MIP.........$15.00
Minicar, #TF1125, Cosmos, spaceship, MIP $15.00
Motorized Autobot Defense Base, #TF1205, Omega Supreme,
    rocket launcher base, MIP..$140.00
Triple Charger, #TF1151, Blitzwing, tank/plane, MIP $45.00
Triple Charger, #TF1153, Astrotrain, shuttle/train, MIP.$45.00
Watch, #TF1207, Autoceptor, Kronoform, watch car, MIP .$25.00
Watch, #TF1209, Deceptor, Kronoform, watch jet, MIP .$25.00
Watch, #TF1211, Listen 'n Fun, w/tape & yel Cliffjumper,
    MIP $35.00

SERIES 3, 1986

Aerialbot, #TF 1273, Superion, gift set, MIP..................$180.00
Aerialbot, #TF1263, Air Raid (1), F-14 jet, MIP.............$20.00
Aerialbot, #TF1265, Skydive (2), F-15 jet, MIP...............$20.00
Aerialbot, #TF1267, Fireflight (3), Phantom jet, MIP $20.00
Aerialbot, #TF1271, Silverbolt (5), Concorde, MIP $50.00
Autobot Car, #TF1333, Blurr, futuristic car, MIP............$60.00
Autobot Car, #TF1335, Kup, pickup truck, MIP $60.00
Autobot Car, #TF1337, Hot Rod, red race car, MIP $90.00
Autobot City Commander, #TF1367, Reflector, Spectro,
    Viewfinder & Spyglass into camera, mail-in, MIP.....$60.00
Autobot City Commander, #TF1369, STARS Control Center,
    action cb, mail-in, MIP..$60.00

Autobot City Commander, #TF1365, Ultras Magnus, car carrier, MIP, $50.00.

Battlecharger, #TF1311, Runamuch, Corvette, MIP $15.00
Battlecharger, #TF1313, Runabout, Trans Am, MIP........$15.00
Cassette, #TF1315, Ratbat & Frenzy, bat & bl robot, MIP ..$15.00
Cassette, #TF1317, Rewind & Steeljaw, gold weapons, blk robot & lion, MIP..$10.00
Cassette, #TF1318, Rewind & Steeljaw, silver weapons, blk robot & lion, MIP..$15.00
Cassette, #TF1319, Ramhorn & Eject, gold weapons, rhino & gray robot, MIP..$15.00
Cassette, #TF1320, Ramhorn & Eject, gold weapons, rhino & gray robot, MIP..$15.00
Combaticon, #TF1287, Brawl (1), tank, MIP..................$15.00
Combaticon, #TF1289, Swindle (2), jeep, MIP..............$15.00
Combaticon, #TF1291, Blast Off (3), shuttle, MIP..........$15.00
Combaticon, #TF1293, Vortex (4), helicopter, MIP........$15.00
Combaticon, #TF1295, Onslaught (5), missile transport, MIP..$30.00
Combaticon, #TF1297, Bruticus, Combaticon gift set, MIP...$300.00
Decepticon City Commander, #TF1363, Galvatron, laser cannon, MIP..$100.00
Heroes, #TF1131, Rodimus Prime, futuristic RV, MIP.....$60.00
Heroes, #TF1329, Wreck-Car, futuristic motorcycle, MIP ..$50.00
Jet, #TF1353, Scourge, hovercraft, MIP..........................$60.00
Jet, #TF1355, Cyclonus, space jet, MIP $60.00
Minicar, #TF1252, Wheelie, futuristic car, MIP..............$20.00
Minicar, #TF1253, Outback, brn jeep, MIP....................$15.00
Minicar, #TF1255, Tailgate, wht Firebird, MIP..............$15.00
Minicar, #TF1257, Hubcap, yel race car, MIP..................$15.00
Minicar, #TF1259, Pipes, bl semi cab, MIP....................$15.00
Minicar, #TF1261, Swerve, red truck, MIP......................$15.00
Motorized Autobot Space Shuttle Robot, #TF1359, Sky Lynz shuttle, MIP $90.00
Motorized Decepticon City/Battle Station, #TF1357, Trypticon, dinosaur w/Brunt, robot tank & Full Tilt, MIP $130.00
Predacon, #TF1339, Razorclaw (1), lion, MIP..................$60.00
Predacon, #TF1341, Rampage (2), tiger, MIP $60.00
Predacon, #TF1343, Divebomb (3), vulture, MIP $50.00
Predacon, #TF1345, Tantrum (4), bull, MIP....................$50.00
Predacon, #TF1347, Headstrong (5), rhino, MIP $50.00
Predacon, #TF1348, Predaking, Predacon gift set (Japan only), MIP..$350.00

Sharkticon, #TF1351, Gnaw, futuristic shark, MIP $50.00
Stunticon, #TF1275, Dead End (1), Porsche, MIP...........$15.00
Stunticon, #TF1277, Breakdown (2), Countach, MIP $15.00
Stunticon, #TF1279, Wildrider (3), Ferrari, MIP $15.00
Stunticon, #TF1281, Drag Strip (4), Indy car, MIP..........$15.00
Stunticon, #TF1283, Motormaster (5), tractor trailer, MIP..$40.00
Stunticon, #TF1285, Menasor, Stunticon gift set, MIP .$300.00
Triple Changer, #TF1321, Springer, armored car/helicopter, MIP..$80.00
Triple Changer, #TF1323, Sandstorm, dune buggy/helicopter, MIP..$40.00
Triple Changer, #TF1325, Broadside, aircraft carrier/plane, MIP..$40.00
Triple Changer, #TF1327, Octane, tanker truck/jumbo jet, MIP..$35.00

SERIES 4, 1987

Cassette, #TF1441, Slugfest & Overkill, Stegosaurus & Tyrannosaurus, MIP $15.00
Clone, #TF1443, Pounce & Wingspan, puma & eagle, MIP...$40.00
Clone, #TF1445, Fastlane & Cloudraker, dragster & spaceship, MIP..$40.00
Double Spy, #TF1447, Punch-Counterpunch, Fiero, MIP..$40.00
Duocon, #TF1437, Battletrap, jeep/helicopter, MIP.........$20.00
Duocon, #TF1439, Flywheels, jet/tank, MIP....................$20.00
Headmaster Autobot, #TF1477, Chromedome w/Stylor, futuristic car, MIP..$55.00
Headmaster Autobot, #TF1479, Hardhead w/Duros, tank, MIP..$40.00
Headmaster Autobot, #TF1481, Highbrow w/Gort, helicopter, MIP..$40.00
Headmaster Autobot, #TF1483, Brainstorm w/Arcana, jet, MIP..$40.00
Headmaster Base, #TF1497, Scorponok w/Lord Zarak & Fasttrack, scorpion, mini-tank, MIP $80.00
Headmaster Base, #TF1499, Fortress Maximus w/Cerebros & Spike, Gasket, Grommet, battle station/city, MIP ..$300.00
Headmaster Decepticon, #TF1485, Skullrunner w/Grax, alligator, MIP..$35.00
Headmaster Decepticon, #TF1487, Mindwipe w/Vorath, bat, MIP..$35.00
Headmaster Decepticon, #TF1489, Weirdwolf w/Monzo, wolf, MIP..$35.00
Headmaster Horrocon, #TF1491, Apeface w/Spasma, jet/ape, MIP..$40.00
Headmaster Horrorcon, #TF1493, Snapdragon w/Krunk, jet/dinosaur, MIP..$40.00
Monsterbot, #TF1461, Grotusque, tiger, MIP..................$30.00
Monsterbot, #TF1463, Doublecross, 2-headed dragon, MIP..$30.00
Monsterbot, #TF1465, Repugnus, insect, MIP..................$30.00
Sixchanger, #TF1495, Sixshot, starfighter jet, winged wolf, lazer pistol, armored carrier, tank, MIP $70.00
Targetmaster Autobot, #TF1449, Pointblank w/Peacemaker, race car & gun, MIP $30.00
Targetmaster Autobot, #TF1451, Sureshot w/Spoilsport, off-road buggy & gun, MIP..$30.00

Targetmaster Autobot, #TF1453, Crosshairs w/Pinpointer, truck & gun, MIP $30.00

Targetmaster Autobot, #TF1455, Hot Rod & Firebolt, race car & gun, MIP $45.00

Targetmaster Autobot, #TF1457, Kup & Recoil, pickup truck & gun, MIP $35.00

Targetmaster Autobot, #TF1459, Blurr w/Haywire, futuristic car & gun, MIP $45.00

Targetmaster Decepticon, #TF1469, Misfire w/Aimless, spaceship & gun, MIP $30.00

Targetmaster Decepticon, #TF1471, Slugslinger w/Caliburst, twin jet & gun, MIP $30.00

Targetmaster Decepticon, #TF1475, Scourve w/Fracas, hovercraft & gun, MIP $35.00

Technobot, #TF1425, Afterburner (1), motorcycle, MIP ..$10.00

Technobot, #TF1426, Afterburner, w/decoy, MIP $15.00

Technobot, #TF1427, Nosecone (2), drill tank, MIP.......$10.00

Technobot, #TF1428, Nosecone, w/decoy, MIP...............$15.00

Technobot, #TF1429, Stafe (3), fighter plane, MIP.........$10.00

Technobot, #TF1430, Stafe, w/decoy, MIP.....................$15.00

Technobot, #TF1431, Lightspeed (4), race car, MIP........$10.00

Technobot, #TF1432, Lightspeed, w/decoy, MIP $15.00

Technobot, #TF1433, Scattershot (5), spaceship, MIP $30.00

Terrocon, #TF1413, Rippersnapper (1), lizard, MIP.........$10.00

Terrocon, #TF1414, Rippersnapper, w/decoy, MIP $15.00

Terrocon, #TF1415, Sinnertwin (2), 2-headed dog, MIP.$10.00

Terrocon, #TF1416, Sinnertwin, w/decoy, MIP $15.00

Terrocon, #TF1417, Cutthroat (3), vulture, MIP............$10.00

Terrocon, #TF1418, Cutthroat, w/decoy, MIP $15.00

Terrocon, #TF1419, Blot (4), monster, MIP...................$10.00

Terrocon, #TF1420, Blot, w/decoy, MIP........................$15.00

Terrocon, #TF1421, Hun-grr (5), 2-headed dragon, MIP.$30.00

Terrocon, #TF1423, Abominus, Terrocon gift set, MIP....$70.00

Throttlebot, #TF1401, Goldbug, VW bug, MIP $10.00

Throttlebot, #TF1402, Goldbug, w/decoy, MIP...............$15.00

Throttlebot, #TF1403, Freeway, Corvette, MIP $10.00

Throttlebot, #TF1404, Freeway, w/decoy, MIP................$15.00

Throttlebot, #TF1405, Chase, Ferrari, MIP $10.00

Throttlebot, #TF1406, Chase, w/decoy, MIP...................$15.00

Throttlebot, #TF1407, Wideload, dump truck, MIP $10.00

Throttlebot, #TF1408, Wideload, w/decoy, MIP..............$15.00

Throttlebot, #TF1409, Rollbar, jeep, MIP $10.00

Throttlebot, #TF1410, Rollbar, w/decoy, MIP.................$15.00

Throttlebot, #TF1411, Searchlight, race car, MIP............$10.00

Throttlebot, #TF1412, Searchlight, w/decoy, MIP...........$15.00

Series 5, 1988

Cassette, #TF1539, Squawkalk & Beastbox, hawk & gorilla, MIP $15.00

Cassette, #TF1541, Grand Slam & Raindance, tank & jet, MIP .$15.00

Firecon, #TF1507, Cindersaur, dinosaur, MIP $10.00

Firecon, #TF1509, Flamefeather, monster bird, MIP $10.00

Firecon, #TF1561, Sparkstalker, monster, MIP.................$10.00

Headmaster Autobot, #TF1555, Hosehead w/Lug, fire engine, MIP $30.00

Headmaster Autobot, #TF1557, Siren w/Quig, fire chief car, MIP $25.00

Headmaster Autobot, #TF1559, Nightbeat w/Muzzle, race car, MIP $25.00

Headmaster Decepticon, #TF1561, Horri-Bull w/Kreb, bull, MIP $25.00

Headmaster Decepticon, #TF1563, Fangry w/Brisko, winged wolf, MIP $25.00

Headmaster Decepticon, #TF1565, Squeezeplay w/Lokos, crab, MIP $25.00

Powermaster Autobot, #TF1567, Getaway w/Rev, MR2, MIP..$35.00

Powermaster Autobot, #TF1569, Joyride w/Hotwire, off-road buggy, MIP $35.00

Powermaster Autobot, #TF2571, Slapdash w/Lube, Indy car, MIP $35.00

Powermaster Autobot Leader, #TF1617, Optimus Prime w/HiQ, tractor trailer, MIP..$80.00

Powermaster Decepticon, #TF1573, Darkwing w/Throttle, dk gray jet, MIP $40.00

Powermaster Decepticon, #TF1575, Dreadwind w/Hi-Test, lt gray jet, MIP $40.00

Powermaster Mercenary, #TF1613, Doubledealer w/Knok (robot) & Skar (bat), missile launcher, MIP..............$65.00

Pretender, #TF1577, Landmine, race car w/shell, MIP.....$25.00

Pretender, #TF1579, Cloudburst, jet w/shell, MIP...........$25.00

Pretender, #TF1581, Waverider, submarine w/shell, MIP ..$25.00

Pretender, #TF1583, Skullgrin, tank w/shell, MIP............$25.00

Pretender, #TF1585, Bomb-burst, spaceship w/shell, MIP $25.00

Pretender, #TF1587, Submarauder, submarine w/shell, MIP ..$25.00

Pretender, #TF1589, Groundbreaker, race car w/shell, MIP .$25.00

Pretender, #TF1591, Sky High, jet w/shell, MIP $25.00

Pretender, #TF1593, Splashdown, sea skimmer w/shell, MIP..$25.00

Pretender, #TF1595, Iguanus, motorcycle w/shell, MIP ...$25.00

Pretender, #TF1597, plane w/shell, MIP........................$25.00

Pretender, #TF1599, Finback, sea skimmer w/shell, MIP .$25.00

Pretender Beast, #TF1601, Chainclaw, bear w/shell, MIP ..$20.00

Pretender Beast, #TF1603, Catilla, sabertooth tiger w/shell, MIP $20.00

Pretender Beast, #TF1605, Carnivac, wolf w/shell, MIP ..$20.00

Pretender Beast, #TF1607, Snarler, boar w/shell, MIP $20.00

Pretender Vehicle, #TF1609, Gunrunner, red jet w/vehicle shell, MIP $40.00

Pretender Vehicle, #TF1611, Roadgrabber, purple jet w/vehicle shell, MIP..$40.00

Seacon, #TF1513, Overbite (1), shark, MIP....................$15.00

Seacon, #TF1515, Seawing (2), manta ray, MIP............$15.00

Seacon, #TF1517, Nautilator (3), lobster, MIP................$15.00

Seacon, #TF1519, Skalor (4), fish, MIP..........................$15.00

Seacon, #TF1521, Tentakil (5), squid, MIP.....................$15.00

Seacon, #TF1523, Snaptrap (6), turtle, MIP $35.00

Seacon, #TF1525, Pirancon, Seacon gift set, MIP..........$150.00

Sparkbot, #TF1501, Fizzle, off-road buggy, MIP............$10.00

Sparkbot, #TF1503, Sizzle, funny car, MIP.....................$10.00

Sparkbot, #TF1505, Guzzle, tank, MIP $10.00

Targetmaster Autobot, #TF1543, Scoop w/Tracer & Holepunch, front-end loader & 2 guns, MIP $20.00

Targetmaster Autobot, #TF1545, Landfill w/Flintlock & Silencer, dump truck & 2 guns, MIP..................$20.00

Targetmaster Autobot, #TF1547, Quickmix w/Boomer & Ricochet, cement mixer & 2 guns, MIP $20.00

Targetmaster Decepticon, #TF1549, Quake w/Tiptop & Heater, tank & 2 guns, MIP $20.00
Targetmaster Decepticon, #TF1551, Spinster w/Singe & Hairsplitter, helicopter & 2 guns, MIP......................$20.00
Targetmaster Decepticon, #TF1553, Needlenose w/Sunbeam & Zigzag, jet & 2 guns, MIP $20.00
Tiggerbot, #TF1527, Backstreet, race car, MIP.................$15.00
Tiggerbot, #TF1529, Override, motorcycle, MIP..............$15.00
Tiggerbot, #TF1531, Dogfight, plane, MIP.....................$15.00
Triggercon, #TF1533, Ruckus, dune buggy, MIP $15.00
Triggercon, #TF1535, Windsweeper, B-1 bomber, MIP ...$15.00
Triggercon, #TF1537, Crankcase, jeep, MIP.....................$15.00

Series 6, 1989

Legends, K-Mart Exclusive, #TF1727, Bumblebee, VW bug, MIP .$30.00
Legends, K-Mart Exclusive, #TF1729, Jazz Porsche, MIP .$40.00
Legends, K-Mart Exclusive, #TF1731, Grimlock, dinosaur, MIP $40.00
Legends, K-Mart Exclusive, #TF1733, Starscream, jet, MIP ..$45.00
Mega Pretender, #TF1717, Vroom, dragster w/shell, MIP.....$35.00
Mega Pretender, #TF1719, Thunderwing, jet w/shell, MIP ..$35.00
Mega Pretender, #TF1721, Crossblades, helicopter w/shell, MIP $25.00
Micromaster Base, #TF1679, Skyhopper & Micromaster, helicopter & F-15, MIP $35.00
Micromaster Base, #TF1681, Groundshaker & Micromaster, self-propelled cannon & stealth fighter, MIP.............$35.00
Micromaster Base, #TF1735, Skystalker, Space Shuttle Base & Micromaster Porsche, MIP $55.00
Micromaster Base, #TF1737, Countdown, Rocket Base & Micromaster Lunar Rover, MIP................................$60.00
Micromaster Patrol, #TF1651, Off-Road Series, 4 different, MIP, ea $10.00
Micromaster Patrol, #TF1657, Sports Car Patrol Series, 4 different, MIP, ea $10.00
Micromaster Patrol, #TF1661, Battle Patrol Series, 4 different, MIP, ea...$10.00
Micromaster Station, #TF1671, Greasepit, pickup w/gas station, MIP $20.00
Micromaster Station, #TF1675, Ironworks, semi w/construction site, MIP...$20.00
Micromaster Transport, #TF1663, Overload, car carrier, MIP $15.00
Micromaster Transport, #TF1665, Flattop, aircraft carrier, MIP .$15.00
Micromaster Transport, #TF1667, Roughstuff, military transport, MIP...$15.00
Pretender, #TF1697, Pincher, scorpion w/shell, MIP $20.00
Pretender, #TF1699, Longtooth, hovercraft w/shell, MIP...$20.00
Pretender, #TF1701, Stranglehold, rhino w/shell, MIP $20.00
Pretender, #TF1705, Bludgeon, tank w/shell, MIP $30.00
Pretender, #TF1707, Doubleheader, twin jet w/shell, MIP ..$20.00
Pretender Classic, #TF1709, Bumblebee, VG bug w/shell, MIP...$30.00
Pretender Classic, #TF1711, Grimlock, dinosaur w/shell, MIP.$30.00
Pretender Classic, #TF1713, Starscream, jet w/shell, MIP.$30.00
Pretender Classic, #TF1715, Jazz, Porsche w/shell, MIP ...$30.00
Pretender Monster, #TF1683, Icepick (1), MIP...............$12.00
Pretender Monster, #TF1685, Bristleback (2), MIP $12.00

Pretender Monster, #TF1687, Wildfly (3), MIP $12.00
Pretender Monster, #TF1695, Monstructor, Pretender Monster gift set, not produced, MIP......................$1,000.00
Ultra Pretender, #TF1727, Skyhammer, race car w/figure & vehicle, MIP..$40.00
Ultra Pretender, #TF1725, Roadblock, tank w/figure & vehicle, MIP $40.00

Series 7, 1990

Action Master, #TF1781, Soundwave: Soundwave (bat), Wingthing, MIP...$15.00
Action Master, #TF1785, Grimlock: Grimlock, Anti-Tank Cannon (tank gun), MIP $15.00
Action Master, #TF1789, Rad: Rad, Lionizer (lion), MIP ..$15.00
Action Master, #TF1793, Devastator: Devastator, Scorpulator (scorpion), MIP.....................................$15.00
Action Master, #TF1799, Blaster: Blaster, Flight-Pack (jet pack), MIP $15.00
Action Master, #TF1805, Shockwave: Shockwave, Fistfight (mini-robot), MIP.....................................$15.00
Action Master, #TF1809, Inferno: Inferno, Hydro-Pack (water laser backpack), MIP $15.00
Action Master, #TF1817, Prowl: Prowl, Turbo Cycle, MIP ..$30.00
Action Master, #TF1821, Over-Run: Over-Run, Attack Copter, MIP $30.00
Action Master, #TF1825, Wheeljack: Wheeljack, Turbo Racer, MIP $35.00
Action Master, #TF1829, Gutcruncher: Gutcruncher, Stratotronic Jet, MIP $35.00
Action Master, #TF1833, Optimus Prime: Optimus Prime, Armored Convoy, MIP $65.00
Action Master, #TF1873, Skyfall: Skyfall, Top-Heavy Rhino, MIP $10.00
Micromaster Combiner, #TF1763, Battle Squad: Meltdown, Half-Track, Direct Hit, Power Punch, Fireshot & Vanguish, MIP $15.00
Micromaster Combiner, #TF1767, Metro Squad: Wheel Blaze, Road Burner, Oiler, Slide, Power Run & Strikedown, MIP......$15.00
Micromaster Combiner, #TF1771, Tanker Truck: Tanker Truck, Pipeline & Gusher, MIP................................$15.00
Micromaster Combiner, #TF1775, Missile Launcher: Missile Launcher, Retro & Surge, MIP $15.00
Micromaster Combiner, #TF1777, Anti-Aircraft Base: Anti-Aircraft Base, Blackout & Spaceshot, MIP......................$15.00
Micromaster Patrol, #TF 1759, Hot Rod Patrol: Big Daddy, Trip-Up, Greaser & Hubs, MIP..............................$7.00
Micromaster Patrol, #TF1751, Race Track Patrol: Barricade, Roller Force, Ground Hog & Motorhead, MIP...........$7.00
Micromaster Patrol, #TF1755, Air Patrol: Thread Bolt, Eagle Eye, Sky High & Blaze Master, MIP.........................$7.00
Micromaster Patrol, #TF1761, Military Patrol: Bombshock, Tracer, Dropshot & Growl, MIP $7.00

Generation 2, Series 1, 1992-93

Autobot Car, #TF1863, Jazz, Porsche, MIP.....................$25.00
Autobot Car, #TF1867, Inferno, fire truck, MIP $25.00

Autobot Leader, #TF1879, Optimus Prime w/Roller, tractor trailer w/electronic sound-effect box, MIP.................$35.00

Autobot Minicar, #TF1881, Bumblebee, metallic VW bug, MIP...$10.00

Autobot Minicar, #TF1883, Hubcap, metallic, MIP $10.00

Autobot Minicar, #TF1887, Seaspray, metallic hovercraft, MIP...$10.00

Autobot Obliterator (Europe only), Spark, MIP.............$45.00

Photo courtesy David Kolodny-Nagy.

Autobot, Spark, missile-firing base and light-up eyes, 1992, MIP, $35.00.

Color Change Transformer, #TF1905, Deluge, MIP $15.00

Color Change Transformer, #TF1911, Gobots, MIP $15.00

Constructicon (orange version), #TF1851, Bonecrusher (1), bulldozer, MIP...$7.00

Constructicon (orange version), #TF1855, Scrapper (3), front-end loader, MIP $7.00

Constructicon (orange version), #TF1859, Long Haul (5), dump truck, MIP...$7.00

Constructicon (yel version), #TF1851, Bonecrusher (1), bull-dozer, MIP...$6.00

Constructicon (yel version), #TF1855, Scrapper (3), front-end loader, MIP $6.00

Constructicon (yel version), #TF1859, Long Haul (5), dump truck, MIP...$6.00

Decepticon Obliterator (Europe only), Colossus, MIP.....$45.00

Photo courtesy David Kolodny-Nagy.

Decepticon, Colossus, missile-firing base and light-up eyes, 1992, MIP, $35.00.

Decepticon Jet, #TF1875, Starscream, gray jet w/electronic light & sound-effect box, MIP $30.00

Decepticon Leader, #TF1913, Megatron, gr tank w/electronic sound-effect treads, MIP $45.00

Dinobot, #TF1869, Grimlock, bl Tyrannosaurus, MIP $25.00

Dinobot, #TF1870, Grimlock, turq Tyrannosaurus, MIP .$50.00

Dinobot, #TF1873, Snarl, orig gray Stegosaurus, MIP......$30.00

Dinobot, #TF1873, Snarl, red Stegosaurus, MIP.............$25.00

Small Autobot Car, #TF1899, Skram, MIP......................$6.00

Small Autobot Car, #TF1903, Turbofire, MIP..................$6.00

Small Decepticon Jet, #TF1889, Afterburner, MIP $6.00

Small Decepticon Jet, #TF1891, Eagle Eye, MIP $6.00

Small Decepticon Jet, #TF1893, Terradive, MIP...............$6.00

Small Decepticon Jet, #TF1895, Windrazor, MIP.............$6.00

GENERATION 2, SERIES 2, 1994

Aerialbot, #TF1915, Skydive (1), F-15, MIP $7.00

Aerialbot, #TF1919, Firefight (3), Phantom, MIP..............$7.00

Aerialbot, #TF1923, Silverbolt (5), Concorde, MIP $18.00

Combaticon, #TF1927, Brawl (1), tank, MIP $7.00

Combaticon, #TF1931, Blast Off (3), shuttle, MIP $7.00

Combaticon, #TF1935, Onslaught (5), missile transport, MIP.$18.00

Dreadwing w/Smokescreen 80115, MIP $25.00

Heroes, #TF1953, Autobot Hero Optimus Prime, MIP $15.00

Heroes, #TF1955, Decepticon Hero Megatron, MIP........$15.00

Laser Rod Transformer, #TF1937, Electro, 1993, MIP $15.00

Laser Rod Transformer, #TF1941, Jolt, 1993, MIP...........$15.00

Rotor Force, #TF1945, Leadfoot, MIP...............................$7.00

Rotor Force, #TF1947, Manta Ray, MIP $7.00

Rotor Force, #TF1951, Ransack, MIP $7.00

Stunticon, BotCon '94 Exclusive, #TF1925, Breakdown (2), Countach, MIP.......................................$100.00

Watch, #TF1957, Superion, MIP.....................................$12.00

Watch, #TF1961, Ultra Magnus, MIP $12.00

Watch, #TF1965, Scorpia, MIP.......................................$12.00

BOOTLEG/UNLICENSED TRANSFORMERS

Action Master Blue Streak w/Action Master Optimus Prime's Vehicle, K2 ....$30.00

Action Master Jazz, gray & purple or gray & ultramarine bl, K2, ea $5.00

Action Master Rad, orange & purple, K2.........................$5.00

Blitzwing, plastic, K2..$6.00

Dai-Atlas (Dai-Atris), same as orig Japanese toy except for recolored stickers, battery-op, K2 ....$25.00

Dino King, oversized version from Victory series, K2 ....$25.00

Generation 3 Inferno, plastic, yel arms & legs, K2..............$6.00

G2 Combaticon Blast-Off, giant size, K2 ....$10.00

Mini Max, sm version of Fortress Maximus, spike forms head, 7", K2...$15.00

Power Master Decepticon Jet, different colors than orig, K2 ...$15.00

Sky Garry, remake of robot from Star Convoy series, no micro-masters or shuttles, K2 ....$10.00

Star Saber, Brainmaster from Japanese Victory series, no com-ponets to form super robot, K2 ....$15.00

Superion, lg firearm, gold helmet, 13", K2 ....$25.00

Trolls

The first trolls to come to the United States were modeled after a 1952 design by Marti and Helena Kuuskoski of Tampere, Finland. The first trolls to be mass produced in America were molded from wood carvings made by Thomas Dam of Denmark. As the demand for these trolls increased, several US manufacturers were licensed to produce them. The most noteworthy of these were Uneeda Doll Company's Wishnik line and Inga Scandia House True Trolls. Thomas Dam continued to import his Dam Things line. Today trolls are enjoying a renaissance as baby boomers try to recapture their childhood. As a result, values are rising.

The troll craze from the '60s spawned many items other than just dolls such as wall plaques, salt and pepper shakers, pins, squirt guns, rings, clay trolls, lamps, Halloween costumes, animals, lawn ornaments, coat racks, notebooks, folders, and even a car.

In the '70s, '80s, and '90s, new trolls were produced. While these trolls are collectible to some, the avid troll collector still prefers those produced in the '60s. Remember, trolls must be in mint condition to receive top dollar.

For more information, we recommend *Collector's Guide to Trolls* by Pat Petersen.

Advisor: Roger Inouye (I1).

Ballerina, Dam, bright red hair, gr eyes, orig outfit, MIP, I1..**$55.00**
Batman, felt clothes, blond hair, 3", EX **$25.00**
Boy & Girl, Sun Rubber, 1964, pnt-on clothes, orange hair, EX, I1, pr, from $125 to..**$150.00**
Boy w/Club, Wishnik, pnt-on clothes, molded club, blk hair, orange eyes, 3", NM, I1 ....**$65.00**
Bride-Nik, Uneeda Wishnik, MOC, T1...........................**$20.00**

Caveman, 'Ughie Ughie,' Scandia House Ent., NM, $20.00.

Clown, Dam, 1965, pnt-on clothes, yel eyes & red nose, 5½", NM, I1, from $175 to **$250.00**

Cook-Nik, Uneeda Wishnik, 1970s, bendable, 5", M (VG+ card) **$2.00**
Donkey, Dam, wht mane & tail, lg amber eyes, 9", G, I1 ..**$50.00**
Eskimo, Dam, 1965, red & wht pnt-on clothes, brn hair & eyes, 5½", EX..**$75.00**
Giraffe, Dam, 1960s, amber eyes, gray hair, orig tag, 12", EX, H4...**$125.00**
Good Luck-Nik, Uneeda Wishnik, 1970s, M (orig tube pkg) **$15.00**
Horse, Dam, 1964, long mane & tail, felt saddle, NM, F8..**$45.00**
Indian Dress, Wishnik, Black w/blk rooted hair, blk eyes, 3½", EX, I1 ....**$75.00**
Judge, Uneeda Wishnik, gray hair, orange eyes, 5½", EX, I1 .**$30.00**
Kool-Aid Troll, pk hair, 5", M...**$15.00**
Leprechaun, 1969, w/jacket, EX, B10................................**$25.00**
Lion, Dam, lg version, VG, H4 ....**$100.00**
Moonitik, Uneeda Wishnik, mohair body w/rubber feet & shake eyes, 18", extremely rare, I1......................................**$100.00**
Nursenik, Uneeda Wishnik, 1970s, NM, H4 ....**$25.00**
Nursenik, Uneeda Wishnik, 1970s, NMOC, H4 ....**$50.00**
Pick-Nik, Uneeda, Wishnik, 1970s, bendable, 5", M (EX+ card)..**$20.00**
Playboy Bunny, unmarked, blk & wht felt ears & outfit, blond hair, clip hands, 3½", EX, I1 ....**$15.00**
Tailed Troll, Dam, 1965, burlap outfit w/belt & charms, gray hair, brn eyes, M, I1, from $150 to..........................**$250.00**
Two-Headed Troll, pk & gr hair, VG+, H4 ....**$35.00**
Viking, Dam, 1967, wht felt dress w/bl belt, wht hair, brn eyes, 5½", NM, I1, from $150 to.....................................**$200.00**
Voodoo Doll, 1960s, cloth outfit, wht hair, red ruby eyes, M .**$15.00**
Werewolf Monster, 1960s, 3", I1 ....**$40.00**

MISCELLANEOUS

Bank, Silvestre Bros, 1964, glazed ceramic, 18", M, I1 ...**$150.00**
Carrying Case, Ideal, w/molded waterfall, M, I1 ....**$25.00**
Cookie Cutter, Mills, 3½", extremely rare, M, I1 ....**$50.00**
Greeting Card, Am Greeting Corp, 1965, w/3" troll tied on card, rare, I1..**$100.00**
Lamp, Wishnik, complete, 18", rare, I1 ....**$250.00**
Outfit, any style, MIP, I1, ea...**$15.00**
Pencil Topper, astronaut troll, Scandia House Ent, 1½", MIP, I1..**$45.00**
Playhouse, Wishnik Mini Trolls, Ideal, 1960s, EX, B10 ...**$20.00**
Salt & Pepper Shakers, girl & boy, ceramic w/rabbit fur hair, pnt features, 3½", rare, I1, from $150 to.........................**$250.00**

View-Master and Tru-Vue

View-Master, the invention of William Gruber, was introduced to the public at the 1939-1940 New York World's Fair and the Golden Gate Exposition in California. Since then, View-Master reels, packets, and viewers have been produced by five different companies — the original Sawyers Company, G.A.F (1966), View-Master International (1981), Ideal Toys, and Tyco Toys (the present owners). Because none of the noncartoon single reels and three-reel packets have been made since 1980, these have become collectors' items. Also highly sought after are the 3-reel sets featuring popular TV and cartoon characters. The market is divided between those who simply collect View-Master as a field all its own and collectors of character-related memorabilia who will often pay much higher prices for reels about Barbie, Batman, The Addams Family, etc. Our values tend to follow the more conservative approach.

The first single reels were dark blue with a gold sticker and came in attractive gold-colored envelopes. They appeared to have handwritten letters. These were followed by tan reels with a blue circular stamp. Because these were produced for the most part after 1945 and paper supplies were short during WWII, they came in a variety of front and back color combinations, tan with blue, tan with white, and some were marbleized. Since print runs were low during the war, these early singles are much more desirable than the printed white ones that were produced by the millions from 1946 until 1957. Three-reel packets, many containing story books, were introduced in 1955, and single reels were phased out. Nearly all viewers are very common and have little value except for the very early ones, such as the Model A and Model B. Blue and brown versions of the Model B are especially rare. Another desirable viewer, unique in that it is the only focusing model ever made, is the Model D. For more information we recommend *View-Master Single Reels, Volume I*, by Roger Nazeley. Note: though the market was down by a substantial percentage at one point, it appears to have recovered, and prices are now fairly stable.

    Advisor: Roger Nazeley (N4).

    Other Sources: C1, M15

A-B-C Circus, B-585, 1974, MIP, N4 .... $15.00
Adventures of Tarzan, #975, w/book, M, B10 .... $7.00
Airplanes of the World, B-773, MIP, N4 .... $20.00
Alice in Wonderland, B-360, MIP, B10 .... $15.00
Alice in Wonderland, FT-20, MIP, B10 .... $12.00
America's Man in Space, B-657, MIP, B10/N4 .... $18.00
American Indian, B-725, MIP, B10 .... $15.00
Apollo Moon Landing, B-663, MIP, B10 .... $15.00
Apple's Way, B-558, MIP (sealed), B10 .... $25.00
Apple's Way, B-558, 1974, MIP, N4 .... $18.00
Archies, B-574, MIP (sealed), B10 .... $32.00
Aristocats, B-365, 1970, MIP, N4 .... $8.00
Arizona, ARIZ-1, M, B10 .... $4.00
Babes in Toyland, B-375, 1961, NMIP, F8 .... $36.00
Bad News Bears in Breaking Training, H-77, 1977, MIP, N4 .$20.00
Bambi, B-400, MIP (sealed), B10 .... $18.00
Barbie's Around the World Trip, B-500, 1965, MIP, N4 .$35.00
Batman, B-492, MIP, B10 .... $25.00
Batman Forever, #4160, MIP (sealed), B10 .... $6.00
Beautiful Cypress Gardens, Florida, A-961, MIP, N4 .... $14.00
Bedknobs & Broomsticks, B-366, 1971, MIP, N4 .... $20.00
Beverly Hillbillies, B-570, 1963, MIP, N4 .... $45.00
Bible Heroes, B-852, 1967, MIP, N4 .... $10.00
Big Blue Marble, B-587, MIP (sealed), B10 .... $26.00
Big Blue Marble, B-587, 1976, MIP, N4 .... $20.00
Birth of Jesus, B-875, MIP, B10 .... $12.00
Bonanza, B-471, 1st issue, 1964, MIP, N4 .... $35.00

Brave Eagle, B-466, 1955, MIP, N4 .... $30.00
Buck Rogers in the 25th Century, J-1, MIP, B10 .... $18.00
Bugs Bunny, B-531, MIP, B10 .... $14.00
Bugs Bunny in Big Top Bunny, B-549, MIP (sealed), B10..$22.00
California Wildflowers, #291, M, B10 .... $4.00
Canada, #A-090, MIP, B10 .... $15.00
Captain Kangaroo, B-560, 1957, MIP, N4 .... $30.00
Casper the Friendly Ghost, B-533, MIP, B10 .... $20.00
Casper's Ghostland, B-545, 1969, MIP, N4 .... $18.00
Cat From Outer Space, J-22, 1978, MIP, N4 .... $18.00
Charlotte's Web, B-321, 1973, MIP, N4 .... $6.00
Children's Zoo, B-617, MIP (sealed), B10 .... $18.00
Christmas Carol, B-380, MIP (sealed), B10 .... $22.00
Christmas Story, B-383, MIP, from $9 to $12.00
Cinderella, B-318, MIP, B10 .... $12.00
City Beneath the Sea, B-496, 1971, MIP, N4 .... $40.00
Close Encounters of the Third Kind, J-47, 1977, MIP, N4 ..$20.00
Daktari, B-498, MIP (sealed), B10 .... $45.00
Daniel Boone, B-479, MIP, B10 .... $30.00
Dark Shadows, B-503, 1968, MIP, N4 .... $100.00
Dennis the Menace, B-539, MIP, B10 .... $22.00
Disneyworld Fantasyland, A-948, MIP (sealed), B10 .... $22.00
Disneyworld Liberty Square, A-950, MIP (sealed), B10 ...$18.00
Donald Duck, B-525, 1957, MIP, N4 .... $14.00
Dr Shrinker & Wonderbug, H-2, 1977, MIP, N4 .... $18.00
Dukes of Hazzard, L-17, 1980, MIP, N4 .... $20.00
Easter Story, EA1-3, MIP, B3 .... $10.00
Eight Is Enough, K-76, 1980, MIP, N4 .... $22.00
Emergency!, B-597, MIP, B10 .... $18.00
Family Affair, B-571, 1969, MIP, N4 .... $38.00
Fangface, K-66, 1980, NMIP, J7 .... $15.00
Fat Albert & the Cosby Kids, B-554, 1974, MIP, N4 .... $4.00
Flash Gordon in Planet Mongo, B-583, 1976, MIP, N4 ...$15.00
Flintstones, B-514, MIP, from $15 to $20.00
Flintstones, Beasts of Bedrock, L-6, 1980, MIP, N4 .... $8.00
Flipper, B-485, 1966, MIP, from $15 to $20.00
For the Love of Benji, H-54, 1977, MIP, N4 .... $12.00
Gene Autry & Wonder Horse Champion, #950, M, B10 ...$5.00
Godzilla, J-23, MIP (sealed), B10 .... $30.00
Golden Book Favorites, H-14, 1977, MIP, N4 .... $18.00
Goldilocks & the Three Bears, B-317, MIP (sealed), B10 ..$22.00
Great Smokies National Park, A-889, 1950, MIP, N4 ..... $10.00
Green Hornet, B-488, 1966, MIP, N4 .... $75.00
Grizzly Adams, 1978, MIP (sealed), C1 .... $24.00
Hair Bear Bunch in No Space Like Home, B-552, 1972, MIP,
    N4 .... $8.00
Hansel & Gretel, FT-2, w/book, M, B10 .... $5.00
Happy Days, B-586, 1974, MIP, N4 .... $18.00
Hardy Boys, H-69, 1977, MIP, N4 .... $14.00
Hare & the Tortoise, B-309, MIP (sealed), B10 .... $20.00
Harlem Globetrotters, H-69, 1977, MIP, from $15 to $20.00
Hawaii Five-O, B-590, MIP (sealed), B10 .... $28.00
Hearst Castle, A-190, MIP, B10 .... $18.00
Herbie Rides Again, B-578, 1974, MIP, N4 .... $18.00
History of Flight, B-865, MIP, B10 .... $15.00
Hopalong Cassidy & Topper, #955, M, B10 .... $5.00
Horses, H-5, MIP (sealed), B10 .... $18.00
Huckleberry Hound & Yogi Bear, B-512, 1960, MIP, N4...$16.00

Indians of the Southwest, B-721, MIP, B10 ....$15.00
Inspector Gadget, BD-232, MIP, N4 ....$8.00
It's a Bird Charlie Brown, B-556, 1973, MIP, N4 ....$14.00
Jody McCrea in Johnny Moccasin, B-468, 1957, MIP, N4 ..$45.00
Joe Forrester, BB-454, M (sealed), B10 ....$25.00
Julia, B-572, 1969, MIP, N4 ....$26.00
Jungle Book, B-363, MIP, B10 ....$15.00
King Kong, B-392, MIP (sealed), B10 ....$35.00
KISS, Canadian issue, 1978, 3-reel set, MIP, J6 ....$85.00
Knight Rider, 4054, 1982, MIP, N4 ....$12.00
Land of the Giants, B-494, 1968, MIP, N4 ....$60.00
Land of the Lost, B-579, 1974, MIP, N4 ....$26.00
Lassie & Timmie, B-477, MIP, B10......................................$20.00
Lassie Look Homeward, B-480, 1965, MIP, N4 ....$20.00
Lassie Rides the Log Flume, B-489, 1968, MIP, N4 ....$15.00
Laverne & Shirley, J-20, 1978, MIP, N4 ....$15.00
Legend of Indiana Jones, #4092, 1989, MIP, N4 ....$6.00
Life & Times of Grizzly Adams, J-10, 1978, MIP, N4 ....$14.00
Little Black Sambo, FT-8, M, B10 ....$10.00
Little Drummer Boy, B-871, MIP, B10 ....$18.00
Little Orphan Annie, J-21, 1978, MIP, C1 ....$25.00
Little Red Riding Hood, B-310, MIP (sealed), B10 ....$22.00
Lost in Space, B-482, 1967, MIP, N4 ....$90.00
Love Bug, B-501, MIP (sealed), B10 ....$22.00
M*A*S*H, J-11, 1978, MIP, N4..$20.00
Man From UNCLE, B-484, 1966, MIP, N4 ....$38.00
Marineland of Florida, A-964, MIP, B10 ....$14.00
Mary Poppins, B-376, 1964, MIP, N4 ....$15.00
Mickey Mouse, B-528, MIP, B10 ....$15.00
Mickey Mouse Club Mouseketeers, B-524, 1956, MIP, N4 .$45.00
Mighty Mouse, B-526, 1968, NMIP $10.00
Million Dollar Duck, B-506, MIP (sealed), B10 ....$30.00
Mod Squad, B-478, 1968, MIP, N4 ....$30.00
Monkees, B-493, 1967, MIP, N4 ....$30.00
Mork & Mindy, K-67, 1979, MIP, N4..................................$18.00
Mount Vernon, A-812, MIP (sealed), B10 ....$24.00
Movie Stars Hollywood USA I, #740, M, B10.....................$10.00
New York World's Fair, #88, M, B10.....................................$7.00
Niagara Falls, A-655, MIP, N4 ....$14.00
Night Before Christmas, B-382, 1962, MIP, N4 ....$10.00
Partridge Family, B-592, 1973, MIP, N4 ....$65.00
Peanuts, B-536, MIP (sealed), B10......................................$15.00
Peter Pan, B-372, MIP, B10..$12.00
Pikes Peak & Colorado Springs, A-321, MIP, B10 ....$15.00
Pink Panther, J-12, 1978, MIP, from $8 to.........................$12.00
Pinocchio, B-311, MIP, B10..$16.00
Planet of the Apes, B-507, 1967, MIP, N4 ....$30.00
Popeye, B-516, MIP, B10...$12.00
Poseidon Adventure, B-391, 1972, MIP, N4 ....$28.00
Prehistoric Animals, B-619, MIP, B10................................$22.00
Project Apollo, B-658, MIP, B10 ....$25.00
Quick Draw McGraw, B-534, 1961, MIP, N4......................$18.00
Raggedy Ann & Andy, B-406, 1971, MIP, N4 ....$15.00
Ren & Stimpy, #1084, M (sealed), B10 ....$7.00
Rescuers, H-26, 1978, MIP, N4...$14.00
Resurrection Part 1, Easter Story, EA-1, w/book, M, B10...$5.00
Robin Hood, B-342, MIP (sealed), B10 ....$25.00
Robin Hood, B-371, MIP, N4..$25.00

Rocky Mountain National Park, A-322, MIP, N4............$10.00
Rookies, B-452, 1975, MIP, N4...$20.00
Roy Rogers — The Holdup, #946, M, B10............................$5.00
Roy Rogers King of the Cowboys & Trigger, #945, M, B10..$5.00
Rudolph the Red-Nosed Reindeer, B-870, MIP, B10 ....$15.00
Rudolph the Red-Nosed Reindeer, FT-25, w/book, M, B10..$5.00
San Diego Zoo, Packet No 1, A-173, MIP, B10................$15.00
Scooby & Scrappy-Doo, B-553, 1980, MIP, N4 ....$18.00
Search, B-591, 1973, MIP, N4...$30.00
Seven Wonders of the World, B-901, MIP, B10...............$14.00
Shaggy DA, B-368, MIP (sealed), B10 ....$20.00
Shazam!, B-550, 1975, MIP, N4 ....$8.00
Six Million Dollar Man, B-559, 1974, MIP, from $15 to..$20.00
Sleeping Beauty, B-308, MIP, B10 ....$15.00
Sleeping Beauty, FT-10, w/book, M, B10 ....$5.00
Snoopy & the Red Baron, B-544, 1969, MIP, N4.............$12.00
Snow White & the Seven Dwarfs, FT-4, w/book, M, B10..$5.00
Snow White & the Seven Dwarfs, K-69, 1980, MIP, N4 .$15.00
Spider-Woman, The Enforcer Strikes, L-7, 1980, MIP, N4 ..$5.00
Star Trek, B-499, 1968, MIP $30.00
Star Trek: Mr Spock's Time Trek, B-555, MIP, B10 ....$30.00
Star Trek: The Motion Picture, K-57, 1979, MIP, N4......$20.00
Statue of Liberty, A-648, MIP, B10.....................................$18.00
Strange Animals of the World, B-615, MIP, B10 ....$15.00
Superman II, L-46, MIP, N4..$20.00
Superman Meets Computer Crook, B-584, 1976, MIP, N4 ..$14.00
SWAT, B-453, 1975, MIP, N4..$20.00
Tarzan of the Apes, B-580, 1950, MIP, N4 ....$35.00
Time Tunnel, B-491, 1966, MIP, N4 ....$50.00
Tom Corbett Space Cadet, B-581, 1954, MIP, N4 ....$25.00
Treasure Island, BB-432, MIP (sealed), B10 ....$25.00

Tru-Vue 3-Dimension viewer, MIB, $25.00.

Tweety & Sylvester, J-28, MIP, B10 ....$14.00
Ugly Duckling, FT-9, w/book, M, B10 ....$5.00
Universal Studios Scenic Tour, Packet No 1, A-241, MIP,
   N4 ....$25.00
Voltron, Defenders of the Universe, #1055, MIP (sealed),
   B10...$8.00
Walt Disney World, Fantasyland, A-948, MIP, N4..........$10.00

Walt Disney's Cartoon Theatre, Sawyers View-Master, 1960s, w/electric projector & 10 reels, 15", VG, M8 ....$35.00
Welcome Back Kotter, J-19, MIP (sealed), B10................$22.00
Westward Expansion, B-812, MIP (sealed), B10 ....$25.00
White House, A-793, MIP, B10..$20.00
Who Framed Roger Rabbit?, #4086, MIP, N4 ....$15.00
Wild Animals of Africa, B-618, MIP, B10 ....$15.00
Wild Bill Hickok & Jingles in Proud Sol, B-4732, M, B10.$5.00
Winnie the Pooh & the Blustery Day, K-37, 1979, MIP, N4...$10.00
Winnie the Pooh & the Honey Tree, B-364, MIP, B10 ...$15.00
Wizard of Oz, B-361, MIP, N4..$20.00
Wolfman, J-30, 1978, MIP, N4 ....$16.00
Wonderful World of Peanuts, B-536, 1966, MIP, N4 ....$8.00
Wonders of the Deep, B-612, 1954, MIP, from $10 to $14.00
World of Liddle Kiddles, B-577, 1970, MIP, N4...............$75.00
X-Men, Captive Hearts, #1085, MIP (sealed), B10 ....$8.00
Yellowstone National Park, A-306, MIP, N4......................$8.00
Yellowstone South, A-306, MIP, B10 ....$15.00
Zorro, B-469, 1958, MIP, N4...$40.00
101 Dalmatians, B-532, 1961, MIP, N4 ....$6.00
20,000 Leagues Under the Sea, B-370, MIP (sealed), B10...$35.00

Western

No friend was ever more true, no brother more faithful, no acquaintance more real to us than our favorite cowboys of radio, TV, and the silver screen. They were upright, strictly moral, extrememly polite, and tireless in their pursuit of law and order in the American West. How unfortunate that such role models are practically extinct nowadays.

This is an area of strong collector interest right now, and prices are escalating. For more information and some wonderful pictures, we recommend *Character Toys and Collectibles, First* and *Second Series*, by David Longest and *Guide to Cowboy Character Collectibles* by Ted Hake. New publications include *The Lone Ranger* by Lee Felbinger and *The W.F. Cody Buffalo Bill Collector's Guide* by James W. Wojtowicz. With the expection of Hake's, all are published by Collector Books.

Advisors: Donna and Ron Donnelly (D7).

See also Advertising Signs, Ads, and Displays; Books; Cereal Boxes; Character and Promotional Drinking Glasses; Character Clocks and Watches; Coloring, Activity, and Paint Books; Guns; Lunch Boxes; Premiums; Windups, Friction, and Other Mechanicals; and other specific categories.

Annie Oakley, doll, in western clothing, 25", VG, I2 ......$25.00
Bonanza, cup, 1960s, litho tin, features Adam, 3½" dia, EX, T2...$30.00
Bonanza, Foto Fantastiks Coloring Set, Eberhard Faber, 1965, complete, M (EX box), A..$100.00
Bonanza, sweatshirt, Norwich, 1960-63, wht cotton w/portraits, logo & map, child sz, scarce, VG+, A $150.00
Cheyenne, play cowboy gloves, fringed w/name & image of horse head, unused, M, P6...$40.00
Dale Evans, skirt, 1950s, cream w/brn vinyl fringe & trim, image of Dale riding Buttermilk on front, child-sz, VG, J5 ..$65.00

Daniel Boone, Fess Parker Cartoon Kit, Colorforms, 1964, complete, M (EX box), A..$85.00
Daniel Boone, Rub-Ons, Hasbro, 1964, transfers applied, NM (NM box), A..$15.00
Davy Crocket, doll, Reliable/Toronto, rubber head & hands w/cloth outfit, coonskin cap, shoes & knife sheath, 10", EX, A $175.00
Davy Crockett, bank, dime register, metal box w/canted corners, press-down trap, 2½" sq, EX, A................................$300.00
Davy Crockett, bank, plaster figure, VG, T1 ....$125.00

Davy Crockett, child's spoon and fork set, EX, $15.00.

Davy Crockett, coonskin cap, 1950s, image of Davy on top, EX $25.00
Davy Crockett, doll, Reliable Mfg/Canadian, rubber, flannel clothes & coonskin cap, rare, EX $150.00

Davy Crockett, flashlight, 1950s, litho tin w/red plastic top, 3", EX, J5 ....$25.00

Davy Crockett, guitar, Peter Puppet/WDP, fiberboard w/color decal, w/pick & songbook, 25", EX (EX box), ...$195.00

Davy Crockett, stamp/storybook, Simon & Schuster, 1950s, complete, unused, EX, J5/M8, from $15 to $25.00

Davy Crockett, Thunderbird Moccasin Kit, Blaine, 1950s, complete, NM (EX box), A $175.00

Davy Crockett, toy watch, Japan, w/sm metal crossed pistols, NMOC, A...$75.00

Davy Crockett, wallet, NM, C10 ....$65.00

Gabby Hayes, hat, wool, EX+, J2 ....$135.00

Gabby Hayes, Sheriff's Set, 1950s, unused, NMOC, J2 ....$80.00

Gene Autry, drum set, 3-pc set w/cb figure of Autry seated on lg drum, NMIB, A...$1,145.00

Gene Autry, flip book, Handy w/a Lasso, #1 in series of Pocket Television Theatre, blk & wht photos, EX, J5, from $50 to..$75.00

Gene Autry, outfit, Leslie Henry, 1940s, brn suede vest & chaps, red felt trim, w/images, NM (VG box), J5, from $200 to..$300.00

Gunsmoke, outfit, Matt Dillon, Kaynee, complete, EX+ (EX+ display box for 6 outfits), A.......................................$155.00

Gunsmoke, outfit, Matt Dillon, Seneca, 1958, complete, M (EX box), A..$125.00

Gunsmoke, pencil case, Hasbro, 1961, bl cb w/full-color decal of Matt Dillon, snap opening, 4x9", EX, T2...................$30.00

Gunsmoke, tablet, 1950s, Amanda Blake as Miss Kitty on cover, unused, NM, J2 ....$25.00

Gunsmoke, tablet, 1950s, James Arness as Matt Dillon on cover, unused, EX, A $18.00

High Chaparral, tablet, 1967, full-color photo cover, unused, minor water stain o/w VG+, A...................................$18.00

Hopalong Cassidy, bedspread, 1950, chenille, image of Hoppy w/lasso on Topper jumping fence at the Bar 20 Ranch, VG $250.00

Hopalong Cassidy, bedspread, 1950, chenille, NM, C10 ..$300.00

Hopalong Cassidy, bicycle horn, w/handlebar clamp, C10 .$200.00

Hopalong Cassidy, chaps, 1950s, blk suede w/image of Hoppy, G, pr $45.00

Hopalong Cassidy, Chuck Wagon Set, ceramic plate, bowl & mug w/images of Hoppy & Topper, EXIB, A............$300.00

Hopalong Cassidy, figures, Ideal, 1950, plastic, Hoppy in blk on wht Topper w/blk reins, M (EX box), A.................$300.00

Hopalong Cassidy, folder, Whitman, 1950, cb w/Hoppy & Topper on front & back, complete w/paper & envelopes, NM, A $100.00

Hopalong Cassidy, iron-on transfer, 1950s, blk steer head w/Deputy below, Hopalong Cassidy on either side, 2x7", EX, J5 ....$25.00

Hopalong Cassidy, jacket, Pied Piper/Dallas, ca 1950, blk w/Hoppy & Topper patch, wht trim, child sz, EX+, A $200.00

Hopalong Cassidy, linoleum floor, bust images of Hoppy, Topper & names against desert scene, 9x12', scarce, EX, A...$885.00

Hopalong Cassidy, mask, Traveler Trading Co, rubber, 8", EX+ (EX box), A $300.00

Hopalong Cassidy, milk bottle, Melville, 1950s, glass w/red graphics, 4", VG, J5 ....$25.00

Hopalong Cassidy, money clip, Bar 20 w/dial, C10 ....$75.00

Hopalong Cassidy, neckerchief slide, steer head, lg, C10 .$60.00

Hopalong Cassidy, necktie, Glick, 1950, blk silk w/full-color image of Hoppy & Topper, metal longhorn clasp, NM, A $125.00

Hopalong Cassidy, outfit, Sun Valley, w/blk shirt & pants, hat, red neckerchief w/metal holder, leather boots, NM, A......$435.00

Hopalong Cassidy, party plate, C10 ....$15.00

Hopalong Cassidy, pencil, 1950s, name etched in silver, originally came in pencil case, unused, EX, J5 ....$15.00

Hopalong Cassidy, pennant, C10......................................$25.00

Hopalong Cassidy, plate, ceramic w/fired-on image of Hoppy & Topper, inscr To My Friend Hoppy, 9" dia, M, A......$85.00

Hopalong Cassidy, pocketknife, 1950s, blk & wht, 3½", VG, J5 ....$45.00

Hopalong Cassidy, spurs, metal w/name screened on leather, EX+, A $225.00

Hopalong Cassidy, sweater, gr, child sz, unworn, C10....$150.00

Hopalong Cassidy, sweater, image and lettering in shades of brown on tan, NM, $225.00.

Hopalong Cassidy, tablet, C10 ....$35.00

Hopalong Cassidy, tie rack, EX $225.00

Hopalong Cassidy, vest, 1950s, blk suede w/image of Hoppy, VG $95.00

Hopalong Cassidy, wallet, 1950, leather w/image of Hoppy & Topper on metal front, w/Special Agent card, EX (EX box), A $275.00

Lone Ranger, arcade toy, Durham, 1974, EX, J2...............$60.00

Lone Ranger, bedspread, chenille, gr w/image of Lone Ranger & Silver, reads Hi-Yo Silver, 95x72", EX, A $165.00

Lone Ranger, binoculars, Harrison/TLR, 1949, NM, A .$100.00

Lone Ranger, binoculars, Harrison/TLR, 1949, NM (EX box), A...$225.00

Lone Ranger, Chuck Wagon Lantern, Dietz, 8", NMIB, A...$130.00

Lone Ranger, figure, Dollcraft TLR, pnt compo, standing w/guns drawn, wearing chaps & felt mask, 10", NMIB........$800.00

Lone Ranger, mask & neckerchief, VG+, J2 ....$115.00

Lone Ranger, outfit, mk TLR, complete w/hat, mask & bandana, EX (box top only)...$195.00

Lone Ranger, paint box, Milton Bradley, 1938, M, A $80.00

Lone Ranger, party horn, tin, 5", NM, J2..........................$30.00

Lone Ranger, pen, Everlast, 1950, mk The Lone Ranger TLR Inc w/plastic figural end, M, A................................$120.00

Lone Ranger, pencil box, Am Pencil, 1949, simulated blk leather over cb w/image of Lone Ranger & Silver, 5x9", NM, T2................................$50.00

Lone Ranger, Water Gun Playset, HG Toys, 1981, complete, MIB, M17................................$50.00

Maverick, TV Eras-O-Picture Book, Hasbro, 1959, no crayons o/w complete & NM, A................................$25.00

Maverick, wallet & key case, Warner Bros, 1958, blk plastic w/mc image of James Garner, photo ID on key case, NM+, A................................$100.00

Range Rider, chair, 1956, wood folding-type w/image on blk fabric bk, wht fringe on bottom, 24", scarce, EX+, T2 ...$80.00

Range Rider, tablet, 1950s, full-color image & facsimile signature on cover, 10x8", EX, T2................................$10.00

Rifleman, hat, Tex-Felt, 1958, red felt w/photo image of Chuck Conners on fabric label, NMIB, A................................$75.00

Rifleman, outfit, Pla-Master, 1959, flannel & corduroy w/felt hat, complete, M (NM box), A................................$250.00

Rin-Tin-Tin, magic pictures, Trans-O-Graph, 1956, unused, NMIB, J2................................$45.00

Rin-Tin-Tin, outfit, Pla-Master, 1955, Corporal Rusty 101st Cavalry, complete, scarce, NM (EX box), T2..........$130.00

Roy Rogers, bank, bronze boot w/Roy & Trigger emb on sides, 1950s, 6", EX................................$165.00

Roy Rogers, bank, ceramic, Roy on rearing Trigger, names on base, 8", NM, A................................$275.00

Roy Rogers, binoculars, decaled, 5", NM, A...................$100.00

Roy Rogers, book bag, 1950s, brn vinyl w/shoulder strap, Roy & Trigger pictured on front, VG, J5................................$65.00

Roy Rogers, Bunkhouse Boots, box only, style 2775, cb w/head image of Roy, 10x4", EX, A................................$130.00

Roy Rogers, camera & binocular set, Herbert George, complete w/paperwork & photo, NM (NM box), A................$675.00

Roy Rogers, Fix-It Stagecoach, Ideal, 1955, EX (EX box), H4................................$250.00

Roy Rogers, Fix-It Stagecoach, Ideal, 1955, missing some parts o/w VG, J2................................$100.00

Roy Rogers, Horse Trailer and Jeep, Ideal, 1950s, NM (EX box), A, $250.00.

Roy Rogers, fountain pen, name on side in script, C10..$150.00

Roy Rogers, hunting knife w/sheath & compass, EX, C10................................$450.00

Roy Rogers, jacket, brn leather w/fringe, silk lining, Roy Rogers/Trigger King of the Cowboys & image on label, VG, A................................$185.00

Roy Rogers, neckerchief slide, hat, yel plastic, C10..........$75.00

Roy Rogers, outfit, cowboy, Merit Playsuits, 1950s, complete, NM (EX box), A................................$450.00

Roy Rogers, outfit, cowboy, Yankeeboy, 1950s, tan pant styled like chaps, vest & folding cloth hat, EX (G box) $275.00

Roy Rogers, outfit, cowgirl, Merit Playsuits, 1950s, complete, NM (EX box)................................$265.00

Roy Rogers, paint-by-number set, Avalon, 1950s, oils, unused, EXIB................................$165.00

Roy Rogers, pants & chaps, 1950s, brn & orange, EX, J5.$65.00

Roy Rogers, pull toy, NN Hill Brass Co, wood, lithoed image of Roy on Trigger, w/bell, 9", NM, A................................$275.00

Roy Rogers, Quick Shooter Hat, Ideal, MIB, A.............$385.00

Roy Rogers, scarf, 1950s, silk, image on yel w/red border, 24x24", NM, A................................$75.00

Roy Rogers, shirt, RR Frontier Shirts, 1950s, western plaid w/embroidered design of Roy & Trigger, rare, NM, A..$50.00

Roy Rogers, slippers, 1950s, leather cowboy-boot style, image of Roy rearing on Trigger w/gr lettering, EX, J5...........$175.00

Roy Rogers, tablet, VG+, J2................................$30.00

Roy Rogers, tent, 1950s, name & image of Roy on Trigger, full-sz, complete, unused, NMIB, A................................$275.00

Roy Rogers, wall plaque, chalkware, emb image of Roy on rearing Trigger, signed Many Happy Trails..., 8x7", EX+, A ..$275.00

Roy Rogers & Dale Evans, Colorforms Dress-Up Kit, 1950s, w/2 9" dolls & mc stick-on clothing, complete, EXIB, J5 ......$150.00

Texas Ranger, outfit, Leslie Henry, box only, VG, J2.......$35.00

Wild Bill Hickok, outfit, Yankeeboy, 1948, complete, MIB, A................................$195.00

Wyatt Earp, guitar, 24", EX, J2................................$120.00

Wyatt Earp, paint-by-number set, Life & Legend of Wyatt Earp, Transogram, 1958, unused, M (EX box), A................$50.00

Wyatt Earp, spur set, Selcol, plastic, NMOC.................$50.00

Wyatt Earp, tablet, Hugh O'Brien on cover, M, J2..........$25.00

Zorro, bowl, Melmac, wht w/Zorro image, part of a set, EX, W6................................$35.00

Zorro, bracelet, Banntalite, w/light, EX, W6.....................$25.00

Zorro, cape, Carnival Creations, w/card, EX, W6............$65.00

Zorro, cup, Melmac, wht w/Zorro image, part of a set, EX ..$25.00

Zorro, figure, ceramic, WDP, 1958, EX, W6....................$125.00

Zorro, flashlight, 1958, blk plastic w/wrist strap, 2" dia, light not working o/w EX, F8................................$35.00

Zorro, gloves w/ring, M, W6................................$60.00

Zorro, hat & mask, Benay Albee, w/orig $1.19 price tag, EX, W6................................$80.00

Zorro, key chain/flashlight, 1950s, plastic, EX, W6..........$60.00

Zorro, Pencil Craft By Numbers, Hassenfeld Bros/WDP, EXIB, W6................................$75.00

Zorro, ring, silver & blk, EX, W6................................$15.00

Zorro, rug, 1950s, full-color cotton pile, EX, W6............$185.00

Zorro, sword, WDP, EX, W6................................$20.00

Zorro, wallet, brn or wht vinyl w/Zorro & horse, EX, W6, ea..$70.00

Windups, Friction, and Other Mechanicals

Windup toys represent a fun and exciting field of collecting — our fascination with them stems from their simplistic but exciting actions and brightly colored lithography, and especially the comic character or personality-related examples are greatly in demand by collectors today. Though most were made through the years of the '30s through the '50s, they carry their own weight against much earlier toys and are considered very worthwhile investments. Various types of mechanisms were used — some are key wound while others depend on lever action to tighten the mainspring and release the action of the toy. Tin and celluloid were used in their production, and although it is sometimes possible to repair a tin windup, experts advise against investing in a celluloid toy whose mechanism is not working, since the material is usually too fragile to withstand the repair.

Many of the boxes that these toys came in are almost as attractive as the toys themselves and can add considerably to their value.

If you especially enjoy windup and friction motorcycle toys, Sally Gibson-Downs and Christine Gentry have written a collectors' guide called *Motorcycle Toys, Antique and Contemporary*, published by Collector Books.

Advisors: Richard Trautwein (T3); Scott Smiles (S10).

See also Aeronautical; Automobiles and Other Replica Vehicles; Boats; Chein; Lehmann; Marx; Robots and Space Toys; Strauss.

Amos 'N Andy Acrobat Toy, 1930s, hand controls cause figures to do tricks on platform, pnt wood, 12", EX, from $190 to..$240.00

Amos Andra Creeping Baby, CBS copyright, 1940s, plastic, 5", rare, EX (G box w/Amos 'N Andy graphics), A...$1,000.00

Photo courtesy June Moon.

Auto Speedway, Automatic Toy Co., 1930s, NMIB, J6, $225.00.

Bambo the Monk, Unique Art, EXIB, J2 ....$275.00

Billiard Table, Ranger Steel, 2 full-figure men take turns hitting balls, litho tin, 5x10" table, EX, A $275.00

Black Boy on Velocipede, Stevens & Brown, 1870, cloth-dressed figure on CI velocipede w/spoke wheels, EX $2,000.00

Blacksmith, Girard, flat-sided jtd man sharpening tool at grinding wheel on rectangular base, litho tin, 4½", EX, A.......$150.00

Boy on Tricycle, 1890, litho tin w/compo figure, 10½" L, EX, A.....................$1,100.00

Busy Bee, Walt Disney, plastic & celluloid, 7", EX, J2 ...$450.00

Capital Hill Racer, Unique Art, 16", VG (G-box).........$225.00

Charleston Trio, 1921, jigger dances, boy plays violin & dog w/cane jumps atop cabin, litho tin, 10", EX (worn box) $1,200.00

Charlie Chaplin Walker, B&R, 1925, advances & swings cane, tin w/lead feet, 8½", EX+, A.................................$1,050.00

Cop-Cycle, Nosco, red cycle w/sidecar & 2 figures, plastic, friction, 5", NM (worn box), A $265.00

Dancing Cinderella & Prince, Irwin/WDP, 1950s, plastic, 5", NMIB.....................$150.00

Dancing Dude, Mattel, cowboy in cloth clothes dances atop litho tin stage, hand-crank, 8", NMIB, A $150.00

Donald Duck & Pluto Hand Car #1107, Lionel, 1930s, G, A .$450.00

Donald Duck and Pluto Hand Car, Lionel, EX, $1,000.00.

Elgin Clown Circus, ca 1920, several combinations of clowns performing, pnt tin, extremely rare, NM, A.........$8,250.00

FBI Riot Squad Car, Courtland, advances w/sound, litho tin w/mounted hood weapon, 7", NM (EX box), A $175.00

Felix the Cat, Lindstrom, plush over tin, glass eyes & button nose, 11", EX, A $550.00

Futurmatic Airport, Automatic Toy, plane circles tower & lands on base, litho tin, 15x15" base, NM (EX box), A ...$225.00

Gasoline Tanker, Courtland, litho tin w/blk rubber tires, 12", VG (G box), A.....................$150.00

GI Joe & His Jouncing Jeep, Unique Art, 1941, forward & reverse action, litho tin, 7", G+, A $150.00

GI Joe & His K-9 Pups, Unique Art, walks while carrying litho pups in cages, 9", NM, from $250 to $275.00

Goose, Unique Art, hops forward w/nodding head, litho tin, 9", VG, A $75.00

Hee Haw, Unique Art, 1930, driver on 2-wheeled donkey cart, litho tin, 10¼", VG $225.00

Hobo Train, Unique Art, 1925, train advances as dog pulls on hobo's shirt on roof, litho tin, 8", NM $700.00

Hoky & Poky, Wyandotte, clowns operating handcar, litho tin, 7", NM (EX box) $400.00

Home Run King, Selrite, batter mounted on rectangular base lithoed w/ball diamond spins & hits ball on tee, 7", G .$450.00

Howdy Doody Band, Unique Art, Bob Smith plays piano while Howdy dances, litho tin, 8", EX.....................$1,000.00

Humphrey Mobile, Wyandotte, 1950, litho tin, 9", EX..$400.00

Humphrey Mobile, Wyandotte, 1950, litho tin, 9", EX (EX box)..$500.00

Ice-Cream Scooter, Courtland, driver rings bell mounted on hood of scooter wagon, litho tin, 6½", M $275.00

Jazzbo Jim, Unique Art, ca 1920, litho tin, 10", EXIB, A .$600.00

Jumpin' Jeep, Unique Art, litho tin, EX+, T1 ....$225.00

Li'l Abner & His Dogpatch Band, Unique Art, 1945, characters around piano, litho tin, 7", NM, from $650 to $750.00

Lincoln Tunnel, Unique Art, vehicles travel road to tunnels, litho tin, 24", EX (G- box), A.....................$400.00

Lincoln Tunnel, Unique Art, 24", EX $300.00

Loop de Loop Carnival Ride, Wolverine, car navigates track & loops in center of base, litho tin, 19" base, NMIB...$475.00

Mammy, Lindstrom, advances & vibrates, litho tin, 8", EX ..$275.00

Mammy, Lindstrom, litho tin, 8", G $125.00

Mickey Mouse Hand Car, Lionel, 1930s, Mickey & Minnie work hdl, 8", EX+, A.....................$525.00

Motor Racer w/Rider, US Plastics, 1950s, friction, 5", NM (EX box), A.....................$100.00

Mickey Mouse Scooter Jockey, Mayco, 1950s, advances with nodding head and waving arm, plastic, 6", EX, from $150.00 to $200.00.

Officer Stop-Go the Whistling Traffic Cop, Marks Bros, 1930s, litho tin figure on wood, 12", EX (VG box), A $450.00

Police Motorcycle, Unique Art, litho tin, 8½", EX........$350.00

Pump-Mobile, Nylint, figure advances on 4-wheeled cart, litho tin, 9", EX (VG box), A.....................$350.00

Racer #13, Mohawk, litho tin, w/driver, 7", VG, A........$135.00

Rodeo Joe, Unique Art, cowboy in bucking jeep, litho tin, 7", NM (EX box).....................$375.00

Rodeo Joe, Unique Art, cowboy in bucking jeep, litho tin, 7", EX, A $225.00

Scooter Girl, Buffalo Toys, 1937, girl in swimsuit drives scooter, litho tin, 7", scarce, NM (EX box) $825.00

Sedan, Mohawk Toy Co, red, yel & blk, wht rubber tires w/spoke wheels, 5", scarce, EX, A $975.00

See-Saw Motion Toy, Gibbs, 2 tin figures on rod that spins up & down pole, 14", EX $250.00
Silver Meteor Train, 1930s, silver & bl litho tin, 18", MIB, A $150.00

Photo courtesy Dunbar Gallery.

Skeeter-Bug, Lindstrom, lithographed tin, NMIB, $300.00.

Sky Rangers, Unique Art, plane & blimp circle lighthouse, litho tin, 8", EX (EX box) $495.00
Speedway, 1920s, track undulates causing cars to race around grandstand, litho tin, 14" dia track, VG, A $450.00
Streak Racer, Buffalo Toys, red metal w/half-figure driver, pull rod for action, 21", VG, A.....................................$200.00
Sweeping Mammy, Lindstrom, figure moves around w/sweeping action, litho tin, 7½", EX (EX box), A....................$350.00
Taxi Cab, Irwin, yel & red plastic, 12", EX (EX box), A..$175.00
Three Little Pigs Acrobats, Borgfeldt, 3 celluloid pigs swinging on metal bars, 10¾", EX, A.......................................$700.00
Zilotone, Wolverine, clown w/rod moves end to end as music plays, complete w/6 interchangeable disks, EXIB, from $700 to..$800.00

ENGLISH

Airplane Carousel, mk Made in England, 2 litho tin airplanes w/celluloid props, pressed-steel base, 6", VG, A $100.00
Circus Truck, Wells, litho tin w/animals on both sides, 9½", EX, A $150.00
Delivery Van, Tri-ang Minic, gr tin w/blk plastic wheels, key missing, 3¼", VG, A $150.00
English Sports Car, Meccano, open w/interchangeable body, red & bl w/chrome grille, wht rubber tires, w/up, 8", EX, A $425.00
Fire & Ladder Truck, Wells, w/4 firemen & elevating ladder, litho tin, w/up, 14", VG, A $550.00
Gyro Cycle, Tri-ang, prewar, rider on cycle, litho tin & compo, 8", MIB $600.00
Mickey Mouse Duet, Salco, 1950, Minnie dances atop piano as Mickey plays, diecast w/crank, VG (VG box), A $400.00
Mickey Mouse Handcar, Wells, 1935, celluloid Mickey & Minnie figures w/tin arms, 6 sections of track, 13", NMIB, A ..$850.00
Road Roller, Tri-ang Minic, gr & gray plastic, w/up, 5½", EX (VG box), A $85.00
Rolls Royce, Wells, bl, cream & gray, auto club insignias over front bumper, VG, A..$400.00
Tanker Truck, Tri-ang Minic/L Bros Ltd, red & bl, 5¾", EX, A $200.00

FRENCH

Acrobat Cart, rider & horse w/acrobat on 2 wheels, pulling toy causes acrobat to do tricks & plink-plunk music, 6", A..$275.00
Auto Transport, Bonnet, auto w/cloth top & 4 disk wheels pulls cloth-covered 2-wheeled trailer, w/driver, 14", EX, A ..$350.00
Auto Transport, Martin, ca 1920, truck w/driver pulling canvas-topped 2-wheeled wagon, 10½", EXIB, A $1,400.00
Bear Climbing Pole, Martin, wht cloth- & fur-covered bear realistically climbs pole, 14", EXIB, A $1,875.00
Bear Performing, blk-pnt tin bear w/ruffled collar dances around rod, 8", VG+, A...$300.00
Bear Performing (L'Ours Martin), Martin, wht fur-covered bear w/rod behind head, 8", EX (EX box), A $1,870.00
Bell Ringer, Martin, jtd flat figure rings bell on post on oblong base, rubber-band driven, pnt tin & lead, 7¼", G, A $325.00
Bird on a Branch, rocks back & forth on branch, string-activated, pnt tin, 8", VG, A..$225.00
Black Man Playing Banjo, gr w/gold trim, legs & hand move, plink-plunk music, 6½", G+, A $550.00
Black Man Playing Bass Fiddle, standing on trapezoid-shaped base w/plink-plunk music, 9½", EX, A.................$1,325.00
Black Man Pushing Fruit Cart, Martin, mk FM, cloth-dressed man leans on flat 4-wheeled cart, pnt & litho tin, 8", VG, A..$950.00
Black Man Seated on Wheels, eccentric wheel rocks him as he moves forward, pnt tin, 6", VG, A $700.00
Black Minstrel Seated, figure in top hat shakes bells & claps cymbals w/feet, pnt tin, 7", VG+, rpt, A...................$700.00
Boy on Scooter, Bonnet, mk VBE, cloth-dressed boy on pnt tin scooter, 9", VG+, A $1,375.00
Boy Pushing Cart, Martin, cloth-dressed boy pushes 2-wheeled cart w/package mk Tres Tres Presse, pnt tin, 8", EX..........$1,000.00
Boy Sitting Backward on Chair, Martin, boy in red cloth jacket & blk pants on straight-backed chair mk FM, 7", EX, A.$2,000.00
Boy Twirling Balls, no cap, rocks torso as he spins arms, pnt tin, 8½", EX, A $550.00
Boy Twirling Balls, w/cap, pnt tin, 10", EX, A $900.00
Boy Twirling Balls, w/cap, pnt tin, 10", VG, A $400.00
Bus, Joustra, 1930s, red & bl w/wht striping, battery-op lights, 12", VG+, A $325.00
Cat Pushing Mice in Cage, dressed cat walks & pushes 2-wheeled cage as 2 mice jump around, pnt tin, 8½", G, A.....$1,050.00
Champion, Rossignol, Buffalo Bill-type figure shoots rifle at target on box, lever action, pnt tin, 9", NMIB, A $1,875.00
Chinese Man Pulling Rickshaw, Creation, pnt compo & tin, 6½", NMIB, A...$400.00
Chinese Warrior w/Swords, Martin, hat mk FM, figure in bl & blk period costume wields swords, pnt tin & wire, 7" VG $1,000.00
Citroen B2 Taxi, 1925, blk w/simulated cane body, hub wheels, tin, 14½", G, A $2,075.00
City Bus, JP, gr litho tin w/wht top, destinations listed on sides, 10½", EX, A $1,100.00
Clown & Duck Roundego, clown bobs up & down as duck pops in & out of base, pnt tin, 8½" wide, G+, A $775.00
Clown Acrobat on Rings, clown rotates & does overhead flips while rotating on base w/plink-plunk music, 6", VG, A...........$700.00

Clown Banjo Player, cloth-dressed pnt-tin figure w/banjo spins around on stool, plink-plunk music, 7½", VG, A...$1,050.00

Clown Banjo Player, pnt-tin figure seated on chair w/leg crossed strums on banjo, plink-plunk music, 6", rpt, EX, A.$700.00

Clown Clarinetist, seated on drum, rocks head & arms while playing, plink-plunk music, pnt tin, 6½", rpt, EX, A.........$650.00

Clown Curtsying, cloth-dressed clown pulls on sides of his suit, pnt tin, 7½", G, A...$350.00

Clown Doing Splits, cloth-dressed clown goes up & down doing splits, pnt tin, 10", rpt, EX, A...$900.00

Clown Playing Bass Fiddle, pnt-tin & stained figure standing on crank base, plink-plunk music, 8", VG, A...$650.00

Clown Trombonist, clown straddles drum-like base while 'playing' trombone, plink-plunk music, pnt tin, 8½", VG+, A.$1,000.00

Clown Twirling Balls, rotates arms while balls twirl from rod attached to stomach on platform, pnt tin, 9", G+, A.....$600.00

Clown Twirling Parasol, clown rotates as parasol spins on its side on ground, pnt tin, 5½", VG, A...$475.00

Clown Twirling Star, lg gr & yel litho tin star twirls from clown's stomach, pnt tin, 5", G, A...$525.00

Clown Twirling Star w/3 Bells, gold star twirls on clown's stomach, pnt tin, 9", VG, A...$1,325.00

Clown Twirling Star w/8 Bells, lg lithoed star twirls from clown's stomach, pnt tin, 9", EX, A...$1,980.00

Clown Twirling Star w/8 Bells, lg lithoed star twirls on nose, pnt tin, 10½", VG, A...$1,375.00

Clown Viola Player, clown in cloth suit plays & moves glass eyes to plink-plunk music, pnt tin w/compo head, 11", EX, A...$3,850.00

Clown Violinist, seated, nods head & bows as he claps cymbals on feet, plink-plunk music, pnt tin, 7½", VG+, A ..$700.00

Clown Violinist, standing, plink-plunk music, cloth-dressed pnt tin, bsk head w/glass eyes, 13", VG+, A...$3,400.00

Clown w/Cymbals Balancing Wine Bottles on Spinning Tray, tray rod balanced on nose, pnt tin, 12½", rpt, EX, A....$2,550.00

Clown w/Duck, clown faces lg quacking duck that flaps wings as they move back & forth, pnt tin, 10", rpt on duck, G, A.......$525.00

Clown w/Fly Swatter & Flies, cloth-dressed figure swatts at flies hovering near his face, pnt tin, 8", EX, A...$100.00

Clown w/Hoop & Ball, wooden ball spins as hoop rotates & revolves around clown, pnt tin, 5½", G, A...$275.00

Clown w/Large Hoop, rotating hoop revolves around clown while playing plink-plunk music, pnt tin, 6", G, A.$225.00

Clown Zilophonist, cloth-dressed clown alternately raises arms, plink-plunk music, pnt tin, 5½", G+, A...$500.00

Clowns on Seesaw, legs outstretched on plank attached to drum on base, w/plink-plunk music, pnt tin, 10" L, G, A.......$1,320.00

Clowns on 4-Wheeled Platform w/Bells, 2 clowns waving bells while facing each other, pnt tin, 7¾", VG, A.........$800.00

Couple Dancing, Martin, cloth-dressed couple dance & spin, pnt tin, wire & lead, 7½", VG+, A...$650.00

Course de Taureau (Bull Fighter), Martin, bull & matador attached to base by rods, rubber-band drive, 8", EXIB, A...$1,320.00

Donald Duck (Donald le Canard), Donald as a caballero bounces around, plastic, 6½", NM (EX box), A......$285.00

Drunkard (Le Pouchard), Martin, cloth-dressed figure shakes bottle & raises glass to mouth, 8", EX (EX box), A $1,100.00

Dump Truck, Bonnet, open cab w/side-dump bed, disk wheels, w/driver, pnt & emb tin, 7¾", VG+, A...$450.00

English Bobbie, Martin, cloth-dressed figure in blk uniform & helmet w/nightstick, pnt tin, wire & lead, 7½", VG+, A.$825.00

English Soldier Presents Arms, Martin, cloth-uniformed figure in red top, blk pants & gray helmet nods head, 8", VG, A...$950.00

Exposition Universalle 1889, Martin, Chinese man pulls lady w/fan in rickshaw, inertia wheel, pnt tin, 7½", VG, A ...$900.00

Exposition Universalle 1889, Martin, man pushes lady w/fan in 3-wheeled chair, inertia wheel, litho tin, 7", EX+, A....$1,925.00

Farmer w/Scythe (Le Faucher), Martin, cloth-dressed figure realistically uses scythe, 7", VG+ (damaged box), A .$1,870.00

Fire Engine, Delahaye, 1900, red-pnt tin w/top-& rear-mounted reels, 2 cloth-dressed compo figures, 15", EXIB, A ..$4,620.00

Fireman Climbing Ladder, Martin, figure in blk & gold helmet climbs triangular ladder, pnt tin, 7½", EX...$850.00

Fireman Pushing Hose Reel, Martin, on/off switch on back of figure in blk uniform & gold helmet, pnt tin, 8", EX, A...$900.00

Fisherman, Martin, cloth-dressed figure sitting atop rock manipulating rod w/fish, pnt tin, 7", EX, A...$1,825.00

Flying Boy, boy flies in circle when suspended on string, pnt tin, 6", rpl paper prop, G, A...$325.00

Flying Carpet, couple on carpet fly in circle when suspended on string, pnt tin, 5½", rpl paper prop, VG, A...$600.00

Flying Geese, 2 geese fly in circle when suspended on string, pnt tin, 8", rpl paper props, VG, A...$300.00

Flying Pigeon, molded wings flap as prop turns, pnt emb tin, 9", rpl paper prop, VG, A...$285.00

French Sentinel, Martin, cloth-uniformed figure in bl coat, red hat & pants walks w/dbl-prop action, 7½", EX...$675.00

Girl Skipping Rope, figure attached to rod on rnd base jumps in realistic motion, pnt tin, 6", VG+, A...$775.00

Hansom Cab, Martin, emb FM, horse w/jtd legs, pnt tin, 9" ..$350.00

Horse Race, 2 horses w/jockeys race around base w/weathervane & emb w/numbers 1-12, pnt tin, 8" wide, G+, A.$1,150.00

International Circus Set, cloth-dressed clown balances on 2 ladders, w/additional props, litho tin & wood, MIB, A...$1,020.00

Lady Chasing Mouse, Martin, lady in gray cloth dress w/wht bonnet waves broom & rocks back as mouse jumps, 8", EX..$2,000.00

Lady Doing Cakewalk, Martin, lady in cloth dress moves arms & dances forward, pnt tin, wire & lead, 7½", rare, G+, A...$2,100.00

Lady Lifting Baby, figure dances around lifting baby up & down in realistic manner, pnt tin, 7", VG+, A...$825.00

Lady on Roller Skates, figure in long dress & hat moves feet as she advances, pnt tin, 7", VG, A...$850.00

Lady Pushing Baby Carriage, Bonnet, cloth-dressed figure & baby, pnt-tin carriage, 7", EXIB, A...$1,050.00

Lady Pushing Cart (La Petite Marchande), Martin, cloth-dressed lady pushing pnt-tin 2-wheeled cart, 7", EX+ (EX+ box), A...$1,050.00

Lady Pushing Cart (Le Petite Marchande), Martin, 7", VG+, A...$700.00

Lady Pushing Fruit Cart, Creation, pnt compo & tin, 6", NMIB, A...$350.00

Lady Sweeping, Martin, cloth-dressed figure w/molded headscarf sweeps back & forth, pnt tin, wire & lead, 7", EX, A..$1,100.00

Lady w/Basket & Umbrella, figure in full skirt advances while rocking torso, pnt tin, 6½", VG+, A $400.00

Lady w/Broom & Basket on Her Back, stooped figure advances, pnt tin, 6", VG+, A $450.00

Lady w/Broom & Hair Bow, figure sweeps while advancing in erratic pattern, pnt tin, 7", VG+, A $800.00

Lady w/Fan, figure slowly dances around while moving upper torso, pnt tin, 7¼", VG, A $850.00

Lady w/Muff, Martin, pnt-tin figure in cloth coat w/fur collar & muff advances slowly w/rocking motion, 8", VG+, A $1,050.00

Lady w/Muff, Martin, pnt-tin figure w/flocked hat & muff advances slowly w/rocking motion, 8", VG, A $800.00

Lady w/Umbrella, stooped figure advances & rocks back & forth, pnt tin, 6½", rpt, EX, A..$400.00

Lawyer Behind Desk (L/Eminent Avocat), Martin, cloth-dressed figure addresses court, pnt & litho tin, 9", EX+, A ..$2,875.00

Man on Tricycle, Martin (?), mc jtd figure on blk trike, pnt tin & lead, 4", EX+, A $550.00

Man Riding Goat on Rockers, gray jtd goat rocks back & forth while man holds onto horns, pnt tin, 7", rstr, EX, A ..$300.00

Man Sweeping, Martin, cloth-dressed figure twists from waist swinging broom, pnt tin, wire & lead, 7", rare, G....$850.00

Man Swinging Around Pole, man clasps legs together as he rotates around pole, pnt tin, 15", VG+, A............$1,650.00

Man Tumbling (Le Petit Culbuteur), Martin, cloth-dressed figure does somersaults, pnt tin, 9", EX (EX box), A $1,375.00

Marble-Drop Toy (Le Treuil), Martin, marbles descend pole causing man to turn crank, pnt tin, 25", VG (VG box), A........$700.00

Marble-Drop Toy (Le Treuil), Martin, pnt tin, 25", EX (EX box), A $1,000.00

Marechal Ferrand, Martin, 2 men working forge w/anvil, pnt & litho tin, 6½", some overpnt on legs, EX, A.........$2,750.00

Motorcycle w/Policeman, 1930s, full-figure driver in red uniform, cream cycle, 3¾", VG+, from $200 to............$250.00

Motorcycle w/Sidecoach, red-pnt tin early type w/gold trim, enclosed coach, rubber tires w/spoke wheels, 9¼", EX, A..........$2,860.00

Oriental Soldier, Martin, free-standing figure in gold costume & cap holds weapon, pnt tin, wire & lead, 8", VG, A.$775.00

Pianist, Martin, cloth-dressed figure rocks as hands move over keyboard, plink-plunk music, pnt tin, 5¼", EX, A........$1,050.00

Pigeon, Bonnet, pnt emb tin, eccentric wheels, 8", VG+, A..$250.00

Porter Pulling 2-Wheeled Cart, Martin, red & blk striped cart w/inertia wheel, litho & pnt tin, 6½", VG, A $580.00

Porter Pushing 2-Wheeled Cart, Martin, porter pushing cart w/lg box, inertia wheel, spirit-pnt & litho tin, 5", EX, A ..$700.00

Renault Garage w/Auto, CIJ/France, wooden garage mounted on wooded base, w/red & tan litho tin coupe, rare, NMIB, A $1,925.00

Soldier w/Rifle & Bayonet, Martin, figure in tan cloth uniform, helmet & cartridge belt, pnt tin, wire, 7½", EX, A .$900.00

Squirrel in a Cage, Martin, mk FM, squirrel runs in cage attached to tan & red housing on flat base, pnt tin, 9", VG+, A...$400.00

Torpedo Convertible, JEP, mc tin roadster w/driver, 10½", EXIB, A $2,530.00

Touring Car, ca 1900, aqua-pnt tin w/blk slanted & vented hood, wht rubber tires, red spokes, 2 cloth figures, 12", M, A...$14,300.00

Tractor, Bonnet, resembles open car w/4 disk wheels, w/driver, pnt emb tin, 6" L, G+, A...$150.00

Violin Player (Le Gai Violinist), Martin, cloth-dressed man in top hat plays violin, 8", EX (EX box), A $1,200.00

Washer Woman, Martin, cloth-dressed figure in molded headscarf scrubs w/1 hand, pnt tin, wire & lead, 7", VG..$900.00

GERMAN

Africa Cart, G&K, Black man pops out of 2-wheeled cart pulled by another man, litho tin, 6½", EX, A $1,025.00

Airplanes Circle Tower, US Zone, 2 litho tin planes circle silo-type tower w/lithoed airport, 4½" W, EX+, A.........$135.00

Beetle Crawling, Gunthermann, beetle crawls in realistic motion, 7½", NMIB, A $350.00

Billiards Player, ca 1900, man in gray suit takes aim at cluster of pockets at end of long table, litho tin, 11", EX, A.$1,300.00

Black Clarinet Player w/Monkey Violinist, Gunthermann, mk SawG, monkey bows & man rocks, plink-plunk music, 8", VG+, A $1,150.00

Black Patriotic Minstrels, 2 jtd flat figures dance & stick out tongues, plink-plunk music, crank action, 7½", EX, A.$350.00

BMW Convertible, Schuco #1048, red, 4½", NM, A $225.00

BMW Convertible, Schuco #2002, maroon, 5½", missing windshield o/w VG...$150.00

Bonzo on Scooter, Gunthermann, litho tin, 7½", EX, A..$1,600.00

Boy Feeding Bird on Wheeled Platform, lever action, pnt tin, 7", G+, A...$275.00

Boy on Skies w/Propeller, Bing, prop pushes boy in hooded fur coat on short skies, celluloid, cloth & tin, 7", VG, A $3,850.00

Boy w/Little Girl, Schuco, boy raises & lowers girl overhead, tin & celluloid w/cloth clothes, 5", EX, A....................$325.00

Bullfighter, matador lifts sword to bull on 4-wheeled platform, 9½", EX, A $350.00

Bully Bulldog, US Zone, litho tin, 8", scarce, NMIB......$450.00

Busy Lizzy, lady bent forward mopping, litho tin, 6½", VG, A...$450.00

Carousel, Gunthermann, 3 tin horses w/riders & flying chairs w/riders on perforated base, umbrella top, 11", EX, A $2,200.00

Carousel, 3 tin horses & riders on perforated tin base, perforated top w/flag, plink-plunk music, 13", VG, A $500.00

Cat & Mouse Chase, 1930s, cat & mouse chase each other around base, litho tin, 4", rare, EX (EX box), A......$300.00

Cat Pulling Kittens in 2-Wheeled Cart w/Hood, 2 kittens in cart jump as cart is pulled, pnt & litho tin, 9", EX, A $650.00

Cat Sitting, early 1900s, mouth opens, tail wags, papier-mache covered w/gray mohiar, glass eyes, w/up, 6", fur loss, A.......$100.00

Cat Sitting, early 1900s, pull ring & mouth opens to meow, papier-mache covered w/stenciled wool fur, w/up, 7", VG, A...$250.00

Charlie Chaplin, articulated figure dances when base-mounted crank is turned, litho tin, 6½", EX+, A $1,320.00

Charlie Chaplin, tips hat, blinks eyes & speaks on phone while seated on bell box that rings, litho tin, 7", EX, A...$1,350.00

Charlie Chaplin Walker, Schuco, litho tin w/CI shoes, 8½", EX $900.00

Chicken Flapping Wings, mk Bavaria, yel chicken on 2 blk wheels, 6½", VG (orig box) $350.00

Clown Driving Car, Gunthermann, mk SG, clown in car w/Irish mail-type hdl, pnt & litho tin, 6", VG+, A..........$1,500.00

Clown Juggler, Schuco, juggles 4 balls in circular pattern, tin w/cloth clothes, 5", NM (G box), A.......................$425.00

Clown on Barrel, clown stands on hands as barrel rolls back & forth, litho tin, 7", EX, A...$500.00

Clown Pushing Clown on 2 Balls, sm clown holds legs of lg clown while pushing, pnt tin, 7½", VG+, A........$2,200.00

Clown Riding Donkey, mk Made in Germany/USA Pend, donkey bucks clown on 2-wheeled mechanism, litho tin, 9", EX, A...$825.00

Clown Riding Donkey Cart, Gama, w/revolving umbrella, litho tin, 8", G, A..$275.00

Clown Riding Pig, Stock, clown on pig wearing circus skirted blanket, orig string harness, litho tin, 5", EX...........$700.00

Clown Seated w/Parasol, clown spins around on dome base, pnt tin, 6½", VG+, A...$650.00

Clown w/Big Nose, standing figure w/hands in pockets vibrates & turns head, litho tin, 8", VG, A.......................$1,250.00

Clown w/Dog, Gunthermann, clown sitting on bottom w/knees up & heels on floor playing w/dog, pnt & litho tin, 9", EX, A...$2,300.00

Clown w/Pig on Platform, clown jumps up & down as platform moves forward, litho tin, 6", EX, A......................$1,000.00

Clown w/Spinning Ball on Head, clown dances in circle w/ball spinning on head, 7¾", VG, A..............................$500.00

Clown w/2 Dogs on Wheeled Frame, Tipp, dogs gallop as clown's arm moves w/reins, litho tin, 8", EX, A...$1,550.00

Clowns (2) Balancing on Hands on Horizontal Ladder, Gunthermann, mk SG, plink-plunk music base, pnt tin, 8½", G+, A...$1,750.00

Command Car AD2000, Schuco, blow on roof w/whistle or push lever & car advances, 6", missing whistle o/w NM (G box), A...$250.00

Coupe 3000, Schuco, gr, complete w/accessories, 4", EX+ (G box), A...$150.00

Cowboy, US Zone, upper half of body turns side to side, eyes move, litho tin, 9", NM, A...$500.00

Dodgem Car, Lindstrom, 1930s, couple travels in red car w/rubber bumper, litho tin, 9½", EX...............................$150.00

Dog Pushing Car, Stock, dog pushes open car w/driver, spoke wheels, eccentric wheel imparts action, 7¼", EX, A ..$900.00

Dog Somersaulting (Salto), Gunthermann, dog does back flips, litho tin, 5", EX (EX box) $375.00

Donald Duck, Nifty, 1960s-70s, travels in circle, mouth opens as head bobs & quacks, tin, cloth clothes, 8½", EXIB.$400.00

Donald Duck, Schuco, 1930s, moves as bill opens, tin body w/plastic bill & limbs, 6", MIB.................................$875.00

Donald Duck, Schuco, 1960, moves as bill opens, tin body w/plastic bill & limbs, 6", MIB, A.............................$400.00

Donald Duck Race Car, 1930s, litho tin w/rubber wheels, 4", G, A...$200.00

Double-Decker Bus, Bing, gr w/yel trim & spoke wheels, rear stairs lead to bench seats, litho tin, 12", VG $3,500.00

Double-Decker Bus, Orobr, red w/silver sidestep & spoked wheels, rear steps lead to bench seats, litho tin, 6", G $300.00

Drinking Monk, Schuco, figure raises & lowers stein, litho tin w/cloth clothes, 5", EX, A.......................................$250.00

Drinking Mouse, Schuco, mouse raises & lowers stein & staggers in circles, cloth w/tin feet, 5", EX, A.......................$200.00

Ducks (3) on Wheels, 2 rear ducks rock as all 3 roll forward, 5½", EX...$330.00

Elephant Organ Grinder, Ri Co, elephant pushes organ, stops & begins grinding w/trunk, plink-plunk music, tin, 8", EX, A.......$1,875.00

Famous Clown Juggler, sways & juggles 3 sets of rings, plastic & celluloid w/cloth clothes, 9", NM (EX box) $250.00

Ferris Wheel, late 19th C, 3 horses & riders on rods rotate w/crank plink-plunk mechanism, 8", G, A..............$235.00

Fire Chief Car, Hoge, 1930s, 13", NM, $575.00.

Fire Engine, Orobr, litho tin open vehicle w/4 firemen, spoked wheels, 6", EX, A..$2,300.00

Ford Hot Rod 1036, Schuco, 1932, red, litho tin, 3½", scarce, EX+, A...$200.00

Frog Jumping, Gunthermann, frog leans forward then jumps, cloth & litho tin w/glass eyes, 3½", EX, A $225.00

Funny Face (similar to Marx's Harold Lloyd), changes facial expressions as he walks, litho tin, 7", very rare, G, A.............$350.00

Garage & Touring Car, Orobr, w/driver, litho tin, garage: 6x6", car: 6", garage missing doors o/w EX, A...................$275.00

Garage w/Auto, Schuco, doors open when telephone receiver is pressed, 6x3x3", EX, A $150.00

Gik-Gak, Ebrel, chick on 2-wheeled box rocks back & forth as box is pulled by mother hen, litho tin, 9½", G+, A...$250.00

Girl w/Baby Carriage, mk DRGM, carriage rolls as girl lifts leg & baby lifts bottle, crying sound, litho tin, 7", EX, A...$1,550.00

Go-Cart, Schuco #1055, w/driver, advances w/sound, tin & plastic, 6", M (G box), A..$425.00

Harold Lloyd Hand Toy, figural head on plunger changes expressions & bell rings when pushed down, litho tin, 6", VG, A...$250.00

Heine, boy w/tousled brn hair, yel plaid jacket & gr pants rides yel Irish mail w/red wheels, litho tin, 6", EX+, A....$225.00

Hi-Way Henry, c Oscar Hitl, litho tin, 10", EX, A.....$2,500.00

Hobo, Gama/US Zone, waddles, litho tin, 7", EX $175.00

Hopsa, Schuco, mouse spins while lifting smaller mouse, tin w/cloth clothes, 4½", NM (EX box), from $300 to .$400.00

Horses on 4-Wheeled Platform, 3 horses w/riders gallop, litho tin, 6", EX, A...$350.00

Howdy Doody Acrobat, Arnold, Howdy Doody performs on high bar, compo w/cloth clothes, 12", VG, A..........$250.00

Jazzi Jim, Distler, dapper Black figure standing while playing concertina, litho tin, 7½", EXIB, A.....................$3,100.00

Jenny & Benny, Nifty, Jenny the mule bucks & moves as the Black boy Benny rides, celluloid figure, 6½", EXIB, A $525.00

Jiggs in His Jazz Car, Nifty, Jiggs steers & moves his head as car goes in circles, litho tin, 6½", EX, A $2,000.00

Juggling Clown, Schuco, vibrates around while juggling 4 balls, litho tin & cloth, 5", EX, A..$400.00

Lady at Piano, figure swings from side to side w/hands on keyboard, plays plink-plunk music, litho tin, 5", EX, A ..$400.00

Lady in Goose Cart, Stock, cart moves as goose flaps wings & lady raises arms, litho tin, 9½", EX, from $600 to ...$675.00

Lady in 2-Wheeled Horse Cart, Stock, horse moves as lady w/whip moves arms up & down, litho tin, 7½", EX, A..............$600.00

Limousine, Bing, convertible w/side lamps, glass windshield, rust w/yel striping, yel spoke wheels, w/driver, 12", EX.....$3,000.00

Limousine, Carette, open front w/enclosed rear, railed top, gray w/red & bl trim, spoke wheels, 4 figures, 12½", M.....$6,800.00

Limousine, Carette, open front w/enclosed rear, railed top, lt yel w/bl trim, red spoke wheels, w/driver, 16", EX, A...$9,500.00

Limousine, Distler, 1920, enclosed sedan, dk bl w/aqua trim, rear folding rack, bl spoke wheels, w/driver, 12", NM, A..$4,500.00

Limousine, G&K, convertible, metal spoke wheels, driver & animated lady passenger w/fan, 6", EX $750.00

Limousine, Gunthermann, open front w/convertible rear, brn w/yel trim, NP tires w/red spokes, w/driver, 10", EX, A.......$1,500.00

Limousine, Karl Bub, C-style open driver's seat w/enclosed rear, red & blk w/blk spoke wheels, w/driver, 14", EX, A.........$1,875.00

Limousine, mk EBO Motor on grille, w/driver, orig Kaufmann & Baer store tag, 7", VG, A...$300.00

Limousine, Orobr, enclosed sedan, red & gray w/wht top, blk fenders & running boards, disk wheels, w/driver, 9", EX.....$900.00

Limousine, Tipp, enclosed sedan, bl w/yel top, running boards & trim, disk wheels w/orange hubs, w/driver, 10", EX, A $525.00

Limousine Saloon Taxi, Bing, open-sided front w/enclosed rear, railed top, w/meter, maroon w/orange trim, 13", M, A...........$3,300.00

Lobster, claws move as red lobster moves erratically, pnt tin, 8½", EX, A $500.00

Loop the Loop, Technofix, racer navigates track, Vacuform plastic track & litho tin racer, NM (VG box) $250.00

MAC 700 Motorcycle, Arnold, w/sidecar, driver mounts & dismounts, red & blk version, litho tin, 8", M $1,200.00

MAC 700 Motorcycle, Arnold, 1948, w/sidecar, driver mounts & dismounts, dk bl version, litho tin, 8", G, A $600.00

Maggie & Jiggs, Nifty, 2 figures facing each other on tin band w/4 spoke wheels, 7", EX, from $850 to................$2,000.00

Man at Grindstone, figure operates stone w/foot treadle as he puts knife to wheel, plink-plunk music, pnt tin, 7", VG, A.$400.00

Man in Tails Jumping, Gunthermann, mk SG, jumps & moves forward, pnt tin, 7" $600.00

Man on Skies, mustached figure pushes self along w/pole, pnt tin, 7", VG+, A $1,325.00

Mercedes Race Car, Schuco, #1050, 1930s, 6", EX, A ...$175.00

Mercedes 190-SL Coupe, Schuco #1044, salmon & cream, 4", EX, A $200.00

Merry-Go-Round, early, mk V&R, 4 gondolas w/figures swing around base w/flags at top, 12½", VG, A $5,000.00

Mickey Mouse Slate Dancer, 1931, crank-op/steam-powered, litho tin, 6½", rare, VG, A $11,000.00

Micro Racer #1042, Schuco, red, 3", EX.........................$300.00

Minnie Mouse Mascot, Schuco, fabric w/plastic face & shoes, 4", NM (EX box), A $150.00

Mickey Mouse Drummer (Open Mouth), Nifty, lithographed tin, plunger activated, 6½", NM, $2,750.00.

Monkey Driving Car, Distler, dressed monkey moves hat back & forth as car goes in circles, litho tin, 6", EX, A........$600.00

Monkey Drummer, Distler, uniformed monkey standing on sq platform drumming, litho tin, 7½", EX, A...............$400.00

Monkey Drummer (Tambourineur), Schuco, advances & plays drum, litho tin & cloth, 5", M (EX box), A $250.00

Monkey on Tricycle, Arnold, dressed monkey steers & pedals trike, litho tin, 3½", G, A $175.00

Monkey on Tricycle, Arnold, dressed monkey steers & pedals trike, litho tin, 3½", EX, A $300.00

Monkey Riding in Open Touring Car, Schuco, plush monkey in glasses, felt hat & scarf, litho-tin w/disk wheels, 7", EX, A...........$9,025.00

Motorcycle Racers, Fischer (?), 2 riders on cycles go around base w/red flag, pnt & litho tin, 10" wide, NMIB, A ...$3,500.00

Motorcycle w/Driver, Gunthermann, 1910, red w/spoke wheels & splash board, 7", M..$3,000.00

Motorcycle w/Driver, Technofix, travels in circular pattern, litho tin, 7½", NM (VG box), from $300 to $375.00

Motorcycle w/Driver, Technofix, travels in circular pattern, litho tin, 7½", EX $250.00

Motorcycle w/Driver, US Zone, #GF207, red & tan litho tin, 5", VG+, A...$225.00

Motorcycle w/Driver & Rear Passenger, Gely, yel & red litho tin, hub wheels, 6", EX, A......................................$1,850.00

Motorcycle w/Driver & Rear Passenger, US Zone, brn w/litho spoked wheels, rider turns at waist, 6", EX $1,200.00

Motorcycle w/Sidecar, Driver & Passenger, CKO/DRGM, #K-342, passenger shoots machine gun, litho tin, 4", from $250 to......$300.00

Motorcycle w/Sidecar, Driver & Passenger, Geppert & Kelch, 1920, gray, red trim, lady w/parasol in chair-type car, EX, A $3,740.00

Motorcycle w/Sidecar, Driver & Passenger, Muller & Kaderer, 1914, bl w/spoke wheels, lady in boat-type car, 8", EX, A...$5,500.00

Motorcycle w/Sidecar, Woman Driver & Passenger, Tipp, brn & blk litho tin, boat-type car, 10", EX...................$1,500.00

Motorcycle w/Sidecar & Driver, Geppert & Kelch, 1920, red litho tin w/spoke wheels, boat-type car mk G&K, 6½", EX, A...$3,400.00

Motorcycle w/Sidecar & Driver, Tipp, litho tin, 7", VG, A ...$400.00

Motorcycle w/Sidecar & Driver, Tipp, litho tin, 7½", EX, A .$775.00

Mouse Cart, 2 wheels pull 2 tumbling mice, litho tin, 6", EX, A..$450.00

Mutt & Jeff, Gunthermann, mk SG, piggyback pose on wheeled mechanism, litho tin, 6½", EX, A $3,850.00

Nodding Man, early 20th C, compo head w/pnt features, felt suit w/vest & lg bow tie, head nods when wound, 49", G, A............$3,225.00

Old Timer Renault, Schuco, 7", EX (EX box), A...........$100.00

Packard Coupe, Orobr, red w/blk top & running boards, rumble seat w/rear spare, red disk wheels, litho tin, NM, A .$4,950.00

Paddy's Pride, Stock, pig pulling driver in 2-wheeled cart, litho tin, 8", MIB, A..$2,200.00

Parrot, bird rolls forward on 3 wheels, pnt tin, 9", VG, A..$200.00

Pigeon, mk Bavaria, nods head as it rolls forward, internal bellows, pnt tin, 7¼", VG, A...$150.00

Powerful Katrinka, copyright 1923, lg lady advances & lifts Jimmy figure from wheelbarrow, litho tin, 7", EX, A..........$2,000.00

Punch & Judy, DRGM/US Zone, devil & Punch battle back & forth while Judy watches, litho tin, 9", M, from $400 to $450.00

Race Track w/Pit Stop, US Zone, 2 racers travel track & enter pit stop, litho tin, 17" oval track, EX (EX box), A ..$250.00

Racer, Hess, early gr & blk 2-seater w/front crank, brass wheels, hood opens, w/driver, 6¼", EX, A............................$825.00

Roosters Fighting, 2 roosters on 4-wheeled platform w/back-&-forth action, litho tin, 10", EX, A $250.00

Safety First, Distler, street scene on sq base w/various vehicles, pedestrians & passengers, etc, 9" sq, EX (EX+ box), A.........$2,600.00

Santa Claus Sparkler, 1915, push hdl & Santa appears w/sack of toys, litho tin, 6½", rare, NM, A..............................$250.00

Schuco Garage w/Kommando Anno 2000, litho tin garage w/exterior phone & blk 2-door car, 5¾x6½", MIB, A $250.00

Sedan, Distler, w/driver, bl & gray tin w/Dunlop tires, 11", VG, A..$900.00

Soldier in German Helmet w/Backpack & Rifle Kneeling, bends on knee then stands to shoot rifle, pnt tin, 7", rpt, EX, A...$825.00

Soldiers in Horse-Drawn 2-Wheeled Cart, Orobr, on/off lever, litho tin, 7", VG+, A..$400.00

Solisto Clown Drummer, Schuco, tin w/cloth clothes, celluloid face, 4½", NM (EX box), A $500.00

Solisto Clown Violinist, Schuco, tin w/cloth clothes, celluloid face, 4½", VG, A..$175.00

Solisto Clown Violinist, Schuco, tin w/cloth clothes, celluloid face, 4½", NM, A..$300.00

Sparkling Motorcycle, Arnold, advances w/sparks, tires mk Union Cord, litho tin, 7½", EX $450.00

Spirit of St Louis Plane, Schuco, litho tin w/felt-bodied pilot, friction, 4" wingspan, not working o/w EX $1,400.00

Stake Truck, Bing, open cab w/floor-mounted steering wheel, gray litho tin w/red seat, orange spoke wheels, 11", EX ..$2,850.00

Super Sport Convertible, PN, litho tin w/blk rubber tires, friction, 11", EX (VG box), A $125.00

Taxi, Carette, red body w/blk back, spoke wheels, w/driver, litho tin, 13", EX, A...$700.00

Telecar, JNF, cream convertible advances forward, 10", EX..$200.00

Telestreering Car, Schuco #3000, tin car w/12 pylons & steering-wheel control, MIB, A $225.00

Three Little Pigs Drummer, Schuco, 4", rare, NM (EX box), A, $1,000.00.

Three Little Pigs Flutist, Schuco, 4", rare, M (NM box), A $1,400.00

Three Little Pigs Violinist, Schuco, 4", rare, M (EX+ box), A $1,200.00

Tippy Dog, Schuco, 1930, blk dog w/ball in mouth, 5", EX (VG box), A..$175.00

Tippy Dog, Schuco, 1930, blk dog w/ball in mouth, 5", NM (NM box) $275.00

Toonerville Trolley, Nifty, 1922, litho tin, 7", EX, A $950.00

Touring Car, Carette, open 4-seat w/side lamps, wht litho tin w/gold trim, red spoke wheels, 4 figures, 13", EX, A $3,750.00

Touring Car, Carette, open 4-seat w/side lamps, wht-pnt tin w/blk seats, wht spoke wheels, w/driver, 13", M, A.............$8,800.00

Touring Car, Gunthermann, open 4-seat w/no side lamps, red litho tin w/blk trim, simulated doors, w/driver, 10", EX, A $1,050.00

Touring Car, Gunthermann (?), open 4-seat w/side lamps, red litho tin w/blk & yel trim, doors open, w/driver, 12", EX, A $1,100.00

Touring Car, Karl Bub, open 4-seat, gray litho tin w/blk running boards & bl trim, w/driver, 10", EX, A $1,100.00

Touring Rider, Gunthermann, boy w/jtd legs pedals bike w/spring power & chain drive, hand-pnt, 8½", VG, A.........$1,200.00

Traffic Cop, Schuco #4520, circles & raises arm as discs in base change color, pnt tin, 5", NM (EX box) $375.00

Traffic Cop, Schuco #4520, pnt tin, 5", EX (box bottom only) $275.00

Tramway Co Trolley Car, litho tin w/spoked wheels, 6½", VG, A..$275.00

Tricycle w/Policeman, Gunthermann, figure rings bell as cycle moves, litho tin, 10", VG+, A $8,000.00

Tumbling Mouse, Schuco, mouse tumbles forward, felt over tin, 4", VG, A...$100.00

Turtle Crawling, mk DRGM, realistic movements, 7½", EX .$275.00

Vis-A-Vis, red w/bl print interior, blk rear fenders, litho-spoked wheels, w/driver, litho tin, 4½", VG+, A $275.00

Volkswagen Convertible, CKO, unique flip-over design converts from coupe to convertible, compo driver, 6½", EX, A..$425.00

Volkswagen Coupe Micro Racer, #1046, wht, 4", NM, A ..$100.00

Wanderer Sports Car, Distler, 3 speeds, bl w/blk rubber tires, 9½", EX (VG box), A $400.00

Zeppelins & Airplanes Roundego, 3 zeppelins & 3 planes move around base w/2 Am flags atop, pnt tin, 11½", EX ..$5,000.00

Zeppelins Roundego, 2 zeppelins rotate from canopy on oblong base, plink-plunk music, crank-op, litho tin, 10", EX, A $1,425.00

Italian

Ferrari, Fara S Martino Dececco, 1950s, red-pnt aluminum w/fold-down windshield, open seat, blk tires, 21", M, A.....$4,400.00

Superman Telecomando Flying Figure, Cosmec, 1978, string attaches to plastic figure w/hand-held controller, 9", MIB, J5 ....$85.00

Japanese

Aerial Ladder Truck, K, mk MFD, turn screw & ladder rises, litho tin, friction, 12", MIB, A $135.00

American Circus Truck, w/tiger in back, litho tin, friction, 5", scarce, NM (EX box), A..$225.00

Animal House, TPS, rabbit swings, bear & monkey see-saw & various animals appear in tree house, litho tin, 6", EX+ $250.00

Automatic Racing Game, Haji, grandstand w/3 racers, push lever for action, litho tin, 2" cars, NM (EX box).....$200.00

Babes in Toyland, Linemar, soldier advances & plays drum, litho tin, 6", NM (EX box), from $400 to.........................$450.00

Baby Bicycle, dog running along side bell trike w/boy holding silk flag, celluloid & tin, 5", EXIB, A.......................$225.00

Baby Carriage Merry-Go-Round, girl pushing carriage w/twirling canopy, celluloid & tin, 7", EXIB..............................$200.00

Ball & Kitty, 1960s, hits ball w/paw, wht plush, 6", NM (NM box), T2 ....$30.00

Ball-Playing Giraffe, TPS, bounces ball up & down wire, litho tin, 8½", NM (EX box) $325.00

Baseball Catcher, Occupied Japan, catcher w/NY on sleeve dances around while looking for ball, 5½", VG+, from $150 to..$180.00

Batman, Billiken, litho tin w/vinyl cape, 8", MIB, T1....$100.00

Batmobile, ASC, advances w/sound, litho tin figure w/vinyl head, friction, 14", scarce, NMIB............................$850.00

Bear Golfer, TPS, bear hits ball over bridge into net, litho tin, 4", NM (M box), A $300.00

Begging Dog, Occupied Japan, NM, J2 ....$100.00

Ben Hur Trotter, AHI, gladiator in chariot w/metal whip being pulled by comical horse w/rubber ears, 7", NM (EX+ box), A...$250.00

Bestmaid Jolly Duck, yel celluloid duck pecks at gr litho tin duck, 8", NMIB, A $100.00

Black Boy & Girl w/Bananas, girl on 4-wheeled platform next to boy on 3-wheeled platform, celluloid & tin, 6", NMIB, A...$1,100.00

Bobo the Magician, TN, lifts hat to reveal egg, rabbit & chick, litho tin, 9", NM (EX box).......................................$500.00

Boy & Girl, 2 separate doll-like figures vibrate, celluloid w/cloth costumes, 6½", EX+, A $100.00

Boy Driving Race Car, toddler-type figure in go-cart, litho tin friction, 6", EX, A $75.00

Boy on Stick Horse, boy stands on 4-wheeled mechanism, celluloid & tin, 10", EX, A...$400.00

Boy on Tricycle, celluloid boy pedals litho tin trike, 5", VG+, A...$100.00

Boy Riding Donkey, celluloid, articulated donkey w/lg front wheel & 2 sm rear wheels, 7", G, A $100.00

Boy w/Suitcase, Occupied Japan, boy in red coat & bl cap carries brn suitcase, 4½", EX, A $150.00

Broderick Crawford Highway Patrol, policemen fire pistols w/moving arms, litho tin, friction, 8", NM $170.00

Bump Car w/Pop-Up Clown, clown pops up when car hits solid object, litho tin, 7", EX (EX box), from $175 to......$200.00

Bunny Cycle, Japan, 1950s, dressed wht litho tin bunny w/ears back pedals litho tin tricycle as bell rings, 5", EX+, A..........$250.00

Bunny Cycle, Toyland/Japan, 1950, celluloid bunny pedals pressed-steel tricycle as bell rings, 5", NM (NM box)...............$375.00

Calypso Joe the Drummer, Linemar, native rocks & plays drum, litho tin, 6", scarce, MIB, A $500.00

Casper the Ghost, Linemar, advances w/bobbing head, litho tin, 5", rare, NM (EX box), from $725 to....................$1,000.00

Champion Acrobat Car, Occupied Japan, red racer w/driver flips over to gr racer w/driver, tin, 5", rare, NM (G- box) .$250.00

Champion Rider #10, Yonezawa, travels in circular motion w/engine noise, litho tin, 5", MIB, A $125.00

Charlie McCarthy, prewar, articulated celluloid figure, 7", missing cane o/w EX, A $650.00

Circus Boy, boy in mc clown costume rings bell & holds placard, litho tin, 6", MIB...$375.00

Circus Bugler, TPS, clown rocks on stilts while blowing horn, tin w/cloth costume, scarce, 10", NM (EX box), A .$525.00

Circus Bugler, TPS, scarce, 10", NM (G- box), A..........$300.00

Circus Clown on Horse, K, advances & sways while rolling drum, celluloid & litho tin, 8" L, NM (EX box), A.$550.00

Circus Motorcycle, TN, advances & makes U-turn, litho tin, 6", M (EX+ box) $350.00

Circus Parade, TPS, elephant pulls 3 performing clowns, litho tin, 11", VG $225.00

Clown & Elephant w/Twirling Canopy, clown & elephant on ball atop 4-wheeled mechanism, celluloid & tin, 12½", EX $250.00

Clown & Monkey w/Twirling Canopy, figures & beaded canopy atop 4-wheeled mechanism, celluloid & tin, 7½", NM, A $225.00

Clown Doing Handstand, waddles back & forth on hands, celluloid & tin w/cloth costume, bells on feet, 6½", EX+ .$175.00

Clown Drummer, Alps, mc clown playing snare & parade drum, litho tin, 8", EX, A $400.00

Clown Juggler w/Monkey, TPS, clown balances monkey on his head w/several actions, litho tin, 9", rare, NMIB, A..$750.00

Clown Magician, TN, lifts hat to reveal rabbit, tin w/cloth clothes, 7", NM (NM box), A...............................$425.00

Clown on Donkey, Alps, celluloid clown w/spinning cb box on nose rides litho tin donkey, 8", VG+, A $200.00

Clown on Pig, see Mechanical Pig

Clown Trainer & His Acrobatic Dog, TPS, poodle jumps through hoop, litho tin, 4", NM (EX box), from $275 to........$300.00

Comical Ape, Toyland Toys, performs somersaults, celluloid w/hand-pnt features, 4", NM (VG box)...................$175.00

Comical Clara, TPS, advances in twisting motion w/moving head, litho tin, 5", scarce, NM (NM box), A $900.00

Communication Truck, MT, gr w/equipment & lights on bed, friction w/battery-op lights, 12", NM (VG box), A.$150.00

Concrete Mixer Truck, Cragstan, litho tin w/blk rubber tires, friction, 8", VG (worn box), A................................$50.00

Cook ? Boy, Showa/Occupied Japan, Black waiter in wht hat & top w/bl pants holding plate of food, celluloid, 5", NMIB, A...$400.00

Couple in Donkey Cart, man waves hat & she holds accordion in gr cart w/bell, pk donkey, celluloid & tin, 8", EX+ $200.00

Covered Wagon, 2 horses pull cloth-covered wagon that encloses ringing bell, w/driver, celluloid & tin, 8½", EX, A...$100.00

Cowboy on Rocking Horse, 1950s, lithographed tin, 6½", NM, from $95.00 to $115.00.

Photo courtesy June Moon.

Cowboy w/Trick Lasso, Occupied Japan, cowboy w/hand on hip spins lasso, celluloid, 4", NM, A $175.00

Cragstan Fast Freight, litho tin tractor-trailer, friction, 20", MIB, A...$250.00

Cunningham Special, Linemar, 1950s, bl & wht racer, litho tin, friction, 6", MIB, A $175.00

Cycling Quacky Duck, pedals cycle & talks, litho tin w/red, wht & bl cloth clothes, 6", NM (EX box), A..................$275.00

Dancing Couple, Occupied Japan, couple dances & twirls, celluloid, 4", MIB...$250.00

Dancing Couple, prewar, couple dances & twirls, celluloid, 6", EXIB, A $350.00

Dancing Jigilo, AM, clown made up of balls spins atop globe w/side-wheels, celluloid, 10½", EXIB, A $500.00

Dandy, Mikuni, dapper clown w/cane tips hat & rolls eyes, litho tin, 9½", EX (VG box)..$250.00

Deluxe Open Zephyr, Y, 1950s, red & yel litho tin, friction, 11", EX (NM box)..$275.00

Dino (Flintstones), Linemar, 1961, walks, mouth opens, purple w/pk & gr, on/off switch, litho tin, 7", NM, A $825.00

Disney Flivver, Linemar, 1955, Donald Duck driver in yel car w/Disney characters, 5½", NMIB, A.......................$850.00

Dizzy Clown w/Musical Balls, CK, rabbit twirls atop globe, celluloid, 12½", EX (EX box w/image of boy clown), A .$300.00

Dog Chasing Puppy, Mikuni, mama dog chases puppy, litho tin, 8", EX (EX box)...$175.00

Dog w/Ball, dog standing upright in jacket & hat holds ball while opening mouth & moving arms, celluloid, 8", EX, A...$150.00

Donald Duck, Linemar, litho tin, friction, 3", NM, A....$135.00

Donald Duck Acrobat, Gym-Toys by Linemar, Donald performs on high bar, 8", NM (EX box) $385.00

Donald Duck Acrobat, Linemar, Donald performs on high bar, celluloid, 6½", NM, A..$200.00

Donald Duck Climbing Fireman, Linemar, 1955, Donald climbs ladder on platform, litho tin, 14", NM (G box) $725.00

Donald Duck Climbing Fireman, Linemar, 1955, litho tin, 14", EX, from $300 to $375.00

Donald Duck Dipsy Car, Linemar, advances w/erratic action, litho tin, 5", MIB...$1,000.00

Donald Duck Driver, Linemar, litho tin car & figure w/name & image of Pluto on door w/other characters, 6½", EX, A.............$350.00

Donald Duck Drummer, Linemar, advances & plays drum, nods head, litho tin, 6", VG, A $275.00

Donald Duck Tricycle, MT, Donald pedals tricycle in circular pattern, litho tin & plastic, 7", NM (NM box), A ..$350.00

Donald Duck, see also Disney Flivver

Drummer Boy, advances while playing drum, litho tin w/vinyl head, 6", EX (VG box), A.......................................$100.00

Drummer Boy w/Bell, boy behind table w/twirling beaded canopy beats drum & taps bell, celluloid & tin, 11", EX, A...$275.00

Duck & Bulldog, dog chases duck attached by spring rod as it appears to fly, litho tin, friction, 8", MIB.................$200.00

Duck the Mail Man, TPS, advances in erratic motion w/2 nodding ducks in packages, litho tin, 4", NM (EX box), A $1,000.00

Elephant & Clowns, prewar, advances as clown on back plays saxaphone & clown on trunk waves, celluloid, 7", MIB, A.$400.00

Elephant w/2 Riders, elephant moves & vibrates w/boy on back & 1 on trunk, celluloid, 7", VG+, A.......................$275.00

Ferdinand the Bull, Linemar, 1950s, litho tin w/rubber ears & tail, 5", NM (worn box), A $350.00

Ferris Wheel Truck, TN, Ferris wheel spins as truck advances, litho tin, friction, 8½", NM (EX box), A $225.00

Fire Car, SSS, advances w/sound, litho tin w/4 firemen & driver, friction, 6½", NM (EX box), A...............................$250.00

Fire Engine, K, extension ladder raises w/bell sound, litho tin, friction, 14½", NM (EX box), A.............................$175.00

Firing Cycle No 2, military cycle w/2 seated soldiers, 1 w/gun, 4", EX (worn box) $395.00

Fishing Bear, TN, raises & lowers fly rod w/boot attached to hook, litho tin & celluloid, 7", NM (EX box) $125.00

Fishing Bear, TPS, fish bounces in & out of bear's net, litho tin, 7", EX, (VG box), A...$150.00

Flintstone Turnover Tank, Linemar, 1961, Fred forces tank to turn over, litho tin, 4", EX, from $775 to................$825.00

Flintstone Turnover Tank, Linemar, 1961, litho tin, 4", MIB, from $925 to..$1,200.00

Flower (Bambi), Linemar, 1940s, litho tin, friction, 3", M, M8...$100.00

Fred Astaire Dancer, Occupied Japan, celluloid figure in cloth clothes standing under Hollywood & Vine street sign, 8", EX+..$350.00

Fred Flintstone on Dino, Linemar, 1962, litho tin w/vinyl-headed figure, 8½", EX+, from $275 to....................$325.00

G-Man Car, MT, 1950s, gun mounted on hood, litho tin, friction, 5", M, A $100.00

G-Man Car, MT, 1950s, gun mounted on hood, litho tin, friction, 5", NM (NM box), A...............................$200.00

Gas Station, KT, 2-bay station w/1 red & 1 gr airflow sedan, car lift at side of station, 11", NM, A $3,080.00

Good Flavor Ice Cream Truck, KO, mystery action, litho tin, 7", NM (NM box), A...$550.00

Goofy, Linemar, 1950s, head moves up & down & tail spins, 5½", EXIB, A..................................$450.00

Graham Paige No 3, litho tin, 6", EXIB, A....................$175.00

Graham Sedan (1932), bl litho tin w/wht trim, chrome runners, headlights, grille & bumper, w/spare, 11", EX, A ..$2,200.00

Grand-Pa's New Car, Yonezawa, drivers bounces & car separates as it advances, litho tin, 5½", NM (EX box), A $300.00

Greyhound Bus, Cragstan, mk Greyhound Lines, litho tin, friction, 9", MIB, A..................................$225.00

Greyhound Scenicruiser, litho tin w/blk rubber tires, w/Express destination plate, friction, 12", NM (NM box), A $75.00

Handstand Clown, MM, advances on hands & juggles ball on feet, tin & celluloid w/cloth clothes, 10", M, A $350.00

Happy Chick Car, Yonezawa, 1957, advances as rooster bounces up & down, tin, friction, 5", NM (EX box), from $300 to..................................$350.00

Happy Grandpa, Y, tin, unused, MIB............................$150.00

Happy Hippo, TPS, bump-&-go action, native on back dangles bunch of bananas in hippo's face, litho tin, 6", NM, A..$375.00

Happy Skater Bear, TPS, pushes off right leg & skates, litho tin, 6½", NM (EX box), A..................................$400.00

Happy Tar (Drunken Sailor), Occupied Japan, figure wabbles while clutching bottle & glass, celluloid, 6", NMIB, A...........$350.00

Happy the Violinist, TPS, clown w/long legs in cloth suit plays violin, litho tin, 9½", MIB, from $300 to $350.00

Harley-Davidson Motorcycle, TN, piston action, friction, 4½", EXIB, A $550.00

Henry & Brother, prewar, Henry pulls little brother on cart behind him, celluloid, 7", NM..............................$1,000.00

Henry & Porter, Borgfeldt, ca 1938, 1-pc Henry w/articulated Black boy on 2-wheeled platform, 8", no suitcase o/w EXIB, A..$2,400.00

Henry & the Elephant, Borgfeldt, 1930s, boy on vibrating elephant w/wiggling ears & Henry on trunk, celluloid, 8", EX, A..$975.00

Herman the Mouse, Linemar/Harvey Famous Comics, advances in hopping motion w/bobbing head, litho tin, 5", rare, NMIB, A $3,600.00

Hollywood & Vine, Occupied Japan, cloth-dressed drunk standing under street sign, celluloid & tin, VG+, A........$125.00

Honey Bee, Ace, bee w/pot of honey advances w/flapping wings, litho tin, 7", MIB, A..................................$150.00

Honeymoon Express, Linemar, unused, MIB..................$250.00

Hopping Cary the Crow, Linemar, 1950s, lithographed tin, 4", NMIB, from $175.00 to $275.00.

Hoop Clown, Linemar, advances in hoop w/swinging arms & bell sound, litho tin, 4" clown, scarce, NM (NM box), A.$850.00

Horse & Carriage, horse pulls carriage w/driver & lady passenger, umbrella & balls spin, litho tin, 7", NM, A $200.00

Horse Race, H, 3 jockeys on horses bounce up & down on platform, litho tin, 8", EX (EX box), A..................$450.00

Horse Race, 2 jockeys on horses gallop atop 3-wheeled mechanism, celluloid & tin, 6", EX, A..................$100.00

Horse Racing, Y, child-like cowboy & Indian on horses atop wheel-drive mechanism, celluloid & tin, 4", EX, A...$275.00

Howdy Doody & Clarabell Delivery Wagon, Linemar, 1950s, litho tin w/celluloid face, friction, 6", rare, NM (EX box), A $4,500.00

Howdy Doody Clock-A-Doodle, Bandai, full-figure Howdy swings under clock w/several other actions, tin, 10", NMIB, A..$2,600.00

Huckleberry Hound Go-Mobile, Linemar, 1961, litho tin w/blk rubber tires, friction, 6½", EX $175.00

Hunter Truck, Y, truck advances as lion pushes rear door open & hunter tries to shut it, tin, friction, 9", NMIB.....$250.00

Isetta, Bandai, tin w/plastic windshield, 2-tone gr, friction, 6½", scarce, NM (EX box), A..................................$350.00

Isuzu 500 Dump Truck, ATC, press lever for hydraulic-type action, yel, red & blk tin w/rubber tires, 9", NM (NM box), A..$175.00

Jack-O-Panda, Modern Toys, bear on horse, tin, unused, MIB..$200.00

Jazzbo Jim, Linemar, rare White version, man plays fiddle & dances atop cabin roof, litho tin, 7", NM $750.00

Jeep w/Hood, Bandai, plastic & tin w/blk rubber tires, friction, 7", NM (EX box), A..................................$100.00

Jiminy Cricket, Linemar, litho tin figure w/top hat & umbrella, 6", NM (worn box), A..................................$800.00

Joe the Xylophone Player, TPS, clown w/big belly plays xylophone, litho tin, 5", M (EX box), from $450 to.......$575.00

Joker (Batman), Billiken, 8", MIB, T1 ....$100.00

Jolly Cat, wht kitten chases mouse on spinning ball as blk cat rides pole of twirling canopy, celluloid, 9", EX, A...$350.00

Jolly Farmer, KT, farmer pulls on pig's tail, tin & celluloid, EX (EX box), from $200 to $275.00

Kitchen Wagon Delivery Van, H, advances w/ringing bell, litho tin, friction, 9½", VG, A..................................$125.00

Lady Bug & Tortoise w/Babies, TPS, turtle flips over to reveal ladybug, litho tin, 7", NM (EX box), from $100 to....$175.00

Learn-to-Drive Car, Linemar, car travels w/nonfall action as tiger's head moves, litho tin, 7", scarce, NM (EX box), A....$175.00

Lenox Ave & 125 St Tap Dancer, Occupied Japan, Black celluloid figure w/cloth clothes under street sign, 8", NM, A.....$325.00

Lion Teaser, monkey rides on lion's back & waves bone in front of him, celluloid, 8", NM (NM box), A....................$375.00

Lucky Pup (101 Dalmatians), Linemar, sits up w/moving paws & twirling tail, plush over tin, 5", scarce, EX (VG box), A..$700.00

Lucky Sledge, Occupied Japan, boy rides sled as it advances & spins, celluloid & tin, 4½", MIB, A $175.00

Mama Kangaroo & Playful Baby, TPS, baby jumps up & down in pouch, litho tin, 6½", MIB, A $200.00

Marching Drummer, Fukuda, litho tin uniformed figure w/celluloid head & rollers attached to feet, 8¾", EX, A.....$225.00

Marionette Theatre, CK, 2 figures perform & dance, hand-pnt celluloid figures on metal base, NM (EX box), A..**$1,100.00**

Mary & Her Little Lamb, Mary & lamb on separate 4-wheeled platforms, celluloid & tin, 4½", EXIB......................**$275.00**

Mechanical Pig, clown riding pig, celluloid, 3½", NM (box missing flap), from $250 to..**$350.00**

Merry-Go-Round Truck, TN, carousel spins w/bell noise as truck advances, friction, litho tin, 8", EX (VG box), A....**$275.00**

Merry-Go-Round Truck, TN, carousel spins w/bell noise as truck advances, friction, litho tin, 8", NM (EX box), A...**$350.00**

Merry-Go-Round w/Music, giraffe atop dome w/spinning zoo animals, celluloid, 11", NMIB, from $350 to **$450.00**

Mickey Mouse, see also Skating Mickey Mouse; Twirling Tail Mickey; Walt Disney's Mechanical Tricycle

Mickey Mouse Acrobat, Gym-Toys by Linemar, Mickey performs on high bar, 10", VG (worn box), A..............**$350.00**

Mickey Mouse Dipsy Car, Linemar, advances w/erratic action, litho tin, 6", VG, A..**$350.00**

Mickey Mouse Driver, Linemar, litho tin car w/plastic figure, name & image of Pluto on door & other characters, VG, A.**$200.00**

Mickey Mouse on Galloping Horse, 1938, celluloid Mickey w/lasso on articulated wooden horse w/wheels, w/up, 19", EX, A..**$2,200.00**

Mickey Mouse on Rocking Horse, early, wood w/celluloid figure, w/up, 8", VG, A..**$1,500.00**

Mickey Mouse on Trapeze, Borgfeldt, performs acrobats, celluloid, 3", NM (EX box), A **$3,000.00**

Mickey Mouse on Tricycle, Illco, 1970s, mc plastic w/metal bell, 6½", EX, M8..**$75.00**

Mickey Mouse Walker, jtd celluloid figure, 8", G, A......**$450.00**

Mickey Mouse Whirligig, STS/Borgfeldt, 10", EX (VG box), A...**$5,000.00**

Mickey Mouse Xylophone Player, Linemar, Mickey plays xylophone, litho tin, 7", VG, A **$425.00**

Mickey Mouse Xylophone Player, Linemar, rocks & plays xylophone, litho tin, 6", EX+ (orig box), A................**$1,200.00**

Mickey's Delivery w/Donald Driver, Linemar, ca 1940, Donald pedals 3-wheeled cart, celluloid & tin, friction, 6", EX, A **$425.00**

Mickey's Delivery w/Pluto Driver, Linemar, ca 1940, Pluto pedals 3-wheeled cart, celluloid & tin, friction, 6", EX, A ...**$425.00**

Mickey's Mousketeers Moving Van, Linemar, tractor-trailer, 12½", EX+ **$900.00**

Military Police Jeep, Asahitoy, litho tin w/driver, friction, 11½", EX (VG box), A **$100.00**

Minnie Mouse Cart Pulled by Pluto, 1930s, Minnie in 3-wheeled cart, celluloid & litho tin, 8½", VG+, A **$1,150.00**

Monkey Basketball Player, monkey in litho uniform shoots at basket, litho tin, 8", EX **$125.00**

Monkey Guitarist, Occupied Japan, dressed monkey on stump strums guitar w/bell-like music, celluloid & tin, 8", EX, A..**$200.00**

Monkey the Sheriff, TN, rocks & moves pistols, litho tin & plush, 6", EX (EX box), A **$125.00**

Mother Pushing Carriage, Haji, advances w/bell sound, litho tin, 6", EX..**$200.00**

Mounted Cavalryman w/Cannon, TPS, bounces on horse, cannon attached w/rope, litho tin, 5", scarce, NM (EX box) ...**$425.00**

MP Auto Bi Cycle, TN, litho tin Indian cycle w/driver, friction, 6", NM (NM box) **$950.00**

New X Car, red litho tin, friction, 6", NMIB...................**$75.00**

News Puppy, TN, advances & waves newspaper w/ringing bell, litho tin, 6½", NM (EX box), A **$350.00**

Ninkimono the Balancing Clown, MT, cb body w/celluloid head & hands, brn, tan & red felt outfit, 12", EXIB, A....**$200.00**

Obstinate Donkey, KT, clown pulls on kneeling donkey's tail, celluloid, 7", EXIB, A **$250.00**

Old Smoky Joe, MT, w/fireman driver, advances w/sparks, litho tin, friction, 8", needs new flint o/w NM (EX box), A **$125.00**

Photo courtesy June Moon.

Pango-Pango African Dancer, TPS, vibrates around with shield and spear, lithographed tin, 6", NM (EX box), $350.00.

Peace Corps Man, SY, patriotic figure carries suitcase w/ringing bell in chest, litho tin, 7", VG (EX box), A **$225.00**

Peace Corps Man, SY, patriotic figure carries suitcase w/ringing bell in chest, litho tin, 7", NM (NM box) **$375.00**

Performing Seal w/Monkey & Fish, TPS, seal advances as monkey holds fish over his head, litho tin, 5", scarce, NMIB...**$425.00**

Peter Clown, CK, prewar, performs somersaults, celluloid, 6", NM (EX box), A **$135.00**

Piano Pooch, MM, puppy plays piano mk Spring Melody, litho tin & plush, 8", scarce, NM (NM box), A...............**$350.00**

Pig w/Horn & Chicks, 2 chicks under twirling canopy behind pig atop 4-wheeled mechanism, celluloid & tin, 9½", EX+ **$200.00**

Piggy Cook, Y, shakes salt into pan w/egg, egg flips in air & lands back in pan, litho tin, 5½", MIB **$275.00**

Pinocchio, see Walking Pinocchio

Pioneer Spirit Prairie Schooner, Alps, litho tin, friction w/battery-op lanterns, 11", NM (EX box), A **$200.00**

Playful Pluto & Goofy, Linemar, figures vibrate w/spinning tails, litho tin w/rubber tails, NM (scarce cartoon box), A............**$1,900.00**

Playland Express, Y, train & trolley circle tracks w/plane above, carnival & animal scenes on base, 8" base, NMIB, A **$125.00**

Playland Roller Coaster, Cragstan, bus-type vehicles travel track, litho tin, 20", NM (EX box), A **$225.00**

Pluto the Drum Major, Linemar, rocks while blowing party horn & shaking bell, litho tin, 6", EX, A..........................**$400.00**

Pluto, see also Playful Pluto; Mickey's Delivery; Minnie Mouse Cart

Police Patrol Cycle, TN, advances w/sound & sparks, litho tin, friction, 8", NM (EX box), from $200 to $300.00

Poor Pete, little Black boy w/watermelon waddles around as dog bites his rear, celluloid, 5½", NM, A $455.00

Popeye, 1929, arms move as head moves up & down, celluloid, 9", NM (G box), A $2,000.00

Popeye & Olive Oyl Ball Toss, Linemar, Popeye & Olive Oyl bounce ball back & forth on base, tin, 19" L, EX (G box), A $1,450.00

Popeye Basketball Player, Linemar, litho tin, 9", EX......$750.00

Popeye on Tricycle, Linemar, bell rings as Popeye pedals trike, litho tin, 4", EX $950.00

Popeye Transit Co, Linemar, lithoed tractor-trailer, friction, 13", NM $1,200.00

Popeye Turnover Tank, Linemar, Popeye figure forces tank to turn over, litho tin, 4", EX $500.00

Popeye, see also Skating Popeye

Power Shovel, Linemar, tin, friction, 8", EX, J2 ....$100.00

Prehistoric Dinosaur, Linemar, advances w/clicking sound, litho tin, 9", NM (VG box) $350.00

Rescue Ladder Car, 1930s model w/long nose & ladder mounted on top, red w/bl, yel & chrome trim, rare, 11½", EX, A...$3,000.00

Ridem Cowboy, MT, full-figure cowboy w/lariat rides bucking bronco, litho tin, 4", EX (VG box) $200.00

Romance Car, KO, litho tin w/celluloid figures, friction, 7", scarce, NM (EX box), A $1,500.00

Sammy Skeleton, Mikuni, advances in rocking motion, litho tin, 6", M $175.00

Sampson the Strong Man, TPS, weight lifter lifts barbell, litho tin, 5½", EX (G box)...$500.00

Santa Claus, Alps, sways side to side & rings bell, litho tin & plush, 10", MIB, A..$125.00

Santa Claus, TN, Santa turns head, rings bell & waves Merry Christmas sign, litho tin, 6", EX (EX box), A $175.00

Santa Claus Cycle, Suzuki, Santa pedals tricycle w/bell, litho tin w/celluloid figure, 4½", MIB $100.00

Santa Fe Train, SE, train moves w/whistle sound, litho tin, unused, 14", MIB, A $75.00

Scratcher Dog, MT, advances w/twirling tail & scratches face w/leg, celluloid w/HP features, 5", EX (EX box), A.$200.00

See Saw Rabbit & Boy, MM, boy & rabbit rotate around base, litho tin w/celluloid figures, 6", EX (G box), A $125.00

Shingun, TN, prewar, soldier marches w/rifle, litho tin & celluloid, 8½", MIB, A...$575.00

Shogun Warrior Robot, walker w/movable head & arms, vivid litho tin w/vinyl head, 9½", EX+ (VG box in Japanese), A..$200.00

Sight-Seeing Bus, mc litho w/chrome trim, friction, unused, 16½", NM, A...$350.00

Skating Mickey Mouse, Linemar, advances in realistic motion, litho tin w/cloth pants, 6", VG, A $650.00

Skating Popeye, Linemar, skates in realistic motion, litho tin w/cloth clothes, NM $1,000.00

Skier, Occupied Japan, 2 mc child skiers w/poles, celluloid & tin, 6½", EX (EX box) $300.00

Skipping Bear, TN, jumps rope & nods head, litho tin, 5", NM (NM box) $150.00

Skipping Puppy, TN, puppy jumps rope, litho tin, 5", NM (EX box)..$100.00

Photo courtesy June Moon.

Shy Anne, Linemar, lithographed tin with cloth outfit, NM, from $400.00 to $450.00.

Sky Wanderer, Asahitoy, helicopter & USAF jet revolve around tower, litho tin & celluloid, 7" tower, EX (EX box), A..$325.00

Snapping Alligator, S&E, tin, EXIB $200.00

Soldier w/Machine Gun, TN, tin, 6", NM.....................$125.00

Space Dog, KO, advances w/several facial actions, tin, 7", EX+ (EX box), A $850.00

Sparking Combat Car, Modern Toys, friction, MIP (sealed), J2 ....$50.00

Speed King Racer #7, SAN, early 1950s, advances w/sound, litho tin w/driver, friction, 5", NM (EX box) $275.00

Station Wagon & Boat on Trailer, silver, wht & gold litho tin, friction, unused, 11", MIB, A...................................$225.00

Super Boat S-6021, 1950s, litho tin cabin cruiser, MIB, A ..$100.00

Super Electric Train, K, mk Super Express, advances w/bell sound, litho tin, friction, 13", EX (EX box), A........$100.00

Superman Turnover Tank, Linemar, figure causes tank to turn over, litho tin, 4", NM (G scarce box) $1,000.00

Symphony Sam, My Friend Toys, mohair & plush monkey in tuxedo as orchestra conductor, 4½", VG (G box), A.$75.00

Tank Carrier w/Net, Toymaster, US Army truck carries tank w/net over it, friction, tin, 8", MIB, A....................$100.00

Teacup Merry-Go-Round, MM, 3 bears in cups spin w/twirling umbrella above, plush, tin & plastic, 8", NM (EX box), A...$125.00

Teeter-Totter, prewar, Black baby girls seesaw as umbrella spins above, celluloid & tin, 8", rare, EX, from $450 to ...$550.00

Television Car, Alps, litho tin w/TV screen in trunk, friction, 6", EX (VG box), from $200 to...............................$260.00

Thumper (Bambi), Linemar, 1940s, litho tin, friction, 3", M ..$200.00

Tom & Jerry Handcar, MT, Tom or Jerry, litho tin & plastic, 8", EXIB, A, ea..$225.00

Town-to-Town Bareback Rider & Clown, celluloid clown on ball & rider rotate around wooden spool w/bells, 10", EX, A $650.00

Trumpet Player, TN, man plays trumpet w/several other actions, tin w/cloth clothes, 10", G, A $150.00

Tumbling Clown, SK, celluloid figure w/cloth costume somersaults, 4½", NM (EX box)......................................$250.00

Turtle Family, TM, NMIB, J2................................$75.00

Twirling Tail Mickey, Linemar, vibrates around w/twirling tail, litho tin, 6", EX, A $300.00

Uncle Scrooge, Linemar/WDP, litho tin, 6", EX, P6......$350.00

Vacationland Express, Linemar, plane flies above train station w/2 trains, litho tin, 5x5" base, EX (VG box), A $200.00

Wagon Fantasyland, TPS, beetle pulls leaf w/monkey driver & 2 squirrels, litho tin, 12", MIB, A..................................$350.00

Walking Duck, Daito, knock-off of Donald in red & yel checked vest w/2 'Nephews' following, 9", NM (EX box), A ...$475.00

Walking Pinocchio, Linemar, advances w/moving arms, litho tin w/rubber nose, 6", NM (NM box).............................$525.00

Walking Pinocchio, Linemar, litho tin, 6", VG.............$300.00

Walking Santa, Occupied Japan, advances w/step-over action, celluloid w/metal feet, 6", scarce, M (EX box), A ...$625.00

Walt Disney's Mechanical Tricycle, Linemar, Mickey pedals tricycle w/bell, litho tin & celluloid, 4", NM (EX box), A..$575.00

Walt Disney's Television Car, Linemar, litho tin, friction, 8", NMIB, A..$425.00

Western Hero, child-like cowboy on horse chasing bull atop 4-wheeled mechanism, celluloid & tin, 6½", NMIB, A..$275.00

White-Faced Roller Skating Clown, litho tin w/cloth clothes, 6", scarce, VG, from $375 to $400.00

Wild Roaring Bull & Boy, Mukini, boy pulls bull by the tail, litho tin, 9", NM (EX box), from $275 to................$300.00

Wimpy Walker, unlicensed figure in blk hat, coat & shoes w/bl & blk striped pants, red tie, celluloid, 7", NMIB, A $1,750.00

Wimpy Walker, unlicensed figure in blk hat, coat & shoes w/bl & blk striped pants, red tie, celluloid, 7", VG+, A..$575.00

World Circus, M, advances as seal spins ball & clown w/cane spins on top, litho tin, friction, 9", NM (EX box), A...........$225.00

World Circus Truck, M, advances as clown on roof spins & seal balances ball, litho tin, friction, 9", NM (EX box), A .$400.00

Xylophone Player, Occupied Japan, man in tuxedo plays xylophone, celluloid, 6", M (VG box) $200.00

SPANISH

Bears on Motorcycle, Rico, mk RSA, big bear driver w/2 sm bear passengers, litho tin, 9", VG+, A..........................$1,600.00

Bugatti Racer #I-970, Paya, bl tin w/yel & red trim, w/cut-out hood vents, spoke wheels & spare, w/driver, 18½", M, A...$5,500.00

Charlie Chaplin, 1950s, figure in famous pose w/valise labeled Juguetes Roman, plastic, 6½", EX+, A.......................$75.00

Harley-Davidson Police Motorcycle, Sanchis, red & wht plastic w/driver in bl uniform, 10", EX+ (EX box), A.........$300.00

Racer #3, bump-&-go action, driver w/movable head, litho tin, 9", NMIB, A...$250.00

Wyandotte

Though the Wyandotte Company (Michigan) produced toys of all types, included here are only the heavy-gauge pressed-steel cars, trucks, and other vehicles they made through the 1930s and '40s.

See also Aeronautical; Boats; Character, TV, and Movie Collectibles; Windups, Friction, and Other Mechanicals.

Auto Carrier with Steam Shovel, 22½", G, A, $250.00.

Boat-Tail Racer, w/wheel covers, red, 8½", G, A...........$175.00

Cabriolet Sedan, red & wht w/NP grille, wooden wheels, 6", NM...$165.00

Car Carrier, dbl-decker w/2 cars, 9", EX, A $100.00

Car Carrier, orange w/yel wheels, no cars, 21", EX, A....$200.00

Circus Truck & Trailer, red cab w/2 cages containing paper animals, 19", EX, A $800.00

Circus Truck & Trailer, 1930s, Greatest Show on Earth on backplate, 11", EX, A $500.00

Construction Truck, 2-tone cab w/Wyandotte decals, side dump, metal wheels, 17", NMIB, A $250.00

Construction Truck w/Steam Shovel, 1940s, wht, bl & yel w/blk tires, NM...$400.00

Coupe, 1930s, gr w/blk fenders, wht rubber tires, 6½", NM, A...$145.00

Dump Truck, gr w/chrome grille & bumper, covered wheels, 14", G, A...$75.00

Dump Truck, yel, red & blk, 16", VG, A......................$100.00

Dump Truck w/Shovel, red & yel tin & plastic w/balloon tires, 11", MIB, A..$200.00

Fire Truck, rider, w/seat, steering wheel & siren mounted on hood, removable mirror, 30", EX, A $125.00

Fire Truck w/Water Pump & Hose, mk #5, complete w/extension ladder, 10", NM (EX box), A $200.00

Flash Strat-O-Wagon, 1940, red, wht & bl futuristic wagon w/fins, litho rocket ship, 6", NM (VG box), A........$175.00

Green Valley Ranch Semi, red, open stake bed, VG......$100.00

Haulaway Truck, complete w/2 plastic cars, 8½", EX (EX box), A..$165.00

Moving Van, Cargo Lines, w/Indian logo on cab doors, 25", VG, A..$125.00

Moving Van, Wyandotte Van Lines Coast To Coast... on sides, red, wht & bl w/blk rubber tires, 8", NM (G- box), A........$175.00

Oil Tanker, ca 1938, red w/hinged ramp back door, 1-pc bumper, grille & headlights, rubber tires, 10½", EX, A............$200.00

Painter's Truck, #126, red, wht & bl w/Jiffy's Painting & Decorating decal, 10", NM (EX box), A $325.00

Stake Truck, 1930s, red & gr w/bl grille, wooden wheels, 12½", EX $165.00

Stake Truck, 1930s, red w/blk fenders & chassis, rubber wheels, 9½", G, A $145.00

Tank Truck, 1930s, gr w/wooden wheels, 10", EX, A.....$115.00

Tow Truck, 2-tone, w/W logo, VG $100.00

US Army Medical Corps, covered wheels, chrome grille, EX $185.00

Woodie Sports Car, red and yellow, roof flips up and down, trunk opens, 12½", EX (original box), $185.00.

Woodie Station Wagon, maroon w/wood-look panels, lady driver lithoed in window, tin w/rubber tires, 24", EX+, A $525.00
Wyandotte Construction Co Dump Truck, 2-tone, VG..$225.00

Yo-Yos

Yo-Yos are starting to attract toy collectors, especially those with special features such as Hasbro's 'Glow-Action' and Duncan's 'Whistler.'

Advisor: Lucky Meisenheimer (M3).

Alox Mfg, Flying Disc, wood, 1950s, 2⅛", M, M3 ....$15.00
Avon, Garfield, plastic, MIP, M20 ....$10.00
Avon, Teenage Mutant Ninja Turtles, MIP, M20............$10.00
Champion, Style #44, return top, red, VG, M20 ....$12.00
Cheerio, Pro 99, EX, M3..$35.00
Duncan, Beginner, #1044 or #44, wood, MIP, M20, ea....$25.00
Duncan, Beginner, Bosco Bear advertising, sm, G, M20.....$7.00
Duncan, Cattle Brand, late 1970s, MOC, M3.....................$8.00
Duncan, Glow Imperial, orange letters, MIP, M3.............$12.00

Duncan Whistling Yo-Yos, 1930s, lithographed tin, EX, $75.00 each.

Duncan, Glow Imperial, red letters, early 1970s, MIP, M3.$8.00
Duncan, Imperial, Kool-Aid premium, MIP $10.00
Duncan, Magic Motion, 1975, Hulk, MIP $25.00
Duncan, Shrieking, Sonic Satellite, #500, MIP, M20 .....$35.00
Duncan, Super Yo-Yo, tournament, natural wood w/gr stripe, VG, M20...$15.00
Festival, Be a Sport Series, 1970s, M (M pkg), M3 ....$20.00
Festival, Disney (Goofy), 1970s, MOC, M3.....................$15.00
Festival, Disney (Mickey, Pluto or Donald), 1970s, MOC, M3, ea...$12.00
Hasbro, Glow Action, 1968, MOC, M3, from $10 to......$15.00
Hi-Ker, flat-top, NM, M3 ....$35.00
Spectra Star, Freddy Krueger, 1980s, MOC, M3 ....$6.00
Spectra Star, Ghostbusters, 1980s, MOC, M3 ....$7.00
Spectra Star, Pee Wee Herman, 1980s, MOC, M3 ....$8.00
Spectra Star, Radical Curve Ball #1502, 1988, MIP $6.00
Spirello, heavy pressed cb, red & wht spiral, VG, M20 ....$15.00
Whirl King, top standard model, G, M20 ....$10.00

Dealer Codes

Most of our description lines contain a letter/number code just before the suggested price. They correspond with the names of the following collectors and dealers who sent us their current selling list to be included in this addition. If you're interested in buying a item in question, don't hesitate to call or write them. We only ask that you consider the differences in time zones, and try to call at a convenient time. If you're corresponding, please send a self-addressed, stamped envelope for their reply. **Because our data was entered several months ago, many of the coded items will have already sold,** but our dealers tell us that they are often able to restock some of the same merchandise over and over. Some said that they had connections with other dealers around the country and might be able to locate a particular toy for you. But please bear in mind that because they may have had to pay more to restock their shelves, they may also have to charge a little more than the price quoted in their original sales list. We must stress that these people are not appraisers, so please do not ask them to price your toys.

If you have lists of toys for sale that you would like for us to use in the next edition, please send them to us at the address as soon as possible. We will process incoming lists as they arrive and because our space is limited, the earlier you send it, the better. Please do not ask us to include you in our Categories of Special Interest unless you contribute useable information. Not only are we limited on available space, it isn't fair to those who do. If you would like to advertise with us but cannot contribute listings, display ads are available (see page 482 for rates). We will hold a previously assigned dealer code over for you who are our contributors/advisors from year to year as long as we know you are interested in keeping it, but if we haven't heard from you by February 1, we will reassign that code to someone else. Because the post office prefers your complete 9-digit zip code, please send us that information for our files.

Direct your correspondence to:

Huxford Enterprises, Inc., 1202 7th St., Covington, IN 47932

(A1)
Stan and Sally Alekna
4724 Kernan Mill Lane East
Jacksonville, FL 32224
904-992-9525

(A2)
Jane Anderson
R.R. 5, Box 5525
Saylorsburg, PA 18353

(A3)
Avalon Comics
Larry Curcio
P.O. Box 821
Medford, MA 02155
617-391-5614

(A4)
Bob Armstrong
15 Monadnock Rd.
Worcester, MA 01609

(A5)
Geneva Addy
P.O. Box 124
Winterset, IA 50273

(A6)
Jerry Alingh
505 5th Ave. #302
Des Moines, Iowa 50309

(A7)
Matt and Lisa Adams
1234 Harbor Cove
Woodstock, GA 30189
770-516-6874

(B1)
Richard Belyski
P.O. Box 124
Sea Cliff, NY 11579
516-676-1183
e-mail: peznews@juno.com

(B2)
Larry Blodget
Box 753
Rancho Mirage, CA 92270

(B3)
Bojo
Bob Gottuso
P.O. Box 1403
Cranberry Twp., PA 16066
Phone or FAX 412-776-0621

(B4)
Dick Borgerding
RJB Toys
720 E Main
Flushing, MI 48433
810-659-9859

(B6)
Jim Buskirk
3009 Oleander Ave.
San Marcos, CA 92069
619-599-1054

(B7)
Danny Bynum
P.O. Box 440818
Houston, TX 77244-0818
713-531-5711

(B8)
Stanley A. and Robert S. Block
P.O. Box 51
Trumbull, CT 06611
203-261-3223 or 203-775-0138

(B10)
Tom Bremer
P.O. Box 49
Newark, NY 14513
Phone or FAX 315-331-8146

(B11)
Sue and Marty Bunis
RR 1, Box 36
Bradford, NH 03221-9102

(B12)
Bromer Booksellers, Inc.
607 Boylston St.
Boston, MA 02116
617-247-2818 or FAX 617-247-2975

(B13)
Mark Bergin
P.O. Box 3073
Peterborough, NH 03458-3073
603-924-2079 or FAX 603-924-2022

(B14)
Scott Bruce
P.O. Box 481
Cambridge, MA 02140
e-mail: scott@flake.com

(C1)
Casey's Collectible Corner
HCR Box 31, Rt. 3
N Blenheim, NY 12131
607-588-6464

(C2)
Mark E. Chase and Michael Kelley
Collector Glass News
P.O. Box 308
Slippery Rock, PA 16057
412-946-2838
FAX 412-946-9012

(C3)
Ken Clee
Box 11412
Philadelphia, PA 19111
215-722-1979

(C4)
Arlan Coffman
1223 Wilshire Blvd., Ste. 275
Santa Monica, CA 90403
310-453-2507

(C5)
Joe Corea, New Jersey Nostalgia
Hobby
401 Park Ave.
Scotch Plains, NJ 07076
908-322-2676 or FAX 908-322-4079

(C6)
Cotswold Collectibles
P.O. Box 249
Clinton, WA 98236
360-579-1223; FAX 360-579-1287

(C9)
Marilyn Cooper
P.O. Box 55174
Houston, TX 77255; 713-465-7773
Author of *The Pictorial Guide to Toothbrush Holders*

(C10)
Bill Campbell
1221 Littlebrook Lane
Birmingham, AL 35235
205-853-8227; FAX 405-658-6986

(C11)
Jim Christoffel
409 Maple
Elburn, IL 60119; 708-365-2914

(C12)
Joel J. Cohen
Cohen Books and Collectibles
P.O. Box 810310
Boca Raton, FL 33481
561-487-7888; FAX 561-487-3117
e-mail: cohendisney@prodigy.com

(C13)
Brad Cassity
1350 Stanwix
Toledo, OH 43614
419-385-9910

(C14)
Cynthia's Country Store
The Wellington Mall #15-A
12794 W Forest Hill Blvd.
Wellington, FL 33414
561-793-0554
FAX 561-795-4222 (24 hrs)
e-mail: cynbears@aol.com
website: http://www.thecrier.com/ccs

(C15)
Rosalind Cranor
P.O. Box 859
Blacksburg, VA 24063

(C17)
John and Michele Casino
633 Franklin Ave., Suite #169
Nutley, NJ 07110
201-759-2520

(C18)
Classic Golf & Collectibles
P.O. Box 8
Lake Havasu City, AZ 86406-0008
520-855-9623

(D2)
Marl Davidson (Marl & B)
10301 Braden Run
Bradenton, FL 34202
941-751-6275
FAX 941-751-5463

(D3)
Larry DeAngelo
516 King Arthur Dr.
Virginia Beach, VA 23464
804-424-1691

(D4)
John DeCicco
57 Bay View Dr.
Shrewsbury, MA 01545
508-797-0023

(D6)
Doug Dezso
864 Patterson Ave.
Maywood, NJ 07607
201-488-1311

(D7)
Ron and Donna Donnelly
Saturday Heroes
6302 Championship Dr.
Tuscaloosa, AL 35405

(D8)
George Downes
Box 572
Nutley, NJ 07110
201-935-3388

(D9)
Gordy Dutt
P.O. Box 201
Sharon Center, OH 44274-0201
330-239-1657
FAX 330-239-2991

(D10)
Dunbar's Gallery
Leila and Howard Dunbar
76 Haven St.
Milford, MA 01757
508-634-8697
FAX 508-634-8696

(D11)
Larry Doucet
2351 Sultana Dr.
Yorktown Heights, NY 10598
914-245-1320

(D12)
Doris' Dolls & Collectibles
325 E. 10th St.
Mt. Vernon, IN 47620
Phone or FAX 812-838-5290

(D13)
Dr. Doors Miniatures
3111 S. Valley View, Suite O-104
Las Vegas, NV 89102
702-362-2722

(E3)
Alan Edwards
Toys From the Crypt
P.O. Box 3294
Shawnee, KS 66203
913-383-1242

(F1)
Figures
Anthony Balasco
P.O. Box 19482
Johnston, RI 02919
401-946-5720
FAX 401-942-7980

(F2)
Paul Fideler
20 Shadow Oak Dr., Apt. #18
Sudbury, MA 01776
617-386-0228 (24 hours)

(F3)
Paul Fink's Fun and Games
P.O. Box 488
59 S Kent Rd.
Kent, CT 06757
203-927-4001

(F4)
Mike and Kurt Fredericks
145 Bayline Cir.
Folsom, CA 95630
916-985-7986

(F5)
Fun House Toy Co.
G.F. Ridenour
P.O. Box 343
Bradfordwoods, PA 15015-0343
412-935-1392 (FAX capable)

(F7)
Finisher's Touch Antiques
Steve Fisch, proprietor
10 W Main St.
Wappingers Falls, NY 12590
914-298-8882
FAX 914-298-8945

(F8)
52 Girls Collectibles
P.O. Box 36
Morral, OH 43337
614-465-6062

(F9)
Donald Friedman
660 W Grand Ave.
Chicago, IL 60610
708-656-3700 (day) or
312-226-4741 (evening & weekends)
FAX 708-656-6292

(G1)
Gary's Trains
186 Pine Springs Camp Road
Boswell, PA 15531
814-629-9277

(G2)
Mark Giles
510 E Third St.
Ogalala, NE 69153
308-284-4360

(G5)
John F. Green Inc.
1821 W. Jacaranda Pl.
Fullerton, CA 92633-USA
714-526-5467
800-807-4759

(G6)
Carol Karbowiak Gilbert
2193 14 Mile Rd. 206
Sterling Height, MI 48310

(G7)
PAK-RAT
Andy Galbus
900 8th St. NW
Kasson, MN 55944-1079
507-634-2093
e-mail: lhpakrat@polaristel.net

(G8)
Joan Stryker Grubaugh
2342 Hoaglin Rd.
Van Wert, OH 45891
419-622-4411 or FAX 419-622-3026

(G16)
Candelaine (Candace Gunther)
Pasadena, CA 91103-2320
818-796-4568; FAX 818-796-7172
e-mail: Candelaine@aol.com.

(H1)
The Hamburgs
Happy Memories Antique Toy Co.
P.O. Box 1305
Woodland Hills, CA 91365
818-346-9884 or 818-346-1269
FAX 818-346-0215

(H3)
George Hardy
1670 Hawkwood Ct.
Charlottesville, VA 22901
804-295-4863; FAX 804-295-4898
Internet: georgeh@comet.net
http://www.comet.net/personal/
georgeh/

(H4)
Jerry and Ellen L. Harnish
110 Main St.
Bellville, OH 44813
Phone or FAX 419-886-4782
after 7 PM Eastern time

(H6)
Phil Helley
Old Kilbourne Antiques
629 Indiana Ave.
Wisconsin Dells, WI 53965
608-254-8770

(H7)
Jacquie and Bob Henry
Antique Treasures and Toys
Box 17
Walworth, NY 14568
315-986-1424

(H8)
Homestead Collectibles
Art and Judy Turner
R.D. 2, Rte. 150
P.O. Box 173-E
Mill Hall, PA 17751
717-726-3597
FAX 717-726-4488

(H9)
Pamela E. Apkarian-Russell, The
Halloween Queen
C.J. Russell & The Halloween
Queen Antiques
P.O. Box 499
Winchester, NH 03470
603-239-8875

(H10)
Don Hamm
712 N. Townsend St.
Syracuse, NY 13203
315-478-7035

(H11)
M.R. Huber, the SNO-PEA
Trader
Norman and Marilyn Huber, Buyers
931 Emerson St.
Thousand Oaks, CA 91362
805-497-0119
FAX 1-800-SNO-OPY-2

(H12)
Roslyn L. Herman
124-16 84th Rd.
Kew Gardens, New York 11415
718-846-3496 or 718-846-8491

(H13)
Tim Hunter
1668 Golddust
Sparks, NV 89436
702-626-5029

(I1)
Roger Inouye
765 E Franklin
Pomona, CA 91766

(I2)
Terri Ivers
Terri's Toys and Nostalgia
419 S 1st St.
Ponca City, OK 74601
405-762-(TOYS) 8697 or
405-762-5174 (no collect calls please);
FAX 405-765-2657 or
e-mail: tivers@pcok.com

(I3)
Dan Iannotti
212 W. Hickory Grove Rd.
Bloomfield Hills, MI 48302-1127

(J1)
Bill Jackameit
200 Victoria Dr.
Bridgewater, VA 22812
703-828-4359 (Mon-Thurs,
7 pm-9 pm EST)

(J2)
Ed Janey
2920 Meadowbrook Dr. SE
Cedar Rapids, IA 52403
319-362-5213

(J3)
Dana Johnson Enterprises
P.O. Box 1824
Bend, OR 97709-1824
503-382-8410

(J5)
Just Kids Nostalgia
310 New York Avenue
Huntington, NY 11743
516-423-8449
FAX 516-423-4326

(J6)
June Moon
245 N Northwest Hwy.
Park Ridge, IL 60068
847-825-1411 (24-hr phone)
FAX 847-825-6090

(J7)
Jim's TV Collectibles
P.O. Box 4767
San Diego, CA 92164
Phone/FAX 619-462-1953

(J8)
Jeff and Bob's Fun Stuff
7324 Reseda Blvd #168
Reseda, CA 91335
818-705-3368

(K1)
K-3 Inc.
Bendees Only; Simpson Mania
2335 NW Thurman
Portland, OR 97210
503-222-2713

(K2)
David Kolodny-Nagy
May through Jan:
3701 Connecticut Ave. NW #500
Washington, DC 20008
202-364-8753

(K3)
Ilene Kayne
1308 S Charles St.
Baltimore, MD 21230
410-685-3923
e-mail: Ilenegold@aol.com

(K4)
Debby and Marty Krim
P.O. Box 2273
W Peabody, MA 01960
508-535-3140
FAX 508-535-7522

(K5)
Kerry and Judy's Toys
7370 Eggleston Rd.
Memphis, TN 38125-2112
901-757-1722
FAX 901-757-0126
e-mail: kjtoys@memphisonline.com

(K6)
Keith and Donna Kaonis
60 Cherry Ln.
Huntington, NY 11743
516-261-8337
FAX 516-261-8235

(L1)
Jean-Claude H. Lanau
740 Thicket Ln.
Houston, TX 77079
713-497-6034 (after 7:00 pm, CST)

(L2)
John and Eleanor Larsen
523 Third St.
Colusa, CA 95932
916-458-4769 (after 4 pm)

(L4)
Tom Lastrapes
P.O. Box 2444
Pinellas Park, FL 34664
813-545-2586

(L5)
Stephen Leonard
Box 127
Albertson, LI, NY 11507
516-742-0979

(L6)
Kathy Lewis
187 N Marcello Ave
Thousand Oaks, CA 91360
805-499-8101

(L7)
Terry and Joyce Losonsky
7506 Summer Leave Ln.
Columbia, MD 21046-2455
301-381-3358

(M1)
Mark and Val Macaluso
3603 Newark Rd.
Marion, NY 14505
315-926-4349
FAX 315-926-4853

(M2)
John McKenna
801-803 W Cucharres
Colorado Springs, CO 80905
719-630-8732

(M3)
Lucky Meisenheimer
7300 Sand Lake Commons Blvd.
Orlando, FL 32819
407-354-0478

(M4)
Bill Mekalian
550 E Chesapeake Cir.
Fresno, CA 93720
209-434-3247

(M5)
Mike's General Store
52 St. Annes Rd.
Winnipeg, Manitoba, Canada
R2M-2Y3
204-255-3463
FAX 204-253-4124

(M6)
Paul David Morrow
1045 Rolling Point Ct.
Virginia Beach, VA 23456-6371

(M7)
Judith A. Mosholder
186 Pine Springs Camp Road
Boswell, PA 15531
814-629-9277

(M8)
The Mouse Man Ink
P.O. Box 3195
Wakefield, MA 01880
Phone or FAX 617-246-3876

(M9)
Steven Meltzer
670 San Juan Ave. #B
Venice, CA 90291
310-396-6007

(M10)
Gary Metz
263 Key Lakewood Dr.
Moneta, VA 24121
540-721-2091
FAX 504-721-1782

(M11)
Michael and Polly McQuillen
McQuillen's Collectibles
P.O. Box 11141
Indianapolis, IN 46201-0141
317-322-8518

(M14)
Ken Mitchell
710 Conacher Dr.
Willowdale, Ontario
Canada M2M 3N6
416-222-5808 ANYTIME

(M15)
Marcia's Fantasy
Marcia Fanta
R.R.#1, Box 107
Tappen, ND 58487-9635
701-327-4441

(M16)
Gene Mack
408 Yorkshire Blvd.
Syracuse, NY 13219
315-487-9023

(M17)
Mrs. Miller's Memorabilia
70a Greenwich Ave., Box #116
New York, NY 10011
212-614-9774 (leave message)

(M18)
Nancy McMichael
P.O. Box 53262
Washington DC 20009

(M19)
Model Auto
P.O. Box 79253
Houston, TX 77279
Phone or FAX 713-468-4461
(phone evenings; FAX anytime)

(M20)
Bruce Middleton
5 Lloyd Rd.
Newburgh, NY 12550
914-564-2556

(M21)
Peter Muldavin
173 W 78th St., Apt. 5-F
New York, NY 10024
212-362-9606
http://members.aol.com/kiddie78s/

(N1)
Natural Way/dba Russian Toy Co.
820 Massachusetts
Lawrence, KS 66044
913-841-0100

(N2)
Norman's Olde & New Store
Philip Norman
126 W Main St.
Washington, NC 27889-4944
919-946-3448

(N3)
Neil's Wheels, Inc.
Box 354
Old Bethpage, NY 11804
516-293-9659; FAX 516-420-0483

(N4)
Roger Nazeley
4921 Castor Ave.
Philadelphia, PA 19124
FAX 215-288-8030

(O1)
Olde Tyme Toy Shop
120 S Main St.
Fairmount, IN 46928
317-948-3150 or FAX 317-948-4257

(P2)
Dawn Parrish
20460 Samual Dr.
Saugus, CA 91350-3812
805-263-TOYS

(P3)
American Pie Collectibles
John and Sheri Pavone
29 Sullivan Rd.
Peru, NY 12972
518-643-0993; toll Free 888-458-
2200 or FAX 518-643-8152
e-mail: apc1@worldnet.att.net
website: http://www.serftech.com/apc
Mastercard, Visa, Discover

(P4)
Plymouth Rock Toy Co.
38 Russell St.
Plymouth, MA 02360
508-746-2842 or
508-830-1880 (noon-11 PM EDT)
FAX 508-830-0364

(P5)
Gary Pollastro
5047 84th Ave. SE
Mercer, WA 98040
206-232-3199

(P6)
Judy Posner
R.D. 1, Box 273
Effort, PA 18330
717-629-6583
(or winter) 4195 South Tamiami
Trail
Suite #183
Venice, FL 34293
941-497-7149

(P8)
Diane Patalano
P.O. Box 144
Saddle River, NJ 07458
201-327-2499

(P10)
Bill and Pat Poe
220 Dominica Circle E
Niceville, FL 32578-4068
904-897-4163
FAX 904-897-2606
e-mail: mcpoes@aol.com or
anem34a@prodigy.com

(P11)
The Phoenix Toy Soldier Co.
Bob Wilson
16405 North 9th Place
Phoenix, AZ 85022
602-863-2891

(P12)
Michael Paquin, That Toy Guy
72 Penn Blvd.
E Lansdowne, PA 19050
610-394-8697 (10 am - 10 pm EST)
FAX 610-259-8626 (24 hr)

(P13)
Lorraine Punchard
8201 Pleasant Ave. South
Bloomington, MN 55420
612-888-1079

(R1)
David Richter
6817 Sutherland Dr.
Mentor, OH 44060-3917

(R2)
Rick Rann, Beatlelist
P.O. Box 877
Oak Park, IL 60303
708-442-7907

(R3)
Jim Rash
135 Alder Ave.
Egg Harbor Twp., NJ 08234-9302
609-646-4125 (evenings)

(R4)
Robert Reeves
104 Azalea Dr.
St. Mathews, SC 29135
803-578-5939 (leave message)

(R5)
Reynolds Toys
Charlie Reynolds
2836 Monroe St.
Falls Church, VA 22042
703-533-1322

(R6)
David E. Riddle
P.O. Box 13141
Tallahassee, FL 32308
904-877-7207

(R7)
Leo E. Rishty, Toy Doctor
77 Alan Loop
Staten Island, NY 10304

(S1)
Sam Samuelian, Jr.
700 Llanfair Rd.
Upper Darby, PA 19082
215-566-7248

(S5)
Son's a Poppin' Ranch
John Rammacher
1610 Park Ave.
Orange City, FL 32763-8869
904-775-2891

(S6)
Bill Stillman
Scarfone & Stillman Vintage Oz
P.O. Box 167
Hummelstown, PA 17036
717-566-5538

(S7)
Nate Stoller
960 Reynolds Ave.
Ripon, CA 95366
209-599-5933

(S10)
Scott Smiles
848 SE Atlantic Dr.
Lantana, FL 33462-4702
561-582-4947

(S12)
Nancy Stewart Books
1188 NW Weybridge Way
Beaverton, OR 97006
503-645-9779

(S14)
Cindy Sabulis
P.O. Box 642
Shelton, CT 06484
203-926-0176

(S15)
Jim and Nancy Schaut
P.O. Box 10781
Glendale AZ 85318-0781
602-878-4293

(S16)
Bill Smith
56 Locust ST.
Douglas, MA 01516
508-476-2015

(S18)
The Silver Bullet
Terry and Kay Klepey
P.O. Box 553
Forks, WA 98331
360-327-3726

(S19)
Craig and Donna Stifter
P.O. Box 6514
Naperville, IL 60540
630-789-5780

(S20)
Pat and Kris Secor
P.O. Box 158
Clarksville, AR 72830
501-754-5746

(S21)
Stad's
815 N 12th St.
Allentown, PA 18102
610-770-1140 (days)
FAX 610-770-1740

(S22)
Carole & Richard Smyth
Carole Smyth Antiques
P.O. Box 2068
Huntington, NY 11743

(S24)
Mark and Lynda Suozzi
P.O. Box 102
Ashfield, MA 01330
Phone or FAX 413-628-3241
(9am to 5pm)

(S25)
Steve Stevenson
11117 NE 164th Pl.
Bothell, WA 98011-4003
206-488-2603
FAX 206-488-2841

(T1)
Jon Thurmond
Collector Holics
15006 Fuller
Grandview, MO 64030
816-322-0906

(T2)
Toy Scouts, Inc.
Bill Bruegman
137 Casterton Ave.
Akron, OH 44303
216-836-0668
FAX 216-869-8668

(T3)
Richard Trautwein
Toys N Such
437 Dawson St.
Sault Ste. Marie, MI 49783
906-635-0356

(T4)
Toy Talk
2509 Brookside Drive
Lancaster, PA 17601
717-898-2932

(T5)
Bob and Marcie Tubbs
6405 Mitchell Hollow Rd.
Charlotte, NC 28277
704-541-5839

(T6)
TV Collector
P.O. Box 1088
Easton, MA 02334
508-238-1179 or
FAX by pre-set agreement

(V1)
Norm Vigue
62 Bailey St.
Stoughton, MA 02072
617-344-5441

(V2)
Marci Van Ausdall
P.O. Box 946
Quincy, CA 95971

(W1)
Dan Wells Antique Toys
7008 Main St.
Westport, KY 40077
502-225-9925
FAX 502-225-0019
e-mail: dwatcatDan@aol.com

(W2)
Adrienne Warren
1032 Feather Bed Lane
Edison, NJ 08820

(W4)
Randy Welch
27965 Peach Orchard Rd.
Easton, MD 21601-8203
410-822-5441

(W5)
Linda and Paul Woodward
14 Argo Drive
Sewell, NJ 08080-1908
609-582-1253

(W6)
John D. Weatherhead
5224 S. Guerin Pass
New Berlin, WI 53151
414-425-8810
FAX 414-425-7844

(W7)
Larry and Mary White
108 Central St.
Rowley, MA 10969

(Y1)
Henri Yunes
971 Main St., Apt. 2
Hackensack, NJ 07601
201-488-2236

(Y2)
Mary Young
Box 9244
Dayton, OH 45409
937-298-4838

Categories of Special Interest

If you would like to be included in this section, send us a list of your 'for sale' merchandise. These listings are complimentary to those who participate in the preparation of this guide by doing so. Please understand that the people who are listed here want to buy and sell. They are not appraisers. Read the paragraph under the title *Dealer Codes* for more information. If you have no catalogs or lists but would like to advertise with us, see the display ad rate sheet on page 482.

Action Figures
Also GI Joe, Star Wars and Super Heroes
John DiCicco
57 Bay View Dr.
Shrewsbury, MA 01545
508-797-0023

Captain Action, Star Wars, Secret Wars and other character-related Western, TV, movie, comic or paperback tie-ins
George Downes
Box 572
Nutley, NJ 07110
201-935-3388

Figures
Anthony Balasco
P.O. Box 19482
Johnston, RI 02919
401-946-5720;
FAX 401-942-7980

GI Joe, Captain Action and other character-related TV, advertising, Marx and Mego figures; send $2 for sales catalog
Jerry and Ellen Harnish
110 Main St.
Bellville, OH 44813
Phone or FAX 419-886-4782

Advertising
Gary Metz
263 Key Lakewood Dr.
Moneta, VA 24121
540-721-2091 or FAX 504-721-1782

Also general line
Mike's General Store
52 St. Annes Rd.
Winnipeg, Manitoba, Canada
R2M 2Y3
204-255-3463;
FAX 204-253-4124

Advertising figures, novelty radios, Barbies, promotional watches, character toys and more
Michael Paquin, That Toy Guy
72 Penn Blvd.
E Lansdowne, PA 19050
610-394-8697 (10 am - 10 pm EST)
or FAX 610-259-8626 (24 hrs)

Coca-Cola and Pepsi-Cola toys
Craig and Donna Stifter
P.O. Box 6514
Naperville, IL 60540
630-789-5780

M&M Toppers
Ken Clee
P.O. Box 11412
Phil., PA 19111; 215-722-1979

Automobilia
Especially model kits, promotional model cars, books and literature
Model Auto
P.O. Box 79253
Houston, TX 77279
Phone or FAX 713-468-4461
(phone evenings; FAX anytime)

Banks
Ertl; sales lists available
Homestead Collectibles
Art and Judy Turner
R.D. 2, Rte. 150
P.O. Box 173-E
Mill Hall, PA 17751
717-726-3597 or
FAX 717-726-4488

Modern mechanical banks: Reynolds, John Wright, James Capron, Book of Knowledge, Richards, Wilton; sales lists available
Dan Iannotti
212 W. Hickory Grove Rd.
Bloomfield Hills, MI 48302-1127

Also children's sadirons, Black Americana dolls and memorabilia
Diane Patalano
Country Girls Appraisal and Liquidation Service
P.O. Box 144
Saddle River, NJ 07458
201-327-2499

Penny banks (limited editions): new, original, mechanical, still or figural; also bottle openers
Reynolds Toys
Charlie Reynolds
2836 Monroe St.
Falls Church, VA 22042
703-533-1322

Antique tin and iron mechanical penny banks; no reproductions or limited editions; cast-iron architectural bank buildings in Victorian form. Buy and sell list available upon request
Mark and Lynda Suozzi
P.O. Box 102
Ashfield, MA 01330
Phone/FAX 413-628-3241 (9 am – 5 pm). Mail order and shows only

Ertl; First Gear
Toy Talk
2509 Brookside Dr.
Lancaster, PA 17601
717-898-2932

Barbie and Friends
Wanted: Mackies, holiday and porcelain as well as vintage Barbies; buying and selling ca 1959 dolls to present issues
Marl Davidson (Marl & B)
10301 Braden Run
Bradenton, FL 34202
941-751-6275;
FAX 941-751-5463

Especially NRFB dolls ca 1980 to present, also Barbie Hallmark ornaments
Doris Gerton (Doris' Dolls & Collectibles)
325 E 10th St.
Mt. Vernon, IN 47620
Phone or FAX 812-835-5290

Battery-Operated
Tom Lastrapes
P.O. Box 2444
Pinellas Park, FL 34664
813-545-2586

Also general line
Mike Roscoe
3351 Lagrange
Toledo, OH 43608
419-244-6935

Boats and Toy Motors
Also Japanese wood toys
Dick Borgerding
RJB Toys
720 E Main St.
Flushing, MI 48433
810-659-9859

Books
Little Golden Books, Wonder Books, many others; 20-page list available
Ilene Kayne
1308 S Charles St.
Baltimore, MD 21230
410-685-3923
e-mail: Ilenegold@aol.com

Specializing in Little Golden Books and look-alikes
Steve Santi
19626 Ricardo Ave.
Hayward, CA 94541; 510-481-2586.
Author of *Collecting Little Golden Books, Volumes I and II*. Also publishes newsletter, *Poky Gazette*, primarily for Little Golden Book collectors

Children's Books
Nancy Stewart Books
1188 NW Weybridge Way
Beaverton, OR 97006
503-645-9779

Breyer
Carol Karbowiak Gilbert
2193 14 Mile Rd. 206
Sterling Height, MI 48310
Author of *Breyer Value List*; available by sending $6.50 (includes shipping and handling) with information on models made through 1995 with their catalog numbers and colors

Bubble Bath Containers
Including foreign issues; also character collectibles, character bobbin' head nodders, and Dr. Dolittle; write for information or send SASE for Bubble Bath Bulletin
Matt and Lisa Adams
1234 Harbor Cove
Woodstock, GA 30189
770-516-6874

Building Blocks and Construction Toys
Arlan Coffman
1223 Wilshire Blvd., Ste. 275
Santa Monica, CA 90403
310-453-2507

Anchor Stone Building Sets by Richter
George Hardy
1670 Hawkwood Ct.
Charlottesville, VA 22901
804-295-4863;
FAX 804-295-4898

California Raisins
Ken Clee
Box 11412
Philadelphia, PA 19111
215-722-1979

California Raisins (PVC); buying collections, old store stock and closeouts
Larry DeAngelo
516 King Arthur Dr.
Virginia Beach, VA 23464
804-424-1691

John D. Weatherhead
5224 S. Guerin Pass
New Berlin, WI 53151
414-425-8810
FAX 414-425-7844

Candy Containers
Jeff Bradfield
Corner of Rt. 42 and Rt. 257
Dayton, VA 22821
703-879-9961

Also Tonka, Smith-Miller, Shafford black cats, German nodders
Doug Dezso
864 Patterson Ave.
Maywood, NJ 07607
201-488-1311

Cast Iron
Pre-war, large-scale cast-iron toys and early American tinplate toys
John McKenna
801-803 W Cucharres
Colorado Springs, CO 80905
719-630-8732

Victorian bell toys, horse-drawn wagons, fire toys, carriages, penny banks, pull toys, animated coin-operated machines. Buy and sell, list available upon request, mail order and shows only
Mark and Lynda Suozzi
P.O. Box 102
Ashfield, MA 01330
Phone/FAX 413-628-3241
(9 am – 5 pm)

Cereal Boxes and Premiums
Scott Bruce, Mr. Cereal Box
P.O. Box 481
Cambridge, MA 02140
e-mail: scott@flake.com

Character and Promotional Glasses
Especially fast-foods and sports glasses; publishers of Collector Glass News
Mark Chase and Michael Kelly
P.O. Box 308
Slippery Rock, PA 16057
412-946-2838; FAX 412-946-9012

Character Clocks and Watches
Also radio premiums and decoders, P-38 airplane-related items from World War II, Captain Marvel and Hoppy items, Lone Ranger books with jackets, selected old comic books, toys and cap guns; buys and sells Hoppy and Roy items
Bill Campbell
Kirschner Medical Corp.
1221 Littlebrook Ln.
Birmingham, AL 35235
205-853-8227; FAX 405-658-6986

Character Collectibles
All characters, TV stuff, monsters, Toy Story, Disney, etc. Extensive lists available
Jerry Alingh
505 5th Ave #302
Des Moines, IA 50309

Dolls, rock 'n roll personalities (especially the Beatles), related character items and miscellaneous toys
BOJO
Bob Gottuso
P.O. Box 1403
Cranberry Twp., PA 16066
Phone or FAX 412-776-0621

Children's plastic character cups by F&F, Deka, etc.; also related advertising and catalogs; SASE required when requesting information
Cheryl and Lee Brown
7377 Badger Ct.
Indianapolis, IN 46260

1940s-'60s character items such as super heroes, TV and cartoon items, games, playsets, lunch boxes, model kits, comic books and premium rings
Bill Bruegman
Toy Scouts, Inc.
137 Casterton Ave.
Akron, OH 44303
216-836-0668;
FAX 216-869-8668

Hanna-Barbera, Warner Bros, Disney, vintage TV and 'toons; also collectible dolls of the '60s and '70s
John and Michele Casino
633 Franklin Ave., Suite #169
Nutley, NJ 07110
201-759-2520

TV, radio and comic collectibles; sports and non-sports cards; silver and golden age comics
Casey's Collectible Corner
HCR Box 31, Rt. 3
N Blenheim, NY 12131
607-588-6464

Disney, especially books and animation art
Cohen Books and Collectibles
Joel J. Cohen
P.O. Box 810310
Boca Raton, FL 33481
561-487-7888; FAX 561-487-3117
e-mail: cohendisney@prodigy.com

Early Disney, Western heroes, premiums and other related collectibles
Ron and Donna Donnelly
Saturday Heroes
6302 Championship Dr.
Tuscaloosa, AL 35405

Dick Tracy collectibles; free appraisals of DT items with SASE and photo or detailed description
Larry Doucet
2351 Sultana Dr.
Yorktown Heights, NY 10598
914-245-1320

Large comprehensive catalog available by subscription ($2 for sample copy, $10 per yr for 4 issues, 1st class); 100% satisfaction guaranteed
52 Girls Collectibles
P.O. Box 36
Morral, OH 43337
614-465-6062

Rocketeer memorabilia
Don Hamm
712 N. Townsend St.
Syracuse, NY 13203
315-478-7035

Snoopy/Peanuts classics, new and old
M.R. Huber, The SNO-PEA Trader
931 Emerson St.
1000 Oaks, CA 91362
805-497-0119 or
FAX 1-800-SNO-OPY-2

Any and all, also Hartland figures
Terri Ivers
Terri's Toys & Nostalgia
419 S 1st St.
Ponca City, OK 74601
405-762-(TOYS) 8697 or 405-762-5174; FAX 405-765-2657;
e-mail: tivers@pcok.com

Characters from comic strips/comic books, related memorabilia
Jeff and Bob's Fun Stuff
7324 Reseda Blvd #168
Reseda, CA 91335
818-705-3368

TV characters and shows, original network stills from 1955-85, soundtrack albums from 1950-90
Jim's TV Collectibles
P.O. Box 4767
San Diego, CA 92764
Phone or FAX 619-462-1953

Games, models, action figures, dolls, general line; especially Nightmare Before Christmas
June Moon
245 N Northwest Hwy
Park Ridge, IL 60068
847-825-1411 (24-hour phone)
FAX 847-825-6090
Open 2 to 6 PM Tues - Sat

TV, Western, Space, Beatles; auction as well as set-price catalogs available
Just Kids Nostalgia
310 New York Ave.
Huntington, NY 11743
516-423-8449; FAX 516-423-4326

Especially bendy figures and the Simpsons
K-3 Inc.
Bendees Only; Simpson Mania
2335 NW Thurman
Portland, OR 97210
503-222-2713

Auction house with consignments welcomed; specializing in western Hartlands, airplanes, boats, cars, trucks, robots, windups, battery-ops, dolls, character items and playset figures
Kerry and Judy's Toys
7370 Eggleston Rd.
Memphis, TN 31825-2112
901-575-1722

Western stars of radio, movies, and TV
Gene Mack
408 Yorkshire Blvd.
Syracuse, NY 13219
315-487-9023 (anytime)

Disney and other character collectibles
Kathy and Skip Matthews
Second Childhood Antiques & Collectibles
1154 Grand Ave.
Astoria, OR 97103
503-325-6543

Any and all, also gum cards, sports, movie posters, etc.
Mrs. Miller's Memorabilia
70a Greenwich Ave., Box 116
New York, NY 10011
212-614-9774 (leave message)

Especially Disney; send $5 for annual subscription (6 issues) for sale catalogs
The Mouse Man Ink
P.O. Box 3195
Wakefield, MA 01880
Phone or FAX 617-246-3876

General line, especially Raggedy Ann, Disneyana, Star Wars, GI Joe
Olde Tyme Toy Shop
Jim May and Debra Coleman
120 S Main St.
Fairmount, IN 46928
317-948-3150 or FAX 317-948-4257
Also tin windups, cast iron, old toy stock, cap pistols and trains

Especially pottery, china, ceramics, salt and pepper shakers, cookie jars, tea sets and children's china; with special interest in Black Americana and Disneyana; illustrated sale lists available
Judy Posner
R.D. #1, Box 273
Effort, PA 18330
717-629-6583
(or winter)
4195 South Tamiami Trail
Suite #183
Venice, FL 34293
941-497-7149

Buying, selling and trading original Beatles memorabilia
Rick Rann, Beatlelist
P.O. Box 877
Oak Park, IL 60303
708-442-7907

Also battery-ops, character clocks and novelties
Sam Samuelian, Jr.
700 Llanfair Rd.
Upper Darby, PA 19082
215-566-7248

Lone Ranger collector, buy and sell; publisher of Silver Bullet Newsletter (see Clubs, Newsletters, and Other Publications)
The Silver Bullet
Terry and Kay Klepey
P.O. Box 553
Forks, WA 98331
360-327-3726

Wizard of Oz memorabilia; quarterly mail/phone bid auctions available for $2; always buying Oz
Bill Stillman
Scarfone and Stillman Vintage Oz
P.O. Box 167
Hummelstown, PA 17036
717-566-5538

General line; extensive inventory. Anything and everything
Jon Thurmond
Collector Holics
15006 Fuller
Grandview, MO 64030
816-322-0906

Especially tinplate toys and cars, battery-op toys and toy trains
Richard Trautwein
Toys N Such
437 Dawson St.
Sault Ste. Marie, MI 49783
906-635-0356

TV, movie, rock 'n roll, comic character, commercials, radio, theater, etc., memorabilia of all kinds; Send $4 for sale catalog. We are not interested in buying items. All inquiries must include SASE for reply unless ordering catalog
TV Collector
P.O. Box 1088
Easton, MA 02334
508-238-1179 or
FAX by pre-set agreement

Games, premiums, cartoon personalities, Dick Tracy, Popeye, Buck Rogers, Flash Gordon, Tarzan, Lone Ranger and others
Norm Vigue
62 Bailey St.
Stoughton, MA 02072
617-344-5441

Especially Garfield, Smurfs, comic/character collectibles, dolls, monsters, premiums, etc. Lists available
Adrienne Warren
1032 Feather Bed Lane
Edison, NJ 08820
908-381-7083 (EST)

Children's Play Dishes
Author of book
Lorraine Punchard
8201 Pleasant Ave. South
Bloomington, MN 55420
612-888-1079

Chinese Tin Toys
Also buying and selling antiques, old toys and collectibles; custom refinishing and quality repairing
Finisher's Touch Antiques
Steve Fisch, proprietor
10 W Main St.
Wappingers Falls, NY 12590
914-298-8882; FAX 914-298-8945

Comic Books
Also Western pulps, Big Little Books, magazines, Mad and other humor publications; large catalog available
Avalon Comics
Larry Curcio
P.O. Box 821
Medford, MA 02155
617-391-5614

Also Sunday comics, books, pulp magazines, premiums, character collectibles, non-sports cards and more
Ken Mitchell
710 Conacher Dr.
Wilowdale, Ontario
Canada M2M 3N6
416-222-5808 (anytime)

Cracker Jack
Author of *Cracker Jack Toys*
Larry and Mary White
108 Central St.
Rowley, MA 10969

Dakins
Jim Rash
135 Alder Ave.
Egg Harbor Twp., NJ 08234-9302

Diecast
Matchbox, extensive lists available
Classic Golf & Collectibles
P.O. Box 8
Lake Havasu City, AZ 86406-0008
520-855-9623

Buying complete or partial collections of die-cast banks, promos, and any Nascar products
Dr. Doors Miniatures
3111 S. Valley View, Suite O-104
Las Vegas, NV 89102
702-362-2722

Especially Dinky; also selling inexpensive restorable diecast as well as reproduction parts and decals for many diecast brands
Paul Fideler
20 Shadow Oak Dr., Apt. #18
Sudbury, MA 01776
617-386-0228 (24 hours); FAX
617-386-0159 (24 hours)

Especially English-made toy vehicles
Mark Giles
510 E Third St.
Ogalala, NE 69153
308-284-4360

Especially Matchbox and other small-scale cars and trucks
Bill Jackameit
200 Victoria Dr.
Bridgewater, VA 22812
703-828-4359 (Monday-Thursday, 7 pm-9 pm EST)

Especially Matchbox, Hot Wheels, Majorette
Dana Johnson Enterprises
P.O. Box 1824
Bend, OR 97709-1824
503-382-8410
Author/publisher of *Matchbox Blue Book, Hot Wheels Blue Book* and *Collecting Majorette Toys* (prices updated yearly)

Especially Dinky; also obsolete French, German, Italian and English-made vehicles
Jean-Claude Lanau
740 Thicket Ln.
Houston, TX 77079
713-4971-6034

Matchbox of all types including Dinky, Commando, Convoys, Harley-Davidson, Indy/Formula 1, and Looney Tunes; also Corgi, Hartoy, Hot Wheels, Tomica, and Tyco slot cars
Neil's Wheels, Inc.
Box 354
Old Bethpage, NY 11804
516-293-9659; FAX 516-420-0483

Also pressed steel trucks and comic character toys
Jim and Nancy Schaut
P.O. Box 10781
Glendale, AZ 85318-0781
602-878-4293

Ertl, banks, farm, trucks and construction
Son's a Poppin' Ranch
John Rammacher
1610 Park Ave.
Orange City, FL 32763-8869
904-775-2891

All types; also action figures such as GI Joe, Johnny West, Matt Mason and others
Robert Reeves
104 Azalea Dr.
St. Mathews, SC 29135
803-578-5939 (leave message)

Especially Soviet-made toys (marked USSR or CCCP)
David E. Riddle
P.O. Box 13141
Tallahassee, FL 32308
905-877-7207

Hot Wheels
Steve Stevenson
11117 NE 164th Pl.
Bothell, WA 98011-4003
206-488-2603 or
FAX 206-488-2841

Hot Wheels, Matchbox and all obsolete toy cars, trucks and airplanes
Dan Wells Antiques Toys
7008 Main St.
Westport, KY 40077
502-225-9925;
FAX 502-225-0019
e-mail: dwatcatDan@aol.com

Dolls
Strawberry Shortcake dolls, accessories and related items
Geneva Addy
P.O. Box 124
Winterset, IA 50273
515-462-3027

Hard plastic and composition, Ginny and accessories, pincushion dolls, doll dishes; catalogs available
Roslyn L. Herman
124-16 84th Rd.
Kew Gardens, NY 11415
718-846-3496 or 718-846-8491

Chatty Cathy and Mattel
Kathy Lewis
187 N Marcello Ave.
Thousand Oaks, CA 91360
805-499-8101
Author of book: *Chatty Cathy Dolls, An Identification and Value Guide*

Ad dolls, Barbies and other Mattel dolls, premiums, character memorabilia, modern dolls, related items
Marcia Fanta
Marcia's Fantasy
RR 1, Box 107
Tappen, ND 58487-9635
701-327-4441

Gerber Baby dolls; author of book ($44 postpaid)
Joan S. Grubaugh
2342 Hoaglin Rd.
Van Wert, OH 45891
419-622-4411 or
FAX 419-622-3026

Holly Hobbie dolls and collectibles
Kathe Conley
51 Spencer Rd.
Airville, PA 17302
717-862-3162; FAX per Winchester Group, 410-866-3125

Liddle Kiddles and other small dolls from the late '60s and early '70s
Dawn Parrish
20460 Samual Dr.
Saugus, CA 91350-3812
805-263-TOYS

Dolls from the 1960s-70s, including Liddle Kiddles, Barbie, Tammy, Tressy, etc. Co-author of The Collector's Guide to Tammy, the Ideal Teen (Collector Books)
Cindy Sabulis
P.O. Box 642
Shelton, CT 06484
203-926-0176

Betsy McCall
Marci Van Ausdall
P.O. Box 946
Quincy, CA 95971

Celebrity and character dolls
Henri Yunes
971 Main St., Apt. 2
Hackensack, NJ 07601
201-488-2236

Dollhouse Furniture
Renwal, Ideal, Marx, etc.
Judith A. Mosholder
186 Pine Springs Camp Road
Boswell, PA 15531
814-629-9277

Dollhouses
Tin and fiberboard dollhouses and plastic furniture from all eras
Bob and Marcie Tubbs
6405 Mitchell Hollow Rd.
Charlotte, NC 28277
704-541-5839

Elvis Presley Collectibles
Rosalind Cranor
P.O. Box 859
Blacksburg, VA 24063
Author of books: *Elvis Collectibles, Best of Elvis Collectibles*

Ertl
Also Tonka, construction and logging toys, pressed steel, diecast toy trucks, Smokey Bear items
Glen Brady
P.O. Box 3933
Central Point, OR 97502
503-772-0350

Fast Food
Early Big Boy, Royal Castle, McDonald's® items
Allan Bradley Music (BMI)
Allan Licht
484 S. Grand
Orange, CA 92866
714-633-2628
Also '50s & '60s toys; Batman; Superman; '60s & '70s cereal boxes

All restaurants
Jim Christoffel
409 Maple
Elburn, IL 60119
708-365-2914

All restaurants and California Raisins
Ken Clee
Box 11412
Philadelphia, PA 19111
215-722-1979

McDonald's® only, especially older or unusual items
John and Eleanor Larsen
523 Third St.
Colusa, CA 95932
916-458-4769

McDonald's®
Terry and Joyce Losonsky
7506 Summer Leave Lane
Columbia, MD 21046-2455
410-381-3358
Authors of *Illustrated Collector's Guide to McDonald's® Happy Meals® Boxes, Premiums, and Promotionals* ($9 plus $2 postage), *McDonald's® Happy Meal® Toys in the USA* and *McDonald's® Happy Meal® Toys Around the World* (both full color, $24.95 each plus $3 postage), and *Illustrated Collector's Guide to McDonald's® McCAPS®* ($4 plus $2 postage)

Source for catalog: McDonald's® Collectibles and Other Fast-Food Toys and Memorabilia
Bill and Pat Poe
220 Dominica Circle E
Niceville, FL 32578-4068
904-897-4163;
FAX 904-897-2606
e-mail: mcpoes@aol.com or anem34a@prodigy.com
Send $3.00 for catalogs (2 each year, in January and July); see Clubs, Newsletters, and Other Publications for information on McDonald's® club

Fisher-Price
Brad Cassity
1350 Stanwix
Toledo, OH 43614
419-385-9910 (FAX capable, please call first)

Games
Victorian, cartoon, comic, TV and nostalgic themes
Paul Fink's Fun & Games
P.O. Box 488
59 S Kent Rd.
Kent, CT 06757
203-927-4001

Paul David Morrow
1045 Rolling Point Ct.
Virginia Beach, VA 23456-6371

Circa 1900 to modern
Bill Smith
56 Locust St.
Douglas, MA 01516
508-476-2015

Gas-Powered Toys
Airplanes, cars and boats; publishes Gas Toy Collector newsletter
Danny Bynum
P.O. Box 440818
Houston, TX 77244-0818
713-531-5711

GI Joe
Also diecast and Star Wars
Cotswold Collectibles
P.O. Box 249
Clinton, WA 98236
360-579-1223
FAX 360-579-1287

Guns
Pre-WWII American spring-air BB guns, all Red Ryder BB guns, cap guns with emphasis on Western six-shooters; especially wanted are pre-WWII cast iron six-guns
Jim Buskirk
3009 Oleander Ave.
San Marcos, CA 92069
619-599-1054

Parts for 1940 cast-iron and 1950 diecast guns: steer-head grips, 2-pc silver or silver and brass bullets for Nicholas paint 6-shooter and spitfire rifle
ED Drew
7530 146th Ave. NE
Redmond, WA 98052
206-885-7378

Specializing in cap guns
Happy Memories Antique Toy Co.
The Hamburgs
P.O. Box 1305
Woodland Hills, CA 91365
818-346-9884 or 818-346-1269
FAX 818-346-0215

Also model kits, toy soldiers and character toys and watches; character watch service available
Plymouth Rock Toy Co.
38 Russell St.
Plymouth, MA 02360
508-746-2842 or 508-830-1880 (noon to 11 pm EDT); FAX 508-830-0364

Hartland Plastics, Inc.
Issues price guide
Gail Fitch
1733 N. Cambridge Ave.
Milwaukee, WI 53202

Specializing in Western Hartlands
Kerry and Judy's Toys
7370 Eggleston Rd.
Memphis, TN 38125-2112
901-757-1722

Halloween Collectibles
Also postcards
Pamela E. Apkarian-Russell
C.J. Russell and The Halloween Queen Antiques
P.O. Box 499
Winchester, NH 03470
603-239-8875

Lunch Boxes
Also Little House on the Prairie items, Star Trek and Star Wars unusual items
PAK-RAT
Andy Galbus
900 8th St. NW
Kasson, MN 55944-1079
507-634-2093
e-mail: lhpakrat@polaristel.net

Norman's Olde and New Store
Philip Norman
126 W Main St.
Washington, NC 27889-4944
919-946-3448

Also characters such as cowboys, TV shows, cartoons and more
Terri's Toys
Terri Ivers
419 S First St.
Ponca City, OK 74601
405-762-8697 or 405-762-5174
FAX 405-765-2657
e-mail: tivers@pcok.com

Marbles
Block's Box is the longest continuously running absentee marble auction service in the country; catalogs issued
Stanley A. & Robert S. Block
P.O. Box 51
Trumbull, CT 06611
203-261-3223 or 203-926-8448
internet: bblock@well.com
web: http://pages.prodigy.com/marbles/mcc.html
Prodigy: BWVR62A

Marionettes and Puppets
Steven Meltzer
670 San Juan Ave. #B
Venice, CA 90281
310-396-6007

Marx
Figures, playsets and character toy; send 3 32¢ stamps for extensive sales lists
G.F. Ridenour
Fun House Toy Co.
P.O. Box 343
Bradfordwoods, PA 15015-0343
412-935-1392 (FAX capable)

Model Kits
Specializing in figures and science fiction
Gordy Dutt
P.O. Box 201
Sharon Center, OH 44274-0201
330-239-1657 or 330-239-2991

Also action figures, monsters (especially Godzilla and Japan automated toys), Star Trek and non-sports cards
Alan Edwards
Toys From the Crypt
P.O. Box 3294
Shawnee, KS 66203
913-383-1242

From and of science fiction, TV, movies, figures, space, missiles, comics, etc.
John F. Green Inc.
1821 W. Jacaranda Pl
Fullerton, CA 92633
714-526-5467; 800-807-4759

Character, space, monster, Western, radio and cereal premiums and toys; GI Joe, Captain Action, tin toys and windups
Ed Janey
2920 Meadowbrook Dr. SE
Cedar Rapids, IA 52403
319-362-5213

Also plastic toys and radio, movie or TV tie-ins, movie posters
John and Sheri Pavone
29 Sullivan Rd.
Peru, NY 12972
518-643-0993 Toll Free 888-458-2200 or FAX 518-643-8152
e-mail: apc1@worldnet.att.net
Website: http://www.serftech.com/apc
Mastercard Visa Discover

Non-Sport Trading Cards
Send $1 for our 40-page catalog of non-sport cards ca 1970 to date; dealers send large SASE for our 10-page wholesale and closeout list
Mark and Val Macaluso
3603 Newark Rd.
Marion, NY 14505
315-926-4349; FAX 315-926-4853

Paper Dolls
Author of books
Mary Young
Box 9244
Dayton, OH 45409
937-298-4838

Paper Lithographed Toys
Rare 18th-, 19th-, and 20th-century games, paper dolls, books, etc.
Bromer Booksellers, Inc.
607 Boylston St.
Boston, MA 02116
617-247-2818; FAX 617-247-2975

Antique McLoughlin games, Bliss and Reed boats, toy wagons, Ten Pin sets, cube blocks, puzzles and Victorian dollhouses. Buy and sell; lists available upon request. Mail order and shows only
Mark and Linda Suozzi
P.O. Box 102
Ashfield, MA 01330
Phone or FAX 413-628-3241 (9am to 5pm)

Pedal Cars
Also specializing in Maytag collectibles
Nate Stoller
960 Reynolds Ave.
Ripon, CA 95366
510-481-2586

Penny Toys
Jane Anderson
R.R. 5, Box 5525
Saylorsburg, PA 18353

Pez Candy Dispensers
Richard Belyski
P.O. Box 124
Sea Cliff, NY 11579
e-mail: peznews@juno.com

Plastic Figures
Also Dakins, cartoon and advertising figures, and character squeeze toys
Jim Rash
135 Alder Ave.
Egg Harbor Twp., NJ 08234-9302
609-649-4125

Stad's
815 N 12th St.
Allentown, PA 18102
610-770-1140 (days) or FAX 610-770-1740

Playsets
Also GI Joe, Star Trek and dinosaurs
Mike and Kurt Fredericks
145 Bayline Circle
Folsom, CA 95630-8077

Political Toys
Michael and Polly McQuillen
McQuillen's Collectibles
P.O. Box 11141
Indianapolis, IN 46201
317-322-8518

Promotional Vehicles
'50s and '60s models (especially Ford); also F&F Post Cereal cars; author of 2 books on promotional model cars, both available directly from him
Larry Blodget
Box 753
Rancho Mirage, CA 92270
619-862-1979

Puzzles
Wood jigsaw type, from before 1950
Bob Armstrong
15 Monadnock Rd.
Worcester, MA 01609

Specializing in advertising puzzles
Donald Friedman
660 W Grand Ave
Chicago, IL 60610
Day phone: 708-656-3700
Evenings and weekends:
312-226-4741
FAX 708-656-6292

Radio Premiums
Also Fisher-Price; lists available
Pat and Kris Secor
P.O. Box 158
Clarksville, AR 72830
501-754-5746

Radios
Authors of several books on antique, novelty, and transistor radios
Sue and Marty Bunis
RR 1, Box 36
Bradford, NH 03221-9102

Ramp Walkers
Specializing in walkers, ramp-walking figures, and tin windups
Randy Welch
Raven'tiques
27965 Peach Orchard Rd.
Easton, MD 21601-8203
410-822-5441

Records
78 rpm children's records and picture disks; buys, sells, and trades records as well as makes cassette recordings for a small fee
Peter Muldavin
173 W 78th St., Apt. 5-F
New York, NY 10024
212-362-9606
http://members.aol.com/kiddie78s/

Russian and East European Toys
Wooden Matrioskha dolls, toys of tin, plastic, diecast metal; military theme and windups
Natural Way/dba Russian Toy Co.
820 Massachusetts
Lawrence, KS 66044
913-841-0100

Specializing in Russian toys
David E. Riddle
P.O. Box 13141
Tallahassee, FL 32308
904-877-7207

Sand Toys
Jane Anderson
Rt. 1, Box 1030
Saylorsburg, PA 18353

Authors of book; send $25 plus $3 for postage for a signed copy. New York residents please add 8¼% sales tax.
Carole and Richard Smyth
Carole Smyth Antiques
P.O. Box 2068
Huntington, NY 11743

Schoenhut
Publishers of *Inside Collector and Antique Doll World*
Keith and Donna Kaonis
60 Cherry Ln.
Huntington, NY 11743
516-261-8337 or
FAX 516-261-8235

Slot Cars
Especially HO scale from the 1960s to the present; also vintage diecast
Joe Corea
New Jersey Nostalgia Hobby
401 Park Ave.
Scotch Plains, NJ 07076
908-322-2676
FAX 908-322-4079

Specializing in slots and model racing from the '60s-'70s; especially complete race sets in original boxes
Gary Pollastro
5047 84th Ave. SE
Mercer, WA, 98040
206-232-3199

Snow Domes
Broad assortment from states, cities, tourist attractions, novelties, also glass domes; list available
Nancy McMichael
P.O. Box 53262
Washington DC 20009
Editor of *Snow Biz*, quarterly newsletter, see Clubs, Newsletters and Other Publications

Soldiers
Barclay, Manoil, Grey Iron, Jones, dimestore types and others; also Syrocco figures
Stan and Sally Alekna
4724 Kernan Mill Lane E
Jacksonville, FL 32224
904-992-9525

Recasts, conversions, diorama work; price list available
Bryan and Val Davis
3132 E. Prince Rd.
Tucson, AZ 85716
502-323-2598 (9 am - 7 pm, Mountain Standard)

Auburn, Airfix, Atlantic, etc; also Marx plastic figures, playsets and accessories; lists available with SASE
Phoenix Toy Soldier Co.
Bob Wilson
16405 North 9th Place
Phoenix, AZ 85022
602-863-2891

Sports Bobbin' Head Dolls
Tim Hunter
1668 Golddust
Sparks, NV 89436
702-626-5029

Star Wars
Also vehicles, model kits, GI Joes, games, ad figures, View-Master, non-sports cards, Star Trek, advertising, antiques, fine art and much more
June Moon
Jim and Nancy Frugoli
245 N Northwest Hwy
Park Ridge, IL 60068
847-825-1411 (24-hr phone);
FAX 847-825-6090
Open 2 to 6 PM Tues - Sat

Steiff
Also Schucos and children's things
Candelaine (Candice Gunther)
Pasadena, CA 91103-2320
818-796-4568; FAX 818-796-7172
e-mail: Candelaine@aol.com.

Especially limited editions, '50s and antique. Other teddies and reference books.
Cynthia's Country Store
The Wellington Mall #15-A
12794 W Forest Hill Blvd
Wellington, FL 33414
561-793-0554; FAX 561-795-4222
e-mail: cynbears@aol.com
web: http://www.thecrier.com/ccs

Particularly bears; also Schucos and dolls
Bunny Walker
Box 502
Bucyrus, OH 44820
419-562-8355

Tonka
Also candy containers and German nodders
Doug Dezso
864 Patterson Ave.
Maywood, NJ 07607
201-488-1311

Toothbrush Holders
Also Pez
Marilyn Cooper
P.O. Box 55174
Houston, TX 77255

Tootsietoys
David Richter
6817 Sutherland Dr.
Mentor, OH 44060-3917
Author of *Collector's Guide to Tootsietoys*

Tops and Other Spinning Toys
Yo-yos, advertising spinners, gyroscopes, spinning games, Victorian figural tops; any unique spinning toy. Buy, sell, trade
Bruce Middleton
5 Lloyd Rd.
Newburgh, NY 12550
914-564-2556

Trains
Lionel, American Flyer and Plasticville
Gary's Trains
186 Pine Springs Camp Road
Boswell, PA 15531
814-629-9277

Also Fisher-Price, Tonka toys and diecast vehicles
Bill Mekalian
550 E Chesapeake Cir.
Fresno, CA 93720
209-434-3247

Buying American Flyer S gauge. Toys of all types for sale. Satisfaction guaranteed; color photos with SASE; shipping extra. No return calls on sold items; phone until midnight
Linda and Paul Woodward
14 Argo Drive
Sewell, NJ 08080-1908
609-582-1253

Toy mall; general line (toys on 2nd floor)
Bo-Jo's Antique Mall
3400 Summer Avenue
Memphis, TN 38122
901-323-2050

Transformers

Specializing in Transformers, Robotech, Shogun Warriors, Gadaikins, and any other robot; want to buy these MIP — also selling
David Kolodny-Nagy
3701 Connecticut Ave. NW
Apt. #500
Washington, DC 20008
202-364-8753
For copy of *BotCon Transformer Comic Book, Comic Smorgasbord Special*, send $3 + $1.50 for single issues, $2.50 each for 10 or more + $2. Also available: *Transformers: BotCon '94 Ten-Year Retrospective* (130+ pages) at $15 + $2

Trolls
Roger Inouye
765 E. Franklin Ave.
Pomona, CA 91766

View-Master
Also games, slot cars, Pez, lunch boxes, Halloween costumes, dolls, premiums, TV Guides, Mad magazines
Tom Bremer
P.O. Box 49
Newark, NY 14513
Phone or FAX 315-331-8146

Roger Nazeley
4921 Castor Ave.
Phil., PA 19124
FAX 215-288-8030

Windups
Also Occupied Japan celluloid toys
Barry Hardin
1834 NW 39th Terrace
Gainesville, FL 32605-3536
352-372-5182

Especially German and Japan tin toys, Cracker Jack, toothbrush holders, radio premiums, pencil sharpeners and comic strip toys
Phil Helley
Old Kilbourne Antiques
629 Indiana Ave.
Wisconsin Dells, WI 53965
608-254-8770

Also pressed steel toys, battery-ops, candy containers, dolls and children's things, games, soldiers, Noah's ark, space, robots, etc.
Jacquie and Bob Henry
Antique Treasures and Toys
Box 17
Walworth, NY 14568-0017
315-986-1424

Fine character windups; also Black Americana
Stephen Leonard
Box 127
Albertson, LI, NY 11507
516-742-0979

Also friction and battery operated; fast-food toys, displays
Scott Smiles
848 SE Atlantic Dr.
Lantana, FL 33462-4702
561-582-4947

Yo-Yos
Lucky Meisenheimer
7300 Sand Lake Commons Blvd.
Orlando, FL 32819
407-354-0478

Clubs, Newsletters, and Other Publications

There are hundreds of clubs, newsletters, and magazines available to toy collectors today. Listed here are some devoted to specific areas of interest. You can obtain a copy of many newsletters simply by requesting a sample.

Action Figure News & Toy Review
James Tomlinson, Editor
556 Monroe Turnpike
Monroe, CT 06458
203-452-7286
FAX 203-452-0410

Action Toys Newsletter
P.O. Box 31551
Billings, MT 59107
406-248-4121

American Game Collectors Assn.
49 Brooks Ave.
Lewiston, MA 04240

American International Matchbox Collectors & Exchange Club News
(Monthly)
Dottie Colpitts
532 Chestnut St.
Lynn, MA 01904
617-595-4135

Anchor Block Foundation
908 Plymouth St.
Pelham, NY 10303; 914-738-2935

Antique Advertising Association
P.O. Box 1121
Morton Grove, IL 60053
708-446-0904

Antique & Collectors Reproduction News
Mark Cherenka
Circulation Department
P.O. Box 71174
Des Moines, IA 50325
800-227-5531. Monthly newsletter showing differences between old originals and new reproductions; subscription: $32 per year

Antique Trader Weekly
Kyle D. Husfloen, Editor
P.O. Box 1050
Dubuque, IA 52004
Sub. $32 (52 issues) per year

The Autograph Review (newsletter)
Jeffrey Morey
305 Carlton Rd.
Syracuse, NY 13207
315-474-3516

Autographs & Memorabilia
P.O. Box 224
Coffeyville, KS 67337
316-251-5308
6 issues per year on movie and sports memorabilia

Barbie Bazaar (magazine)
5617 Sixth Ave., Dept NY593
Kenosha, WI 53140
414-658-1004; FAX 414-658-0433. 6 issues for $25.95

Barbie Talks Some More!
Jacqueline Horning
7501 School Rd.
Cincinnati, OH 45249

The Baum Bugle
The International Wizard of Oz Club
Fred M. Meyer
220 N 11th St.
Escanaba, MI 49829

Berry-Bits
Strawberry Shortcake Collectors' Club
Peggy Jimenez
1409 72nd St.
N Bergen, NJ 07047

Beyond the Rainbow Collector's Exchange
P.O. Box 31672
St. Louis, MO 63131

Big Little Times
Big Little Book Collectors Club of America
Larry Lowery
P.O. Box 1242
Danville, CA 94526
415-837-2086

Bojo
P.O. Box 1203
Cranberry Township, PA 16033-2203; 412-776-0621 (9 am to 9 pm EST). Issues fixed-price catalog containing Beatles and Rock 'n' Roll memorabilia

Buckeye Marble Collectors Club
Betty Barnard
472 Meadowbrook Dr.
Newark, Oh 43055
614-366-7002

Bulletin
Doll Collectors of America
14 Chestnut Rd.
Westford, MA 01886
617-692-8392

Canadian Toy Collectors Society
Gary A. Fry
P.O. Box 636
Maple, Ontario, Canada L6A 1S5

Candy Container Collectors of America
P.O. Box 352
Chelmsford, MA 01824-0352
or Jeff Bradfield
90 Main St.
Dayton, VA 22821

The Candy Gram newsletter
Candy Container Collectors of America
Douglas Dezso
864 Paterson, Ave.
Maywood, NJ 07607
201-845-7707

Captain Action Collectors Club
P.O. Box 2095
Halesite, NY 11743
516-423-1801. Send SASE for newsletter information

Cast Iron Toy Collectors of America
Paul McGinnis
1340 Market St.
Long Beach, CA 90805

Cat Collectors Club
33161 Wendy Dr.
Sterling Heights, MI 48310
Subscription: $18 per year

Cat Talk
Marilyn Dipboye
31311 Blair Dr.
Warren, MI 48092; 313-264-0285

Century Limited
Toy Train Collectors Society
160 Dexter Terrace
Tonawanda, NY 14150
716-694-3771

Children's Cups America
Cheryl and Lee Brown
7377 Badger Ct.
Indianapolis, IN 46260
Newsletter, information share, free ad space; send SASE

Coca-Cola Collectors Club International
P.O. Box 49166
Atlanta, GA 30359
Annual dues: $25

Collecting Tips Newsletter
c/o Meredith Williams
P.O. Box 633
Joplin, MO 64802
417-781-3855 or 417-624-2518. 12 issues per year focusing on fast-food collectibles

Collector Glass News
P.O. Box 308
Slippery Rock, PA 16057
412-946-2838 or FAX 412-946-9012. 6 issues per year focusing on character glasses, $15 per year

The Cookie Jar Collector's Club News
Louise Messina Daking
595 Cross River Rd.
Katonah, NY 10536
914-232-0383
FAX 914-232-0384

Cookie Jarrin' With Joyce: The Cookie Jar Newsletter
R.R. 2, Box 504
Walterboro, SC 29488

Cynthia's Country Store
Wellington Mall #15A
12794 West Forest Hill Blvd.
West Palm Beach, FL 33414
FAX or Phone 407-793-0554
Specializing in Steiff new, discontinued and antique. Publishes quarterly Steiff and bear-related newsletter and limited edition yearly price guide. $15 per year for both. Call or FAX for information or if you have any questions. Also specializes in pieces by R. John Wright, other bear manufacturers, toy soldiers and some old toys. Many Steiff color catalogs and books available.

Dark Shadows Collectibles Classified
Sue Ellen Wilson
6173 Iroquois Trail
Mentor, OH 44060
216-946-6348. For collectors of both old and new series

Dionne Quint Collectors Club
(see also Quint News)
Jimmy Rodolfos
P.O. Box 2527
Woburn, MA 01888
617-933-2219

Doll Castle News Magazine
P.O. Box 247
Washington, NJ 07882; 908-689-7042 or FAX 908-689-6320; Subscription: $16.95 per year or $31.95 for 2 years; issued 6 times a year, serves general interests of doll and miniature collectors as well as dollmaking

Doll Investment Newsletter
P.O. Box 1982
Centerville, MA 02632

Doll News
United Federation of Doll Clubs
P.O. Box 14146
Parkville, MO 64152

Dollhouse & Miniature Collectors Quarterly
Sharon Unger, Editor
P.O. Box 16
Bellaire, MI 49615
$20.00 for 4 issues per year, 45-50 pages of information, buy & sell ads, pricing information.

Dunbar's Gallery
76 Haven St.
Milford, MA 01757
508-634-8697
FAX 508-634-8698. Specializing in quality advertising, Halloween, toys, coin-operated machines; holding cataloged auctions occasionally, lists available

Ephemera News
The Ephemera Society of America, Inc.
P.O. Box 37, Schoharie, NY 12157; 518-295-7978

The Ertl Replica
Ertl Collectors Club
Mike Meyer, Editor
Hwys 136 & 20
Dyersville, IA 52040; 319-875-2000

The Fisher-Price Collector's Club
This club issues a quarterly newsletter packed with information and ads for toys. For more information write to:
Fisher-Price Club, CC Jeanne Kennedy
1442 N. Ogden
Mesa, AZ 85205

FLAKE, The Breakfast Nostalgia Magazine
P.O. Box 481
Cambridge, MA 02140; 617-492-5004. Bimonthly illustrated issue devoted to one hot collecting area such as Disney, etc., with letters, discoveries, new releases, and ads; single issue: $4 ($6 foreign); annual: $20 ($28 foreign); free 25-word ad with new subscription

Friends of Hoppy Club and Newsletter
Laura Bates
6310 Friendship Dr.
New Concord, OH 43762-9708;
614-826-4850

Game Times
American Game Collectors Assn.
Joe Angiolillo, Pres.
4628 Barlow Dr.
Bartlesville, OK 74006

Garfield Collectors Society Newsletter
c/o David L. Abrams, Editor
744 Foster Ridge Rd.
Germantown, TN 38138-7036;
901-753-1026

Gas Toy Collector
P.O. Box 440818
Houston, TX 77244-0818
Membership: $15 per year; sample issue $1.00

Gene Autry Star Telegram
Gene Autry Development Assn.
Chamber of Commerce
P.O. Box 158
Gene Autry, OK 73436

Ginny Doll Club News
Jeanne Niswonger
305 W Beacon Rd.
Lakeland, FL 33803
813-687-8015

Gone With the Wind Collectors Club Newsletter
8105 Woodview Rd.
Ellicot City, MD 21043
301-465-4632

Good Bears of the World
Terri Stong
P.O. Box 13097
Toledo, OH 43613

Grandma's Trunk
P.O. Box 404
Northport, MI 49670
Subscription: $8 per year for 1st class or $5 per year for bulk rate

Headquarters Quarterly, for GI Joe Collectors
Joe Bodnarchuk
62 McKinley Ave.
Kenmore, NY 14217-2414

Hello Again, Old-Time Radio Show Collector
Jay A. Hickerson
P.O. Box 4321
Hamden, CT 06514; 203-248-2887; FAX 203-281-1322. Sample copy upon request with SASE

Highballer for Toy Train Collectors
c/o Lou Bohn
109 Howedale Dr.
Rochester, NY 14616-1543

Hobby News
J.L.C. Publications
Box 258
Ozone Park, NY 11416

Hopalong Cassidy Fan Club International
Laura Bates
6310 Friendship Dr.
New Concord, OH 43762
614-826-4850; Subscription: $15 (USA) or $20 (Canada and overseas); includes quarterly newsletter and information on annual Cambridge, Ohio, festival

Hopalong Cassidy Newsletter
Hopalong Cassidy Fan Club
P.O. Box 1361
Boyes Hot Springs, CA 95416

Ideal Doll & Toy Collectors Club
P.O. Box 623
Lexington, MA 02173; 617-862-2994

International Figure Kit Club
Gordy's
P.O. Box 201
Sharon Center, OH 44274-0201; 330-239-1657; FAX 330-239-2991

International Wizard of Oz Club Inc.
P.O. Box 95
Kinderhook, IL 62345

Kit Builders Magazine
Gordy's
P.O. Box 201
Sharon Center, OH 44274-0201; 216-239-1657; FAX 216-239-2991

Madame Alexander Fan Club Newsletter
Earl Meisinger
11 S 767 Book Rd.
Naperville, IL 60564

Marble Mania
Marble Collectors Society of America
Stanley Block
P.O. Box 222
Trumbull, CT 06611
203-261-3223

Martha's Kidlit Newsletter
Box 1488A
Ames, IA 50010
A bimonthly publication for children's books collectors. Subscription: $25 per year

Matchbox USA
Charles Mack
62 Saw Mill Rd.
Durham, CT 06422
203-349-1655

McDonald's® Collecting Tips
Meredith Williams
Box 633
Joplin, MO 64802
Send SASE for information

McDonald's® Collector Club
Joyce Terry Losonsky
7506 Summer Leave Ln.
Columbia, MD 21046-2455; 301-381-3358. Authors of *Illustrated Collector's Guide to McDonald's® Happy Meal® Boxes, Premiums, & Promotions®* ($9 plus $2 postage), and *Illustrated Collector's Guide to McDonald's® McCAPS®* ($3 plus $2), both available from the authors.

McDonald's® Collector Club 'Sunshine Chapter'
Bill and Pat Poe, founders
c/o Dominica Circle. E.
Niceville, FL 32578-4068; 904-897-4163; FAX 904-897-2606
e-mail: mcpoes@aol.com or anem34a@prodigy.com

McDonald's® Collector Club Newsletter
c/o Tenna Greenberg
5400 Waterbury Rd.
Des Moines, IA 50312
515-279-0741

Model & Toy Collector Magazine
Toy Scouts, Inc.
137 Casterton Ave.
Akron, OH 44303; 216-836-0668; FAX 216-869-8668

Modern Doll Club Journal
Jeanne Niswonger
305 W Beacon Rd.
Lakeland, FL 33803

The Mouse Club East (Disney collectors)
P.O. Box 3195
Wakefield, MA 01880
Family membership: $25 (includes newsletters and 2 shows per year)

The Mouse Club (newsletter)
Kim and Julie McEuen
2056 Cirone Way
San Jose, CA 95124; 408-377-2590; FAX 408-379-6903

Movie Advertising Collector (magazine)
George Reed
P.O. Box 28587
Phil., PA 19149

NAOLH Newsletter
National Assn. for Outlaw & Lawman History
Hank Clark
P.O. Box 812
Waterford, CA 95386
209-874-2640

NAPAC Newsletter
National Assn. of Paper and Advertising Collectors
P.O. Box 500
Mt. Joy, PA 17552; 717-653-4300

National Fantasy Fan Club (for Disney collectors)
Dept. AC, Box 19212
Irvine, CA 92713. Membership: $20 per year, includes newsletters, free ads, chapters, conventions, etc.

National Headquarters News
Train Collectors Assn.
300 Paradise Ln.
Strasburg, PA 17579

Novelty Salt and Pepper Club
c/o Irene Thornburg, Membership Coordinator
581 Joy Rd.
Battle Creek, MI 49017
Publishes quarterly newsletter and annual roster. Annual dues: $20 in USA, Canada, and Mexico; $25 for all other countries

Old Toy Soldier
The Journal for Collectors
209 N Lombard Ave.
Oak Park, IL 60302; 708-383-6525 or FAX 708-383-2182. Subscription: $35 per year for 6 issues (1st class U.S. mail); current sample copy available by sending $3. Written for collectors by collectors, this magazine shares useful information on military and civilian toy figures and the companies that produced them

On Line With Betsy McCall
Marci Van Ausdall
P.O. Box 946
Quincy, CA 95971. Subscription: $10 per year for 4 issues

Paper Collectors' Marketplace
470 Main St., P.O. Box 128
Scandinavia, WI 54977; 715-467-2379. Subscription: $17.95 (12 issues) per year in USA; Canada and Mexico add $15 per year

Paper Doll News
Emma Terry
P.O. Box 807
Vivian, LA 71082

Paper Pile Quarterly
P.O. Box 337
San Anselmo, CA 94979-0337
415-454-5552. Subscription: $12.50 per yr in USA and Canada

The Pencil Collector
American Pencil Collectors Soc.
Robert J. Romey, Pres.
2222 S Millwood
Wichita, KS 67213; 316-263-8419

Pepsi-Cola Collectors Club Newsletter
Pepsi-Cola Collectors Club
Bob Stoddard
P.O. Box 1275
Covina, CA 91722
714-593-8750
Membership: $15

Pez Collector's News
Richard and Marianne Belyski, Editors
P.O. Box 124
Sea Cliff, NY 11579
Phone or FAX 516-676-1183
e-mail: peznews@juno.com

Piece by Piece
Frances Main, Editor
P.O. Box 12823
Kansas City, KS 66112-9998; for Springbok puzzle collectors; subscription: $8 per year

Plastic Figure & Playset Collector
5894 Lakeview Ct. E
Onalaska, WI 54650

The Pokey Gazette, A Little Golden Book collector newsletter
Steve Santi
19626 Ricardo Ave.
Hayward, CA 94541
510-481-2586

The Prehistoric Times
Mike and Kurt Fredericks
145 Bayline Circle
Folsom, CA 95630; 916-985-7986
For collectors of dinosaur toys; 6
issues (1 yr), $19

The Prize Insider Newsletter, for
Cracker Jack collectors
Larry White
108 Central St.
Rowley, MA 01969
508-948-8187

The Puppet Collector's Newsletter
Steven Meltzer
670 San Juan Ave. #B
310-396-6007

Quint News (see also Dionne
Quint Collectors Club)
Dionne Quint Collectors
P.O. Box 2527
Woburn, MA 01888
617-933-2219

Record Collectors Monthly
(newspaper)
P.O. Box 75
Mendham, NJ 07945; 201-543-
9520; FAX 201-543-6033

Roy Rogers-Dale Evans Collec-
tors Assn.
Nancy Horsley
P.O. Box 1166
Portsmouth, OH 45662

Schoenhut Collectors Club
For membership information:
Patricia J. Girbach
1003 W Huron St.
Ann Arbor, MI 48103-4217

*The Shirley Temple Collectors
News*
8811 Colonial Rd.
Brooklyn, NY 11209
Dues: $20 per year; checks
payable to Rita Dubas

The Silent Film Newsletter
Gene Vazzana
140 7th Ave.
New York, NY 10011
Subscription $18, send $2.50 for
sample copy

The Silver Bullet
Terry and Kay Klepey
P.O. Box 553
Forks, WA 98331; 206-327-3726.
Subscription $10 per year, sample
issue $4; also licensed mail-order
seller of memorabilia and appraiser

Smurf Collectors Club
24ACH, Cabot Rd. W
Massapequa, NY 11758. Membership includes newsletters. LSASE
for information

Snow Biz
c/o Nancy McMichael
P.O. Box 53262
Washington, DC 20009
Quarterly newsletter (subscription $10 per year) and collector's
club, annual meeting/swap meet

Steiff Life
Steiff Collectors Club
Beth Savino
c/o The Toy Store
7856 Hill Ave.
Holland, OH 43528
419-865-3899 or 800-862-8697

The Survivors (Transformer Club)
For membership information:
Send name and address along
with SASE or e-mail address to:
Liane Elliot
6202 34th St. NW
Gig Harbor, WA 98335-7205
e-mail: tetra@eskimo.com

The Television History Magazine
William J. Flechner
700 E Macoupin St.
Staunton, IL 62088
618-635-2712

Toy Collector Club of America
(for Ertl toys)
P.O. Box 302
Dyersville, IA 52040
800-452-3303

Toy Dish Collectors
Abbie Kelly
P.O. Box 351
Camillus, NY 13031
315-487-7415

*Toy Gun Collectors of America
Newsletter*
Jim Buskirk, Editor and Publisher
3009 Oleander Ave.
San Marcos, CA 92069
619-599-1054
Published quarterly, covers cap
guns, spring air BB guns and other
toy guns. Dues: $15 per year;
SASE for information

Toy Shop
700 E State St.
Iola, WI 54990
715-445-2214; subscription (3rd
class) $23.95 for 26 issues

Toy Trader
100 Bryant St.
Dubuque, Iowa 52003
1-800-364-5593; subscription in
US $24 for 12 issues

Toychest
Antique Toy Collectors of America, Inc.
2 Wall St., 13th Floor
New York, NY 10005
212-238-8803

Toys & Prices (magazine)
700 E State St.
Iola, WI 54990-0001
715-445-2214
FAX 715-445-4087
Subscription: $14.95 per year

The Trick or Treat Trader
CJ Russell and the Halloween
Queen Antiques
P.O. Box 499, 4 Lawrence St. and
Rt. 10
Winchester, NH, 03470
Subscription is $15 a year for 4
issues or $4 for a sample

Trainmaster (newsletter)
P.O. Box 1499
Gainesville, FL 32602
904-377-7439 or 904-373-4908.
FAX 904-374-6616

Troll Monthly
5858 Washington St.
Whitman, MA 02382
800-858-7655 or 800-85-Troll

Turtle River Farm Toys
Rt. 1, Box 44
Manvel, ND 58256-9763

The TV Collector
Diane L. Albert
P.O. Box 1088
Easton, MA 02334-1088
508-238-1179
Send $4 for sample copy

View-Master Reel Collector
Roger Nazeley
4921 Castor Ave.
Phil., PA 19124
215-743-8999

Western & Serials Club
Rt. 1, Box 103
Vernon Center, NM 56090
507-549-3677

The Working Class Hero (Beatles
newsletter)
3311 Niagara St.
Pittsburgh, PA 15213-4223
Published 3 times per year; send
SASE for information

The Wrapper
Bubble Gum & Candy Wrapper
Collectors
P.O. Box 573
St. Charles, IL 60174
708-377-7921

The Yellow Brick Road Fantasy
Museum & Gift Shop
Rt. 49 and Yellow Brick Rd.
Chesterton, IN 46304
219-926-7048

Yo-Yo Times
P.O. Box 1519-SCT
Herndon, VA 22070

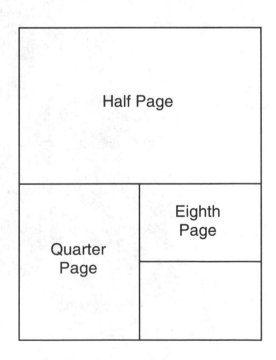

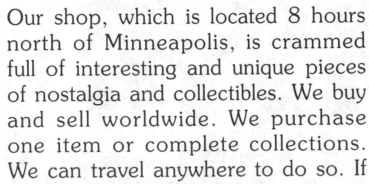

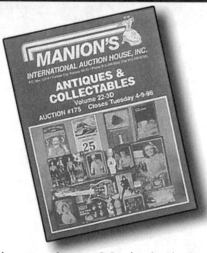

Index to Advertisers